Paperback Oxford Large Print Dictionary

Edited by
Julia Elliott

OXFORD
UNIVERSITY PRESS

OXFORD
UNIVERSITY PRESS

Great Clarendon Street, Oxford OX2 6DP

Oxford University Press is a department of the University of Oxford.
It furthers the University's objective of excellence in research, scholarship, and education by publishing worldwide in

Oxford New York

Auckland Bangkok Buenos Aires Cape Town Chennai
Dar es Salaam Delhi Hong Kong Istanbul Karachi Kolkata
Kuala Lumpur Madrid Melbourne Mexico City Mumbai Nairobi
São Paulo Shanghai Taipei Tokyo Toronto

Published in the United States
by Oxford University Press Inc., New York

British Library Cataloguing in Publication Data
Data available

Library of Congress Cataloging in Publication Data
Data available

ISBN 0-19-861348-2

10 9 8 7 6 5 4 3

Designed by George Hammond
Typeset in Stone Serif and Arial
by Morton Word Processing Ltd
Printed in Great Britain by
Clays Ltd, Bungay, Suffolk

Preface

The *Paperback Oxford Large Print Dictionary* is a compact and up-to-date dictionary presented in a large, clear type. The text, which is based on that of the *Oxford English Minidictionary*, draws on extensive research into current English carried out by the Oxford Dictionaries Department. In the light of this research new words, senses, and phrases have been selected for inclusion and the most important and frequent meanings placed first in each entry. The definitions are written in a style that is concise and easy to understand.

The large type and generous spacing and margins make this an ideal dictionary for adults and schoolchildren seeking a text that is clear and easy to read. It is especially suitable for people with sight problems.

In producing this dictionary, the editors have worked closely with the Royal National Institute of the Blind, who have approved and made recommendations on all aspects of design and layout.

Pronunciation

A guide to pronunciation is given for any word that is difficult to pronounce, or difficult to recognize when read, or spelt in the same way as another word but pronounced differently. Pronunciations are not given for easy words that are familiar to everyone.

Words are broken up into small units, usually of one syllable. The syllable that is spoken with most stress in a word of two or more syllables is shown in bold, like this.

The sounds represented are as follows:

a	*as in* cat	g	*as in* gets
ă	*as in the first syllable in* ago	h	*as in* hat
ah	*as in* calm	i	*as in* pin
air	*as in* hair	I	*as in* eye
ar	*as in* bar	j	*as in* jam
aw	*as in* law	k	*as in* king
ay	*as in* say	l	*as in* leg
b	*as in* bat	m	*as in* man
ch	*as in* chin	n	*as in* not
d	*as in* day	ng	*as in* sing, finger
e	*as in* bed	nk	*as in* thank
ĕ	*as in the second syllable in* taken	o	*as in* top
ee	*as in* meet	ŏ	*as in the second syllable in* lemon
eer	*as in* beer	oh	*as in* most
er	*as in* her	oi	*as in* join
ew	*as in* few	oo	*as in* soon
ewr	*as in* pure	oor	*as in* poor
f	*as in* fat	or	*as in* corn
		ow	*as in* cow

p	*as in* pen	uu	*as in* book
r	*as in* red	v	*as in* van
s	*as in* sit	w	*as in* will
sh	*as in* shop	y	*as in* yes, *or, when preceded by a consonant,* I *as in* cry
t	*as in* top	yoo	*as in* unit
th	*as in* thin	yoor	*as in* Europe
th	*as in* this	yr	*as in* fire
u	*as in* cup	z	*as in* zebra
ŭ	*as in the second syllable in* circus		

Abbreviations

ABBREV	abbreviation	PL	plural
ADJ	adjective	PREP	preposition
ADV	adverb	PRON	pronoun
CONJ	conjunction		

Labels

Unless otherwise stated, the words and senses in this dictionary are all part of standard English. Some words, however, are appropriate only to certain situations, or are found only in certain contexts or varieties of English, and where this is the case a label (or a combination of labels) is used.

For example, the labels [INFORMAL], [ARCHAIC], and [POETIC] refer to a particular level of use in the language; in the case of [OFFENSIVE], [DEROGATORY], and [VULGAR SLANG], the labels act as warnings that the term in question may cause offence.

The [US] label indicates that a word is used in US English but is not standard in British English.

Subject labels, such as [MUSIC], [PHYSICS], and [CRICKET], indicate that a word or phrase is associated with a particular subject field or specialist activity.

Note on trade marks and proprietary status

This book includes some words which are or are asserted to be proprietary names or trade marks. Their inclusion does not imply that they have acquired for legal purposes a non-proprietary or general significance, nor is any other judgement implied concerning their legal status.

In cases where the editor has some evidence that a word is used as a proprietary name or trade mark this is indicated by the label [TRADE MARK], but no judgement concerning the legal status of such words is made or implied thereby.

Aa

A (also **a**) NOUN (PL **As** or **A's**) the first letter of the alphabet.
ABBREV **1** amperes. **2** (**Å**) angstroms.

a DETERMINER **1** used in mentioning someone or something not previously referred to; the indefinite article; one, any. **2** in, to, or for each; per: *60 words a minute.*

AA ABBREV **1** Automobile Association. **2** Alcoholics Anonymous.

aardvark NOUN an African animal with a long snout.

aback ADV (**taken aback**) surprised and disturbed.

abacus /a-bă-kŭs/ NOUN an instrument for counting, consisting of a frame with beads sliding on wires or rods.

abandon VERB leave (a place or person) without intending to return; give up. NOUN lack of inhibition.
abandonment NOUN

abandoned ADJ careless, wild, or undisciplined.

abase VERB humiliate, degrade.
abasement NOUN

abashed ADJ embarrassed, ashamed.

abate VERB become less intense.
abatement NOUN

abattoir /ab-ă-twar/ NOUN a slaughterhouse.

abbess NOUN a woman who is the head of an abbey of nuns.

abbey NOUN a building occupied by a community of monks or nuns; a church or house that was formerly an abbey.

abbot NOUN a man who is

the head of an abbey of monks.

abbreviate VERB shorten.

abbreviation NOUN a shortened form of a word or phrase.

ABC NOUN **1** the alphabet. **2** the basic facts of a subject.

abdicate VERB **1** renounce the throne. **2** fail to fulfil (a duty).
abdication NOUN

abdomen NOUN the part of the body containing the digestive organs.
abdominal ADJ

abduct VERB take (someone) away by force.
abduction NOUN
abductor NOUN

aberrant ADJ not normal or acceptable.

aberration NOUN a deviation from what is normal or acceptable.

abet VERB (**abets**, **abetting**, **abetted**) encourage or assist in wrongdoing.
abettor NOUN

abeyance NOUN (**in abeyance**) not currently occurring or in use.

abhor VERB (**abhors**, **abhorring**, **abhorred**) detest.

abhorrence NOUN hatred.

abhorrent ADJ detestable.

abide VERB **1** (**abide by**) accept (a rule or decision). **2** tolerate. **3** endure, last. **4** [ARCHAIC] live, dwell.

ability NOUN (PL **abilities**) **1** the power to do something. **2** skill.

abject ADJ **1** wretched. **2** without pride or self-respect.
abjectly ADV

abjure VERB renounce; repudiate.

ablaze ADJ burning fiercely.

able ADJ **1** capable of doing something. **2** skilled.
ably ADV

ablutions PLURAL NOUN the act of washing oneself.

abnegate VERB renounce.

abnormal ADJ not normal.
abnormality NOUN
abnormally ADV

aboard ADV & PREP on board a ship etc.

abode NOUN a house or home.

abolish VERB put an end to (a custom or law).

abolition NOUN

abominable ADJ very bad or wicked.
abominably ADV

abominate VERB detest.

abomination NOUN a hated thing.

aboriginal ADJ **1** existing in a country from its earliest times.
2 (**Aboriginal**) relating to the native peoples of Australia. NOUN (**Aboriginal** or **Aborigine**) a member of one of the native peoples of Australia.

abort VERB **1** expel (a foetus) prematurely.
2 bring to an early end because of a problem.

abortion NOUN the premature expulsion of a foetus from the womb.

abortionist NOUN a person who performs abortions.

abortive ADJ unsuccessful.

abound VERB be plentiful.

about PREP & ADV **1** in connection with.
2 approximately. **3** in the surrounding area.
be about to be on the point of.

about-turn (also **about-face**) NOUN a turn to face the other way; a reversal of policy.

above PREP & ADV at a higher level than; greater than; superior to.
above board legitimate, honest.

abracadabra EXCLAMATION a word said when performing magic.

abrasion NOUN the action or process of scraping or wearing away; an area of scraped skin.

abrasive ADJ tending to rub or scrape; harsh. NOUN a substance used for grinding or polishing.

abreast ADV side by side.
abreast of up to date with.

abridge VERB shorten (a text etc.).
abridgement NOUN

abroad ADV in or to a foreign country; over a wide area.

abrogate VERB repeal, abolish.
abrogation NOUN

abrupt ADJ **1** sudden.
2 curt. **3** steep.
abruptly ADV
abruptness NOUN

abscess NOUN a pus-filled swelling.

abscond VERB leave secretly or illegally.

abseil /ab-sayl/ VERB descend using a rope fixed at a higher point.

absence NOUN **1** the state of being absent. **2** lack.

absent ADJ /ab-sĕnt/ not present; not paying attention. VERB /ab-**sent**/ (**absent oneself**) stay away.
absent-minded forgetful or distracted.

absentee NOUN a person who is absent from work, school, etc.
absenteeism NOUN

absinthe /ab-sinth/ NOUN a green liqueur.

absolute ADJ complete; unrestricted.

absolutely ADV completely, entirely. EXCLAMATION used for emphasis or to express agreement.

absolution NOUN formal forgiveness of sins.

absolutism NOUN the principle that those in government should have unlimited power.
absolutist NOUN

absolve VERB clear of blame or guilt.

absorb VERB take in, soak up; assimilate; hold the attention of.

absorbent ADJ able to absorb moisture.
absorbency NOUN

absorption NOUN the process of absorbing or being absorbed.

abstain VERB **1** refrain from doing something enjoyable. **2** choose not to vote.
abstainer NOUN

abstemious /ab-stee-mi-ŏs/ ADJ not indulging in something enjoyable.
abstemiously ADV
abstemiousness NOUN

abstention NOUN **1** a decision not to vote. **2** the act of abstaining.

abstinence NOUN the act of abstaining from something enjoyable.

abstract ADJ /ab-strakt/ **1** existing in thought or theory but not materially. **2** (of art) not representing things pictorially. VERB /ăb-**strakt**/ take out or remove. NOUN

/ab-strakt/ a summary. **abstraction** NOUN

abstracted ADJ preoccupied.

abstruse ADJ hard to understand, obscure.

absurd ADJ completely unreasonable or inappropriate. **absurdity** NOUN **absurdly** ADV

abundant ADJ plentiful; having plenty of something. **abundance** NOUN **abundantly** ADV

abuse VERB /ă-**bewz**/ **1** ill-treat; insult. **2** misuse. NOUN /ă-**bewss**/ **1** ill-treatment; insults. **2** wrongful use.

abusive ADJ **1** insulting, offensive. **2** cruel, violent. **abusively** ADV

abut VERB (**abuts**, **abutting**, **abutted**) be next to or touching.

abysmal /ă-**biz**-măl/ ADJ very bad.

abyss /ăb-**is**/ NOUN a deep or bottomless chasm.

AC ABBREV alternating current.

a/c ABBREV account.

academia /a-kă-**dee**-mi-ă/ NOUN the academic community.

academic ADJ **1** of a college or university; scholarly. **2** of theoretical interest only. NOUN a person who studies or teaches in a college or university. **academically** ADV

academy NOUN (PL **academies**) **1** a place of study or training in a special field. **2** a society of scholars, artists, or scientists.

acanthus NOUN a plant with decorative spiny leaves.

accede /ak-**seed**/ VERB (**accede to**) **1** agree to. **2** take up (an office or position).

accelerate VERB begin or cause to move more quickly. **acceleration** NOUN

accelerator NOUN **1** a foot pedal which controls the speed of a vehicle. **2** an apparatus for accelerating charged particles.

accent NOUN /**ak**-sĕnt/ **1** a way of pronouncing a language. **2** a written mark indicating the

a

pronunciation of a part of a word. **3** a particular emphasis. VERB /ak-**sent**/ **1** pronounce with an accent. **2** emphasize.

accentuate VERB emphasize; make prominent.
accentuation NOUN

accept VERB **1** agree to receive or do. **2** regard as valid or correct. **3** resign oneself to.
acceptance NOUN

acceptable ADJ approved of; satisfactory.
acceptability NOUN
acceptably ADV

access NOUN a way in; the opportunity to use something; the right to see or enter. VERB enter (a place); open (a computer file).

accessible ADJ able to be reached or obtained; easily understood or enjoyed.
accessibility NOUN

accession NOUN **1** the gaining of a rank or position. **2** an addition.

accessory NOUN (PL **accessories**) **1** something added as a supplement or decoration. **2** someone who helps in or knows about a crime.

accident NOUN **1** an unplanned event causing damage or injury. **2** chance, absence of intention.

accidental ADJ happening by accident.
accidentally ADV

acclaim VERB praise enthusiastically and publicly.
NOUN enthusiastic public praise.

acclamation NOUN enthusiastic praise.

acclimatize (also **acclimatise**) VERB make or become used to new conditions.
acclimatization NOUN

accolade NOUN an award or honour.

accommodate VERB **1** provide lodging or room for. **2** adapt to.

accommodating ADJ willing to fit in with others.

accommodation NOUN a place to live.

accompany VERB (**accompanies**, **accompanying**,

a

accompanied) **1** go with. **2** play an instrumental part supporting (a singer or instrument).
accompaniment NOUN
accompanist NOUN

accomplice NOUN a person who helps another commit a crime.

accomplish VERB succeed in doing or achieving.
accomplishment NOUN

accomplished ADJ highly skilled.

accord VERB **1** give (power or recognition) to. **2** (**accord with**) be in harmony with. NOUN agreement, harmony.
of one's own accord without being asked.

accordance NOUN conformity.

according ADV (**according to**) **1** as stated by. **2** following or agreeing with.
accordingly ADV

accordion NOUN a musical instrument with bellows and keys or buttons.

accost VERB approach and speak to.

account NOUN **1** a statement of money paid or owed; a credit arrangement with a bank or firm. **2** a description of an event. VERB (**account for**) **1** explain. **2** form, make up.
on account of because of.

accountable ADJ obliged to account for one's actions.
accountability NOUN

accountant NOUN a person who keeps or inspects business accounts.
accountancy NOUN

accoutrements /ă-koo-trĕ-mĕnts/ ([US] **accouterments**) PLURAL NOUN items of equipment.

accredited ADJ officially recognized or authorized.

accretion NOUN growth by a build-up of layers; an addition.

accrue VERB (**accrues, accruing, accrued**) accumulate.
accrual NOUN

accumulate VERB acquire more and more of; increase in amount.
accumulation NOUN

accumulator NOUN **1** a

a

rechargeable electric battery. **2** a series of bets with winnings restaked.

accurate ADJ free from error.
accuracy NOUN
accurately ADV

accusative NOUN the grammatical case expressing the direct object.

accuse VERB represent (someone) as responsible for a crime or fault.
accusation NOUN
accuser NOUN

accustom VERB (**be accustomed to**) be used to.

ace NOUN **1** a playing card with a single spot. **2** [INFORMAL] an expert. **3** an unreturnable serve in tennis.

acerbic /ă-ser-bik/ ADJ sharp and direct.
acerbity NOUN

acetate /a-si-tayt/ NOUN a synthetic textile fibre produced from cellulose.

acetic acid /ă-see-tik, ă-set-ik/ NOUN the acid that gives vinegar its characteristic taste.

acetone /a-si-tohn/ NOUN a colourless liquid used as a solvent.

acetylene /ă-set-ĭleen/ NOUN a gas which burns with a bright flame, used in welding.

ache NOUN a dull continuous pain.
VERB suffer such a pain.

achieve VERB succeed through effort or skill in doing, reaching, or gaining.
achievable ADJ
achievement NOUN
achiever NOUN

Achilles heel NOUN a person's weak point.

Achilles tendon NOUN the tendon attaching the calf muscles to the heel.

acid NOUN a chemical substance that contains hydrogen and has a pH of less than 7. ADJ having the properties of an acid; sharp-tasting; (of words) bitter or cutting.
acidic ADJ
acidity NOUN
acidly ADV

acidify VERB (**acidifies, acidified, acidifying**) make or become acid.

acid rain NOUN rain made

acid by pollution.

acknowledge VERB **1** admit the truth of. **2** confirm receipt of or thanks for. **3** greet. **acknowledgement** NOUN

acme /ak-mi/ NOUN the height of perfection.

acne /ak-ni/ NOUN an eruption of pimples.

acolyte /a-kŏ-lIt/ NOUN an assistant or follower.

acorn NOUN the oval nut of the oak tree.

acoustic /ă-koo-stik/ ADJ relating to sound. NOUN (**acoustics**) the qualities of a space that affect the way sound carries.

acquaint VERB make aware of or familiar with; (**be acquainted with**) know personally.

acquaintance NOUN a slight knowledge; a person one knows.

acquiesce VERB accept without protest. **acquiescence** NOUN **acquiescent** ADJ

acquire VERB gain possession of.

acquisition NOUN something acquired; the action of acquiring.

acquisitive ADJ eager to acquire things. **acquisitiveness** NOUN

acquit VERB (**acquits, acquitting, acquitted**) **1** declare to be not guilty. **2** (**acquit oneself**) behave or perform in a particular way. **acquittal** NOUN

acre /ay-ker/ NOUN a measure of land area equal to 4,840 sq. yds (0.405 hectare). **acreage** NOUN

acrid ADJ bitter.

acrimonious ADJ angry and bitter. **acrimony** NOUN

acrobat NOUN a performer of acrobatics.

acrobatic ADJ involving spectacular gymnastic feats. NOUN (**acrobatics**) acrobatic feats.

acronym /ak-rŏ-nim/ NOUN a word formed from the initial letters of others.

acropolis NOUN the citadel of an ancient Greek city, built on high ground.

across PREP & ADV **1** from one side to the other of. **2** on the other side of.

acrostic NOUN a poem or

puzzle in which certain letters in each line form a word or words.

acrylic /ă-kri-lik/ NOUN a synthetic material made from an organic substance.

act VERB **1** do something; take effect; behave; (**act as**) perform the function of; (**acting**) temporarily doing the duties of another. **2** play (a part); be an actor. NOUN **1** something done. **2** a law made by parliament. **3** a pretence. **4** a section of a play.

actinium NOUN a radioactive element.

action NOUN **1** the process of doing or functioning; a thing done. **2** a lawsuit. **3** armed conflict.

actionable ADJ giving cause for a lawsuit.

activate VERB cause to act or work.
activation NOUN
activator NOUN

active ADJ **1** functioning. **2** energetic.
actively ADV

activist NOUN a person who campaigns for political or social change.
activism NOUN

activity NOUN (PL **activities**) **1** an action or pursuit. **2** lively action.

actor NOUN a person whose profession is acting.

actress NOUN a female actor.

actual ADJ existing in fact or reality.

actuality NOUN reality.

actually ADV in fact, really.

actuary NOUN (PL **actuaries**) an insurance expert who calculates risks and premiums.
actuarial ADJ

actuate VERB cause to function.

acuity /ă-kyoo-i-ti/ NOUN sharpness of thought, vision, or hearing.

acumen NOUN shrewdness.

acupuncture NOUN the insertion of fine needles into the skin as a medical treatment.
acupuncturist NOUN

acute ADJ **1** intense; (of an illness) short but severe. **2** quick to understand. **3** (of the senses) highly developed. **4** (of an angle)

less than 90°.
acutely ADV
acuteness NOUN

acute accent NOUN the accent (´).

AD ABBREV indicating the number of years after Christ's birth (from Latin *Anno Domini* 'in the year of the Lord').

adage /ad-ĭj/ NOUN a saying expressing a general truth.

adagio /ă-dah-jee-oh/ ADV [MUSIC] in slow time.

adamant ADJ not yielding to requests or arguments.

Adam's apple NOUN the projection of cartilage at the front of the neck.

adapt VERB make or become suitable for new use or conditions.
adaptation NOUN

adaptable ADJ able to be adapted or to adapt oneself.
adaptability NOUN

adaptor NOUN a device for connecting pieces of equipment, or for connecting several electric plugs to one socket.

add VERB **1** join to an existing item to increase or enlarge it. **2** say as a further remark. **3** put (numbers) together to calculate a total.

addendum NOUN (PL **addenda**) a section added to a book.

adder NOUN a poisonous snake.

addict NOUN a person who is addicted to something.

addicted ADJ **1** physically dependent on a particular substance. **2** devoted to a particular activity.
addiction NOUN
addictive ADJ

addition NOUN the action or process of adding; a thing added.

additional ADJ added, extra.
additionally ADV

additive NOUN a substance added.

addled ADJ **1** (of an egg) rotten. **2** muddled.

address NOUN **1** particulars of where a person lives or where mail should be delivered. **2** a speech. VERB **1** write the address on (mail). **2** speak to. **3** apply (oneself) to a task.

addressee NOUN a person to whom a letter etc. is addressed.

adduce VERB cite as evidence.

adenoids PLURAL NOUN a mass of tissue between the back of the nose and the throat.

adept ADJ very skilful. NOUN a skilful person.

adequate ADJ satisfactory in quantity or quality.
adequacy NOUN
adequately ADV

adhere VERB (**adhere to**) stick firmly to.
adherence NOUN

adherent NOUN a supporter of a person or theory.

adhesion NOUN the process of sticking to something.

adhesive ADJ sticking, sticky. NOUN an adhesive substance.

ad hoc ADV & ADJ created or done for a particular purpose.

adieu /ă-dew/ EXCLAMATION goodbye.

ad infinitum ADV endlessly; forever.

adipose ADJ fatty.

adjacent ADJ close by or adjoining.

adjective NOUN a word ascribing characteristics to a noun.
adjectival ADJ

adjoin VERB be next to or joined with.

adjourn VERB move (a meeting etc.) to another place or time.
adjournment NOUN

adjudge VERB decide judicially.

adjudicate VERB make a formal judgement on an issue or for a competition.
adjudication NOUN
adjudicator NOUN

adjunct NOUN an additional part.

adjure VERB command; urge.

adjust VERB **1** alter slightly. **2** become used to a new situation.
adjustable ADJ
adjustment NOUN

adjutant NOUN an army officer assisting in administrative work.

ad lib ADV without preparation. ADJ (of a

speech or performance) improvised. VERB (**ad-lib**) (**ad-libs**, **ad-libbing**, **ad-libbed**) improvise.

administer VERB **1** organize or put into effect. **2** give or hand out.

administrate VERB organize; administer. **administrator** NOUN

administration NOUN management of public or business affairs. **administrative** ADJ

admirable ADJ worthy of admiration. **admirably** ADV

admiral NOUN a naval officer of the highest rank.

admire VERB **1** respect highly. **2** look at with pleasure. **admiration** NOUN **admirer** NOUN

admissible ADJ able to be admitted or allowed. **admissibility** NOUN

admission NOUN **1** a statement admitting something. **2** entrance or right of entrance into a place. **3** a person admitted into hospital.

admit VERB (**admits**, **admitting**, **admitted**) **1** reluctantly state as true. **2** allow to enter. **3** receive into a hospital for treatment. **4** accept as valid.

admittance NOUN admission to a private place.

admixture NOUN a mixture.

admonish VERB **1** reprimand. **2** urge or warn. **admonition** NOUN

ad nauseam ADV to a tedious or sickening extent.

ado /ă-**doo**/ NOUN commotion, fuss.

adobe /ă-**doh**-bi/ NOUN a kind of clay used to make sun-dried bricks.

adolescent ADJ between childhood and adulthood. NOUN an adolescent boy or girl. **adolescence** NOUN

adopt VERB **1** bring up (another's child) as one's own. **2** choose to follow (a course of action). **3** take up (a position). **adoption** NOUN

adoptive ADJ related by

a

adoption.

adorable ADJ lovable or charming.

adore VERB **1** love deeply. **2** worship.
adoration NOUN

adorn VERB make more attractive; decorate.
adornment NOUN

adrenal glands PLURAL NOUN two glands that produce adrenalin, located close to the kidneys.

adrenalin /ă-dren-ă-lin/ (also **adrenaline**) NOUN a hormone that increases the heartrate.

adrift ADJ & ADV drifting; without guidance or purpose.

adroit ADJ skilful.

adsorb VERB attract and hold (a gas or liquid) to a surface.

adulation NOUN excessive praise.
adulatory ADJ

adult ADJ fully grown. NOUN an adult person or animal.
adulthood NOUN

adulterate VERB make impure by adding a substance.
adulteration NOUN

adulterer NOUN a person who commits adultery.

adultery NOUN sex between a married person and someone who is not their husband or wife.
adulterous ADJ

adumbrate VERB indicate; foreshadow.

advance VERB **1** move forward; make or cause to make progress. **2** pay (money) as a loan or before it is due. NOUN **1** a forward movement; an improvement. **2** a loan or forward payment. **3** (**advances**) romantic or sexual approaches to someone.
advancement NOUN

advanced ADJ **1** far on in development or time. **2** not elementary.

advantage NOUN **1** something that puts one in a favourable position. **2** a benefit.
take advantage of **1** exploit. **2** make use of.

advantageous ADJ beneficial.

advent NOUN **1** an arrival.

2 (**Advent**) the season before Christmas.

adventure NOUN an exciting experience or undertaking.
adventurer NOUN
adventurous ADJ

adverb NOUN a word qualifying a verb, adjective, or other adverb.

adversary NOUN (PL **adversaries**) an opponent.
adversarial ADJ

adverse ADJ unfavourable; harmful.
adversely ADV

adversity NOUN (PL **adversities**) misfortune; hardship.

advertise VERB **1** promote (a product or service) in order to increase sales. **2** publicize (a job vacancy).

advertisement NOUN a notice, display, short film, etc. promoting a product or publicizing a job vacancy.

advice NOUN a suggestion to someone about their best course of action.

advisable ADJ prudent and sensible.
advisability NOUN

advise VERB **1** give advice to; recommend. **2** inform.
adviser NOUN

advisory ADJ giving advice.

advocate NOUN /**ad**-vŏ-kăt/ **1** a person who recommends a policy. **2** a person who speaks in court on behalf of another. VERB /**ad**-vŏ-kayt/ recommend.
advocacy NOUN

adze ([US] **adz**) NOUN an axe with a blade at right angles to the handle.

aegis /**ee**-jiss/ NOUN protection, sponsorship.

aeolian /ee-**oh**-li-ăn/ ADJ relating to wind.

aeon /**ee**-ŏn/ (also **eon**) NOUN an immense time.

aerate VERB introduce air into.

aerial ADJ **1** existing or taking place in the air. **2** involving the use of aircraft. NOUN a structure for transmitting or receiving radio or television signals.

aero- COMBINING FORM relating to air; relating to

a

aircraft.

aerobatics PLURAL NOUN spectacular feats performed by an aircraft in flight.
aerobatic ADJ

aerobic ADJ relating to the increased intake of oxygen into the body through exercise. NOUN (**aerobics**) vigorous exercises designed to increase oxygen intake.

aerodynamic ADJ relating to aerodynamics; having a shape that allows quick movement through the air.
aerodynamically ADV

aerodynamics NOUN the science concerned with the movement of objects through the air.

aerofoil NOUN an aircraft wing, fin, or tailplane giving lift in flight.

aeronautics NOUN the science or practice of building or flying aircraft.
aeronautical ADJ

aeroplane NOUN a powered flying vehicle with fixed wings.

aerosol NOUN a substance sealed in a pressurized container and released as a fine spray.

aerospace NOUN the branch of technology concerned with aviation and space flight.

aesthete /ees-theet/ ([US] also **esthete**) NOUN a person who appreciates art and beauty.

aesthetic /ess-**the**-tik/ ([US] also **esthetic**) ADJ relating to beauty and the appreciation of beauty. NOUN **1** the principles followed by an artist or artistic movement. **2** (**aesthetics**) the study or philosophy of beauty and its appreciation.
aesthetically ADV

aesthetics NOUN the study of beauty and its appreciation.

aetiology /ee-ti-**ol**-ŏji/ ([US] **etiology**) NOUN **1** a set of causes. **2** the study of causation.

afar ADV to or from a distance.

affable ADJ polite and friendly.
affability NOUN
affably ADV

affair NOUN **1** an event or series of events. **2** a person's rightful concerns. **3** a temporary sexual relationship.

affect VERB **1** have an effect on. **2** touch the feelings of. **3** pretend to feel, have, etc.

affectation NOUN an artificial and pretentious manner.

affected ADJ seeking to impress; pretentious.

affection NOUN fondness, liking.

affectionate ADJ showing affection.
affectionately ADV

affidavit NOUN a written statement sworn on oath to be true.

affiliate VERB connect as a subordinate member or branch.
affiliation NOUN

affinity NOUN (PL **affinities**) a close resemblance or attraction.

affirm VERB state firmly or publicly.
affirmation NOUN

affirmative ADJ agreeing with or to a statement or request. NOUN a statement indicating agreement.

affix VERB /ă-**fiks**/ attach. NOUN /**a**-fiks/ a prefix or suffix.

afflict VERB cause pain or suffering to.
affliction NOUN

affluent ADJ wealthy.
affluence NOUN

afford VERB **1** (**can afford**) have enough money or resources for. **2** give, provide (an opportunity, view, etc.).

afforest VERB convert (land) into forest.
afforestation NOUN

affray NOUN a public fight or riot.

affront NOUN an open insult. VERB insult, offend.

aficionado /ă-fi-shŏ-**nah**-do/ NOUN a person who knows a lot about something.

afloat ADV & ADJ floating; on a boat.

afoot ADV & ADJ in progress.

aforementioned, **aforesaid** ADJ mentioned previously.

afraid ADJ frightened.
I'm afraid expressing polite regret.

afresh ADV in a fresh or

a

new way.

African ADJ of Africa or its people. NOUN an African person.

Afrikaans NOUN a language of South Africa, developed from Dutch.

Afrikaner NOUN an Afrikaans-speaking white person in South Africa.

aft ADV at or towards the rear of a ship or aircraft.

after PREP **1** in the time or position following. **2** in pursuit of. **3** in reference to. CONJ & ADV in the time following.

afterbirth NOUN the placenta discharged from the womb after childbirth.

after-effect NOUN an effect persisting after its cause has gone.

aftermath NOUN the consequences of an unpleasant event.

afternoon NOUN the time between noon and evening.

aftershave NOUN an astringent lotion used after shaving.

afterthought NOUN something thought of or added later.

afterwards ADV at a later time.

Aga NOUN [TRADE MARK] a large cooking stove.

again ADV **1** once more. **2** returning to a previous position or condition. **3** in addition.

against PREP **1** in opposition or resistance to. **2** in contrast to. **3** in or into contact with.

agate NOUN a stone with bands of colour.

age NOUN **1** the length of time that a person or thing has existed. **2** a particular stage in someone's life. **3** a historical period. **4** (**an age** or **ages**) a very long time. VERB (**ages**, **ageing** or **aging**, **aged**) grow old or older.

aged ADJ **1** /ayjd/ of a specified age. **2** /ay-jid/ old.

ageism NOUN prejudice on grounds of age.
ageist NOUN & ADJ

ageless ADJ not growing or seeming to grow old.

agency NOUN (PL **agencies**) **1** an organization

providing a particular service. **2** action or intervention.

agenda NOUN a list of items to be discussed or things to be dealt with.

agent NOUN **1** a person who provides a particular service. **2** a spy. **3** a person or thing producing an effect.

agent provocateur /*azh*-ahn prŏ-vok-ă-**ter**/ NOUN a person who tempts others to do something illegal.

agglomerate VERB collect into a mass.
agglomeration NOUN

aggrandize (also **aggrandise**) VERB increase the power or reputation of.
aggrandizement NOUN

aggravate VERB **1** make worse. **2** [INFORMAL] annoy.
aggravation NOUN

aggregate NOUN /ag-ri-găt/ **1** a whole combining several elements. **2** crushed stone used in making concrete.
ADJ /ag-ri-găt/ formed by combination or addition.
VERB /ag-ri-gayt/ combine, unite.

aggression NOUN hostile action or attitudes.

aggressive ADJ **1** hostile. **2** excessively forceful.
aggressively ADV

aggressor NOUN a person who initiates an attack.

aggrieved ADJ having a grievance.

aghast ADJ filled with horror.

agile ADJ nimble, quick-moving.
agility NOUN

agitate VERB **1** worry, disturb; campaign to raise concern. **2** shake briskly.
agitation NOUN
agitator NOUN

AGM ABBREV annual general meeting.

agnostic NOUN a person who believes that one cannot know whether or not God exists.
agnosticism NOUN

ago ADV in the past.

agog ADJ eager, expectant.

agonize (also **agonise**) VERB (**agonizes**, **agonizing**, **agonized**) worry intensely; (**agonizing**) very painful or worrying.

agony NOUN (PL **agonies**) extreme suffering.

agoraphobia NOUN an irrational fear of open or public places.
agoraphobic NOUN & ADJ

agrarian ADJ relating to agriculture.

agree VERB (**agrees**, **agreeing**, **agreed**) **1** have the same opinion about something. **2** (**agree to**) consent to. **3** (**agree with**) be consistent with. **4** (**agree with**) be good for.

agreeable ADJ **1** pleasant. **2** willing to agree.
agreeably ADV

agreement NOUN **1** the sharing of opinion or feelings. **2** an arrangement agreed between people. **3** consistency.

agriculture NOUN the science or practice of farming.
agricultural ADJ

agronomy NOUN soil management and crop production.

aground ADV & ADJ (of a ship) on or on to the bottom in shallow water.

ague /ay-gyoo/ NOUN [ARCHAIC] an illness involving fever and shivering.

ahead ADV further forward in position or time.

ahoy EXCLAMATION a seaman's shout for attention.

AI ABBREV **1** artificial intelligence. **2** artificial insemination.

aid NOUN help, support; food or money given to a country in need of help.
VERB give help to.

aide NOUN an assistant to a political leader.

Aids (also **AIDS**) NOUN a disease which breaks down the sufferer's natural defences against infection, caused by the HIV virus. (Short for *acquired immune deficiency syndrome*.)

aikido /I-kee-doh/ NOUN a Japanese martial art.

ail VERB [ARCHAIC] cause someone to suffer or have problems.

aileron NOUN a hinged flap on an aircraft wing.

ailment NOUN a slight illness.

aim VERB point, send, or direct towards a target; intend, try. NOUN the aiming of something; an intention.

aimless ADJ without a purpose.
aimlessly ADV
aimlessness NOUN

ain't CONTRACTION [INFORMAL] am not, is not, are not; has not, have not.

air NOUN **1** the invisible mixture of gases surrounding the earth. **2** a manner; an impression given; (**airs**) an affectation of superiority. **3** a melody. VERB **1** express (an opinion) publicly. **2** expose to air to dry or ventilate.
airless ADJ

air bag NOUN a safety device in a vehicle that fills with air in a collision to protect the driver or passenger.

airborne ADJ carried by air; (of aircraft) in flight.

airbrick NOUN a brick perforated to allow ventilation.

airbrush NOUN a device for spraying paint.

air conditioning NOUN a system controlling the humidity and temperature of air in a building or vehicle.
air-conditioned ADJ

aircraft NOUN (PL **aircraft**) a machine capable of flight in air.

aircraft carrier NOUN a ship acting as a base for aircraft.

aircrew NOUN the crew of an aircraft.

airfield NOUN an area for the take-off and landing of aircraft.

air force NOUN a branch of the armed forces using aircraft.

air gun NOUN a gun with a missile propelled by compressed air.

airlift NOUN the large-scale transport of supplies by aircraft. VERB transport in this way.

airline NOUN a company providing an air transport service.

airliner NOUN a passenger aircraft.

airlock NOUN **1** a stoppage of the flow in a pipe, caused by an air bubble.

2 an airtight compartment giving access to a pressurized chamber.

airmail NOUN mail carried by aircraft.

airman NOUN a member of an air force, especially one below the rank of officer.

airplane NOUN [US] an aeroplane.

airport NOUN a complex of buildings and runways for the take-off and landing of aircraft.

airship NOUN a powered aircraft kept airborne by a gas-filled chamber.

airspace NOUN the air and skies above a particular country.

airstrip NOUN a strip of ground for take-off and landing of aircraft.

airtight ADJ not allowing air to enter or escape.

airwaves PLURAL NOUN the radio frequencies used for broadcasting.

airway NOUN **1** a regular route used by aircraft. **2** the passage by which air reaches the lungs.

airworthy ADJ (**airworthier**, **airworthiest**) (of an aircraft) fit to fly.
airworthiness NOUN

airy ADJ (**airier**, **airiest**) **1** spacious and well ventilated. **2** carefree and casual.
airily ADV

aisle /Il/ NOUN **1** a passage between rows of seats. **2** a side part of a church.

ajar ADV & ADJ (of a door) slightly open.

aka ABBREV also known as.

akimbo ADV with hands on hips and elbows pointed outwards.

akin ADJ related; similar.

alabaster NOUN a translucent white mineral.

à la carte ADJ & ADV (of a menu or meal) offering or ordered as separate items from a menu.

alacrity NOUN eager readiness.

à la mode ADJ & ADV in fashion.

alarm NOUN **1** fear and anxiety. **2** a warning sound or signal; a device to wake someone at a set time. VERB cause alarm to.

alarmist NOUN a person who exaggerates a danger. ADJ causing needless alarm.

alas EXCLAMATION an exclamation of sorrow or regret.

albatross NOUN a large seabird.

albino NOUN (PL **albinos**) a person or animal with no pigmentation in the hair, skin, or eyes.

album NOUN **1** a blank book for holding photographs, stamps, etc. **2** a collection of recordings issued as a single item.

albumen NOUN egg white.

albumin NOUN a protein found in egg white, milk, blood, etc.

alchemy NOUN a medieval form of chemistry that sought to turn common metals into gold.
alchemist NOUN

alcohol NOUN a colourless inflammable liquid, the intoxicant in wine, beer, etc.; drink containing this.

alcoholic ADJ containing or relating to alcohol. NOUN a person addicted to drinking alcohol.
alcoholism NOUN

alcopop NOUN a ready-mixed soft drink with alcohol added.

alcove NOUN a recess in a wall.

al dente /al **den**-tay/ ADJ (of pasta) cooked so as to be still firm.

alder NOUN a catkin-bearing tree of the birch family.

alderman NOUN [HISTORICAL] a senior member of an English county or borough council.

ale NOUN beer.

alert ADJ watchful, observant. VERB warn, make aware.

A level NOUN advanced level, the highest level in the GCE examinations.

alfalfa NOUN a plant used for fodder.

alfresco ADV & ADJ in the open air.

algae PLURAL NOUN simple plants with no true stems or leaves.

algebra NOUN a branch of mathematics using letters and symbols to represent quantities.

a

algebraic ADJ

algorithm NOUN a step by step procedure for calculation.

alias NOUN a false name. ADV also called.

alibi NOUN evidence that an accused person was elsewhere when a crime was committed.

alien NOUN **1** a person who is not a citizen of the country where he or she lives. **2** a being from another world. ADJ **1** foreign; unfamiliar. **2** extraterrestrial.

alienate VERB cause to become unfriendly or unsympathetic.

alienation NOUN a state of isolation or estrangement.

alight[1] VERB get down from a vehicle; land, settle.

alight[2] ADJ & ADV on fire; shining brightly.

align VERB **1** bring into the correct position. **2** ally (oneself).
alignment NOUN

alike ADJ like one another. ADV in the same way.

alimentary canal NOUN the passage along which food passes through the body.

alimony /a-li-mŏ-ni/ NOUN money paid by a divorced person to their former spouse.

alive ADJ **1** living; lively. **2** (**alive to**) aware of.

alkali NOUN a substance that has a pH greater than 7 and that neutralizes acids.
alkaline ADJ

all DETERMINER the whole number, amount, or extent of. PRON everyone, everything.
ADV completely.
all in 1 including everything. **2** [INFORMAL] exhausted. **all out** using all one's strength. **all right 1** unhurt. **2** satisfactory.

allay VERB lessen (fears).

all-clear NOUN a signal that danger is over.

allegation NOUN a claim that someone has done something illegal or wrong.

allege VERB claim that someone has done something illegal or wrong.

allegedly ADV according to allegation.

allegiance NOUN loyal support.

allegory NOUN (PL **allegories**) a story with an underlying meaning.
allegorical ADJ

allegro ADV [MUSIC] briskly.

alleluia (also **hallelujah**) EXCLAMATION & NOUN praise to God.

allergen NOUN a substance causing an allergic reaction.

allergic ADJ having or caused by an allergy.

allergy NOUN (PL **allergies**) a condition in which the body reacts badly to certain foods and other substances.

alleviate VERB ease (pain or distress).
alleviation NOUN

alley NOUN (PL **alleys**) a narrow passageway; a long narrow area for bowling skittles.

alliance NOUN an association formed for mutual benefit.

allied ADJ **1** joined in alliance. **2** (**allied with**) combined with.

alligator NOUN a large reptile similar to a crocodile.

alliteration NOUN the occurrence of the same sound at the start of adjacent words.
alliterative ADJ

allocate VERB assign or give to.
allocation NOUN

allot VERB (**allots**, **allotting**, **allotted**) distribute; give as a share.

allotment NOUN **1** a small piece of land rented for cultivation. **2** an allotted share.

allotrope NOUN one of the forms of an element that exists in different physical forms.

allow VERB **1** permit; enable, make possible. **2** (**allow for**) take into consideration. **3** set aside for a purpose. **4** admit.

allowance NOUN **1** a permitted amount. **2** a sum of money paid regularly.
make allowances be tolerant or lenient.

alloy NOUN a mixture of two or more metals.

a

VERB **1** mix (metals) to make an alloy. **2** spoil by adding something undesirable.

allude VERB (**allude to**) hint at.

allure VERB entice, attract. NOUN attractiveness.

allusion NOUN an indirect reference to something.

alluvium NOUN a deposit left by flood water.
alluvial ADJ

ally NOUN /al-I/ (PL **allies**) a country or person in alliance with another. VERB /ăl-I/ make (oneself) an ally; join, combine.

almanac (also **almanack**) NOUN **1** an annually published calendar containing information on important dates, astronomical data, etc. **2** a yearbook of a particular activity.

almighty ADJ **1** all-powerful. **2** [INFORMAL] enormous.

almond NOUN an oval nut.

almost ADV very nearly.

alms /ahmz/ PLURAL NOUN [HISTORICAL] charitable donations of money or food to the poor.

almshouse NOUN [HISTORICAL] a house built by charity for poor people.

aloe NOUN a plant with bitter juice.

aloe vera NOUN a lotion for the skin obtained from a kind of aloe.

aloft ADV high up; upwards.

alone ADJ not with others; without company or help. ADV only, uniquely.

along PREP & ADV **1** moving in a constant direction on; extending horizontally on or beside. **2** into company with others: *bring him along.*

alongside ADV & PREP close to the side of.

aloof ADJ unfriendly, distant.
aloofness NOUN

alopecia /a-lŏ-pee-shă/ NOUN abnormal loss of hair.

aloud ADV so as to be heard; audibly.

alpaca NOUN a long-haired mammal related to the llama.

alpha NOUN the first letter

of the Greek alphabet (Α, α).

alphabet NOUN a set of letters in a fixed order representing the sounds of a language.
alphabetical ADJ
alphabetically ADV

alpine ADJ of high mountains. NOUN a plant growing in mountains or rocky areas.

already ADV before this time; as early as this.

Alsatian NOUN a large dog of a breed often used for police work.

also ADV in addition, besides.

altar NOUN a table used in religious services.

altarpiece NOUN a painting behind an altar.

alter VERB make or become different.
alteration NOUN

altercation NOUN a noisy dispute.

alternate VERB /**awl**-ter-nayt/ occur or do in turn repeatedly; change repeatedly between two states. ADJ /awl-**ter**-năt/ **1** every other, every second. **2** (of two things) repeatedly following and replacing each other.
alternately ADV
alternation NOUN

alternating current NOUN an electric current that reverses its direction many times a second.

alternative ADJ **1** available as another choice. **2** unconventional. NOUN a choice, another option.
alternatively ADV

alternator NOUN a dynamo producing an alternating current.

although CONJ despite the fact that.

altimeter NOUN an instrument in an aircraft showing altitude.

altitude NOUN height above sea or ground level.

alto NOUN (PL **altos**) the highest adult male or lowest female voice; a musical instrument with the second or third highest pitch in its group.

altogether ADV **1** completely. **2** taking everything into consideration.

altruism NOUN unselfishness.
altruist NOUN
altruistic ADJ

alum NOUN a compound used in dyeing and tanning.

aluminium NOUN a lightweight silvery-grey metallic element.

always ADV at all times; whatever the circumstances.

Alzheimer's disease /alts-hy-merz/ NOUN a disorder causing mental deterioration in middle or old age.

am 1st person singular present of **BE**.

a.m. ABBREV before noon (Latin *ante meridiem*).

amalgam NOUN **1** a blend. **2** an alloy of mercury used in dentistry.

amalgamate VERB unite, combine.
amalgamation NOUN

amass VERB heap up; collect.

amateur NOUN a person who does something as a pastime rather than as a profession.

amateurish ADJ unskilful.

amatory ADJ relating to love.

amaze VERB astonish; overwhelm with wonder.
amazement NOUN

Amazon NOUN a member of a legendary tribe of female warriors; a very tall, strong woman.

ambassador NOUN a senior diplomat representing his or her country abroad.

amber NOUN yellowish fossilized resin; a yellowish colour.

ambidextrous ADJ able to use either hand equally well.

ambience NOUN atmosphere, feeling.

ambient ADJ **1** surrounding. **2** (of music) used to create atmosphere.

ambiguous ADJ having two or more possible meanings.
ambiguity NOUN
ambiguously ADV

ambit NOUN scope, bounds.

ambition NOUN a strong desire to achieve something.
ambitious ADJ

ambitiously ADV

ambivalent ADJ having mixed feelings.
ambivalence NOUN

amble VERB walk at a leisurely pace. NOUN a leisurely walk.

ambrosia NOUN the food of the mythical Greek and Roman gods; delicious food or drink.
ambrosial ADJ

ambulance NOUN a vehicle equipped to carry sick or injured people to hospital.

ambush NOUN a surprise attack by people lying in wait. VERB attack in this way.

ameba American spelling of **AMOEBA**.

ameliorate /ă-mee-lĭŏ-rayt/ VERB make (something) better.
amelioration NOUN

amen EXCLAMATION (in prayers) so be it.

amenable ADJ
1 cooperative.
2 (**amenable to**) able to be treated in a particular way.
amenability NOUN
amenably ADV

amend VERB make minor improvements to.
amendment NOUN

amends PLURAL NOUN (**make amends**) make up for a wrongdoing.

amenity NOUN (PL **amenities**) a pleasant or useful feature of a place.

American ADJ of the USA or its people. NOUN an American person.

American football NOUN a form of football played with an oval ball and an H-shaped goal on a field marked as a gridiron.

American Indian NOUN a member of the native peoples of America.

Americanism NOUN an American word or phrase.

americium NOUN an artificially made radioactive metallic element.

amethyst /a-mĕ-thist/ NOUN a precious stone, a purple or violet quartz.

amiable ADJ likeable; friendly.
amiability NOUN
amiably ADV

amicable ADJ friendly.

amicably ADV

amid, **amidst** PREP in the middle of; during.

amino acid NOUN an organic acid found in proteins.

amiss ADV wrongly, inappropriately. ADJ not quite right.

amity NOUN friendly relations.

ammeter NOUN an instrument that measures electric current.

ammonia NOUN a strong-smelling gas; a solution of this in water.

ammonite NOUN an extinct sea creature with a spiral shell.

ammunition NOUN a supply of bullets, shells, etc.

amnesia NOUN loss of memory.
amnesiac ADJ & NOUN

amnesty NOUN (PL **amnesties**) a general pardon.

amniocentesis /amni-oh-sen-**tee**-sis/ NOUN (PL **amniocenteses**) a test for foetal abnormality involving the withdrawal of a sample of amniotic fluid from the womb.

amniotic fluid NOUN the fluid surrounding the foetus in the womb.

amoeba /ă-**mee**-bă/ ([US] also **ameba**) NOUN (PL **amoebae** or **amoebas**) a single-celled organism capable of changing shape.

amok (also **amuck**) ADV (**run amok**) be out of control.

among, **amongst** PREP **1** surrounded by. **2** being one of (a larger group). **3** shared by, between.

amoral /ay-**mo**-răl/ ADJ not concerned about right or wrong; without morals.

amorous ADJ showing sexual desire.

amorphous ADJ shapeless.

amortize (also **amortise**) VERB pay off (a debt) gradually.

amount NOUN a total of anything; a quantity. VERB (**amount to**) add up to; be equivalent to.

amp NOUN [INFORMAL] **1** an ampere. **2** an amplifier.

ampere /**am**-pair/ NOUN a unit of electric current.

ampersand NOUN the sign

& (= and).

amphetamine NOUN a stimulant drug.

amphibian NOUN an animal, such as a frog, that can live both in water and on land. **amphibious** ADJ

amphitheatre ([US] **amphitheater**) NOUN a semicircular unroofed building with tiers of seats round a central arena.

ample ADJ plentiful, quite enough; large. **amply** ADV

amplifier NOUN a device that makes sounds or radio signals louder.

amplify VERB (**amplifies, amplifying, amplified**) **1** make louder; intensify. **2** add details to (a statement). **amplification** NOUN

amplitude NOUN breadth; abundance.

ampoule /am-pool/ NOUN a small sealed container.

amputate VERB cut off by surgical operation. **amputation** NOUN

amuck variant of **AMOK**.

amulet NOUN something worn as a charm against evil.

amuse VERB cause to laugh or smile; make time pass pleasantly for. **amusement** NOUN

an DETERMINER the form of *a* used before vowel sounds.

anabolic steroid NOUN a synthetic hormone used to build up muscle.

anachronism /ă-na-krŏ-ni-zĕm/ NOUN something that belongs or seems to belong to another time. **anachronistic** ADJ

anaconda NOUN a large snake of South America.

anaemia /ă-nee-miă/ ([US] **anemia**) NOUN lack of haemoglobin in the blood.

anaemic ([US] **anemic**) ADJ suffering from anaemia; lacking in vitality.

anaerobic ADJ not requiring air or oxygen.

anaesthetic /an-is-**thet**-ik/ ([US] **anesthetic**) NOUN a drug or gas that causes loss of sensitivity to pain.

anaesthetist /ă-nees-thĕ-tist/ ([US] **anesthetist**) NOUN a medical specialist who administers anaesthetics. **anaesthetize** VERB (also **anesthetise**)

anagram NOUN a word or phrase formed by rearranging the letters of another.

anal /ay-năl/ ADJ of the anus.

analgesic NOUN a pain-relieving drug.

analogous ADJ comparable.

analogue ([US] also **analog**) NOUN an analogous thing. ADJ using a variable physical property to represent information, rather than binary digits.

analogy NOUN (PL **analogies**) a comparison; a partial likeness.

analyse ([US] **analyze**) VERB examine the structure or composition of; psychoanalyse. **analyst** NOUN

analysis NOUN (PL **analyses**) an examination of the structure or composition of something.

analytical (also **analytic**) ADJ of or using analysis. **analytically** ADV

anarchist NOUN a person who believes that government should be abolished. **anarchism** NOUN

anarchy NOUN a state of disorder due to lack of rule or control; a society with no government. **anarchic** ADJ

anathema /ă-nath-ĕmă/ NOUN a detested thing.

anathematize (also **anathematise**) VERB condemn, curse.

anatomy NOUN (PL **anatomies**) bodily structure; the study of the structure of the human body. **anatomical** ADJ **anatomically** ADV **anatomist** NOUN

ANC ABBREV African National Congress.

ancestor NOUN a person from whom one is descended.

ancestral ADJ inherited from one's ancestors.

ancestry NOUN (PL **ancestries**) one's ancestors or origins.

anchor NOUN a heavy object for mooring a ship to the sea bottom. VERB moor with an anchor; fix firmly.

anchorage NOUN a place where ships may anchor.

anchorman NOUN a person who presents a television or radio programme.

anchovy NOUN (PL **anchovies**) a small strong-tasting fish.

ancient ADJ very old.

ancillary /an-**sil**-ă-ri/ ADJ helping in a subsidiary way.

and CONJ together with, added to.

andante /an-**dan**-tai/ ADV [MUSIC] in moderately slow time.

androgynous ADJ partly male and partly female.

anecdotal ADJ not backed up by facts.

anecdote NOUN a short entertaining account of something that really happened.

anemia etc. US spelling of **ANAEMIA** etc.

anemone /ă-**ne**-mŏ-nee/ NOUN a plant with white, red, or purple flowers.

anesthetic etc. US spelling of **ANAESTHETIC** etc.

aneurysm /**a**-newr-iz-ĕm/ NOUN a swelling of an artery.

anew ADV **1** making a new start. **2** again.

angel NOUN **1** a winged messenger of God represented in human form. **2** a kind person; [INFORMAL] a benefactor.
angelic ADJ

angelica NOUN candied stalks of a fragrant plant.

angelus NOUN a Roman Catholic prayer said at morning, noon, and sunset.

anger NOUN a strong feeling of displeasure. VERB make angry.

angina /an-**jI**-nă/ (in full **angina pectoris**) NOUN pain in the chest caused by an inadequate supply of blood to the heart.

angle[1] NOUN **1** the space between two lines or surfaces at the point where they meet; a corner; a slant. **2** a point of view. VERB present from

a

a particular viewpoint; place obliquely.

angle² VERB fish with line and bait as a sport; try to obtain something by hinting.
angler NOUN
angling NOUN

Anglican ADJ relating to the Church of England. NOUN a member of the Church of England.
Anglicanism NOUN

Anglicize (also **Anglicise**) VERB make English in character.

Anglo- COMBINING FORM English, British.

Anglo-Saxon NOUN **1** a person living in England between the 5th century and the Norman Conquest. **2** the language of these people.

angora NOUN yarn from the hair of a long-haired goat.

angry ADJ (**angrier**, **angriest**) feeling or showing anger.
angrily ADV

angst NOUN severe anxiety.

angstrom NOUN a unit of length equal to one hundred-millionth of a centimetre.

anguish NOUN severe physical or mental pain.
anguished ADJ

angular ADJ having angles or sharp corners; forming an angle.

anhydrous /an-**hI**-drŭs/ ADJ containing no water.

aniline /**a**-ni-leen/ NOUN an oily liquid used in making dyes and plastics.

animal NOUN a living being with sense organs, able to move voluntarily; a mammal, as opposed to a fish, bird, etc. ADJ relating to animals; physical rather than spiritual.

animate VERB /**an**-i-mayt/ bring life or energy to. ADJ /**an**-i-măt/ living.
animated ADJ

animation NOUN **1** liveliness. **2** the technique of filming a sequence of drawings or positions of models to give the appearance of movement.
animator NOUN

animism NOUN the belief that all natural things have a living soul.

animosity NOUN hostility.

animus NOUN hostility, dislike.

anion NOUN an ion with a negative charge.

aniseed NOUN a seed used as a flavouring.

ankle NOUN the joint connecting the foot with the leg.

anklet NOUN a chain or band worn round the ankle.

annals PLURAL NOUN a record of events year by year.

anneal VERB toughen (metal or glass) by heat and slow cooling.

annex /ă-neks/ VERB **1** take possession of (territory). **2** add as a subordinate part.
annexation NOUN

annexe /a-neks/ NOUN an extension to a building.

annihilate VERB destroy completely.
annihilation NOUN

anniversary NOUN (PL **anniversaries**) the date on which an event took place in a previous year.

annotate VERB add explanatory notes to.
annotation NOUN

announce VERB make known publicly.
announcement NOUN
announcer NOUN.

annoy VERB make slightly angry; harass.
annoyance NOUN

annual ADJ yearly. NOUN **1** a plant that lives for one season. **2** a book published in yearly issues.
annually ADV

annuity NOUN (PL **annuities**) a sum of money paid each year.

annul VERB (**annuls**, **annulling**, **annulled**) declare invalid; cancel.
annulment NOUN

annular ADJ ring-shaped.

Annunciation NOUN the announcement by the angel Gabriel to the Virgin Mary that she was to be the mother of Christ.

anode NOUN a positively charged electrode.

anodize (also **anodise**) VERB coat (metal) with a protective layer by electrolysis.

anodyne /**an**-o-dIn/ ADJ inoffensive but dull.

a

NOUN a painkilling drug.

anoint VERB dab or smear with water or oil as part of a religious ceremony.

anomaly NOUN (PL **anomalies**) something that differs from the norm.
anomalous ADJ

anon ADV [ARCHAIC] soon.

anon. ABBREV anonymous.

anonymous ADJ of unknown or undisclosed name or authorship.
anonymity NOUN
anonymously ADV

anorak NOUN a waterproof jacket with a hood.

anorexia (in full **anorexia nervosa**) NOUN a condition characterized by an obsessive desire to lose weight.
anorexic ADJ & NOUN

another DETERMINER & PRON **1** one more. **2** different from the one already mentioned.

answer NOUN **1** something said or written in response to a question or statement. **2** the solution to a problem. VERB **1** give an answer. **2** provide a solution to. **3** correspond to (a description). **4** (**answer to**) have to explain one's actions to. **5** (**answer for**) be responsible for.

answerable ADJ having to account for something or be responsible to someone.

ant NOUN a small insect that lives in highly organized groups.

antacid ADJ reducing excess acid in the stomach.

antagonism NOUN hostility.

antagonist NOUN an opponent.
antagonistic ADJ

antagonize (also **antagonise**) VERB make (someone) hostile.

Antarctic ADJ relating to the region surrounding the South Pole.

ante NOUN a stake put up by a poker player at the beginning of a hand.

ante- PREFIX before.

anteater NOUN a long-nosed mammal that eats ants and termites.

antecedent NOUN something that predates

or precedes something else; (**antecedents**) a person's ancestors. ADJ coming before.

antechamber NOUN an ante-room.

antedate VERB **1** precede in time. **2** give an earlier date to.

antediluvian ADJ of the time before the biblical Flood; [INFORMAL] old, old-fashioned.

antelope NOUN a deer-like mammal.

antenatal ADJ before birth; of or during pregnancy.

antenna NOUN **1** (PL **antennae**) an insect's feeler. **2** (PL **antennas**) a radio or television aerial.

anterior ADJ further forward in position or time.

ante-room NOUN a small room leading to a main one.

anthem NOUN **1** a piece of music sung by a choir in a religious service. **2** a song adopted by a country as an expression of identity.

anther NOUN a part of a flower's stamen containing pollen.

anthology NOUN (PL **anthologies**) a collection of poems or other pieces of writing.

anthracite NOUN a form of coal burning with little flame or smoke.

anthrax NOUN a serious disease of sheep and cattle, transmissible to humans.

anthropoid ADJ relating to apes that resemble humans.

anthropology NOUN the study of the origin and customs of human beings.
anthropological ADJ
anthropologist NOUN

anthropomorphic ADJ attributing human form or character to a god or animal.
anthropomorphism NOUN

anti- PREFIX opposed to; counteracting.

antibiotic NOUN a medicine that kills bacteria.

antibody NOUN (PL **antibodies**) a protein formed in the blood in reaction to a harmful substance, which it then destroys.

anticipate VERB **1** expect, look forward to. **2** deal with or respond to in advance.
anticipation NOUN
anticipatory ADJ

anticlimax NOUN a dull ending where a climax was expected.

anticlockwise ADJ & ADV in the direction opposite to clockwise.

antics PLURAL NOUN ridiculous or amusing behaviour.

anticyclone NOUN an area of high atmospheric pressure around which air slowly circulates, producing fine weather.

antidepressant NOUN a drug counteracting mental depression.

antidote NOUN a substance that counteracts the effects of a poison; a thing that counteracts something unpleasant.

antifreeze NOUN a substance added to water to prevent freezing.

antigen /an-ti-jĕn/ NOUN a substance stimulating the production of antibodies.

anti-hero NOUN (PL **anti-heroes**) a central fictional character who lacks conventional heroic qualities.

antihistamine NOUN a drug counteracting the effect of histamine, used to treat allergies.

antimacassar NOUN a protective covering for a chair-back.

antimony NOUN a silvery-white metallic element.

antipathy NOUN (PL **antipathies**) strong dislike.
antipathetic ADJ

antiperspirant NOUN a substance applied to the skin to reduce sweating.

Antipodes /an-tip-ŏdeez/ PLURAL NOUN (**the Antipodes**) Australia and New Zealand.
Antipodean ADJ

antiquarian ADJ relating to the collection and study of antiques and rare books.

antiquated ADJ very old-fashioned or outdated.

antique ADJ belonging to

the distant past. NOUN an old and usually valuable object.

antiquity NOUN (PL **antiquities**) **1** ancient times. **2** an object dating from ancient times.

anti-Semitic ADJ hostile to Jews.
anti-Semitism NOUN

antiseptic ADJ preventing the growth of organisms that cause disease or infection. NOUN an antiseptic substance.

antisocial ADJ behaving in a way that is unacceptable to others.

antithesis NOUN (PL **antitheses**) an opposite; a contrast.
antithetical ADJ

antler NOUN a branched horn of a deer.

antonym /**an**-tŏ-nim/ NOUN a word opposite to another in meaning.

anus /ay-nŭs/ NOUN the opening through which solid waste leaves the body.

anvil NOUN an iron block on which metal is hammered and shaped.

anxiety NOUN (PL **anxieties**) the state of feeling troubled and uneasy.

anxious ADJ **1** troubled and uneasy. **2** (**anxious to**) eager to.
anxiously ADV

any DETERMINER & PRON **1** one or some: *have you any bread?* **2** whichever or whatever: *any one will do.* ADV at all: *he wasn't any good at football.*

anybody PRON any person.

anyhow ADV **1** anyway. **2** in a disorganized or untidy way.

anyone PRON any person or people.

anything PRON a thing of any kind.

anyway ADV **1** used to add a further point: *it's too late, anyway.* **2** used to dismiss objections or difficulties: *I did it anyway.* **3** used to introduce a new topic.

anywhere ADV in or to any place. PRON any place.

AOB ABBREV any other business.

aorta /ay-**or**-tă/ NOUN the main artery carrying blood from the heart.

a

apace ADV swiftly.

apart ADV **1** separated by a distance. **2** into pieces.

apartheid /ă-par-tayt/ NOUN a former policy of racial segregation in South Africa.

apartment NOUN a set of rooms; [US] a flat.

apathy NOUN lack of interest or enthusiasm. **apathetic** ADJ

ape NOUN an animal related to the monkeys but with no tail, such as a chimpanzee or gorilla. VERB imitate, mimic.

aperitif NOUN an alcoholic drink taken as an appetizer.

aperture NOUN an opening; the variable opening by which light enters a camera.

apex NOUN the highest point or level.

aphasia NOUN loss of the ability to use language, resulting from brain damage.

aphid /ay-fid/ NOUN a small insect that feeds on the sap of plants.

aphorism /a-fŏr-iz-ĕm/ NOUN a short saying expressing a general truth.

aphrodisiac NOUN a substance arousing sexual desire.

apiary NOUN (PL **apiaries**) a place where bees are kept.

apiece ADV to, for, or by each.

aplomb /ă-plom/ NOUN calm self-confidence.

apocalypse /ă-po-kă-lips/ NOUN a catastrophic event in which everything is destroyed. **apocalyptic** ADJ

Apocrypha PLURAL NOUN the books of the Old Testament, not accepted as part of the Hebrew scriptures.

apocryphal /ă-po-krŭ-făl/ ADJ of doubtful authenticity.

apogee /a-pŏ-jee/ NOUN **1** the point in the orbit of the moon or a satellite at which it is furthest from the earth. **2** the highest point reached.

apologetic ADJ expressing regret for having done wrong. **apologetically** ADV

a

apologize (also **apologise**) VERB make an apology.

apology NOUN (PL **apologies**) **1** a statement of regret for having done wrong or hurt someone. **2** (**an apology for**) a poor example of.

apoplectic ADJ **1** [INFORMAL] overcome with anger. **2** [DATED] relating to apoplexy.

apoplexy NOUN **1** [DATED] a stroke. **2** [INFORMAL] incapacity caused by extreme anger.

apostasy /ă-pos-tă-si/ NOUN abandonment of a belief or principle.

apostate /a-pos-tayt/ NOUN a person who renounces a former belief.

a posteriori ADJ (of reasoning) proceeding from effect to cause.

Apostle NOUN **1** (**Apostle**) each of the twelve chief disciples of Christ. **2** a strong supporter of a policy or cause.

apostrophe /ă-pos-trŏ-fi/ NOUN the sign ('), used to show the possessive case or omission of a letter.

apothecary NOUN (PL **apothecaries**) [ARCHAIC] a person who prepared and sold medicines.

apotheosis NOUN (PL **apotheoses**) the highest point or level.

appal ([US] **appall**) VERB (**appals**, **apalling**, **apalled**) horrify.
appalling ADJ

apparatus NOUN equipment for scientific or other work.

apparel NOUN clothing.

apparent ADJ **1** clearly seen or understood. **2** seeming real, but not necessarily so.
apparently ADV

apparition NOUN a ghost.

appeal VERB **1** make a serious or earnest request. **2** refer a decision by a court of law to a higher court. **3** be attractive. NOUN **1** an act of appealing. **2** attractiveness.

appear VERB **1** become visible. **2** seem, give an impression.
appearance NOUN

appease VERB pacify (someone) by giving

what they ask for.
appeasement NOUN

append VERB add at the end.

appendage NOUN a thing attached or appended.

appendectomy NOUN (PL **appendectomies**) the surgical removal of the appendix.

appendicitis NOUN inflammation of the appendix.

appendix NOUN (PL **appendices** or **appendixes**) **1** a small tube of tissue attached to the lower end of the large intestine. **2** a section of additional information at the end of a book.

appertain VERB be relevant.

appetite NOUN a natural desire for food; an enthusiasm.

appetizer (also **appetiser**) NOUN a small item of food or a drink taken before a meal.

appetizing (also **appetising**) ADJ stimulating the appetite.

applaud VERB show approval by clapping; express approval.
applause NOUN

apple NOUN a round fruit with green or red skin and crisp flesh.

appliance NOUN a piece of equipment for a specific task.

applicable ADJ appropriate; relevant.
applicability NOUN

applicant NOUN a person who applies for something.

application NOUN **1** a formal request. **2** sustained hard work. **3** the action of applying something. **4** a computer program designed for a particular purpose.

applicator NOUN a device for inserting or spreading something.

applied ADJ used in a practical way.

appliqué /ap-lee-kay/ NOUN decorative needlework in which pieces of fabric are attached to a background.

apply VERB (**applies**, **applying**, **applied**) **1** make a formal request. **2** bring into operation. **3** be relevant. **4** spread over a surface. **5** (**apply oneself**) concentrate on a task.

appoint VERB **1** choose (a person) for a job; decide on (a time or place). **2** (**appointed**) equipped or furnished in a specified way.

appointment NOUN **1** an arrangement to meet. **2** a job. **3** (**appointments**) furniture or fittings.

apportion VERB share out.

apposite /a-pŏ-zIt/ ADJ appropriate.

appraise VERB estimate the value or quality of. **appraisal** NOUN

appreciable ADJ considerable. **appreciably** ADV

appreciate VERB **1** recognize the good qualities of; understand; be grateful for. **2** increase in value. **appreciation** NOUN **appreciative** ADJ

apprehend VERB **1** seize, arrest. **2** perceive, understand.

apprehension NOUN **1** anxiety. **2** understanding.

apprehensive ADJ worried, afraid. **apprehensively** ADV

apprentice NOUN a person learning a skilled trade from an employer. **apprenticeship** NOUN

apprise VERB (**apprise of**) inform.

approach VERB **1** come near to. **2** make a request or suggestion to. **3** start to deal with (a task). NOUN an act or manner of approaching; a path leading to a place.

approachable ADJ easy to talk to.

approbation NOUN approval.

appropriate ADJ /ă-**proh**-pri-ăt/ suitable, proper. VERB /ă-**proh**-pri-ayt/ take and use; set aside for a special purpose. **appropriately** ADV **appropriation** NOUN

approval NOUN the opinion that something is good; official acceptance.

approve VERB **1** regard something as good or acceptable. **2** formally authorize or accept.

approx. ABBREV approximate(ly).

approximate ADJ /ă-**prok**-sim-ăt/ almost but not quite exact. VERB /ă-**prok**-sim-ayt/ be very similar.
approximately ADV
approximation NOUN

APR ABBREV annual percentage rate (of interest).

après-ski /ap-ray-**skee**/ NOUN social activities following a day's skiing.

apricot NOUN a fruit with soft orange-yellow flesh.

April NOUN the fourth month of the year.

a priori ADJ & ADV using facts or theory rather than observation as a basis for assuming a result or effect.

apron NOUN **1** a garment worn over the front of the body to protect clothes. **2** part of a theatre stage in front of the curtain. **3** an area on an airfield for manoeuvring and loading aircraft.

apropos /ap-rŏ-**poh**/ ADV concerning.

apse NOUN a recess with an arched or domed roof in a church.

apt ADJ **1** appropriate. **2** (**apt to**) having a tendency to.
aptly ADV
aptness NOUN

aptitude NOUN natural ability.

aqualung NOUN a portable breathing apparatus for divers.

aquamarine NOUN a bluish-green gemstone.

aquaplane VERB (of a vehicle) slide uncontrollably on a wet road surface.

aquarium NOUN (PL **aquariums** or **aquaria**) a water-filled tank in which fish and other water creatures are kept.

aquatic ADJ relating to water; living in water.

aqueduct NOUN a channel or bridge-like structure carrying water over a valley or land.

aqueous /ay-kwi-ŭs/ ADJ relating to or containing water.

aquifer NOUN a layer of water-bearing rock or soil.

aquiline ADJ like an eagle; (of a nose) curved like an eagle's beak.

Arab NOUN a member of a Semitic people of the Middle East and North Africa.
Arabian NOUN & ADJ

arabesque NOUN **1** a ballet position in which one leg is lifted and extended backwards. **2** an ornamental design of intertwined lines.

Arabic NOUN the language of the Arabs. ADJ relating to the Arabs or Arabic.

Arabic numeral NOUN any of the numerals 0, 1, 2, 3, 4, 5, 6, 7, 8, and 9.

arable ADJ (of land) suitable for growing crops.

arachnid NOUN a creature of a class including spiders, scorpions, mites, and ticks.

arbiter NOUN a person who settles a dispute.

arbitrary ADJ based on random choice.
arbitrarily ADV

arbitrate VERB act as arbitrator.
arbitration NOUN

arbitrator NOUN a person chosen to settle a dispute.

arboreal /ah-**bor**-ree-ăl/ ADJ of or living in trees.

arboretum NOUN (PL **arboretums** or **arboreta**) a place where trees are grown for study and display.

arbour ([US] **arbor**) NOUN a shady place with a canopy of trees or climbing plants.

arc NOUN **1** a curve forming part of the circumference of a circle. **2** a curving movement through the air. **3** a luminous electric current crossing a gap between terminals.

arcade NOUN a series of arches supporting a roof or wall; a covered walk between shops, stalls, etc.

arcane ADJ mysterious.

arch¹ NOUN a curved structure spanning an opening or supporting a bridge, roof, etc.; the inner side of the foot. VERB form an arch.

arch² ADJ playfully suggesting one is not revealing everything.

a

archly ADV

archaeology ([US] **archeology**) NOUN the study of earlier civilizations through the examination of remains of buildings, objects, etc.
archaeological ADJ
archaeologist NOUN

archaic ADJ belonging to former or ancient times.
archaism NOUN

archangel NOUN an angel of high rank.

archbishop NOUN a chief bishop.

archdeacon NOUN a priest ranking next below bishop.

archduke NOUN [HISTORICAL] the son of an Austrian Emperor.

archer NOUN a person who shoots with a bow and arrows.
archery NOUN

archetype /ar-ki-typ/ NOUN a typical example; an original model.
archetypal ADJ

archipelago /ah-ki-pe-lă-goh/ NOUN (PL **archipelagos** or **archipelagoes**) a group of islands; the sea round this.

architect NOUN a designer of buildings.

architecture NOUN the designing of buildings.
architectural ADJ

architrave /ah-ki-trayv/ NOUN a moulded frame round a doorway or window.

archive /ar-kyv/ NOUN a collection of historical documents.

archivist /ar-kiv-ist/ NOUN a person trained to manage an archive.

archway NOUN an arched entrance or passage.

Arctic ADJ relating to regions around the North Pole.

ardent ADJ passionate, enthusiastic.
ardently ADV

ardour ([US] **ardor**) NOUN passion; enthusiasm.

arduous ADJ difficult and tiring.

are 2nd person singular present and 1st, 2nd and 3rd person plural present of **BE**.

area NOUN **1** a part of a place, object, or surface; the extent or measurement of a surface. **2** a subject or range of activity.

arena NOUN a level area surrounded by seating, for sport or entertainment; an area of activity.

arête NOUN a sharp mountain ridge.

argon NOUN an inert gas.

argot /ar-goh/ NOUN jargon, slang.

arguable ADJ able to be argued or disagreed with. **arguably** ADV

argue VERB **1** express disagreement; exchange angry words. **2** give reasons for an opinion.

argument NOUN **1** a discussion involving disagreement; a quarrel. **2** a reason put forward; a chain of reasoning.

argumentative ADJ given to arguing.

aria NOUN a song for a solo voice in an opera.

arid ADJ dry and parched as a result of no rain. **aridity** NOUN

arise VERB (**arises**, **arising**, **arose**; PAST PARTICIPLE **arisen**) **1** come into existence or to people's notice. **2** stand up.

aristocracy NOUN (PL **aristocracies**) the hereditary upper classes. **aristocrat** NOUN **aristocratic** ADJ

arithmetic NOUN the use of numbers in counting and calculation.

ark NOUN **1** (in the Bible) the ship built by Noah to escape the Flood. **2** a chest housing the holy scrolls in a synagogue; (**Ark of the Covenant**) the chest which contained the laws of the ancient Israelites.

arm NOUN **1** an upper limb of the body. **2** a raised side part of a chair. **3** a division of an organization. **4** (**arms**) weapons. VERB equip with weapons; make (a bomb) ready to explode.

armada NOUN a fleet of warships.

armadillo NOUN (PL **armadillos**) a mammal of South America with a body encased in bony plates.

Armageddon NOUN a final disastrous conflict; (in the Bible) the last battle

a

between good and evil before the Day of Judgement.

armament NOUN military weapons.

armature NOUN the rotating coil of a dynamo or electric motor.

armchair NOUN an upholstered chair with supports for the sitter's arms.

armistice NOUN an agreement to stop fighting.

armorial ADJ relating to heraldry.

armour ([US] **armor**) NOUN metal coverings formerly worn in battle to protect the body; (**armour plate**) a metal layer covering a military vehicle or ship.
armoured ADJ

armoury ([US] **armory**) NOUN (PL **armouries**) a place where weapons are kept.

armpit NOUN the hollow under the arm at the shoulder.

army NOUN (PL **armies**) **1** an organized force for fighting on land. **2** a vast group.

arnica NOUN a plant substance used to treat bruises.

aroma NOUN a pleasant smell.
aromatic ADJ

aromatherapy NOUN the use of essential plant oils for healing.

arose past of **ARISE**.

around ADV & PREP **1** on every side. **2** in or to many places throughout an area. ADV **1** so as to face in the opposite direction. **2** approximately. **3** available or present.

arouse VERB waken; stir; stimulate.

arpeggio NOUN /ah-pe-jee-oh/ (PL **arpeggios**) the notes of a musical chord played in succession.

arraign /ă-rayn/ VERB call someone to court to answer a charge.
arraignment NOUN

arrange VERB **1** put tidily or into order. **2** organize or plan. **3** adapt (a piece of music).
arrangement NOUN

arrant ADJ utter, complete.

array NOUN **1** a display or wide range. **2** an

arrangement of troops. **3** fine clothing. VERB **1** display, arrange. **2** (**be arrayed in**) be dressed in.

arrears PLURAL NOUN money owed and overdue for repayment; work whose completion is overdue.

arrest VERB **1** seize (someone) by legal authority. **2** stop, delay. NOUN the legal seizure of an offender.

arrival NOUN the process of arriving; a person or thing that has arrived.

arrive VERB reach a destination; (of a particular moment) come about.

arrogant ADJ exaggerating one's importance or abilities; proud.
arrogance NOUN
arrogantly ADV

arrogate VERB take or claim for oneself without justification.

arrow NOUN a straight shaft with a sharp point, shot from a bow; a sign shaped like this.

arrowroot NOUN an edible starch obtained from a plant.

arse ([US] **ass**) NOUN [VULGAR SLANG] the buttocks or anus.

arsenal NOUN a place where weapons are stored or made.

arsenic NOUN a semi-metallic element; a strongly poisonous compound of this.

arson NOUN the intentional and unlawful setting on fire of a building.
arsonist NOUN

art NOUN **1** the expression of creative skill in a visual form such as painting or sculpture; paintings and sculptures. **2** (**the arts**) subjects other than sciences; creative activities (e.g. painting, music, writing). **3** a skill.

artefact ([US] **artifact**) NOUN a man-made object.

artery NOUN (PL **arteries**) a large blood vessel carrying blood away from the heart; a major road or route.
arterial ADJ

artesian well NOUN a well that is bored vertically into oblique strata so that water rises through natural pressure.

a

artful ADJ cunningly clever.
artfully ADV

arthritis NOUN a condition in which there is pain and stiffness in the joints.
arthritic ADJ

arthropod NOUN an animal with a segmented body and jointed limbs (such as an insect or crustacean).

artichoke NOUN **1** (also **globe artichoke**) a plant with a flower of leaf-like scales eaten as a vegetable. **2** (**Jerusalem artichoke**) a type of sunflower with a root eaten as a vegetable.

article NOUN **1** an individual object. **2** a piece of writing in a newspaper or journal. **3** a clause in an agreement. VERB (**be articled**) (of a solicitor, accountant, etc.) be employed as a trainee.

articulate ADJ /ar-**tik**-yoo-lăt/ able to express oneself coherently; (of speech) clear and coherent. VERB /ar-**tik**-yoo-layt/ **1** speak or express clearly. **2** form a joint; connect by joints.
articulately ADV
articulation NOUN

articulated lorry NOUN a lorry with sections connected by a flexible joint.

artifact US spelling of **ARTEFACT**.

artifice NOUN a skilful deception.

artificial ADJ made as a copy of or to replace something natural.
artificiality NOUN
artificially ADV

artillery NOUN (PL **artilleries**) large guns used in fighting on land; a branch of an army using these.

artisan NOUN a skilled manual worker, a craftsperson.

artist NOUN **1** a person who creates works of art, especially paintings. **2** a person skilled at a particular task. **3** a professional entertainer.
artistry NOUN

artiste /ar-**teest**/ NOUN a professional entertainer.

artistic ADJ **1** relating to

art or artists. **2** having creative skill.
artistically ADV

artless ADJ simple and natural.
artlessly ADV

artwork NOUN pictures and diagrams in published material.

arty ADJ (**artier**, **artiest**) [INFORMAL] displaying an obvious interest in the arts.

as ADV used in comparisons to refer to extent or amount. CONJ **1** while. **2** in the way that. **3** because. **4** even though. PREP in the role of.

asafoetida (also **asafetida**) NOUN a strong-smelling spice.

asap ABBREV as soon as possible.

asbestos NOUN a soft fibrous mineral substance used to make fireproof material.

asbestosis NOUN a lung disease caused by inhaling asbestos particles.

ascend VERB go up; climb, rise.

ascendant ADJ rising.

ascension NOUN an ascent; (**the Ascension**) the ascent of Christ to heaven.

ascent NOUN the action of going up; an upward slope.

ascertain /as-ser-**tayn**/ VERB find out.
ascertainable ADJ

ascetic ADJ abstaining from pleasures and luxuries. NOUN an ascetic person.
asceticism NOUN

ASCII ABBREV [COMPUTING] American Standard Code for Information Interchange.

ascorbic acid NOUN vitamin C.

ascribe VERB attribute.
ascription NOUN

asepsis NOUN an aseptic condition.

aseptic ADJ free from harmful bacteria.
aseptically ADV

asexual ADJ without sex or sexual organs; not having sexual feelings.
asexually ADV

ash NOUN **1** a tree with silver-grey bark. **2** powder that remains after something has burnt.

ashamed ADJ feeling shame.

ashen ADJ pale as ashes; grey.

ashlar NOUN masonry made of large square-cut stones.

ashore ADV to or on the shore.

ashram NOUN (originally in India) a place of religious retreat.

Asian ADJ relating to Asia or its people. NOUN an Asian person.

Asiatic ADJ relating to Asia.

aside ADV to or on one side. NOUN a remark made so that only certain people will hear.

asinine /a-si-nIn/ ADJ very silly.

ask VERB **1** say something so as to get an answer or information. **2** make a request; (**ask for**) request to speak to. **3** invite.

askance ADV with a suspicious or disapproving look.

askew ADV & ADJ not straight or level.

asleep ADV & ADJ in or into a state of sleep.

asp NOUN a small viper.

asparagus NOUN a plant whose shoots are used as a vegetable.

aspect NOUN **1** a feature or part of something. **2** the appearance of something. **3** the direction in which a building faces.

aspen NOUN a poplar tree.

asperity NOUN harshness.

aspersion NOUN a derogatory remark.

asphalt NOUN a black tar-like substance mixed with gravel for surfacing roads.

asphyxia /ăs-fix-i-ă/ NOUN suffocation.

asphyxiate VERB suffocate.
asphyxiation NOUN

aspic NOUN a savoury jelly.

aspidistra NOUN an ornamental plant.

aspirant NOUN a person aiming to achieve something.

aspirate NOUN /ass-pi-răt/ the sound of *h*. VERB /ass-pi-rayt/ pronounce with an *h*.

aspiration NOUN an

earnest desire or ambition.
aspirational ADJ

aspire VERB have a hope or ambition.

aspirin NOUN a drug that relieves pain and reduces fever.

ass NOUN **1** a donkey. **2** [INFORMAL] a stupid person. **3** [US] spelling of **ARSE**.

assail VERB attack violently.

assailant NOUN an attacker.

assassin NOUN a killer of an important person.

assassinate VERB kill (an important person) by violent means.
assassination NOUN

assault NOUN a violent attack. VERB make an assault on.

assay NOUN the testing of a metal to see how pure it is. VERB make an assay of.

assemble VERB bring or come together; put together the parts of.

assembly NOUN an assembled group; a body of people with law-making powers.

assent NOUN agreement. VERB express agreement.

assert VERB **1** state; declare to be true. **2** exercise (rights or authority). **3** (**assert oneself**) behave forcefully.
assertion NOUN

assertive ADJ forthright and self-assured.
assertiveness NOUN

assess VERB decide the amount or value of; estimate the worth or likelihood of.
assessment NOUN
assessor NOUN

asset NOUN **1** a property with money value. **2** a useful or valuable thing, person, or quality.

assiduous ADJ showing care and thoroughness.
assiduity NOUN
assiduously ADV
assiduousness NOUN

assign VERB allot to a person or purpose; designate to perform a task.

assignation NOUN an arrangement to meet.

assignment NOUN a task assigned.

a

assimilate VERB absorb or be absorbed into the body, into a larger group, or into the mind as knowledge.
assimilation NOUN

assist VERB help.
assistance NOUN

assistant NOUN a helper; a person employed as a subordinate; a person who serves customers in a shop.

assizes PLURAL NOUN [HISTORICAL] a county court which sat at regular intervals.

associate VERB /ă-soh-si-ayt/ **1** connect in one's mind; (**be associated**) occur together, be linked. **2** mix socially; (**associate oneself**) be involved with something. NOUN /ă-soh-si-ăt/ a business companion, a partner.

association NOUN **1** a group organized for a shared purpose; a link, a connection. **2** feelings or ideas commonly connected with another idea.

assonance NOUN the rhyming of vowel sounds.
assonant ADJ

assorted ADJ of several sorts.

assortment NOUN a collection composed of several sorts.

assuage /ă-swayj/ VERB soothe; satisfy (a desire).

assume VERB **1** accept as true without proof. **2** take on (a responsibility, quality, etc.).

assumption NOUN something assumed to be true.

assurance NOUN **1** an assertion, a promise. **2** self-confidence. **3** life insurance.

assure VERB **1** declare confidently to. **2** make certain. **3** cover by life insurance.

assured ADJ **1** sure, confident. **2** certain, guaranteed.

assuredly ADV certainly.

asterisk NOUN a star-shaped symbol (*).

astern ADV at or towards the rear of a ship or aircraft.

asteroid NOUN one of many small rocky bodies orbiting the sun between

Mars and Jupiter.

asthma NOUN a chronic condition causing difficulty in breathing.
asthmatic ADJ & NOUN

astigmatism NOUN a defect in the curvature of the eye, preventing proper focusing.
astigmatic ADJ

astonish VERB surprise very greatly.
astonishment NOUN

astound VERB shock or greatly surprise.

astral ADJ relating to the stars.

astray ADV & ADJ away from the proper path.

astride ADV & PREP with one leg on each side of.

astringent ADJ **1** causing tissue to contract. **2** harsh, severe. NOUN an astringent lotion.
astringency NOUN

astro- COMBINING FORM of the stars.

astrology NOUN the study of the supposed influence of stars on human affairs.
astrologer NOUN
astrological ADJ

astronaut NOUN a person trained to travel in a spacecraft.

astronomical ADJ **1** relating to astronomy. **2** [INFORMAL] enormous in amount.
astronomically ADV

astronomy NOUN the study of stars and planets and their movements.
astronomer NOUN

astrophysics NOUN the study of the physical nature of stars and planets.
astrophysicist NOUN

astute ADJ good at making accurate judgements, shrewd.
astutely ADV
astuteness NOUN

asunder ADV apart.

asylum NOUN **1** refuge, protection. **2** [DATED] an institution for people who are mentally ill.

asymmetrical (also **asymmetric**) ADJ lacking symmetry.
asymmetrically ADV

at PREP expressing: **1** location or time. **2** a point on a scale. **3** a state or condition.

atavistic ADJ reverting to

something ancient or inherited from the earliest humans.
atavism NOUN

ataxia NOUN difficulty in controlling body movements.

ate past of **EAT**.

atheist NOUN a person who does not believe in God.
atheism NOUN

athlete NOUN a person who competes in track and field events; a person who is good at sports.

athlete's foot NOUN an infectious fungal condition of the foot.

athletic ADJ **1** strong, fit, and active. **2** relating to athletics. NOUN (**athletics**) track and field sports.
athletically ADV
athleticism NOUN

atlas NOUN a book of maps.

ATM ABBREV automated teller machine.

atmosphere NOUN **1** the mixture of gases surrounding a planet; air. **2** a unit of pressure. **3** the feeling given by a place, situation, etc.
atmospheric ADJ

atoll NOUN a ring-shaped coral reef enclosing a lagoon.

atom NOUN the smallest particle of a chemical element; a very small quantity.

atomic ADJ relating to atoms; relating to nuclear energy or weapons.

atomic bomb NOUN a bomb deriving its power from nuclear fission.

atomic energy NOUN energy obtained from nuclear fission.

atomize (also **atomise**) VERB reduce to atoms or fine particles.
atomization NOUN
atomizer NOUN

atonal /ay-**toh**-năl/ ADJ (of music) not written in any key.
atonality NOUN

atone VERB make amends for a fault.
atonement NOUN

atrium NOUN (PL **atria** or **atriums**) **1** either of the two upper heart cavities. **2** the central court of an ancient Roman house. **3** a glazed central hall rising through several stories.

atrocious ADJ very bad.
atrociously ADV

atrocity NOUN (PL **atrocities**) wickedness; a cruel act.

atrophy VERB (**atrophies**, **atrophying**, **atrophied**) waste away from lack of use or nourishment. NOUN the condition of atrophying.

attach VERB **1** fasten; join. **2** ascribe or be ascribed. **3** (**be attached to**) be working with. **4** (**attached to**) fond of.
attachment NOUN

attaché /ă-**tash**-ay/ NOUN a person attached to an ambassador's staff.

attaché case NOUN a small case for carrying documents.

attack NOUN a violent attempt to hurt or defeat a person; strong criticism; a sudden onset of illness. VERB make an attack; hurt or criticize.
attacker NOUN

attain VERB achieve.
attainable ADJ
attainment NOUN

attar NOUN a fragrant oil from rose petals.

attempt VERB try. NOUN an effort.

attend VERB **1** be present at; accompany. **2** take notice; (**attend to**) deal with, look after.
attendance NOUN

attendant NOUN an assistant; a person providing service in a particular place. ADJ occurring with something; accompanying.

attention NOUN **1** the concentration of one's mind on something; notice; care. **2** a straight standing position in military drill.

attentive ADJ paying attention; considerate, helpful.
attentively ADV
attentiveness NOUN

attenuate VERB make thin or weaker.
attenuation NOUN

attest VERB provide proof of; declare true or genuine.
attestation NOUN

attic NOUN a room in the

roof space or top storey of a house.

attire NOUN clothes.
VERB clothe.

attitude NOUN **1** a way of thinking. **2** a position of the body. **3** [INFORMAL] self-confident or aggressive behaviour.

attorney NOUN (PL **attorneys**) a person appointed to act for another in legal matters; [US] a lawyer.

attract VERB cause to come somewhere or do something by offering advantage; arouse interest or liking in.
attraction NOUN

attractive ADJ pleasing in appearance.
attractively ADV
attractiveness NOUN

attribute NOUN /**at**-ri-bewt/ a characteristic quality.
VERB /ă-**tri**-bewt/ (**attribute to**) regard as belonging to or caused by.
attributable ADJ
attribution NOUN

attrition NOUN gradual wearing down or away through prolonged attack, pressure, or friction.

attune VERB make or become sensitive.

atypical ADJ not typical.
atypically ADV

aubergine /**oh**-ber-*zh*een/ NOUN a purple fruit eaten as a vegetable.

auburn ADJ (of hair) reddish brown.

auction NOUN a public sale where articles are sold to the highest bidder.
VERB sell by auction.

auctioneer NOUN a person who conducts an auction.

audacious ADJ daring.
audaciously ADV
audacity NOUN

audible ADJ loud enough to be heard.
audibly ADV

audience NOUN **1** a group of listeners or spectators. **2** a formal interview.

audio NOUN sound or the reproduction of sound.

audio tape NOUN a magnetic tape for recording sound; a recording on this.

audio-visual ADJ using both sight and sound.

audit NOUN an official examination of accounts.

VERB make an audit of.
auditor NOUN

audition NOUN a test of a performer's ability for a particular part. VERB test or be tested in an audition.

auditorium NOUN (PL **auditoriums** or **auditoria**) the part of a theatre or hall where the audience sits.

auditory ADJ relating to hearing.

au fait /oh fay/ ADJ (**au fait with**) having good knowledge of (a subject).

auger /or-gĕ/ NOUN a tool for boring, with a spiral point.

augment VERB add to, increase.
augmentation NOUN

augur VERB be an omen or sign.

augury NOUN (PL **auguries**) an omen or sign.

August NOUN the eighth month.

august /aw-gust/ ADJ majestic.

auk /ork/ NOUN a northern seabird.

aunt NOUN the sister or sister-in-law of one's father or mother.

au pair NOUN a young person from overseas who helps with childcare and housework in return for board and lodging.

aura NOUN the atmosphere surrounding a person or thing.

aural /or-ăl, ow-răl/ ADJ relating to the ear.
aurally ADV

aureole (also **aureola**) NOUN a halo; a circle of light.

au revoir /oh rĕ-vwah/ EXCLAMATION goodbye (until we meet again).

auspices PLURAL NOUN (**under the auspices of**) with the support of.

auspicious ADJ conducive to success; being an omen of success.
auspiciously ADV
auspiciousness NOUN

austere ADJ severely simple and plain.
austerity NOUN

Australasian ADJ relating to Australasia, a region consisting of Australia, New Zealand, and the neighbouring islands of

a

the SW Pacific.

Australian NOUN a person from Australia. ADJ relating to Australia.

authentic ADJ genuine, known to be true. **authentically** ADV **authenticity** NOUN

authenticate VERB prove the authenticity of. **authentication** NOUN

author NOUN the writer of a book etc.; an originator of something. **authorship** NOUN

authoritarian ADJ favouring complete obedience to authority. **authoritarianism** NOUN

authoritative ADJ **1** reliably accurate or true. **2** self-confident and commanding respect. **authoritatively** ADV

authority NOUN (PL **authorities**) **1** power to enforce obedience; a person with this. **2** a person with specialized knowledge.

authorize (also **authorise**) VERB give official permission for. **authorization** NOUN

autistic /or-tis-tik/ ADJ suffering from a mental disorder that prevents normal communication and relationships. **autism** NOUN

auto- COMBINING FORM self; own.

autobiography NOUN (PL **autobiographies**) the story of a person's life written by that person. **autobiographical** ADJ

autocracy NOUN (PL **autocracies**) rule by an autocrat.

autocrat NOUN a ruler with unrestricted power. **autocratic** ADJ **autocratically** ADV

autocue NOUN [TRADE MARK] a device showing a speaker's script on a television screen unseen by the audience.

autograph NOUN a person's signature. VERB write one's name in or on.

autoimmune ADJ (of diseases) caused by antibodies produced against substances naturally present in the body.

automate VERB introduce

automation to (a process).

automatic ADJ functioning without human intervention; done without thinking. NOUN an automatic machine or firearm.
automatically ADV

automation NOUN the use of automatic equipment.

automaton NOUN (PL **automatons** or **automata**) a robot.

automobile NOUN [US] a car.

automotive ADJ concerned with motor vehicles.

autonomous ADJ self-governing.
autonomy NOUN

autopilot NOUN a device for keeping an aircraft or ship on a set course automatically.

autopsy NOUN (PL **autopsies**) a post-mortem.

autumn NOUN the season between summer and winter.
autumnal ADJ

auxiliary ADJ giving help or support. NOUN (PL **auxiliaries**) a helper.

auxiliary verb NOUN [GRAMMAR] a verb used in forming the tenses of other verbs.

avail VERB be of use or help; (**avail oneself of**) make use of.
to no avail without success.

available ADJ ready to be used; obtainable.
availability NOUN

avalanche NOUN a mass of snow sliding down a mountain.

avant-garde /av-ahn-gard/ ADJ new, experimental, progressive. NOUN (**the avant-garde**) a group of innovators in the arts.

avarice NOUN greed for wealth or material things.
avaricious ADJ

avenge VERB take vengeance for.
avenger NOUN

avenue NOUN a wide tree-lined road; a method of approach.

aver VERB (**avers**, **averring**, **averred**) state as true.

average NOUN a value

arrived at by adding several quantities together and dividing by the number of these quantities; a standard regarded as usual. ADJ found by making an average; ordinary, usual.

averse ADJ having a strong dislike.

aversion NOUN a strong dislike.

avert VERB **1** turn away. **2** ward off.

aviary NOUN (PL **aviaries**) a large cage or building for keeping birds.

aviation NOUN the practice or science of flying an aircraft.

avid ADJ having a strong desire.
avidly ADV

avionics NOUN electronics in aviation.

avocado NOUN (PL **avocados**) a pear-shaped tropical fruit.

avocet NOUN a wading bird with a long upturned bill.

avoid VERB keep oneself away from; refrain from.
avoidable ADJ
avoidance NOUN

avoirdupois /av-wah-dyou-**pwah**/ NOUN a system of weights based on a pound of 16 ounces.

avow VERB declare.
avowal NOUN

avuncular ADJ of or like a kind uncle.

AWACS ABBREV airborne warning and control system.

await VERB wait for; be in store for.

awake VERB (**awakes**, **awaking**, **awoke**; PAST PARTICIPLE **awoken**) wake. ADJ not asleep; alert.

awaken VERB stop sleeping; stir up (a feeling).

award VERB give by official decision as a prize or penalty. NOUN something awarded; the action of awarding.

aware ADJ having knowledge or realization.
awareness NOUN

awash ADJ covered or flooded with water.

away ADV **1** to or at a distance; into non-existence. **2** constantly: *toiling away*. ADJ (of a match) played on an opponent's ground.

awe NOUN great respect mixed with fear. VERB fill with awe.

aweigh ADJ (of an anchor) raised clear of the sea bottom.

awesome ADJ causing awe.

awful ADJ **1** extremely bad or unpleasant. **2** [INFORMAL] used for emphasis: *an awful lot.*

awfully ADV **1** very much; extremely. **2** very badly.

awhile ADV for a short time.

awkward ADJ **1** difficult to use, do, or handle; inconvenient; clumsy. **2** uncooperative. **3** embarrassed; embarrassing. **awkwardly** ADV **awkwardness** NOUN

awl NOUN a tool for making holes in leather or wood.

awning NOUN a canvas shelter.

awoke, **awoken** past and past participle of **AWAKE**.

AWOL ABBREV absent without leave.

awry /ă-ry/ ADV & ADJ **1** twisted to one side. **2** wrong, amiss.

axe ([US] **ax**) NOUN a chopping tool with a sharp blade. VERB (**axes**, **axing**, **axed**) remove by abolishing or dismissing.

axiom NOUN an accepted general principle. **axiomatic** ADJ

axis NOUN (PL **axes**) a line through the centre of an object, round which it rotates if spinning. **axial** ADJ

axle NOUN a rod on which wheels turn.

ayatollah NOUN a Muslim religious leader in Iran.

aye (also **ay**) EXCLAMATION [ARCHAIC] or [DIALECT] yes. NOUN a vote in favour.

Aztec NOUN a member of an Indian people ruling Mexico before the Spanish conquest in the 16th century.

azure NOUN a deep, bright blue colour.

b

Bb

B (also **b**) NOUN (PL **Bs** or **B's**) the second letter of the alphabet. ABBREV **1** (**b.**) born. **2** (of pencil lead) black.

BA ABBREV Bachelor of Arts.

baa VERB (**baas**, **baaing**, **baaed**) bleat.

babble VERB chatter indistinctly or foolishly; (of a stream) murmur. NOUN babbling talk or sound.

babe NOUN a baby; [INFORMAL] an attractive young woman.

babel NOUN a confused noise.

baboon NOUN a large monkey.

baby NOUN (PL **babies**) a very young child or animal. ADJ small of its kind.
babyish ADJ

babysit VERB (**babysits**, **babysitting**, **babysat**) look after a child while its parents are out.
babysitter NOUN

baccalaureate /bak-ă-lor-i-ăt/ NOUN the final school examination in France.

baccarat /bak-er-ah/ NOUN a gambling card game.

bachelor NOUN **1** an unmarried man. **2** used in names of university degrees.

bacillus /ba-si-lŭs/ NOUN (PL **bacilli**) a rod-shaped bacterium.

back NOUN the surface or part furthest from the front; the rear part of the human body from shoulders to hips; the corresponding part of an animal's body; a defensive player positioned near the goal in football etc. ADV **1** at or towards the rear; in or

into a previous time, position, or state. **2** in return: *ring me back.* VERB **1** support, help. **2** move backwards. **3** lay a bet on. ADJ **1** situated at the back. **2** of or relating to the past: *back numbers.*
back down withdraw a claim or argument. **back out** withdraw from a commitment. **back up** **1** support. **2** make a copy of (a computer disc).
backer NOUN

backache NOUN a pain in one's back.

back-bencher NOUN an ordinary MP not holding a senior office.

backbiting NOUN spiteful talk.

backbone NOUN the column of small bones down the centre of the back.

backchat NOUN [INFORMAL] a rude or cheeky response.

backcloth NOUN a painted cloth at the back of a stage or scene.

backdate VERB declare to be valid from a previous date.

backdrop NOUN a backcloth; a background.

backfire VERB **1** make an explosion in an exhaust pipe. **2** produce an undesired effect.

backgammon NOUN a board game played with draughts and dice.

background NOUN the back part of a scene or picture; the circumstances surrounding something.

backhand NOUN a backhanded stroke.

backhanded ADJ **1** performed with the back of the hand turned forwards. **2** said with underlying sarcasm.

backhander NOUN **1** a backhanded stroke. **2** [INFORMAL] a bribe.

backlash NOUN a hostile reaction.

backlist NOUN a publisher's list of books available.

backlog NOUN arrears of work.

backpack NOUN a rucksack.

back-pedal VERB (**back-pedals**, **back-pedalling**, **back-pedalled**; [US] **back-**

b

pedaling, back-pedaled) reverse one's previous action or opinion.

back seat NOUN an inferior position or status.
back-seat driver a passenger who gives unwanted advice to a driver.

backside NOUN [INFORMAL] the buttocks.

backslide VERB slip back from good behaviour into bad.

backspace VERB move a computer cursor or typewriter carriage one space back.

backspin NOUN a backward spinning movement of a ball.

backstage ADJ & ADV behind a theatre stage.

backstreet NOUN a side street. ADJ secret and illegal.

backstroke NOUN a swimming stroke performed on the back.

backtrack VERB retrace one's route; reverse one's opinion.

back-up NOUN a support, a reserve; [COMPUTING] a copy of data made in case of loss or damage.

backward ADJ **1** directed to the rear. **2** having made less than normal progress. **3** diffident. ADV backwards.
backwardness NOUN

backwards ADV towards the back; with the back foremost; in reverse.

backwash NOUN **1** receding waves created by a ship etc. **2** a reaction.

backwater NOUN **1** a part of a river that is stagnant because not reached by the current. **2** a place unaffected by progress.

backwoods PLURAL NOUN a remote or backward region.

backyard NOUN a yard behind a house; (**one's own backyard**) the area surrounding one's home.

bacon NOUN salted or smoked meat from a pig.

bacterium NOUN (PL **bacteria**) a microscopic organism, often causing disease.
bacterial ADJ
bacteriological ADJ

bacteriology NOUN

bad ADJ (**worse**, **worst**) **1** of poor quality; having undesirable characteristics. **2** wicked; naughty. **3** harmful; serious. **4** decayed.
badness NOUN

bade past of **BID²**.

badge NOUN something worn to show membership, rank, etc.

badger NOUN a large burrowing animal with a black and white striped head. VERB pester.

badly ADV **1** in an unsatisfactory, undesirable, or evil way. **2** very intensely.
badly off in a difficult situation, especially financially.

badminton NOUN a game played with rackets and a shuttlecock over a high net.

baffle VERB be too difficult for; puzzle.
bafflement NOUN

bag NOUN **1** a flexible container. **2** (**bags**) [INFORMAL] a large amount. **3** [INFORMAL] an unpleasant or annoying woman. VERB (**bags**, **bagging**, **bagged**) [INFORMAL] take or reserve for oneself.

bagatelle NOUN **1** a board game in which balls are struck into holes. **2** something trivial. **3** a short piece of music.

baggage NOUN luggage.

baggy ADJ (**baggier**, **baggiest**) hanging in loose folds.

bagpipes PLURAL NOUN a wind instrument with air stored in a bag and pressed out through pipes.

baguette /ba-get/ NOUN a long thin French loaf.

bail¹ NOUN **1** the release of an accused person before trial, on condition that money is left with the court, to be returned when the person attends trial. **2** money paid to release an accused person. VERB set free on payment of bail.

bail² (also **bale**) VERB **1** scoop water out of (a boat). **2** (**bail out**) make an emergency jump by parachute from an aircraft. **3** (**bail out**) rescue from a difficulty.

bailey NOUN the outer wall of a castle.

bailiff NOUN a person who delivers writs and seizes the property of people who owe money for rent.

bailiwick NOUN a district over which a bailiff has authority.

bairn NOUN [SCOTTISH] & [NORTHERN ENGLISH] a child.

bait NOUN food etc. placed to attract prey; an attraction, an inducement. VERB **1** place bait on or in. **2** torment; taunt.

baize NOUN thick woollen green cloth.

bake VERB cook or harden by dry heat.

baker NOUN a person who bakes or sells bread.
bakery NOUN

baker's dozen NOUN thirteen.

baking powder NOUN a mixture used to make cakes rise.

balaclava NOUN a woollen hat covering the head and neck, with a hole for the face.

balalaika /bal-ă-lI-kă/ NOUN a Russian guitar-like instrument.

balance NOUN **1** an even distribution of weight; stability; proportion. **2** the difference between credits and debits; a remainder. **3** a weighing apparatus. **4** the regulating apparatus of a clock. VERB **1** make or stay stable, without falling. **2** compare.

balcony NOUN (PL **balconies**) a projecting platform with a rail or parapet; the upper floor of seats in a theatre etc.

bald ADJ **1** with the scalp wholly or partly hairless; (of tyres) with the tread worn away. **2** without details.
baldness NOUN

balderdash NOUN nonsense.

balding ADJ becoming bald.

bale¹ NOUN a large quantity of paper, hay, cotton, etc. tied or wrapped in a bundle. VERB make into bales.

bale² variant of **BAIL²**.

baleful ADJ menacing,

destructive.
balefully ADV

balk variant of **BAULK**.

ball NOUN **1** a spherical object used in games; a rounded part or mass; (**balls**) [VULGAR SLANG] testicles. **2** a formal social gathering for dancing.
on the ball alert, aware.

ballad NOUN a song telling a story.

ballast NOUN heavy material placed in a ship's hold to steady it; coarse stones as the base of a railway or road.

ball bearing NOUN a ring of small steel balls reducing friction between moving parts of a machine; one of these balls.

ballcock NOUN a valve attached to a floating ball, controlling the water level in a cistern.

ballerina NOUN a female ballet dancer.

ballet NOUN an artistic dance form performed to music.
balletic ADJ

ballistic missile NOUN a powered missile, directed at its launch, then falling by gravity to its target.

ballistics PLURAL NOUN the study of projectiles and firearms.
ballistic ADJ

balloon NOUN a rubber bag inflated with air or lighter gas. VERB swell like such a bag.

ballot NOUN a system of secret voting in which votes are recorded on slips of paper.
VERB (**ballots**, **balloting**, **balloted**) ask (a group) to vote by ballot.

ballpark NOUN **1** a baseball ground. **2** [INFORMAL] an area or range. ADJ [INFORMAL] approximate.

ballpoint NOUN a pen with a tiny ball as its writing point.

ballroom NOUN a large room where dances are held.

ballyhoo NOUN [INFORMAL] a fuss.

balm NOUN a fragrant ointment or herb; a soothing influence.

balmy ADJ (**balmier**, **balmiest**) **1** (of air or weather) pleasantly

b

warm. **2** variant of **BARMY**.

baloney (also **boloney**) NOUN [INFORMAL] nonsense.

balsa NOUN lightweight wood from a tropical American tree.

balsam NOUN a scented resin used as a soothing oil.

baluster NOUN a short pillar in a balustrade.

balustrade NOUN a row of short pillars supporting a rail or coping.

bamboo NOUN a giant tropical grass with hollow stems.

bamboo shoot NOUN the young shoot of bamboo, eaten as a vegetable.

bamboozle VERB [INFORMAL] trick or mystify.

ban VERB (**bans**, **banning**, **banned**) forbid officially. NOUN an order banning something.

banal /bă-nahl/ ADJ commonplace, uninteresting.
banality NOUN

banana NOUN a curved yellow fruit.

band[1] NOUN **1** a flat strip or loop. **2** a range of values or wavelengths.

band[2] NOUN an organized group of people; a set of musicians. VERB form a group.

bandage NOUN a strip of material for binding a wound. VERB bind with this.

bandanna NOUN a large coloured neckerchief.

B. & B. ABBREV bed and breakfast.

bandit NOUN a member of a band of robbers.

bandstand NOUN a covered outdoor platform for a band playing music.

bandwagon NOUN (**climb on the bandwagon**) join a fashionable or successful movement or trend.

bandy[1] VERB (**bandies**, **bandying**, **bandied**) spread (gossip); exchange (words).

bandy[2] ADJ (**bandier**, **bandiest**) (of legs) curving apart at the knees.

bane NOUN a cause of annoyance or misfortune.

bang NOUN a sudden loud sharp noise; a sharp blow. VERB strike, especially noisily; close or put down noisily; make a banging noise. ADV with a bang.

banger NOUN **1** a firework that explodes noisily; [INFORMAL] a noisy old car. **2** [INFORMAL] a sausage.

bangle NOUN a bracelet of rigid material.

banish VERB condemn to exile; dismiss from one's presence or thoughts. **banishment** NOUN

banister (also **bannister**) NOUN the uprights and handrail of a staircase; a single upright.

banjo NOUN (PL **banjos**) a guitar-like musical instrument with a circular body.

bank NOUN **1** a slope at the side of a river; a raised mass of earth etc. **2** a row of lights, switches, etc. **3** an establishment for the safe keeping of money; a stock or store. VERB **1** build up into a mound or bank. **2** tilt sideways. **3** place (money) in a bank. **4** (**bank on**) rely on.

banker's order NOUN an instruction to a bank to pay money or deliver property.

banknote NOUN a printed strip of paper issued as currency.

bankrupt ADJ unable to pay one's debts. NOUN a bankrupt person. VERB make bankrupt. **bankruptcy** NOUN

banner NOUN a flag; a piece of cloth bearing a slogan.

bannister variant of **BANISTER**.

banns PLURAL NOUN an announcement of a forthcoming marriage.

banquet NOUN an elaborate ceremonial meal.

banshee NOUN a spirit whose wail is said to foretell a death.

bantam NOUN a small chicken.

bantamweight NOUN a weight in boxing between featherweight and flyweight.

banter NOUN good-humoured joking.

b

VERB joke in this way.

Bantu NOUN (PL **Bantu** or **Bantus**) a member of a group of African peoples; their languages.

> **Bantu** is an offensive word in S. African English when used in reference to an individual person.

bap NOUN a large soft bread roll.

baptism NOUN a religious rite of sprinkling with water as a sign of purification, usually with name-giving.
baptismal ADJ

Baptist NOUN a member of a Protestant sect believing in adult baptism by total immersion in water.

baptize (also **baptise**) VERB perform baptism on; give a nickname to.

bar NOUN **1** a length of solid rigid material. **2** a stripe. **3** a counter or room where alcohol is served. **4** a barrier. **5** one of the short units into which a piece of music is divided. **6** (**the Bar**) barristers or their profession. **7** a unit of atmospheric pressure. VERB (**bars**, **barring**, **barred**) **1** fasten with bars. **2** forbid, exclude; obstruct. PREP apart from.

barb NOUN **1** a backward-pointing part of an arrow, fish-hook, etc. **2** a wounding remark.

barbarian NOUN an uncivilized person.

barbaric ADJ **1** primitive. **2** savagely cruel.

barbarity NOUN savage cruelty.

barbarous ADJ **1** uncivilized. **2** cruel.
barbarism NOUN
barbarously ADV

barbecue NOUN an open-air meal where food is cooked on a frame above an open fire; this frame. VERB cook on a barbecue.

barbed ADJ having barbs; (of a remark) hurtful.

barbed wire NOUN wire with sharp points at intervals along it.

barber NOUN a men's hairdresser.

barbican NOUN an outer defence to a city or castle; a double tower over a gate or bridge.

barbiturate NOUN a sedative drug.

bar code NOUN a pattern of printed stripes used as a machine-readable code.

bard NOUN a poet.
bardic ADJ

bare ADJ **1** not clothed or covered; not adorned. **2** scanty, just sufficient. VERB reveal.

bareback ADV & ADJ on horseback without a saddle.

barefaced ADJ shameless, undisguised.

barely ADV only just, hardly.

bargain NOUN **1** an agreement where each side does something for the other. **2** something obtained cheaply. VERB **1** discuss the terms of an agreement. **2** (**bargain on/for**) rely on, expect.

barge NOUN a large flat-bottomed boat used on rivers and canals. VERB move forcefully; (**barge in**) intrude.

baritone NOUN a male voice between tenor and bass.

barium NOUN a white metallic element.

bark NOUN **1** a sharp harsh sound made by a dog. **2** the outer layer of a tree. VERB **1** make the sharp harsh sound of a dog; utter in a sharp commanding voice. **2** scrape skin off (one's shin) accidentally.

barley NOUN a cereal plant; its grain.

barley sugar NOUN a sweet made of boiled sugar.

barmaid NOUN a woman serving at a bar.

barman NOUN a man serving at a bar.

bar mitzvah NOUN a Jewish ceremony in which a boy of 13 takes on the responsibilities of an adult.

barmy ADJ (**barmier**, **barmiest**) [INFORMAL] crazy.

barn NOUN a simple roofed farm building used for storage.

barnacle NOUN a shellfish that attaches itself to objects under water.

barney NOUN (PL **barneys**) [INFORMAL] a noisy argument.

barometer NOUN an instrument measuring atmospheric pressure, used in forecasting weather.
barometric ADJ

baron NOUN **1** a member of a low rank of nobility. **2** an influential businessman.
baronial ADJ

baroness NOUN a woman of the rank of baron; a baron's wife or widow.

baronet NOUN the holder of a title below baron but above knight.
baronetcy NOUN

baroque /bă-**rok**/ ADJ of the ornate architectural or musical style of the 17th and 18th centuries; complicated, elaborate. NOUN this style.

barque /bahk/ NOUN a sailing ship.

barrack VERB shout protests; jeer at.

barracks PLURAL NOUN buildings for soldiers to live in.

barracuda NOUN a large voracious tropical sea fish.

barrage NOUN **1** a heavy bombardment. **2** an artificial barrier across a river.

barre NOUN a horizontal bar used for support in ballet exercises.

barrel NOUN **1** a cylindrical container with flat ends. **2** the tube-like part of a gun.

barrel organ NOUN a mechanical instrument producing music by a pin-studded cylinder acting on pipes or keys.

barren ADJ **1** not fertile or fruitful. **2** bleak; pointless; worthless.
barrenness NOUN

barricade NOUN a barrier. VERB block or defend with a barricade.

barrier NOUN something that prevents access or progress.

barring PREP except for, apart from.

barrister NOUN a lawyer representing clients in court.

barrow NOUN **1** a wheelbarrow; a cart pushed or pulled by hand. **2** a prehistoric burial mound.

barter VERB engage in trade by exchange of goods. NOUN trade of this type.

basal /bay-săl/ ADJ of or at the base of something.

basalt /ba-sawlt/ NOUN a dark rock of volcanic origin.

base NOUN **1** the lowest part; a part on which a thing rests or is supported; a starting point. **2** the main place where a person works or stays. **3** headquarters; a centre of organization. **4** a substance capable of combining with an acid to form a salt. **5** each of four stations to be reached by a batter in baseball. **6** the number on which a system of counting is based. VERB make something the foundation or supporting evidence for. ADJ dishonourable; of inferior value.

baseball NOUN a team game in which the batter has to hit the ball and run round a circuit.

baseless ADJ without foundation.

basement NOUN a storey below ground level.

bash [INFORMAL] VERB strike violently; attack. NOUN a violent blow.

bashful ADJ shy.
bashfully ADV
bashfulness NOUN

basic ADJ **1** forming an essential foundation. **2** without elaboration or luxury.
basically ADV

basil NOUN a sweet-smelling herb.

basilica NOUN an oblong hall or church with an apse at one end.

basilisk NOUN a mythical reptile said to cause death by its glance or breath.

basin NOUN **1** a washbasin. **2** a round open container for food or liquid; a sunken place where water collects; an area drained by a river.

basis NOUN (PL **bases**) **1** a foundation or support. **2** a system of proceeding: *on a regular basis.*

bask VERB sit or lie comfortably exposed to pleasant warmth.

basket NOUN a container for holding or carrying things, made of interwoven cane or wire.

basketball NOUN a team game in which the aim is to throw the ball through a high hooped net.

basketwork NOUN material woven in the style of a basket.

Basque /bahsk/ NOUN a member of a people living in the western Pyrenees; their language.

bas-relief NOUN a carving with figures standing out slightly from the background.

bass¹ /bayss/ ADJ deep-sounding; of the lowest pitch in music. NOUN the lowest male voice.

bass² /bass/ NOUN (PL **bass**) an edible fish.

bassoon NOUN a woodwind instrument with a deep tone.

bast NOUN the inner bark of the lime tree used as fibre for matting.

bastard NOUN **1** [ARCHAIC] an illegitimate child. **2** [INFORMAL] an unpleasant person or thing.

baste VERB **1** moisten with fat during cooking. **2** sew together temporarily with loose stitches.

bastion NOUN a projecting part of a fortified place; a stronghold.

bat NOUN **1** a wooden implement for hitting a ball in games; a batsman. **2** a flying animal with a mouse-like body. **3** (**old bat**) [INFORMAL] an unpleasant woman. VERB (**bats**, **batting**, **batted**) perform or strike with the bat in cricket etc.

batch NOUN a set of people or things dealt with as a group.

bated ADJ (**with bated breath**) very anxiously.

bath NOUN a large tub that one lies in to wash the body; a wash in this. VERB wash in a bath.

bathe VERB **1** immerse in or clean with liquid. **2** swim for pleasure. NOUN a swim. **bather** NOUN

bathos /bay-thos/ NOUN an anticlimax; a descent from an important thing to a trivial one.

bathetic ADJ

bathroom NOUN a room containing a bath, shower, washbasin, etc.

batik NOUN a method of printing textiles by waxing the areas not to be dyed.

batman NOUN a soldier acting as an officer's personal servant.

baton NOUN a short stick, especially one used by a conductor.

batsman NOUN a player batting in cricket etc.

battalion NOUN an army unit of several companies.

batten NOUN a bar of wood or metal holding something in place.
VERB fasten with battens.

batter VERB hit hard and often. NOUN **1** a beaten mixture of flour, eggs, and milk, used in cooking. **2** a player batting in baseball.

battering ram NOUN an iron-headed beam formerly used for breaking through walls or gates.

battery NOUN (PL **batteries**) **1** a device containing and supplying electric power. **2** a group of big guns; an artillery unit. **3** a set of similar or connected units of equipment; a series of small cages for intensive rearing of livestock. **4** unlawful violent blows.

battle NOUN a fight between large organized forces; a contest.
VERB engage in a battle, struggle.

battleaxe NOUN a heavy axe used as a weapon in ancient times; [INFORMAL] an aggressive woman.

battlefield NOUN the scene of a battle.

battlements PLURAL NOUN a parapet with openings for firing from.

battleship NOUN a warship of the most heavily armed kind.

batty ADJ (**battier**, **battiest**) [INFORMAL] crazy.

bauble NOUN a small coloured sphere used for decoration; a valueless ornament.

baulk (also **balk**) VERB **1** (**baulk at**) be reluctant to accept. **2** hinder.

b **bauxite** /bork-sIt/ NOUN a mineral from which aluminium is obtained.

bawdy ADJ (**bawdier**, **bawdiest**) rude in an amusing way. **bawdiness** NOUN

bawl VERB **1** shout; weep noisily. **2** (**bawl out**) [INFORMAL] reprimand.

bay NOUN **1** part of the sea within a wide curve of the shore. **2** a recess. **3** a laurel, especially a type used as a herb. **4** the deep cry of a large dog or of hounds in pursuit. VERB (of a dog) give a deep howling cry. ADJ (of a horse) reddish brown. **at bay** forced to face attackers.

bayonet NOUN a stabbing blade fixed to a rifle.

bay window NOUN a window projecting from an outside wall.

bazaar NOUN **1** a market in an eastern country. **2** a sale of goods to raise funds.

bazooka NOUN a portable weapon firing anti-tank rockets.

BBC ABBREV British Broadcasting Corporation.

BC ABBREV (of a date) before Christ.

be VERB **1** exist; occur; be present. **2** have a specified quality, position, or condition. AUXILIARY VERB used to form tenses of other verbs.

beach NOUN a flat area of shoreline. VERB bring on shore from water.

beachcomber NOUN a person who salvages things on a beach.

beachhead NOUN a fortified position set up on a beach by an invading army.

beacon NOUN a fire on a hill, serving as a signal.

bead NOUN a small piece of glass, stone, etc. threaded with others to make a necklace; a rounded drop of liquid on a surface.

beading NOUN a decorative rounded trim of wood or fabric.

beadle NOUN (formerly) a minor parish official.

beady ADJ (**beadier**, **beadiest**) (of eyes) small

and bright.

beagle NOUN a small hound.

beak NOUN **1** a bird's horny projecting jaws; any similar projection. **2** [INFORMAL] a magistrate.

beaker NOUN a tall cup; a tumbler.

beam NOUN **1** a long piece of timber or metal carrying the weight of part of a building. **2** a ray of light or other radiation. **3** a bright smile. **4** a ship's breadth. VERB **1** send out (radio signals). **2** shine brightly; smile radiantly.

bean NOUN a plant with kidney-shaped seeds in long pods; a seed of this or of coffee.
full of beans [INFORMAL] very cheerful.

beanfeast NOUN [INFORMAL] a celebratory party.

bear[1] NOUN a large heavy animal with thick fur; a child's toy resembling this.

bear[2] VERB (**bears**, **bearing**, **bore**; PAST PARTICIPLE **borne**) **1** carry; support; shoulder (responsibilities etc.). **2** endure, tolerate. **3** be fit for (specified treatment): *does not bear repeating.* **4** produce (children, young, or fruit). **5** take a specified direction.
bear down exert pressure; (**bear down on**) approach (someone) purposefully. **bear in mind** remember. **bear up** remain cheerful in difficult circumstances. **bring to bear** exert; make use of.

bearable ADJ endurable.

beard NOUN the hair around a man's chin. VERB confront boldly.

bearing NOUN **1** a way of standing, moving, or behaving. **2** relevance. **3** a compass direction. **4** a device in a machine reducing friction where a part turns.

bearskin NOUN a tall furry cap worn by some troops.

beast NOUN **1** a large animal. **2** [INFORMAL] an unpleasant person or thing.

beastly ADJ (**beastlier**, **beastliest**) [INFORMAL] very

unpleasant.
beastliness NOUN

beat VERB (**beats**, **beating**, **beat**; PAST PARTICIPLE **beaten**) **1** hit repeatedly; (**beat up**) assault violently. **2** move or pulsate rhythmically. **3** defeat or overcome. **4** mix (cooking ingredients) vigorously. NOUN **1** an accent in music; the sound of a drum being struck; a pulsation of the heart; a movement of a bird's wing. **2** an area regularly patrolled by a policeman.
beat it [INFORMAL] go away. **beat up** assault violently.

beatific /bee-ă-ti-fik/ ADJ showing great happiness.
beatifically ADV

beatify /bee-a-ti-fI/ VERB (**beatifies**, **beatifying**, **beatified**) (in the RC Church) declare (a dead person) blessed, as the first step in canonization.
beatification NOUN

beatitude /bee-a-ti-tyood/ NOUN blessedness.

beauteous ADJ [LITERARY] beautiful.

beautician NOUN a person who gives beauty treatment.

beautiful ADJ **1** having beauty; very pleasing to the senses. **2** excellent.
beautifully ADV

beautify VERB (**beautifies**, **beautifying**, **beautified**) make beautiful.
beautification NOUN

beauty NOUN (PL **beauties**) a combination of qualities giving pleasure to the sight, mind, etc.; a beautiful person; an excellent specimen of something.

beaver NOUN an amphibious rodent that builds dams.
beaver away work hard.

becalmed ADJ (of a sailing ship) unable to move because there is no wind.

because CONJ for the reason that.

beck[1] NOUN [NORTHERN ENGLISH] a stream.

beck[2] NOUN (**at someone's beck and call**) always ready to do whatever a particular person asks.

beckon VERB make a summoning gesture.

become VERB (**becomes**, **becoming**, **became**; PAST PARTICIPLE **become**) **1** turn into; begin to be. **2** suit; befit.
becoming ADJ

becquerel /**bek**-er-el/ NOUN a unit of radioactivity.

bed NOUN **1** a thing to sleep or rest on; a framework with a mattress and coverings. **2** a flat base; a foundation; the bottom of a sea or river etc. **3** an area of ground planted with flowers.

bedclothes PLURAL NOUN sheets, blankets, etc.

bedding NOUN bedclothes; straw for animals to sleep on.

bedding plant NOUN a plant grown to be planted when in flower and discarded at the end of the season.

bedevil VERB (**bedevils**, **bedevilling**, **bedevilled**; [US] **bedeviling**, **bedeviled**) afflict with difficulties.

bedfellow NOUN **1** a person sharing one's bed. **2** a close associate.

bedlam NOUN a scene of noisy confusion.

Bedouin /**bed**-oo-in/ (also **Beduin**) NOUN (PL **Bedouin**) a member of a nomadic Arab people of the desert.

bedpan NOUN a pan for use as a toilet by a person confined to bed.

bedraggled ADJ limp and untidy.

bedridden ADJ permanently confined to bed through illness.

bedrock NOUN **1** solid rock beneath loose soil. **2** basic facts or principles.

bedroom NOUN a room for sleeping in.

bedsitter (also **bedsit**, **bed-sitting room**) NOUN a room used for both living and sleeping in.

bedsore NOUN a sore developed by lying in bed in one position for a long time.

bedspread NOUN a covering for a bed.

bedstead NOUN the framework of a bed.

Beduin variant of **BEDOUIN**.

bee NOUN an insect that produces honey.

b

beech NOUN a tree with smooth grey bark and pale wood.

beef NOUN **1** meat from an ox, bull, or cow. **2** muscular strength. **3** [INFORMAL] a complaint. VERB [INFORMAL] complain.

beefburger NOUN a fried or grilled cake of minced beef.

beefeater NOUN a warder in the Tower of London.

beefy ADJ (**beefier**, **beefiest**) [INFORMAL] having a solid muscular body.

beehive NOUN a structure in which bees live.

beeline NOUN (**make a beeline for**) go straight or rapidly towards.

been past participle of **BE**.

beep NOUN a short high-pitched sound. VERB make a beep.

beer NOUN an alcoholic drink made from malt and hops.
beery ADJ

beeswax NOUN a yellow substance secreted by bees, used as polish.

beet NOUN a plant with a fleshy root used as a vegetable (**beetroot**) or for making sugar (**sugar beet**).

beetle NOUN **1** an insect with hard wing-covers. **2** a tool for ramming or crushing. VERB [INFORMAL] move hurriedly.

beetling ADJ overhanging; projecting.

beetroot NOUN the dark red root of a beet eaten as a vegetable.

befall VERB (**befalls**, **befalling**, **befell**; PAST PARTICIPLE **befallen**) happen; happen to.

befit VERB (**befits**, **befitting**, **befitted**) be proper for.

before ADV, PREP, & CONJ during the time preceding; in front of; in preference to.

beforehand ADV in advance.

befriend VERB be friendly towards.

befuddle VERB confuse.

beg VERB (**begs**, **begging**, **begged**) **1** ask humbly or solemnly for something; ask for food or money as charity. **2** (of a dog) sit up expectantly with forepaws off the ground.

beg the question assume the truth of a thing to be proved.

beget VERB (**begets**, **begetting**, **begot** or **begat**; PAST PARTICIPLE **begotten**) be the father of; give rise to.

beggar NOUN a person who lives by asking for charity. VERB reduce to poverty.

beggarly ADJ mean and insufficient.

begin VERB (**begins**, **beginning**, **began**; PAST PARTICIPLE **begun**) **1** perform the first or earliest part of (an activity); be the first to do a thing. **2** come into existence.

beginner NOUN a person beginning to learn a skill.

beginning NOUN a first part; a source or origin.

begrudge VERB be unwilling to give or allow.

beguile VERB charm, especially deceptively.

begum /bay-gum/ NOUN the title of a married Muslim woman.

behalf NOUN (**on behalf of**) as the representative of; in the interests of.

behave VERB act in a specified way; (also **behave oneself**) act in a polite and proper way.

behaviour ([US] **behavior**) NOUN a way of behaving.

behead VERB cut the head off.

beheld past and past participle of **BEHOLD**.

behind ADV & PREP **1** at or to the back or far side of. **2** further back than. **3** in support of. **4** responsible for. **5** late in doing.

behold VERB (**beholds**, **beholding**, **beheld**) see, observe.

beholden ADJ indebted.

behove VERB be a duty of; befit.

beige NOUN a light fawn colour.

being present participle of **BE**. NOUN existence; a thing that exists and has life, a person.

belabour ([US] **belabor**) VERB **1** attack. **2** argue (a point) at excessive length.

belated ADJ coming very late or too late.

b

belatedly ADV

belay VERB secure (a rope) by winding it round something.

belch VERB expel wind noisily from the stomach through the mouth. NOUN an act of belching.

beleaguer VERB besiege; harass.

belfry NOUN (PL **belfries**) a place in a tower where bells are housed.

belie VERB (**belies**, **belying**, **belied**) contradict; fail to confirm.

belief NOUN a feeling that something exists or is true; something believed.

believe VERB **1** accept as true or as speaking truth. **2** (**believe in**) have faith in the truth or existence of. **3** think, suppose.
believer NOUN

belittle VERB disparage.

bell NOUN **1** a cup-shaped metal instrument that makes a ringing sound when struck. **2** a device making a ringing or buzzing sound as a signal.

belladonna NOUN deadly nightshade; a medicinal drug made from this.

belle NOUN a beautiful woman.

bellicose ADJ eager to fight.

belligerent ADJ **1** aggressive. **2** engaged in a war.
belligerence NOUN
belligerently ADV

bellow NOUN a loud deep sound made by a bull; a deep shout. VERB make this sound.

bellows PLURAL NOUN an apparatus for pumping air into something.

belly NOUN (PL **bellies**) the abdomen; the stomach.

bellyful NOUN (**have a bellyful of**) [INFORMAL] have more than enough of.

belong VERB **1** be rightly placed or assigned; fit in a particular environment; (**belong to**) be a member of. **2** (**belong to**) be owned by.

belongings PLURAL NOUN personal possessions.

beloved ADJ dearly loved.

below ADV & PREP at or to a lower level than.

belt NOUN a strip of leather, cloth, etc. worn round

b

the waist; a long narrow strip or region. VERB **1** put a belt round. **2** [INFORMAL] hit. **3** [INFORMAL] rush. **below the belt** unfair.

bemoan VERB express unhappiness about.

bemused ADJ bewildered. **bemusement** NOUN

bench NOUN **1** a long seat of wood or stone; a long table for working on. **2** the office of judge or magistrate.

benchmark NOUN a surveyor's mark; a standard, a criterion.

bend VERB (**bends**, **bending**, **bent**) make or become curved; stoop; turn in a new direction; distort (rules). NOUN a curve, a turn. **bendy** ADJ

bender NOUN [INFORMAL] a wild drinking spree.

beneath ADV & PREP **1** below, underneath. **2** not worthy of.

benediction NOUN a spoken blessing.

benefactor NOUN a person who gives financial or other help.

beneficent ADJ doing good; actively kind. **beneficence** NOUN

beneficial ADJ resulting in good; advantageous. **beneficially** ADV

beneficiary NOUN (PL **beneficiaries**) one who receives a benefit or legacy.

benefit NOUN **1** an advantage or profit. **2** a state payment to someone in need. VERB (**benefits**, **benefiting**, **benefited**; [US] **benefitting**, **benefitted**) profit from something; give an advantage to.

benevolent ADJ kind, helpful. **benevolence** NOUN **benevolently** ADV

benighted ADJ in darkness; ignorant.

benign /bi-**nIn**/ ADJ kind, mild; (of a tumour) not malignant.

bent past & past participle of **BEND**. NOUN a natural skill or liking. **bent on** determined to do or attain.

benzene NOUN a liquid obtained from petroleum and coal tar, used as a solvent, fuel, etc.

b

bequeath VERB leave in one's will.

bequest NOUN a legacy.

berate VERB scold.

bereave VERB (**be bereaved**) be deprived of a close relative or friend through death. **bereavement** NOUN

bereft ADJ deprived; deserted and lonely.

beret /be-ray/ NOUN a round flat cap with no peak.

beriberi NOUN a disease caused by lack of vitamin B.

berk NOUN [INFORMAL] a stupid person.

berry NOUN (PL **berries**) a small round juicy fruit with no stone.

berserk /bĕ-zerk/ ADJ wild and frenzied.

berth NOUN **1** a bunk or sleeping place in a ship or train. **2** a place for a ship to tie up at a wharf. VERB moor at a berth. **give a wide berth to** keep a safe distance from.

beryl NOUN a transparent green gem.

beryllium NOUN a light metallic element.

beseech VERB (**beseeches**, **beseeching**, **besought**) ask in a pleading way.

beset VERB (**besets**, **besetting**, **beset**) trouble persistently; surround, hem in.

beside PREP **1** at the side of. **2** compared with. **beside oneself** distraught. **beside the point** irrelevant.

besides PREP **1** in addition to. **2** apart from. ADV also.

besiege VERB lay siege to.

besmirch VERB make dirty; dishonour.

besom /bee-zŏm/ NOUN a broom made from a bundle of twigs tied to a handle.

besotted ADJ so much in love that one stops acting sensibly.

besought past & past participle of **BESEECH**.

bespeak VERB (**bespeaks**, **bespeaking**, **bespoke**; PAST PARTICIPLE **bespoken**) **1** be evidence of. **2** reserve in advance.

bespoke ADJ made to order.

best ADJ most excellent or desirable; most beneficial. ADV **1** better than any others. **2** to the highest degree. NOUN (**the best**) something that is of the highest quality.
the best part of most of.

bestial ADJ of or like a beast; savage.
bestiality NOUN

bestir VERB (**bestirs**, **bestirring**, **bestirred**) (**bestir oneself**) exert oneself.

best man NOUN a bridegroom's chief attendant.

bestow VERB present as a gift.
bestowal NOUN

bestride VERB (**bestrides**, **bestriding**, **bestrode**; PAST PARTICIPLE **bestridden**) stand astride over.

bet VERB (**bets**, **betting**, **bet** or **betted**) **1** stake money on the outcome of a future event. **2** [INFORMAL] feel certain. NOUN an act of betting; the amount staked.

beta NOUN the second letter of the Greek alphabet (**Β**, **β**).

beta blocker NOUN a drug used to control heartbeat rhythms and treat high blood pressure.

betake VERB (**betakes**, **betaking**, **betook**; PAST PARTICIPLE **betaken**) (**betake oneself**) [FORMAL] go.

bête noire /bet **nwar**/ NOUN (PL **bêtes noires**) something greatly disliked.

betide VERB happen or happen to.

betimes ADV early.

betoken VERB be a sign of.

betray VERB act treacherously towards (one's country) by helping an enemy; be disloyal to; reveal (something) without meaning to.
betrayal NOUN

betrothed ADJ engaged to be married. NOUN (**one's betrothed**) the person to whom one is engaged.
betrothal NOUN

better ADJ **1** of a higher standard or quality. **2** recovered from illness. ADV in a more satisfactory way. NOUN (**one's betters**)

b

one's superiors. VERB outdo, surpass; (**better oneself**) reach a higher position in society. **better off** having more money; being in a more desirable situation. **the better part of** more than half. **get the better of** overcome; outwit.

between PREP **1** in the space or time bounded by (two limits); separating; to and from. **2** indicating division or difference. **3** indicating connection or collision; indicating a shared action or outcome. ADV between points or limits.

bevel NOUN a sloping edge. VERB (**bevels**, **bevelling**, **bevelled**; [US] **beveling**, **beveled**) give a sloping edge to.

beverage NOUN a drink.

bevvy NOUN (PL **bevvies**) [INFORMAL] an alcoholic drink.

bevy NOUN (PL **bevies**) a large group.

bewail VERB lament (a misfortune).

beware VERB be on one's guard.

bewilder VERB puzzle, confuse.
bewilderment NOUN

bewitch VERB put under a magic spell.

beyond PREP at or to the far side of (a point in space or time); more advanced than; greater than; too hard for. ADV at or to the far side.

bhaji /**bah**-jee/ NOUN an Indian dish of vegetables fried in batter.

b.h.p. ABBREV brake horsepower.

bi- COMBINING FORM two; twice.

biannual ADJ happening twice a year.

bias NOUN **1** a feeling based on prejudice rather than sound reason. **2** (in bowls) a tendency to swerve caused by a bowl's irregular shape. **3** a direction diagonal to the weave of a fabric. VERB (**biases**, **biasing**, **biased**) give a bias to; influence.

bib NOUN a covering put under a young child's chin to protect its clothes while it is feeding.

Bible NOUN the Christian or Jewish scriptures; [INFORMAL] a book regarded as authoritative.

biblical ADJ of or in the Bible.

bibliography NOUN (PL **bibliographies**) a list of books about a subject or by a specified author.
bibliographer NOUN
bibliographical ADJ

bibliophile NOUN a book-lover.

bicarbonate NOUN a salt containing a double proportion of carbon dioxide.

bicentenary NOUN (PL **bicentenaries**) a 200th anniversary.

bicentennial ADJ happening every 200 years. NOUN a bicentenary.

biceps /bI-seps/ NOUN the large muscle at the front of the upper arm.

bicker VERB quarrel about unimportant things.

bicycle NOUN a two-wheeled vehicle driven by pedals. VERB ride a bicycle.

bid[1] VERB (**bids, bidding, bid**) **1** offer (a price) for something, especially at an auction. **2** (**bid for**) offer to do work for a stated price. **3** (**bid for**) try to get. NOUN an act of bidding.

bid[2] VERB (**bids, bidding, bid** or **bade**; PAST PARTICIPLE **bid**) **1** utter (a greeting or farewell). **2** [ARCHAIC] command.

biddable ADJ obedient.

bide VERB [ARCHAIC] stay in a place.
bide one's time wait patiently for an opportunity.

bidet /bee-day/ NOUN a low basin used for washing the genital and anal regions.

biennial ADJ happening every two years. NOUN a plant that flowers and dies in its second year.
biennially ADV

bier /beer/ NOUN a movable stand for a coffin.

biff NOUN [INFORMAL] a sharp blow. VERB hit (a person).

bifocals PLURAL NOUN spectacles with lenses that have two segments, assisting both distant and close focusing.

b

bifurcate VERB split into two branches.
bifurcation NOUN

big ADJ (**bigger**, **biggest**) of great size, amount, or intensity; important; serious.

bigamy NOUN the crime of marrying someone else while already married.
bigamist NOUN
bigamous ADJ

bigot NOUN a person who is prejudiced and intolerant of differing views.
bigoted ADJ
bigotry NOUN

bijou /bee-zhoo/ ADJ small and elegant.

bike NOUN [INFORMAL] a bicycle or motorcycle.
biker NOUN

bikini NOUN a woman's two-piece swimming costume.

bilateral ADJ **1** involving two parties. **2** having two sides.
bilaterally ADV

bile NOUN **1** a bitter fluid which aids digestion, produced by the liver. **2** anger or hatred.

bilge NOUN **1** a ship's bottom; water collecting there. **2** [INFORMAL] nonsense.

bilharzia /bil-hahts-i-ă/ NOUN a disease caused by a tropical parasitic flatworm.

bilingual ADJ written in or able to speak two languages.

bilious ADJ **1** sick, especially from trouble with the bile or liver. **2** spiteful, bad-tempered.
biliousness NOUN

bill NOUN **1** a written statement of charges to be paid. **2** a draft of a proposed law. **3** a programme of entertainment. **4** [US] a banknote. **5** a poster. **6** a bird's beak.

billboard NOUN a hoarding for advertisements.

billet NOUN a lodging for troops. VERB (**billets**, **billeting**, **billeted**) (**be billeted**) (of a soldier) stay in a particular place.

billhook NOUN a tool with a broad curved blade for lopping trees.

billiards NOUN a game played on a table, with

three balls which are struck with cues into pockets at the edge of the table.

billion NOUN a thousand million.

billow NOUN a great wave. VERB rise or move like waves; swell out.

bimbo NOUN (PL **bimbos**) [INFORMAL] an attractive but unintelligent young woman.

bin NOUN a large rigid container or receptacle. VERB (**bins**, **binning**, **binned**) discard.

binary ADJ composed of or involving two things.

binary digit NOUN either of the two digits (0 and 1) of the **binary system**, a number system used in computing.

bind VERB (**binds**, **binding**, **bound**) **1** firmly tie, wrap, or fasten. **2** hold together; unite. **3** secure a cover round (a book); cover the edge of (cloth). **4** place under an obligation. NOUN [INFORMAL] something irritating or tedious.

binding NOUN **1** a book cover. **2** braid etc. used to bind an edge.

binge NOUN [INFORMAL] a bout of excessive eating and drinking.

bingo NOUN a gambling game using cards marked with numbered squares.

binocular ADJ using two eyes. NOUN (**binoculars**) an instrument with lenses for both eyes, for viewing distant objects.

bio- COMBINING FORM of living things.

biochemistry NOUN the chemistry of living organisms.
biochemical ADJ
biochemist NOUN

biodegradable ADJ able to be decomposed by bacteria.

biodiversity NOUN the variety of living things in an environment.

biography NOUN (PL **biographies**) the story of a person's life.
biographer NOUN
biographical ADJ

biology NOUN the study of the life and structure of living things.
biological ADJ
biologist NOUN

b

bionic ADJ having electronically operated artificial body parts.

biopic NOUN [INFORMAL] a biographical film.

biopsy NOUN (PL **biopsies**) an examination of tissue taken from the body.

biorhythm NOUN a recurring cycle in the functioning of an organism.

biotechnology NOUN the use of micro-organisms and biological processes in industrial production.

bipartisan ADJ involving two parties.

bipartite ADJ consisting of two parts; involving two groups.

biped NOUN an animal that walks on two feet.

biplane NOUN an aeroplane with two pairs of wings.

birch NOUN a tree with thin peeling bark.

bird NOUN **1** a feathered egg-laying animal, usually able to fly. **2** [INFORMAL] a young woman or girlfriend.

birdie NOUN [GOLF] a score of one stroke under par for a hole.

biro NOUN (PL **biros**) [TRADE MARK] a ballpoint pen.

birth NOUN the emergence of young from its mother's body; origin, ancestry.

birth control NOUN contraception.

birthday NOUN the anniversary of the day of one's birth.

birthmark NOUN a coloured mark on the skin which is there from birth.

birthright NOUN a right or privilege possessed from birth; a basic human right.

biscuit NOUN a small, flat, crisp cake.

bisect VERB divide into two equal parts.

bisexual ADJ sexually attracted to members of both sexes. NOUN a bisexual person.
bisexuality NOUN

bishop NOUN a Christian minister who is in charge of a diocese.

bishopric NOUN the position or diocese of a bishop.

bismuth NOUN a metallic

element resembling lead.

bison NOUN (PL **bison**) a wild ox; a buffalo.

bistro NOUN (PL **bistros**) a small informal restaurant.

bit[1] NOUN **1** a small piece or quantity; a short time or distance. **2** the mouthpiece of a bridle. **3** a tool for drilling or boring. **4** [COMPUTING] a binary digit.

bit[2] past of **BITE**.

bitch NOUN **1** a female dog. **2** [INFORMAL] a spiteful woman; something difficult or unpleasant. VERB [INFORMAL] make spiteful comments.
bitchiness NOUN
bitchy ADJ

bite VERB (**bites**, **biting**, **bit**; PAST PARTICIPLE **bitten**) **1** cut with the teeth to eat or injure. **2** take hold on a surface. NOUN **1** an act of biting; a wound made by this. **2** a small meal.

biting ADJ causing a smarting pain; sharply critical.

bitter ADJ **1** tasting sharp or sour, not sweet. **2** resentful. **3** very distressing. **4** piercingly cold. NOUN beer which is flavoured with hops and is slightly bitter.
bitterly ADV
bitterness NOUN

bittern NOUN a marsh bird.

bitty ADJ (**bittier**, **bittiest**) lacking unity, disconnected.

bitumen NOUN a black substance made from petroleum, used for covering roads and roofs.
bituminous ADJ

bivalve NOUN a shellfish with a hinged double shell.

bivouac /**bi**-voo-ak/ NOUN a temporary camp without tents or other cover. VERB (**bivouacks**, **bivouacking**, **bivouacked**) camp in a bivouac.

bizarre ADJ strikingly odd in appearance or effect.

blab VERB (**blabs**, **blabbing**, **blabbed**) talk indiscreetly.

black ADJ **1** of the very darkest colour, like coal. **2** having a dark skin. **3** (of tea or coffee) without milk. **4** gloomy; hostile; evil; (of humour)

b

macabre. NOUN **1** a black colour or thing. **2** a person who has dark skin.

in the black with a credit balance, not in debt.

black out 1 lose consciousness. **2** cover windows so that no light can penetrate.

blackberry NOUN (PL **blackberries**) an edible dark berry growing on a prickly bush.

blackbird NOUN a European songbird, the male of which is black.

blackboard NOUN a dark board for writing on with chalk.

black economy NOUN (PL **black economies**) unofficial and untaxed business activity.

blacken VERB **1** make or become black. **2** damage (someone's reputation).

black eye NOUN a bruised eye.

blackguard /blag-ard/ NOUN a dishonourable man.

blackhead NOUN a small dark lump blocking a pore in the skin.

black hole NOUN a region in outer space from which matter and radiation cannot escape.

blackleg NOUN a person who works while fellow workers are on strike.

blacklist NOUN a list of people considered untrustworthy or unacceptable.

blackmail VERB extort money from (someone) by threatening to reveal compromising information. NOUN the offence of doing this.
blackmailer NOUN

black market NOUN illegal trading in officially controlled goods.

blackout NOUN a temporary loss of consciousness.

black pudding NOUN a sausage of blood and suet.

black sheep NOUN a member of a family regarded as a disgrace.

blacksmith NOUN a person who makes and repairs things in iron.

bladder NOUN **1** the sac in

which urine collects in the body. 2 an inflatable bag.

blade NOUN the flattened cutting part of a knife or sword; the flat part of an oar or propeller; a long narrow leaf of grass.

blame VERB hold responsible for a fault. NOUN responsibility for a fault.
blameless ADJ
blameworthy ADJ

blanch VERB 1 make or become white or pale. 2 immerse (vegetables) briefly in boiling water; peel (almonds) by scalding.

blancmange /blă-monj/ NOUN a jelly-like dessert made with cornflour and milk.

bland ADJ 1 lacking strong qualities and therefore uninteresting. 2 showing little emotion.
blandly ADV

blandishments PLURAL NOUN flattering or coaxing words.

blank ADJ 1 not marked or decorated. 2 showing no interest, understanding, or reaction. NOUN a blank space; a cartridge containing no bullet.

blank cheque NOUN a cheque with the amount left for the payee to fill in.

blanket NOUN a warm covering made of woollen or similar material; a thick covering mass. VERB (**blankets**, **blanketing**, **blanketed**) cover with a thick layer.

blank verse NOUN verse without rhyme.

blare VERB make a loud harsh sound. NOUN such a sound.

blarney NOUN charming and persuasive talk.

blasé /blah-zay/ ADJ unimpressed with something because of overfamiliarity.

blaspheme VERB talk irreverently about sacred things.
blasphemer NOUN
blasphemous ADJ
blasphemy NOUN

blast NOUN 1 a wave of air from an explosion; a strong gust. 2 a loud note on a whistle or horn. VERB 1 blow up with

b

explosives; (**blast off**) (of a spacecraft) take off. **2** produce a loud sound. **3** [INFORMAL] criticize severely. **4** blight, shrivel.

blatant /blay-tănt/ ADJ very obvious; shameless.
blatantly ADV

blather (also **blether**) VERB chatter foolishly.

blaze NOUN **1** a bright flame or fire; a bright light; an outburst or display. **2** a white mark on an animal's face; a mark chipped in the bark of a tree to mark a route. VERB burn or shine brightly.
blaze a trail mark out a route; pioneer.

blazer NOUN a loose-fitting jacket, especially in the colours or bearing the badge of a school, team, etc.

blazon VERB display or proclaim publicly. NOUN a description of a coat of arms.

bleach VERB whiten by sunlight or chemicals. NOUN a bleaching substance; a chemical used to sterilize sinks, drains, etc.

bleak ADJ cold and cheerless; not hopeful or encouraging.
bleakly ADV
bleakness NOUN

bleary ADJ (**blearier**, **bleariest**) (of eyes) tired and unfocused.
blearily ADV
bleariness NOUN

bleat NOUN the cry of a sheep or goat. VERB utter this cry; speak or complain feebly.

bleed VERB (**bleeds**, **bleeding**, **bled**) lose blood from the body; draw fluid from; extort money from.

bleep NOUN a short high-pitched sound. VERB make this sound, especially as a signal.
bleeper NOUN

blemish NOUN a flaw or defect. VERB spoil the appearance of.

blench VERB flinch.

blend VERB mix smoothly; mingle. NOUN a mixture.

blender NOUN an appliance for puréeing food.

bless VERB make holy; call on God to protect; (**be blessed with**) be fortunate in having.

blessed /bleṣ-id/ ADJ **1** holy and protected by God. **2** bringing welcome pleasure and relief.
blessedly ADV

blessing NOUN **1** God's favour; a prayer for this. **2** approval, support. **3** something one is glad of.

blether variant of **BLATHER**.

blew past of **BLOW**.

blight NOUN a disease or fungus that withers plants; a malignant influence. VERB affect with blight; spoil.

blind ADJ **1** unable to see. **2** lacking discernment; not guided by reason. **3** (of a road etc.) hidden. VERB make blind; rob of judgement. NOUN a screen for a window.
bake blind bake a pastry case with no filling.
blindly ADV
blindness NOUN

blindfold NOUN a cloth used to cover the eyes and block the sight. VERB cover the eyes of (a person) with this.

blink VERB open and shut one's eyes rapidly; shine unsteadily. NOUN an act of blinking; a quick gleam.

blinker NOUN a leather piece fixed to a bridle to prevent a horse from seeing sideways. VERB obstruct the sight or understanding of.

blip NOUN **1** a slight error or deviation. **2** a short high-pitched sound; a small image on a radar screen.

bliss NOUN perfect happiness.
blissful ADJ
blissfully ADV

blister NOUN a bubble-like swelling on the skin; a raised swelling on a surface. VERB raise a blister on; be affected with blister(s).

blithe ADJ casual and carefree.
blithely ADV

blitz NOUN a sudden intensive attack; an energetic and concerted effort. VERB attack in a blitz.

blizzard NOUN a severe snowstorm.

bloat VERB swell with fat, gas, or liquid.

bloater NOUN a salted

smoked herring.

b **blob** NOUN a drop of liquid; a round mass.

bloc NOUN a group of parties or countries who combine for a purpose.

block NOUN **1** a solid flat-sided piece of a hard substance. **2** a large building divided into flats or offices; a group of buildings enclosed by roads. **3** a large quantity of related items treated as a unit. **4** an obstacle. VERB obstruct; prevent the movement or use of.

blockade NOUN the blocking of access to a place, to prevent entry of goods. VERB set up a blockade of.

blockage NOUN an obstruction.

blockbuster NOUN [INFORMAL] a very successful book or film.

blockhead NOUN [INFORMAL] a stupid person.

block letters PLURAL NOUN plain capital letters.

bloke NOUN [INFORMAL] a man.

blonde (also **blond**) ADJ fair-haired; (of hair) fair. NOUN a woman with fair hair.

blood NOUN **1** the red liquid circulating in the bodies of animals. **2** family, descent. VERB give a first taste of blood to (a hound); initiate (a person).

in cold blood deliberately and ruthlessly.

blood count NOUN the number of corpuscles in a sample of blood.

blood-curdling ADJ horrifying.

bloodhound NOUN a large dog with a keen sense of smell, formerly used in tracking.

bloodless ADJ without bloodshed.

bloodlessly ADV

bloodshed NOUN the killing or wounding of people.

bloodshot ADJ (of eyes) red from dilated veins.

blood sports PLURAL NOUN sports involving killing.

bloodstock NOUN thoroughbred horses.

bloodstream NOUN blood circulating in the body.

bloodsucker NOUN a

creature that sucks blood; [INFORMAL] a person who extorts money.

bloodthirsty ADJ eager for bloodshed.

blood vessel NOUN a tubular structure conveying blood within the body.

bloody ADJ (**bloodier**, **bloodiest**) **1** covered in blood. **2** involving much bloodshed. ADJ & ADV expressing anger; used for emphasis. VERB stain with blood.

bloody-minded ADJ [INFORMAL] deliberately uncooperative.

bloom 1 a flower. **2** youthful beauty; perfection. VERB **1** bear flowers. **2** be healthy and attractive.

bloomer NOUN **1** [INFORMAL] a blunder. **2** a long loaf with diagonal marks. **3** (**bloomers**) loose knee-length knickers.

blossom NOUN the flowers of a fruit tree. VERB produce blossom; develop and flourish.

blot NOUN a stain of ink etc.; an eyesore; a disgrace. VERB (**blots**, **blotting**, **blotted**) **1** make a blot on. **2** soak up with absorbent material. **3** (**blot out**) erase, obscure, destroy.

blotch NOUN a large irregular mark.
blotchy ADJ

blotto ADJ [INFORMAL] very drunk.

blouse NOUN a garment like a fitted shirt, worn by women.

blouson NOUN a short full jacket gathered at the waist.

blow VERB (**blows**, **blowing**, **blew**; PAST PARTICIPLE **blown**) **1** send out a current of air or breath; move as a current of air; carry on air or breath. **2** break open with explosives. **3** play (a wind instrument). **4** use air to shape (glass). **5** (of a fuse) burn out. **6** [INFORMAL] spend, squander. **7** [INFORMAL] bungle; waste (an opportunity). NOUN **1** a wind; an act of blowing. **2** a stroke with the hand or a weapon; a shock, disappointment, or setback.

b

blow up **1** explode; shatter. **2** inflate; enlarge; exaggerate. **3** [INFORMAL] lose one's temper.

blowfly NOUN (PL **blowflies**) a fly that lays its eggs on meat.

blowout NOUN a release of air or gas from a tyre, oil well, etc.

blowpipe NOUN a tube through which an arrow or dart is blown.

blowsy /blow-zi/ (also **blowzy**) ADJ (**blowsier**, **blowsiest**) (of a woman) plump and untidy.

blowtorch (also **blowlamp**) NOUN a portable burner with a very hot flame for removing old paint.

blowy ADJ (**blowier**, **blowiest**) windy.

blub VERB (**blubs**, **blubbing**, **blubbed**) [INFORMAL] sob.

blubber NOUN whale fat. VERB [INFORMAL] sob noisily.

bludgeon NOUN a heavy stick used as a weapon. VERB strike with a bludgeon; compel forcefully.

blue ADJ **1** of the colour of the sky on a sunny day. **2** [INFORMAL] unhappy. **3** [INFORMAL] indecent. NOUN **1** a blue colour or thing. **2** (**blues**) melancholy jazz melodies; a state of depression. VERB [INFORMAL] spend (money) recklessly.
out of the blue unexpectedly.
bluish ADJ

bluebell NOUN a plant with blue bell-shaped flowers.

blue-blooded ADJ of aristocratic descent.

bluebottle NOUN a large fly with a metallic blue body.

blueprint NOUN a design plan; a model.

bluestocking NOUN a serious intellectual woman.

bluff VERB pretend; deceive. NOUN **1** an act of bluffing. **2** a broad steep cliff or headland. ADJ **1** with a broad steep front. **2** frank and direct.

blunder VERB move clumsily and uncertainly; make a mistake. NOUN a stupid mistake.

blunderbuss NOUN an old type of gun firing many

balls at one shot.

blunt ADJ **1** without a sharp edge or point. **2** speaking or expressed plainly. VERB make or become blunt.
bluntly ADV
bluntness NOUN

blur NOUN something perceived indistinctly. VERB (**blurs**, **blurring**, **blurred**) make or become indistinct.

blurb NOUN a written description promoting something.

blurt VERB say suddenly and without thinking.

blush VERB become red-faced from shame or embarrassment. NOUN an instance of blushing; a pink tinge.

blusher NOUN a cosmetic giving a rosy colour to cheeks.

bluster VERB **1** blow in gusts. **2** make aggressive but empty threats. NOUN blustering talk.
blustery ADJ

BMA ABBREV British Medical Association.

BO ABBREV body odour.

boa /boh-ă/ NOUN a large snake that winds itself around and crushes its prey.

boar NOUN a wild pig; a male pig.

board NOUN **1** a long piece of sawn wood; a flat piece of wood or stiff material. **2** daily meals supplied in return for payment or services. **3** a committee. VERB **1** get on (a ship, aircraft, etc.). **2** receive accommodation and meals for payment. **3** cover or block with boards.
go by the board (of a plan) be abandoned. **on board** on or in a ship, aircraft, or other vehicle.

boarder NOUN a person who boards with someone; a resident pupil.

boarding house NOUN a house at which board and lodging can be obtained for payment.

boarding school NOUN a school where pupils live during term time.

boardroom NOUN a room where a board of directors meets.

boast VERB **1** talk with pride about one's

b

achievements or possessions. **2** possess (a desirable feature). NOUN a boastful statement; a thing one is proud of.
boastful ADJ
boastfully ADV
boastfulness NOUN

boat NOUN a vehicle for travelling on water. **burn one's boats** do something irreversible. **push the boat out** be extravagant. **rock the boat** destabilize a situation.

boater NOUN a flat-topped straw hat.

boatman NOUN a man who hires out boats or provides transport by boat.

boatswain /boh-sŭn/ (also **bosun**, **bo'sun**) NOUN a ship's officer in charge of rigging, boats, etc.

bob VERB (**bobs**, **bobbing**, **bobbed**) move quickly up and down; curtsy briefly. NOUN **1** a bobbing movement. **2** a hairstyle in which the hair is cut at an even length all round.

bobbin NOUN a small spool holding thread or wire in a machine.

bobble NOUN a small woolly ball as an ornament.

bobsleigh NOUN a mechanically steered sledge with two sets of runners.

bode VERB be a portent of, foreshadow.

bodice NOUN the part of a dress from shoulder to waist; an undergarment for this part of the body.

bodily ADJ of the body; physical, material. ADV **1** by taking hold of the body. **2** in one mass or whole.

body NOUN (PL **bodies**) **1** the physical form of a person or animal. **2** a corpse. **3** the main part of something. **4** a collection; a group. **5** a distinct object.

body blow NOUN a severe setback.

bodyguard NOUN a personal guard for an important person.

bodywork NOUN the outer shell of a motor vehicle.

Boer NOUN a member of the Dutch people who

settled in South Africa.

boffin NOUN [INFORMAL] a person engaged in scientific research.

bog NOUN an area of soft, permanently wet ground. VERB (**bogs**, **bogging**, **bogged**) (**bog down**) make or become stuck and unable to progress.
bogginess NOUN
boggy ADJ

bogey NOUN (PL **bogeys**) **1** [GOLF] a score of one stroke over par at a hole. **2** (also **bogy**) something causing fear.

boggle VERB be amazed or alarmed.

bogus ADJ false.

bohemian ADJ socially unconventional.

boil VERB bubble up with heat; heat (liquid) until it does this; cook in boiling water. NOUN an inflamed swelling producing pus.

boiler NOUN a container in which water is heated.

boiler suit NOUN a pair of overalls worn for rough work.

boisterous ADJ cheerfully noisy or rough.
boisterously ADV

bold ADJ **1** confident and courageous. **2** (of a colour or design) strong and vivid.
boldly ADV
boldness NOUN

bole NOUN the trunk of a tree.

bolero /bo-**lair**-oh/ NOUN (PL **boleros**) **1** a Spanish dance. **2** a woman's short jacket with no fastening.

boll NOUN a round seed capsule of cotton, flax, etc.

bollard NOUN a short thick post.

bollocks [VULGAR SLANG] PLURAL NOUN testicles. EXCLAMATION rubbish, nonsense.

boloney variant of **BALONEY**.

bolshie (also **bolshy**) ADJ [INFORMAL] deliberately uncooperative.

bolster NOUN a long pad placed under a pillow. VERB support, prop.

bolt NOUN **1** a sliding bar for fastening a door; a strong metal pin used with a nut to hold things together. **2** a shaft of lightning. **3** a roll of

b

cloth. **4** an arrow from a crossbow. VERB **1** fasten with a bolt. **2** run away. **3** gulp (food) hastily.

bolt hole NOUN a place into which one can escape.

bomb NOUN a case of explosive or incendiary material to be set off by impact or a timing device. VERB **1** attack with bombs. **2** [INFORMAL] move quickly. **3** [INFORMAL] be a failure.
cost a bomb [INFORMAL] be very expensive.

bombard VERB attack with artillery; attack with questions etc.
bombardment NOUN

bombardier NOUN a rank of non-commissioned officer in an artillery regiment.

bombastic ADJ using pompous words.
bombast NOUN

bomber NOUN an aircraft that carries and drops bombs; a person who places bombs.

bombshell NOUN a great shock.

bona fide /boh-nă fy-di/ ADJ genuine.

bonanza NOUN a sudden increase in wealth or luck.

bond NOUN **1** something that unites or restrains; a binding agreement; an emotional link. **2** a document issued by a government or public company acknowledging that money has been lent to it and will be repaid with interest. VERB join with a bond; feel connected.

bondage NOUN slavery, captivity.

bone NOUN each of the hard parts making up the vertebrate skeleton. VERB remove bones from.
bone up on [INFORMAL] study intensively.

bonfire NOUN a fire built in the open air.

bongo NOUN (PL **bongos** or **bongoes**) each of a pair of small drums played with the fingers.

bonhomie /bon-ŏ-mi/ NOUN cheerful friendliness.

bonk VERB **1** make an abrupt thudding sound; bump. **2** [INFORMAL] have sexual intercourse. NOUN **1** a thudding sound. **2** [INFORMAL] an act of sexual intercourse.

bonnet NOUN **1** a hat with strings that tie under the chin. **2** a hinged cover over the engine of a motor vehicle.

bonny ADJ (**bonnier**, **bonniest**) [SCOTTISH] & [NORTHERN ENGLISH] attractive and healthy looking.

bonsai NOUN the art of growing trees as ornamental miniatures.

bonus NOUN an extra payment or benefit.

bon voyage /bon vwa-yah*zh*/ EXCLAMATION an expression of good wishes to a person starting a journey.

bony ADJ (**bonier**, **boniest**) like bones; having many bones; so thin that the bones show.

boo EXCLAMATION an exclamation of disapproval; an exclamation to startle someone. VERB say or shout 'boo' to.

boob [INFORMAL] NOUN **1** a blunder. **2** a woman's breast. VERB make an embarrassing mistake.

booby NOUN (PL **boobies**) a foolish person.

booby prize NOUN a prize given to a competitor with the lowest score.

booby trap NOUN a disguised bomb; a trap set as a practical joke.

boogie VERB (**boogies**, **boogieing**, **boogied**) dance to fast rock or pop music.

book NOUN **1** a written or printed work set out on pages that are bound together in a cover; a main division of a literary work. **2** a record of bets made. VERB **1** reserve, buy, or engage in advance. **2** record details of (an offender).

bookcase NOUN a piece of furniture with shelves for books.

bookie NOUN [INFORMAL] a bookmaker.

bookkeeping NOUN the systematic recording of business transactions.

booklet NOUN a small thin book.

bookmaker NOUN a

person whose business is the taking of bets.

bookmark NOUN a strip of paper etc. to mark a place in a book.

bookworm NOUN **1** [INFORMAL] a person fond of reading. **2** a grub that eats holes in books.

boom VERB **1** make a deep resonant sound. **2** have a period of prosperity. NOUN **1** a booming sound. **2** a period of prosperity. **3** a pivoted beam at the foot of a sail; a pole carrying a microphone or film camera. **4** a floating barrier.

boomerang NOUN an Australian missile of curved wood that can be thrown so as to return to the thrower.

boon NOUN a benefit.

boor NOUN an ill-mannered person.
boorish ADJ
boorishness NOUN

boost VERB improve or increase; support, encourage.
NOUN encouragement, help; an increase.

booster NOUN **1** a small supplementary dose of a vaccine. **2** a rocket giving extra speed to a spacecraft as it takes off.

boot NOUN **1** a shoe covering both foot and ankle. **2** the luggage compartment at the back of a car. **3** (**the boot**) [INFORMAL] dismissal.
VERB **1** kick. **2** start up (a computer).

bootee NOUN a baby's woollen boot.

booth NOUN a small enclosed compartment; a stall or stand.

bootleg ADJ smuggled, illicit.
bootlegger NOUN
bootlegging NOUN

booty NOUN stolen goods.

booze [INFORMAL] VERB drink alcohol. NOUN alcoholic drink.
boozer NOUN
boozy ADJ

borax NOUN a compound of boron used in detergents.

border NOUN a boundary, an edge; a flower bed round part of a garden.
VERB put or be a border to; (**border on**) come

close to being.

borderline NOUN a line marking a boundary.

bore[1] past of **BEAR**.

bore[2] VERB **1** tire by dullness. **2** make (a hole) with a revolving tool. NOUN **1** a tedious person or thing. **2** the hollow inside of a gun barrel; its diameter. **3** a hole bored. **4** a tidal wave in an estuary.
boredom NOUN

boric ADJ of boron.

born ADJ **1** existing as a result of birth. **2** naturally having a specified ability: *he's a born engineer.*

born-again ADJ having converted to Christianity.

borne past participle of **BEAR**.

boron NOUN a chemical element.

borough NOUN a town or district with rights of local government.

borrow VERB take (something needed) from someone, with the intention of returning it.
borrower NOUN

borstal NOUN a former name for a prison for young offenders.

borscht (also **borsch**) NOUN beetroot soup.

bosom NOUN the breast.

boss NOUN **1** [INFORMAL] an employer; a person in charge. **2** a projecting knob. VERB [INFORMAL] give orders to in a domineering way.

boss-eyed ADJ blind in one eye; cross-eyed.

bossy ADJ (**bossier**, **bossiest**) fond of giving orders.

bosun, **bo'sun** variants of **BOATSWAIN**.

botany NOUN the study of plants.
botanical ADJ
botanist NOUN

botch VERB do (a task) badly.

both DETERMINER & PRON two people or things regarded together; applying to each of two.

bother VERB **1** take the trouble to do something; (**bother with** or **about**) feel concern about or interest in. **2** disturb or worry. NOUN trouble and fuss; a cause of this.

bothersome ADJ

b **bottle** NOUN a narrow-necked container for liquid. VERB store in bottles; preserve in jars.

bottleneck NOUN a narrow point or junction in a road where congestion occurs.

bottom NOUN **1** the lowest part or point; the ground under a stretch of water. **2** the buttocks. ADJ lowest in position, rank, or degree.
bottomless ADJ

botulism NOUN poisoning caused by bacteria in food.

bougainvillea /boo-gĕn-vi-lee-ă/ NOUN a tropical shrub with large red or purple bracts.

bough NOUN a main branch of a tree.

bought past & past participle of **BUY**.

bouillon /boo-yawn/ NOUN a stock or thin clear soup.

boulder NOUN a large rounded stone.

boulevard NOUN a wide street.

bounce VERB **1** move quickly up or away from a surface after hitting it; move up and down; move in a light, lively manner. **2** [INFORMAL] (of a cheque) be sent back by a bank as worthless. NOUN an instance of bouncing; a bouncing movement; resilience, liveliness.

bouncer NOUN a person employed to eject or bar troublemakers from a club etc.

bound[1] past and past participle of **BIND**.

bound[2] VERB **1** run with a leaping movement. **2** form the boundary of. **3** (**be bound to**) be certain to. NOUN **1** a leap. **2** a boundary; a limitation. ADJ heading in a specified direction.
out of bounds outside where one is permitted to be.

boundary NOUN (PL **boundaries**) the limit of an area or the line marking it; a hit to the boundary in cricket.

boundless ADJ unlimited.

bountiful ADJ giving generously; abundant.
bountifully ADV

bounty NOUN (PL **bounties**)

generosity; a generous gift.
bounteous ADJ

bouquet /boo-**kay**/ NOUN **1** a bunch of flowers. **2** the scent of a wine or perfume.

bouquet garni /boo-kay gar-ni/ NOUN (PL **bouquets garnis**) a bunch of herbs for flavouring stews etc.

bourbon /**ber**-bŏn/ NOUN an American whisky made from maize and rye.

bourgeois /**boor**-*zh*wah/ ADJ conventionally middle class.

bourgeoisie /boor-*zh*wah-**zi**/ NOUN the bourgeois class.

bout NOUN **1** a period of exercise, work, or illness. **2** a boxing contest.

boutique NOUN a small shop selling fashionable clothes.

bovine ADJ **1** relating to cattle or oxen. **2** dull and stupid.

bow¹ /boh/ NOUN **1** a weapon for shooting arrows. **2** a rod with horsehair stretched between its ends, for playing a violin etc. **3** a knot with two loops, for fastening or decoration.

bow² /bow/ NOUN an inclination of the head or body in greeting, respect, etc. VERB bend in this way; cause to bend downwards under weight; submit.

bow³ /bow/ NOUN the front end of a boat or ship.

bowdlerize (also **bowdlerise**) VERB remove sections considered improper from (a book etc.).
bowdlerization NOUN

bowel NOUN the intestines; (**bowels**) the innermost parts.

bower NOUN a leafy shelter.

bowl NOUN **1** a round, deep dish for food or liquid; the hollow rounded part of a spoon etc. **2** a heavy ball weighted to roll in a curve; (**bowls**) a game played with such balls; a ball used in skittles. VERB **1** send rolling along the ground; go fast and smoothly. **2** send a ball to a batsman; dismiss (a batsman) by knocking bails off with the ball.

b

3 (**bowl over**) knock down; overwhelm with surprise or emotion.

bowler NOUN **1** a person who bowls in cricket; a person who plays bowls or takes part in bowling. **2** (in full **bowler hat**) a hard felt hat with a rounded top.

bowling NOUN bowls, skittles, or a similar game.

box NOUN **1** a container with a flat base and sides, usually square and with a lid; a space enclosed by straight lines on a page or screen; a compartment at a theatre; [INFORMAL] television. **2** a facility at a newspaper office or post office for receiving replies to an advertisement or letters. **3** a small evergreen shrub; its wood. VERB **1** put into a box. **2** fight with the fists as a sport.
boxing NOUN

boxer NOUN **1** a person who engages in the sport of boxing. **2** a dog of a breed resembling a bulldog.

boxer shorts PLURAL NOUN men's loose underpants like shorts.

box office NOUN an office for booking seats at a theatre etc.

boxroom NOUN a small spare room.

boy NOUN a male child.
boyhood NOUN
boyish ADJ

boycott VERB refuse to deal with or trade with. NOUN an act of boycotting.

boyfriend NOUN a person's regular male companion or lover.

bra NOUN a woman's undergarment worn to support the breasts.

brace NOUN **1** a device that holds things together or in position; (**braces**) straps to keep trousers up, passing over the shoulders; a wire device worn in the mouth to straighten the teeth. **2** a pair. VERB give support or firmness to.

bracelet NOUN an ornamental band or chain worn on the arm.

bracing ADJ invigorating.

bracken NOUN a large fern.

bracket NOUN **1** any of the

marks used in pairs to enclose and separate off words or figures: (), [], {}. **2** a group or category falling within certain limits. **3** a support for a shelf or lamp, projecting from a wall. VERB enclose in brackets; group together.

brackish ADJ slightly salty.

bract NOUN a brightly coloured leaf-like part of a plant.

brag VERB (**brags**, **bragging**, **bragged**) boast.

braggart NOUN a person who brags.

Brahman (also **Brahmin**) NOUN a member of the highest Hindu caste, the priestly caste.

braid NOUN **1** a woven ornamental trimming. **2** a plait of hair. VERB **1** trim with braid. **2** plait.

Braille NOUN a system of representing letters etc. by raised dots which blind people read by touch.

brain NOUN the mass of soft grey matter in the skull, the centre of the nervous system; (also **brains**) the mind, intelligence.

brainchild NOUN a person's invention or plan.

brainstorm NOUN **1** a violent mental disturbance; a sudden mental lapse. **2** a spontaneous discussion in search of new ideas; [US] a clever idea.

brainwash VERB pressurize (someone) into changing their beliefs by means other than rational argument.

brainwave NOUN an electrical impulse in the brain; [INFORMAL] a bright idea.

brainy ADJ (**brainier**, **brainiest**) [INFORMAL] clever.

braise VERB cook slowly with little liquid in a closed container.

brake NOUN a device for reducing speed or stopping motion. VERB stop or slow by the use of this.

bramble NOUN a prickly shrub on which

blackberries grow.

b **bran** NOUN the ground inner husks of grain, sifted from flour.

branch NOUN **1** a part of a tree growing out from the trunk. **2** a division of a road, river, etc.; a subdivision of a subject; a local shop or office belonging to a large organization. VERB send out or divide into branches.

brand NOUN **1** goods of a particular make. **2** an identifying mark made on skin with hot metal. VERB mark with a brand.

brandish VERB wave, flourish.

brand new ADJ completely new.

brandy NOUN (PL **brandies**) a strong alcoholic spirit distilled from wine or fermented fruit juice.

brash ADJ aggressively self-assertive.
brashly ADV
brashness NOUN

brass NOUN a yellow alloy of copper and zinc; musical instruments made of this; a memorial tablet made of this; [INFORMAL] money. ADJ made of brass.

brasserie /bra-sĕ-ree/ NOUN an informal licensed restaurant.

brassica NOUN a plant of the cabbage family.

brassière /bras-i-air/ NOUN a bra.

brassy ADJ (**brassier, brassiest**) **1** like brass. **2** bold and vulgar.
brassiness NOUN

brat NOUN [INFORMAL] a badly behaved child.

bravado NOUN a show of boldness.

brave ADJ able to face and endure danger or pain. VERB face and endure bravely. NOUN [DATED] an American Indian warrior.
bravely ADV
bravery NOUN

bravo EXCLAMATION well done!

bravura NOUN brilliant style and technique in performing.

brawl NOUN a noisy quarrel or fight. VERB take part in a brawl.

brawn NOUN **1** muscular strength. **2** pressed meat

from a pig's or calf's head.

brawny ADJ (**brawnier**, **brawniest**) muscular.

bray NOUN a donkey's cry; a harsh, loud sound. VERB make this cry or sound.

brazen ADJ **1** shameless, impudent. **2** [LITERARY] made of brass. VERB (**brazen it out**) behave (after doing wrong) as if unashamed.
brazenly ADV

brazier NOUN a basket-like stand for holding burning coals.

breach NOUN **1** failure to observe a rule or contract. **2** separation, estrangement. **3** a gap in a defence. VERB break through; make a breach in.

bread NOUN food made of baked dough of flour and liquid, usually leavened by yeast.

breadline NOUN (**on the breadline**) living in extreme poverty.

breadth NOUN width, broadness.

breadwinner NOUN the member of a family who earns money to support the others.

break VERB (**breaks**, **breaking**, **broke**; PAST PARTICIPLE **broken**) **1** separate or cause to separate as a result of a blow or strain; suffer a fracture in (a limb); interrupt (a sequence or habit). **2** fail to keep (a promise or law). **3** crush, defeat. **4** reveal (bad news). **5** surpass (a record). **6** (of a wave) fall on the shore. **7** (of a boy's voice) deepen at puberty. **8** (of the weather) change for the worse. NOUN **1** a gap; an interruption of continuity; a rest, a holiday. **2** a fracture. **3** a sudden dash. **4** [INFORMAL] an opportunity. **5** points scored consecutively in snooker.
break down 1 cease to function; collapse; give way to emotion. **2** analyse, separate. **break even** have equal profits and costs. **break in 1** force entry. **2** accustom a horse to being ridden.
breakable ADJ

b

breakage NOUN the action of breaking; something broken.

breakdown NOUN **1** a mechanical failure; a collapse of health or mental stability. **2** an analysis.

breaker NOUN a heavy ocean wave that breaks on the coast.

breakfast NOUN the first meal of the day.

breakneck ADJ dangerously fast.

breakthrough NOUN a sudden major advance in an undertaking.

breakwater NOUN a wall built out into the sea to break the force of waves.

breast NOUN the upper front part of the body; either of the two milk-producing organs on a woman's chest. VERB move forwards against or through; reach the top of (a hill).

breastbone NOUN the bone down the upper front of the body.

breaststroke NOUN a swimming stroke performed on one's front with circular arm and leg movements.

breath NOUN air drawn into and sent out of the lungs in breathing; a slight movement of wind.
hold one's breath temporarily cease breathing; be in suspense. **out of breath** panting after exercise. **under one's breath** in a whisper.
breathy ADJ

breathalyser ([US] [TRADE MARK] **Breathalyzer**) NOUN a device measuring the alcohol in a person's breath.
breathalyse VERB ([US] **breathalyze**)

breathe VERB draw (air) into the lungs and send it out again.

breather NOUN a pause for rest; a short period in fresh air.

breathless ADJ out of breath.

breathtaking ADJ amazing.

bred past and past participle of **BREED**.

breech NOUN the back part

of a gun barrel, where it opens.

breeches PLURAL NOUN trousers reaching to just below the knees.

breed VERB (**breeds**, **breeding**, **bred**) produce offspring; control the mating of (animals) to produce young with particular qualities; train, rear; give rise to. NOUN a variety of animals within a species; a sort.
breeder NOUN

breeding NOUN good manners resulting from training or background.

breeze NOUN a light wind.
breezy ADJ

breeze block NOUN a lightweight building block.

brethren PLURAL NOUN [ARCHAIC] brothers.

Breton NOUN a person from Brittany; the language of Brittany.

breve NOUN **1** a mark (˘) over a short vowel. **2** (in music) a long note.

breviary NOUN (PL **breviaries**) a book of prayers to be said by Roman Catholic priests.

brevity NOUN briefness; conciseness.

brew VERB **1** make (beer) by boiling and fermentation; make (tea) by infusion. **2** (of an unpleasant situation) begin to develop. NOUN a liquid or amount brewed.

brewer NOUN a person whose trade is brewing beer.

brewery NOUN (PL **breweries**) a place where beer is made commercially.

briar (also **brier**) NOUN a thorny bush, especially a wild rose.

bribe VERB pay (someone) to act in one's favour; offer gifts as an inducement. NOUN something offered in an attempt to bribe.
bribery NOUN

bric-a-brac NOUN odd items of ornaments, furniture, etc.

brick NOUN a block of baked or dried clay used to build walls; a rectangular block.
VERB block with a brick structure.

b

brickbat NOUN a missile hurled at someone; a criticism.

bricklayer NOUN a person who builds structures with bricks.

bridal ADJ of a bride or wedding.

bride NOUN a woman on her wedding day or when newly married.

bridegroom NOUN a man on his wedding day or when newly married.

bridesmaid NOUN a girl or unmarried woman attending a bride.

bridge NOUN **1** a structure providing a way over a river, road, etc.; a connection between two points or groups. **2** the captain's platform on a ship. **3** the bony upper part of the nose. **4** a card game developed from whist. VERB make or be a bridge over.

bridgehead NOUN a fortified area established in enemy territory, especially on the far side of a river.

bridgework NOUN a dental structure covering a gap.

bridle NOUN a harness on a horse's head. VERB **1** put a bridle on; restrain. **2** draw up one's head in pride or scorn.

bridle path (also **bridleway**) NOUN a path for riders or walkers.

brief ADJ lasting only for a short time; concise; short. NOUN a set of instructions and information, especially to a barrister about a case. VERB inform or instruct in advance.
briefly ADV
briefness NOUN

briefcase NOUN a case for carrying documents.

briefs PLURAL NOUN short pants or knickers.

brier variant of **BRIAR**.

brig NOUN a square-rigged sailing vessel with two masts.

brigade NOUN an army unit forming part of a division; [INFORMAL] a group with a shared purpose or interest.

brigadier NOUN an officer commanding a brigade or of similar status.

brigand NOUN a member of

a band of robbers.

bright ADJ **1** giving out or reflecting much light; shining. **2** clever. **3** cheerful; encouraging.
brightly ADV
brightness NOUN

brighten VERB make or become brighter.

brilliant ADJ **1** very bright, sparkling. **2** very clever. NOUN a cut diamond with many facets.
brilliance NOUN
brilliantly ADV

brim NOUN the edge of a cup or hollow; the projecting edge of a hat. VERB (**brims**, **brimming**, **brimmed**) be full to the brim.

brimstone NOUN [ARCHAIC] sulphur.

brindled ADJ brown with streaks of another colour.

brine NOUN salt water.

bring VERB (**brings**, **bringing**, **brought**) cause to come or move in a particular direction; accompany; cause to be in a particular state. **bring about** cause to happen. **bring off** achieve. **bring on** cause. **bring oneself** force oneself to do something. **bring out 1** produce, publish. **2** make more obvious. **bring up** look after and educate.

brink NOUN the edge of a steep place or of a stretch of water; the point just before an event or state.

brinkmanship NOUN a policy of pursuing a dangerous course to the brink of catastrophe.

briny ADJ of brine or sea water; salty. NOUN (**the briny**) [INFORMAL] the sea.

briquette /bri-ket/ NOUN a block of compressed coal dust.

brisk ADJ **1** energetic; moving quickly. **2** slightly abrupt.
briskly ADV

brisket NOUN a joint of beef from the breast.

bristle NOUN a short stiff hair; one of the stiff pieces of hair or wire in a brush. VERB (of hair) stand upright as a result of anger or fear; show indignation; be thickly set with something.

b

British ADJ of Britain or its people.

Briton NOUN a British person.

brittle ADJ hard but easily broken.
brittleness NOUN

broach VERB **1** raise (a subject) for discussion. **2** open, pierce.

broad ADJ **1** wide, large from side to side; extensive, inclusive. **2** in general terms; not precise or detailed. **3** (of humour) rather coarse. **4** (of an accent) strong.

broadcast VERB (**broadcasts**, **broadcasting**, **broadcast**; PAST PARTICIPLE **broadcast** or **broadcasted**) **1** send out by radio or television; make generally known. **2** sow (seed) by scattering. NOUN a broadcast programme.
broadcaster NOUN

broaden VERB make or become broader.

broadly ADV in general; with few exceptions.

broad-minded ADJ not easily shocked.

broadsheet NOUN a large-sized, serious newspaper.

broadside NOUN the firing of all guns on one side of a ship; a strongly worded criticism.

brocade NOUN a fabric woven with raised patterns.

broccoli NOUN a vegetable with tightly-packed green or purple flower heads.

brochure /**broh**-shewr/ NOUN a booklet or leaflet giving information.

broderie anglaise /broh-dĕ-ri **ong**-layz/ NOUN open embroidery on white cotton or linen.

brogue NOUN **1** a strong shoe with ornamental perforated bands. **2** a strong regional accent.

broil VERB grill (meat etc.).

broiler NOUN a chicken suitable for broiling.

broke past of **BREAK**. ADJ [INFORMAL] having spent all one's money; bankrupt.

broken past participle of **BREAK**. ADJ (of a language) badly spoken by a foreigner.

broken-hearted ADJ overwhelmed with grief.

broker NOUN an agent who

buys and sells on behalf of others. VERB arrange, negotiate (a deal).

brolly NOUN (PL **brollies**) [INFORMAL] an umbrella.

bromide NOUN a compound used to calm nerves.

bromine NOUN a dark red poisonous liquid element.

bronchial ADJ relating to the branched tubes into which the windpipe divides.

bronchitis NOUN inflammation of the bronchial tubes.

bronco NOUN (PL **broncos**) a wild or half-tamed horse of the western US.

brontosaurus NOUN a large plant-eating dinosaur.

bronze NOUN an alloy of copper and tin; something made of this; its colour. VERB make suntanned.

brooch /brohch/ NOUN an ornament fastened to clothing with a hinged clasp.

brood NOUN young produced at one hatching or birth; a family. VERB **1** sit on (eggs) and hatch them. **2** think long, deeply, and with sadness or regret.

broody ADJ (**broodier**, **broodiest**) **1** (of a hen) wanting to brood; [INFORMAL] (of a woman) wanting children. **2** thoughtful and unhappy.

brook NOUN a small stream. VERB [FORMAL] tolerate, allow.

broom NOUN **1** a long-handled brush. **2** a shrub with yellow flowers.

broomstick NOUN the handle of a broom.

Bros. ABBREV Brothers.

broth NOUN a stock or thin soup.

brothel NOUN a house where people pay to have sex with prostitutes.

brother NOUN **1** a man or boy in relation to other children of his parents. **2** a male colleague or friend. **3** a male fellow Christian or member of a religious order.
brotherly ADJ

brotherhood NOUN the

b

relationship of brothers; comradeship; an association with a common interest.

brother-in-law NOUN (PL **brothers-in-law**) the brother of one's husband or wife; the husband of one's sister.

brought past and past participle of **BRING**.

brow NOUN **1** an eyebrow; a forehead. **2** the summit of a hill.

browbeat VERB (**browbeats**, **browbeating**, **browbeat**; PAST PARTICIPLE **browbeaten**) intimidate.

brown ADJ of a colour between orange and black, like earth or wood. NOUN a brown colour or thing. VERB **1** make or become brown. **2** (**be browned off**) [INFORMAL] be irritated or depressed.

browse VERB **1** look around casually; read or scan superficially. **2** (of an animal) feed on leaves or grass.

bruise NOUN an injury that discolours skin without breaking it. VERB cause a bruise on.

bruiser NOUN [INFORMAL] a tough aggressive person.

brunch NOUN a meal combining breakfast and lunch.

brunette NOUN a woman with brown hair.

brunt NOUN the chief impact of something bad.

brush NOUN **1** an implement for smoothing hair, painting, etc., consisting of bristles set into a block; an act of using this; a light touch. **2** a fox's tail. **3** a dangerous or unpleasant encounter. **4** undergrowth. VERB clean or arrange with a brush; touch lightly in passing. **brush aside** dismiss. **brush off** reject, snub. **brush up** improve one's knowledge.

brushwood NOUN undergrowth; cut or broken twigs.

brusque /broosk/ ADJ curt and offhand.

Brussels sprout NOUN the edible bud of a kind of cabbage.

brutal ADJ cruel, without mercy.
brutality NOUN
brutally ADV

brutalize (also **brutalise**) VERB make brutal; treat brutally.

brute NOUN **1** an animal. **2** a brutal person; [INFORMAL] an unpleasant person or thing. ADJ without reason; merely physical.
brutish ADJ

BS ABBREV British Standard(s).

BSc ABBREV Bachelor of Science.

BSE ABBREV bovine spongiform encephalopathy, a fatal brain disease in cattle.

BSI ABBREV British Standards Institution.

BST ABBREV British Summer Time.

bubble NOUN a thin sphere of liquid enclosing air or gas; an air-filled cavity. VERB **1** rise in bubbles; contain bubbles. **2** show great liveliness.
bubbly ADJ

bubonic plague NOUN a plague characterized by swollen lymph nodes in the armpit or groin.

buccaneer NOUN a pirate; an adventurer.

buck NOUN **1** the male of a deer, hare, or rabbit. **2** an article placed before the dealer in a game of poker. **3** [US] & [AUSTRALIAN] a dollar. VERB **1** (of a horse) jump with the back arched. **2** [INFORMAL] resist, oppose, or reverse.
buck up 1 cheer up. **2** hurry. **pass the buck** shift the responsibility (and possible blame).

bucket NOUN an open container with a handle, for carrying liquid; (**buckets**) [INFORMAL] a large amount of liquid. VERB [INFORMAL] rain heavily.

buckle NOUN a device through which a belt or strap is threaded to secure it. VERB **1** fasten with a buckle. **2** crumple under pressure. **3** (**buckle down to**) set about doing.

buckram NOUN stiffened cloth used in binding books and in upholstery.

bucolic ADJ rustic.

bud NOUN a leaf or flower

b

that is not yet open. VERB (**buds, budding, budded**) produce buds; begin to develop.

Buddhism NOUN an Asian religion based on the teachings of Buddha.
Buddhist ADJ & NOUN

budding ADJ beginning to develop or be successful.

buddleia NOUN a tree or shrub with purple or yellow flowers.

buddy NOUN (PL **buddies**) [US] [INFORMAL] a friend.

budge VERB move slightly.

budgerigar NOUN an Australian parakeet often kept as a pet.

budget NOUN a plan of income and expenditure; the amount of money someone has available. VERB allow or provide for in a budget.

budgie NOUN [INFORMAL] a budgerigar.

buff NOUN **1** a fawn colour. **2** [INFORMAL] an expert and enthusiast. VERB polish with soft material.
in the buff [INFORMAL] naked.

buffalo NOUN (PL **buffaloes** or **buffalo**) a wild ox; a North American bison.

buffer NOUN **1** a shock absorber at the end of a railway line or on a vehicle. **2** something that lessens the effect of impact.

buffet[1] /**buuf**-ay/ NOUN a meal where guests serve themselves; a counter where food and drink are served.

buffet[2] /**buff**-it/ VERB strike repeatedly.

buffoon NOUN a person who plays the fool.
buffoonery NOUN

bug NOUN **1** a small insect; [INFORMAL] a micro-organism causing illness; [INFORMAL] an infection; [INFORMAL] a fault in a computer system. **2** [INFORMAL] a hidden microphone. VERB (**bugs, bugging, bugged**) [INFORMAL] **1** install a hidden microphone in. **2** annoy.

bugbear NOUN something feared or disliked.

bugger [VULGAR SLANG] EXCLAMATION damn. NOUN **1** an unpleasant person or thing; a person of a specified type. **2** a person who commits buggery.

buggery NOUN anal intercourse.

buggy NOUN (PL **buggies**) a small light vehicle; a lightweight folding pushchair.

bugle NOUN a brass instrument like a small trumpet.
bugler NOUN

build VERB (**builds**, **building**, **built**) **1** construct by putting parts or material together. **2** (**build up**) establish gradually; increase. NOUN bodily shape.
builder NOUN

building NOUN a structure with a roof and walls.

building society NOUN a financial organization that pays interest on people's investments and lends money for mortgages.

bulb NOUN the rounded base of the stem of certain plants; something shaped like this; the glass part giving light in an electric lamp.
bulbous ADJ

bulge NOUN a rounded swelling. VERB form a bulge, swell.

bulimia (in full **bulimia nervosa**) NOUN an eating disorder marked by bouts of overeating followed by vomiting and fasting.
bulimic ADJ

bulk NOUN mass; something large and heavy; the majority. VERB be or seem large or important; increase the size of.

bulkhead NOUN a partition in a ship etc.

bulky ADJ (**bulkier**, **bulkiest**) taking up much space.

bull NOUN **1** the male of the ox, whale, elephant, etc. **2** the bullseye of a target. **3** a pope's official edict. **4** [INFORMAL] nonsense.

bulldog NOUN a powerful dog with a short thick neck.

bulldozer NOUN a powerful tractor with a device for clearing ground.

bullet NOUN **1** a small missile fired from a rifle or revolver. **2** a small solid circle printed before each item in a list.

b **bulletin** NOUN a short official statement of news.

bullfighting NOUN the sport of baiting and killing bulls.
bullfight NOUN

bullion NOUN gold or silver in bulk or bars.

bullock NOUN a castrated bull.

bullseye NOUN the centre of a target.

bullshit NOUN [VULGAR SLANG] nonsense.

bully NOUN (PL **bullies**) a person who hurts or intimidates others who are weaker. VERB (**bullies**, **bullying**, **bullied**) behave as a bully towards.

bulrush NOUN a rush with a velvety head.

bulwark NOUN **1** a defensive wall; a defence. **2** the part of a ship's side extending above deck level.

bum NOUN [INFORMAL] **1** the buttocks. **2** a tramp; an idler.

bumble VERB move or act clumsily or incompetently.

bumblebee NOUN a large bee.

bumf (also **bumph**) NOUN [INFORMAL] documents, papers.

bump VERB **1** knock or collide with. **2** proceed with a jolting movement. NOUN **1** a knock or collision; the dull sound of this. **2** a swelling; a raised area on a surface. **3** a jolt.
bumpy ADJ

bumper NOUN a horizontal bar at the front or back of a motor vehicle to lessen the damage in a collision. ADJ unusually large or successful.

bumpkin NOUN a country person with awkward manners.

bumptious ADJ conceited.

bun NOUN **1** a small cake or bread roll. **2** a coil of hair held at the back of the head.

bunch NOUN a number of things grouped or held together. VERB form or be formed into a bunch.

bundle NOUN **1** a collection of things loosely held or wrapped together.

2 [INFORMAL] a large amount of money. VERB **1** make into a bundle. **2** move or push hurriedly.

bung NOUN a stopper for a jar or barrel. VERB **1** block, close. **2** [INFORMAL] throw, put.

bungalow NOUN a house with only one storey.

bungee jumping NOUN the sport of jumping from a height while attached to an elasticated rope (a **bungee**).

bungle VERB spoil through lack of skill; mismanage. NOUN a bungled attempt. **bungler** NOUN

bunion NOUN a painful swelling at the base of the big toe.

bunk NOUN a shelf-like bed. **do a bunk** [INFORMAL] run away.

bunker NOUN **1** a container for fuel. **2** a sandy hollow forming an obstacle on a golf course. **3** a reinforced underground shelter.

bunkum NOUN [INFORMAL] nonsense.

Bunsen burner NOUN a small adjustable gas burner used in laboratories.

bunting NOUN **1** a bird related to the finches. **2** a string of decorative flags.

buoy /boy/ NOUN an anchored floating object serving as a navigation mark.
buoy up **1** keep afloat. **2** make cheerful.

buoyant /boy-ănt/ ADJ **1** able to float. **2** cheerful. **buoyancy** NOUN

bur (also **burr**) NOUN a prickly seed case that clings to fur and clothing.

burble VERB make a gentle murmuring sound; speak in a confused and rambling manner.

burden NOUN something carried; an obligation causing hardship. VERB load; oppress.

bureau /bew-roh/ NOUN (PL **bureaux** or **bureaus**) **1** a writing desk with drawers. **2** an office, a department.

bureaucracy /bew-**rok**-ră-si/ NOUN (PL **bureaucracies**) government by unelected officials; excessive

b

administration.
bureaucratic ADJ

bureaucrat NOUN a government official.

burgeon /ber-jĕn/ VERB begin to grow rapidly.

burger NOUN [INFORMAL] a hamburger.

burglar NOUN a person who breaks into a building in order to steal.
burglary NOUN
burgle VERB

burgundy NOUN (PL **burgundies**) a red wine; a deep red colour.

burial NOUN the burying of a corpse.

burlesque NOUN a mocking imitation. VERB parody.

burly ADJ (**burlier**, **burliest**) having a strong heavy body.
burliness NOUN

burn¹ VERB (**burns**, **burning**, **burned** or **burnt**) be on fire; produce heat or light; damage or destroy by fire, heat, or acid; use (fuel); feel hot and painful; feel passionate emotion. NOUN a mark or injury made by burning.

burn² NOUN [SCOTTISH] a stream.

burner NOUN a part that shapes the flame in a lamp, cooker, etc.

burning ADJ **1** intense. **2** (of an issue) keenly discussed.

burnish VERB polish by rubbing.

burnt past and past participle of **BURN**.

burp [INFORMAL] VERB make a belch. NOUN a belch.

burr NOUN **1** a whirring sound; the strong pronunciation of 'r'; a country accent using this. **2** variant of **BUR**. VERB make a whirring sound.

burrow NOUN a hole dug by an animal for shelter. VERB dig a burrow; advance by tunnelling; inquire or search thoroughly.

bursar NOUN a person who manages the finances and other business of a college or school.

bursary NOUN (PL **bursaries**) a scholarship or grant given to a student.

burst VERB (**bursts**,

bursting, **burst**) break suddenly and violently apart; force or be forced open; be very full; appear or come suddenly and forcefully; suddenly begin to do something. NOUN an instance of breaking; a brief violent or energetic outbreak; a spurt.

bury VERB (**buries**, **burying**, **buried**) put underground; place (a dead body) in the earth or a tomb; cover, conceal; involve (oneself) deeply, be absorbed.

bus NOUN (PL **buses**; [US] **busses**) a large motor vehicle for public transport by road. VERB (**buses**, **busing**, **bused** or **busses**, **bussing**, **bussed**) travel or transport by bus.

busby NOUN (PL **busbies**) a tall fur hat.

bush NOUN **1** a shrub. **2** uncultivated land or the vegetation on it; an untidy clump of hair.
beat about the bush talk without coming to the point.

bushy ADJ (**bushier**, **bushiest**) covered with bushes; growing thickly.

business NOUN **1** an occupation, profession, or trade; something that is someone's duty or concern. **2** trade, commerce; a commercial establishment. **3** [INFORMAL] a set of events, an affair.

businesslike ADJ practical, systematic, efficient.

businessman (also **businesswoman**) NOUN a person engaged in trade or commerce.

busk VERB play music in the street for donations.
busker NOUN

busman's holiday NOUN leisure time spent doing something similar to one's work.

bust NOUN a woman's chest measured around the breasts; a sculptured head, shoulders, and chest. VERB [INFORMAL] burst, break.
go bust [INFORMAL] become bankrupt.

bustle VERB make a show of activity or hurry. NOUN **1** excited activity. **2** [HISTORICAL] padding to puff out the top of a skirt at the back.

bust-up NOUN [INFORMAL] a quarrel.

busy ADJ (**busier, busiest**) having much to do; occupied; full of activity. **busily** ADV

busybody NOUN (PL **busybodies**) a meddlesome person.

but CONJ introducing contrast; however; except. PREP apart from. ADV merely, only.

butane NOUN an inflammable gas used in liquid form as fuel.

butch ADJ [INFORMAL] ostentatiously and aggressively masculine.

butcher NOUN a person who cuts up and sells animal flesh for food; a savage killer. VERB slaughter for food; kill brutally.
butchery NOUN

butler NOUN a chief manservant.

butt NOUN **1** a cask. **2** the thick end of a tool or weapon; a cigarette stub. **3** [INFORMAL] the buttocks. **4** a target for ridicule or teasing. **5** (**butts**) a shooting range. VERB **1** push with the head; (**butt in**) interrupt. **2** meet or place end to end.

butter NOUN a pale yellow fatty food substance made from milk and used as a spread. VERB **1** spread with butter. **2** (**butter up**) [INFORMAL] flatter.

buttercup NOUN a wild plant with yellow cup-shaped flowers.

butterfly NOUN (PL **butterflies**) **1** an insect with four large often brightly coloured wings. **2** a frivolous person. **3** a swimming stroke with both arms lifted at the same time.

buttermilk NOUN the liquid left after butter is churned from milk.

butterscotch NOUN a hard toffee-like sweet.

buttock NOUN either of the two fleshy rounded parts of the human body that form the bottom.

button NOUN **1** a disc or knob sewn to a garment and used as a fastener. **2** a knob pressed to operate a device. VERB fasten with buttons.

buttonhole NOUN a slit through which a button is passed to fasten clothing; a flower worn in the buttonhole of a lapel. VERB accost and detain in conversation.

buttress NOUN a support built against a wall; something that supports. VERB reinforce, prop up.

butty NOUN (PL **butties**) [INFORMAL] a sandwich.

buxom ADJ (of a woman) plump, large-breasted.

buy VERB (**buys**, **buying**, **bought**) **1** obtain in exchange for money. **2** [INFORMAL] accept as true. NOUN [INFORMAL] a purchase.
buyer NOUN

buzz NOUN **1** a vibrating humming sound; [INFORMAL] a telephone call. **2** [INFORMAL] a thrill; an exciting atmosphere. VERB **1** make a buzzing sound. **2** be full of activity; move quickly. **3** [INFORMAL] fly close to at high speed.

buzzard NOUN a large hawk.

buzzer NOUN a device that produces a buzzing sound as a signal.

buzzword NOUN [INFORMAL] a fashionable technical word.

by PREP **1** beside; near. **2** through the agency or means of. **3** not later than. **4** during. **5** indicating extent or margin: *by far the best.* **6** past; via. ADV going past.
by and by before long.
by and large on the whole.

bye[1] NOUN **1** [CRICKET] a run scored from a ball not hit by the batsman. **2** the transfer of a competitor to a higher round in the absence of an opponent.

bye[2] EXCLAMATION [INFORMAL] goodbye.

by-election NOUN an election of an MP to replace one who has died or resigned.

bygone ADJ belonging to the past.
let bygones be bygones forgive past offences.

by-law NOUN a regulation made by a local authority or corporation.

byline NOUN a line naming

the writer of a newspaper article.

bypass NOUN **1** a road taking traffic round a town. **2** an operation providing an alternative passage for blood. VERB provide with a bypass; go round, avoid.

by-product NOUN something produced incidentally while making something else.

byre NOUN a cowshed.

byroad NOUN a minor road.

bystander NOUN a person who is nearby when something happens.

byte NOUN a unit of information stored in a computer, equal to eight bits.

byway NOUN a minor road.

byword NOUN a famous or typical example; a familiar saying.

Cc

C (also **c**) NOUN (PL **Cs** or **C's**) **1** the third letter of the alphabet. **2** the Roman numeral for 100. ABBREV **1** Celsius; centigrade. **2** (**c**) cent(s). **3** (**c**) circa. **4** (**c.**) century.

cab NOUN **1** a taxi. **2** a compartment for the driver of a train, lorry, etc.

cabal /kă-**bahl**/ NOUN a group involved in a plot; a small, exclusive, influential group.

cabaret /**kab**-ă-ray/ NOUN entertainment provided in a nightclub or restaurant.

cabbage NOUN a vegetable with a round head of green or purple leaves.

cabby NOUN (PL **cabbies**) [INFORMAL] a taxi driver.

caber NOUN a roughly trimmed tree trunk thrown as a trial of strength.

cabin NOUN a compartment in a ship or aircraft; a small hut.

cabinet NOUN **1** a cupboard with drawers or shelves. **2** (**the Cabinet**) the group of ministers chosen to be responsible for government policy.

cabinetmaker NOUN a maker of high-quality furniture.

cable NOUN **1** a thick rope of fibre or wire; a set of insulated wires for carrying electricity or signals. **2** a telegram.

cable car NOUN a vehicle pulled by a moving cable, for carrying passengers up and down mountains.

cable television NOUN television transmission by cable to subscribers.

cabriolet /**kab**-ree-oh-lay/ NOUN a car with a folding top; a light two-wheeled carriage with a hood.

C

cacao NOUN the bean from which cocoa and chocolate are made.

cache /kash/ NOUN a hidden store; a hiding place. VERB store secretly.

cachet /kash-ay/ NOUN **1** prestige. **2** a distinguishing mark.

cackle NOUN the clucking of hens; chattering talk; a loud silly laugh. VERB utter a cackle.

cacophony /ka-ko-fŏ-nee/ NOUN (PL **cacophonies**) a discordant mixture of sounds.
cacophonous ADJ

cactus NOUN (PL **cacti** or **cactuses**) a fleshy plant, often with prickles, from a hot dry climate.

cad NOUN [DATED] a dishonourable man.

cadaver NOUN a corpse.

cadaverous ADJ gaunt and pale.

caddie (also **caddy**) NOUN a golfer's attendant carrying clubs. VERB act as caddie.

caddy NOUN (PL **caddies**) a small box for tea.

cadence NOUN **1** the rise and fall of the voice in speech. **2** a sequence of notes ending a musical phrase.

cadenza NOUN an elaborate passage for a solo instrument or singer.

cadet NOUN a young trainee in the armed forces or police.

cadge VERB ask for as a gift; beg.

cadmium NOUN a metallic element.

cadre /kah-drĕ/ NOUN a small group of specially trained people; an activist in a revolutionary organization.

caecum /see-kŭm/ ([US] **cecum**) NOUN (PL **caeca**) a small pouch at the first part of the large intestine.

Caesarean section ([US] **Cesarean, Cesarian**) NOUN an operation to deliver a child by an incision through the walls of the mother's abdomen and womb.

caesium /see-zi-ŭm/ ([US]

cesium) NOUN a soft metallic element.

café NOUN a small informal tea shop or restaurant.

cafeteria NOUN a self-service restaurant.

cafetière /ka-fĕ-**tyair**/ NOUN a coffee pot with a plunger to keep the ground coffee separate from the liquid.

caffeine NOUN a stimulant found in tea and coffee.

caftan variant of **KAFTAN**.

cage NOUN an enclosure of wire or with bars, especially for birds or animals. VERB confine in a cage.

cagey ADJ (**cagier**, **cagiest**) [INFORMAL] secretive, reticent.
cagily ADV
caginess NOUN

cagoule /kă-**gool**/ NOUN a light hooded waterproof jacket.

cahoots NOUN (**in cahoots with**) [INFORMAL] in league with.

caiman variant of **CAYMAN**.

cairn NOUN a mound of stones as a memorial or landmark.

cajole VERB coax.
cajolery NOUN

Cajun /**kay**-jĕn/ ADJ in the style of French Louisiana.

cake NOUN **1** a sweet food made from a baked mixture of flour, eggs, sugar, and fat. **2** a flat compact mass. VERB form a crust on.

calamine NOUN a soothing skin lotion containing zinc carbonate.

calamity NOUN (PL **calamities**) a disaster.
calamitous ADJ
calamitously ADV

calcify VERB (**calcifies**, **calcifying**, **calcified**) harden by a deposit of calcium salts.
calcification NOUN

calcium NOUN a whitish metallic element.

calculate VERB **1** reckon mathematically; estimate. **2** intend, plan.
calculation NOUN

calculating ADJ ruthlessly scheming.

calculator NOUN an electronic device for mathematical calculations.

calculus NOUN (PL

C

calculuses or **calculi**) **1** a branch of mathematics dealing with rates of variation. **2** a stone formed in the body.

caldron variant of **CAULDRON**.

Caledonian ADJ of Scotland.

calendar NOUN a chart showing dates of days of the year.

calendar year NOUN 1 January to 31 December inclusive.

calf NOUN (PL **calves**) **1** the young of cattle, elephants, whales, etc. **2** the fleshy back of the human leg below the knee.

calibrate VERB mark the units of measurement on or check the accuracy of (a gauge).
calibration NOUN

calibre ([US] **caliber**) NOUN **1** degree of quality or ability. **2** the diameter of a gun, tube, or bullet.

calico NOUN unbleached cotton cloth.

caliper (also **calliper**) NOUN **1** a metal support for a weak leg. **2** (also **calipers**) a measuring instrument with hinged legs.

caliph /kay-lif/ NOUN (formerly) a Muslim ruler.

calk variant of **CAULK**.

call VERB (**calls, calling, called**) **1** shout to someone to attract their attention; summon. **2** (of a bird) utter a characteristic cry. **3** telephone. **4** pay a visit. **5** name; describe or address in a specified way. NOUN **1** a shout; a summons. **2** a bird's cry. **3** a telephone communication. **4** a brief visit.
call off cancel. **call on** visit. **call the shots** (or **tune**) control the action.
caller NOUN

calligraphy NOUN decorative handwriting.
calligrapher NOUN

callisthenics (US **calisthenics**) PLURAL NOUN exercises to develop strength and grace.

callous ADJ feeling no pity or sympathy.
callously ADV
callousness NOUN

callow ADJ immature and inexperienced.

callus NOUN a patch of hardened skin.

calm ADJ **1** not excited or agitated. **2** not windy or disturbed by wind.
NOUN a calm condition.
VERB make calm.
calmly ADV
calmness NOUN

Calor gas NOUN [TRADE MARK] liquefied butane stored under pressure in containers.

calorie NOUN a unit of heat; a unit of the energy-producing value of food.

calorific ADJ of heat or calories.

calumniate VERB slander.

calumny NOUN (PL **calumnies**) slander.

calve VERB give birth to a calf.

Calvinism NOUN a branch of Protestantism following the teachings of John Calvin.
Calvinist NOUN

calypso NOUN (PL **calypsos**) a West Indian song with syncopated music.

calyx NOUN (PL **calyxes** or **calyces**) a ring of leaves (sepals) covering a flower bud.

cam NOUN a projecting part on a wheel or shaft changing rotary to to-and-fro motion.

camaraderie NOUN comradeship.

camber NOUN a slight convex curve given to the surface of a road.

cambric NOUN thin linen or cotton cloth.

camcorder NOUN a combined video and sound recorder.

came past of **COME**.

camel NOUN a large animal with one hump or two; its fawn colour.

camellia NOUN an evergreen flowering shrub.

cameo NOUN (PL **cameos**) **1** a piece of jewellery with a portrait carved in low relief on a background of a different colour. **2** a small part in a play or film taken by a famous actor or actress.

camera NOUN an apparatus for taking

photographs or film pictures.

camiknickers PLURAL NOUN a woman's one-piece undergarment combining camisole and knickers.

camisole NOUN a woman's bodice-like undergarment with shoulder straps.

camomile (also **chamomile**) NOUN an aromatic herb.

camouflage /ka-mĕ-flah*zh*/ NOUN concealment of an animal by means of its natural colouring; concealment by the use of special covering or clothing. VERB conceal in this way.

camp NOUN **1** a place with temporary accommodation in tents; a complex of buildings for troops, holidaymakers, or people in custody. **2** a group of people with the same ideals. VERB sleep in a tent; stay temporarily in a makeshift place. ADJ exaggeratedly effeminate.

campaign NOUN a connected series of military operations; an organized course of action to achieve a goal. VERB conduct or take part in a campaign.
campaigner NOUN

campanology NOUN the art of bell-ringing.

camp bed NOUN a portable folding bed.

camper NOUN a person who is camping; a large vehicle with beds, cooking facilities, etc.

camphor NOUN a strong-smelling white substance used in medicine and mothballs.

campsite NOUN a place for camping.

campus NOUN the grounds of a university or college.

camshaft NOUN a shaft carrying cams.

can[1] NOUN a cylindrical metal container for holding liquid or preserving food. VERB (**cans**, **canning**, **canned**) preserve in a can.

can[2] AUXILIARY VERB (**can**, **could**) be able or allowed to.

Canadian NOUN a person from Canada. ADJ relating to Canada.

canal NOUN an artificial

watercourse; a duct in the body.

canapé /kan-ă-pay/ NOUN a small piece of bread or pastry with savoury topping.

canard NOUN a false rumour.

canary NOUN (PL **canaries**) a small yellow songbird, often kept as a pet.

cancan NOUN a lively high-kicking stage dance.

cancel VERB (**cancels**, **cancelling**, **cancelled**; [US] **canceling**, **canceled**) **1** declare that (something arranged) will not take place; put an end to. **2** mark (a ticket or stamp) to prevent reuse. **3** neutralize, negate. **cancellation** NOUN

cancer NOUN a malignant tumour; a disease in which these form. **cancerous** ADJ

candela NOUN a unit measuring the brightness of light.

candelabrum (also **candelabra**) NOUN (PL **candelabra**; [US] **candelabras** or **candelabrums**) a large branched candlestick or stand for lights.

candid ADJ frank. **candidly** ADV

candidate NOUN a person applying for a job, standing for election, or taking an examination. **candidacy** NOUN **candidature** NOUN

candied ADJ encrusted or preserved in sugar.

candle NOUN a stick of wax enclosing a wick which is burnt to give light. **hold a candle to** compare or compete with.

candlestick NOUN a holder for a candle.

candour ([US] **candor**) NOUN frankness.

candy NOUN (PL **candies**) [US] sweets, a sweet.

candyfloss NOUN a fluffy mass of spun sugar.

candy-striped ADJ patterned with stripes of white and a colour.

cane NOUN a stem of a tall reed or grass; a light walking stick; a stick used for corporal punishment. VERB beat with a cane.

C

canine /kay-nyn/ ADJ of dogs. NOUN (in full **canine tooth**) a pointed tooth between the incisors and molars.

canister NOUN a small metal container.

canker NOUN a disease of animals or plants; a persistent corrupting influence.

cannabis NOUN a drug obtained from the hemp plant.

canned ADJ preserved in a can.

cannelloni PLURAL NOUN rolls of pasta with a savoury filling.

cannibal NOUN a person who eats human flesh.
cannibalism NOUN

cannibalize (also **cannibalise**) VERB use parts from (a machine) to repair another.

cannon NOUN (PL usually **cannon**) a large heavy gun formerly used in warfare; an automatic heavy gun that fires shells.

cannonade NOUN continuous gunfire.

cannot negative form of CAN².

canny ADJ (**cannier**, **canniest**) **1** shrewd. **2** [SCOTTISH] & [NORTHERN ENGLISH] pleasant, attractive.
cannily ADV

canoe NOUN a light boat propelled by paddling. VERB (**canoes**, **canoeing**, **canoed**) go in a canoe.
canoeist NOUN

canon NOUN **1** a member of the clergy in a cathedral. **2** a general rule or principle. **3** a set of writings accepted as genuine.
canonical ADJ

canonize (also **canonise**) VERB declare officially to be a saint.
canonization NOUN

canoodle VERB [INFORMAL] kiss and cuddle.

canopy NOUN (PL **canopies**) an ornamental cloth suspended or draped over a bed or throne; a roof-like covering or shelter.

cant NOUN insincere talk; jargon.

cantabile /kan-tah-bi-lay/ ADV [MUSIC] smooth and

flowing.

cantankerous ADJ bad-tempered. **cantankerously** ADV

cantata NOUN a choral composition.

canteen NOUN **1** a restaurant for employees. **2** a case of cutlery.

canter NOUN a gentle gallop. VERB go at a canter.

cantilever NOUN a projecting beam or girder supporting a structure.

canto NOUN (PL **cantos**) a division of a long poem.

canton NOUN a political division of Switzerland.

canvas NOUN a strong coarse cloth; a painting on this.

canvass VERB **1** ask for votes. **2** propose (a plan) for discussion.

canyon NOUN a deep gorge.

CAP ABBREV Common Agricultural Policy.

cap NOUN **1** a soft brimless hat, often with a peak; a headdress worn as part of a uniform; a cover or top; an upper limit. **2** an explosive device for a toy pistol. VERB (**caps**, **capping**, **capped**) put a lid on; cover; set an upper limit to; surpass.

capable ADJ **1** able or fit to do something. **2** competent, efficient. **capability** NOUN **capably** ADV

capacious ADJ roomy.

capacitance NOUN the ability to store an electric charge.

capacitor NOUN a device storing a charge of electricity.

capacity NOUN (PL **capacities**) **1** the amount that something can contain. **2** ability to do something. **3** a role or function.

caparison /kă-pa-ri-sŏn/ VERB deck out. NOUN finery.

cape NOUN **1** a short cloak. **2** a coastal promontory.

caper VERB jump about friskily. NOUN **1** a frisky movement; [INFORMAL] a foolish or illicit activity. **2** (**capers**) the pickled buds of a bramble-like shrub.

capillary NOUN (PL **capillaries**) a very fine

hair-like tube or blood vessel.

C

capillary action (also **capillarity**) NOUN the rise or fall of a liquid in a narrow tube.

capital ADJ **1** chief, very important. **2** (of a letter of the alphabet) of the kind used to begin a name or sentence. **3** involving the death penalty. NOUN **1** the chief town of a country etc. **2** a capital letter. **3** money with which a business is started. **4** the top part of a pillar.

capitalism NOUN a system in which trade and industry are controlled by private owners.

capitalist NOUN a person who invests in trade and industry; a supporter of capitalism.

capitalize (also **capitalise**) VERB **1** convert into or provide with capital; (**capitalize on**) make advantageous use of. **2** write as or with a capital letter.
capitalization NOUN

capitation NOUN a fee paid per person.

capitulate VERB surrender, yield.
capitulation NOUN

capo NOUN (PL **capos**) a device fitted across the strings of an instrument to raise their pitch.

capon /kay-pŏn/ NOUN a domestic cock castrated and fattened.

cappuccino /ka-poo-chee-noh/ NOUN (PL **cappuccinos**) coffee made with frothy steamed milk.

caprice /kă-prees/ NOUN a whim; a short lively piece of music.

capricious ADJ acting on whims; unpredictable.
capriciously ADV
capriciousness NOUN

capsicum NOUN a sweet pepper.

capsize VERB (of a boat) overturn.

capstan NOUN a revolving post or spindle on which a cable etc. winds.

capsule NOUN **1** a small soluble gelatin case enclosing medicine for swallowing. **2** a detachable compartment of a spacecraft. **3** a plant's seed case.

captain NOUN a person commanding a ship or aircraft; the leader of a group or team; a naval officer next below rear admiral; an army officer next below major. VERB be captain of.
captaincy NOUN

caption NOUN a short title or heading; an explanation for an illustration.

captious ADJ fond of finding fault.

captivate VERB capture the fancy of; charm.
captivation NOUN

captive ADJ taken prisoner; unable to escape. NOUN a captive person or animal.
captivity NOUN

captor NOUN a person who has taken a captive.

capture VERB **1** gain control of by force; take prisoner. **2** record accurately in words or pictures. **3** store (data) in a computer. NOUN the action of capturing.

car NOUN a motor vehicle for a small number of passengers; a compartment in a cable railway, lift, etc.

carafe /kă-**raf**/ NOUN a glass bottle for serving wine or water.

caramel NOUN brown syrup made from heated sugar; toffee tasting like this.
caramelize VERB (also **caramelise**)

carapace NOUN the upper shell of a tortoise.

carat NOUN a unit of purity of gold; a unit of weight for precious stones.

caravan NOUN **1** a vehicle equipped for living in, able to be towed by a horse or car. **2** a group travelling together across a desert.
caravanning NOUN

caraway NOUN a plant with spicy seeds used as flavouring.

carbine NOUN an automatic rifle.

carbohydrate NOUN an energy-producing compound (e.g. starch) in food.

carbolic NOUN a kind of disinfectant.

C

carbon NOUN a chemical element occurring as diamond, graphite, and charcoal, and in all living matter.

carbonate NOUN a compound releasing carbon dioxide when mixed with acid. VERB dissolve carbon dioxide in (a liquid).

carbon copy NOUN a copy made with carbon paper; an exact copy.

carbon dating NOUN a method of deciding the age of something by measuring the decay of radiocarbon in it.

carboniferous ADJ producing coal.

carbon paper NOUN paper coated with carbon, used to make copies of typed or written matter.

carborundum NOUN a compound of carbon and silicon, used for grinding and polishing things.

carboy NOUN a large round bottle surrounded by a protective framework.

carbuncle NOUN **1** a severe abscess. **2** a garnet cut in a round knob shape.

carburettor ([US] **carburetor**) NOUN a device mixing air and petrol in a motor engine.

carcass (also **carcase**) NOUN the dead body of an animal; the framework or basic structure of something.

carcinogen /kah-**sin**-ŏ-jin/ NOUN a cancer-producing substance.
carcinogenic ADJ

carcinoma /kah-si-**noh**-mă/ NOUN (PL **carcinomata** or **carcinomas**) a cancerous tumour.

card NOUN a piece of cardboard or thick paper; this used to send a message or greeting; this printed with someone's identifying details; a playing card; a credit card; (**cards**) any card game. VERB clean or comb (wool) with a wire brush or toothed instrument.
on the cards [INFORMAL] probable.

cardamom NOUN a spice.

cardboard NOUN thin board made from paper pulp. ADJ (of a fictional character) unconvincing, lacking depth.

cardiac ADJ of the heart.

cardigan NOUN a knitted garment that buttons down the front.

cardinal ADJ chief, most important. NOUN a senior Roman Catholic priest who has the power to elect the Pope.

cardinal number NOUN a number denoting quantity rather than order (1, 2, 3, etc.); contrast **ordinal**.

cardiogram NOUN a record of heart movements.

cardiograph NOUN an instrument recording heart movements.

cardiology NOUN the study of diseases of the heart.
cardiological ADJ
cardiologist NOUN

card sharp (also **card sharper**) NOUN a swindler at card games.

care NOUN **1** the provision of welfare and protection. **2** serious attention and thought; caution to avoid damage or loss. VERB **1** feel concern or interest; (**care for**) look after. **2** (**care for**) feel affection for; like, enjoy.

careen VERB tilt or keel over.

career NOUN the way someone makes their living over a significant period of their life; the progress and development of a person or thing. VERB move swiftly or wildly.

careerist NOUN a person intent on advancement in a career.

carefree ADJ light-hearted and free from worry.

careful ADJ showing attention or caution.
carefully ADV

careless ADJ showing insufficient attention or concern.
carelessly ADV
carelessness NOUN

carer NOUN a person who looks after a sick or disabled person at home.

caress NOUN a gentle loving touch. VERB touch gently and lovingly.

caretaker NOUN a person employed to look after a building.

C

careworn ADJ showing signs of prolonged worry.

cargo NOUN (PL **cargoes** or **cargos**) goods carried on a ship, aircraft, etc.

Caribbean ADJ relating to the Caribbean Sea and its islands.

caribou NOUN (PL **caribou**) a North American reindeer.

caricature NOUN a portrayal exaggerating someone's characteristics for comic effect. VERB portray in this way.
caricaturist NOUN

caries /kair-eez/ NOUN decay of a tooth or bone.

carillon /kă-**ril**-yŏn/ NOUN a set of bells sounded mechanically; a tune played on these.

carmine ADJ & NOUN vivid crimson.

carnage NOUN great slaughter.

carnal ADJ of the body or flesh, not spiritual.
carnally ADV

carnation NOUN a plant with fragrant red, pink, or white flowers.

carnelian variant of **CORNELIAN**.

carnival NOUN a public festival, usually with a procession.

carnivore NOUN an animal feeding on flesh.
carnivorous ADJ

carob NOUN a chocolate substitute made from the pods of a Mediterranean evergreen tree.

carol NOUN a Christmas hymn. VERB (**carols**, **carolling**, **carolled**; [US] **caroling**, **caroled**) sing carols; sing joyfully.

carotene NOUN an orange-coloured pigment found in carrots, tomatoes, etc.

carotid /kă-**rot**-id/ NOUN an artery carrying blood to the head.

carouse /kă-**rowz**/ VERB drink and be merry.
carouser NOUN

carousel /ka-roo-**sel**/ NOUN
1 [US] a merry-go-round.
2 a rotating conveyor, especially for luggage at an airport.

carp NOUN a freshwater fish. VERB keep finding fault.

carpal ADJ relating to the bones in the wrist.

carpel NOUN the part of a flower in which the seeds develop.

carpenter NOUN a person who makes or repairs wooden objects and structures.
carpentry NOUN

carpet NOUN a textile fabric for covering a floor; a covering. VERB (**carpets, carpeting, carpeted**) **1** cover with a carpet. **2** [INFORMAL] reprimand.
on the carpet [INFORMAL] being reprimanded.

carport NOUN a roofed open-sided shelter for a car.

carriage NOUN **1** a section of a train; a horse-drawn vehicle. **2** transport of goods. **3** a person's way of standing and moving. **4** a part of a machine that carries other parts into position.

carriage clock NOUN a small portable clock with a handle on top.

carriageway NOUN the part of the road on which vehicles travel.

carrier NOUN a person or thing carrying something; a company transporting goods; a bag with handles for shopping.

carrion NOUN dead decaying flesh.

carrot NOUN **1** a tapering orange root vegetable. **2** [INFORMAL] an incentive.

carry VERB (**carries, carrying, carried**) **1** move (something) to another place, supporting its weight; have on one's person; transmit (a disease). **2** support; assume (responsibility). **3** entail (a consequence). **4** take (a process) to a particular point. **5** approve (a measure); gain the support of. **6** stock (goods). **7** be audible at a distance.
carry on 1 continue. **2** [INFORMAL] behave excitedly. **3** [INFORMAL] have a love affair. **carry out** put into practice. **get carried away** lose self-control.

cart NOUN a wheeled vehicle for carrying loads. VERB carry, transport.

carte blanche /kart **blahnsh**/ NOUN full power

C

to do as one thinks best.

cartel NOUN a manufacturers' or producers' union to control prices.

carthorse NOUN a horse of heavy build.

cartilage NOUN the firm elastic tissue in skeletons of vertebrates; gristle.

cartography NOUN the science or practice of drawing maps.
cartographer NOUN
cartographic ADJ

carton NOUN a cardboard or plastic container.

cartoon NOUN **1** a humorous drawing. **2** a film consisting of an animated sequence of drawings. **3** a sketch for a painting.
cartoonist NOUN

cartridge NOUN **1** a case containing explosive for firearms. **2** a sealed cassette.

cartridge paper NOUN thick strong paper.

cartwheel NOUN a handspring with limbs spread like the spokes of a wheel.

carve VERB cut (hard material) to make (an object or pattern); cut (meat) into slices for eating.

carvery NOUN (PL **carveries**) a restaurant where meat is served from a joint as required.

Casanova NOUN a man noted for his love affairs.

cascade NOUN a waterfall; something falling like this; a large quantity of related things. VERB fall like a waterfall.

case NOUN **1** an instance of something occurring; an instance of a disease. **2** a lawsuit; a set of arguments supporting a position. **3** a container or protective covering; a suitcase. **4** the form of a noun, adjective, or pronoun indicating its grammatical role in a sentence; this role. VERB **1** enclose in a case. **2** [INFORMAL] examine (a building etc.) in preparation for a crime.
in case to provide for a particular possibility.

casement NOUN a window opening on vertical hinges.

cash NOUN money in the form of coins or banknotes. VERB give or obtain cash for (a cheque etc.).
cash in on get profit or advantage from.

cashew NOUN an edible nut.

cashier NOUN a person employed to handle money. VERB dismiss from military service in disgrace.

cashmere NOUN very fine soft wool; fabric made from this.

casino NOUN (PL **casinos**) a public building or room for gambling.

cask NOUN a barrel for liquids.

casket NOUN a small usually ornamental box for valuables; [US] a coffin.

cassava NOUN the edible starchy root of a tropical tree.

casserole NOUN a covered dish in which meat etc. is cooked and served; food cooked in this. VERB cook in a casserole.

cassette NOUN a small case containing a reel of magnetic tape or film.

cassis NOUN a blackcurrant-flavoured usually alcoholic syrup.

cassock NOUN a long robe worn by clergy and choristers.

cassowary NOUN (PL **cassowaries**) a large flightless bird.

cast VERB (**casts**, **casting**, **cast**) **1** throw; cause (light or shadow) to appear on a surface; direct (eyes or thoughts). **2** register (a vote). **3** shape (molten metal) in a mould; produce (a sculpture) by casting. **4** give a part to (an actor); allocate parts in (a film or play). **5** cause (a magic spell) to take effect. NOUN **1** a throw of dice, a fishing line, etc. **2** an object made by casting molten metal. **3** a set of actors in a play or film. **4** a type, a quality: *an inquiring cast of mind*. **5** a slight squint. **6** (also **plaster cast**) bandage stiffened with plaster of Paris.

castanets PLURAL NOUN a

C

pair of shell-shaped pieces of wood, clicked in the hand to accompany Spanish dancing.

castaway NOUN a shipwrecked person.

caste NOUN a social class in the Hindu system.

castellated ADJ having turrets or battlements.

caster variant of **CASTOR**.

castigate VERB reprimand severely.
castigation NOUN

casting vote NOUN a deciding vote when those on each side are equal.

cast iron NOUN a hard alloy of iron cast in a mould. ADJ (**cast-iron**) made of cast iron; unbreakable, unchangeable.

castle NOUN a large fortified residence.

cast-off NOUN a discarded thing.

castor (also **caster**) NOUN **1** a small swivelling wheel on a leg of furniture. **2** a small container with a perforated top for sprinkling sugar etc.

castor oil NOUN a purgative and lubricant oil from the seeds of a tropical plant.

castor sugar NOUN finely granulated white sugar.

castrate VERB remove the testicles of.
castration NOUN

castrato NOUN (PL **castrati**) [HISTORICAL] a male singer castrated to retain a soprano or alto voice.

casual ADJ **1** relaxed, not worried. **2** happening by chance. **3** not regular or permanent; not serious or formal.
casually ADV
casualness NOUN

casualty NOUN (PL **casualties**) **1** a person killed or injured; something lost or destroyed. **2** (in full **casualty department**) part of a hospital treating accident victims.

casuistry NOUN **1** clever but unsound argument. **2** the application of moral rules to particular instances.
casuist NOUN

cat NOUN a small furry domesticated animal; a

wild animal related to this.

cataclysm NOUN a violent upheaval or disaster.
cataclysmic ADJ

catacomb /kat-ă-koom/ NOUN an underground gallery with recesses for tombs.

catafalque /kat-ă-falk/ NOUN a platform for the coffin of a distinguished person before or during a funeral.

catalepsy NOUN (PL **catalepsies**) a seizure or trance in which the body goes rigid.
cataleptic ADJ

catalogue ([US] **catalog**) NOUN a systematic list of items. VERB (**catalogues**, **cataloguing**, **catalogued**; [US] **catalogs**, **cataloging**, **cataloged**) list in a catalogue.

catalyse ([US] **catalyze**) VERB subject to the action of a catalyst.
catalysis NOUN

catalyst NOUN a substance that aids a chemical reaction while remaining unchanged.

catalytic converter NOUN part of an exhaust system that reduces the harmful effects of pollutant gases.

catamaran NOUN a boat with parallel twin hulls.

catapult NOUN a device with elastic fitted to a forked stick for shooting small stones. VERB hurl from or as if from a catapult.

cataract NOUN **1** a large waterfall. **2** an opaque area clouding the lens of the eye.

catarrh /kă-**tah**/ NOUN inflammation of a mucous membrane, especially of the nose, with a watery discharge.

catastrophe /kă-tas-trŏ-fi/ NOUN a sudden great disaster.
catastrophic ADJ
catastrophically ADV

catcall NOUN a shout or whistle of mockery or disapproval.

catch VERB **1** grasp and hold (a moving object). **2** capture; detect. **3** be in time for (a train etc.). **4** become infected with. **5** hear; understand. **6** succeed in expressing.

C

7 hit. NOUN 1 an act of catching; something caught or worth catching. 2 a fastener for a door or window. 3 [INFORMAL] a hidden drawback.
catch on [INFORMAL] 1 become popular. 2 understand. **catch out** detect in a mistake. **catch up** reach those ahead of one; complete arrears of work.

catch-22 NOUN a dilemma in which either choice will cause suffering.

catching ADJ infectious.

catchment area NOUN an area from which rainfall drains into a river; an area from which a hospital draws patients or a school draws pupils.

catchphrase NOUN a well-known sentence or phrase.

catchword NOUN a word or phrase used to sum up a concept.

catchy ADJ (**catchier**, **catchiest**) (of a tune) pleasant and easy to remember.

catechism NOUN a series of questions and answers on the principles of a religion.

catechize (also **catechise**) VERB (**catechizes**, **catechizing**, **catechized**) put a series of questions to.

categorical ADJ unconditional, absolute.
categorically ADV

categorize (also **categorise**) VERB place in a category.
categorization NOUN

category NOUN (PL **categories**) a class of things.

cater VERB supply food; provide what is needed or wanted.
caterer NOUN

caterpillar NOUN the larva of a butterfly or moth.

caterwaul /ka-tĕ-worl/ VERB make a cat's howling cry.

catgut NOUN material used for instrument strings etc., made from horse or sheep gut.

catharsis NOUN (PL **catharses**) a release of strong feeling or tension.
cathartic ADJ

cathedral NOUN the

principal church of a diocese.

Catherine wheel NOUN a rotating firework.

catheter NOUN a tube inserted into the bladder to extract urine.

cathode NOUN an electrode by which current leaves a device.

cathode ray tube NOUN a vacuum tube in which beams of electrons produce a luminous image on a fluorescent screen.

catholic ADJ **1** all-embracing, universal. **2** (**Catholic**) Roman Catholic. NOUN (**Catholic**) a Roman Catholic.
Catholicism NOUN

cation /kat-I-ŏn/ NOUN a positively charged ion.

catkin NOUN a hanging flower of willow, hazel, etc.

catnap NOUN a short nap.

catseye NOUN [TRADE MARK] each of a series of reflective studs on a road.

cattery NOUN (PL **catteries**) a place where cats are kept while their owners are away.

cattle PLURAL NOUN cows, bulls, and oxen.

catty ADJ (**cattier**, **cattiest**) spiteful.
cattily ADV
cattiness NOUN

catwalk NOUN a narrow platform extending into an auditorium, used in fashion shows.

caucus /kor-kŭs/ NOUN a group with shared interests within a political party; [US] a meeting of party leaders.

caught past and past participle of **CATCH**.

caul NOUN a membrane enclosing a foetus in the womb.

cauldron (also **caldron**) NOUN a large deep cooking pot.

cauliflower NOUN a cabbage with a large white flower head.

caulk (also **calk**) NOUN a waterproof sealant.

causal ADJ relating to or acting as a cause.

causality NOUN the relation between cause and effect.

cause NOUN **1** something that brings about

something else; a reason, a motive. **2** a principle or movement supported. VERB bring about, give rise to.
causation NOUN

cause célèbre /kohz se-lebr/ NOUN (PL **causes célèbres**) an issue arousing great interest.

causeway NOUN a raised road across low or wet ground.

caustic ADJ **1** able to burn by chemical action. **2** sarcastic. NOUN a caustic substance.
caustically ADV

caustic soda NOUN sodium hydroxide.

cauterize (also **cauterise**) VERB burn (tissue) to destroy infection or stop bleeding.
cauterization NOUN

caution NOUN **1** care to avoid danger or error. **2** a warning. VERB warn; reprimand.

cautionary ADJ conveying a warning.

cautious ADJ having or showing caution.
cautiously ADV

cavalcade NOUN a procession.

cavalier ADJ casual or offhand. NOUN (**Cavalier**) [HISTORICAL] a supporter of Charles I in the English Civil War.

cavalry NOUN (PL **cavalries**) mounted troops; troops in armoured vehicles.

cave NOUN a natural hollow in a cliff or hillside or underground.
cave in collapse; give way.

caveat /kav-i-at/ NOUN a warning.

caveman NOUN a person of prehistoric times living in a cave.

cavern NOUN a large cave.

cavernous ADJ like a cavern, large and hollow.

caviar NOUN the pickled roe of sturgeon or other large fish.

cavil VERB (**cavils**, **cavilling**, **cavilled**; [US] **caviling**, **caviled**) raise petty objections. NOUN a petty objection.

caving NOUN the sport of exploring caves.

cavity NOUN (PL **cavities**) a

hollow within a solid object.

cavort VERB leap about excitedly.

caw NOUN the harsh cry of a rook or crow. VERB utter this cry.

cayenne NOUN a hot red pepper.

cayman (also **caiman**) NOUN (PL **caymans**) a South American alligator.

CB ABBREV citizens' band (radio frequencies).

CBE ABBREV Commander of the Order of the British Empire.

CBI ABBREV Confederation of British Industry.

cc (also **c.c.**) ABBREV **1** carbon copy or copies. **2** cubic centimetre(s).

CCTV ABBREV closed-circuit television.

CD ABBREV compact disc.

CD-ROM NOUN a compact disc holding data for display on a computer screen.

cease VERB come to an end; stop doing something; discontinue.

ceasefire NOUN a period when fighting with guns etc. stops.

ceaseless ADJ not ceasing.

cecum US spelling of **CAECUM**.

cedar NOUN a large spreading evergreen tree.

cede VERB surrender (territory etc.).

cedilla NOUN a mark (¸) written under the letter *c* to show that it is pronounced as *s*.

ceilidh /kay-li/ NOUN [SCOTTISH] & [IRISH] an informal gathering for traditional music and dancing.

ceiling NOUN the upper interior surface of a room; an upper limit.

celandine NOUN a small wild plant with yellow flowers.

celebrant NOUN an officiating priest.

celebrate VERB mark (an occasion) with festivities or other special activity. **celebration** NOUN

celebrated ADJ famous.

celebrity NOUN (PL **celebrities**) a famous person; fame.

celerity NOUN [LITERARY] swiftness.

celery NOUN a plant with edible crisp stems.

celestial ADJ of the sky; of heaven.

celibate ADJ abstaining from sexual intercourse. **celibacy** NOUN

cell NOUN **1** a small room for a prisoner or monk; a compartment in a honeycomb. **2** a microscopic unit of living matter. **3** a small group as a nucleus of political activity. **4** a device for producing electric current chemically.

cellar NOUN an underground room; a stock of wine.

cello /che-loh/ NOUN (PL **cellos**) a bass instrument of the violin family. **cellist** NOUN

cellophane NOUN [TRADE MARK] a thin transparent wrapping material.

cellular ADJ **1** of living cells. **2** woven with an open mesh.

cellular phone (or **radio**) NOUN a system of mobile communication over an area served by several short-range radio stations.

cellulite NOUN a lumpy form of fat producing puckering of the skin.

celluloid NOUN transparent plastic formerly used for cinema film.

cellulose NOUN a substance in plant tissues, used in making plastics.

Celsius ADJ of a centigrade scale with 0° as the freezing point and 100° as the boiling point of water.

Celt NOUN a member of an ancient European people or their descendants. **Celtic** ADJ

cement NOUN a substance of lime and clay used to make mortar or concrete; an adhesive; a substance for filling cavities in teeth. VERB join with cement; unite firmly.

cemetery NOUN (PL **cemeteries**) a burial ground other than a churchyard.

cenotaph NOUN a monument to people buried elsewhere.

censer NOUN a container for burning incense.

censor NOUN a person who examines material that is to be published and bans unacceptable parts. VERB examine and alter in this way.
censorial ADJ
censorship NOUN

censorious ADJ severely critical.

censure NOUN hostile criticism and rebuke. VERB criticize harshly; express disapproval of.

census NOUN an official count of the population.

cent NOUN a 100th part of a dollar or other currency; a coin worth this.

centaur NOUN (in mythology) a creature with the upper body of a man and the lower body of a horse.

centenarian NOUN a person 100 years old or more.

centenary NOUN (PL **centenaries**) a 100th anniversary.

centennial ADJ of a centenary. NOUN a centenary.

center US spelling of **CENTRE**.

centigrade ADJ using the Celsius scale of temperature.

centigram (also **centigramme**) NOUN a 100th of a gram.

centilitre ([US] **centiliter**) NOUN a 100th of a litre.

centime NOUN a 100th of a franc.

centimetre ([US] **centimeter**) NOUN a 100th of a metre, about 0.4 inch.

centipede NOUN a small crawling creature with many legs.

central ADJ of, at, or forming a centre; most important.
centrality NOUN
centrally ADV

central heating NOUN heating generated by a central boiler and conducted through pipes and radiators.

centralize (also **centralise**) VERB bring under the control of a central authority.
centralization NOUN

C

central nervous system NOUN the brain and the spinal cord.

centre ([US] **center**) NOUN **1** a point or part in the middle of something; a position avoiding extremes. **2** a place where a specified activity takes place; a point where something begins or is most intense. VERB (**centres**, **centring**, **centred**; [US] **centers**, **centering**, **centered**) **1** have or cause to have something as a major concern or theme. **2** place in the middle; base at a particular place.

centrefold NOUN the two middle pages of a magazine or newspaper.

centrifugal ADJ moving away from the centre.

centripetal ADJ moving towards the centre.

centurion NOUN a commander in the ancient Roman army.

century NOUN (PL **centuries**) **1** a period of 100 years; this reckoned from the traditional date of the birth of Christ. **2** 100 runs at cricket.

cephalic ADJ of the head.

cephalopod NOUN a mollusc with tentacles (e.g. an octopus).

ceramic ADJ made of fired clay. NOUN (**ceramics**) the art of making ceramic articles; these articles.

cereal NOUN a grass plant with edible grain; this grain; breakfast food made from it.

cerebellum NOUN (PL **cerebellums** or **cerebella**) a small part of the brain at the back of the skull.

cerebral ADJ of the brain; intellectual.
cerebrally ADV

cerebral palsy NOUN lack of muscle control resulting from brain damage before or at birth.

cerebrum NOUN (PL **cerebra**) the main part of the brain.

ceremonial ADJ of or used in ceremonies; formal.
ceremonially ADV

ceremonious ADJ done in a formal and grand way.

ceremoniously ADV

ceremony NOUN (PL **ceremonies**) a formal occasion at which special acts are performed. **stand on ceremony** behave formally.

cerise /se-reez/ ADJ & NOUN light clear red.

cerium NOUN a metallic element.

certain ADJ **1** definite, reliable. **2** feeling sure. **3** specific but not named: *certain people disagreed.*

certainly ADV of course; yes.

certainty NOUN (PL **certainties**) conviction; definite truth or reliability; something that is certain.

certifiable ADJ able or needing to be certified.

certificate NOUN an official document attesting certain facts.

certify VERB (**certifies**, **certifying**, **certified**) declare formally; recognize as meeting certain standards; declare insane.

certitude NOUN a feeling of certainty.

cerulean /se-roo-lee-ăn/ ADJ deep blue like a clear sky.

cervical ADJ relating to the cervix.

cervical smear NOUN a specimen of cells taken from the cervix for medical examination.

cervix NOUN (PL **cervices**) the narrow neck-like passage between the womb and the vagina.

Cesarean, **Cesarian** US spelling of **CAESAREAN**.

cesium US spelling of **CAESIUM**.

cessation NOUN the stopping of something.

cession NOUN the giving up of rights or territory.

cesspit (also **cesspool**) NOUN an underground tank or covered pit for sewage.

cetacean /si-tay-shăn/ NOUN a member of the whale family.

cf. ABBREV compare with.

CFC ABBREV chlorofluorocarbon, a gas used in refrigerators and aerosols that harms the ozone layer.

chafe VERB **1** warm by

C

rubbing; make or become sore by rubbing. **2** make or become irritated or impatient.

chafer NOUN a large beetle.

chaff NOUN **1** corn husks separated from seed. **2** banter. VERB banter, tease.

chaffinch NOUN a pink-breasted finch.

chagrin NOUN annoyance and embarrassment.

chain NOUN **1** a series of connected metal links; a connected series or sequence; a group of hotels or shops owned by the same company. **2** a unit of measurement (66 feet). VERB fasten with a chain.

chain reaction NOUN a series of events in which each causes the next.

chainsaw NOUN a saw with teeth set on a circular chain.

chair NOUN **1** a movable seat for one person, usually with a back and four legs. **2** the position of a chairperson; the position of a professor. VERB act as chairperson of.

chairlift NOUN a series of chairs on a cable for carrying people up a mountain.

chairman (also **chairwoman**) NOUN a person who presides over a meeting or board of directors.

chairperson NOUN a chairman or chairwoman.

chaise longue /shayz lawng/ NOUN (PL **chaises longues** or **chaise longues**) a sofa with a backrest at only one end.

chalcedony /kal-**sed**-ŏ-nee/ NOUN a type of quartz.

chalet /**sha**-lay/ NOUN a Swiss hut or cottage; a small cabin in a holiday camp.

chalice NOUN a large goblet.

chalk NOUN white soft limestone; a piece of this or similar coloured substance used for drawing.
chalky ADJ

challenge NOUN **1** an invitation to take part in a contest or to prove

something. **2** a demanding task. VERB **1** raise doubt as to whether (something) is true. **2** invite to do something difficult or take part in a fight. **3** call on (someone) to prove their identity.
challenger NOUN

chamber NOUN a hall used for meetings of a council, parliament, etc.; [ARCHAIC] a room, a bedroom; (**chambers**) rooms used by a barrister; an enclosed space, a cavity.

chamberlain NOUN an official managing a sovereign's or noble's household.

chambermaid NOUN a woman employed to clean hotel bedrooms.

chamber music NOUN music written for a small group of players.

chamber pot NOUN a bowl used as a toilet.

chameleon /kă-mee-li-ŏn/ NOUN a small lizard that changes colour according to its surroundings.

chamfer /cham-fĕ/ VERB bevel the edge of.

chamois NOUN **1** /sham-wah/ a small mountain antelope. **2** /sha-mi/ a piece of soft leather used for cleaning windows, cars, etc.

chamomile variant of **CAMOMILE**.

champ VERB munch noisily; make a chewing action.
champ at the bit show impatience.

champagne NOUN a sparkling white French wine.

champion NOUN **1** a person who defeats all others in a competition. **2** a person who fights or speaks in support of another or of a cause. VERB support. ADJ [DIALECT] excellent.
championship NOUN

chance NOUN **1** a possibility, an opportunity; a degree of likelihood. **2** development of events without planning or obvious reason. VERB **1** try (something uncertain or dangerous). **2** do, find, or see by accident. ADJ unplanned, happening by chance.

C

chancel NOUN the part of a church near the altar.

chancellor NOUN the government minister in charge of the nation's budget; a state or law official of various other kinds; the non-resident head of a university. **chancellorship** NOUN

chancy ADJ (**chancier**, **chanciest**) [INFORMAL] risky, uncertain.

chandelier NOUN a hanging light with branches for several bulbs or candles.

chandler NOUN a dealer in ropes, canvas, etc. for ships.

change VERB **1** make or become different. **2** exchange, substitute, replace; go from one of two (trains, sides, etc.) to the other. **3** get or give small money or different currency for. NOUN **1** the process of changing. **2** money in small units or returned as balance.
change one's mind adopt a new opinion or plan.
changeable ADJ

changeling NOUN a child believed to have been substituted secretly for another.

channel NOUN **1** a stretch of water connecting two seas; a passage for water. **2** a medium of communication. **3** a band of broadcasting frequencies. VERB (**channels**, **channelling**, **channelled**; [US] **channeling**, **channeled**) direct to a particular end or by a particular route.

chant NOUN a repeated rhythmic phrase called out or sung to music; a melody for psalms. VERB sing, intone; shout rhythmically and repeatedly.

chanter NOUN the melody-pipe of bagpipes.

chanterelle NOUN a yellow edible funnel-shaped fungus.

chantry NOUN (PL **chantries**) a chapel founded for priests to sing Masses for the founder's soul.

chaos NOUN great disorder. **chaotic** ADJ **chaotically** ADV

chap NOUN [INFORMAL] a man.

VERB (**chaps**, **chapping**, **chapped**) (of the skin) split or crack.

chapatti NOUN (in Indian cookery) a flat cake of wholemeal bread.

chapel NOUN a place used for Christian worship, other than a cathedral or parish church; a place with a separate altar within a church.

chaperone NOUN an older woman looking after a young unmarried woman on social occasions. VERB act as chaperone to.

chaplain NOUN a clergyman of an institution, private chapel, ship, regiment, etc.
chaplaincy NOUN

chapter NOUN **1** a division of a book; a period of time. **2** the canons of a cathedral.

char NOUN **1** [INFORMAL] a charwoman. **2** [INFORMAL] tea. VERB (**chars**, **charring**, **charred**) make or become black by burning.

charabanc /sha-ră-bang/ NOUN an early form of bus with bench seats.

character NOUN **1** the distinctive qualities of someone or something; moral strength. **2** a person in a novel, play, or film; an individual and original person. **3** a physical characteristic. **4** a printed or written letter or sign.

characteristic ADJ typical of and helping to identify a person or thing. NOUN a typical and identifying feature.
characteristically ADV

characterize (also **characterise**) VERB (**characterizes**, **characterizing**, **characterized**) **1** describe the character of. **2** be a characteristic of.
characterization NOUN

charade /shă-**rahd**/ NOUN **1** an absurd pretence. **2** (**charades**) a game involving guessing words from acted clues.

charcoal NOUN a black substance made by burning wood slowly.

charge NOUN **1** the price asked for goods or services. **2** an accusation. **3** responsibility and care;

someone or something for which one is responsible. **4** a rushing attack. **5** the electricity contained in a substance. **6** a quantity of explosive. VERB **1** ask for (a specified price) from (someone). **2** accuse formally. **3** entrust with a task or responsibility. **4** rush forward in attack. **5** give an electric charge to. **6** load with explosive.
in charge in command.
take charge take control.

charge card NOUN a credit card issued by a large shop.

chargé d'affaires NOUN (PL **chargés d'affaires**) an ambassador's deputy.

charger NOUN **1** a cavalry horse. **2** a device for charging a battery.

chariot NOUN a two-wheeled horse-drawn vehicle used in ancient times in battle and in racing.

charioteer NOUN a driver of a chariot.

charisma /kă-riz-mă/ NOUN the power to inspire devotion and enthusiasm; great charm.

charismatic ADJ having charisma; (of worship) emphasizing spontaneity and divine inspiration.
charismatically ADV

charitable ADJ **1** relating to charities. **2** lenient, kind.
charitably ADV

charity NOUN (PL **charities**) **1** an organization helping the needy; gifts or voluntary work for the needy. **2** kindness and tolerance in judging others.

charlatan NOUN a person falsely claiming to be an expert.

charm NOUN **1** the power to attract, delight, or fascinate. **2** an act, object, or words believed to have magic power; a small ornament worn on a bracelet etc. VERB **1** delight; influence by personal charm. **2** control by magic.
charmer NOUN

charming ADJ delightful.

charnel house NOUN a place containing corpses or bones.

chart NOUN **1** a table, graph, or diagram; a map for navigators. **2** (**the charts**) a weekly list of the current best-selling pop records. VERB record or show on a chart.

charter NOUN **1** an official document granting rights. **2** the hiring of an aircraft etc. for a special purpose. VERB **1** grant a charter to. **2** let or hire (an aircraft, ship, or vehicle).

chartered ADJ (of an accountant, engineer, etc.) qualified according to the rules of an association holding a royal charter.

charter flight NOUN a flight by a chartered aircraft as opposed to a scheduled flight.

chartreuse /shah-**trerz**/ NOUN a green or yellow liqueur.

charwoman NOUN a woman employed to clean a house.

chary ADJ (**charier**, **chariest**) cautious.
charily ADV
chariness NOUN

chase VERB go quickly after in order to capture, overtake, or drive away. NOUN an act of chasing, a pursuit; (**the chase**) the sport of hunting.

chaser NOUN a drink taken after a drink of another kind.

chasm /kaz-ŭm/ NOUN a deep opening in the earth.

chassis /**sha**-see/ NOUN (PL **chassis**) the base frame of a vehicle.

chaste ADJ **1** not having sexual intercourse outside marriage or at all. **2** simple in style, not ornate.
chastely ADV
chastity NOUN

chasten VERB subdue, restrain; punish, discipline.

chastise VERB punish; reprimand severely.
chastisement NOUN

chat NOUN an informal conversation. VERB (**chats**, **chatting**, **chatted**) have a chat.

chateau /**sha**-toh/ NOUN (PL **chateaux**) a French castle or large country house.

chatelaine /**sha**-tĕ-layn/

NOUN [DATED] the mistress of a large house.

C

chattel NOUN a movable possession.

chatter VERB **1** talk quickly and continuously about unimportant matters. **2** (of teeth) rattle together. NOUN chattering talk; a series of short high-pitched sounds.
chatterer NOUN

chatterbox NOUN [INFORMAL] a talkative person.

chatty ADJ (**chattier**, **chattiest**) fond of chatting; (of a letter etc.) informal and lively.
chattily ADV
chattiness NOUN

chauffeur /shoh-fer/ NOUN a person employed to drive a car. VERB be a driver for.

chauvinism /shoh-vin-izm/ NOUN prejudiced belief in the superiority of one's own race, sex, etc.
chauvinist NOUN
chauvinistic ADJ

cheap ADJ low in cost or value; poor in quality; contemptible; worthless.
cheaply ADV
cheapness NOUN

cheapen VERB make or become cheap; degrade.

cheapskate NOUN [INFORMAL] a stingy person.

cheat VERB act dishonestly or unfairly to win profit or advantage; trick, deprive by deceit. NOUN a person who cheats; a deception.

check VERB **1** examine, test, verify. **2** stop; slow the motion of. **3** (**check in** or **out**) register one's arrival or departure. NOUN **1** an inspection. **2** a hindrance; a control or restraint. **3** the exposure of a chess king to capture. **4** [US] a bill in a restaurant; a cheque. **5** a pattern of squares or crossing lines.
checked ADJ

checker NOUN **1** variant of **CHEQUER**. **2** (**checkers**) [US] the game of draughts. **3** a person who checks things.

checkmate NOUN the situation in chess where capture of a king is inevitable; complete defeat, deadlock. VERB put into checkmate; defeat, foil.

C

checkout NOUN a desk where goods are paid for in a supermarket.

checkpoint NOUN a place where security checks are made on travellers, especially at a border.

cheek NOUN **1** the side of the face below the eye. **2** bold or impudent speech. VERB speak cheekily to.
cheek by jowl close together.

cheeky ADJ (**cheekier**, **cheekiest**) mischievously impudent.
cheekily ADV

cheep NOUN a weak shrill cry like that of a young bird. VERB make this cry.

cheer NOUN **1** a shout of applause. **2** cheerfulness. VERB **1** applaud with a cheer, utter a cheer. **2** (**cheer up**) make or become more cheerful.

cheerful ADJ **1** happy, optimistic. **2** expressing or inspiring cheerfulness.
cheerfully ADV
cheerfulness NOUN

cheerio EXCLAMATION [INFORMAL] goodbye.

cheerless ADJ gloomy, dreary.

cheery ADJ (**cheerier**, **cheeriest**) cheerful.
cheerily ADV
cheeriness NOUN

cheese NOUN **1** food made from pressed milk curds. **2** a thick, smooth, sweet spread.
cheesy ADJ

cheeseburger NOUN a hamburger with cheese on it.

cheesecake NOUN **1** an open tart filled with flavoured cream cheese or curd cheese. **2** [INFORMAL] the portrayal of women in a sexually attractive manner.

cheesecloth NOUN a thin loosely-woven cotton fabric.

cheesed off ADJ [INFORMAL] bored, exasperated.

cheese-paring ADJ stingy. NOUN stinginess.

cheetah NOUN a swift large animal of the cat family.

chef NOUN a professional cook.

chef-d'oeuvre /shay-dervr/ NOUN (PL **chefs-d'oeuvre**) a masterpiece.

chemical ADJ relating to

chemistry or chemicals. NOUN a substance obtained by or used in a chemical process.
chemically ADV

chemise /shĕ-**meez**/ NOUN a woman's loose-fitting undergarment or nightdress.

chemist NOUN **1** a person authorized to sell medicinal drugs; a shop where such drugs and items such as toiletries are sold. **2** an expert in chemistry.

chemistry NOUN (PL **chemistries**) **1** the study of substances and their reactions; its application in forming new substances; the structure and properties of a substance. **2** complex emotional interaction between people.

chemotherapy /kee-moh-**the**-ră-pi/ NOUN treatment of cancer by drugs.

chenille /shĕ-**neel**/ NOUN a fabric with a velvety pile.

cheque ([US] **check**) NOUN a written order to a bank to pay out money from an account; a printed form for this.

cheque card (also **banker's card**) NOUN a card guaranteeing payment of cheques.

chequer (also **checker**) NOUN a pattern of squares, especially of alternating colours.

chequered ADJ **1** marked with a chequer pattern. **2** having frequent changes of fortune.

cherish VERB **1** take loving care of. **2** cling to (hopes etc.).

cheroot /shĕ-**root**/ NOUN a cigar with two open ends.

cherry NOUN (PL **cherries**) a small round red fruit with a stone; a tree bearing this or grown for its ornamental flowers; bright red.

cherub NOUN **1** (PL **cherubim** or **cherubs**) an angelic being. **2** (in art) a chubby infant with wings; an angelic child.
cherubic ADJ

chess NOUN a game of skill for two players using 32 pieces on a chequered board.

chest NOUN **1** a large strong box. **2** the upper front surface of the body.

chestnut NOUN **1** a nut which can be roasted and eaten; the tree on which it grows. **2** reddish brown; a horse of this colour. **3** an old joke or anecdote.

chest of drawers NOUN a piece of furniture with drawers for clothes etc.

cheval glass /shĕ-val/ NOUN a tall mirror mounted on a frame so that it can be tilted.

chevron NOUN a V-shaped symbol.

chew VERB work or grind between the teeth.

chewing gum NOUN flavoured gum used for prolonged chewing.

chewy ADJ (**chewier**, **chewiest**) tough; needing or suitable for chewing. **chewiness** NOUN

chez /shay/ PREP at the home of.

chiaroscuro /ki-a-rŏ-**skoor**-oh/ NOUN the use of contrasting light and shade in painting etc.

chic /sheek/ ADJ stylish and elegant. NOUN stylishness, elegance.

chicane /shi-**kayn**/ NOUN a sharp double bend on a motor-racing track.

chicanery NOUN trickery.

chick NOUN a newly hatched young bird.

chicken NOUN **1** a young domestic fowl; its flesh as food. **2** [INFORMAL] a coward. ADJ [INFORMAL] cowardly. VERB (**chicken out**) [INFORMAL] withdraw through cowardice.

chickenpox NOUN an infectious illness with a rash of small red blisters.

chickpea NOUN a yellowish seed eaten as a vegetable.

chicory NOUN a blue-flowered plant grown for its salad leaves and its root which is used as a flavouring with coffee.

chide VERB (**chides**, **chiding**, **chided** or **chid**) [ARCHAIC] rebuke.

chief NOUN a leader, a ruler; the person with the highest rank. ADJ most important; highest in rank.

chiefly ADV mainly.

chieftain NOUN the chief of a clan or tribe.

chiffon /shif-on/ NOUN a thin almost transparent fabric.

chignon /sheen-yon/ NOUN a coil of hair worn at the back of the head.

chihuahua /chi-wah-wă/ NOUN a very small smooth-haired dog.

chilblain NOUN a painful swelling on a foot or hand caused by exposure to cold.

child NOUN (PL **children**) a young human being; a son or daughter.
childhood NOUN
childless ADJ

childbirth NOUN the process of giving birth to a child.

childish ADJ appropriate to a child; silly and immature.

childlike ADJ simple and innocent.

chili US spelling of **CHILLI**.

chill NOUN **1** an unpleasant coldness. **2** a feverish cold. **3** unfriendliness. ADJ chilly. VERB **1** make cold; cool in a refrigerator. **2** [INFORMAL] relax.

chilli ([US] **chili**) NOUN (PL **chillies**) a hot-tasting dried pod of red or green pepper.

chilly ADJ (**chillier**, **chilliest**) rather cold; unfriendly in manner.

chime NOUN the sound of a tuned set of bells; such a set. VERB ring as a chime.
chime in put in a remark.

chimera /ky-meer-ă/ NOUN a legendary monster with a lion's head, goat's body, and serpent's tail; a fantasy, an impossible dream.

chimney NOUN (PL **chimneys**) a structure for carrying off smoke or gases from a fire or furnace.

chimney breast NOUN a projecting wall surrounding a chimney.

chimney pot NOUN a short pipe on top of a chimney.

chimp NOUN [INFORMAL] a chimpanzee.

chimpanzee NOUN an African ape.

chin NOUN the protruding

part of the face below the mouth.

china NOUN fine earthenware, porcelain; things made of this.

chinchilla NOUN a small squirrel-like South American animal; its grey fur.

chine NOUN **1** an animal's backbone. **2** (in southern England) a ravine.

Chinese NOUN (PL **Chinese**) **1** a person from China. **2** the language of China. ADJ relating to China.

chink NOUN **1** a narrow opening, a slit. **2** the sound of glasses or coins striking together. VERB make this sound.

chinless ADJ [INFORMAL] weak or feeble in character.

chinoiserie /shin-wah-zĕ-ree/ NOUN imitation Chinese motifs as decoration.

chintz NOUN glazed cotton cloth used for furnishings.

chip NOUN **1** a small piece cut or broken off something hard; a small hole left by breaking off such a piece. **2** a fried oblong strip of potato. **3** a counter used in gambling. VERB (**chips**, **chipping**, **chipped**) cut (small pieces) off (hard material); break, flake. **chip in** [INFORMAL] **1** interrupt. **2** make a contribution. **chip on one's shoulder** a long-held grievance.

chipboard NOUN board made of compressed wood chips.

chipmunk NOUN a striped squirrel-like animal of North America.

chipolata NOUN a small sausage.

chippings PLURAL NOUN chips of stone etc. for surfacing a path or road.

chiropody /ki-rop-ŏdi/ NOUN treatment of minor ailments of the feet. **chiropodist** NOUN

chiropractic /ky-rŏ-prak-tik/ NOUN treatment of certain physical disorders by manipulation of the joints. **chiropractor** NOUN

chirp NOUN a short sharp sound made by a small

bird or grasshopper. VERB make this sound.

chirpy ADJ (**chirpier**, **chirpiest**) [INFORMAL] lively and cheerful.

chisel NOUN a tool with a sharp bevelled end for shaping wood or stone etc. VERB (**chisels**, **chiselling**, **chiselled**; [US] **chiseling**, **chiseled**) cut with this.

chit NOUN **1** a young and impudent girl. **2** a short written note.

chitterlings PLURAL NOUN the small intestines of a pig, cooked as food.

chivalry NOUN an honourable code of behaviour adopted by medieval knights; polite behaviour by a man towards a woman. **chivalrous** ADJ

chive NOUN a herb with onion-flavoured leaves.

chivvy VERB (**chivvies**, **chivvying**, **chivvied**) urge, nag, pester.

chloride NOUN a compound of chlorine and another element.

chlorinate VERB treat or sterilize with chlorine. **chlorination** NOUN

chlorine NOUN a chemical element in the form of a poisonous gas, sometimes added to water as a disinfectant.

chlorofluorocarbon *see* **CFC**.

chloroform NOUN a liquid giving off vapour that causes unconsciousness when inhaled.

chlorophyll /klor-ŏ-fil/ NOUN green colouring matter in plants.

choc ice NOUN a bar of ice cream coated with chocolate.

chock NOUN a block or wedge for preventing a wheel from moving.

chock-a-block ADJ & ADV [INFORMAL] crammed, crowded together.

chocolate NOUN an edible substance made from cacao seeds; a sweet made or coated with this; a drink made with this; a dark brown colour.

choice NOUN an act of choosing; the right or opportunity to choose; a variety from which to choose; a person or thing chosen. ADJ of especially good quality.

choir NOUN an organized band of singers, especially in church; part of a church where these sit, the chancel.

choirboy NOUN a boy singer in a church choir.

choke VERB stop (a person) breathing by squeezing or blocking the windpipe; have difficulty breathing; clog, smother. NOUN a valve controlling the flow of air into a petrol engine.

choker NOUN a close-fitting necklace.

cholera NOUN a serious often fatal disease caused by bacteria.

choleric ADJ easily angered.

cholesterol NOUN a fatty substance in the blood which, in high concentrations, is thought to cause hardening of arteries.

chomp VERB munch noisily.

choose VERB (**chooses**, **choosing**, **chosen**) select out of a number of things; decide (on).

choosy ADJ (**choosier**, **choosiest**) [INFORMAL] excessively fastidious. **choosiness** NOUN

chop VERB (**chops**, **chopping**, **chopped**) cut by a blow with an axe or knife; cut into small pieces; hit with a short downward movement. NOUN **1** a downward cutting blow. **2** a thick slice of meat, usually including a rib.

chopper NOUN **1** a chopping tool. **2** [INFORMAL] a helicopter.

choppy ADJ (**choppier**, **choppiest**) (of the sea) full of short broken waves.

chopstick NOUN each of a pair of sticks used as eating utensils in China, Japan, etc.

chop suey NOUN a Chinese dish of meat fried with vegetables.

choral ADJ for or sung by a choir.

chorale NOUN a choral composition using the words of a hymn.

chord NOUN **1** a

C

combination of notes sounded together. **2** a straight line joining two points on a curve.
strike (or **touch**) **a chord** appeal to the emotions.

chore NOUN a routine or irksome task.

choreography /ko-ri-og-ră-fi/ NOUN the composition of stage dances.
choreographer NOUN
choreographic ADJ

chorister NOUN a member of a choir.

chortle NOUN a loud chuckle. VERB utter a chortle.

chorus NOUN **1** a group of singers; a group of singing dancers in a musical etc.; an utterance by many people simultaneously. **2** the refrain of a song. VERB say (the same thing) as a group.

chose, **chosen** past and past participle of **CHOOSE**.

choux pastry /shoo/ NOUN very light pastry enriched with eggs.

chow NOUN a long-haired dog of a Chinese breed.

chowder NOUN a thick soup usually containing clams or fish.

chow mein /mayn/ NOUN a Chinese dish of fried noodles and shredded meat etc.

christen VERB admit to the Christian Church by baptism; name.

Christendom NOUN all Christians or Christian countries.

Christian ADJ of or believing in Christianity; [INFORMAL] kind, humane. NOUN a believer in Christianity.

Christianity NOUN a religion based on the teachings of Christ.

Christian name NOUN an individual's distinguishing name, a first name.

Christian Science NOUN a religious system by which health and healing are sought by Christian faith, without medical treatment.

Christmas NOUN a festival held annually on 25 December in celebration of Christ's birth.

Christmas tree NOUN an evergreen tree decorated at Christmas.

chromatic ADJ of colour; in colours.
chromatically ADV

chromatic scale NOUN a music scale proceeding by semitones.

chromatography NOUN separation of substances by slow passage through material that absorbs them at different rates.

chrome NOUN **1** chromium plating. **2** a yellow pigment made from a compound of chromium.

chromium NOUN a metallic element that does not rust.

chromosome NOUN a thread-like structure carrying genes in animal and plant cells.

chronic ADJ **1** constantly present or recurring; having a chronic disease or habit. **2** [INFORMAL] very bad.
chronically ADV

chronicle NOUN a record of events. VERB record in a chronicle.
chronicler NOUN

chronological ADJ following the order in which things happened.
chronologically ADV

chronology NOUN arrangement of events in order of occurrence.

chronometer NOUN a time-measuring instrument.

chrysalis NOUN (PL **chrysalises**) a form of an insect in the stage between larva and adult insect; the case enclosing this.

chrysanthemum NOUN a garden plant flowering in autumn.

chubby ADJ (**chubbier**, **chubbiest**) round and plump.
chubbiness NOUN

chuck VERB **1** [INFORMAL] throw carelessly; discard. **2** touch gently under the chin. NOUN **1** part of a lathe holding the drill; part of a drill holding the bit. **2** a cut of beef from neck to ribs.

chuckle VERB laugh quietly. NOUN a quiet laugh.

chuff VERB (of an engine) work with a regular puffing noise.

chuffed ADJ [INFORMAL] pleased.

chug VERB (**chugs**, **chugging**, **chugged**) (of a boat etc.) make repeated dull short sounds while moving.

chum NOUN [INFORMAL] a close friend.
chummy ADJ

chump NOUN [INFORMAL] a stupid person.

chunk NOUN a thick piece; [INFORMAL] a substantial amount.

chunky ADJ (**chunkier**, **chunkiest**) **1** containing chunks. **2** short and thick or sturdy.
chunkiness NOUN

chunter VERB [INFORMAL] **1** grumble monotonously. **2** move slowly.

church NOUN a building for public Christian worship; (**the Church**) Christians collectively.

churchwarden NOUN a parish representative assisting with church business.

churchyard NOUN enclosed land round a church, used for burials.

churlish ADJ ill-mannered, surly.
churlishly ADV
churlishness NOUN

churn NOUN a machine in which milk is beaten to make butter; a very large milk can. VERB beat (milk) or make (butter) in a churn; move and turn violently.
churn out produce large quantities of (something) without thought or care.

chute NOUN a sloping channel down which things can be slid or dropped.

chutney NOUN (PL **chutneys**) a seasoned mixture of fruit, vinegar, spices, etc.

Ci ABBREV curie.

CIA ABBREV (in the USA) Central Intelligence Agency.

ciabatta /chă-**bah**-tă/ NOUN an Italian bread made with olive oil.

ciao /chow/ EXCLAMATION [INFORMAL] a greeting on meeting or parting.

cicada /si-**kah**-dă/ NOUN a

chirping insect resembling a grasshopper.

cicatrice /si-kă-tris/ (also **cicatrix** /-triks/) NOUN a scar.

CID ABBREV Criminal Investigation Department.

cider NOUN a fermented drink made from apples.

cigar NOUN a roll of tobacco wrapped in tobacco leaves for smoking.

cigarette NOUN a roll of shredded tobacco in thin paper for smoking.

cinch NOUN [INFORMAL] a very easy task; a certainty.

cinder NOUN a piece of partly burnt coal or wood.

cine- COMBINING FORM cinematographic.

cinema NOUN a theatre where films are shown; films as an art form or industry.

cinematography NOUN the process of making and projecting moving pictures.
cinematographic ADJ

cinnamon NOUN a spice.

cipher (also **cypher**) NOUN **1** a code; a key to a code. **2** a person of no importance.

circa PREP about, approximately.

circle NOUN **1** a perfectly round plane figure. **2** a curved tier of seats at a theatre etc. **3** a group with similar interests or shared acquaintances.
VERB move in a circle; form a circle round.

circuit NOUN **1** a roughly circular route returning to its starting point. **2** an itinerary regularly followed. **3** the path of an electric current.

circuitous /sir-kew-it-ŭs/ ADJ roundabout, indirect.
circuitously ADV

circuitry NOUN electric circuits.

circular ADJ shaped like or moving round a circle.
NOUN a letter or leaflet sent to a large number of people.
circularity NOUN

circulate VERB move or cause to move around an area; pass from one place or person to another.

circulation NOUN

C

1 movement through a system or area; the movement of blood round the body. 2 the number of copies sold of a newspaper.
circulatory ADJ

circumcise VERB cut off the foreskin of.
circumcision NOUN

circumference NOUN the boundary of a circle; the distance round this.

circumflex accent NOUN a mark (ˆ) placed over a vowel in some languages to change its sound.

circumlocution NOUN an evasively or pointlessly lengthy way of saying something.
circumlocutory ADJ

circumnavigate VERB sail completely round.
circumnavigation NOUN
circumnavigator NOUN

circumscribe VERB restrict; draw a line round.

circumspect ADJ cautious and watchful, wary.
circumspection NOUN
circumspectly ADV

circumstance NOUN an occurrence or fact relevant to an event or situation.

circumstantial ADJ (of evidence) suggesting but not proving something.

circumvent VERB evade (a difficulty etc.).
circumvention NOUN

circus NOUN a travelling show with performing animals, acrobats, etc.

cirrhosis /si-**roh**-sis/ NOUN a disease of the liver.

cirrus /sir-rŭs/ NOUN (PL **cirri**) a high wispy white cloud.

cistern NOUN a tank for storing water.

citadel NOUN a fortress overlooking a city.

cite VERB quote; mention as an example.
citation NOUN

citizen NOUN 1 a person with full rights in a country. 2 an inhabitant of a city.
citizenship NOUN

citrus NOUN a tree or fruit of a group including lemon, orange, etc.
citric ADJ

city NOUN (PL **cities**) 1 an important town; a town

with special rights given by charter and containing a cathedral. **2** (**the City**) the financial and commercial institutions of the City of London.

civet (in full **civet cat**) NOUN a catlike animal of central Africa; a musky substance obtained from its glands.

civic ADJ of a city or citizenship.

civil ADJ **1** of citizens; not of the armed forces or the Church. **2** polite and obliging.
civilly ADV

civil engineering NOUN the design and construction of roads, bridges, etc.

civilian NOUN a person who is not in the armed forces.

civility NOUN (PL **civilities**) politeness; a polite remark.

civilization (also **civilisation**) NOUN **1** an advanced stage of social development; progress towards this. **2** the culture and way of life of a particular area or period.

civilize (also **civilise**) VERB (**civilises**, **civilising**, **civilised**) **1** cause to improve to a developed stage of society. **2** (**civilized**) polite and well-mannered.

civil servant NOUN a person who works in the civil service.

civil service NOUN the departments that carry out the work of the government.

civil war NOUN war between citizens of the same country.

civvies PLURAL NOUN [INFORMAL] ordinary clothes, not uniform.

CJD ABBREV Creutzfeldt-Jakob Disease, a fatal degenerative brain disease.

cl ABBREV centilitre(s).

clack NOUN a short sharp sound as of two hard objects hitting each other. VERB make this sound.

clad ADJ [ARCHAIC] clothed.

cladding NOUN protective or insulating covering.

claim VERB **1** demand as

C

one's right. **2** assert. NOUN **1** a demand; a right to something. **2** an assertion.

claimant NOUN a person making a claim.

clairvoyance NOUN the power of seeing the future.
clairvoyant NOUN & ADJ

clam NOUN a shellfish with a hinged shell.
clam up (**clams**, **clamming**, **clammed**) [INFORMAL] refuse to talk.

clamber VERB climb with difficulty.

clammy ADJ (**clammier**, **clammiest**) unpleasantly moist and sticky.

clamour NOUN ([US] **clamor**) a loud confused noise; a loud protest etc. VERB (**clamours**, **clamouring**, **clamoured**) shout loudly; demand or protest vehemently.
clamorous ADJ

clamp NOUN a device for holding things tightly; a device for immobilizing an illegally parked car. VERB grip with a clamp; fix firmly; immobilize (an illegally parked car) with a clamp.
clamp down on become firmer about; put a stop to.

clan NOUN a group of families with a common ancestor.
clannish ADJ

clandestine ADJ kept secret, done secretly.

clang NOUN a loud ringing metallic sound. VERB make a clang.

clanger NOUN [INFORMAL] a blunder.

clangour ([US] **clangor**) NOUN a clanging noise.

clank NOUN a sound like metal striking metal. VERB make a clank.

clap VERB (**claps**, **clapping**, **clapped**) **1** strike the palms of one's hands loudly together, especially in applause. **2** place (a hand) quickly over a part of one's face; slap on the back. NOUN **1** an act of clapping. **2** a sharp noise of thunder.
clapped out [INFORMAL] worn out.

clapper NOUN the tongue or striker of a bell.

clapperboard NOUN a device of hinged boards

struck together at the start of filming to synchronize the starting of picture and sound machinery.

claptrap NOUN pretentious talk; nonsense.

claret NOUN a dry red wine.

clarify VERB (**clarifies**, **clarifying**, **clarified**) **1** make more intelligible. **2** remove impurities from (fats) by heating.
clarification NOUN

clarinet NOUN a woodwind instrument.
clarinettist NOUN

clarion ADJ loud, rousing.

clarity NOUN clearness.

clash NOUN a violent confrontation, a conflict; discordant sounds or colours. VERB come into conflict; be incompatible; be discordant.

clasp NOUN a device for fastening things, with interlocking parts; a grasp, a handshake. VERB grasp tightly; embrace closely; fasten with a clasp.

class NOUN **1** a set of people or things with shared characteristics; a standard of quality; a social rank; a set of students taught together. **2** [INFORMAL] excellence; style. VERB assign to a particular category.

classic ADJ **1** of recognized high quality. **2** typical. **3** simple in style. NOUN **1** a classic author or work etc. **2** (**classics**) the study of ancient Greek and Roman literature, history, etc.
classicism NOUN
classicist NOUN

classical ADJ **1** of ancient Greek and Roman civilization. **2** traditional in form and style.
classically ADV

classify VERB (**classifies**, **classifying**, **classified**) **1** arrange systematically; class. **2** designate as officially secret.
classifiable ADJ
classification NOUN
classified ADJ

classless ADJ without distinctions of social class.

classroom NOUN a room where a class of students

is taught.

classy ADJ (**classier**, **classiest**) [INFORMAL] of high quality; stylish.

clatter NOUN a rattling sound. VERB make a clatter.

clause NOUN **1** a single part in a treaty, law, or contract. **2** a distinct part of a sentence, with its own verb.

claustrophobia NOUN abnormal fear of being in an enclosed space.
claustrophobic ADJ

clavichord NOUN an early keyboard instrument.

clavicle NOUN the collarbone.

claw NOUN a pointed nail on an animal's or bird's foot; a claw-like device for grappling or holding things. VERB scratch or clutch with a claw or hand.

clay NOUN stiff sticky earth, used for making bricks and pottery.
clayey ADJ

clay pigeon NOUN a breakable disc thrown up as a target for shooting.

clean ADJ free from dirt or impurities; not soiled or used; not indecent or obscene. VERB make clean.
cleaner NOUN
cleanly ADV

cleanly /klen-li/ ADJ (**cleanlier**, **cleanliest**) attentive to cleanness, with clean habits.
cleanliness NOUN

cleanse /klenz/ VERB make clean; rid of undesirable elements.
cleanser NOUN

clear ADJ **1** easily perceived or understood. **2** transparent. **3** free of obstructions. **4** free from blemishes, doubts, or anything undesirable. VERB **1** free or become free from obstacles etc. **2** prove innocent. **3** get past or over. **4** give official approval for. **5** make as net profit.
clear off [INFORMAL] go away. **clear out 1** empty, tidy. **2** [INFORMAL] go away.
clearly ADV

clearance NOUN **1** the action or process of clearing. **2** official permission. **3** space allowed for one object to pass another.

clearing NOUN a space cleared of trees in a forest.

clearway NOUN a road where vehicles must not stop.

cleat NOUN a projecting piece for fastening ropes to.

cleavage NOUN a split, a separation; the hollow between full breasts.

cleave¹ VERB (**cleaves**, **cleaving**, **cleaved** or **cleft** or **clove**; PAST PARTICIPLE **cleft** or **cloven**) [LITERARY] split, divide.

cleave² VERB stick, cling.

cleaver NOUN a chopping tool.

clef NOUN a symbol on a stave in music, showing the pitch of notes.

cleft ADJ split. NOUN a split, a cleavage.

cleft lip NOUN a split in the upper lip, present from birth.

cleft palate NOUN a split in the roof of the mouth, present from birth.

clematis NOUN a climbing plant with showy flowers.

clemency NOUN mercy.
clement ADJ

clementine NOUN a small variety of orange.

clench VERB close (the teeth or fingers) tightly.

clerestory NOUN (PL **clerestories**) an upper row of windows in a large church.

clergy NOUN people ordained for religious duties.
clergyman NOUN

cleric NOUN a member of the clergy.

clerical ADJ **1** of routine office work. **2** of clergy.

clerk NOUN a person employed to do written work in an office.

clever ADJ quick at learning and understanding things; showing skill.
cleverly ADV
cleverness NOUN

cliché /klee-shay/ NOUN an overused phrase or idea.
clichéd ADJ

click NOUN a short sharp sound. VERB **1** make or cause to make such a sound; press (a button on a computer mouse). **2** [INFORMAL] quickly

C

become friendly. 3 [INFORMAL] become intelligible.

client NOUN a person using the services of a professional person.

clientele /klee-ahn-**tel**/ NOUN clients collectively.

cliff NOUN a steep rock face, especially on a coast.

cliffhanger NOUN an ending to an episode of a serial that leaves the audience in suspense.

climate NOUN the regular weather conditions of an area.
climatic ADJ

climax NOUN the most intense or exciting point; the culmination.
climactic ADJ

climb VERB go up; rise. NOUN an ascent; a route for ascent; an increase.
climber NOUN

clime NOUN [LITERARY] a climate; a region.

clinch VERB settle conclusively; fasten; grapple. NOUN a close hold or embrace.
clincher NOUN

cling VERB (**clings**, **clinging**, **clung**) hold on tightly; stick.

cling film NOUN thin polythene wrapping that adheres to surfaces.

clinic NOUN a place or session at which medical treatment is given; a private or specialized hospital.

clinical ADJ 1 of or used in the treatment of patients. 2 unemotional and efficient.
clinically ADV

clink NOUN 1 a sharp ringing sound. 2 [INFORMAL] prison. VERB make this sound.

clinker NOUN fused coal ash.

clip NOUN 1 a device for holding things together or in place. 2 an act of cutting; an excerpt. 3 [INFORMAL] a sharp blow. VERB (**clips**, **clipping**, **clipped**) 1 fasten with a clip. 2 cut with shears or scissors. 3 [INFORMAL] hit sharply.

clipper NOUN 1 a fast sailing ship. 2 (**clippers**) an instrument for clipping.

clipping NOUN a piece

clipped off; a newspaper cutting.

clique /kleek/ NOUN a small exclusive group.
cliquey ADJ
cliquish ADJ

clitoris NOUN the small erectile part of the female genitals.

cloak NOUN an outer garment that fastens at the neck and hangs loosely from the shoulders. VERB cover, conceal.

cloakroom NOUN **1** a room where outer garments can be left. **2** a lavatory.

clobber [INFORMAL] NOUN equipment; belongings. VERB hit hard; defeat heavily.

cloche /klosh/ NOUN a translucent cover for protecting plants.

clock NOUN an instrument indicating time.
clock in or **on, out** or **off** register one's time of arrival or departure.
clock up [INFORMAL] reach, register (a speed or total).

clockwise ADV & ADJ moving in the direction of the hands of a clock.

clockwork NOUN a mechanism with a spring and interlocking wheels, used to drive a clock or other device.
like clockwork smoothly and easily; predictably.

clod NOUN a lump of earth.

clog NOUN a wooden-soled shoe. VERB (**clogs**, **clogging**, **clogged**) cause an obstruction in; become blocked.

cloister NOUN a covered walk round an open court in a monastery, cathedral, etc.

cloistered ADJ shut away, sheltered, secluded.

clone NOUN a group of organisms or cells produced asexually from one ancestor; an identical copy. VERB produce (a clone); make an identical copy of.

close ADJ /klohss/ **1** near in space or time. **2** very affectionate or intimate. **3** airless, humid. **4** detailed, careful. **5** secretive; stingy. ADV /klohss/ in or into a near position; leaving little space. VERB /klohz/ **1** move so as to cover an opening; bring two parts of (something) together. **2** bring or come to an end. **3** come nearer together. NOUN **1** /klohz/ an ending. **2** /klohss/ a street closed at one end; the precinct surrounding a cathedral.

closely ADV

closeness NOUN

closet NOUN a tall cupboard; a small room. VERB (**closets, closeting, closeted**) shut away in private conference or study. ADJ secret, unacknowledged.

close-up NOUN a photograph etc. showing a subject at close range.

closure NOUN the action of closing; conclusion.

clot NOUN **1** a thickened mass of liquid. **2** [INFORMAL] a stupid person. VERB (**clots, clotting, clotted**) form clots.

cloth NOUN **1** woven or felted material; a piece of this for cleaning etc. **2** the clergy; the clerical profession.

clothe VERB put clothes on; provide with clothes.

clothes PLURAL NOUN things worn to cover the body.

clothier NOUN a maker or seller of clothes or cloth.

clothing NOUN clothes for the body.

clotted cream NOUN very thick cream, thickened by scalding.

cloud NOUN **1** a visible mass of watery vapour floating in the sky; a mass of smoke or dust. **2** something spoiling happiness or peace. VERB **1** (**cloud over**) become covered with clouds. **2** become less clear. **3** show sadness or gloom.

cloudburst NOUN a sudden violent rain storm.

cloudy ADJ (**cloudier, cloudiest**) covered with clouds; (of liquid) not transparent.

cloudiness NOUN

clout [INFORMAL] NOUN **1** a blow. **2** influence. VERB hit.

clove[1] past of **CLEAVE**[1].

clove[2] NOUN **1** a dried bud of a tropical tree, used as a spice. **2** one division of a compound bulb such as garlic.

clove hitch NOUN a knot used to fasten a rope round a pole etc.

cloven hoof NOUN a divided hoof like that of sheep, cows, etc.

clover NOUN a flowering plant with three-lobed leaves.
in clover in luxury.

clown NOUN a person who does comical tricks. VERB perform or behave as a clown.

cloy VERB sicken by glutting with sweetness or pleasure.

club NOUN **1** a group who meet for social or sporting purposes; their premises; an organization offering benefits to subscribers. **2** a heavy stick used as a weapon; a stick with a wooden or metal head, used in golf. **3** (**clubs**) one of the four suits in a pack of playing cards, marked with black trefoils. VERB (**clubs**, **clubbing**, **clubbed**) **1** strike with a club. **2** go to nightclubs.
club together join together to collect a sum of money.

club class NOUN a class of air travel designed for business travellers.

cluck NOUN the throaty cry of a hen. VERB utter a cluck.

clue NOUN something that helps solve a puzzle or problem.

clump NOUN a cluster, a mass. VERB **1** tread heavily. **2** form into a clump.

clumsy ADJ (**clumsier**, **clumsiest**) moving or done without grace or skill; awkward to handle.
clumsily ADV
clumsiness NOUN

clung past and past participle of **CLING**.

cluster NOUN a small close group. VERB form a cluster.

clutch VERB grasp tightly. NOUN **1** a tight grasp. **2** a device for connecting and disconnecting moving parts. **3** a set of eggs laid at one time; chickens hatched from these.

clutter NOUN things lying about untidily. VERB crowd untidily.

cm ABBREV centimetre(s).

C

CND ABBREV Campaign for Nuclear Disarmament.

Co. ABBREV **1** company. **2** county.

co- COMBINING FORM joint, jointly.

c/o ABBREV care of.

coach NOUN **1** a long-distance bus; a horse-drawn carriage; a railway carriage. **2** a private tutor; an instructor in sports. VERB train, teach.

coagulate /koh-ag-yoo-layt/ VERB change from liquid to semi-solid; clot.
coagulant NOUN
coagulation NOUN

coal NOUN a hard black mineral burnt as fuel.

coalesce VERB form a single mass; combine.
coalescence NOUN

coalfield NOUN an area where coal is mined.

coalition NOUN a union, especially a temporary union of political parties.

coal tar NOUN tar produced when gas is made from coal.

coarse ADJ **1** composed of large particles; rough in texture. **2** crude, vulgar.
coarsely ADV
coarseness NOUN

coarse fish NOUN any freshwater fish other than salmon and trout.

coarsen VERB make or become coarse.

coast NOUN the seashore and land near it. VERB move easily without using power.
coastal ADJ

coaster NOUN **1** a ship trading along a coast. **2** a mat for a glass.

coastguard NOUN an officer of an organization that keeps watch on the coast.

coat NOUN a long outer garment with sleeves; the fur or hair covering an animal's body; a covering layer. VERB cover with a layer.

coating NOUN a covering layer.

coat of arms NOUN a design on a shield as the emblem of a family or institution.

coax VERB persuade gently; manipulate carefully or slowly.

coaxial /koh-aks-i-ăl/ ADJ (of cable) containing two

conductors, one surrounding but insulated from the other.

cob NOUN **1** a sturdy short-legged horse. **2** a hazelnut. **3** the central part of an ear of maize. **4** a small round loaf. **5** a male swan.

cobalt NOUN a metallic element; a deep blue pigment made from this.

cobber NOUN [AUSTRALIAN] [INFORMAL] a friend, a mate.

cobble NOUN a rounded stone formerly used for paving roads. VERB mend or assemble roughly.

cobbler NOUN a shoe-mender.

cobra NOUN a poisonous snake of India and Africa.

cobweb NOUN a spider's web.

cocaine NOUN a drug used illegally as a stimulant.

coccyx /**kok**-siks/ NOUN the bone at the base of the spinal column.

cochineal /ko-chi-**neel**/ NOUN red food colouring made from dried insects.

cock NOUN **1** a male bird. **2** a stopcock. **3** a firing lever in a gun. **4** [VULGAR SLANG] a penis. VERB **1** tilt (the head etc.); bend. **2** set (a gun) for firing.

cockade NOUN a knot of ribbons, rosette, etc. worn on a hat as part of a uniform.

cock-a-hoop ADJ very pleased, triumphant.

cockatoo NOUN (PL **cockatoos**) a crested parrot.

cockatrice NOUN a basilisk; a dragon with a cock's head.

cockerel NOUN a young male fowl.

cock-eyed ADJ [INFORMAL] **1** crooked. **2** absurd, crazy.

cockle NOUN an edible shellfish.

cockney NOUN (PL **cockneys**) a person from the East End of London; their accent or dialect.

cockpit NOUN **1** the compartment for the pilot in a plane, or for the driver in a racing car. **2** a pit for cockfighting.

cockroach NOUN a beetle-like insect.

cockscomb NOUN the crest of a male fowl.

C

cocksure ADJ overconfident.

cocktail NOUN a mixed alcoholic drink; a dish of mixed small pieces of food; a mixture.

cocky ADJ (**cockier**, **cockiest**) conceited and arrogant.
cockily ADV

cocoa NOUN powdered cacao seeds; a drink made from this.

coconut NOUN the nut of a tropical palm.

cocoon NOUN a silky sheath round a chrysalis; a protective wrapping. VERB wrap in something soft and warm; protect, cherish.

cod NOUN a large edible sea fish.

coda NOUN the final part of a musical composition.

coddle VERB **1** cherish and protect. **2** cook (eggs) in water just below boiling point.

code NOUN **1** a system of words or symbols used to represent others for secrecy; a sequence of numbers or letters for identification. **2** a set of laws, standards, etc.

codeine /koh-deen/ NOUN a painkilling drug.

codicil NOUN an appendix to a will.

codify VERB (**codifies**, **codifying**, **codified**) arrange (laws etc.) into a code.
codification NOUN

co-education NOUN education of boys and girls in the same classes.
co-educational ADJ

coefficient NOUN a multiplier; the constant multiplying the variable in an algebraic expression.

coelacanth /seel-ă-kanth/ NOUN a large sea fish formerly thought to be extinct.

coerce VERB compel by threats or force.
coercion NOUN
coercive ADJ

coeval /koh-eev-ăl/ ADJ of the same age or epoch.

coexist VERB exist together, especially harmoniously.
coexistence NOUN
coexistent ADJ

C. of E. ABBREV Church of

England.

coffee NOUN the seeds of a tropical shrub, roasted and ground for making a drink; this drink; a pale brown colour.

coffee table NOUN a small low table.

coffer NOUN a large strong box for holding money and valuables; (**coffers**) financial resources.

coffin NOUN a long box in which a corpse is laid for burial or cremation.

cog NOUN one of a series of projections on the edge of a wheel, engaging with those of another.

cogent ADJ logical and convincing.
cogency NOUN
cogently ADV

cogitate VERB think deeply.
cogitation NOUN

cognac /**kon**-yak/ NOUN French brandy.

cognate ADJ akin, related.

cognition NOUN the process of gaining knowledge through thought or perception.
cognitive ADJ

cognizant ADJ aware; having knowledge.
cognizance NOUN

cognoscente /kon-yŏ-**shen**-ti/ NOUN (PL **cognoscenti**) a connoisseur.

cohabit VERB live together as man and wife.
cohabitation NOUN

cohere VERB hold firmly together; form a whole.

coherent ADJ connected logically; articulate; forming a consistent whole.
coherence NOUN
coherently ADV

cohesion NOUN the action of holding together or forming a whole.
cohesive ADJ
cohesively ADV

cohort NOUN a tenth part of a Roman legion; a group or set of people.

coiffure /kwa-**fyoor**/ NOUN a hairstyle.

coil VERB wind into a spiral. NOUN **1** something wound in a spiral; one ring or turn in this. **2** a contraceptive device inserted into the womb.

coin NOUN a piece of metal money. VERB **1** make

C

(coins) by stamping metal; [INFORMAL] get (money) in large quantities as profit. **2** invent (a word or phrase).

coinage NOUN **1** coins, a system of coins; the making of coins. **2** a coined word or phrase.

coincide VERB occupy the same portion of time or space; be in agreement or identical.

coincidence NOUN **1** the chance occurrence of events which are similar or interrelate to affect developments. **2** the fact of two or more things coinciding.
coincidental ADJ
coincidentally ADV

coir /koi-ĕ/ NOUN fibre from coconut husks.

coitus NOUN sexual intercourse.

coke NOUN **1** a solid substance left after gas and tar have been extracted from coal, used as fuel. **2** [INFORMAL] cocaine.

col NOUN the lowest point in a ridge between two mountain peaks.

colander NOUN a perforated container for draining food.

cold ADJ **1** at or having a low temperature. **2** not affectionate; not enthusiastic. **3** not prepared or rehearsed.
NOUN **1** low temperature; a cold condition. **2** an illness causing catarrh and sneezing.
coldly ADV
coldness NOUN

cold-blooded ADJ **1** having a blood temperature varying with that of the surroundings. **2** unfeeling, ruthless.

cold feet PLURAL NOUN [INFORMAL] loss of confidence.

cold-shoulder VERB treat with deliberate unfriendliness.

cold turkey NOUN [INFORMAL] an unpleasant state experienced by a drug addict after the sudden withdrawal of the drug.

cold war NOUN hostility between nations without fighting.

coleslaw NOUN a salad of shredded raw cabbage in

a dressing.

coley NOUN an edible fish.

colic NOUN severe abdominal pain.

colitis NOUN inflammation of the colon.

collaborate VERB work in partnership.
collaboration NOUN
collaborator NOUN
collaborative ADJ

collage /kol-ah*zh*/ NOUN a picture formed by fixing various items to a backing; this art form.

collagen NOUN a protein substance found in bone and tissue.

collapse VERB fall down suddenly; lose strength suddenly; fold. NOUN an instance of something collapsing; a breakdown or failure.

collapsible ADJ made so as to fold up.

collar NOUN **1** a band round the neck of a garment. **2** a band holding part of a machine. **3** a cut of bacon from near the head. VERB [INFORMAL] seize or apprehend.

collate VERB **1** collect and combine. **2** compare in detail.
collation NOUN
collator NOUN

collateral ADJ additional but subordinate. NOUN security for repayment of a loan.
collaterally ADV

colleague NOUN a fellow worker in a business or profession.

collect VERB bring or come together; obtain specimens of, especially as a hobby; fetch. ADV & ADJ [US] (of a telephone call) paid for by the person receiving it. NOUN a short prayer.
collectable (or **collectible**) ADJ & NOUN
collector NOUN

collected ADJ calm and controlled.

collection NOUN the action of collecting; a set of objects or money collected.

collective ADJ of or denoting a group taken or working as a unit.
collectively ADV

collective noun NOUN [GRAMMAR] a noun (singular in form) denoting a group (e.g.

army, herd).

colleen NOUN [IRISH] a girl.

C

college NOUN an educational establishment for higher or professional education; an organized body of professional people.
collegiate ADJ

collide VERB (of two moving things) bump into each other; (**collide with**) strike against when moving.

collie NOUN a breed of dog often used as a sheepdog.

colliery NOUN (PL **collieries**) a coal mine.

collision NOUN the striking of one thing against another when at least one is moving.

collocate VERB place (words) together.
collocation NOUN

colloquial ADJ suitable for informal speech or writing.
colloquialism NOUN
colloquially ADV

collusion NOUN an agreement made for a deceitful or fraudulent purpose.

cologne /kŏ-**lohn**/ NOUN a light perfume.

colon NOUN **1** a punctuation mark (:). **2** the lower part of the large intestine.
colonic ADJ

colonel /**ker**-nĕl/ NOUN an army officer next below brigadier.

colonial ADJ of a colony or colonies. NOUN an inhabitant of a colony.

colonialism NOUN a policy of acquiring or maintaining colonies.

colonize (also **colonise**) VERB (**colonizes**, **colonizing**, **colonized**) acquire as a colony; establish a colony in.
colonist NOUN
colonization NOUN

colonnade NOUN a row of columns.

colony NOUN (PL **colonies**) a country under the control of and occupied by settlers from another country; a group of settlers; people of shared nationality or occupation living as a community; a community of animals or plants of one kind.

C

color, **colorful**, etc. US spelling of **COLOUR**, **COLOURFUL**, etc.

coloration (also **colouration**) NOUN arrangement or scheme of colour; colouring.

coloratura NOUN elaborate ornamentation of a vocal melody; a singer (especially a soprano) skilled in such singing.

colossal ADJ immense. **colossally** ADV

colossus NOUN (PL **colossi** or **colossuses**) an immense statue.

colostomy NOUN (PL **colostomies**) an operation to form an opening from the colon onto the surface of the abdomen, through which the bowel can empty.

colour ([US] **color**) NOUN **1** the effect on something's appearance of the way it reflects light; pigment, paint. **2** (usually **colours**) the flag of a ship or regiment. VERB **1** put colour on. **2** blush. **3** give a special character or bias to (an outlook, account, etc.).

colourant (also **colorant**) NOUN a dye etc.

colour-blind ADJ unable to distinguish between certain colours.

coloured ([US] **colored**) ADJ **1** having a colour. **2** wholly or partly of non-white descent.

colourful ([US] **colorful**) ADJ **1** full of colour. **2** vivid, lively; (of language) rude. **colourfully** ADV

colourless ([US] **colorless**) ADJ without colour; lacking vividness.

colt NOUN a young male horse.

column NOUN **1** a round pillar; something resembling this. **2** a vertical division of a page; material printed in this. **3** a long narrow formation of troops, vehicles, etc.

columnist NOUN a journalist who regularly writes a column of comments.

coma NOUN deep unconsciousness.

comatose ADJ in a coma; [INFORMAL] very lethargic.

comb NOUN **1** an object

with a row of fine teeth for tidying hair. **2** a fowl's fleshy crest. VERB tidy with a comb; search thoroughly.

combat NOUN fighting, especially between armed forces. VERB (**combats, combating, combatted**) oppose; try to stop or destroy.

combatant NOUN a person or nation engaged in fighting.

combative ADJ ready or eager to fight or argue.

combe variant of **COOMB**.

combination NOUN **1** the process of combining or being combined; a set of united but distinct elements. **2** (**combinations**) [DATED] an undergarment covering the body and legs.

combination lock NOUN a lock controlled by a series of positions of dials.

combine VERB /kŏm-**byn**/ (**combines, combining, combined**) put together; join, unite. NOUN /**kom**-byn/ **1** a combination of people or firms acting together. **2** (in full **combine harvester**) a combined reaping and threshing machine.

combining form NOUN a word or partial word used in combination with another to form a different word, e.g. *Anglo-*.

combustible ADJ capable of catching fire.

combustion NOUN the process of burning; the process in which substances combine with oxygen and produce heat.

come VERB (**comes, coming, came**) move towards the speaker or a place or point; arrive; occur; pass into a specified state; originate from a specified place; have a specified place in an ordering. **come about** happen. **come across 1** find by chance. **2** make a particular impression. **come by** obtain. **come into** inherit. **come off** be successful. **come**

out become known; cease to be secretive. **come round 1** recover consciousness. **2** be persuaded. **come to** recover consciousness. **come up** occur; arise for discussion.

comeback NOUN **1** a return to a former successful position. **2** a retort.

comedian NOUN a humorous entertainer.

comedienne NOUN a female comedian.

comedown NOUN a fall in status.

comedy NOUN (PL **comedies**) an amusing book, film, or play; the amusing aspect of a series of events etc.

comely ADJ (**comelier**, **comeliest**) [ARCHAIC] attractive.
comeliness NOUN

comestibles PLURAL NOUN [FORMAL] food.

comet NOUN a mass of ice and dust with a long tail, moving round the solar system.

comeuppance NOUN (**get one's comeuppance**) [INFORMAL] get the punishment or fate one deserves.

comfort NOUN a state of ease and contentment; relief of suffering or grief; a person or thing giving this. VERB relieve the grief of.
comforter NOUN

comfortable ADJ **1** providing or enjoying physical or mental ease. **2** adequate; easy.
comfortably ADV

comfy ADJ (**comfier**, **comfiest**) [INFORMAL] comfortable.

comic ADJ causing amusement; of comedy. NOUN **1** a comedian. **2** a children's paper with a series of strip cartoons.
comical ADJ
comically ADV

comic strip NOUN a sequence of drawings telling a story.

comma NOUN a punctuation mark (,).

command NOUN **1** an order, an instruction; authority; forces or a district under a commander. **2** skill in using something. VERB **1** give an order to; have authority over. **2** be in a position to receive.

commandant NOUN an officer in command of a military establishment.

commandeer VERB seize for use.

commander NOUN a person in command; a naval officer next below captain; a police officer next below commissioner.

commandment NOUN a rule to be strictly observed.

commando NOUN (PL **commandos**) a member of a military unit specially trained for making raids and assaults.

commemorate VERB keep in the memory by a celebration or memorial.
commemoration NOUN
commemorative ADJ

commence VERB begin.
commencement NOUN

commend VERB **1** praise. **2** [FORMAL] entrust.
commendation NOUN

commendable ADJ worthy of praise.
commendably ADV

commensurable ADJ measurable by the same standard.
commensurably ADV

commensurate ADJ proportionate, corresponding.

comment NOUN an expression of opinion; an explanatory note. VERB make a comment.

commentary NOUN (PL **commentaries**) **1** the making of comments; a set of notes on a text. **2** an account of an event, given as it occurs.

commentator NOUN a person who gives a commentary on an event.
commentate VERB

commerce NOUN all forms of trade and business.

commercial ADJ of or engaged in commerce; intended to make a profit. NOUN a radio or television advertisment.
commercially ADV

commercialize (also **commercialise**) VERB (**commercializes**, **commercializing**, **commercialized**) operate (a business etc.) so as to

make a profit.
commercialization NOUN

commiserate VERB sympathize; express pity.
commiseration NOUN

commissariat NOUN a military department supplying food.

commission NOUN **1** a task, an instruction; an order for a piece of work; a group of people given official authority to do something. **2** a sum paid to an agent selling goods or services. **3** a warrant conferring the rank of officer in the armed forces. **4** the committing of an offence. VERB **1** order or authorize the production of. **2** bring into working order.
in commission ready for service. **out of commission** not in working order.

commissionaire NOUN a uniformed attendant at the door of a theatre, business premises, etc.

commissioner NOUN a member of, or a person appointed by, a commission; a government official in charge of a district abroad.

commit VERB (**commits**, **committing**, **committed**) **1** do, carry out (a crime etc.). **2** bind to a course of action. **3** entrust, consign.

commitment NOUN dedication; an obligation; a binding pledge.

committal NOUN **1** the committing of someone to prison etc. **2** a burial.

committee NOUN a group of people appointed to attend to special business or manage the affairs of a club etc.

commode NOUN **1** a seat containing a chamber pot. **2** a chest of drawers.

commodious ADJ roomy.

commodity NOUN (PL **commodities**) an article to be bought and sold; something valuable.

commodore NOUN a naval officer next below rear admiral; a president of a yacht club.

common ADJ **1** found or done often; not rare. **2** generally or widely shared. **3** ordinary, undistinguished. **4** vulgar. NOUN an area of unfenced grassland for public use.

commoner NOUN one of the common people, not a noble.

common law NOUN an unwritten law based on custom and former court decisions.

commonly ADV usually, frequently.

Common Market NOUN the European Community.

commonplace ADJ ordinary; lacking originality. NOUN something widely recognized; a trite remark.

common room NOUN a room shared by students or workers for social purposes.

common sense NOUN normal good sense in practical matters.

commonwealth NOUN an independent state; a federation of states; (**the Commonwealth**) an association of Britain and independent states formerly under British rule.

commotion NOUN uproar, confusion, disturbance.

communal ADJ shared among a group.
communally ADV

commune VERB /kŏ-**mewn**/ communicate mentally or spiritually. NOUN /**kom**-yoon/ **1** a group (not all of one family) sharing accommodation and goods. **2** a district of local government in France etc.

communicable ADJ able to be made known or transmitted to others.

communicant NOUN a person who receives Holy Communion.

communicate VERB **1** exchange news and information; pass on (information); transmit, convey. **2** (**communicating**) (of two rooms) having a connecting door.
communicator NOUN

communication NOUN the sharing or imparting of information; a letter or message; (**communications**) means of communicating or of travelling.

communicative ADJ talkative; willing to give information.

communion NOUN **1** the sharing of thoughts and feelings. **2** (**Holy Communion**) a Christian sacrament in which bread and wine are made holy are shared.

communiqué /kŏ-**mew**-ni-kay/ NOUN an official announcement or statement.

communism NOUN a social system based on common ownership of property, means of production, etc.; a political doctrine or movement seeking a form of this.
communist NOUN & ADJ

community NOUN (PL **communities**) **1** a body of people living in one place or united by origin, interests, etc.; the public, society. **2** similarity or identity.

commute VERB **1** travel regularly between one's home and workplace. **2** exchange, replace; make (a sentence) less severe.
commuter NOUN

compact ADJ /kŏm-**pakt**/ closely or neatly packed together; concise. VERB /kŏm-**pakt**/ compress. NOUN /**kom**-pakt/ **1** a small flat case for face powder. **2** a pact, a contract.

compact disc NOUN a small disc on which music or other digital information is stored.

companion NOUN a person living or travelling with another; a thing designed to complement another.
companionship NOUN

companionable ADJ sociable.

companionway NOUN a staircase from a ship's deck to cabins etc.

company NOUN (PL **companies**) **1** the fact of being with other people; companionship; a group of people. **2** a commercial business. **3** a subdivision of an infantry battalion.

comparable ADJ able to be compared; similar.
comparability NOUN
comparably ADV

C

comparative ADJ involving comparison; based on or judged by comparing; of the grammatical form expressing 'more'. NOUN a comparative form of a word.
comparatively ADV

compare VERB **1** assess the similarity of. **2** declare to be similar. **3** be of equal quality with something.
beyond compare outstanding, unparalleled.

comparison NOUN the action or process of comparing.

compartment NOUN a partitioned space.
compartmental ADJ

compass NOUN **1** a device showing the direction of the magnetic or true north. **2** range, scope. **3** (**compasses**) a hinged instrument for drawing circles.

compassion NOUN a feeling of sympathetic pity.
compassionate ADJ
compassionately ADV

compatible ADJ able to exist or be used together; consistent.
compatibility NOUN
compatibly ADV

compatriot NOUN a fellow countryman.

compel VERB (**compels**, **compelling**, **compelled**) force.

compelling ADJ very interesting, fascinating; irresistible; very convincing.

compendious ADJ giving much information concisely.

compendium NOUN (PL **compendia** or **compendiums**) a summary; a collection of information etc.

compensate VERB make payment to (a person) in return for loss or damage; counterbalance, offset something.
compensation NOUN
compensatory ADJ

compère /kom-pair/ NOUN a person who introduces performers in a variety show. VERB act as compère.

compete VERB try to win something by defeating others; take part in a competition.

competence NOUN ability, efficiency.

competent ADJ skilled and efficient.
competently ADV

competition NOUN an event in which people try to outdo others; the activity of competing; one's rivals in a competition.

competitive ADJ involving competition; enjoying competition, anxious to win.
competitively ADV
competitiveness NOUN

competitor NOUN one who competes.

compile VERB collect and arrange into a list or book; make (a book) in this way.
compilation NOUN
compiler NOUN

complacent ADJ not worrying about one's abilities, a situation, etc.; self-satisfied.
complacency NOUN
complacently ADV

complain VERB express dissatisfaction.
complainant NOUN

complaint NOUN **1** a declaration of dissatisfaction or annoyance. **2** an illness.

complaisant ADJ willing to please others.
complaisance NOUN

complement NOUN a thing that completes or balances something else; the full number required. VERB form a complement to.
complementary ADJ

complete ADJ having all its parts, entire; finished; total, absolute. VERB make complete; fill in (a form).
completely ADV
completeness NOUN
completion NOUN

complex ADJ made up of many parts; complicated, hard to understand. NOUN **1** a complex whole; a group of buildings. **2** a set of repressed or complicated feelings affecting behaviour.
complexity NOUN

complexion NOUN the colour and texture of the skin of the face; the general character of things.

compliant ADJ

complying, obedient.
compliance NOUN

C

complicate VERB make complicated.

complicated ADJ difficult because complex and confused.

complication NOUN the fact of being complicated; a factor causing this; a secondary disease aggravating an existing one.

complicity NOUN involvement in wrongdoing.

compliment NOUN a polite expression of praise. VERB pay a compliment to.

complimentary ADJ **1** expressing a compliment. **2** free of charge.

compline NOUN (in the Roman Catholic Church) the last service of the day.

comply VERB (**complies, complying, complied**) act in accordance with a request.

component NOUN one of the parts of which a thing is composed.

comport VERB (**comport oneself**) conduct oneself, behave.

compose VERB **1** create (a work of music); write (a letter, poem, etc.). **2** (of parts) make up (a whole). **3** prepare (a text) for printing. **4** (**composed**) calm and in control of one's feelings.
composer NOUN

composite ADJ made up of parts.

composition NOUN **1** the way something is made up; its structures and elements. **2** the process of composing. **3** a musical work; a piece of written work; a painting. **4** a compound artificial substance.

compositor NOUN a typesetter.

compos mentis ADJ sane.

compost NOUN decayed organic matter used as fertilizer.

composure NOUN calmness.

compote NOUN fruit in syrup.

compound ADJ /kom-pownd/ made up of

two or more elements. NOUN /**kom**-pownd/ **1** a compound substance. **2** a fenced-in enclosure. VERB /kŏm-**pownd**/ **1** combine; make by combining. **2** make worse.

comprehend VERB grasp mentally, understand.

comprehensible ADJ intelligible. **comprehensibility** NOUN **comprehensibly** ADV

comprehension NOUN understanding.

comprehensive ADJ including much or all. NOUN (in full **comprehensive school**) a school providing secondary education for children of all abilities. **comprehensively** ADV **comprehensiveness** NOUN

compress VERB /kŏm-**press**/ squeeze; force into less space. NOUN /**kom**-press/ a pad to stop bleeding or to reduce inflammation. **compression** NOUN **compressor** NOUN

comprise VERB consist of.

compromise NOUN a settlement reached by concessions on each side. VERB **1** make a settlement in this way. **2** expose to suspicion, scandal, or danger.

comptroller /kŏn-**troh**-ler/ NOUN (in titles) a financial controller.

compulsion NOUN pressure to do something; an irresistible urge.

compulsive ADJ **1** resulting from or driven by an irresistible urge. **2** fascinating, gripping. **compulsively** ADV

compulsory ADJ required by a law or rule. **compulsorily** ADV

compunction NOUN regret, scruple.

compute VERB calculate; use a computer. **computation** NOUN

computer NOUN an electronic device for analysing or storing data, making calculations, etc.

computerize (also **computerise**) VERB (**computerizes**, **computerizing**, **computerized**) equip with, perform, or operate by computer. **computerization** NOUN

C

comrade NOUN a companion, an associate. **comradeship** NOUN

con VERB (**cons, conning, conned**) [INFORMAL] trick, cheat. NOUN **1** [INFORMAL] a confidence trick. **2** (in the phrase **pros and cons**) a disadvantage; an argument against something.
pros and cons *see* **PRO**.

concatenation NOUN a connected series.

concave ADJ curving inwards like the inner surface of a ball.

conceal VERB hide, keep secret.
concealment NOUN

concede VERB **1** admit to be true; grant (a privilege etc.). **2** admit defeat in (a contest); yield.

conceit NOUN **1** excessive pride in oneself. **2** a fanciful idea or figure of speech.

conceited ADJ vain, arrogant.

conceivable ADJ able to be imagined or grasped.
conceivably ADV

conceive VERB **1** become pregnant (with). **2** form (an idea etc.) in the mind.

concentrate VERB **1** focus all one's attention. **2** gather together in a small area; make less dilute. NOUN a concentrated substance.
concentrated ADJ
concentration NOUN

concentration camp NOUN a prison camp for political prisoners etc., especially associated with Nazi Germany.

concentric ADJ (of circles) having the same centre.
concentrically ADV

concept NOUN an idea, a general notion.
conceptual ADJ

conception NOUN **1** the conceiving of a child. **2** the devising of a plan; a concept.

conceptualize (also **conceptualise**) VERB (**conceptualizes, conceptualizing, conceptualized**) form a concept of.
conceptualization NOUN

concern VERB **1** be about. **2** be relevant to; involve. **3** make anxious. NOUN

1 anxiety. 2 something in which one is interested or involved. 3 a business, a firm.

concerned ADJ anxious.

concerning PREP on the subject of.

concert NOUN a musical entertainment.

concerted ADJ done in combination; jointly arranged or carried out; done in a determined way.

concertina NOUN a portable musical instrument with bellows and buttons.
VERB (**concertinas**, **concertinaing**, **concertinaed**) fold up like concertina bellows.

concerto /kŏn-**chair**-toh/ NOUN (PL **concertos** or **concerti**) a musical composition for solo instrument and orchestra.

concession NOUN something granted; the granting or yielding of something; an allowance or reduced price.

conch NOUN a shellfish with a spiral shell.

conciliate VERB make less hostile or angry.
conciliation NOUN
conciliatory ADJ

concise ADJ expressed in few words.
concisely ADV
conciseness NOUN

conclave NOUN a private meeting.

conclude VERB 1 end; settle finally. 2 reach an opinion by reasoning.

conclusion NOUN 1 an ending. 2 an opinion reached.

conclusive ADJ decisive; settling an issue.
conclusively ADV

concoct VERB prepare from ingredients; invent.
concoction NOUN

concomitant ADJ accompanying, associated.

concord NOUN agreement, harmony.

concordance NOUN 1 an index of the words in a text. 2 [FORMAL] agreement.

concordant ADJ in agreement.

concourse NOUN 1 a large open area at a railway station etc. 2 [FORMAL] a

C

crowd.

concrete NOUN a mixture of gravel and cement etc., used for building. ADJ material, physical, not abstract; definite. VERB cover or fix with concrete.

concubine NOUN (in some societies) a woman who lives with a man but has lower status than his wife or wives.

concur VERB (**concurs**, **concurring**, **concurred**) **1** agree in opinion. **2** happen together, coincide.
concurrence NOUN
concurrent ADJ
concurrently ADV

concuss VERB affect with concussion.

concussion NOUN temporary unconsciousness caused by a blow on the head.

condemn VERB **1** express strong disapproval of; declare unfit for use. **2** sentence; doom; prove guilty.
condemnation NOUN

condensation NOUN **1** water from humid air collecting as droplets on a cold surface. **2** the conversion of gas or vapour to liquid.

condense VERB **1** make denser or briefer. **2** change from gas or vapour to liquid.

condescend VERB behave patronizingly; do something one believes to be beneath one.
condescending ADJ
condescension NOUN

condiment NOUN a seasoning for food.

condition NOUN **1** the state something is in; (**conditions**) circumstances. **2** something that is necessary if something else is to exist or occur. VERB **1** influence, determine; train, accustom. **2** bring into the desired condition.

conditional ADJ subject to specified conditions.
conditionally ADV

conditioner NOUN a substance that improves the condition of hair, fabric, etc.

condole VERB express sympathy.
condolence NOUN

condom NOUN a contraceptive sheath.

condominium NOUN [US] a building containing flats which are individually owned.

condone VERB forgive or overlook (a fault etc.).

condor NOUN a large vulture.

conducive ADJ (**conducive to**) helping or contributing towards.

conduct VERB /kŏn-**dukt**/ **1** lead, guide; be the conductor of. **2** manage; carry out. **3** transmit (heat or electricity). NOUN /**kon**-dukt/ behaviour; a way of conducting business etc.

conduction NOUN the conducting of heat or electricity.
conductive ADJ
conductivity NOUN

conductor NOUN **1** a person who directs an orchestra's or choir's performance. **2** a substance that conducts heat or electricity. **3** a person collecting fares on a bus.

conduit NOUN **1** a channel for liquid. **2** a tube protecting electric wires.

cone NOUN **1** an object with a circular base, tapering to a point. **2** a dry scaly fruit of a pine or fir.

coney (also **cony**) NOUN (PL **coneys**) a rabbit; its fur.

confection NOUN an elaborate sweet dish; an elaborately constructed thing.

confectioner NOUN a maker or seller of confectionery.

confectionery NOUN sweets, cakes, and pastries.

confederacy NOUN (PL **confederacies**) a league of states.

confederate ADJ joined by treaty or agreement. NOUN a member of a confederacy; an accomplice.

confederation NOUN a union of states, people, or organizations.

confer VERB (**confers**, **conferring**, **conferred**) **1** grant (a title etc.). **2** hold a discussion.

conference NOUN a meeting for discussion.

C

confess VERB acknowledge, admit; declare one's sins to a priest.

confession NOUN an acknowledgement of a fact, sin, guilt, etc.; a statement of beliefs.

confessional NOUN an enclosed stall in a church for hearing confessions.

confessor NOUN a priest who hears confessions and gives counsel.

confetti NOUN bits of coloured paper thrown at a bride and bridegroom.

confidant NOUN a person in whom one confides.

confidante NOUN a woman in whom one confides.

confide VERB **1** tell someone about a secret. **2** [DATED] entrust to someone.

confidence NOUN **1** trust; certainty; boldness. **2** something told in secret.

confidence trick NOUN a swindle worked by gaining a person's trust.

confident ADJ feeling confidence.
confidently ADV

confidential ADJ to be kept secret; entrusted with secrets.
confidentiality NOUN
confidentially ADV

configuration NOUN an arrangement, a form.

confine VERB keep within limits; keep shut up.

confinement NOUN **1** the state of being confined. **2** [DATED] the time of childbirth.

confines PLURAL NOUN boundaries.

confirm VERB **1** establish the truth of; make definite. **2** administer the rite of confirmation to.
confirmatory ADJ

confirmation NOUN **1** the action of confirming or state of being confirmed. **2** a Christian rite admitting a baptized person to full church membership.

confiscate VERB take or seize by authority.
confiscation NOUN

conflagration NOUN a great fire.

conflate VERB combine into one.
conflation NOUN

conflict NOUN /**kon**-flikt/ a fight, a struggle; disagreement.
VERB /kŏn-**flikt**/ clash; be incompatible.

confluence NOUN a place where two rivers unite.
confluent ADJ

conform VERB comply with rules, standards, or conventions.
conformity NOUN

conformist NOUN a person who conforms to rules or custom.
conformism NOUN

confound VERB surprise and confuse; prove wrong; defeat.

confront VERB be or come or bring face to face with; face boldly.
confrontation NOUN

confuse VERB **1** bewilder. **2** mix up, identify wrongly. **3** make muddled or unclear.
confusion NOUN

confute VERB prove wrong.
confutation NOUN

conga NOUN a dance in which people form a long winding line.

congeal VERB coagulate, solidify.

congenial ADJ suited or pleasing to one's tastes.
congenially ADV

congenital ADJ being so from birth.
congenitally ADV

conger NOUN a large sea eel.

congested ADJ over full; blocked up; (of the nose) blocked with mucus.
congestion NOUN

conglomerate NOUN /kŏn-**glom**-er-ăt/ a number of things grouped together; a corporation formed from a merger of firms.
ADJ /kŏn-**glom**-ĕr-ăt/ massed together. VERB /kŏn-**glom**-er-ayt/ gather into a mass; form a conglomerate.
conglomeration NOUN

congratulate VERB express pleasure at the success or achievements of.
congratulation NOUN
congratulatory ADJ

congregate VERB flock together.

congregation NOUN people assembled at a church service.

congress NOUN a formal meeting of delegates for discussion; (**Congress**) a law-making assembly in the USA.
congressional ADJ

congruent ADJ
1 consistent. **2** [GEOMETRY] of identical shape and size.
congruence NOUN

conical ADJ cone-shaped.

conifer NOUN a tree bearing cones.
coniferous ADJ

conjecture NOUN an opinion based on incomplete information; a guess. VERB form a conjecture.

conjugal ADJ relating to marriage.

conjugate VERB [GRAMMAR] give the different forms of (a verb).
conjugation NOUN

conjunction NOUN **1** a word such as *and* or *or*, that connects others. **2** a combination; simultaneous occurrence.

conjunctivitis NOUN inflammation of the membrane connecting the eyeball and eyelid.

conjure VERB produce as though by magic; summon, evoke.

conjuror (also **conjurer**) NOUN a person who performs sleight-of-hand tricks for entertainment.

conk [INFORMAL] NOUN the nose; the head. VERB hit.
conk out break down.

connect VERB join, be joined; associate mentally; put into contact by telephone; (of a train, coach, or flight) arrive so that passengers are in time to catch another.
connective ADJ
connector NOUN

connection NOUN **1** a link or relationship; the action of connecting; a connecting train etc. **2** (**connections**) influential friends or relatives.

connive VERB **1** (**connive at** or **in**) secretly allow (a wrongdoing). **2** conspire.
connivance NOUN

connoisseur /kon-ŏ-ser/ NOUN an expert judge in matters of taste.

connote VERB (of a word) imply in addition to its

literal meaning.
connotation NOUN

conquer VERB overcome in war or by effort.
conqueror NOUN

conquest NOUN the action of conquering; a territory gained in this way; a person whose affection or favour has been won.

conscience NOUN a sense of right and wrong guiding a person's actions.

conscientious ADJ **1** diligent in one's duty. **2** relating to conscience.
conscientiously ADV
conscientiousness NOUN

conscientious objector NOUN a person who refuses to serve in the armed forces for moral reasons.

conscious ADJ **1** awake and alert; aware. **2** intentional.
consciously ADV
consciousness NOUN

conscript VERB /kŏn-**skript**/ summon for compulsory military service. NOUN /**kon**-skript/ a conscripted person.
conscription NOUN

consecrate VERB make sacred.
consecration NOUN

consecutive ADJ following in unbroken sequence.
consecutively ADV

consensus NOUN general agreement.

consent VERB agree; give permission. NOUN permission; agreement.

consequence NOUN **1** a result or effect. **2** importance.

consequent ADJ resulting.

consequential ADJ **1** resulting. **2** important.
consequentially ADV

consequently ADV as a result.

conservancy NOUN (PL **conservancies**) **1** an authority controlling a river etc. **2** official conservation.

conservation NOUN the action or process of conserving; preservation of the natural environment; preservation and repair of historical sites and artefacts.

C

conservationist NOUN a person who seeks to preserve the natural environment.

conservative ADJ **1** opposed to change; (**Conservative**) of the Conservative Party. **2** (of an estimate) purposely low for the sake of caution. NOUN a conservative person; (**Conservative**) a member of the Conservative Party.
conservatively ADV
conservatism NOUN

Conservative party NOUN a British political party promoting free enterprise and private ownership.

conservatoire NOUN a school of music or other arts.

conservator NOUN a person involved in conservation.

conservatory NOUN (PL **conservatories**) a structure with a glass roof and walls, attached to a house.

conserve VERB /kŏn-**serv**/ keep from harm, decay, or loss. NOUN /**kon**-serv/ jam.

consider VERB **1** think carefully about. **2** believe; think. **3** take into account.

considerable ADJ great in amount or importance.
considerably ADV

considerate ADJ careful not to hurt or inconvenience others.
considerately ADV

consideration NOUN **1** careful thought; a factor taken into account in making a decision; thoughtfulness towards others. **2** a payment or reward.

considering PREP taking into account.

consign VERB deliver, send; put for disposal.

consignment NOUN **1** a batch of goods sent to someone. **2** the action of consigning.

consist VERB (**consist of**) be composed of.

consistency NOUN (PL **consistencies**) **1** the state of being consistent. **2** the degree of thickness or solidity of semi-liquid matter.

consistent ADJ **1** unchanging. **2** not conflicting; free from contradictions. **consistently** ADV

console¹ /kŏn-**sohl**/ VERB comfort in time of sorrow.

consolation NOUN comfort received after a loss or disappointment; a source of this.

console² /**kon**-sohl/ NOUN a panel holding controls for electronic equipment.

consolidate VERB **1** make stronger or more secure. **2** combine. **consolidation** NOUN

consommé /kŏn-**som**-ay/ NOUN clear soup.

consonant NOUN a sound made by obstructing the breath, a sound other than a vowel; a letter representing this. ADJ in agreement.

consort NOUN /**kon**-sort/ a husband or wife, especially of a monarch. VERB /kŏn-**sort**/ associate with someone.

consortium NOUN (PL **consortia** or **consortiums**) a group of firms acting together.

conspicuous ADJ easily seen, attracting attention. **conspicuously** ADV

conspiracy NOUN (PL **conspiracies**) a secret plan made by a group; the action of conspiring.

conspire VERB **1** plot secretly in a group to do something wrong. **2** (of events) combine to produce an effect as though deliberately. **conspirator** NOUN **conspiratorial** ADJ

constable NOUN a police officer of the lowest rank.

constabulary NOUN (PL **constabularies**) a police force.

constancy NOUN **1** faithfulness. **2** the quality of being unchanging.

constant ADJ occurring continuously or repeatedly; unchanging; faithful. NOUN an unvarying quantity. **constantly** ADV

constellation NOUN a group of stars.

consternation NOUN great surprise and anxiety or dismay.

C

constipation NOUN difficulty in emptying the bowels.
constipated ADJ

constituency NOUN (PL **constituencies**) a body of voters who elect a representative; an area represented in this way.

constituent ADJ forming part of a whole. NOUN **1** a constituent part. **2** a member of a constituency.

constitute VERB **1** be (a part) of a whole. **2** be or be equivalent to.

constitution NOUN **1** the principles by which a state is organized. **2** the general condition of the body. **3** the composition of something.

constitutional ADJ of or in accordance with a constitution. NOUN [DATED] a walk taken for exercise.

constrain VERB compel, oblige.

constraint NOUN a restriction; self-control.

constrict VERB make or become narrower; squeeze; restrict.
constriction NOUN
constrictor NOUN

construct VERB /kŏn-**strukt**/ make by placing parts together. NOUN /**kon**-strukt/ something constructed, especially in the mind.

construction NOUN **1** the process of constructing; a thing constructed. **2** an interpretation. **3** the arrangement of words in a sentence etc.

constructive ADJ (of criticism etc.) helpful, giving advice.
constructively ADV

construe VERB interpret.

consul NOUN an official representative of a state in a foreign city.
consular ADJ

consulate NOUN a consul's position or premises.

consult VERB seek information or advice from.
consultation NOUN

consultant NOUN a specialist consulted for professional advice.
consultancy NOUN

consultative ADJ of or for consultation; advisory.

consume VERB eat or drink; use up; (of fire) destroy; absorb, obsess.

consumer NOUN a person who buys or uses goods or services.

consummate VERB /**kon**-sŭ-mayt/ accomplish; complete (especially marriage by sexual intercourse). ADJ /**kon**-sum-măt/ highly skilled, perfect.
consummation NOUN

consumption NOUN **1** the action of consuming. **2** [DATED] tuberculosis.

consumptive [DATED] ADJ suffering from tuberculosis. NOUN a consumptive person.

cont. ABBREV continued.

contact NOUN the state or condition of touching; communication; an electrical connection; a person who may be contacted for information or help. VERB get in touch with.

contact lens NOUN a small lens worn directly on the eyeball to correct the vision.

contagion NOUN the spreading of disease by contact.
contagious ADJ

contain VERB **1** have within itself; include. **2** control, restrain.

container NOUN a receptacle; a metal box of standard design for transporting goods.

containment NOUN the action of keeping something harmful under control.

contaminate VERB pollute.
contaminant NOUN
contamination NOUN

contemplate VERB **1** gaze at. **2** consider as a possibility; intend; meditate.
contemplation NOUN

contemplative ADJ meditative; of religious meditation.

contemporaneous ADJ existing or occurring at the same time.

contemporary ADJ **1** living or occurring at the same time. **2** modern.

C

NOUN (PL **contemporaries**) a person of the same age or living at the same time.

contempt NOUN despising or being despised; disrespectful disregard or disobedience.

contemptible ADJ deserving contempt.

contemptuous ADJ showing contempt.
contemptuously ADV

contend VERB **1** struggle; compete. **2** assert, argue.
contender NOUN

content¹ /kŏn-**tent**/ ADJ satisfied with what one has. NOUN satisfaction. VERB satisfy.
contented ADJ
contentment NOUN

content² /**kon**-tent/ NOUN (also **contents**) what is contained in something; the subject matter of a book etc.

contention NOUN **1** disagreement, conflict. **2** an assertion.

contentious ADJ quarrelsome; disputed heatedly.

contest VERB /kŏn-**test**/ compete for or in; oppose; argue about. NOUN /**kon**-test/ a struggle for victory; a competition.
contestant NOUN

context NOUN what precedes or follows a word or statement and fixes its meaning; circumstances.
contextual ADJ

contiguous ADJ adjacent, touching.
contiguity NOUN

continent¹ NOUN one of the earth's main land masses.
continental ADJ

continent² ADJ able to control the excretion of one's urine and faeces; self-restrained.
continence NOUN

contingency NOUN (PL **contingencies**) a possible but unpredictable occurrence.

contingent ADJ **1** subject to chance. **2** depending on other circumstances. **3** not logically necessary. NOUN a body of troops contributed to a larger group.

continual ADJ constantly or frequently recurring.
continually ADV

continue VERB **1** not cease; remain in existence, in a place or condition. **2** resume; extend.
continuance NOUN
continuation NOUN

continuo NOUN (PL **continuos**) [MUSIC] an accompaniment providing a bass line.

continuous ADJ without interval, uninterrupted.
continuity NOUN
continuously ADV

continuum NOUN (PL **continua**) a sequence with gradual development from one extreme to another.

contort VERB force or twist out of normal shape.
contortion NOUN

contortionist NOUN a performer who can twist his or her body dramatically.

contour NOUN an outline; a line on a map showing height above sea level.

contra- PREFIX against.

contraband NOUN goods that have been imported or exported illegally.

contraception NOUN the prevention of pregnancy, birth control.

contraceptive ADJ preventing conception. NOUN a contraceptive drug or device.

contract NOUN /**kon**-trakt/ a formal agreement. VERB /kŏn-**trakt**/ **1** make or become smaller or shorter. **2** make a contract; arrange by contract for (work) to be done. **3** catch (an illness).
contractor NOUN
contractual ADJ

contractable ADJ (of a disease) able to be contracted.

contractible ADJ able to be shrunk or drawn together.

contractile ADJ able to contract or to produce contraction.

contraction NOUN making or becoming smaller; a shortened form of a word or words; a shortening of the uterine muscles during childbirth.

contradict VERB say that (a statement) is untrue or (a person) is wrong; conflict with.
contradiction NOUN

C

contradictory ADJ inconsistent; containing inconsistencies.

contraflow NOUN a flow (especially of traffic) in a direction opposite to and alongside the usual flow.

contralto NOUN (PL **contraltos**) the lowest female voice.

contraption NOUN a strange device or machine.

contrapuntal ADJ of or in counterpoint.

contrariwise ADV on the other hand; in the opposite way.

contrary /kon-tră-ri/ ADJ **1** opposite in nature, tendency, or direction. **2** /kŏn-**trair**-i/ [INFORMAL] perverse, doing the opposite of what is desired. NOUN the opposite.
contrary to conflicting with. **on the contrary** as the opposite of what was just stated.
contrarily ADV
contrariness NOUN

contrast NOUN /**kon**-trahst/ a striking difference; a comparison drawing attention to this. VERB /kŏn-**trahst**/ be strikingly different; point out the difference between (two things).

contravene VERB break (a rule etc.).
contravention NOUN

contretemps /**kon**-trĕ-tahn/ NOUN (PL **contretemps**) a minor disagreement.

contribute VERB give to a common fund or effort; help to cause something.
contribution NOUN
contributor NOUN
contributory ADJ

contrite ADJ remorseful.
contritely ADV
contrition NOUN

contrivance NOUN the action of contriving something; something skilfully made to serve a purpose; artificiality.

contrive VERB skilfully make or bring about; manage to do.

contrived ADJ artificial; feeling false.

control NOUN the power to direct, influence, or restrain something; a means of restraining or regulating; a standard for checking the results of an experiment. VERB (**controls**, **controlling**, **controlled**) influence; regulate; restrain.

controversial ADJ causing controversy.
controversially ADV

controversy NOUN (PL **controversies**) a prolonged and heated disagreement.

controvert VERB deny the truth of.
controvertible ADJ

contumacy /kon-tyoo-mă-see/ NOUN stubborn refusal to obey.
contumacious ADJ

contusion NOUN a bruise.

conundrum NOUN a riddle, a puzzle.

conurbation NOUN a large urban area formed where towns have spread and merged.

convalesce VERB regain health after illness.
convalescence NOUN
convalescent ADJ & NOUN

convection NOUN the transmission of heat within a liquid or gas by movement of heated particles.

convene VERB call together; assemble.
convener (or **convenor**) NOUN

convenience NOUN **1** ease, lack of effort; something contributing to this. **2** a lavatory.

convenient ADJ involving little trouble or effort; easily accessible.
conveniently ADV

convent NOUN a community of nuns; their residence.

convention NOUN **1** an accepted custom; behaviour generally considered correct. **2** an assembly. **3** a formal agreement.
conventional ADJ
conventionally ADV

converge VERB come to or towards the same point.
convergence NOUN
convergent ADJ

conversant ADJ (**conversant with**) having knowledge of.

conversation NOUN informal talk between people.
conversational ADJ
conversationally ADV

C

converse¹ VERB /kŏn-**vers**/ hold a conversation.

converse² /**kon**-verss/ ADJ opposite, contrary. NOUN the opposite, the reverse.
conversely ADV

convert VERB /kŏn-**vert**/ change or cause to change from one form or use to another; cause to change an attitude or belief. NOUN /**kon**-vert/ a person persuaded to adopt a new faith or other belief.
conversion NOUN
converter (or **convertor**) NOUN

convertible ADJ able to be converted. NOUN a car with a folding or detachable roof.

convex ADJ curved like the outer surface of a ball.
convexity NOUN

convey VERB transport, carry; communicate; express.

conveyance NOUN 1 transport; a means of transport. 2 the transfer of ownership of property.

conveyancing NOUN the branch of law concerned with transferring ownership of property.

conveyor NOUN a person or thing that conveys; (in full **conveyor belt**) a continuous moving belt conveying objects.

convict VERB /kŏn-**vikt**/ prove or declare guilty. NOUN /**kon**-vikt/ a convicted person in prison.

conviction NOUN 1 a firm belief; confidence. 2 the action or process of convicting.

convince VERB make (a person) feel certain that something is true.

convivial ADJ sociable and lively.

convocation NOUN an assembly; the summoning of an assembly.

convoke VERB summon to assemble.

convoluted ADJ complicated; intricately coiled.
convolution NOUN

convolvulus NOUN a twining plant with trumpet-shaped flowers.

convoy NOUN ships or vehicles travelling under escort or together. VERB escort (ships etc.) for protection.

convulse VERB suffer violent muscle spasms; cause violent movement in; throw into upheaval.

convulsion NOUN a violent involuntary movement of the body; (**convulsions**) uncontrollable laughter.
convulsive ADJ

cony variant of **CONEY**.

coo VERB make a soft murmuring sound like a dove. NOUN this sound. EXCLAMATION an expression of surprise.

cooee EXCLAMATION a cry to attract attention.

cook VERB **1** prepare (food) by heating; undergo this process. **2** [INFORMAL] falsify (accounts etc.). NOUN a person who cooks, especially as a job.
cook up [INFORMAL] invent (a story etc.).

cooker NOUN a stove for cooking food.

cookery NOUN the art and practice of cooking.

cookie NOUN [US] a sweet biscuit.

cool ADJ **1** fairly cold. **2** calm; not enthusiastic or friendly. **3** [INFORMAL] sophisticated; excellent. **4** [INFORMAL] emphasizing an amount: *a cool five thousand.* NOUN **1** low temperature. **2** [INFORMAL] calmness; sophistication. VERB make or become cool.
coolly ADV
coolness NOUN

coolant NOUN fluid for cooling machinery.

cool bag (also **cool box**) NOUN an insulated container for keeping food cool.

coolie NOUN [DATED] a labourer in Eastern countries.

coomb /koom/ (also **combe**) NOUN a valley in a hillside.

coop NOUN a cage for poultry. VERB confine, shut in.

co-op NOUN [INFORMAL] a cooperative society; a shop run by this.

cooper NOUN a person who makes or repairs casks and barrels.

cooperate VERB work together for a common

end.
cooperation NOUN

cooperative ADJ helpful; involving mutual help; (of a firm etc.) run collectively, based on economic cooperation. NOUN a farm or firm etc. run on this basis.

co-opt VERB appoint to a committee by invitation of existing members, not election.

coordinate VERB /koh-**ord**-i-nayt/ arrange the elements of (a complex whole) to achieve efficiency; negotiate and work with others. ADJ /koh-**ord**-i-năt/ equal in importance. NOUN /koh-**ord**-i-năt/ **1** any of the numbers used to indicate the position of a point. **2** (**coordinates**) matching items of clothing.
coordination NOUN
coordinator NOUN

coot NOUN a waterbird.

cop [INFORMAL] NOUN a police officer. VERB (**cops**, **copping**, **copped**) catch or arrest.
cop it get into trouble.
cop out avoid doing something that one ought to.

cope VERB deal effectively with something difficult.

copeck variant of **KOPEK**.

copier NOUN a copying machine.

coping NOUN the sloping top row of masonry of a wall.

copious ADJ abundant, plentiful.
copiously ADV

copper NOUN **1** a reddish-brown metallic element; a coin containing this; its colour. **2** [INFORMAL] a police officer. ADJ made of or coloured like copper.

copper-bottomed ADJ reliable, especially financially; genuine.

copperplate NOUN neat round handwriting.

coppice (also **copse**) NOUN a group of small trees and undergrowth.

Coptic ADJ of the Egyptian branch of the Christian Church.

copula NOUN [GRAMMAR] the verb *be*.

copulate VERB have sexual intercourse.
copulation NOUN

copy NOUN (PL **copies**) a

thing made to look like another; a specimen of a book etc.; matter to be printed in a newspaper etc. VERB (**copies**, **copying**, **copied**) make a copy of; imitate.

copyright NOUN the sole right to publish a work. VERB secure copyright for.

copywriter NOUN a person who writes advertising copy.

coquette NOUN a woman who flirts.
coquetry NOUN
coquettish ADJ

coracle NOUN a small wicker boat.

coral NOUN a hard red, pink, or white substance built by tiny sea creatures; a reddish-pink colour.

cor anglais /kor **ahng**-lay/ NOUN (PL **cors anglais**) a woodwind instrument.

corbel NOUN a stone or wooden support projecting from a wall.

cord NOUN **1** long thin flexible material made from twisted strands; a piece of this; an anatomical structure like this. **2** corduroy.

cordial ADJ warm and friendly. NOUN a fruit-flavoured drink.
cordially ADV

cordite NOUN a smokeless explosive.

cordless ADJ (of an electrical appliance or telephone) working without connection to a mains supply.

cordon NOUN **1** a line of police, soldiers, etc., enclosing something. **2** a fruit tree pruned to grow as a single stem.
cordon off enclose with a cordon; isolate.

cordon bleu /kor-don **bler**/ ADJ of the highest class in cookery.

corduroy NOUN cloth with velvety ridges.

core NOUN the central or most important part; the tough central part of an apple etc., containing seeds. VERB remove the core from.

co-respondent NOUN the person with whom the respondent in a divorce suit is said to have committed adultery.

C

corgi NOUN a dog of a small breed with short legs.

coriander NOUN a fragrant herb.

cork NOUN the light tough bark of a Mediterranean oak; a piece of this used as a float; a bottle stopper. VERB stop up with a cork.

corkage NOUN a restaurant's charge for serving wine brought from elsewhere.

corked ADJ (of wine) contaminated by a decayed cork.

corkscrew NOUN a device with a spiral rod for extracting corks from bottles; a spiral thing.

corm NOUN a bulb-like underground stem from which buds grow.

cormorant NOUN a large black seabird.

corn NOUN **1** wheat, oats, or maize; grain. **2** [INFORMAL] triteness. **3** a small painful area of hardened skin on the foot.

cornea NOUN the transparent outer covering of the eyeball.

corneal ADJ

cornelian (also **carnelian**) NOUN a reddish or white semi-precious stone.

corner NOUN **1** an angle where two lines or sides meet; the area around this. **2** a free kick or hit from the corner of the field in football or hockey. **3** an awkward position. VERB **1** force into a position from which there is no escape. **2** drive round a corner. **3** obtain a monopoly of (a commodity).

cornerstone NOUN a basis; a vital foundation.

cornet NOUN **1** a brass instrument like a small trumpet. **2** a cone-shaped wafer holding ice cream.

cornflour NOUN fine flour made from maize.

cornflower NOUN a blue-flowered plant.

cornice NOUN an ornamental moulding round the top of an indoor wall.

Cornish ADJ relating to Cornwall. NOUN the

ancient language of Cornwall.

cornucopia NOUN a horn-shaped container overflowing with fruit and flowers, symbolizing abundance; a plentiful supply.

corny ADJ (**cornier**, **corniest**) [INFORMAL] sentimental; hackneyed.

corolla NOUN the petals of a flower.

corollary NOUN (PL **corollaries**) a proposition that follows logically from another.

corona NOUN (PL **coronae**) a ring of light round the sun or moon.

coronary ADJ of the arteries supplying blood to the heart. NOUN (PL **coronaries**) a blockage in one of these arteries, caused by a blood clot.

coronation NOUN the ceremony of crowning a monarch or consort.

coroner NOUN an officer holding inquests.

coronet NOUN a small crown.

corpora pl. of **CORPUS**.

corporal NOUN a non-commissioned officer next below sergeant. ADJ of the body.

corporal punishment NOUN punishment by whipping or beating.

corporate ADJ shared by members of a group; united in a group.

corporation NOUN a group in business or elected to govern a town.

corporeal /kor-**por**-ee-ăl/ ADJ having a body; tangible.
corporeally ADV

corps /kor/ NOUN (PL **corps**) a military unit; an organized body of people.

corpse NOUN a dead body.

corpulent ADJ fat.
corpulence NOUN

corpus NOUN (PL **corpora**) a collection of writings.

corpuscle NOUN a blood cell.

corral NOUN [US] an enclosure for cattle. VERB (**corrals**, **corralling**, **coralled**) put or keep in a corral.

correct ADJ **1** true; free from errors. **2** conforming to an accepted standard

of behaviour. VERB mark or rectify errors in; put right; reprove.
correctly ADV
correctness NOUN

correction NOUN the action or process of correcting; an alteration correcting something; [DATED] punishment.

corrective ADJ designed to correct something undesirable. NOUN a corrective measure.

correlate VERB be systematically related; analyse such a relation between (two things).
correlation NOUN

correspond VERB **1** be similar, equivalent, or in harmony. **2** write letters to each other.

correspondence NOUN **1** similarity. **2** the action or fact of corresponding; letters sent or received.

correspondent NOUN **1** a person who writes letters. **2** a person employed by a newspaper or television news station to gather news and send reports.

corridor NOUN a passage in a building or train giving access to rooms or compartments; a strip of territory giving access to somewhere.

corrie NOUN a round hollow on a mountainside.

corroborate VERB support, confirm.
corroboration NOUN
corroborative ADJ

corrode VERB destroy (a metal etc.) gradually by chemical action.
corrosion NOUN
corrosive ADJ

corrugated ADJ shaped into alternate ridges and grooves.
corrugation NOUN

corrupt ADJ **1** accepting bribes, dishonest; immoral. **2** (of a text) full of errors. VERB **1** bribe; influence into bad habits.

corruption NOUN **1** bribery; dishonesty. **2** [ARCHAIC] decay.

corsair NOUN a pirate ship; a pirate.

corset NOUN a close-fitting undergarment worn to shape or support the body.

cortège /kor-tay*zh*/ NOUN a funeral procession.

C

cortex NOUN (PL **cortices**) the outer part of the brain; an outer layer of tissue.
cortical ADJ

cortisone NOUN a hormone used in treating allergies.

corvette NOUN a small fast gunboat.

cos ABBREV cosine.

cosh NOUN a weighted weapon for hitting people. VERB hit with a cosh.

cosine /koh-sIn/ NOUN [MATHEMATICS] the ratio of the side adjacent to an acute angle (in a right-angled triangle) to the hypotenuse.

cosmetic NOUN a substance for beautifying the complexion etc. ADJ improving the appearance; superficial.

cosmic ADJ of the universe.

cosmic rays (also **cosmic radiation**) PLURAL NOUN radiation from outer space.

cosmogony NOUN (PL **cosmogonies**) the branch of science concerned with the origin of the universe.

cosmology NOUN the science or theory of the universe.
cosmological ADJ

cosmonaut NOUN a Russian astronaut.

cosmopolitan ADJ free from national prejudices; including people from all parts of the world. NOUN a cosmopolitan person.

cosmos NOUN the universe.

Cossack NOUN a member of a people of southern Russia, Ukraine, and Siberia, famous as horsemen.

cosset VERB (**cossets**, **cosseting**, **cosseted**) pamper.

cost VERB **1** (past and past participle **cost**) have as its price; involve the sacrifice or loss of; require (someone) to do or give something. **2** (past and past participle **costed**) estimate the cost of. NOUN what a thing costs.

costal ADJ of the ribs.

co-star NOUN a celebrity

performing with another of equal status.

C

costermonger NOUN a person selling fruit etc. from a barrow in the street.

costly ADJ (**costlier**, **costliest**) expensive.

costume NOUN a style of clothes, especially that of a historical period; garments for a special activity.

cosy ([US] **cozy**) ADJ (**cosier**, **cosiest**) **1** warm and comfortable. **2** mutually advantageous. NOUN (PL **cosies**) a cover to keep a teapot etc. hot.
cosy up to 1 snuggle up to. **2** [INFORMAL] ingratiate oneself with.
cosily ADV
cosiness NOUN

cot NOUN a child's bed with high sides.

cot death (also **SIDS**) NOUN the unexplained death of a sleeping baby.

coterie /**koh**-ter-ee/ NOUN a select group.

cottage NOUN a small simple house, especially in the country.

cottage cheese NOUN soft white lumpy cheese made from curds.

cottage pie NOUN a dish of minced meat topped with mashed potato.

cotton NOUN a soft white substance round the seeds of a tropical plant; this plant; thread or fabric made from cotton.
cotton on [INFORMAL] understand.

cotton wool NOUN fluffy wadding, originally made from raw cotton, used to clean wounds etc.

cotyledon /ko-ti-**lee**-dŏn/ NOUN the first leaf growing from a seed.

couch NOUN a sofa. VERB express in a specified way.

couchette /koo-**shet**/ NOUN a railway carriage with seats convertible into sleeping berths.

couch potato NOUN [INFORMAL] a person who takes very little exercise and watches a lot of television.

cougar /**koo**-ger/ NOUN [US] a puma.

cough VERB expel air etc. from the lungs with a

sudden sharp sound. NOUN the act or sound of coughing; an illness causing coughing. **cough up** [INFORMAL] say or give something reluctantly.

could past of **CAN²**.

coulomb /koo-lom/ NOUN a unit of electric charge.

council NOUN a formal group meeting regularly for debate and administration; the body governing a town.

councillor ([US] **councilor**) NOUN a member of a council.

council tax NOUN a UK local tax based on property value.

counsel NOUN **1** advice. **2** (PL **counsel**) a barrister. VERB (**counsels, counselling, counselled**; [US] **counseling, counseled**) advise; give professional psychological help to. **counsellor** NOUN

count VERB **1** find the total of; say numbers in order. **2** include. **3** be important. **4** regard in a specified way. NOUN **1** an act of counting; a total reached by counting. **2** a point to consider; a charge. **3** a foreign nobleman. **count on** rely on.

countdown NOUN counting seconds backwards to zero; the final period before an important event.

countenance NOUN **1** the face; an expression. **2** [FORMAL] approval. VERB give approval to.

counter NOUN **1** a flat-topped fitment over which goods are sold or business transacted with customers. **2** a small disc used in board games. ADV in the opposite direction; in conflict. ADJ responding; opposed. VERB speak or act against. **under the counter** (of trade) secret and illegal.

counter- PREFIX retaliatory; rival; opposite; corresponding.

counteract VERB reduce or prevent the effects of. **counteraction** NOUN

counter-attack NOUN an attack made in response to an opponent's attack. VERB make a counter-attack.

C

counterbalance NOUN a weight or influence balancing or neutralizing another. VERB act as a counterbalance to.

counterblast NOUN a powerful retort.

counterfeit ADJ forged, not genuine. NOUN a forgery. VERB forge.

counterfoil NOUN a section of a cheque or receipt kept as a record by the person issuing it.

countermand VERB cancel.

counterpane NOUN a bedspread.

counterpart NOUN a person or thing corresponding to another.

counterpoint NOUN [MUSIC] a technique of combining melodies; a contrasting theme or element.

counterproductive ADJ having the opposite of the desired effect.

countersign VERB add a second signature to (a document already signed by one person).

countersink VERB (**countersinks**, **countersinking**, **countersunk**) sink (a screwhead) into a shaped cavity so that the surface is level.

countertenor NOUN a male alto.

countess NOUN a count's or earl's wife or widow; a woman with the rank of count or earl.

countless ADJ too many to be counted.

countrified (also **countryfied**) ADJ rustic in appearance etc.; unsophisticated.

country NOUN (PL **countries**) **1** a nation with its own government and territory; its people; the state of which one is a member; a region. **2** land outside large towns.
go to the country call a general election.

countryman (also **countrywoman**) NOUN **1** a person living in the country. **2** a person of one's own country.

countryside NOUN a rural district.

county NOUN (PL **counties**) **1** a major administrative division of some countries. **2** families of high social class long established in a county.

coup /koo/ NOUN a very successful action; a coup d'état.

coup de grâce /koo dĕ grahs/ NOUN (PL **coups de grâce**) a finishing stroke.

coup d'état /koo day-**tah**/ NOUN (PL **coups d'état**) the sudden, violent, and illegal overthrow of a government.

coupé ([US] **coupe**) NOUN a closed two-door car with a sloping back.

couple NOUN two people or things; a married or romantically involved pair. VERB fasten or link together; copulate.

couplet NOUN two successive rhyming lines of verse.

coupling NOUN a connecting device.

coupon NOUN a form or ticket entitling the holder to something; an entry form for a football pool.

courage NOUN the ability to control fear when facing danger or pain. **courageous** ADJ **courageously** ADV

courgette /kor-**zhet**/ NOUN a small vegetable marrow.

courier /**ku**-ree-ĕ/ NOUN **1** a messenger carrying documents. **2** a person employed to guide and assist tourists.

course NOUN **1** onward progress; a direction taken or intended. **2** a series of lessons or treatments. **3** an area on which golf is played or a race takes place. **4** a layer of stone etc. in a building. **5** one part of a meal. VERB **1** move or flow freely. **2** pursue (hares etc.) with hounds.
a matter of course a regular and unremarkable procedure. **in course of** undergoing; during. **of course** certainly; naturally; without doubt. **on course for** heading for; likely to achieve.

court NOUN **1** a body of

people hearing legal cases; the place where they meet. **2** a courtyard; an area for playing squash, tennis, etc. **3** a sovereign's establishment with attendants. VERB try to win the love or support of; risk (danger etc.).

courteous /**ker**-tee-ŭs/ ADJ polite.
courteously ADV
courteousness NOUN

courtesan /**kor**-ti-zan/ NOUN [LITERARY] a prostitute with high-class clients.

courtesy /**ker**-tĕ-see/ NOUN politeness.

courtier NOUN a sovereign's companion or attendant at court.

courtly ADJ (**courtlier, courtliest**) dignified and polite.

court martial NOUN (PL **courts martial** or **court martials**) a court trying offences against military law; a trial by this. VERB (**court-martial**) (**court-martials, court-martialling, court-martialled**; [US] **court-martials, court-martialing, court-martialed**) try by such a court.

courtship NOUN the action of courting; a period during which a couple develop a romantic relationship.

courtyard NOUN a space enclosed by walls or buildings.

couscous /**koos**-koos/ NOUN a North African dish of crushed wheat.

cousin (also **first cousin**) NOUN a child of one's uncle or aunt.
second cousin a child of one's parent's cousin.

couture /koo-**tyewr**/ NOUN the design and making of fashionable clothes.

couturier /koo-**tyewr**-ee-ay/ NOUN a designer of fashionable clothes.

cove NOUN a small bay.

coven /**kuv**-ĕn/ NOUN an assembly of witches.

covenant /**kuv**-ĕ-nănt/ NOUN a formal agreement, a contract. VERB make a covenant.

cover VERB **1** be or place something over; conceal or protect in this way; disguise. **2** deal with (a subject); report on for a

newspaper etc. **3** be enough to pay for; protect by insurance. **4** travel over (a distance). **5** keep a gun aimed at. **6** take over someone's job temporarily. NOUN **1** a thing that covers; a wrapper, envelope, or binding of a book; a shelter or protection; a disguise. **2** protection by insurance. **3** a place laid at a meal.
cover up conceal (a thing or fact).
cover-up NOUN

coverage NOUN **1** treatment of a subject by the media. **2** an area covered.

covering letter NOUN an explanatory letter enclosed with goods.

coverlet NOUN a cover lying over other bedclothes.

covert NOUN thick undergrowth where animals hide. ADJ concealed, done secretly.
covertly ADV

covet VERB (**covets, coveting, coveted**) desire (a thing belonging to another person).
covetous ADJ

covey /**ku**-vee/ NOUN (PL **coveys**) a group of game birds.

C

cow NOUN **1** a fully grown female of cattle or certain other large animals (e.g. the elephant or whale). **2** [INFORMAL] an unpleasant woman. VERB intimidate.

coward NOUN a person who lacks courage.
cowardly ADJ

cowardice NOUN lack of courage.

cowboy NOUN **1** a man in charge of cattle on a ranch. **2** [INFORMAL] a person with careless or dishonest methods in business.

cower VERB crouch or shrink in fear.

cowl NOUN a monk's hood or hooded robe; a hood-shaped covering on a chimney.

cowling NOUN a removable metal cover on an engine.

cowrie NOUN a type of seashell.

cowslip NOUN a wild plant with small yellow

flowers.

cox NOUN a coxswain. VERB act as cox of (a racing boat).

coxcomb NOUN [DATED] a conceited person.

coxswain /**kok**-sŭn/ NOUN **1** a person who steers a boat. **2** a senior petty officer in the Royal Navy.

coy ADJ pretending to be shy or embarrassed.
coyly ADV

coyote /koy-**oh**-ti/ NOUN a North American wolf-like wild dog.

coypu NOUN a beaver-like aquatic rodent.

cozy US spelling of **COSY**.

CPS ABBREV Crown Prosecution Service.

CPU ABBREV [COMPUTING] central processing unit.

crab NOUN a ten-legged shellfish.

crab apple NOUN a small sour apple.

crabbed ADJ **1** (also **crabby**) bad-tempered. **2** (of handwriting) hard to read.

crack NOUN **1** a line where a thing is broken but not separated; a narrow opening; a sharp blow. **2** a sudden sharp noise. **3** [INFORMAL] a joke. **4** a strong form of cocaine. VERB **1** break without separating; knock sharply; give way under strain; (of a voice) suddenly change in pitch. **2** make or cause to make the sound of a crack. **3** [INFORMAL] solve (a problem). **4** [INFORMAL] tell (a joke). ADJ excellent. **crack down on** [INFORMAL] take severe measures against. **crack up** [INFORMAL] **1** have an emotional breakdown. **2** praise. **have a crack at** [INFORMAL] attempt.

crackdown NOUN severe measures against something.

cracker NOUN **1** a small explosive firework; a paper tube giving an explosive crack when pulled apart, containing a small gift. **2** a thin dry biscuit.

crackers ADJ [INFORMAL] crazy.

crackle VERB make or cause to make a series of light cracking sounds.

NOUN these sounds.

crackling NOUN crisp skin on roast pork.

crackpot [INFORMAL] NOUN an eccentric person. ADJ mad.

cradle NOUN **1** a baby's bed usually with rockers; a place where something originates. **2** a supporting structure. VERB hold or support gently.

craft NOUN **1** a skill; an occupation requiring this. **2** cunning, deceit. **3** (PL **craft**) a ship or boat.

craftsman NOUN a worker skilled in a craft.
craftsmanship NOUN

crafty ADJ (**craftier**, **craftiest**) cunning, using underhand methods.
craftily ADV
craftiness NOUN

crag NOUN a steep or rugged rock.

craggy ADJ (**craggier**, **craggiest**) rugged.

cram VERB (**crams**, **cramming**, **crammed**) **1** force into too small a space; overfill. **2** study intensively for an examination.

cramp NOUN **1** a painful involuntary tightening of a muscle. **2** a metal bar with bent ends for holding things together. VERB keep within too narrow limits.

crampon NOUN a spiked plate worn on boots for climbing on ice.

crane NOUN **1** a large wading bird. **2** a machine for lifting and moving heavy objects. VERB stretch (one's neck) to see something.

cranium NOUN (**craniums** or **crania**) the skull.

crank NOUN **1** an L-shaped device for converting to-and-fro into circular motion. **2** an eccentric person. VERB turn (a crank) to start (an engine).
cranky ADJ

crankshaft NOUN a shaft driven by a crank.

cranny NOUN (PL **crannies**) a crevice.

crap [VULGAR SLANG] NOUN faeces; nonsense, rubbish. VERB (**craps**, **crapping**, **crapped**) defecate.

craps PLURAL NOUN [US] a

gambling game played with a pair of dice.

crash NOUN a loud noise of collision or breakage; a violent collision; a financial collapse. VERB **1** make a crash; be or cause to be involved in a crash; move noisily. **2** [INFORMAL] gatecrash. ADJ involving intense effort to achieve something rapidly: *a crash course.*

crash helmet NOUN a padded helmet worn especially by a motorcyclist to protect the head in a crash.

crashing ADJ [INFORMAL] great, absolute: *a crashing bore.*

crash-land VERB (of an aircraft) land in an emergency, causing damage.

crass ADJ gross; very stupid; insensitive.

crate NOUN a packing case made of wooden slats; a container divided into individual units for bottles. VERB pack in crate(s).

crater NOUN a bowl-shaped cavity; the mouth of a volcano.

cravat NOUN a short scarf; a necktie.

crave VERB feel an intense longing (for); [DATED] ask earnestly for.

craven ADJ cowardly.

craving NOUN an intense longing.

craw NOUN a bird's crop.

crawfish NOUN = **CRAYFISH.**

crawl VERB **1** move on hands and knees or with the body on the ground; move very slowly. **2** [INFORMAL] seek favour by servile behaviour. NOUN a crawling movement or pace; an overarm swimming stroke.
crawling with very crowded with.
crawler NOUN

crayfish NOUN (PL **crayfish**) a freshwater shellfish like a small lobster.

crayon NOUN a stick of coloured wax etc. for drawing. VERB draw or colour with crayons.

craze NOUN a temporary enthusiasm.

crazy ADJ (**crazier, craziest**) insane; very foolish; [INFORMAL] madly

eager.
crazily ADV
craziness NOUN

crazy paving NOUN paving made of irregular pieces.

creak NOUN a harsh squeak. VERB make this sound.
creaky ADJ

cream NOUN the fatty part of milk; its colour, yellowish white; a cream-like ointment etc.; the best part. ADJ yellowish white. VERB beat to a creamy consistency. **cream off** take (the best part of something).
creamy ADJ

cream cheese NOUN a soft rich cheese.

cream cracker NOUN a crisp unsweetened biscuit.

creamery NOUN (PL **creameries**) a factory producing butter and cheese.

cream of tartar NOUN a compound of potassium used in baking powder.

crease NOUN **1** a line made in cloth or paper by crushing or pressing. **2** a line marking the limit of the bowler's or batsman's position in cricket. VERB make a crease in; develop creases.

create VERB **1** bring into existence; produce by what one does; give a specified title to. **2** [INFORMAL] make a fuss.
creation NOUN
creator NOUN

creative ADJ involving creation or invention; showing imagination and originality.
creatively ADV
creativity NOUN

creature NOUN an animal; a person.

crèche /kresh/ NOUN a day nursery.

credence NOUN belief.

credentials PLURAL NOUN qualifications, qualities, etc.; documents attesting to these.

credible ADJ believable.
credibly ADV
credibility NOUN

credit NOUN **1** a system of deferring payment for purchases. **2** a record in an account of a sum received; having money in one's bank account. **3** acknowledgement or honour for an achievement; a source of honour or pride. **4** a unit of study counting towards a degree. **5** (**credits**) acknowledgements of contributors to a film. VERB (**credits**, **crediting**, **credited**) **1** attribute. **2** enter in an account. **3** believe.

creditable ADJ deserving praise.
creditably ADV

credit card NOUN a plastic card containing machine-readable magnetic code, allowing the holder to make purchases on credit.

creditor NOUN a person to whom money is owed.

credulous ADJ too ready to believe things; gullible.
credulity NOUN

creed NOUN a set of beliefs or principles.

creek NOUN a narrow inlet of water, especially on a coast; [US] a tributary.

creep VERB (**creeps**, **creeping**, **crept**) **1** move slowly, quietly, and stealthily; develop or increase gradually; (of a plant) grow along the ground or a wall etc. **2** (of skin) have an unpleasant sensation through fear or disgust. NOUN **1** [INFORMAL] an unpleasant person. **2** slow and stealthy or imperceptible movement. **3** (**the creeps**) [INFORMAL] a nervous sensation.

creepy ADJ (**creepier**, **creepiest**) [INFORMAL] frightening; disturbing.

cremate VERB burn (a corpse) to ashes.
cremation NOUN

crematorium NOUN (PL **crematoria** or **crematoriums**) a place where corpses are cremated.

crème de la crème /krem dĕ la **krem**/ NOUN the very best.

crème de menthe /krem dĕ **month**/ NOUN a peppermint-flavoured liqueur.

crenellated ADJ having battlements.
crenellation NOUN

Creole /kree-ohl/ NOUN a

descendant of European settlers in the West Indies or South America; their dialect; a hybrid language.

creosote NOUN a brown oily liquid distilled from coal tar, used as a preservative for wood.

crêpe NOUN **1** /krayp/ a fabric with a wrinkled surface. **2** /krep/ a pancake.

crept past and past participle of **CREEP**.

crepuscular ADJ of or like twilight; active at twilight.

crescendo /kri-**shen**-doh/ ADV gradually becoming louder. NOUN (PL **crescendos** or **crescendi**) a gradual increase in loudness.

crescent NOUN a narrow curved shape tapering to a point at each end; a curved street of houses.

cress NOUN a plant with small leaves used in salads.

crest NOUN **1** a tuft or outgrowth on a bird's or animal's head; a plume on a helmet. **2** the top of a slope or hill; a white top of a large wave. **3** a design above a shield on a coat of arms.

crestfallen ADJ disappointed at failure.

cretaceous /kri-**taysh**-ŭs/ ADJ chalky.

cretin NOUN **1** [DATED] a person who is physically and mentally disabled because of a lack of thyroid hormone. **2** [OFFENSIVE] a stupid person.
cretinous ADJ

crevasse NOUN a deep open crack, especially in a glacier.

crevice NOUN a narrow gap in a surface.

crew[1] NOUN the people working a ship or aircraft; a group working together; a gang. VERB act as a crew member (of).

crew[2] past of **CROW**.

crew cut NOUN a very short haircut.

crib NOUN **1** a rack for fodder; a model of the manger scene at Bethlehem; a cot. **2** [INFORMAL] a translation of a text for students' use. VERB (**cribs**, **cribbing**, **cribbed**) [INFORMAL] copy unfairly; plagiarize.

C

cribbage NOUN a card game.

crick NOUN a sudden painful stiffness in the neck or back.

cricket NOUN **1** an outdoor game for two teams of 11 players with ball, bats, and wickets. **2** a brown insect resembling a grasshopper.
cricketer NOUN

crier (also **cryer**) NOUN an official making public announcements.

crikey EXCLAMATION [INFORMAL] an exclamation of astonishment.

crime NOUN a serious offence, an act that breaks a law; illegal acts.

criminal NOUN a person guilty of a crime. ADJ of or involving crime.
criminality NOUN
criminally ADV

criminology NOUN the study of crime.
criminologist NOUN

crimp VERB press into ridges.

crimson NOUN a deep red colour.

cringe VERB cower; behave obsequiously.

crinkle VERB form small creases or wrinkles. NOUN a small crease or wrinkle.

crinoline NOUN a light framework formerly worn to make a long skirt stand out.

cripple NOUN a disabled or lame person. VERB make lame; weaken seriously.

crisis NOUN (PL **crises**) a time of intense danger or difficulty; the decisive moment in an illness.

crisp ADJ **1** firm, dry, and brittle. **2** cold and bracing. **3** brisk and decisive. NOUN a thin slice of potato fried crisp.
crisply ADV
crispness NOUN
crispy ADJ

crispbread NOUN a thin crisp unsweetened biscuit.

criss-cross NOUN a pattern of intersecting lines. ADJ & ADV in this pattern. VERB form a criss-cross pattern (on).

criterion NOUN (PL **criteria**) a standard of judgement.

critic NOUN **1** a person who points out faults. **2** a person who appraises artistic works and performances.

critical ADJ **1** looking for faults. **2** of literary or artistic criticism. **3** of or at a crisis.
critically ADV

criticism NOUN **1** the pointing out of faults. **2** an evaluation of literary or artistic work.

criticize (also **criticise**) VERB **1** find fault with. **2** analyse and evaluate.

critique NOUN an analysis and assessment.

croak NOUN a deep hoarse cry or sound like that of a frog. VERB **1** utter or speak with a croak. **2** [INFORMAL] die.

crochet /kroh-shay/ NOUN lacy fabric produced from thread worked with a hooked needle. VERB (**crochets**, **crocheting**, **crocheted**) make by or do such work.

crock NOUN **1** an earthenware pot; a broken piece of this. **2** [INFORMAL] a weak or disabled person; a worn-out vehicle etc.

crockery NOUN household china.

crocodile NOUN **1** a large predatory amphibious tropical reptile. **2** a line of people walking in pairs.

crocodile tears PLURAL NOUN insincere sorrow.

crocus NOUN a small spring-flowering plant.

croft NOUN a small rented farm in Scotland.

crofter NOUN the tenant of a croft.

croissant /krwa-son/ NOUN a rich crescent-shaped roll.

crone NOUN an old and ugly woman.

crony NOUN (PL **cronies**) a close friend or companion.

crook NOUN **1** a hooked stick; an angle. **2** [INFORMAL] a criminal. VERB bend (a finger).

crooked ADJ **1** not straight. **2** [INFORMAL] dishonest.
crookedly ADV

croon VERB sing softly or sentimentally.
crooner NOUN

crop NOUN **1** a plant

C

cultivated on a large scale for its produce; a harvest from this; a group or amount produced at one time. **2** a pouch in a bird's gullet where food is broken up for digestion. **3** the handle of a whip. **4** a very short haircut.
VERB (**crops, cropping, cropped**) **1** cut or bite off. **2** produce or gather as harvest.
crop up occur unexpectedly.

cropper NOUN (**come a cropper**) [INFORMAL] fall heavily; fail badly.

croquet /**kroh**-kay/ NOUN a game played on a lawn with balls driven through hoops with mallets.

croquette /kroh-**ket**/ NOUN a small ball of potato etc. fried in breadcrumbs.

crosier (also **crozier**) NOUN a bishop's hooked staff.

cross NOUN **1** a mark or shape formed by two intersecting lines or pieces; an upright post with a transverse bar, formerly used in crucifixion. **2** an unavoidable affliction. **3** a hybrid; a mixture of two things. **4** a transverse blow or pass of a ball.
VERB **1** go or extend across; draw a line across; mark (a cheque) so that it must be paid into a named account.
2 intersect or cause to intersect; mark with a cross. **3** (of a letter) be dispatched while a letter from the addressee is already in the post.
4 cause to interbreed.
5 oppose the wishes of.
ADJ annoyed.
at cross purposes misunderstanding or with different aims.
crossly ADV
crossness NOUN

crossbar NOUN a horizontal bar between uprights.

cross bench NOUN a seat in the House of Lords for members independent of any political party.

crossbow NOUN a mechanical bow fixed across a wooden support.

cross-breed NOUN an animal produced by interbreeding.
cross-bred ADJ

cross-check VERB verify (figures etc.) by an alternative method.

cross-dressing NOUN the wearing of clothing typical of the opposite sex.

cross-examine VERB question (a witness in court) to check a testimony already given. **cross-examination** NOUN

cross-eyed ADJ squinting.

crossfire NOUN gunfire crossing another line of fire.

crossing NOUN a place where things cross; a journey across water; moving across something; a place to cross a road, border, etc.

crosspatch NOUN [INFORMAL] a bad-tempered person.

cross-ply ADJ (of a tyre) having fabric layers with cords lying crosswise.

cross reference NOUN a reference to another place in the same book.

crossroads NOUN a place where roads intersect.

cross section NOUN a surface or shape revealed by cutting across something; a representative sample.

crosswise (also **crossways**) ADV in the form of a cross; intersecting; diagonally.

crossword NOUN a puzzle in which intersecting words have to be inserted into a grid of squares.

crotch NOUN the fork between the legs where they join the trunk; a fork in a tree etc.

crotchet NOUN a note in music, half a minim.

crotchety ADJ peevish, irritable. **crotchetiness** NOUN

crouch VERB stoop low with the legs tightly bent. NOUN this position.

croup /kroop/ NOUN **1** an inflammation of the windpipe in children, causing coughing and breathing difficulty. **2** the rump of a horse etc.

croupier /kroop-i-ay, kroop-i-ĕ/ NOUN a person who rakes in stakes and pays out winnings at a gaming table.

crouton NOUN a small piece of fried or toasted bread as a garnish.

crow NOUN **1** a large black bird. **2** a cock's call; a triumphant cry. VERB (**crows**, **crowing**, **crowed** or **crew**) utter a cock's cry; express triumph and glee.

crowbar NOUN an iron bar with a bent end, used as a lever.

crowd NOUN a large group. VERB fill completely or excessively; move or gather in a crowd.

crown NOUN **1** a monarch's ceremonial headdress; (**the Crown**) the supreme governing power in a monarchy. **2** the top of a head, hill, etc. VERB **1** place a crown on (a new monarch). **2** form the top of; be the climax of. **3** [INFORMAL] hit on the head.

Crown prince, Crown princess NOUN the heir to a throne.

crozier variant of **CROSIER**.

cruces pl. of **CRUX**.

crucial ADJ very important, decisive.
crucially ADV

crucible NOUN a container in which metals are melted.

crucifix NOUN a model of a cross with a figure of Christ on it.

crucifixion NOUN the execution of someone by crucifying them; (**the Crucifixion**) that of Christ.

cruciform ADJ cross-shaped.

crucify VERB (**crucifies**, **crucifying**, **crucified**) put to death by nailing or binding to a cross; cause anguish to.

crude ADJ in a natural or raw state; roughly made; offensively coarse or rude.
crudely ADV
crudity NOUN

crudités PLURAL NOUN sliced mixed raw vegetables to dip into a sauce.

cruel ADJ (**crueller** or **crueler**, **cruellest** or **cruelest**) deliberately causing suffering; hard-hearted; harsh.
cruelly ADV

cruelty NOUN

cruet NOUN a set of containers for salt, pepper, etc. at the table.

cruise VERB **1** sail for pleasure or on patrol. **2** travel at a moderate economical speed. **3** [INFORMAL] search for casual sexual partners. NOUN a cruising voyage.

cruiser NOUN a fast warship; a motor boat with a cabin.

crumb NOUN a small fragment of bread etc.; a tiny piece.

crumble VERB break or fall apart into small fragments; gradually decline. NOUN a pudding of stewed fruit topped with a crumbly mixture of flour, fat, and sugar.

crumbly ADJ (**crumblier, crumbliest**) easily crumbled.

crummy ADJ (**crummier, crummiest**) [INFORMAL] of poor quality.

crumpet NOUN **1** a flat soft yeast cake eaten toasted. **2** [INFORMAL] a sexually attractive person.

crumple VERB **1** crush or become crushed into creases. **2** collapse.

crunch VERB crush noisily with the teeth; make a muffled grinding sound. NOUN **1** the sound of crunching. **2** [INFORMAL] a crucial point or situation.

crunchy ADJ (**crunchier, crunchiest**) crisp; making a crunching sound when crushed.

crupper NOUN a strap looped under a horse's tail from the saddle.

crusade NOUN a medieval Christian military expedition to recover the Holy Land from Muslims; a campaign for a cause. VERB take part in a crusade.

crusader NOUN

crush VERB press so as to break, injure, or wrinkle; pound into fragments; defeat or subdue completely. NOUN **1** a crowded mass of people. **2** [INFORMAL] an infatuation.

crust NOUN a hard outer layer, especially of bread.

crustacean /krust-aysh-ŭn/ NOUN a creature with a hard shell (e.g. a lobster).

crusty ADJ (**crustier, crustiest**) **1** with a crisp crust. **2** irritable.

C

crutch NOUN **1** a support for a lame person. **2** the crotch.

crux NOUN (PL **cruces** or **cruxes**) a vital part of a problem; a difficult point.

cry NOUN (PL **cries**) **1** a loud inarticulate shout expressing emotion; a call; an appeal. **2** a spell of weeping. VERB (**cries, crying, cried**) **1** shed tears. **2** call loudly; scream; appeal.
cry off [INFORMAL] fail to do what one has arranged to.

cryer variant of **CRIER**.

cryogenics /krI-oh-jen-iks/ NOUN a branch of physics dealing with very low temperatures.
cryogenic ADJ

crypt /kript/ NOUN a room below the floor of a church.

cryptic ADJ hard to interpret; puzzling.

cryptogram NOUN something written in cipher.

cryptography NOUN the study of ciphers.
cryptographer NOUN

crystal ADJ a glass-like mineral; high-quality glass; a symmetrical piece of a solidified substance.

crystalline ADJ **1** like or made of crystal. **2** [LITERARY] clear.

crystallize (also **crystallise**) VERB (**crystallizes, crystallizing, crystallized**) **1** form into crystals; make or become definite in form. **2** preserve (fruit) in sugar.
crystallization NOUN

CSE ABBREV Certificate of Secondary Education.

CS gas NOUN a gas causing tears and choking, used to control riots etc.

cu. ABBREV cubic.

cub NOUN **1** the young of foxes, lions, etc. **2** (**Cub**, in full **Cub Scout**) a member of the junior branch of the Scout Association.

cubby hole NOUN a very small room or space.

cube NOUN **1** a solid object with six equal square

sides. **2** the product of a number multiplied by itself twice. VERB **1** find the cube of (a number). **2** cut into cubes.

cube root NOUN a number which produces a given number when cubed.

cubic ADJ cube-shaped; (of measurements) of three dimensions.

cubicle NOUN a small area partitioned off in a large room.

cubism NOUN a style of painting in which objects are shown as geometrical shapes.
cubist NOUN

cuckold NOUN a man whose wife commits adultery. VERB make a cuckold of.

cuckoo NOUN a bird that lays its eggs in other birds' nests.

cucumber NOUN a long green-skinned fruit eaten as salad.

cud NOUN food that cattle bring back from the stomach into the mouth and chew again.

cuddle VERB hug lovingly; nestle together. NOUN a gentle hug.
cuddly ADJ

cudgel NOUN a short thick stick used as a weapon. VERB (**cudgels**, **cudgelling**, **cudgelled**; [US] **cudgeling**, **cudgeled**) beat with a cudgel.

cue NOUN **1** a signal to do something, especially for an actor to begin a speech. **2** a long rod for striking balls in billiards etc. VERB (**cues**, **cueing**, **cued**) **1** give a signal to (someone). **2** use a billiards cue.

cuff NOUN **1** a band of cloth round the edge of a sleeve. **2** a blow with the open hand. VERB strike with the open hand.
off the cuff [INFORMAL] without preparation.

cuff link NOUN a device of two linked discs etc. to hold cuff edges together.

cuisine /kwi-zeen/ NOUN a style of cooking.

cul-de-sac NOUN a street closed at one end.

culinary ADJ of or for cooking.

cull VERB gather, select; select and kill (animals)

to reduce numbers.

culminate VERB reach a climax.
culmination NOUN

culottes /kyuu-lots/ PLURAL NOUN women's trousers styled to resemble a skirt.

culpable ADJ deserving blame.
culpability NOUN
culpably ADV

culprit NOUN a person who has committed an offence.

cult NOUN a system of religious worship; excessive admiration of a person or thing.

cultivate VERB **1** prepare and use (land) for crops; produce (crops) by tending them. **2** develop (a skill etc.) by practice. **3** try to win the friendship or support of.
cultivation NOUN
cultivator NOUN

culture NOUN **1** a developed understanding of literature, art, music, etc.; the art, customs, etc. of a particular country or society. **2** artificial rearing of bacteria; bacteria grown for study. VERB grow in artificial conditions.
cultural ADJ
culturally ADV

culvert NOUN a drain under a road.

cum PREP as well as; also used as: *a bedroom-cum-study.*

cumbersome ADJ heavy and awkward to carry or use.

cumin (also **cummin**) NOUN a spice.

cummerbund NOUN a sash for the waist.

cumquat variant of **KUMQUAT**.

cumulative ADJ increasing by additions.
cumulatively ADV

cumulus /kyoo-myuu-lŭs/ NOUN (PL **cumuli**) clouds formed in heaped-up rounded masses.

cuneiform /kyoo-ni-form/ NOUN ancient writing done in wedge-shaped strokes cut into stone etc.

cunning ADJ skilled at deception, crafty; ingenious. NOUN craftiness; ingenuity.
cunningly ADV

cup NOUN **1** a drinking vessel usually with a

handle at the side; a cup-shaped trophy. **2** wine or fruit juice with added flavourings. VERB (**cups**, **cupping**, **cupped**) form (one's hands) into a cup-like shape.

cupboard NOUN a recess or piece of furniture with a door, in which things may be stored.

cupidity NOUN greed for gain.

cupola NOUN a small dome.

cupreous /kyoo-pree-ŭs/ ADJ of or like copper.

cur NOUN a mongrel dog; [INFORMAL] a contemptible person.

curaçao /kewr-ăs-oh/ NOUN an orange-flavoured liqueur.

curacy NOUN (PL **curacies**) the position of curate.

curare /kyoo-**rah**-ri/ NOUN a vegetable poison that induces paralysis.

curate NOUN a member of the clergy who assists a parish priest.

curate's egg NOUN [INFORMAL] something that is good only in parts.

curator NOUN a person in charge of a museum or other collection.

curb NOUN a means of restraint. VERB restrain.

curdle VERB form or cause to form curds.

curds PLURAL NOUN the thick soft substance formed when milk turns sour.

cure VERB **1** restore to health; get rid of (a disease or trouble etc.). **2** preserve by salting, drying, etc. NOUN a substance or treatment curing disease; restoration to health.

curette /kyou-**ret**/ NOUN a surgical scraping instrument.
curettage NOUN

curfew NOUN a law requiring people to stay indoors after a stated time; this time.

curie NOUN a unit of radioactivity.

curio NOUN (PL **curios**) an unusual and interesting object.

curiosity NOUN (PL **curiosities**) **1** desire to find something out. **2** a curio.

curious ADJ **1** eager to

learn or know something. **2** strange, unusual.
curiously ADV
curiousness NOUN

curium NOUN a radioactive metallic element.

curl VERB take or cause to take a curved or spiral shape. NOUN a curled thing or shape; a coiled lock of hair.
curly ADJ

curler NOUN a small tube round which hair is wound to make it curl.

curlew NOUN a wading bird with a long curved bill.

curlicue NOUN a curly ornamental line.

curling NOUN a game like bowls played on ice.

curmudgeon NOUN a bad-tempered person.

currant NOUN **1** a dried grape used in cookery. **2** a small round edible berry; a shrub producing this.

currency NOUN (PL **currencies**) **1** money in use in a particular area. **2** the state of being widely used or known.

current ADJ **1** belonging to the present time. **2** in general use. NOUN a body of water or air moving in one direction; a flow of electricity.
currently ADV

curriculum NOUN (PL **curricula**) a course of study.

curriculum vitae NOUN a brief account of one's career.

curry NOUN (PL **curries**) a savoury dish cooked with hot spices. VERB (**curries**, **currying**, **curried**) **1** make into such a dish. **2** groom (a horse) with a curry-comb.
curry favour win favour by flattery.

curry-comb NOUN a rubber comb for grooming horses.

curse NOUN a call for evil to come on a person or thing; something causing suffering or annoyance; an offensive word expressing anger. VERB utter a curse (against); afflict.
cursed ADJ

cursive ADJ (of handwriting) written with the characters joined.

cursor NOUN a movable indicator on a VDU screen.

cursory ADJ hasty and not thorough.
cursorily ADV

curt ADJ noticeably or rudely brief.
curtly ADV
curtness NOUN

curtail VERB cut short, reduce.
curtailment NOUN

curtain NOUN a piece of cloth hung as a screen, especially at a window.

curtsy (also **curtsey**) NOUN (PL **curtsies**) a woman's movement of respect, made by bending the knees. VERB (**curtsies**, **curtsying**, **curtsied**) make a curtsy.

curvaceous ADJ (of a woman) having a shapely curved figure.

curvature NOUN the fact of being curved; a curved form.

curve NOUN a line or surface with no part straight or flat. VERB form (into) a curve.
curvy ADJ

curvilinear ADJ contained by or consisting of curved lines.

cushion NOUN a stuffed bag used for sitting or leaning on; a support or protection; a body of air supporting a hovercraft. VERB protect with a pad; lessen the impact of.

cushy ADJ (**cushier**, **cushiest**) [INFORMAL] pleasant and easy.

cusp NOUN **1** a pointed part where curves meet. **2** a point of transition, especially between astrological signs.

cuss [INFORMAL] NOUN a curse; a difficult person. VERB curse.

cussed /cuss-id/ ADJ [INFORMAL] stubborn.

custard NOUN a sweet sauce made with milk and eggs or flavoured cornflour.

custodian NOUN a guardian, a keeper.

custody NOUN **1** protective care. **2** imprisonment.

custom NOUN **1** the usual way of behaving or acting. **2** regular dealing by customers.

C

3 (**customs**) duty on imported goods.

customary ADJ usual.
customarily ADV

customer NOUN a person buying goods or services from a shop etc.

cut VERB (**cuts**, **cutting**, **cut**) **1** open, wound, divide, or shape by pressure of a sharp edge; remove or reduce in this way. **2** intersect. **3** divide (a pack of cards). **4** avoid or ignore. **5** have (a tooth) coming through the gum. NOUN **1** an act of cutting; an incision or wound. **2** a piece cut off; [INFORMAL] a share. **3** a reduction. **4** a style of cutting.
a cut above superior to. **cut off** isolated. **cut out for** suited to.

cute ADJ [INFORMAL] **1** attractive, endearing. **2** clever.
cutely ADV
cuteness NOUN

cuticle NOUN the skin at the base of a nail.

cutlass NOUN a short curved sword.

cutler NOUN a maker of cutlery.

cutlery NOUN table knives, forks, and spoons.

cutlet NOUN a lamb or veal chop from behind the neck; a flat cake of minced meat or nuts and breadcrumbs etc.

cut-throat ADJ ruthless, unscrupulous. NOUN a murderer.

cutting ADJ (of remarks) hurtful. NOUN **1** a passage cut through high ground for a railway etc. **2** a piece of a plant for replanting. **3** a piece cut out of a newspaper etc.

cuttlefish NOUN a sea creature that ejects black fluid when attacked.

CV ABBREV curriculum vitae.

cwt ABBREV hundredweight.

cyan /sI-ăn/ NOUN a greenish-blue colour.

cyanide NOUN a strong poison.

cyber- COMBINING FORM relating to electronic communication and virtual reality.

cybernetics NOUN the science of systems of control and

communication in animals and machines.

cycle NOUN **1** a recurring series of events. **2** a bicycle or motorcycle. VERB ride a bicycle.
cyclist NOUN

cyclic (also **cyclical**) ADJ recurring regularly.
cyclically ADV

cyclone NOUN a violent wind rotating round a central area.
cyclonic ADJ

cyclotron /sIk-lŏ-tron/ NOUN an apparatus for accelerating charged particles in a spiral path.

cygnet /sig-nĕt/ NOUN a young swan.

cylinder NOUN an object with straight sides and circular ends.
cylindrical ADJ
cylindrically ADV

cymbal NOUN a brass plate struck against another or with a stick as a percussion instrument.

cynic NOUN a person who believes people's motives are usually bad or selfish.
cynical ADJ
cynically ADV
cynicism NOUN

cynosure /sin-o-syewr, sIn-o-syewr/ NOUN a centre of attention.

cypher variant of **CIPHER**.

cypress NOUN an evergreen tree.

cyst /sist/ NOUN a growth on the body containing fluid or soft matter.

cystic ADJ of the bladder or gall bladder.

cystic fibrosis NOUN a hereditary disease usually resulting in respiratory infections.

cystitis NOUN inflammation of the bladder.

cytology /sI-to-lŏ-ji/ NOUN the study of biological cells.

czar variant of **TSAR**.

Dd

d

D (also **d**) NOUN (PL **Ds** or **D's**) **1** the fourth letter of the alphabet. **2** the Roman numeral for 500. ABBREV (**d**) (of pre-decimal currency) penny or pence.

DA ABBREV [US] district attorney.

dab VERB (**dabs**, **dabbing**, **dabbed**) wipe with quick strokes using something absorbent; apply with quick strokes. NOUN a quick stroke; a small amount applied.

dabble VERB **1** splash about gently or playfully. **2** work at something in a casual or superficial way.

dab hand NOUN [INFORMAL] an expert.

da capo ADV [MUSIC] repeat from the beginning.

dacha NOUN a Russian country cottage.

dachshund NOUN a small dog with a long body and short legs.

dad NOUN [INFORMAL] father.

daddy NOUN (PL **daddies**) [INFORMAL] father.

daddy-long-legs NOUN [INFORMAL] a long-legged flying insect.

dado /day-doh/ NOUN (PL **dados**) the lower part of a wall decorated differently from the upper part.

daffodil NOUN a yellow flower with a trumpet-shaped central part.

daft ADJ [INFORMAL] silly, crazy.

dagger NOUN a short pointed two-edged weapon used for stabbing.

dago /day-goh/ NOUN (PL **dagos** or **dagoes**) [INFORMAL], [OFFENSIVE] a person from southern Europe (especially Spain or Italy).

daguerreotype /dă-ger-rŏ-tIp/ NOUN an early kind of photograph.

Dáil /doil/ (in full **Dáil Éireann**) NOUN the lower House of Parliament in the Republic of Ireland.

daily ADJ happening or appearing on every day or every weekday. ADV once a day. NOUN (PL **dailies**) **1** a daily newspaper. **2** [INFORMAL] a domestic cleaner.

dainty ADJ (**daintier**, **daintiest**) **1** delicate, small, and pretty. **2** fastidious.
daintily ADV
daintiness NOUN

dairy NOUN (PL **dairies**) a place where milk and its products are processed or sold.

dais /day-iss/ NOUN a low platform, especially at the end of a hall.

daisy NOUN (PL **daisies**) a flower with many ray-like petals.

daisy wheel NOUN a device with radiating spokes ending in letters, used in printers.

dal variant of **DHAL**.

dale NOUN a valley.

dally VERB (**dallies**, **dallying**, **dallied**) idle, dawdle; flirt.
dalliance NOUN

Dalmatian NOUN a dog of a large white breed with dark spots.

dam NOUN **1** a barrier built across a river to hold back water. **2** the mother of an animal, especially a mammal. VERB (**dams**, **damming**, **dammed**) build a dam across; obstruct, hold back.

damage NOUN **1** harm, injury, especially reducing something's value, usefulness, or attractiveness. **2** (**damages**) money as compensation for injury. VERB cause damage to.

damask NOUN a fabric woven with a pattern visible on either side.

dame NOUN **1** (**Dame**) the title of a woman with an order of knighthood. **2** [US] [INFORMAL] a woman.

damn VERB **1** (**be damned**) be condemned to hell.

d

2 strongly condemn or criticize. EXCLAMATION [INFORMAL] expressing anger. ADJ [INFORMAL] used to emphasize anger.

damnable ADJ hateful, annoying.
damnably ADV

damnation NOUN eternal punishment in hell. EXCLAMATION [INFORMAL] an exclamation of annoyance.

damp ADJ slightly wet. NOUN moistness. VERB **1** dampen. **2** restrain, discourage. **3** reduce the vibration and volume of (a piano string etc.).
dampness NOUN

dampen VERB **1** make or become damp. **2** make less strong or intense.
dampener NOUN

damper NOUN **1** something that depresses or subdues. **2** a pad silencing a piano string. **3** a metal plate controlling the draught in a flue.

damsel NOUN [ARCHAIC] a young woman.

damson NOUN a small purple plum.

dance VERB move with rhythmical steps and gestures, usually to music; move in a quick or lively way. NOUN a piece of dancing; music for this; a social gathering for dancing.
dance attendance on follow about and help dutifully.
dancer NOUN

D and C ABBREV dilatation and curettage, a minor operation to clean the womb.

dandelion NOUN a wild plant with bright yellow flowers.

dandified ADJ like a dandy.

dandle VERB dance or nurse (a child) in one's arms.

dandruff NOUN flakes of dead skin from the scalp.

dandy NOUN (PL **dandies**) a man who pays excessive attention to his appearance. ADJ [INFORMAL] excellent.

Dane NOUN a person from Denmark.

danger NOUN likelihood of harm or death; something causing this.

dangerous ADJ causing or involving danger.
dangerously ADV

dangle VERB hang or swing loosely; hold out temptingly.
dangler NOUN
dangly ADJ

Danish ADJ relating to Denmark. NOUN the language of Denmark.

dank ADJ damp and cold.
dankly ADV
dankness NOUN

dapper ADJ neat and precise in dress or movement.

dapple VERB mark with patches of colour or shade.

dapple grey ADJ (of a horse etc.) grey or white with darker spots.

dare VERB be bold enough (to do something); challenge to do something risky. NOUN this challenge.
I dare say I think it likely.

daredevil NOUN a recklessly daring person. ADJ recklessly daring.

daring ADJ bold. NOUN boldness.
daringly ADV

dark ADJ **1** with little or no light; closer to black than to white; having dark hair or skin. **2** gloomy, tragic; evil. **3** hidden, mysterious. NOUN absence of light; night.
darkly ADV
darkness NOUN

darken VERB make or become dark.

dark horse NOUN a successful competitor of whom little is known.

darkroom NOUN a darkened room for processing photographs.

darling NOUN a loved or lovable person or thing; a favourite. ADJ beloved, lovable; favourite.

darn VERB mend (a hole in fabric) by weaving thread across it. NOUN a darned area in material. ADJ (also **darned**) [INFORMAL] damn.

dart NOUN **1** a small pointed missile; (**darts**) a game in which such missiles are thrown at a target. **2** a sudden run. **3** a tuck shaping a garment. VERB run suddenly; send out (a glance etc.) rapidly.

dartboard NOUN a target in the game of darts.

dash VERB **1** run rapidly. **2** strike or throw violently against something; destroy (hopes etc.). NOUN **1** a rapid run, a rush. **2** a small amount of liquid etc. added to something. **3** a punctuation mark (-) marking a pause or break in the sense or representing omitted letters. **4** flamboyance and liveliness. **5** a dashboard.

dashboard NOUN the instrument panel of a motor vehicle.

dashing ADJ stylish; spirited, gallant.

dastardly ADJ [DATED] wicked, vile.

DAT ABBREV digital audio tape.

data NOUN facts collected for reference or analysis; facts to be processed by computer.

data bank NOUN a large store of computerized data.

database NOUN an organized store of computerized data.

date[1] NOUN **1** a specified day of a month or year; the day or year of something's occurrence; the period to which something belongs. **2** [INFORMAL] an appointment to meet someone socially or romantically; [US] the person to be met. VERB **1** establish the date of; originate from a specified date; mark with a date; become or show to be old-fashioned. **2** [INFORMAL] go out with (a romantic partner).
to date until now.

date[2] NOUN a small brown edible fruit.

dated ADJ old-fashioned.

date rape NOUN the rape of a woman by a person with whom she is on a date.

dative NOUN the grammatical case expressing the indirect object.

datum NOUN (PL **data**) an item of data.

daub /dorb/ VERB smear roughly. NOUN a crudely painted picture; a smear.

daughter NOUN a female in relation to her parents.

daughter-in-law NOUN (PL **daughters-in-law**) a son's wife.

daunt VERB intimidate, discourage.

dauntless ADJ fearless and determined.

dauphin /**doh**-fah, **dor**-fin/ NOUN the title of the eldest son of former kings of France.

davit NOUN a small crane on a ship.

dawdle VERB walk slowly; idle.
dawdler NOUN

dawn NOUN the first light of day; a beginning. VERB grow light; begin; be realized or understood.
dawning NOUN

day NOUN **1** a period of 24 hours; the part of this when the sun is above the horizon; the part of this spent working. **2** a time, a period.
in one's day at an earlier and better point in one's life.

daybreak NOUN the first light of day.

daydream NOUN pleasant idle thoughts. VERB have daydreams.

daze VERB cause to feel stunned or bewildered. NOUN a dazed state.

dazzle VERB blind temporarily with bright light; impress with splendour.
dazzlement NOUN

dB ABBREV decibel(s).

DC ABBREV direct current.

DDT ABBREV a chlorinated hydrocarbon used as an insecticide.

de- PREFIX implying removal or reversal.

deacon NOUN a member of the clergy ranking below priest; a lay person attending to church business in Nonconformist churches.

dead ADJ **1** no longer alive. **2** lacking sensation or emotion; lacking excitement; lacking resonance. **3** no longer functioning; no longer relevant. **4** total, absolute. ADV absolutely; exactly.

dead beat ADJ [INFORMAL] tired out.

deaden VERB make less

intense; deprive of sensation or sensitivity; deprive of vitality.

d

dead end NOUN a cul-de-sac; an occupation with no prospect of development or progress.

dead heat NOUN a race in which two or more competitors finish exactly even.

dead letter NOUN a law or rule no longer observed.

deadline NOUN a time limit.

deadlock NOUN a state when no progress can be made. VERB bring to such a state.

deadly ADJ (**deadlier**, **deadliest**) **1** causing death. **2** absolute: *in deadly earnest.* **3** [INFORMAL] very boring. ADV **1** so as to appear dead. **2** extremely.
deadliness NOUN

deadpan ADJ expressionless.

deaf ADJ wholly or partly unable to hear; refusing to listen.
deafen VERB
deafness NOUN

deal VERB (**deals**, **dealing**, **dealt**) **1** distribute (playing cards) to players; hand out; inflict (a blow, a misfortune, etc.). **2** engage in trade. NOUN **1** a bargain, a transaction. **2** an act of dealing cards. **3** fir or pine timber.
a great deal a large amount. **a raw deal** [INFORMAL] unfair or harsh treatment. **big deal** [INFORMAL] an ironic expression of contempt.
deal with 1 take action about. **2** have as a topic.

dealer NOUN a person who deals; a trader.

dean NOUN **1** a clergyman who is head of a cathedral chapter. **2** a university official.

deanery NOUN (PL **deaneries**) a dean's residence.

dear ADJ **1** much loved, cherished. **2** expensive. NOUN a dear person. EXCLAMATION an exclamation of surprise or distress.
dearly ADV
dearness NOUN

dearth /derth/ NOUN a scarcity, a lack.

death NOUN the process of dying; the state of being dead; an end; ruin.

death duty NOUN (PL **death duties**) a tax levied on property after the owner's death.

deathly ADJ (**deathlier**, **deathliest**) as of death: *a deathly hush.*

death trap NOUN a very dangerous place.

death-watch beetle NOUN a beetle whose larvae bore into wood and make a ticking sound.

deb NOUN [INFORMAL] a debutante.

debacle /day-**bah**-kl/ NOUN an utter and ignominious failure.

debar VERB (**debars**, **debarring**, **debarred**) exclude.

debase VERB lower in quality or value.
debasement NOUN

debatable ADJ questionable.

debate NOUN a formal discussion. VERB discuss formally; consider.

debauchery NOUN over-indulgence in harmful or immoral pleasures.
debauched ADJ

debenture /di-**bent**-chĕ/ NOUN a long-term security bearing a fixed rate of interest.

debilitate VERB weaken.
debilitation NOUN

debility NOUN physical weakness.

debit NOUN an entry in an account for a sum owing. VERB (**debits**, **debiting**, **debited**) enter as a debit, charge.

debonair ADJ having a carefree self-confident manner.

debouch /di-**bowsh**, di-**boosh**/ VERB come out from a narrow into an open area.

debrief VERB question to obtain facts about a completed mission.

debris /**deb**-ree/ NOUN scattered broken pieces or rubbish.

debt /det/ NOUN something owed.
in debt owing something.

debtor NOUN a person who owes money.

debunk VERB [INFORMAL]

show up as exaggerated or false.

debut /day-bew/ NOUN a first public appearance.

debutante NOUN a young upper-class woman making her first formal appearance in society.

deca- COMBINING FORM ten.

decade NOUN a ten-year period.

decadent ADJ in a state of moral deterioration.
decadence NOUN

decaffeinated ADJ with caffeine removed.

decagon NOUN a geometric figure with ten sides.

Decalogue NOUN the Ten Commandments.

decamp VERB go away suddenly or secretly.

decant VERB pour (liquid) into another container, leaving sediment behind.

decanter NOUN a bottle into which wine may be decanted before serving.

decapitate VERB behead.
decapitation NOUN

decarbonize (also **decarbonise**) VERB remove carbon deposit from (an engine).

decathlon NOUN an athletic contest involving ten events.

decay VERB rot; decline, deteriorate. NOUN rot; deterioration.

decease NOUN [FORMAL] death.

deceased ADJ [FORMAL] dead.

deceit NOUN deception.
deceitful ADJ
deceitfully ADV

deceive VERB **1** cause to believe something that is not true. **2** be sexually unfaithful to.
deceiver NOUN

decelerate VERB reduce the speed (of).
deceleration NOUN

December NOUN the twelfth month.

decennial /di-sen-i-ăl/ ADJ happening every tenth year; lasting ten years.
decennially ADV

decent ADJ **1** conforming to accepted standards of propriety; respectable, fitting. **2** of an acceptable standard. **3** [INFORMAL] kind, generous.
decency NOUN
decently ADV

decentralize (also **decentralise**) VERB transfer from central to local control.
decentralization NOUN

deception NOUN the action of deceiving; a trick.

deceptive ADJ misleading.
deceptively ADV

deci- COMBINING FORM one-tenth.

decibel NOUN a unit for measuring the intensity of sound.

decide VERB make up one's mind; settle (a contest or argument).

decided ADJ having firm opinions; clear, definite.
decidedly ADV

deciduous ADJ (of a tree) shedding its leaves annually.

decimal ADJ reckoned in tens or tenths. NOUN a decimal fraction.

decimal currency NOUN currency with each unit 10 or 100 times the value of the one next below it.

decimal fraction NOUN a fraction based on powers of ten, shown as figures after a dot.

decimalize (also **decimalise**) VERB convert into a decimal.
decimalization NOUN

decimal point NOUN the dot used in a decimal fraction.

decimate VERB destroy a large proportion of; (in ancient Rome) destroy one tenth of.
decimation NOUN

decipher VERB make out the meaning of (code, bad handwriting).

decision NOUN a conclusion or resolution reached after consideration; the ability to decide quickly and confidently.

decisive ADJ **1** settling an issue definitively. **2** able to decide quickly and confidently.
decisively ADV
decisiveness NOUN

deck NOUN **1** a floor or storey of a ship or bus. **2** the part of a cassette or record player that holds and plays the cassettes or records. VERB decorate, dress up.

d

deckchair NOUN a folding canvas chair.

declaim VERB speak or say impressively.
declamation NOUN
declamatory ADJ

declare VERB announce openly or formally; state firmly.
declaration NOUN
declaratory ADJ

declassify VERB (**declassifies**, **declassifying**, **declassified**) cease to classify as officially secret.
declassification NOUN

declension NOUN [GRAMMAR] a class of nouns and adjectives having the same inflectional forms.

decline VERB **1** decrease in size or number; lose strength or quality. **2** refuse politely. **3** slope downwards. NOUN a gradual decrease or loss of strength.

declivity NOUN (PL **declivities**) a downward slope.

declutch VERB disengage the clutch of a motor.

decoction NOUN an essence extracted by boiling; extracting this.
decoct VERB

decode VERB put (a coded message) into plain language; make (an electronic signal) intelligible.
decoder NOUN

décolleté ADJ having a low neckline.

decompose VERB **1** decay, become rotten. **2** break down or cause to break down into component elements.
decomposition NOUN

decompress VERB **1** reduce air pressure in or on. **2** expand (computer data) so it can be processed.
decompression NOUN

decongestant NOUN a medicinal substance that relieves congestion.

decontaminate VERB free from radioactivity, germs, etc.
decontamination NOUN

decor /day-kor, de-kor/ NOUN the style of decoration used in a room.

decorate VERB **1** make

attractive by adding ornaments; paint or paper the walls of. **2** confer a medal or award on.
decoration NOUN

decorative ADJ ornamental.
decoratively ADV

decorator NOUN a person who paints and papers rooms etc. professionally.

decorous ADJ decent; restrained.
decorously ADV

decorum /di-**kor**-ŭm/ NOUN correctness and dignity of behaviour.

decoy NOUN a person or animal used to lure others into a trap.
VERB lure by a decoy.

decrease VERB make or become smaller or fewer.
NOUN the process of decreasing; the extent of this.

decree NOUN an order given by a government or other authority.
VERB order by decree.

decrepit ADJ made weak by age or use; dilapidated.

decriminalize (also **decriminalise**) VERB cease to treat (an action) as criminal.

decry VERB (**decries**, **decrying**, **decried**) denounce publicly.

dedicate VERB devote to a cause or task; address (a book etc.) to a person as a tribute.
dedication NOUN

dedicated ADJ serious in one's commitment to a task; exclusively set aside for a particular purpose.

deduce VERB arrive at (a conclusion) by reasoning; infer.
deducible ADJ

deduct VERB subtract.

deduction NOUN **1** the action of deducting; something deducted. **2** the action of deducing; a conclusion deduced.

deductive ADJ based on reasoning.

deed NOUN **1** something done, an act. **2** a legal document.

deem VERB [FORMAL] consider to be of a specified character.

deep ADJ **1** extending or situated far down or in

d

from the top or surface. **2** intense, extreme. **3** profound. **4** low-pitched.
deep in fully absorbed in.
deepen VERB
deeply ADV
deepness NOUN

deer NOUN (PL **deer**) a hoofed animal, the male of which usually has antlers.

deerstalker NOUN a cloth cap with a peak in front and at the back.

deface VERB spoil or damage the surface of.
defacement NOUN

de facto ADJ existing in fact, whether by right or not.

defame VERB attack the good reputation of.
defamation NOUN
defamatory ADJ

default VERB fail to fulfil an obligation, especially to pay debts or appear in court. NOUN **1** failure to fulfil an obligation. **2** a pre-selected option adopted by a computer program unless otherwise instructed.
by default in the absence of competition or other options. **in default of** in the absence of.
defaulter NOUN

defeat VERB win victory over; cause to fail. NOUN the action of defeating; the state of being defeated.

defeatist NOUN a person who pessimistically expects or accepts failure.
defeatism NOUN

defecate VERB discharge faeces from the body.
defecation NOUN

defect NOUN /**dee**-fekt/ an imperfection. VERB /di-**fekt**/ desert one's country or cause.
defection NOUN
defector NOUN

defective ADJ imperfect, faulty; incomplete.
defectively ADV
defectiveness NOUN

defence ([US] **defense**) NOUN **1** the action of defending against attack; military measures or resources for protecting a country. **2** arguments against an accusation.
defenceless ADJ
defencelessness NOUN

defend VERB **1** protect from

attack. **2** uphold by argument; represent (the defendant).
defender NOUN

defendant NOUN a person accused or sued in a lawsuit.

defensible ADJ able to be defended.
defensibility NOUN
defensibly ADV

defensive ADJ **1** intended for defence. **2** sensitive to criticism.
defensively ADV
defensiveness NOUN

defer VERB (**defers, deferring, deferred**) **1** postpone. **2** yield to a person's wishes or authority.
deferment NOUN
deferral NOUN

deference NOUN polite respect.
deferential ADJ
deferentially ADV

defiance NOUN resistance, disobedience.
defiant ADJ
defiantly ADV

deficiency NOUN (PL **deficiencies**) a lack, a shortage; an imperfection.

deficient ADJ not having enough; insufficient, inadequate.

deficit NOUN an amount by which a total falls short of what is required.

defile VERB make dirty or impure, pollute. NOUN a narrow pass or gorge.

define VERB **1** state precisely; give the meaning of. **2** mark the boundary of.

definite ADJ clearly and firmly decided or stated; certain, unambiguous; with a clear shape or outline.
definitely ADV

definite article NOUN [GRAMMAR] the word *the*.

definition NOUN a statement of precise meaning; distinctness, clearness of outline.

definitive ADJ settling something finally and authoritatively; most authoritative.
definitively ADV

deflate VERB collapse or cause to collapse through release of air; make less confident; reduce the price levels in (an

economy).
deflation NOUN

deflect VERB turn aside.
deflection (or **deflexion**) NOUN
deflector NOUN

deflower VERB [LITERARY] deprive of virginity.

defoliate VERB remove the leaves of.
defoliant NOUN
defoliation NOUN

deforest VERB clear of trees.
deforestation NOUN

deform VERB distort the shape of.
deformed ADJ

deformity NOUN (PL **deformities**) abnormality of shape, especially of a part of the body.

defraud VERB deprive by fraud.

defray VERB provide money to pay (costs).

defrost VERB remove ice from (a refrigerator); thaw.

deft ADJ skilful and quick.
deftly ADV

defunct ADJ no longer existing or functioning.

defuse VERB remove the fuse from (an explosive); reduce the dangerous tension in (a situation).

defy VERB (**defies**, **defying**, **defied**) resist, disobey; challenge; make difficult or impossible: *defies belief.*

degenerate VERB /di-**jen**-er-ayt/ become worse physically, mentally, or morally. ADJ /di-**jen**-er-ăt/ having degenerated. NOUN /di-**jen**-er-ăt/ a degenerate person.
degeneracy NOUN
degeneration NOUN

degrade VERB **1** treat disrespectfully, humiliate; [ARCHAIC] reduce to a lower rank. **2** decompose.
degradation NOUN

degree NOUN **1** the extent to which something is true or present; a stage in a series. **2** a unit of measurement for angles or temperature. **3** an award given by a university or college.

dehumanize (also **dehumanise**) VERB remove human qualities from; make impersonal.
dehumanization NOUN

dehydrate VERB lose or cause to lose a large

amount of moisture; preserve (food) by doing this.
dehydration NOUN
dehydrator NOUN

deify VERB (**deifies**, **deifying**, **deified**) treat as a god.
deification NOUN

deign /dayn/ VERB condescend.

deity NOUN (PL **deities**) a divine being.

déjà vu /day-*zh*ah **voo**/ NOUN a feeling of having experienced a present situation before.

dejected ADJ in low spirits.

dejection NOUN lowness of spirits.

de jure /dee **joo**-ri/ ADV rightfully, by right. ADJ rightful.

delay VERB make late; be slow; postpone. NOUN the action of delaying; time lost by delaying.

delayering NOUN the reduction of the number of levels in the hierarchy of an organization.

delectable ADJ delicious, delightful.
delectably ADV

delectation NOUN [FORMAL] enjoyment.

delegate NOUN /**del**-i-găt/ a representative. VERB /**del**-i-gayt/ entrust (a task or power) to an agent.

delegation NOUN a group of representatives; the action of delegating.

delete VERB strike out (a word etc.); remove.
deletion NOUN

deleterious ADJ harmful.

delft NOUN glazed earthenware.

deliberate ADJ /di-**lib**-er-ăt/ **1** intentional. **2** slow and careful. VERB /di-**lib**-er-ayt/ engage in careful discussion or consideration (of).
deliberately ADV
deliberation NOUN

delicacy NOUN (PL **delicacies**) **1** the quality of being delicate. **2** discretion and tact. **3** a high-quality or expensive food.

delicate ADJ **1** fine, intricate. **2** fragile; prone to illness or injury. **3** requiring or showing tact.
delicately ADV

delicatessen NOUN a shop selling speciality groceries, cheeses, cooked meats, etc.

d

delicious ADJ delightful, especially to taste or smell.
deliciously ADV

delight NOUN great pleasure; a source of this. VERB please greatly; feel delight.
delightful ADJ
delightfully ADV

delimit VERB determine the limits or boundaries of.
delimitation NOUN

delineate VERB outline.
delineation NOUN
delineator NOUN

delinquent ADJ guilty of persistent lawbreaking. NOUN a delinquent person.
delinquency NOUN

deliquesce /de-li-kwes/ VERB become liquid, melt.

delirium NOUN a disordered state of mind, especially during fever; wild excitement.
delirious ADJ
deliriously ADV

deliver VERB **1** take to an addressee or purchaser; hand over; utter (a speech etc.); aim (a blow or attack). **2** rescue, set free. **3** assist in the birth of.
deliverer NOUN
delivery NOUN

deliverance NOUN rescue, freeing.

dell NOUN a small wooded hollow.

delta NOUN **1** the fourth letter of the Greek alphabet (Δ, δ). **2** a triangular patch of deposited earth at the mouth of a river, formed by its diverging outlets.

delude VERB deceive, mislead.

deluge NOUN a flood; a heavy fall of rain; a large quantity of something coming at the same time. VERB flood; overwhelm.

delusion NOUN a false belief or impression.
delusory ADJ

delusive ADJ giving a false impression.

de luxe ADJ of superior quality; luxurious.

delve VERB search deeply.

demagogue NOUN a political leader who wins support by appealing to

popular feelings and prejudices.
demagogic ADJ
demagogy NOUN

demand NOUN a firm or official request; customers' desire for goods or services; a claim. VERB make a demand for; need.

demanding ADJ **1** difficult, requiring great skill or effort. **2** expecting a lot from other people.

demarcation NOUN the marking of a boundary or limits, especially of work for different trades.

demean VERB lower the dignity of.

demeanour ([US] **demeanor**) NOUN the way a person behaves.

demented ADJ driven mad, crazy.

dementia NOUN a mental disorder.

demerara NOUN brown raw cane sugar.

demesne /dĕ-**mayn**/ NOUN a landed estate.

demi- PREFIX half.

demilitarize (also **demilitarise**) VERB remove military forces from.
demilitarization NOUN

demise NOUN death; failure.

demisemiquaver NOUN a note equal to half a semiquaver.

demo NOUN (PL **demos**) [INFORMAL] a demonstration.

demob [INFORMAL] VERB (**demobs**, **demobbing**, **demobbed**) demobilize. NOUN demobilization.

demobilize VERB (also **demobilise**) release from military service.
demobilization NOUN

democracy NOUN (PL **democracies**) government by all the people, usually through elected representatives; a country governed in this way.
democratic ADJ
democratically ADV

democrat NOUN a person favouring democracy.

demography NOUN the statistical study of human populations.
demographic ADJ

demolish VERB pull or knock down; destroy.
demolition NOUN

d

demon NOUN a devil, an evil spirit; a cruel person; an energetic and forceful person.
demoniac ADJ
demoniacal ADJ
demonic ADJ

demonstrable ADJ able to be proved; clearly apparent.
demonstrability NOUN
demonstrably ADV

demonstrate VERB **1** prove, show clearly; give an exhibition of. **2** take part in a public protest.
demonstrator NOUN

demonstration NOUN **1** the action of proving or exhibiting. **2** a public protest.

demonstrative ADJ **1** showing feelings openly. **2** giving proof.
demonstratively ADV

demoralize (also **demoralise**) VERB dishearten.
demoralization NOUN

demote VERB reduce to a lower rank or category.
demotion NOUN

demur VERB (**demurs, demurring, demurred**) show reluctance; raise doubts or objections. NOUN the showing of reluctance; objection.

demure ADJ quiet and modest or pretending to be so.
demurely ADV
demureness NOUN

den NOUN a wild animal's lair; [INFORMAL] a person's small private room.

denary ADJ of ten; decimal.

denationalize (also **denationalise**) VERB privatize.
denationalization NOUN

denature VERB **1** change the properties of. **2** make (alcohol) unfit for drinking.

dendrochronology NOUN the dating of timber by study of the annual growth rings.

deniable ADJ able to be denied.

denial NOUN the action of denying; a statement that a thing is not true.

denier /den-yer/ NOUN a unit of weight for measuring the fineness of yarn.

denigrate VERB disparage;

criticize unfairly. **denigration** NOUN

denim NOUN a strong twilled fabric; (**denims**) trousers made of this.

denizen NOUN [FORMAL] an inhabitant.

denominate VERB [FORMAL] name.

denomination NOUN **1** a branch of the Christian Church or another religion. **2** the face value of a coin or bank note. **3** [FORMAL] a name. **denominational** ADJ

denominator NOUN a number below the line in a vulgar fraction.

denote VERB be a sign or symbol of; indicate. **denotation** NOUN

denouement /day-noo-mahn/ NOUN the final outcome of a play or story.

denounce VERB condemn, criticize; inform against.

dense ADJ **1** thick, closely massed. **2** compressed and hard to understand. **3** [INFORMAL] stupid. **densely** ADV **denseness** NOUN

density NOUN the degree to which something is full or closely packed; the relation of weight to volume.

dent NOUN a hollow left by a blow or pressure. VERB mark with a dent; diminish, discourage.

dental ADJ of or for teeth; of dentistry.

dental floss NOUN thread for cleaning between the teeth.

dentate ADJ toothed, notched.

dentifrice NOUN a paste or powder for cleaning teeth.

dentine NOUN the hard tissue forming the teeth.

dentist NOUN a person qualified to treat decay and malformations of teeth.

dentistry NOUN a dentist's work.

dentition NOUN the arrangement of the teeth.

denture NOUN a plate holding an artificial tooth or teeth.

denude VERB strip of covering or property. **denudation** NOUN

denunciation NOUN the

action of denouncing; a public condemnation.

deny VERB (**denies**, **denying**, **denying**) **1** say that (something) is not true; refuse to admit as belonging or attaching to one. **2** refuse; prevent from having.
deny oneself practise abstinence.

deodorant NOUN a substance that removes or conceals unwanted odours. ADJ deodorizing.

deodorize (also **deodorise**) VERB remove unpleasant smells from.
deodorization NOUN

deoxyribonucleic acid *see* **DNA**.

depart VERB go away, leave.

departed ADJ dead.

department NOUN a section of an organization with a special function or concern.
departmental ADJ

department store NOUN a large shop selling many kinds of goods.

departure NOUN an act of departing; the process of setting out on a new course of action.

depend VERB (**depend on**) **1** be determined by. **2** trust confidently. **3** be unable to do without.

dependable ADJ reliable.

dependant NOUN one who depends on another for support.

dependency NOUN (PL **dependencies**) the state of being dependent; a country controlled by another.

dependent ADJ depending; controlled by another.
dependence NOUN

depict VERB represent in a picture or in words.
depiction NOUN

depilatory ADJ used to remove unwanted hair. NOUN (PL **depilatories**) a depilatory cream.

deplete VERB reduce the number of by overuse.
depletion NOUN

deplorable ADJ shockingly bad.
deplorably ADV

deplore VERB feel or express strong disapproval of.

deploy VERB move into position for action; utilize.
deployment NOUN

depopulate VERB reduce the population of.
depopulation NOUN

deport VERB remove (a person) from a country.
deportation NOUN

deportment NOUN behaviour; bearing.

depose VERB remove from power.

deposit VERB (**deposits**, **depositing**, **deposited**) **1** put down; leave (a layer of earth etc.). **2** entrust for safe keeping; pay into a bank or as a guarantee. NOUN **1** a sum paid into a bank; a first instalment of payment. **2** a layer of sediment etc.
depositor NOUN

depositary NOUN (PL **depositaries**) a person to whom something is entrusted.

deposition NOUN **1** the action of removing someone from power. **2** a sworn statement. **3** the action of depositing.

depository NOUN (PL **depositories**) **1** a storehouse. **2** a depositary.

depot /de-poh/ NOUN a storage area, especially for vehicles; [US] a bus or railway station.

depraved ADJ morally corrupt.
deprave VERB

depravity NOUN moral corruption, wickedness.

deprecate VERB **1** express disapproval of. **2** disclaim politely.
deprecation NOUN
deprecatory ADJ

depreciate VERB diminish in value; belittle.
depreciation NOUN
depreciatory ADJ

depredations PLURAL NOUN acts that cause harm or damage.

depress VERB **1** cause to feel dispirited. **2** press down. **3** reduce the strength or activity of.
depressant ADJ & NOUN

depression NOUN **1** sadness, gloominess. **2** a long period of inactivity in trading. **3** the action of pressing down; a lowering or reduction; a

hollow on a surface; an area of low atmospheric pressure.
depressive ADJ

d **deprive** VERB prevent from using or enjoying something.
deprivation NOUN

depth NOUN **1** distance downwards or inwards from a surface. **2** profundity; detailed treatment; intensity. **3** the deepest or most central part.
in depth thoroughly, in detail. **out of one's depth** in water too deep for one to stand; unable to understand or cope.

depth charge NOUN a bomb that will explode under water.

deputation NOUN a body of people sent to represent others.

depute VERB appoint to act as one's representative.

deputize (also **deputise**) VERB act as deputy.

deputy NOUN (PL **deputies**) a person appointed to act as a substitute or representative.

derail VERB cause (a train) to leave the rails.
derailment NOUN

derange VERB **1** make insane. **2** throw into confusion.
derangement NOUN

derelict ADJ left to fall into ruin.

dereliction NOUN **1** the state of being derelict. **2** failure to do one's duty.

derestrict VERB remove restrictions from.

deride VERB mock, scorn.

de rigueur /dĕ rig-**er**/ ADJ required by custom or etiquette.

derision NOUN scorn, ridicule.
derisive ADJ
derisively ADV

derisory ADJ **1** ridiculously or insultingly small. **2** derisive.

derivative ADJ derived from another source; lacking originality. NOUN something derived from another source; a financial contract whose value is dependent on a variable asset.

derive VERB obtain from a source; originate.

derivation NOUN

dermatitis NOUN inflammation of the skin.

dermatology NOUN the study of the skin and its diseases.
dermatologist NOUN

derogatory ADJ disparaging.

derrick NOUN a crane with a pivoted arm; a framework over an oil well etc.

derris NOUN an insecticide made from the root of a tropical plant.

derv NOUN fuel for diesel engines.

dervish NOUN a member of a Muslim religious order known for their whirling dance.

desalinate VERB remove salt from (especially sea water).
desalination NOUN

descant NOUN a treble accompaniment to a main melody.

descend VERB go or come down; stoop to unworthy behaviour; make an attack or a sudden visit.
be descended from have as one's ancestor(s).

descendant NOUN a person descended from another.

descent NOUN an act of descending; a downward route or slope; ancestry.

describe VERB **1** give a description of. **2** mark the outline of (a geometrical figure).

description NOUN **1** a statement of what a person or thing is like. **2** a kind, a sort: *cars of all descriptions.*

descriptive ADJ describing something, especially in a vivid style.

descry VERB (**descries, descrying, descried**) [LITERARY] catch sight of.

desecrate VERB defile (a sacred place or object) by irreverent treatment.
desecration NOUN
desecrator NOUN

desegregate VERB abolish segregation in or of.
desegregation NOUN

deselect VERB **1** reject (an MP) as a candidate for re-election. **2** turn off (a

selected feature) on a list of options on a computer menu.
deselection NOUN

d **desert**[1] /dez-ert/ NOUN a barren uninhabited often sandy area.

desert[2] /di-zert/ VERB abandon; leave one's service in the armed forces without permission.
deserter NOUN
desertion NOUN

deserts /di-zerts/ PLURAL NOUN what one deserves.

deserve VERB be worthy of through one's actions or qualities.
deservedly ADV

deserving ADJ worthy of good treatment or fortune.

déshabillé /day-za-bee-ay/ (also **dishabille**) NOUN the state of being only partly dressed.

desiccate VERB dry out moisture from.
desiccation NOUN

desideratum NOUN (PL **desiderata**) something required.

design NOUN **1** a plan or drawing produced before something is made; the production of such plans and drawings. **2** purpose; deliberate planning. **3** a decorative pattern. VERB prepare a design for; plan, intend.
have designs on aim to acquire, especially illicitly.
designedly ADV
designer NOUN

designate VERB /dez-ig-nayt/ appoint to a position; officially assign a status to. ADJ /dez-ig-năt/ appointed but not get installed.
designation NOUN

designing ADJ scheming, crafty.

desirable ADJ **1** arousing desire, attractive. **2** advisable, beneficial.
desirability NOUN

desire NOUN a feeling of wanting something strongly; sexual appetite; a thing desired. VERB feel a desire for.

desirous ADJ desiring.

desist VERB cease, stop.

desk NOUN a piece of furniture for reading or writing at; a counter; a section of a newspaper office etc.

desktop NOUN **1** the working surface of a desk. **2** (in full **desktop computer**) a computer small enough for use on a desk.

desolate ADJ deserted, lonely; very unhappy.
desolation NOUN

desolated ADJ feeling very distressed.

despair NOUN complete lack of hope. VERB feel despair.

despatch variant of **DISPATCH**.

desperado NOUN (PL **desperadoes**; [US] **desperados**) a reckless criminal.

desperate ADJ **1** hopeless; very bad or serious; made reckless by despair. **2** feeling an intense desire or need.
desperately ADV
desperation NOUN

despicable ADJ contemptible.
despicably ADV

despise VERB regard as worthless.

despite PREP in spite of.

despoil VERB [LITERARY] plunder.
despoilment NOUN
despoliation NOUN

despondent ADJ dejected and discouraged.
despondency NOUN
despondently ADV

despot NOUN a dictator.
despotic ADJ
despotically ADV
despotism NOUN

dessert /di-zert/ NOUN the sweet course of a meal.

dessertspoon NOUN a medium-sized spoon for eating puddings etc.
dessertspoonful NOUN

destabilize (also **destabilise**) VERB make unstable or insecure.

destination NOUN the place to which a person or thing is going.

destine VERB set apart for a purpose; doom to a particular fate.

destiny NOUN (PL **destinies**) fate; one's future destined by fate.

destitute ADJ extremely poor; without means to live.
destitution NOUN

destroy VERB pull or break down; ruin; kill (an

animal).
destruction NOUN
destructive ADJ

destroyer NOUN **1** a fast warship. **2** a person or thing that destroys.

destruct VERB destroy (especially a rocket) deliberately.

destructible ADJ able to be destroyed.

desuetude NOUN [FORMAL] disuse.

desultory /dez-ŭl-tĕ-ree/ ADJ without purpose or enthusiasm; moving at random between subjects.
desultorily ADV

detach VERB **1** separate, unfasten. **2** send (a group of soldiers) on a separate mission.
detachable ADJ

detached ADJ **1** separate; not connected. **2** free from bias or emotion.

detachment NOUN **1** objectivity. **2** the action of detaching. **3** a group sent on a military mission.

detail NOUN **1** a small individual fact or item; such items collectively. **2** a small military detachment. VERB **1** describe in detail. **2** assign to a special duty.

detain VERB keep in official custody; delay.
detainment NOUN

detainee NOUN a person detained in custody.

detect VERB discover the presence of.
detection NOUN
detector NOUN

detective NOUN a person whose job is to investigate crimes.

détente /day-**tahnt**/ NOUN an easing of tension between nations.

detention NOUN the action of detaining; imprisonment.

deter VERB (**deters**, **deterring**, **deterred**) discourage from action; prevent.

detergent NOUN a cleaning substance, especially other than soap.

deteriorate VERB become worse.
deterioration NOUN

determinant NOUN a decisive factor.

determination NOUN **1** resolution, firmness of purpose. **2** the process of determining something.

determine VERB **1** control. **2** resolve firmly. **3** establish precisely.

determined ADJ full of determination.

determiner NOUN **1** a person or thing that determines. **2** a word that comes before a noun to show how the noun is used (e.g. *a, the, every*).

determinism NOUN a theory that actions are determined by external forces.

deterrent NOUN a thing that deters.
deterrence NOUN

detest VERB dislike intensely.
detestable ADJ
detestation NOUN

dethrone VERB remove from power.

detonate VERB explode or cause to explode.
detonation NOUN
detonator NOUN

detour NOUN a deviation from a direct or intended course.

detoxify VERB (**detoxifies, detoxifying, detoxified**) remove harmful substances from.

detract VERB (**detract from**) cause to seem less valuable or impressive.

detractor NOUN a person who criticizes something.

detriment NOUN harm.
detrimental ADJ
detrimentally ADV

detritus /di-**trI**-tŭs/ NOUN debris; loose stones.

deuce /dyoos/ NOUN **1** a score of 40 all in tennis. **2** [INFORMAL] (in exclamations) the Devil.

deuterium NOUN a heavy form of hydrogen.

Deutschmark /**doich**-mark/ NOUN the former unit of money in Germany.

devalue VERB reduce the value of; disparage.
devaluation NOUN

devastate VERB cause great destruction to; cause severe shock or grief to.
devastation NOUN

devastating ADJ very destructive; shocking and distressing; [INFORMAL] very impressive or effective.

develop VERB (**develops, developing, developed**) **1** make or become larger, more mature, or more advanced; begin to exist or have. **2** make (land etc.) usable or profitable. **3** treat (a film) so as to make a picture visible.
developer NOUN
development NOUN

deviant ADJ deviating from accepted standards. NOUN a deviant person.

deviate VERB diverge from a route, course of action, etc.
deviation NOUN

device NOUN a thing made or used for a purpose; a scheme.

devil NOUN an evil spirit; (**the Devil**) the supreme spirit of evil; a cruel person; a person of mischievous energy or cleverness; [INFORMAL] a difficult person or problem.
devilish ADJ

devilled ([US] **deviled**) ADJ cooked with hot spices.

devilment NOUN mischief.

devilry NOUN wickedness; mischief.

devil's advocate NOUN a person who tests a proposition by arguing against it.

devious ADJ underhand; (of a route) indirect.
deviously ADV
deviousness NOUN

devise VERB plan; invent.
devisor NOUN

devoid ADJ (**devoid of**) completely lacking.

devolution NOUN delegation of power especially from central to local administration.

devolve VERB transfer (power) to a lower level; (of duties etc.) pass to a deputy.

devote VERB give or use exclusively for a particular purpose.

devoted ADJ showing devotion.

devotee NOUN an enthusiast; a worshipper.

devotion NOUN great love, loyalty, or commitment; religious worship; (**devotions**) prayers.
devotional ADJ

devour VERB eat hungrily

or greedily; consume, destroy; take in avidly.
devourer NOUN

devout ADJ earnestly religious; earnest, sincere.
devoutly ADV

dew NOUN drops of condensed moisture forming on cool surfaces at night.
dewy ADJ

dewclaw NOUN a small claw on the inner side of a dog's leg.

dewlap NOUN a fold of loose skin on the throat of cattle etc.

dexterity NOUN skill.
dexterous ADJ (also **dextrous**)
dexterously ADV

dextrose NOUN a form of glucose.

dhal (also **dal**) NOUN an Indian dish of split pulses.

di- PREFIX two; double.

diabetes NOUN a disease in which sugar and starch are not properly absorbed by the body.
diabetic ADJ & NOUN

diabolic ADJ of the Devil.

diabolical ADJ very wicked; [INFORMAL] extremely bad.
diabolically ADV

diabolism NOUN worship of the Devil.

d

diachronic ADJ concerned with the historical development of a subject.

diaconate NOUN the office of deacon; a body of deacons.
diaconal ADJ

diacritic NOUN a sign on a letter indicating a difference in pronunciation, e.g. an accent.

diadem NOUN a crown.

diaeresis ([US] **dieresis**) NOUN a mark over a vowel sounded separately.

diagnose VERB make a diagnosis of.

diagnosis NOUN (PL **diagnoses**) the identification of a disease or condition after observing its symptoms.
diagnostic ADJ
diagnostician NOUN

diagonal ADJ (of a line) joining opposite corners of a square or rectangle; slanting. NOUN a diagonal line.

d

diagonally ADV

diagram NOUN a schematic drawing that shows the parts or operation of something.
diagrammatic ADJ
diagrammatically ADV

dial NOUN the face of a clock or watch; a similar plate or disc with a movable pointer; a movable disc manipulated to connect one telephone with another. VERB (**dials**, **dialling**, **dialled**; [US] **dialing**, **dialed**) select or operate by using a dial or numbered buttons.

dialect NOUN a local form of a language.
dialectal ADJ

dialectic NOUN investigation of truths especially by examining contradictions.
dialectical ADJ

dialogue ([US] **dialog**) NOUN a conversation or discussion.

dialysis NOUN purification of blood by filtering it through a membrane.

diamanté /dee-ă-mon-tay/ ADJ decorated with artificial jewels.

diameter NOUN a straight line from side to side through the centre of a circle or sphere; its length.

diametrical ADJ **1** (of opposites) total, absolute. **2** of or along a diameter.
diametrically ADV

diamond NOUN **1** a very hard brilliant precious stone. **2** a four-sided figure with equal sides and with angles that are not right angles. **3** (**diamonds**) one of the four suits in a pack of playing cards, marked with red diamonds.

diamond wedding NOUN a 60th anniversary.

diaper NOUN [US] a baby's nappy.

diaphanous /dI-af-ă-nŭs/ ADJ almost transparent.
diaphanously ADV

diaphragm /dy-ă-fram/ NOUN **1** the muscular partition between the chest and abdomen. **2** a contraceptive cap fitting over the cervix.

diarrhoea /dy-ă-ree-ă/ ([US] **diarrhea**) NOUN a condition with frequent fluid faeces.

diary NOUN (PL **diaries**) a daily record of events; a book for this or for noting appointments. **diarist** NOUN

diatribe NOUN a violent verbal attack.

dibber (also **dibble**) NOUN a tool to make holes in the ground for young plants.

dice NOUN (PL **dice**) a small cube marked on each side with 1–6 spots, used in games of chance. VERB (**dices**, **dicing**, **diced**) cut into small cubes. **dice with death** take great risks.

dicey ADJ (**dicier**, **diciest**) [INFORMAL] risky, unpredictable.

dichotomy /dy-kot-ŏ-mi/ NOUN (PL **dichotomies**) a division into two absolutely opposed parts. **dichotomous** ADJ

dicky [INFORMAL] ADJ (**dickier**, **dickiest**) weak, unhealthy. NOUN (PL **dickies**) a false shirt-front.

dicta pl. of **DICTUM**.

dictate VERB /dik-**tayt**/ **1** say (words) aloud to be written or recorded. **2** give orders officiously; control, prescribe. NOUN /**dik**-tayt/ (**dictates**) commands. **dictation** NOUN

dictator NOUN a ruler with unrestricted authority; a domineering person. **dictatorship** NOUN

dictatorial ADJ of or like a dictator.

diction NOUN a manner of uttering or pronouncing words.

dictionary NOUN (PL **dictionaries**) a book that lists and gives the meaning of the words of a language; an alphabetically arranged reference book.

dictum NOUN (PL **dicta**) a formal statement; a saying.

did past of **DO**.

didactic ADJ meant or meaning to instruct. **didactically** ADV

diddle VERB [INFORMAL] cheat.

die[1] VERB (**dies**, **dying**, **died**) cease to be alive; cease to exist; [INFORMAL] stop functioning; fade away.

be dying for (or **to**) long for or to.

die² NOUN a device for cutting or moulding metal or for stamping a design on coins etc.

diehard NOUN a stubbornly conservative person.

dieresis US spelling of **DIAERESIS**.

diesel (also **diesel engine**) NOUN an oil-burning engine in which ignition is produced by the heat of compressed air; fuel used in this.

diet NOUN **1** a person's usual food; a special restricted course of food adopted to lose weight or for medical reasons. **2** a congress; a parliamentary assembly in certain countries. VERB (**diets**, **dieting**, **dieted**) restrict what one eats. ADJ designed for a weight-reducing diet; low in sugar and fat.

dietary ADJ

dieter NOUN

dietetic ADJ of diet and nutrition. NOUN (**dietetics**) the study of diet and nutrition.

dietitian (also **dietician**) NOUN an expert in dietetics.

differ VERB be unlike; disagree.

difference NOUN **1** a way in which people or things are not the same; the state of being unlike. **2** a disagreement or dispute. **3** the remainder when one sum is subtracted from another.

different ADJ not the same; distinct; novel.

differently ADV

differential ADJ of, showing, or depending on a difference; distinctive. NOUN **1** an agreed difference in wage-rates. **2** an arrangement of gears allowing a vehicle's wheels to revolve at different speeds when cornering.

differentiate VERB distinguish between; be a difference between; make or become different.

differentiation NOUN

difficult ADJ needing much effort or skill to do, deal with, or understand; hard to please, uncooperative.

difficulty NOUN

diffident ADJ lacking self-confidence.
diffidence NOUN
diffidently ADV

diffract VERB break up (a beam of light) into a series of coloured or dark-and-light bands.
diffraction NOUN
diffractive ADJ

diffuse ADJ /di-fewss/ spread widely, not concentrated. VERB /di-fewz/ spread widely or thinly.
diffusely ADV
diffuser NOUN
diffusion NOUN
diffusive ADJ
diffusible ADJ

dig VERB (**digs**, **digging**, **dug**) **1** break up and move soil; make (a hole etc.) in this way; extract from the ground in this way. **2** push, poke. **3** search for; find. **4** [INFORMAL] like. NOUN **1** an act of digging; an excavation. **2** a poke with the finger etc. **3** [INFORMAL] a cutting remark. **4** (**digs**) [INFORMAL] lodgings.

digest VERB /dy-jest/ break down (food) in the body; absorb into the mind. NOUN /**dy**-jest/ a methodical summary.
digester NOUN
digestible ADJ
digestibility NOUN

digestion NOUN the process or power of digesting food.

digestive ADJ of or aiding digestion.

digger NOUN a person who digs; a mechanical excavator.

digit NOUN **1** any numeral from 0 to 9. **2** a finger or toe.

digital ADJ of or using digits; (of a clock) showing the time by a row of figures; converting information into electrical pulses, as in a computer.
digitally ADV

digital camera NOUN a camera that captures images by digital means.

digitalis NOUN a heart stimulant prepared from foxglove leaves.

dignified ADJ showing dignity.

dignify VERB (**dignifies**, **dignifying**, **dignified**) treat as important or deserving respect.

dignitary NOUN (PL **dignitaries**) a person holding high rank or position.

d

dignity NOUN (PL **dignities**) the state of being worthy of respect; a calm and serious manner; a high rank or position.

digress VERB depart from the main subject temporarily.
digression NOUN
digressive ADJ

dike variant of **DYKE**.

diktat NOUN a firm statement or order.

dilapidated ADJ in disrepair.

dilapidation NOUN disrepair due to neglect.

dilate VERB make or become wider.
dilation, **dilatation** NOUN
dilator NOUN

dilatory /dil-ă-ter-i/ ADJ slow to act; causing delay.

dilemma NOUN a situation in which a difficult choice has to be made.

dilettante /di-li-tan-ti/ NOUN (PL **dilettanti** or **dilettantes**) a person who dabbles in a subject for pleasure.

diligent ADJ working or done with care and effort.
diligence NOUN
diligently ADV

dill NOUN a herb.

dilly-dally VERB (**dilly-dallies**, **dilly-dallying**, **dilly-dallied**) [INFORMAL] waste time by dawdling or being indecisive.

dilute VERB reduce the strength of (fluid) by adding water etc.; reduce the forcefulness of. ADJ diluted.
dilution NOUN

dim ADJ (**dimmer**, **dimmest**) **1** not bright, indistinct. **2** [INFORMAL] stupid. VERB (**dims**, **dimming**, **dimmed**) make or become less bright or distinct.
dimly ADV
dimness NOUN

dime NOUN a 10-cent coin of the USA.

dimension NOUN **1** an aspect or feature. **2** a measurement such as length or breadth; (**dimensions**) size,

extent.
-dimensional ADJ

diminish VERB make or become less.

diminuendo NOUN (PL **diminuendos** or **diminuendi**) [MUSIC] a gradual decrease in loudness.

diminution NOUN a decrease.

diminutive ADJ tiny. NOUN a form of a word suggesting smallness.

dimple NOUN a small dent, especially in the skin. VERB show or cause to show dimples.

din NOUN a loud annoying noise. VERB (**dins, dinning, dinned**) impress (information) on someone by constant repetition.

dinar /dee-nar/ NOUN a unit of money in some Balkan and Middle Eastern countries.

dine VERB eat dinner.
dine out on frequently relate (an experience) at social occasions.
diner NOUN

ding-dong NOUN **1** the sound of bells. **2** [INFORMAL] a fierce argument.

dinghy NOUN (PL **dinghies**) a small open boat or inflatable rubber boat.

dingle NOUN [LITERARY] a deep dell.

dingo NOUN (PL **dingoes**) an Australian wild dog.

dingy ADJ (**dingier, dingiest**) dull, drab.
dingily ADV
dinginess NOUN

dining room NOUN a room in which meals are eaten.

dinky ADJ (**dinkier, dinkiest**) [INFORMAL] attractively small and neat.

dinner NOUN the chief meal of the day; a formal evening meal.

dinner jacket NOUN a man's jacket for formal evening wear.

dinosaur NOUN an extinct prehistoric reptile, often of enormous size.

dint NOUN a dent.
by dint of by means of.

diocese NOUN a district under the care of a bishop.
diocesan ADJ

diode NOUN a semiconductor allowing

the flow of current in one direction only and having two terminals.

dioptre /dy-**op**-ter/ ([US] **diopter**) NOUN a unit of refractive power of a lens.

dioxide NOUN an oxide with two atoms of oxygen to one of a metal or other element.

dip VERB (**dips, dipping, dipped**) **1** plunge briefly into liquid; put (a hand etc.) briefly into something. **2** move or slope downwards; lower; lower the beam of (headlights). NOUN **1** a short swim; a brief immersion; a liquid in which sheep are dipped to guard against infection; a creamy sauce in which crudités etc. are dipped. **2** hollow.
dip into casually read parts of (a book).

diphtheria NOUN an infectious disease with inflammation of the throat.

diphthong NOUN a compound vowel sound (as *ou* in *loud*).

diploma NOUN a certificate awarded on completion of a course of study.

diplomacy NOUN the management of relations between countries; skill and tact in dealing with people.

diplomat NOUN **1** an official representing a country abroad. **2** a tactful person.
diplomatic ADJ
diplomatically ADV

dipper NOUN **1** a diving bird. **2** a ladle.

dipsomania NOUN an uncontrollable craving for alcohol.
dipsomaniac NOUN

diptych /**dip**-tik/ NOUN a pair of pictures on two panels hinged together.

dire ADJ extreme, serious; [INFORMAL] very bad.

direct ADJ **1** straight, without interruptions or diversions; with nothing intervening or mediating; frank. **2** absolute: *the direct opposite*. ADV with no interruption, intermediary, etc. VERB **1** control, manage; order. **2** aim in a particular direction; address (a letter etc.); tell (someone)

how to reach a place; instruct.
directness NOUN

direct action NOUN the use of strikes, public protests, etc. rather than negotiation to achieve one's demands.

direct debit NOUN an instruction to one's bank to make regular payments to a third party.

direction NOUN **1** a course along which someone or something moves; the way something faces. **2** control; (**directions**) instructions.
directional ADJ

directive NOUN an official instruction.

directly ADV **1** in a direct line or manner. **2** immediately. CONJ as soon as.

direct object NOUN [GRAMMAR] the primary object of a transitive verb, the person or thing directly affected.

director NOUN a person in charge of an activity or organization; a member of a board directing a business; one who supervises acting and filming.
directorship NOUN

directorate NOUN a board of directors; a section of a government department dealing with a particular area.

directory NOUN (PL **directories**) a book listing telephone subscribers etc.; a computer file listing other files.

direct speech NOUN speech reported by quoting the exact words spoken.

dirge NOUN a mournful song.

dirham /deer-ĕm/ NOUN the unit of money in Morocco and the United Arab Emirates.

dirigible NOUN an airship. ADJ able to be steered or guided.

dirndl NOUN a full gathered skirt.

dirt NOUN unclean matter; loose soil; excrement; [INFORMAL] scandalous information; obscene material.

dirty ADJ (**dirtier**, **dirtiest**)

marked or covered with dirt; producing dirt or pollution; obscene; dishonourable, unfair. VERB (**dirties**, **dirtying**, **dirtied**) make dirty. ADV [INFORMAL] emphasizing size: *a dirty great rock.*
dirtily ADV
dirtiness NOUN

disability NOUN (PL **disabilities**) a physical or mental incapacity; a legal disadvantage.

disable VERB impair the capacities or activity of; keep from functioning or from doing something.

disabled ADJ having a physical disability.
disablement NOUN

disabuse VERB disillusion.

disadvantage NOUN an unfavourable condition or position in relation to others; something diminishing one's chances of success or effectiveness.
disadvantaged ADJ
disadvantageous ADJ

disaffected ADJ discontented and no longer loyal.
disaffection NOUN

disagree VERB have a different opinion; argue; be inconsistent.
disagree with (of food etc.) make ill.
disagreement NOUN

disagreeable ADJ unpleasant; bad-tempered.
disagreeably ADV

disallow VERB refuse to sanction.

disappear VERB pass from sight or existence.
disappearance NOUN

disappoint VERB fail to fulfil the hopes or expectations of.
disappointment NOUN

disapprobation NOUN disapproval.

disapprove VERB consider something bad or immoral.
disapproval NOUN

disarm VERB **1** deprive of weapons; reduce armed forces. **2** make less hostile; win over.

disarmament NOUN a reduction of a country's forces or weapons.

disarrange VERB make untidy.
disarrangement NOUN

disarray NOUN disorder,

confusion.

disassociate VERB = **DISSOCIATE**.

disaster NOUN a sudden great misfortune or failure.
disastrous ADJ
disastrously ADV

disavow VERB deny any connection with.
disavowal NOUN

disband VERB separate or cause to separate.

disbar VERB (**disbars**, **disbarring**, **disbarred**) deprive (a barrister) of the right to practise law.

disbelieve VERB refuse or be unable to believe.
disbelief NOUN

disburse VERB pay out (money).
disbursement NOUN

disc ([US] **disk**) NOUN **1** a thin, flat round object. **2** a record. **3** a layer of cartilage between vertebrae. **4** (**disk**) a device on which computer data is stored.

discard VERB /dis-**kard**/ reject as useless or unwanted. NOUN /**dis**-kard/ something rejected.

discern VERB perceive with the mind or senses.
discernible ADJ
discernibly ADV
discernment NOUN

discerning ADJ with good judgement or understanding.

discharge VERB **1** dismiss; release; free from obligation. **2** allow (liquid etc.) to flow out; unload. **3** pay (a debt); fulfil (an obligation). NOUN the action of discharging; material flowing from something.

disciple NOUN a pupil or follower; one of the original followers of Christ.

disciplinarian NOUN a person who enforces strict discipline.

disciplinary ADJ of or for discipline.

discipline NOUN **1** controlled and obedient behaviour; training and punishment producing this. **2** a branch of learning. VERB train to be orderly; punish.

disc jockey NOUN a person who introduces and plays pop records on the radio or at a disco.

d

disclaim VERB refuse to acknowledge.

disclaimer NOUN a denial of responsibility.

disclose VERB reveal.
disclosure NOUN

disco NOUN (PL **discos**) a place where recorded pop music is played for dancing; equipment for playing this.

discolour ([US] **discolor**) VERB become a less attractive colour; stain.
discoloration NOUN

discomfit VERB (**discomfits**, **discomfiting**, **discomfited**) make uneasy; embarrass.
discomfiture NOUN

discomfort NOUN lack of physical or mental ease; slight pain.

discommode VERB [FORMAL] inconvenience.

disconcert VERB upset the self-confidence of, unsettle.

disconnect VERB break the connection of; cut off the power supply of.
disconnection NOUN

disconsolate ADJ very unhappy.
disconsolately ADV

discontent NOUN dissatisfaction.
discontented ADJ

discontinue VERB put an end to; cease.
discontinuance NOUN

discontinuous ADJ having gaps or breaks.
discontinuity NOUN

discord NOUN
1 disagreement, quarrelling.
2 inharmonious noise.
discordance NOUN
discordant ADJ

discotheque NOUN a disco.

discount NOUN /dis-kownt/ an amount of money taken off something's full price. VERB /dis-**kownt**/
1 reduce the price of.
2 disregard as unreliable.

discourage VERB dishearten; deter, dissuade.
discouragement NOUN

discourse NOUN /**dis**-korss/ communication, debate; a treatise or lecture. VERB /dis-**korss**/ speak or write authoritatively.

discourteous ADJ impolite.

discourteously ADV
discourtesy NOUN

discover VERB find; learn; be the first to find.
discovery NOUN

discredit VERB (**discredits**, **discrediting**, **discredited**) damage the reputation of; cause to be disbelieved. NOUN damage to a reputation.

discreditable ADJ bringing discredit.

discreet ADJ unobtrusive; cautious; not giving away secrets.
discreetly ADV

discrepancy NOUN (PL **discrepancies**) a difference; a failure to match.

discrete ADJ separate, distinct.
discretely ADV

discretion NOUN **1** the quality of being discreet. **2** the freedom to decide something.

discretionary ADJ done or used at a person's discretion.

discriminate VERB distinguish; make an unfair difference in one's treatment of people.
discrimination NOUN
discriminatory ADJ

discriminating ADJ having good judgement.

discursive ADJ (of writing) flowing and wide-ranging.

discus NOUN a heavy disc thrown in an athletic contest.

discuss VERB examine by argument; talk or write about.
discussion NOUN

disdain NOUN the feeling that someone or something does not deserve respect. VERB treat with disdain.
disdainful ADJ
disdainfully ADV

disease NOUN an illness, an unhealthy condition.
diseased ADJ

disembark VERB leave or cause to leave a ship, train, etc.
disembarkation NOUN

disembodied ADJ (of a voice) with no obvious physical source.

disembowel VERB (**disembowels**, **disembowelling**, **disembowelled**; [US]

disemboweling, **disemboweled**) take out the entrails of. **disembowelment** NOUN

d

disenchant VERB disappoint, disillusion. **disenchantment** NOUN

disenfranchise (also **disfranchise**) VERB deprive of the right to vote. **disenfranchisement** NOUN

disengage VERB detach; release. **disengagement** NOUN

disentangle VERB free from tangles or confusion; separate. **disentanglement** NOUN

disestablish VERB deprive (an organization, especially a Church) of an official connection with the state.

disfavour ([US] **disfavor**) NOUN dislike, disapproval.

disfigure VERB spoil the appearance of. **disfigurement** NOUN

disfranchise variant of **DISENFRANCHISE**.

disgorge VERB eject, pour forth. **disgorgement** NOUN

disgrace NOUN loss of respect resulting from dishonourable action. VERB bring disgrace on. **disgraceful** ADJ **disgracefully** ADV

disgruntled ADJ annoyed, resentful. **disgruntlement** NOUN

disguise VERB conceal the identity of. NOUN a means of concealing one's identity; the state of being disguised.

disgust NOUN a feeling that something is offensive or unpleasant; loathing. VERB cause disgust in. **disgusting** ADJ

dish NOUN **1** a shallow bowl, especially for food; food prepared according to a recipe. **2** [INFORMAL] an attractive person. **dish out** serve (food); [INFORMAL] distribute casually. **dish up** serve (food).

dishabille variant of **DÉSHABILLÉ**.

disharmony NOUN lack of harmony.

dishearten VERB cause to lose hope or confidence.

dished ADJ concave.

dishevelled ([US]

disheveled) ADJ ruffled and untidy.
dishevelment NOUN

dishonest ADJ not honest.
dishonestly ADV
dishonesty NOUN

dishonour ([US] **dishonor**) NOUN shame or disgrace. VERB **1** bring dishonour to. **2** fail to honour (an agreement etc.).

dishonourable ([US] **dishonorable**) ADJ bringing shame or disgrace.
dishonourably ADV

dishwasher NOUN a machine for washing dishes.

dishy ADJ (**dishier**, **dishiest**) [INFORMAL] attractive.

disillusion VERB rid of pleasant but mistaken beliefs.
disillusionment NOUN

disincentive NOUN something that discourages an action or effort.

disinclination NOUN unwillingness.

disinclined ADJ reluctant.

disinfect VERB clean by destroying harmful bacteria.
disinfection NOUN

disinfectant NOUN a substance used for disinfecting things.

disinformation NOUN deliberately misleading information.

disingenuous ADJ insincere.

disinherit VERB deprive of an inheritance.
disinheritance NOUN

disintegrate VERB break into small pieces.
disintegration NOUN

disinter VERB (**disinters**, **disinterring**, **disinterred**) dig up (something buried).
disinterment NOUN

disinterested ADJ **1** unbiased, impartial. **2** uninterested.
disinterest NOUN

disjointed ADJ lacking coherent connection.

disjunction NOUN lack of agreement between connected things.

disk [US] & [COMPUTING] variant of **DISC**.

diskette NOUN [COMPUTING] a small floppy disk.

dislike NOUN distaste, hostility. VERB feel dislike for.

dislocate VERB 1 disturb the arrangement or position of (a joint in the body). 2 disrupt.
dislocation NOUN

dislodge VERB remove from an established position.

disloyal ADJ not loyal.
disloyally ADV
disloyalty NOUN

dismal ADJ gloomy; [INFORMAL] very bad.
dismally ADV

dismantle VERB take to pieces.

dismay NOUN a feeling of shock and distress. VERB cause to feel this.

dismember VERB remove the limbs of; split into pieces.
dismemberment NOUN

dismiss VERB send away from one's presence or employment; disregard.
dismissal NOUN

dismissive ADJ treating something as unworthy of consideration.
dismissively ADV

dismount VERB get off a thing on which one is riding.

disobedient ADJ not obedient.
disobediently ADV
disobedience NOUN

disobey VERB disregard orders.

disobliging ADJ uncooperative, unhelpful.
disoblige VERB

disorder NOUN 1 untidiness. 2 a breakdown of discipline. 3 an ailment. VERB disarrange, disrupt.
disorderly ADJ
disorderliness NOUN

disorganized (also **disorganised**) ADJ not properly planned or arranged; muddled.
disorganization NOUN

disorientate (also **disorient**) VERB cause (a person) to lose his or her sense of direction.
disorientation NOUN

disown VERB refuse to acknowledge; reject all connection with.

disparage VERB belittle; criticize.
disparagement NOUN

disparate ADJ different in kind.
disparately ADV

disparity NOUN (PL **disparities**) a great difference.

dispassionate ADJ unemotional and objective.
dispassionately ADV

dispatch (also **despatch**) VERB **1** send off to a destination or for a purpose. **2** complete (a task) quickly. **3** kill. NOUN **1** the action of dispatching. **2** promptness. **3** an official report; a news report.

dispatch box NOUN a container for carrying official documents.

dispatch rider NOUN a messenger who travels by motorcycle.

dispel VERB (**dispels**, **dispelling**, **dispelled**) drive or clear away.

dispensable ADJ not essential.

dispensary NOUN (PL **dispensaries**) a place where medicines are dispensed.

dispensation NOUN **1** exemption. **2** a system of government, organization, etc. **3** distribution.

dispense VERB deal out; prepare and give out (medicine).
dispense with do without; abandon.
dispenser NOUN

disperse VERB go or send in different directions; scatter.
dispersal NOUN
dispersion NOUN

dispirited ADJ dejected.
dispiriting ADJ

displace VERB take the place of; move from its place or home.
displacement NOUN

display VERB show, make conspicuous. NOUN the displaying of a quality or feeling; a thing or collection of things displayed; a performance or event for public entertainment.

displease VERB irritate; annoy.

displeasure NOUN annoyance.

disport (also **disport oneself**) VERB frolic; enjoy

oneself.

disposable ADJ **1** designed to be thrown away after use. **2** (of money) available for use.
disposability NOUN

disposal NOUN **1** the action of disposing of something.
2 arrangement.
at one's disposal available for one's use.

dispose VERB **1** place, arrange. **2** make willing or ready to do something.
dispose of get rid of. **be well disposed** be friendly or favourable.

disposition NOUN **1** a person's character; a tendency. **2** arrangement.

dispossess VERB deprive (someone) of something they own.
dispossession NOUN

disproportionate ADJ relatively too large or too small.
disproportionately ADV

disprove VERB show to be false.

disputable ADJ questionable.
disputably ADV

disputant NOUN a person engaged in a dispute.

disputation NOUN an argument, a debate.

disputatious ADJ fond of arguing.

dispute VERB argue, debate; question the truth of; compete for. NOUN a debate; a disagreement.

disqualify VERB (**disqualifies**, **disqualifying**, **disqualified**) cause or judge to be ineligible or unsuitable.
disqualification NOUN

disquiet NOUN uneasiness, anxiety. VERB make uneasy.

disquisition NOUN a long elaborate discussion or explanation.

disregard VERB pay no attention to. NOUN lack of attention.

disrepair NOUN bad condition caused by lack of repair.

disreputable ADJ not respectable.
disreputably ADV

disrepute NOUN a bad reputation.

disrespect NOUN lack of respect.
disrespectful ADJ
disrespectfully ADV

disrobe VERB get undressed.

disrupt VERB interrupt the flow, continuity, or organization of.
disruption NOUN
disruptive ADJ

dissatisfaction NOUN lack of satisfaction or of contentment.

dissatisfied ADJ not pleased or contented.

dissect VERB cut apart so as to examine the internal structure.
dissection NOUN
dissector NOUN

dissemble VERB conceal one's feelings etc.
dissemblance NOUN

disseminate VERB spread widely.
dissemination NOUN

dissension NOUN disagreement that gives rise to strife.

dissent VERB disagree, especially with a widely or officially held view. NOUN disagreement.
dissenter NOUN

dissertation NOUN a lengthy essay.

disservice NOUN an unhelpful or harmful action.

dissident NOUN a person who opposes official policy. ADJ opposing official policy.
dissidence NOUN

dissimilar ADJ unlike.
dissimilarity NOUN
dissimilitude NOUN

dissimulate VERB conceal, disguise.
dissimulation NOUN

dissipate VERB dispel; fritter away.

dissipated ADJ living a dissolute life.

dissipation NOUN **1** a dissipated lifestyle. **2** dispersal, squandering.

dissociate VERB regard as separate; declare to be unconnected.
dissociation NOUN

dissolute ADJ lacking moral restraint or self-discipline.

dissolution NOUN the dissolving of an assembly or partnership.

dissolve VERB make or become liquid or

dispersed in liquid; disappear gradually; disperse (an assembly); end (a partnership, especially marriage).

d

dissonant ADJ lacking harmony.
dissonance NOUN
dissonantly ADV

dissuade VERB deter by argument.
dissuasion NOUN

distaff NOUN a cleft stick holding wool etc. in spinning.
the distaff side the mother's side of the family.

distance NOUN **1** the length of space or time between two points; the state of being far away; a far point or part. **2** the full length (of a race etc.). VERB separate, make remote.

distant ADJ **1** far away; at a specified distance. **2** cool, aloof.
distantly ADV

distaste NOUN dislike, disapproval.

distasteful ADJ arousing distaste.
distastefully ADV

distemper NOUN **1** a disease of dogs. **2** a kind of paint for use on walls. VERB paint with distemper.

distend VERB swell or cause to swell from internal pressure.
distension NOUN

distil ([US] **distill**) VERB (**distils**, **distilling**, **distilled**; [US] **distills**) treat or make by distillation; undergo distillation; capture the essence of.

distillation NOUN the process of vaporizing and condensing a liquid so as to purify it or to extract elements; something distilled.

distiller NOUN one who makes alcoholic liquor by distillation.

distillery NOUN (PL **distilleries**) a place where alcohol is distilled.

distinct ADJ **1** different in kind. **2** clearly perceptible; definite.
distinctly ADV

distinction NOUN **1** a contrast or difference; difference in treatment or attitude. **2** excellence; an honour; a high grade in an examination.

distinctive ADJ distinguishing, characteristic.
distinctively ADV

distinguish VERB 1 perceive a difference; be a characteristic of, differentiate. 2 discern.
distinguish oneself behave in a notable and admirable way.
distinguishable ADJ

distinguished ADJ commanding respect; famous for great achievements.

distort VERB pull out of shape; misrepresent.
distortion NOUN

distract VERB draw away the attention of.

distracted ADJ preoccupied, unable to concentrate.

distraction NOUN 1 something that distracts; an entertainment. 2 extreme distress and agitation.

distraint NOUN seizure of a debtor's possessions as payment for the debt.
distrain VERB

distraught ADJ nearly crazy with grief or worry.

distress NOUN 1 unhappiness; pain; hardship. 2 = **DISTRAINT**. VERB 1 make unhappy. 2 make (wood or furniture) look old and worn.
in distress in danger and needing help.

distribute VERB divide and share out; spread over an area.
distribution NOUN
distributive ADJ

distributor NOUN a person or thing that distributes; a device in an engine for passing electric current to the spark plugs.

district NOUN an area (of a country, county, or city) with a particular feature or regarded as an administrative unit.

distrust NOUN lack of trust; suspicion. VERB feel distrust in.
distrustful ADJ
distrustfully ADV

disturb VERB interfere with the arrangement of; break the rest or privacy of; make anxious.
disturbance NOUN

disturbed ADJ mentally or

emotionally unstable or abnormal.

disuse NOUN a state of not being used.

disused ADJ no longer used.

ditch NOUN a long narrow trench for drainage. VERB **1** make or repair ditches. **2** [INFORMAL] abandon.

dither VERB hesitate indecisively.

ditto NOUN (in lists) the same again.

ditty NOUN (PL **ditties**) a short simple song.

diuretic NOUN a drug that causes more urine to be excreted.

diurnal ADJ of or in the day.

diva NOUN a famous female singer.

divan NOUN a couch without a back or arms; a bed resembling this.

dive VERB plunge head first into water; swim under water using breathing apparatus; move quickly downwards or in a specified direction. NOUN **1** an act of diving. **2** [INFORMAL] a disreputable nightclub etc.

diver NOUN a person who dives or swims under water; a diving bird.

diverge VERB separate and go in different directions; depart from a path etc. **divergence** NOUN **divergent** ADJ

diverse ADJ of differing kinds.

diversify VERB (**diversifies, diversifying, diversified**) make or become more varied; (of a company) enlarge its range of products. **diversification** NOUN

diversion NOUN **1** the action of diverting; an alternative route avoiding a closed road. **2** a recreation or entertainment.

diversity NOUN (PL **diversities**) the state of being varied; a wide range.

divert VERB **1** turn from a course or route. **2** entertain; distract.

divest VERB (**divest of**) deprive of; (**divest oneself of**) free oneself of.

divide VERB **1** separate into

parts or from something else. **2** cause to disagree. **3** find how many times one number contains another; be divisible by a number without remainder. NOUN a divergence; a boundary.

dividend NOUN a sum paid to a company's shareholders out of its profits; a benefit from an action.

divider NOUN **1** a thing that divides. **2** (**dividers**) measuring compasses.

divine ADJ **1** of, from, or like God or a god. **2** [INFORMAL] wonderful. VERB discover by intuition or magic.
divination NOUN
divinely ADV
diviner NOUN

divining rod NOUN a dowser's stick.

divinity NOUN (PL **divinities**) **1** the state of being divine; a god or goddess. **2** theology.

divisible ADJ able to be divided.
divisibility NOUN

division NOUN the action of dividing, the state of being divided; a dividing line, a partition; one of the parts into which something is divided.
divisional ADJ

divisive ADJ tending to cause disagreement.

divisor NOUN a number by which another is to be divided.

divorce NOUN the legal termination of a marriage; separation. VERB end the marriage of (a person) by divorce; separate.

divorcee NOUN a divorced person.

divulge VERB reveal (information).

Diwali NOUN a Hindu festival at which lamps are lit, held between September and November.

DIY ABBREV do-it-yourself.

dizzy ADJ (**dizzier, dizziest**) giddy, feeling confused; causing giddiness.
dizzily ADV
dizziness NOUN

DJ ABBREV **1** disc jockey. **2** dinner jacket.

djellaba /jel-ă-bă/ NOUN an Arab cloak.

DM ABBREV Deutschmark.

d

DNA NOUN deoxyribonucleic acid, a substance in animal and plant cells that carries genetic information.

D notice NOUN an official order not to publish specific items for security reasons.

do VERB (**does**, **doing**, **did**; PAST PARTICIPLE **done**) **1** perform, complete; work at, deal with; provide, make. **2** act, proceed; fare. **3** be suitable or acceptable. AUXILIARY VERB used to form the present or past tense, in questions, for emphasis, or to avoid repeating a verb just used. NOUN (PL **dos** or **do's**) [INFORMAL] a party. **do away with** abolish. **do for** [INFORMAL] destroy, ruin. **do in** [INFORMAL] kill; injure; tire out. **do out** [INFORMAL] redecorate. **do out of** [INFORMAL] deprive of unfairly. **do up** **1** fasten; wrap. **2** [INFORMAL] redecorate. **do without** manage without. **to do with** concerning; connected with.

docile ADJ submissive, easily managed.
docilely ADV
docility NOUN

dock NOUN **1** an enclosed body of water where ships are loaded, unloaded, or repaired. **2** an enclosure for the prisoner in a criminal court. **3** a weed with broad leaves. VERB **1** (of a ship) come into dock; bring into dock. **2** (of a spacecraft) join with another craft in space. **3** deduct, take away; cut short.

docker NOUN a labourer who loads and unloads ships in a dockyard.

docket NOUN a document listing goods delivered; a voucher. VERB (**dockets**, **docketing**, **docketed**) label with a docket.

dockyard NOUN the area and buildings round a shipping dock.

doctor NOUN **1** a person qualified to give medical treatment. **2** a person holding a doctorate. VERB **1** tamper with, falsify; adulterate. **2** [INFORMAL] treat medically; castrate or spay (an animal);

repair.

doctorate NOUN the highest degree at a university.
doctoral ADJ

doctrinaire ADJ very strict in applying beliefs or principles.

doctrine NOUN a principle or the beliefs of a religious, political, or other group.
doctrinal ADJ

docudrama NOUN a television drama based on real events.

document NOUN a piece of written, printed, or electronic material giving information or evidence. VERB **1** record. **2** provide written evidence for.
documentation NOUN

documentary ADJ **1** consisting of documents. **2** giving a factual report. NOUN (PL **documentaries**) a documentary film.

dodder VERB totter because of age or frailty.
doddery ADJ

dodecagon NOUN a geometric figure with twelve sides.

dodge VERB avoid by a quick sideways movement; move in this way; evade. NOUN a dodging movement; [INFORMAL] a cunning trick.
dodger NOUN

dodgem NOUN a small electric car driven in an enclosure with the aim of bumping into others as a funfair amusement.

dodo NOUN (PL **dodos**) a large extinct bird.

DoE ABBREV Department of the Environment.

doe NOUN the female of the deer, hare, or rabbit.

does 3rd person singular present of **DO**.

doff VERB [DATED] take off (one's hat).

dog NOUN **1** a four-legged carnivorous wild or domesticated animal; the male of this or of the fox or wolf. **2** (**the dogs**) [INFORMAL] greyhound racing. VERB (**dogs**, **dogging**, **dogged**) follow persistently.
go to the dogs [INFORMAL] deteriorate shockingly.

dog cart NOUN a two-wheeled cart with back-to-back seats.

dog collar NOUN [INFORMAL] a clerical collar fastening at the back of the neck.

d

dog-eared ADJ with page-corners crumpled through use.

dogfish NOUN a small shark.

dogged /dog-id/ ADJ persistent, undeterred.
doggedly ADV

doggerel NOUN bad verse.

doggo ADV (**lie doggo**) [INFORMAL] remain motionless to escape detection.

doggy ADJ of or like a dog. NOUN (also **doggie**) (PL **doggies**) a child's word for a dog.

doggy bag NOUN [INFORMAL] a bag for taking home leftovers from a restaurant etc.

doghouse NOUN [US] a dog's kennel.
in the doghouse [INFORMAL] in disgrace or disfavour.

dogma NOUN doctrines put forward by authority to be accepted without question.

dogmatic ADJ not admitting doubt or questions.
dogmatically ADV

do-gooder NOUN a well-meaning but unrealistic or interfering person.

dog rose NOUN a wild hedge-rose.

dogsbody NOUN (PL **dogsbodies**) [INFORMAL] a drudge.

doh NOUN [MUSIC] the first note of a major scale, or the note C.

doily (also **doyley**) NOUN (PL **doilies**) a small ornamental lace or paper mat.

Dolby NOUN [TRADE MARK] a system for reducing unwanted sounds in a tape recording.

doldrums PLURAL NOUN inactivity; depression; an equatorial region of the Atlantic with little or no wind.

dole NOUN [INFORMAL] unemployment benefit.
dole out distribute.

doleful ADJ mournful.
dolefully ADV
dolefulness NOUN

doll NOUN a small model of a human figure,

especially as a child's toy.
dolled up [INFORMAL] finely dressed.

dollar NOUN the unit of money in the USA and various other countries.

dollop NOUN [INFORMAL] a mass of a soft substance.

dolly NOUN (PL **dollies**) **1** a child's name for a doll. **2** a movable platform for a cine-camera.

dolmen NOUN a megalithic structure of a large flat stone laid on two upright ones.

dolomite NOUN a type of limestone rock.
dolomitic ADJ

dolour ([US] **dolor**) NOUN [LITERARY] sorrow.
dolorous ADJ

dolphin NOUN a sea animal like a large porpoise, with a beak-like snout.

dolt NOUN [DATED] a stupid person.
doltish ADJ

domain NOUN an area under a person's control; a field of activity.

dome NOUN a rounded roof with a circular base; something shaped like this.
domed ADJ

domestic ADJ of home or household; of one's own country; domesticated. NOUN a servant in a household.
domestically ADV

domesticate VERB train (an animal) to live with humans; accustom to household work and home life.
domestication NOUN

domesticity NOUN family life.

domicile NOUN [FORMAL] a place of residence.
domiciliary ADJ

dominant ADJ dominating.
dominance NOUN

dominate VERB have a commanding influence over; be most influential or conspicuous in; tower over.
domination NOUN

domineer VERB control people arrogantly.

dominion NOUN authority to rule, control; a ruler's territory.

domino NOUN (PL **dominoes**) a small

oblong piece marked with 0-6 pips, used in the game of **dominoes**, where the aim is to match pieces with the same value.

don VERB (**dons, donning, donned**) put on. NOUN **1** a head, fellow, or tutor of a college. **2** (**Don**) a Spanish title put before a man's Christian name. **donnish** ADJ

donate VERB give as a donation.

donation NOUN a gift (especially of money) to a fund or institution.

done past participle of **DO**. ADJ [INFORMAL] socially acceptable.

donkey NOUN (PL **donkeys**) a long-eared animal of the horse family.

donkey jacket NOUN a thick weatherproof jacket.

donkey's years PLURAL NOUN [INFORMAL] a very long time.

donkey work NOUN [INFORMAL] drudgery.

Donna NOUN the title of an Italian, Spanish, or Portuguese lady.

donor NOUN one who gives or donates something.

donut US spelling of **DOUGHNUT**.

doodle NOUN a drawing made absent-mindedly. VERB draw absent-mindedly.

doom NOUN a grim fate; death or ruin. VERB destine to a grim fate.

doomsday NOUN the day of the Last Judgement.

door NOUN a hinged, sliding, or revolving barrier at the entrance to a room, building, etc.; a doorway.

doorway NOUN an entrance to a room, building, etc.

dope [INFORMAL] NOUN **1** a drug; a narcotic. **2** information. **3** a stupid person. VERB drug.

dopey (also **dopy**) ADJ (**dopier, dopiest**) [INFORMAL] half asleep; stupid.

dormant ADJ temporarily inactive; with physical functions slowed down. **dormancy** NOUN

dormer NOUN an upright window under a small

gable on a sloping roof.

dormitory NOUN (PL **dormitories**) a room with several beds in a school, hostel, etc.

dormitory town NOUN a town from which most residents travel to work elsewhere.

Dormobile NOUN [TRADE MARK] a motor caravan.

dormouse NOUN (PL **dormice**) a mouse-like animal that hibernates.

dorsal ADJ of or on the back.

dosage NOUN the size of a dose.

dose NOUN an amount of medicine to be taken at one time; an amount of radiation received. VERB give a dose of medicine to.

doss VERB [INFORMAL] **1** sleep in rough accommodation. **2** idle.
dosser NOUN

dosshouse NOUN [INFORMAL] a cheap hostel.

dossier NOUN a set of documents about a person or event.

DoT ABBREV Department of Transport.

dot NOUN a small round mark. VERB (**dots**, **dotting**, **dotted**) mark with dots; scatter here and there. **dot the i's and cross the t's** [INFORMAL] make sure that all details are correct. **on the dot** [INFORMAL] exactly on time.

dotage NOUN senility.

dote VERB (**dote on**) be extremely and uncritically fond of.

dot matrix printer NOUN a computer printer that forms letters etc. from a number of tiny dots.

dotty ADJ (**dottier**, **dottiest**) [INFORMAL] slightly mad; infatuated.
dottily ADV
dottiness NOUN

double ADJ consisting of two equal parts; twice the usual size; occurring twice; for two people. ADV twice as much. NOUN **1** a double quantity or thing. **2** a person very like another. **3** (**doubles**) a game with two players on each side. VERB **1** make or become twice as much or as many; fold in two; act two parts; have two uses. **2** go back in the

d

direction one came from.
at the double very fast.
see double see two images of something when there is only one of it.
doubly ADV

double bass NOUN the largest and lowest-pitched instrument of the violin family.

double-breasted ADJ (of a coat) with fronts overlapping.

double chin NOUN a chin with a roll of fat below.

double cream NOUN thick cream with a high fat content.

double-cross VERB cheat, deceive.

double-dealing NOUN deceit, especially in business.

double-decker NOUN a bus with two decks.

double Dutch NOUN [INFORMAL] incomprehensible talk.

double entendre /doobl ahn-**tahndr**/ NOUN a phrase with two meanings, one of which is usually indecent.

double figures PLURAL NOUN numbers from 10 to 99.

double glazing NOUN two sheets of glass in a window, designed to reduce heat loss.

double negative NOUN [GRAMMAR] a statement containing two negative expressions which neutralize each other to give a positive meaning, e.g. *I didn't do nothing,* logically meaning *I did something.*

doublet NOUN **1** each of a pair of similar things. **2** [HISTORICAL] a man's short close-fitting jacket.

double take NOUN a delayed reaction just after one's first reaction.

doubletalk NOUN talk with deliberately ambiguous meaning.

double time NOUN a rate of pay equal to double the standard rate, paid e.g. for working on holidays.

double whammy NOUN [INFORMAL] a twofold blow or setback.

doubloon NOUN a former Spanish gold coin.

doubt NOUN a feeling of uncertainty or disbelief. VERB feel uncertain of the truth or existence of; disbelieve.
doubter NOUN

doubtful ADJ feeling doubt; not known for certain; unlikely.
doubtfully ADV

doubtless ADJ certainly.

douche /doosh/ NOUN a jet of water applied to the body for cleaning or medical purposes; a device for applying this. VERB spray with or use a douche.

dough /doh/ NOUN **1** a thick mixture of flour etc. and liquid, for baking. **2** [INFORMAL] money.
doughy ADJ

doughnut /doh-nut/ ([US] **donut**) NOUN a small cake of fried sweetened dough.

doughty /dow-ti/ ADJ (**doughtier**, **doughtiest**) brave and determined.

dour /door/ ADJ stern, gloomy-looking.
dourly ADV
dourness NOUN

douse /dowss/ VERB **1** drench with a liquid. **2** extinguish (a light).

dove NOUN **1** a bird with a thick body and short legs. **2** a person favouring negotiation rather than violence.

dovecote (also **dovecot**) NOUN a shelter for domesticated pigeons.

dovetail NOUN a wedge-shaped joint interlocking two pieces of wood. VERB combine easily and conveniently.

dowager /dow-ij-ĕ/ NOUN a woman holding a title or property from her dead husband.

dowdy ADJ (**dowdier**, **dowdiest**) not smart or fashionable.
dowdily ADV
dowdiness NOUN

dowel NOUN a headless wooden or metal pin holding pieces of wood or stone together.

dowelling ([US] **doweling**) NOUN rods for cutting into dowels.

down¹ ADV **1** to, in, or at a lower place or position. **2** to or at a lower level of intensity; to a smaller

d

size. **3** from an earlier to a later point in time or order. **4** in or into a worse or weaker position. **5** in writing. **6** as payment or partial payment at the time of purchase. PREP from a higher to a lower point of; at a point further along; along, throughout. ADJ **1** directed downwards; travelling away from a central place. **2** depressed. **3** (of a computer system) not functioning. VERB [INFORMAL] **1** knock down. **2** swallow. NOUN [INFORMAL] a period of misfortune or depression. **down to** attributable to; the responsibility of. **down under** [INFORMAL] in the Antipodes, especially Australia or New Zealand.

down² NOUN **1** very fine soft furry feathers or short hairs. **2** an area of open undulating land; (**downs**) chalk uplands.

down-and-out ADJ destitute. NOUN a destitute person.

downbeat ADJ **1** gloomy. **2** relaxed, understated. NOUN [MUSIC] an accented beat.

downcast ADJ dejected; (of eyes) looking downwards.

downfall NOUN a loss of prosperity or power; something causing this.

downgrade VERB reduce to a lower grade.

downhearted ADJ discouraged and depressed.

downhill ADJ & ADV towards the bottom of a slope; becoming worse.

download VERB transfer (data) from one computer to another or to a disk.

downmarket ADJ & ADV of or towards lower prices and quality.

downpour NOUN a heavy fall of rain.

downright ADJ utter; complete. ADV extremely.

downshift VERB change to a less profitable but more relaxed way of life.

downside NOUN a negative aspect.

downsize VERB reduce the number of staff employed by a company.

Down's syndrome NOUN

a congenital disorder characterized by a broad face, sloping eyes, and learning difficulties.

downstairs ADV & ADJ to or on a lower floor. NOUN the ground floor.

downstream ADJ & ADV in the direction in which a stream or river flows.

down-to-earth ADJ sensible and practical.

downtown ADJ & ADV [US] in or towards the central part of a city.

downtrodden ADJ oppressed.

downward (also **downwards**) ADJ moving or leading down. ADV towards what is lower, less important, or later.

downwind ADV & ADJ in the direction in which the wind is blowing.

downy ADJ (**downier**, **downiest**) covered with or resembling soft down.

dowry NOUN (PL **dowries**) property or money brought by a bride to her husband on marriage.

dowse /dowz/ VERB search for underground water or minerals by using a stick which dips when these are present.
dowser NOUN

doxology NOUN (PL **doxologies**) a formula of praise to God.

doyen /doi-ĕn/ NOUN (FEMININE **doyenne**) /doi-yen/ the most important or highly regarded person in a particular field.

doyley variant of **DOILY**.

doze VERB sleep lightly. NOUN a short light sleep.

dozen NOUN a set of twelve; (**dozens**) very many.
talk nineteen to the dozen talk very fast.

dozy ADJ (**dozier**, **doziest**) not fully awake or alert.

D.Phil ABBREV Doctor of Philosophy.

DPP ABBREV Director of Public Prosecutions.

Dr ABBREV Doctor.

drab ADJ (**drabber**, **drabbest**) dull and unexciting; not brightly coloured.

drachma NOUN (PL **drachmas** or **drachmae**) the former unit of money in Greece.

draconian ADJ harsh,

strict.

draft NOUN **1** a preliminary written version; a plan or sketch. **2** a written order to a bank to pay money. **3** [US] military conscription. **4** US spelling of **DRAUGHT**. VERB **1** prepare a draft of. **2** [US] conscript for military service.

draftsman US spelling of **DRAUGHTSMAN**.

drafty US spelling of **DRAUGHTY**.

drag VERB (**drags**, **dragging**, **dragged**) **1** pull or bring with effort; (of time) pass slowly. **2** trail on the ground. **3** search (water) with nets or hooks. NOUN **1** something that impedes progress; [INFORMAL] something irritating or tedious. **2** [INFORMAL] women's clothes worn by men. **3** [INFORMAL] an act of inhaling on a cigarette.

dragnet NOUN a net for dragging water.

dragon NOUN **1** a mythical reptile able to breathe out fire. **2** a bad-tempered and intimidating person.

dragonfly NOUN (PL **dragonflies**) a long-bodied insect with gauzy wings.

dragoon NOUN a cavalryman or (formerly) mounted infantryman. VERB force into action.

drag race NOUN an acceleration race between cars over a short distance.

drain VERB **1** draw liquid out of; become dry; draw off (liquid) by channels or pipes; flow away. **2** gradually deprive of strength or resources. **3** drink all the contents of. NOUN **1** a channel or pipe carrying off water or liquid waste. **2** something that deprives one of energy or resources.

drainage NOUN the action of draining; a system of drains.

drake NOUN a male duck.

dram NOUN a small drink of spirits.

drama NOUN a play; plays and acting; an exciting series of events; a striking and exciting quality.

dramatic ADJ **1** of plays and acting. **2** exciting,

striking, impressive. **dramatically** ADV

dramatist NOUN a writer of plays.

dramatize (also **dramatise**) VERB present in dramatic form. **dramatization** NOUN

drank past of **DRINK**.

drape VERB spread (covers) loosely over something. NOUN (**drapes**) [US] curtains.

drastic ADJ having an extreme or violent effect. **drastically** ADV

drat EXCLAMATION [INFORMAL] an expression of annoyance.

dratted ADJ [INFORMAL] cursed; wretched; damn.

draught ([US] **draft**) NOUN **1** a current of air in a confined space. **2** an amount of liquid swallowed at one time; [ARCHAIC] a medicinal drink. **3** (**draughts**) a game played with 24 round pieces on a chessboard. **4** the depth of water needed to float a ship. ADJ used for pulling loads.

draught beer NOUN beer drawn from a cask.

draughtsman ([US] **draftsman**) NOUN **1** a person who draws plans or diagrams. **2** a person who drafts legal documents.

draughty ([US] **drafty**) ADJ (**draughtier**, **draughtiest**) letting in cold currents of air. **draughtiness** NOUN

draw VERB (**draws**, **drawing**, **drew**; PAST PARTICIPLE **drawn**) **1** create a picture or diagram by marking a surface. **2** pull; take out or from a store; take in (breath). **3** attract. **4** finish a contest with scores equal. **5** pick lots to decide an outcome. **6** make one's way, come: *draw near*. **7** write out (a cheque). **8** require (a specified depth) in which to float. **9** infuse. **10** (of a chimney) allow an upward current of air, enabling a fire to burn. NOUN **1** a lottery; an act of drawing lots. **2** a contest with equal closing scores. **3** something that attracts. **4** an act of inhaling. **draw in** (of days) become shorter. **draw on** use as a resource. **draw out** 1 prolong; (of days) become longer. 2 encourage to talk. **draw up** 1 come to a halt. 2 compose (a contract etc.).

drawback NOUN a disadvantage.

drawbridge NOUN a bridge over a moat, hinged so it can be raised.

drawer NOUN 1 a lidless compartment sliding horizontally into and out of a piece of furniture. 2 a person who draws. 3 a person who writes a cheque. 4 (**drawers**) knickers, underpants.

drawing NOUN a picture made with a pencil or pen.

drawing pin NOUN a pin for fastening paper to a surface.

drawing room NOUN a formal sitting room.

drawl VERB speak slowly with drawn-out vowel sounds. NOUN a drawling manner of speaking.

drawn past participle of **DRAW**. ADJ looking strained from tiredness or worry.

drawstring NOUN a string that can be pulled to close an opening.

dray NOUN a low cart for heavy loads.

dread NOUN great fear. VERB fear greatly. ADJ greatly feared.

dreadful ADJ very bad or unpleasant.
dreadfully ADV

dream NOUN a series of pictures or events in a sleeping person's mind; something greatly desired; something unreal or impossible. VERB (**dreams**, **dreaming**, **dreamed** or **dreamt**) have a dream while asleep; have an ambition or desire; think of or contemplate something as possible.
dream up invent or imagine (something foolish or improbable).
dreamer NOUN

dreamy ADJ (**dreamier**, **dreamiest**) 1 absorbed in a day dream; distracted, vague. 2 [INFORMAL] very attractive or pleasant.
dreamily ADV

dreaminess NOUN

dreary ADJ (**drearier**, **dreariest**) depressingly dull; gloomy.
drearily ADV
dreariness NOUN

dredge VERB **1** clear (an area of water) of (mud or silt). **2** sprinkle (food) with flour or sugar.

dredger NOUN **1** a machine or boat for dredging. **2** a container with a perforated lid for sprinkling flour or sugar.

dregs PLURAL NOUN sediment at the bottom of a drink; a last small remnant; the least useful, attractive, or valuable part.

drench VERB wet all through.

dress NOUN **1** a woman's or girl's garment with a bodice and skirt. **2** clothing. VERB **1** clothe oneself; clothe. **2** put a dressing on. **3** decorate; arrange.
dress up 1 put on fancy dress. **2** put on smart or formal clothes.

dressage /dress-ah*zh*/ NOUN exercises to show off a horse's obedience and deportment.

dress circle NOUN the first gallery in a theatre.

dresser NOUN **1** a person who helps actors with their costumes. **2** a person who dresses in a particular style: *a smart dresser*. **3** a sideboard with shelves above for dishes etc.

dressing NOUN **1** a sauce for salad. **2** a protective covering for a wound. **3** fertilizer etc. spread over land.

dressing down NOUN [INFORMAL] a scolding.

dressing gown NOUN a loose robe worn when one is not fully dressed.

dressing table NOUN a table topped by a mirror, used while dressing or applying make-up.

dressmaker NOUN a person whose job is making women's clothes.
dressmaking NOUN

dress rehearsal NOUN a final rehearsal, in full costume, of a dramatic production.

dress shirt NOUN a man's shirt for formal wear.

d

dressy ADJ (**dressier**, **dressiest**) stylish, smart; wearing stylish clothes.

drew past of **DRAW**.

d

drey NOUN (PL **dreys**) a squirrel's nest.

dribble VERB **1** flow or cause to flow in drops; have saliva flowing from the mouth. **2** (in football etc.) move the ball forward with slight touches. NOUN a thin stream of liquid; saliva running from the mouth.

dried ADJ (of food) preserved by removal of moisture.

drier (also **dryer**) NOUN a device for drying things.

drift VERB be carried by a current of water or air; go casually or aimlessly; pass gradually into a particular state. NOUN **1** a drifting movement. **2** a mass of snow piled up by the wind. **3** the general meaning of a speech etc.

drifter NOUN an aimless person.

driftwood NOUN wood floating on the sea or washed ashore.

drill NOUN **1** a tool or machine for boring holes or sinking wells. **2** training in military exercises; (**the drill**) the correct procedure. **3** a strong twilled cotton fabric. VERB **1** use a drill; make (a hole) with a drill. **2** train, be trained.

drily (also **dryly**) ADV **1** with irony. **2** without moisture.

drink VERB (**drinks**, **drinking**, **drank**; PAST PARTICIPLE **drunk**) swallow (liquid); consume alcoholic drink, especially in excess; express good wishes in a toast. NOUN a liquid for drinking; alcoholic liquor.
drink in watch or listen to eagerly.
drinker NOUN

drink-driver NOUN a person who drives having drunk more than the legal limit of alcohol.

drip VERB (**drips**, **dripping**, **dripped**) **1** fall or let fall in drops. **2** be conspicuously full of or covered in. NOUN **1** a regular fall of drops of liquid; the sound of this;

(also **drip feed**) an apparatus for administering a liquid at a very slow rate into the body, especially intravenously. **2** [INFORMAL] an ineffectual person.

drip-dry ADJ (of clothes) capable of drying without creasing if hung up wet after washing. VERB (**drip-dries**, **drip-drying**, **drip-dried**) dry (clothes) in this way.

dripping NOUN fat melted from roast meat.

drive VERB (**drives**, **driving**, **drove**; PAST PARTICIPLE **driven**) **1** operate (a vehicle), controlling its direction and speed; travel or convey in a private vehicle. **2** propel or carry forcefully; provide the energy to work (a machine); hit (a ball) hard; urge onwards; compel; cause to work too hard. **3** make (a bargain). NOUN **1** a journey in a private vehicle. **2** an innate urge or motive; determination; an organized effort to achieve something; the transmission of power to machinery. **3** a short road leading to a house etc.
drive at try to convey as a meaning.

drive-in ADJ (of a cinema etc.) able to be used without getting out of one's car.

drivel NOUN silly talk, nonsense.

driver NOUN **1** a person who drives. **2** a golf club for striking the ball from a tee.

drizzle NOUN very fine drops of rain. VERB rain very lightly.

droll ADJ strange and amusing.
drollery NOUN
drolly ADV

dromedary NOUN a camel with one hump, bred for riding.

drone NOUN **1** a deep humming sound. **2** a male bee. **3** an idle person living off others. VERB make a humming sound; speak monotonously.

drool VERB **1** slaver, dribble. **2** [INFORMAL] show gushing appreciation.

d

droop VERB bend or hang down limply. NOUN a drooping attitude.
droopy ADJ

drop NOUN **1** a small rounded mass of liquid; a very small amount of liquid; (**drops**) liquid medicine measured in drops. **2** a fall; letting something fall; an abrupt slope. **3** something that drops, e.g. a stage curtain. VERB (**drops, dropping, dropped**) **1** let (something) fall; fall vertically; [INFORMAL] collapse from weariness; make or become lower, weaker, or smaller. **2** give up (a habit); discard, reject; [INFORMAL] stop associating with. **3** utter casually. **4** set down (a passenger or load).
drop in pay a casual visit. **drop off** fall asleep. **drop out** cease to participate.

droplet NOUN small drop of liquid.

dropout NOUN a person who abandons a course of study or rejects conventional society.

dropper NOUN a device for measuring out drops of medicine etc.

droppings PLURAL NOUN animal dung.

dropsy NOUN [DATED] oedema.
dropsical ADJ

dross NOUN rubbish, worthless matter; scum on molten metal.

drought /drowt/ NOUN a long spell of dry weather; a shortage of water.

drove[1] past of **DRIVE**.

drove[2] NOUN a flock or herd; a crowd.

drover NOUN a person who drives cattle.

drown VERB **1** kill or be killed by suffocating in water or other liquid; submerge; deaden (grief etc.) with drink. **2** (of a sound) be louder than (another sound) and make it inaudible.

drowse VERB be lightly asleep.

drowsy ADJ (**drowsier, drowsiest**) sleepy, lethargic.
drowsily ADV
drowsiness NOUN

drub VERB (**drubs, drubbing, drubbed**)

thrash; [INFORMAL] defeat thoroughly.

drudge NOUN a person who does laborious or menial work.
drudgery NOUN

drug NOUN a substance used in medicine or as a stimulant or narcotic. VERB (**drugs**, **drugging**, **drugged**) treat with drugs; add a drug to.

drugstore NOUN [US] a chemist's shop also selling toiletries etc.

Druid NOUN an ancient Celtic priest.
Druidic, **Druidical** ADJ

drum NOUN a round frame with a membrane stretched across, used as a percussion instrument; a sound of or as of this; a cylindrical object. VERB (**drums**, **drumming**, **drummed**) play a drum; make a continuous rhythmic noise; tap (one's fingers etc.) repeatedly on a surface.
drum up obtain by canvassing or requesting.

drum majorette NOUN a female member of a parading group.

drummer NOUN a person who plays drums.

drumstick NOUN **1** a stick for beating a drum. **2** the lower part of a cooked fowl's leg.

drunk past participle of **DRINK**. ADJ deprived of the control of one's faculties by alcohol. NOUN a drunken person.

drunkard NOUN a person who is often drunk.

drunken ADJ intoxicated; often in this condition.
drunkenly ADV
drunkenness NOUN

dry ADJ (**drier**, **driest**)
1 without moisture or liquid; thirsty.
2 uninteresting. **3** (of humour) subtle, understated. **4** not allowing the sale of alcohol. **5** (of wine etc.) not sweet. **6** (of bread) without butter etc. VERB (**dries**, **drying**, **dried**) make or become dry; preserve (food) by removing its moisture; wipe tears from (the eyes).
dry up 1 dry washed dishes etc. **2** [INFORMAL] stop talking; decrease and stop.

d

dryness NOUN

dryad NOUN a wood nymph.

dry-clean VERB clean with solvents without using water.

dryer variant of **DRIER**.

dryly variant of **DRILY**.

dry rot NOUN decay of wood that is not ventilated.

dry run NOUN [INFORMAL] a rehearsal.

drystone wall NOUN a wall built without mortar.

DSS ABBREV Department of Social Security.

DTI ABBREV Department of Trade and Industry.

DTP ABBREV desktop publishing.

dual ADJ composed of two parts; double.
duality NOUN

dual carriageway NOUN a road with a central strip separating traffic travelling in opposite directions.

dub VERB (**dubs**, **dubbing**, **dubbed**) **1** give (a film) a soundtrack in a language other than the original. **2** give a nickname to. **3** confer a knighthood on.

dubbin NOUN a thick grease for softening and waterproofing leather.

dubiety NOUN [LITERARY] doubt; uncertainty.

dubious ADJ **1** hesitant; uncertain. **2** suspect, questionable.
dubiously ADV

ducal ADJ of a duke.

ducat NOUN a former gold coin of various European countries.

duchess NOUN a woman with the rank of duke; a duke's wife or widow.

duchy NOUN (PL **duchies**) the territory of a duke.

duck NOUN **1** a water bird with a broad blunt bill and webbed feet; the female of this. **2** a batsman's score of 0. **3** a quick dip or lowering of the head. VERB **1** push (a person) or dip one's head under water. **2** lower one's head or body to avoid a blow or so as not to be seen; avoid (a blow); [INFORMAL] evade (a duty).

duckboards PLURAL NOUN boards forming a narrow path over mud etc.

duckling NOUN a young duck.

duct NOUN a channel or tube conveying liquid or air; a vessel in the body carrying secreted or excreted matter.
ductless ADJ

ductile ADJ (of metal) able to be drawn into fine strands; easily moulded.
ductility NOUN

dud [INFORMAL] NOUN something that fails to work; an ineffectual person. ADJ useless; counterfeit.

dude NOUN [US] [INFORMAL] a fellow; a dandy.

dudgeon NOUN a feeling of offence: *in high dudgeon.*

due ADJ **1** expected or scheduled at a particular time. **2** owed, to be paid; deserved. **3** deserving; entitled to expect. NOUN **1** what is owed to or deserved by someone. **2** (**dues**) fees. ADV directly, exactly: *due north.*
due to because of, caused by.

duel NOUN a fight or contest between two people or sides. VERB (**duels**, **duelling**, **duelled**; [US] **dueling**, **dueled**) fight a duel.
duellist NOUN

duenna NOUN an older women chaperoning a younger one.

duet NOUN a musical composition for two performers.

duff ADJ [INFORMAL] worthless; incorrect.

duffel coat NOUN a heavy woollen coat with a hood.

duffer NOUN [INFORMAL] an inefficient or stupid person.

dug[1] past and past participle of **DIG**.

dug[2] NOUN an udder, a teat.

dugong /dew-gong/ NOUN an Asian sea mammal.

dugout NOUN **1** an underground shelter. **2** a canoe made from a hollowed tree trunk.

duke NOUN a nobleman of the highest hereditary rank; a ruler of certain small states.

dulcet ADJ sounding

sweet.

dulcimer NOUN a musical instrument with strings struck with hand-held hammers.

dull ADJ **1** not interesting or exciting. **2** not bright or resonant; not sharp. **3** stupid. VERB make or become less intense, sharp, or bright.
dully ADV
dullness NOUN

dullard NOUN a stupid person.

duly ADV as is required or appropriate; as might be expected.

dumb ADJ **1** unable to speak; silent. **2** [INFORMAL] stupid.
dumb down [INFORMAL] make or become less intellectually challenging.
dumbly ADV
dumbness NOUN

> The use of **dumb** to mean 'unable to speak' is found offensive by many people.

dumb-bell NOUN a short bar with weighted ends, lifted to exercise muscles.

dumbfound VERB astonish.

dumdum bullet NOUN a soft-nosed bullet that expands on impact.

dummy NOUN (PL **dummies**) **1** a model of the human figure used to display clothes or in an exhibition; a model of something used as a substitute. **2** a rubber teat for a baby to suck. **3** [INFORMAL] a stupid person.

dummy run NOUN a trial or rehearsal.

dump VERB **1** deposit as rubbish; put down carelessly; [INFORMAL] end a relationship with; sell (unsaleable goods) abroad at a lower price. **2** [COMPUTING] copy (data) to a different location; print out the contents of (a store). NOUN **1** a site for depositing rubbish or waste; a temporary store; [INFORMAL] a dull or unpleasant place. **2** [COMPUTING] an act of dumping data; a printout.

dumpling NOUN a ball of dough cooked in stew or

with fruit inside.

dun NOUN a greyish brown colour.

dunce NOUN a person slow at learning.

dune NOUN a mound of drifted sand.

dung NOUN animal excrement.

dungarees PLURAL NOUN overalls of coarse cotton cloth.

dungeon NOUN a strong underground cell for prisoners.

dunk VERB dip (bread etc.) into soup or a drink before eating it.

duo NOUN (PL **duos**) a pair of performers; a duet.

duodecimal ADJ reckoned in twelves or twelfths.

duodenum /dyoo-ŏ-dee-nŭm/ NOUN the part of the intestine next to the stomach.
duodenal ADJ

dupe VERB deceive, trick. NOUN a duped person.

duple ADJ (in music) having two beats to the bar.

duplex ADJ having two elements.

duplicate NOUN /dew-pli-kăt/ an exact copy. ADJ /dew-pli-kăt/ exactly like something specified; having two identical parts; doubled. VERB /dew-pli-kayt/ make or be an exact copy of; do (work already done) again unnecessarily.
duplication NOUN
duplicator NOUN

duplicity NOUN deceitfulness.

durable ADJ lasting; withstanding damage. NOUN (**durables**) goods that can be kept without immediate consumption or replacement.
durably ADV
durability NOUN

duration NOUN the time during which a thing continues.

duress NOUN the use of force or threats.

during PREP throughout; at a point in the duration of.

dusk NOUN a darker stage of twilight.

dusky ADJ (**duskier**, **duskiest**) darkish in colour.
duskiness NOUN

d

dust NOUN fine particles of earth or other matter. VERB **1** wipe dust from the surface of. **2** cover lightly with a powdered substance.

dustbin NOUN a bin for household rubbish.

dust bowl NOUN an area denuded of vegetation and reduced to desert.

duster NOUN a cloth for wiping dust from things.

dust jacket (also **dust cover**) NOUN a paper cover used to protect a book.

dustman NOUN a person employed to empty dustbins.

dustpan NOUN a container into which dust is brushed from a floor.

dusty ADJ (**dustier, dustiest**) **1** covered with dust. **2** like dust; (of colours) dull.
dustiness NOUN

Dutch ADJ relating to the Netherlands. NOUN the language of the Netherlands.
go Dutch share the cost of a meal.

Dutch courage NOUN false courage obtained by drinking alcohol.

dutiable ADJ on which customs or other duties must be paid.

dutiful ADJ obedient and conscientious.
dutifully ADV

duty NOUN (PL **duties**) **1** a moral or legal obligation; a task that one is required to perform. **2** a tax on imports etc.
on duty at work.

duvet /doo-vay/ NOUN a thick soft bed quilt.

dwarf NOUN (PL **dwarfs** or **dwarves**) a mythical human-like being of small size and with magic powers; a person or thing much below the usual size. VERB (**dwarfs, dwarfing, dwarfed**) **1** cause to seem small by comparison. **2** stunt.

dwell VERB (**dwells, dwelling, dwelt** or **dwelled**) [FORMAL] live as an inhabitant.
dwell on write, speak, or think at length about.
dweller NOUN

dwelling NOUN [FORMAL] a house etc. to live in.

dwindle VERB gradually

become less or smaller.

dye NOUN a substance used to colour something. VERB (**dyes**, **dyeing**, **dyed**) make (something) a particular colour with dye.

dying present participle of **DIE**.

dyke (also **dike**) NOUN a wall or embankment to prevent flooding; a drainage ditch.

dynamic ADJ characterized by constant change or activity; energetic, forceful; [PHYSICS] of force producing motion. **dynamically** ADV

dynamics NOUN **1** the branch of mechanics dealing with the motion of bodies under the action of forces; forces stimulating growth and change. **2** the variations in volume in a musical work.

dynamism NOUN energizing power.

dynamite NOUN a powerful explosive made of nitroglycerine. VERB blow up with dynamite.

dynamo NOUN (PL **dynamos**) a small generator producing electric current.

dynasty NOUN (PL **dynasties**) a line of hereditary rulers. **dynastic** ADJ

dysentery NOUN a disease causing severe diarrhoea.

dysfunctional ADJ **1** not operating properly. **2** unable to deal with normal social relations. **dysfunction** NOUN

dyslexia NOUN a condition causing difficulty in reading and spelling. **dyslexic** ADJ & NOUN

dyspepsia NOUN indigestion. **dyspeptic** ADJ & NOUN

dysprosium NOUN a metallic element.

dystrophy NOUN wasting of a part of the body. *See also* **MUSCULAR DYSTROPHY**.

Ee

E (also **e**) NOUN (PL **Es** or **E's**) the fifth letter of the alphabet. ABBREV **1** east, eastern. **2** [INFORMAL] the drug Ecstasy.

e- COMBINING FORM involving electronic communication.

each DETERMINER & PRON every one of two or more, regarded separately. ADV to or for each one individually.

eager ADJ full of desire, interest, or enthusiasm.
eagerly ADV
eagerness NOUN

eagle NOUN a large, keen-sighted bird of prey.

ear NOUN **1** the organ of hearing; the external part of this; the ability to distinguish sounds accurately. **2** the seed-bearing part of corn.

eardrum NOUN a membrane inside the ear, vibrating when sound waves strike it.

earl NOUN a British nobleman ranking between marquess and viscount.
earldom NOUN

early ADJ (**earlier**, **earliest**) & ADV before the usual or expected time; near the beginning of a series, period, etc.

earmark NOUN a distinguishing mark. VERB designate for a particular purpose.

earn VERB get or deserve for work or merit; (of invested money) gain as interest.
earner NOUN

earnest ADJ showing serious feeling or intention. NOUN a sign or guarantee of future actions etc.
in earnest seriously.

earnestly ADV
earnestness NOUN

earphone NOUN a device worn on the ear to receive radio or telephone communications or to listen privately to a radio etc.

earring NOUN a piece of jewellery worn on the ear.

earshot NOUN the distance over which something can be heard.

earth NOUN **1** (also **Earth**) the planet we live on; its surface; soil. **2** a connection of an electrical circuit to ground. **3** a fox's den. VERB connect (an electrical circuit) to ground.
cost the earth [INFORMAL] be very expensive. **run to earth** find after a long search.

earthen ADJ made of earth or of baked clay.

earthenware NOUN pottery made of coarse baked clay.

earthly ADJ **1** of this earth, of man's life on it. **2** [INFORMAL] used to emphasize a negative: *no earthly reason.*

earthquake NOUN a violent movement of part of the earth's crust.

earthwork NOUN a large defensive bank built of earth.

earthworm NOUN a worm living in the soil.

earthy ADJ (**earthier**, **earthiest**) **1** (of humour etc.) unrefined, uninhibited. **2** like soil.

earwig NOUN a small insect with pincers at the end of its body.

ease NOUN lack of difficulty; freedom from anxiety or pain. VERB **1** make or become less severe or intense. **2** move gradually and carefully; make (something) happen easily.

easel NOUN a frame to support a painting, blackboard, etc.

easement NOUN [FORMAL] a right of way over another's property.

east NOUN the point on the horizon where the sun rises; the direction in which this lies; an eastern part or region. ADJ & ADV in or towards the east; (of wind) from the east.

Easter NOUN a spring festival commemorating Christ's resurrection.

e

easterly ADJ towards the east; blowing from the east.

eastern ADJ of or in the east.

easterner NOUN a person from the east.

easternmost ADJ furthest east.

eastward ADJ towards the east.
eastwards ADV

easy ADJ (**easier**, **easiest**) achieved without great effort; free from worries or problems; relaxed, not awkward. ADV [INFORMAL] in an easy way.
take it easy go slowly; relax.
easily ADV
easiness NOUN

easy chair NOUN a large comfortable chair.

easy-going ADJ relaxed in manner; not strict.

eat VERB (**eats**, **eating**, **ate**; PAST PARTICIPLE **eaten**) chew and swallow (food); have a meal; use up, consume; erode, destroy. NOUN (**eats**) [INFORMAL] light food.

eatable ADJ fit to be eaten. NOUN (**eatables**) items of food.

eating disorder NOUN any of a range of psychological disorders characterized by abnormal eating habits.

eau de Cologne /oh-dĕ-kŏ-**lohn**/ NOUN (PL **eaux de Cologne**) a delicate perfume.

eaves PLURAL NOUN the overhanging edge of a roof.

eavesdrop VERB (**eavesdrops**, **eavesdropping**, **eavesdropped**) listen secretly to a private conversation.
eavesdropper NOUN

ebb NOUN **1** the movement of the tide out to sea. **2** a decline. VERB **1** flow away. **2** decline.
at a low ebb in a poor or weak state.

ebonite NOUN vulcanite.

ebony NOUN the hard black wood of a tropical tree. ADJ black as ebony.

ebullient ADJ full of high

spirits.
ebullience NOUN
ebulliently ADV

EC ABBREV European Community.

eccentric ADJ **1** unconventional and strange. **2** not concentric; (of an orbit or wheel) not circular. NOUN an eccentric person.
eccentrically ADV
eccentricity NOUN

ecclesiastical ADJ of the Church or clergy.

ECG ABBREV electrocardiogram.

echelon /esh-ĕ-lon/ NOUN **1** a level in a hierarchy. **2** a wedge-shaped formation of troops etc.

echo NOUN (PL **echoes**) a repetition of sound caused by reflection of sound waves; a close imitation. VERB (**echoes, echoing, echoed**) resound, be repeated by echo; repeat (someone's words); be very like.

eclair NOUN a finger-shaped pastry cake with cream filling.

eclampsia NOUN a condition involving convulsions, affecting women in pregnancy.

eclectic ADJ choosing or accepting from various sources.

eclipse NOUN the blocking of light from one heavenly body by another; a loss of influence or prominence. VERB cause an eclipse of; outshine.

ecliptic NOUN the sun's apparent path.

eclogue NOUN a short pastoral poem.

eco- COMBINING FORM relating to ecology.

eco-friendly ADJ not harmful to the environment.

ecology NOUN the study of how animals, plants, and other organisms relate to one another and to their surroundings.
ecological ADJ
ecologically ADV
ecologist NOUN

economic ADJ **1** of economics or the economy. **2** profitable, not wasteful.

economical ADJ thrifty, avoiding waste.

economically ADV

economics NOUN the science of the production and use of goods or services; (as PL) the financial aspects of a region or group.
economist NOUN

economize (also **economise**) VERB reduce one's expenses.

economy NOUN (PL **economies**) **1** a country's system of using its resources to produce wealth. **2** careful management of resources. ADJ (of a product) giving the best value for money; economical to use.

ecosystem NOUN a system of interacting organisms and their environment.

ecru NOUN a light fawn colour.

ecstasy NOUN (PL **ecstasies**) **1** intense delight. **2** (**Ecstasy**) an illegal amphetamine-based drug.
ecstatic ADJ
ecstatically ADV

ECT ABBREV electroconvulsive therapy.

ectopic pregnancy NOUN an unsuccessful pregnancy in which the egg develops outside the womb.

ecu (also **Ecu**) former term for **EURO**.

ecumenical ADJ of the whole Christian Church; seeking worldwide Christian unity.

eczema NOUN a skin disease causing scaly itching patches.

eddy NOUN (PL **eddies**) a circular movement in water or air etc. VERB swirl in eddies.

edelweiss /ay-dĕl-vys/ NOUN an alpine plant.

edema US spelling of **OEDEMA**.

edge NOUN **1** the outer limit of an area or object; a rim; the area next to a steep drop. **2** the sharpened side of a blade; the narrow side of a thin, flat object. **3** a position of advantage: *I had the edge over him.* **4** a sharp or anxious note; an exciting quality. VERB **1** provide with a border. **2** move slowly and carefully.

on edge tense, nervous.

edgeways (also **edgewise**) ADV with the edge forwards or outwards.

get a word in edgeways say something with difficulty because someone else hardly stops talking.

edging NOUN a decorative border.

edgy ADJ (**edgier**, **edgiest**) tense and irritable.

edgily ADV

edginess NOUN

edible ADJ suitable for eating.

edibility NOUN

edict /ee-dikt/ NOUN an order issued by someone in authority.

edifice NOUN a large building.

edify VERB (**edifies**, **edifying**, **edified**) improve morally or intellectually.

edification NOUN

edit VERB (**edits**, **editing**, **edited**) prepare (written material) for publication; choose and arrange material for (a film etc.).

edition NOUN a version of a published text; all the copies of a text etc. issued at one time; one instance of a regular broadcast programme; a version or copy.

editor NOUN a person responsible for the contents of a newspaper etc. or a section of this; a person who edits.

editorial ADJ of an editor. NOUN a newspaper article giving the editor's comments.

educate VERB train the mind, character, and abilities of; teach.

education NOUN

educational ADJ

edutainment NOUN material or an activity intended both to entertain and to inform.

Edwardian ADJ relating to the reign of Edward VII (1901–10). NOUN a person who lived during this period.

EEC ABBREV European Economic Community.

EEG ABBREV electroencephalogram.

eel NOUN a snake-like fish.

e

eerie ADJ (**eerier**, **eeriest**) mysterious and frightening.
eerily ADV
eeriness NOUN

efface VERB rub out, obliterate; make inconspicuous.
effacement NOUN

effect NOUN **1** a change produced by an action or cause; an impression; (**effects**) lighting, sound, etc. in a film, broadcast, etc. **2** the state of being operative. **3** (**effects**) property. VERB bring about, cause.

effective ADJ **1** achieving the intended result; operative. **2** fulfilling a function in fact though not officially.
effectively ADV
effectiveness NOUN

effectual ADJ effective.
effectually ADV

effeminate ADJ (of a man) feminine in appearance or manner.
effeminacy NOUN
effeminately ADV

effervescent ADJ fizzy, bubbling; vivacious, high-spirited.
effervesce VERB
effervescence NOUN

effete ADJ having lost vitality; feeble.
effeteness NOUN

efficacious ADJ producing the desired result.
efficaciously ADV
efficacy NOUN

efficient ADJ producing results with little waste of effort; competent, organized.
efficiency NOUN
efficiently ADV

effigy NOUN (PL **effigies**) a model of a person.

effloresce VERB **1** (of a substance) lose moisture and turn to powder. **2** reach a peak of development.
efflorescence NOUN

effluent NOUN outflow, sewage.

effluvium NOUN (PL **effluvia**) an unpleasant or harmful smell or outflow.

effort NOUN a vigorous attempt; use of energy, hard work.
effortless ADJ

effrontery NOUN bold insolence.

effusion NOUN an outpouring.

effusive ADJ expressing emotion in an unrestrained way.
effusively ADV
effusiveness NOUN

e.g. ABBREV for example (Latin *exempli gratia*).

egalitarian ADJ believing in the principle of equal rights for all people. NOUN an egalitarian person.
egalitarianism NOUN

egg NOUN an oval or round object laid by a female bird, reptile, etc., containing an embryo; an ovum; a hen's egg as food.
egg on urge, encourage.

egghead NOUN [INFORMAL] an intellectual person.

eggplant NOUN [US] an aubergine.

eggshell NOUN the shell of an egg. ADJ **1** (of china) fragile. **2** (of paint) with a slightly glossy finish.

ego NOUN self; self-esteem.

egocentric ADJ self-centred.

egoism NOUN self-centredness.
egoist NOUN
egoistic ADJ

egotism NOUN the practice of talking too much about oneself, conceit.
egotist NOUN
egotistic ADJ
egotistical ADJ

egregious /i-gree-jŭs/ ADJ outstandingly bad, shocking.

egress /ee-gress/ NOUN departure; a way out.

Egyptian NOUN a person from Egypt. ADJ relating to Egypt.

Egyptology NOUN the study of Egyptian antiquities.
Egyptologist NOUN

eider NOUN a large northern duck.

eiderdown NOUN a quilt stuffed with soft material.

eight ADJ & NOUN one more than seven (8, VIII).
eighth ADJ & NOUN

eighteen ADJ & NOUN one more than seventeen (18, XVIII).
eighteenth ADJ & NOUN

eighty ADJ & NOUN ten times eight (80, LXXX).
eightieth ADJ & NOUN

einsteinium NOUN a

radioactive metallic element.

eisteddfod /I-sted-vĕd, I-steth-vĕd/ NOUN a Welsh festival of music, poetry, and dance.

either CONJ & ADV **1** used before the first of two alternatives specified. **2** used to indicate a similarity or link with a statement just made. DETERMINER & PRONOUN one or the other of two people or things; each of two.

ejaculate VERB **1** utter suddenly. **2** eject (semen).
ejaculation NOUN

eject VERB throw or force out.
ejection NOUN
ejector NOUN

eke VERB (**eke out**) make (a supply of something) last longer by careful use; make (a living) laboriously.

elaborate ADJ /i-lab-ĕr-ăt/ complicated, with many parts or details; exaggerated, emphasized. VERB /i-lab-ĕr-ayt/ develop in detail; add detail to.
elaborately ADV
elaboration NOUN

elan /ay-lan/ NOUN vivacity, vigour.

elapse VERB (of time) pass, go by.

elastic ADJ going back to its original length or shape after being stretched or squeezed; adaptable. NOUN cord or material made elastic by interweaving strands of rubber etc.
elasticity NOUN

elated ADJ very happy and excited.
elate VERB
elation NOUN

elbow NOUN the joint between the forearm and upper arm; the part of a sleeve covering this; a sharp bend. VERB thrust with one's elbow; clear one's way by pushing with one's elbows.

elbow grease NOUN [INFORMAL] vigorous polishing, hard work.

elbow room NOUN [INFORMAL] enough space to move or work in.

elder ADJ older. NOUN **1** an older person; an official in certain Churches. **2** a tree with small dark berries.

elderly ADJ old.

eldest ADJ first-born, oldest.

eldorado NOUN (PL **eldorados**) a place of prosperity and abundance.

elect VERB choose by vote; decide on a course of action. ADJ chosen; elected but not yet in office.

election NOUN an occasion when representatives, office-holders, etc. are chosen by vote; the action of electing.

electioneer VERB take part in an election campaign.

elective ADJ **1** working by elections; chosen by election. **2** optional.

elector NOUN a person entitled to vote in an election.
electoral ADJ

electorate NOUN a body of electors.

electric ADJ of, producing, or worked by electricity.

electrical ADJ of electricity.
electrically ADV

electrician NOUN a person whose job is to deal with electrical equipment.

electricity NOUN a form of energy occurring in certain particles; a supply of electric current.

electrics PLURAL NOUN electrical fittings.

electrify VERB (**electrifies**, **electrifying**, **electrified**) charge with electricity; convert to the use of electric power; cause a sudden thrill to.
electrification NOUN

electrocardiogram NOUN a record of the electric current generated by heartbeats.

electroconvulsive therapy NOUN treatment of mental illness by electric shocks producing convulsions.

electrocute VERB kill by electric shock.
electrocution NOUN

electrode NOUN a solid conductor through which electricity enters or leaves a vacuum tube etc.

electroencephalogram NOUN a record of the

electrical activity of the brain.

electrolysis NOUN the decomposition of a substance by the application of an electric current; the destruction of hair-roots etc. by this process.

electrolyte NOUN a solution that conducts an electric current.

electromagnet NOUN a magnet consisting of a metal core magnetized by a current-carrying coil round it.

electromagnetic ADJ of the interrelation of electric and magnetic fields.
electromagnetically ADV
electromagnetism NOUN

electromotive ADJ producing an electric current.

electron NOUN a particle with a negative electric charge.

electronic ADJ **1** having many small components, e.g. microchips, that control an electric current; concerned with electronic equipment; carried out using a computer or other electronic device. **2** of electrons.
electronically ADV

electronics NOUN the branch of physics and technology concerned with the behaviour of electric currents in electronic equipment; (as PL) electronic circuits or devices.

electronic tagging NOUN the attaching of electronic markers to people or goods enabling them to be traced.

electron microscope NOUN a very powerful microscope using a focused beam of electrons instead of light.

electroplate VERB coat (metal) with a thin layer of silver etc. by electrolysis.

elegant ADJ graceful and stylish, tasteful.
elegantly ADV
elegance NOUN

elegy NOUN (PL **elegies**) a sorrowful poem.
elegiac ADJ

element NOUN **1** a part or aspect, especially an essential one; a small

amount; (**elements**) basic principles of a subject. **2** a substance that cannot be broken down into other substances; earth, air, fire, and water, regarded as basic. **3** (**the elements**) weather, especially when bad. **4** a wire that gives out heat in an electrical appliance.
in one's element in a situation or activity that suits one perfectly.
elemental ADJ

elementary ADJ dealing with the simplest facts of a subject.

elephant NOUN a very large animal with a trunk and ivory tusks.

elephantine ADJ huge.

elevate VERB raise to a higher position or level.

elevation NOUN **1** the action of elevating; altitude. **2** one side of a building etc.; a drawing of this.

elevator NOUN [US] a lift.

eleven ADJ & NOUN one more than ten (11, XI).
eleventh ADJ & NOUN

elevenses NOUN [INFORMAL] a mid-morning snack.

elf NOUN (PL **elves**) an imaginary small being with magic powers.

elfin ADJ (of a face etc.) small and delicate.

elicit VERB draw out (a response).

eligible ADJ **1** qualified or having the right to something. **2** desirable as a marriage partner.
eligibility NOUN

eliminate VERB get rid of; exclude.
elimination NOUN
eliminator NOUN

elision NOUN omission of part of a word in pronunciation.

elite /ay-leet/ NOUN a group regarded as superior and favoured.

elitism /ay-leet-izm/ NOUN dominance by a selected group; the belief that society should be run by an elite.
elitist NOUN & ADJ

elixir NOUN a liquid used for medicinal or magical purposes.

Elizabethan ADJ relating to the reign of Elizabeth I (1558–1603). NOUN a person who lived during this period.

elk NOUN a large deer.

ellipse NOUN a regular oval.

ellipsis NOUN (PL **ellipses**) omission of words; dots indicating this.

elliptical ADJ **1** shaped like an ellipse. **2** with a word or words omitted.
elliptically ADV

elm NOUN a tree with rough serrated leaves; its wood.

elocution NOUN the art of clear and expressive speech; a style of speaking.
elocutionary ADJ

elongate VERB lengthen.

elope VERB run away secretly with a lover to get married.
elopement NOUN

eloquence NOUN fluent and persuasive use of language.
eloquent ADJ
eloquently ADV

else ADV **1** in addition. **2** instead, other.
or else otherwise, if not.

elsewhere ADV in another place.

elucidate VERB throw light on, explain.
elucidation NOUN

elude VERB escape skilfully from; escape the memory or understanding of; be unattainable by.
elusive ADJ

elver NOUN a young eel.

emaciated ADJ thin from illness or starvation.
emaciation NOUN

email NOUN the sending of electronic messages from one computer user to another via a network. VERB mail or send using email.

emanate VERB issue, originate from a source.
emanation NOUN

emancipate VERB liberate, free from restraint.
emancipation NOUN

emasculate VERB deprive of force, weaken.
emasculation NOUN

embalm VERB preserve (a corpse) by using spices or chemicals.
embalmment NOUN

embankment NOUN a bank or stone structure to keep a river from spreading or to carry a railway.

embargo NOUN (PL **embargoes**) an official ban on trade or another activity. VERB (**embargoes**, **embargoing**, **embargoed**) impose an official ban on.

embark VERB board a ship. **embark on** begin (an undertaking). **embarkation** NOUN

embarrass VERB cause to feel awkward or ashamed; cause financial difficulties to. **embarrassment** NOUN

embassy NOUN (PL **embassies**) the official residence or offices of an ambassador.

embattled ADJ prepared for war; beset by conflicts or problems.

embed (also **imbed**) VERB (**embeds**, **embedding**, **embedded**) fix firmly in a surrounding mass.

embellish VERB ornament; invent exciting details for (a story). **embellishment** NOUN

embers PLURAL NOUN small pieces of live coal or wood in a dying fire.

embezzle VERB take (company funds etc.) fraudulently for one's own use. **embezzlement** NOUN **embezzler** NOUN

embittered ADJ resentful, bitter. **embitterment** NOUN

emblem NOUN a symbol; a design used as a badge etc.

emblematic ADJ serving as an emblem. **emblematically** ADV

embody VERB (**embodies**, **embodying**, **embodied**) **1** give a tangible or visible form to. **2** include. **embodiment** NOUN

embolden VERB make bold.

embolism NOUN obstruction of a blood vessel by a clot or air bubble.

emboss VERB decorate by a raised design; mould in relief.

embrace VERB **1** hold closely in one's arms as a sign of affection; hold each other in this way. **2** accept, adopt; include. NOUN an act of embracing, a hug.

embrocation NOUN liquid for rubbing on the body to relieve aches.

embroider VERB ornament with needlework; embellish (a story).
embroidery NOUN

embroil VERB involve in an argument or quarrel etc.

embryo NOUN (PL **embryos**) an animal developing in a womb or egg; something in an early stage of development.
embryology NOUN
embryonic ADJ

emend VERB alter to remove errors.
emendation NOUN
emendatory ADJ

emerald NOUN a bright green precious stone; its colour.

emerge VERB come up or out into view; become known; recover from a difficult situation.
emergence NOUN
emergent ADJ

emergency NOUN (PL **emergencies**) a serious situation needing prompt attention.

emeritus ADJ retired and retaining a title as an honour.

emery NOUN a coarse abrasive.

emery board NOUN a strip of cardboard coated with emery, used for filing the nails.

emetic ADJ causing vomiting. NOUN an emetic substance.

emigrate VERB leave one country and go to settle in another.
emigrant NOUN
emigration NOUN

émigré /em-i-gray/ NOUN an emigrant, especially a political exile.

eminence NOUN **1** fame, superiority; an important person; (**Eminence**) a title of a cardinal.
2 [FORMAL] a hill.

eminent ADJ famous, distinguished.
eminently ADV

emir /em-eer/ NOUN a Muslim ruler.

emirate NOUN the territory of an emir.

emissary NOUN (PL **emissaries**) a person sent to conduct negotiations.

emit VERB (**emits**, **emitting**, **emitted**) send out (light, heat, fumes, etc.); utter.
emission NOUN
emitter NOUN

emollient ADJ softening; soothing. NOUN a cream to soften the skin.

emolument NOUN [FORMAL] a fee; a salary.

emotion NOUN an intense feeling; feeling contrasted with reason.

emotional ADJ of emotions; readily feeling or showing emotion; expressing strong feelings.
emotionally ADV

emotive ADJ rousing emotion.

empathize (also **empathise**) VERB share and understand another's feelings.

empathy NOUN the ability to share and understand another's feelings.

emperor NOUN a male ruler of an empire.

emphasis NOUN (PL **emphases**) special importance or prominence; stress on a sound or word; intensity of expression.

emphasize (also **emphasise**) VERB stress; treat as important; make more noticeable.

emphatic ADJ using or showing emphasis.
emphatically ADV

emphysema /em-fi-see-mă/ NOUN enlargement of the air sacs in the lungs, causing breathlessness.

empire NOUN a group of countries ruled by a supreme authority; a large organization controlled by one person or group.

empirical ADJ based on observation or experiment, not on theory.
empirically ADV
empiricism NOUN
empiricist NOUN

emplacement NOUN a platform for a gun or battery of guns.

employ VERB give work to; make use of.
employer NOUN
employment NOUN

employee NOUN a person employed by another in

return for wages.

emporium NOUN (PL **emporia** or **emporiums**) a large shop selling a variety of goods.

empower VERB authorize, enable.

empress NOUN a female ruler of an empire; the wife of an emperor.

empty ADJ (**emptier**, **emptiest**) **1** containing nothing; without occupants. **2** having no meaning or value. VERB make or become empty. NOUN [INFORMAL] an empty glass or bottle.
emptiness NOUN

EMU ABBREV Economic and Monetary Union.

emu NOUN a large flightless Australian bird resembling an ostrich.

emulate VERB match or surpass; imitate.
emulation NOUN

emulsify VERB (**emulsifies**, **emulsifying**, **emulsified**) convert or be converted into emulsion.
emulsification NOUN
emulsifier NOUN

emulsion NOUN **1** finely dispersed droplets of one liquid in another. **2** a light-sensitive coating on photographic film. **3** a type of paint.

enable VERB give the means or authority to do something.

enact VERB **1** make into a law. **2** play (a part or scene).
enactment NOUN

enamel NOUN **1** a glass-like coating for metal or pottery. **2** glossy paint. **3** the hard outer covering of teeth. VERB (**enamels**, **enamelling**, **enamelled**; [US] **enameling**, **enameled**) coat with enamel.

enamoured ([US] **enamored**) ADJ fond.

en bloc /ahn **blok**/ ADV as a whole, all at the same time.

encamp VERB settle in a camp.

encampment NOUN a camp.

encapsulate VERB **1** enclose (as) in a capsule. **2** summarize.
encapsulation NOUN

encase VERB enclose in a case.

encephalitis NOUN inflammation of the brain.

enchant VERB delight; bewitch.
enchanter NOUN
enchantment NOUN
enchantress NOUN

encircle VERB surround.
encirclement NOUN

enclave NOUN a small territory wholly within the boundaries of another.

enclose VERB **1** shut in on all sides. **2** include with other contents.

enclosure NOUN **1** an enclosed area; the action of enclosing; the fencing off of land. **2** something placed in an envelope together with a letter.

encode VERB put into code; put (data) into computerized form.
encoder NOUN

encomium NOUN (PL **encomiums** or **encomia**) a formal expression of praise.

encompass VERB **1** encircle. **2** include.

encore /ong-kor/ NOUN a repeated or additional performance. EXCLAMATION a call for this. VERB call for (a performance) to be repeated.

encounter VERB meet by chance; be faced with. NOUN a chance meeting; a battle.

encourage VERB give hope, confidence, or stimulus to; urge.
encouragement NOUN

encroach VERB intrude on someone's territory or rights.
encroachment NOUN

encrust VERB cover with a crust of hard material.
encrustation NOUN

encumber VERB be a burden to, hamper.
encumbrance NOUN

encyclical NOUN a pope's letter for circulation to all bishops.

encyclopedia (also **encyclopaedia**) NOUN a book containing information on many subjects.
encyclopedic ADJ

end NOUN **1** the point after which something no longer exists or happens; a furthest or final part or point; a remnant. **2** death. **3** a goal. VERB bring or come to an end. **end up** eventually reach a particular place or state. **make ends meet** earn enough money to support oneself. **on end** continuing for a long time: *it rained for days on end.*

endanger VERB cause danger to.

endear VERB cause to be loved.

endearment NOUN words expressing love.

endeavour ([US] **endeavor**) VERB try hard to achieve something. NOUN a serious attempt to achieve something; hard work and effort.

endemic ADJ commonly found in a specified area or people.

ending NOUN the final part.

endive NOUN a curly-leaved plant used in salads; [US] chicory.

endless ADJ without end; continual; [INFORMAL] countless. **endlessly** ADV

endocrine gland NOUN a gland secreting hormones into the blood.

endorse VERB **1** declare approval of. **2** sign (a cheque) on the back. **3** record an offence on (a driving licence). **endorsement** NOUN

endow VERB provide with a permanent income or property. **endowed with** possessing (a desirable quality). **endowment** NOUN

endurance NOUN the power of enduring.

endure VERB experience and survive (pain or hardship); tolerate; last. **endurable** ADJ

enema NOUN liquid injected into the rectum, especially to empty the bowels.

enemy NOUN (PL **enemies**) one who is hostile to and seeks to harm another.

energetic ADJ possessing, showing, or requiring a great deal of energy. **energetically** ADV

energize (also **energise**) VERB give energy to; supply electricity to.

energy NOUN the strength and vitality needed for vigorous activity; the ability of matter or radiation to do work; power derived from physical resources to provide light, heat, etc.

enervate VERB cause to lose vitality.
enervation NOUN

enfant terrible /ahn-fahn te-**reebl**/ NOUN (PL **enfants terribles**) a person who embarrasses others by unconventional behaviour.

enfeeble VERB make weak.
enfeeblement NOUN

enfold VERB surround; embrace.

enforce VERB compel obedience to (a law etc.); force to happen or be done.
enforceable ADJ
enforcement NOUN

enfranchise VERB give the right to vote.
enfranchisement NOUN

engage VERB **1** occupy, involve; employ. **2** promise. **3** come into contact; move (part of a machine) into working position; begin a battle with.
engage in occupy oneself with.

engaged ADJ **1** having promised to marry a specified person. **2** occupied; in use.

engagement NOUN **1** a promise to marry a specified person. **2** an appointment. **3** the action of engaging or state of being engaged. **4** a battle.

engaging ADJ charming.

engender VERB give rise to.

engine NOUN a machine with moving parts that converts energy into motion; a railway locomotive.

engineer NOUN a person skilled in engineering; one in charge of machines and engines. VERB design and build (a machine); contrive to bring about (an event).

engineering NOUN the application of science for the design and building of machines and structures.

English NOUN the language

of Britain, the USA, and several other countries; (**the English**) the people of England. ADJ of England or its language.
Englishman NOUN
Englishwoman NOUN

engrave VERB cut (a design) into a hard surface; ornament in this way.
engraver NOUN

engraving NOUN a print made from an engraved metal plate.

engross VERB absorb the attention of.
engrossed ADJ

engulf VERB swamp.

enhance VERB increase the quality, value, or extent of.
enhancement NOUN

enigma NOUN a mysterious person or thing.
enigmatic ADJ
enigmatically ADV

enjoy VERB **1** take pleasure in. **2** possess and benefit from.
enjoy oneself have a pleasant time.
enjoyable ADJ
enjoyment NOUN

enlarge VERB make or become larger.
enlarge on say more about.
enlargement NOUN
enlarger NOUN

enlighten VERB make more knowledgeable or comprehending.
enlightenment NOUN

enlist VERB enrol for military service; secure (support, service).
enlistment NOUN

enliven VERB make more interesting or cheerful.
enlivenment NOUN

en masse /ahn **mass**/ ADV all together; in a group.

enmesh VERB entangle.

enmity NOUN hostility; hatred.

ennoble VERB give a noble rank to.
ennoblement NOUN

ennui /ahn-**wee**/ NOUN boredom.

enormity NOUN (PL **enormities**) **1** great wickedness. **2** great size.

enormous ADJ very large.

enough DETERMINER & PRON as much or as many as necessary. ADV to the required degree; to a moderate degree.

enquire VERB ask.
enquiry NOUN

enrage VERB make furious.

enrapture VERB delight intensely.

enrich VERB **1** enhance; make more rewarding, nourishing, etc. **2** make wealthier.
enrichment NOUN

enrol ([US] **enroll**) VERB (**enrols**, **enrolling**, **enrolled**; [US] **enrolls**) admit as or become a member.
enrolment NOUN

en route /ahn **root**/ ADV on the way.

ensconce VERB establish securely or comfortably.

ensemble /ahn-**sahmbl**/ NOUN a thing viewed as a whole; a group of performers; an outfit.

enshrine VERB preserve and respect.
enshrinement NOUN

ensign NOUN a military or naval flag.

enslave VERB take away the freedom of.
enslavement NOUN

ensnare VERB snare; trap.

ensue VERB happen afterwards or as a result.

en suite /ahn **sweet**/ ADV & ADJ (of a bedroom and bathroom) adjoining and forming a single unit.

ensure VERB make certain (that); secure.

entail VERB involve as a necessary part or consequence.

entangle VERB tangle; entwine and trap.
entanglement NOUN

entente /on-**tont**/ (also **entente cordiale**) NOUN friendly understanding between countries.

enter VERB **1** go or come in or into; become involved in; register as a competitor (in). **2** record (information) in a book, computer, etc.

enteritis NOUN inflammation of the intestines.

enterprise NOUN a bold undertaking; boldness; a business activity.

enterprising ADJ full of initiative.

entertain VERB **1** amuse. **2** offer hospitality to. **3** consider (an idea etc.).
entertainer NOUN
entertainment NOUN

enthral ([US] **enthrall**) VERB (**enthrals**, **enthralling**, **enthralled**; [US] **enthralls**) hold spellbound.
enthralment NOUN

enthrone VERB place on a throne; install in a position of power.
enthronement NOUN

enthuse VERB fill with or show enthusiasm.

enthusiasm NOUN eager liking or interest.

enthusiast NOUN a person who is full of enthusiasm for something.
enthusiastic ADJ
enthusiastically ADV

entice VERB attract by offering something pleasant; tempt.
enticement NOUN

entire ADJ complete.
entirely ADV

entirety NOUN (**the entirety**) the whole; (**in its entirety**) as a whole.

entitle VERB **1** give (a person) a right or claim. **2** give (a book etc.) a particular title.
entitlement NOUN

entity NOUN (PL **entities**) a distinct and individual thing.

entomology NOUN the study of insects.
entomological ADJ
entomologist NOUN

entourage /**on**-toor-ahzh/ NOUN people accompanying an important person.

entr'acte /**on**-trakt/ NOUN an interval between acts of a play.

entrails PLURAL NOUN intestines.

entrance[1] /**en**-trăns/ NOUN a door, passage, etc., through which one enters; the action of coming in; a right of admission, the fee for this.

entrance[2] /en-**trahns**/ VERB fill with intense delight.

entreat VERB request earnestly or emotionally.
entreaty NOUN

entrée /**on**-tray/ NOUN **1** a dish served between the fish and meat courses of a meal. **2** the right of admission.

entrench VERB establish firmly.
entrenchment NOUN

entrepreneur /on-trĕ-prĕ-**ner**/ NOUN a person

who sets up a business at considerable risk. **entrepreneurial** ADJ

entropy NOUN a measure of the amount of a system's thermal energy not available for conversion into mechanical work.

entrust VERB give as a responsibility; place in a person's care.

entry NOUN (PL **entries**) **1** an act of entering; an entrance. **2** an item entered in a record. **3** an entrant to a competition.

entwine VERB twist together.

E-number NOUN E followed by a number, the EU designation for permitted food additives.

enumerate VERB mention (items) one by one. **enumeration** NOUN

enunciate VERB pronounce; state clearly. **enunciation** NOUN

envelop VERB (**envelops**, **enveloping**, **enveloped**) wrap up; surround. **envelopment** NOUN

envelope NOUN a paper holder for a letter, with a sealable flap.

enviable ADJ desirable enough to arouse envy. **enviably** ADV

envious ADJ full of envy. **enviously** ADV

environment NOUN **1** surroundings, setting. **2** the natural world. **environmental** ADJ **environmentally** ADV

environmentalist NOUN a person seeking to protect the natural environment.

environs PLURAL NOUN the surrounding area or district.

envisage VERB imagine; foresee.

envoy NOUN a messenger, especially to a foreign government.

envy NOUN (PL **envies**) discontent aroused by another's possessions or success; the object of this: *he is the envy of us all.* VERB (**envies**, **envying**, **envied**) feel envy of.

enzyme NOUN a protein formed in living cells and assisting chemical processes.

eon variant of **AEON**.

e

epaulette NOUN an ornamental shoulder-piece on a uniform.

ephemera /e-fem-ĕ-ră/ PLURAL NOUN things of only short-lived usefulness.

ephemeral ADJ lasting only a short time.

epic NOUN a long poem, story, or film about heroic deeds or history. ADJ of or like an epic; on a grand or heroic scale.

epicene /e-pi-seen/ ADJ appropriate to either sex.

epicentre ([US] **epicenter**) NOUN the point on the earth's surface above the focus of an earthquake.

epicure NOUN a person who enjoys fine food and drink.
epicurean ADJ & NOUN

epidemic NOUN an outbreak of a disease etc. spreading through a community.

epidemiology NOUN the study of the spread of diseases.

epidermis NOUN the outer layer of the skin.

epidural NOUN a spinal anaesthetic affecting the lower part of the body, especially used in childbirth.

epiglottis NOUN a cartilage that covers the larynx in swallowing.

epigram NOUN a short witty saying.
epigrammatic ADJ

epilepsy NOUN a disorder of the nervous system, causing fits.
epileptic ADJ & NOUN

epilogue NOUN a short concluding section of a book etc.

episcopal ADJ of or governed by bishops.

episcopalian ADJ relating to the government of a church by bishops. NOUN a supporter of the episcopalian system.

episiotomy /e-pi-si-o-tŏ-mi/ NOUN (PL **episiotomies**) a cut made at the opening of the vagina during childbirth.

episode NOUN an event forming one part of a sequence; one part of a serial.
episodic ADJ

epistle NOUN [FORMAL] a letter.
epistolary ADJ

epitaph NOUN words in memory of a dead person, especially inscribed on a tomb.

epithet NOUN a descriptive word.

epitome /i-pit-ŏ-mi/ NOUN **1** a perfect example. **2** a summary.

epitomize (also **epitomise**) VERB be a perfect example of.
epitomization NOUN

epoch /ee-pok/ NOUN a period marked by particular characteristics.

eponymous /e-pon-i-mŭs/ ADJ after whom something is named.

equable ADJ **1** calm, not easily angered. **2** free from extremes.
equably ADV

equal ADJ the same in size, amount, value, etc.; having the same rights or status; free from discrimination or disadvantage. NOUN a person or thing of the same status or quality as another. VERB (**equals, equalling, equalled**; [US] **equaling, equaled**) be the same as in number or amount; match, rival.
equal to able to deal with.
equality NOUN
equally ADV

equalize (also **equalise**) VERB make or become equal; match an opponent's score.
equalization NOUN

equalizer (also **equaliser**) NOUN something that equalizes; a goal making scores even.

equal opportunity NOUN absence of discrimination in the competition for jobs etc.

equanimity NOUN calmness of mind or temper.

equate VERB consider to be equal or equivalent.

equation NOUN a mathematical statement that two expressions are equal.

equator NOUN an imaginary line round the earth at an equal distance from the North and South Poles.
equatorial ADJ

equerry NOUN (PL **equerries**) an officer

attending the British royal family.

equestrian ADJ of horse riding; on horseback.

equidistant ADJ at an equal distance.

equilateral ADJ having all sides equal.

equilibrium NOUN (PL **equilibria**) a balanced state.

equine /ek-wyn/ ADJ of or like a horse.

equinox NOUN the time of year when night and day are of equal length.
equinoctial ADJ

equip VERB (**equips**, **equipping**, **equipped**) supply with what is needed.

equipage NOUN [HISTORICAL] a carriage, horses, and attendants.

equipment NOUN the tools etc. needed for a purpose; the supply of these.

equipoise NOUN equilibrium.

equitable ADJ fair and just.
equitably ADV

equitation NOUN [FORMAL] the practice of horse riding.

equity NOUN **1** fairness, impartiality. **2** (**equities**) stocks and shares not bearing fixed interest.

equivalent ADJ equal in amount, value, meaning, etc. NOUN an equivalent thing.
equivalence NOUN

equivocal ADJ ambiguous.
equivocally ADV

equivocate VERB use words ambiguously.
equivocation NOUN

ER ABBREV Queen Elizabeth (Latin *Elizabetha Regina*).

era NOUN a period of history.

eradicate VERB wipe out.
eradicable ADJ
eradication NOUN

erase VERB rub out.
eraser NOUN
erasure NOUN

erbium NOUN a soft metallic element.

ere /air/ PREP & CONJ [LITERARY] before.

erect ADJ upright; (of the penis) rigid from sexual excitement. VERB set upright; construct.
erection NOUN

erectile ADJ capable of

becoming erect.

erg NOUN a unit of work or energy.

ergo ADV therefore.

ergonomics NOUN the study of people's efficiency in their working environment.
ergonomic ADJ

ERM ABBREV Exchange Rate Mechanism.

ermine NOUN a stoat; its white winter fur.

erode VERB wear away gradually.
erosion NOUN
erosive ADJ

erogenous ADJ (of part of the body) sensitive to sexual stimulation.

erotic ADJ of or arousing sexual desire.
erotically ADV

eroticism NOUN the quality of being erotic.

err VERB (**errs**, **erring**, **erred**) make a mistake; do wrong.

errand NOUN a short journey to do a job for someone.

errant ADJ [FORMAL] misbehaving.

erratic ADJ irregular, uneven.
erratically ADV

erratum NOUN (PL **errata**) an error in printing or writing.

erroneous ADJ incorrect.
erroneously ADV

error NOUN a mistake; the state of being wrong.

ersatz ADJ used as a substitute.

erstwhile ADJ former.

eructation NOUN [FORMAL] the action of belching.

erudite ADJ learned.
erudition NOUN

erupt VERB (of a volcano) eject lava; burst out; express an emotion violently.
eruption NOUN

erythrocyte /e-rith-ro-sIt/ NOUN a red blood cell.

escalate VERB increase in intensity or extent.
escalation NOUN

escalator NOUN a moving staircase.

escalope NOUN a thin slice of boneless meat, especially veal.

escapade NOUN a piece of reckless or mischievous conduct.

escape VERB get free (from); avoid (danger);

leak from a container; fail to be remembered by. NOUN an act or means of escaping.

escapee NOUN one who escapes.

escapement NOUN a mechanism regulating a clock movement.

escapism NOUN a tendency to ignore the realities of life.
escapist NOUN & ADJ

escapologist NOUN an entertainer whose act involves escaping from bonds etc.
escapology NOUN

escarpment NOUN a steep slope at the edge of a plateau etc.

eschew VERB [LITERARY] abstain from, avoid.

escort NOUN /ess-kort/ a group of people or vehicles accompanying another as a protection or honour; a person accompanying someone of the opposite sex to a social event. VERB /i-**skort**/ act as escort to.

escritoire /es-kri-**twah**/ NOUN a writing desk with drawers.

escudo NOUN (PL **escudos**) a former unit of money in Portugal.

escutcheon NOUN **1** a shield bearing a coat of arms. **2** the protective plate around a keyhole or door handle.

Eskimo NOUN (PL **Eskimos** or **Eskimo**) a member of a people living near the Arctic coast of America and eastern Siberia; their language.

> The Eskimos of North America prefer the term **Inuit**.

esophagus US spelling of **OESOPHAGUS**.

esoteric ADJ intended only for a few people with special knowledge or interest.

ESP ABBREV extrasensory perception.

espadrille NOUN a canvas shoe with a sole of plaited fibre.

espalier NOUN a tree trained on a trellis against a wall.

esparto NOUN a coarse grass used in making paper.

especial ADJ special.

especially ADV **1** more than any other; particularly, individually. **2** to a great extent.

Esperanto NOUN an artificial international language.

espionage NOUN the practice of spying.

esplanade NOUN a promenade.

espouse VERB **1** support (a cause). **2** [ARCHAIC] marry.
espousal NOUN

espresso (also **expresso**) NOUN (PL **espressos**) strong coffee made by forcing steam through powdered coffee beans.

esprit de corps /es-pree dĕ **kor**/ NOUN loyalty uniting a group.

espy VERB (**espies, espying, espied**) [LITERARY] catch sight of.

Esq. ABBREV Esquire, a courtesy title placed after a man's surname.

essay NOUN /ess-ay/ a short literary composition in prose. VERB /e-**say**/ [FORMAL] attempt.

essence NOUN the qualities or elements making something what it is; a concentrated extract.
of the essence critically important.

essential ADJ **1** absolutely necessary. **2** central to something's nature. NOUN something absolutely necessary; (**the essentials**) the basic facts.
essentially ADV

establish VERB set up; make permanent or secure; prove.

established ADJ officially recognized as the national Church.

establishment NOUN **1** the action of establishing something. **2** an organization; its staff; (**the Establishment**) influential people in a social system.

estate NOUN landed property; a residential or industrial district planned as a unit; property left at someone's death.

estate car NOUN a car with a door at the back and extended luggage space.

esteem VERB think highly of. NOUN a favourable opinion, respect.

esthete, **esthetic** US spelling of **AESTHETE**, **AESTHETIC**.

estimable ADJ worthy of esteem.

estimate VERB /ess-ti-mayt/ make an approximate judgement of (something's quantity, value, etc.). NOUN /ess-ti-măt/ such a judgement.
estimation NOUN

estrange VERB cause to be no longer friendly or loving.
estrangement NOUN

estrogen US spelling of **OESTROGEN**.

estuary NOUN (PL **estuaries**) the mouth of a large river, affected by tides.
estuarine ADJ

et al. ABBREV and others (Latin *et alia*).

etc. ABBREV et cetera, and other similar things.

etch VERB **1** produce (a picture) by engraving (a metal plate) with acid. **2** impress deeply on the mind.
etcher NOUN
etching NOUN

eternal ADJ existing always; unchanging.
eternally ADV

eternity NOUN (PL **eternities**) infinite time; the endless period of life after death; [INFORMAL] a long time.

ethanol NOUN alcohol.

ether NOUN **1** the upper air. **2** a liquid used as an anaesthetic and solvent.

ethereal ADJ light, delicate, and other-worldly.
ethereally ADV

ethic NOUN a moral principle or framework; (**ethics**) moral principles; the discussion of these.

ethical ADJ of ethics; morally correct.
ethically ADV

ethnic ADJ of a group sharing a common origin, culture, or language.
ethnically ADV
ethnicity NOUN

ethnic cleansing NOUN the mass expulsion or killing of members of one ethnic group in an area by those of another.

ethnology NOUN the study of human races and their characteristics.
ethnological ADJ
ethnologist NOUN

ethos /ee-thoss/ NOUN the characteristic spirit and beliefs of a community.

ethylene NOUN a hydrocarbon occurring in natural gas, used in manufacturing polythene.

etiolated /ee-ti-ŏi-lay-tĕd/ ADJ pale through being deprived of light.
etiolation NOUN

etiology US spelling of **AETIOLOGY**.

etiquette NOUN conventions of behaviour accepted as polite.

étude NOUN a short musical composition.

etymology NOUN (PL **etymologies**) an account of a word's origin and development.
etymological ADJ
etymologist NOUN

EU ABBREV European Union.

eucalyptus (also **eucalypt**) NOUN (PL **eucalyptuses** or **eucalypti**) a tree, native to Australia, with leaves that yield a strong-smelling oil.

Eucharist NOUN the Christian sacrament commemorating the Last Supper, in which bread and wine are consumed; this bread and wine.
Eucharistic ADJ

eugenics NOUN the science of controlling breeding to produce a healthier, more intelligent, etc. race.

eulogy NOUN (PL **eulogies**) a speech or work praising someone.
eulogistic ADJ
eulogize VERB (also **eulogise**)

eunuch NOUN a castrated man.

euphemism NOUN a mild expression substituted for an improper or blunt one.
euphemistic ADJ
euphemistically ADV

euphony NOUN pleasantness of sounds, especially in words.

euphoria NOUN excited happiness.
euphoric ADJ

e

euphorically ADV

Eurasian ADJ of Europe and Asia; of mixed European and Asian parentage. NOUN a Eurasian person.

eureka /yoor-**eek**-ă/ EXCLAMATION a cry of joy or satisfaction (announcing a discovery etc.).

eurhythmics ([US] **eurythmics**) NOUN physical exercises to music.

euro NOUN the single European currency, which replaced some national currencies in 2002.

Euro- COMBINING FORM European.

European ADJ of Europe or its people. NOUN a European person.

europium NOUN a soft metallic element.

eurythmics US spelling of **EURHYTHMICS**.

Eustachian tube /yoo-stay-shăn/ NOUN the passage between the ear and the throat.

euthanasia NOUN painless killing, especially of someone with a terminal illness.

evacuate VERB **1** send from a dangerous to a safer place. **2** empty. **evacuation** NOUN

evacuee NOUN an evacuated person.

evade VERB avoid by cleverness or trickery.

evaluate VERB find out or state the value of; assess. **evaluation** NOUN

evanescent ADJ [LITERARY] quickly fading. **evanesce** VERB **evanescence** NOUN

evangelical ADJ **1** of the gospel. **2** of a branch of Protestantism emphasizing biblical authority. **3** zealously advocating something. **evangelicalism** NOUN

evangelist NOUN any of the authors of the four Gospels; a person who tries to convert others. **evangelism** NOUN **evangelistic** ADJ

evaporate VERB turn (liquid) into vapour; (of something abstract) disappear. **evaporation** NOUN

evasion NOUN the action of evading something; an

evasive answer or excuse.

evasive ADJ evading; not frank.
evasively ADV
evasiveness NOUN

eve NOUN an evening, day, or time just before a special event.

even ADJ **1** level; regular; equally balanced. **2** exactly divisible by two. **3** not easily upset or annoyed. VERB make or become even. ADV used for emphasis or in comparisons: *even faster.*
evenly ADV
evenness NOUN

evening NOUN the latter part of the day, before nightfall.

evensong NOUN an evening service in the Church of England.

event NOUN something that happens; an organized social occasion; an item in a sports programme.

eventful ADJ full of exciting events.

eventual ADJ ultimate, final.

eventuality NOUN (PL **eventualities**) a possible event.

eventually ADV in the end, at last.

ever ADV **1** at any time: *have you ever been there?* **2** always.

evergreen ADJ (of a plant) having green leaves throughout the year. NOUN an evergreen plant.

everlasting ADJ lasting forever or for a very long time.

evermore ADV for all the future.

every DETERMINER each without exception; all possible; indicating an interval at which something regularly occurs: *every three months.*
every other each alternate.

everybody PRON every person.

everyday ADJ used or occurring on ordinary days; ordinary.

everyone PRON everybody.

everything PRON all things; all that is important.

everywhere ADV in every

place.

evict VERB expel (a tenant) by legal process.
eviction NOUN
evictor NOUN

e **evidence** NOUN signs of something's truth or existence; statements made in a law court to support a case. VERB be evidence of.
be in evidence be conspicuous.
evidential ADJ

evident ADJ obvious to the eye or mind.
evidently ADV

evil ADJ morally bad; harmful; very unpleasant. NOUN wickedness; something wicked.
evilly ADV

evince VERB [FORMAL] show, indicate.

eviscerate /i-vis-ĕ-rayt/ VERB [FORMAL] disembowel.
evisceration NOUN

evoke VERB **1** cause someone to think of. **2** elicit (a response).
evocation NOUN
evocative ADJ

evolution NOUN the process of developing into a different form; the origination of living things by such development.
evolutionary ADJ

evolve VERB develop or work out gradually.
evolvement NOUN

ewe NOUN a female sheep.

ewer NOUN a water jug.

ex PREP **1** (of goods) as sold from (a factory etc.). **2** without, excluding. NOUN [INFORMAL] a former husband, wife, or partner.

ex- PREFIX **1** out, away. **2** thoroughly. **3** former.

exacerbate /ig-zass-er-bayt/ VERB make worse.
exacerbation NOUN

exact ADJ completely accurate; giving all details. VERB insist on and obtain.
exactness NOUN

exacting ADJ making great demands; requiring great effort.

exactitude NOUN exactness.

exactly ADV **1** without vagueness or discrepancy. **2** expressing total agreement.

exaggerate VERB represent as greater than is the case.
exaggeration NOUN
exaggerator NOUN

exalt VERB regard or praise highly; raise in rank.

exaltation NOUN **1** extreme happiness. **2** the action of exalting.

exam NOUN [INFORMAL] an examination.

examination NOUN an inspection or investigation; a formal test of knowledge or ability.

examine VERB look at closely; question as a formal test of knowledge.
examiner NOUN

examinee NOUN a person being tested in an examination.

example NOUN something seen as typical of its kind or of a general rule; a person or thing worthy of imitation.
make an example of punish as a warning to others.

exasperate VERB annoy greatly.
exasperation NOUN

excavate VERB make (a hole) by digging; dig out; reveal (buried remains) by digging (a site).
excavation NOUN
excavator NOUN

exceed VERB be greater than; go beyond the limit of.

exceedingly ADV very.

excel VERB (**excels**, **excelling**, **excelled**) be very good at something.
excel oneself do better than one ever has.

Excellency NOUN the title of an ambassador, governor, etc.

excellent ADJ extremely good.
excellence NOUN
excellently ADV

except PREP not including. VERB exclude.

excepting PREP except.

exception NOUN something that does not follow a general rule.
take exception to object to.

exceptionable ADJ [FORMAL] open to objection.

exceptional ADJ very unusual; outstandingly

good.
exceptionally ADV

excerpt NOUN /**ek**-serpt/ an extract from a book, film, etc. VERB /ek-**serpt**/ make (a short extract).

excess NOUN too large an amount of something; the amount by which one quantity exceeds another; lack of moderation. ADJ exceeding a limit.

excessive ADJ too much.
excessively ADV

exchange VERB give or receive in place of another thing. NOUN **1** an act or the action of exchanging; giving money for its equivalent in another currency; a brief conversation. **2** a place for trading a particular commodity. **3** a centre where telephone lines are connected.
exchangeable ADJ

exchequer /eks-**chek**-ĕ/ NOUN a national treasury.

excise NOUN /**ek**-syz/ duty or tax on certain goods and licences. VERB /ek-**syz**/ cut out or away.
excision NOUN

excitable ADJ easily excited.
excitability NOUN
excitably ADV

excitation NOUN arousing, being aroused.

excite VERB **1** cause strong feelings of enthusiasm and eagerness in. **2** arouse sexually. **3** give rise to.
excitation NOUN
excitement NOUN

exclaim VERB cry out suddenly.

exclamation NOUN a sudden utterance, especially expressing an emotion.
exclamatory ADJ

exclamation mark NOUN a punctuation mark (!) placed after an exclamation.

exclude VERB keep out from a place, group, privilege, etc.; omit, ignore as irrelevant; make impossible.
exclusion NOUN

exclusive ADJ **1** excluding something. **2** limited to one or a few people; catering only for the wealthy. NOUN a story published in only one newspaper.
exclusive of not

including. **exclusive to** found only in.
exclusively ADV
exclusiveness NOUN

excommunicate VERB officially exclude from a Church or its sacraments.
excommunication NOUN

excoriate VERB **1** strip skin from. **2** [FORMAL] criticize severely.
excoriation NOUN

excrement NOUN faeces.

excrescence NOUN an outgrowth on an animal or plant; an unnecessary or unattractive addition.

excreta PLURAL NOUN matter (especially faeces) excreted from the body.

excrete VERB expel (waste matter) from the body or tissues.
excretion NOUN
excretory ADJ

excruciating ADJ intensely painful or unpleasant.

excursion NOUN a short journey, especially for pleasure.

excuse VERB /ek-**skewz**/ **1** justify, defend (an action etc.); forgive. **2** exempt. NOUN /ek-**skewss**/ a reason put forward to justify a fault; a pretext.
excusable ADJ

ex-directory ADJ deliberately not listed in a telephone directory.

execrable ADJ very bad or unpleasant.
execrably ADV

execrate VERB express loathing for.
execration NOUN

execute VERB **1** carry out (an order); produce or perform (a work of art). **2** put (a condemned person) to death.
execution NOUN

executioner NOUN an official who executes condemned people.

executive NOUN a person or group with managerial powers, or with authority to put government decisions into effect. ADJ having such power or authority.

executor NOUN a person appointed to carry out the terms of a will.

exemplar NOUN a typical example, a model.

exemplary ADJ **1** serving as a desirable model.

2 serving as a warning to others.

exemplify VERB (**exemplifies**, **exemplifying**, **exemplified**) serve as an example of.
exemplification NOUN

exempt ADJ free from an obligation etc. imposed on others. VERB make exempt.
exemption NOUN

exercise NOUN **1** physical activity. **2** a task designed to practise a skill. **3** use of one's powers or rights. VERB **1** use (a right etc.). **2** take or cause to take physical exercise. **3** occupy the thoughts of.

exercise book NOUN a book for writing in.

exert VERB **1** apply or bring to bear (a force, influence, or quality.). **2** (**exert oneself**) make a physical or mental effort.

exertion NOUN **1** physical or mental effort. **2** applying a force etc.

exeunt /eks-iunt/ VERB (as a stage direction) they (actors) leave the stage.

exfoliate VERB come off in scales or layers; remove dead layers of skin from.
exfoliation NOUN

ex gratia /eks gray-shă/ ADJ & ADV done or given as a favour, without legal obligation.

exhale VERB breathe out; give off in vapour.
exhalation NOUN

exhaust VERB **1** tire out. **2** use up completely. NOUN waste gases from an engine etc; a device through which they are expelled.
exhaustible ADJ

exhaustion NOUN **1** extreme tiredness. **2** the action of exhausting or the state of being exhausted.

exhaustive ADJ attending to every detail.
exhaustively ADV

exhibit VERB put on show publicly; display (a quality etc.). NOUN a thing on public show.
exhibitor NOUN

exhibition NOUN **1** a public show; a display of a quality etc. **2** a scholarship at a college.

exhibitionism NOUN a tendency to behave in a way designed to attract attention.
exhibitionist NOUN

exhilarate VERB make joyful or lively.
exhilaration NOUN

exhort VERB urge or advise earnestly.
exhortation NOUN
exhortative ADJ

exhume VERB dig up (a buried corpse).
exhumation NOUN

exigency (also **exigence**) NOUN (PL **exigencies**) an urgent need.

exigent ADJ [FORMAL] demanding, taxing.

exiguous ADJ [FORMAL] very small, scanty.

exile NOUN banishment or long absence from one's country or home, especially as a punishment; an exiled person. VERB send into exile.

exist VERB have being; occur; live, survive.
existence NOUN
existent ADJ

existentialism NOUN a philosophical theory emphasizing individuals' freedom to choose their actions.
existentialist NOUN & ADJ

exit NOUN a way out; a departure; an actor's going off stage. VERB go away; (as a stage direction) he or she leaves the stage.

exodus NOUN a departure of many people.

ex officio /eks ŏ-**fish**-i-oh/ ADV & ADJ because of one's official position.

exonerate VERB show to be blameless.
exoneration NOUN

exorbitant ADJ (of a price) unreasonably high.
exorbitantly ADV
exorbitance NOUN

exorcize (also **exorcise**) VERB drive out (an evil spirit) by prayer; free (a person or place) of an evil spirit.
exorcism NOUN
exorcist NOUN

exotic ADJ belonging to a distant foreign country; attractively unusual, striking.
exotically ADV

exotica NOUN strange or

rare objects.

expand VERB **1** make or become larger; give a more detailed account. **2** become less reserved.
expandable ADJ
expansion NOUN

expanse NOUN a wide area or extent.

expansive ADJ **1** covering a wide area. **2** genial and communicative.
expansiveness NOUN

expatiate /eks-pay-shi-ayt/ VERB speak or write at length about a subject.
expatiation NOUN

expatriate NOUN a person living outside their native country.

expect VERB **1** believe that (a person or thing) will come or (a thing) will happen; require, see as due; suppose, believe. **2** [INFORMAL] be pregnant.

expectant ADJ **1** filled with anticipation. **2** pregnant.
expectancy NOUN
expectantly ADV

expectation NOUN a belief that something will happen; a hope.

expectorant NOUN a medicine for causing a person to expectorate.

expectorate VERB cough and spit phlegm; spit.
expectoration NOUN

expedient ADJ advantageous rather than right or just. NOUN a means of achieving something.
expediency NOUN

expedite VERB help or hurry the progress of.

expedition NOUN a journey for a purpose; people and equipment for this.
expeditionary ADJ

expeditious ADJ speedy and efficient.
expeditiously ADV

expel VERB (**expels, expelling, expelled**) **1** deprive of membership; force to leave. **2** force out (breath etc.).

expend VERB spend; use up.

expendable ADJ not causing serious loss if abandoned.

expenditure NOUN the expending of money etc.; an amount expended.

expense NOUN money

spent on something; something on which one spends money; (**expenses**) the amount spent doing a job; reimbursement of this.

expensive ADJ involving great expenditure; costing or charging more than average.
expensively ADV
expensiveness NOUN

experience NOUN practical involvement in an activity, event, etc.; knowledge or skill gained through this; an event or action from which one learns. VERB undergo, be involved in.

experienced ADJ having had much experience.

experiment NOUN a scientific test to find out or prove something; a trial of something new. VERB conduct an experiment.
experimentation NOUN

experimental ADJ of or used in experiments; still being tested.
experimentally ADV

expert NOUN a person who has great knowledge or skill in a particular area. ADJ having or involving such knowledge or skill.
expertly ADV

expertise NOUN expert knowledge or skill.

expiate VERB make amends for.
expiation NOUN
expiatory ADJ

expire VERB **1** die; cease to be valid. **2** breathe out (air).
expiration NOUN

expiry NOUN termination of validity.

explain VERB make clear, show the meaning of; account for.
explanation NOUN
explanatory ADJ

expletive NOUN a violent exclamation, an oath.

explicable ADJ able to be explained.
explicability NOUN

explicit ADJ speaking or stated plainly.
explicitly ADV
explicitness NOUN

explode VERB **1** expand and break or cause to expand and break with a loud noise; show sudden violent emotion; increase suddenly. **2** destroy the

credibility of (a theory etc.).
explosion NOUN

exploit NOUN /**eks**-ployt/ a notable deed. VERB /eks-**ployt**/ make full use of; use selfishly and unfairly.
exploitable ADJ
exploitation NOUN
exploiter NOUN

explore VERB travel into (a country etc.) in order to learn about it; examine.
exploration NOUN
exploratory ADJ
explorer NOUN

explosive ADJ able or liable to explode; likely to cause controversy. NOUN an explosive substance.

exponent NOUN **1** a person who holds and argues for a theory etc. **2** a raised figure beside a number indicating how many times the number is to be multiplied by itself.

exponential ADJ **1** of a mathematical exponent. **2** (of an increase) more and more rapid.

export VERB /eks-**port**/ send (goods etc.) to another country for sale; transfer (data) from one computer system to another. NOUN /**eks**-port/ the action of exporting; a thing exported.
exportation NOUN
exporter NOUN

expose VERB leave uncovered or unprotected; subject to a risk etc.; allow light to reach (film etc.); reveal.
exposure NOUN

exposé /eks-**poh**-zay/ NOUN a media report revealing something discreditable.

exposition NOUN **1** an account and explanation. **2** a large exhibition.

expostulate VERB protest, argue.
expostulation NOUN
expostulatory ADJ

expound VERB explain in detail.

express VERB **1** convey (feelings etc.) by words or gestures; represent by symbols. **2** squeeze out (liquid or air).
ADJ **1** definitely stated; precisely identified.
2 travelling or operating at high speed. NOUN a fast train or bus making few stops. ADV by express train or special delivery service.

expressible ADJ

expression NOUN **1** the action of expressing. **2** a look on someone's face conveying feeling. **3** a word or phrase.

expressionism NOUN a style of art seeking to express feelings rather than represent objects realistically.
expressionist NOUN

expressive ADJ conveying feelings etc. clearly; expressing something.
expressively ADV

expressly ADV precisely, definitely.

expresso variant of **ESPRESSO**.

expressway NOUN [US] an urban motorway.

expropriate VERB (especially of the state) deprive (an owner) of (property).
expropriation NOUN

expulsion NOUN the action of expelling or being expelled.
expulsive ADJ

expunge VERB wipe out.

expurgate VERB remove (objectionable matter) from (a book etc.).
expurgation NOUN
expurgator NOUN
expurgatory ADJ

exquisite ADJ **1** extremely beautiful and delicate. **2** acute; keenly felt.
exquisitely ADV

extant ADJ still existing.

extemporize (also **extemporise**) VERB speak, perform, or produce without preparation.
extemporization NOUN

extend VERB **1** make longer or larger; stretch and straighten (part of the body); reach over an area. **2** offer.
extendable ADJ (also **extendible**, **extensible**).

extension NOUN **1** a part added to and enlarging something. **2** the action of extending. **3** a subsidiary telephone; its number. **4** the items to which a concept applies.

extensive ADJ large in area or scope.
extensively ADV

extensor NOUN a muscle that extends a part of the body.

extent NOUN the area

covered by something; scope, scale; the degree to which something is true.

extenuate VERB make (an offence) seem less serious or more forgivable.
extenuation NOUN

exterior ADJ on or coming from the outside. NOUN an outer surface or appearance.

exterminate VERB destroy completely; kill.
extermination NOUN
exterminator NOUN

external ADJ of or on the outside. NOUN an outward or superficial feature.
externally ADV

externalize (also **externalise**) VERB express, see, or present as existing outside oneself.

extinct ADJ with no living members; no longer active or alight.

extinction NOUN the state of being or becoming extinct.

extinguish VERB put out (a light or flame); put an end to.

extinguisher NOUN a device for discharging liquid chemicals or foam to extinguish a fire.

extirpate VERB root out, destroy.
extirpation NOUN

extol VERB (**extols**, **extolling**, **extolled**) praise enthusiastically.

extort VERB obtain by force or threats.
extortion NOUN
extortioner NOUN

extortionate ADJ excessively high in price, exorbitant.
extortionately ADV

extra ADJ additional, more than is usual or expected. ADV more than usually; in addition. NOUN an additional item; a person employed as one of a crowd in a film.

extra- PREFIX outside, beyond.

extract VERB /eks-**trakt**/ take out or obtain by force or effort; obtain by chemical treatment etc.; select (a passage from a book etc.). NOUN /**eks**-trakt/ a passage quoted from a book, film, etc.; the concentrated essence of a substance.
extractor NOUN

extraction NOUN **1** the action of extracting. **2** ancestry, origin.

extra-curricular ADJ not part of the normal curriculum.

extradite VERB hand over (an accused person) for trial in the country where a crime was committed.
extraditable ADJ
extradition NOUN

extramarital ADJ occurring outside marriage.

extramural ADJ for students who are not members of a university.

extraneous ADJ **1** irrelevant. **2** of external origin.
extraneously ADV

extraordinary ADJ **1** very unusual or surprising. **2** special, extra.
extraordinarily ADV

extrapolate VERB extend (a conclusion etc.) beyond what is known, on the basis of available data.
extrapolation NOUN

extrasensory ADJ achieved by some means other than the known senses.

extraterrestrial ADJ of or from outside the earth or its atmosphere.

extravagant ADJ spending or using excessively; very expensive; going beyond what is reasonable.
extravagance NOUN
extravagantly ADV

extravaganza NOUN a lavish spectacular display.

extreme ADJ **1** very great or intense; reaching a very high degree; very severe; drastic or immoderate; (of a sport) involving great physical danger. **2** furthest, outermost. NOUN an extreme point; one end of a scale; a very high degree.
extremely ADV

extremist NOUN a person holding extreme views.
extremism NOUN

extremity NOUN (PL **extremities**) **1** an extreme degree; extreme hardship or danger. **2** an outermost point; (**the extremities**) the hands and feet.

extricate VERB free from an entanglement or difficulty.
extricable ADJ
extrication NOUN

e

extrinsic ADJ not intrinsic; extraneous.
extrinsically ADV

extrovert NOUN a lively sociable person.
extroversion NOUN

extrude VERB thrust or squeeze out.
extrusion NOUN
extrusive ADJ

exuberant ADJ **1** full of high spirits. **2** growing profusely.
exuberance NOUN
exuberantly ADV

exude VERB ooze; give off like sweat or a smell.
exudation NOUN

exult VERB feel or show delight.
exultant ADJ
exultation NOUN

eye NOUN **1** the organ of sight; the iris of this; the region round it; the power of seeing. **2** something compared to an eye in shape, centrality, etc. VERB (**eyes**, **eyeing**, **eyed**) look at, watch.

eyeball NOUN the whole of the eye within the eyelids.

eyebrow NOUN the fringe of hair on the ridge above the eye socket.

eyelash NOUN one of the hairs fringing the eyelids.

eyelet NOUN a small hole through which a lace can be threaded.

eyelid NOUN either of the two folds of skin that can be moved together to cover the eye.

eyeliner NOUN a cosmetic applied in a line around the eye.

eye-opener NOUN [INFORMAL] something that brings enlightenment or great surprise.

eyepiece NOUN the lens to which the eye is applied in a telescope or microscope etc.

eyeshadow NOUN a cosmetic applied to the skin round the eyes.

eyesight NOUN the ability to see; the range of vision.

eyesore NOUN an ugly thing.

eye tooth NOUN a canine

tooth in the upper jaw, below the eye.

eyewash NOUN [INFORMAL] insincere talk; nonsense.

eyewitness NOUN a person who saw something happen.

eyrie /eer-i/ NOUN an eagle's nest; a high and inaccessible place.

e

Ff

F (also **f**) NOUN (PL **Fs** or **F's**) the sixth letter of the alphabet. ABBREV **1** Fahrenheit. **2** [MUSIC] forte. **3** (of pencil lead) fine.

FA ABBREV Football Association.

fable NOUN a story not based on fact, often with a moral.

fabled ADJ famous; legendary.

fabric NOUN **1** woven or knitted cloth. **2** the essential structure of a building etc.

fabricate VERB **1** invent (a story etc.). **2** construct.
fabrication NOUN
fabricator NOUN

fabulous ADJ **1** extraordinarily great. **2** mythical. **3** [INFORMAL] very good.
fabulously ADV

facade /fŭ-sahd/ NOUN the front of a building; an outward appearance, especially a misleading one.

face NOUN **1** the front of the head; an expression on its features; a grimace: *make a face.* **2** an aspect. **3** a surface; a side of a mountain; the surface of a coal seam. **4** the dial of a clock. VERB **1** have one's face or front towards; confront boldly. **2** put a facing on.
lose face become less respected.

facecloth NOUN a small towelling cloth for washing the face and body.

faceless ADJ **1** impersonal, not identifiable. **2** without character.

facelift NOUN an operation tightening the skin of the face to remove wrinkles; an alteration that improves the appearance.

facet NOUN one of many sides of a cut stone or jewel; one aspect.

facetious ADJ inappropriately humorous about serious subjects.
facetiously ADV
facetiousness NOUN

facia /fay-shă/ (also **fascia**) NOUN **1** the instrument panel of a vehicle. **2** a nameplate over a shop front.

facial ADJ of the face. NOUN a beauty treatment for the face.

facile /fa-syl/ ADJ misleadingly simple; superficial, glib.

facilitate VERB make easy or easier.
facilitation NOUN

facility NOUN (PL **facilities**) **1** space etc. for doing something; an amenity or resource. **2** absence of difficulty.

facing NOUN an outer covering; a layer of material at the edge of a garment for strengthening, contrast, neatening, etc.

facsimile /fak-sim-i-li/ NOUN an exact copy of a document etc.

fact NOUN something known to be true.
facts of life information about sex and reproduction. **in fact** actually.

faction NOUN **1** an organized group within a larger one; dissension between such groups. **2** a blend of fact and fiction in a book etc.
factious ADJ

factitious ADJ (of a quality, emotion, etc.) artificial.

factor NOUN **1** a circumstance that contributes towards a result. **2** a number by which a given number can be divided exactly.

factory NOUN (PL **factories**) a building in which goods are manufactured.

factotum NOUN a general servant or assistant.

factual ADJ based on or containing facts.
factually ADV

f

faculty NOUN (PL **faculties**) **1** a mental or physical power. **2** a department teaching a specified subject in a university or college.

fad NOUN a craze, a whim.

f

faddy ADJ (**faddier**, **faddiest**) having petty likes and dislikes, especially about food.

fade VERB lose or cause to lose colour, freshness, or vigour; disappear gradually.

faeces /fee-seez/ ([US] **feces**) PLURAL NOUN waste matter discharged from the bowels.
faecal ADJ

faff NOUN [INFORMAL] fuss; pointless activity.
faff about fuss; dither.

fag [INFORMAL] VERB (**fags**, **fagging**, **fagged**) toil; make tired. NOUN **1** a tiring or tedious task. **2** a cigarette.

faggot NOUN **1** ([US] **fagot**) a tied bundle of sticks or twigs. **2** a ball of chopped seasoned liver etc., baked or fried.

fah NOUN [MUSIC] the fourth note of a major scale, or the note F.

Fahrenheit ADJ of a temperature scale with the freezing point of water at 32° and boiling point at 212°.

faience /fy-ahns/ NOUN painted glazed earthenware.

fail VERB **1** be unsuccessful; declare to be unsuccessful. **2** neglect one's duty; disappoint (someone relying on one). **3** become weak; cease functioning; become bankrupt. NOUN a mark too low to pass an examination.

failing NOUN a weakness or fault. PREP if (a thing) does not happen.

failure NOUN lack of success; a deficiency; a person or thing that fails.

fain ADV [ARCHAIC] willingly.

faint ADJ **1** indistinct, not clear or intense. **2** weak; about to faint. VERB collapse unconscious. NOUN the act or state of fainting.
faintly ADV
faintness NOUN

faint-hearted ADJ timid.

fair NOUN **1** a funfair. **2** a gathering for a sale of goods, often with entertainments; an exhibition of commercial goods. ADJ **1** light in colour; having light-coloured hair. **2** (of weather) fine; (of wind) favourable. **3** just, unbiased. **4** of moderate quality or amount. ADV without cheating.

fairground NOUN an open space where a fair is held.

fairing NOUN a streamlining structure added to a ship, vehicle, etc.

fairly ADV **1** justly. **2** to some extent; quite.

fairway NOUN **1** a navigable channel. **2** part of a golf course between tee and green.

fairy NOUN (PL **fairies**) an imaginary small being with magical powers.

fairy godmother NOUN a benefactress providing help in times of difficulty.

fairyland NOUN an ideally beautiful place.

fairy lights PLURAL NOUN strings of small coloured lights used as decorations.

fait accompli /fayt ŭ-kom-**plee**/ NOUN something already done and not reversible.

faith NOUN reliance, trust; belief in religious doctrine.
break (or **keep**) **faith** be disloyal (or loyal).

faithful ADJ **1** loyal. **2** true, accurate.
faithfully ADV
faithfulness NOUN

faith healing NOUN healing achieved through religious belief rather than medicine.
faith healer NOUN

faithless ADJ disloyal.

fake NOUN a person or thing that is not genuine. ADJ counterfeit. VERB make an imitation of; pretend.
faker NOUN

fakir /fay-keer/ NOUN a Muslim or Hindu religious ascetic living on alms.

falcon NOUN a small long-winged hawk.

falconry NOUN the breeding and training of hawks.
falconer NOUN

fall VERB (**falls**, **falling**, **fell**; PAST PARTICIPLE **fallen**) **1** move downwards without control; lose one's balance; (of land) slope downwards. **2** decrease. **3** pass into a specified state. **4** lose power; be captured or conquered; die in battle. **5** (of the face) show distress. **6** occur. NOUN **1** an instance of falling; the distance or amount of this; something fallen; (**falls**) a waterfall. **2** [US] autumn.
fall back on have recourse to. **fall for** [INFORMAL] **1** fall in love with. **2** be deceived by. **fall out 1** quarrel. **2** happen. **fall short** be inadequate. **fall through** (of a plan) fail.

fallacy NOUN (PL **fallacies**) unsound reasoning; a false belief.
fallacious ADJ

fallible ADJ liable to make mistakes.
fallibility NOUN

Fallopian tube NOUN either of the two tubes from the ovary to the womb.

fallout NOUN airborne radioactive debris.

fallow ADJ (of farmland) ploughed but left unplanted to restore its fertility.

false ADJ **1** not true; incorrect; not genuine, sham. **2** unfaithful.
play false cheat, deceive.
falsely ADV
falseness NOUN

falsehood NOUN a lie; the state of being untrue.

falsetto NOUN (PL **falsettos**) a voice above one's natural range.

falsify VERB (**falsifies**, **falsifying**, **falsified**) **1** alter fraudulently. **2** prove to be false.
falsification NOUN

falsity NOUN falseness; falsehood.

falter VERB become weaker; move or function unsteadily; speak hesitantly.

fame NOUN the state of being famous.
famed ADJ

familial ADJ of a family.

familiar ADJ **1** well known. **2** having knowledge or experience. **3** friendly, intimate; too informal.
familiarity NOUN
familiarly ADV

familiarize (also **familiarise**) VERB make familiar.
familiarization NOUN

family NOUN (PL **families**) parents and their children; a person's children; a set of relatives; a group of related plants, animals, or things.

famine NOUN extreme scarcity of food.

famished ADJ [INFORMAL] extremely hungry.

famous ADJ **1** known about by many people. **2** [INFORMAL] excellent.
famously ADV

fan NOUN **1** a hand-held or mechanical device to create a current of air. **2** an enthusiastic admirer or supporter. VERB (**fans**, **fanning**, **fanned**) **1** cool with a fan; make (a fire etc.) stronger by fanning. **2** spread from a central point.

fanatic NOUN a person with excessive enthusiasm for something.
fanatical ADJ
fanatically ADV
fanaticism NOUN

fan belt NOUN a belt driving a fan that cools a car engine.

fancier NOUN a person with special knowledge and love of something specified.

fanciful ADJ imaginative; imaginary.
fancifully ADV

fancy NOUN (PL **fancies**) **1** imagination; something imagined, an unfounded idea. **2** a desire, a whim. ADJ (**fancier**, **fanciest**) ornamental, elaborate. VERB (**fancies**, **fancying**, **fancied**) **1** imagine; suppose. **2** [INFORMAL] feel a desire for (something); be attracted to (someone).

fancy dress NOUN a costume representing an animal, historical character, etc., worn for a party.

fanfare NOUN a short ceremonious sounding of trumpets.

f

fang NOUN a long sharp tooth; a snake's tooth that injects venom.

fanlight NOUN a small window above a door or larger window.

fantasia NOUN an improvisatory musical composition.

fantasize (also **fantasise**) VERB daydream.

fantastic ADJ 1 imaginative; bizarre, exotic. 2 [INFORMAL] excellent.
fantastically ADV

fantasy NOUN (PL **fantasies**) 1 imagination; a daydream; fiction involving magic and adventure. 2 a fantasia.

FAQ ABBREV [COMPUTING] frequently asked questions.

far ADV at, to, or by a great distance; for a long way; by a great deal.
ADJ distant, remote.

farad NOUN a unit of electrical capacitance.

farce NOUN a light comedy; an absurd situation.
farcical ADJ
farcically ADV

fare NOUN 1 the price charged for a passenger to travel; a passenger paying this. 2 food provided. VERB get on or be treated in a specified way.

Far East NOUN China, Japan, and other countries of east Asia.

farewell EXCLAMATION goodbye. NOUN a parting; parting good wishes.

far-fetched ADJ unconvincing, very unlikely.

farinaceous /fa-ri-nay-shŭs/ ADJ starchy.

farm NOUN a unit of land used for raising crops or livestock. VERB grow crops, raise livestock; use (land) for this.
farm out subcontract (work) to others.
farmer NOUN

farmhouse NOUN a farmer's house.

farmstead NOUN a farm and its buildings.

farmyard NOUN an enclosed area round farm buildings.

farrago /fŭ-rah-goh/ NOUN (PL **farragos** or **farragoes**) a confused mixture.

farrier NOUN a smith who shoes horses.

farrow VERB give birth to (piglets). NOUN a litter of pigs.

fart VERB [INFORMAL] send out wind from the anus.

farther, **farthest** variants of **FURTHER**, **FURTHEST**.

farthingale NOUN [HISTORICAL] a hooped petticoat.

fascia variant of **FACIA**.

fascinate VERB irresistibly interest and attract.
fascination NOUN

fascism /fash-izm/ NOUN a system of extreme right-wing dictatorship.
fascist NOUN & ADJ
fascistic ADJ

fashion NOUN **1** a popular trend; the production and marketing of new styles of clothing. **2** a way of doing something. VERB make into a particular shape.

fashionable ADJ currently popular; following popular trends.
fashionably ADV

fast[1] ADJ **1** moving or able to move quickly; working or done quickly; allowing quick movement. **2** (of a clock etc.) showing a time ahead of the correct one. **3** firmly fixed. ADV **1** quickly. **2** securely, tightly; soundly.

fast[2] VERB go without food. NOUN a period without eating.

fastback NOUN a car with a long sloping back.

fasten VERB fix firmly, tie or join together; be closed or done up.

fastener (also **fastening**) NOUN a device to close or secure something.

fast food NOUN food that is sold pre-prepared for a quick meal.

fastidious ADJ attentive to details; hard to please; easily disgusted.
fastidiously ADV
fastidiousness NOUN

fastness NOUN a stronghold, a secure refuge.

fat NOUN a greasy substance occurring in animal bodies and certain seeds; this as used in cooking or an element in diet;

excess of this in the body, corpulence.
ADJ (**fatter**, **fattest**) excessively plump; containing much fat; thick; substantial.
fat chance [INFORMAL] no chance.
fatness NOUN
fatty ADJ

fatal ADJ causing death or disaster.
fatally ADV

fatalist NOUN a person believing that whatever happens is predestined and inescapable.
fatalism NOUN
fatalistic ADJ

fatality NOUN (PL **fatalities**) a death caused by accident or in war etc.

fate NOUN a power thought to control all events; a person's destiny.

fated ADJ destined by fate.

fateful ADJ leading to great, usually unpleasant, events.
fatefully ADV

father NOUN a male parent or ancestor; a founder, an originator; a title of certain priests. VERB beget; originate.
fatherhood NOUN
fatherless ADJ
fatherly ADJ

father-in-law NOUN (PL **fathers-in-law**) the father of one's wife or husband.

fatherland NOUN one's native country.

fathom NOUN a measure (1.82 m) of the depth of water. VERB understand.
fathomable ADJ

fathomless ADJ **1** too deep to measure. **2** incomprehensible.

fatigue NOUN **1** tiredness. **2** weakness in metal etc., caused by stress. **3** a soldier's non-military task; (**fatigues**) soldiers' clothes for specific tasks. VERB tire or weaken.

fatstock NOUN livestock fattened for slaughter as food.

fatten VERB make or become fat.

fatuous ADJ foolish, silly.
fatuously ADV
fatuousness NOUN

fatwa NOUN a ruling made by an Islamic leader.

faucet /for-sit/ NOUN [US] a tap.

fault NOUN **1** a defect, an imperfection.

2 responsibility for something wrong; a weakness or offence. **3** a break in layers of rock. VERB criticize, find defects in.
at fault responsible for a mistake etc.
faultless ADJ
faulty ADJ

faun NOUN a Roman god of the countryside with a goat's legs and horns.

fauna NOUN (PL **faunas** or **faunae**) the animals of an area or period.

faux pas /foh **pah**/ NOUN (PL **faux pas**) an embarrassing social blunder or breach of etiquette.

favour ([US] **favor**) NOUN **1** liking, approval. **2** a kind or helpful act beyond what is due. **3** favouritism. VERB **1** like, approve of, support. **2** gratify. **3** [INFORMAL] resemble (a parent etc.).

favourable ([US] **favorable**) ADJ **1** showing approval; giving consent. **2** advantageous. **3** (of weather) fine; (of a wind) in the right direction.
favourably ADV

favourite ([US] **favorite**) ADJ liked above others. NOUN a favoured person or thing; a competitor expected to win.

favouritism ([US] **favoritism**) NOUN unfairly generous treatment of one at the expense of others.

fawn NOUN **1** a deer in its first year. **2** light yellowish brown. ADJ fawn-coloured. VERB try to win favour by obsequiousness; (of a dog) show extreme affection.

fax NOUN transmission of exact copies of documents by electronic scanning; a copy produced in this way; a machine for sending and receiving faxes. VERB transmit (a document) by this process.

fay NOUN [LITERARY] a fairy.

faze VERB [INFORMAL] disconcert; daunt.

FBI ABBREV (in the USA) Federal Bureau of Investigation.

FC ABBREV Football Club.

fealty NOUN [HISTORICAL]

f

loyalty, allegiance.

fear NOUN an unpleasant sensation caused by nearness of danger or pain. VERB **1** be afraid (of). **2** used to express regret.

fearful ADJ **1** terrible. **2** feeling fear. **3** [INFORMAL] very great or bad.
fearfully ADV

fearless ADJ feeling no fear.
fearlessly ADV
fearlessness NOUN

fearsome ADJ frightening.

feasible ADJ able to be done, possible.
feasibility NOUN
feasibly ADV

feast NOUN a large elaborate meal; an annual religious celebration. VERB eat heartily; give a feast to.

feat NOUN a remarkable achievement.

feather NOUN each of the structures with a central shaft and fringe of fine strands, growing from a bird's skin. VERB turn (an oar) to pass through the air edgeways.
a feather in one's cap an achievement to be proud of. **feather one's nest.** make money dishonestly.
feathery ADJ

feather-bed VERB (**feather-beds**, **feather-bedding**, **feather-bedded**) make things financially easy for.

feathered ADJ covered or decorated with feathers.

featherweight NOUN a very lightweight thing or person; a boxing weight between bantamweight and lightweight.

feature NOUN **1** a distinctive part of the face. **2** a noticeable attribute or aspect. **3** a newspaper article on a particular topic. **4** a full-length cinema film. VERB have as a feature; be a feature of or in.

febrile /fee-bryl/ ADJ feverish; tense and excited.

February NOUN the second month.

feces US spelling of **FAECES**.

feckless ADJ incompetent and irresponsible.
fecklessness NOUN

fecund ADJ fertile.

fecundity NOUN

fed past and past participle of **FEED**.

federal ADJ of a system in which states unite under a central authority but are independent in internal affairs.
federalism NOUN
federalist NOUN
federally ADV

federate VERB /**fed**-er-ayt/ unite on a federal basis or for a common purpose. ADJ /**fed**-er-ŭt/ united in this way.

federation NOUN a federated society or group of states.

fed up ADJ [INFORMAL] annoyed and resentful.

fee NOUN a sum payable for professional services, or for a privilege.

feeble ADJ weak; ineffective.
feebly ADV
feebleness NOUN

feed VERB (**feeds**, **feeding**, **fed**) give (food) to (a person or animal); eat; supply (a necessary resource) to (someone or something). NOUN food for animals; an act of feeding.

feedback NOUN return of part of a system's output to its source, causing a whistling sound; return of information about a product, a piece of work, etc. to the producer.

feeder NOUN **1** a person or thing that feeds; a feeding apparatus in a machine. **2** a road, railway line, etc. linking outlying areas to a central system.

feel VERB (**feels**, **feeling**, **felt**) **1** perceive or examine by touch; give a specified sensation when touched. **2** experience an emotion or sensation. **3** have an opinion or belief. NOUN the sense of touch; an act of touching; a sensation given by something touched.
feel like be inclined to have or do.

feeler NOUN **1** a long slender organ of touch in certain animals. **2** a tentative suggestion.

feeling NOUN **1** an emotion; (**feelings**) emotional susceptibilities; sympathy, sensitivity. **2** a belief not based on reason. **3** the power of sensation.

feet pl. of **FOOT**.

feign /fayn/ VERB pretend.

feint /faynt/ NOUN a sham attack made to divert attention. VERB make a feint. ADJ (of paper) printed with faint ruled lines.

feisty /fI-sti/ ADJ (**feistier**, **feistiest**) [INFORMAL] boldly determined and energetic.

feldspar (also **felspar**) NOUN a white or red mineral.

felicitate VERB congratulate.
felicitation NOUN

felicitous ADJ well chosen, apt.
felicitously ADV
felicitousness NOUN

felicity NOUN (PL **felicities**) happiness; an apt or pleasing feature.

feline ADJ of cats; catlike. NOUN an animal of the cat family.

fell[1] past of **FALL**.

fell[2] NOUN a stretch of moor or hilly land, especially in northern England. VERB cut or knock down.

fellow NOUN **1** [INFORMAL] a man or boy. **2** an associate or equal; a thing like another. **3** a member of a learned society or governing body of a college.

fellowship NOUN **1** friendly association with others. **2** a society. **3** the position of a college fellow.

felon NOUN a person who has committed a serious violent crime.
felony NOUN

felspar variant of **FELDSPAR**.

felt[1] past and past participle of **FEEL**.

felt[2] NOUN cloth made by matting and pressing fibres. VERB make into felt; cover with felt.

felt-tip pen (also **felt-tipped pen**) NOUN a pen with a writing point made of fibre.

female ADJ **1** of the sex that can bear offspring or produce eggs; (of plants) fruit-bearing. **2** (of a machine part etc.) hollow. NOUN a female animal or plant.

feminine ADJ **1** of, like, or traditionally considered suitable for women. **2** [GRAMMAR] of the gender of nouns and adjectives conventionally regarded as female.
femininity NOUN

feminist NOUN a supporter of women's claims to be given rights equal to those of men.
feminism NOUN

femme fatale /fam fŭ-tahl/ NOUN (PL **femmes fatales**) a dangerously seductive woman.

femur NOUN (PL **femurs** or **femora**) the thigh bone.
femoral ADJ

fen NOUN a low-lying marshy or flooded tract of land.

fence NOUN **1** a barrier round the boundary of a field or garden etc. **2** [INFORMAL] a person who deals in stolen goods. VERB **1** surround with a fence. **2** engage in the sport of fencing.

fencing NOUN **1** the sport of fighting with swords, especially foils. **2** fences; their material.

fend VERB **1** (**fend for oneself**) look after and provide for oneself. **2** (**fend off**) ward off.

fender NOUN **1** a low frame bordering a fireplace. **2** a pad hung over a moored vessel's side to protect against bumping. **3** [US] the mudguard or bumper of a motor vehicle.

fennel NOUN an aniseed-flavoured plant.

fenugreek NOUN a plant with fragrant seeds used for flavouring.

feral ADJ wild.

ferment VERB /fer-**ment**/ undergo fermentation; cause fermentation in; stir up (unrest or excitement). NOUN /**fer**-mĕnt/ excitement, agitation.

fermentation NOUN a chemical change caused by an organic substance, producing effervescence and heat.

fermium NOUN a radioactive metallic element.

fern NOUN a flowerless plant with feathery green leaves.

f

ferny ADJ

ferocious ADJ fierce, savage.
ferociously ADV
ferocity NOUN

ferrel variant of **FERRULE**.

ferret NOUN a small animal of the weasel family. VERB (**ferrets**, **ferreting**, **ferreted**) search tenaciously, rummage.
ferrety ADJ

ferric (also **ferrous**) ADJ of or containing iron.

Ferris wheel NOUN a giant revolving vertical wheel with passenger cars for funfair rides.

ferroconcrete NOUN concrete reinforced with steel.

ferrule (also **ferrel**) NOUN a metal cap strengthening the end of a stick or tube.

ferry NOUN (PL **ferries**) a boat for transporting passengers and goods; the service it provides; the place where it operates. VERB (**ferries**, **ferrying**, **ferried**) convey in a ferry; transport.

fertile ADJ able to produce vegetation, fruit, or young; capable of developing into a new plant or animal; productive, inventive.
fertility NOUN

fertilize (also **fertilise**) VERB **1** introduce pollen or sperm into. **2** add fertilizer to.
fertilization NOUN

fertilizer (also **fertiliser**) NOUN material added to soil to make it more fertile.

fervent ADJ showing intense feeling.
fervency NOUN
fervently ADV

fervid ADJ fervent.
fervidly ADV

fervour ([US] **fervor**) NOUN intensity of feeling.

fester VERB **1** make or become septic. **2** (of ill-feeling) continue and grow worse.

festival NOUN **1** a day or period of celebration. **2** a series of concerts, plays, etc.

festive ADJ of or suitable for a festival; cheerful.
festively ADV
festiveness NOUN

festivity NOUN (PL

festivities) a festive occasion; celebration.

festoon NOUN a hanging chain of flowers or ribbons etc. VERB decorate with hanging ornaments.

feta NOUN a white salty Greek cheese.

fetch VERB **1** go for and bring back; cause to come. **2** be sold for (a specified price).

fetching ADJ attractive.

fête /fayt/ NOUN an outdoor entertainment or sale, especially in aid of charity; [US] a festival. VERB honour and entertain lavishly.

fetid (also **foetid**) ADJ stinking.

fetish NOUN an object worshipped as having magical powers; something given excessive respect.

fetlock NOUN a horse's leg above and behind the hoof.

fetter NOUN a shackle for the ankles; a restraint. VERB put into fetters; restrict, hinder.

fettle NOUN condition: *in fine fettle.*

fetus US spelling of **FOETUS**.

feud NOUN a state of lasting hostility. VERB be involved in a feud.

feudalism NOUN a medieval social system involving a strict hierarchy in which lower orders gave services to higher in return for land or protection.
feudal ADJ
feudalistic ADJ

fever NOUN an abnormally high body temperature; a disease causing this; nervous excitement.
fevered ADJ
feverish ADJ
feverishly ADV

few DETERMINER, PRON, & ADJ (**a few**) a small number of, some; not many. NOUN (**the few**) a select minority.
a few some. **a good few** a fairly large number.

fey ADJ uncanny; clairvoyant.
feyness NOUN

fez NOUN (PL **fezzes**) a high flat-topped red cap worn by some Muslim men.

ff. ABBREV **1** the following pages. **2** (**ff**) [MUSIC] fortissimo.

fiancé, **fiancée** NOUN a man (*fiancé*) or woman (*fiancée*) one is engaged to marry.

fiasco NOUN (PL **fiascos**) a total and ludicrous failure.

fiat /fy-at/ NOUN an order; an authorization.

fib NOUN a trivial lie. VERB (**fibs**, **fibbing**, **fibbed**) tell a fib.
fibber NOUN

fibre ([US] **fiber**) NOUN **1** a thread-like strand; a substance formed of fibres; fibrous material in food, roughage.
2 strength of character.
fibrous ADJ

fibreglass ([US] **fiberglass**) NOUN material made of or containing glass fibres.

fibre optics NOUN transmission of information by light along thin flexible glass fibres.

fibril NOUN a small fibre.

fibroid ADJ consisting of fibrous tissue. NOUN a benign fibroid tumour.

fibrositis NOUN rheumatic pain in tissue other than bones and joints.

fibula NOUN (PL **fibulae** or **fibulas**) the bone on the outer side of the shin.

fiche /feesh/ NOUN (PL **fiche** or **fiches**) a microfiche.

fickle ADJ inconstant, not loyal.
fickleness NOUN

fiction NOUN literature describing imaginary events and people; an invented story.
fictional ADJ

fictitious ADJ imaginary, not true or real.

fiddle [INFORMAL] NOUN **1** a violin. **2** a swindle. VERB **1** fidget with something. **2** falsify (figures etc.).
fiddler NOUN

fiddlesticks EXCLAMATION [INFORMAL] nonsense.

fiddly ADJ (**fiddlier**, **fiddliest**) [INFORMAL] awkward or complicated.

fidelity NOUN **1** faithfulness, loyalty. **2** accuracy in a copy etc.

fidget VERB (**fidgets**, **fidgeting**, **fidgeted**) make small restless movements; be or make uneasy. NOUN a person

who fidgets.
fidgety ADJ

fiduciary ADJ held or given in trust. NOUN (PL **fiduciaries**) a trustee.

fief /feef/ NOUN [HISTORICAL] an estate held by a noble under feudalism.

field NOUN **1** an enclosed area of open ground, especially for pasture or cultivation; a sports ground. **2** an area rich in a natural product. **3** a sphere of action or interest. **4** all the competitors in a race or contest. VERB **1** (in cricket etc.) stop and return the ball to prevent scoring. **2** put (a team) into a contest.

field day NOUN an opportunity for successful unrestrained action.

fielder NOUN (in cricket etc.) a member of the side not batting.

field events NOUN athletic contests other than races.

field glasses PLURAL NOUN binoculars.

field marshal NOUN an army officer of the highest rank.

fieldwork NOUN practical research done outside libraries and laboratories.
fieldworker NOUN

fiend /feend/ NOUN **1** an evil spirit; a cruel or mischievous person. **2** [INFORMAL] a devotee or addict: *a fitness fiend.*

fiendish ADJ cruel; extremely difficult.
fiendishly ADV

fierce ADJ violent, aggressive; intense; powerful and destructive.
fiercely ADV
fierceness NOUN

fiery ADJ (**fierier**, **fieriest**) **1** consisting of or like fire. **2** passionate, intense.
fierily ADV
fieriness NOUN

fiesta NOUN a festival in Spanish-speaking countries.

fife NOUN a small shrill flute.

fifteen ADJ & NOUN one more than fourteen (15, XV).
fifteenth ADJ & NOUN

fifth ADJ & NOUN the next after fourth.
fifthly ADV

fifty ADJ & NOUN five times ten (50, L).
fiftieth ADJ & NOUN

fifty-fifty ADJ & ADV half-and-half, equally.

fig NOUN a soft, sweet pear-shaped fruit.

f

fig. ABBREV figure.

fight VERB (**fights**, **fighting**, **fought**) struggle (against), especially in physical combat or war; strive to obtain or accomplish something; argue. NOUN an act of fighting; a struggle; a boxing match.

fighter NOUN one who fights; an aircraft designed for attacking others.

figment NOUN something that exists only in the imagination.

figurative ADJ metaphorical.
figuratively ADV

figure NOUN **1** a number; an amount of money; a numerical symbol; (**figures**) arithmetic. **2** bodily shape; a representation of a person or animal. **3** a well-known person. **4** a geometric shape; a diagram or illustration; a pattern. VERB **1** appear; play a part. **2** calculate; [US] [INFORMAL] suppose, think.

figured ADJ with a woven pattern.

figurehead NOUN a carved image at the prow of a ship; a leader with only nominal power.

figure of speech NOUN an expression used for effect rather than literally.

figurine NOUN a statuette.

filament NOUN a slender thread; a fine wire giving off light in an electric lamp.

filbert NOUN a hazelnut.

filch VERB [INFORMAL] steal (something small).

file NOUN **1** a folder or box for keeping documents; its contents. **2** a set of data in a computer. **3** a line of people or things one behind another. **4** a tool with a rough surface for smoothing things. VERB **1** place (a document) in a file; place on record. **2** march in a long line. **3** shape or smooth (a surface) with a file.

filial ADJ of or due from a son or daughter.
filially ADV

filibuster VERB delay the passage of a bill by making long speeches. NOUN delaying progress in this way.

filigree NOUN ornamental work of fine gold or silver wire.

filings PLURAL NOUN thin chips removed with a file.

Filipino NOUN (PL **Filipinos**; FEMININE **Filipina**, PL **Filipinas**) a person from the Philippines; the language of the Philippines. ADJ relating to the Philippines.

fill VERB **1** make or become full; stop up (a cavity). **2** occupy; appoint someone to (a vacant post). NOUN enough of a substance to fill a container.
fill in 1 complete (a form etc.). **2** act as someone's substitute. **3** tell (someone) more details. **fill out 1** put on weight. **2** [US] complete (a form etc.). **fill up** fill completely. **one's fill** as much as one wants or can bear.

filler NOUN a thing or material used to fill a gap or increase bulk.

fillet NOUN a piece of boneless meat or fish. VERB (**fillets**, **filleting**, **filleted**) remove bones from.

filling NOUN a substance used to fill a cavity etc. ADJ (of food) satisfying hunger.

filling station NOUN a place selling petrol to motorists.

fillip NOUN a stimulus or incentive.

filly NOUN (PL **fillies**) a young female horse.

film NOUN **1** a thin flexible strip of light-sensitive material for taking photographs. **2** a story told through a sequence of images projected on a screen. **3** a thin layer. VERB photograph with a cine-camera or video camera; make a film of.
film over become covered with a thin layer of something.

filmstrip NOUN a series of transparencies in a strip for projection.

filmy ADJ (**filmier**, **filmiest**) thin and almost transparent.

filo /fee-loh/ NOUN pastry in very thin sheets.

Filofax NOUN [TRADE MARK] a loose-leaf notebook for recording appointments, addresses, etc.

filter NOUN **1** a device or substance for holding back impurities in liquid or gas passing through it; a screen for absorbing or modifying light or electrical or sound waves. **2** an arrangement allowing traffic to filter. VERB **1** pass through a filter; remove (impurities) in this way; pass gradually in or out. **2** (of traffic) be allowed to turn while traffic going straight on is held up.

filth NOUN disgusting dirt; obscenity.
filthily ADV
filthiness NOUN
filthy ADJ

filtrate NOUN a filtered liquid.
filtration NOUN

fin NOUN a thin projection from a fish's body, used for propelling and steering itself; a similar projection to improve the stability of aircraft etc.

final ADJ coming at the end of a series or process; allowing no dispute. NOUN the last contest in a series; the last edition of a day's newspaper; (**finals**) examinations at the end of a degree course.
finally ADV

finale /fi-**nah**-li/ NOUN the closing section of a performance or musical composition.

finalist NOUN a competitor in a final.

finality NOUN the quality or fact of being final.

finalize (also **finalise**) VERB complete; put in definitive form.
finalization NOUN

finance NOUN management of money; (**finances**) money resources. VERB fund.
financial ADJ
financially ADV

financier NOUN a person

engaged in financing businesses.

finch NOUN a small bird.

find VERB (**finds**, **finding**, **found**) **1** discover; learn. **2** reach; obtain: *find time to write.* **3** judge (something) to have a particular quality; declare a verdict. NOUN something found, especially something valuable.

find out detect; learn, discover.

finder NOUN

fine¹ ADJ **1** of very high quality; satisfactory; acceptable; in good health. **2** bright, free from rain etc. **3** thin; in small particles; subtle. **4** (of feelings) noble, refined. ADV very well.

finely ADV

fineness NOUN

fine² NOUN a sum of money to be paid as a penalty. VERB punish with a fine.

finery NOUN showy clothes etc.

finesse NOUN delicate manipulation; tact.

finger NOUN each of the five parts extending from each hand; any of these other than the thumb; an object compared to a finger; a measure (about 20 mm) of alcohol in a glass. VERB touch or feel with the fingers.

fingerboard NOUN a flat strip on a stringed instrument against which the strings are pressed with the fingers to produce different notes.

fingerprint NOUN an impression of the ridges on the pad of a finger, used for identification.

fingerstall NOUN a sheath to cover an injured finger.

finial NOUN an ornament at the apex of a gable, pinnacle, etc.

finicky (also **finicking**) ADJ fussy; detailed and fiddly.

finish VERB **1** bring or come to an end; consume the whole or the remains of; reach the end of a race etc. **2** complete; put final touches to. NOUN **1** the final part or stage; the end of a race. **2** the way in which something is made; a surface appearance.

finish off 1 complete. **2** consume; kill.

finisher NOUN

finite /fI-nIt/ ADJ limited.

Finn NOUN a person from Finland.

Finnish NOUN the language of Finland. ADJ relating to Finland.

fiord variant of **FJORD**.

fir NOUN an evergreen cone-bearing tree.

fire NOUN **1** combustion; destructive burning; fuel burned to provide heat; a gas or electrical heater. **2** the firing of guns. **3** passionate feeling. VERB **1** send a bullet or shell from (a gun); launch (a missile). **2** [INFORMAL] dismiss from a job. **3** excite. **4** supply fuel to. **5** bake (pottery) in a kiln.

firearm NOUN a gun, pistol, etc.

firebrand NOUN a person who causes trouble and unrest.

firebreak NOUN an obstacle to the spread of fire.

fire brigade NOUN an organized body of people employed to extinguish fires.

firecracker NOUN [US] an explosive firework.

firedamp NOUN an explosive mixture of methane and air in mines.

firedog NOUN an iron support for logs in a fireplace.

fire engine NOUN a vehicle with equipment for putting out fires.

fire escape NOUN a special staircase or apparatus for escape from a burning building.

firefighter NOUN a person whose job is to put out fires.

firefly NOUN (PL **fireflies**) a phosphorescent beetle.

fireman NOUN a firefighter; a member of a fire brigade.

fireplace NOUN a recess with a chimney for a domestic fire.

fireside NOUN the area round a fireplace.

firework NOUN a device containing chemicals that explode producing spectacular colours etc.

firing squad NOUN a group ordered to shoot a condemned person.

firkin NOUN a small barrel.

firm ADJ not yielding when pressed or pushed; securely in place; (of a hold etc.) steady and strong; not giving way to argument, intimidation, etc. ADV firmly. VERB make or become firm. NOUN a business company.

firmament NOUN [LITERARY] the sky with the stars etc.

first ADJ coming before all others in time, order, or importance. NOUN **1** the first thing or occurrence; the first day of a month. **2** a top grade in an examination. ADV before all others or another; before doing something else; for the first time. **at first** at the beginning.

first aid NOUN basic treatment given for an injury etc. before a doctor arrives.

first class NOUN a group or division considered the best; the best accommodation in a train, ship, etc. ADJ & ADV (**first-class**) relating to the first class; (of mail) delivered most quickly.

first cousin *see* **COUSIN**.

first-hand ADV & ADJ directly from the original source.

firstly ADV as the first point or consideration.

first name NOUN a personal name.

first-rate ADJ excellent.

firth NOUN a narrow inlet of the sea in Scotland.

fiscal ADJ of public revenue.

fish NOUN (PL **fish** or **fishes**) a cold-blooded vertebrate living wholly in water; its flesh as food. VERB try to catch fish; do this in (an area of water); reach into a receptacle to find something; say something to elicit a compliment etc.

fishery NOUN (PL **fisheries**) a place where fish are reared commercially; an area of sea where fishing is done; fishing as an industry.

fishmeal NOUN ground dried fish used as a fertilizer or animal feed.

fishmonger NOUN a shopkeeper who sells fish.

f

fishnet ADJ (of fabric) of a coarse open mesh.

fishy ADJ (**fishier**, **fishiest**) **1** like fish. **2** [INFORMAL] arousing suspicion.

fissile ADJ tending to split; capable of undergoing nuclear fission.

fission NOUN the action of splitting into two or more parts; the splitting of an atomic nucleus, with great release of energy.

fissure NOUN a cleft.

fist NOUN a tightly closed hand.

fisticuffs PLURAL NOUN fighting with fists.

fistula NOUN (PL **fistulae** or **fistulas**) an abnormal or surgically made passage in the body.

fit ADJ (**fitter**, **fittest**) **1** suitable; right and proper; competent or qualified. **2** in good health. VERB (**fits**, **fitting**, **fitted**) **1** be the right size and shape for; try on and adjust; be small or few enough to get into a space. **2** fix in place; join or be joined. **3** make or be appropriate; make competent. NOUN **1** the way a garment etc. fits. **2** a sudden outburst of emotion, activity, etc.; a sudden attack of convulsions or loss of consciousness.
fitness NOUN

fitful ADJ irregular; occurring in short periods.
fitfully ADV

fitment NOUN a piece of fixed furniture.

fitter NOUN **1** a person who supervises the fitting of clothes. **2** a mechanic.

fitting ADJ right and proper. NOUN **1** the process of having a garment fitted. **2** (**fittings**) items of furniture fixed in a house but removable when the owner moves.

five ADJ & NOUN one more than four (5, V).

fiver NOUN [INFORMAL] a five-pound note.

fix VERB **1** fasten securely in position; direct (the eyes or attention) steadily. **2** repair. **3** agree on, settle. **4** [INFORMAL] arrange, deal with; influence (a result etc.) dishonestly. NOUN **1** [INFORMAL] an awkward

situation. **2** [INFORMAL] a dose of something to which one is addicted. **3** [INFORMAL] a solution to a problem, especially a makeshift one. **4** a position determined by taking bearings.
fix up [INFORMAL] organize; provide for.

fixated ADJ having an obsession.

fixation NOUN **1** an obsession. **2** the action of fixing.

fixative NOUN a substance for keeping things in position, or preventing fading or evaporation.

fixedly ADV without changing or wavering.

fixity NOUN the state of being unchanging or permanent.

fixture NOUN a thing fixed in position; [INFORMAL] a firmly established person or thing.

fizz VERB **1** (of liquid) produce bubbles of gas with a hissing sound. **2** [INFORMAL] be exciting and lively. NOUN bubbliness; the sound of this; [INFORMAL] an effervescent drink.
fizziness NOUN
fizzy ADJ

fizzle VERB hiss or splutter feebly.
fizzle out end feebly.

fjord /fi-ord/ (also **fiord**) NOUN a narrow inlet of sea between cliffs, especially in Norway.

fl. ABBREV **1** floruit. **2** fluid.

flab NOUN [INFORMAL] flabbiness, fat.

flabbergast VERB [INFORMAL] astound.

flabby ADJ (**flabbier**, **flabbiest**) fat and limp, not firm.
flabbiness NOUN

flaccid /flas-sid/ ADJ soft, loose, and limp.
flaccidly ADV

flag NOUN a piece of cloth attached by one edge to a staff or rope as a signal or symbol; a device used as a marker. VERB (**flags**, **flagging**, **flagged**) **1** mark or signal (as) with a flag. **2** become tired or weak.

flag day NOUN a day on which small emblems are sold for a charity.

flagellate /fla-jĕ-layt/ VERB whip, flog.
flagellant NOUN

flagellation NOUN

flageolet /fla-jĕ-**let**/ NOUN a small wind instrument.

flagged ADJ paved with flagstones.

flagon NOUN a large bottle for wine or cider; a container with a handle, lip, and lid for serving wine.

f

flagrant /**flay**-grŭnt/ ADJ (of an offence or offender) very bad and obvious. **flagrantly** ADV

flagship NOUN an admiral's ship; the most important product of an organization etc.

flagstone NOUN a large paving stone.

flail NOUN an implement formerly used for threshing grain. VERB thrash or swing about wildly.

flair NOUN natural ability.

flak NOUN **1** anti-aircraft shells. **2** harsh criticism.

flake NOUN a thin, flat piece of something. VERB come off in flakes; break (food) into flakes.
flake out [INFORMAL] faint; fall asleep from exhaustion.

flakiness NOUN
flaky ADJ

flambé /**flom**-bay/ ADJ (of food) served covered in flaming alcohol.

flamboyant ADJ showy in appearance or manner. **flamboyance** NOUN **flamboyantly** ADV

flame NOUN a hot, glowing quantity of burning gas coming from something on fire; an orange-red colour. VERB burn with flames; be bright, become bright red.
fan the flames make a feeling more intense. **old flame** [INFORMAL] a former sweetheart.

flamenco NOUN (PL **flamencos**) a Spanish style of singing and dancing.

flamingo NOUN (PL **flamingos** or **flamingoes**) a wading bird with long legs and pink feathers.

flammable ADJ able to be set on fire.
flammability NOUN

flan NOUN an open pastry or sponge case with filling.

flange /flanj/ NOUN a

projecting rim.
flanged ADJ

flank NOUN a side, especially of the body between ribs and hip; a side of an army etc. VERB be on either side of.

flannel NOUN **1** soft, slightly raised fabric. **2** a facecloth. **3** (**flannels**) trousers of flannel. **4** [INFORMAL] evasive and meaningless talk. VERB (**flannels**, **flannelling**, **flannelled**; [US] **flanneling**, **flanneled**) [INFORMAL] talk meaninglessly to avoid an issue.

flannelette NOUN a heavy brushed cotton fabric.

flap VERB (**flaps**, **flapping**, **flapped**) **1** move (wings, arms, etc.) up and down; flutter or sway. **2** [INFORMAL] be anxious, panic. NOUN **1** a piece of cloth, metal, etc., covering an opening and moving (as) on a hinge. **2** a flapping movement. **3** [INFORMAL] a panic.

flapjack NOUN a biscuit made with oats.

flare VERB **1** blaze suddenly; burst into activity or anger. **2** grow wider towards one end; dilate. NOUN **1** a sudden blaze; a device producing flame as a signal or illumination. **2** a flared shape. **3** (**flares**) trousers with legs widening from the knee down.

flash VERB **1** give out a sudden bright light; cause to shine briefly; show suddenly, briefly, or ostentatiously. **2** move or send rapidly. NOUN a sudden burst of flame or light; a bright patch; a sudden, brief show of wit, feeling, etc.; a brief news item; a very short time; a device producing a brief bright light in photography. ADJ [INFORMAL] ostentatiously expensive, smart, etc.
a flash in the pan a success that is not repeated or continued.

flashback NOUN a scene in a story, film, etc., set at a time earlier than the main narrative.

flasher NOUN [INFORMAL] a man who indecently exposes himself.

flash flood NOUN a sudden destructive flood.

flashing NOUN a strip of metal covering a joint in a roof etc.

flashlight NOUN an electric torch.

flashpoint NOUN **1** a point at which violence often flares up. **2** the temperature at which a vapour ignites.

flashy ADJ (**flashier**, **flashiest**) ostentatiously smart, expensive, etc.
flashily ADV
flashiness NOUN

flask NOUN a narrow-necked bottle; a vacuum flask.

flat ADJ (**flatter**, **flattest**) **1** level, even, without irregularities; broad and shallow; horizontal. **2** lacking enthusiasm or energy; monotonous; having lost effervescence; having lost power to generate electric current. **3** absolute: *a flat refusal;* (of a price) unvarying. **4** [MUSIC] below the correct or normal pitch; (of a note) a semitone lower than a specified note. ADV **1** so as to be flat. **2** [INFORMAL] absolutely, definitely. NOUN **1** a flat surface or object; level ground. **2** a set of rooms on one floor, used as a residence. **3** [MUSIC] a note lowered by a semitone.
flat out at top speed; with maximum effort.

flatfish NOUN a sea fish with a flattened body and both eyes on one side.

flatmate NOUN a person with whom one shares a flat.

flatten VERB make or become flat.

flatter VERB compliment insincerely; represent as or cause to appear more attractive than is the case.
flatterer NOUN
flattery NOUN

flatulent ADJ causing or suffering from formation of gas in the digestive tract.
flatulence NOUN

flaunt VERB display ostentatiously; show off.

flautist /flor-tist/ NOUN a flute-player.

flavour ([US] **flavor**) NOUN a distinctive taste; a special characteristic. VERB give

flavour to.
flavourless ADJ

flavouring ([US] **flavoring**) NOUN a substance used to give flavour to food.

flaw NOUN an imperfection. VERB spoil, weaken.
flawed ADJ
flawless ADJ

flax NOUN a blue-flowered plant; a textile fibre from its stem.

flaxen ADJ made of flax; [LITERARY] pale yellow like dressed flax.

flay VERB **1** strip off the skin or hide of. **2** criticize severely.

flea NOUN a small jumping blood-sucking insect.

flea market NOUN a market for second-hand goods.

fleck NOUN a very small mark; a speck. VERB mark with flecks.

fled past and past participle of **FLEE**.

fledged ADJ (of a young bird) with fully grown wing-feathers; able to fly.
fully (or **newly**) **fledged** completely (or recently) trained, appointed, etc. in a particular capacity.

fledgeling (also **fledgling**) NOUN a bird just fledged.

flee VERB (**flees**, **fleeing**, **fled**) run or hurry away (from).

fleece NOUN a sheep's woolly hair. VERB [INFORMAL] rob by trickery.
fleecy ADJ

fleet NOUN a navy; ships sailing together; vehicles or aircraft under one command or ownership. ADJ [LITERARY] swift and nimble.
fleetness NOUN

fleeting ADJ passing quickly, brief.

flesh NOUN **1** the soft substance of animal bodies; meat; the body as opposed to the mind or soul. **2** the pulpy part of fruits and vegetables.
flesh and blood human nature; a real person.
flesh out add details to.
one's own flesh and blood a relative.

fleshy ADJ (**fleshier**, **fleshiest**) **1** plump. **2** thick, pulpy. **3** like flesh.

fleur-de-lis /fler dĕ **lee**/ (also **fleur-de-lys**) NOUN (PL

fleurs-de-lis) a heraldic design of a lily with three petals.

flew past of **FLY**.

flex NOUN a flexible insulated wire for carrying electric current. VERB bend; move (a muscle) so that it bends a joint.
flexion NOUN

flexible ADJ able to bend easily; adaptable, changing readily.
flexibility NOUN
flexibly ADV

flexitime NOUN a system of working a set number of hours but with variable starting and finishing times.

flibbertigibbet NOUN a gossiping or frivolous person.

flick NOUN **1** a quick, sharp, small movement; a light blow. **2** [INFORMAL] a cinema film. VERB move, strike, or remove with a flick.

flicker VERB burn or shine unsteadily; make small rapid movements; occur or appear briefly. NOUN an unsteady light; a tiny movement; a brief or slight occurrence.

flier variant of **FLYER**.

flight NOUN **1** the action of flying; a journey through air or space; the path of an object moving through the air; a group of birds or aircraft. **2** a series of stairs. **3** feathers etc. on a dart or arrow. **4** the action of running away; escape.

flight deck NOUN **1** the cockpit of a large aircraft. **2** the deck of an aircraft carrier.

flightless ADJ unable to fly.

flight recorder NOUN an electronic device in an aircraft recording details of its flight.

flighty ADJ (**flightier**, **flightiest**) unreliable, irresponsible.
flightily ADV
flightiness NOUN

flimsy ADJ (**flimsier**, **flimsiest**) light and thin; fragile; unconvincing.
flimsily ADV
flimsiness NOUN

flinch VERB make a nervous movement in pain or fear; shrink from something.

fling VERB (**flings**, **flinging**, **flung**) throw violently or forcefully. NOUN a spell of indulgence in pleasure; a brief sexual relationship.

flint NOUN very hard stone; a piece of a hard alloy producing sparks when struck.

flintlock NOUN an old type of gun.

flip VERB (**flips**, **flipping**, **flipped**) **1** turn over or cause to turn over suddenly and swiftly. **2** [INFORMAL] lose one's self-control. NOUN a sudden sharp movement. ADJ [INFORMAL] glib, flippant.

flippant ADJ not showing proper seriousness.
flippancy NOUN
flippantly ADV

flipper NOUN a sea animal's limb used in swimming; a large flat rubber attachment to the foot for underwater swimming.

flirt VERB behave in a frivolously amorous way; consider an idea etc. without committing oneself to it. NOUN a person who flirts.
flirtation NOUN
flirtatious ADJ
flirtatiously ADV

flit VERB (**flits**, **flitting**, **flitted**) **1** move swiftly and lightly. **2** leave one's home, especially secretly. NOUN [INFORMAL] an act of leaving one's home.

flitch NOUN a side of bacon.

flitter VERB flit about. NOUN a flittering movement.

float VERB **1** rest or drift on the surface of liquid; be supported in air; move aimlessly. **2** make (a suggestion) to test reactions. **3** offer the shares of (a company) for sale. **4** (of currency) have a variable rate of exchange. NOUN **1** a thing designed to float on liquid. **2** money for minor expenditure or giving change. **3** a small vehicle.

floatation variant of **FLOTATION**.

flocculent ADJ like tufts of wool.

flock NOUN **1** a number of animals or birds together; a large number of people; a congregation. **2** a tuft of wool or cotton; wool or cotton waste as stuffing. VERB gather or go in a group.

floe NOUN a sheet of floating ice.

f

flog VERB (**flogs**, **flogging**, **flogged**) **1** beat severely. **2** [INFORMAL] sell.
flogging NOUN

flood NOUN an overflow of water on a place usually dry; a great outpouring; a large quantity; the inflow of the tide. VERB cover with flood water; overflow; arrive in great quantities; overwhelm.

floodlight NOUN a lamp producing a broad bright beam. VERB (**floodlights**, **floodlighting**, **floodlit**) illuminate with this.

floor NOUN **1** the lower surface of a room. **2** a storey. **3** the right to speak in a debate: *have the floor*. VERB **1** provide with a floor. **2** [INFORMAL] knock down; baffle.

flooring NOUN material for a floor.

floor show NOUN a cabaret.

floozie (also **floozy**) NOUN (PL **floozies**) [INFORMAL] a woman regarded as promiscuous.

flop VERB (**flops**, **flopping**, **flopped**) **1** hang or fall heavily and loosely. **2** [INFORMAL] be a failure. NOUN **1** a flopping movement or sound. **2** [INFORMAL] a failure.

floppy ADJ (**floppier**, **floppiest**) not firm or stiff.

floppy disk NOUN a magnetic disk for storing machine-readable data.

flora NOUN (PL **florae** or **floras**) the plants of an area or period.

floral ADJ of flowers.

floret NOUN each of the small flowers of a composite flower.

florid ADJ **1** red, flushed. **2** over-elaborate.
floridity NOUN

florin NOUN a former British coin worth two shillings; a Dutch guilder.

florist NOUN a person who sells flowers.

floruit VERB indicating when a person was alive and working (Latin, meaning 'he/she flourished').

floss NOUN **1** a mass of silky fibres. **2** dental floss.
flossy ADJ

flotation (also **floatation**) NOUN the action of floating; the sale of new shares in a company to the public.

flotilla NOUN a small fleet.

flotsam NOUN floating wreckage.
flotsam and jetsam odds and ends.

flounce VERB go in an impatient annoyed manner. NOUN **1** a flouncing movement. **2** a deep frill.
flounced ADJ

flounder VERB move clumsily, as in mud; become confused; be in difficulty. NOUN a small flatfish.

flour NOUN fine powder made from grain, used in cooking. VERB sprinkle with flour.
floury ADJ

flourish VERB **1** grow vigorously; prosper, be successful. **2** wave dramatically. NOUN a dramatic gesture; an ornamental curve; a fanfare.

flout VERB disobey (a law etc.) contemptuously.

flow VERB **1** glide along as a stream; move steadily; (of hair etc.) hang loosely. **2** be supplied and drunk in large quantities: *wine flowed at the party.* NOUN a flowing movement; a continuous stream; its speed.
go with the flow follow a general tendency.

flow chart NOUN a diagram showing the sequence of events in a process.

flower NOUN **1** the part of a plant where fruit or seed develops, usually brightly coloured and decorative; a plant grown for this. **2** the best among a group of people. VERB produce flowers.

flowered ADJ ornamented with a design of flowers.

flowerpot NOUN a pot in which plants are grown.

flowery ADJ **1** full of flowers. **2** full of ornamental phrases.

flown past participle of **FLY**.

flu NOUN influenza.

fluctuate VERB vary irregularly.
fluctuation NOUN

f

flue NOUN a smoke-duct in a chimney; a channel for conveying heat.

fluent ADJ speaking or spoken smoothly and readily.
fluency NOUN
fluently ADV

fluff NOUN a soft mass of fibres or down. VERB **1** make (something) appear fuller and softer. **2** [INFORMAL] bungle, do unsuccessfully.
fluffiness NOUN
fluffy ADJ

fluid ADJ flowing easily; not fixed or settled. NOUN a liquid.
fluidity NOUN
fluidly ADV

fluid ounce NOUN one-twentieth (in the USA, one-sixteenth) of a pint (about 28 ml, in the USA 35 ml).

fluke NOUN **1** a lucky accident. **2** the barbed arm of an anchor etc.; a lobe of a whale's tail. **3** a flat parasitic worm. **4** a flatfish.

flummery NOUN **1** nonsense, empty compliments. **2** a type of pudding.

flummox VERB [INFORMAL] baffle.

flung past and past participle of **FLING**.

flunk VERB [US] [INFORMAL] fail.

flunkey (also **flunky**) NOUN (PL **flunkeys** or **flunkies**) a liveried servant; a person who does menial work.

fluorescent ADJ taking in radiations and sending them out as light.
fluoresce VERB
fluorescence NOUN

fluoridate VERB add fluoride to (a water supply) to combat tooth decay.
fluoridation NOUN

fluoride NOUN a compound of fluorine with metal.

fluorine NOUN a pungent corrosive gas.

fluorspar NOUN a colourless mineral.

flurry NOUN (PL **flurries**) a short rush of wind, rain, or snow; a commotion.

flush VERB 1 make or become red; blush. 2 clean or dispose of with a flow of water. 3 drive out from cover. NOUN 1 a blush. 2 a rush of emotion. 3 an act of cleaning something with a rush of water. ADJ 1 level, even with another surface. 2 [INFORMAL] wealthy.

fluster VERB make agitated and confused. NOUN a flustered state.

flute NOUN 1 a wind instrument consisting of a pipe with holes along it and a mouth-hole at the side. 2 an ornamental groove. 3 a tall narrow wine glass.

flutter VERB move wings hurriedly; wave or flap quickly; (of the heart) beat irregularly. NOUN 1 a fluttering movement; a state of nervous excitement. 2 [INFORMAL] a small bet.

fluvial ADJ of or found in rivers.

flux NOUN 1 the action of flowing; a discharge; continuous change. 2 a substance mixed with a solid to lower its melting point.

fly VERB (**flies**, **flying**, **flew**; PAST PARTICIPLE **flown**) 1 move through the air on wings or in an aircraft; be thrown through the air; control the flight of. 2 display (a flag); flutter, be blown about. 3 (of time) pass rapidly. 4 [ARCHAIC] run away. NOUN (PL **flies**) 1 a two-winged insect. 2 (also **flies**) a fastening down the front of trousers. **a fly in the ointment** something that spoils a situation or thing. **no flies on someone** [INFORMAL] used of an alert and astute person. **with flying colours** with great credit or success.

flyblown ADJ tainted by flies' eggs.

flyer (also **flier**) NOUN 1 a thing that flies; an airman or airwoman; something that moves fast. 2 a small handbill advertising something.

flying ADJ able to fly.

flying buttress NOUN a buttress based on a structure separate from the wall it supports.

flying fish NOUN a tropical fish with wing-like fins for gliding through the air.

flying fox NOUN a large fruit-eating bat.

f

flying saucer NOUN an unidentified flying object, supposedly a craft from outer space.

flying squad NOUN a group of police etc. organized to reach an incident quickly.

flyleaf NOUN (PL **flyleaves**) a blank leaf at the beginning or end of a book.

flyover NOUN a bridge carrying one road or railway over another.

fly-post VERB display (posters etc.) in unauthorized places.

flysheet NOUN an outer cover for a tent.

fly-tip VERB (**fly-tips**, **fly-tipping**, **fly-tipped**) dump waste illegally.

flyweight NOUN a weight below bantamweight, in amateur boxing between 48 and 51 kg.

flywheel NOUN a heavy wheel revolving on a shaft to regulate machinery.

FM ABBREV frequency modulation.

foal NOUN the young of a horse or related animal. VERB give birth to a foal.

foam NOUN **1** a mass of small bubbles; a bubbly substance prepared for shaving etc. **2** spongy rubber or plastic. VERB form or produce foam.
foamy ADJ

fob NOUN a chain for a watch; an ornament hanging from it; a tab on a key ring.
fob off (**fobs**, **fobbing**, **fobbed**) give (something inferior) to (someone); deceitfully pacify.

focal ADJ of or at a focus.

fo'c's'le variant of **FORECASTLE**.

focus NOUN (PL **focuses** or **foci**) **1** the centre of interest or activity; concentration of attention. **2** clear visual definition; the distance at which an object is most clearly seen; an adjustment on a lens to produce a clear image. **3** a point where rays meet. VERB (**focuses**, **focusing**, **focused** or **focusses**, **focussing**, **focussed**) **1** adjust the focus of; bring into focus. **2** concentrate.

fodder NOUN food for animals.

foe NOUN an enemy.

foetid variant of **FETID**.

foetus /fee-tŭs/ ([US] **fetus**) NOUN (PL **foetuses**) a developed embryo in a womb or egg.
foetal ADJ

fog NOUN thick mist. VERB (**fogs**, **fogging**, **fogged**) cover or become covered with fog or condensed vapour; make obscure.
fogginess NOUN
foggy ADJ

fogey (also **fogy**) NOUN (PL **fogeys** or **fogies**) an old-fashioned person.

foghorn NOUN a device making a deep sound to warn ships of hidden rocks etc. in fog.

foible NOUN a harmless peculiarity in a person's character.

foil NOUN **1** a very thin flexible sheet of metal. **2** a person or thing emphasizing another's qualities by contrast. **3** a long thin sword with a button on the point. VERB thwart, frustrate.

foist VERB cause a person to accept (an inferior or unwelcome thing).

fold VERB **1** bend (something thin and flat) so that one part of it lies over another. **2** wrap; clasp. **3** mix (an ingredient) gently into a mixture. **4** [INFORMAL] (of a business etc.) fail, cease operating. **5** enclose (sheep) in a fold. NOUN **1** a shape or line made by folding. **2** a pen for sheep; a close and protected community.

folder NOUN **1** a folding cover for loose papers. **2** [US] a leaflet.

foliage NOUN leaves.

foliate ADJ decorated with leaves.

folio NOUN (PL **folios**) a folded sheet of paper making two leaves of a book; a book of such pages; the page-number of a book.

folk NOUN (PL **folk** OR **folks**) 1 [INFORMAL] people; relatives. 2 folk music. ADJ (of music, song, etc.) in the traditional style of a country or region.

folklore NOUN the traditional beliefs and tales of a community.

folksy ADJ (**folksier**, **folksiest**) 1 in the style of traditional culture, especially artificially. 2 informal and friendly.

follicle NOUN a very small cavity containing a hair-root.

follow VERB 1 go or come after; go along (a route); happen after. 2 act according to (instructions etc.); accept the ideas of. 3 pay close attention to; take an interest in. 4 be a consequence or conclusion.
follow suit follow someone's example.
follow up investigate further.
follower NOUN

following NOUN a body of believers or supporters. ADJ 1 about to be mentioned. 2 next in time. PREP as a sequel to.

folly NOUN (PL **follies**) 1 foolishness, a foolish act. 2 an impractical ornamental building.

foment VERB stir up (trouble).

fond ADJ 1 liking someone or something; doting. 2 (of hope) unlikely to be fulfilled.
fondly ADV
fondness NOUN

fondant NOUN a soft sugary sweet.

fondle VERB stroke lovingly.

fondue NOUN a dish in which small pieces of food are dipped into hot sauce or oil.

font NOUN 1 a basin in a church, holding water for baptism. 2 (also **fount**) a size and style of printing type.

fontanelle ([US] **fontanel**) NOUN a soft spot where the bones of an infant's skull have not yet grown together.

food NOUN a substance (especially solid) that can be taken into the body of an animal or plant to maintain its life.

foodie NOUN [INFORMAL] a gourmet.

food processor NOUN a machine for chopping and mixing food.

foodstuff NOUN a substance used as food.

fool NOUN **1** a foolish person. **2** a creamy fruit-flavoured pudding. VERB trick, deceive; behave frivolously, joke.

foolery NOUN foolish behaviour.

foolhardy ADJ recklessly bold.

foolish ADJ lacking good sense or judgement; ridiculous.
foolishly ADV
foolishness NOUN

foolproof ADJ unable to go wrong or be misused.

foolscap NOUN a large size of paper.

foot NOUN (PL **feet**) **1** the part of the leg below the ankle; a lower end; a base. **2** a measure of length = 12 inches (30.48 cm). **3** a unit of rhythm in verse. VERB [INFORMAL] pay (a bill).
foot it travel on foot. **put one's foot down** [INFORMAL] be firm in dealing with bad behaviour.

footage NOUN **1** a length of film. **2** length measured in feet.

foot-and-mouth disease NOUN a contagious viral disease of cattle.

football NOUN a large round or elliptical inflated ball; a game played with this.
footballer NOUN

football pools PLURAL NOUN a form of gambling on the results of football matches.

footfall NOUN the sound of footsteps.

foothills PLURAL NOUN low hills near the bottom of a mountain or range.

foothold NOUN a place just wide enough for one's foot; a secure position as a basis for progress.

footing NOUN **1** a secure grip with one's feet: *I lost my footing*. **2** a way of operating; a position: *put us on an equal footing*.

footlights PLURAL NOUN a row of lights along the

front of a stage floor.

footling /foot-ling/ ADJ [INFORMAL] trivial.

footloose ADJ independent, without responsibilities.

footman NOUN a manservant, usually in livery.

footnote NOUN a note printed at the bottom of a page.

footpath NOUN a path for pedestrians; a pavement.

footplate NOUN the platform for the crew of a locomotive.

footprint NOUN an impression left by a foot or shoe.

footsie NOUN [INFORMAL] flirtatious touching of another's feet with one's own.

footsore ADJ with feet sore from walking.

footstep NOUN a step; the sound of this.

footstool NOUN a stool for resting the feet on while sitting.

footwear NOUN shoes, socks, etc.

footwork NOUN a manner of moving or using the feet in sports etc.

fop NOUN an affectedly fashionable man.
foppery NOUN
foppish ADJ

for PREP **1** in support of; on behalf of. **2** to be received or used by. **3** relating to, in respect of. **4** having as a purpose, goal, or destination; on account of. **5** in place of; as a price or penalty of; representing. **6** over (a period or distance).
CONJ [LITERARY] because.

forage /fo-rij/ VERB search for food. NOUN **1** fodder. **2** a search.

foray NOUN a sudden attack, a raid. VERB make a foray.

forbade past of **FORBID**.

forbear VERB (**forbears**, **forbearing**, **forbore**; PAST PARTICIPLE **forborne**) refrain (from).

forbearing ADJ patient, tolerant.
forbearance NOUN

forbid VERB (**forbids**, **forbidding**, **forbade**; PAST PARTICIPLE **forbidden**) order not to do something; refuse to allow.

forbidding ADJ daunting, uninviting.

force NOUN **1** strength, power; someone or something exerting an influence; [PHYSICS] an influence tending to cause movement. **2** violent compulsion. **3** validity. **4** a body of troops or police; an organized group. VERB **1** make one's way by effort or violence. **2** compel. **3** strain; produce with an effort.

forceful ADJ powerful; assertive, strong-willed.
forcefully ADV
forcefulness NOUN

forcemeat NOUN finely chopped seasoned meat used as stuffing.

forceps PLURAL NOUN pincers used in surgery etc.

forcible ADJ done by force.
forcibly ADV

ford NOUN a shallow place where a stream may be crossed by wading or driving through. VERB cross (a stream etc.) in this way.

fore ADJ found or placed in front.
to the fore in front; in or to a noticeable position.

forearm NOUN /**for**-arm/ the arm from the elbow downwards. VERB /for-**arm**/ arm or prepare in advance against possible danger.

forebear (also **forbear**) NOUN an ancestor.

foreboding NOUN a feeling that trouble is coming.

forecast VERB (**forecasts**, **forecasting**, **forecast** or **forecasted**) predict (future weather, events, etc.). NOUN a statement that does this.
forecaster NOUN

forecastle /**fohk**-sŭl/ (also **fo'c's'le**) NOUN the forward part of certain ships.

foreclose VERB take possession of property when a loan secured on it is not repaid.
foreclosure NOUN

forecourt NOUN an open area in front of a building.

forefather (also **foremother**) NOUN an ancestor.

forefinger NOUN the finger next to the thumb.

forefoot NOUN (PL **forefeet**) an animal's front foot.

forefront NOUN the very front.

f

foregather (also **forgather**) VERB [FORMAL] assemble.

forego variant of **FORGO**.

foregoing ADJ preceding.

foregone conclusion NOUN a predictable result.

foreground NOUN the part of a scene etc. that is nearest to the observer.

forehand NOUN (in tennis etc.) a stroke played with the palm of the hand turned forwards. ADJ played in this way.

forehead NOUN the part of the face above the eyes.

foreign ADJ of, from, or in a country that is not one's own; relating to other countries; strange, out of place.

foreigner NOUN a person born in or coming from another country.

foreknowledge NOUN knowledge of a thing before it occurs.

foreleg NOUN an animal's front leg.

forelock NOUN a lock of hair just above the forehead.

foreman NOUN a worker supervising others; the president and spokesman of a jury.

foremost ADJ most advanced in position or rank; most important. ADV first; in the most important position.

forename NOUN a first name.

forenoon NOUN [US] the morning.

forensic /fŏ-**ren**-sik/ ADJ of or used in law courts.

forensic medicine NOUN medical knowledge used in police investigations etc.

foreplay NOUN stimulation preceding sexual intercourse.

forerunner NOUN a person or thing coming before and foreshadowing another.

foresee VERB (**foresees**, **foreseeing**, **foresaw**; PAST PARTICIPLE **foreseen**) be aware of or realize beforehand.

foreseeable ADJ

foreshadow VERB be an advance sign of (a future event etc.).

foreshore NOUN the part of the shore between high and low water marks.

foreshorten VERB show or portray (an object) as shorter than it is, as an effect of perspective.

foresight NOUN the ability to foresee and prepare for future needs.

foreskin NOUN the fold of skin covering the end of the penis.

forest NOUN a large area covered with trees and undergrowth.

forestall VERB prevent or foil by taking action first.

forester NOUN a person in charge of a forest or of growing timber.

forestry NOUN the science of planting and caring for forests.

foretaste NOUN a sample or indication of what is to come.

foretell VERB (**foretells**, **foretelling**, **foretold**) forecast.

forethought NOUN careful planning for the future.

forever (also **for ever**) ADV **1** for all time. **2** continually.

forewarn VERB warn beforehand.

foreword NOUN an introduction to a book.

forfeit NOUN something that has to be paid or given up as a penalty. VERB give or lose as a forfeit. ADJ forfeited. **forfeiture** NOUN

forgather variant of **FOREGATHER**.

forgave past of **FORGIVE**.

forge NOUN a blacksmith's workshop; a furnace where metal is heated. VERB **1** shape (metal) by heating and hammering. **2** make a fraudulent copy of. **3** force one's way. **forger** NOUN

forgery NOUN (PL **forgeries**) the action of forging; something forged.

forget VERB (**forgets**, **forgetting**, **forgot**; PAST PARTICIPLE **forgotten** or [US] **forgot**) cease to remember or think about.

forget oneself behave improperly or uncontrolledly.

forgetful ADJ tending to forget.
forgetfully ADV
forgetfulness NOUN

forget-me-not NOUN a plant with small blue flowers.

forgive VERB (**forgives**, **forgiving**, **forgave**; PAST PARTICIPLE **forgiven**) cease to feel angry or bitter towards or about.
forgivable ADJ
forgiveness NOUN

forgo (also **forego**) VERB (**forgoes**, **forgoing**, **forwent**; PAST PARTICIPLE **forgone**) give up; go without.

fork NOUN **1** a pronged implement for holding food or tool for digging. **2** a point where a road, river, etc., divides; one of its branches. VERB **1** (of a road etc.) divide into two branches; follow one branch. **2** lift or dig with a fork.
fork out [INFORMAL] give money.
forked ADJ

forklift truck NOUN a truck with a forked device for lifting and carrying loads.

forlorn ADJ left alone and unhappy.
forlornly ADV

forlorn hope NOUN a desperate enterprise.

form NOUN **1** shape, appearance; structure. **2** a type or variety; the way in which something exists: *what form did it take?* **3** correct behaviour. **4** a document with blank spaces for information. **5** a school class or year. **6** a bench. VERB create; shape; develop; be the parts of, constitute.

formal ADJ **1** following rules of custom or polite behaviour; of or for official occasions; stiff, prim. **2** of structure or appearance as opposed to content.
formally ADV

formaldehyde /for-**mal**-di-hId/ NOUN a colourless gas used in solution as a preservative and disinfectant.

formalin NOUN a solution of formaldehyde in water, used as a preservative for biological specimens.

formalism NOUN excessive attention to prescribed form or outward appearance.

formality NOUN (PL **formalities**) the state of being formal; (**a formality**) a thing done only because required by a rule.

formalize (also **formalise**) VERB make official.
formalization NOUN

format NOUN the way something is arranged; the shape and size of a book; [COMPUTING] a structure for the processing etc. of data. VERB (**formats**, **formatting**, **formatted**) arrange in a format; prepare (a disk) to receive data.

formation NOUN the action of forming or the process of being formed; a structure or pattern.

formative ADJ influencing development; relating to development.

former ADJ of an earlier period; mentioned first of two.

formerly ADV in former times.

formic acid NOUN a colourless acid in fluid emitted by ants.

formidable ADJ inspiring fear or awe; difficult to achieve.
formidably ADV

formula NOUN (PL **formulae** or **formulas**) **1** symbols showing chemical constituents or a mathematical statement. **2** a fixed series of words for use on social or ceremonial occasions. **3** a list of ingredients. **4** a classification of a racing car.
formulaic ADJ

formulate VERB **1** create, devise. **2** express precisely.
formulation NOUN

fornicate VERB [FORMAL] have sexual intercourse outside marriage.
fornication NOUN
fornicator NOUN

forsake VERB (**forsakes**, **forsaking**, **forsook**; PAST PARTICIPLE **forsaken**) withdraw one's help or companionship from; give up, abandon.

forsooth ADV [ARCHAIC] indeed.

forswear VERB (**forswears, forswearing, forswore**; PAST PARTICIPLE **forsworn**) [FORMAL] renounce.

forsworn ADJ [FORMAL] having sworn falsely.

fort NOUN a fortified building.

forte /for-tay/ NOUN something at which a person excels. ADV [MUSIC] loudly.

forth ADV **1** outwards and forwards. **2** onwards from a point in time.
back and forth to and fro.

forthcoming ADJ **1** about to occur or appear. **2** communicative.

forthright ADJ frank, outspoken.

forthwith ADV immediately.

fortification NOUN a defensive wall or building; the action of fortifying.

fortify VERB (**fortifies, fortifying, fortified**) **1** strengthen against attack. **2** strengthen, invigorate. **3** increase the alcohol content or nutritive value of.

fortissimo ADV [MUSIC] very loudly.

fortitude NOUN courage in bearing pain or trouble.

fortnight NOUN a period of two weeks.

fortnightly ADJ & ADV done, produced, or occurring every two weeks.

Fortran NOUN a computer programming language used especially for scientific work.

fortress NOUN a fortified building or town.

fortuitous ADJ happening by chance.
fortuitously ADV

fortunate ADJ lucky.
fortunately ADV

fortune NOUN **1** chance seen as affecting people's lives; luck; (**fortunes**) what happens to someone. **2** a large amount of money.

fortune-teller NOUN a person who claims to foretell future events in people's lives.

forty ADJ & NOUN four times ten (40, XL).
fortieth ADJ & NOUN

forty winks PLURAL NOUN [INFORMAL] a short sleep.

forum NOUN a place or meeting where a public discussion is held.

forward ADV towards the front; in the direction one is facing or moving; onward, making progress; towards the future; so as to happen sooner. ADJ **1** facing the front or the line of motion. **2** bold, presumptuous. **3** having made faster than usual progress; advanced. **4** concerning the future. NOUN an attacking player in football, hockey, etc. VERB **1** send on (a letter etc.) to another destination. **2** help, advance (interests).
forwardness NOUN

forwards ADV forward.

fosse NOUN a long fortification ditch.

fossil NOUN the petrified remains or traces of a prehistoric animal or plant.
fossilization NOUN (also **fossilisation**)
fossilize VERB (also **fossilise**)

fossil fuel NOUN fuel such as coal or gas, formed from the remains of living organisms.

foster VERB **1** encourage or help the development of. **2** bring up (a child that is not one's own).

foster child NOUN a child brought up by parents other than its own.

foster parent NOUN a person who fosters a child.

fought past and past participle of **FIGHT**.

foul ADJ **1** causing disgust; very bad; dirty. **2** wicked; against the rules of a game. ADV unfairly. NOUN an action that breaks the rules of a game. VERB **1** make dirty. **2** commit a foul against (a sporting opponent). **3** (of a ship) collide with (another); obstruct, entangle.
foully ADV
foulness NOUN

found¹ past and past participle of **FIND**.

found² VERB **1** establish (an institution etc.); set on a base or basis. **2** melt and mould (metal or glass); make (an object) in this way.

foundation NOUN **1** a base, a lowest layer; an underlying principle. **2** the action of founding; an institution etc. that is founded.

f

founder VERB stumble or fall; (of a ship) sink; fail completely. NOUN a person who has founded an institution etc.

foundling NOUN a deserted child of unknown parents.

foundry NOUN (PL **foundries**) a workshop where metal or glass founding is done.

fount NOUN **1** [LITERARY] a fountain; a source. **2** variant of **FONT** (*sense* 2).

fountain NOUN **1** an ornamental structure pumping out a jet of water. **2** a source.

fountainhead NOUN a source.

fountain pen NOUN a pen with a container supplying ink to the nib.

four ADJ & NOUN one more than three (4, IV).

fourfold ADJ & ADV four times as great or as many; having four parts.

four-poster NOUN a bed with four posts that support a canopy.

foursome NOUN a party of four people.

fourteen ADJ & NOUN one more than thirteen (14, XIV).
fourteenth ADJ & NOUN

fourth ADJ next after the third. NOUN **1** a fourth thing, class, etc. **2** a quarter.
fourthly ADV

four-wheel drive NOUN motive power acting on all four wheels of a vehicle.

fowl NOUN a bird kept to supply eggs and meat.

fox NOUN **1** a wild animal of the dog family with a bushy tail; its fur. **2** [INFORMAL] a cunning person. VERB [INFORMAL] baffle, deceive.

foxglove NOUN a tall plant with flowers like glove-fingers.

foxhole NOUN a small trench as a military shelter.

foxhound NOUN a hound

bred to hunt foxes.

foxtrot NOUN a dance with slow and quick steps; music for this.

foyer /foi-yay/ NOUN an entrance hall of a theatre, cinema, or hotel.

fracas /fra-kah/ NOUN (PL **fracas**) a noisy quarrel or disturbance.

fraction NOUN a number that is not a whole number; a small part or amount.
fractional ADJ
fractionally ADV

fractious ADJ irritable; hard to control.
fractiously ADV
fractiousness NOUN

fracture NOUN a break, especially in a bone; the process of breaking. VERB break.

fragile ADJ easily broken or damaged; delicate.
fragility NOUN

fragment NOUN /frag-měnt/ a piece broken off something; an isolated part. VERB /frag-**ment**/ break into fragments.
fragmentation NOUN

fragmentary ADJ consisting of fragments.

fragrance NOUN a pleasant smell.
fragrant ADJ

frail ADJ weak; fragile.
frailty NOUN

frame NOUN **1** a rigid structure supporting other parts; a basis for a system, theory, etc.; a person's body. **2** a rigid structure surrounding a picture, window, etc. **3** a single exposure on a cinema film. **4** a single game of snooker. VERB **1** put or form a frame round. **2** construct. **3** [INFORMAL] arrange false evidence against.
frame of mind a temporary state of mind.

framework NOUN a supporting frame.

franc NOUN a unit of money in Switzerland (formerly in France, Belgium, etc.).

franchise NOUN **1** the right to vote in public elections. **2** authorization to sell a company's goods or services in a certain area. VERB grant a franchise to.

francium NOUN a radioactive metallic

element.

Franco- COMBINING FORM French.

frank ADJ honest in expressing one's thoughts and feelings. VERB mark (a letter etc.) to show that postage has been paid.
frankly ADV
frankness NOUN

frankfurter NOUN a smoked sausage.

frankincense NOUN a sweet-smelling gum burnt as incense.

frantic ADJ wildly agitated or excited.
frantically ADV

fraternal ADJ of a brother or brothers.
fraternally ADV

fraternity NOUN (PL **fraternities**) **1** a group of people with a common interest. **2** brotherhood.

fraternize (also **fraternise**) VERB associate with others in a friendly way.
fraternization NOUN

fratricide NOUN the killing of one's own brother or sister; a person who does this.
fratricidal ADJ

Frau /frow/ NOUN the title of a German married woman.

fraud /frord/ NOUN criminal deception; a dishonest trick; a person carrying this out.
fraudulence NOUN
fraudulent ADJ
fraudulently ADV

fraught /frort/ ADJ causing or suffering anxiety.
fraught with filled with, involving.

Fräulein /**froi**-lyn/ NOUN the title of a German unmarried woman.

fray VERB (of fabric, rope, etc.) unravel, become worn; (of nerves) be strained. NOUN a fight, a conflict.

frazzle NOUN [INFORMAL] an exhausted state: *worn to a frazzle.*
frazzled ADJ

freak NOUN **1** an abnormal person, thing, or event. **2** [INFORMAL] an enthusiast for something specified.
freak out [INFORMAL] behave or cause to behave wildly and irrationally.
freakish ADJ

freaky ADJ

freckle NOUN a light brown spot on the skin. VERB spot or become spotted with freckles. **freckled** ADJ

free ADJ (**freer**, **freest**) **1** not captive, confined, or restricted; not in another's power. **2** not busy or taken up; not in use; not prevented from doing something. **3** not subject to something; without. **4** costing nothing. **5** giving or spending without restraint. ADV at no cost. VERB **1** set free. **2** rid of something undesirable. **a free hand** authority to do what one thinks fit. **make free with** use or handle carelessly and without restraint. **freely** ADV

freebie NOUN [INFORMAL] something provided free.

freebooter NOUN a pirate.

freedom NOUN **1** the state of being free; independence. **2** unrestricted use. **3** honorary citizenship. **4** [ARCHAIC] familiarity.

free fall NOUN unrestricted falling under the force of gravity, especially the part of a parachute descent before the parachute opens.

Freefone (also **Freephone**) NOUN [TRADE MARK] a system whereby an organization pays for incoming calls made by customers.

freehand ADJ (of drawing) done by hand without ruler or compasses etc.

freehold NOUN the holding of land or a house etc. in absolute ownership. ADJ owned in this way. **freeholder** NOUN

free house NOUN a public house not controlled by one brewery.

freelance ADJ self-employed and working for different companies on particular assignments. NOUN (also **freelancer**) a freelance worker.

freeloader NOUN [INFORMAL] a person who lives off others' generosity.

Freemason NOUN a member of a fraternity for mutual help, with elaborate secret rituals.

Freemasonry NOUN

Freephone variant of **FREEFONE.**

Freepost NOUN a system in which postage is paid by the addressee.

free-range ADJ (of hens) allowed to range freely in search of food; (of eggs) from such hens.

freestyle NOUN a swimming race allowing any stroke.

freeway NOUN [US] a motorway.

freewheel VERB ride a bicycle without pedalling.

freeze VERB (**freezes**, **freezing**, **froze**; PAST PARTICIPLE **frozen**) **1** change or be changed from liquid to solid by extreme cold; (of weather etc.) be so cold that water turns to ice; become or make blocked or rigid with ice; be or make very cold; **2** preserve (food etc.) at a very low temperature. **3** become motionless; stop (a moving image); hold (prices or wages) at a fixed level; prevent (assets) from being used; anaesthetize. NOUN **1** the freezing of prices etc. **2** [INFORMAL] a very cold spell.
freezing ADJ

freeze-dry VERB (**freeze-drys**, **freeze-drying**, **freeze-dried**) preserve by freezing and evaporating ice in a vacuum.

freezer NOUN a refrigerated container for preserving and storing food.

freight /frayt/ NOUN goods transported in bulk; a charge for transport. VERB transport (goods).

freighter /fray-tĕ/ NOUN a ship or aircraft carrying mainly freight.

freightliner NOUN [TRADE MARK] a train carrying goods in containers.

French ADJ relating to France. NOUN the language of France.

French bread NOUN white bread in a long crisp loaf.

French dressing NOUN a salad dressing of oil and vinegar.

French fries PLURAL NOUN potato chips.

French horn NOUN a brass wind instrument with a

coiled tube.

French leave NOUN [INFORMAL] absence without permission.

French polish NOUN polish producing a high gloss on wood.

French window NOUN a window reaching to the ground, used also as a door.

frenetic ADJ wild, agitated, uncontrolled.
frenetically ADV

frenzy NOUN (PL **frenzies**) a state of wild excitement or agitation.
frenzied ADJ

frequency NOUN (PL **frequencies**) **1** the rate at which something occurs or is repeated; frequent occurrence. **2** [PHYSICS] the number of cycles of a carrier wave per second; a band or group of these.

frequent ADJ /free-kwĕnt/ happening or appearing often. VERB /fri-**kwent**/ go frequently to, be often in (a place).
frequently ADV

fresco NOUN (PL **frescos** or **frescoes**) a picture painted on a wall or ceiling before the plaster is dry.

fresh ADJ **1** new; not faded or stale; not tired. **2** (of food) not tinned, frozen, etc. **3** (of water) not salty. **4** refreshing; vigorous. **5** [INFORMAL] impudent.
freshen VERB
freshener NOUN
freshly ADV
freshness NOUN

fresher (also **freshman**) NOUN [INFORMAL] a first-year university student.

freshwater ADJ of fresh water, not of the sea.

fret VERB (**frets**, **fretting**, **fretted**) **1** feel or cause to feel anxious. **2** erode, wear away. NOUN each of the ridges on the fingerboard of a guitar etc.

fretful ADJ distressed or irritable.
fretfully ADV

fretsaw NOUN a narrow saw used for fretwork.

fretwork NOUN woodwork cut in decorative patterns.

friable /frI-ă-bĕl/ ADJ easily crumbled.
friability NOUN

friar NOUN a member of certain religious orders of men.

friary NOUN (PL **friaries**) a building occupied by friars.

f

fricassée NOUN a dish of pieces of meat served in a thick white sauce. VERB (**fricassées**, **fricasséeing**, **fricasséed**) make a fricassée of.

friction NOUN **1** the action of rubbing; resistance of one surface to another that moves over it. **2** conflict of people who disagree.
frictional ADJ

Friday NOUN the day following Thursday.

fridge NOUN [INFORMAL] a refrigerator.

fried past and past participle of **FRY**.

friend NOUN a person (other than a relative or lover) with whom one is on terms of mutual affection; a supporter of a cause; a person on the same side in a conflict.
friendship NOUN

friendly ADJ (**friendlier**, **friendliest**) kind, pleasant; (of people or their relationship) affectionate; (of a game) not part of a serious competition; favourable, not harmful.
friendliness NOUN

frieze /freez/ NOUN a band of decoration round a wall.

frigate NOUN a small fast naval ship.

fright NOUN sudden great fear; an experience of this.
look a fright [INFORMAL] be very untidy or grotesque.

frighten VERB make afraid; deter through fear.

frightened ADJ afraid.

frightful ADJ very bad or unpleasant; [INFORMAL] extreme (especially of something bad).
frightfully ADV
frightfulness NOUN

frigid ADJ intensely cold; very cold in manner; unresponsive sexually.
frigidity NOUN

frill NOUN a gathered or pleated strip of material attached at one edge to a garment etc. for decoration; [INFORMAL] an

unnecessary extra feature or luxury.
frilled ADJ
frilly ADJ

fringe NOUN **1** an ornamental edging of hanging threads; front hair cut short to hang over the forehead. **2** the outer part of an area, group, etc. ADJ (of theatre etc.) unconventional. VERB give or form a fringe to.

fringe benefit NOUN a benefit provided in addition to wages.

frippery NOUN showy or unnecessary finery or ornament.

frisbee NOUN [TRADE MARK] a plastic disc for skimming through the air as an outdoor game.

frisk VERB **1** leap or skip playfully. **2** feel over or search (a person) for concealed weapons etc. NOUN **1** a playful leap or skip. **2** a search by frisking.

frisky ADJ (**friskier**, **friskiest**) lively, playful.
friskily ADV
friskiness NOUN

frisson /free-son/ NOUN a thrill.

frith variant of **FIRTH**.

fritter VERB waste (money or time) on trivial things. NOUN a fried batter-coated slice of fruit or meat etc.

frivolous ADJ not serious; purely for or interested in pleasure.
frivolity NOUN
frivolously ADV

frizz VERB form (hair) into a mass of small curls; curl in this way. NOUN such curls.
frizziness NOUN
frizzy ADJ

frizzle VERB sizzle while frying; fry (food) until crisp.

frock NOUN a woman's or girl's dress.

frock coat NOUN a man's long-skirted coat, not cut away in front.

frog NOUN a small amphibian with long web-footed hind legs.
frog in one's throat [INFORMAL] hoarseness.

frogman NOUN a swimmer with a rubber suit and oxygen supply for working under water.

frogmarch VERB hustle (a person) forcibly, holding

the arms.

frogspawn NOUN the eggs of a frog, surrounded by transparent jelly.

frolic VERB (**frolicks**, **frolicking**, **frolicked**) play about in a lively way. NOUN such play.

from PREP **1** having as the starting point, source, material, or cause. **2** as separated, distinguished, or unlike.

fromage frais /from-a*zh* fray/ NOUN a smooth low-fat soft cheese.

frond NOUN a long leaf or leaf-like part of a fern, palm tree, etc.

front NOUN **1** the side or part normally nearer or towards the spectator or line of motion; any side of a building. **2** a battle line. **3** an outward appearance; a cover for secret activities. **4** a boundary between warm and cold air-masses. **5** a promenade at a seaside resort. ADJ of or at the front. VERB **1** face, have the front towards; give (an object) a front of a specified type. **2** lead (a group etc.). **3** act as a cover for secret activities.
in front at the front.

frontage NOUN the front of a building; land bordering this.

frontal ADJ of or on the front.

frontbencher NOUN an MP entitled to sit on the front benches in Parliament, reserved for ministers and the Shadow Cabinet.

frontier NOUN a boundary between countries.

frontispiece NOUN an illustration opposite the title-page of a book.

front-runner NOUN the contestant most likely to win.

frost NOUN small white ice crystals on grass etc.; a period cold enough for these to form. VERB cover or be covered with frost.

frostbite NOUN injury to body tissues due to freezing.
frostbitten ADJ

frosted ADJ (of glass) having its surface roughened to make it opaque.

frosting NOUN [US] sugar

icing.

frosty ADJ (**frostier**, **frostiest**) **1** cold with frost; covered with frost. **2** unfriendly.
frostily ADV
frostiness NOUN

froth NOUN **1** a mass of small bubbles. **2** trivial ideas or talk.
VERB produce froth.
frothy ADJ

frown VERB wrinkle one's brow in thought or disapproval. NOUN a frowning movement or look.
frown on disapprove of.

frowsty /frŏw-sti/ ADJ (**frowstier**, **frowstiest**) stuffy, oppressive.

frowzy /frow-zi/ (also **frowsy**) ADJ (**frowzier**, **frowziest**) scruffy, dingy.

froze, **frozen** past and past participle of **FREEZE**.

fructose NOUN a sugar found in honey and fruit.

frugal ADJ economical; simple and costing little.
frugality NOUN
frugally ADV

fruit NOUN **1** the seed-containing part of a plant; this used as food. **2** (**fruits**) the product of labour. VERB produce fruit.
bear fruit have good results.

fruiterer NOUN a shopkeeper selling fruit.

fruitful ADJ producing much fruit or good results.
fruitfully ADV
fruitfulness NOUN

fruition /froo-ish-ŏn/ NOUN the fulfilment of a hope, plan, or project.

fruitless ADJ producing little or no result.
fruitlessly ADV
fruitlessness NOUN

fruit machine NOUN a coin-operated gambling machine.

fruity ADJ (**fruitier**, **fruitiest**) **1** like or containing fruit. **2** (of a voice) deep and rich.
fruitiness NOUN

frump NOUN a dowdy woman.
frumpish ADJ
frumpy ADJ

frustrate VERB prevent from achieving something or from being achieved.

frustration NOUN

fry[1] VERB (**fries**, **frying**, **fried**) cook or be cooked in very hot fat; be very hot. NOUN a fried meal.
fryer NOUN

fry[2] NOUN (PL **fry**) young fish.
small fry unimportant or powerless people.

ft ABBREV foot or feet (as a measure).

FTSE ABBREV Financial Times Stock Exchange 100 share index.

fuchsia /few-shŭ/ NOUN a plant with drooping flowers.

fuck VERB [VULGAR SLANG] have sexual intercourse (with).
fuck off go away.

fucking ADJ & ADV [VULGAR SLANG] damned.

fuddle VERB confuse or stupefy, especially with alcoholic drink.

fuddy-duddy NOUN (PL **fuddy-duddies**) [INFORMAL] a person who has old-fashioned views.

fudge NOUN **1** a soft sweet made of milk, sugar, and butter. **2** a makeshift way of dealing with a problem. VERB present or deal with in an inadequate and evasive way.

fuel NOUN material burnt as a source of energy; something that increases anger etc. VERB (**fuels**, **fuelling**, **fuelled**; [US] **fueling**, **fueled**) supply with fuel.

fug NOUN [INFORMAL] a stuffy atmosphere in a room etc.
fugginess NOUN
fuggy ADJ

fugitive NOUN a person who is fleeing or escaping. ADJ passing or vanishing quickly.

fugue /fewg/ NOUN a musical composition using repeated themes in increasingly complex patterns.

fulcrum /fuul-krŭm/ NOUN (PL **fulcra** or **fulcrums**) the point of support on which a lever pivots.

fulfil ([US] **fulfill**) VERB (**fulfils**, **fulfilling**, **fulfilled**; [US] **fulfills**) accomplish, carry out (a task); satisfy, do what is required by (a contract etc.).
fulfil oneself develop and

use one's abilities fully.
fulfilment NOUN

full ADJ **1** holding or containing as much as is possible; having a lot of something; obsessed with something. **2** complete. **3** plump; (of a garment) using much material in folds or gathers; (of a tone) deep and mellow. ADV directly; very.
fully ADV
fullness NOUN

fullback NOUN (in football etc.) a defensive player positioned near the goal.

full-blooded ADJ vigorous, hearty.

full-blown ADJ fully developed.

full moon NOUN the moon with the whole disc illuminated.

full-scale ADJ (of a model etc.) the same size as what it represents.

full stop NOUN a dot used as a punctuation mark at the end of a sentence or abbreviation; a complete stop.

fulminate VERB protest loudly and bitterly.
fulmination NOUN

fulsome ADJ excessively flattering.

fumble VERB use one's hands clumsily; grope about.

fume NOUN pungent smoke or vapour. VERB **1** emit fumes; subject to fumes. **2** be very angry.

fumigate VERB disinfect with chemical fumes.
fumigation NOUN
fumigator NOUN

fun NOUN light-hearted amusement.
make fun of cause people to laugh at.

function NOUN **1** the special activity or purpose of a person or thing. **2** an important ceremony. **3** (in mathematics) a relation involving variables; a quantity whose value depends on varying values of others. VERB perform a function; work, operate.

functional ADJ of uses or purposes; practical, not decorative; working, operating.
functionally ADV

functionary NOUN (PL **functionaries**) an official.

fund NOUN a sum of money for a special purpose; (**funds**) financial resources; a stock, a supply. VERB provide with money.

fundamental ADJ basic; essential. NOUN a fundamental fact or principle.
fundamentally ADV

fundamentalist NOUN a person who upholds a strict or literal interpretation of traditional religious beliefs.
fundamentalism NOUN

fundholder NOUN a medical practice controlling its own budget.

funeral NOUN a ceremony of burial or cremation.

funerary ADJ of or used for a burial or funeral.

funereal ADJ mournful, dismal.

funfair NOUN a fair consisting of amusements and sideshows.

fungicide NOUN a substance that kills fungus.
fungicidal ADJ

fungus NOUN (PL **fungi**) a plant without green colouring matter (e.g. a mushroom or mould).
fungal ADJ
fungous ADJ

funicular /fyoo-**nik**-guu-lŭ/ ADJ (of a railway) operating by cable up and down a mountainside.

funk NOUN [INFORMAL] dance music with a heavy rhythmical beat.
funky ADJ

funnel NOUN **1** a tube with a wide top for pouring liquid into small openings. **2** a chimney on a steam engine or ship. VERB (**funnels**, **funnelling**, **funnelled**; [US] **funneling**, **funneled**) guide (as) through a funnel.

funny ADJ (**funnier**, **funniest**) **1** causing amusement. **2** puzzling, odd.
funnily ADV

funny bone NOUN [INFORMAL] the part of the elbow where a very sensitive nerve passes.

fur NOUN **1** the short fine hair of certain animals; a skin with this used for clothing. **2** a coating on the inside of a kettle etc. VERB (**furs**, **furring**, **furred**) cover or become covered with fur.

furbish VERB clean up; renovate.

furious ADJ very angry; intense, violent.
furiously ADV

furl VERB roll up and fasten (a piece of fabric).

furlong NOUN an eighth of a mile.

furlough /fer-loh/ NOUN leave of absence.

furnace NOUN an enclosed fireplace for intense heating or smelting.

furnish VERB **1** equip with furniture. **2** supply (someone) with (something).

furnishings PLURAL NOUN furniture and fitments etc.

furniture NOUN movable articles (e.g. chairs, beds) for use in a room.

furore /few-**ror**-i/ ([US] **furor**) NOUN an outbreak of public anger or excitement.

furrier /**fu**-ri-ĕ/ NOUN a person who deals in furs.

furrow NOUN a long cut in the ground; a groove. VERB make furrows in.

furry ADJ (**furrier**, **furriest**) like fur; covered with fur.
furriness NOUN

further ADV & ADJ (also **farther**) **1** at, to, or over a greater distance; more distant. **2** to a greater extent. **3** in addition. VERB help the progress of.

furtherance NOUN assistance, advancement.

further education NOUN education provided for people above school age but usually below degree level.

furthermore ADV moreover.

furthest (also **farthest**) ADJ most distant. ADV at, to, or by the greatest distance.

furtive ADJ stealthy, secretive.
furtively ADV
furtiveness NOUN

fury NOUN (PL **furies**) wild anger, rage; violence.

furze NOUN gorse.

fuse VERB **1** blend (metals etc.); become blended;

unite. **2** (of an electrical appliance) stop working when a fuse melts. **3** fit (an appliance) with a fuse. NOUN **1** a strip of wire placed in an electric circuit to melt and interrupt the current when the circuit is overloaded. **2** (also **fuze**) a length of easily burnt material for igniting a bomb or explosive.
fusibility NOUN
fusible ADJ

fuselage NOUN the body of an aeroplane.

fusilier /fyoo-zi-**leer**/ NOUN a soldier of certain regiments.

fusillade NOUN a continuous discharge of firearms.

fusion NOUN **1** the process or result of joining two or more things together to form a whole. **2** the union of atomic nuclei, with release of energy. **3** music that is a mixture of different styles.

fuss NOUN unnecessary excitement or activity; a vigorous protest. VERB show excessive concern; move about restlessly; disturb.

fussy ADJ (**fussier**, **fussiest**) **1** hard to please. **2** with much unnecessary detail or decoration.
fussily ADV
fussiness NOUN

fustian NOUN thick twilled cotton cloth.

fusty ADJ (**fustier**, **fustiest**) **1** smelling stale and stuffy. **2** old-fashioned.
fustiness NOUN

futile ADJ pointless, useless.
futilely ADV
futility NOUN

futon /foo-ton/ NOUN a Japanese quilted mattress laid on the floor for use as a bed; this with a wooden frame convertible into a sofa.

future NOUN **1** time still to come; what may happen then. **2** a prospect of success. **3** (**futures**) goods or shares bought at an agreed price but paid for later. ADJ of time to come.
in future from now on.

futuristic ADJ with very modern technology or design.
futuristically ADV

fuze variant of **FUSE** (in sense 2 of the noun).

fuzz NOUN **1** a fluffy or frizzy mass; a blur. **2** [INFORMAL] the police.

fuzzy ADJ (**fuzzier**, **fuzziest**) **1** fluffy or frizzy. **2** indistinct.
fuzzily ADV
fuzziness NOUN

Gg

g

G (also **g**) NOUN (PL **Gs** or **G's**) the seventh letter of the alphabet. ABBREV **1** the force exerted by the earth's gravitational field. **2** (**g**) grams.

gabble VERB talk quickly and indistinctly.

gable NOUN a triangular upper part of a wall, between sloping roofs.
gabled ADJ

gad VERB (**gads**, **gadding**, **gadded**) (**gad about**) [INFORMAL] go about idly in search of pleasure.

gadabout NOUN [INFORMAL] an idle pleasure-seeker.

gadfly NOUN (PL **gadflies**) a fly that bites cattle.

gadget NOUN a small mechanical device or tool.
gadgetry NOUN

gadolinium NOUN a metallic element.

Gaelic /gay-lik, ga-lik/ NOUN the Celtic language of the Scots or Irish.

gaff NOUN a hooked stick for landing large fish.

gaffe NOUN an embarrassing blunder.

gaffer NOUN [INFORMAL] **1** a person in charge of others. **2** an old man.

gag NOUN **1** something put over a person's mouth to silence them. **2** a joke. VERB (**gags**, **gagging**, **gagged**) **1** put a gag on; deprive of freedom of speech. **2** retch.

gaga /gah-gah/ ADJ [INFORMAL] slightly mad; senile.

gage US spelling of **GAUGE**.

gaggle NOUN a flock of geese; [INFORMAL] a disorderly group.

gaiety NOUN (PL **gaieties**) light-hearted and cheerful mood or behaviour.

gaily ADV **1** cheerfully. **2** thoughtlessly.

gain VERB **1** obtain, secure; acquire gradually; profit. **2** reach (a place). **3** increase in value. **4** (of a clock) become fast. NOUN an increase in wealth or value; something gained. **gain on** get nearer to (someone or something pursued).

gainful ADJ profitable. **gainfully** ADV

gainsay VERB (**gainsays, gainsaying, gainsaid**) [FORMAL] deny, contradict.

gait NOUN a manner of walking or running.

gaiter NOUN a covering for the lower leg.

gala /gah-lă/ NOUN an occasion with special entertainments; a sports gathering, especially for swimming.

galaxy NOUN (PL **galaxies**) a system of stars, especially (**the Galaxy**) the one containing the sun and the earth. **galactic** ADJ

gale NOUN a very strong wind; a noisy outburst.

gall /gawl/ NOUN **1** boldness, impudence. **2** [ARCHAIC] bile. **3** something very hurtful. **4** a sore made by rubbing; an abnormal growth on a plant. VERB make sore by rubbing; annoy.

gallant ADJ brave; chivalrous. **gallantly** ADV **gallantry** NOUN

gall bladder NOUN an organ attached to the liver, storing bile.

galleon NOUN a large Spanish sailing ship of the 15th-17th centuries.

galleria /ga-lĕ-**ree**-ă/ NOUN a group of small shops under one roof.

gallery NOUN (PL **galleries**) **1** a building for displaying works of art. **2** a balcony in a theatre or hall. **3** a long room or passage.

galley NOUN (PL **galleys**) **1** an ancient ship, usually rowed by slaves. **2** a kitchen on a boat or aircraft. **3** (also **galley proof**) a printer's proof before division into pages.

Gallic ADJ **1** French. **2** of

ancient Gaul.

galling /gawl-ing/ ADJ annoying.

gallium NOUN a metallic element.

gallivant VERB [INFORMAL] go about looking for fun.

gallon NOUN a measure for liquids = 8 pints (4.546 litres, or 3.785 litres in the USA).

gallop NOUN a horse's fastest pace; a ride at this pace. VERB (**gallops**, **galloping**, **galloped**) go at a gallop; go fast.

gallows NOUN a framework with a noose for hanging criminals.

gallstone NOUN a small hard mass forming in the gall bladder.

Gallup poll NOUN [TRADE MARK] an assessment of public opinion by questioning a sample group.

galore ADV in plenty.

galosh NOUN a rubber overshoe.

galvanize (also **galvanise**) VERB 1 stimulate into activity. 2 coat (iron or steel) with zinc.

galvanometer NOUN an instrument measuring electric current.

gambit NOUN an opening move; [CHESS] an opening involving the sacrifice of a pawn.

gamble VERB play games of chance for money; risk (money etc.) in hope of gain. NOUN an act of gambling; a risky undertaking.
gambler NOUN

gambol VERB (**gambols**, **gambolling**, **gambolled**; [US] **gamboling**, **gamboled**) jump about playfully.

game NOUN 1 a form of play or sport; a period of play with a closing score. 2 [INFORMAL] a secret plan: *what's your game?* 3 wild animals hunted for sport or food; their flesh as food. ADJ 1 willing, eager. 2 [DATED] lame.
gamely ADV

gamekeeper NOUN a person employed to protect and breed game.

gamelan /gam-ĕ-lan/ NOUN a SE Asian percussion orchestra.

gamesmanship NOUN the

art of winning games by upsetting an opponent's confidence.

gamete NOUN a reproductive cell.

gamine /ga-meen/ NOUN a girl with mischievous or boyish charm.

gamma NOUN the third letter of the Greek alphabet (Γ, γ); a third-class mark.

gammon NOUN cured or smoked ham.

gammy ADJ [INFORMAL] lame, injured.

gamut /gam-ŭt/ NOUN the whole range or scope: *the whole gamut of emotions.*

gamy ADJ (**gamier**, **gamiest**) smelling or tasting of game kept till it is high.

gander NOUN **1** a male goose. **2** [INFORMAL] a look, a glance.

gang NOUN an organized group, especially of criminals or workers.
gang up (on) form a group (to intimidate someone).

gangling ADJ tall and awkward.

ganglion NOUN (PL **ganglia** or **ganglions**) **1** a group of nerve cells. **2** a cyst on a tendon.

gangplank NOUN a plank for walking to or from a boat.

gang rape NOUN the rape of one person by several men.

gangrene NOUN decay of body tissue.
gangrenous ADJ

gangster NOUN a member of a gang of violent criminals.

gangway NOUN **1** a passage, especially between rows of seats. **2** a movable bridge from a ship to land.

gannet NOUN a large seabird; [INFORMAL] a greedy person.

gantry NOUN (PL **gantries**) an overhead framework supporting railway signals, road signs, a crane etc.

gaol etc. variant of **JAIL** etc.

gap NOUN **1** a space, an opening; an interval. **2** a deficiency; a wide difference.
gappy ADJ

g

gape VERB open one's mouth wide; be wide open.

garage NOUN a building for storing a vehicle; an establishment selling petrol or repairing and selling vehicles.

garb NOUN clothing. VERB clothe.

garbage NOUN rubbish.

garbled ADJ (of a message or story) distorted or confused.

garden NOUN a piece of cultivated ground by a house; (**gardens**) ornamental public grounds. VERB tend a garden.
gardener NOUN

gargantuan ADJ gigantic.

gargle VERB wash the throat with liquid held there by breathing out through it. NOUN an act of gargling; a liquid for this.

gargoyle NOUN a waterspout in the form of a grotesque carved face on a building.

garish /gair-ish/ ADJ too bright and harsh.
garishly ADV

garland NOUN a wreath of flowers as a decoration. VERB decorate with garlands.

garlic NOUN an onion-like plant.
garlicky ADJ

garment NOUN a piece of clothing.

garner VERB gather, collect.

garnet NOUN a red semi-precious stone.

garnish VERB decorate (food). NOUN something used for garnishing.

garotte variant of **GARROTTE**.

garret NOUN an attic.

garrison NOUN troops stationed in a town or fort; the building they occupy. VERB guard (a town etc) with a garrison.

garrotte (also **garotte**; [US] **garrote**) NOUN a wire or a metal collar used to strangle a victim. VERB strangle with this.

garrulous ADJ talkative.
garrulously ADV
garrulousness NOUN

garter NOUN a band worn round the leg to keep up a stocking; (**the Garter**) the highest order of English knighthood.

gas NOUN (PL **gases**) **1** an air-like substance (not a solid or liquid); such a substance used as fuel. **2** [US] petrol. VERB (**gasses**, **gassing**, **gassed**) **1** attack or kill with poisonous gas. **2** [INFORMAL] talk at length.

gas chamber NOUN a room filled with poisonous gas to kill people.

gaseous /gay-see-ŭs, ga-see-ŭs/ ADJ of or like a gas.

gash NOUN a long deep cut. VERB make a gash in.

gasify VERB (**gasifies**, **gasifying**, **gasified**) change into gas.

gasket NOUN a piece of rubber etc. sealing a joint between metal surfaces. **blow a gasket** [INFORMAL] lose one's temper.

gas mask NOUN a device worn over the face as protection against poisonous gas.

gasoline NOUN [US] petrol.

gasp VERB draw in breath sharply; speak breathlessly. NOUN a sharp intake of breath.

gastric ADJ of the stomach.

gastro-enteritis NOUN inflammation of the stomach and intestines.

gastropod NOUN a mollusc, such as a snail, that moves by means of a single muscular foot.

gate NOUN **1** a movable barrier in a wall or fence; an entrance. **2** the number of spectators paying to attend a sporting event; the amount of money taken.

-gate COMBINING FORM denoting a scandal involving deception and concealment.

gateau /gat-oh/ NOUN (PL **gateaux** or **gateaus**) a large rich cream cake.

gatecrash VERB go to (a private party) uninvited. **gatecrasher** NOUN

gateway NOUN an opening closed by a gate; a means of entry or access.

gather VERB **1** come or bring together; collect; pick up; summon up: *gather strength.* **2** conclude, infer. **3** draw (fabric) together in folds by running a thread through it. NOUN a small fold in a garment.

gathering NOUN people assembled.

gauche /gohsh/ ADJ socially awkward.
gaucherie NOUN

gaucho /gow-choh/ NOUN (PL **gauchos**) a South American cowboy.

gaudy /gaw-di/ ADJ (**gaudier, gaudiest**) showy or bright, but tasteless.
gaudily ADV
gaudiness NOUN

gauge /gayj/ ([US] **gage**) NOUN **1** a measuring device; a standard measure of thickness etc. **2** the distance between the rails of a railway track. VERB estimate; measure.

gaunt /gawnt/ ADJ lean and haggard; grim, desolate.

gauntlet NOUN a glove with a long wide cuff. **run the gauntlet** be exposed to something dangerous or unpleasant.

gauss /gowss/ NOUN (PL **gauss**) a unit of magnetic flux density.

gauze /gawz/ NOUN thin transparent fabric; fine wire mesh.
gauzy ADJ

gave past of **GIVE**.

gavel NOUN a mallet used by an auctioneer or chairman to call for attention.

gawky ADJ (**gawkier, gawkiest**) awkward and ungainly.

gay ADJ **1** homosexual. **2** [DATED] merry, light-hearted; brightly coloured. NOUN a homosexual person.
gayness NOUN

gaze VERB look long and steadily. NOUN a long steady look.

gazebo /gă-zee-boh/ NOUN (PL **gazebos**) a summer house with a wide view.

gazelle NOUN a small antelope.

gazette NOUN an official journal of an institution; the title of some newspapers.

gazetteer NOUN an index of places, rivers, etc.

gazump VERB [INFORMAL] make a higher offer for a

property than (someone whose offer had been accepted).

GB ABBREV Great Britain.

Gb ABBREV gigabyte(s).

GBH ABBREV grievous bodily harm.

GC ABBREV George Cross.

GCE ABBREV General Certificate of Education.

GCSE ABBREV General Certificate of Secondary Education.

GDP ABBREV gross domestic product.

gear NOUN **1** a set of toothed wheels working together to change the speed of machinery; a particular adjustment of these: *top gear.* **2** [INFORMAL] equipment; belongings, clothes. VERB **1** design or adjust the gears in (a machine). **2** intend or direct to a particular purpose.
in gear with the gear mechanism engaged.

gearbox NOUN a case enclosing a gear mechanism.

gecko NOUN (PL **geckos**) a tropical lizard.

geese pl. of **GOOSE**.

Geiger counter /gy-ger/ NOUN a device for measuring radioactivity.

geisha /gay-shă/ NOUN a Japanese hostess trained to entertain men.

gel /jel/ NOUN a jelly-like substance. VERB set; become firm or fixed.

gelatin (also **gelatine**) NOUN a clear substance made by boiling bones and used in making jelly etc.
gelatinous ADJ

geld VERB castrate.

gelding NOUN a castrated horse.

gelignite NOUN an explosive containing nitroglycerine.

gem NOUN a precious stone; something of great beauty or excellence.

gender NOUN **1** the state of being male or female. **2** the classification of nouns as masculine, feminine, or neuter.

gene NOUN each of the factors controlling heredity, carried by a chromosome.

genealogy NOUN (PL **genealogies**) a line of

g

descent; the study of family pedigrees.
genealogical ADJ
genealogist NOUN

genera pl. of **GENUS**.

general ADJ **1** of or involving all or most parts, things, or people; not detailed or specific. **2** (in titles) chief. NOUN an army officer next below field marshal.
in general 1 mostly, with few exceptions. **2** as a whole, all together: *things in general.*
generally ADV

general election NOUN an election of parliamentary representatives from the whole country.

generality NOUN (PL **generalities**) **1** a general statement; the state of being general. **2** the majority.

generalize (also **generalise**) VERB **1** speak in general terms. **2** make generally available.
generalization NOUN

general practitioner NOUN a community doctor treating cases of all kinds.

generate VERB bring into existence, produce.

generation NOUN **1** all the people born at roughly the same time; one stage in the descent of a family; a period of about 30 years. **2** the action of producing or generating.
generational ADJ

generator NOUN a machine converting mechanical energy into electricity.

generic /jĕn-e-rik/ ADJ of a whole genus or group.
generically ADV

generous ADJ giving freely; large, plentiful.
generosity NOUN
generously ADV

genesis NOUN a beginning or origin.

genetic ADJ of genes or genetics; of origin. NOUN (**genetics**) the science of heredity.
genetically ADV
geneticist NOUN

genetic engineering NOUN manipulation of DNA to change hereditary features.

genetic fingerprinting NOUN identifying

individuals by their DNA patterns.

genial /jee-ni-ăl/ ADJ kind and cheerful; (of climate etc.) pleasantly mild.
geniality NOUN
genially ADV

genie NOUN (PL **genii**) a spirit in Arabian folklore.

genital ADJ of animal reproduction or sex organs. NOUN (**genitals** or **genitalia**) the external sex organs.

genitive NOUN the grammatical case expressing possession or source.

genius NOUN (PL **geniuses**) exceptionally great intellectual or creative power; a person with this.

genocide NOUN deliberate extermination of a race of people.

genre /*zh*ahnr/ NOUN a style of art or literature.

genteel ADJ polite and refined, often affectedly so.
genteelly ADV
gentility NOUN

gentian /jen-shăn/ NOUN an alpine plant with deep blue flowers.

Gentile NOUN a non-Jewish person.

gentle ADJ kind and mild; (of climate etc.) moderate, not harsh.
gentleness NOUN
gently ADV

gentleman NOUN (PL **gentlemen**) a well-mannered man; a man of good social position.
gentlemanly ADJ

gentrify VERB (**gentrifies**, **gentrifying**, **gentrified**) alter (an area) to conform to middle-class tastes.

gentry NOUN people next below nobility.

genuflect VERB bend the knee and lower the body, especially in worship.

genuine ADJ really what it is said to be.
genuinely ADV
genuineness NOUN

genus NOUN (PL **genera**) a group of similar animals or plants, usually containing several species; a kind.

geocentric ADJ having the earth as a centre; as

g

viewed from the earth's centre.

geode /jee-ohd/ NOUN a cavity lined with crystals; a rock containing this.

geodesy /jee-o-de-si/ NOUN the study of the earth's shape and size.

g **geography** NOUN the study of the earth's physical features, climate, etc.; the features and arrangement of a place.
geographer NOUN
geographical ADJ
geographically ADV

geology NOUN the study of the earth's structure; the rocks etc. of a district.
geological ADJ
geologically ADV
geologist NOUN

geometry NOUN the branch of mathematics dealing with lines, angles, surfaces, and solids.
geometric ADJ
geometrical ADJ
geometrically ADV

Georgian ADJ relating to the time of the Georges, kings of England, especially 1714–1830.

geranium NOUN a cultivated flowering plant.

gerbil NOUN a rodent with long hind legs, often kept as a pet.

geriatric ADJ of old people. NOUN an old person; (**geriatrics**) the branch of medicine dealing with the diseases and care of old people.

germ NOUN **1** a micro-organism causing disease. **2** a portion of an organism capable of developing into a new organism; a basis from which a thing may develop.

German NOUN a person from Germany; the language of Germany. ADJ relating to Germany.

germane ADJ relevant.

Germanic ADJ **1** of the Scandinavians, Anglo-Saxons, or Germans. **2** having characteristics commonly associated with Germans.

germanium NOUN a semi-metallic element.

German measles (also **rubella**) NOUN a disease like mild measles.

germinate VERB begin or cause to grow.
germination NOUN

gerontology NOUN the study of ageing.

gerrymander VERB arrange boundaries of (a constituency) to gain unfair electoral advantage.

gerund NOUN [GRAMMAR] a verbal noun (ending in *-ing* in English).

Gestapo NOUN the German secret police of the Nazi regime.

gestation NOUN the period when a foetus is developing in the womb.

gesticulate VERB make expressive movements with the hands and arms.
gesticulation NOUN

gesture NOUN **1** a movement designed to convey a meaning. **2** something done to display good intentions etc., with no practical value. VERB make a gesture.

get VERB (**gets**, **getting**, **got**; [US] **gotten**) **1** come to possess; receive; succeed in attaining. **2** fetch. **3** experience (pain etc.); catch (a disease). **4** bring or come into a specified state; arrive or bring somewhere. **5** persuade, induce, or order: *get him to come.* **6** capture. **7** [INFORMAL] understand. **8** [INFORMAL] annoy.
get by manage to survive. **get off** [INFORMAL] be acquitted. **get on** **1** make progress. **2** be friendly. **3** [INFORMAL] grow old. **get over** recover from. **get round** **1** overcome (a difficulty). **2** persuade. **get up** **1** get out of bed; stand up. **2** organize, arrange. **get up to** [INFORMAL] be involved in (something secret or disreputable).

getaway NOUN an escape after a crime.

get-together NOUN a social gathering.

get-up NOUN [INFORMAL] an outfit.

geyser /gee-zer/ NOUN **1** a spring spouting hot water or steam. **2** a water heater.

ghastly ADJ (**ghastlier**, **ghastliest**) **1** causing

horror; [INFORMAL] very unpleasant. **2** very pale.
ghastliness NOUN

ghee /gee/ NOUN clarified butter used in Indian cooking.

gherkin NOUN a small pickled cucumber.

g

ghetto NOUN (PL **ghettos**) an area in which members of a minority racial etc. group are segregated.

ghetto blaster NOUN [INFORMAL] a large portable stereo radio etc.

ghost NOUN an apparition of a dead person; a faint trace. VERB write as a ghost writer.

ghostly ADJ like a ghost; eerie.
ghostliness NOUN

ghostwriter NOUN a person who writes a book etc. for another to pass off as his or her own.

ghoul /gool/ NOUN an evil spirit said to rob graves and eat corpses; a person morbidly interested in death and injury.
ghoulish ADJ

GHQ ABBREV general headquarters.

giant NOUN (in fairy tales) a being of superhuman size; an abnormally large person, animal, or thing; a person of outstanding ability. ADJ very large.

gibber VERB make meaningless sounds in shock or terror.

gibberish NOUN unintelligible talk; nonsense.

gibbet NOUN a gallows.

gibbon NOUN a long-armed ape.

gibe (also **jibe**) VERB jeer. NOUN a jeering remark.

giblets /jib-lits/ PLURAL NOUN the liver, heart, gizzard, and neck of a chicken, turkey, etc.

giddy ADJ (**giddier**, **giddiest**) having or causing the feeling that everything is spinning; excitable, flighty.
giddiness NOUN

gift NOUN **1** something given or received without payment; [INFORMAL] a very easy task. **2** a natural talent.

gifted ADJ having great natural ability.

gig /gig/ NOUN **1** a light two-wheeled horse-drawn carriage. **2** [INFORMAL] a live performance by popular or jazz musicians.

giga- COMBINING FORM one thousand million, 10^9.

gigantic ADJ very large.

giggle VERB laugh quietly. NOUN such a laugh.
giggly ADJ

gigolo /jig-ŏ-loh/ NOUN (PL **gigolos**) a man paid by a woman to be her escort or lover.

gild VERB cover with a thin layer of gold or gold paint.

gill /jil/ NOUN one-quarter of a pint.

gills /gilz/ NOUN **1** the organ with which a fish breathes. **2** the vertical plates on the underside of a mushroom.

gilt ADJ gilded. NOUN **1** gold leaf or paint used in gilding. **2** a gilt-edged investment.

gilt-edged ADJ (of an investment etc.) very safe.

gimbals /jim-bălz/ PLURAL NOUN a device for keeping instruments horizontal on a ship.

gimcrack /jim-krak/ ADJ cheap and poorly made.

gimlet /gim-lit/ NOUN a small tool with a screw-like tip for boring holes.

gimmick NOUN a trick or device to attract attention.
gimmicky ADJ

gin NOUN an alcoholic spirit flavoured with juniper berries.

ginger NOUN a hot-tasting root, used as a spice. ADJ reddish-yellow in colour. **ginger up** stimulate or enliven.

gingerbread NOUN ginger-flavoured cake.

ginger group NOUN a group urging a more active policy.

gingerly ADV in a cautious manner.

gingham /ging-ăm/ NOUN cotton fabric with a checked or striped pattern.

gingivitis /jin-ji-vy-tiss/ NOUN inflammation of the gums.

ginseng /jin-seng/ NOUN a medicinal plant with a

fragrant root.

gipsy variant of **GYPSY**.

giraffe NOUN a long-necked African animal.

gird VERB [LITERARY] encircle with a belt or band.

girder NOUN a metal beam supporting a structure.

g

girdle NOUN a belt; an elastic corset; something surrounding something else. VERB surround; encircle.

girl NOUN a female child; a young woman.
girlhood NOUN

girlfriend NOUN a female friend; a woman with whom someone has a romantic relationship.

giro /jy-roh/ NOUN (PL **giros**) a banking system in which payment can be made by transferring credit from one account to another; a cheque or payment made by this.

girth NOUN the measurement round something, especially someone's stomach; a band under a horse's belly holding a saddle in place.

gist /jist/ NOUN the essential points or general sense of a speech etc.

gîte /*zh*eet/ NOUN (in France) a holiday cottage.

give VERB (**gives**, **giving**, **gave**, **given**) **1** hand over; cause (someone) to receive (something); devote to a cause; cause (someone) to experience (something); make available. **2** do; utter. **3** yield under pressure; be flexible. NOUN elasticity. **give and take** mutual compromise. **give away** reveal unintentionally. **give in** acknowledge defeat. **give out** **1** announce; distribute. **2** be used up or exhausted. **give over** [INFORMAL] cease. **give up** hand over; sacrifice; abandon hope or an effort. **give way** yield; allow other traffic to go first.
giver NOUN

giveaway NOUN [INFORMAL] **1** a free gift. **2** an unintentional disclosure.

given past participle of **GIVE**. ADJ **1** specified. **2** having a tendency: *given to swearing.* PREP taking into account, considering: *given the circumstances*. NOUN something already existing, known, or assumed.

given name NOUN a first name.

gizmo NOUN (PL **gizmos**) [INFORMAL] a gadget.

gizzard NOUN a bird's second stomach, in which food is ground.

glacé /gla-say/ ADJ preserved in sugar.

glacial /glay-see-ăl/ ADJ of or from glaciers; icy, very cold.

glaciated ADJ covered with or affected by a glacier.
glaciation NOUN

glacier /gla-see-ĕ, glay-see-ĕ/ NOUN a mass or river of ice moving very slowly.

glad ADJ pleased, joyful.
gladly ADV
gladness NOUN

gladden VERB make glad.

glade NOUN an open space in a forest.

gladiator NOUN a man trained to fight at public shows in ancient Rome.
gladiatorial ADJ

glamour ([US] **glamor**) NOUN alluring beauty; attractive exciting qualities.
glamorize VERB (also **glamorise**)
glamorous ADJ
glamorously ADV

glance VERB **1** look briefly. **2** strike something and bounce off at an angle; (of light) reflect off a surface. NOUN a brief look.

gland NOUN an organ that secretes substances to be used or expelled by the body.
glandular ADJ

glare VERB stare angrily or fiercely; shine with a harsh dazzling light. NOUN a fierce stare; a harsh light.

glaring ADJ conspicuous.

glasnost /glaz-nost/ NOUN (in the former Soviet Union) a policy of more openness in news reporting etc.

glass NOUN **1** a hard brittle transparent substance; a drinking container made of this; a mirror. **2** (**glasses**) spectacles; binoculars.
glassy ADJ

g

glass ceiling NOUN an unacknowledged barrier to advancement in a profession.

glasshouse NOUN **1** a greenhouse. **2** [INFORMAL] a military prison.

glaucoma /glow-**koh**-mă/ NOUN a condition causing gradual loss of sight.

glaze VERB **1** fit or cover with glass. **2** coat with a glossy surface. **3** (of eyes etc.) lose brightness and animation. NOUN a shiny surface or coating.
glazed ADJ

glazier NOUN a person whose job is to fit glass in windows.

gleam NOUN a briefly shining light; a brief or faint show of a quality. VERB shine brightly; reflect light.

glean VERB pick up (grain left by harvesters); collect, gather.
gleaner NOUN
gleanings PLURAL NOUN

glebe NOUN [HISTORICAL] a portion of land allocated to, and providing revenue for, a clergyman.

glee NOUN lively or triumphant joy.
gleeful ADJ
gleefully ADV

glen NOUN a narrow valley.

glib ADJ (**glibber**, **glibbest**) articulate but insincere or superficial.

glide VERB move smoothly; fly in a glider or aircraft without engine power. NOUN a gliding movement.

glider NOUN an aeroplane with no engine.

glimmer NOUN a faint gleam. VERB gleam faintly.

glimpse NOUN a brief view. VERB catch a glimpse of.

glint NOUN a brief flash of light. VERB send out a glint.

glisten VERB shine like something wet.

glitch NOUN [INFORMAL] a malfunction; a setback.

glitter VERB shine with a shimmering or sparkling light. NOUN shimmering or sparkling light; tiny pieces of sparkling material.

glitterati /glit-tĕ-**rah**-tee/ PLURAL NOUN [INFORMAL] rich famous people.

glitz NOUN [INFORMAL] superficial glamour and

ostentation.
glitzy ADJ

gloaming NOUN [LITERARY] twilight.

gloat VERB exult in one's own success or another's misfortune.

global ADJ worldwide; of or affecting an entire group.
globally ADV

global warming NOUN an increase in the temperature of the earth's atmosphere.

globe NOUN a ball-shaped object, especially one with a map of the earth on it; the world.

globetrotter NOUN [INFORMAL] a person who travels widely.
globetrotting NOUN & ADJ

globular ADJ globe-shaped.

globule NOUN a small round drop.

globulin NOUN a protein found in animal and plant tissue.

glockenspiel /glok-ĕn-shpeel/ NOUN a musical instrument of metal bars or tubes struck by hammers.

gloom NOUN **1** semi-darkness. **2** depression, sadness.
gloomily ADV
gloomy ADJ

glorify VERB (**glorifies**, **glorifying**, **glorified**) **1** praise highly; worship. **2** make (something) seem grander than it is.
glorification NOUN

glorious ADJ having or bringing glory; beautiful, splendid.
gloriously ADV

glory NOUN (PL **glories**) fame, honour, and praise; beauty, splendour; a source of fame and pride. VERB take pride or pleasure in something.

gloss NOUN **1** a shine on a smooth surface. **2** a translation or explanation.
gloss over try to conceal (a fault etc.).
glossily ADV
glossiness NOUN
glossy ADJ

glossary NOUN (PL **glossaries**) a list of technical or special words with definitions.

glottis NOUN the opening at the upper end of the windpipe between the

vocal cords.
glottal ADJ

glove NOUN a covering for the hand with separate divisions for fingers and thumb.

glow VERB send out light and heat without flame; have a warm or flushed look or colour; feel deep pleasure. NOUN a glowing state.

glower /glow-ĕ/ VERB scowl.

glow-worm NOUN a beetle that can give out a greenish light.

glucose NOUN a form of sugar found in fruit juice.

glue NOUN a sticky substance used for joining things. VERB (**glues**, **gluing**, **glued**) fasten with glue.
glued to [INFORMAL] paying close attention to.
gluey ADJ

glue-sniffing NOUN the inhalation of glue fumes for their narcotic effects.

glum ADJ (**glummer**, **glummest**) sad and gloomy.
glumly ADV
glumness NOUN

glut VERB (**gluts**, **glutting**, **glutted**) supply or fill to excess. NOUN an excessive supply.

gluten NOUN a protein found in cereals.

glutinous ADJ glue-like, sticky.

glutton NOUN a greedy person; one who is eager for something.
gluttonous ADJ
gluttony NOUN

glycerine /gli-sĕ-reen/ ([US] **glycerin**) NOUN a thick sweet liquid used in medicines etc.

glycerol NOUN = **GLYCERINE**.

gm ABBREV gram(s).

GMT ABBREV Greenwich Mean Time.

gnarled ADJ knobbly; twisted and misshapen.

gnash VERB (of teeth) strike together; grind (one's teeth).

gnat /nat/ NOUN a small biting fly.

gnaw VERB bite persistently at something hard.

gnome NOUN a dwarf in fairy tales.

gnomic /noh-mik/ ADJ

expressed in or using brief maxims.

gnomon /noh-mon/ NOUN the rod of a sundial.

gnostic /noss-tik/ ADJ of or having mystical knowledge.

GNP ABBREV gross national product.

gnu /noo/ NOUN a large heavy antelope.

GNVQ ABBREV General National Vocational Qualification.

go VERB (**goes**, **going**, **went**; PAST PARTICIPLE **gone**) **1** move, travel. **2** depart; (of time) pass. **3** pass into a specified state; proceed in a specified way: *the party went well.* **4** be regularly kept in a particular place; fit into a space. **5** (of a machine etc.) function; (of a bell etc.) sound. **6** cease functioning; die. **7** (of a story etc.) have a particular content. NOUN (PL **goes**) [INFORMAL] **1** an attempt; a turn to do something. **2** energy. **go back on** fail to keep (a promise). **go for 1** like, be attracted by; choose. **2** [INFORMAL] attack. **go into** study, investigate. **go off 1** explode. **2** (of food etc.) become stale or bad. **3** [INFORMAL] begin to dislike. **go on 1** continue. **2** happen. **go out** be extinguished. **go round** be enough for everyone. **go under** collapse, fail. **go with** harmonize with. **make a go of** [INFORMAL] be successful in. **on the go** [INFORMAL] active. **to go** [US] (of food) to be taken away for eating.

goad NOUN a pointed stick for driving cattle; a stimulus to activity. VERB provoke to action.

go-ahead [INFORMAL] NOUN permission to proceed. ADJ enterprising.

goal NOUN **1** a structure or area into which players send the ball to score a point in certain games; a point scored. **2** something aimed at; an ambition.

goalie NOUN [INFORMAL] a goalkeeper.

goalkeeper NOUN a player whose job is to keep the ball out of the goal.

goalpost NOUN either of the posts marking the

limit of a goal.
move the goalposts unfairly alter conditions or rules of a procedure once it has started.

goat NOUN a horned animal, sometimes domesticated for milk etc.
get someone's goat [INFORMAL] irritate someone.

gobble VERB **1** eat quickly and greedily. **2** make a throaty sound like a turkeycock.

gobbledegook NOUN [INFORMAL] unintelligible language.

go-between NOUN a messenger or negotiator.

goblet NOUN a drinking glass with a stem and a foot.

goblin NOUN a mischievous ugly elf.

go-cart variant of **GO-KART**.

god NOUN a superhuman being worshipped as having power over nature and human affairs; a person or thing greatly admired or adored; (**God**) the creator and ruler of the universe in Christian, Jewish, and Muslim teaching.

godchild NOUN (PL **godchildren**) a child in relation to its godparent(s).

god-daughter NOUN a female godchild.

goddess NOUN a female deity.

godfather NOUN **1** a male godparent. **2** a head of an illegal organization, especially the Mafia.

God-fearing ADJ sincerely religious.

godforsaken ADJ with no merit or attractiveness.

godhead NOUN divine nature; a deity.

godmother NOUN a female godparent.

godparent NOUN a person who represents a child at baptism and takes responsibility for its religious education.

godsend NOUN a very helpful thing, person, or event.

godson NOUN a male godchild.

go-getter NOUN [INFORMAL] an aggressively

enterprising person.

goggle VERB stare with wide-open eyes.

goggles PLURAL NOUN spectacles for protecting the eyes.

goitre /goy-ter/ ([US] **goiter**) NOUN an enlarged thyroid gland causing a swelling on the neck.

go-kart (also **go-cart**) NOUN a miniature racing car.

gold NOUN a chemical element; a yellow metal of high value; coins or articles made of this; its colour; a gold medal (awarded as first prize); something very valuable. ADJ made of or coloured like gold.

golden ADJ **1** gold. **2** precious, excellent; very happy: *golden days*.
golden boy (or **girl**) [INFORMAL] a very popular or successful man (or woman).

golden handshake NOUN a generous cash payment given on redundancy or early retirement.

golden jubilee NOUN the 50th anniversary of a sovereign's reign.

golden wedding NOUN the 50th anniversary of a wedding.

goldfield NOUN an area where gold is mined.

goldfish NOUN (PL **goldfish** or **goldfishes**) a small reddish carp kept in a bowl or pond.

gold leaf NOUN gold beaten into a very thin sheet.

gold rush NOUN a rush to a newly discovered goldfield.

goldsmith NOUN a person who makes gold articles.

gold standard NOUN something setting the standard of excellence for things of its type.

golf NOUN a game in which a ball is struck with clubs into a series of holes.
golfer NOUN

golf course (also **golf links**) NOUN an area of land on which golf is played.

golliwog NOUN a black-faced soft doll with fuzzy hair.

gonad /goh-nad/ NOUN an animal organ producing

gametes.

gondola NOUN a boat with high pointed ends, used on canals in Venice.

gondolier NOUN a man who propels a gondola with a pole.

gone past participle of **GO**.

g

gong NOUN a metal plate that resounds when struck; [INFORMAL] a medal.

gonorrhoea /gon-ŏ-**ree**-ă/ ([US] **gonorrhea**) NOUN a venereal disease with a discharge from the genitals.

goo NOUN [INFORMAL] a sticky wet substance.

good ADJ (**better**, **best**) **1** to be desired or approved of; pleasing, welcome. **2** having the right or necessary qualities; performing a particular function well; beneficial. **3** morally correct; kind; well behaved. **4** (of food etc.) enjoyable. **5** valid. **6** complete, thorough: *a good wash.* **7** [INFORMAL] at least as many as: *a good twenty minutes.* NOUN **1** that which is morally right. **2** benefit, advantage. **3** (**goods**) movable property; articles for trade; items to be transported.
as good as almost. **good at** talented at.

goodbye EXCLAMATION & NOUN an expression used when parting.

good-for-nothing ADJ worthless. NOUN a worthless person.

Good Friday NOUN the Friday before Easter, commemorating the Crucifixion.

goodie variant of **GOODY**.

goodness NOUN the quality of being good; the wholesome or beneficial part of food.

goodwill NOUN friendly feeling; the established popularity of a business, treated as a saleable asset.

goody (also **goodie**) NOUN (PL **goodies**) [INFORMAL] **1** a good person in a story etc. **2** something pleasant, especially to eat.

goody-goody NOUN (PL **goody-goodies**) [INFORMAL] a smugly virtuous person.

gooey ADJ (**gooier**, **gooiest**) [INFORMAL] wet and sticky.

goose NOUN (PL **geese**) a web-footed bird larger than a duck; the female of this.

gooseberry NOUN (PL **gooseberries**) **1** an edible berry growing on a thorny bush. **2** [INFORMAL] an unwelcome third person in the company of two lovers.

gooseflesh (also **goose pimples**) NOUN bristling bumpy skin caused by cold or fright.

goose-step VERB march without bending the knees. NOUN (**goose step**) this style of marching.

gopher NOUN **1** an American burrowing rodent. **2** [COMPUTING] a system for searching for information on the Internet.

gore NOUN **1** blood from a wound. **2** a triangular or tapering section of a skirt or sail. VERB pierce with a horn or tusk.

gorge NOUN a narrow steep-sided valley. VERB eat greedily.

gorgeous ADJ beautiful; richly coloured or decorated; [INFORMAL] very pleasant or attractive. **gorgeously** ADV

gorgon NOUN a mythical monster able to turn people into stone; an intimidating woman.

gorilla NOUN a large powerful ape.

gorse NOUN a wild evergreen thorny shrub with yellow flowers.

gory ADJ (**gorier**, **goriest**) covered with blood; involving bloodshed.

gosling NOUN a young goose.

go-slow NOUN a form of industrial action in which work is delayed or slowed down.

gospel NOUN **1** the teachings of Christ; (**Gospel**) any of the first four books of the New Testament. **2** something regarded as definitely true.

gossamer NOUN a fine piece of cobweb.

gossip NOUN casual talk about other people's affairs; a person fond of such talk. VERB (**gossips**, **gossiping**, **gossiped**) engage in gossip.

got past and past participle of **GET**.

Gothic ADJ **1** of an architectural style of the 12th-16th centuries, with pointed arches. **2** (of a novel etc.) in a horrific style popular in the 18th-19th centuries.

gotten [US] = **GOT**.

gouache /goo-ash, gwash/ NOUN a method of painting with opaque pigments in water thickened with a gluey substance.

gouge /gowj, gooj/ NOUN a chisel with a concave blade. VERB cut out with a gouge; scoop or force out.

goulash NOUN a stew of meat and vegetables, seasoned with paprika.

gourd NOUN a fleshy fruit of a climbing plant; a container made from its dried rind.

gourmand /goor-mond/ NOUN a food lover; a glutton.

gourmet /goor-may/ NOUN a connoisseur of good food and drink.

gout NOUN a disease causing inflammation of the joints.

govern VERB conduct the policy etc. of (a country, its people), rule; control, influence, direct.
governor NOUN

governance NOUN the action of governing.

governess NOUN a woman employed to teach children in a private household.

government NOUN the governing body of a state; the system by which a state is governed.
governmental ADJ

gown NOUN a long dress; a loose overgarment; an official robe.

GP ABBREV general practitioner.

grab VERB (**grabs**, **grabbing**, **grabbed**) grasp suddenly; take greedily. NOUN a sudden clutch or attempt to seize something; a mechanical device for gripping things.

grace NOUN **1** elegance of movement. **2** courtesy; an attractive manner.

3 mercy; undeserved favour, especially from God. 4 a short prayer of thanks for a meal. VERB honour (a place etc.) with one's presence; be an ornament to.

graceful ADJ 1 moving elegantly. 2 polite, charming.
gracefully ADV

graceless ADJ inelegant.

gracious ADJ kind and pleasant, especially towards inferiors.
graciously ADV
graciousness NOUN

gradation NOUN a series of changes; a stage in such a series.

grade NOUN 1 a level of rank or quality; a mark indicating standard of work. 2 [US] a class in school. VERB arrange in grades; assign a grade to.
make the grade [INFORMAL] be successful.

gradient NOUN a slope; the angle of a slope.

gradual ADJ taking place by degrees, not sudden.
gradually ADV

graduate NOUN /**grad**-yoo-ăt/ a person who has a university degree. VERB /**grad**-yoo-ayt/ 1 obtain a university degree. 2 arrange in a series or according to a scale; change (colour etc.) by small stages.
graduation NOUN

graffiti PLURAL NOUN words or drawings scribbled or sprayed on a wall.

graft NOUN 1 a plant shoot fixed into a cut in another plant to form a new growth; living tissue transplanted surgically. 2 [INFORMAL] hard work. 3 [INFORMAL] bribery, corrupt practice. VERB 1 insert (a graft) in a plant; transplant (tissue); join, add. 2 [INFORMAL] work hard.

grain NOUN 1 small seed(s) of a food plant such as wheat or rice; these plants; a small hard particle; a very small amount. 2 a unit of weight (about 65 mg). 3 the pattern of fibres in wood etc.
against the grain contrary to one's natural inclination.
grainy ADJ

g

gram (also **gramme**) NOUN one-thousandth of a kilogram.

grammar NOUN the whole system and structure of a language; rules for and use of words in their correct form and relationships; a book analysing this.

grammatical ADJ conforming to the rules of grammar.
grammatically ADV

grampus NOUN a dolphin-like sea animal.

gran NOUN [INFORMAL] grandmother.

granary NOUN (PL **granaries**) a storehouse for grain.

grand ADJ large and imposing; ambitious; chief of its kind; [INFORMAL] excellent. NOUN **1** a grand piano. **2** [INFORMAL] a thousand dollars or pounds.
grandly ADV
grandness NOUN

grandchild NOUN (PL **grandchildren**) a child of one's son or daughter.

granddad NOUN [INFORMAL] grandfather.

granddaughter NOUN a female grandchild.

grandeur /gran-dewr/ NOUN splendour, grandness.

grandfather NOUN a male grandparent.

grandfather clock NOUN a clock in a tall wooden case.

grandiloquent ADJ using pompous language.
grandiloquence NOUN

grandiose ADJ imposing; planned on a large scale.

grandma NOUN [INFORMAL] grandmother.

grandmother NOUN a female grandparent.

grandpa NOUN [INFORMAL] grandfather.

grandparent NOUN a parent of one's father or mother.

grand piano NOUN a large piano with horizontal strings.

grand slam NOUN the winning of all the major championships in a sport in one season.

grandson NOUN a male grandchild.

grandstand NOUN the principal stand for spectators at a sports ground.

grange NOUN a country house with farm buildings.

granite NOUN a hard grey stone.

granny (also **grannie**) NOUN (PL **grannies**) [INFORMAL] grandmother.

granny flat NOUN [INFORMAL] part of a house made into self-contained accommodation for a relative.

grant VERB **1** give or allow as a privilege. **2** admit to be true. NOUN a sum of money given from public funds for a particular purpose.
take for granted 1 fail to appreciate or be grateful for. **2** assume to be true.

granular ADJ like or consisting of grains.

granulated ADJ formed into grains.

granule NOUN a small grain.

grape NOUN a green or purple berry growing in clusters, used for making wine.

grapefruit NOUN a large round yellow citrus fruit.

grapevine NOUN a vine bearing grapes.
on the grapevine [INFORMAL] by a rumour spread unofficially.

graph NOUN a diagram showing the relationship between quantities.

graphic ADJ **1** of drawing, painting, or engraving. **2** giving a vivid description. NOUN (**graphics**) diagrams used in calculation and design; drawings; computer images.

graphical ADJ **1** in the form of a graph. **2** of visual art or computer graphics.
graphically ADV

graphic equalizer NOUN a device controlling individual frequency bands of a stereo system.

graphite NOUN a form of carbon.

graphology NOUN the study of handwriting.
graphologist NOUN

grapnel NOUN a small anchor with several hooks; a hooked device for dragging a river bed.

grapple VERB wrestle;

struggle.

grappling iron NOUN a grapnel.

grasp VERB **1** seize and hold. **2** understand. NOUN **1** a firm hold or grip. **2** an understanding.

g

grasping ADJ greedy, avaricious.

grass NOUN **1** a plant with green blades; a species of this (e.g. a cereal plant); ground covered with grass. **2** [INFORMAL] marijuana. **3** [INFORMAL] an informer. VERB **1** cover with grass. **2** [INFORMAL] act as an informer.
grassy ADJ

grasshopper NOUN a jumping insect that makes a chirping noise.

grassland NOUN a wide grass-covered area with few trees.

grass roots PLURAL NOUN the fundamental level or source; ordinary people, rank-and-file members.

grass widow NOUN a wife whose husband is absent for some time.

grate NOUN a metal framework keeping fuel in a fireplace. VERB **1** shred finely by rubbing against a jagged surface. **2** make a harsh noise; have an irritating effect.

grateful ADJ valuing a kindness or benefit received; thankful.
gratefully ADV

grater NOUN a device for grating food.

gratify VERB (**gratifies**, **gratifying**, **gratified**) give pleasure to; satisfy (wishes).
gratification NOUN

grating NOUN a screen of spaced bars placed across an opening.

gratis ADJ & ADV free of charge.

gratitude NOUN thankfulness and appreciation of a kindness or benefit received.

gratuitous ADJ **1** without reason, uncalled for. **2** free of charge.
gratuitously ADV

gratuity NOUN (PL **gratuities**) money given for services rendered, a tip.

grave[1] NOUN a hole dug to bury a corpse.

grave² ADJ **1** causing anxiety, serious. **2** solemn.
gravely ADV

grave accent /grahv/ NOUN the accent (`).

gravel NOUN small stones, used for paths etc.

gravelly ADJ **1** like or consisting of gravel. **2** rough-sounding.

graven image NOUN a carved figure of a god used as an idol.

gravestone NOUN a stone placed over a grave.

graveyard NOUN a burial ground.

gravitate VERB move or be attracted towards a person, place, or thing.

gravitation NOUN movement towards a centre of gravity.
gravitational ADJ

gravity NOUN **1** the force that attracts bodies towards the centre of the earth. **2** seriousness; solemnity.

gravy NOUN (PL **gravies**) juice from cooked meat; a sauce made from this.

gravy train NOUN [INFORMAL] an easy way of making money.

gray US spelling of **GREY**.

graze VERB **1** feed on growing grass; pasture animals in (a field); [INFORMAL] frequently eat snacks. **2** injure by scraping the skin; touch or scrape lightly in passing. NOUN a grazed place on the skin.

grease NOUN a fatty or oily substance; a lubricant. VERB put grease on.
greasy ADJ

greasepaint NOUN make-up used by actors.

great ADJ much above average in size, amount, or intensity; of outstanding ability or character; important; [INFORMAL] very good.
greatness NOUN

great- COMBINING FORM (of a family relationship) one generation removed in ancestry or descent.

greatly ADV very much.

grebe NOUN a diving bird.

Grecian ADJ Greek.

Grecian nose NOUN a straight nose.

greed NOUN excessive

desire for food, wealth, power, etc.
greedily ADV
greedy ADJ

Greek NOUN a person from Greece; the ancient or modern language of Greece. ADJ relating to Greece.

g

green ADJ **1** of the colour of growing grass; covered with growing grass; consisting of fresh green vegetables. **2** concerned with protecting the environment. **3** unripe; inexperienced, naive. NOUN a green colour; a piece of grassy public land; (**greens**) green vegetables.
greenish ADJ
greenness NOUN

green belt NOUN an area of open land round a town.

green card NOUN **1** (in the UK) an international insurance document for motorists. **2** (in the US) a work and residence permit.

greenery NOUN green foliage or plants.

green fingers PLURAL NOUN [INFORMAL] skill in growing plants.

greenfly NOUN (PL **greenfly**) a small green insect that sucks juices from plants.

greengage NOUN a round plum with a greenish skin.

greengrocer NOUN a shopkeeper selling vegetables and fruit.

greenhorn NOUN [INFORMAL] an inexperienced person.

greenhouse NOUN a glass building for rearing plants.

greenhouse effect NOUN the trapping of the sun's radiation by pollution in the atmosphere, causing a rise in temperature.

greenhouse gas NOUN a gas contributing to the greenhouse effect.

green light NOUN [INFORMAL] a signal or permission to proceed.

Green Paper NOUN a preliminary report of government proposals.

green room NOUN a room in a theatre used by actors when off stage.

greenstick fracture NOUN a bent and partially

broken bone.

greet VERB address politely on meeting; welcome; react to; become apparent to (sight or hearing).
greeting NOUN

gregarious ADJ fond of company; living in flocks.
gregariousness NOUN

gremlin NOUN an imaginary mischievous spirit blamed for mechanical faults; [INFORMAL] a fault or problem.

grenade NOUN a small bomb thrown by hand or fired from a rifle.

grenadine NOUN a sweet syrup.

grew past of **GROW**.

grey ([US] **gray**) ADJ of the colour between black and white; dull, depressing. NOUN a grey colour; a grey or white horse.
grey area a problem or situation that has no clear rules or definition.
greyish ADJ
greyness NOUN

greyhound NOUN a slender smooth-haired dog noted for its swiftness.

grey matter NOUN [INFORMAL] intelligence.

grid NOUN a grating; a system of numbered squares for map references; a network of lines, power cables, etc.; a gridiron.

gridiron NOUN a framework of metal bars for cooking on; a field for American football, marked with parallel lines.

gridlock NOUN a traffic jam affecting intersecting streets; a situation in which no progress can be made.

grief NOUN deep sorrow.
come to grief meet with disaster; fail.

grievance NOUN a cause for complaint.

grieve VERB cause grief to; feel grief.

grievous ADJ [FORMAL] very serious or distressing.
grievous bodily harm the offence of inflicting serious injury.
grievously ADV

griffin (also **griffon**, **gryphon**) NOUN a mythological creature with an eagle's head and wings and a lion's body.

griffon NOUN **1** a small terrier-like dog. **2** a vulture. **3** a griffin.

grill NOUN **1** a device on a cooker for radiating heat downwards; food cooked on this. **2** a grille. VERB **1** cook under a grill or on a gridiron. **2** [INFORMAL] question closely and severely.

grille (also **grill**) NOUN a grating; a grid protecting a vehicle's radiator.

grim ADJ (**grimmer**, **grimmest**) stern, severe; forbidding; disagreeable.
grimly ADV
grimness NOUN

grimace NOUN a contortion of the face in pain or amusement. VERB make a grimace.

grime NOUN ingrained dirt. VERB blacken with grime.
grimily ADV
griminess NOUN
grimy ADJ

grin VERB (**grins**, **grinning**, **grinned**) smile broadly. NOUN a broad smile.

grind VERB (**grinds**, **grinding**, **ground**) **1** crush into grains or powder. **2** sharpen or smooth by friction; rub together gratingly. **3** oppress cruelly. NOUN hard or tedious work.

grindstone NOUN a revolving disc for sharpening or grinding things.

grip VERB (**grips**, **gripping**, **gripped**) hold firmly; hold the attention of; affect deeply. NOUN **1** a firm grasp; a method of holding; a part that is held. **2** understanding of or skill in something. **3** a travelling bag.

gripe VERB [INFORMAL] grumble. NOUN **1** [INFORMAL] a complaint. **2** colic pain.

gripping ADJ very interesting or exciting; enthralling.

grisly ADJ (**grislier**, **grisliest**) causing fear, horror, or disgust.

grist NOUN grain to be ground.
grist to the mill something that one can exploit.

gristle NOUN tough inedible tissue in meat.
gristly ADJ

grit NOUN **1** particles of stone or sand. **2** [INFORMAL] courage and endurance. VERB (**grits**, **gritting**, **gritted**) **1** clench (the teeth) to aid endurance or restraint. **2** spread grit on (a road etc.). **3** make a grating sound.
grittiness NOUN
gritty ADJ

grizzle VERB [INFORMAL] whimper, whine; complain.

grizzled ADJ grey-haired.

groan VERB make a long deep sound in pain or disapproval; make a deep creaking sound. NOUN such a sound.
groan under be oppressed by.

grocer NOUN a shopkeeper selling food and household goods.

grocery NOUN (PL **groceries**) a grocer's shop; (**groceries**) a grocer's goods.

grog NOUN a drink of spirits mixed with water.

groggy ADJ (**groggier**, **groggiest**) [INFORMAL] weak and unsteady, especially after illness.
groggily ADV

groin NOUN **1** the place where the thighs join the abdomen. **2** a curved edge where two vaults meet. **3** US spelling of **GROYNE**.

grommet NOUN **1** a ring to protect a rope etc. passing through a hole in a panel. **2** a tube placed through the eardrum to drain the ear.

groom NOUN **1** a person employed to look after horses. **2** a bridegroom. VERB **1** clean and brush (an animal); make neat and tidy. **2** prepare (a person) for a career or position.

groove NOUN a long narrow channel; the track for a stylus on a gramophone record; a fixed routine. VERB cut grooves in.

grope VERB feel about as one does in the dark.

gross ADJ **1** unattractively large or fat. **2** vulgar; [INFORMAL] repulsive. **3** (of income etc.) total, without deductions. NOUN (PL **gross**) twelve dozen. VERB produce or earn as total profit.
grossly ADV

g

grossness NOUN

grotesque /groh-tesk/ ADJ very odd or ugly. NOUN a comically distorted figure; a design using fantastic forms.
grotesquely ADV
grotesqueness NOUN

grotto NOUN (PL **grottoes** or **grottos**) a picturesque cave.

grouch [INFORMAL] VERB grumble. NOUN a grumbler; a complaint.
grouchy ADJ

ground[1] past and past participle of **GRIND**.

ground[2] NOUN **1** the solid surface of the earth; an area of this; land of a specified type or used for a specified purpose; (**grounds**) land belonging to a large house. **2** (**grounds**) the reason or justification for a belief or action. **3** (**grounds**) coffee dregs. VERB **1** prevent (an aircraft or a pilot) from flying. **2** give a basis to. **3** instruct thoroughly in a subject.

ground glass NOUN glass made opaque by grinding.

grounding NOUN basic training.

groundless ADJ without basis or good reason.

groundnut NOUN a peanut.

ground rent NOUN rent paid by the owner of a building to the owner of the land on which it is built.

groundsheet NOUN a waterproof sheet for spreading on the ground.

groundsman NOUN a person employed to look after a sports ground.

groundswell NOUN **1** slow heavy waves. **2** a forceful build-up of public opinion.

groundwork NOUN preliminary or basic work.

group NOUN a number of people or things near, categorized, or working together. VERB form or gather into group(s); classify.

grouse NOUN **1** a game bird. **2** [INFORMAL] a complaint. VERB [INFORMAL] grumble.

grout /growt/ NOUN thin fluid mortar. VERB fill with

grout.

grove NOUN a group of trees.

grovel VERB (**grovels**, **grovelling**, **grovelled**; [US] **groveling**, **groveled**) crawl face downwards; behave humbly; apologize profusely.

grow VERB (**grows**, **growing**, **grew**; PAST PARTICIPLE **grown**) **1** increase in size or amount; allow (hair etc.) to grow. **2** exist as a living plant; cultivate (crops etc.). **3** develop a specified characteristic, become: *grow fat.*
grow on gradually start to appeal to. **grow up** become adult; start to behave maturely.
grower NOUN

growl VERB make a low threatening sound as a dog does. NOUN this sound.

grown past participle of **GROW**. ADJ adult, fully developed.

grown-up ADJ adult. NOUN [INFORMAL] an adult.

growth NOUN the process of growing; something that grows or has grown; a tumour.

groyne ([US] **groin**) NOUN a solid structure built out into the sea to prevent erosion.

grub NOUN **1** the worm-like larva of certain insects. **2** [INFORMAL] food. VERB (**grubs**, **grubbing**, **grubbed**) **1** dig the surface of soil; dig up by the roots. **2** rummage.

grubby ADJ (**grubbier**, **grubbiest**) dirty.
grubbiness NOUN

grudge NOUN a feeling of resentment or ill will. VERB begrudge, resent.

gruel NOUN thin oatmeal porridge.

gruelling ([US] **grueling**) ADJ very tiring.

gruesome ADJ horrifying.

gruff ADJ (of the voice) low and hoarse; (of a person) appearing bad-tempered.
gruffly ADV
gruffness NOUN

grumble VERB **1** complain in a bad-tempered way. **2** rumble. NOUN **1** a complaint. **2** a rumbling sound.
grumbler NOUN

grumpy ADJ (**grumpier**, **grumpiest**) bad-tempered.
grumpily ADV
grumpiness NOUN

grunge NOUN a style of rock music with a raucous guitar sound; torn and untidy clothing as a fashion associated with this.

g

grunt NOUN a gruff snorting sound made or like that made by a pig. VERB make this sound.

gryphon variant of **GRIFFIN**.

G-string NOUN a narrow strip of cloth covering the genitals, attached to a string round the waist.

G-suit NOUN a pressurized suit worn by astronauts and some pilots.

guano /gwah-noh/ NOUN the dung of seabirds, used as manure.

guarantee NOUN a formal promise to do something or that a thing is of a specified quality; something offered as security; a guarantor. VERB give or be a guarantee (of).

guarantor NOUN the giver of a guarantee.

guard VERB watch over to protect, prevent escape, etc.; take precautions. NOUN **1** a person guarding someone or something; a railway official in charge of a train; a protective part or device. **2** a state of watchfulness; a defensive posture in boxing, cricket, etc.

guarded ADJ cautious, discreet.

guardian NOUN one who guards or protects; a person undertaking legal responsibility for an orphan.
guardianship NOUN

guardsman NOUN a soldier of a Guards regiment.

guava /gwah-vă/ NOUN a tropical fruit.

gudgeon NOUN **1** a small freshwater fish. **2** a pivot; a socket for a rudder; a metal pin.

guerrilla /gĕ-**ril**-lă/ (also **guerilla**) NOUN a member of a small fighting force, taking independent irregular action.

guess VERB form an

opinion without definite knowledge; think likely. NOUN an opinion formed by guessing.

guesstimate (also **guestimate**) NOUN [INFORMAL] an estimate based on guesswork and reasoning.

guesswork NOUN the action of guessing.

guest NOUN a person entertained at another's house, or staying at a hotel; a visiting performer.

guest house NOUN a private house offering accommodation to paying guests.

guestimate variant of **GUESSTIMATE**.

guffaw NOUN a coarse noisy laugh. VERB laugh in this way.

guidance NOUN the action of guiding; advice or information.

guide NOUN **1** a person who shows others the way; one employed to point out sights to travellers. **2** a thing helping one to make a decision; a book of information, maps, etc.; a structure marking the correct position or direction of something. VERB act as a guide to.

guidebook NOUN a book of information about a place.

guild NOUN a society for mutual aid or with a common purpose; [HISTORICAL] an association of craftsmen or merchants.

guilder NOUN a former unit of money of the Netherlands.

guile NOUN treacherous cunning, craftiness. **guileless** ADJ

guillotine NOUN **1** a machine for beheading criminals; a machine for cutting paper or metal. **2** the fixing of times for voting in Parliament, to prevent a lengthy debate. VERB behead, cut, or limit with a guillotine.

guilt NOUN the fact of having committed an offence; a feeling that one is to blame. **guiltless** ADJ

guilty ADJ (**guiltier**, **guiltiest**) having done wrong; having committed a particular

g

offence; feeling or showing guilt.
guiltily ADV

guinea NOUN a former British coin worth 21 shillings (£1.05).

guinea pig NOUN **1** a small domesticated rodent. **2** [INFORMAL] a person or thing used as a subject for an experiment.

guise /gIz/ NOUN a false outward appearance; a pretence.

guitar NOUN a stringed musical instrument.
guitarist NOUN

gulf NOUN **1** a large area of sea partly surrounded by land. **2** a deep ravine; a wide difference in opinion.

gull NOUN a seabird with long wings. VERB fool, deceive.

gullet NOUN the passage by which food goes from mouth to stomach.

gullible ADJ easily deceived.
gullibility NOUN
gullibly ADV

gully NOUN (PL **gullies**) a narrow channel cut by water or carrying rainwater from a building.

gulp VERB swallow (food etc.) hastily or greedily; make a gulping movement. NOUN the act of gulping; a large mouthful of liquid gulped.

gum NOUN **1** the firm flesh in which teeth are rooted. **2** a sticky substance exuded by certain trees; adhesive; chewing gum. VERB (**gums**, **gumming**, **gummed**) smear or stick together with gum.
gummy ADJ

gumboots PLURAL NOUN [DATED] rubber boots, wellingtons.

gumdrop NOUN a hard gelatin sweet.

gumption NOUN [INFORMAL] resourcefulness, spirit.

gum tree NOUN a tree that exudes gum, especially a eucalyptus.

gun NOUN a weapon that fires shells or bullets from a metal tube; a device forcing out a substance through a tube. VERB (**guns**, **gunning**, **gunned**) **1** shoot (someone) with a

gun. **2** [INFORMAL] accelerate.
gun for 1 pursue with hostility. **2** try determinedly to achieve.
jump the gun [INFORMAL] act prematurely. **stick to one's guns** [INFORMAL] refuse to give way to criticism.

gunboat diplomacy NOUN foreign policy combining diplomacy with the threat of force.

gunfire NOUN the firing of guns.

gunge [INFORMAL] NOUN an unpleasantly sticky and messy substance. VERB clog or coat with this.
gungy ADJ

gunman NOUN a person armed with a gun.

gunnel variant of **GUNWALE**.

gunner NOUN an artillery soldier; a member of an aircraft crew operating a gun.

gunnery NOUN the construction and operating of large guns.

gunny NOUN coarse material for making sacks.

gunpowder NOUN an explosive of saltpetre, sulphur, and charcoal.

gunrunning NOUN the smuggling of firearms.
gunrunner NOUN

gunshot NOUN a shot fired from a gun; the range of a gun

gunsmith NOUN a maker and repairer of small firearms.

gunwale /**gun**-ăl/(also **gunnel**) NOUN the upper edge of a boat's side.

gurdwara /gerd-**wah**-ră/ NOUN a Sikh temple.

gurgle VERB make a low bubbling sound.
NOUN such a sound.

Gurkha NOUN a Hindu of Nepal; a Nepalese soldier serving in the British army.

guru NOUN (PL **gurus**) a Hindu spiritual teacher; a revered teacher.

gush VERB **1** (of liquid) flow out suddenly and in large quantities. **2** express excessive or insincere enthusiasm. VERB **1** a gushing stream.
2 effusiveness.

gusset NOUN a piece of

cloth inserted to strengthen or enlarge a garment.
gusseted ADJ

gust NOUN a sudden rush of wind, rain, or smoke. VERB blow in gusts.
gusty ADJ

g

gusto NOUN zest, enthusiasm.

gut NOUN **1** the belly; the intestine; thread made from animal intestines; (**guts**) the internal parts or essence of something. **2** (**guts**) [INFORMAL] courage, determination. VERB (**guts**, **gutting**, **gutted**) remove the guts from (fish); remove or destroy the internal parts of (a building etc.).
gut reaction [INFORMAL] an emotional rather than reasoned response.

gutsy ADJ (**gutsier**, **gutsiest**) [INFORMAL] **1** brave, spirited. **2** greedy.

gutta-percha NOUN a rubbery substance made from the juice of various Malaysian trees.

gutter NOUN a trough round a roof, or a channel beside a road, for carrying away rainwater. VERB (of a candle) burn unsteadily.
the gutter a life of poverty.

guttersnipe NOUN a street urchin.

guttural ADJ throaty, harsh-sounding.
gutturally ADV

guv NOUN an informal address to a man.

guy NOUN **1** [INFORMAL] a man. **2** an effigy of Guy Fawkes burnt on 5 Nov. **3** a rope or chain to keep a thing steady or secured. VERB imitate mockingly.

guzzle VERB eat or drink greedily.

gybe ([US] **jibe**) VERB (of a sail or boom) swing across the wind; (of a boat) change course in this way. NOUN this movement.

gym NOUN [INFORMAL] a gymnasium; gymnastics.

gymkhana NOUN a horse riding competition.

gymnasium NOUN (PL **gymnasia** or **gymnasiums**) a room equipped for physical training and gymnastics.

gymnast NOUN an expert

in gymnastics.

gymnastics PLURAL NOUN exercises involving physical agility and coordination.
gymnastic ADJ

gynaecology /gy-ni-kol-ŏ-ji/ ([US] **gynecology**) NOUN the study of the physiological functions and diseases of women.
gynaecological ADJ
gynaecologist NOUN

gypsum NOUN a chalk-like mineral used in building etc.

gypsy (also **gipsy**) NOUN (PL **gypsies**) a member of a travelling people.

gyrate VERB move in circles or spirals, revolve.
gyration NOUN

gyratory ADJ gyrating; following a circular or spiral path.

gyrocompass NOUN a navigation compass using a gyroscope.

gyroscope NOUN a device used to keep navigation instruments steady, consisting of a disc rotating on an axis.
gyroscopic ADJ

Hh

h

H (also **h**) NOUN (PL **Hs** or **H's**) the eighth letter of the alphabet. ABBREV **1** (**h**) hours. **2** (of pencil lead) hard.

ha EXCLAMATION an exclamation of triumph. ABBREV hectare(s).

habeas corpus /hay-bee-ăs/ NOUN an order requiring a person to be brought to court after arrest.

haberdasher NOUN a seller of sewing materials.
haberdashery NOUN

habit NOUN **1** a regular way of behaving; [INFORMAL] an addiction. **2** a long, loose garment, especially as worn by a monk or nun.

habitable ADJ suitable for living in.

habitat NOUN an animal's or plant's natural environment.

habitation NOUN the action of inhabiting; [FORMAL] a place to live in.

habitual ADJ done regularly or constantly; usual.
habitually ADV

habituate VERB accustom.

hacienda NOUN a ranch or large estate in South America.

hack NOUN **1** a writer producing dull and unoriginal work. **2** a horse for ordinary riding. VERB **1** cut, chop, or hit roughly. **2** [INFORMAL] gain unauthorized access to computer files. **3** ride on horseback for pleasure.

hacker NOUN [INFORMAL] a person who habitually gains unauthorized access to computer files.

hacking ADJ (of a cough) dry and frequent.

hackles PLURAL NOUN the hairs on the back of an animal's neck, raised in alarm or hostility.

hackneyed ADJ (of a phrase etc.) overused and lacking impact.

hacksaw NOUN a saw for metal.

had past and past participle of **HAVE**.

haddock NOUN (PL **haddock**) an edible sea fish.

haematology /heem-ă-tol-ŏ-ji/ ([US] **hematology**) NOUN the study of blood. **haematologist** NOUN

haemoglobin /heem-ŏ-gloh-bin/ ([US] **hemoglobin**) NOUN the red oxygen-carrying substance in blood.

haemophilia /heem-ŏ-fil-i-ă/ ([US] **hemophilia**) NOUN failure of the blood to clot causing excessive bleeding. **haemophiliac** NOUN

haemorrhage /hem-ŏ-rij/ ([US] **hemorrhage**) NOUN heavy bleeding. VERB bleed heavily.

haemorrhoids /hem-ŏ-roidz/ ([US] **hemorrhoids**) PLURAL NOUN varicose veins at or near the anus.

haft NOUN the handle of a knife or dagger.

hag NOUN an ugly old woman.

haggard ADJ looking pale and exhausted.

haggis NOUN a Scottish dish made from offal boiled in a sheep's stomach.

haggle VERB argue about the price or terms of a deal.

ha-ha NOUN a concealed ditch that marks a boundary without interrupting a view.

haiku /hy-koo/ NOUN a Japanese three-line poem of 17 syllables.

hail NOUN a shower of frozen rain; a shower of blows, questions, etc. VERB **1** pour down as or like hail. **2** call out to; welcome or acclaim. EXCLAMATION [ARCHAIC] an expression of greeting or acclamation.

hailstone NOUN a pellet of frozen rain.

hair NOUN one of the fine thread-like strands

growing from the skin; these strands on a person's head. **let one's hair down** [INFORMAL] behave uninhibitedly. **not turn a hair** not be at all worried or surprised. **split hairs** make overly fine distinctions.

h

haircut NOUN an act of cutting someone's hair; the style in which someone's hair is cut.

hairdo NOUN (PL **hairdos**) [INFORMAL] an arrangement of the hair.

hairdresser NOUN a person who cuts and arranges hair. **hairdressing** NOUN

hairgrip NOUN a springy hairpin.

hairline NOUN **1** the edge of the hair on the forehead etc. **2** a very narrow crack or line.

hairpin NOUN a U-shaped pin for keeping hair in place.

hairpin bend NOUN a sharp U-shaped bend.

hair-raising ADJ terrifying.

hair trigger NOUN a trigger operated by the slightest pressure.

hairy ADJ (**hairier, hairiest**) **1** covered with hair. **2** [INFORMAL] frightening and difficult. **hairiness** NOUN

Haitian /**hay**-shăn/ NOUN a person from Haiti. ADJ relating to Haiti.

hajji (also **haji**) NOUN a Muslim who has been to Mecca on pilgrimage.

haka /**ha**-kă/ NOUN a Maori war dance with chanting.

hake NOUN (PL **hake**) an edible sea fish.

halal /hă-**lahl**/ NOUN meat from an animal killed according to Muslim law.

halcyon /**hal**-si-ŏn/ ADJ (of a period) happy and peaceful.

hale ADJ strong and healthy.

half NOUN (PL **halves**) **1** each of two equal parts into which something is divided. **2** half a pint, half a pound, etc. **3** [INFORMAL] a child's fare on a bus etc. ADJ & PRON amounting to half of something. ADV to the extent of a half; partly. **half a dozen** six. **half and**

half half one thing and half another.

halfback NOUN a player between forwards and fullback(s).

half board NOUN bed, breakfast, and evening meal at a hotel etc.

half-brother NOUN a brother with whom one has only one parent in common.

half-caste NOUN [OFFENSIVE] a person of mixed race.

half-hearted ADJ not very enthusiastic.

half-life NOUN the time taken for radioactivity to reach half its original level.

half mast NOUN the position of a flag lowered in mourning.

half nelson NOUN a wrestling hold.

halfpenny /hayp-ni/ NOUN (PL **halfpennies** for single coins, **halfpence** for a sum of money) [HISTORICAL] a coin worth half a penny.

half-sister NOUN a sister with whom one has only one parent in common.

half-term NOUN a short holiday halfway through a school term.

half-timbered ADJ (of a house etc.) built with a timber frame and brick or plaster filling.

half-time NOUN the interval between two halves of a game.

half-tone NOUN a black and white illustration with grey shades shown by dots.

half-volley NOUN (in tennis etc.) the return of the ball as soon as it bounces.

halfway ADJ & ADV at a point equidistant between two others.

halfwit NOUN [INFORMAL] a stupid person.
half-witted ADJ

halibut NOUN (PL **halibut**) a large edible flatfish.

halitosis /hal-i-**toh**-sis/ NOUN breath that smells unpleasant.

hall NOUN **1** the room or space inside the front entrance of a house. **2** a large room or building for meetings, concerts, etc. **3** a large country house.

hallelujah variant of ALLELUIA.

hallmark NOUN an official mark on precious metals to indicate their standard; a distinguishing characteristic. **hallmarked** ADJ

h

hallo variant of **HELLO**.

hallow VERB make holy; honour as holy.

Hallowe'en NOUN 31 Oct., eve of All Saints' Day.

hallucinate VERB experience hallucinations.

hallucination NOUN an illusion of seeing or hearing something. **hallucinatory** ADJ

hallucinogenic ADJ causing hallucinations. **hallucinogen** NOUN

halo NOUN (PL **haloes**) (in a painting) a circle of light surrounding the head of a sacred figure.

halogen NOUN any of a group of various non-metallic elements including chlorine and iodine.

halon /hay-lon/ NOUN a gaseous compound of halogens used to extinguish fires.

halt VERB come or bring to a stop. NOUN a temporary stop; a minor stopping place on a railway. ADJ [ARCHAIC] lame.

halter NOUN a strap round the head of a horse for leading or holding it.

halting ADJ slow and hesitant. **haltingly** ADV

halve VERB divide equally between two; reduce by half.

halyard /hal-yăd/ NOUN a rope for raising or lowering a sail or flag.

ham NOUN **1** smoked or salted meat from a pig's thigh. **2** (**hams**) the thighs and buttocks. **3** a bad actor. **4** [INFORMAL] an amateur radio operator. VERB (**hams, hamming, hammed**) [INFORMAL] overact.

hamburger NOUN a flat round cake of minced beef.

ham-fisted ADJ [INFORMAL] clumsy.

hamlet NOUN a small village.

hammer NOUN **1** a tool with a head for hitting nails etc. **2** a metal ball attached to a wire, thrown in an athletic contest. VERB hit or beat with a hammer; hit something forcefully; impress (an idea etc.) on people.

hammock NOUN a hanging bed of canvas or netting.

hamper NOUN a large lidded basket for carrying food etc. on a picnic; a selection of food packed as a gift. VERB keep from moving or acting freely.

hamster NOUN a small domesticated rodent.

hamstring NOUN a tendon at the back of a knee or hock. VERB (**hamstrings**, **hamstringing**, **hamstrung**) cripple by cutting the hamstring(s); cripple the activity of.

hand NOUN **1** the part of the arm below the wrist. **2** a pointer on a clock, dial, etc. **3** control, influence; (**a hand**) help. **4** a manual worker. **5** the cards dealt to a player in a card game; a round of a game. **6** [INFORMAL] a round of applause. **7** a person's handwriting. **8** a unit of measurement of a horse's height. VERB give, pass. **at hand** close by. **hand out** distribute. **hands down** easily; decisively. **on hand** available. **out of hand** out of control. **to hand** within reach.

handbag NOUN a small bag to hold a purse and personal articles.

handball NOUN **1** a game similar to fives, in which the ball is hit with the hand. **2** the intentional touching of the ball with the hand or arm in football (a foul).

handbill NOUN a printed notice circulated by hand.

handbook NOUN a small book giving useful facts.

handcuff NOUN a metal ring linked to another, for securing a prisoner's wrists. VERB put handcuffs on.

handful NOUN **1** a quantity that fills the hand; a few. **2** [INFORMAL] a person hard to deal with or control.

handicap NOUN

1 something that makes progress difficult. **2** a disadvantage imposed on a superior competitor to equalize chances; a race etc. in which handicaps are imposed. **3** a physical or mental disability. VERB (**handicaps**, **handicapping**, **handicapped**) be a handicap to; place at a disadvantage.

> When used in reference to people with physical and mental disabilities, the word **handicapped** may cause offence; it is better to use **disabled**.

handkerchief NOUN (PL **handkerchiefs** or **handkerchieves**) a small square of cloth for wiping the nose etc.

handle NOUN a part by which a thing is held, carried, or controlled. VERB touch or move with the hands; deal with; manage.

handlebar NOUN a steering bar of a bicycle etc.

handler NOUN a person in charge of a trained dog etc.

handout NOUN a quantity of financial aid; information etc. given free of charge.

handrail NOUN a rail beside stairs etc. for people to hold for support.

handshake NOUN the act of shaking hands as a greeting etc.

handsome ADJ (**handsomer**, **handsomest**) **1** good-looking; striking, imposing. **2** (of a sum etc.) ample, substantial; generous.
handsomely ADV

handstand NOUN an act of balancing upside down on one's hands.

handwriting NOUN writing by hand with a pen or pencil; a person's particular style of writing.

handy ADJ (**handier**, **handiest**) **1** ready to hand; convenient; easy to use. **2** skilled with one's hands.
come in handy [INFORMAL] prove to be useful.
handily ADV

handiness NOUN

handyman NOUN a person who does minor repairs etc.

hang VERB (**hangs**, **hanging**, **hung**; in sense 2 **hangs**, **hanging**, **hanged**) **1** support or be supported from above; fasten to a wall; remain static in the air. **2** kill or be killed by suspension on a rope tied round the neck. NOUN the way something hangs.
get the hang of [INFORMAL] learn how to do. **hang about** loiter. **hang back** hesitate; remain behind. **hang on 1** hold tightly. **2** [INFORMAL] wait. **3** depend on. **hang out** [INFORMAL] spend time relaxing.

hangar NOUN a building for aircraft.

hangdog ADJ shamefaced.

hanger NOUN a shaped piece of wood, metal, etc. to hang a garment on.

hang-glider NOUN an unpowered flying device for one person, consisting of a frame with a fabric aerofoil above it.

hang-gliding NOUN the sport of flying in a hang-glider.

hangings PLURAL NOUN draperies hung on walls.

hangman NOUN a person whose job is to hang people condemned to death.

hangnail NOUN torn skin at the base of a fingernail.

hangover NOUN unpleasant after-effects from drinking too much alcohol.

hank NOUN a coil or length of thread.

hanker VERB crave, feel a longing.

hanky NOUN (PL **hankies**) [INFORMAL] a handkerchief.

Hanukkah /han-oo-kă/ NOUN a Jewish festival of lights, beginning in December.

haphazard ADJ done or chosen at random.
haphazardly ADV

hapless ADJ unlucky.

happen VERB take place; occur by chance.
happen on find by chance. **happen to** be the fate or experience of.

h

happy ADJ (**happier**, **happiest**) **1** pleased, contented. **2** fortunate. **happy medium** a satisfactory compromise. **happily** ADV **happiness** NOUN

happy-go-lucky ADJ cheerfully casual.

harangue VERB lecture earnestly and at length.

harass VERB worry or annoy continually; make repeated attacks on. **harassment** NOUN

harbour ([US] **harbor**) NOUN a place for ships to moor in shelter. VERB **1** keep (a thought etc.) in one's mind. **2** shelter.

hard ADJ **1** firm to the touch; rigid, not easily cut or dented; (of a person) strong-minded; severe; (of information) reliable. **2** difficult; requiring effort; harsh; causing suffering. **3** powerful; (of drinks) strongly alcoholic; (of drugs) strong and addictive; (of currency) not likely to drop suddenly in value; (of water) containing minerals that prevent soap from lathering freely. ADV **1** with effort, diligently; with force. **2** so as to be firm: *the cement set hard.* **hard of hearing** slightly deaf. **hard up** [INFORMAL] short of money. **the hard sell** aggressive salesmanship. **hardness** NOUN

hardbitten ADJ tough and cynical.

hardboard NOUN stiff board made of compressed wood pulp.

hard-boiled ADJ **1** (of eggs) boiled until the yolk and white are set. **2** (of people) callous.

hard copy NOUN material produced in printed form from a computer.

harden VERB make or become hard or hardy.

hard-headed ADJ practical, not sentimental.

hard-hearted ADJ unfeeling.

hardly ADV only with difficulty; scarcely.

hardship NOUN severe suffering.

hard shoulder NOUN an

extra strip of road beside a motorway, for use in an emergency.

hardware NOUN **1** tools and household implements sold by a shop. **2** machinery used in a computer system.

hardwood NOUN the hard heavy wood of deciduous trees.

hardy ADJ (**hardier**, **hardiest**) capable of enduring cold or harsh conditions.
hardiness NOUN

hare NOUN a field animal like a large rabbit.
VERB run rapidly.

hare-brained ADJ wild and foolish, rash.

harelip NOUN a cleft lip.

> The term **harelip** is often considered offensive; use **cleft lip** instead.

harem /har-eem/ NOUN the women's quarters in a Muslim household; the wives of a polygamous man.

hark VERB [LITERARY] listen.
hark back recall something from the past.

harlequin NOUN a character in traditional pantomime. ADJ variegated like this character's costume.

harm NOUN damage, injury. VERB cause harm to.
harmful ADJ
harmless ADJ

harmonica NOUN a mouth organ.

harmonium NOUN a musical instrument like a small organ.

harmonize (also **harmonise**) VERB **1** add notes to (a melody) to form chords. **2** make consistent; go well together.
harmonization NOUN

harmony NOUN (PL **harmonies**) the combination of musical notes to form chords; pleasing tuneful sound; agreement, peace; consistency.
harmonic ADJ
harmonious ADJ
harmoniously ADV

harness NOUN straps and fittings by which a horse is controlled; fastenings for a parachute etc. VERB put (a horse) in harness,

h

attach to a cart etc.; control and use (resources).

harp NOUN a musical instrument with strings in a triangular frame.
harp on [INFORMAL] talk repeatedly about.
harpist NOUN

harpoon NOUN a spear-like missile with a rope attached. VERB spear with a harpoon.

harpsichord NOUN a piano-like instrument.

harpy NOUN (PL **harpies**) a grasping unscrupulous woman.

harridan NOUN a bad-tempered old woman.

harrier NOUN **1** a hound used for hunting hares. **2** a falcon.

harrow NOUN a heavy frame with metal spikes or discs for breaking up soil. VERB **1** draw a harrow over (soil). **2** distress greatly.
harrowing ADJ

harry VERB (**harries, harrying, harried**) harass.

harsh ADJ disagreeably rough to touch, hear, etc.; severe, cruel; grim.
harshly ADV
harshness NOUN

hart NOUN an adult male deer.

harvest NOUN the gathering of crop(s); the season for this; a season's yield of a natural product. VERB gather (a crop).
harvester NOUN

has 3rd person singular present of **HAVE**.

has-been NOUN [INFORMAL] a person who is no longer important.

hash NOUN **1** a dish of chopped recooked meat. **2** [INFORMAL] hashish.
make a hash of [INFORMAL] do or make badly, make a mess of.

hashish NOUN cannabis.

hasp /hahsp/ NOUN a metal plate fitting over a U-shaped staple as part of a door fastening.

hassle [INFORMAL] NOUN inconvenience, annoyance; harassment. VERB harass; bother.

hassock NOUN a thick firm cushion for kneeling on in church.

haste NOUN hurry.

hasten VERB hurry; cause to go faster.

hasty ADJ (**hastier**, **hastiest**) hurried; acting or done too quickly.
hastily ADV
hastiness NOUN

hat NOUN a covering for the head.

hatch[1] NOUN an opening in a deck, ceiling, etc., to allow passage.

hatch[2] VERB emerge from an egg; cause to do this; devise (a plot).

hatch[3] VERB shade (an area) with close parallel lines.
hatching NOUN

hatchback NOUN a car with a back door that opens upwards.

hatchery NOUN (PL **hatcheries**) a place for hatching eggs, especially for fish.

hatchet NOUN a small axe.
bury the hatchet stop quarrelling.

hatchway NOUN an opening in a ship's deck for loading cargo.

hate NOUN hatred. VERB feel hatred towards; dislike greatly.

hateful ADJ arousing hatred.

hatred NOUN intense dislike.

hat-trick NOUN three successes in a row, especially in sports.

haughty /hor-ti/ ADJ (**haughtier**, **haughtiest**) proud and looking down on others.
haughtily ADV
haughtiness NOUN

haul VERB **1** pull or drag forcibly. **2** transport by truck etc. NOUN a quantity of goods stolen.
a long haul a long way to travel.

haulage NOUN transport of goods.

haulier NOUN a person or firm transporting goods by road.

haulm /horm/ NOUN a stalk or stem.

haunch NOUN the fleshy part of the buttock and thigh; a leg and loin of meat.

haunt VERB (of a ghost) appear regularly at or to; frequent (a place); linger in the mind of. NOUN a place often visited by a particular person.

haute couture /oht koo-tewr/ NOUN high fashion.

haute cuisine /oht kwi-zeen/ NOUN high-class cookery.

have VERB (**has**, **having**, **had**) **1** possess; hold; contain. **2** experience; suffer from (an illness etc.). **3** cause to be or be done: *have the house painted.* **4** be obliged or compelled: *I have to go.* **5** give birth to. **6** allow, tolerate. **7** [INFORMAL] cheat. AUXILIARY VERB used with the past participle to form past tenses: *he has gone.*

have had it [INFORMAL] be past recovery or survival. **have it out** [INFORMAL] discuss a problem frankly. **have on 1** be wearing. **2** have as an engagement. **3** [INFORMAL] tease, try to fool. **haves and have-nots** [INFORMAL] people with and without wealth or privilege. **have up** [INFORMAL] bring (someone) to trial.

haven NOUN a refuge; a small harbour.

haversack NOUN a strong bag carried on the back or shoulder.

havoc NOUN great destruction or disorder.

haw NOUN a hawthorn berry.

hawk NOUN **1** a bird of prey. **2** a person who favours an aggressive policy.

hawser NOUN a heavy rope or cable for mooring or towing a ship.

hawthorn NOUN a thorny tree with small red berries.

hay NOUN grass cut and dried for fodder.

hay fever NOUN an allergy caused by pollen and dust.

haystack NOUN a pile of hay stacked in a large block shape for storing.

haywire ADJ (**go haywire**) [INFORMAL] go out of control.

hazard NOUN a risk, a danger; an obstacle. VERB risk; venture.

hazardous ADJ

haze NOUN thin mist.

hazel NOUN **1** a tree with small edible nuts. **2** light

brown.
hazelnut NOUN

hazy ADJ (**hazier**, **haziest**) misty; indistinct; vague.
hazily ADV
haziness NOUN

HB ABBREV (of a pencil lead) hard black.

H-bomb NOUN a hydrogen bomb.

he PRON the male previously mentioned. NOUN a male.

head NOUN **1** the part of the body containing the eyes, nose, mouth, and brain. **2** the intellect. **3** the front or top end of something. **4** something shaped like a head. **5** a leader, a chief; a head teacher. **6** a person considered as a unit: *six pounds a head.* **7** (**heads**) the side of a coin showing a head, turned upwards after being tossed. **8** a body of water or steam confined for exerting pressure. **9** the foam on top of beer. VERB **1** lead, control, be at the head of; give a heading to. **2** move in a specified direction. **3** (in football) strike (the ball) with one's head.
come to a head reach a crisis. **head off** go in front of (someone), forcing them to turn.

headache NOUN a continuous pain in the head; [INFORMAL] a worrying problem.

headdress NOUN an ornamental covering worn on the head.

header NOUN **1** a heading of the ball in football. **2** [INFORMAL] a headlong fall or dive.

headgear NOUN a hat or headdress.

headhunt VERB seek to recruit (senior staff) from another firm.

heading NOUN **1** a word or words at the top of written matter as a title; a division of a subject. **2** a direction, a bearing.

headlamp NOUN a headlight.

headland NOUN a promontory.

headlight NOUN a powerful light on the front of a vehicle etc.

headline NOUN a heading in a newspaper;

(**headlines**) a summary of broadcast news.

headlong ADJ & ADV falling or plunging with the head first; in a hasty and rash way.

headmaster NOUN a man who is a head teacher.

headmistress NOUN a woman who is a head teacher.

head-on ADJ & ADV involving the front of a vehicle; involving direct confrontation.

headphones PLURAL NOUN a set of earphones for listening to audio equipment.

headquarters PLURAL NOUN a place from which an organization is controlled.

headstone NOUN a memorial stone set up at the head of a grave.

headstrong ADJ self-willed and obstinate.

head teacher NOUN the principal teacher in a school, responsible for organizing it.

headway NOUN progress.

headwind NOUN a wind blowing from directly in front.

heady ADJ (**headier**, **headiest**) intoxicating; exciting.

heal VERB make or become healthy after injury; cure.
healer NOUN

health NOUN the state of being well and free from illness; mental or physical condition: *poor health*.

health centre NOUN a doctors' surgery with several doctors, a nurse, a pharmacy, etc.

health farm NOUN an establishment offering controlled regimes of diet, exercise, massage, etc. to improve health.

health visitor NOUN a trained nurse who visits invalids at home.

healthy ADJ (**healthier**, **healthiest**) having or showing good health; producing good health; functioning well.
healthily ADV
healthiness NOUN

heap NOUN **1** a number of things or articles lying one on top of another. **2** (**heaps**) [INFORMAL] plenty.

VERB pile or become piled in a heap; load with large quantities.

hear VERB (**hears**, **hearing**, **heard**) perceive (sounds) with the ear; be informed of; pay attention to; judge (a legal case). **hear from** be contacted by. **hear! hear!** I agree. **hearer** NOUN

hearing NOUN **1** ability to hear. **2** an opportunity to state one's case; a trial in court.

hearing aid NOUN a small sound amplifier worn by a partially deaf person to improve the hearing.

hearsay NOUN rumour or gossip.

hearse /hers/ NOUN a vehicle carrying the coffin at a funeral.

heart NOUN **1** the muscular organ that keeps blood circulating. **2** the centre of a person's emotions or inner thoughts; courage; enthusiasm. **3** a central or essential part. **4** a figure representing a heart. **5** (**hearts**) one of the four suits in a pack of playing cards, marked with red hearts. **at heart** really, fundamentally. **break a person's heart** cause someone overwhelming grief. **by heart** memorized thoroughly. **a heart of gold** a generous or compassionate nature.

heartache NOUN deep sorrow.

heart attack (also **heart failure**) NOUN sudden failure of the heart to function normally.

heartbeat NOUN the pulsation of the heart.

heartbreak NOUN overwhelming grief.

heartbroken ADJ very sad.

heartburn NOUN a burning sensation in the lower part of the chest from indigestion.

hearten VERB encourage.

heartfelt ADJ felt deeply, sincere.

hearth NOUN the floor of a fireplace; the fireside.

heartless ADJ not feeling pity or sympathy. **heartlessly** ADV

heart-rending ADJ very distressing.

heart-searching NOUN

examination of one's own feelings and motives.

heart-throb NOUN [INFORMAL] an attractive person inspiring romantic feelings.

heart-to-heart ADJ frank and personal. NOUN a conversation of this nature.

heart-warming ADJ emotionally moving and encouraging.

heartwood NOUN the dense, hardest, inner part of a tree trunk.

hearty ADJ (**heartier**, **heartiest**) **1** vigorous; enthusiastic; heartfelt. **2** (of a meal or an appetite) large.
heartily ADV
heartiness NOUN

heat NOUN **1** the state of being hot; high temperature; a source of this; [PHYSICS] energy produced by movement of molecules. **2** intense feeling. **3** a preliminary contest in a sporting competition. VERB make or become hot.
on heat (of female mammals) ready to mate.

heated ADJ (of a person or discussion) angry.
heatedly ADV

heater NOUN a device supplying heat.

heath NOUN flat uncultivated land with low shrubs; a shrub typically growing on this.

heathen NOUN a person who does not believe in an established religion. ADJ of or relating to heathens.

heather NOUN an evergreen shrub with purple, pink, or white flowers.

heatstroke NOUN an illness caused by overexposure to sun.

heatwave NOUN a long period of hot weather.

heave VERB (**heaves**, **heaving**, **heaved**) **1** lift or haul with great effort; throw. **2** utter (a sigh). **3** rise and fall like waves. **4** [INFORMAL] retch. NOUN an act of heaving.
heave in sight (past **hove**) come into view.
heave to (past **hove**) bring a ship to a standstill with its head to

the wind.

heaven NOUN **1** the abode of God; a place or state of bliss. **2** (**the heavens**) [LITERARY] the sky.

heavenly ADJ **1** of heaven; divine; [INFORMAL] very pleasing. **2** of the sky.

heavy ADJ (**heavier, heaviest**) **1** having great weight; requiring physical effort. **2** unusually great, forceful, or intense. **3** dense, thick; (of food) hard to digest. **4** serious; oppressive; sad.
heavy going a situation in which it is hard to make headway.
heavily ADV
heaviness NOUN

heavy-hearted ADJ sad.

heavy industry NOUN industry producing metal or heavy machines etc.

heavy metal NOUN a type of loud rock music.

heavyweight NOUN **1** the heaviest weight in boxing. **2** [INFORMAL] an influential person.

Hebrew NOUN a member of an ancient people living in what is now Israel and Palestine; their language in its ancient or modern form.
Hebraic ADJ

heckle VERB interrupt (a public speaker) with aggressive questions or abuse.
heckler NOUN

hectare NOUN a unit of area, 10,000 sq. metres (2.471 acres).

hectic ADJ full of frantic activity.
hectically ADV

hectogram NOUN 100 grams.

hector VERB intimidate by bullying.

hedge NOUN a barrier formed by closely growing bushes or shrubs. VERB **1** surround with a hedge; make or trim hedges. **2** avoid giving a direct answer or commitment.

hedgehog NOUN a small animal covered in stiff spines.

hedgerow NOUN bushes etc. forming a hedge.

hedonism NOUN the pursuit of pleasure as the

chief good.
hedonist NOUN
hedonistic ADJ

heed VERB pay attention to. NOUN careful attention.
heedful ADJ
heedless ADJ
heedlessly ADV

heel NOUN **1** the back part of the foot; part of a shoe supporting this; (**heels**) high-heeled shoes. **2** [INFORMAL], [DATED] a scoundrel. VERB **1** make or repair the heel(s) of. **2** (of a boat) tilt to one side.
down at heel shabby. **take to one's heels** run away.

hefty ADJ (**heftier, heftiest**) large, heavy, and powerful.
heftily ADV
heftiness NOUN

hegemony /hi-jem-ŏ-ni/ NOUN dominance, especially of one country over others.

Hegira /hej-i-ră/ (also **Hejira**) NOUN Muhammad's flight from Mecca (AD 622), from which the Muslim era is reckoned.

heifer /hef-er/ NOUN a young cow.

height NOUN **1** measurement from base to top or foot to head; distance above ground or sea level. **2** the quality of being tall; a high place; the highest degree of something.

heighten VERB make or become higher or more intense.

heinous /hay-nŭss, hee-nŭs/ ADJ very wicked.

heir /air/ NOUN a person entitled to inherit property or a rank etc.

heiress /air-ess/ NOUN a female heir.

heirloom /air-loom/ NOUN a possession handed down in a family for several generations.

Hejira variant of **HEGIRA**.

held past and past participle of **HOLD**.

helical ADJ like a helix.

helicopter NOUN an aircraft with horizontally rotating overhead rotors.

heliport NOUN a helicopter station.

helium NOUN a light colourless gas that does not burn.

helix /hee-liks/ NOUN (PL **helices**) a spiral.

hell NOUN a place of

punishment for the wicked after death; a place or state of misery. EXCLAMATION an exclamation of anger.
hell for leather very fast.
hellish ADJ

hell-bent ADJ recklessly determined.

Hellenic ADJ Greek.

hello (also **hallo**, **hullo**) EXCLAMATION & NOUN (PL **hellos**) an exclamation used in greeting or to call attention.

helm NOUN the tiller or wheel by which a ship's rudder is controlled.

helmet NOUN a hard protective hat.

helmsman NOUN a person controlling a ship's helm.

help VERB **1** make a task etc. easier for (someone); improve or ease; benefit. **2** serve with food. **3** avoid; stop oneself: *I can't help laughing.* NOUN the action of helping; someone or something that helps.
help oneself take what one wants.
helper NOUN

helpful ADJ giving help, useful.
helpfully ADV
helpfulness NOUN

helping NOUN a portion of food served.

helpless ADJ unable to manage without help; powerless.
helplessly ADV
helplessness NOUN

helpline NOUN a telephone service providing help with problems.

helter-skelter ADV in disorderly haste. NOUN a spiral slide at a funfair.

hem NOUN an edge (of cloth) turned under and sewn down. VERB (**hems**, **hemming**, **hemmed**) sew a hem on.
hem in surround and restrict.

hematology etc. US spelling of **HAEMATOLOGY** etc.

hemisphere NOUN half a sphere; half of the earth.
hemispherical ADJ

hemlock NOUN a poisonous plant.

hemp NOUN **1** the cannabis plant, the fibre of which is used to make rope, fabrics, etc. **2** the drug cannabis.

hen NOUN a female bird, especially of the domestic fowl.

hence ADV **1** for this reason. **2** from this time. **3** [ARCHAIC] from here.

henceforth (also **henceforward**) ADV from this time on, in future.

henchman NOUN a supporter, a follower.

henna NOUN a reddish dye used especially on the hair.
hennaed ADJ

hen party NOUN (PL **hen parties**) [INFORMAL] a party for women only.

henpecked ADJ [INFORMAL] (of a man) nagged by his wife.

henry NOUN (PL **henries** or **henrys**) [PHYSICS] a unit of electric inductance.

hepatic ADJ of the liver.

hepatitis NOUN inflammation of the liver.

heptagon NOUN a geometric figure with seven sides.
heptagonal ADJ

heptathlon NOUN an athletic contest involving seven events.

her PRON the objective case of *she*. ADJ belonging to a female already mentioned.

herald VERB be a sign of; proclaim the approach of. NOUN a person or thing heralding something.

heraldry NOUN the study of coats of arms.
heraldic ADJ

herb NOUN a plant used as a flavouring or in medicine.

herbaceous /her-bay-shŭs/ ADJ soft-stemmed.

herbaceous border NOUN a border containing especially perennial plants.

herbal ADJ of herbs. NOUN a book about herbs.

herbalist NOUN a dealer in medicinal herbs.

herbicide NOUN a substance used to destroy plants.

herbivorous ADJ feeding on plants.
herbivore NOUN

herculean /her-kyoo-lee-ăn/ ADJ needing or showing great strength or effort.

herd NOUN a group of

animals feeding or staying together; a mob. VERB move or cause to move in a group; look after (livestock).

herdsman NOUN a man who looks after livestock.

here ADV in, at, or to this place; at this point.

hereabouts ADV near here.

hereafter ADV [FORMAL] from now on.
the hereafter life after death.

hereby ADV [FORMAL] by this means; as a result of this.

hereditary ADJ inherited; holding a position by inheritance.

heredity NOUN inheritance of characteristics from parents.

herein ADV [FORMAL] in this document, book, or matter.

heresy NOUN (PL **heresies**) a belief, especially a religious one, contrary to orthodox doctrine.

heretic NOUN a person who believes in a heresy.
heretical ADJ
heretically ADV

hereto ADV [FORMAL] to this.

herewith ADV [FORMAL] with this.

heritage NOUN inherited property; a nation's historic buildings etc.

hermaphrodite NOUN a creature with male and female sexual organs.

hermetic ADJ airtight, sealed.
hermetically ADV

hermit NOUN a person living in solitude.

hermitage NOUN a hermit's dwelling.

hernia NOUN a protrusion of part of an organ through the wall of the cavity (especially the abdomen) containing it.

hero NOUN (PL **heroes**) a man admired for his brave deeds; the chief male character in a story.

heroic ADJ very brave; grand in scale. NOUN (**heroics**) bold or dramatic behaviour or talk.
heroically ADV

heroin NOUN a powerful addictive drug derived from morphine.

heroine NOUN a woman admired for her brave

deeds; the chief female character in a story.

heroism NOUN heroic conduct.

heron NOUN a long-legged wading bird.

herpes /her-peez/ NOUN a viral disease causing blisters.

h **Herr** NOUN (PL **Herren**) the title of a German man, corresponding to Mr.

herring NOUN an edible North Atlantic fish.

herringbone NOUN a zigzag pattern or arrangement.

hers POSSESSIVE PRONOUN belonging to her.

herself PRON the emphatic and reflexive form of *she* and *her*.

hertz NOUN (PL **hertz**) [PHYSICS] a unit of frequency of electromagnetic waves.

hesitant ADJ uncertain, reluctant.
hesitancy NOUN
hesitantly ADV

hesitate VERB pause doubtfully; be reluctant.
hesitation NOUN

hessian NOUN a strong coarse cloth of hemp or jute.

heterodox ADJ not in accordance with what is generally accepted or believed.

heterogeneous /het-ĕ-ro-jee-nee-ŭs/ ADJ made up of people or things of various sorts.
heterogeneity NOUN

heterosexual ADJ sexually attracted to people of the opposite sex. NOUN a heterosexual person.
heterosexuality NOUN

hew VERB (**hews**, **hewing**, **hewn** or **hewed**) chop or cut with an axe etc.; cut into shape.

hex NOUN a magic spell; a curse.

hexadecimal ADJ [COMPUTING] of a number system using 16 rather than 10 as a base.

hexagon NOUN a geometric figure with six sides.
hexagonal ADJ

hexagram NOUN a six-pointed star formed of two intersecting triangles.

hey EXCLAMATION an

exclamation of surprise or inquiry, or calling attention.

heyday NOUN the time of someone's or something's greatest success.

HGV ABBREV heavy goods vehicle.

HH ABBREV (of pencil lead) extra hard.

hi EXCLAMATION an informal greeting or call to attract attention.

hiatus /hy-**ay**-tus/ NOUN (PL **hiatuses**) a break or gap in a sequence.

hibernate VERB spend the winter in a sleep-like state.
hibernation NOUN

Hibernian ADJ Irish; relating to Ireland. NOUN an Irish person.

hiccup (also **hiccough**) NOUN a sudden stopping of breath with a 'hic' sound; [INFORMAL] a temporary setback. VERB (**hiccups**, **hiccuping**, **hiccuped**; **hiccoughs**, **hiccoughing**, **hiccoughed**) suffer from a hiccup.

hide VERB (**hides**, **hiding**, **hid**; PAST PARTICIPLE **hidden**) put or keep out of sight; keep secret; conceal oneself. NOUN **1** a hiding place used when birdwatching etc. **2** an animal's skin.

hidebound ADJ rigidly conventional.

hideous ADJ very ugly.
hideously ADV
hideousness NOUN

hideout NOUN a hiding place.

hiding NOUN [INFORMAL] a severe beating.

hierarchy /**hI**-ĕ-rah-ki/ NOUN a system with grades ranking one above another.
hierarchical ADJ

hieroglyphics /hI-ĕ-rŏ-**glif**-iks/ PLURAL NOUN writing consisting of pictorial symbols.
hieroglyph NOUN
hieroglyphic ADJ

hi-fi ADJ high-fidelity, reproducing sound accurately. NOUN a set of hi-fi equipment.

higgledy-piggledy ADJ & ADV in complete confusion.

high ADJ **1** extending far

upwards or a specified distance upwards; far above ground or sea level. **2** greater or more intense than normal. **3** great in status. **4** (of a sound) not deep or low. **5** (of an opinion) favourable. **6** (of meat) slightly decomposed. **7** [INFORMAL] excited; under the influence of drugs.
NOUN **1** a high level; an area of high pressure. **2** [INFORMAL] a euphoric state. ADV in, at, or to a high level.
high time at or past the time when something should happen.

highbrow ADJ intellectual, cultured. NOUN a highbrow person.

higher education NOUN education at university etc.

highfalutin (also **highfaluting**) ADJ [INFORMAL] pompous, pretentious.

high-handed ADJ using authority arrogantly.

highlands PLURAL NOUN a mountainous region.
highland ADJ
highlander NOUN

highlight NOUN **1** an outstandingly good part of something. **2** a bright area in a picture; a light streak in the hair.
VERB emphasize.

highlighter NOUN a coloured marker pen.

highly ADV **1** to a high degree. **2** favourably: *highly regarded.*

highly strung ADJ nervous, easily upset.

high-rise ADJ (of a building) with many storeys.

high road NOUN a main road; the best or most direct way to achieve something.

high school NOUN a secondary school.

high seas PLURAL NOUN the sea outside a country's territorial waters.

high season NOUN the busiest season at a hotel etc.

high-spirited ADJ lively.

high street NOUN the principal shopping street of a town.

high tea NOUN an early evening meal with tea and cooked food.

high-tech (also **hi-tech**)

ADJ involving advanced technology and electronics.

high tide (also **high water**) NOUN the tide at its highest level.

highway NOUN a public road; a main route.

highwayman NOUN a person who robbed travellers in former times.

hijack VERB illegally seize control of (a vehicle or aircraft in transit). NOUN an instance of hijacking. **hijacker** NOUN

hike NOUN **1** a long walk. **2** a sharp increase in price etc. VERB **1** go for a hike. **2** lift or raise (clothing). **3** raise (a price) **hiker** NOUN

hilarious ADJ very funny; boisterous and merry. **hilariously** ADV **hilarity** NOUN

hill NOUN a raised part of the earth's surface, lower than a mountain; a slope in a road etc.

hillock NOUN a small hill.

hilt NOUN the handle of a sword or dagger. **to the hilt** completely.

him PRON the objective case of *he*.

himself PRON the emphatic and reflexive form of *he* and *him*.

hind[1] ADJ situated at the back.

hind[2] NOUN a female deer.

hinder VERB obstruct, make difficulties for.

Hindi NOUN the most widely spoken language of northern India.

hindmost ADJ furthest behind.

hindrance NOUN something that hinders; difficulty, obstruction.

hindsight NOUN wisdom about an event after it has occurred.

Hinduism NOUN the principal religion and philosophy of India. **Hindu** ADJ & NOUN

Hindustani NOUN a group of languages of NW India.

hinge NOUN a movable joint such as that on a door or lid. VERB attach or be attached by hinge(s). **hinge on** depend on.

hint NOUN a slight or indirect suggestion; a

piece of practical information; a slight trace. VERB suggest, indicate.

hinterland NOUN remote areas away from the coast; the area beyond a major town or port.

hip NOUN **1** the projection of the pelvis on each side of the body. **2** the fruit of the rose.

hip hop NOUN a style of popular music featuring rap with electronic backing; culture associated with this.

hippie variant of **HIPPY**.

hippopotamus NOUN (PL **hippopotamuses** or **hippopotami**) a large African river animal with a thick skin.

hippy (also **hippie**) NOUN (PL **hippies**) a young person rejecting convention and supporting peace and free love.

hire VERB purchase the temporary use of. NOUN the action of hiring. **hire out** grant temporary use of for payment.

hireling NOUN a hired helper.

hire purchase NOUN a system of purchase by payment in instalments.

hirsute /herss-yoot/ ADJ [FORMAL] hairy.

his ADJ & POSSESSIVE PRONOUN belonging to a male already mentioned.

Hispanic ADJ relating to Spain or the Spanish-speaking countries of Central and South America. NOUN a Spanish-speaking person living in the US.

hiss NOUN a sound like 's'. VERB make this sound; utter with a hiss; express disapproval in this way.

histamine NOUN a substance in the body, associated with allergic reactions.

histology NOUN the study of organic tissues.

historian NOUN an expert on history.

historic ADJ **1** important in the development of events. **2** relating to history.

historical ADJ of or concerned with history; belonging to the past.

historically ADV

history NOUN (PL **histories**) the study of past events; the past; someone's or something's past; a narrative.
make history do something important and memorable.

histrionic ADJ excessively dramatic. NOUN (**histrionics**) exaggeratedly theatrical behaviour.

hit VERB (**hits, hitting, hit**) **1** strike with a blow or missile; strike forcefully against. **2** affect badly. **3** reach (a target etc.). NOUN **1** a blow, a stroke; a shot that hits its target. **2** [INFORMAL] a success.
hit it off [INFORMAL] like one another.

hitch VERB **1** move (something) with a jerk. **2** [INFORMAL] hitch-hike; obtain (a lift). **3** tether, fasten. NOUN **1** a temporary problem or setback. **2** a kind of knot.
get hitched [INFORMAL] marry.

hitch-hike VERB travel by seeking free lifts in passing vehicles.
hitch-hiker NOUN

hi-tech variant of **HIGH-TECH**.

hither ADV [ARCHAIC] to or towards this place.

hitherto ADV until this time.

hit list NOUN a list of prospective victims.

HIV ABBREV human immunodeficiency virus.

hive NOUN **1** a structure in which bees live. **2** (**hives**) a skin eruption, especially nettlerash.
hive off separate from a larger group.

HM ABBREV Her (or His) Majesty or Majesty's.

HMS ABBREV Her (or His) Majesty's Ship.

HNC ABBREV Higher National Certificate.

HND ABBREV Higher National Diploma.

hoard VERB save and store away. NOUN a store, especially of valuable things.

hoarding NOUN a large board for displaying advertisements.

hoar frost NOUN white frost.

hoarse ADJ (of a voice)

rough and dry-sounding.
hoarsely ADV
hoarseness NOUN

hoary ADJ (**hoarier**, **hoariest**) grey with age; (of a joke etc.) old.

hoax VERB deceive jokingly. NOUN a joking deception.
hoaxer NOUN

h

hob NOUN a cooking surface with hotplates.

hobble VERB **1** walk lamely. **2** fasten the legs of (a horse) to limit its movement. NOUN **1** a hobbling walk. **2** a rope etc. used to hobble a horse.

hobby NOUN (PL **hobbies**) something done for pleasure in one's spare time.

hobby horse NOUN **1** a stick with a horse's head, as a toy. **2** [INFORMAL] a favourite topic.

hobgoblin NOUN an imp.

hobnail NOUN a heavy-headed nail for boot-soles.

hobnob VERB (**hobnobs**, **hobnobbing**, **hobnobbed**) [INFORMAL] mix socially with people of a higher class etc.

Hobson's choice NOUN no alternative to the thing offered.

hock NOUN **1** the middle joint of an animal's hind leg. **2** German white wine. VERB [INFORMAL] pawn.

hockey NOUN a field game played with curved sticks and a small hard ball.

hocus-pocus NOUN mystifying and often deceptive talk or behaviour.

hod NOUN **1** a trough on a pole for carrying mortar or bricks. **2** a tall container for coal.

hodgepodge variant of **HOTCHPOTCH**.

hoe NOUN a tool for loosening soil or scraping up weeds. VERB (**hoes**, **hoeing**, **hoed**) dig or scrape with a hoe.

hog NOUN **1** a castrated male pig reared for meat. **2** [INFORMAL] a greedy person. VERB (**hogs**, **hogging**, **hogged**) [INFORMAL] take greedily.
go the whole hog [INFORMAL] do something thoroughly.

Hogmanay NOUN [SCOTTISH] New Year's Eve.

hoick [INFORMAL] VERB lift or bring out with a jerk. NOUN a jerky pull.

hoi polloi NOUN ordinary people.

hoist VERB raise or haul up. NOUN an apparatus for hoisting things.

hoity-toity ADJ haughty.

hokum NOUN [INFORMAL] sentimental or unreal material in a story; nonsense.

hold VERB (**holds**, **holding**, **held**) **1** keep or support in one's hands or arms; contain; support in position; bear the weight of. **2** keep in one's possession; detain, keep captive. **3** remain unmoved or unbroken under pressure; remain true or valid. **4** consider to be of a particular nature. **5** arrange and take part in: *hold a meeting*. NOUN **1** an act, manner, or means of holding; a means of exerting influence. **2** a storage cavity below a ship's deck.
hold on wait; endure. **hold out 1** resist, survive, last; persist in making a demand. **2** offer. **hold up 1** delay. **2** rob with violence. **hold with** [INFORMAL] approve of.
holder NOUN

holdall NOUN a large soft travel bag.

holding NOUN **1** land held by lease. **2** (**holdings**) stocks, property, etc. owned by someone.

hold-up NOUN **1** a delay. **2** a robbery.

hole NOUN **1** a hollow in a surface; a burrow; an opening; a tear in cloth etc. **2** [INFORMAL] an unpleasant place; an awkward situation. VERB make a hole in.
holey ADJ

holiday NOUN a period of recreation. VERB spend a holiday.

holism NOUN treatment of the whole person rather than just particular isolated symptoms.
holistic ADJ

hollow ADJ **1** empty within, not solid; sunken; echoing as if in something hollow. **2** worthless. NOUN a cavity;

a sunken place; a valley. VERB make hollow.
hollowly ADV
hollowness NOUN

holly NOUN an evergreen shrub with prickly leaves and red berries.

holmium NOUN a metallic element.

holocaust NOUN destruction or slaughter on a mass scale.

hologram NOUN a three-dimensional photographic image.

holography NOUN the study of holograms.

holster NOUN a leather case holding a pistol or revolver.

holy ADJ (**holier**, **holiest**) dedicated to God; pious, virtuous.
holiness NOUN

homage NOUN things said or done as a mark of respect or loyalty.

home NOUN **1** the place where one lives. **2** an institution where people needing care may live. **3** the finishing point in a race. ADJ of one's home or country; (of a match) played on a team's own ground. ADV at or to one's home; to the point aimed at. VERB make its way home or to a target.
homeless ADJ
homelessness NOUN

homeland NOUN one's native land.

homely ADJ (**homelier**, **homeliest**) **1** simple but comfortable. **2** [US] plain, not beautiful.
homeliness NOUN

homeopathy US spelling of **HOMOEOPATHY**.

home page NOUN [COMPUTING] an individual's or organization's introductory document on the World Wide Web.

homesick ADJ longing for home.

home truth NOUN an unpleasant truth about oneself.

homeward ADJ & ADV going towards home.
homewards ADV

homework NOUN work set for a pupil to do away from school.

homicide NOUN the killing of one person by another.
homicidal ADJ

homily NOUN (PL **homilies**) a moralizing lecture.

hominid NOUN a member of the family of primates which includes humans and their prehistoric ancestors.

homoeopathy /hohm-i-op-ăthi/ ([US] **homeopathy**) NOUN treatment of a disease by very small doses of a substance that would produce symptoms of the same disease in a healthy person.
homoeopath NOUN
homoeopathic ADJ

homogeneous /hom-ŏ-jeen-ee-ŭs/ ADJ of the same kind, uniform.
homogeneity NOUN
homogeneously ADV

homogenize (also **homogenise**) VERB treat (milk) so that cream does not separate and rise to the top.

homograph (also **homonym**) NOUN a word spelt the same way as another.

homophobia NOUN hatred or fear of homosexuals.
homophobe NOUN
homophobic ADJ

homophone NOUN a word with the same sound as another.

Homo sapiens /hoh-moh sap-i-enz/ NOUN modern humans.

homosexual ADJ feeling or involving sexual attraction to people of the same sex. NOUN a homosexual person.
homosexuality NOUN

hone VERB sharpen on a whetstone.

honest ADJ truthful, trustworthy; fairly earned.
honesty NOUN

honestly ADV **1** in an honest way. **2** really (emphasizing an opinion).

honey NOUN (PL **honeys**) **1** a sweet substance made by bees from nectar. **2** [INFORMAL] darling.

honey bee NOUN the common hive-bee.

honeycomb NOUN a bees' wax structure holding their honey and eggs; a pattern of six-sided sections.

honeydew NOUN **1** a sticky substance on plants, secreted by aphids. **2** a variety of melon.

honeyed ADJ flattering, pleasant.

honeymoon NOUN a holiday for a newly married couple; an initial period of goodwill. VERB spend a honeymoon.

honeysuckle NOUN a climbing shrub with fragrant pink and yellow flowers.

honk NOUN the cry of a wild goose; the harsh sound of a car horn. VERB make this noise.

honor US spelling of **HONOUR**.

honorarium NOUN (PL **honorariums** or **honoraria**) a voluntary payment made where no fee is legally required.

honorary ADJ **1** given as an honour, without the usual requirements. **2** (of an office-holder) unpaid.

honour ([US] **honor**) NOUN **1** great respect or public regard; a mark of this, a privilege. **2** honesty, integrity. VERB **1** respect; confer a mark of honour on. **2** keep (an agreement); pay (a cheque).

honourable ([US] **honorable**) ADJ honest; deserving honour. **honourably** ADV

honours degree NOUN a degree of a higher standard than a pass.

hood NOUN **1** a covering for the head and neck. **2** a hood-like thing or cover; a folding roof over a car; [US] a car bonnet. **3** [US] [INFORMAL] a gangster or gunman.

hoodlum NOUN a hooligan or gangster.

hoodoo NOUN bad luck; something causing this.

hoodwink VERB deceive.

hoof NOUN (PL **hoofs** or **hooves**) the horny part of a horse's foot.

hook NOUN **1** a curved device for catching hold of or hanging things on; a bent piece of metal for catching fish; a curved implement for reaping etc. **2** a short blow made with the elbow bent. VERB **1** attach with a hook. **2** catch with a hook. **3** bend or be bent into a hooked shape.

off the hook 1 (of a telephone) off its rest. 2 [INFORMAL] no longer in difficulty.

hookah NOUN an oriental tobacco pipe with a long tube passing through water.

hooked ADJ 1 hook-shaped. 2 [INFORMAL] addicted.

hook-up NOUN an interconnection of broadcasting equipment.

hookworm NOUN a parasitic worm with hook-like mouthparts.

hooligan NOUN a young ruffian.
hooliganism NOUN

hoop NOUN a circular band of metal or wood; a metal croquet arch.

hoopla NOUN a game in which rings are thrown to encircle a prize.

hoopoe NOUN a crested bird.

hooray variant of **HURRAH**.

hoot NOUN 1 an owl's cry; the sound of a hooter; a cry of laughter or disapproval. 2 [INFORMAL] an amusing person or thing. VERB utter or make a hoot.

hooter NOUN a siren or steam whistle; a car horn.

Hoover NOUN [TRADE MARK] a vacuum cleaner. VERB (**hoover**) clean with a vacuum cleaner.

hop¹ VERB (**hops, hopping, hopped**) 1 jump on one foot; (of an animal) jump with all feet together. 2 [INFORMAL] make a short journey; move quickly to a new position. NOUN a hopping movement; a short journey.
on the hop [INFORMAL] unprepared.

hop² NOUN a plant used to flavour beer.

hope NOUN expectation of something desired; something giving grounds for this; something hoped for. VERB feel hope.
hopeful ADJ

hopefully ADV 1 in a hopeful way. 2 it is to be hoped.

hopeless ADJ 1 without hope. 2 inadequate, incompetent.
hopelessly ADV

hopelessness NOUN

hopper NOUN **1** a container with an opening at the base for discharging its contents. **2** one who hops.

hopscotch NOUN a game involving hopping over marked squares.

horde NOUN a large group or crowd.

horizon NOUN **1** the line at which earth and sky appear to meet. **2** the limit of someone's knowledge or interests.

horizontal ADJ parallel to the horizon; going across rather than up and down.
horizontally ADV

hormone NOUN a substance produced by the body or a plant to stimulate growth or an organ's functions.
hormonal ADJ

horn NOUN **1** a hard pointed growth on the heads of certain animals; the substance of this; something resembling these growths. **2** a wind instrument with a trumpet-shaped end; a device for sounding a warning signal.
horned ADJ

hornblende NOUN a dark mineral constituent of granite etc.

hornet NOUN a large wasp.

hornpipe NOUN a lively solo dance traditionally performed by sailors.

horn-rimmed ADJ (of glasses) with frames of horn or similar material.

horny ADJ (**hornier, horniest**) **1** of or like horn; hardened and calloused. **2** [INFORMAL] sexually excited.

horology NOUN the measurement of time; the making of clocks.
horologist NOUN

horoscope NOUN a forecast of events based on the positions of stars.

horrendous ADJ horrifying.
horrendously ADV

horrible ADJ causing horror; very unpleasant.
horribly ADV

horrid ADJ horrible.

horrific ADJ horrifying.
horrifically ADV

horrify VERB (**horrifies, horrifying, horrified**)

arouse horror in.

horror NOUN intense shock and fear or disgust; a terrible event or situation; [INFORMAL] a naughty child.

hors d'oeuvre /or **dervr**/ NOUN food served as an appetizer.

horse NOUN **1** a four-legged animal with a mane and tail. **2** a padded structure for vaulting over in a gym.
horse around [INFORMAL] fool about.

horseback NOUN (**on horseback**) riding on a horse.

horsebox NOUN a vehicle for transporting horses.

horse chestnut NOUN a brown shiny nut; the tree bearing this.

horsefly NOUN (PL **horseflies**) a large biting fly.

horseman (also **horsewoman**) NOUN a rider on horseback.
horsemanship NOUN

horseplay NOUN boisterous play.

horsepower NOUN (PL **horsepower**) a unit for measuring the power of an engine.

horseradish NOUN a plant with a hot-tasting root, used to make sauce.

horse sense NOUN [INFORMAL] common sense.

horseshoe NOUN a U-shaped strip of metal nailed to a horse's hoof; something shaped like this.

horsy (also **horsey**) ADJ (**horsier**, **horsiest**) **1** of or like a horse. **2** interested in horses.

horticulture NOUN the art of garden cultivation.
horticultural ADJ
horticulturist NOUN

hose NOUN **1** (also **hosepipe**) a flexible tube for conveying water. **2** stockings and socks.
VERB water or spray with a hosepipe.

hosiery NOUN stockings, socks, etc.

hospice NOUN a hospital or home for the terminally ill.

hospitable ADJ friendly and welcoming.
hospitably ADV

hospital NOUN an

institution for treatment of sick or injured people.

hospitality NOUN friendly and generous entertainment of guests.

hospitalize (also **hospitalise**) VERB send or admit to a hospital. **hospitalization** NOUN

h

host NOUN **1** a person entertaining guests; a place or person providing facilities for visitors. **2** an organism on which another lives as a parasite. **3** a large number of people or things. VERB act as host at (an event).

hostage NOUN a person held as security that the holder's demands will be satisfied.

hostel NOUN a place providing cheap accommodation for a particular group of people.

hostess NOUN a woman entertaining guests.

hostile ADJ unfriendly; of an enemy; opposed to something.

hostility NOUN (PL **hostilities**) enmity, unfriendliness; (**hostilities**) acts of warfare.

hot ADJ **1** at or having a high temperature. **2** producing a burning sensation when tasted. **3** passionate; eager, excited; angry; arousing strong feelings. **4** (of news) fresh; [INFORMAL] popular. **hot air** [INFORMAL] empty talk designed to impress. **hot up** (**hots, hotting, hotted**) [INFORMAL] make or become hotter or more intense. **in hot water** [INFORMAL] in trouble.

hotbed NOUN a place encouraging vice, intrigue, etc.

hotchpotch (also **hodgepodge**) NOUN a confused mixture.

hot-desking NOUN the sharing of office desks by workers on a rota.

hot dog NOUN a hot sausage in a bread roll.

hotel NOUN an establishment providing rooms and meals for tourists and travellers.

hotelier NOUN a hotel-keeper.

hotfoot ADV in eager haste.

hothead NOUN an impetuous person. **hot-headed** ADJ

hothouse NOUN a heated greenhouse; an environment encouraging rapid development.

hotline NOUN a direct telephone line for speedy communication.

hotly ADV **1** angrily; passionately. **2** closely and quickly: *hotly pursued.*

hotplate NOUN a heated surface on a cooker or hob.

hotting NOUN [INFORMAL] joyriding in stolen cars.

hoummos variant of **HUMMUS**.

hound NOUN a dog used in hunting. VERB pursue, harass.

hour NOUN **1** one twenty-fourth part of a day and night. **2** a point in time. **3** (**hours**) time fixed or set aside for work or an activity.

hourglass NOUN two connected glass globes containing sand that takes an hour to pass from the upper to the lower.

houri /hoor-i/ NOUN a beautiful young woman of the Muslim paradise.

hourly ADJ done or occurring once an hour; reckoned by the hour. ADV **1** once an hour. **2** very frequently.

house NOUN /howss/ **1** a building for people to live in, or for a specific purpose; a household; a family or dynasty. **2** a legislative assembly; a business firm; a theatre audience or performance. **3** a style of popular dance music using drum machines. VERB /howz/ provide accommodation or storage space for; encase.

on the house (of drinks in a bar etc.) provided free of charge.

house arrest NOUN detention in one's own home.

houseboat NOUN a boat fitted up as a dwelling.

housebound ADJ unable to leave one's house, especially through illness.

housebreaker NOUN a burglar.
housebreaking NOUN

housecoat NOUN a woman's dressing gown.

household NOUN the occupants of a house regarded as a unit.

h

householder NOUN a person owning or renting a house or flat.

household word (also **household name**) NOUN a widely known saying or name.

housekeeper NOUN a person employed to look after a household.

housekeeping NOUN management of household affairs; money to be used for this.

housemaster NOUN a male teacher in charge of a school boarding house.

housemistress NOUN a female teacher in charge of a school boarding house.

house-proud ADJ giving great attention to the appearance of one's home.

house-trained ADJ (of a pet) trained to be clean in the house.

house-warming NOUN a party to celebrate moving into a new home.

housewife NOUN (PL **housewives**) a woman managing a household.

housework NOUN the work of cleaning and cooking etc. in a house.

housing NOUN **1** accommodation. **2** a rigid case enclosing machinery.

hove *see* **HEAVE**.

hovel NOUN a small miserable dwelling.

hover VERB (of a bird, aircraft, etc.) remain in one place in the air; wait close by, linger.

hovercraft NOUN a vehicle supported by air thrust downwards from its engines.

how ADV **1** by what means, in what way. **2** to what extent or degree. **3** of what kind, in what condition: *how was the holiday?*

howdah /how-dă/ NOUN a seat with a canopy on an

elephant's back.

however ADV 1 nevertheless, despite this. 2 in whatever way, to whatever extent.

howitzer NOUN a short gun firing shells at high elevation.

howl NOUN a long loud wailing cry or sound. VERB make or utter with a howl; weep loudly.

howler NOUN [INFORMAL] a stupid mistake.

hoyden NOUN [DATED] a boisterous girl.

h.p. ABBREV 1 hire purchase. 2 horsepower.

HQ ABBREV headquarters.

HRH ABBREV Her (or His) Royal Highness.

HRT ABBREV hormone replacement therapy.

hub NOUN the central part of a wheel; the centre of activity.

hubbub NOUN a confused noise of voices.

hubcap NOUN the cover for the hub of a car wheel.

hubris /hew-bris/ NOUN arrogant pride.

huddle VERB crowd into a small place. NOUN a close group or mass.

hue NOUN a colour, a tint.
hue and cry public outcry or outrage.

huff NOUN a fit of annoyance. VERB blow, breathe heavily.
huffily ADV
huffy ADJ

hug VERB (**hugs**, **hugging**, **hugged**) 1 squeeze in one's arms; hold closely. 2 keep close to: *hug the shore.* NOUN an embrace.

huge ADJ extremely large.
hugely ADV

hula hoop /hoo-lă/ NOUN a large hoop for spinning round the body.

hulk NOUN the body of an old ship; a large clumsy-looking person or thing.

hulking ADJ [INFORMAL] large and clumsy.

hull NOUN 1 the framework of a ship. 2 the pod of a pea or bean; the cluster of leaves on a strawberry. VERB remove the hulls of (beans, strawberries, etc.).

hullabaloo NOUN [INFORMAL] an uproar.

hullo variant of **HELLO**.

hum VERB (**hums**, **humming**, **hummed**) 1 make a low continuous

h

sound; sing with closed lips. **2** [INFORMAL] be in a state of activity. NOUN a humming sound.

human ADJ of human beings; not impersonal or insensitive. NOUN a human being, a person.
humanly ADV

humane ADJ kind-hearted, merciful.
humanely ADV

humanism NOUN a system of thought emphasizing human rather than divine matters and seeking rational solutions to human problems.
humanist NOUN
humanistic ADJ

humanitarian ADJ promoting human welfare and reduction of suffering.
humanitarianism NOUN

humanity NOUN **1** human nature; the human race. **2** kindness. **3** (**humanities**) arts subjects.

humanize (also **humanise**) VERB make human; make humane.

human resources PLURAL NOUN the department of an organization dealing with the management and training of employees.

humble ADJ **1** having a low opinion of one's importance or worth. **2** of low rank; not large or expensive. VERB lower the rank of; make less proud.
humbly ADV

humbug NOUN **1** hypocritical talk or behaviour. **2** a hard usually peppermint-flavoured sweet.

humdrum ADJ dull, commonplace.

humerus NOUN (PL **humeri**) the bone in the upper arm.
humeral ADJ

humid ADJ (of air) damp.
humidity NOUN

humidify VERB (**humidifies**, **humidifying**, **humidified**) increase the moisture in (air).
humidifier NOUN

humiliate VERB cause to feel ashamed and foolish.
humiliation NOUN

humility NOUN a humble attitude of mind.

hummock NOUN a hump in the ground.

hummus (also **hoummos**) NOUN a paste of ground chickpeas, sesame oil, lemon juice, and garlic.

humour ([US] **humor**) NOUN **1** the quality of being amusing; the ability to perceive and enjoy this. **2** a state of mind. VERB keep (a person) contented by doing as he or she wishes.
humorous ADJ
humorously ADV

hump NOUN a rounded projecting part; a curved deformity of the spine. VERB **1** form into a hump. **2** [INFORMAL] hoist and carry.

humpback NOUN a hunchback; a whale with a hump on its back.

humpback bridge NOUN a small steeply arched bridge.

humus /hyoo-mŭs/ NOUN rich dark organic material in soil, formed by decay of dead leaves and plants.

hunch VERB draw (one's shoulders) up; bend one's body forward. NOUN **1** an intuitive feeling. **2** a hunched position.

hunchback NOUN a person with a humped back.

> The term **hunchback** is often considered offensive.

hundred NOUN ten times ten (100, C).
hundredth ADJ & NOUN

hundredfold ADJ & ADV 100 times as much or as many.

hundredweight NOUN a measure of weight, 112 lb (50.802 kg), or in America 100 lb (45.359 kg); a metric unit of weight equal to 50 kg.

hung past and past participle of **HANG**. ADJ (of a council, parliament, etc.) with no party having a clear majority.

Hungarian NOUN a person from Hungary; the language of Hungary. ADJ relating to Hungary.

hunger NOUN **1** discomfort and weakness felt when one has not eaten for some time; lack of food. **2** a strong desire. VERB feel a strong desire.

hunger strike NOUN refusal of food as a form

of protest.

hung-over ADJ suffering from a hangover.

hungry ADJ (**hungrier**, **hungriest**) feeling hunger; causing hunger. **hungrily** ADV

hunk NOUN **1** a large piece broken off. **2** [INFORMAL] an attractive man.

hunt VERB **1** pursue (wild animals) for food or sport; pursue with hostility; seek; search. **2** (of an engine) run unevenly. NOUN an act of hunting; a hunting group.

hunter NOUN one who hunts; a horse used for hunting.

hurdle NOUN a portable fencing panel; a frame to be jumped over in a race; an obstacle, a difficulty. VERB jump over (a hurdle). **hurdler** NOUN

hurl VERB throw violently.

hurly-burly NOUN bustling activity.

hurrah (also **hurray**, **hooray**) EXCLAMATION & NOUN an exclamation of joy or approval.

hurricane NOUN a violent storm-wind.

hurricane lamp NOUN a lamp with the flame protected from the wind.

hurried ADJ done with great haste. **hurriedly** ADV

hurry VERB (**hurries**, **hurrying**, **hurried**) move or act with great haste; cause to do this. NOUN great haste.

hurt VERB (**hurts**, **hurting**, **hurt**) cause pain, injury, or grief to; feel pain; offend. NOUN injury, harm, or distress.

hurtful ADJ causing distress.

hurtle VERB move or cause to move rapidly.

husband NOUN a married man in relation to his wife. VERB use economically, try to save.

husbandry NOUN **1** farming. **2** economical management of resources.

hush VERB make or become silent. NOUN silence. **hush up** suppress discussion of or information about.

husk NOUN the dry outer covering of certain seeds and fruits. VERB remove the husk from.

husky ADJ (**huskier**, **huskiest**) **1** (of a voice) low and hoarse. **2** strong, burly. NOUN (PL **huskies**) an Arctic sledge-dog.
huskily ADV
huskiness NOUN

hustings NOUN a meeting for political candidates to address voters.

hustle VERB push roughly; force to move hurriedly. NOUN busy movement and activity.

hut NOUN a small simple or roughly made house or shelter.

hutch NOUN a box-like cage for rabbits.

hyacinth NOUN a plant with fragrant bell-shaped flowers.

hyaena variant of **HYENA**.

hybrid NOUN the offspring of two different species or varieties; something made by combining different elements. ADJ composed of different elements.

hybridize (also **hybridise**) VERB cross-breed; produce hybrids.
hybridism NOUN
hybridization NOUN

hydrant NOUN a pipe from a water main in a street to which a hose can be attached.

hydrate NOUN a chemical compound of water with another substance.

hydraulic /hI-**dror**-lik/ ADJ **1** operated by pressure of fluid conveyed in pipes. **2** hardening under water. NOUN (**hydraulics**) the science of hydraulic operations.
hydraulically ADV

hydride NOUN a compound of hydrogen with an element.

hydrocarbon NOUN a compound of hydrogen and carbon.

hydrochloric acid NOUN a corrosive acid containing hydrogen and chlorine.

hydrodynamic ADJ of the forces exerted by liquids in motion.

hydroelectric ADJ using water-power to produce electricity.

hydrofoil NOUN a boat with a structure that raises its hull out of the water when in motion.

hydrogen NOUN an odourless gas, the lightest element.

hydrogen bomb NOUN a powerful bomb releasing energy by fusion of hydrogen nuclei.

h

hydrolysis NOUN decomposition by chemical reaction with water.
hydrolytic ADJ

hydrometer NOUN a device measuring the density of liquids.

hydrophobia NOUN abnormal fear of water; rabies.

hydroponics NOUN the process of growing plants in water impregnated with chemicals rather than in soil.

hydrostatic ADJ of the pressure and other characteristics of liquid at rest.

hydrotherapy NOUN therapeutic exercise in water.

hydrous ADJ containing water.

hyena (also **hyaena**) NOUN a wolf-like animal with a howl that sounds like laughter.

hygiene /hI-jeen/ NOUN cleanliness as a means of preventing disease.
hygienic ADJ
hygienically ADV
hygienist NOUN

hymen NOUN the membrane partly closing the opening of the vagina of a virgin girl or woman.

hymn NOUN a song used in religious worship.

hype NOUN [INFORMAL] intensive promotion of a product.

hyper- PREFIX **1** excessively. **2** [COMPUTING] relating to hypertext.

hyperactive ADJ abnormally active.
hyperactivity NOUN

hyperbola /hI-per-bŏ-lă/ NOUN (PL **hyperbolas** or **hyperbolae**) the curve produced by a cut made through a cone at an angle with the base greater than that of the side of the cone.

hyperbole NOUN /hy-per-bŏ-li/ an exaggerated statement.

hyperglycaemia /hy-per-gly-see-mi-ă/ ([US] **hyperglycemia**) NOUN excess glucose in the blood.

hypermarket NOUN a very large supermarket.

hypersonic ADJ of speeds more than five times that of sound.

hypertension NOUN abnormally high blood pressure.

hypertext NOUN [COMPUTING] a system allowing simultaneous use of, and cross reference between, several texts.

hyperventilation NOUN abnormally rapid breathing.
hyperventilate VERB

hyphen NOUN a sign (-) used to join words together or mark the division of a word at the end of a line.

hyphenate VERB join or divide with a hyphen.
hyphenation NOUN

hypnosis NOUN the production of a sleep-like condition in a person who then obeys suggestions.
hypnotic ADJ
hypnotically ADV

hypnotism NOUN hypnosis.
hypnotist NOUN

hypnotize (also **hypnotise**) VERB control by or as though by hypnosis.

hypo- PREFIX under; below normal.

hypo-allergenic ADJ unlikely to cause an allergic reaction.

hypochondria NOUN the state of constantly imagining that one is ill.
hypochondriac NOUN

hypocrisy NOUN (PL **hypocrisies**) the practice of pretending to higher standards or beliefs than is the case; insincerity.

hypocrite NOUN a person guilty of hypocrisy.
hypocritical ADJ
hypocritically ADV

hypodermic ADJ injected beneath the skin; used for such injections. NOUN a hypodermic syringe.

hypotension NOUN

abnormally low blood pressure.

hypotenuse /hI-pot-ĕ-nyooz/ NOUN the longest side of a right-angled triangle.

hypothermia NOUN the condition of having an abnormally low body temperature.

hypothesis NOUN (PL **hypotheses**) a supposition put forward as a basis for reasoning or investigation.

hypothetical ADJ supposed but not necessarily true.
hypothetically ADV

hysterectomy /his-tĕr-ek-tŏm-i/ NOUN (PL **hysterectomies**) the surgical removal of the womb.

hysteria NOUN wild uncontrollable emotion.
hysterical ADJ
hysterically ADV

hysterics PLURAL NOUN an outburst of hysteria; [INFORMAL] uncontrollable laughter.

Hz ABBREV hertz.

Ii

I[1] (also **i**) NOUN (PL **Is** or **I's**) **1** the ninth letter of the alphabet. **2** the Roman numeral for one.

I[2] PRON used by a speaker or writer to refer to himself or herself.

iambic /I-**am**-bik/ ADJ (of verse) consisting of syllables that are alternately stressed and unstressed.

Iberian /I-**beer**-i-ăn/ ADJ of the peninsula comprising Spain and Portugal.

ibex NOUN (PL **ibex** or **ibexes**) a mountain goat.

ibid. ABBREV in a source just referred to.

ice NOUN **1** frozen water; an ice cream. **2** [INFORMAL] diamonds. VERB cover with icing.
break the ice start a conversation, relieve shyness. **ice over** become covered with ice. **ice up** become blocked with ice.

iceberg NOUN a mass of ice floating in the sea.

icebox NOUN the freezing compartment in a fridge; [US] a fridge.

ice cream NOUN a sweet creamy frozen food.

Icelandic NOUN the language of Iceland. ADJ relating to Iceland.

ichthyology /ik-thi-**ol**-ŏ-ji/ NOUN the study of fishes.
ichthyologist NOUN

icicle NOUN a piece of ice hanging downwards.

icing NOUN a mixture of powdered sugar and liquid or fat used to decorate cakes.

icon (also **ikon**) NOUN a sacred painting or mosaic; a greatly admired person; [COMPUTING] a graphic symbol on a computer screen.

iconoclast NOUN a person

who attacks established traditions.
iconoclasm NOUN
iconoclastic ADJ

icy ADJ (**icier**, **iciest**) covered with ice; very cold; very unfriendly.
icily ADV
iciness NOUN

ID ABBREV identification.

idea NOUN a plan etc. formed in the mind; an opinion; a mental impression; a vague belief.

ideal ADJ satisfying one's idea of what is perfect. NOUN a person or thing regarded as perfect; an aim, principle, or standard.
ideally ADV

idealist NOUN a person with high ideals.
idealism NOUN
idealistic ADJ

idealize (also **idealise**) VERB regard or represent as perfect.

identical ADJ the same; exactly alike.
identically ADV

identification NOUN the action of identifying; something used as a proof of identity.

identify VERB (**identifies**, **identifying**, **identified**) **1** recognize as being a specified person or thing; reveal the identity of; associate (someone) closely with someone or something else. **2** feel sympathy for someone.
identifiable ADJ
identifiably ADV

identikit NOUN a set of pictures of features that can be put together to form a likeness of a person.

identity NOUN (PL **identities**) **1** the fact of being who or what someone or something is. **2** a close similarity; a feeling of understanding.

ideogram NOUN a symbol or picture representing an idea, e.g. Chinese characters or road signs.

ideology NOUN (PL **ideologies**) ideas that form the basis of a political or economic theory.
ideological ADJ

idiocy NOUN (PL **idiocies**) extreme stupidity.

idiom NOUN a phrase

whose meaning cannot be deduced from the words in it; an expression natural to a language.

idiomatic ADJ using idioms; sounding natural.
idiomatically ADV

idiosyncrasy NOUN (PL **idiosyncrasies**) a way of behaving distinctive of a particular person.
idiosyncratic ADJ

idiot NOUN [INFORMAL] a very stupid person.
idiotic ADJ
idiotically ADV

idle ADJ not employed or in use; lazy; aimless. VERB be idle; move slowly and aimlessly; (of an engine) run slowly in neutral gear.
idleness NOUN
idler NOUN
idly ADV

idol NOUN an image worshipped as a god; an idolized person or thing.

idolatry NOUN worship of idols.
idolater NOUN
idolatrous ADJ

idolize (also **idolise**) VERB love or admire excessively.

idyll /id-il/ NOUN a peaceful or romantic scene; a description of this, usually in verse.
idyllic ADJ
idyllically ADV

i.e. ABBREV that is (Latin *id est*).

if CONJ **1** on condition that; supposing that.
2 whether: *ask if they can come.* NOUN a condition or supposition.

iffy ADJ (**iffier**, **iffiest**) [INFORMAL] uncertain; of doubtful quality.

igloo NOUN a dome-shaped Eskimo snow house.

igneous ADJ (of rock) formed by volcanic action.

ignite VERB set fire to; catch fire.

ignition NOUN the action of igniting; a mechanism producing a spark to ignite the fuel in an engine.

ignoble ADJ **1** not honourable. **2** of low status.
ignobly ADV

ignominy /ig-nŏ-mi-ni/ NOUN disgrace,

humiliation.
ignominious ADJ
ignominiously ADV

ignoramus NOUN (PL **ignoramuses**) an ignorant person.

ignorant ADJ lacking knowledge; [INFORMAL] behaving rudely through not knowing good manners.
ignorance NOUN
ignorantly ADV

ignore VERB take no notice of.

iguana NOUN a large tropical lizard.

ikon variant of **ICON**.

ileum NOUN a part of the small intestine.

ilk NOUN (**of that ilk**) of that kind.

ill ADJ **1** in poor health, sick. **2** of poor quality. **3** harmful; unfavourable. ADV badly, wrongly. NOUN harm; a misfortune or problem.
ill at ease uncomfortable, embarrassed.

ill-advised ADJ unwise.

illegal ADJ against the law.
illegality NOUN
illegally ADV

illegible ADJ not readable.
illegibility NOUN
illegibly ADV

illegitimate ADJ **1** born of parents not married to each other. **2** contrary to a law or rule.
illegitimacy NOUN
illegitimately ADV

ill-gotten ADJ gained by evil or unlawful means.

illicit ADJ unlawful, not allowed.
illicitly ADV

illiterate ADJ unable to read and write; uneducated.
illiteracy NOUN

ill-mannered ADJ having bad manners.

illness NOUN the state of being ill; a particular form of ill health.

illogical ADJ not logical.
illogically ADV

ill-treat VERB treat badly or cruelly.
ill-treatment NOUN

illuminate VERB light up; decorate with lights; explain, clarify (a subject).
illumination NOUN

illumine VERB [LITERARY] light up; enlighten.

illusion NOUN a false belief; a deceptive appearance; an error of perception.

illusionist NOUN a conjuror.

illusory (also **illusive**) ADJ based on illusion; not real.

illustrate VERB supply (a book etc.) with drawings or pictures; make clear by example(s) or picture(s); serve as an example of.
illustration NOUN
illustrative ADJ
illustrator NOUN

illustrious /il-**lus**-tri-ŭs/ ADJ well known and respected.

ill will NOUN hostility, unkind feeling.

image NOUN a picture or other representation; an optical appearance produced in a mirror or through a lens; a mental picture; a reputation; a simile or metaphor.

imaginary ADJ existing only in the imagination, not real.

imagination NOUN the ability to form ideas and images in the mind; the part of the mind that does this.
imaginative ADJ
imaginatively ADV

imagine VERB form a mental image of; think, suppose; guess.
imaginable ADJ

imago /i-**may**-goh/ NOUN (PL **imagines** or **imagos**) an insect in its fully developed adult stage.

imam /i-**mahm**/ NOUN a leader of prayers in a mosque.

imbalance NOUN lack of balance.

imbecile NOUN [INFORMAL] a stupid person.

imbed variant of **EMBED**.

imbibe VERB [FORMAL] drink; absorb (ideas).

imbroglio /im-**broh**-ly-oh/ NOUN (PL **imbroglios**) a confused or embarrassing situation.

imbue VERB fill with feelings, qualities, or emotions.

IMF ABBREV International Monetary Fund.

imitable ADJ able to be imitated.

imitate VERB try to act or be like; copy.
imitation NOUN

imitator NOUN

imitative ADJ imitating; not original.

immaculate ADJ spotlessly clean and tidy; free from blemish or fault.
immaculately ADV

immanent ADJ inherent; present in everything.
immanence NOUN

i

immaterial ADJ **1** having no physical substance. **2** of no importance.

immature ADJ **1** not fully grown. **2** childish, irresponsible.
immaturity NOUN

immeasurable ADJ too large or extreme to measure.
immeasurably ADV

immediate ADJ **1** done or occurring without delay. **2** nearest, with nothing between.
immediacy NOUN

immediately ADV **1** without delay. **2** directly, with nothing in between. CONJ as soon as.

immemorial ADJ extremely old.

immense ADJ extremely great.
immensely ADV
immensity NOUN

immerse VERB put completely into liquid; involve deeply in an activity etc.

immersion NOUN the action of immersing.

immersion heater NOUN an electric device heating a water tank.

immigrate VERB come to live permanently in a foreign country.
immigrant ADJ & NOUN
immigration NOUN

imminent ADJ about to occur.
imminence NOUN
imminently ADV

immiscible /im-miss-i-bĕl/ ADJ (of liquids) not able to be mixed.

immobile ADJ not moving; unable to be moved.
immobility NOUN
immobilize VERB (also **immobilise**)
immobilization NOUN (also **immobilisation**)

immoderate ADJ excessive.
immoderately ADV

immolate VERB kill as a sacrifice.

immoral ADJ morally wrong.
immorality NOUN
immorally ADV

immortal ADJ living forever, not mortal; famous for all time.
immortality NOUN
immortalize VERB (also **immortalise**)

immovable ADJ unable to be moved; unyielding.
immovably ADV

immune ADJ resistant to infection; exempt from an obligation etc.; not affected.
immunity NOUN
immunize VERB (also **immunise**)
immunization NOUN (also **immunisation**)

immunodeficiency NOUN a reduction in normal resistance to infection.

immunology NOUN the study of resistance to infection.
immunological ADJ
immunologist NOUN

immure VERB imprison, shut in.

immutable ADJ unchangeable.
immutability NOUN
immutably ADV

imp NOUN a small devil; a mischievous child.

impact NOUN /**im**-pakt/ a collision, the force of this; a strong effect.
VERB /im-**pakt**/ **1** collide forcefully with something. **2** press firmly. **3** (**impact on**) have a strong effect on.

impair VERB damage, weaken.
impairment NOUN

impale VERB fix or pierce with a pointed object.

impalpable ADJ not easily understood; unable to be felt by touch.
impalpably ADV

impart VERB make (information) known; give (a quality).

impartial ADJ not favouring one side more than another.
impartiality NOUN
impartially ADV

impassable ADJ impossible to travel on or over.

impasse /**am**-pahss/ NOUN a

deadlock.

impassioned ADJ passionate.

impassive ADJ not feeling or showing emotion.
impassively ADV
impassivity NOUN

impatient ADJ
1 intolerant, easily irritated. **2** not ready to wait; eager.
impatience NOUN
impatiently ADV

i

impeach VERB **1** accuse of a serious crime against the state and bring for trial. **2** question, challenge (a privilege etc.).
impeachment NOUN

impeccable ADJ faultless.
impeccability NOUN
impeccably ADV

impecunious ADJ having little or no money.

impedance /im-peed-ăns/ NOUN resistance of an electric circuit to the flow of current.

impede VERB hinder.

impediment NOUN a hindrance or obstruction; a defect in speech, e.g. a lisp or stammer.

impel VERB (**impels**, **impelling**, **impelled**) urge or force to do something; drive forward.

impending ADJ imminent.

impenetrable ADJ
1 impossible to enter or pass through.
2 incomprehensible.
impenetrability NOUN
impenetrably ADV

imperative ADJ **1** essential, vital. **2** giving a command. NOUN **1** an essential thing. **2** a command; the grammatical case used for commands.

imperceptible ADJ too slight to be noticed.
imperceptibly ADV

imperfect ADJ **1** flawed, faulty; not complete.
2 [GRAMMAR] (of a tense) implying action going on and not completed.
imperfection NOUN
imperfectly ADV

imperial ADJ **1** of an empire or emperor; majestic. **2** (of measures) belonging to the British official non-metric system.
imperially ADV

imperialism NOUN the policy of having or

extending an empire.
imperialist NOUN
imperialistic ADJ

imperil VERB (**imperils**, **imperilling**, **imperilled**; [US] **imperiling**, **imperiled**) endanger.

imperious ADJ arrogantly giving orders.
imperiously ADV
imperiousness NOUN

impermeable ADJ not able to be penetrated by liquid.

impersonal ADJ **1** not showing or influenced by personal feeling. **2** not existing as a person.
impersonality NOUN
impersonally ADV

impersonate VERB pretend to be (another person).
impersonation NOUN
impersonator NOUN

impertinent ADJ **1** disrespectful, rude. **2** [FORMAL] irrelevant.
impertinence NOUN
impertinently ADV

imperturbable ADJ not excitable, calm.

impervious ADJ impermeable.
impervious to not able to be penetrated or influenced by.
imperviousness NOUN

impetigo /im-pi-**ty**-goh/ NOUN a contagious skin disease.

impetuous ADJ acting or done quickly and recklessly.
impetuosity NOUN
impetuously ADV

impetus NOUN a moving or driving force.

impiety NOUN (PL **impieties**) lack of reverence.

impinge VERB make an impact; encroach.

impious ADJ not reverent, especially towards a god; wicked.
impiously ADV

implacable ADJ unable to be placated; relentless.
implacability NOUN
implacably ADV

implant VERB /im-**plahnt**/ insert (tissue or a device) into a living thing; fix (an idea) in the mind.
NOUN /**im**-plahnt/ something implanted.
implantation NOUN

implausible ADJ not persuasive, improbable.

implausibly ADV

implement NOUN a tool. VERB put (a decision etc.) into effect.
implementation NOUN

implicate VERB show or cause to be involved in a crime etc.

implication NOUN **1** a thing suggested or indirectly stated. **2** the fact of being involved in something.

implicit ADJ **1** implied but not stated. **2** absolute; total and unquestioning.
implicitly ADV

implode VERB collapse violently inwards.
implosion NOUN

implore VERB beg, ask earnestly.

imply VERB (**implies, implying, implied**) convey without stating directly.

impolite ADJ bad-mannered, rude.

impolitic ADJ unwise; risky.

imponderable ADJ difficult or impossible to assess. NOUN an imponderable thing.

import VERB /im-**port**/ bring from abroad or from an outside source. NOUN /**im**-port/ **1** something imported; the action of importing. **2** meaning; importance.
importation NOUN
importer NOUN

important ADJ having great significance or value; having a high and influential position.
importance NOUN

importunate ADJ making annoyingly persistent requests.
importunity NOUN

importune VERB make insistent requests to; (of a prostitute) solicit.

impose VERB force (something unwelcome) on someone; put (a restriction, tax, etc.) into effect.
impose on take unfair advantage of.

imposing ADJ impressive.

imposition NOUN the action of imposing something; a burden imposed unfairly.

impossible ADJ not able to exist, occur, or be done; very hard to deal with.

impossibility NOUN
impossibly ADV

impostor NOUN a person who fraudulently pretends to be someone else.

imposture NOUN fraudulently pretending to be someone else.

impotent ADJ powerless; (of a male) unable to copulate successfully.
impotence NOUN

impound VERB **1** take (property) into legal custody. **2** shut up, imprison.

impoverish VERB cause to become poor; exhaust the strength or fertility of.
impoverishment NOUN

impracticable ADJ not able to be put into practice.

impractical ADJ not showing realism or common sense; not sensible or useful.

imprecation NOUN [FORMAL] a spoken curse.

imprecise ADJ not precise.

impregnable ADJ safe against attack.
impregnability NOUN

impregnate VERB **1** introduce sperm or pollen into and fertilize. **2** saturate with a substance.
impregnation NOUN

impresario /im-pri-**sah**-ri-oh/ NOUN (PL **impresarios**) an organizer of public entertainment.

impress VERB **1** cause to feel admiration. **2** make a mark on (something) with a seal etc.; fix (an idea) in the mind.

impression NOUN **1** an idea or opinion about someone or something; an effect produced on the mind. **2** an imitation done for entertainment. **3** a mark impressed on a surface.
under the impression believing (something).

impressionable ADJ easily influenced.

impressionism NOUN a style of art giving a general impression without detail.
impressionist NOUN
impressionistic ADJ

impressive ADJ inspiring admiration; grand or

awesome.
impressively ADV
impressiveness NOUN

imprint NOUN /im-print/ **1** a mark made by pressing on a surface. **2** a publisher's name etc. on a title-page. VERB /im-**print**/ impress or stamp (a mark) on a surface.

imprison VERB put into prison; keep in confinement.
imprisonment NOUN

improbable ADJ not likely to be true or to happen.
improbability NOUN
improbably ADV

improbity /im-**proh**-bi-ti/ NOUN [FORMAL] dishonesty.

impromptu ADJ & ADV without preparation or rehearsal.

improper ADJ not conforming to accepted rules or standards; not decent or modest.
improperly ADV
impropriety NOUN

improve VERB make or become better.
improvement NOUN

improvident ADJ not providing for future needs.
improvidence NOUN
improvidently ADV

improvise VERB perform (drama, music etc.) without preparation or a script; make from whatever materials are at hand.
improvisation NOUN

imprudent ADJ unwise, rash.
imprudence NOUN
imprudently ADV

impudent ADJ disrespectful.
impudence NOUN
impudently ADV

impugn /im-**pewn**/ VERB express doubts about the truth or honesty of.

impulse NOUN **1** a sudden urge to do something. **2** a driving force. **3** a pulse of electrical energy.

impulsion NOUN a strong urge; a driving force.

impulsive ADJ acting or done on impulse, without prior thought.
impulsively ADV
impulsiveness NOUN

impunity NOUN freedom from punishment or injury.

impure ADJ **1** mixed with

another substance. **2** dirty; morally wrong.

impurity NOUN (PL **impurities**) the state of being impure; a substance that makes another impure.

impute VERB attribute (a fault) to someone.
imputation NOUN

in PREP **1** enclosed or surrounded by; within (limits of space or time); contained by. **2** having as a condition etc.: *in love.* **3** having as a language or medium: *in English, in writing.* **4** into. ADV so as to be enclosed or surrounded; reaching a destination; entering a position etc. ADJ **1** at home. **2** [INFORMAL] fashionable.
in for about to experience. **in on** sharing (a secret). **ins and outs** [INFORMAL] details. **in so far as** to the extent that. **in with** [INFORMAL] friendly with.

in. ABBREV inch(es).

inability NOUN the state of being unable to do something.

in absentia ADV in his, her, or their absence.

inaccessible ADJ hard or impossible to reach; unfriendly.

inaccurate ADJ not accurate.
inaccuracy NOUN
inaccurately ADV

inaction NOUN lack of action.

inactive ADJ not active; not working or taking effect.
inactivity NOUN

inadequate ADJ not of sufficient quantity or quality; weak and incompetent.
inadequacy NOUN
inadequately ADV

inadmissible ADJ not allowable.

inadvertent ADJ unintentional.
inadvertency NOUN
inadvertently ADV

inalienable ADJ not able to be given or taken away.

inane ADJ silly, lacking sense.
inanely ADV
inanity NOUN

inanimate ADJ lacking animal life; showing no

sign of being alive.

inappropriate ADJ unsuitable.
inappropriately ADV
inappropriateness NOUN

inarticulate ADJ not expressed in words; unable to speak distinctly; unable to express ideas clearly.
inarticulacy NOUN
inarticulately ADV

i

inasmuch ADV (**inasmuch as**) seeing that, because.

inattentive ADJ not paying attention.
inattentively ADV

inaudible ADJ unable to be heard.
inaudibly ADV

inaugurate /in-org-ewr-ayt/ VERB begin, introduce (a policy etc.); admit formally to office; open (a building etc.) formally.
inaugural ADJ
inauguration NOUN

inboard ADJ & ADV in or into the interior of a boat.

inborn ADJ existing in a person or animal from birth; natural.

inbred ADJ **1** produced by inbreeding. **2** inborn.

inbreeding NOUN breeding from closely related individuals.

inbuilt ADJ essentially and naturally part of something.

Inc. ABBREV incorporated.

incalculable ADJ unable to be calculated; unpredictable.
incalculably ADV

incandescent ADJ glowing with heat; [INFORMAL] very angry.
incandescence NOUN

incantation NOUN words or sounds uttered as a magic spell.

incapable ADJ unable to do something; helpless.
incapability NOUN

incapacitate VERB prevent from functioning, disable.

incapacity NOUN mental or physical inability to do something; legal disqualification.

incarcerate /in-kahs-ĕr-ayt/ VERB imprison.
incarceration NOUN

incarnate /in-kah-năt/ ADJ embodied, especially in human form.
incarnation NOUN

embodiment, especially in human form; (**the Incarnation**) that of God as Christ.

incautious ADJ rash.

incendiary ADJ designed to cause fire; tending to provoke conflict. NOUN an incendiary bomb.

incense¹ /**in**-sens/ NOUN a substance burnt to produce fragrant smoke, especially in religious ceremonies.

incense² /in-**sens**/ VERB make angry.

incentive NOUN something that encourages action or effort; a payment to stimulate output.

inception NOUN the beginning of something.

incessant ADJ not ceasing.
incessantly ADV

incest NOUN sexual intercourse between very closely related people.
incestuous ADJ

inch NOUN a measure of length (= 2.54 cm). VERB move gradually.

inchoate /in-koh-ăt, in-**koh**-ayt/ ADJ **1** not fully developed. **2** confused, incoherent.

incidence NOUN **1** the rate at which a thing occurs. **2** [PHYSICS] the falling of a ray, line, etc. on a surface.

incident NOUN an event, especially one causing trouble.

incidental ADJ **1** minor, not essential. **2** occurring as a consequence of something else.

incidentally ADV **1** used to introduce a further or unconnected remark. **2** as a chance occurrence.

incidental music NOUN background music composed for a film.

incinerate VERB burn to ashes.
incineration NOUN
incinerator NOUN

incipient /in-**sip**-i-ĕnt/ ADJ in its early stages; beginning.

incise VERB make a cut in; engrave.
incision NOUN

incisive ADJ clear and decisive.
incisively ADV
incisiveness NOUN

incisor NOUN a sharp-edged front tooth.

incite VERB urge on to action; stir up.
incitement NOUN

incivility NOUN (PL **incivilities**) rudeness.

inclement ADJ (of weather) unpleasant.

inclination NOUN **1** a tendency; a liking or preference. **2** a slope; the process of bending.

i

incline VERB /in-**klIn**/ lean; bend. NOUN /**in**-klIn/ a slope.
inclined to **1** having a tendency to. **2** wanting to, preferring to.

include VERB **1** contain as part of a whole; regard as part of something. **2** put in as part of a group or set.
inclusion NOUN

inclusive ADJ including all charges, services, etc.; (of language) designed to be non-sexist.
inclusive of including.
inclusively ADV
inclusiveness NOUN

incognito /in-kog-**nee**-toh/ ADJ & ADV with one's identity kept secret.

incoherent ADJ disconnected; unclear, confused.
incoherence NOUN
incoherently ADV

incombustible ADJ not able to be burnt.

income NOUN money received as wages, interest, etc.

incoming ADJ coming in.

incommunicado /in-kom-yoo-ni-**kah**-doh/ ADJ not allowed or not wishing to communicate with others.

incomparable ADJ beyond comparison; without an equal.
incomparably ADV

incompatible ADJ conflicting, inconsistent; unable to exist together.
incompatibility NOUN

incompetent ADJ lacking skill; not legally qualified to do something.
incompetence NOUN

incomplete ADJ not complete.

incomprehensible ADJ not able to be understood.
incomprehensibly ADV
incomprehension NOUN

inconceivable ADJ

unable to be imagined; most unlikely.

inconclusive ADJ not fully convincing; not decisive.
inconclusively ADV

incongruous ADJ out of keeping, inappropriate.
incongruity NOUN
incongruously ADV

inconsequential ADJ unimportant.
inconsequentially ADV

inconsiderable ADJ of small size or value.

inconsiderate ADJ not thinking of others' feelings or convenience.
inconsiderately ADV

inconsistent ADJ not consistent.
inconsistency NOUN

inconsolable ADJ not able to be comforted.
inconsolably ADV

inconstant ADJ frequently changing; irregular; disloyal.
inconstancy NOUN

incontestable ADJ indisputable.

incontinent ADJ unable to control one's excretion of urine and/or faeces.
incontinence NOUN

incontrovertible ADJ indisputable, undeniable.
incontrovertibly ADV

inconvenience NOUN difficulty and discomfort; a cause of this. VERB cause inconvenience to.

inconvenient ADJ difficult or troublesome.
inconveniently ADV

incorporate VERB **1** include as a part. **2** form (a company etc.) into a corporation.
incorporation NOUN

incorrect ADJ **1** not right or true. **2** not in accordance with standards.
incorrectly ADV

incorrigible ADJ not able to be reformed or improved.
incorrigibly ADV

incorruptible ADJ **1** not susceptible to bribery. **2** not subject to decay.

increase VERB /in-**kreess**/ make or become greater in size, amount, or intensity. NOUN /**in**-kreess/ a rise in amount, size, or intensity.

increasingly ADV more

and more.

incredible ADJ unbelievable; very surprising.
incredibly ADV

incredulous ADJ unbelieving, showing disbelief.
incredulity NOUN
incredulously ADV

i

increment NOUN an increase; an added amount.
incremental ADJ

incriminate VERB cause to appear guilty; imply the guilt of.
incrimination NOUN
incriminatory ADJ

incrustation NOUN a crust or deposit formed on a surface.

incubate VERB hatch (eggs) by warmth; cause (bacteria etc.) to develop.
incubation NOUN

incubator NOUN an apparatus for incubating eggs or bacteria; an enclosed heated compartment in which a premature baby can be kept.

inculcate /in-kul-kayt/ VERB implant (ideas or habits) by constant urging.

incumbent ADJ forming an obligation or duty. NOUN the holder of an office, especially a rector or a vicar.

incur VERB (**incurs**, **incurring**, **incurred**) bring (something unpleasant) on oneself.

incurable ADJ unable to be cured.

incursion NOUN a brief invasion, a raid.

indebted ADJ owing money or gratitude.

indecent ADJ offending against standards of decency; improper, inappropriate.
indecency NOUN
indecently ADV

indecent assault NOUN sexual assault not involving rape.

indecent exposure NOUN exposing one's genitals in public.

indecipherable ADJ unable to be read or interpreted.

indecision NOUN inability to decide, hesitation.

indecorous ADJ improper;

not in good taste.

indeed ADV in truth, really.

indefatigable /in-di-fat-ig-ă-bĕl/ ADJ untiring.

indefensible ADJ **1** not justifiable. **2** not able to be defended.

indefinable ADJ unable to be defined or described clearly.

indefinite ADJ not clearly stated or fixed; vague; (of time) not limited.

indefinite article NOUN [GRAMMAR] each of the words *a* and *an*.

indefinitely ADV for an unlimited period; to an unlimited extent.

indelible ADJ (of a mark) unable to be removed or washed away; (of ink) making such a mark.
indelibly ADV

indelicate ADJ slightly indecent; tactless.
indelicacy NOUN
indelicately ADV

indemnify VERB (**indemnifies, indemnifying, indemnified**) protect or insure (a person) against penalties that he or she might incur; compensate.
indemnification NOUN

indemnity NOUN (PL **indemnities**) protection against penalties incurred by one's actions; money paid as compensation.

indent VERB **1** start (a line of text) inwards from a margin; form recesses in (a surface). **2** place an official order for goods etc.
indentation NOUN

indenture NOUN a written contract, especially of apprenticeship. VERB bind by this.

independent ADJ **1** not ruled or controlled by another. **2** not relying on another; not connected, separate.
independence NOUN
independently ADV

indescribable ADJ too extreme, unusual, etc., to be described.
indescribably ADV

indestructible ADJ unable to be destroyed.

indeterminable ADJ impossible to discover or decide.

indeterminate ADJ not

known; vague, not fixed or definite.
indeterminacy NOUN

index NOUN (PL **indexes** or **indices**) **1** a list (usually alphabetical) of names, subjects, etc., with references. **2** an indicator of something; a figure indicating the current level of prices etc. compared with a previous level. **3** [MATHEMATICS] the exponent of a number. VERB **1** record in an index. **2** adjust (wages etc.) according to a price index.

indexation NOUN the practice of making wages and benefits index-linked.

index finger NOUN the finger next to the thumb.

index-linked ADJ (of wages and benefits) increased in line with the cost-of-living index.

Indian NOUN **1** a person from India. **2** an American Indian. ADJ **1** relating to India. **2** relating to American Indians.

> Avoid using **Indian** or **Red Indian** in reference to American native peoples; use **American Indian** instead.

Indian ink NOUN deep black ink.

Indian summer NOUN dry sunny weather in autumn.

India rubber NOUN natural rubber.

indicate VERB point out; be a sign of; state briefly.
indication NOUN
indicative ADJ

indicator NOUN a thing that indicates; a pointer; a flashing light on a vehicle showing when it is going to turn.

indices pl. of **INDEX**.

indict /in-**dyt**/ VERB make a formal accusation against.
indictable ADJ
indictment NOUN

indifferent ADJ **1** showing no interest or sympathy. **2** neither good nor bad; not very good.
indifference NOUN
indifferently ADV

indigenous /in-**dij**-i-nŭs/ ADJ native.

indigent /**in**-dij-ĕnt/ ADJ poor.
indigence NOUN

indigestible ADJ difficult or impossible to digest.

indigestion NOUN discomfort caused by difficulty in digesting food.

indignant ADJ feeling or showing indignation.
indignantly ADV

indignation NOUN anger aroused by something unjust or wicked.

indignity NOUN (PL **indignities**) humiliating treatment or circumstances.

indigo /**in**-di-goh/ NOUN a deep blue dye or colour.

indirect ADJ not direct.
indirectly NOUN

indirect object NOUN [GRAMMAR] a word or phrase referring to someone or something indirectly affected by an action, e.g. *him* in *give it to him*.

indirect speech NOUN = **REPORTED SPEECH**.

indirect taxes PLURAL NOUN taxes paid on goods and services, not on income or capital.

indiscernible ADJ unable to be perceived.

indiscreet ADJ incautious; revealing secrets.
indiscreetly ADV
indiscretion NOUN

indiscriminate ADJ done or acting at random; not making a careful choice.
indiscriminately ADV

indispensable ADJ essential.

indisposed ADJ **1** slightly ill. **2** unwilling.
indisposition NOUN

indisputable ADJ undeniable.
indisputably ADV

indissoluble ADJ firm and lasting; not able to be destroyed.

indistinct ADJ unclear; obscure.
indistinctly ADV

indistinguishable ADJ unable to be told apart.

indium NOUN a metallic element.

individual ADJ single, separate; of or for one person or thing; original, not influenced by others.

NOUN one person, animal, or plant considered separately; a person. **individuality** NOUN **individually** ADV

individualist NOUN a person who is very independent in thought or action. **individualism** NOUN

indivisible ADJ not able to be divided.

i

Indo- COMBINING FORM Indian (and).

indoctrinate VERB teach (someone) to accept a set of beliefs uncritically. **indoctrination** NOUN

indolent ADJ lazy. **indolence** NOUN **indolently** ADV

indomitable ADJ impossible to subdue or defeat. **indomitably** ADV

indoor ADJ situated, used, or done inside a building. ADV (**indoors**) inside a building.

indubitable ADJ that cannot reasonably be doubted. **indubitably** ADV

induce VERB **1** persuade. **2** give rise to; bring on (childbirth) artificially.

inducement NOUN an incentive; a bribe.

induct VERB admit formally to a post or organization; install (a clergyman) ceremonially into a benefice.

inductance NOUN the property of producing an electric current by induction.

induction NOUN **1** the process or action of inducting. **2** the process or action of inducing something, especially childbirth. **3** a method of reasoning in which a general rule or conclusion is drawn from particular cases. **4** the production of an electric or magnetic state by proximity of an electrified or magnetic object.

inductive ADJ **1** (of reasoning) proceeding from the individual to the general. **2** of electric or magnetic induction.

indulge VERB satisfy (a desire); allow (someone) to have what they want. **indulge in** allow oneself

(something pleasant).
indulgence NOUN

indulgent ADJ indulging a person's wishes too freely; kind, lenient.
indulgently ADV

industrial ADJ of, for, or full of industries.
industrially ADV

industrial action NOUN a strike or similar protest.

industrial estate NOUN an area of land developed for business and industry.

industrialism NOUN an economic system in which manufacturing industries are predominant.

industrialist NOUN an owner or manager of an industrial business.

industrialized (also **industrialised**) ADJ full of industries.

industrial relations PLURAL NOUN relations between management and workers.

industrious ADJ hard-working.
industriously ADV

industry NOUN (PL **industries**) the manufacture or production of goods; a branch of business activity; hard work.

inebriated ADJ drunk.

inedible ADJ not edible, not suitable for eating.

ineducable ADJ incapable of being educated.

ineffable ADJ too great or extreme to be described.

ineffective ADJ not producing the desired effect.
ineffectively ADV

ineffectual ADJ ineffective; unable to deal with a role or situation.
ineffectually ADV

inefficient ADJ not efficient; wasteful.
inefficiency NOUN
inefficiently ADV

inelegant ADJ lacking elegance or refinement.
inelegantly ADV

ineligible ADJ not eligible or qualified.

ineluctable ADJ inescapable, unavoidable.

inept ADJ clumsy, unskilful.
ineptitude NOUN
ineptly ADV

ineptness NOUN

inequality NOUN (PL **inequalities**) lack of equality.

inequitable ADJ unfair, unjust.
inequitably ADV

inert ADJ without power to move; without active properties; not moving or taking action.
inertly ADV
inertness NOUN

inertia /in-er-shă/ NOUN **1** the state of being inert; slowness to act. **2** the property by which matter continues in its existing state of rest or line of motion unless acted on by a force.

inertia reel NOUN a reel allowing a seat belt to unwind freely unless pulled suddenly.

inescapable ADJ unavoidable.
inescapably ADV

inessential ADJ not essential. NOUN an inessential thing.

inestimable ADJ too great to be estimated.
inestimably ADV

inevitable ADJ unavoidable, sure to happen or appear.
inevitability NOUN
inevitably ADV

inexact ADJ not exact.
inexactitude NOUN
inexactly ADV

inexcusable ADJ unable to be excused or justified.

inexhaustible ADJ available in unlimited quantity.

inexorable ADJ impossible to prevent; impossible to persuade.
inexorably ADV

inexpensive ADJ not expensive.

inexperienced ADJ lacking experience.
inexperience NOUN

inexpert ADJ not expert, unskilful.
inexpertly ADV

inexplicable ADJ impossible to explain.
inexplicability NOUN
inexplicably ADV

inexpressible ADJ unable to be expressed in words.
inexpressibly ADV

in extremis ADJ at the point of death; in an emergency.

inextricable ADJ

impossible to disentangle; impossible to escape from.
inextricably ADV

infallible ADJ incapable of being wrong; never failing.
infallibility NOUN
infallibly ADV

infamous /in-fă-mŭs/ ADJ having a bad reputation.
infamously ADV
infamy NOUN

infancy NOUN early childhood, babyhood; an early stage of development.

infant NOUN a child during the earliest stage of its life.

infanticide NOUN the killing or killer of an infant soon after its birth.

infantile ADJ of infants or infancy; very childish.

infantry NOUN troops who fight on foot.

infatuated ADJ filled with intense unreasoning love.
infatuation NOUN

infect VERB affect or contaminate with a disease or its germs; affect with one's feeling.

infection NOUN the process of infecting; the state of being infected; a disease spread in this way.

infectious ADJ (of disease) able to spread by air or water; infecting others.
infectiously ADV
infectiousness NOUN

infer VERB (**infers**, **inferring**, **inferred**) work out from evidence; conclude.
inference NOUN

inferior ADJ of lower rank, status, or quality; of low standard. NOUN a person inferior to another.
inferiority NOUN

infernal ADJ **1** of hell. **2** [INFORMAL] detestable, tiresome.
infernally ADV

inferno NOUN (PL **infernos**) a raging fire; an intensely hot place; hell.

infertile ADJ unable to have offspring; (of soil) not producing vegetation.
infertility NOUN

infest VERB be present in (a place) in large numbers, especially

harmfully.
infestation NOUN

infidel NOUN a person who does not believe in a religion.

infidelity NOUN (PL **infidelities**) unfaithfulness, especially adultery.

infighting NOUN conflict within an organization.

infill (also **infilling**) NOUN material used to fill a hole; buildings constructed to fill a gap.

infiltrate VERB make one's way into (a group etc.) secretly and gradually.
infiltration NOUN
infiltrator NOUN

infinite ADJ having no end or limit; very great, very many.
infinitely ADV

infinitesimal ADJ very small.
infinitesimally ADV

infinitive NOUN the form of a verb not indicating tense, number, or person (e.g. *to go*).

infinity NOUN (PL **infinities**) the state of being infinite; an infinite number, space, or time.

infirm ADJ weak from age or illness.
infirmity NOUN

infirmary NOUN (PL **infirmaries**) a hospital.

inflame VERB **1** provoke or intensify (feelings). **2** cause inflammation in.

inflammable ADJ easily set on fire.
inflammability NOUN

inflammation NOUN redness, heat, and pain in a part of the body.

inflammatory ADJ arousing strong feeling or anger.

inflatable ADJ able to be inflated. NOUN an object needing to be inflated before use.

inflate VERB **1** swell or cause to swell by filling with air or gas. **2** increase excessively and artificially; exaggerate.

inflation NOUN **1** the process of inflating; the state of being inflated. **2** a general increase in prices and fall in the purchasing power of money.
inflationary ADJ

inflect VERB **1** change the

pitch of (a voice) in speaking. **2** [GRAMMAR] change the ending or form of (a word).
inflection NOUN

inflexible ADJ impossible to bend; unwilling to yield or compromise; unable to be changed.
inflexibility NOUN
inflexibly ADV

inflict VERB cause (something painful or unpleasant) to be suffered.
infliction NOUN

inflorescence NOUN flowering; the complete flower head of a plant.

influence NOUN power to produce an effect, especially on character, beliefs, or actions; a person or thing with this power. VERB exert influence on.

influential ADJ having great influence.
influentially ADV

influenza NOUN a viral disease causing fever, muscular pain, and catarrh.

influx NOUN an arrival of large numbers of people or things.

inform VERB **1** give information to; reveal criminal activities to the authorities. **2** be an essential principle or quality of.

informal ADJ relaxed; unofficial; casual; without ceremony.
informality NOUN
informally ADV

informant NOUN a giver of information.

information NOUN facts told or discovered.

information technology (also **information science**) NOUN the study and use of computers, microelectronics, etc. for storing and transferring information.

informative ADJ giving information.
informatively ADV

informed ADJ having a good knowledge of something.

informer NOUN a person who reveals criminal activity to the authorities.

infra dig ADJ [INFORMAL] beneath one's dignity.

infrared ADJ of or using radiation with a wavelength longer than that of visible light rays.

infrastructure NOUN the basic structural parts of something; roads, sewers, etc. regarded as a country's basic facilities.

infrequent ADJ not frequent.
infrequently ADV

infringe VERB break (a rule or agreement); encroach.
infringement NOUN

infuriate VERB make very angry.

infuse VERB **1** fill (with a quality). **2** soak (tea or herbs) to bring out flavour.

infusion NOUN **1** a drink etc. made by infusing leaves. **2** the introduction of a new element into something.

ingenious ADJ clever at inventing things; cleverly contrived.
ingeniously ADV
ingenuity NOUN

ingenuous /in-jen-you-ŭs/ ADJ innocent, guileless; naive.
ingenuously ADV
ingenuousness NOUN

ingest VERB take in as food.

inglenook NOUN a space for sitting within a very large fireplace.

inglorious ADJ **1** shameful. **2** not famous.

ingot NOUN a brick-shaped lump of cast metal.

ingrained ADJ deeply embedded in a surface or in a person's character.

ingratiate VERB bring (oneself) into a person's favour, especially to gain advantage.

ingratitude NOUN lack of gratitude.

ingredient NOUN any of the parts in a mixture.

ingress NOUN the action of going in; the right of entry; an entrance.

ingrowing ADJ (of a toenail) growing abnormally into the flesh.

inhabit VERB live in as one's home.
inhabitable ADJ
inhabitant NOUN

inhalant NOUN a medicinal substance to be inhaled.

inhale VERB breathe in (air,

smoke, gas, etc.).
inhalation NOUN

inhaler NOUN a device for administering a vapour to be inhaled to relieve asthma etc.

inherent ADJ existing in a thing as a natural or permanent quality.
inherently ADV

inherit VERB receive from a predecessor, especially from someone who has died; receive (a characteristic) from one's parents.
inheritance NOUN
inheritor NOUN

inhibit VERB restrain, prevent; cause inhibitions in.
inhibited ADJ
inhibitor NOUN

inhibition NOUN a sense of embarrassment and self-consciousness keeping one from behaving naturally.

inhospitable ADJ not hospitable; (of a place) with a harsh climate or landscape.

in-house ADJ & ADV within an organization.

inhuman (also **inhumane**) ADJ brutal, extremely cruel.
inhumanity NOUN
inhumanly ADV

inimical ADJ hostile; harmful.
inimically ADV

inimitable ADJ impossible to imitate.
inimitably ADV

iniquity NOUN (PL **iniquities**) great injustice; wickedness.
iniquitous ADJ

initial NOUN the first letter of a word or name. VERB (**initials**, **initialling**, **initialled**; [US] **initialing**, **initialed**) mark or sign with initials. ADJ first, existing at the beginning.
initially ADV

initiate VERB /in-**ish**-i-ayt/ **1** cause (a process etc.) to begin. **2** admit to membership of a secret group; introduce to a skill or activity. NOUN /in-**ish**-i-ăt/ someone who has been admitted to a secret society etc.
initiation NOUN
initiator NOUN
initiatory ADJ

initiative NOUN **1** the

i

capacity to invent and initiate ideas. **2** a position from which one can act to forestall others. **3** a fresh approach to a problem.

inject VERB **1** force (liquid) into the body with a syringe. **2** introduce (a new element) into a situation etc.
injection NOUN

injudicious ADJ unwise.
injudiciously ADV

injunction NOUN an authoritative order, especially one made by a judge.

injure VERB cause injury to.

injurious ADJ harmful.

injury NOUN (PL **injuries**) harm, damage; a wound, broken bone, etc.; unjust treatment.

injustice NOUN lack of justice; an unjust action.

ink NOUN coloured liquid used in writing, printing, etc. VERB apply ink to.
inky ADJ

inkling NOUN a slight suspicion.

inlaid past of **INLAY**.

inland ADJ & ADV in or towards the interior of a country.

in-laws PLURAL NOUN [INFORMAL] one's relatives by marriage.

inlay VERB /in-lay/ (**inlays**, **inlaying**, **inlaid**) decorate (a surface) by setting pieces of another material in it so that the surfaces are flush. NOUN /**in**-lay/ inlaid material or design.

inlet NOUN **1** an arm of the sea etc. extending inland. **2** a way in (e.g. for water into a tank).

in loco parentis ADV acting in the place of a parent.

inmate NOUN a person living in a prison or other institution.

in memoriam PREP in memory of (a dead person).

inmost ADJ furthest inward.

inn NOUN a public house, especially one in the country offering accommodation.

innards PLURAL NOUN [INFORMAL] the stomach and bowels; the inner parts.

innate ADJ inborn; natural.
innately ADV

inner ADJ nearer to the centre or inside; interior, internal.

inner city NOUN the central area of a city.

innermost ADJ furthest inward.

innings NOUN (in cricket) a batsman's or side's turn at batting.

innocent ADJ **1** not guilty; not intended to cause harm; morally pure. **2** without experience or knowledge, especially of something bad.
innocence NOUN
innocently ADV

innocuous ADJ harmless.
innocuously ADV

innovate VERB introduce something new.
innovation NOUN
innovative ADJ
innovator NOUN

innuendo /in-yoo-**end**-oh/ NOUN (PL **innuendoes** or **innuendos**) a remark indirectly suggesting something discreditable or indecent.

innumerable ADJ too many to be counted.

innumerate ADJ without knowledge of basic arithmetic.
innumeracy NOUN

inoculate VERB protect against disease with vaccines or serums.
inoculation NOUN

inoperable ADJ unable to be cured by surgical operation.

inoperative ADJ not functioning.

inopportune ADJ happening at an unsuitable time.

inordinate ADJ excessive; disproportionate.
inordinately ADV

inorganic ADJ of mineral origin, not organic.
inorganically ADV

inpatient NOUN a patient staying in a hospital during treatment.

input NOUN something put in or contributed for use or processing; the putting or feeding in of something. VERB (**inputs**, **inputting**, **input** or **inputted**) supply (data etc.) to a computer.

inquest NOUN a judicial investigation, especially of a sudden death.

inquire VERB make an inquiry.

inquiry NOUN (PL **inquiries**) an investigation.

inquisition NOUN an act of detailed or relentless questioning.
inquisitor NOUN
inquisitorial ADJ

i

inquisitive ADJ curious; prying.
inquisitively ADV
inquisitiveness NOUN

inroad NOUN a hostile attack.
make inroads on (or **into**) encroach on; use up.

insalubrious /in-să-loob-ri-ŭs/ ADJ unhealthy, unwholesome.

insane ADJ mad; extremely foolish.
insanely ADV
insanity NOUN

insanitary ADJ dirty and unhygienic.

insatiable ADJ impossible to satisfy.
insatiability NOUN
insatiably ADV

inscribe VERB write or carve (words) on a surface; write a dedication on or in; [GEOMETRY] draw (a figure) inside another.

inscription NOUN words inscribed.

inscrutable ADJ baffling, impossible to interpret.
inscrutability NOUN
inscrutably ADV

insect NOUN a small creature with six legs, no backbone, and a segmented body.

insecticide NOUN a substance for killing insects.

insectivorous ADJ insect-eating.

insecure ADJ **1** not firmly fixed or attached. **2** lacking confidence.

inseminate VERB insert semen into.
insemination NOUN

insensible ADJ **1** unconscious; unaware. **2** imperceptible.
insensibility NOUN
insensibly ADV

insensitive ADJ not sensitive.
insensitively ADV
insensitivity NOUN

inseparable ADJ impossible to separate or treat separately; (of friends) reluctant to part.
inseparability NOUN
inseparably ADV

insert VERB /in-**sert**/ put into something else; include or enclose. NOUN /**in**-sert/ something inserted, especially pages inserted in a magazine etc.
insertion NOUN

in-service ADJ (of training) for people working in the profession concerned.

inset NOUN /**in**-set/ a small picture included in a larger one; an insert in a magazine; a thing fitted in something else. VERB /in-**set**/ (**insets**, **insetting**, **inset**) put in as an inset; decorate with an inset.

inshore ADJ & ADV at sea but near or towards the shore.

inside NOUN the inner part of something; the inner side or surface; [INFORMAL] a position giving access to confidential information; (**insides**) the stomach and bowels. ADJ on or from the inside. ADV on, in, or to the inside; [INFORMAL] in prison. PREP within, contained by; into; in less than (a specified time).
inside out 1 with the inner side turned outwards; utterly changed. **2** thoroughly: *know the subject inside out.*

insider dealing NOUN the illegal practice of using confidential information to gain advantage in buying stocks and shares.

insidious ADJ imperceptibly spreading or developing with harmful effect.
insidiously ADV
insidiousness NOUN

insight NOUN intuitive perception and understanding.

insignia PLURAL NOUN symbols of authority or office; an identifying badge.

insignificant ADJ trivial, not worth considering.
insignificance NOUN
insignificantly ADV

insinuate VERB **1** indirectly suggest something

discreditable. **2** gradually and artfully manoeuvre (something, especially oneself) into position.
insinuation NOUN
insinuator NOUN

insipid ADJ lacking flavour, interest, or liveliness.
insipidity NOUN

insist VERB demand or state emphatically.

i

insistent ADJ insisting; forcing itself on one's attention.
insistence NOUN
insistently ADV

in situ /in sit-yoo/ ADV in its original place.

insolent ADJ disrespectful, arrogant.
insolence NOUN
insolently ADV

insoluble ADJ **1** impossible to solve. **2** unable to be dissolved.

insolvent ADJ unable to pay one's debts.
insolvency NOUN

insomnia NOUN inability to sleep.
insomniac NOUN

insouciant /in-soo-si-ĕnt/ ADJ carefree, unconcerned.
insouciance NOUN

inspect VERB examine critically or officially.
inspection NOUN

inspector NOUN **1** a person who inspects. **2** a police officer above sergeant.

inspiration NOUN the process of being inspired; a person or thing that inspires; a sudden clever idea.
inspirational ADJ

inspire VERB **1** stimulate to activity; encourage (a feeling); cause to feel uplifted. **2** inhale.

inst. ABBREV instant, of the current month.

instability NOUN lack of stability.

install VERB place (a person) into office ceremonially; set in position and ready for use; establish.

installation NOUN the process of installing; an apparatus etc. installed.

instalment ([US] **installment**) NOUN one of the regular payments made to clear a debt paid over a period of time; one part of a serial.

instance NOUN an example; a particular case. VERB mention as an example.

instant ADJ happening or done immediately; (of food) quickly and easily prepared. NOUN an exact moment; a very short time.
instantly ADV

instantaneous /in-stăn-tay-ni-ŭs/ ADJ occurring or done instantly.
instantaneously ADV

instead ADV as an alternative.

instep NOUN the middle part of the foot.

instigate VERB bring about (an action); urge to act.
instigation NOUN
instigator NOUN

instil ([US] **instill**) VERB (**instils**, **instilling**, **instilled**; [US] **instills**) introduce (ideas etc.) into a person's mind gradually.

instinct NOUN an inborn impulse; a natural tendency or ability.
instinctive ADJ
instinctively ADV

institute NOUN an organization for promotion of a specified activity; its premises. VERB set up; establish.

institution NOUN **1** an institute. **2** a home in which people with special needs are cared for. **3** an established rule or custom. **4** the process of instituting; the action of being instituted.
institutional ADJ

institutionalize (also **institutionalise**) VERB **1** establish as a custom etc. **2** place in a residential institution.
institutionalized ADJ

instruct VERB **1** teach a subject or skill to. **2** give instructions to.
instructor NOUN

instruction NOUN **1** the process of teaching. **2** an order; (**instructions**) an explanation of how to do or use something.
instructional ADJ

instructive ADJ informative, enlightening.
instructively ADV

instrument NOUN **1** a tool for delicate work. **2** a

measuring device of an engine or vehicle. **3** a device for producing musical sounds.

instrumental ADJ **1** serving as a means. **2** performed on musical instruments.

instrumentalist NOUN a player of a musical instrument.

insubordinate ADJ disobedient, rebellious.
insubordination NOUN

insubstantial ADJ lacking reality or solidity.

insufferable ADJ intolerable.
insufferably ADV

insufficient ADJ not enough; inadequate.
insufficiency NOUN
insufficiently ADV

insular ADJ **1** of an island. **2** narrow-minded.
insularity NOUN

insulate VERB **1** cover with a substance that prevents the passage of electricity, sound, or heat. **2** protect from outside influences, pressures, etc.
insulation NOUN
insulator NOUN

insulin NOUN a hormone controlling the body's absorption of sugar.

insult VERB /in-**sult**/ speak or act so as to offend (a person). NOUN /**in**-sult/ an insulting remark or action.
insulting ADJ

insuperable ADJ impossible to overcome.
insuperably ADV

insupportable ADJ unbearable.

insurance NOUN a contract to provide compensation for loss, damage, or death; a sum payable as a premium or in compensation; a safeguard against loss or failure.

insure VERB protect by insurance.
insurer NOUN

insurgent ADJ rebellious, rising in revolt. NOUN a rebel.
insurgency NOUN

insurmountable ADJ too great to be overcome.

insurrection NOUN a rebellion.
insurrectionist NOUN

intact ADJ undamaged, complete.

intake NOUN an amount of a substance taken into the body; people entering an establishment at a particular time; the action of taking in.

intangible ADJ unable to be touched or grasped; vague, indefinable.

integer NOUN a whole number, not a fraction.

integral ADJ necessary to make a whole complete.

integrate VERB combine (parts) into a whole; bring or come into full membership of a community.
integration NOUN

integrity NOUN **1** the quality of being honest and morally upright. **2** the state of being whole or unified.

intellect NOUN the mind's power of reasoning and acquiring knowledge.

intellectual ADJ of the intellect; appealing to the intellect; having a strong intellect. NOUN an intellectual person.
intellectually ADV

intelligence NOUN **1** mental ability to learn and understand things. **2** information, especially that of military value; people collecting this.

intelligent ADJ having great mental ability.
intelligently ADV

intelligentsia NOUN educated and cultured people.

intelligible ADJ able to be understood.
intelligibility NOUN
intelligibly ADV

intend VERB have in mind as what one wishes to achieve; plan a particular use or destiny for (someone or something).

intense ADJ **1** extreme; in a high degree. **2** having strong feelings.
intensely ADV
intensity NOUN

intensifier NOUN [GRAMMAR] a word used to give emphasis, e.g. *really* in *I'm really hot.*

intensify VERB (**intensifies**, **intensifying**, **intensified**) make or become more intense.
intensification NOUN

intensive ADJ **1** achieving

a great deal in a short time; concentrated. **2** intended to achieve the highest level of production possible in an area. **3** making much use of something specified: *labour-intensive.*
intensively ADV
intensiveness NOUN

intensive care NOUN medical treatment with constant attention for a seriously ill patient.

intent NOUN intention.
ADJ with concentrated attention.
intent on determined to.
intently ADV
intentness NOUN

intention NOUN what one intends to do.

intentional ADJ done on purpose.
intentionally ADV

inter VERB (**inters, interring, interred**) bury (a dead body).

inter- PREFIX between, among.

interact VERB have an effect on each other.
interaction NOUN
interactive ADJ

inter alia ADV among other things.

interbreed VERB (**interbreeds, interbreeding, interbred**) breed with each other, cross-breed.

intercede /in-tĕ-**seed**/ VERB intervene on someone's behalf.

intercept VERB stop or catch between a starting point and destination.
interception NOUN
interceptor NOUN

intercession NOUN the action of interceding.

interchange VERB /in-tĕ-**chaynj**/ **1** (of two people) exchange (things). **2** cause to change places.
NOUN /**in**-tĕ-chaynj/ **1** a process of interchanging. **2** a road junction designed so that streams of traffic do not cross on the same level.
interchangeable ADJ

intercom NOUN an electrical device allowing one-way or two-way communication.

Interconnect VERB connect with each other.
interconnection NOUN

intercontinental ADJ

between continents.

intercourse NOUN **1** dealings between people or countries. **2** sexual intercourse, copulation.

interdenominational ADJ involving more than one religious denomination.

interdependent ADJ dependent on each other.

interdict /in-tĕ-dikt/ NOUN a formal prohibition.

interdisciplinary ADJ involving different branches of knowledge.

interest NOUN **1** the state of wanting to know about something; something about which one feels this; the quality of arousing someone's curiosity or holding their attention. **2** money paid for use of money borrowed. **3** advantage: *in my own interest.* **4** a share in an undertaking. VERB arouse the curiosity of; be interesting to.

interested ADJ **1** feeling interest. **2** not impartial.

interesting ADJ arousing interest.

interface NOUN **1** a place where interaction occurs. **2** [COMPUTING] a program or apparatus connecting two machines or enabling a user to use a program.

interfere VERB **1** prevent something's progress or proper functioning. **2** become involved in others' affairs without invitation.
interfere with molest sexually.

interference NOUN the action of interfering; disturbance of radio signals.

interferon NOUN a protein preventing the development of a virus.

intergalactic ADJ between galaxies.

interim NOUN an intervening period. ADJ of or in such a period; temporary.

interior ADJ inner. NOUN the inner part; the inside.

interject VERB put in (a remark) when someone is speaking.

interjection NOUN a remark interjected; an exclamation.

interlace VERB weave or lace together.

interlink VERB link together.

interlock VERB (of two things) fit into each other. NOUN a fine machine-knitted fabric.

interloper NOUN an intruder.

interlude NOUN **1** an interval. **2** music or other entertainment provided during an interval.

intermarry VERB (**intermarries**, **intermarrying**, **intermarried**) (of members of different groups) marry one another; (of close relations) marry.
intermarriage NOUN

intermediary NOUN (PL **intermediaries**) a mediator, a messenger. ADJ intermediate.

intermediate ADJ coming between two things in time, place, or order; having achieved a basic level in a subject or skill.

interment NOUN burial.

intermezzo /in-tĕ-mets-oh/ NOUN (PL **intermezzos** or **intermezzi**) a short piece of music.

interminable ADJ endless; very long.
interminably ADV

intermission NOUN an interval; a pause.

intermittent ADJ occurring at irregular intervals.
intermittently ADV

intern VERB confine (especially an enemy alien). NOUN (also **interne**) [US] a resident junior doctor at a hospital.

internal ADJ of or in the inside; inside the body; of a country's domestic affairs; applying within an organization.
internally ADV

internal-combustion engine NOUN an engine producing power from fuel exploded within a cylinder.

internalize (also **internalise**) VERB learn, absorb into the mind.

international ADJ

between countries; involving several countries. NOUN a sports contest between players of different countries; one of these players.
internationally ADV

interne variant of **INTERN** (noun).

internecine /in-tĕ-nee-syn/ ADJ destructive to both sides in a conflict; of conflict within a group.

internee NOUN an interned person.

Internet NOUN an international computer network with information accessible to the public via modem links.

internment NOUN the process of interning; the state of being interned.

interplay NOUN interaction.

interpolate /in-ter-pŏ-layt/ VERB insert; add to a text; interject.
interpolation NOUN

interpose VERB **1** place between one thing and another. **2** intervene between opponents.

interpret VERB explain the meaning of; understand in a particular way; act as interpreter.
interpretation NOUN
interpretative ADJ
interpretive ADJ

interpreter NOUN a person who orally translates speech between people speaking different languages.

interracial ADJ involving different races.

interregnum NOUN a period between the rule of two successive rulers.

interrelated ADJ related to each other.

interrogate VERB question closely.
interrogation NOUN
interrogator NOUN

interrogative ADJ forming a question; used in questions.
interrogatively ADV

interrupt VERB break the continuity of; break the flow of (speech etc.) by a remark.
interruption NOUN

intersect VERB divide or cross by passing or lying across.

intersection NOUN

intersperse VERB insert here and there; vary by adding something different at intervals.

interstate ADJ between states, especially of the USA.

interval NOUN a time between events; a break in activity; the time between acts of a play etc.; a space between two things; a difference in musical pitch.
at intervals with spaces or time in between.

intervene VERB **1** become involved in a situation to change its course; form an obstacle or delay. **2** occur between events.
intervention NOUN

interview NOUN a formal conversation with someone, designed to extract information or assess their suitability for a position. VERB hold an interview with.
interviewee NOUN
interviewer NOUN

interweave VERB (**interweaves**, **interweaving**, **interwove**; PAST PARTICIPLE **interwoven**) weave together; blend.

intestate /in-tes-tayt/ ADJ not having made a valid will.
intestacy NOUN

intestine NOUN a long tubular section of the alimentary canal between the stomach and anus.
intestinal ADJ

intimate[1] /in-ti-măt/ ADJ **1** closely acquainted or familiar; having a sexual relationship (especially outside marriage); private and personal. **2** (of knowledge) thorough, detailed. NOUN an intimate friend.
intimacy NOUN
intimately ADV

intimate[2] /in-ti-mayt/ VERB make known, especially by hinting.
intimation NOUN

intimidate VERB influence by frightening.
intimidation NOUN

into PREP **1** to the inside of, to a point within. **2** so as to touch: *he bumped into me*. **3** becoming, developing into; resulting in: *changed into a frog*. **4** concerned with, focussing on: *an inquiry* *into the incident.* **5** dividing (a number) mathematically. **6** [INFORMAL] interested in, enthusiastic about.

intolerable ADJ unbearable.
intolerably ADV

intonation NOUN the rise and fall of the voice in speaking.

intone VERB chant, especially on one note.

intoxicate VERB make drunk; make greatly excited.
intoxication NOUN

intra- PREFIX within.

intractable ADJ hard to deal with or control.
intractability NOUN

intramural ADJ **1** within the walls of an institution etc. **2** part of ordinary university work.

intransigent ADJ stubborn.
intransigence NOUN
intransigently ADV

intransitive ADJ [GRAMMAR] (of a verb) not followed by a direct object.

intrauterine ADJ within the uterus.

intravenous ADJ in or administered into a vein.
intravenously ADV

in tray NOUN a tray holding documents that need attention.

intrepid ADJ fearless, brave.
intrepidly ADV

intricate ADJ very complicated.
intricacy NOUN
intricately ADV

intrigue VERB /in-**treeg**/ **1** arouse the curiosity of. **2** plot secretly. NOUN /**in**-treeg/ a plot; a secret love affair.
intriguing ADJ

intrinsic ADJ existing in a thing as a natural or permanent quality; essential.
intrinsically ADV

introduce VERB **1** make (a person) known to another; present to an audience. **2** bring into use. **3** insert. **4** occur at the start of.

introduction NOUN the action of introducing or being introduced; an introductory part; a thing newly brought in; a book or activity introducing a newcomer to a subject of study.

introductory ADJ introducing a person or thing; preliminary.

introspection NOUN examination of one's own thoughts and feelings.
introspective ADJ

introvert NOUN an introspective and shy person.
introverted ADJ

intrude VERB come or join in without being invited or wanted.
intrusion NOUN
intrusive ADJ

intruder NOUN a person who intrudes; a burglar.

intuition NOUN the power of knowing without learning or reasoning; a belief based on instinct or emotion.
intuitive ADJ
intuitively ADV

Inuit /in-yoo-it/ NOUN (PL **Inuit** or **Inuits**) a North American Eskimo.

inundate VERB flood; overwhelm.

inure VERB **1** accustom, especially to something unpleasant. **2** (in law) take effect.

invade VERB enter (territory) with hostile intent; crowd into, encroach on; penetrate harmfully.
invader NOUN

invalid¹ /in-vă-lid/ NOUN a person suffering from ill health.

invalid² /in-val-id/ ADJ not valid.

invalidate VERB make no longer valid.

invaluable ADJ having a value too great to be measured.

invariable ADJ not variable, always the same.
invariably ADV

invasion NOUN a hostile or harmful intrusion.
invasive ADJ

invective NOUN abusive language.

invent VERB make or design (something new); make up (a lie, a story).
inventor NOUN

invention NOUN something invented; the action of inventing.

inventive ADJ able to invent things.

inventiveness NOUN

inventory NOUN (PL **inventories**) a detailed list of goods or furniture.

inverse ADJ opposite, contrary.
inverse proportion a relation such that one item decreases to the extent that the other increases.
inversely ADV

invert VERB turn upside down; reverse the position, order, or relationship of.
inversion NOUN

invertebrate NOUN an animal having no backbone. ADJ relating to invertebrates.

inverted commas PLURAL NOUN quotation marks.

invest VERB **1** use (money, time, etc.) to earn interest or bring profit. **2** confer rank or office on. **3** endow with a quality.
investment NOUN
investor NOUN

investigate VERB study carefully; inquire into.
investigation NOUN
investigative ADJ
investigator NOUN

investiture NOUN the action of investing a person with honours or rank; a ceremony at which this takes place.

inveterate ADJ habitual; firmly established.

invidious ADJ liable to cause resentment.
invidiously ADV

invigilate VERB supervise examination candidates.
invigilator NOUN

invigorate VERB fill with vigour; give strength or courage to.

invincible ADJ unconquerable.

inviolable ADJ never to be broken or dishonoured.

inviolate ADJ not violated; safe.

invisible ADJ not able to be seen.
invisibility NOUN
invisibly ADV

invite VERB ask (a person) politely to come or to do something; ask for; risk provoking: *his behaviour invited criticism.*
invitation NOUN

inviting ADJ pleasant and tempting.
invitingly ADV

in vitro ADJ & ADV in a test tube or other laboratory environment.

invocation NOUN the action of invoking; an incantation used to summon supernatural forces.

invoice NOUN a bill for goods or services. VERB send an invoice to.

invoke VERB call for the help or protection of; summon (a spirit).

involuntary ADJ done without intention.
involuntarily ADV

involve VERB have as a part or consequence; cause to participate; require.
involvement ADJ

involved ADJ **1** concerned in something; in a relationship with someone. **2** complicated.

invulnerable ADJ not vulnerable.
invulnerability NOUN

inward ADJ situated on or going towards the inside; in the mind or spirit. ADV towards the inside.
inwardly ADV
inwards ADV

inward-looking ADJ self-absorbed or insular.

iodine NOUN a chemical used in solution as an antiseptic.

ion NOUN an electrically charged atom that has lost or gained an electron.
ionic ADJ

ionize (also **ionise**) VERB convert or be converted into ions.

ionosphere NOUN the ionized region of the atmosphere.
ionospheric ADJ

iota NOUN **1** a Greek letter (**I**, ι). **2** a very small amount: *not an iota of difference.*

IOU NOUN a signed paper given as a receipt for money borrowed.

ipso facto ADV by that very fact.

IQ ABBREV intelligence quotient.

IRA ABBREV Irish Republican Army.

irascible /irr-ass-i-bĕl/ ADJ hot-tempered.
irascibly ADV

irate ADJ angry.
irately ADV

ire NOUN [LITERARY] anger.

iridescent /irr-id-ess-ĕnt/ ADJ shimmering with many colours.
iridescence NOUN

iridium NOUN a metallic element.

iris NOUN **1** the coloured part of the eyeball, round the pupil. **2** a plant with showy flowers.

Irish NOUN (also **Irish Gaelic**) the Celtic language of Ireland. ADJ relating to Ireland.

irk VERB annoy, be tiresome to.

irksome ADJ irritating.

iron NOUN **1** a strong hard metal; a tool made of this. **2** an implement with a flat base heated for smoothing cloth. **3** (**irons**) fetters. ADJ made of iron; as strong as iron. VERB smooth (clothes etc.) with an iron.
iron out remove (creases) by ironing; solve (problems).

ironmonger NOUN a shopkeeper selling tools and household implements.

irony NOUN (PL **ironies**) the expression of a meaning through words whose literal sense is the opposite; the development of events in the opposite way to that intended or expected.
ironic ADJ
ironical ADJ
ironically ADV

irradiate VERB **1** expose to radiation. **2** illuminate.
irradiation NOUN

irrational ADJ not guided by reason.

irrecoverable ADJ unable to be recovered.
irrecoverably ADV

irredeemable ADJ unable to be set right or saved.

irrefutable ADJ impossible to disprove.
irrefutably ADV

irregular ADJ **1** not even or smooth. **2** contrary to rules or custom.
irregularity NOUN
irregularly ADV

irrelevant ADJ not relevant.
irrelevance NOUN
irrelevantly ADV

irreparable ADJ unable to be repaired.
irreparably ADV

irreplaceable ADJ impossible to replace.

irrepressible ADJ impossible to control or subdue.
irrepressibly ADV

irreproachable ADJ blameless, faultless.
irreproachably ADV

irresistible ADJ too strong or attractive to be resisted.
irresistibility NOUN
irresistibly ADV

irresolute ADJ unable to make up one's mind.
irresolutely ADV

irrespective ADJ (**irrespective of**) regardless of.

irresponsible ADJ not showing a proper sense of responsibility.
irresponsibility NOUN
irresponsibly ADV

irretrievable ADJ impossible to retrieve or put right.

irreverent ADJ lacking respect.
irreverence NOUN
irreverently ADV

irreversible ADJ impossible to alter or undo.
irreversibly ADV

irrevocable ADJ unalterable, irreversible.
irrevocably ADV

irrigate VERB supply (land) with water by streams, pipes, etc.
irrigation NOUN

irritable ADJ easily annoyed, bad-tempered.
irritability NOUN
irritably ADV

irritant NOUN a substance that irritates the skin; a source of annoyance.

irritate VERB **1** annoy. **2** cause to itch.
irritation NOUN

irrupt VERB make a violent entry.

is 3rd person singular present of **BE**.

-ish COMBINING FORM approximately, roughly: *eightish;* rather, somewhat: *greyish.*

isinglass /Iz-ing-glahs/ NOUN gelatin obtained from fish.

Islam NOUN the Muslim religion.
Islamic ADJ

island NOUN a piece of land surrounded by water.

islander NOUN an inhabitant of an island.

isle NOUN an island.

islet NOUN a small island.

ism NOUN [INFORMAL] a set of ideas, a movement. COMBINING FORM (**-ism**) a prejudice based on a specified factor.

isobar NOUN a line on a map, connecting places with the same atmospheric pressure.
isobaric ADJ

isolate VERB place apart or alone; separate from others or from a compound.
isolation NOUN

isolationism NOUN the policy of holding aloof from other countries or groups.
isolationist NOUN

isomer /I-sŏ-mĕ/ NOUN one of two or more substances whose molecules have the same atoms arranged differently.

isosceles /I-sos-i-leez/ ADJ (of a triangle) having two sides equal.

isotherm NOUN a line on a map, connecting places with the same temperature.

isotope NOUN one of two or more forms of a chemical element differing in their atomic weight.
isotopic ADJ

ISP ABBREV Internet service provider.

issue NOUN **1** a topic or problem for discussion. **2** the action of supplying an item for sale, use, etc.; a quantity issued; one edition of a magazine etc. **3** [FORMAL] children. **4** the action of flowing out. **5** [DATED] an outcome, a result. VERB **1** supply for use; supply (someone) with something. **2** publish. **3** come or flow out; result.
at issue being discussed or disputed.

isthmus /isth-mŭs, iss-mŭs/ NOUN (PL **isthmuses**) a narrow strip of land connecting two larger masses of land.

IT ABBREV information technology.

it PRON **1** the thing mentioned or being

discussed. **2** used as the subject of an impersonal verb: *it is raining.* **3** used to identify someone: *it's me.*

Italian NOUN a person from Italy; the language of Italy. ADJ relating to Italy.

italic ADJ (of type) sloping like *this*. NOUN (**italics**) italic type.

italicize (also **italicise**) VERB print in italics.

itch NOUN a tickling sensation in the skin, causing a desire to scratch; a restless desire. VERB feel an itch; be the site or cause of an itch: *my skin itched.*

itchy ADJ

item NOUN **1** a single thing in a list or collection; a single piece of news. **2** [INFORMAL] a couple in a romantic relationship.

itemize (also **itemise**) VERB list; state the individual items of.

itemization NOUN

iterate VERB repeat.

iterative ADJ

itinerant ADJ travelling.

itinerary NOUN (PL **itineraries**) a route, a list of places to be visited on a journey.

its POSSESSIVE PRONOUN of the thing mentioned; belonging to it.

itself PRON the emphatic and reflexive form of *it*.

ITV ABBREV Independent Television.

IUD ABBREV intrauterine device, a contraceptive coil placed inside the womb.

IVF ABBREV in vitro fertilization.

ivory NOUN (PL **ivories**) a hard creamy-white substance forming the tusks of an elephant etc.; its colour; (**ivories**) [INFORMAL] piano keys. ADJ creamy white.

ivory tower NOUN a place providing seclusion from the harsh realities of life.

ivy NOUN (PL **ivies**) an evergreen climbing plant.

Jj

J (also **j**) NOUN (PL **Js** or **J's**) the tenth letter of the alphabet. ABBREV joule(s).

jab VERB (**jabs**, **jabbing**, **jabbed**) poke roughly with something pointed. NOUN a rough poke; [INFORMAL] an injection.

jabber VERB talk rapidly, often unintelligibly.

jack NOUN **1** a portable device for raising heavy weights off the ground. **2** a playing card next below queen. **3** a ship's small flag showing nationality. **4** an electrical connection with a single plug. **5** a small ball aimed at in bowls.
jack up raise with a jack.

jackal NOUN a dog-like wild animal.

jackass NOUN **1** a male ass. **2** a stupid person.

jackboot NOUN a military boot reaching above the knee.

jackdaw NOUN a bird of the crow family.

jacket NOUN **1** a short coat. **2** an outer covering; the skin of a potato.

jackknife NOUN (PL **jackknives**) a large folding knife. VERB (of an articulated vehicle) fold against itself in an accident.

jackpot NOUN a large prize of money that has accumulated until won.
hit the jackpot [INFORMAL] have a great and sudden success.

Jacobean /jak-ŏ-**bee**-ăn/ ADJ of the reign of James I of England (1603–25).

Jacobite NOUN a supporter of James II of England or of the exiled Stuarts.

jacuzzi /jă-**koo**-zee/ NOUN [TRADE MARK] a large bath

with underwater jets of water.

jade NOUN a hard green, blue, or white stone; a green colour.

jaded ADJ tired and bored.

jagged /jagg-id/ ADJ having rough sharp projections.

jaguar NOUN a large animal of the cat family.

jail (also **gaol**) NOUN prison. VERB put into jail.

jailbird (also **gaolbird**) NOUN [INFORMAL] a prisoner or former prisoner.

jailer (also **gaoler**) NOUN a person in charge of a jail or its prisoners.

Jainism NOUN a religion of India.
Jain NOUN

jalopy /jă-lop-i/ NOUN (PL **jalopies**) [INFORMAL] an old battered car.

jam VERB (**jams**, **jamming**, **jammed**) **1** pack tightly into a space. **2** push roughly or forcibly into position. **3** block through crowding. **4** become or make unable to function because a part has stuck. **5** (**jam on**) apply (brakes) forcibly. **6** block a radio transmission by causing interference. **7** [INFORMAL] improvise with other musicians. NOUN **1** an instance of being jammed. **2** [INFORMAL] a difficult situation. **3** [INFORMAL] an improvised performance by musicians. **4** a thick sweet substance made by boiling fruit with sugar.

jamb NOUN the side post of a door or window.

jamboree NOUN a large party; a rally.

jangle NOUN a harsh metallic sound. VERB make or cause to make this sound; upset or be upset by discord.

janitor NOUN the caretaker of a building.

January NOUN the first month.

Japanese NOUN a person from Japan; the language of Japan. ADJ relating to Japan.

japanned ADJ coated with a hard black varnish.

jar[1] NOUN a cylindrical glass or earthenware container; [INFORMAL] a glass of beer.

jar² VERB (**jars, jarring, jarred**) strike with a painful shock; have a painful or disagreeable effect.

jardinière /*zh*ar-din-**yair**/ NOUN a large ornamental pot for growing plants.

jargon NOUN words or expressions developed for use within a particular group of people and hard for others to understand.

jasmine NOUN a shrub with white or yellow flowers.

jasper NOUN a kind of quartz.

jaundice NOUN a condition in which the skin becomes abnormally yellow.

jaundiced ADJ **1** affected by jaundice. **2** filled with resentment.

jaunt NOUN a short pleasure trip.

jaunty ADJ (**jauntier, jauntiest**) cheerful, self-confident.
jauntily ADV
jauntiness NOUN

javelin NOUN a light spear thrown in sport (formerly as a weapon).

jaw NOUN **1** the bones forming the framework of the mouth; (**jaws**) the gripping parts of a tool. **2** [INFORMAL] lengthy talk. VERB [INFORMAL] talk lengthily.

jay NOUN a bird of the crow family.

jaywalking NOUN crossing a road carelessly.
jaywalker NOUN

jazz NOUN a type of music involving improvisation, strong rhythm, and syncopation. VERB (**jazz up**) make more lively.

JCB NOUN [TRADE MARK] a mechanical excavator.

jealous ADJ envying and resenting another's success; suspiciously protecting possessions or a relationship.
jealously ADV
jealousy NOUN

jeans PLURAL NOUN denim trousers.

jeep NOUN [TRADE MARK] a small sturdy motor vehicle with four-wheel drive.

jeer VERB laugh or shout rudely or scornfully (at). NOUN a jeering shout.

jehad variant of **JIHAD**.

Jehovah NOUN the name of God in the Old Testament.

jejune ADJ superficial; not satisfying; dull.

jell VERB set as a jelly; [INFORMAL] (of plans etc.) become clear and fixed.

jelly NOUN (PL **jellies**) a soft solid food made of liquid set with gelatin; a substance of similar consistency; jam made of strained fruit juice.

jellyfish NOUN a sea animal with a jelly-like body.

jemmy NOUN (PL **jemmies**) a short crowbar used by a burglar.

jenny NOUN (PL **jennies**) a female donkey.

jeopardize /jep-er-dyz/ (also **jeopardise**) VERB endanger.

jeopardy /jep-er-di/ NOUN danger.

jerk NOUN a sudden sharp movement or pull. VERB move, pull, or stop with a jerk.
jerkily ADV
jerkiness NOUN
jerky ADJ

jerkin NOUN a sleeveless jacket.

jerry-built ADJ hastily and poorly built.

jerrycan NOUN a large can for petrol or water.

jersey NOUN (PL **jerseys**) a knitted woollen pullover with sleeves; machine-knitted fabric.

jest NOUN a joke. VERB make jokes.

jester NOUN a clown at a medieval court.

Jesuit NOUN a member of the Society of Jesus, a Roman Catholic religious order.

jet[1] NOUN a hard black mineral; glossy black.

jet[2] NOUN **1** a stream of water, gas, or flame from a small opening; a burner on a gas cooker. **2** an engine or aircraft using jet propulsion. VERB (**jets**, **jetting**, **jetted**) **1** spurt out in a jet. **2** travel by jet aircraft.

jet lag NOUN delayed tiredness etc. after a long flight.

jet-propelled ADJ propelled by jet engines.

jet propulsion NOUN forward movement

provided by engines sending out jets of gas at the back.

jetsam NOUN goods jettisoned by a ship and washed ashore.

jet-skiing NOUN the sport of riding in a small jet-propelled vehicle that skims across water.

jettison VERB throw overboard; eject; discard.

jetty NOUN (PL **jetties**) a small pier; a staircase for boarding an aircraft; a breakwater.

Jew NOUN a person of Hebrew descent or whose religion is Judaism. **Jewish** ADJ

jewel NOUN a precious stone cut or set as an ornament; a highly valued person or thing. **jewelled** ADJ

jeweller ([US] **jeweler**) NOUN a person who makes or deals in jewels or jewellery.

jewellery (also **jewelry**) NOUN jewels or similar ornaments to be worn.

Jewry NOUN the Jewish people.

jib NOUN a triangular sail stretching forward from a mast; a projecting arm of a crane. VERB (**jibs**, **jibbing**, **jibbed**) (of a horse) refuse to proceed. **jib at** object to.

jibe **1** variant of **GIBE**. **2** US spelling of **GYBE**.

jiffy NOUN [INFORMAL] a moment.

Jiffy bag NOUN [TRADE MARK] a padded envelope.

jig NOUN **1** a lively dance. **2** a device that holds something and guides tools working on it. VERB (**jigs**, **jigging**, **jigged**) move quickly up and down.

jiggery-pokery NOUN [INFORMAL] trickery.

jiggle VERB rock or shake lightly.

jigsaw NOUN **1** (also **jigsaw puzzle**) a picture cut into pieces to be shuffled and reassembled for amusement. **2** a machine fretsaw.

jihad /ji-hahd/ (also **jehad**) NOUN (in Islam) a holy war.

jilt VERB abandon (a lover).

jingle VERB make or cause to make a ringing or

clinking sound. NOUN **1** this sound. **2** a simple rhyme, especially one used in advertising.

jingoism NOUN excessive patriotism and contempt for other countries. **jingoistic** ADJ

jinx NOUN [INFORMAL] an influence causing bad luck.

jitters PLURAL NOUN [INFORMAL] nervousness. **jittery** ADJ

jiu-jitsu variant of **JU-JITSU**.

jive NOUN a lively dance to jazz music. VERB dance in this style.

Jnr. ABBREV Junior.

job NOUN a piece of work; a paid position of employment; a duty or responsibility; [INFORMAL] a difficult task, difficulty: *I had a job getting here.*

jobber NOUN [HISTORICAL] a principal or wholesaler dealing on the Stock Exchange, not with the public.

jobbing ADJ doing single pieces of work for payment.

jobcentre NOUN (in the UK) a government office displaying information about available jobs.

jobless ADJ out of work.

job lot NOUN miscellaneous articles sold together.

jockey NOUN (PL **jockeys**) a person who rides in horse races. VERB manoeuvre to gain advantage.

jockstrap NOUN a protective support for the male genitals, worn while taking part in sports.

jocose ADJ [FORMAL] joking.

jocular ADJ joking. **jocularity** NOUN **jocularly** ADV

jocund ADJ [FORMAL] merry, cheerful.

jodhpurs /jod-pŭz/ PLURAL NOUN trousers used for horse riding that fit closely below the knee.

jog VERB (**jogs**, **jogging**, **jogged**) **1** run at a steady gentle pace; carry on steadily and uneventfully. **2** nudge, knock; stimulate (someone's memory). NOUN **1** a steady run. **2** a nudge.

jogger NOUN

joggle VERB shake slightly. NOUN a slight shake.

jogtrot NOUN a slow regular trot.

joie de vivre /*zh*wah dĕ **veevr**/ NOUN great enjoyment of life.

join VERB **1** unite, connect, be connected. **2** become a member of; come into the company of. NOUN a place where things join.
join up enlist in the forces.

joiner NOUN a maker of wooden doors, windows, etc.
joinery NOUN

joint NOUN **1** a join; a structure where bones fit together; a large piece of meat. **2** [INFORMAL] a marijuana cigarette. **3** [INFORMAL] an establishment for meeting, eating, etc. ADJ shared by two or more people. VERB connect with a joint; cut into joints.
out of joint dislocated; in disorder.
jointly ADV

jointure NOUN an estate settled on a widow for her lifetime.

joist NOUN one of the beams supporting a floor or ceiling.

jojoba /hŏ-**hoh**-bă/ NOUN a plant with seeds containing oil used in cosmetics.

joke NOUN something said or done to cause laughter; [INFORMAL] a ridiculous person or thing. VERB make jokes.

joker NOUN **1** a person who jokes. **2** an extra playing card with no fixed value.

jollification NOUN time spent having fun.

jollity NOUN (PL **jollities**) lively celebration, being jolly.

jolly ADJ (**jollier**, **jolliest**) happy and cheerful; [INFORMAL] enjoyable. ADV [INFORMAL] very.
jolly along keep (a person) in good humour.

jolt VERB shake or dislodge with a jerk; move jerkily; surprise or shock into action. NOUN a jolting movement; a shock.

josh VERB [INFORMAL] tease playfully.

joss stick NOUN a thin stick that burns with a

smell of incense.

jostle VERB push roughly.

jot NOUN a very small amount. VERB (**jots**, **jotting**, **jotted**) write down briefly.

jotter NOUN a notepad.

joule /jool/ NOUN a unit of energy.

journal NOUN a daily record of events; a newspaper or periodical.

j

journalese NOUN [INFORMAL] a clichéd style of writing associated with newspapers.

journalist NOUN a person employed to write for a newspaper or magazine.
journalism NOUN

journey NOUN (PL **journeys**) an act of travelling from one place to another. VERB make a journey.

journeyman NOUN a reliable worker.

joust VERB [HISTORICAL] fight on horseback with lances.

jovial ADJ cheerful and good-humoured.
joviality NOUN
jovially ADV

jowl NOUN the lower part of the cheek; an animal's dewlap.

joy NOUN great pleasure; something causing delight.
joyful ADJ
joyfully ADV
joyfulness NOUN

joyous ADJ [LITERARY] very happy.
joyously ADV
joyousness NOUN

joyride NOUN [INFORMAL] a fast and dangerous drive in a stolen car.
joyriding NOUN

joystick NOUN an aircraft's control lever; a device for moving a cursor on a VDU screen.

JP ABBREV Justice of the Peace.

Jr. ABBREV Junior.

jubilant ADJ joyful, rejoicing.
jubilantly ADV
jubilation NOUN

jubilee NOUN a special anniversary.

Judaic /joo-day-ik/ ADJ of Jews or Judaism.

Judaism NOUN the religion of the Jewish people.

judder VERB shake noisily or violently. NOUN this movement.

judge NOUN a public officer appointed to hear and try cases in law courts; a person who decides who has won a contest; a person able to give an authoritative opinion.
VERB try (a case) in a law court; act as judge of.

judgement (also **judgment**) NOUN the ability to make wise decisions; an opinion or conclusion; a judge's decision on a case.

judgemental (also **judgmental**) ADJ of judgement; severe, critical.

judicial ADJ of the administration of justice; of a judge or judgement.
judicially ADV

judiciary NOUN (PL **judiciaries**) the whole body of judges in a country.

judicious ADJ judging wisely, showing good sense.
judiciously ADV

judo NOUN a Japanese system of unarmed combat.

jug NOUN **1** a container with a handle and a shaped lip, for holding and pouring liquids.
2 [INFORMAL] prison.
jugful NOUN

juggernaut NOUN a very large transport vehicle; an overwhelmingly powerful object or institution.

juggle VERB toss and catch several objects skilfully for entertainment; manipulate skilfully.
juggler NOUN

jugular vein NOUN either of the two large veins in the neck.

juice NOUN the liquid in fruits and vegetables; fluid secreted by an organ of the body; [INFORMAL] electrical energy; petrol.

juicy ADJ (**juicier**, **juiciest**) full of juice; [INFORMAL] exciting, scandalous.

ju-jitsu (also **jiu-jitsu**, **ju-jutsu**) NOUN a Japanese system of unarmed combat.

jukebox NOUN a coin-operated record player.

julep NOUN a drink of spirits and water flavoured especially with mint.

julienne NOUN a dish of vegetables cut into thin strips.

July NOUN the seventh month.

jumble VERB mix in a confused way. NOUN jumbled articles; items for a jumble sale.

jumble sale NOUN a sale of second-hand articles to raise money for charity.

jumbo NOUN (PL **jumbos**) [INFORMAL] something that is very large of its kind; (also **jumbo jet**) a very large jet aircraft.

jump VERB move up off the ground etc. by movement of the legs; make a sudden upward movement; cross (an obstacle) with a jump; omit, pass over. NOUN **1** a jumping movement; a sudden increase or change. **2** an obstacle to be jumped.
jump at seize or accept eagerly. **jump the queue** obtain something without waiting one's turn.

jumper NOUN **1** a knitted garment for the upper part of the body; [US] a pinafore dress. **2** one who jumps; a short wire used to shorten or temporarily close an electrical circuit.

jump lead NOUN a cable for carrying electric current from one battery to another.

jumpsuit NOUN a one-piece garment for the whole body.

jumpy ADJ (**jumpier**, **jumpiest**) [INFORMAL] nervous.

junction NOUN a join; a place where roads or railway lines meet.

junction box NOUN a box containing a junction of electric cables.

juncture NOUN **1** a particular point in time or the development of events. **2** a join.

June NOUN the sixth month.

jungle NOUN **1** a tropical forest; a mass of tangled vegetation. **2** a scene of ruthless struggle.

junior ADJ younger in age; lower in rank or authority; of or for younger people. NOUN a junior person.

juniper NOUN an evergreen shrub.

junk NOUN **1** [INFORMAL] useless or discarded articles, rubbish. **2** a flat-bottomed ship with sails, used in the China seas.

junket NOUN a sweet custard-like food made of milk and rennet.

junk food NOUN food with low nutritional value.

junkie NOUN [INFORMAL] a drug addict.

junk mail NOUN [INFORMAL] unrequested advertising matter sent by post.

junk shop NOUN [INFORMAL] a shop selling cheap second-hand goods.

junta /**huun**-tă, **jun**-tă/ NOUN a military or political group ruling a country after seizing power.

jurisdiction NOUN the authority to administer justice or exercise power.

jurisprudence NOUN the theory or philosophy of law.

jurist NOUN an expert in law.

juror NOUN a member of a jury.

jury NOUN (PL **juries**) a group of people sworn to give a verdict on a case in a court of law.

jury-rigged ADJ with makeshift rigging.

just ADJ fair to all concerned; morally right; deserved, appropriate. ADV **1** exactly. **2** very recently. **3** by a small amount, barely. **4** only, merely. **5** very, absolutely: *just fine.*
just now very recently.
just so very tidy, immaculate.
justly ADV

justice NOUN **1** just behaviour or treatment; legal proceedings. **2** a judge.

Justice of the Peace NOUN a non-professional magistrate.

justifiable ADJ able to be defended as reasonable or acceptable.
justifiably ADV

justify VERB (**justifies**, **justifying**, **justified**) **1** show to be right or reasonable; be sufficient reason for. **2** adjust (a line of type) to fill a space neatly.
justification NOUN

jut VERB (**juts**, **jutting**, **jutted**) (**jut out**) protrude; thrust forward.

jute NOUN fibre from the bark of certain tropical plants, used to make ropes etc.

juvenile ADJ of or for young people; childish, immature; (of an animal) not adult. NOUN a young person or animal.

juvenile delinquent NOUN a young offender, too young to be held legally responsible for his or her actions.

juxtapose VERB put (things) side by side. **juxtaposition** NOUN

Kk

K (also **k**) NOUN (PL **Ks** or **K's**) the eleventh letter of the alphabet. ABBREV **1** kelvin(s). **2** [INFORMAL] one thousand.

kaftan (also **caftan**) NOUN a long tunic worn by men in the Near East; a long loose dress.

kaiser /**kI**-zĕ/ NOUN [HISTORICAL] an emperor of Germany or Austria.

Kalashnikov NOUN a Russian rifle or sub-machine gun.

kale NOUN a green vegetable.

kaleidoscope /kă-**lI**-dŏ-skohp/ NOUN a tube containing coloured fragments reflected to produce changing patterns as the tube is rotated.
kaleidoscopic ADJ

kamikaze /ka-mi-**kah**-zi/ NOUN (in the Second World War) a Japanese explosive-laden aircraft deliberately crashed on its target. ADJ reckless, suicidal.

kangaroo NOUN an Australian mammal with a pouch to carry its young and strong hind legs for jumping.

kangaroo court NOUN a court formed unofficially by a group to settle disputes among themselves.

kaolin /**kay**-ŏ-lin/ NOUN fine white clay used in porcelain and medicine.

kapok /**kay**-pok/ NOUN a fluffy fibre used as padding.

kaput /kă-**puut**/ ADJ [INFORMAL] broken; ruined.

karaoke /kari-**oh**-ki/ NOUN entertainment in which people sing popular songs to pre-recorded backing tracks.

karate /kă-**rah**-ti/ NOUN a Japanese system of unarmed combat using hands and feet to deliver blows.

karma NOUN (in Buddhism and Hinduism) a person's actions as affecting his or her next reincarnation.

kayak /**ky**-ak/ NOUN a light covered canoe.

Kb ABBREV kilobyte(s).

kebab NOUN small pieces of meat etc. cooked on a skewer.

kedge NOUN an anchor.

kedgeree NOUN a cooked dish of fish, rice, hard-boiled eggs, etc.

keel NOUN a timber or steel structure along the base of a ship.
keel over capsize; [INFORMAL] collapse, fall over.

keen ADJ **1** eager, enthusiastic. **2** sharp; quick, intelligent; (of eyesight etc.) powerful; (of wind etc.) very cold.
keen on fond of, interested in.
keenly ADV
keenness NOUN

keep VERB (**keeps, keeping, kept**) **1** retain possession of; reserve for future use; detain. **2** remain or cause to remain in a specified state or position; continue doing something: *keep talking.* **3** provide with food and other necessities; own and look after (animals); manage (a shop etc.). **4** fulfil (a promise). **5** prevent; restrain oneself: *I couldn't keep from laughing.* NOUN **1** a person's food and other necessities. **2** a strongly fortified structure in a castle.
keep off avoid; abstain from. **keep on** continue. **keep up** progress at the same pace as others.

keeper NOUN a person who keeps or looks after something.

keeping NOUN custody, charge.
in keeping with appropriate to.

keepsake NOUN something kept in memory of the giver.

keg NOUN a small barrel.

kelp NOUN a type of seaweed.

kelvin NOUN a degree of the **Kelvin scale** of temperature with zero at absolute zero (–273.15°C).

kennel NOUN a shelter for a dog; (**kennels**) a boarding place for dogs.

kept past and past participle of **KEEP**.

keratin NOUN a protein forming the basis of horn, nails, and hair.

kerb NOUN a stone edging to a pavement.

kerchief NOUN a piece of fabric worn over the head.

kerfuffle NOUN [INFORMAL] a fuss, a commotion.

kernel NOUN a seed within a husk, nut, or fruit stone; the central or important part.

kerosene (also **kerosine**) NOUN paraffin oil.

kestrel NOUN a small falcon.

ketch NOUN a two-masted sailing boat.

ketchup NOUN a thick tomato sauce.

kettle NOUN a container with a spout and handle, for boiling water.

kettledrum NOUN a drum with a membrane stretched over a large metal bowl.

key NOUN **1** a piece of shaped metal for moving the bolt of a lock, winding a clock, etc.; something giving access or insight; a list of answers; an explanatory list of symbols on a map etc. **2** a button on a panel for operating a typewriter etc.; a lever pressed by the finger on a piano etc. **3** a system of related notes in music. ADJ of crucial importance.
keyed up nervously tense.

keyboard NOUN a set of keys on a piano, typewriter, or computer. VERB enter (data) using a keyboard.
keyboarder NOUN

keyhole NOUN a hole for a key in a lock.

keyhole surgery NOUN surgery carried out through a very small incision.

k

keynote NOUN **1** the note on which a key in music is based. **2** the prevailing idea of a speech, conference etc.

keypad NOUN a small device with buttons for operating electronic equipment, a telephone, etc.

key ring NOUN a ring on which keys are threaded for safe keeping.

k

keystone NOUN the central stone of an arch, locking others into position.

keystroke NOUN a single depression of a key on a keyboard.

keyword NOUN the key to a cipher etc.; a very significant word or concept.

kg ABBREV kilogram(s).

KGB ABBREV the secret police of the former Soviet Union.

khaki /**kah**-ki/ NOUN a dull greenish- or yellowish-brown colour; fabric or clothing of this colour.

khan /kahn/ NOUN the title of rulers and officials in central Asia.

kHz ABBREV kilohertz.

kibbutz NOUN (PL **kibbutzim**) a communal settlement in Israel.

kick VERB **1** strike or propel with the foot. **2** (of a gun) recoil when fired. **3** [INFORMAL] give up (an addictive habit). NOUN **1** an act of kicking; a blow with the foot. **2** [INFORMAL] a thrill.
kick out [INFORMAL] expel, dismiss. **kick up a fuss** [INFORMAL] protest noisily and violently.

kick-off NOUN the start of a football game.

kick-start NOUN a lever pressed with the foot to start a motorcycle. VERB start (an engine) using this; provide initial impetus for.

kid NOUN a young goat; [INFORMAL] a child. VERB (**kids**, **kidding**, **kidded**) [INFORMAL] tease, deceive. ADJ made of leather from a kid's skin.

kidnap VERB (**kidnaps**, **kidnapping**, **kidnapped**; [US] **kidnaping**, **kidnaped**) carry off (a person) illegally to obtain a ransom.
kidnapper NOUN

kidney NOUN (PL **kidneys**) either of a pair of organs that remove waste products from the blood and secrete urine.

kill VERB **1** cause the death of; put an end to. **2** spend (time) unprofitably when waiting. NOUN an act of killing; an animal killed by a hunter.
killer NOUN

killjoy NOUN [INFORMAL] a person who spoils others' enjoyment.

kiln NOUN an oven for hardening or drying pottery or hops, or burning lime.

kilo NOUN (PL **kilos**) a kilogram.

kilo- COMBINING FORM one thousand.

kilobyte NOUN [COMPUTING] 1,024 bytes.

kilocalorie NOUN the amount of heat needed to raise the temperature of 1kg of water by 1°C.

kilogram NOUN a unit of weight or mass in the metric system (2.205 lb).

kilohertz NOUN a unit of frequency of electromagnetic waves, = 1,000 cycles per second.

kilojoule NOUN 1,000 joules.

kilometre NOUN 1,000 metres (0.62 mile).

kilovolt NOUN 1,000 volts.

kilowatt NOUN 1,000 watts.

kilt NOUN a knee-length pleated skirt of tartan, as traditionally worn by Highland men.

kimono NOUN (PL **kimonos**) a loose Japanese robe worn with a sash.

kin NOUN a person's relatives.

kind NOUN a class of similar people or things. ADJ gentle and considerate towards others.
in kind 1 (of payment) in goods etc., not money. **2** (of a response) similar, in the same way.
kind-hearted ADJ
kindness NOUN

kindergarten NOUN a school for very young children.

kindle VERB light (a fire); arouse, stimulate (a feeling).

kindling NOUN small pieces of wood for lighting fires.

kindly ADJ (**kindlier, kindliest**) kind. ADV in a kind way; please (used in polite requests).
kindliness NOUN

kindred NOUN a person's relatives. ADJ related; of a similar kind.

kinetic ADJ of movement.

king NOUN **1** a male ruler of a country; a man or thing regarded as supreme. **2** the most important chess piece; a playing card next above queen.

kingdom NOUN **1** a country ruled by a king or queen. **2** one of the divisions into which natural objects are classified.

kingfisher NOUN a bird with bright blue feathers that dives to catch fish.

kingpin NOUN an indispensable person or thing.

king-size (also **king-sized**) ADJ extra large.

kink NOUN a sharp twist in something straight; a flaw; a mental peculiarity. VERB form or cause to form a kink or kinks.

kinky ADJ (**kinkier, kinkiest**) **1** having kinks. **2** [INFORMAL] given to or involving unusual sexual behaviour.

kinsfolk PLURAL NOUN a person's relatives.
kinsman NOUN
kinswoman NOUN

kiosk NOUN a booth where newspapers or refreshments are sold, or one containing a public telephone.

kip NOUN [INFORMAL] a sleep.

kipper NOUN a smoked herring.

kirk NOUN [SCOTTISH] a church.

kirsch /keersh/ NOUN a liqueur made from cherries.

kismet NOUN destiny, fate.

kiss VERB touch with the lips as a sign of love or affection or in greeting. NOUN an act of kissing.
the kiss of life mouth-to-mouth resuscitation.

kissogram NOUN a novelty greeting delivered with a kiss.

kit NOUN a set of tools; a set of parts to be assembled; the clothing for a particular activity. VERB (**kits**, **kitting**, **kitted**) equip with kit.

kitbag NOUN a bag for holding kit.

kitchen NOUN a room where meals are prepared.

kitchenette NOUN a small kitchen.

kitchen garden NOUN a garden for vegetables, fruit, and herbs.

kite NOUN **1** a light framework with fabric stretched over it, attached to a string for flying in the wind. **2** a large hawk.

Kitemark NOUN an official mark on goods approved by British Standards.

kith and kin NOUN relatives.

kitsch /kich/ NOUN objects etc. seen as in poor taste because garish, sentimental, or vulgar.

kitten NOUN a young cat; the young of a rabbit or ferret.

kitty NOUN (PL **kitties**) a communal fund.

kiwi NOUN a flightless New Zealand bird.

kJ ABBREV kilojoule(s).

klaxon NOUN [TRADE MARK] an electric horn.

Kleenex NOUN [TRADE MARK] a paper handkerchief.

kleptomania NOUN a compulsive desire to steal.
kleptomaniac NOUN

km ABBREV kilometre(s).

knack NOUN the ability to do something skilfully.

knacker NOUN a person who buys and slaughters old horses, cattle, etc. VERB [INFORMAL] **1** tire out. **2** damage.

knapsack NOUN a bag worn strapped on the back.

knave NOUN **1** [ARCHAIC] a dishonest man. **2** a jack in playing cards.

knead VERB press and stretch (dough) with the hands; massage.

knee NOUN the joint between the thigh and the lower leg; part of a garment covering this; a person's lap. VERB (**knees**, **kneeing**, **kneed**) hit with the knee.

kneecap NOUN the small bone over the front of

the knee. VERB (**kneecaps**, **kneecapping**, **kneecapped**) shoot in the knee as a punishment.

knee-jerk ADJ (of a reaction) automatic and predictable.

kneel VERB (**kneels**, **kneeling**, **knelt** or **kneeled**) support oneself on one's knees.

knees-up NOUN [INFORMAL] a lively party.

k

knell NOUN the sound of a bell tolled after a death.

knelt past and past participle of **KNEEL**.

knew past of **KNOW**.

knickerbockers PLURAL NOUN loose breeches gathered at the knee.

knickers PLURAL NOUN **1** underpants. **2** [US] knickerbockers.

knick-knack NOUN a small worthless ornament.

knife NOUN (PL **knives**) a cutting or spreading instrument with a blade and handle. VERB stab with a knife.

knight NOUN **1** a man given a rank below baronet, with the title 'Sir'. **2** a chess piece shaped like a horse's head. **3** [HISTORICAL] a mounted soldier in armour. VERB confer a knighthood on.

knighthood NOUN the rank of knight.

knit VERB (**knits**, **knitting**, **knitted** or **knit**) **1** make a garment from yarn formed into interlocking loops on long needles. **2** become united; (of a broken bone) grow together, heal; tighten (one's eyebrows) in a frown.
knitter NOUN
knitting NOUN

knob NOUN a rounded lump; a round door handle.
knobbly ADJ

knock VERB **1** hit with an audible sharp blow; strike a door to attract attention. **2** collide with; injure by hitting; drive in a particular direction with a blow. **3** [INFORMAL] criticize. NOUN a sharp blow; the sound of this; an injury caused by this; a setback.
knock about 1 treat roughly. **2** [INFORMAL] travel

casually. **knock down** force to the ground with a blow or collision. **knock off** [INFORMAL] **1** finish work. **2** produce (a piece of work) quickly. **3** steal. **knock out 1** strike unconscious. **2** eliminate from a competition. **knock up 1** rouse by knocking at a door. **2** [INFORMAL] make hurriedly.

knock-down ADJ [INFORMAL] (of a price) very low.

knocker NOUN a hinged device for knocking on a door.

knock-kneed ADJ having knees that bend inwards.

knock-on effect NOUN a secondary, indirect effect.

knockout NOUN **1** an act of knocking someone out. **2** a tournament in which the loser in each round is eliminated. **3** [INFORMAL] an outstanding person or thing.

knock-up NOUN a practice game at tennis etc.

knoll NOUN a small hill.

knot NOUN **1** a fastening made by tying a piece of thread, rope, etc.; a tangle; a cluster. **2** a hard round spot in timber formed where a branch joins the trunk. **3** a unit of speed used by ships and aircraft, = one nautical mile per hour. VERB (**knots**, **knotting**, **knotted**) tie or fasten with a knot; entangle.

knotty ADJ (**knottier**, **knottiest**) **1** full of knots. **2** puzzling, difficult.

know VERB (**knows**, **knowing**, **knew**; PAST PARTICIPLE **known**) **1** have in one's mind or memory; feel certain; have learned. **2** be acquainted, familiar, or friendly with (a person, place, etc.). **in the know** [INFORMAL] having inside information. **known as** called, referred to as (a particular name).

know-how NOUN practical knowledge or skill.

knowing ADJ aware, cunning; showing that one has secret knowledge: *a knowing look* **knowingly** ADV

knowledge NOUN information about or

awareness of something; the sum of what is known.

knowledgeable ADJ intelligent; well informed.

knuckle NOUN a finger joint; an animal's leg joint as meat.
knuckle under yield, submit.

knuckleduster NOUN a metal device worn over the knuckles to increase the effect of a blow.

koala NOUN a bear-like Australian tree-climbing animal.

kohl NOUN black powder used as eye make-up.

kola variant of **COLA**.

kookaburra NOUN an Australian giant kingfisher with a harsh cry.

kopek (also **copeck** or **kopeck**) NOUN a Russian coin, one-hundredth of a rouble.

Koran NOUN the sacred book of Islam.

kosher /koh-shĕ/ ADJ **1** conforming to Jewish dietary laws. **2** [INFORMAL] genuine, legitimate.

kowtow VERB [INFORMAL] behave with exaggerated respect.

k.p.h. ABBREV kilometres per hour.

kremlin NOUN a citadel in a Russian town; (**the Kremlin**) the Russian government.

krill NOUN tiny plankton crustaceans that are eaten by whales etc.

krona NOUN the unit of money in Sweden (PL **kronor**) and Iceland (PL **kronur**).

krone NOUN (PL **kroner**) the unit of money in Denmark and Norway.

krugerrand NOUN a South African gold coin.

krypton NOUN a colourless, odourless gas.

kudos NOUN honour and glory.

kumquat (also **cumquat**) NOUN a tiny variety of orange.

kung fu NOUN a Chinese form of unarmed combat.

Kurd NOUN a member of a people of SW Asia.
Kurdish ADJ

kV ABBREV kilovolt(s).

Ll

L (also **l**) NOUN **1** the twelfth letter of the alphabet. **2** the Roman numeral for 50. ABBREV **1** learner driver. **2** (**l**) litre(s).

lab NOUN [INFORMAL] a laboratory.

label NOUN a piece of card, cloth, etc., attached to something and carrying information about it. VERB (**labels**, **labelling**, **labelled**; [US] **labeling**, **labeled**) attach a label to; regard or describe as belonging to a specified category.

labia PLURAL NOUN the folds of the female genitals.

labial ADJ of the lips.

labor etc. US spelling of **LABOUR** etc.

laboratory NOUN (PL **laboratories**) a room or building equipped for scientific work.

laborious ADJ needing or showing much effort. **laboriously** ADV

labour ([US] **labor**) NOUN **1** work, exertion; workers. **2** contractions of the womb at childbirth. VERB work hard; move with effort; explain (a point) at unnecessary length.

laboured ([US] **labored**) ADJ done with great effort; not spontaneous.

labourer ([US] **laborer**) NOUN a person employed to do manual work.

Labour Party NOUN a British political party formed to represent the interests of ordinary working people.

Labrador NOUN a large dog.

laburnum NOUN a tree with hanging clusters of yellow flowers.

labyrinth /lab-i-rinth/ NOUN a maze.

labyrinthine ADJ

lace NOUN **1** decorative fabric made by looping thread in patterns. **2** a cord threaded through holes or hooks to pull opposite edges of a garment etc. together. VERB **1** fasten with laces. **2** intertwine. **3** add alcohol to (a dish or drink).

lacerate VERB tear (flesh).
laceration NOUN

lachrymose /lak-rim-ohs/ ADJ [FORMAL] tearful.

lack NOUN an absence or insufficiency of something; not having something. VERB be without (something needed or wanted).

lackadaisical ADJ lacking vigour or determination, unenthusiastic.

lackey NOUN (PL **lackeys**) a footman, a servant; a servile follower.

lacking ADJ absent, missing, not available; without something; deficient.

lacklustre ([US] **lackluster**) ADJ lacking brightness, enthusiasm, or conviction.

laconic ADJ using few words.
laconically ADV

lacquer NOUN a hard glossy varnish. VERB coat with lacquer.

lacrosse NOUN a game similar to hockey played using sticks with small nets on the ends.

lactation NOUN secretion of milk for suckling.
lactate VERB

lactic acid NOUN acid found in sour milk and produced in the muscles during exercise.

lactose NOUN a sugar present in milk.

lacuna NOUN (PL **lacunas** or **lacunae**) a gap; a place where something is missing.

lacy ADJ (**lacier**, **laciest**) of or like lace.

lad NOUN a boy; [INFORMAL] a young man with sexist attitudes and unrestrained behaviour.

ladder NOUN a set of crossbars between uprights, used for climbing up; a series of ascending stages in a career etc.; a vertical ladder-like flaw where stitches become undone in tights or a stocking. VERB make (a ladder) in tights or a stocking.

laden ADJ loaded.

ladle NOUN a deep long-handled spoon for transferring liquids. VERB transfer with a ladle.

lady NOUN (PL **ladies**) a woman; a well-mannered woman; a woman of noble birth; (**Lady**) the title of wives, widows, or daughters of certain noblemen.

ladybird NOUN a small flying beetle, usually red with black spots.

lady-in-waiting NOUN a woman attending a queen or princess.

ladylike ADJ appropriate to a well-born or well-mannered woman.

ladyship NOUN (**Her/Your Ladyship**) the title used in addressing a Lady.

lag¹ VERB (**lags**, **lagging**, **lagged**) fall behind, fail to keep up. NOUN a delay.

lag² VERB (**lags**, **lagging**, **lagged**) cover (a boiler etc.) with insulating material.

lager NOUN a light-coloured beer.

lager lout NOUN [INFORMAL] a drunken rowdy youth.

laggard NOUN a person who makes slow progress.

lagging NOUN material used to lag a boiler etc.

lagoon NOUN a salt-water lake beside the sea.

lah NOUN [MUSIC] the sixth note of a major scale, or the note A.

laid past and past participle of **LAY²**.

laid-back ADJ [INFORMAL] easy-going, relaxed.

lain past participle of **LIE²**.

lair NOUN a place where a wild animal rests; a hiding-place.

laird NOUN [SCOTTISH] a landowner.

laissez-faire /less-ay-fair/ NOUN a policy of non-interference, especially in politics or economics.

laity /lay-i-ti/ NOUN lay people, not clergy.

lake NOUN a large body of water surrounded by land; a large pool of liquid.

lam VERB (**lams**, **lamming**, **lammed**) [INFORMAL] hit hard.

lama /**lah**-mă/ NOUN a Buddhist priest in Tibet and Mongolia.

lamb NOUN **1** a young sheep; its flesh as food. **2** a gentle or endearing person. VERB give birth to a lamb.

lambaste /lam-**bayst**/ (also **lambast**) VERB reprimand severely.

lame ADJ **1** unable to walk normally. **2** unconvincing, feeble. VERB make lame, disable.
lamely ADV
lameness NOUN

lamé /**lah**-may/ NOUN a fabric interwoven with gold or silver thread.

lament NOUN an expression of grief; a song or poem expressing grief. VERB feel or express grief or regret (for).
lamentation NOUN

lamentable /**lam**-ent-ă-bĕl/ ADJ regrettable, deplorable.
lamentably ADV

laminate /**lam**-in-ăt/ NOUN laminated material.

laminated ADJ made of layers joined one on another.

lamp NOUN a device for giving light.

lampoon NOUN a piece of writing that attacks a person with ridicule. VERB ridicule in a lampoon.

lamp-post NOUN a tall post with a light on top as street illumination.

lamprey NOUN (PL **lampreys**) a small eel-like water animal.

lampshade NOUN a shade on a lamp screening its light.

lance NOUN a long spear. VERB prick or cut open with a lancet.

lance corporal NOUN an army rank below corporal.

lancet NOUN **1** a surgeon's pointed two-edged knife. **2** a tall narrow pointed arch or window.

land NOUN **1** the part of the earth's surface not covered by water;

ground, soil; an area of ground as property or for a particular use. **2** a country or state. VERB **1** come or bring ashore; come or bring down from the air. **2** [INFORMAL] succeed in obtaining or achieving. **3** [INFORMAL] come or cause to come into a specified state: *landed him in trouble.* **4** [INFORMAL] inflict (a blow).

landed ADJ **1** owning land. **2** consisting of land: *landed estates.*

landfall NOUN the approach to land after a journey by sea or air.

landfill NOUN disposal of waste material by burying it, especially to refill excavated pits; this material.

landing NOUN **1** the process of coming or bringing ashore or to ground; a place for this. **2** a level area at the top of a flight of stairs.

landing stage NOUN a platform for coming ashore from a boat.

landlady NOUN (PL **landladies**) **1** a woman who lets land or a house or room to a tenant. **2** a woman who runs a public house.

landlocked ADJ surrounded by land.

landlord NOUN **1** a person who lets land or a house or room to a tenant. **2** a person who runs a public house.

landlubber NOUN [INFORMAL] a person not accustomed to sailing.

landmark NOUN a conspicuous feature of a landscape; an event marking an important stage or turning point.

landscape NOUN the scenery of an area of land; a picture of this. VERB lay out (an area) attractively with natural-looking features.

landslide NOUN **1** a fall of earth and rock from a mountain or cliff. **2** an overwhelming majority of votes.

landslip NOUN a landslide.

lane NOUN a narrow road, track, or passage; a division of a road for a single line of traffic; a track to which ships or aircraft etc. must keep; one of the parallel strips for runners etc. in a race.

language NOUN words and their use; a system of this used by a nation or group; gestures or symbols used for communication.

languid /lang-gwid/ ADJ lacking vigour or vitality.

languish /lang-gwish/ VERB lose or lack vitality; live under miserable conditions.

languor /lang-gĕ/ NOUN tiredness, laziness, lack of energy.
languorous ADJ

lank ADJ (of hair) long, limp, and straight.

lanky ADJ (**lankier**, **lankiest**) tall and thin.
lankiness NOUN

lanolin NOUN a fat extracted from sheep's wool, used in ointments.

lantern NOUN **1** a lamp protected by a transparent case, carried by a handle. **2** a structure at the top of a tower, with windows on all sides.

lanthanum NOUN a metallic element.

lanyard /lan-yăd/ NOUN a short rope for securing sails etc. on a ship; a cord for hanging a whistle etc. round the neck or shoulder.

lap NOUN **1** a flat area over the thighs of a seated person. **2** a single circuit of a racecourse; a section of a journey. VERB (**laps**, **lapping**, **lapped**) **1** take up (liquid) by movements of the tongue. **2** (of water) wash against something with a gentle sound. **3** be one or more laps ahead of (a competitor).
lap up take or accept eagerly.

laparoscope /lap-ă-rŏ-skohp/ NOUN a fibre-optic instrument inserted through the abdomen to view the internal organs.
laparoscopy NOUN

lapdog NOUN a small pampered dog.

lapel /lă-pell/ NOUN a flap folded back at the front of a coat etc.

lapidary /lap-id-ă-ri/ ADJ **1** (of language) concise

and elegant. **2** of stones and gems.

lapis lazuli NOUN a blue semi-precious stone.

Lapp NOUN a person from Lapland; their language.

> The people prefer to be called **Sami**.

lapse NOUN **1** a temporary failure of concentration, memory, etc.; a decline in standard. **2** the passage of time. VERB **1** (of a right or privilege) become invalid. **2** pass into an inferior state; fail to maintain one's standard.

laptop NOUN a portable computer.

larch NOUN a deciduous tree of the pine family.

lard NOUN a white greasy substance prepared from pig-fat. VERB **1** put strips of fat bacon in or on (meat) before cooking. **2** use too many quotations, figures of speech, etc., in (speech or writing).

larder NOUN a storeroom for food.

large ADJ of great size or extent.
at large 1 free to roam about. **2** as a whole, in general.
largeness NOUN

largely ADV to a great extent.

largesse /lah-jess/ (also **largess**) NOUN money or gifts generously given.

lariat /la-ri-ăt/ NOUN a lasso.

lark NOUN **1** a small brown bird, a skylark. **2** [INFORMAL] something done for fun.
lark about [INFORMAL] behave playfully.

larva NOUN (PL **larvae**) an insect in the first stage of its life after coming out of the egg.
larval ADJ

laryngitis NOUN inflammation of the larynx.

larynx /la-rinks/ NOUN the part of the throat containing the vocal cords.

lasagne /lă-zan-yă/ NOUN a dish of pasta layered with sauces of cheese, meat, tomato, etc.

lascivious /lă-siv-i-ŭs/ ADJ lustful.
lasciviously ADV
lasciviousness NOUN

laser NOUN a device

emitting an intense narrow beam of light.

lash VERB **1** strike with a whip; beat against; (of an animal) move (its tail) quickly to and fro. **2** tie down. NOUN **1** the flexible part of a whip; a blow with this. **2** an eyelash.
lash out 1 strike at someone; attack someone verbally. **2** [INFORMAL] spend lavishly.

lashings PLURAL NOUN [INFORMAL] a lot.

lass (also **lassie**) NOUN [SCOTTISH] & [NORTHERN ENGLISH] a girl, a young woman.

lassitude NOUN tiredness, lack of energy.

lasso /lă-soo/ NOUN (PL **lassos** or **lassoes**) a rope with a noose for catching cattle. VERB (**lassoes**, **lassoing**, **lassoed**) catch with a lasso.

last[1] ADJ **1** coming after all others, final; lowest in importance. **2** most recent. ADV **1** most recently. **2** finally. NOUN the last person or thing; all that remains of something. VERB continue; survive, endure; (of resources) be enough for a period of time.
at last, at long last after much delay. **in the last resort** if all else fails. **the last straw** the final thing making a situation unbearable.
lasting ADJ

last[2] NOUN a foot-shaped block used in making and repairing shoes.

lastly ADV finally.

last post NOUN a military bugle call sounded at sunset or military funerals.

last word NOUN **1** the final statement in a dispute. **2** the latest, most fashionable example of something.

latch NOUN a bar lifted from its catch by a lever, used to fasten a gate etc; a spring-lock that catches when a door is closed. VERB fasten with a latch.
on the latch closed but not locked.

latchkey NOUN a key of an outer door.

latchkey child NOUN a child left at home without adult supervision.

late ADJ **1** happening or coming after the proper or expected time. **2** far on in a day or night or period. **3** dead; no longer holding a position. **4** (**latest**) most recent. ADV **1** after the proper or expected time. **2** at or until a late time.
of late lately.
lateness NOUN

lately ADV recently.

latent ADJ existing but not active or developed or visible.
latency NOUN

lateral ADJ of, at, to, or from the side(s).
laterally ADV

latex /lay-teks/ NOUN a milky fluid from the rubber tree; a similar synthetic substance.

lath NOUN (PL **laths**) a narrow thin strip of wood in a trellis or partition wall.

lathe NOUN a machine for holding and turning pieces of wood or metal while they are worked.

lather NOUN froth from soap and water; frothy sweat. VERB cover with or form lather.

Latin NOUN the language of the ancient Romans. ADJ of or in Latin; of a people whose language is based on Latin, e.g. French or Spanish.

Latin America NOUN the parts of Central and South America where Spanish or Portuguese is the main language.

latitude NOUN **1** the distance of a place from the equator, measured in degrees; a region. **2** freedom from restrictions.
latitudinal ADJ

latrine NOUN a lavatory in a camp or barracks.

latter ADJ towards the end, in the final stages; recent.
the latter the second of two things to be mentioned.

latter-day ADJ modern, recent.

latterly ADV **1** recently. **2** towards the end of a period.

lattice NOUN a framework of crossed strips.

laudable ADJ praiseworthy.

laudanum /lord-ă-nŭm/ NOUN opium prepared for use as a sedative.

laudatory /lord-ă-tŏ-ri/ ADJ praising.

laugh VERB make sounds and facial movements expressing amusement or scorn. NOUN the act or manner of laughing; [INFORMAL] an amusing incident or person.

laughable ADJ ridiculous.

laughing stock NOUN a person or thing that is ridiculed.

laughter NOUN the act or sound of laughing.

launch VERB send (a ship) into the water; send (a rocket) into the air; start (an enterprise); introduce (a new product). NOUN **1** the process of launching something. **2** a large motor boat.

launder VERB **1** wash and iron (clothes etc.). **2** transfer (money acquired illegally) to conceal its origin.

launderette NOUN an establishment fitted with washing machines to be used for a fee.

laundry NOUN (PL **laundries**) a place where clothes etc. are laundered; clothes etc. for washing.

laurel NOUN an evergreen shrub; (**laurels**) victories or honours gained.

lava NOUN flowing or hardened molten rock from a volcano.

lavatory NOUN (PL **lavatories**) a fixture into which urine and faeces are discharged; a room equipped with this.

lavender NOUN a shrub with fragrant purple flowers; light purple.

lavish ADJ generous; plentiful; luxurious and extravagant. VERB give generously.
lavishly ADV
lavishness NOUN

law NOUN a rule established by authority; a set of such rules; their influence or operation; a statement of what always happens in certain circumstances.

law-abiding ADJ obeying the law.

law court NOUN a room or

building in which legal trials are held.

lawful ADJ permitted or recognized by law.
lawfully ADV
lawfulness NOUN

lawless ADJ disregarding the law.
lawlessness NOUN

lawn NOUN **1** an area of closely cut grass in a garden or park. **2** fine woven cotton fabric.

lawnmower NOUN a machine for cutting grass.

lawn tennis NOUN tennis played with a soft ball on outdoor grass or a hard court.

lawrencium NOUN a radioactive metallic element.

lawsuit NOUN the process of bringing a dispute before a court of law for settlement.

lawyer NOUN a person qualified in legal matters.

lax ADJ slack, not strict or severe.
laxity NOUN

laxative ADJ stimulating the bowels to empty. NOUN a laxative drug or other substance.

lay[1] ADJ not ordained into the clergy; non-professional.

lay[2] VERB (**lays**, **laying**, PAST and PAST PARTICIPLE **laid**) **1** set down carefully; arrange for use; put cutlery etc. on (a table) for a meal. **2** cause to be in a certain condition: *laid him open to suspicion.* **3** (of a bird) produce (eggs). NOUN the appearance of a landscape.
lay bare expose, reveal. **lay into** [INFORMAL] thrash; scold harshly. **lay off** **1** discharge (workers) temporarily. **2** [INFORMAL] stop doing something. **lay on** provide. **lay out** **1** spread out, arrange; prepare (a body) for burial. **2** [INFORMAL] knock unconscious. **3** [INFORMAL] spend (a sum of money). **lay up** **1** store. **2** put (someone) out of action through illness. **lay waste** devastate.

lay[3] past of **LIE[2]**.

layabout NOUN a lazy person.

lay-by NOUN (PL **lay-bys**) an area beside the road where vehicles may stop.

layer NOUN **1** one of several sheets or thicknesses of a substance covering a surface. **2** a shoot fastened down to take root while attached to the parent plant. **3** a hen that lays eggs. VERB **1** arrange in layers. **2** propagate (a plant) using layers.

layette NOUN an outfit for a newborn baby.

lay figure NOUN an artist's jointed model of the human body.

layman NOUN someone not ordained as a clergyman; someone without professional knowledge of a subject.

layout NOUN an arrangement of parts etc. according to a plan.

laze VERB spend time idly.

lazy ADJ (**lazier**, **laziest**) unwilling to work or use energy; done without effort or care.
lazily ADV
laziness NOUN

lb ABBREV pound(s) weight.

lbw ABBREV [CRICKET] leg before wicket.

LCD ABBREV **1** [COMPUTING] & [ELECTRONICS] liquid crystal display. **2** lowest common denominator.

LEA ABBREV Local Education Authority.

lea NOUN [LITERARY] a piece of meadow or arable land.

leach VERB remove (soluble minerals etc.) from soil through the action of liquid percolating through it; be drained away in this way.

lead¹ /leed/ VERB (**leads**, **leading**, **led**) **1** go in front of and cause to follow one; guide. **2** be a reason or motive for (someone), influence. **3** be a route or means of access; result or culminate in something. **4** be in command of; be ahead of or superior to. **5** pass (one's life). NOUN **1** a leading position; the state of being ahead. **2** a clue. **3** the chief part in a play or film; a person playing this. **4** a strap or cord for leading a dog. **5** a wire conveying electric current.

lead on mislead, deceive.
lead up to be an introduction to; result in; immediately precede.

lead² /led/ NOUN **1** a heavy grey metal; a lump of lead used for sounding depths. **2** graphite in a pencil.

leaden /led-ĕn/ ADJ **1** heavy, slow-moving. **2** dull grey like lead; [ARCHAIC] made of lead.

leader NOUN **1** a person who leads. **2** a newspaper article giving editorial opinions.
leadership NOUN

leading question NOUN a question worded to prompt the desired answer.

leaf NOUN (PL **leaves**) **1** a flat (usually green) organ growing from the stem or root of a plant. **2** a single thickness of paper, a page; a very thin sheet of metal. **3** a hinged flap or extra section of a table.
leaf through turn over the leaves of (a book).

leaflet NOUN **1** a printed sheet of paper giving information. **2** a small leaf of a plant.

leaf mould NOUN soil or compost consisting of decayed leaves.

leafy ADJ (**leafier**, **leafiest**) having many leaves.

league NOUN **1** a group of people or countries united for a purpose; an association of sports clubs that compete against one another. **2** a class, a standard: *in a league of his own.*
in league with conspiring with.

leak VERB (of liquid, gas, etc.) pass through a crack; (of a container) lose contents through a crack or hole; disclose (secrets) or be disclosed. NOUN an escape of liquid or gas through a crack; a crack or hole through which this happens; an escape of an electric charge; a disclosure of secret information.
leakage NOUN
leaky ADJ

lean¹ VERB (**leans**, **leaning**, **leaned** or **lent**) put or be in a sloping position; rest or cause to rest against something for support.

lean on 1 depend on. **2** [INFORMAL] intimidate, put under pressure.

lean² ADJ thin, having no superfluous fat; (of meat) with little fat; (of a period) characterized by hardship. NOUN the lean part of meat.
leanness NOUN

leaning NOUN a tendency, an inclination.

lean-to NOUN a shed etc. against the side of a building.

l **leap** VERB (**leaps**, **leaping**, **leaped** or **leapt**) jump vigorously. NOUN a vigorous jump.
leap at seize (an opportunity) eagerly.

leapfrog NOUN a game in which each player vaults over another who is bending down. VERB (**leapfrogs**, **leapfrogging**, **leapfrogged**) perform this vault (over); overtake another; pass over (an obstacle).

leap year NOUN a year with an extra day (29 Feb.), occurring once every four years.

learn VERB (**learns**, **learning**, **learned** or **learnt**) gain knowledge of or skill in; become aware of; memorize.
learner NOUN

learned /ler-nid/ ADJ having or showing great learning.

learning NOUN knowledge obtained by study.

lease NOUN a contract allowing the use of land or a building for a specified time.
VERB obtain or grant (property) by lease.
leasehold NOUN
leaseholder NOUN

leash NOUN a dog's lead.

least DETERMINER & PRON (**the least**) smallest in amount, extent, or significance. ADV to the smallest extent or degree.
at least 1 not less than. **2** if nothing else; anyway.

leather NOUN material made by treating animal skins; a piece of soft leather for polishing.
VERB [INFORMAL] thrash.

leatherette NOUN imitation leather.

leathery ADJ tough like leather.

leave VERB (**leaves**,

leaving, **left**) 1 go away (from); go away finally or permanently. 2 allow to remain; not take with one; abandon, desert; deposit, entrust to someone; bequeath. 3 cause to remain in a specified state: *leave the door open*. NOUN permission; permission to be absent from duty; the period for which this lasts.
leave out not insert or include.

leaven /lev-ĕn/ NOUN a substance such as yeast, causing dough to rise; a transforming and improving influence. VERB add leaven to; transform.

lecher NOUN a lecherous man.

lechery NOUN excessive sexual desire, lustfulness.
lecherous ADJ

lecithin NOUN a compound found in plants and animals, used as a food emulsifier and stabilizer.

lectern NOUN a stand with a sloping top from which a bible etc. is read.

lecture NOUN a speech giving information about a subject; a lengthy reproof or warning. VERB give a lecture or lectures; reprove at length.
lecturer NOUN

led past and past participle of **LEAD**[1].

ledge NOUN a narrow horizontal projection or shelf.

ledger NOUN a book used for keeping accounts.

lee NOUN shelter from the wind given by a hill, building, etc.; the sheltered side of such an object.

leech NOUN a small blood-sucking worm.

leek NOUN a vegetable with an onion-like flavour.

leer VERB look slyly, maliciously, or lustfully. NOUN a leering look.

lees PLURAL NOUN sediment in wine.

leeward ADJ & NOUN on or towards the side away from the wind.

leeway NOUN a degree of freedom of action.

left[1] past and past participle of **LEAVE**.

left[2] ADJ & ADV of, on, or towards the side of the body which is on the west when one is facing north. NOUN **1** the left side or region; the left hand or foot. **2** people supporting socialism or a more extreme form of socialism than others in their group.

left-handed ADJ using the left hand more easily than the right.

leftovers PLURAL NOUN things remaining when the rest is finished.

leg NOUN **1** each of the limbs on which a person, animal, etc. stands or moves; part of a garment covering a person's leg; a support of a table, chair, etc. **2** one section of a journey or contest.
leg it [INFORMAL] run away.

legacy NOUN (PL **legacies**) something left to someone in a will, or handed down by a predecessor.

legal ADJ of or based on law; authorized or required by law.
legalistic ADJ
legality NOUN
legally ADV

legal aid NOUN help from public funds towards the cost of legal action.

legalize (also **legalise**) VERB make permissible by law.
legalization NOUN

legate NOUN an envoy.

legatee NOUN the recipient of a legacy.

legation NOUN a diplomatic minister and staff; their headquarters.

legato ADV [MUSIC] smoothly and evenly.

legend NOUN **1** a story handed down from the past; such stories collectively. **2** a very famous person. **3** an inscription on a coin or medal; an explanation of the symbols on a map.

legendary ADJ of or described in legend; famous.

legerdemain /lej-er-dĕ-mayn/ NOUN skilful use of the hands in conjuring; trickery.

leggings PLURAL NOUN a close-fitting stretchy garment covering the legs.

legible ADJ clear enough to be deciphered, readable.

legibility NOUN
legibly ADV

legion NOUN a division of the ancient Roman army; a huge crowd. ADJ very numerous.

legionnaire NOUN a member of a legion.

legionnaires' disease NOUN a form of bacterial pneumonia.

legislate VERB make laws.
legislator NOUN

legislation NOUN laws collectively.

legislative ADJ making laws.

legislature NOUN a country's legislative assembly.

legitimate ADJ **1** in accordance with a law or rule; justifiable. **2** born of parents married to each other.
legitimacy NOUN
legitimization NOUN (also **legitimisation**)
legitimize VERB (also **legitimise**)

legless ADJ **1** without legs. **2** [INFORMAL] drunk.

legume NOUN a plant of the family bearing seeds in pods.
leguminous ADJ

leisure NOUN time free from work.
at leisure not busy. **at one's leisure** when one has time.

leisured ADJ having plenty of leisure.

leisurely ADJ & ADV without hurry.

leitmotif /lyt-moh-teef/ (also **leitmotiv**) NOUN a recurrent theme in a musical or literary work, associated with a particular person or idea.

lemming NOUN a mouse-like Arctic rodent (said to rush headlong into the sea and drown in its migration).

lemon NOUN **1** a yellow oval fruit with acid juice; the tree bearing this; a pale yellow colour. **2** [INFORMAL] a stupid or unsatisfactory person or thing.

lemonade NOUN a lemon-flavoured fizzy drink.

lemur NOUN a nocturnal monkey-like animal of Madagascar.

lend VERB (**lends**, **lending**, **lent**) give (something) to (someone) for temporary

use; provide (money) temporarily in return for payment of interest; add (an effect) to (something).
lend a hand [INFORMAL] help. **lend itself to** be suitable for.
lender NOUN

length NOUN **1** the measurement or extent from end to end; the state of being long; the full extent; the length of something as a unit of measurement: *six lengths of the pool;* a piece of cloth etc. **2** an extreme effort: *go to great lengths.*
at length 1 in great detail. **2** at last, after a long time.

l

lengthen VERB make or become longer.

lengthways (also **lengthwise**) ADV & ADJ in the direction of a thing's length.

lengthy ADJ (**lengthier**, **lengthiest**) very long.
lengthily ADV

lenient ADJ merciful, not severe.
lenience NOUN
leniently ADV

lens NOUN a piece of glass or similar substance shaped for use in an optical instrument; the transparent part of the eye, behind the pupil.

Lent NOUN the Christian period of fasting and repentance before Easter.

lent past and past participle of **LEND**.

lentil NOUN a kind of bean.

leonine ADJ of or like a lion.

leopard /lep-erd/ NOUN a large spotted animal of the cat family.

leotard /lee-ŏ-tahd/ NOUN a close-fitting stretchy garment worn by dancers, gymnasts, etc.

leper NOUN a person with leprosy.

leprechaun NOUN (in Irish folklore) a small, mischievous sprite.

leprosy NOUN an infectious disease affecting the skin and nerves and causing deformities.
leprous ADJ

lesbian NOUN a homosexual woman.
ADJ of lesbians.
lesbianism NOUN

lese-majesty /leez/ NOUN

an insult to a ruler; treason.

lesion /lee-*zhŏn*/ NOUN a region in an organ or tissue that is damaged by injury or disease.

less DETERMINER & PRON a smaller amount of; not as much. ADV to a smaller extent. PREP minus.

lessee NOUN a person holding property by lease.

lessen VERB make or become less.

lesser ADJ not so great or important as the other.

lesson NOUN **1** an amount of teaching given at one time; something to be learnt by a pupil; an experience by which one can learn. **2** a passage from the Bible read aloud.

lessor NOUN a person who lets property on lease.

lest CONJ [FORMAL] for fear that.

let VERB (**lets, letting, let**) **1** allow, not forbid; allow to pass: *let me through.* **2** allow someone to use (accommodation) in return for payment. AUXILIARY VERB used in requests, commands, suggestions, or assumptions: *let's try.* NOUN **1** (in tennis etc.) an obstruction of the ball nullifying a service. **2** a period during which property is let: *a short let.* **let alone 1** refrain from interfering with. **2** used to introduce something more extreme and unlikely. **let down 1** disappoint. **2** deflate (a tyre etc.). **let go** stop holding on (to). **let off 1** fire or explode (a weapon, firework, etc.). **2** punish lightly; excuse. **let on** [INFORMAL] reveal a secret. **let out 1** utter; reveal. **2** make (a garment) looser. **let up** [INFORMAL] relax; become less intense or severe.

-let COMBINING FORM small; young.

lethal ADJ causing death.

lethargy NOUN extreme lack of energy or vitality. **lethargic** ADJ

letter NOUN **1** a symbol representing a speech sound. **2** a written message sent by post;

(**letters**) literature. **3** the precise terms or interpretation of something: *the letter of the law.* VERB write or provide with letters.

letter box NOUN a slit in a door, with a movable flap, through which letters are delivered; a postbox.

letterhead NOUN a printed heading on stationery.

lettuce NOUN a plant with broad crisp leaves used as salad.

leucocyte /loo-ko-sIt/ NOUN a white blood cell.

leukaemia /loo-kee-mi-ă/ ([US] **leukemia**) NOUN a disease in which leucocytes multiply uncontrollably.

levee /le-vi/ NOUN an embankment against floods; [US] a quay.

level ADJ **1** flat and even; without bumps or hollows. **2** horizontal. **3** at the same height or in the same relative position as something: *he drew up level with me.* **4** steady; unchanging. NOUN **1** a position on a scale; a degree: *unemployment levels.* **2** a height reached: *flood levels.* **3** an instrument to test a horizontal line.
VERB (**levels**, **levelling**, **levelled**; [US] **leveling**, **leveled**) **1** make or become level; knock down (a building). **2** aim (a gun).
on the level [INFORMAL] honest.

level crossing NOUN a place where a road and railway cross at the same level.

level-headed ADJ sensible.

lever NOUN a bar pivoted on a fixed point to lift something; a pivoted handle used to operate machinery; a means of power or influence.
VERB use a lever; lift by this.

leverage NOUN the action or power of a lever; power, influence.

leveret /lev-ĕr-et/ NOUN a young hare.

leviathan /lĕ-vI-ă-thăn/ NOUN something of enormous size and power.

levitate VERB rise or cause

to rise and float in the air.
levitation NOUN

levity NOUN flippancy; humorous treatment of something serious.

levy VERB (**levies**, **levying**, **levied**) impose (a tax, fee, or fine). NOUN (PL **levies**) a tax; an act of levying a tax etc.

lewd ADJ treating sexual matters vulgarly; lascivious.
lewdly ADV
lewdness NOUN

lexical ADJ of words.

lexicography NOUN the compiling of dictionaries.
lexicographer NOUN

lexicon NOUN a dictionary; a vocabulary.

liability NOUN (PL **liabilities**) **1** the state of being legally responsible. **2** a debt. **3** a person or thing putting one at a disadvantage.

liable ADJ **1** held responsible by law; legally obliged to pay a tax etc. **2** likely to do something.

liaise /lee-ayz/ VERB establish a cooperative link or relationship.

liaison /lee-**ayz**-on/ NOUN **1** communication and cooperation. **2** an illicit sexual relationship.

liana /lee-**ah**-nă/ NOUN a climbing plant of tropical forests.

liar NOUN a person who tells lies.

libation NOUN a drink-offering to a god.

libel NOUN a published false statement that damages a person's reputation; the act of publishing it. VERB (**libels**, **libelling**, **libelled**; [US] **libeling**, **libeled**) publish a libel against.
libellous ADJ

liberal ADJ **1** tolerant; respecting individual freedom; (in politics) favouring moderate social reform. **2** generous. **3** (of an interpretation) not strict or exact.
liberally ADV

liberalize (also **liberalise**) VERB make less strict.
liberalization NOUN

liberate VERB set free.
liberated ADJ
liberation NOUN
liberator NOUN

libertarian NOUN a person favouring absolute liberty of thought and action.

libertine NOUN a person who behaves without moral principles or a sense of responsibility.

liberty NOUN (PL **liberties**) freedom; a right or privilege; scope to act as one pleases.
at liberty free; permitted to do something. **take liberties** behave with undue freedom or familiarity.

libido /li-bee-doh/ NOUN (PL **libidos**) sexual desire.

librarian NOUN a person in charge of or assisting in a library.

library NOUN (PL **libraries**) a collection of books (or records, films, etc.) for consulting or borrowing; a room or building containing these.

libretto NOUN (PL **librettos** or **libretti**) the words of an opera.

lice pl. of **LOUSE**.

licence ([US] **license**) NOUN **1** an official permit to own or do something; permission. **2** freedom to do as one likes.

license VERB grant a licence to or for. NOUN US spelling of **LICENCE**.

licensee NOUN a holder of a licence.

licentious ADJ sexually immoral.
licentiousness NOUN

lichen /ly-kĕn/ NOUN a low-growing dry plant that grows on rocks etc.

lick VERB **1** pass the tongue over; (of waves or flame) touch lightly. **2** [INFORMAL] defeat; thrash. NOUN **1** an act of licking; [INFORMAL] a slight application (of paint etc.). **2** [INFORMAL] a fast pace.

licorice variant of **LIQUORICE**.

lid NOUN a hinged or removable cover for a box, pot, etc.; an eyelid.

lido NOUN (PL **lidos**) a public open-air swimming pool or bathing beach.

lie[1] NOUN a statement the speaker knows to be untrue. VERB (**lies, lying, lied**) tell a lie.

lie[2] VERB (**lies, lying, lay;**

PAST PARTICIPLE **lain**) **1** have or put one's body in a flat or resting position; be at rest on something. **2** be in a specified state; be situated. NOUN the pattern or direction in which something lies. **lie in** lie in bed late in the morning. **lie low** stay hidden.

liege /leej/ NOUN [HISTORICAL] **1** a feudal superior. **2** a vassal.

lien /leen, **lee**-ĕn/ NOUN [LAW] the right to hold another person's property until a debt on it is paid.

lieu /lew/ NOUN (**in lieu**) instead.

lieutenant /lef-**ten**-ănt; [US] loo-**ten**-ănt/ NOUN an army officer next below captain; a naval officer next below lieutenant commander; a chief assistant.

life NOUN (PL **lives**) **1** the ability of animals and plants to function and grow; the state of being alive; living things. **2** the time for which an individual is alive; the time for which an object lasts. **3** a way of living. **4** vitality, enthusiasm; excitement. **5** a biography. **6** [INFORMAL] a sentence of imprisonment for life.

lifebelt NOUN a belt of buoyant material to keep a person afloat.

lifeboat NOUN a boat for rescuing people at sea; a ship's boat for emergency use.

lifebuoy NOUN a buoyant device to keep a person afloat.

life cycle NOUN a series of changes undergone by an organism during its life.

lifeguard NOUN an expert swimmer employed to rescue bathers in danger.

life jacket NOUN a buoyant or inflatable jacket for keeping a person afloat in water.

lifeless ADJ dead; unconscious; not animated; without living things.

lifelike ADJ exactly like a real person or thing.

lifeline NOUN a rope thrown to a swimmer in danger; something essential to safety.

lifelong ADJ lasting all one's life.

life sciences PLURAL NOUN biology and related subjects.

life-size (also **life-sized**) ADJ (of a model etc.) of the same size as the person or thing represented.

lifestyle NOUN a way of spending one's life. ADJ (of a product etc.) designed to appeal to customers with a particular lifestyle.

life support NOUN the artificial maintenance of the body's functions after physical failure or in a hostile environment.

lifetime NOUN the duration of a person's life.

lift VERB **1** raise; turn to face upwards; move upwards; make larger, louder, or higher. **2** pick up and move; remove (legal restrictions etc.); [INFORMAL] steal. **3** raise (someone's spirits) or be raised. NOUN **1** an apparatus for moving people and goods from one floor of a building to another. **2** an act or manner of lifting. **3** a free ride in a motor vehicle. **4** a feeling of encouragement.

lift-off NOUN vertical take-off of a spacecraft etc.

ligament NOUN a tough flexible tissue holding bones together.

ligature NOUN a thing used for tying; thread used in surgery.

light[1] NOUN **1** a kind of radiation that stimulates sight; brightness; a source of illumination. **2** understanding, enlightenment. **3** a lighter or paler part or area of something. **4** a way of regarding something: *viewed the activities in a favourable light.* VERB (**lights**, **lighting**, **lit** or **lighted**) **1** illuminate, provide with light; switch on (an electric light). **2** ignite, set burning. ADJ **1** well lit; not dark. **2** (of a colour) pale. **bring** (or **come**) **to light** reveal (or be revealed). **in the light of** when (something) is taken into account. **light on** discover by chance. **light up** brighten; put lights on at dusk; light a cigarette.

light² ADJ **1** having little weight, not heavy; easy to lift; of less than usual or average weight. **2** not serious or profound; not solemn, sad, or worried. **3** (of sleep) not deep, easily broken. **4** (of food) easy to digest.
make light of treat as unimportant. **travel light** take little luggage.
lightly ADV
lightness NOUN

lighten¹ VERB shed light on; make or become brighter.

lighten² VERB make or become less heavy.

lighter NOUN **1** a device for lighting cigarettes and cigars. **2** a flat-bottomed boat for carrying ships' cargoes ashore.

light-fingered ADJ apt to steal.

light-headed ADJ dizzy and slightly faint.

light-hearted ADJ cheerful, not serious.

lighthouse NOUN a tower with a beacon light to warn or guide ships.

light industry NOUN the manufacture of small or light articles.

lighting NOUN a means of providing light; the light itself.

lightning NOUN a flash of bright light produced from cloud by natural electricity. ADJ very quick.

light pen NOUN a light-emitting device for reading bar codes; a pen-shaped device held to a computer screen to pass information to the computer.

lights PLURAL NOUN the lungs of certain animals, used as animal food.

lightship NOUN a moored ship with a light, serving as a lighthouse.

lightweight ADJ not heavy; not important or influential; trivial, not serious or intellectual. NOUN a lightweight person; a boxing weight between featherweight and welterweight.

light year NOUN the distance light travels in one year, about 6 million million miles.

lignite NOUN a brown coal of a woody texture.

like¹ PREP resembling, similar to; in the same way as; typical of. ADJ similar, the same. CONJ [INFORMAL] **1** in the same way that. **2** as though. ADV [INFORMAL] in a way, rather. NOUN a person or thing resembling another.

like² VERB **1** find pleasant, enjoy. **2** want, wish for. NOUN (**likes**) things one likes or prefers.

l

likeable (also **likable**) ADJ pleasant, easy to like.

likelihood NOUN a probability.

likely ADJ (**likelier, likeliest**) **1** such as may reasonably be expected to occur or be true. **2** seeming to be suitable or have a chance of success. ADV probably. **likeliness** NOUN

liken VERB point out the likeness of (one thing to another).

likeness NOUN the state of being like; a copy, a portrait.

likewise ADV **1** also. **2** in a similar way.

liking NOUN a fondness. **to one's liking** suiting one's taste.

lilac NOUN a shrub with fragrant purple or white flowers; pale purple. ADJ pale purple.

lilt NOUN **1** a rise and fall of the voice when speaking. **2** a pleasant swinging rhythm in a tune. **lilting** ADJ

lily NOUN (PL **lilies**) a plant growing from a bulb, with large flowers.

limb NOUN an arm, leg, or wing; a large branch of a tree.

limber ADJ supple. **limber up** exercise in preparation for athletic activity.

limbo¹ NOUN a state of waiting unable to act or take a decision.

limbo² NOUN (PL **limbos**) a West Indian dance in which the dancer bends back to pass under a bar.

lime NOUN **1** a white substance used in making cement etc. **2** a round yellowish-green fruit like a lemon; its colour. **3** a tree with heart-shaped leaves.

limelight NOUN the focus of public attention.

limerick NOUN a humorous poem with five lines.

limestone NOUN rock from which lime is obtained.

limit NOUN a point beyond which something does not continue; a restriction; the greatest amount allowed. VERB set or serve as a limit to.
off limits out of bounds; not allowed.
limitation NOUN

limousine NOUN a large luxurious car.

limp VERB walk or proceed lamely. NOUN a limping walk. ADJ not stiff or firm; wilting.
limply ADV
limpness NOUN

limpet NOUN a small shellfish that sticks tightly to rocks.

limpid ADJ (of liquids) clear.

linchpin NOUN **1** a pin passed through the end of an axle to secure a wheel. **2** a person or thing vital to an enterprise.

linctus NOUN a soothing cough mixture.

line NOUN **1** a long narrow mark; an outline as a feature of a design; a wrinkle. **2** a length of cord, rope, wire, etc., for a particular purpose; a telephone connection. **3** a row of people or things; a row of words; a brief letter; (**lines**) an actor's part. **4** a series of generations. **5** a railway track or route; a company providing ships, aircraft, or buses on a route. **6** an area or branch of activity: *my line of work*. **7** a series of military field works. VERB **1** stand on either side of (a road etc.). **2** mark with lines. **3** cover the inside surface of.
line one's pockets make money, especially dishonestly. **line up** arrange or be arranged in a row.

lineage /lin-ee-ij/ NOUN descent from an ancestor; one's ancestry.

lineal ADJ of or in a line.

linear ADJ extending along a line; formed with

straight lines; progressing from one stage to another in a series of steps: *linear narrative.*

linen NOUN cloth made of flax; household articles (e.g. sheets, tablecloths) formerly made of this.

liner NOUN **1** a passenger ship or aircraft. **2** a removable lining.

linesman NOUN **1** an umpire's assistant at the boundary line. **2** a workman who maintains railway, electrical, or telephone lines.

ling NOUN heather.

linger VERB stay longer than necessary; take a long time doing something.

lingerie /lahn-*zh*er-ee/ NOUN women's underwear.

lingua franca NOUN (PL **lingua francas**) a common language used among people whose native languages are different.

linguist NOUN a person who is skilled in languages or linguistics.

linguistic ADJ of language. NOUN (**linguistics**) the study of language.
linguistically ADV

liniment NOUN an embrocation.

lining NOUN a layer of material or another substance covering an inner surface.

link NOUN **1** a connection; a means of contact; a person acting as messenger or intermediary. **2** each ring of a chain. VERB connect; intertwine; represent as connected.
linkage NOUN

lino NOUN [INFORMAL] linoleum.

linocut NOUN a design cut in relief on a block of linoleum; a print made from this.

linoleum NOUN a smooth covering for floors.

linseed NOUN the seed of flax, a source of oil.

lint NOUN **1** a soft fabric for dressing wounds. **2** short fibres shed from a fabric.

lintel NOUN a horizontal timber or stone over a doorway.

lion NOUN a large flesh-eating animal of the cat family.

lionize (also **lionise**) VERB treat as a celebrity.
lionization NOUN

lip NOUN **1** either of the fleshy edges of the mouth-opening. **2** the edge of a container or opening; a slight projection for pouring from. **3** [INFORMAL] impudence.
pay lip service express approval but fail to act on it.

liposuction NOUN removal of fat from under the skin by suction, used in cosmetic surgery.

lip-read VERB understand what is said from lip movements.

lipsalve NOUN ointment for the lips.

lipstick NOUN a cosmetic for colouring the lips.

liquefy VERB (**liquefies, liquefying, liquefied**) make or become liquid.
liquefaction NOUN

liqueur /lik-yoor/ NOUN a strong sweet alcoholic spirit.

liquid NOUN a flowing substance like water or oil. ADJ **1** in the form of liquid. **2** (of assets) easy to convert into cash.

liquidate VERB **1** close down (a business) and divide its assets among creditors. **2** convert (assets) into cash. **3** pay off (a debt). **4** [INFORMAL] kill.
liquidation NOUN
liquidator NOUN

liquidity NOUN a company's possession of liquid assets.

liquidize (also **liquidise**) VERB reduce to a liquid.

liquidizer (also **liquidiser**) NOUN a machine for puréeing vegetables etc.

liquor NOUN **1** alcoholic drink. **2** juice from cooked food.

liquorice ([US] **licorice**) NOUN a black substance used in medicine and as a sweet.

lira NOUN (PL **lire**) a unit of money in Turkey (and formerly Italy).

lisp NOUN a speech defect in which *s* and *z* are

pronounced like *th*. VERB speak or utter with a lisp.

lissom ADJ slim and supple.

list[1] NOUN a number of connected items or names following one another. VERB make a list of; include in a list.

list[2] VERB (of a ship) lean over to one side. NOUN a listing position.

listen VERB make an effort to hear; pay attention; take notice of and act on what is said.
listen in overhear a conversation; listen to a broadcast.
listener NOUN

listeria NOUN a type of bacteria causing food poisoning.

listless ADJ without energy or enthusiasm.
listlessly ADV
listlessness NOUN

lit past and past participle of **LIGHT[1]**.

litany NOUN (PL **litanies**) a set form of prayer; a long monotonous recital.

liter US spelling of **LITRE**.

literal ADJ taking the basic meaning of a word, not a metaphorical or exaggerated one.
literally ADV

literary ADJ of or associated with literature.

literate ADJ able to read and write.
literacy NOUN

literati PLURAL NOUN people interested in and knowledgeable about literature.

literature NOUN great novels, poetry, and plays; books on a particular subject; printed matter giving information etc.

lithe ADJ supple, agile.

lithium NOUN a light metallic element.

litho NOUN [INFORMAL] lithography; a lithograph.

lithography NOUN the process of printing from a plate treated so that ink sticks only to the design.
lithograph NOUN
lithographic ADJ

litigant NOUN a person involved in or initiating a lawsuit.

litigate VERB carry on a lawsuit; contest in law.

litigation NOUN

litigious /lit-ij-ŭs/ ADJ fond of litigation.

litmus NOUN a substance turned red by acids and blue by alkalis.

litotes /lI-toh-teez/ NOUN an ironic understatement.

litre ([US] **liter**) NOUN a metric unit of capacity (1.76 pints) for measuring liquids.

litter NOUN **1** rubbish left lying about. **2** young animals born at one birth. **3** material used as bedding for animals or to absorb their excrement. **4** [HISTORICAL] a vehicle consisting of a curtained seat carried on men's shoulders. VERB **1** scatter as litter; make untidy by litter. **2** give birth to (a litter).

little ADJ small in size, amount, or degree; young, younger. DETERMINER & PRON not much. ADV to a small extent; hardly.

littoral ADJ of or by the shore.

liturgy NOUN (PL **liturgies**) a set form of public worship.

liturgical ADJ

live[1] /lyv/ ADJ **1** alive. **2** burning; unexploded; charged with electricity. **3** (of broadcasts) transmitted while actually happening.

live[2] /liv/ VERB **1** be or remain alive. **2** have one's home in a particular place. **3** spend one's life in a particular way; have a full and exciting life. **live down** live until (scandal etc.) is forgotten. **live on 1** eat (a type of food) as one's regular diet. **2** have (an amount of money) to buy necessities.

livelihood NOUN a means of earning or providing enough food etc. to sustain life.

lively ADJ (**livelier**, **liveliest**) full of energy or action.

liveliness NOUN

liven VERB make or become lively.

liver NOUN a large organ in the abdomen, secreting bile.

liveried ADJ wearing livery.

livery NOUN (PL **liveries**) a distinctive uniform; a colour scheme in which a company's vehicles are painted.

livestock NOUN farm animals.

livid ADJ **1** [INFORMAL] furiously angry. **2** bluish grey.

living ADJ **1** alive; current, in use. **2** used as a home rather than for work. NOUN **1** an income; the means of earning it. **2** a particular life style.

living room NOUN a room for general daytime use.

lizard NOUN a reptile with four legs and a long tail.

llama /lah-mă/ NOUN a South American animal related to the camel.

load NOUN **1** a thing or quantity carried; a burden of responsibility or worry; the amount of work someone has to do. **2** the amount of electric current supplied by a source. **3** (**loads**) [INFORMAL] a great deal. VERB **1** put a load in or on; burden. **2** put ammunition into (a gun) or film into (a camera); put (data) into (a computer). **3** bias towards a particular outcome.
loaded ADJ

loaf NOUN (PL **loaves**) **1** a quantity of bread baked as one piece; a similarly shaped mass of other food. **2** [INFORMAL] one's brains. VERB spend time idly, saunter about.
loafer NOUN

loam NOUN rich soil.

loan NOUN a sum of money that is lent; the action of lending something. VERB lend.
on loan being borrowed.

loan shark NOUN [INFORMAL] a person lending money at very high rates of interest.

loath ADJ unwilling.

loathe VERB feel hatred and disgust for.
loathing NOUN
loathsome ADJ

lob VERB (**lobs**, **lobbing**, **lobbed**) throw or hit (a ball) slowly in a high arc. NOUN a lobbed ball.

lobar ADJ of a lobe, especially of the lung.

lobby NOUN (PL **lobbies**) **1** a porch, entrance hall, or ante-room. **2** a body of people seeking to influence legislation. VERB (**lobbies**, **lobbying**, **lobbied**) seek to persuade (an MP etc.) to support one's cause.

lobbyist NOUN a person who lobbies an MP etc.

lobe NOUN a flat rounded part or projection; the lower soft part of the ear.

lobotomy NOUN (PL **lobotomies**) an incision into the frontal lobe of the brain.

lobster NOUN a shellfish with large claws; its flesh as food.

local ADJ of or affecting a particular place or small area; (of a telephone call) relatively cheap because made to somewhere nearby. NOUN **1** an inhabitant of a particular district. **2** [INFORMAL] one's nearest public house.
locally ADV

locale /loh-**kahl**/ NOUN the scene of an event.

local government NOUN the administration of a district by representatives elected locally.

locality NOUN (PL **localities**) the position of something; an area or neighbourhood.

localize (also **localise**) VERB confine within an area; decentralize.
localization NOUN

locate VERB discover the position of; situate in a particular place; set in a particular context.

location NOUN a place where something is situated; the action of locating something.
on location (of filming) in a setting away from the film studio.

loch NOUN [SCOTTISH] a lake; an arm of the sea.

loci pl. of **LOCUS**.

lock NOUN **1** a device (opened by a key) for fastening a door or lid etc. **2** a section of a canal enclosed by gates, where the water level can be changed. **3** a wrestling hold. **4** the extent to which a vehicle's front wheels can be turned using the steering wheel. **5** a piece of hair that hangs together; (**locks**) [LITERARY] a person's hair.

l

VERB fasten with a lock; shut into a locked place; make or become rigidly fixed.
lockable ADJ

locker NOUN a lockable cupboard where things can be stowed securely.

locket NOUN a small ornamental case worn on a chain round the neck.

lockjaw NOUN tetanus.

lockout NOUN the exclusion of employees from their workplace during a dispute.

locksmith NOUN a maker and mender of locks.

lock-up NOUN lockable premises, especially a garage; a place where prisoners can be kept temporarily.

locomotion NOUN the ability to move from place to place.

locomotive NOUN a powered railway vehicle used for pulling trains. ADJ of or effecting locomotion.

locum NOUN [INFORMAL] a temporary stand-in for a doctor, clergyman, etc.

locus NOUN (PL **loci**) **1** a particular position; something's location. **2** [MATHEMATICS] a line or curve etc. formed by certain points or by the movement of a point or line.

locust NOUN a grasshopper that devours vegetation.

lode NOUN a vein of metal ore.

lodestar NOUN a star (especially the pole star) used as a guide in navigation.

lodestone NOUN an oxide of iron used as a magnet.

lodge NOUN **1** a cabin for use by hunters, skiers, etc.; a gatekeeper's house; a porter's room at the entrance to a building. **2** the members or meeting place of a branch of certain societies. **3** a beaver's or otter's lair. VERB **1** provide with sleeping quarters or temporary accommodation; live as a lodger. **2** present (a complaint, appeal, etc.) to an authority. **3** make or become fixed or embedded.

lodger NOUN a person

paying for accommodation in another's house.

lodging NOUN a place where one lodges; (**lodgings**) a room or rooms rented for living in.

loft NOUN a space under a roof; a gallery in a church. VERB hit, throw, or kick (a ball) in a high arc.

lofty ADJ (**loftier**, **loftiest**) very tall; noble, exalted; proud, aloof.
loftily ADV

log NOUN **1** a piece cut from a trunk or branch of a tree. **2** a systematic record; a logbook. **3** a device for gauging a ship's speed. **4** a logarithm. VERB (**logs**, **logging**, **logged**) enter (facts) in a logbook.
log on or **off, log in** or **out** open or close one's on-line access to a computer system.

loganberry NOUN (PL **loganberries**) a large dark red fruit resembling a raspberry.

logarithm NOUN one of a series of numbers set out in tables, used to simplify calculations.

logbook NOUN a book for recording details of a journey.

loggerheads PLURAL NOUN (**at loggerheads**) in strong disagreement.

logic NOUN a science or method of reasoning; correct reasoning.

logical ADJ of or according to logic; following naturally and sensibly; reasonable; reasoning correctly.
logicality NOUN
logically ADV

logician NOUN a person skilled in logic.

logistics PLURAL NOUN the organization of supplies and services; the coordination of a large operation.
logistical ADJ

logo /loh-goh/ NOUN (PL **logos**) a design used as an emblem.

-logy COMBINING FORM the science or study of a particular subject.

loin NOUN the side and back of the body between the ribs and hip bone.

loincloth NOUN a cloth worn round the body at the hips.

loiter VERB linger, stand about idly.
loiterer NOUN

loll VERB sit, lie, or stand in a relaxed way; hang loosely.

lollipop NOUN a large usually flat boiled sweet on a small stick.

lollipop lady (also **lollipop man**) NOUN [INFORMAL] a person whose job is to help children cross a road by holding up a sign on a pole to stop the traffic.

lollop VERB (**lollops**, **lolloping**, **lolloped**) move in clumsy bounds.

lolly NOUN [INFORMAL] **1** a lollipop. **2** money.

lone ADJ solitary.

lonely ADJ (**lonelier**, **loneliest**) **1** solitary; sad because one lacks friends. **2** (of a place) remote, unfrequented.
loneliness NOUN

loner NOUN a person who prefers not to associate with others.

lonesome ADJ lonely.

long¹ ADJ of great length; of a specified length. ADV for a long time; throughout a specified period.
as or **so long as** provided that.

long² VERB feel an intense desire.

long distance ADJ travelling or operated between distant places.

longevity /lon-jev-i-ti/ NOUN long life.

long face NOUN a dismal expression.

longhand NOUN ordinary writing, not shorthand or typing etc.

longing NOUN an intense wish.

longitude NOUN the distance east or west (measured in degrees on a map) from the Greenwich meridian.

longitudinal ADJ **1** running lengthwise rather than across. **2** of longitude.
longitudinally ADV

long johns PLURAL NOUN [INFORMAL] close-fitting underpants with long legs.

long-life ADJ (of milk etc.) treated to prolong its shelf life.

long-lived ADJ living or lasting for a long time.

long-range ADJ effective over long distances; relating to a long period of future time.

longshoreman NOUN [US] a docker.

long shot NOUN a venture or guess very unlikely to succeed.

long-sighted ADJ able to see clearly only what is at a distance.

long-standing ADJ having existed for a long time.

long-suffering ADJ bearing provocation patiently.

long-term ADJ of or for a long period.

long ton *see* **TON**.

long wave NOUN a radio wave of a wavelength above a kilometre and frequency less than 300 kHz.

longways (also **longwise**) ADV lengthways.

long-winded ADJ talking or writing at tedious length.

loo NOUN [INFORMAL] a lavatory.

loofah NOUN the dried pod of a gourd, used as a rough sponge.

look VERB **1** use or direct one's eyes in order to see, search, or examine. **2** seem. NOUN **1** an act of looking. **2** the appearance of something; a facial expression; (**looks**) a person's attractiveness. **look after** take care of; attend to. **look down on** despise. **look forward to** await eagerly. **look into** investigate. **look on** watch without being involved. **look out** be vigilant. **look round** go round and inspect (a building etc.). **look up** **1** search for information about. **2** [INFORMAL] make contact with (someone). **3** (of a prospect) improve. **look up to** admire and respect.

looker NOUN a person with a specified appearance.

lookout NOUN **1** an

observation post; a person keeping watch. **2** [INFORMAL] a likely outcome. **3** [INFORMAL] a person's own concern.

loom VERB appear, especially close at hand or threateningly. NOUN an apparatus for weaving cloth.

loop NOUN a curve that is U-shaped or that crosses itself; something forming this shape. VERB form into a loop; be loop-shaped.
loop the loop fly an aircraft in a vertical circle.

loophole NOUN a means of evading a rule or contract.

loose ADJ **1** not securely fixed in place; not tethered or shut up. **2** (of a garment) not fitting closely; (of a translation etc.) not exact; (of a walk) easy, relaxed. VERB set free; unfasten; relax.
at a loose end with nothing to do. **on the loose** having escaped from confinement.
loosely ADV
looseness NOUN

loose box NOUN a stall for a horse.

loose-leaf ADJ with each page removable.

loosen VERB make or become loose or looser.

loot NOUN goods taken from an enemy or by theft. VERB take loot (from); take as loot.

lop VERB (**lops, lopping, lopped**) cut off (branches) from a tree.

lope VERB run with a long bounding stride. NOUN this stride.

lop-eared ADJ with drooping ears.

lopsided ADJ with one side lower, smaller, or heavier than the other.

loquacious /lŏ-kway-shŭs/ ADJ talkative.
loquacity NOUN

lord NOUN a nobleman; the title of certain peers or high officials; a master or ruler; (**Lord**) God or Christ.
lord it over behave in an arrogantly superior way towards.

lordship NOUN the title used of a man with the rank of lord.

lore NOUN a body of

traditions and knowledge.

lorgnette /lorn-yet/ NOUN eyeglasses held on a long handle.

lorry NOUN (PL **lorries**) a large motor vehicle for transporting heavy loads.

lose VERB (**loses**, **losing**, **lost**) **1** cease to have; be deprived of. **2** become unable to find. **3** fail to win (a game etc.); waste, fail to use or take advantage of; earn less (money) than previously. **4** [INFORMAL] cause (someone) to be unable to follow one's argument.
lose heart become discouraged. **lose oneself** become absorbed in something. **lose one's way** be unable to find the right direction to go in. **lose out** be deprived of an opportunity. **lose weight** become thinner and lighter.
loser NOUN

loss NOUN the losing of someone or something; someone or something lost; a feeling of sadness after losing a valued person or thing.
at a loss 1 not knowing what to do. **2** making less money than has been spent.

loss-leader NOUN an article sold at a loss to attract customers.

lost past and past participle of **LOSE**. ADJ **1** unable to find one's way; not knowing where one is. **2** gone and not recoverable.
be lost on be unnoticed or unappreciated by. **lost in** absorbed in.

lot PRON (**a lot**, **lots**) [INFORMAL] a large number or amount. ADV (**a lot**, **lots**) [INFORMAL] very much, greatly. NOUN **1** [INFORMAL] a group or set of people or things. **2** an item for sale at an auction. **3** each of a set of objects drawn at random to make a decision; a person's luck or condition in life. **4** a plot of land.
the lot [INFORMAL] the total number or quantity.

lotion NOUN a medicinal or cosmetic liquid applied to the skin.

lottery NOUN (PL **lotteries**) a system of raising money by selling numbered tickets and giving prizes to holders of numbers drawn at random; something where the outcome is governed by luck.

lotus NOUN (PL **lotuses**) a tropical water lily; a mythical fruit.

loud ADJ **1** making a great deal of noise, easily heard. **2** gaudy, garish. ADV loudly.
loudly ADV
loudness NOUN

loudhailer NOUN an electronically operated megaphone.

loudspeaker NOUN an apparatus that converts electrical impulses into audible sound.

lough /lok/ NOUN [IRISH] = **LOCH**.

lounge VERB loll; sit or stand about idly. NOUN a sitting room; a waiting room at an airport etc.

lounge suit NOUN a man's ordinary suit for day wear.

lour /low-ĕ/ (also **lower**) VERB frown, scowl; (of clouds) look dark and threatening.

louse NOUN (PL **lice**) a small parasitic insect; (PL **louses**) [INFORMAL] a contemptible person.

lousy ADJ (**lousier**, **lousiest**) **1** [INFORMAL] very bad. **2** infested with lice.

lout NOUN a clumsy ill-mannered person.
loutish ADJ

louvre /loo-vĕ/ (also **louver**) NOUN each of a set of overlapping slats arranged to let in air but exclude light or rain.
louvred ADJ

lovable ADJ endearing, inspiring love.

love NOUN **1** deep, intense affection; sexual passion; a beloved person or thing. **2** (in games) no score, nil. VERB feel love for; like or enjoy greatly. **in love** feeling (especially sexual) love for another person. **make love** have sexual intercourse.

love affair NOUN a romantic or sexual relationship between people who are in love.

lovelorn ADJ pining with unrequited love.

lovely ADJ (**lovelier**, **loveliest**) beautiful, attractive; delightful.
loveliness NOUN

lover NOUN **1** a person in love with another or having a love affair. **2** a person who likes something specified.

loving ADJ feeling or showing love.
lovingly ADV

low[1] ADJ **1** of little height from top to bottom; not far above the ground or sea level; of less than average amount or intensity. **2** ranking below others, inferior. **3** dishonourable. **4** depressed. NOUN a low point; an area of low atmospheric pressure. ADV in, at, or to a low level.

low[2] VERB (of cattle) make a deep mooing sound.

lowbrow ADJ [INFORMAL] not intellectual or cultured.

low-down [INFORMAL] ADJ dishonourable. NOUN relevant information.

lower[1] VERB let downwards; reduce the height, pitch, or degree of.

lower[2] variant of **LOUR**.

lower case NOUN letters that are not capitals.

low-key ADJ not elaborate or ostentatious; restrained.

lowlands PLURAL NOUN low-lying land.
lowland ADJ
lowlander NOUN

lowly ADJ (**lowlier**, **lowliest**) of humble rank or condition.

low-rise ADJ (of a building) having few storeys.

low season NOUN the season that is least busy in a resort, hotel, etc.

low-tech ADJ using relatively simple technology.

loyal ADJ firm in one's allegiance.
loyally ADV
loyalty NOUN

loyalist NOUN a person who is loyal, especially while others revolt.

lozenge NOUN **1** a small medicinal tablet to be dissolved in the mouth. **2** a diamond-shaped figure.

LP ABBREV long-playing (record).

LSD NOUN a powerful hallucinogenic drug.

Ltd. ABBREV Limited.

lubricant NOUN a lubricating substance.

lubricate VERB oil or grease (machinery etc.) to allow smooth movement.
lubrication NOUN

lubricious /loo-**bri**-shŭs/ ADJ **1** lewd. **2** slippery.

lucerne NOUN a clover-like fodder plant.

lucid ADJ clearly expressed; sane.
lucidity NOUN
lucidly ADV

luck NOUN good or bad fortune; chance thought of as a force bringing this.

luckless ADJ unlucky.

lucky ADJ (**luckier**, **luckiest**) having, bringing, or resulting from good luck.
luckily ADV

lucky dip NOUN a game in which people draw small prizes at random from a container; a process determined by chance.

lucrative ADJ profitable, producing much money.

lucre /**loo**-ker/ NOUN money.

Luddite NOUN a person opposing the introduction of new technology or working methods.

ludicrous ADJ ridiculous.
ludicrously ADV

lug VERB (**lugs**, **lugging**, **lugged**) drag or carry with great effort. NOUN an ear-like projection; [INFORMAL] an ear.

luge NOUN a light toboggan, ridden sitting upright.

luggage NOUN suitcases and bags holding a traveller's possessions.

lugubrious /luu-**goo**-bree-ŭs/ ADJ dismal, mournful.
lugubriously ADV

lukewarm ADJ only slightly warm; not enthusiastic.

lull VERB send to sleep; cause to feel deceptively confident; (of a storm etc.) become quiet. NOUN a period of quiet or inactivity.

lullaby NOUN (PL **lullabies**) a soothing song for sending a child to sleep.

lumbago /lum-**bay**-goh/ NOUN rheumatic pain in muscles of the lower back.

lumbar ADJ of the lower back.

lumber NOUN useless or unwanted articles, especially furniture; [US] timber sawn into planks. VERB **1** move heavily and awkwardly. **2** [INFORMAL] burden with something unwanted.

lumberjack NOUN [US] a person who cuts or transports lumber.

luminary NOUN (PL **luminaries**) **1** a natural light-giving body, especially the sun or moon. **2** an eminent person.

luminescent ADJ emitting light without heat.
luminescence NOUN

luminous ADJ emitting light, glowing in the dark.
luminosity NOUN
luminously ADV

lump NOUN a hard or compact mass; a swelling. VERB treat as alike, group together indiscriminately.

lumpectomy NOUN (PL **lumpectomies**) the surgical removal of a lump from the breast.

lumpy ADJ (**lumpier**, **lumpiest**) full of or covered in lumps.
lumpiness NOUN

lunacy NOUN (PL **lunacies**) insanity; great folly.

lunar ADJ of the moon.

lunar month NOUN the period between new moons (29½ days).

lunate ADJ crescent-shaped.

lunatic NOUN an insane person; a very foolish or reckless person.

lunch NOUN a midday meal. VERB eat lunch.

luncheon NOUN [FORMAL] lunch.

luncheon meat NOUN tinned cured meat ready for serving.

luncheon voucher NOUN a voucher given to an employee as part of their pay, exchangeable for food.

lung NOUN either of the pair of breathing-organs in the chest.

lunge NOUN **1** a sudden forward movement of the body; a thrust. **2** a long rope attached to a horse while it is being trained. VERB make a lunge forward.

lupine /loo-pIn/ ADJ like a wolf.

lupus NOUN a skin disease producing ulcers.

l

lurch VERB make an unsteady swaying movement. NOUN such a movement.
leave in the lurch leave (a person) in difficulties.

lure VERB entice. NOUN an enticement; a bait to attract wild animals.

lurid ADJ in glaring colours; vividly shocking or sensational.
luridly ADV

lurk VERB lie in ambush; (of something bad) be latent but threatening.

luscious /lu-shŭs/ ADJ delicious; voluptuously attractive.
lusciously ADV
lusciousness NOUN

lush ADJ (of grass etc.) growing thickly and strongly; very rich, luxurious.
lushly ADV
lushness NOUN

lust NOUN intense sexual desire; any intense desire. VERB feel lust.
lustful ADJ
lustfully ADV

lustre ([US] **luster**) NOUN soft brightness of a surface; brilliance, glory; a metallic glaze on pottery.
lustrous ADJ

lusty ADJ (**lustier**, **lustiest**) strong and vigorous.
lustily ADV

lute NOUN a guitar-like instrument with a rounded body.
lutenist NOUN

lutetium NOUN a metallic element.

lux NOUN a unit of illumination.

luxuriant ADJ growing profusely.
luxuriance NOUN
luxuriantly ADV

luxuriate VERB enjoy or indulge in as a luxury.

luxurious ADJ very comfortable and elegant; giving self-indulgent pleasure.
luxuriously ADV
luxuriousness NOUN

luxury NOUN (PL **luxuries**) great comfort and extravagance; something unnecessary but very pleasant.

lychee NOUN a sweet white fruit with a brown spiny skin.

lychgate NOUN a roofed gateway to a churchyard.

Lycra NOUN [TRADE MARK] an elastic fabric.

lye NOUN an alkaline solution used for cleaning.

lying present participle of LIE[1], LIE[2].

lymph /limf/ NOUN a colourless fluid containing white blood cells.
lymphatic ADJ

lymphatic system NOUN the network of vessels carrying lymph, protecting against infection.

lymphoma /lim-foh-mă/ NOUN (PL **lymphomas** or **lymphomata**) a tumour of the lymph glands.

lynch VERB (of a mob) kill (someone) for an alleged offence, without trial.

lynx NOUN (PL **lynx** or **lynxes**) a wild animal of the cat family.

lyre NOUN an ancient musical instrument with strings in a U-shaped frame.

lyric ADJ (of poetry) expressing the poet's feelings. NOUN a lyric poem; (**lyrics**) the words of a song.

lyrical ADJ resembling or using language suitable for lyric poetry; [INFORMAL] expressing oneself enthusiastically.
lyrically ADV

lyricist /li-ri-sist/ NOUN a person who writes lyrics.

Mm

M (also **m**) NOUN (PL **Ms** or **M's**) **1** the thirteenth letter of the alphabet. **2** the Roman numeral for 1,000. ABBREV **1** motorway. **2** (**m**) metre(s). **3** (**m**) miles. **4** (**m**) million(s).

MA ABBREV Master of Arts.

ma'am NOUN madam.

mac (also **mack**) NOUN [INFORMAL] a mackintosh.

macabre /mă-kah-brĕ/ ADJ disturbingly interested in or involving death and injury.

macadam NOUN layers of broken stone used in road-making.

macadamize (also **macadamise**) VERB surface with macadam.

macaroni NOUN tube-shaped pasta.

macaroon NOUN a small almond biscuit.

macaw NOUN an American parrot.

mace NOUN **1** a ceremonial staff. **2** a spice.

macerate /mas-ĕ-rayt/ VERB soften by soaking.

Mach /mahk/ (in full **Mach number**) NOUN the ratio of the speed of a moving body to the speed of sound.

machete /mă-she-ti/ NOUN a broad heavy knife.

machiavellian ADJ elaborately cunning or deceitful.

machinations PLURAL NOUN clever scheming.

machine NOUN an apparatus with several parts, using mechanical power to perform a particular task; an efficient group of powerful people. VERB produce or work on with a machine.

machine code NOUN a computer language that

controls the computer directly, interpreting instructions passing between the software and the machine.

machine gun NOUN an automatic gun firing bullets in rapid succession.

machine-readable ADJ in a form that a computer can process.

machinery NOUN **1** machines; the parts of a machine. **2** the organisation or structure of something.

machine tool NOUN a power-driven engineering machine such as a lathe.

machinist NOUN a person who works machinery.

machismo /mă-kiz-moh/ NOUN aggressive masculine pride.

macho /ma-choh/ ADJ aggressively masculine.

mack variant of **MAC**.

mackerel NOUN (PL **mackerel** or **mackerels**) an edible sea fish.

mackintosh (also **macintosh**) NOUN a raincoat.

macramé /mă-krah-mi/ NOUN the art of knotting cord in patterns.

macro NOUN [COMPUTING] a single instruction that expands automatically into a set of instructions for a particular task.

macro- COMBINING FORM large-scale; large; long.

macrobiotic ADJ of a dietary system comprising wholefoods grown in close harmony with nature.

macrocosm NOUN the universe; a large complex whole.

mad ADJ (**madder**, **maddest**) **1** not sane; extremely foolish; [INFORMAL] frantic, frenzied. **2** [INFORMAL] very enthusiastic. **3** [INFORMAL] angry.
madly ADV
madness NOUN

madam NOUN a polite form of address to a woman; [INFORMAL] a precocious girl.

Madame /mă-**dahm**/ NOUN (PL **Mesdames**) a title or form of address for a French-speaking woman, corresponding to Mrs or madam.

madcap ADJ wildly impulsive.

mad cow disease NOUN [INFORMAL] = **BSE**.

madden VERB make mad or angry.

madder NOUN a red dye.

made past and past participle of **MAKE**.

Madeira NOUN **1** a fortified wine from Madeira. **2** rich plain cake.

Mademoiselle /ma-dĕ-mwă-**zel**/ NOUN (PL **Mesdemoiselles**) a title or form of address for an unmarried French-speaking woman, corresponding to Miss or madam.

madonna NOUN a picture or statue of the Virgin Mary.

madrigal NOUN a part-song for unaccompanied voices.

maelstrom /**mayl**-strŏm/ NOUN a powerful whirlpool; a scene of confusion.

maestro /**my**-stroh/ NOUN (PL **maestri** or **maestros**) a great musical conductor or composer; a master of any art.

Mafia NOUN an organized international body of criminals, originating in Sicily; (**mafia**) a sinister secret group.

magazine 1 an illustrated periodical; a regular television or radio programme including a variety of items. **2** a chamber holding cartridges in a gun, slides in a projector, etc. **3** a store for arms or explosives.

magenta ADJ & NOUN purplish red.

maggot NOUN a larva, especially of the bluebottle.

magic NOUN the supposed art of controlling things by supernatural power; an exciting or delightful quality. ADJ using or used in magic.

like magic very effectively.

magical ADJ

magically ADV

magician NOUN a person with magical powers; a conjuror.

magisterial /maj-is-**teer**-i-ăl/ ADJ **1** authoritative; domineering. **2** of a magistrate.

magistrate NOUN an official or citizen with authority to hold preliminary hearings and judge minor cases.
magistracy NOUN

magma NOUN molten rock under the earth's crust.

magnanimous ADJ noble and generous, not petty.
magnanimity NOUN
magnanimously ADV

magnate NOUN a wealthy and influential business person.

magnesia NOUN a compound of magnesium used in medicine.

magnesium NOUN a white metallic element that burns with an intensely bright flame.

magnet NOUN **1** a piece of iron or steel that can attract iron and point north when suspended. **2** a powerful attraction.

magnetic ADJ **1** having the properties of a magnet; involving magnetism. **2** fascinating, attractive.
magnetically ADV

magnetic tape NOUN a strip of plastic coated with magnetic particles, used in recording, computers, etc.

magnetism NOUN **1** the properties and effects of magnetic substances. **2** great charm and attraction.

magnetize (also **magnetise**) VERB make magnetic.

magneto /mag-nee-toh/ NOUN (PL **magnetos**) a small electric generator using magnets.

magnificent ADJ **1** impressively beautiful, elaborate, or extravagant. **2** very good.
magnificence NOUN
magnificently ADV

magnify VERB (**magnifies, magnifying, magnified**) **1** make (an object) seem larger than it is, especially by using a lens; increase the volume or intensity of; exaggerate. **2** [ARCHAIC] praise.
magnification NOUN

magnitude NOUN largeness, size; importance.

magnolia NOUN a tree with large white or pink flowers.

magnum NOUN a wine bottle of twice the standard size.

magpie NOUN a black and white bird of the crow family.

Magyar NOUN a member of the people now predominant in Hungary; the Hungarian language.

maharaja (also **maharajah**) NOUN [HISTORICAL] an Indian prince.

maharanee (also **maharani**) NOUN a maharaja's wife or widow.

maharishi NOUN a Hindu man of great wisdom.

mahatma NOUN (in India etc.) a title of a man revered for his holiness and wisdom.

mah-jong (also **mah-jongg**) NOUN a Chinese game played with 136 or 144 pieces (tiles).

mahogany NOUN a very hard reddish-brown wood.

mahout /mă-**howt**/ NOUN an elephant-driver.

maid NOUN a female servant.

maiden NOUN [ARCHAIC] a young unmarried woman, a virgin. ADJ **1** unmarried. **2** first: *a maiden voyage.*
maidenhood NOUN
maidenly ADJ

maiden name NOUN a woman's family name before she married.

maiden over NOUN an over in cricket with no runs scored.

maidservant NOUN a female servant.

mail NOUN **1** post, letters; messages transmitted by computer from one user to another. **2** body-armour made of metal rings or chains. VERB send by post or electronic mail.

mailbox NOUN [US] a letter box.

mail order NOUN purchase of goods selected from a catalogue and ordered by post.

mailshot NOUN advertising material sent to potential

customers.

maim VERB injure so that a part of the body is useless.

main ADJ chief in size or importance. NOUN a main pipe or channel conveying water, gas, or (usually **mains**) electricity.
in the main on the whole, generally.
mainly ADV

main clause NOUN [GRAMMAR] a clause that can stand as a complete sentence.

mainframe NOUN a large computer.

mainland NOUN a country or continent without its adjacent islands.

mainline VERB [INFORMAL] take drugs intravenously.

mainmast NOUN a ship's principal mast.

mainsail NOUN the lowest sail or the sail set on the after part of the mainmast.

mainspring NOUN the chief spring of a watch or clock; the chief motivating force of a movement etc.

mainstay NOUN the cable securing a mainmast; something on which something else depends.

mainstream NOUN the dominant trend of opinion or style etc.

maintain VERB **1** cause to continue, keep in existence; keep repaired and in good condition; bear the expenses of. **2** assert.

maintenance NOUN the action of maintaining something; the provision of money for living expenses; money paid to a former spouse after a divorce.

maiolica /mI-ol-ik-ă/ (also **majolica**) NOUN white pottery decorated with metallic colours.

maisonette NOUN part of a house (usually not all on one floor) used as a separate dwelling.

maître d'hôtel NOUN (PL **maîtres d'hotel**) a hotel manager; a head waiter.

maize NOUN a tall cereal plant bearing grain on large cobs; its grain.

majestic ADJ stately and

dignified, imposing. **majestically** ADV

majesty NOUN (PL **majesties**) impressive stateliness; sovereign power; (**Majesty**) the title of a king or queen.

majolica variant of **MAIOLICA**.

major ADJ **1** important, serious. **2** greater. NOUN an army officer next below lieutenant colonel. VERB (**major in**) [US] specialize in (a subject) at college.

majorette NOUN = **DRUM MAJORETTE**.

major general NOUN an army officer next below lieutenant general.

majority NOUN (PL **majorities**) **1** the greater number of a group; the number by which votes for one party exceed those for the next. **2** the age at which someone is legally considered adult.

make VERB (**makes**, **making**, **made**) **1** form, bring into being, create; prepare, produce. **2** cause to become of a specified nature; compose, be constituents of: *they make a good couple.* **3** earn (a sum of money). **4** perform (a specified action); arrange (an agreement). **5** compel to do something. **6** consider or calculate as being a specified number, age, etc. **7** put bedding on (a bed). **8** arrive at (a place). NOUN a brand of goods. **make do** manage with something inadequate or unsatisfactory. **make for** **1** try to reach. **2** tend to result in. **make good** **1** be successful. **2** repair or pay compensation for. **make it** [INFORMAL] **1** be successful. **2** arrive in time. **make off** leave hastily. **make off with** steal. **make out** **1** decipher; interpret, understand. **2** write out (a document). **3** pretend, claim. **make over** **1** transfer ownership of. **2** remodel, transform. **make up** **1** constitute. **2** invent. **3** compensate for; complete (an amount). **4** become reconciled after a quarrel. **5** apply cosmetics to the face (of). **make up to** [INFORMAL] try to win favour with. **on the make**

[INFORMAL] trying to make profits unscrupulously. **maker** NOUN

make-believe NOUN pretence.

makeshift ADJ acting as a temporary substitute.

make-up NOUN **1** cosmetics applied to the face. **2** the composition of something; a person's character.

makeweight NOUN something added to make up for a deficiency.

mal- COMBINING FORM bad, badly; faulty.

malachite /mal-ă-kyt/ NOUN a green mineral.

maladjusted ADJ unable to adapt to a social environment.

maladminister VERB manage (business or public affairs) badly or improperly.

maladroit ADJ bungling, clumsy.

malady NOUN (PL **maladies**) an illness.

malaise NOUN a feeling of illness, discomfort, or uneasiness.

malapropism /mall-ă-prop-iz-ĕm/ NOUN a comical confusion of words.

malaria NOUN a disease causing recurring fever. **malarial** ADJ

Malay NOUN a member of a people of Malaysia and Indonesia; their language.

malcontent NOUN a dissatisfied and rebellious person.

male ADJ of the sex that can fertilize egg cells produced by a female; of or characteristic of men; (of a plant) producing pollen, not seeds; (of a machine part) for insertion into a corresponding hollow part. NOUN a male person, animal, or plant.

malediction NOUN a curse. **maledictory** ADJ

malefactor /mal-i-fak-ter/ NOUN [FORMAL] a wrongdoer.

malevolent ADJ wishing harm to others. **malevolence** NOUN **malevolently** ADV

malfeasance /mal-feez-ăns/ NOUN [FORMAL] misconduct.

malformation NOUN the state of being abnormally

shaped or formed.
malformed ADJ

malfunction NOUN faulty functioning. VERB function faultily.

malice NOUN a desire to harm others.
malicious ADJ
maliciously ADV

malign /mă-**lyn**/ ADJ harmful; showing malice. VERB say unpleasant and untrue things about.
malignity NOUN
malignly ADV

malignant ADJ **1** (of a tumour) growing harmfully and uncontrollably. **2** malevolent.
malignancy NOUN
malignantly ADV

m

malinger VERB pretend illness to avoid work.
malingerer NOUN

mall /mal, morl/ NOUN a large enclosed shopping precinct; a sheltered walk or promenade.

mallard NOUN a wild duck, the male of which has a glossy green head.

malleable ADJ able to be hammered or pressed into shape; easy to influence.
malleability NOUN

mallet NOUN a hammer, usually of wood; an instrument for striking the ball in croquet or polo.

malmsey NOUN a strong sweet wine.

malnutrition NOUN weakness resulting from lack of nutrition.

malodorous ADJ stinking.
malodour NOUN

malpractice NOUN wrongdoing; improper professional behaviour.

malt /morlt/ NOUN barley or other grain prepared for brewing or distilling; whisky made with this.

maltreat VERB treat cruelly.
maltreatment NOUN

mamba NOUN a poisonous snake.

mammal NOUN a member of the class of animals that suckle their young.
mammalian ADJ

mammary ADJ of the breasts.

mammography NOUN the use of X-rays to detect tumours in the breasts.

mammoth NOUN a large extinct elephant.
ADJ huge.

man NOUN (PL **men**) **1** an adult male person; a male servant or employee; an ordinary soldier, not an officer. **2** a human being; the human race. **3** a small figure used in a board game. VERB (**mans, manning, manned**) provide (a place etc.) with people to work in or defend it.
man to man directly, frankly.

manacle NOUN a shackle for the wrists or ankles.
manacled ADJ

manage VERB **1** be in charge of, control; supervise (staff). **2** cope successfully with a task; succeed in doing or producing; succeed in dealing with.
manageable ADJ

management NOUN the action of managing; the people who manage a business.

manager NOUN a person in charge of a business etc.
managerial ADJ

manageress NOUN a woman in charge of a business etc.

mañana /man-**yahn**-ă/ ADV at some indefinite time in the future.

manatee NOUN a large tropical aquatic mammal.

mandarin NOUN **1** a senior influential official. **2** a variety of small orange. **3** (**Mandarin**) the literary and official form of the Chinese language.

mandate NOUN an official order or permission to perform certain tasks.
VERB give a mandate to.

mandatory ADJ compulsory.

mandible NOUN a jaw or jaw-like part.

mandolin NOUN a musical instrument like a lute.

mandrake NOUN a poisonous plant with a root said to resemble the human form.

mandrel NOUN a shaft holding work in a lathe.

mane NOUN long hair on the neck of a horse or lion.

maneuver US spelling of **MANOEUVRE**.

manful ADJ brave, resolute.
manfully ADV

manganese NOUN a hard brittle grey metallic element or its black oxide.

mange NOUN a skin disease affecting hairy animals.

manger NOUN an open trough for horses or cattle to feed from.

mangetout /mornz*h*-**too**/ NOUN a variety of pea, eaten with the pod.

mangle NOUN a clothes wringer. VERB damage by cutting or crushing roughly; mutilate.

m

mango NOUN (PL **mangoes** or **mangos**) a tropical fruit.

mangrove NOUN a tropical tree growing in swamps.

mangy ADJ (**mangier**, **mangiest**) having mange; shabby.

manhandle VERB **1** move by human effort alone. **2** treat roughly.

manhole NOUN an opening through which someone can enter a drain etc. to inspect it.

manhood NOUN the state of being a man; men collectively; qualities associated with men.

man-hour NOUN one hour's work by one person.

manhunt NOUN an organized search for a person, especially a criminal.

mania NOUN violent madness; an extreme enthusiasm for something.

maniac NOUN a person behaving wildly; a fanatical enthusiast.

maniacal ADJ of or like a mania or maniac.

manic ADJ showing wild excitement; frantically busy; of or affected by mania.

manicure NOUN cosmetic care of the hands and fingernails. VERB apply such treatment to.
manicurist NOUN

manifest ADJ clear and unmistakable. VERB show clearly, give signs of. NOUN a list of cargo or passengers carried by a ship or aircraft.
manifestation NOUN

manifestly ADV

manifesto NOUN (PL **manifestos**) a public declaration of policy.

manifold ADJ [FORMAL] many and varied; having many elements. NOUN (in a machine) a pipe or chamber with several openings.

manikin NOUN **1** a very small person. **2** a jointed model of the human body.

manila NOUN brown paper used for envelopes and wrapping paper.

manipulate VERB **1** handle or control skilfully; treat (a part of the body) by moving it by hand. **2** control or influence (someone) unscrupulously.
manipulation NOUN
manipulative ADJ
manipulator NOUN

mankind NOUN human beings in general.

manly ADJ (**manlier**, **manliest**) brave, strong; considered suitable for a man.
manliness NOUN

man-made ADJ artificial, not produced or occurring naturally.

mannequin NOUN a dummy used to display clothes in a shop window; someone acting as a model.

manner NOUN **1** the way in which something is done or happens; [LITERARY] a sort or kind: *what manner of man?* **2** a person's way of behaving towards others; (**manners**) polite social behaviour.
in a manner of speaking in a sense.

mannered ADJ **1** having manners of a specified kind. **2** stilted, unnatural.

mannerism NOUN a distinctive personal habit or way of doing something.

manoeuvre /măn-oo-vĕ/ ([US] **maneuver**) NOUN **1** a skilful movement; a crafty plan. **2** (**manoeuvres**) large-scale exercises of troops etc. VERB **1** guide or manipulate. **2** perform or carry out manoeuvres.
manoeuvrability NOUN
manoeuvrable ADJ

manor NOUN a large

country house, usually with lands.
manorial ADJ

manpower NOUN the number of people available for work or service.

manqué /mahn-kay/ ADJ having failed to become something that one might have: *an artist manqué.*

manse NOUN a church minister's house, especially in Scotland.

manservant NOUN (PL **menservants**) a male servant.

mansion NOUN a large stately house.

manslaughter NOUN the act of killing a person unlawfully but not intentionally.

mantelpiece NOUN the shelf above a fireplace.

mantilla NOUN a lace veil worn over the hair and shoulders.

mantis NOUN (PL **mantis** or **mantises**) a grasshopper-like insect.

mantle NOUN a loose cloak; a covering.

mantra NOUN a phrase repeated to aid concentration during meditation; a statement or slogan frequently repeated.

manual ADJ of the hands; done or operated by the hand(s); working with one's hands. NOUN a handbook.
manually ADV

manufacture VERB make or produce (goods) on a large scale by machinery; invent (a story). NOUN the process of manufacturing.
manufacturer NOUN

manure NOUN animal dung used as fertilizer. VERB apply manure to.

manuscript NOUN a book or document written by hand or typed, not printed.

Manx ADJ relating to the Isle of Man.

many DETERMINER, PRON, & ADJ a large number of. NOUN (**the many**) the majority of people.

Maori /mow-ri/ NOUN (PL **Maori** or **Maoris**) a member of the aboriginal people of New Zealand; their language.

map NOUN a representation of the earth's surface or a part of it; a diagram showing the arrangement of something.
VERB (**maps**, **mapping**, **mapped**) make a map of.
map out plan in detail.

maple NOUN a tree with broad leaves and winged fruits.

mar VERB (**mars**, **marring**, **marred**) disfigure; spoil.

maracas PLURAL NOUN club-like gourds containing beads etc., shaken as a musical instrument.

marathon NOUN a long-distance running race; a long-lasting or gruelling task of a specified kind.

marauding ADJ going about in search of plunder.
marauder NOUN

marble NOUN **1** crystalline limestone that can be polished; a piece of sculpture made of this. **2** a small ball of glass or clay used in children's games. VERB give a veined or mottled appearance to.

March NOUN the third month.

march VERB walk in a regular rhythm or an organized column; walk purposefully; force to walk somewhere quickly; progress steadily. NOUN the act of marching; the distance covered by marching; a piece of music suitable for marching to; progress.
marcher NOUN

marches PLURAL NOUN border regions.

marchioness /mah-shĕn-ess/ NOUN the wife or widow of a marquess; a woman with the rank of marquess.

mare NOUN the female of the horse or a related animal.

margarine NOUN a substance made from animal or vegetable fat and used like butter.

marge NOUN [INFORMAL] margarine.

margin NOUN **1** an edge or border; a blank space around the edges of a page. **2** an amount by which something is won or falls short.

marginal ADJ **1** of or in a margin. **2** slight, unimportant.

marginalize (also **marginalise**) VERB make or treat as insignificant.

marginally ADV very slightly.

marguerite NOUN a large daisy.

marigold NOUN a plant with golden daisy-like flowers.

marijuana /ma-ri-**wah**-nă/ (also **marihuana**) NOUN dried hemp, smoked as a hallucinogenic drug.

marina NOUN a harbour for yachts and pleasure boats.

marinade NOUN a flavoured liquid in which savoury food is soaked before cooking. VERB soak in a marinade.

marinate VERB marinade.

marine ADJ of the sea; of shipping. NOUN a soldier trained to serve on land or sea.

mariner NOUN [FORMAL] a sailor, a seaman.

marionette NOUN a puppet worked by strings.

marital ADJ of marriage.

maritime ADJ living or found near the sea; of seafaring.

marjoram NOUN a fragrant herb.

mark NOUN **1** a small area on a surface different in colour from the rest; a distinguishing feature. **2** a symbol; an indication of something's presence. **3** a point awarded for a correct answer; the total of such points achieved by someone in a test etc. **4** a target. **5** a particular model of a vehicle or other product: *a Mark 10 Jaguar*. **6** a Deutschmark. VERB **1** make a mark on; stain or be stained. **2** write a word or symbol on (something) to indicate ownership, destination, etc.; show the position of; identify, indicate as being of a particular nature. **3** assess the merit of (school or college work). **4** notice, pay attention to. **5** (in football etc.) keep close to (an opponent) to prevent them from gaining the ball.

mark time move the feet as though marching but without advancing.
quick off the mark reacting quickly.

marked ADJ clearly noticeable.
markedly ADV

marker NOUN a person or object that marks something; a broad felt-tipped pen.

market NOUN **1** a place or gathering for the sale of provisions, livestock, etc. **2** demand for a commodity. VERB (**markets**, **marketing**, **marketed**) advertise; offer for sale.
on the market offered for sale.
marketable ADJ

marketeer NOUN a specialist in promoting and advertising products.

market garden NOUN a small farm producing vegetables.

marking NOUN the colouring of an animal's skin, feathers, or fur; identifying marks.

marksman NOUN a person who is a skilled shot.
marksmanship NOUN

marl NOUN soil composed of clay and lime, used as a fertilizer.

marmalade NOUN a jam made from citrus fruit, especially oranges.

marmoset NOUN a small bushy-tailed monkey.

maroon NOUN **1** a brownish-red colour. **2** an explosive device used as a warning signal. ADJ brownish red. VERB put and leave (a person) ashore in a desolate place; leave stranded.

marquee /mah-**kee**/ NOUN a large tent used for a party or exhibition etc.

marquess NOUN a nobleman ranking between duke and earl.

marquetry /**mah**-kit-ri/ NOUN inlaid work in wood, ivory, etc.

marquis NOUN a rank in some European nobilities; a marquess.

marram NOUN a type of grass growing in sand.

marriage NOUN the legal union of a man and woman; the act or ceremony of marrying; a combination or blend.

marriageable ADJ suitable or old enough for marriage.

marrow NOUN **1** a soft fatty substance in the cavities of bones. **2** a gourd used as a vegetable.

marry VERB (**marries**, **marrying**, **married**) join in marriage; take as one's spouse; enter into marriage; combine (different things or qualities).

marsh NOUN low-lying watery ground.
marshy ADJ

marshal NOUN a high-ranking officer; an official controlling an event or ceremony. VERB (**marshals**, **marshalling**, **marshalled**; [US] **marshaling**, **marshaled**) arrange in proper order; assemble; guide, lead.

marshmallow NOUN a soft sweet made from sugar, egg white, and gelatin.

marsupial NOUN a mammal that carries its young in a pouch.

mart NOUN a market.

martial ADJ of war, warlike.

martial law NOUN military government suspending ordinary law.

martinet NOUN a person who exerts strict discipline.

martyr NOUN a person who undergoes death or suffering for his or her beliefs; someone who ostentatiously displays their distress to gain sympathy. VERB kill or torment as a martyr.
martyrdom NOUN

marvel NOUN a wonderful thing. VERB (**marvels**, **marvelling**, **marvelled**; [US] **marveling**, **marveled**) feel wonder.

marvellous ([US] **marvelous**) ADJ amazing, extraordinary; very good or pleasing.
marvellously ADV

Marxism NOUN the socialist theories of Karl Marx.
Marxist ADJ & NOUN

marzipan NOUN an edible paste made from ground almonds.

mascara NOUN a cosmetic for darkening the eyelashes.

mascot NOUN an object believed to bring good luck to its owner.

masculine ADJ **1** of, like, or traditionally considered suitable for men. **2** [GRAMMAR] of the gender of nouns and adjectives conventionally regarded as male.
masculinity NOUN

mash NOUN a soft pulp of crushed matter; mashed potatoes. VERB beat into a soft mass.

mask NOUN a covering worn over the face as a disguise or protection. VERB cover with a mask; disguise, screen, conceal.

masochism NOUN pleasure in suffering pain.
masochist NOUN
masochistic ADJ

mason NOUN a person who builds or works with stone.

masonry NOUN stonework.

masque /mahsk/ NOUN a musical drama with mime.

masquerade NOUN a false show or pretence. VERB pretend to be what one is not.

mass NOUN **1** a coherent body of matter with no definite shape; the quantity of matter a body contains. **2** a large group of people or things; (**masses**) [INFORMAL] a large amount. **3** (**the masses**) ordinary people. **4** (usually **Mass**) a celebration of the Eucharist, especially in the RC Church; a form of liturgy used in this. VERB gather or assemble into a mass.

massacre NOUN a great slaughter. VERB slaughter in large numbers.

massage NOUN the rubbing and kneading of parts of the body to reduce pain or stiffness. VERB **1** treat (the body) in this way. **2** manipulate (figures) to give a more acceptable result.

masseur NOUN a man who practises massage professionally.

masseuse NOUN a woman who practises massage professionally.

massif NOUN a compact group of mountain

heights.

massive ADJ large and heavy or solid; huge. **massively** ADV

mass-produce VERB manufacture in large quantities by a standardized process.

mast NOUN **1** a tall pole, especially supporting a ship's sails. **2** the fruit of the beech, oak, chestnut, etc., used as food for pigs.

mastectomy NOUN (PL **mastectomies**) surgical removal of a breast.

m

master NOUN **1** a man who has control of people or things; a male teacher. **2** a person with great skill, a great artist. **3** a recording etc. from which a series of copies is made. **4** (**Master**) the title of a boy not old enough to be called *Mr.* ADJ **1** highly skilled. **2** main, principal. VERB **1** acquire complete knowledge of or expertise in. **2** gain control of; overcome.

masterclass NOUN a class given by a famous musician, artist, etc.

masterful ADJ **1** powerful, commanding. **2** very skilful. **masterfully** ADV

master key NOUN a key that opens several different locks.

masterly ADJ very skilful.

mastermind NOUN a person of outstanding mental ability; the person planning and directing an enterprise. VERB plan and direct.

Master of Arts, **Master of Science** NOUN a university degree, above a first degree but below a PhD.

masterpiece NOUN an outstanding piece of work.

master stroke NOUN a very skilful act of policy.

mastery NOUN **1** thorough knowledge, great skill. **2** control, supremacy.

mastic NOUN **1** gum or resin from certain trees. **2** a type of cement.

masticate VERB chew.

mastitis NOUN inflammation of the breast or udder.

mastoid NOUN a projecting

piece of a bone behind the ear.

masturbate VERB stimulate the genitals with the hand.
masturbation NOUN

mat NOUN a piece of material placed on a floor or other surface as an ornament or to protect it. ADJ variant of **MATT**. VERB (**mats**, **matting**, **matted**) make or become tangled into a thick mass.
matted ADJ

matador NOUN a bullfighter.

match NOUN **1** a short stick tipped with material that catches fire when rubbed on a rough surface. **2** a contest in a game or sport. **3** a person or thing exactly like or corresponding or equal to another. **4** a marriage; a potential marriage partner. VERB **1** correspond, be alike; find something or someone corresponding to. **2** equal in ability, extent, etc. **3** set against each other in a contest.

matchmaking NOUN the attempt to arrange relationships or marriages between other people.
matchmaker NOUN

matchstick NOUN the stick of a match.

matchwood NOUN wood broken into splinters.

mate NOUN **1** a companion or fellow worker; each of a pair of mated animals. **2** a merchant ship's officer. **3** checkmate. VERB (of animals) come together for breeding, copulate; bring (animals) together for breeding.

material NOUN **1** a substance from which something can be made. **2** facts to be used in a book etc.; cloth, fabric. ADJ **1** of matter; of the physical (not spiritual) world. **2** significant, important.
materially ADV

materialism NOUN **1** concentration on material possessions rather than spiritual values. **2** the belief that only the material world exists.
materialist NOUN
materialistic ADJ

materialize (also **materialise**) VERB appear, become visible; become a fact, happen.
materialization NOUN

maternal ADJ of a mother; motherly; related through one's mother.
maternally ADV

maternity NOUN motherhood. ADJ of or for women in pregnancy and childbirth.

math NOUN [US] [INFORMAL] mathematics.

m

mathematician NOUN a person skilled in mathematics.

mathematics NOUN (as SINGULAR) the science of numbers, quantities, and measurements; (as PL) the mathematical aspect of a subject or phenomenon.
mathematical ADJ
mathematically ADV

maths NOUN [INFORMAL] mathematics.

matinee NOUN an afternoon performance in a theatre or cinema.

matinee coat NOUN a baby's jacket.

matins (also **mattins**) NOUN morning prayer.

matriarch /may-tree-ahk/ NOUN the female head of a family or tribe.
matriarchal ADJ

matriarchy NOUN (PL **matriarchies**) a social organization in which a female is head of the family.

matrices pl. of **MATRIX**.

matricide NOUN the killing of one's mother; someone guilty of this.
matricidal ADJ

matriculate VERB enrol at a college or university.
matriculation NOUN

matrimony NOUN marriage.
matrimonial ADJ

matrix /may-triks/ NOUN (PL **matrices** or **matrixes**) **1** an environment in which something develops; a mould in which something is shaped. **2** [MATHEMATICS] a rectangular array of quantities treated as a unit.

matron NOUN **1** a woman in charge of domestic and medical arrangements at a school etc.; [DATED] the woman in charge of nursing in a hospital. **2** a married woman.

matronly ADJ like or characteristic of a staid or dignified married woman.

matt (also **mat**) ADJ dull, not shiny.

matter NOUN **1** physical substance occupying space; a specified type of substance. **2** a situation or affair; a problem, something causing distress. **3** printed material. VERB be important; be of concern to someone.
matter-of-fact practical, unemotional.

mattins variant of **MATINS**.

mattress NOUN a fabric case filled with padding or springy material, used on or as a bed.

maturation NOUN the process of maturing.

mature ADJ fully grown or developed; mentally and emotionally developed, not childish; (of a life assurance policy etc.) due for payment. VERB make or become mature.
maturely ADV
maturity NOUN

matzo NOUN (PL **matzos**) a wafer of unleavened bread.

maudlin /**mord**-lin/ ADJ sentimental in a silly or tearful way.

maul VERB treat roughly, injure by rough handling.

maunder VERB talk in a rambling way.

mausoleum /mor-so-lee-ŭm/ NOUN a magnificent tomb.

mauve /mohv/ ADJ & NOUN pale purple.

maverick NOUN an unorthodox or independent-minded person.

mawkish ADJ sentimental in a sickly way.
mawkishly ADV
mawkishness NOUN

maxim NOUN a sentence giving a general truth or rule of conduct.

maximize (also **maximise**) VERB make as great as possible.
maximization NOUN

maximum NOUN (PL **maxima** or **maximums**)

the greatest amount, extent, or strength possible or recorded. ADJ greatest in amount, extent, or strength.
maximal ADJ

May NOUN the fifth month.

may[1] AUXILIARY VERB used to express a wish, possibility, or permission: *it may be true; may I come in?*

may[2] NOUN hawthorn blossom.

maya NOUN (in Hinduism) illusion, magic.

m **maybe** ADV perhaps.

May Day NOUN 1 May, especially as a festival.

mayday NOUN an international radio distress signal used by ships and aircraft.

mayhem NOUN violent confusion and disorder.

mayonnaise NOUN a cold creamy sauce made with eggs and oil.

mayor NOUN the head of the municipal corporation of a city or borough.
mayoral ADJ
mayoralty NOUN

mayoress NOUN a female mayor; a mayor's wife.

maypole NOUN a tall pole for dancing round on May Day.

maze NOUN a network of paths etc. through which it is hard to find one's way.

Mb ABBREV [COMPUTING] megabyte(s).

MBA ABBREV Master of Business Administration.

MBE ABBREV Member of the Order of the British Empire.

MC ABBREV **1** Master of Ceremonies. **2** Member of Congress.

MD ABBREV **1** Doctor of Medicine (Latin *Medicinae Doctor*). **2** Managing Director.

MDF ABBREV medium density fibreboard.

ME ABBREV myalgic encephalomyelitis, a condition characterized by prolonged fatigue.

me[1] PRON the objective case of *I*.

me[2] NOUN [MUSIC] the third note of a major scale, or the note E.

mea culpa EXCLAMATION an acknowledgement of

error or guilt.

mead NOUN an alcoholic drink made from honey and water.

meadow NOUN a field of grass.

meagre ([US] **meager**) ADJ scanty in amount.

meal NOUN **1** an occasion when food is eaten; the food itself. **2** coarsely ground grain.

mealy ADJ of or like meal.

mealy-mouthed ADJ afraid to speak frankly or straightforwardly.

mean¹ ADJ **1** ungenerous, miserly; unkind; vicious. **2** of poor quality; [DATED] of low rank.
meanly ADV
meanness NOUN

mean² NOUN something midway between two extremes; an average. ADJ calculated as a mean; midway between two extremes.

mean³ VERB (**means**, **meaning**, **meant**) **1** convey, express; signify. **2** intend. **3** result in.
mean much to be considered important by.
mean well have good or kind intentions.

meander /mee-**an**-de/ VERB follow a winding course; wander in a leisurely way. NOUN a winding course; a wide bend in a river.

meaning NOUN what is meant. ADJ expressive.
meaningful ADJ
meaningless ADJ

means NOUN (as SINGULAR or PL) that by which a result is brought about; (as PL) financial resources.
by all means certainly.
by no means certainly not.

means test NOUN an official investigation to establish need before giving financial help from public funds.

meant past and past participle of **MEAN³**.

meantime ADV meanwhile.

meanwhile ADV in the intervening period; at the same time.

measles NOUN an infectious disease producing red spots on the body.

measly ADJ (**measlier**, **measliest**) [INFORMAL]

meagre.

measure VERB find the size, amount, etc. of (something) by comparison with a known standard; be of a specified size; take or give (a measured amount); assess. NOUN **1** a course of action to achieve a purpose; a law. **2** a standard unit used in measuring; a size or quantity found by measuring; a certain quantity or degree: *a measure of freedom.*

m

measure up to reach (a standard).
measurable ADJ
measurably ADV

measured ADJ **1** with a slow steady rhythm. **2** carefully considered.

measurement NOUN the action of measuring; an amount, size, or extent found by measuring.

meat NOUN animal flesh as food.

meaty ADJ (**meatier**, **meatiest**) **1** like meat; full of meat. **2** [INFORMAL] full of interesting subject matter.
meatiness NOUN

mechanic NOUN a skilled workman who uses or repairs machines.

mechanical ADJ of or worked by machinery; done or acting without conscious thought.
mechanically ADV

mechanics NOUN the study of motion and force; the science of machinery; (as PL) the way a thing works.

mechanism NOUN a system of parts in a machine; the way something works or happens.

mechanize (also **mechanise**) VERB equip with machinery; use machines for.
mechanization NOUN

medal NOUN a coin-like piece of metal commemorating an event or awarded for an achievement.

medallion NOUN a pendant shaped like a medal; a circular ornamental design.

medallist ([US] **medalist**) NOUN the winner of a medal.

meddle VERB interfere in people's affairs.
meddler NOUN
meddlesome ADJ

media PLURAL NOUN
1 television, radio, and newspapers as the means of mass communication.
2 plural of **MEDIUM**.

mediaeval variant of **MEDIEVAL**.

medial ADJ situated in the middle.
medially ADV

median ADJ in or passing through the middle.
NOUN a median point in a range of values; a median point or line.

mediate VERB act as peacemaker between opposing sides; bring about (a settlement) in this way.
mediation NOUN
mediator NOUN

medic NOUN [INFORMAL] a doctor.

medical ADJ of the science of medicine. NOUN an examination to assess someone's health or fitness.
medically ADV

medicament NOUN any medicine, ointment, etc.

medicate VERB treat with or add a medicinal substance.

medication NOUN drugs etc. for medical treatment; treatment with these.

medicinal ADJ having healing properties.
medicinally ADV

medicine NOUN the science of the prevention and cure of disease; a substance used to treat disease.

medicine man NOUN a witch doctor.

medieval (also **mediaeval**) ADJ of the Middle Ages.

mediocre ADJ second-rate.
mediocrity NOUN

meditate VERB think deeply; focus one's mind in silence for relaxation or religious purposes.
meditation NOUN
meditative ADJ
meditatively ADV

medium NOUN (PL **media**)
1 a means of doing something; a substance through which

m

something acts or is conveyed; a means of communication; (PL **mediums**) a person claiming to be in contact with the spirits of the dead. **2** a middle quality, state, or size. ADJ roughly halfway between extremes; average.

medium wave NOUN a radio wave between 300 kHz and 3 MHz.

medlar NOUN a fruit like a small brown apple.

medley NOUN (PL **medleys**) an assortment; excerpts of music from various sources.

m

medulla NOUN the inner part of an organ or tissue.
medullary ADJ

meek ADJ quiet and obedient, not protesting.
meekly ADV
meekness NOUN

meerschaum /meer-shăm/ NOUN a tobacco pipe with a white clay bowl.

meet VERB (**meets**, **meeting**, **met**) **1** come into contact (with); make the acquaintance of; assemble, gather; wait for and greet on arrival. **2** satisfy (a requirement etc.). **3** experience. NOUN an assembly for a hunt. ADJ [ARCHAIC] suitable, proper.
meet with receive (a particular response or reaction).

meeting NOUN an instance of two or more people coming together; an assembly for discussion; a sporting event.

mega [INFORMAL] ADJ **1** huge. **2** excellent. ADV extremely.

mega- COMBINING FORM **1** large. **2** one million (as in *megavolts*, *megawatts*). **3** [INFORMAL] extremely; very big.

megabyte NOUN [COMPUTING] 1,048,576 (i.e. 2^{20}) bytes.

megahertz NOUN one million cycles per second, as a unit of frequency of electromagnetic waves.

megalith NOUN a large stone, especially as a prehistoric monument.
megalithic ADJ

megalomania NOUN obsession with power; delusion about one's own power.

megalomaniac ADJ & NOUN

megaphone NOUN a funnel-shaped device for amplifying the voice.

megaton NOUN a unit of explosive power equal to one million tons of TNT.

melamine /mel-ă-meen/ NOUN a resilient plastic, used especially for laminated coatings.

melancholy NOUN mental depression, sadness; gloom. ADJ sad, gloomy; depressing.

melanin NOUN a dark pigment in the skin, hair, etc.

melanoma NOUN a malignant skin tumour.

meld VERB merge, blend.

melee /mel-ay/ NOUN a confused fight; a confused mass or crowd.

mellifluous ADJ sweet-sounding.

mellow ADJ **1** (of fruit) ripe and sweet; (of sound or colour) soft and rich. **2** (of people) having become gentle with age. **3** relaxed, cheerful. VERB make or become mellow.

melodeon (also **melodion**) NOUN a small organ or harmonium.

melodious ADJ tuneful.
melodiously ADV

melodrama NOUN a sensational drama.
melodramatic ADJ
melodramatically ADV

melody NOUN (PL **melodies**) sweet music; the main part in a piece of harmonized music.
melodic ADJ
melodically ADV

melon NOUN a large sweet fruit.

melt VERB **1** make (something solid) liquid, especially by heat; become liquid. **2** make or become less stern; leave unobtrusively, vanish.

meltdown NOUN the melting of an overheated reactor core.

member NOUN a person belonging to a particular group or society; part of a structure; [ARCHAIC] a limb.

membership NOUN the state of being a member; the members of a group; their number.

membrane NOUN a thin flexible skin-like tissue.

membranous ADJ

memento NOUN (PL **mementoes** or **mementos**) a souvenir.

memo NOUN (PL **memos**) [INFORMAL] a memorandum.

memoir /mem-wah/ NOUN a written account of events etc. that one remembers.

memorable ADJ worth remembering, easy to remember.
memorability NOUN
memorably ADV

m

memorandum NOUN (PL **memoranda** or **memorandums**) a note written as a reminder; a written message from one colleague to another.

memorial NOUN an object or custom etc. established to commemorate an event or person(s). ADJ serving as a memorial.

memorize (also **memorise**) VERB learn (a thing) so as to know it from memory.

memory NOUN (PL **memories**) the ability to remember things; a thing remembered; the storage capacity of a computer, RAM.
in memory of as a reminder of or memorial to.

men pl. of **MAN**.

menace NOUN something dangerous; a threatening quality; [INFORMAL] an annoying person. VERB threaten.
menacingly ADV

ménage /may-nahzh/ NOUN a household.

menagerie /men-aj-ĕ-ree/ NOUN a collection of wild animals for exhibition.

mend VERB repair; heal; set right (a dispute etc.) NOUN a repaired place.
on the mend getting better.

mendacious ADJ untruthful.
mendaciously ADV
mendacity NOUN

mendelevium NOUN a radioactive metallic element.

mendicant ADJ depending on charitable donations; engaged in begging. NOUN a member of a mendicant religious order; a beggar.

menfolk NOUN the men of a community or family.

menhir /**men**-heer/ NOUN a tall upright stone set up in prehistoric times.

menial ADJ lowly, degrading. NOUN a person who does menial tasks.
menially ADV

meningitis NOUN inflammation of the membranes covering the brain and spinal cord.

meniscus NOUN the curved surface of a liquid in a tube; a lens convex on one side and concave on the other.

menopause NOUN the time of life when a woman finally ceases to menstruate.
menopausal ADJ

menorah /mi-**nor**-ă/ NOUN a seven-armed candelabrum used in Jewish worship.

menstrual ADJ of menstruation.

menstruate VERB experience a monthly discharge of blood from the womb.
menstruation NOUN

mensuration NOUN measurement; mathematical rules for this.

mental ADJ **1** of, in, or performed by the mind. **2** [INFORMAL] mad.
mental age a person's mental ability expressed as the age at which an average person reaches that ability.
mentally ADV

mentality NOUN (PL **mentalities**) a characteristic attitude of mind.

menthol NOUN a peppermint-flavoured substance, used medicinally.

mentholated ADJ impregnated with menthol.

mention VERB speak or write about briefly; refer to by name. NOUN a reference to someone or something.

mentor NOUN a trusted adviser.

menu NOUN (PL **menus**) a list of dishes to be served; a list of options displayed on a computer screen.

meow (also **miaow**) = **MEW**.

MEP ABBREV Member of the European Parliament.

mercantile /mer-kăn-tIl/ ADJ trading; of trade or merchants.

mercenary ADJ working merely for money or reward; grasping. NOUN (PL **mercenaries**) a professional soldier hired by a foreign country.

mercerized (also **mercerised**) ADJ (of cotton) treated with a slightly glossy substance that adds strength.

m

merchandise NOUN goods bought and sold or for sale. VERB promote sales of (goods).

merchant NOUN a wholesale trader; [US] & [SCOTTISH] a retail trader.

merchantable ADJ saleable.

merchant bank NOUN a bank dealing in commercial loans and the financing of businesses.

merchantman NOUN a merchant ship.

merchant navy NOUN shipping employed in commerce.

merchant ship NOUN a ship carrying merchandise.

merciful ADJ showing mercy; giving relief from pain and suffering.

mercifully ADV in a merciful way; [INFORMAL] to one's great relief, thank goodness.

mercurial ADJ **1** liable to sudden changes of mood. **2** of the element mercury.

mercury NOUN a heavy silvery usually liquid metallic element.
mercuric ADJ

mercy NOUN (PL **mercies**) kindness shown to someone in one's power; something to be grateful for; a fortunate event or circumstance.
at the mercy of wholly in the power of or subject to.
merciless ADJ
mercilessly ADV

mere¹ ADJ no more or no better than what is specified.
merely ADV

mere² NOUN [LITERARY] a

lake.

merest ADJ very small or insignificant.

meretricious /me-rĕ-**trish**-ŭs/ ADJ showily attractive but cheap or insincere.

merge VERB combine into a whole; blend gradually.

merger NOUN the combining of commercial companies etc. into one.

meridian NOUN any of the great semicircles on the globe, passing through the North and South Poles.

meringue /mĕ-**rang**/ NOUN a small cake made from a mixture of sugar and egg white.

merino /mĕ-**ree**-noh/ NOUN (PL **merinos**) a breed of sheep with fine soft wool.

merit NOUN a feature or quality that deserves praise; worthiness.
VERB (**merits, meriting, merited**) deserve.

meritocracy NOUN (PL **meritocracies**) government or control by people selected for ability.

meritorious ADJ deserving praise.

merlin NOUN a small falcon.

mermaid NOUN an imaginary sea creature, a woman with a fish's tail instead of legs.

merry ADJ (**merrier, merriest**) **1** cheerful and lively. **2** [INFORMAL] slightly drunk.
merrily ADV
merriment NOUN

merry-go-round NOUN a roundabout at a funfair; a cycle of activities.

merrymaking NOUN happy celebrations.

mescaline (also **mescalin**) NOUN a hallucinogenic drug.

Mesdames pl. of **MADAME**.

Mesdemoiselles pl. of **MADEMOISELLE**.

mesh NOUN material made of a network of wire or thread; the spacing of the strands in this: *wide mesh*. VERB (of a toothed gearwheel) engage with another; make or become entangled; be in harmony.

mesmerize (also **mesmerise**) VERB dominate the attention or will of.
mesmerizing ADJ

mesolithic ADJ of the period between palaeolithic and neolithic.

meson NOUN an unstable elementary particle.

mess NOUN **1** a dirty or untidy condition; an untidy collection of things; a portion of pulpy food; a difficult or confused situation, trouble. **2** a room where members of the armed forces have meals. VERB (usually **mess up**) make untidy or dirty; muddle, bungle.
mess about behave irresponsibly; potter.
mess someone about cause someone inconvenience.

message NOUN a spoken or written communication; moral or social teaching.

messenger NOUN the bearer of a message.

Messiah NOUN the deliverer expected by Jews; Christ as this.
Messianic ADJ

Messrs pl. of **MR**.

messy ADJ (**messier**, **messiest**) **1** untidy or dirty, slovenly. **2** complicated and difficult.
messily ADV
messiness NOUN

met past and past participle of **MEET**.

metabolism NOUN the process by which food is digested and energy supplied.
metabolic ADJ

metabolize (also **metabolise**) VERB process (food) by metabolism.

metacarpus NOUN (PL **metacarpi**) the set of bones between the wrist and fingers.

metal NOUN **1** any of a class of mineral substances such as gold, silver, iron, etc., or an alloy of these. **2** road metal. VERB (**metals**, **metalling**, **metalled**; [US] **metaling**, **metaled**) make or mend (a road) with road metal.

metallic ADJ of or like metal.

metallically ADV

metallography NOUN the study of the internal structure of metals.

metallurgy NOUN the study of the properties of metals; the science of extracting and working metals.

metamorphic ADJ (of rock) changed in form or structure by heat, pressure, etc; of metamorphosis.

metamorphosis NOUN (PL **metamorphoses**) a change of form or character.
metamorphose VERB

metaphor NOUN the application of a word or phrase to something that it does not apply to literally (e.g. the *evening* of one's life, *food* for thought).
metaphorical ADJ
metaphorically ADV

metaphysics NOUN the branch of philosophy dealing with the nature of existence and knowledge.
metaphysical ADJ

metatarsus NOUN (PL **metatarsi**) the set of bones between the ankle and the toes.

mete VERB (**mete out**) deal out (justice, punishment, etc.).

meteor NOUN a small body of matter entering the earth's atmosphere from outer space and appearing as a streak of light.

meteoric ADJ of meteors; swift and brilliant.
meteorically ADV

meteorite NOUN a meteor fallen to earth.

meteorology NOUN the study of atmospheric conditions in order to forecast weather.
meteorological ADJ
meteorologist NOUN

meter NOUN **1** a device measuring and indicating the quantity supplied, distance travelled, time elapsed, etc. **2** US spelling of **METRE**. VERB measure by a meter.

methadone NOUN a narcotic painkilling drug.

methanal NOUN = **FORMALDEHYDE**.

methane NOUN a colourless inflammable

gas.

methanol NOUN a colourless inflammable liquid hydrocarbon, used as a solvent.

method NOUN a procedure or way of doing something; orderliness.

methodical ADJ orderly, systematic.
methodically ADV

Methodist NOUN a member of a Christian Protestant group originally founded by John and Charles Wesley. ADJ relating to Methodists or their beliefs.
Methodism NOUN

methodology NOUN (PL **methodologies**) a system of methods used in an activity or study.

meths NOUN [INFORMAL] methylated spirit.

methyl NOUN a chemical unit present in methane and many organic compounds.

methylated spirit NOUN a form of alcohol used as a solvent and for heating.

meticulous ADJ careful and precise in attention to details.
meticulously ADV
meticulousness NOUN

métier /met-ee-ay/ NOUN one's profession; what one does best.

metre ([US] **meter**) NOUN **1** a metric unit of length (about 39.4 inches). **2** rhythm in poetry.

metric ADJ of or using the metric system.

metrical ADJ **1** of or composed in rhythmic metre, not prose. **2** of or involving measurement.

metricate VERB convert to a metric system.
metrication NOUN

metric system NOUN a decimal system of weights and measures, using the metre, litre, and gram as units.

metric ton *see* **TON**.

metro NOUN (PL **metros**) an underground railway.

metronome NOUN a device used to indicate tempo while practising music.

metropolis /mĕ-tro-pŏ-lis/ NOUN the chief city of country or region.
metropolitan ADJ

mettle NOUN courage,

strength of character.

mettlesome ADJ spirited, brave.

mew NOUN a cat's characteristic cry. VERB make this sound.

mews NOUN a set of stables converted into houses.

mezzanine NOUN an extra storey set between two others.

mezzo /mets-oh/ ADV (in music) half; moderately: *mezzo forte*. NOUN a mezzo-soprano, a voice between soprano and contralto.

mezzotint /mets-oh-tint/ NOUN a method of engraving.

mg ABBREV milligram(s).

MHz ABBREV megahertz.

miaow (also **meow**) = **MEW**.

miasma /mee-az-mă/ NOUN [LITERARY] an oppressive atmosphere; unwholesome air.

mica /my-kă/ NOUN a mineral substance used as an electrical insulator.

mice pl. of **MOUSE**.

micro- COMBINING FORM extremely small; one-millionth part of (as in *microgram*).

microbe NOUN a micro-organism, especially a bacterium.
microbial ADJ

microbiology NOUN the study of micro-organisms.
microbiologist NOUN

microchip NOUN a small piece of a semiconductor holding a complex electronic circuit.

microclimate NOUN the climatic conditions of a small area, e.g. of part of a garden.

microcomputer NOUN a computer in which the central processor is contained on microchips.

microcosm NOUN something regarded as resembling something else but on a very small scale.

microfiche /my-kroh-feesh/ NOUN (PL **microfiche** or **microfiches**) a small sheet of microfilm.

microfilm NOUN a length of film bearing miniature photographs of documents. VERB make a microfilm of.

microlight NOUN a very

small, light one- or two-seater aircraft.

micromesh NOUN fine-meshed material, especially nylon.

micrometer NOUN an instrument measuring small lengths or angles.

micron NOUN one-millionth of a metre.

micro-organism NOUN an organism invisible to the naked eye.

microphone NOUN an instrument for picking up sound waves for transmitting or amplifying.

microprocessor NOUN an integrated circuit containing the functions of a computer's central processing unit.

microscope NOUN an instrument with lenses that magnify very small things, making them visible.

microscopic ADJ **1** tiny; too small to be seen without a microscope. **2** of or using a microscope.
microscopically ADV

microsurgery NOUN intricate surgery using miniature instruments and a microscope.

microwave NOUN an electromagnetic wave of length between about 50 cm and 1 mm; an oven using such waves to heat food quickly.

mid ADJ in the middle.

midday NOUN noon.

midden NOUN a heap of dung or rubbish.

middle ADJ occurring at an equal distance from extremes or outer limits; intermediate in rank, quality, etc. NOUN the middle point, position, area, etc.; [INFORMAL] the waist and belly.

middle age NOUN the part of life between youth and old age.
middle-aged ADJ

Middle Ages PLURAL NOUN the period of European history from about 1000 to 1453.

middle class NOUN the class of society between upper and working classes.
middle-class ADJ

Middle East NOUN an area

of SW Asia and northern Africa, extending from the Mediterranean to Pakistan.

middleman NOUN a trader buying goods from producers and selling them to consumers.

middleweight NOUN a weight above welterweight, in amateur boxing between 71 and 75 kg.

middling ADJ average in size, amount, rank, or quality.

midfield NOUN the part of a football pitch away from the goals.

midge NOUN a small biting insect.

midget NOUN a very small person or thing.

Midlands PLURAL NOUN the inland counties of central England.
midland ADJ

midnight NOUN 12 o'clock at night.

midriff NOUN the front part of the body just above the waist.

midshipman NOUN a naval rank just below sub-lieutenant.

midst NOUN [LITERARY] the middle.

midway ADV halfway.

midwife NOUN (PL **midwives**) a person trained to assist at childbirth.

mien /meen/ NOUN a person's manner or bearing.

might[1] NOUN great strength or power.

might[2] AUXILIARY VERB **1** used to express possibility, especially what would have been possible under different circumstances: *we might have gone out if it hadn't rained.* **2** used to request permission.

mighty ADJ (**mightier**, **mightiest**) very strong or powerful; [INFORMAL] very great. ADV [INFORMAL] very, extremely.
mightily ADV

migraine NOUN a severe form of headache.

migrant ADJ migrating. NOUN a migrant animal; a person travelling in search of work.

migrate VERB (of animals) regularly move from one area to another each

season; move from one area and settle in another.
migration NOUN
migratory ADJ

mike NOUN [INFORMAL] a microphone.

mil NOUN one-thousandth of an inch.

milage variant of **MILEAGE**.

milch ADJ (of a cow) giving milk.

mild ADJ gentle, not severe; not intense; (of an illness) not serious; (of weather) moderately warm; not strongly flavoured.
mildly ADV
mildness NOUN

mildew NOUN tiny fungi forming a coating on things exposed to damp.
mildewed ADJ

mile NOUN a measure of length, 1760 yds (about 1.609 km).

mileage (also **milage**) NOUN a distance in miles.

milestone NOUN a stone showing the distance to a certain place; a significant event or stage reached.

milieu /meel-yer, meel-yer/ NOUN (PL **milieus** or **milieux**) environment, surroundings.

militant ADJ prepared to take aggressive action in support of a cause. NOUN a militant person.
militancy NOUN

militarism NOUN support for maintaining and using a military force.
militaristic ADJ

military ADJ of soldiers or the army or all armed forces. NOUN (**the military**) the armed forces.

militate VERB be a factor preventing (something).

militia /mil-ish-ă/ NOUN a military force, especially of trained civilians available in an emergency.

milk NOUN a white fluid secreted by female mammals as food for their young; cow's milk; a milk-like liquid. VERB draw milk from; gain all possible advantage from; exploit unfairly.

milkman NOUN a person who delivers milk to

customers.

milksop NOUN a weak or timid man.

milk teeth PLURAL NOUN the first (temporary) teeth in young mammals.

milky ADJ (**milkier**, **milkiest**) of or like milk; containing much milk.

mill NOUN **1** machinery for grinding specified material; a building containing this. **2** a building fitted with machinery for manufacturing.
VERB **1** grind in a mill. **2** produce markings on the edge of (a coin). **3** move about as a confused crowd.
go through the mill undergo an unpleasant experience.

millennium NOUN (PL **millenniums** or **millennia**) a period of 1,000 years; the point at which one period of a thousand years ends and another begins.

millepede variant of **MILLIPEDE**.

miller NOUN someone who owns and works a mill for grinding corn.

millet NOUN a cereal plant; its seeds.

milli- COMBINING FORM one-thousandth part of (as in *milligram, millilitre, millimetre*).

millibar NOUN one-thousandth of a bar, a unit of meteorological pressure.

milliner NOUN a person who makes or sells women's hats.
millinery NOUN

million NOUN one thousand thousand (1,000,000); (**millions**) [INFORMAL] very many.
millionth ADJ & NOUN

millionaire NOUN a person who has over a million pounds, dollars, etc.

millipede (also **millepede**) NOUN a small crawling creature with many legs.

millstone NOUN a heavy circular stone for grinding corn; a heavy burden of responsibility.

milometer NOUN an instrument measuring the distance in miles travelled by a vehicle.

milt NOUN sperm

discharged by a male fish over eggs laid by the female.

mime NOUN the use of silent gestures and facial expressions to tell a story or convey feelings. VERB use mime to recount or convey.

mimic VERB (**mimics**, **mimicking**, **mimicked**) imitate, especially playfully or for entertainment. NOUN a person who is clever at mimicking others.
mimicry NOUN

minaret NOUN a tall slender tower on or beside a mosque.

mince VERB **1** cut (meat) into very small pieces. **2** walk or speak with affected refinement. NOUN minced meat.
not mince one's words be candid in criticism etc.

mincemeat NOUN a mixture of dried fruit, sugar, etc.

mince pie NOUN a small pie containing mincemeat.

mincer NOUN a machine with revolving blades for cutting food into very small pieces.

mind NOUN **1** the ability to be aware of things and to think and reason; the intellect; sanity: *losing my mind.* **2** attention, concentration; memory. VERB **1** be distressed or worried by, object to. **2** remember to do something; take care. **3** look after temporarily.
be minded to be inclined to. **be of one mind** share an opinion. **have it in mind to** intend to. **mind out** take care.

minded ADJ having inclinations or interests of a certain kind: *scientifically minded.*

minder NOUN a person whose job is to have charge of someone or something; [INFORMAL] a bodyguard.

mindful ADJ conscious or aware of something.

mindless ADJ taking or showing no thought; not requiring thought or intelligence.
mindlessly ADV
mindlessness NOUN

mine[1] ADJ & POSSESSIVE

PRONOUN belonging to me.

mine² NOUN **1** an excavation for extracting metal or coal etc; an abundant source. **2** an explosive device laid in or on the ground or in water. VERB **1** extract (minerals) by excavating (an area). **2** lay explosive mines under or in.

minefield NOUN an area where explosive mines have been laid; a situation full of hazards.

miner NOUN a person who works in a mine.

mineral NOUN **1** an inorganic natural substance. **2** a fizzy soft drink. ADJ of or containing minerals.
mineralogist NOUN
mineralogy NOUN

mineral water NOUN water naturally containing dissolved mineral salts or gases.

minestrone NOUN /mi-ni-**stroh**-ni/ soup containing vegetables and pasta.

minesweeper NOUN a ship for clearing away mines laid in the sea.

mingle VERB blend together; mix socially.

mini- COMBINING FORM miniature, small.

miniature ADJ very small, on a small scale. NOUN a small-scale portrait, copy, or model.

miniaturize (also **miniaturise**) VERB make a small version of.

minibus NOUN a small bus for about twelve people.

minicab NOUN a cab like a taxi that can be booked but not hailed in the street.

minicomputer NOUN a computer that is bigger than a microcomputer, but smaller than a mainframe.

minim NOUN a note in music, lasting half as long as a semibreve.

minima pl. of **MINIMUM**.

minimal ADJ very small, the least possible; negligible.
minimally ADV

minimalism NOUN the use of simple basic design forms.
minimalist ADJ & NOUN

minimize (also **minimise**) VERB reduce to a

minimum; represent as small or unimportant.

minimum NOUN (PL **minima** or **minimums**) the smallest amount, extent, or strength possible. ADJ smallest in amount, extent, or strength.
minimal ADJ

minion NOUN a servant or follower.

miniskirt NOUN a very short skirt.

minister NOUN **1** the head of a government department; a senior diplomatic representative. **2** a member of the clergy.
minister to attend to the needs of.
ministerial ADJ

ministration NOUN [FORMAL] help, service.

ministry NOUN (PL **ministries**) **1** a government department headed by a minister. **2** the work of a minister of religion. **3** a period of government under one Prime Minister.

mink NOUN a small stoat-like animal; its valuable fur; a coat made of this.

minnow NOUN a small fish.

minor ADJ lesser; not very important. NOUN a person not yet legally of adult age.

minority NOUN (PL **minorities**) the smaller part of a group or class; a small group differing from or disagreeing with others.

minster NOUN a large church.

minstrel NOUN a medieval singer and musician.

mint¹ NOUN a place authorized to make a country's coins. VERB make (coins).
in mint condition as new.

mint² NOUN a fragrant herb; peppermint, a sweet flavoured with this.
minty ADJ

minuet /min-yoo-**et**/ NOUN a slow stately dance.

minus PREP with the subtraction of; (of temperature) falling below zero by (a specified number of degrees); [INFORMAL] without. ADJ (of a number) negative, less than zero; (of a grade) lower than a specified grade: *B minus*. NOUN the symbol (−), indicating subtraction or a negative value.

minuscule ADJ very small.

minute¹ /min-it/ NOUN **1** one-sixtieth of an hour or degree; a moment of time. **2** (**minutes**) an official summary of the proceedings of a meeting. VERB record (points discussed) in the minutes of a meeting.

minute² /my-**newt**/ ADJ extremely small; very precise and detailed.
minutely ADV
minuteness NOUN

minutiae /min-**yoo**-shi-ee/ PLURAL NOUN very small details.

minx NOUN a mischievous girl.

miracle NOUN an event attributed to supernatural causes because not explicable in terms of natural laws, especially one that is welcomed; a remarkable event or thing.
miraculous ADJ
miraculously ADV

mirage /mi-rahz*h*/ NOUN an optical illusion caused by atmospheric conditions.

MIRAS ABBREV mortgage interest relief at source.

mire NOUN swampy ground; mud.

mirror NOUN glass coated so that reflections can be seen in it. VERB reflect in a mirror; correspond to.

mirth NOUN merriment, laughter.
mirthful ADJ
mirthless ADJ

mis- PREFIX badly, wrongly.

misadventure NOUN an accident, an unlucky occurrence.

misanthrope (also **misanthropist**) NOUN a person who dislikes people in general.
misanthropic ADJ
misanthropy NOUN

misapprehension NOUN a mistaken belief.

misappropriate VERB take dishonestly.
misappropriation NOUN

misbehave VERB behave badly.

miscalculate VERB calculate incorrectly.
miscalculation NOUN

miscarriage NOUN an

abortion occurring naturally.

miscarry VERB (**miscarries, miscarrying, miscarried**) **1** have a miscarriage. **2** (of a plan) go wrong, fail.

miscegenation /mis-i-jin-ay-shŏn/ NOUN interbreeding of races.

miscellaneous ADJ assorted.

miscellany NOUN (PL **miscellanies**) a collection of assorted items.

mischance NOUN misfortune.

m

mischief NOUN playful misbehaviour; harm, trouble: *making mischief.*

mischievous ADJ full of mischief.
mischievously ADV
mischievousness NOUN

misconception NOUN a wrong interpretation.

misconduct NOUN bad behaviour; mismanagement.

misconstrue VERB interpret wrongly.
misconstruction NOUN

miscreant /mis-kree-ănt/ NOUN a wrongdoer.

misdeed NOUN a wrongful act.

misdemeanour ([US] **misdemeanor**) NOUN a misdeed, a wrongdoing.

miser NOUN a person who hoards money and spends as little as possible.
miserliness NOUN
miserly ADJ

miserable ADJ very unhappy; wretchedly poor in quality or surroundings.
miserably ADV

misery NOUN (PL **miseries**) great unhappiness or discomfort; a cause of this; [INFORMAL] someone who is always complaining.

misfire VERB (of a gun or engine) fail to fire correctly; (of a plan etc.) go wrong.

misfit NOUN a person not well suited to his or her environment.

misfortune NOUN bad luck, an unfortunate event.

misgiving NOUN a slight feeling of doubt, fear, or mistrust.

misguided ADJ having or

showing bad judgement.

mishap NOUN an unlucky accident.

misinform VERB give wrong information to.
misinformation NOUN

misinterpret VERB interpret incorrectly.
misinterpretation NOUN

misjudge VERB form a wrong or unfair opinion of; estimate wrongly.

mislay VERB (**mislays**, **mislaying**, **mislaid**) lose temporarily.

mislead VERB (**misleads**, **misleading**, **misled**) cause to form a wrong impression.
misleading ADJ

mismanage VERB manage badly or wrongly.
mismanagement NOUN

misnomer NOUN a wrongly applied name or description.

misogynist /mis-**oj**-in-ist/ NOUN a man who hates women.
misogyny NOUN

misplace VERB put in a wrong place; put (confidence) in someone who does not deserve it; mislay.

misprint NOUN an error in printing.

misquote VERB quote incorrectly.
misquotation NOUN

misread VERB (**misreads**, **misreading**, **misread**) read or interpret incorrectly.

misrepresent VERB represent in a false way.
misrepresentation NOUN

misrule NOUN bad government; disorder, anarchy.

Miss NOUN (PL **Misses**) the title of a girl or unmarried woman.

miss VERB **1** fail to hit or reach; fail to catch; fail to see or hear; be too late to catch (public transport) or meet (someone who has left); fail to take (an opportunity). **2** notice or regret the absence of. NOUN a failure to hit or catch something.
miss out omit, especially accidentally. **miss out on** [INFORMAL] be deprived of.

misshapen ADJ badly shaped.

missile NOUN an object

thrown or fired at a target.

missing ADJ not present; not in its place, lost.

mission NOUN **1** a task that a person or group is sent to perform; this group; a person's aim or vocation. **2** a missionary's headquarters.

missionary NOUN (PL **missionaries**) a person sent to spread religious faith.

misspell VERB (**misspells**, **misspelling**, **misspelt** or **misspelled**) spell incorrectly.

mist NOUN water vapour near the ground or clouding a window etc; a film over the eyes. VERB cover or become covered with mist.

mistake NOUN an incorrect idea or opinion; a misguided or imprudent action. VERB (**mistakes**, **mistaking**, **mistook**; PAST PARTICIPLE **mistaken**) misunderstand; identify wrongly.

mistletoe NOUN a plant with white berries, growing on trees.

mistral NOUN a cold north or north-west wind in southern France.

mistress NOUN a woman who has control of people or things; a female teacher; a man's female lover.

mistrial NOUN a trial invalidated by an error in procedure etc.

mistrust VERB feel no trust in. NOUN lack of trust.
mistrustful ADJ

misty ADJ (**mistier**, **mistiest**) full of mist; indistinct.
mistily ADV
mistiness NOUN

misunderstand VERB (**misunderstands**, **misunderstanding**, **misunderstood**) fail to understand correctly; misinterpret.
misunderstanding NOUN

misuse VERB /mis-**yooz**/ **1** use wrongly. **2** treat badly. NOUN /mis-**yooss**/ wrong use.

mite NOUN a very small spider-like animal; a small creature, especially a child; a very small amount.

mitigate VERB make less intense or severe; make (an offence) less serious.
mitigation NOUN

mitre ([US] **miter**) NOUN **1** the pointed headdress of bishops and abbots. **2** a join between pieces of wood that form a right angle. VERB (**mitres, mitring, mitred**) join in this way.

mitt NOUN a mitten.

mitten NOUN a glove with no partitions between the fingers.

mix VERB **1** combine (different things) or be combined; prepare by combining ingredients. **2** associate socially. **3** be compatible. NOUN a mixture.
mix up mix thoroughly; confuse.
mixer NOUN

mixed ADJ composed of various elements; of or for both sexes.

mixed-up ADJ [INFORMAL] muddled; not well adjusted emotionally.

mixture NOUN something made by mixing; the process of mixing things.

mizzenmast NOUN the mast that is next aft of the mainmast.

ml ABBREV millilitre(s).

mm ABBREV millimetre(s).

MMR ABBREV measles, mumps, and rubella (a vaccination for children).

mnemonic /nim-on-ik/ NOUN a pattern of letters or words used as an aid to memory. ADJ aiding the memory.

moan NOUN a low mournful sound; [INFORMAL] a grumble. VERB utter a moan; [INFORMAL] complain.
moaner NOUN

moat NOUN a deep wide water-filled ditch round a castle etc.

mob NOUN a large disorderly crowd; [INFORMAL] a group. VERB (**mobs, mobbing, mobbed**) crowd round in a disorderly or violent way; (of birds) flock round and attack (a predator).

mobile ADJ able to move or be moved easily. NOUN **1** an ornamental hanging structure whose parts

move in currents of air. **2** a mobile phone.
mobility NOUN

mobile phone NOUN a telephone that can be carried and used over a wide area without a physical connection to a network.

mobilize (also **mobilise**) VERB assemble (troops etc.) for active service.
mobilization NOUN

moccasin NOUN a soft flat-soled leather shoe.

mocha /mo-kă/ NOUN a kind of coffee.

m

mock VERB tease, laugh at; imitate scornfully. ADJ imitation, not authentic.

mockery NOUN (PL **mockeries**) ridicule; an absurd representation of something.

mock-up NOUN a model for testing or study.

MOD ABBREV Ministry of Defence.

mod cons PLURAL NOUN [INFORMAL] modern conveniences; appliances in a house making life easier and more comfortable.

mode NOUN **1** a way of doing something. **2** the current fashion.

model NOUN **1** a three-dimensional reproduction, usually on a smaller scale. **2** someone or something seen as an example of excellence; a pattern to follow. **3** a person employed to pose for an artist or display clothes by wearing them. ADJ exemplary. VERB (**models**, **modelling**, **modelled**; [US] **modeling**, **modeled**) **1** make a model of; shape. **2** work as an artist's or fashion model; display (clothes) in this way.
model oneself on try to imitate.

modem NOUN a device for transmitting computer data via a telephone line.

moderate ADJ /**mod**-er-ăt/ medium; not extreme or excessive. NOUN /**mod**-er-ăt/ a holder of moderate views. VERB /**mod**-er-ayt/ make or become moderate.
moderately ADV

moderation NOUN avoidance of extremes.

in moderation to a reasonable extent, not in excess.

moderator NOUN **1** an arbitrator. **2** a Presbyterian minister presiding over a church assembly.

modern ADJ of present or recent times; in current style.
modernity NOUN

modernist NOUN a person who favours modern ideas or methods.
modernism NOUN

modernize (also **modernise**) VERB adapt to modern ways or needs.
modernization NOUN
modernizer NOUN

modest ADJ **1** not vain or boastful; not elaborate or ostentatious. **2** small, moderate in size, amount, etc. **3** avoiding indecency.
modestly ADV
modesty NOUN

modicum NOUN a small amount.

modify VERB (**modifies, modifying, modified**) **1** make minor changes to, adapt. **2** make or become less extreme.
modification NOUN

modish /moh-dish/ ADJ fashionable.

modulate VERB regulate, moderate; vary in tone or pitch.
modulation NOUN

module NOUN a standardized part or independent unit forming part of a complex structure; a unit of training or education.
modular ADJ

modus operandi NOUN (PL **modi operandi**) a method of working.

m

mogul /moh-gŭl/ NOUN [INFORMAL] an important or influential person.

mohair NOUN yarn made from the fine silky hair of the angora goat.

moiety /moy-i-ti/ NOUN (PL **moieties**) [FORMAL] each of two parts of something.

moist ADJ slightly wet.

moisten VERB make or become moist.

moisture NOUN water or other liquid diffused through a substance or as vapour or condensed on a surface.

moisturize (also **moisturise**) VERB make (skin) less dry.
moisturizer NOUN

molar NOUN a back tooth with a broad top.

molasses NOUN syrup from raw sugar; [US] treacle.

mold etc. US spelling of **MOULD** etc.

mole NOUN **1** a small burrowing animal with dark fur. **2** [INFORMAL] a spy established within an organization. **3** a small dark spot on human skin. **4** a pier or breakwater.

m

molecule NOUN a group of atoms, the smallest unit that can take part in a chemical reaction.
molecular ADJ

molehill NOUN a mound of earth thrown up by a mole.

molest VERB pester, annoy; assault or abuse sexually.
molestation NOUN

mollify VERB (**mollifies, mollifying, mollified**) soothe the anger or anxiety of.

mollusc NOUN an animal with a soft body and often a hard shell.

mollycoddle VERB pamper.

Molotov cocktail NOUN an improvised incendiary bomb, a bottle filled with inflammable liquid.

molt US spelling of **MOULT**.

molten ADJ liquefied by heat.

molto ADV [MUSIC] very.

molybdenum /mo-**lib**-di-nŭm/ NOUN a hard metallic element used in steel.

moment NOUN **1** a point or brief portion of time. **2** [FORMAL] importance.

momentary ADJ lasting only a moment.
momentarily ADV

momentous ADJ of great importance.

momentum NOUN impetus gained by movement.

monarch NOUN a ruler with the title of king, queen, emperor, or empress.
monarchic ADJ
monarchical ADJ

monarchist NOUN a supporter of monarchy.

monarchism NOUN

monarchy NOUN (PL **monarchies**) a form of government with a monarch as the supreme ruler; a country governed in this way.

monastery NOUN (PL **monasteries**) the residence of a community of monks.

monastic ADJ of monks or monasteries.
monasticism NOUN

Monday NOUN the day of the week following Sunday.

monetarism NOUN the theory that inflation is best controlled by limiting the supply of money.
monetarist NOUN & ADJ

monetary ADJ of money or currency.

money NOUN current coins and banknotes; wealth; resources; payment for work; (PL **moneys**) any form of currency.

moneyed ADJ wealthy.

money-spinner NOUN a profitable thing.

Mongol NOUN **1** a person from Mongolia; the language of Mongolia. **2** (**mongol**) [OFFENSIVE] a person suffering from Down's syndrome. ADJ relating to Mongolia.
Mongolian NOUN & ADJ

mongoose NOUN (PL **mongooses**) a stoat-like tropical animal that can attack and kill snakes.

mongrel NOUN an animal (especially a dog) of mixed breed. ADJ of mixed origin or character.

monitor NOUN **1** a device checking or testing the operation of something; a person observing a process to ensure proper procedure. **2** a school pupil with special duties. VERB keep watch over; record and test or control.

monk NOUN a member of a male religious community.

monkey NOUN (PL **monkeys**) a small primate, usually long-tailed and tree-dwelling; [INFORMAL] a mischievous person. VERB (**monkeys**, **monkeying**, **monkeyed**) [INFORMAL] behave mischievously; tamper with something.

monkey nut NOUN a peanut.

monkey puzzle NOUN an evergreen tree with needle-like leaves.

monkey wrench NOUN a wrench with an adjustable jaw.

mono ADJ monophonic.

mono- COMBINING FORM one, alone, single.

monochrome ADJ done in only one colour or in black and white.

monocle NOUN an eyeglass for one eye only.

monocular ADJ with or for one eye.

monoculture NOUN the cultivation of only one crop in an area.

monogamy NOUN the system of being married to only one person at a time.
monogamous ADJ

monogram NOUN letters (especially a person's initials) combined in a design.
monogrammed ADJ

monograph NOUN a scholarly treatise on a single subject.

monolith NOUN a large single upright block of stone; a large impersonal organization etc.
monolithic ADJ

monologue NOUN a long speech.

monomania NOUN an obsession with one idea or interest.
monomaniac NOUN

monophonic ADJ using only one transmission channel for reproduction of sound.

monoplane NOUN an aeroplane with only one set of wings.

monopolize (also **monopolise**) VERB have exclusive control or the largest share of; keep to oneself.
monopolization NOUN

monopoly NOUN (PL **monopolies**) exclusive control of trade in a commodity; exclusive possession of something.

monorail NOUN a railway in which the track is a single rail.

monosodium glutamate NOUN a

substance added to food to enhance its flavour.

monosyllable NOUN a word of one syllable. **monosyllabic** ADJ

monotheism NOUN the doctrine that there is only one God. **monotheist** NOUN **monotheistic** ADJ

monotone NOUN a level unchanging tone of voice.

monotonous ADJ dull because lacking in variety or variation. **monotonously** ADV **monotony** NOUN

monoxide NOUN an oxide with one atom of oxygen.

Monsieur /mŏ-**syer**/ NOUN (PL **Messieurs**) a title or form of address for a French-speaking man, corresponding to Mr or sir.

monsoon NOUN a seasonal wind in South Asia; the rainy season accompanying this.

monster NOUN a large, frightening imaginary creature; something very large; a cruel person; something abnormal in shape. ADJ [INFORMAL] very large.

monstrosity NOUN (PL **monstrosities**) something very large and ugly; something very wrong.

monstrous ADJ outrageous, shocking; huge; ugly and frightening. **monstrously** ADV

montage NOUN /mon-**ta***zh*, mon-tah*zh*/ the making of a composite picture from pieces of others; the technique of selecting and joining sections of film to form a whole.

month NOUN each of the twelve portions into which the year is divided; a period of 28 days.

monthly ADJ & ADV done, produced, or occurring once a month. NOUN (PL **monthlies**) a monthly publication.

monument NOUN an object commemorating a person or event etc.; a structure of historical importance.

monumental ADJ of great

size or importance; of or serving as a monument.

moo NOUN a cow's low deep cry. VERB make this sound.

mooch VERB [INFORMAL] pass one's time aimlessly.

mood NOUN a temporary state of mind or spirits; a fit of bad temper or depression.
in the mood for feeling inclined to.

moody ADJ (**moodier**, **moodiest**) given to unpredictable changes of mood; sulky, gloomy.
moodily ADV
moodiness NOUN

moon NOUN the earth's satellite, made visible by light it reflects from the sun; a natural satellite of any planet. VERB (**moon about** or **around**) behave dreamily.
over the moon [INFORMAL] very happy and excited.

moonlight NOUN light from the moon.
VERB [INFORMAL] have two paid jobs, one by day and the other in the evening.

moonlit ADJ lit by the moon.

moonscape NOUN a landscape that is rocky and barren like the surface of the moon.

moonshine NOUN [INFORMAL] **1** foolish ideas. **2** illicitly distilled alcoholic liquor.

moonstone NOUN a pearly semi-precious stone.

Moor NOUN a member of a Muslim people of north-west Africa.
Moorish ADJ

moor¹ NOUN a stretch of open uncultivated land with low shrubs.

moor² VERB secure (a boat etc.) to a fixed object by means of cable(s).

moorhen NOUN a small waterbird.

moorings PLURAL NOUN the cables or a place for mooring a boat.

moose NOUN (PL **moose**) an elk of North America.

moot point NOUN a debatable or undecided issue.

mop NOUN a pad or bundle of yarn on a stick, used for cleaning things; a thick mass of hair.
VERB (**mops**, **mopping**, **mopped**) clean with a

mop; wipe (one's eyes, forehead, etc.); soak up (liquid) by wiping.

mope VERB be unhappy and listless.

moped NOUN a low-powered motorcycle.

moraine NOUN a mass of stones etc. deposited by a glacier.

moral ADJ concerned with right and wrong conduct; virtuous. NOUN **1** a moral lesson or principle derived from a story etc. **2** (**morals**) a person's standards of behaviour, especially sexual conduct.
morally ADV

morale /mŏ-**rahl**/ NOUN the state of a person's or group's spirits and confidence.

moralist NOUN a person who expresses or teaches moral principles.

morality NOUN (PL **moralities**) moral principles; the extent to which something is right or wrong; a system of values.

moralize (also **moralise**) VERB comment on moral issues, especially self-righteously.

moral support NOUN encouragement.

moral victory NOUN (PL **moral victories**) a defeat in which the defeated party gain credit, stand by their principles, etc.

morass NOUN a boggy area; a complicated situation from which it is hard to escape.

moratorium NOUN (PL **moratoriums** or **moratoria**) a temporary ban on an activity.

morbid ADJ **1** preoccupied with gloomy or unpleasant things. **2** of disease, unhealthy.
morbidity NOUN
morbidly ADV
morbidness NOUN

mordant ADJ (of wit) sharp, biting. NOUN a substance combining with a dye to fix it in material.
mordantly ADV

more DETERMINER & PRON a greater or additional amount or degree. ADV to a greater extent; again; forming the comparative of adjectives and adverbs.

more or less approximately. **no more** never again, no longer.

moreish ADJ [INFORMAL] so pleasant to eat that one wants more.

moreover ADV besides.

mores /mor-ayz/ PLURAL NOUN customs or conventions.

morgue /morg/ NOUN a mortuary.

moribund ADJ on the point of death; in terminal decline.

Mormon NOUN a member of a Christian sect founded in the USA. **Mormonism** NOUN

morning NOUN the part of the day before noon or the midday meal.

morning sickness NOUN nausea felt in early pregnancy.

morocco NOUN goatskin leather.

moron NOUN [INFORMAL] a stupid person. **moronic** ADJ

morose ADJ gloomy and unsociable, sullen. **morosely** ADV **moroseness** NOUN

morphia NOUN [DATED] morphine.

morphine NOUN a pain-killing drug made from opium.

morphology NOUN the study of forms of animals and plants or of words. **morphological** ADJ

morris dance NOUN a traditional English dance performed in a costume decorated with ribbons and bells.

Morse code NOUN a code of signals using short and long sounds or flashes of light.

morsel NOUN a small piece of food; a small amount.

mortal ADJ **1** subject to death. **2** causing death; fought to the death; hostile until death. NOUN a mortal being. **mortally** ADV

mortality NOUN (PL **mortalities**) the state of being mortal; loss of life on a large scale; the death rate.

mortar NOUN **1** a mixture of lime or cement with sand and water for joining bricks or stones. **2** a bowl in which substances are pounded with a pestle. **3** a short cannon.

mortar board NOUN a stiff square cap worn as part of academic dress.

mortgage /mor-gij/ NOUN a loan for the purchase of property, in which the property itself is pledged as security; an agreement effecting this. VERB pledge (property) as security in this way.

mortgagee /mor-gij-ee/ NOUN the borrower in a mortgage.

mortgagor /mor-gij-ĕr/ NOUN the lender in a mortgage.

mortician NOUN [US] an undertaker.

mortify VERB (**mortifies**, **mortifying**, **mortified**) **1** humiliate, embarrass. **2** subdue (bodily desires) by self-discipline. **3** (of flesh) become gangrenous.
mortification NOUN

mortise (also **mortice**) NOUN a hole in one part of a framework shaped to receive the end of another part.

mortise lock NOUN a lock set in a door, not attached to its surface.

mortuary NOUN (PL **mortuaries**) a place where dead bodies are kept temporarily.

mosaic NOUN a pattern or picture made with small pieces of coloured glass or stone.

Moslem ADJ & NOUN = **MUSLIM**.

mosque NOUN a Muslim place of worship.

mosquito NOUN (PL **mosquitoes**) a bloodsucking insect.

moss NOUN a small flowerless plant forming a dense growth in moist places.
mossy ADJ

most DETERMINER & PRON greatest in amount or degree; the majority of. ADV to the greatest extent; very; forming the superlative of adjectives and adverbs.
at most not more than. **for the most part** in most cases. **make the most of** use or enjoy to the best advantage.

mostly ADV for the most part.

MOT ABBREV an annual test of motor vehicles over a certain age, checking safety etc.

motel NOUN a roadside hotel for motorists.

motet NOUN a short religious choral work.

moth NOUN an insect like a butterfly but usually flying at night; a similar insect whose larvae feed on cloth or fur.

mothball NOUN a small ball of a pungent substance for keeping moths away from clothes.

mother NOUN a female parent; the title of the female head of a religious community; the origin of or inspiration for something. VERB look after in a motherly way. **motherhood** NOUN

motherboard NOUN a printed circuit board containing the principal components of a microcomputer.

mother-in-law NOUN (PL **mothers-in-law**) the mother of one's wife or husband.

motherland NOUN one's native country.

motherless ADJ without a living mother.

motherly ADJ showing a mother's kindness. **motherliness** NOUN

mother-of-pearl NOUN a pearly substance lining shells of oysters and mussels etc.

mother tongue NOUN one's native language.

motif /moh-**teef**/ NOUN a pattern; a recurring feature or theme.

motion NOUN **1** the action of moving; movement. **2** a formal proposal put to a meeting for discussion. **3** an emptying of the bowels; faeces. VERB direct (someone) with a gesture.

motionless ADJ not moving.

motion picture NOUN a cinema film.

motivate VERB give a motive to; stimulate the interest of, inspire. **motivation** NOUN

motive NOUN a person's

reason for doing something. ADJ producing movement; being the reason for something.

mot juste /moh *zh*oost/ NOUN (PL **mots justes**) the most appropriate word.

motley ADJ varied, incongruously assorted. NOUN [HISTORICAL] a jester's particoloured costume.

motocross NOUN a motorcycle race over rough ground.

motor NOUN a machine supplying motive power; [INFORMAL] a car. ADJ **1** driven by a motor. **2** producing motion. VERB [INFORMAL] travel by car.

motorbike NOUN a motorcycle.

motorcade NOUN a procession or parade of motor vehicles.

motorcycle NOUN a two-wheeled motor-driven road vehicle.
motorcyclist NOUN

motorist NOUN a car driver.

motorize (also **motorise**) VERB equip with motor(s) or motor vehicles.

motor vehicle NOUN a vehicle with a motor engine, for use on ordinary roads.

motorway NOUN a road designed for fast long-distance traffic.

mottled NOUN patterned with irregular patches of colour.

motto NOUN (PL **mottoes**) a short sentence or phrase expressing an ideal or rule of conduct; a maxim or joke inside a paper cracker.

mould ([US] **mold**) NOUN **1** a hollow container into which a liquid is poured to set in a desired shape; something made in this. **2** a furry growth of tiny fungi on a damp surface. **3** a soft fine earth rich in organic matter. VERB form into a particular shape; influence the development of.

moulder ([US] **molder**) VERB decay, rot away.

moulding ([US] **molding**) NOUN an ornamental strip of plaster or wood.

mouldy ([US] **moldy**) ADJ (**mouldier, mouldiest; moldier, moldiest**)

1 covered with mould; stale. 2 [INFORMAL] dull; depressing, unpleasant.

moult ([US] **molt**) VERB shed feathers, hair, or skin before new growth. NOUN this process.

mound NOUN a pile of earth or stones; a small hill; a large pile.

mount VERB 1 go up (stairs, a hill, etc.); get up on to (a horse etc.); provide with a horse to ride. 2 organize and set in process; establish. 3 grow larger, more numerous, or more intense. 4 fix on or in a support or setting. NOUN 1 a support or setting. 2 a horse for riding. 3 a mountain (used in names).

mountain NOUN a mass of land rising to a great height; a large heap or pile.
move mountains achieve amazing results; make a great effort.

mountain bike NOUN a sturdy bicycle suitable for riding on rough hilly ground.

mountaineer NOUN a person who climbs mountains.
mountaineering NOUN

mountainous ADJ 1 full of mountains. 2 huge.

mourn VERB feel or express sorrow about (a dead person or lost thing).
mourner NOUN

mournful ADJ sorrowful.
mournfully ADV

mourning NOUN dark clothes worn as a symbol of bereavement.

mouse NOUN 1 (PL **mice**) a small rodent with a long tail; a quiet timid person. 2 (PL also **mouses**) a small rolling device for moving the cursor on a VDU screen.

moussaka /moo-**sah**-kă/ NOUN a Greek dish of minced meat and aubergine.

mousse NOUN a frothy creamy dish; a soft gel or frothy preparation.

moustache /mŭs-**tahsh**/ ([US] **mustache**) NOUN hair on the upper lip.

mousy ADJ (**mousier**, **mousiest**) 1 dull greyish brown. 2 quiet and timid.

mouth NOUN /mowth/ the opening in the face

through which food is taken in and sounds uttered; the opening of a bag, cave, cannon, etc; a place where a river enters the sea. VERB /mow*th*/ form (words) soundlessly with the lips; say (something unoriginal)
mouthful NOUN

mouth organ NOUN a small instrument played by blowing and sucking.

mouthpiece NOUN **1** the part of an instrument placed between or near the lips. **2** a spokesperson.

mouthwash NOUN a liquid for cleaning the mouth.

movable ADJ able to be moved.

move VERB **1** go in a specified direction, change position, change the position of; change one's residence. **2** prompt to action; provoke emotion in. **3** make progress; take action. **4** put to a meeting for discussion. NOUN an act of moving; the moving of a piece in chess etc.; a calculated action, an initiative.
get a move on [INFORMAL] hurry up. **move in** take possession of a new home.

movement NOUN **1** an act of moving; the process of moving; the ability to move; activity, bustle; (**movements**) a person's activities and whereabouts. **2** a group with a common cause. **3** a section of a long piece of music.

movie NOUN [US] [INFORMAL] a cinema film.

moving ADJ arousing pity or sympathy.
movingly ADV

mow VERB (**mows**, **mowing**, **mowed**; PAST PARTICIPLE **mown**) cut down (grass) on (an area of ground).
mow down kill or destroy by a moving force.
mower NOUN

mozzarella /mots-ă-**rell**-ă/ NOUN a soft Italian cheese.

MP ABBREV Member of Parliament.

mpg ABBREV miles per gallon.

mph ABBREV miles per hour.

Mr NOUN (PL **Messrs**) the

title prefixed to a man's name.

Mrs NOUN (PL **Mrs**) the title prefixed to a married woman's name.

MS ABBREV **1** multiple sclerosis. **2** (PL **MSS**) manuscript.

Ms NOUN the title prefixed to a married or unmarried woman's name.

MSc ABBREV Master of Science.

MS-DOS [TRADE MARK] Microsoft disk operating system.

much DETERMINER & PRON a large amount, a great quantity. ADV to a great extent; often.
a bit much [INFORMAL] excessive, unreasonable.
too much an intolerable situation or event.

mucilage /myoo-si-lij/ NOUN a sticky substance obtained from plants; an adhesive gum.

muck NOUN dirt, mess; farmyard manure; [INFORMAL] something worthless or unpleasant.
muck about [INFORMAL] behave foolishly. **muck out** clean (a stable).
muck up [INFORMAL] bungle; spoil.
mucky ADJ

muckraking NOUN the seeking out and exposing of scandal.

mucous ADJ like or covered with mucus.

mucus NOUN a slimy substance coating the inner surface of hollow organs of the body.

mud NOUN wet soft earth.
muddy ADJ

muddle VERB confuse, mix up; progress in a haphazard way. NOUN a muddled state or collection.

mudguard NOUN a curved cover above a wheel on a vehicle, protecting the vehicle against spray.

muesli /mooz-li, myooz-li/ NOUN food of mixed crushed cereals, dried fruit, nuts, etc.

muezzin /moo-ez-in/ NOUN a man who proclaims the hours of prayer for Muslims.

muff NOUN a tube-shaped furry covering for the hands. VERB [INFORMAL] bungle.

muffin NOUN a light round yeast cake eaten toasted and buttered; a cup-shaped cake.

muffle VERB wrap for warmth or protection, or to deaden sound; make (a sound) less loud or less distinct.

muffler NOUN a scarf.

mufti /**muf**-tee/ NOUN plain clothes worn by someone who usually wears a uniform.

mug NOUN **1** a large drinking vessel with a handle, for use without a saucer. **2** [INFORMAL] the face. **3** [INFORMAL] a person who is easily outwitted. VERB (**mugs, mugging, mugged**) [INFORMAL] rob (a person) with violence, especially in a public place.
mug up [INFORMAL] revise (a subject) intensively.
mugger NOUN

muggy ADJ (**muggier, muggiest**) (of weather) oppressively damp and warm.
mugginess NOUN

mulberry NOUN (PL **mulberries**) a purple or white fruit resembling a blackberry.

mulch NOUN a mixture of wet straw, leaves, etc., spread on ground to protect plants or retain moisture. VERB cover with mulch.

mule NOUN **1** an animal that is the offspring of a horse and a donkey; a stubborn person. **2** a backless slipper.
mulish ADJ

mull VERB heat (wine etc.) with sugar and spices, as a drink.
mull over think over.

mullah NOUN a Muslim learned in Islamic law.

mullet NOUN a small edible sea fish.

mullion NOUN an upright bar between the sections of a window.

multi- COMBINING FORM many.

multicultural ADJ of or involving several cultural or ethnic groups.

multifarious ADJ very varied and diverse; many and various.
multifariously ADV

multilateral ADJ involving three or more

parties.

multinational ADJ involving several countries. NOUN a company operating in several countries.

multiple ADJ having or involving many parts; numerous. NOUN a quantity divisible by another a number of times without remainder.

multiplex ADJ having many elements; (of a cinema) having several separate screens within one building.

multiplicand NOUN a quantity to be multiplied by another.

multiplicity NOUN (PL **multiplicities**) a large number; a great variety.

multiplier NOUN the number by which a quantity is multiplied.

multiply VERB (**multiplies, multiplying, multiplied**) add (a number) to itself a specified number of times; become or cause to become more numerous. **multiplication** NOUN

multiracial ADJ of or involving people of several races.

multi-speed ADJ progressing at different speeds towards the same goal.

multitasking NOUN [COMPUTING] the performance of different tasks simultaneously.

multitude NOUN a great number of things or people.

multitudinous ADJ very numerous.

mum [INFORMAL] NOUN mother. ADJ silent: *keep mum.*

mumble VERB speak indistinctly. NOUN indistinct speech.

mumbo-jumbo NOUN [INFORMAL] meaningless ritual; deliberately obscure language.

mummify VERB (**mummifies, mummifying, mummified**) preserve (a corpse) by embalming as in ancient Egypt. **mummification** NOUN

mummy NOUN (PL **mummies**) **1** [INFORMAL] mother. **2** a corpse embalmed and wrapped for burial, especially in ancient Egypt.

mumps NOUN a viral disease with painful swellings in the neck.

munch VERB chew vigorously.

mundane ADJ **1** dull, routine. **2** worldly.

municipal ADJ of a town or city or its governing body.

municipality NOUN (PL **municipalities**) a self-governing town or district.

munificent ADJ splendidly generous.
munificence NOUN

munitions PLURAL NOUN weapons, ammunition, etc.

muon NOUN an unstable elementary particle.

mural ADJ of or on a wall. NOUN a painting on a wall.

murder NOUN intentional unlawful killing; [INFORMAL] a very difficult or unpleasant task or experience. VERB kill intentionally and unlawfully.
murderer NOUN

murderous ADJ involving or capable of murder.

murk NOUN darkness, gloom.

murky ADJ (**murkier**, **murkiest**) dark, gloomy; not clear, cloudy; involving dishonesty and deception.

murmur NOUN a low continuous sound; softly spoken words. VERB make a murmur; speak or utter softly.

murrain /**mu**-rin/ NOUN an infectious disease of cattle.

muscle NOUN a strip of fibrous tissue able to move a part of the body by contracting; physical strength; power or influence.
muscle in [INFORMAL] force oneself on others.

Muscovite NOUN a person from Moscow.

muscular ADJ of muscles; having well-developed muscles.
muscularity NOUN

muscular dystrophy NOUN a condition causing progressive wasting of the muscles.

muse VERB be deep in thought. NOUN a poet's source of inspiration.

museum NOUN a place where objects of historical or scientific interest are collected and displayed.

mush NOUN a soft pulp. VERB crush to make this.

mushroom NOUN an edible fungus with a stem and a domed cap. VERB spring up in large numbers; rise and spread in a mushroom shape.

m

mushy ADJ (**mushier**, **mushiest**) **1** soft and pulpy. **2** [INFORMAL] sentimental.
mushiness NOUN

music NOUN vocal or instrumental sounds combined to produce beauty and express emotion; the art of this; the written signs representing this; something very pleasant or welcome to hear.

musical ADJ of or involving music; sweet-sounding; skilled or interested in music. NOUN a play with songs and dancing.
musically ADV

musician NOUN a person skilled in music.

musicology NOUN the study of the history and forms of music.
musicologist NOUN

musk NOUN a substance secreted by certain animals or produced synthetically, used in perfumes.

musket NOUN a long-barrelled gun, formerly used by infantry.

Muslim (also **Moslem**) ADJ of or believing in Muhammad's teaching. NOUN a believer in this faith.

muslin NOUN a thin cotton cloth.

mussel NOUN a bivalve mollusc.

must AUXILIARY VERB **1** used to express necessity, obligation, or insistence. **2** used to express certainty or logical necessity. NOUN [INFORMAL] something that should not be missed or overlooked.

mustache US spelling of **MOUSTACHE**.

mustang NOUN a wild horse of Mexico and California.

mustard NOUN a sharp-tasting yellow condiment made from the seeds of a plant; this plant.

muster VERB gather together, assemble; summon (energy, strength). NOUN a formal gathering of troops.
pass muster be adequate or acceptable.

musty ADJ (**mustier**, **mustiest**) smelling mouldy; stale.
mustiness NOUN

mutable ADJ liable to change; [LITERARY] fickle.
mutability NOUN

mutagen NOUN something causing genetic mutation.

mutant ADJ resulting from mutation. NOUN a mutant form.

mutate VERB undergo mutation.

mutation NOUN a change in form; a change in genetic structure which may be passed on to subsequent generations; a form resulting from such a change.

mute ADJ silent; dumb. NOUN a device muffling the sound of a musical instrument; [DATED] a dumb person. VERB deaden or muffle the sound of.
mutely ADV
muteness NOUN

mutilate VERB injure or disfigure by cutting off a part.
mutilation NOUN

mutineer NOUN a person who mutinies.

mutinous ADJ rebellious, ready to mutiny.
mutinously ADV

mutiny NOUN (PL **mutinies**) a rebellion against authority, especially by members of the armed forces. VERB (**mutinies**, **mutinying**, **mutinied**) engage in mutiny.

mutter VERB speak or utter in a low unclear tone; utter subdued grumbles. NOUN a low indistinct utterance.

mutton NOUN the flesh of sheep as food.

mutual ADJ **1** felt or done

m

by each of two or more people to the other(s): *mutual respect.* **2** common to two or more people: *a mutual friend.*
mutuality NOUN
mutually ADV

Muzak NOUN [TRADE MARK] recorded music played through loudspeakers in public places.

muzzle NOUN **1** the projecting nose and jaws of certain animals; a guard fitted over this to stop an animal biting. **2** the open end of a firearm's barrel. VERB put a muzzle on; prevent from expressing opinions freely.

muzzy ADJ (**muzzier**, **muzziest**) confused, vague, dazed; (of vision or an image) blurred.
muzzily ADV
muzziness NOUN

MW ABBREV megawatt(s).

my ADJ belonging to me.

myalgia /mI-**al**-jă/ NOUN muscle pain.

mycelium /mI-**see**-li-ŭm/ NOUN microscopic thread-like parts of a fungus.

mycology /mI-**ko**-lŏ-ji/ NOUN the study of fungi.

myelin /**mI**-ĕ-lin/ NOUN a substance forming a protective sheath around nerve fibres.

mynah (also **myna**) NOUN a bird of the starling family that can mimic sounds.

myopia /my-**oh**-pi-ă/ NOUN short-sightedness.
myopic ADJ

myriad /**mi**-ree-ăd/ NOUN a vast number.

myrrh /mer/ NOUN a gum resin used in perfumes, medicines, and incense.

myself PRON the emphatic and reflexive form of *I* and *me.*

mysterious ADJ puzzling, hard to explain, enigmatic; (of an atmosphere) strange, secret, eerie.
mysteriously ADV

mystery NOUN (PL **mysteries**) a matter that remains unexplained; the quality of being unexplained or obscure; a story dealing with a puzzling crime.

mystic ADJ having a

hidden or symbolic meaning, especially in religion; inspiring a sense of mystery and awe. NOUN a person who seeks to obtain union with God by spiritual contemplation.
mystical ADJ
mystically ADV
mysticism NOUN

mystify VERB (**mystifies, mystifying, mystified**) puzzle, baffle.
mystification NOUN

mystique /mis-teek/ NOUN an aura of mystery or mystical power.

myth NOUN a traditional tale containing beliefs about ancient times or natural events and usually involving supernatural beings; an imaginary person or thing.
mythical ADJ

mythology NOUN myths; the study of myths.
mythological ADJ

myxomatosis /miks-ŏ-mă-**toh**-sis/ NOUN a fatal viral disease of rabbits.

m

Nn

N (also **n**) NOUN (PL **Ns** or **N's**) the fourteenth letter of the alphabet. ABBREV north, northern.

NAAFI ABBREV Navy, Army, and Air Force Institutes.

naan (also **nan**) NOUN soft flat bread made in India.

nab VERB (**nabs**, **nabbing**, **nabbed**) [INFORMAL] catch (a wrongdoer) in the act, arrest; take, steal.

nadir /na-deer/ NOUN the lowest point.

naevus /nee-vŭs/ ([US] **nevus**) NOUN (PL **naevi**) a red birthmark.

naff ADJ [INFORMAL] lacking taste or style.

nag VERB (**nags**, **nagging**, **nagged**) scold continually; (of pain) be felt persistently. NOUN **1** a person who nags. **2** [INFORMAL] a horse.

nail NOUN **1** a layer of horny substance over the outer tip of a finger or toe. **2** a small metal spike driven into wood as a fastening. VERB **1** fasten with nail(s). **2** [INFORMAL] catch, arrest.

naive /nah-eev/ ADJ showing lack of experience or judgement.
naively ADV
naivety NOUN

naked ADJ without clothes on; without coverings; (of feelings etc.) undisguised.
nakedness NOUN

naked eye NOUN the eye unassisted by a telescope or microscope etc.

namby-pamby ADJ feeble, cowardly, or effeminate.

name NOUN **1** the word(s) by which a person, place, or thing is known or indicated. **2** a reputation; a famous person. VERB give a name to; identify; nominate, specify.

name after call by the same name as.

namely ADV that is to say.

namesake NOUN a person or thing with the same name as another.

nan¹ NOUN [INFORMAL] a grandmother.

nan² variant of **NAAN**.

nanny NOUN (PL **nannies**) a child's nurse.

nano- COMBINING FORM one thousand millionth.

nap NOUN **1** a short sleep, especially during the day. **2** short raised fibres on the surface of cloth or leather. VERB (**naps**, **napping**, **napped**) have a short sleep.

napalm /nay-pahm/ NOUN a jelly-like petrol substance used in incendiary bombs.

nape NOUN the back part of the neck.

naphtha /naf-thă/ NOUN an inflammable oil.

naphthalene NOUN a strong-smelling white substance used as a moth-repellent.

napkin NOUN **1** a piece of cloth or paper used at meals to protect clothes or for wiping one's lips. **2** a nappy.

nappy NOUN (PL **nappies**) a piece of absorbent material worn by a baby to absorb or retain urine and faeces.

narcissism NOUN abnormal self-admiration.
narcissist NOUN
narcissistic ADJ

narcissus NOUN (PL **narcissi**) a flower of the group including the daffodil.

narcosis NOUN a state of drowsiness produced by drugs.

narcotic NOUN a drug affecting mood and behaviour; a drug causing drowsiness.

narrate VERB tell (a story); give an account of.
narration NOUN
narrator NOUN

narrative NOUN a spoken or written account of something; a story. ADJ of or forming a narrative.

narrow ADJ **1** small in width, small from side to side. **2** limited in extent

n

or scope; (of views or beliefs) limited and intolerant or inflexible. VERB make or become narrow.
narrowly ADV
narrowness NOUN

narrow-minded ADJ intolerant.

narwhal NOUN an Arctic whale with a spirally grooved tusk.

NASA ABBREV (in the US) National Aeronautics and Space Administration.

nasal ADJ of the nose; sounding as if breath came out through the nose.
nasally ADV

nascent /nay-sĕnt/ ADJ just coming into existence.
nascency NOUN

nasty ADJ (**nastier**, **nastiest**) unpleasant; unkind; annoying, unwelcome.
nastily ADV
nastiness NOUN

natal /nay-tăl/ ADJ of or from one's birth.

nation NOUN people of mainly common descent and history usually inhabiting a particular country under one government.

national ADJ **1** of a nation; common to a whole nation. **2** owned or supported by the state. NOUN a citizen of a particular country.
nationally ADV

national curriculum NOUN a common programme of study for school pupils in England and Wales.

nationalism NOUN patriotic feeling; a policy of national independence.
nationalist NOUN
nationalistic ADJ

nationality NOUN (PL **nationalities**) **1** the status of belonging to a particular nation. **2** an ethnic group forming part of one or more political nations.

nationalize (also **nationalise**) VERB convert from private to state ownership.
nationalization NOUN

native ADJ belonging to a place by birth; associated by birth; (of a quality etc.) natural, inborn. NOUN a person born in a specified place; a local inhabitant.

nativity NOUN (PL **nativities**) birth; (**the Nativity**) that of Christ; a representation of this in art.

NATO ABBREV North Atlantic Treaty Organization.

natter [INFORMAL] VERB chat in a leisurely way. NOUN a leisurely chat.

natural ADJ **1** of or produced by nature; not man-made; having a specified skill or quality from birth. **2** relaxed, spontaneous. NOUN **1** a person or thing that seems naturally suited for something. **2** [MUSIC] a note that is not a sharp or flat.
naturalness NOUN

natural history NOUN the study of animal and plant life.

naturalism NOUN realism in art and literature.
naturalistic ADJ

naturalist NOUN an expert in natural history.

naturalize (also **naturalise**) VERB admit (a person of foreign birth) to full citizenship of a country; introduce and acclimatize (an animal or plant) into a region to which it is not native.
naturalization NOUN

naturally ADV **1** according to nature. **2** without affectation. **3** of course; as might be expected.

natural science NOUN a science studying the natural or physical world.

nature NOUN **1** the world with all its features and living things; the physical power producing these. **2** a thing's basic features and character, making it what it is; a person's character; a sort, a kind: *things of this nature.*

naturist NOUN a nudist.
naturism NOUN

naught PRON [ARCHAIC] nothing.

naughty ADJ (**naughtier, naughtiest**) **1** behaving badly, disobedient. **2** [INFORMAL] slightly indecent.

naughtily ADV
naughtiness NOUN

nausea NOUN a feeling of sickness; revulsion.

nauseate VERB affect with nausea.

nauseous ADJ causing nausea; suffering from nausea.

nautical ADJ of sailors or seamanship.

nautical mile NOUN a unit of 1,852 metres (approximately 2,025 yds).

nautilus NOUN (PL **nautiluses** or **nautili**) a mollusc with a spiral shell.

naval ADJ of a navy.

nave NOUN the main part of a church.

navel NOUN the small hollow in the abdomen where the umbilical cord was attached; the central point of a place.

navigable ADJ (of a river) suitable for boats to sail in.

navigate VERB **1** plan and direct the course of a ship, aircraft, etc.; travel along a planned course. **2** sail or travel over (water or land) or along (a route).
navigation NOUN
navigator NOUN

navvy /na-vee/ NOUN (PL **navvies**) [DATED] a labourer employed in building a canal, railway, or road.

navy /nay-vee/ NOUN (PL **navies**) **1** a country's warships; the people serving in a naval force. **2** (in full **navy blue**) very dark blue.

NB ABBREV note well (Latin *nota bene*).

NE ABBREV north-east; north-eastern.

Neapolitan NOUN a person from the city of Naples. ADJ relating to Naples.

neap tide NOUN the tide when there is least rise and fall of water.

near ADV **1** at, to, or within a short distance or interval. **2** almost. PREP **1** a short distance or time from. **2** on the verge of. ADJ **1** separated by only a short distance or time; closely related. **2** similar; close to being something specified: *a near disaster.* **3** on the side of a vehicle

normally nearer the kerb. VERB draw near.
nearness NOUN

nearby ADJ & ADV not far away.

nearly ADV **1** almost. **2** closely: *nearly related.*

neat ADJ **1** clean and orderly in appearance or workmanship; skilful. **2** undiluted. **3** [INFORMAL] excellent.
neatly ADV
neatness NOUN

neaten VERB make tidy.

nebula NOUN (PL **nebulae**) a cloud of gas or dust in space.
nebular ADJ

nebulous ADJ indistinct, having no definite form; vague.

necessarily ADV as a necessary result, inevitably.

necessary ADJ **1** required to be done or possessed, essential. **2** inevitable; existing or happening by natural or logical laws or by fate. NOUN (**necessaries**) essential items; (**the necessary**) [INFORMAL] what is required.

necessitate VERB make necessary; involve as a condition or result.

necessitous ADJ poor, needy.

necessity NOUN (PL **necessities**) **1** the state of being required or essential; something essential. **2** the state of being unavoidable; the principle by which something must be so according to logic or natural law.

neck NOUN the narrow part connecting the head to the body; the part of a garment round this; the narrow part of a bottle, cavity, etc.
neck and neck running level in a race.

necklace NOUN a piece of jewellery worn round the neck.

neckline NOUN the outline formed by the edge of a garment at the neck.

necromancy NOUN the supposed art of predicting the future by communicating with the dead.
necromancer NOUN

necrosis /ne-**kroh**-sis/ NOUN

death of bone or tissue.
necrotic ADJ

nectar NOUN a sweet fluid from plants, collected by bees; any delicious drink.

nectarine NOUN a kind of peach with a smooth shiny skin.

née /nay/ ADJ born (used in stating a married woman's maiden name).

need VERB **1** require (something) as essential, not as a luxury. **2** have to, be obliged or required to. NOUN **1** a situation in which something is needed; a thing needed. **2** lack of basic necessities, poverty.

needful ADJ [FORMAL] necessary.

needle NOUN a small thin pointed piece of steel used in sewing; something shaped like this; a pointer of a compass or gauge; the end of a hypodermic syringe. VERB [INFORMAL] annoy, provoke.

needless ADJ unnecessary.
needlessly ADV

needlework NOUN sewing or embroidery.

needy ADJ (**needier**, **neediest**) very poor.

nefarious ADJ wicked or criminal.

negate VERB **1** nullify, make ineffective. **2** make (a statement) negative. **3** deny the existence of.
negation NOUN

negative ADJ **1** expressing denial, refusal, or prohibition; (of the results of a test) indicating that a substance is not present. **2** (of a quantity) less than zero. **3** (of a battery terminal) through which electric current leaves. **4** not optimistic; harmful, not helpful. NOUN **1** a negative statement or word; a negative quality or quantity. **2** a photograph with lights and shades or colours reversed, from which positive pictures can be obtained.
negatively ADV
negativity NOUN

negative equity NOUN a situation in which the value of property falls below the debt outstanding on it.

negative pole NOUN the south-seeking pole of a magnet.

neglect VERB pay insufficient attention to; fail to take proper care of; fail to do something. NOUN the action of neglecting or the state of being neglected.
neglectful ADJ

negligee /neg-li-*zh*ay/ NOUN a woman's light flimsy dressing gown.

negligence NOUN lack of proper care or attention.
negligent ADJ
negligently ADV

negligible ADJ too small to be worth taking into account.

negotiate VERB **1** hold a discussion so as to reach agreement; arrange by such discussion. **2** get past (an obstacle) successfully.
negotiation NOUN
negotiator NOUN

Negress NOUN [OFFENSIVE] a woman or girl of black African origin.

Negro NOUN (PL **Negroes**) a member of a dark-skinned group of peoples that originated in Africa south of the Sahara.
Negroid ADJ

> The terms **Negro** and **Negress** are considered offensive; it is better to say **a black person.**

neigh NOUN a horse's long high-pitched cry.
VERB make this cry.

neighbour ([US] **neighbor**) NOUN a person living next or near to another; a thing situated near another.

neighbourhood ([US] **neighborhood**) NOUN a district.

neighbourhood watch NOUN systematic vigilance by residents to deter crime in their area.

neighbouring ([US] **neighboring**) ADJ situated nearby.

neighbourly ([US] **neighborly**) ADJ kind and friendly towards neighbours.
neighbourliness NOUN

neither DETERMINER & PRON not either. ADV used to

show that a negative statement is true of two things, or also true of something else.

nemesis /nem-i-sis/ NOUN downfall; punishment for arrogance.

neo- PREFIX new.

neoclassical ADJ of a style of art, music, etc. influenced by classical style.

neodymium NOUN a metallic element.

neolithic ADJ of the later part of the Stone Age.

neologism NOUN a new word.

neon NOUN a gas used in illuminated signs.

neonatal ADJ of the newly born.

neophyte /nee-o-fIt/ NOUN a new convert; a novice.

nephew NOUN one's brother's or sister's son.

nephritis /nef-rI-tis/ NOUN inflammation of the kidneys.

nepotism NOUN favouritism shown to relatives or friends in appointing them to jobs.

neptunium NOUN a radioactive metallic element.

nerd NOUN [INFORMAL] an unfashionable person, especially with an obsessive interest in a technical subject.

nerve NOUN **1** a fibre carrying impulses of sensation or movement between the brain and a part of the body. **2** (**nerves**) agitation, anxiety, nervousness. **3** courage and steadiness; [INFORMAL] impudence. **get on someone's nerves** [INFORMAL] irritate someone. **nerve oneself** gather one's strength and courage.

nervous ADJ **1** easily alarmed; slightly afraid or anxious. **2** of the nerves.
nervously ADV
nervousness NOUN

nervy ADJ (**nervier**, **nerviest**) easily alarmed; anxious.
nerviness NOUN

nest NOUN **1** a structure or place in which a bird lays eggs and shelters its young; a breeding place, a lair; a snug place. **2** a set of articles (especially tables) designed to fit inside each other. VERB **1** build or use a nest. **2** fit (an object) inside a larger one.

nest egg NOUN a sum of money saved for future use.

nestle VERB settle oneself comfortably; (of a place) lie in a sheltered and concealed position.

nestling NOUN a bird too young to leave the nest.

net¹ NOUN **1** open-meshed material of cord, wire, etc.; a piece of this for a particular purpose, e.g. catching fish. **2** (**Net**) the Internet. VERB (**nets**, **netting**, **netted**) catch in a net.

net² ADJ (also **nett**) remaining after all deductions; (of weight) not including wrappings etc. VERB (**nets**, **netting**, **netted**) obtain or yield as net profit.

netball NOUN a team game in which a ball has to be thrown into a high net.

nether ADJ lower.

netting NOUN open-meshed fabric.

nettle NOUN a wild plant with leaves that sting when touched. VERB irritate, provoke.

network NOUN an arrangement of intersecting lines; a complex system; a group of interconnected people or broadcasting stations, computers, etc.

networking NOUN interaction and exchange of ideas and information, as a business strategy or to further one's career.

neural ADJ of nerves.

neuralgia NOUN a sharp pain along a nerve. **neuralgic** ADJ

neural network NOUN a computer system modelled on the human brain and nervous system.

neuritis NOUN inflammation of a nerve.

neurology NOUN the study of nerve systems. **neurological** ADJ **neurologist** NOUN

neurosis NOUN (PL **neuroses**) a mental disorder producing depression or abnormal behaviour.

neurotic ADJ of or caused by a neurosis; subject to abnormal anxieties or obsessive behaviour. NOUN a neurotic person.
neurotically ADV

neuter ADJ **1** of a grammatical gender that is neither masculine nor feminine. **2** without developed sexual parts. NOUN **1** the neuter gender; a neuter word. **2** a castrated animal. VERB castrate (an animal).

neutral ADJ **1** not supporting either side in a conflict. **2** without distinctive or positive characteristics. NOUN **1** a neutral person, country, or colour. **2** (also **neutral gear**) a position of a gear mechanism in which the engine is disconnected from driven parts.
neutrality NOUN
neutrally ADV

neutralize (also **neutralise**) VERB make ineffective.
neutralization NOUN

neutrino /nyoo-tree-noh/ NOUN (PL **neutrinos**) an elementary particle with zero electric charge and probably zero mass.

neutron NOUN an elementary particle with no electric charge.

neutron bomb NOUN a nuclear bomb that kills people but does little damage to buildings etc.

never ADV **1** at no time, on no occasion. **2** not at all; [INFORMAL] surely not (expressing surprise or incredulity).
never mind do not worry.

nevermore ADV [LITERARY] at no future time.

nevertheless ADV in spite of this.

nevus US spelling of **NAEVUS**.

new ADJ **1** not existing before, made recently. **2** acquired, discovered, or experienced for the first time; unfamiliar; replacing a former one of the same kind. ADV newly, recently.
newness NOUN

New Age NOUN a set of beliefs replacing Western culture with alternative approaches to religion, medicine, the environment, etc.

newcomer NOUN a person who has arrived recently.

newel NOUN the top or bottom post of the handrail of a stair; the central pillar of a winding stair.

newfangled ADJ objectionably new in method or style.

newly ADV recently, freshly.

newly-wed NOUN a recently married person.

new man NOUN a man who rejects traditional male attitudes and supports women's liberation, shares household chores, etc.

new moon NOUN the moon seen as a crescent.

news NOUN new or interesting information about recent events; a broadcast report of this. **be good news** [INFORMAL] be an asset, be welcome.

newsagent NOUN a shopkeeper who sells newspapers.

newscaster NOUN a newsreader.

newsflash NOUN an item of important news, broadcast as an interruption to another programme.

newsgroup NOUN a group of Internet users exchanging messages about a shared interest.

newsletter NOUN a bulletin issued periodically to members of a society etc.

newspaper NOUN a printed daily or weekly publication containing news reports; the paper forming this.

newsprint NOUN cheap, low-quality paper on which newspapers are printed.

newsreader NOUN a person who reads broadcast news reports.

newsworthy ADJ important or interesting enough to report as news.
newsworthiness NOUN

newt NOUN a small lizard-like amphibious creature.

New Testament *see* **TESTAMENT**.

newton NOUN [PHYSICS] a

unit of force.

new year NOUN the first days of January.

New Year's Day 1 Jan.

next ADJ nearest in position or time; soonest come to. ADV immediately afterwards; on the next occasion; following in a scale: *next tallest.* NOUN the next person or thing.
next to 1 beside. **2** in comparison with. **3** apart from: *the quickest way next to flying.* **4** almost: *next to nothing.*

next door ADV in or to the next house or room. ADJ living next door.

n

next of kin NOUN one's closest relative(s).

nexus NOUN (PL **nexus** or **nexuses**) a link, a connection; a connected group; the central or most important point.

NGO ABBREV non-governmental organization.

NHS ABBREV National Health Service.

niacin NOUN = **NICOTINIC ACID**.

nib NOUN the metal point of a pen.

nibble VERB take small quick or gentle bites (at). NOUN a small quick bite; (**nibbles**) [INFORMAL] small snacks.
nibbler NOUN

Nicam NOUN [TRADE MARK] a digital system used in Britain to produce high-quality stereo television sound.

nice ADJ **1** pleasant, satisfactory. **2** subtle, precise: *a nice distinction;* [ARCHAIC] fastidious.
nicely ADV
niceness NOUN

nicety NOUN (PL **niceties**) a fine detail; precision.
to a nicety exactly.

niche /neesh/ NOUN **1** a shallow recess especially in a wall. **2** a suitable or advantageous position in life or employment.

nick NOUN **1** a small cut or notch. **2** [INFORMAL] prison. VERB **1** make a nick in. **2** [INFORMAL] steal; arrest.
in good nick [INFORMAL] in good condition. **in the nick of time** only just in time.

nickel NOUN **1** a silver-white metallic element used in alloys. **2** [US]

[INFORMAL] a 5-cent piece.

nickelodeon NOUN [US] [INFORMAL] a jukebox.

nickname NOUN a familiar or humorous name given to a person or thing instead of the real name. VERB give a nickname to.

nicotine NOUN a poisonous substance found in tobacco.

nicotinic acid NOUN a vitamin of the B complex.

niece NOUN one's brother's or sister's daughter.

niggardly ADJ stingy; meagre.
niggard NOUN

nigger NOUN [OFFENSIVE] a black person.

niggle VERB cause slight but persistent discomfort; find fault with details.

nigh [ARCHAIC] ADV & PREP near.

night NOUN the period of darkness between sunset and sunrise; the onset of this, nightfall; the late evening.

nightcap NOUN an alcoholic or hot drink taken at bedtime.

nightclub NOUN a club open at night, providing refreshment and entertainment.

nightdress NOUN a woman's or child's loose garment worn in bed.

nightfall NOUN the onset of night.

nightgown NOUN a nightdress.

nightie NOUN [INFORMAL] a nightdress.

nightingale NOUN a small thrush, the male of which sings melodiously.

nightjar NOUN a night-flying bird with a harsh cry.

nightlife NOUN entertainment available in public places at night.

nightly ADJ & ADV happening at night or every night.

nightmare NOUN a frightening dream; a very unpleasant experience.
nightmarish ADJ

night school NOUN instruction or education provided in the evening.

nightshade NOUN a plant with poisonous berries.

nightshirt NOUN a long shirt worn in bed.

nightspot NOUN [INFORMAL] a nightclub.

nihilism /nI-il-iz-ĕm/ NOUN rejection of all religious and moral principles.
nihilist NOUN
nihilistic ADJ

nil NOUN nothing; zero.

nimble ADJ able to move quickly.
nimbly ADV

nimbus NOUN (PL **nimbi** or **nimbuses**) **1** a halo. **2** a rain cloud.

nincompoop NOUN a foolish person.

nine ADJ & NOUN one more than eight (9, IX).
ninth ADJ & NOUN

ninepins NOUN a game of skittles played with nine objects.

nineteen ADJ & NOUN one more than eighteen (19, XIX).
nineteenth ADJ & NOUN

ninety ADJ & NOUN nine times ten (90, XC).
ninetieth ADJ & NOUN

ninny NOUN (PL **ninnies**) [INFORMAL] a foolish person.

niobium NOUN a metallic element.

nip VERB (**nips, nipping, nipped**) **1** pinch or squeeze sharply; bite quickly with the front teeth. **2** [INFORMAL] go quickly. NOUN **1** a sharp pinch, squeeze, or bite. **2** a sharp coldness. **3** a small drink of spirits.

nipple NOUN the small projection at the centre of a breast; the teat of a feeding bottle.

nippy ADJ (**nippier, nippiest**) [INFORMAL] **1** nimble, quick. **2** (of the weather) cold.

nirvana /neer-**vah**-nă/ NOUN (in Buddhism and Hinduism) a state of perfect bliss achieved by the soul.

Nissen hut NOUN a tunnel-shaped hut of corrugated iron.

nit NOUN an egg of a louse or similar parasite.

nit-picking NOUN [INFORMAL] petty fault-finding.

nitrate NOUN a substance formed from nitric acid, especially used as a fertilizer.

nitric acid NOUN a corrosive acid containing nitrogen.

nitrogen NOUN a gas forming about four-fifths of the atmosphere.

nitroglycerine (also **nitroglycerin**) NOUN a powerful explosive.

nitrous oxide NOUN a gas used as an anaesthetic.

nitty-gritty NOUN [INFORMAL] the basic facts or realities of a matter.

nitwit NOUN [INFORMAL] a stupid or foolish person.

No. (also **no.**) ABBREV number.

no DETERMINER not any. EXCLAMATION used as a denial or refusal of something. ADV not at all. NOUN (PL **noes**) a decision or vote against something.

nobble VERB [INFORMAL] **1** try to influence unfairly. **2** obtain dishonestly.

nobelium NOUN a radioactive metallic element.

nobility NOUN (PL **nobilities**) **1** high character. **2** high rank; titled people.

noble ADJ **1** belonging to the aristocracy. **2** having excellent moral qualities; generous, not petty. **3** grand, imposing. NOUN a member of the aristocracy.
nobleness NOUN
nobly ADV

nobleman (also **noblewoman**) NOUN a member of the nobility.

noblesse NOUN nobility.
noblesse oblige /noh-bless o-**bleez*h***/ privilege entails responsibility.

nobody PRON no person. NOUN (PL **nobodies**) a person of no importance.

nocturnal ADJ of, happening in, or active in the night.
nocturnally ADV

nocturne /**nok**-tern/ NOUN a short romantic piece of music.

nod VERB (**nods**, **nodding**, **nodded**) **1** move the head down and up quickly; indicate (agreement or casual greeting) in this way; (of flowers) bend and sway. **2** let the head droop from drowsiness; make a mistake through lack of concentration. NOUN a nodding movement, especially as a sign of agreement.

nod off [INFORMAL] fall asleep.

node NOUN **1** a point in a network where lines intersect. **2** a point on a stem where a leaf or bud grows out. **3** [ANATOMY] a small mass of tissue.
nodal ADJ

nodule NOUN a small rounded lump, a small node.
nodular ADJ

no-fly zone NOUN an area in which specified aircraft are forbidden to fly.

noggin NOUN a small alcoholic drink.

no-go area NOUN an area to which entry is forbidden or restricted.

noise NOUN **1** a sound, especially a loud, unpleasant, or disturbing one. **2** fluctuations accompanying and obscuring an electrical signal.
noiseless ADJ

noisome ADJ [LITERARY] evil-smelling; disgusting.

noisy ADJ (**noisier**, **noisiest**) making much noise; full of noise.
noisily ADV
noisiness NOUN

nomad NOUN a member of a tribe that roams seeking pasture for its animals; a wanderer.
nomadic ADJ

no-man's-land NOUN disputed ground between opposing armies; unowned land.

nom de plume NOUN (PL **noms de plume**) a writer's pseudonym.

nomenclature NOUN the devising of a system of names, e.g. in a science.

nominal ADJ **1** existing in name only. **2** (of a fee) very small. **3** of names.
nominally ADV

nominal value NOUN the face value of a coin etc.

nominate VERB name as candidate for or the future holder of an office; appoint as a place or date.
nomination NOUN
nominator NOUN

nominative NOUN the grammatical case expressing the subject of a verb.

nominee NOUN a person nominated.

non- PREFIX not; an absence of.

nonagenarian /noh-nă-gĕn-air-ee-ăn/ NOUN a person in his or her nineties.

non-aligned ADJ not in alliance with another power.

nonchalant /non-shă-lănt/ ADJ calm and casual.
nonchalance NOUN
nonchalantly ADV

non-committal ADJ not expressing a definite opinion or commitment to a course of action.
non-committally ADV

nonconformist NOUN a person not conforming to established practices; (**Nonconformist**) a member of a Protestant sect not conforming to Anglican practices.

non-contributory ADJ (of a pension) funded by payments by the employer, not the employee; (of a benefit) paid to eligible people regardless of how much tax they have paid.

nondescript ADJ lacking distinctive characteristics.

none PRON not any; no person. ADV to no extent, not at all: *none the worse*.
none too not at all.

nonentity NOUN (PL **nonentities**) an unimportant or uninteresting person.

non-event NOUN an event that was expected to be important or exciting but proves disappointing.

non-existent ADJ not existing.
non-existence NOUN

nonplussed ADJ surprised and confused.

nonsense NOUN words put together in a way that does not make sense; foolish talk, ideas, or behaviour.
nonsensical ADJ

non sequitur NOUN a statement or conclusion that does not follow from the previous statement or argument.

non-starter NOUN a horse entered for a race but not running in it; [INFORMAL] a person or idea with no chance of success.

non-stop ADJ & ADV not ceasing; (of a train etc.) not stopping at places on the way to its destination.

noodles PLURAL NOUN pasta in narrow strips.

nook NOUN a secluded place; a recess.

noon NOUN twelve o'clock in the day.

no one NOUN no person, nobody.

noose NOUN a loop of rope etc. with a knot that tightens when pulled.

nor CONJ and not; and not either: *neither cheap nor convenient.*

n

norm NOUN a standard type; usual behaviour.

normal ADJ conforming to what is standard or usual; free from mental or emotional disorders.
normality NOUN
normally ADV

north NOUN the point or direction to the left of a person facing east; a northern part or region. ADJ & ADV in or towards the north; (of wind) from the north.

north-east NOUN the direction or region halfway between north and east. ADJ & ADV in or towards the north-east; (of a wind) blowing from the north-east.
north-easterly NOUN & ADJ
north-eastern ADJ

northerly ADJ towards or blowing from the north.

northern ADJ of or in the north.

northerner NOUN a person from the north.

northernmost ADJ furthest north.

northward ADJ towards the north.
northwards ADV

north-west NOUN the direction or region halfway between north and west. ADJ & ADV in or towards the north-west; (of a wind) blowing from the north-west.
north-westerly NOUN & ADJ
north-western ADJ

Norwegian NOUN a person from Norway; the language of Norway. ADJ relating to Norway.

Nos. (also **nos.**) ABBREV numbers.

nose NOUN **1** the organ at

the front of the head, used in breathing and smelling; the sense of smell; a talent for detecting something. **2** the front end of an aircraft, car, etc. VERB **1** push the nose against something; sniff (something). **2** investigate, pry. **3** move forward slowly or cautiously.

nosebag NOUN a bag of fodder hung from a horse's head to allow it to eat at will.

nosedive NOUN a steep downward plunge, especially of an aeroplane. VERB make this plunge.

nosh [INFORMAL] NOUN food. VERB eat.

nostalgia NOUN sentimental memory of or longing for things of the past.
nostalgic ADJ
nostalgically ADV

nostril NOUN either of the two external openings in the nose.

nostrum NOUN a remedy prepared by someone unqualified; a pet scheme.

nosy ADJ (**nosier, nosiest**) [INFORMAL] inquisitive, prying.
nosily ADV
nosiness NOUN

not ADV expressing a negative, denial, or refusal.
not at all 1 definitely not. **2** a polite response to thanks.

notable ADJ worthy of notice; remarkable, eminent. NOUN an eminent person.
notably ADV

notary (in full **notary public**) NOUN (PL **notaries**) an official authorized to witness the signing of documents, perform formal transactions, etc.

notation NOUN a system of signs or symbols representing numbers, quantities, musical notes, etc.

notch NOUN **1** a V-shaped cut or indentation. **2** a degree on a scale: *a few notches higher.* VERB make a notch in.
notch up score, achieve.

note NOUN **1** a brief record written down to aid

n

memory; a short or informal letter; a short written comment. **2** a banknote. **3** a musical tone of definite pitch; a symbol representing the pitch and duration of a musical sound; each of the keys on a piano etc. **4** a quality or tone expressing a mood: *a note of anger.* **5** importance, significance. VERB **1** notice; remark on. **2** write down.

notebook NOUN a book with blank pages on which to write notes.

notecase NOUN a wallet for banknotes.

noted ADJ famous, well known.

notelet NOUN a small folded card for a short informal letter.

notepaper NOUN paper for writing letters on.

noteworthy ADJ worthy of notice, remarkable.

nothing NOUN not anything; something unimportant; nought, no amount. ADV not at all: *cared nothing for it.*
for nothing 1 for no payment, at no cost. **2** achieving nothing.
nothing for it no alternative.

notice NOUN **1** attention, observation. **2** information or warning that something is going to happen; the formal announcement of the termination of a job or an agreement. **3** a placard or sheet displayed to give information. **4** a review in a newspaper.
VERB become aware of.
take notice show interest. **take no notice (of)** pay no attention (to).

noticeable ADJ conspicuous, easily noticed.
noticeably ADV

notifiable ADJ (of a disease etc.) having to be reported to authorities.

notify VERB (**notifies, notifying, notified**) inform (someone) of an intention etc.; report.
notification NOUN

notion NOUN **1** a belief, an idea; a concept. **2** an impulse or desire.

notional ADJ hypothetical.
notionally ADV

notorious ADJ famous,

especially for something bad.
notoriety NOUN
notoriously ADV

notwithstanding PREP in spite of. ADV nevertheless.

nougat /**noo**-gah/ NOUN a chewy sweet.

nought NOUN the figure 0; nothing.

noun NOUN a word used as the name of a person, place, or thing.

nourish VERB feed so as to keep alive and healthy; cherish (a feeling).

nourishment NOUN food necessary for life and growth.

nous /nowss/ NOUN [INFORMAL] common sense.

nouveau riche /noo-voh **reesh**/ NOUN people who have become rich recently and make a display of it.

nouvelle cuisine /noo-vel kwi-**zeen**/ NOUN a style of cooking avoiding heavy foods and emphasizing high quality.

nova NOUN (PL **novae** or **novas**) a star that suddenly becomes much brighter for a short time.

novel NOUN a book-length story. ADJ new, unusual.

novelette NOUN a short (especially romantic) novel.

novelist NOUN a writer of novels.

novelty NOUN (PL **novelties**) **1** the quality of being new, unusual, or original. **2** a small toy or ornament.

November NOUN the eleventh month.

novice NOUN a person new to and inexperienced in an activity; a probationary member of a religious order.

now ADV **1** at the present time; immediately. **2** (with no reference to time) used to draw attention to a point or request: *now why didn't I think of that?* CONJ once or because something has happened: *now you're here, let's start.*
for now for the moment, until later. **now and again, now and then** occasionally.

nowadays ADV in present

n

times.

nowhere ADV not anywhere.

noxious ADJ unpleasant and harmful.

nozzle NOUN the vent or spout of a hosepipe etc.

nuance /nyoo-ahns/ NOUN a subtle difference in meaning.

nub NOUN **1** the central or crucial point of a problem. **2** a small lump.

nubile ADJ (of a young woman) sexually mature; sexually attractive.
nubility NOUN

n

nuclear ADJ of a nucleus; of the nuclei of atoms; using energy released in nuclear fission or fusion; possessing or involving nuclear weapons.

nuclear family NOUN (PL **nuclear families**) a couple and their children as a basic social unit.

nucleic acid NOUN either of two complex organic molecules (DNA or RNA) present in all living cells.

nucleon NOUN a proton or neutron.

nucleus NOUN (PL **nuclei**) the central part or thing round which others are collected; the central portion of an atom, seed, or cell.

nude ADJ naked. NOUN a naked figure in a picture etc.
nudity NOUN

nudge VERB poke gently with the elbow to attract attention quietly; push slightly or gradually. NOUN a slight push or poke.

nudist NOUN a person who believes that going unclothed is good for the health.
nudism NOUN

nugget NOUN a rough lump of gold or platinum found in the earth.

nuisance NOUN an annoying person or thing.

nuke VERB [INFORMAL] attack with nuclear weapons.

null ADJ **1** having no legal force. **2** having the value zero.

nullify VERB (**nullifies**, **nullifying**, **nullified**) make legally null; make ineffective, cancel out.
nullification NOUN

numb ADJ deprived of the power of feeling.

VERB make numb.
numbness NOUN

number NOUN **1** a symbol or word indicating quantity, used in calculation and counting; a quantity. **2** a single issue of a magazine; an item in a performance; [INFORMAL] something such as an item of clothing. VERB **1** amount to (a specified number). **2** mark with a number, assign a number to. **3** include as a member of a group.
a number of several.

numberless ADJ too many to count.

number one NOUN the most important person or thing; [INFORMAL] oneself.

number plate NOUN a plate on a motor vehicle, bearing its registration number.

numeral NOUN a symbol representing a number.

numerate ADJ having a good basic understanding of mathematics and science.
numeracy NOUN

numerator NOUN the number above the line in a vulgar fraction.

numerical ADJ of a number or series of numbers.
numerically ADV

numerous ADJ great in number.

numismatics /nyoo-miz-ma-tiks/ NOUN the study of coins and medals.

nun NOUN a member of a female religious community.

nuncio /nun-see-oh/ NOUN (PL **nuncios**) a representative of the Pope.

nunnery NOUN (PL **nunneries**) a residence of a community of nuns.

nuptial ADJ of marriage or a wedding. NOUN (**nuptials**) a wedding ceremony.

nurse NOUN **1** a person trained to look after sick or injured people. **2** [DATED] a person employed to take charge of young children. VERB **1** work as a nurse; act as nurse (to). **2** feed or be fed at the breast or udder. **3** hold carefully; give special care to; harbour (a belief or feeling).

nursery NOUN (PL **nurseries**) **1** a room for young children. **2** a place where plants are reared for sale.

nurseryman (also **nurserywoman**) NOUN a person growing plants at a nursery.

nursery rhyme NOUN a traditional verse for children.

nursery school NOUN a school for children below normal school age.

nursing home NOUN a privately run hospital or home for invalids, especially elderly ones.

n

nurture VERB care for and promote the growth or development of; cherish (a hope, belief, etc.). NOUN the state of being nurtured; upbringing and environment as an influence on character.

nut NOUN **1** a fruit with a hard shell round an edible kernel; this kernel. **2** a small metal ring with a threaded hole, for use with a bolt as a fastening. **3** [INFORMAL] the head. **4** [INFORMAL] a mad or fanatical person.
ADJ (**nuts**) [INFORMAL] crazy.

nutcase NOUN [INFORMAL] a crazy person.

nuthatch NOUN a small climbing bird.

nutmeg NOUN a spice.

nutrient NOUN a nourishing substance.

nutriment NOUN nourishing food.

nutrition NOUN the provision of food for nourishment; the process of taking nourishment; the study of nutrients and nourishment.
nutritional ADJ
nutritionally ADV

nutritious ADJ nourishing.

nutshell NOUN the hard shell of a nut.
in a nutshell expressed very briefly.

nutty ADJ (**nuttier**, **nuttiest**) **1** full of nuts; tasting like nuts. **2** [INFORMAL] crazy.

nuzzle VERB press or rub gently with the nose.

NVQ ABBREV National Vocational Qualification.

NW ABBREV north-west; north-western.

nylon NOUN a very light

strong synthetic fibre.

nymph NOUN **1** a mythological semi-divine maiden. **2** a young insect.

nymphomania NOUN excessive sexual desire in a woman.

nymphomaniac NOUN

Oo

O (also **o**) NOUN (PL **Os** or **O's**) **1** the fifteenth letter of the alphabet. **2** zero.

oaf NOUN a stupid or clumsy person.
oafish ADJ

oak NOUN a deciduous forest tree bearing acorns; its hard wood.
oaken ADJ

oak apple NOUN a growth on oak trees formed by the larvae of wasps.

OAP ABBREV old-age pensioner.

oar NOUN a pole with a flat blade used to row a boat.

oasis NOUN (PL **oases**) **1** a fertile spot in a desert where there is water. **2** a peaceful area or period in the midst of uproar, violence, etc.

oast house NOUN a building containing a kiln for drying hops.

oat NOUN a hardy cereal plant; (**oats**) its grain.

oatcake NOUN a biscuit made of oatmeal.

oath NOUN **1** a solemn promise. **2** a swear word.

oatmeal NOUN **1** ground oats. **2** a greyish-fawn colour.

obdurate ADJ stubborn.
obduracy NOUN
obdurately ADV

OBE ABBREV Order of the British Empire.

obedient ADJ doing what one is told to do.
obedience NOUN
obediently ADV

obeisance /o-bay-săns/ NOUN respect; a bow or curtsy.

obelisk NOUN a tall pillar set up as a monument.

obese ADJ very fat.
obesity NOUN

obey VERB carry out the orders of; act in accordance with (a law etc.).

obfuscate VERB make obscure or unclear.
obfuscation NOUN

obituary NOUN (PL **obituaries**) an announcement of someone's death, often with a short biography.

object NOUN /**ob**-jekt/ **1** something solid that can be seen or touched. **2** a person or thing to which an action or feeling is directed; [GRAMMAR] a noun governed by a transitive verb or a preposition. **3** a goal or purpose. VERB /ob-**jekt**/ express disapproval or disagreement; protest.
no object not influencing or restricting decisions.
objector NOUN

objection NOUN disapproval, opposition; a statement of this; a reason for objecting.

objectionable ADJ unpleasant.
objectionably ADV

objective ADJ **1** not influenced by personal feelings or opinions; actual, not dependent on the mind for existence. **2** [GRAMMAR] of the form of a word used when it is the object of a verb or preposition. NOUN the thing one is trying to achieve, reach, or capture.
objectively ADV
objectiveness NOUN
objectivity NOUN

object lesson NOUN a striking practical example of a principle.

objet d'art /ob-*zh*ay **dar**/ NOUN (PL **objets d'art**) a small decorative or artistic object.

oblation NOUN an offering made to God.

obligate VERB oblige.

obligation NOUN **1** a duty, something to which one is legally or morally bound; the state of being obliged to do something. **2** the state of being indebted for a favour.

obligatory ADJ compulsory, not optional.

oblige VERB **1** require to do something; make legally or morally bound. **2** please or help (someone) by doing as they wish.

obliged ADJ grateful; indebted.

obliging ADJ polite and helpful.
obligingly ADV

oblique /o-bleek/ ADJ 1 slanting, neither parallel nor at right angles. 2 not explicit or direct.
obliquely

obliterate VERB blot out, destroy.
obliteration NOUN

oblivion NOUN the state of being forgotten; the state of being unconscious or unaware.

oblivious ADJ unaware.
obliviously ADV

oblong ADJ rectangular in shape. NOUN an oblong shape.

obloquy /ob-lŏ-kwee/ NOUN criticism, verbal abuse.

obnoxious ADJ very unpleasant.
obnoxiously ADV

oboe NOUN a woodwind instrument of treble pitch, with a double reed.
oboist NOUN

obscene ADJ offensive in its treatment of sexual matters; offending against moral principles; repugnant.
obscenely ADV

obscenity NOUN (PL **obscenities**) the state of being obscene; an obscene word or action.

obscure ADJ not known about, uncertain; not easily understood; not important or well known; not easy to perceive distinctly. VERB conceal; make unclear.
obscurely ADV
obscurity NOUN

obsequies /ob-si-quiz/ PLURAL NOUN funeral rites.

obsequious ADJ excessively respectful, servile.
obsequiously ADV

observance NOUN the keeping of a law, custom, or festival.

observant ADJ quick to notice things.
observantly ADV

observation NOUN 1 the action of watching carefully; the ability to notice significant details. 2 a remark.
under observation being

watched.
observational ADJ

observatory NOUN (PL **observatories**) a building equipped for the observation of stars or weather.

observe VERB **1** perceive; watch carefully; pay attention to. **2** make a remark. **3** comply with (a rule etc.); celebrate (a festival).
observable ADJ
observer NOUN

obsess VERB occupy the thoughts of (someone) continually.

obsession NOUN the state of being obsessed; a persistent idea.
obsessional ADJ
obsessive ADJ
obsessively ADV

obsolescent ADJ becoming obsolete.
obsolescence NOUN

obsolete ADJ out of date, no longer used or of use.

obstacle NOUN something that obstructs progress.

obstetrics NOUN the branch of medicine and surgery dealing with childbirth.
obstetric ADJ
obstetrician NOUN

obstinate ADJ not changing one's mind under pressure or persuasion; (of a problem) hard to overcome or get rid of.
obstinacy NOUN
obstinately ADV

obstreperous ADJ noisy, unruly.
obstreperously ADV
obstreperousness NOUN

obstruct VERB block; hinder the movement or progress of.
obstruction NOUN
obstructive ADJ

obtain VERB **1** get, come into possession of. **2** [FORMAL] be customary or prevalent.
obtainable ADJ

obtrude VERB **1** be annoyingly noticeable, intrude. **2** force (something unwanted) on someone.
obtrusion NOUN

obtrusive ADJ obtruding oneself, unpleasantly noticeable.
obtrusively ADV
obtrusiveness NOUN

obtuse ADJ **1** blunt in

shape; (of an angle) more than 90° but less than 180°. **2** slow at understanding.
obtusely ADV
obtuseness NOUN

obverse NOUN the side of a coin bearing a head or the principal design; an opposite or counterpart.

obviate VERB do away with (a need or problem).

obvious ADJ easy to perceive or understand, self-evident; (of a remark or action) naturally chosen, predictable.
obviously ADV
obviousness NOUN

ocarina NOUN an egg-shaped wind instrument.

occasion NOUN **1** the time at which an event takes place; a special event; a suitable time or opportunity. **2** [FORMAL] a reason or cause. VERB [FORMAL] cause.

occasional ADJ **1** happening sometimes but not frequently. **2** for a particular occasion.
occasionally ADV

occidental ADJ relating to the countries of the West.

occlude VERB stop up, obstruct.
occlusion NOUN

occluded front NOUN an upward movement of a mass of warm air caused by a cold front overtaking it, producing prolonged rainfall.

occult ADJ **1** of supernatural powers or magical practices. **2** secret, known to few.

occupant NOUN a person occupying a place or dwelling.
occupancy NOUN

occupation NOUN **1** a job or profession; a way of spending time. **2** the occupying of a place.

occupational ADJ of or caused by one's employment.

occupational therapy NOUN activities designed to assist recovery from illness or injury.

occupy VERB (**occupies**, **occupying**, **occupied**) **1** be in, live in; fill (a place or space). **2** take control of (a country) by force. **3** keep busy; fill (the mind or thoughts).
occupier NOUN

occur VERB (**occurs**, **occurring**, **occurred**) **1** happen. **2** exist in a particular place.
occur to be thought of by.

occurrence NOUN an incident or event; the fact of something happening or existing; the frequency with which something occurs.

ocean NOUN the sea surrounding the continents of the earth.
oceanic ADJ

oceanography NOUN the study of the ocean.

ochre /oh-kĕ/ ([US] **ocher**) NOUN a type of yellow, red, or brown earth, used as a pigment.

o'clock ADV used in specifying an hour.

octagon NOUN a geometric figure with eight sides.
octagonal ADJ

octahedron NOUN a solid with eight sides.
octahedral ADJ

octane NOUN a hydrocarbon occurring in petrol.

octave NOUN the interval of eight notes between one musical note and the next note of the same name above or below it.

octavo NOUN (PL **octavos**) the size of a book formed by folding a standard sheet three times to form eight leaves.

octet NOUN a group of eight voices or instruments; music for these.

October NOUN the tenth month.

octogenarian NOUN a person in his or her eighties.

octopus NOUN (PL **octopuses**) a sea animal with eight tentacles.

ocular ADJ of, for, or by the eyes.

oculist NOUN a specialist in the treatment of eye disorders and defects.

OD VERB (**OD's**, **OD'ing**, **OD'd**) [INFORMAL] take an overdose of a drug.

odd ADJ **1** unusual, unexpected, strange. **2** (of a number) not exactly divisible by two. **3** occasional, happening rarely. **4** separated from or not part of a set or

pair.
oddly ADV
oddness NOUN

oddity NOUN (PL **oddities**) an unusual person or thing; the quality of being strange.

oddment NOUN an isolated piece or item left over from a larger set.

odds PLURAL NOUN the ratio between the amounts staked by the parties to a bet; the likelihood of something's happening.
at odds with in conflict with. **odds and ends** oddments.

odds-on ADJ with success more likely than failure.

O

ode NOUN a poem addressed to a person or celebrating an event.

odious ADJ hateful.
odiously ADV

odium NOUN widespread hatred or disgust.

odometer NOUN a milometer.

odoriferous /oh-dŏ-**rif**-ĕ-rŭs/ ADJ giving off a smell.

odour ([US] **odor**) NOUN a smell.
in good (or **bad**) **odour** [INFORMAL] in (or out of) favour.
odorous ADJ

odyssey NOUN (PL **odysseys**) a long adventurous journey.

OECD ABBREV Organization for Economic Cooperation and Development.

oedema /i-dee-mă/ ([US] **edema**) NOUN excess fluid in tissues, causing swelling.

oesophagus /i-sof-ă-gŭs/ ([US] **esophagus**) NOUN the tube from the mouth to the stomach.

oestrogen /ee-strŏ-jĕn/ ([US] **estrogen**) NOUN a sex hormone responsible for controlling female bodily characteristics.

of PREP **1** belonging to. **2** helping to form: *part of the body;* made up from: *a group of people.* **3** done, made, etc., by: *the decision of the committee;* done to: *the murder of the boys.* **4** consisting in, equivalent to. **5** expressing direction: *north of the river.* **6** concerning, involving.

off ADV **1** away; so as to be removed or separated:

took off his coat. **2** not at work, absent; cancelled; unavailable. **3** so as to come or bring to an end: *finish off the work.* **4** not functioning, so as to cease functioning. PREP **1** moving away from; leading away from. **2** [INFORMAL] having a temporary dislike for: *off my food.* ADJ **1** characterized by bad performance: *an off day.* **2** (of food) starting to decay. **3** [INFORMAL] unfair, annoying. **4** unwell. **5** of the side of a vehicle furthest from the kerb.
on the off chance just in case.

offal NOUN the edible organs from an animal carcass.

offbeat ADJ [INFORMAL] unusual, unconventional.

off-colour ADJ **1** unwell. **2** slightly indecent.

offcut NOUN a piece of waste material left after cutting off a larger piece.

offence ([US] **offense**) NOUN **1** an illegal act. **2** a feeling of annoyance or resentment.

offend VERB **1** cause to feel indignant or hurt. **2** commit an illegal act.
offender NOUN

offensive ADJ **1** causing offence, insulting; disgusting. **2** used in attacking. NOUN an aggressive action; a campaign.
offensively ADV
offensiveness NOUN

offer VERB present for acceptance or refusal, or for consideration or use; state what one is willing to do, pay, or give; show an intention. NOUN an expression of willingness to do, give, or pay something; an amount offered; a reduction in the price of goods.

offering NOUN a gift; a contribution.

offertory NOUN (PL **offertories**) **1** the offering of bread and wine at the Eucharist. **2** a collection of money at a religious service.

offhand ADJ unceremonious, casual. ADV unceremoniously, casually.

office NOUN **1** a room or building used for clerical

and similar work. **2** a position of authority or trust; tenure of an official position.

officer NOUN **1** a person holding authority in the armed forces; a policeman. **2** a holder of a public office.

official ADJ of or authorized by a public body or authority; formally approved. NOUN a person holding public office.
officially ADV

officialese NOUN [INFORMAL] formal, verbose, and obscure language seen as typical of official documents.

officiate VERB act as an official in charge of an event; perform a religious ceremony.

officious ADJ asserting one's authority, bossy.
officiously ADV
officiousness NOUN

off-licence NOUN a shop with a licence to sell alcohol for consumption away from the premises.

offload VERB unload.

off-putting ADJ repellent; discouraging.

offset VERB (**offsets**, **offsetting**, **offset**) **1** counterbalance, compensate for. **2** place out of line.
NOUN **1** something counterbalancing something else. **2** the amount by which something is out of line. **3** a method of printing using an inked rubber surface.

offshoot NOUN a side shoot on a plant; something that has developed from something else.

offshore ADJ at sea some distance from land; (of wind) blowing from the land to the sea.

offside ADJ & ADV (in football etc.) in a position where one may not legally play the ball.

offspring NOUN (PL **offspring**) a person's child or children; an animal's young.

off-white ADJ not quite pure white.

often ADV many times, frequently; in many cases.

ogee /**oh**-jee/ NOUN a double continuous curve as in an S.

ogle VERB look lustfully at.

ogre NOUN a man-eating giant in fairy tales; a terrifying person.

oh EXCLAMATION an exclamation of surprise, delight, or pain, or used for emphasis.

ohm NOUN a unit of electrical resistance.

OHP ABBREV overhead projector.

oil NOUN **1** a thick slippery liquid that will not dissolve in water. **2** petroleum; a thick liquid derived from it. **3** an oil painting; (**oils**) oil paints. VERB lubricate or treat with oil.
oily ADJ

oilfield NOUN an area where mineral oil is found in the ground.

oil paint NOUN paint made by mixing pigment in oil.
oil painting NOUN

oil rig NOUN a structure for drilling and extracting mineral oil.

oilskin NOUN cloth waterproofed by treatment with oil; (**oilskins**) waterproof clothing made of this.

ointment NOUN a cream rubbed on the skin to heal injuries etc.

OK (also **okay**) ADJ & ADV [INFORMAL] all right.

old ADJ **1** having lived or existed for a long time or a specified time; worn and shabby with age. **2** of an earlier time, former.

old age NOUN the later part of life.

old-fashioned ADJ no longer fashionable.

Old Testament *see* **TESTAMENT**.

old wives' tale NOUN a traditional but unfounded belief.

oleaginous /oh-lee-**aj**-i-nŭs/ ADJ producing or covered in oil; unpleasantly complimentary, obsequious.

O level NOUN = **ORDINARY LEVEL**.

olfactory ADJ concerned with the sense of smell.

oligarchy NOUN government by a small

group; a country governed in this way.
oligarch NOUN
oligarchic ADJ

olive NOUN **1** a small oval fruit from which an oil **olive oil** is obtained; a tree bearing this. **2** a greenish colour. ADJ of this colour; (of the skin) yellowish brown.

olive branch NOUN something done or offered to show one's desire to make peace.

ombudsman /om-buudz-măn/ NOUN an official appointed to investigate people's complaints about maladministration by public authorities.

omega NOUN the last letter of the Greek alphabet (Ω, ω).

omelette NOUN a dish of beaten eggs cooked in a frying pan.

omen NOUN an event regarded as a prophetic sign.

ominous ADJ threatening, suggesting that trouble is imminent.
ominously ADV

omit VERB (**omits**, **omitting**, **omitted**) leave out, not include; neglect (to do something).
omission NOUN

omnibus NOUN **1** a volume containing several works originally published separately. **2** [DATED] a bus.

omnipotent ADJ having unlimited or very great power.
omnipotence NOUN

omnipresent ADJ present everywhere.
omnipresence NOUN

omniscient ADJ knowing everything.
omniscience NOUN

omnivorous ADJ feeding on both plants and animals.

on PREP **1** attached to and supported by, on top of; moving to the surface of: *put it on the table;* coming into contact with: *hit his head on the ceiling.* **2** about, concerning; having as a basis: *depending on availability.* **3** aiming at, directed towards. **4** in the course of (a journey); travelling in (a public vehicle). **5** at (a point in time). **6** added to. **7** taking

(medication). ADV **1** so as to be in contact with or covering something. **2** continuing: *carry on;* further forward, progressing: *move on.* **3** taking place, being presented: *what's on at the theatre?* **4** (of an electric appliance) functioning, so as to function.
not on [INFORMAL] not acceptable. **on and off** from time to time, intermittently.

once ADV **1** on one occasion or for one time only. **2** formerly. CONJ as soon as: *we'll start once he's arrived.*
at once 1 immediately. **2** simultaneously. **once upon a time** at some vague time in the past.

once-over NOUN [INFORMAL] a rapid inspection; a piece of work done quickly.

oncogene /ong-kŏ-jeen/ NOUN a gene that transforms a cell into a cancer cell.

oncology NOUN the study of tumours.

oncoming ADJ approaching.

one NOUN the smallest whole number (1, I); a single person or thing. ADJ single, individual; only, unique, sole; denoting a certain unidentified instance: *one day;* denoting one of two or more; united, identical: *of one mind.* PRON **1** a person, anyone, the speaker as representative of people in general. **2** referring to a type of thing already mentioned: *do you want this book or the other one?*
at one in agreement. **one another** each other. **one by one** separately and in succession.

onerous /oh-nĕ-rŭs/ ADJ burdensome.

oneself PRON the emphatic and reflexive form of *one*.

one-sided ADJ biased; unfairly dealing with only one side of an issue.

one-upmanship NOUN [INFORMAL] the maintaining of an advantage over others.

one-way ADJ allowing movement in one direction only.

ongoing ADJ continuing, in progress.

onion NOUN a vegetable with a bulb that has a strong taste and smell.

online ADJ & ADV controlled by or connected to a computer.

onlooker NOUN a spectator.

only ADJ alone of its kind; single, sole. ADV **1** with no one or nothing besides; no more than: *only ten.* **2** no longer ago than: *only yesterday*. CONJ [INFORMAL] except that, but: *I'd help, only I'm busy.*
only too very much so.

onomatopoeia /on-ŏ-ma-tŏ-pee-ă/ NOUN the formation of words that imitate the sound of what they stand for.
onomatopoeic ADJ

onset NOUN **1** a beginning. **2** [ARCHAIC] an attack.

onshore ADJ (of wind) blowing from the sea to the land.

onslaught NOUN a fierce attack.

onto PREP to a position on; to a place on the surface of.

onus /oh-nŭs/ NOUN a duty or responsibility.

onward ADV & ADJ with an advancing motion; further on.
onwards ADV

onyx /o-niks/ NOUN a stone like marble.

oodles PLURAL NOUN [INFORMAL] a great amount.

oomph NOUN [INFORMAL] energy, vigour; enthusiasm.

ooze VERB trickle or flow out slowly; exude.
NOUN wet mud.

op. ABBREV opus.

opal NOUN an iridescent precious stone.

opalescent ADJ iridescent like an opal.
opalescence NOUN

opaque ADJ impossible to see through; difficult to understand.
opacity NOUN

OPEC /oh-pek/ ABBREV Organization of Petroleum Exporting Countries.

open ADJ **1** able to be entered or passed through; not closed or sealed. **2** not covered; not hidden or disguised. **3** (of

a shop etc.) ready to admit customers. 4 (of a book) with the covers parted. 5 not finally settled or answered. VERB 1 make or become open or more open; unfold, spread out; allow public access to (one's home etc.). 2 establish, begin. **in the open** 1 out of doors. 2 not hidden. **open to** 1 subject to; vulnerable to. 2 ready to accept.
openness NOUN

opencast ADJ (of mining) on the surface of the ground.

open-ended ADJ with no fixed limit.

opener NOUN a device for opening tins, bottles, etc.

open-handed ADJ giving generously.

open house NOUN hospitality to all comers.

opening NOUN 1 a gap. 2 a beginning, an initial part. 3 an opportunity.

open letter NOUN a letter addressed to a person by name but printed in a newspaper.

openly ADV without concealment or deception.

open-plan ADJ (of a room) not divided, without partition walls.

open prison NOUN a prison with few physical restraints on prisoners.

open system NOUN [COMPUTING] a system allowing software and hardware from different manufacturers to be used together.

open verdict NOUN a verdict not specifying whether a suspicious death is due to crime.

opera NOUN a play in which words are sung to music.
operatic ADJ

operable ADJ 1 able to be operated. 2 suitable for treatment by surgery.

opera glasses PLURAL NOUN small binoculars used to give a better view of the stage in a theatre.

operate VERB 1 function; control the functioning of. 2 perform a surgical operation.

operating system NOUN basic software allowing a computer program to run.

operation NOUN **1** the action of operating. **2** an act of surgery performed on a patient. **3** an organized action involving a number of people.

operational ADJ **1** in or ready for use. **2** involved in functioning or activity.

operative ADJ **1** working, functioning. **2** of surgical operations. NOUN a worker, especially in a factory.

operator NOUN a person who operates a machine; one who connects lines at a telephone exchange; one who runs a business or enterprise.

operetta NOUN a short or light opera.

ophthalmic ADJ of or for the eyes.

ophthalmic optician NOUN an optician qualified to prescribe and dispense spectacles.

ophthalmology NOUN the study of the eye and its diseases.
ophthalmologist NOUN

ophthalmoscope NOUN an instrument for examining the eye.

opiate NOUN a sedative containing opium.

opine /o-pIn/ VERB [FORMAL] express or hold as an opinion.

opinion NOUN a belief or judgement held without actual proof; what one thinks on a particular point; one's estimate of someone's or something's merit or value.

opinionated ADJ obstinate and arrogant in asserting one's opinions.

opium NOUN a narcotic drug made from the juice of certain poppies.

opossum NOUN a small tree-living marsupial.

opponent NOUN one who disagrees with or is hostile to another.

opportune ADJ (of a time) favourable; well timed.
opportunely ADV
opportuneness NOUN

opportunist NOUN a person who exploits opportunities for immediate gain, especially

unscrupulously.
opportunism NOUN
opportunistic ADJ

opportunity NOUN (PL **opportunities**) a set of circumstances making it possible to do something.

oppose VERB **1** argue or fight against; compete with. **2** place opposite; contrast with something; bring into opposition.

opposite ADJ **1** on the further side; facing something. **2** totally different, contrasting. NOUN a person or thing totally different from another. ADV in an opposite position. PREP in a position opposite to.

opposition NOUN **1** resistance, disagreement; a group of people who oppose something; (also **the Opposition**) the main parliamentary party opposing the one in power. **2** a difference or contrast.

oppress VERB govern or treat harshly; distress, make anxious.
oppression NOUN
oppressor NOUN

oppressive ADJ exercising power harshly and unjustly; causing distress or anxiety; (of weather) sultry and tiring.
oppressively ADV
oppressiveness NOUN

opprobrious /o-**proh**-bri-ŭs/ ADJ (of language) abusive.

opprobrium /o-**proh**-bri-ŭm/ NOUN harsh criticism; disgrace due to shameful conduct.

opt VERB make a choice.
opt out choose not to participate; (of a school or hospital) withdraw from local authority control.

optic ADJ of the eye or sight.

optical ADJ of or aiding sight; visual.
optically ADV

optical character reader NOUN [COMPUTING] a scanner enabling text to be transferred to computer.

optical fibre NOUN a thin glass fibre used to transmit signals.

optician NOUN a maker or

seller of spectacles.

optics NOUN the study of sight and of light as its medium.

optimal ADJ the best or most favourable.

optimism NOUN a tendency to take a hopeful view of things.
optimist NOUN
optimistic ADJ
optimistically ADV

optimize (also **optimise**) VERB make the best use of.
optimization NOUN

optimum ADJ most likely to lead to a favourable outcome. NOUN (PL **optima** or **optimums**) the most favourable conditions for growth or success.

option NOUN something that is or may be chosen; the freedom or right to choose; a right to buy or sell something at a specified price within a set time.

optional ADJ not compulsory.
optionally ADV

optometrist /op-tom-e-trist/ NOUN an ophthalmic optician.

opulent ADJ ostentatiously luxurious; very wealthy.
opulence NOUN

opus NOUN (PL **opuses** or **opera**) a musical composition numbered as one of a composer's works.

or CONJ used to link alternatives; also known as; otherwise, if not.

oracle NOUN a person or thing regarded as an infallible guide; an ancient shrine where a god was believed to answer questions.

oracular ADJ of an oracle; authoritative; enigmatic, hard to interpret.

oral ADJ **1** spoken not written. **2** of the mouth; taken by mouth. NOUN a spoken examination.
orally ADV

orange NOUN a round juicy citrus fruit with reddish-yellow peel; its colour. ADJ reddish yellow.

orang-utan (also **orang-outang**) NOUN a large ape.

oration NOUN a long speech, especially of a ceremonial kind.

orator NOUN a person who

O

makes public speeches; a skilful speaker.

oratorio NOUN (PL **oratorios**) a musical composition for voices and orchestra, usually with a biblical theme.

oratory NOUN the art of public speaking.
oratorical ADJ

orb NOUN a sphere, a globe.

orbit NOUN **1** the curved path of a planet, satellite, or spacecraft round a star or planet. **2** a sphere of activity or influence. VERB (**orbits**, **orbiting**, **orbited**) move in orbit round.

orbital ADJ **1** of orbits. **2** (of a road) round the outside of a city.

orchard NOUN a piece of land planted with fruit trees.

orchestra NOUN a large body of people playing various musical instruments.
orchestral ADJ

orchestrate VERB **1** compose or arrange (music) for an orchestra. **2** organize, manipulate (a situation or event).
orchestration NOUN

orchid NOUN a showy flower.

ordain VERB **1** appoint ceremonially to the Christian ministry. **2** order or decree authoritatively; determine.

ordeal NOUN a painful or difficult experience.

order NOUN **1** the arrangement of people or things in relation to each other; a sequence followed in determining this arrangement. **2** the following of the proper sequence or arrangement; a state of peace and obedience to law. **3** a command; a request to supply goods etc.; the things supplied; a written instruction. **4** a rank, kind, or quality; a group of plants or animals classified as similar. **5** a monastic organization. VERB **1** give a command; request (something) to be supplied. **2** arrange methodically.
in order 1 properly arranged. **2** in accordance with the rules. **3** able to

function. **in order to** or **that** with the purpose of or intention that. **on order** (of goods) requested but not yet supplied. **out of order** not functioning.

orderly ADJ neatly arranged; disciplined, not unruly. NOUN (PL **orderlies**) an attendant in a hospital; a soldier assisting an officer. **orderliness** NOUN

order paper NOUN a programme of the day's business in Parliament.

ordinal (in full **ordinal number**) NOUN a number defining a thing's position in a series (e.g. *first, second,* etc.); contrast with **cardinal**.

ordinance NOUN a decree.

ordinand NOUN a candidate for ordination.

ordinary ADJ usual, not exceptional. **ordinarily** ADV

Ordinary level (also **O level**) NOUN [HISTORICAL] the lower of the two main levels of GCE examination.

ordination NOUN ceremonial appointment to the Christian ministry.

ordnance NOUN mounted guns; missiles, bombs.

Ordnance Survey NOUN an official surveying organization preparing maps of the British Isles.

ordure NOUN dung.

ore NOUN solid rock or mineral from which metal is obtained.

oregano NOUN a herb.

organ NOUN **1** a keyboard instrument with pipes supplied with wind by bellows. **2** a body part with a specific function. **3** a medium of communication, especially a newspaper.

organic ADJ **1** of or derived from living matter. **2** of bodily organs. **3** (of farming methods) using no artificial fertilizers or pesticides. **4** forming or part of a system where all parts are essential and in harmony. **organically** ADV

organism NOUN a living being; an individual animal or plant.

organist NOUN a person

O

who plays the organ.

organization NOUN the action of organizing; a systematic arrangement or approach; an organized group of people with a shared purpose, e.g. a business.
organizational ADJ

organize (also **organise**) VERB **1** arrange into an ordered whole; form (people) into an association with a common purpose. **2** make arrangements for (an event).
organizer NOUN

orgasm NOUN a climax of sexual excitement.

orgy NOUN (PL **orgies**) a wild party; unrestrained indulgence in a specified activity.
orgiastic ADJ

Orient NOUN the East, the eastern world.

orient (also **orientate**) VERB **1** position (something) relative to the points of the compass. **2** adapt to particular needs or circumstances; guide, direct.
orient oneself find one's position in strange surroundings; become used to a new situation.
orientation NOUN

oriental ADJ relating to the Far East. NOUN [DATED] or [OFFENSIVE] a person of Far Eastern descent.

orienteering NOUN the sport of finding one's way across country with a map and compass.

orifice NOUN an opening, especially in the body.

origami /or-i-**gah**-mi/ NOUN the Japanese decorative art of paper folding.

origin NOUN the point, source, or cause from which a thing begins its existence; a person's ancestry or parentage.

original ADJ **1** existing from the beginning, not replaced or added; first. **2** created by a particular artist etc.; not copied. **3** new and unusual; creative, not dependent on others' ideas. NOUN a model on which copies are based.
originality NOUN
originally ADV

originate VERB bring or come into being.
origination NOUN

originator NOUN

ornament NOUN an object or detail designed to make something more attractive; decoration. VERB decorate with ornaments.
ornamentation NOUN

ornamental ADJ serving as an ornament.
ornamentally ADV

ornate ADJ elaborately ornamented.
ornately ADV
ornateness NOUN

ornithology NOUN the study of birds.
ornithological ADJ
ornithologist NOUN

O

orphan NOUN a child whose parents are dead. VERB make (a child) an orphan.

orphanage NOUN an institution where orphans are cared for.

orthodontics NOUN correction of irregularities in teeth.
orthodontic ADJ
orthodontist NOUN

orthodox ADJ of or holding conventional or currently accepted beliefs, especially in religion.
orthodoxy NOUN

Orthodox Church NOUN the Eastern or Greek Church.

orthography /or-**thog**-ră-fi/ NOUN conventionally correct spelling.
orthographic ADJ

orthopaedics /or-thŏ-**pee**-diks/ ([US] **orthopedics**) NOUN the surgical correction of deformities in bones or muscles.
orthopaedic ADJ
orthopaedist NOUN

oscillate VERB move or swing to and fro.
oscillation NOUN

osier /**oh**-zee-ĕ/ NOUN willow with flexible twigs.

osmium NOUN a hard metallic element.

osmosis /oz-**moh**-sis/ NOUN the diffusion of fluid through a porous partition into another more concentrated fluid.
osmotic ADJ

osprey NOUN (PL **ospreys**) a large bird preying on fish.

osseous /**os**-ee-ŭs/ ADJ like

bone, bony.

ossify VERB (**ossifies**, **ossifying**, **ossified**) turn into bone; become rigid; cease to progress or develop.
ossification NOUN

ostensible ADJ apparent but not true; used as a pretext.
ostensibly ADV

ostentation NOUN a showy display intended to impress people.
ostentatious ADJ
ostentatiously ADV

osteopathy NOUN the treatment of certain conditions by manipulating bones and muscles.
osteopath NOUN
osteopathic ADJ

ostracize (also **ostracise**) VERB exclude from a society or group.
ostracism NOUN

ostrich NOUN a large flightless swift-running African bird.

other ADJ **1** distinct from one already present or mentioned; extra, further. **2** different. NOUN & PRON the one of two people or things not already mentioned or accounted for; (**others**) the members of a group not already accounted for.
other than apart from; differently from. **the other day**, **week**, etc. a few days, weeks, etc., ago.

otherwise ADV **1** in different circumstances. **2** in other respects: *I'm tired, but otherwise I'm fine.* **3** in a different way.

otiose /oh-tee-ohs/ ADJ serving no practical purpose.

OTT ABBREV [INFORMAL] over the top; extravagant, excessive.

otter NOUN a fish-eating water animal.

ottoman NOUN a low seat without back or arms, also serving as a storage box.

OU ABBREV Open University.

ought AUXILIARY VERB **1** expressing duty, desirability, or advisability. **2** expressing strong probability.

Ouija board /wee-jă/ NOUN

[TRADE MARK] a board marked with letters and signs, over which a pointer is moved to indicate supposed messages from spirits.

ounce NOUN a unit of weight, one-sixteenth of a pound (about 28 grams); a very small amount.

our ADJ of or belonging to us.

ours POSSESSIVE PRONOUN belonging to us.

ourselves PRON the emphatic and reflexive form of *we* and *us*.

oust VERB drive out, eject.

O

out ADV **1** so as to leave a place; in or into the open. **2** away from one's home or base. **3** away from land: *out to sea.* **4** so as to be known: *find out;* so as to be heard: *call out.* **5** so as to be extinguished; so as to end or be completed. ADJ **1** not at home; not at work, on strike. **2** known, public. **3** extinguished, not alight. **4** [INFORMAL] not possible. **5** unconscious. **6** in error. NOUN [INFORMAL] a way of escape. VERB [INFORMAL] reveal the homosexuality of (a well-known person). **be out to** aim or intend to. **out and out** complete, thorough. **out of** having none left. **out of date** no longer current, valid, or fashionable. **out of the way 1** remote. **2** (of an obstacle) removed.

out- PREFIX more than, so as to exceed.

outback NOUN the remote inland areas of Australia.

outboard ADJ (of a motor) attached to the outside of a boat.

outbreak NOUN a sudden onset of anger, war, disease, etc.

outbuilding NOUN an outhouse.

outburst NOUN a sudden release of feeling.

outcast NOUN a person driven out of a group or by society.

outclass VERB surpass in quality.

outcome NOUN a consequence.

outcrop NOUN part of an underlying layer of rock that projects on the surface of the ground.

outcry NOUN (PL **outcries**) a loud cry; a strong protest.

outdistance VERB get far ahead of.

outdo VERB (**outdoes**, **outdoing**, **outdid**; PAST PARTICIPLE **outdone**) be or do better than.

outdoor ADJ of or for use in the open air.
outdoors ADV

outer ADJ external; further from the centre or inside.

outermost ADV furthest outward.

outface VERB disconcert (an opponent) by confronting them boldly.

outfit NOUN a set of clothes or equipment.

outfitter NOUN a supplier of equipment or men's clothing.

outflank VERB get round the side of (an enemy).

outgoing ADJ **1** sociable, talkative. **2** leaving an office or position.

outgoings PLURAL NOUN expenditure.

outgrow VERB (**outgrows**, **outgrowing**, **outgrew**; PAST PARTICIPLE **outgrown**) grow too large for; grow faster than; leave behind or cease to be interested in as one grows or matures.

outhouse NOUN a shed, barn, etc.

outing NOUN a pleasure trip.

outlandish ADJ bizarre or unfamiliar; [ARCHAIC] foreign.

outlast VERB last longer than.

outlaw NOUN a fugitive criminal; [HISTORICAL] a criminal punished by being deprived of the law's protection. VERB make illegal; [HISTORICAL] make (someone) an outlaw.

outlay NOUN money etc. spent.

outlet NOUN a way out; a means for giving vent to energies or feelings; a market for goods.

outline NOUN **1** a line showing a thing's shape or boundary. **2** a summary. VERB draw or describe in outline; mark the outline of.

outlook NOUN **1** a person's

attitude to life. **2** a view; the prospect for the future.

outlying ADJ remote, far from the centre.

outmoded ADJ no longer fashionable or accepted.

outnumber VERB exceed in number.

outpace VERB go faster than.

outpatient NOUN a person visiting a hospital for treatment but not staying overnight.

outplacement NOUN assistance in finding new employment, given to workers who have been made redundant.

outpost NOUN a small military camp at a distance from the main army; a remote settlement.

output NOUN the amount of electrical power, work, etc. produced. VERB (**outputs**, **outputting**, **output** or **outputted**) (of a computer) supply (results etc.).

outrage NOUN extreme shock and anger; an action or event provoking this. VERB provoke to shock and anger; blatantly break (a rule etc.).

outrageous ADJ shockingly bad or excessive; exaggerated, improbable, unreasonable.
outrageously ADV

outré /oo-tray/ ADJ eccentric, unseemly.

outrider NOUN a mounted attendant or motorcyclist escorting and guarding a vehicle.

outrigger NOUN a stabilizing strip of wood fixed outside and parallel to a canoe; a canoe with this.

outright ADV **1** totally, altogether. **2** frankly. **3** immediately; not gradually. ADJ **1** total. **2** frank, direct.

outrun VERB (**outruns**, **outrunning**, **outran**; PAST PARTICIPLE **outrun**) run faster or further than.

outset NOUN the beginning.

outside NOUN the outer side, surface, or part. ADJ on or near the outside;

coming from outside a group: *outside advice.* ADV to the outside; outside the boundaries. PREP not within; beyond the boundaries of; not a member of; beyond the scope of.
an outside chance a remote possibility.

outsider NOUN **1** a non-member of a group. **2** a competitor thought to have no chance in a contest.

outsize (also **outsized**) ADJ much larger than average.

outskirts PLURAL NOUN the outer districts.

outsource VERB obtain (goods) by contract from an outside supplier; contract (work) out.

outspoken ADJ very frank.

outstanding ADJ **1** conspicuous; exceptionally good. **2** not yet paid or dealt with.
outstandingly ADV

outstrip VERB (**outstrips**, **outstripping**, **outstripped**) run faster or further than; surpass.

out tray NOUN a tray for documents that have been dealt with.

outvote VERB defeat by a majority of votes.

outward ADJ **1** of or on the outside. **2** (of a journey) going away from a place. ADV towards the outside, away from the centre.
outwardly ADV
outwards ADV

outweigh VERB be of greater weight or importance than.

outwit VERB (**outwits**, **outwitting**, **outwitted**) defeat by one's craftiness.

outwork NOUN work done away from the employer's premises.

ova pl. of **OVUM**.

oval ADJ having an elongated rounded shape. NOUN an oval shape.

ovary NOUN (PL **ovaries**) an organ producing egg cells; that part of a pistil from which fruit is formed.
ovarian ADJ

ovate ADJ egg-shaped.

ovation NOUN enthusiastic

applause.

oven NOUN an enclosed chamber in which things are cooked or heated.

ovenware NOUN dishes for use in an oven.

over PREP **1** in or to a position higher than; directly upwards from. **2** moving across; to or on the other side of. **3** superior to; greater than, more than. **4** during, in the course of. **5** on the subject of. ADV **1** moving outwards or downwards: *lean over*. **2** from one side to another; across a space. **3** repeatedly. **4** at an end. NOUN [CRICKET] a sequence of six balls bowled from one end of the pitch. **get something over with** complete an unpleasant task. **over and above** in addition to.

over- PREFIX **1** excessively; thoroughly. **2** extra; on top, upper.

overall NOUN a garment worn to protect other clothing; (**overalls**) a one-piece garment of this kind covering the body and legs. ADJ total; taking all aspects into account. ADV taken as a whole.

overarm ADJ & ADV (of a throw or stroke in sport) made with the arm brought forward and down from above shoulder level.

overawe VERB overcome with awe.

overbalance VERB lose balance and fall; cause to do this.

overbearing ADJ domineering.

overblown ADJ exaggerated or pretentious.

overboard ADV from a ship into the water. **go overboard** [INFORMAL] be very enthusiastic; be excessive or immoderate.

overcast ADJ covered with cloud.

overcharge VERB ask too high a price from.

overcoat NOUN a warm full-length outdoor coat.

overcome VERB (**overcomes**, **overcoming**, **overcame**; PAST PARTICIPLE **overcome**) succeed in dealing with (a problem); defeat or overwhelm (someone).

overdo VERB (**overdoes**, **overdoing**, **overdid**; PAST PARTICIPLE **overdone**) take to excess; use too much of; cook for too long. **overdo it** tire oneself by overwork.

overdose NOUN a dangerously large dose of a drug. VERB take an overdose.

overdraft NOUN a deficit in a bank account caused by overdrawing.

overdraw VERB (**overdraws**, **overdrawing**, **overdrew**; PAST PARTICIPLE **overdrawn**) draw more money from (a bank account) than it holds.

overdrive NOUN a mechanism providing an extra gear above top gear.

overdue ADJ not paid or arrived etc. by the required or expected time.

overestimate VERB form too high an estimate of.

overflow VERB flow over the edge or limits (of). NOUN an excess or surplus; a pipe to carry off excess water in a bath or sink.

overgrown ADJ **1** covered with weeds. **2** grown beyond the proper size.

overhaul VERB **1** take (a machine) apart to examine and repair it. **2** overtake. NOUN an examination and repair.

overhead ADV above one's head. ADJ situated above one's head. NOUN (**overheads**) the expenses involved in running a business etc.

overhead projector NOUN a projector producing an image from a transparency placed on it, using an overhead mirror.

overhear VERB (**overhears**, **overhearing**, **overheard**) hear accidentally or without the speaker's knowledge.

overjoyed ADJ very happy.

overkill NOUN excessive use or treatment; too much of something.

overland ADJ & ADV by land.

overlap VERB (**overlaps**,

overlapping, **overlapped**) extend beyond the edge of (something) so as to cover part of it; partially coincide. NOUN an instance of something overlapping; a part or amount that overlaps.

overleaf ADV on the other side of a leaf of a book etc.

overload VERB put too great a load on or in. NOUN too great a load or amount.

overlook VERB **1** fail to notice; ignore (a fault); fail to recognize the merits of. **2** have a view over.

overly ADV excessively, too.

overman VERB (**overmans**, **overmanning**, **overmanned**) provide with too many staff or crew.

overnight ADV & ADJ during or for a night.

overpass NOUN a road crossing another by means of a bridge.

overpower VERB overcome by greater strength or numbers.

overpowering ADJ (of heat or feelings) extremely intense.

overrate VERB have too high an opinion of.

overreach VERB (**overreach oneself**) fail through being too ambitious.

overreact VERB respond more emotionally or extremely than is justified.

override VERB (**overrides**, **overriding**, **overrode**; PAST PARTICIPLE **overridden**) overrule; be more important than; interrupt the operation of (an automatic device).

overrule VERB set aside (a decision etc.) by using one's authority.

overrun VERB (**overruns**, **overrunning**, **overran**; PAST PARTICIPLE **overrun**) **1** spread over and occupy in large numbers. **2** exceed (a limit).

overseas ADV in or to a foreign country. ADJ relating to a foreign country.

oversee VERB (**oversees**, **overseeing**, **oversaw**;

PAST PARTICIPLE **overseen**) supervise.
overseer NOUN

overshadow VERB cast a shadow over; be more important or prominent than, distract attention from.

overshoot VERB (**overshoots**, **overshooting**, **overshot**) pass beyond (a target or limit etc.).

oversight NOUN **1** an unintentional omission. **2** supervision.

overspill NOUN an excess; a district's surplus population looking for homes elsewhere.

oversteer VERB (of a car) tend to turn more sharply than was intended. NOUN this tendency.

overstep VERB (**oversteps**, **overstepping**, **overstepped**) go beyond (a limit).

overt ADJ done or shown openly.
overtly ADV

overtake VERB (**overtakes**, **overtaking**, **overtook**; PAST PARTICIPLE **overtaken**) **1** pass while travelling in the same direction. **2** (of misfortune) suddenly affect.

overthrow VERB (**overthrows**, **overthrowing**, **overthrew**; PAST PARTICIPLE **overthrown**) remove forcibly from power. NOUN a removal from power.

overtime NOUN time worked in addition to one's regular working hours; payment for this. ADV in addition to one's regular working hours.

overtone NOUN an additional quality or implication.

overture NOUN an orchestral composition forming a prelude to a performance; (**overtures**) an initial approach or proposal.

overturn VERB **1** turn or cause to turn upside down or onto its side. **2** cancel, reverse (a decision etc.).

overview NOUN a general survey.

overwhelm VERB **1** bury beneath a huge mass. **2** overcome completely;

make helpless with emotion.
overwhelming ADJ

overwrought ADJ in a state of nervous agitation.

oviduct NOUN the tube through which ova pass from the ovary.

oviparous /oh-**vip**-ă-rŭs/ ADJ egg-laying.

ovoid ADJ egg-shaped, oval.

ovulate VERB produce or discharge an egg cell from an ovary.
ovulation NOUN

ovule NOUN a germ cell of a plant.

O

ovum NOUN (PL **ova**) an egg cell; a reproductive cell produced by a female.

owe VERB be under an obligation to pay or repay (money etc.) in return for something received; have (something) through someone else's action: *I owe my life to him.*

owing ADJ owed and not yet paid.
owing to caused by; because of.

owl NOUN a bird of prey with large eyes, usually flying at night.
owlish ADJ

own ADJ belonging to a specified person: *her own home.* VERB possess as one's own; [FORMAL] acknowledge as one's own; admit.
of one's own belonging to oneself. **on one's own** alone; independently.
own up confess.
owner NOUN
ownership NOUN

ox NOUN (PL **oxen**) an animal of or related to the kind kept as domestic cattle; a fully grown bullock.

oxidation NOUN the process of combining with oxygen.

oxide NOUN a compound of oxygen and one other element.

oxidize (also **oxidise**) VERB combine with oxygen; coat with an oxide; make or become rusty.
oxidization NOUN

oxyacetylene ADJ using a very hot flame produced by mixing oxygen and acetylene, especially in metal-cutting and welding.

oxygen NOUN a colourless gas existing in air and necessary for life.

oxygenate VERB supply or mix with oxygen.

oyster NOUN an edible shellfish.

oz. ABBREV ounce(s).

ozone NOUN a colourless toxic gas with a strong odour.

ozone hole NOUN a thinning of the ozone layer in high latitudes, resulting in an increase in ultraviolet light reaching the earth.

ozone layer NOUN a layer of ozone in the stratosphere, absorbing ultraviolet radiation.

Pp

P (also **p**) NOUN (PL **Ps** or **P's**) the sixteenth letter of the alphabet. ABBREV **1** (**p**) page. **2** (in signs) parking. **3** penny or pence.

PA ABBREV **1** personal assistant. **2** public address system.

pa NOUN [INFORMAL] father.

p.a. ABBREV per annum, yearly.

p

pace NOUN **1** a single step in walking or running. **2** a rate of progress. VERB walk steadily or to and fro; measure (a distance) by pacing; lead (one's competitors) in a race, establishing the speed. **pace oneself** do something slowly and steadily so as not to tire oneself too quickly.

pacemaker NOUN **1** a runner etc. who sets the pace for another. **2** a device regulating heart contractions.

pachyderm /pak-i-derm/ NOUN a large thick-skinned mammal such as the elephant.

pacific ADJ peaceable.

pacifist NOUN a person totally opposed to war. **pacifism** NOUN

pacify VERB (**pacifies**, **pacifying**, **pacified**) calm the anger of; establish peace in (an area). **pacification** NOUN

pack NOUN **1** a collection of things wrapped or tied for carrying or selling. **2** a set of playing cards. **3** a group of hounds or wolves. VERB **1** fill (a suitcase, bag, etc.); put (items) into a container. **2** press or crowd together; fill (a space) in this way. **3** cover or protect with something pressed

tightly.
pack it in [INFORMAL] stop what one is doing. **pack off** [INFORMAL] send away. **send packing** [INFORMAL] dismiss abruptly.
packer NOUN

package NOUN **1** a parcel; a box etc. in which goods are packed. **2** [INFORMAL] a package deal. VERB **1** put together in a package. **2** present so as to make more attractive.
packager NOUN
packaging NOUN

package deal NOUN a set of proposals offered or accepted as a whole.

package holiday NOUN a holiday with set arrangements at an inclusive price.

packet NOUN **1** a small package. **2** [INFORMAL] a large sum of money. **3** [DATED] a mailboat.

pact NOUN an agreement, a treaty.

pad NOUN **1** a piece of soft material used to protect against friction, absorb liquid, etc. **2** a set of sheets of paper fastened together at one edge. **3** a soft fleshy part under an animal's paw. **4** a flat surface for use by helicopters or for launching rockets. VERB (**pads, padding, padded**) **1** protect or make softer with a pad. **2** make larger or longer. **3** walk softly or steadily.

padding NOUN soft material used as a pad.

paddle NOUN a short oar with a broad blade. VERB **1** propel by use of a paddle or paddles; row gently. **2** walk with bare feet in shallow water.

paddock NOUN a small field where horses are kept; an enclosure for horses at a racecourse.

padlock NOUN a detachable lock with a U-shaped bar secured through the object fastened. VERB fasten with a padlock.

padre /pah-dray/ NOUN [INFORMAL] a chaplain in the army etc.

paean /pee-ăn/ ([US] **pean**) NOUN a song of triumph or praise.

paediatrics /peed-i-at-riks/ ([US] **pediatrics**) NOUN the branch of

medicine dealing with children's diseases.
paediatric ADJ
paediatrician NOUN

paella /py-el-ă/ NOUN a Spanish dish of rice, seafood, chicken, etc.

pagan NOUN a person holding religious beliefs other than those of an established religion. ADJ relating to pagans or their beliefs.

page NOUN **1** a sheet of paper in a book etc.; one side of this. **2** a young male attendant at a hotel; a boy attendant of a bride; [HISTORICAL] a boy training for knighthood. VERB summon over a public address system; contact using a pager.
page through leaf through (a book).

pageant /paj-ĕnt/ NOUN a public show or procession, especially with people in costume.
pageantry NOUN

pager NOUN a radio device with a bleeper for summoning the wearer.

pagoda NOUN a Hindu or Buddhist temple.

paid past and past participle of **PAY**.
put paid to [INFORMAL] end (hopes or prospects).

pail NOUN a bucket.

pain NOUN **1** physical discomfort caused by injury or disease; mental suffering. **2** (**pains**) careful effort: *he took pains over the job.* VERB cause pain to.

painful ADJ **1** causing or suffering pain. **2** laborious.
painfully ADV

painkiller NOUN a drug for reducing pain.

painless ADJ not causing pain.
painlessly ADV

painstaking ADJ very careful and thorough.

paint NOUN colouring matter for applying in liquid form to a surface; (**paints**) tubes or cakes of paint. VERB **1** coat with paint; apply (liquid) to (a surface). **2** depict with paint; describe.

painter NOUN **1** a person who paints as an artist or decorator. **2** a rope attached to a boat's bow for tying it up.

painting NOUN a painted picture.

pair NOUN a set of two things or people; an article consisting of two parts: *a pair of scissors;* one member of a pair in relation to the other. VERB arrange or be arranged in a pair or pairs.

paisley ADJ patterned with feather-shaped figures.

pajamas US spelling of **PYJAMAS**.

pal NOUN [INFORMAL] a friend.

palace NOUN an official residence of a sovereign, archbishop, or bishop; a splendid mansion.

palaeography /pa-li-og-ră-fi/ ([US] **paleography**) NOUN the study of ancient writing and inscriptions.
palaeographer NOUN

palaeolithic /pa-li-ŏ-lith-ik/ ([US] **paleolithic**) ADJ of the early part of the Stone Age.

palaeontology /pa-li-ŏn-tol-ŏ-ji/ ([US] **paleontology**) NOUN the study of fossil animals and plants.
palaeontologist NOUN

palatable /pal-ă-tă-bĕl/ ADJ pleasant to the taste; acceptable, welcome.

palate NOUN the roof of the mouth; the sense of taste.

palatial /pă-lay-shăl/ ADJ of or like a palace; splendid, grand.

palaver /păl-ah-vĕ/ NOUN [INFORMAL] a fuss.

pale ADJ light in colour; (of the face) having less colour than normal. VERB turn pale; seem less important or prominent.
beyond the pale outside the bounds of acceptable behaviour.
palely ADV
paleness NOUN

paleo- US spelling of words beginning with **palaeo-**.

Palestinian NOUN a member of the Arab population of Palestine. ADJ relating to Palestine.

palette NOUN a board on which an artist mixes colours; a range of colours used.

palette knife NOUN a knife with a flexible blade for spreading paint or for smoothing soft substances in cookery.

palindrome /pal-in-drohm/ NOUN a word or phrase that reads the same backwards as forwards.

paling NOUN a fence made from pointed stakes; a stake.

pall /pawl/ NOUN a cloth spread over a coffin; a heavy dark covering. VERB come to seem less interesting.

palladium NOUN a rare metallic element.

pall-bearer NOUN a person helping to carry or walking beside the coffin at a funeral.

P

pallet NOUN **1** a straw-stuffed mattress; a hard narrow or makeshift bed. **2** a tray or platform for goods being lifted or stored.

palliate /pal-i-ayt/ VERB make (a disease or its symptoms) less severe or painful; make (an offence) seem less serious.
palliative ADJ

pallid ADJ pale, especially from illness.
pallidness NOUN
pallor NOUN

pally ADJ (**pallier**, **palliest**) [INFORMAL] friendly.

palm NOUN **1** the inner surface of the hand. **2** a tree of warm and tropical climates, with large leaves and no branches. VERB conceal in one's hand.
palm off [INFORMAL] fraudulently persuade someone to accept.

palmist NOUN a person who tells people's fortunes from lines in their palms.
palmistry NOUN

palomino /pal-ŏ-mee-noh/ NOUN (PL **palominos**) a golden or cream-coloured horse.

palpable ADJ able to be touched or felt; obvious.
palpably ADV

palpate VERB examine medically by touch.
palpation NOUN

palpitate VERB throb rapidly; quiver with fear or excitement.
palpitation NOUN

palsy NOUN (PL **palsies**) [DATED] paralysis,

especially with involuntary tremors. **palsied** ADJ

paltry ADJ (**paltrier**, **paltriest**) (of a sum) very small; worthless. **paltriness** NOUN

pampas NOUN vast grassy plains in South America.

pamper VERB treat very indulgently.

pamphlet NOUN a leaflet or paper-covered booklet.

pamphleteer NOUN a writer of pamphlets.

pan NOUN a metal or earthenware container with a flat base, used in cooking; any similar container. VERB (**pans**, **panning**, **panned**) **1** [INFORMAL] criticize severely. **2** turn (the camera) horizontally in filming to give a panoramic effect. **3** wash gravel in a pan to separate (gold) from it. **panful** NOUN

pan- COMBINING FORM all, whole.

panacea /pan-ă-**see**-ă/ NOUN a remedy for all kinds of diseases or troubles.

panache /păn-**ash**/ NOUN a confident stylish manner.

panama NOUN a straw hat.

pancake NOUN a thin round cake of fried batter.

pancreas NOUN the gland near the stomach, discharging insulin into the blood. **pancreatic** ADJ

panda NOUN a bear-like black and white animal.

pandemic ADJ (of a disease) occurring over a whole country or the world.

pandemonium /pan-de-**moh**-ni-ŭm/ NOUN uproar.

pander VERB (**pander to**) indulge (a weakness, distasteful desire, or bad habit).

p. & p. ABBREV postage and packing.

pane NOUN a sheet of glass in a window or door.

panegyric /pan-ĕ-**ji**-rik/ NOUN a piece of written or spoken praise.

panel NOUN **1** a piece of wood or glass forming part of a door; a piece of metal forming part of a vehicle's body; any distinct part of a larger surface. **2** a group assembled to discuss or decide something; a list of jurors, a jury. VERB (**panels**, **panelling**, **panelled**; [US] **paneling**, **paneled**) cover or decorate with panels.

panelling ([US] **paneling**) NOUN a series of wooden panels in a wall.

panellist ([US] **panelist**) NOUN a member of a panel.

pang NOUN a sudden sharp pain.

panic NOUN sudden strong fear; frenzied, unthinking action caused by this. VERB (**panics**, **panicking**, **panicked**) affect or be affected with panic.
panic-stricken, **panic-struck** ADJ
panicky ADJ

panjandrum /pan-jan-drŭm/ NOUN a mock title for an important person.

pannier NOUN a large basket carried by a donkey etc.; a bag fitted on a motorcycle or bicycle.

panoply NOUN (PL **panoplies**) a splendid display.

panorama NOUN a view of a wide area or set of events.
panoramic ADJ

pan pipes PLURAL NOUN a musical instrument made of a series of graduated pipes.

pansy NOUN (PL **pansies**) **1** a garden flower. **2** [OFFENSIVE] an effeminate or homosexual man.

pant VERB breathe with short quick breaths; utter breathlessly.

pantaloons PLURAL NOUN baggy trousers gathered at the ankles.

pantechnicon NOUN [DATED] a large van for transporting furniture etc.

pantheism NOUN the doctrine that God is in everything.
pantheist NOUN
pantheistic ADJ

panther NOUN a leopard.

panties PLURAL NOUN [INFORMAL] underpants for women or children.

pantile NOUN a roof tile curved so as to overlap a

neighbouring one.

pantograph NOUN a device for copying a plan etc. on any scale.

pantomime NOUN a Christmas play based on a fairy tale.

pantry NOUN (PL **pantries**) a room for storing china, glass, etc.; a larder.

pants PLURAL NOUN underpants, knickers; [US] trousers.

pap NOUN soft, bland food suitable for infants or invalids; undemanding reading matter.

papacy NOUN (PL **papacies**) the position or authority of the pope.

papal ADJ of the pope or papacy.

paparazzo NOUN (PL **paparazzi**) a freelance photographer who pursues celebrities for pictures.

papaw, **papaya** variants of **PAWPAW**.

paper NOUN **1** a substance manufactured in thin sheets from wood fibre, rags, etc., used for writing on, wrapping, etc. **2** a newspaper. **3** a document; a set of examination questions to be answered in one session; an essay. VERB cover (walls) with wallpaper.

paperback NOUN a book bound in stiff paper or flexible card.

paperweight NOUN a small heavy object for holding loose papers down.

paperwork NOUN clerical or administrative work.

papier mâché /**pap**-ee-ay-**mash**- ay/ NOUN moulded paper pulp used for making small objects.

papoose NOUN [OFFENSIVE] a young North American Indian child.

paprika NOUN red pepper.

papyrus NOUN (PL **papyri**) a reed-like water plant from which the ancient Egyptians made a kind of paper; this paper; a manuscript written on this.

par NOUN **1** [GOLF] the number of strokes needed by a first-class player for a hole or course. **2** the face value of stocks and shares. **below par** not as good or well as usual. **on a par with** equal to in quality or importance. **par for the course** normal, to be expected under the circumstances.

parable NOUN a story told to illustrate a moral.

parabola NOUN a curve like the path of an object that is thrown into the air and falls back to earth.
parabolic ADJ

paracetamol NOUN a drug that relieves pain and reduces fever.

parachute NOUN a device used to slow the descent of a person or object dropping from a great height. VERB descend or drop using a parachute.
parachutist NOUN

parade NOUN **1** a public procession; a formal assembly of troops; an ostentatious display of something. **2** a row of shops; a promenade. VERB march in a parade; display ostentatiously.

paradigm /pa-ră-dym/ NOUN an example; a model.

paradise NOUN heaven; a very beautiful or pleasant place or state.

paradox NOUN a statement that seems self-contradictory but contains a truth.
paradoxical ADJ
paradoxically ADV

paraffin NOUN oil from petroleum or shale, used as fuel.

paragliding NOUN a sport in which someone jumps from a height and glides through the air supported by a canopy resembling a parachute.

paragon NOUN an apparently perfect person or thing.

paragraph NOUN a distinct section of a piece of writing, begun on a new line. VERB arrange in paragraphs.

parakeet NOUN a small parrot.

parallax /pa-ră-laks/ NOUN an apparent difference in an object's position when viewed from different points.
parallactic ADJ

parallel ADJ **1** (of lines or planes) going continuously at the same distance from each other. **2** existing at the same time and corresponding: *parallel worlds.* NOUN **1** someone or something similar to another; a comparison. **2** a line of latitude. VERB (**parallels, paralleling, paralleled**) be parallel to; be comparable to.
parallelism NOUN

parallelogram NOUN a four-sided geometric figure with its opposite sides parallel to each other.

paralyse ([US] **paralyze**) VERB affect with paralysis; bring (work, a system) to a standstill.

paralysis NOUN loss of power of movement.

paralytic ADJ **1** affected with paralysis. **2** [INFORMAL] very drunk.

paramedic NOUN a person trained to do medical work but without a doctor's qualifications.
paramedical ADJ

parameter NOUN a numerical factor forming part of a set that defines a system; a limit defining the scope of an activity.

paramilitary ADJ organized like a military force.

paramount ADJ chief in importance.

paranoia NOUN a mental disorder in which a person has delusions of grandeur or persecution; an abnormal tendency to mistrust others.
paranoiac ADJ
paranoid ADJ

paranormal ADJ supernatural.

parapet NOUN a low wall along the edge of a balcony or bridge.

paraphernalia /pa-ră-fer-**nay**-li-ă/ NOUN numerous belongings or pieces of equipment.

paraphrase VERB express in other words. NOUN a rewording in this way.

paraplegia /pa-ră-**plee**-jă/ NOUN paralysis of the legs and part or all of the trunk.
paraplegic ADJ & NOUN

parapsychology NOUN the study of mental

perceptions that seem outside normal abilities.

paraquat NOUN a poisonous weedkiller.

parasailing (also **parascending**) NOUN a sport in which a person wearing a parachute is towed behind a motor boat or vehicle.

parasite NOUN an animal or plant living on or in another; a person living off another or others and giving no useful return.
parasitic ADJ

parasol NOUN a light umbrella used to give shade from the sun.

paratroops PLURAL NOUN troops trained to parachute into an attack.
paratrooper NOUN

parboil VERB cook partially by boiling.

parcel NOUN **1** something wrapped in paper, to be posted or carried. **2** something considered as a unit. VERB (**parcels, parcelling, parcelled**; [US] **parceling, parceled**) **1** wrap as a parcel. **2** divide into portions.

parched ADJ dried out with heat; [INFORMAL] very thirsty.

parchment NOUN writing material made from animal skins; paper resembling this.

pardon NOUN forgiveness. VERB (**pardons, pardoning, pardoned**) forgive or excuse. EXCLAMATION used to ask a speaker to repeat something.
pardonable ADJ

pare VERB trim the edges of; reduce little by little.

parent NOUN **1** a father or mother. **2** an organization owning and controlling subsidiary ones.
parental ADJ
parenthood NOUN

parentage NOUN ancestry; origin.

parenthesis /pă-ren-thĕ-sis/ NOUN (PL **parentheses**) a word or phrase inserted into a passage; brackets (like these) placed round this.
parenthetic ADJ
parenthetical ADJ

parenting NOUN the process of looking after and bringing up offspring.

par excellence ADV being a supreme example of its kind.

pariah /pă-ry-ă/ NOUN an outcast.

parietal bone /pă-ry-i-tăl/ NOUN each of a pair of bones forming part of the skull.

parings PLURAL NOUN thin strips pared off something.

parish NOUN **1** an area with its own church and clergyman. **2** a local government area within a county.

parishioner NOUN an inhabitant of a parish.

Parisian NOUN a person from Paris. ADJ relating to Paris.

parity NOUN equality.

park NOUN **1** a public garden or recreation ground; the enclosed land of a country house. **2** an area for a specified purpose: *a science park;* an area for parking vehicles: *a car park*. VERB stop and leave (a vehicle) temporarily; [INFORMAL] put down casually.

parka NOUN a hooded windproof jacket.

parking ticket NOUN a notice of a fine for illegal parking.

Parkinson's disease NOUN a disease causing trembling and weakness.

Parkinson's law NOUN the notion that work expands to fill the time available.

parlance /pah-lăns/ NOUN a particular way of expressing oneself.

parley NOUN (PL **parleys**) a discussion to settle a dispute. VERB (**parleys, parleying, parleyed**) hold a parley.

parliament NOUN an assembly that makes a country's laws. **parliamentarian** ADJ & NOUN **parliamentary** ADJ

parlour ([US] **parlor**) NOUN **1** [DATED] a sitting room. **2** a shop or business providing specified goods or services.

parlous ADJ [ARCHAIC] difficult; dangerous.

Parmesan NOUN a hard Italian cheese.

parochial ADJ **1** of a

p

church parish. **2** concerning or interested in only a limited area; narrow. **parochialism** NOUN **parochially** ADV

parody NOUN (PL **parodies**) an imitation using exaggeration for comic effect. VERB (**parodies, parodying, parodied**) make a parody of.

parole NOUN the release of a prisoner before the end of his or her sentence on condition of good behaviour. VERB release in this way.

paroxysm /pa-roks-iz-ĕm/ NOUN an outburst of emotion; a sudden attack of an illness.

parquet /par-kay/ NOUN flooring of wooden blocks arranged in a pattern.

parricide NOUN the killing of one's own parent. **parricidal** ADJ

parrot NOUN a tropical bird with a short hooked bill, able to mimic human speech. VERB (**parrots, parroting, parroted**) repeat mechanically.

parry VERB (**parries, parrying, parried**) ward off (a blow); evade (a question) skilfully.

parse /pahz/ VERB analyse (a sentence) in terms of grammar.

parsec /pah-sek/ NOUN a unit of distance used in astronomy, about 3.25 light years.

parsimonious ADJ mean, stingy. **parsimoniously** ADV **parsimony** NOUN

parsley NOUN a herb with crinkled green leaves.

parsnip NOUN a vegetable with a large yellowish tapering root.

parson NOUN [INFORMAL] a clergyman.

parsonage NOUN a rectory or vicarage.

part NOUN **1** some but not all of something; a portion, a division; a constituent or element; a measure of relative amounts: *one part sugar to three parts flour.* **2** a character assigned to an actor; their words to be learned; the proper behaviour for someone: *not my part to criticize.* VERB

separate, be separated; divide. ADV partly.
in good part without taking offence. **in part** partly. **part with** give up, give away. **take part** join in. **take someone's part** support someone.

partake VERB (**partakes**, **partaking**, **partook**; PAST PARTICIPLE **partaken**) [FORMAL] **1** join in an activity. **2** take a portion, especially of food.
partaker NOUN

partial ADJ **1** favouring one side or person, biased. **2** not complete or total.
be partial to have a strong liking for.
partially ADV

partiality NOUN bias, favouritism; a strong liking.

participate VERB take part in something.
participant NOUN
participation NOUN

participle NOUN [GRAMMAR] a word formed from a verb, as a **past participle** (e.g. *burnt, frightened*), or a **present participle** (e.g. *burning, frightening*).
participial ADJ

particle NOUN a very small portion of matter; a minor part of speech.

particoloured ([US] **particolored**) ADJ coloured partly in one colour, partly in another.

particular ADJ **1** individual, specific, singled out from others. **2** especially great: *particular care*. **3** insisting on high standards in every detail. NOUN a detail; a piece of information.
in particular especially.
particularly ADV

parting NOUN **1** leaving, being separated. **2** a line from which hair is combed in different directions.

partisan NOUN **1** a strong supporter. **2** a guerrilla. ADJ prejudiced in favour of one side.
partisanship NOUN

partition NOUN division into parts; a structure dividing a room or space, a thin wall. VERB divide into parts or by a partition.

partitive ADJ [GRAMMAR] (of a word) denoting part of a group or quantity.

partly ADV to some extent;

not completely.

partner NOUN a person sharing with another or others in an activity; each of a pair; a husband or wife or member of an unmarried couple. VERB be the partner of.
partnership NOUN

part of speech NOUN a word's grammatical class (noun, verb, adjective, etc.).

partridge NOUN a game bird.

part-time ADJ for or during only part of the working week.

parturition /pah-tewr-ish-ŏn/ NOUN [FORMAL] the process of giving birth to young; childbirth.

p

party NOUN (PL **parties**) **1** a social gathering. **2** a formally constituted political group; a group travelling, working, etc. as a unit. **3** one side in an agreement or dispute.

party line NOUN the policy of a political party.

party wall NOUN a wall common to two buildings or rooms.

pascal /pas-kăl/ NOUN a unit of pressure.

paschal /pas-kăl/ ADJ [FORMAL] of the Passover; of Easter.

pass VERB **1** move in a specified direction; change from one state into another. **2** go past, move in front of from one end to the other; overtake; go beyond, excel, outdo. **3** send or transfer to someone else. **4** (of time) elapse; while away (time). **5** be successful in an examination; be acceptable; judge to be acceptable or successful. **6** put (a law) into effect. **7** discharge from the body as excreta. **8** (in a game) refuse one's turn; decline to answer. NOUN **1** an act of moving past or through something. **2** a success in an examination. **3** a permit to enter a place. **4** a route over or through mountains. **5** (in football etc.) an act of passing the ball to another player on one's team.
a pretty pass [INFORMAL] a bad state of affairs. **make**

a pass at [INFORMAL] make sexual advances to. **pass away** die. **pass off as** represent falsely as being. **pass out** become unconscious. **pass over** disregard. **pass up** refrain from doing or taking.

passable ADJ **1** just satisfactory. **2** able to be crossed or travelled on. **passably** ADV

passage NOUN **1** movement through or past something on one's way between places; the right to pass through. **2** a narrow access way, usually with walls on either side; a duct etc. in the body. **3** an extract from a book etc. **4** a journey by sea. **passageway** NOUN

passbook NOUN a book recording a customer's deposits and withdrawals from a bank etc.

passé /pa-say/ ADJ old-fashioned.

passenger NOUN **1** a person (other than the driver, pilot, or crew) travelling in a vehicle, aircraft, etc. **2** a member of a team etc. who contributes less than the others.

passer-by NOUN (PL **passers-by**) a person who happens to be going past.

passim ADV throughout a book, article, etc.

passing ADJ not lasting long; casual.

passion NOUN **1** strong emotion; sexual love; great enthusiasm. **2** (**the Passion**) the sufferings of Christ on the Cross.

passionate ADJ full of passion; intense. **passionately** ADV

passive ADJ acted on and not active; not resisting; lacking initiative or forceful qualities. **passively** ADV **passiveness** NOUN **passivity** NOUN

Passover NOUN a Jewish festival commemorating the escape of Jews from slavery in Egypt.

passport NOUN an official document for use by a person travelling abroad, certifying identity and citizenship; a means of achieving something: *a* *passport to success.*

password NOUN a secret word or phrase used to gain admission, prove identity, etc.

past ADJ belonging to the time before the present; no longer existing or happening. NOUN the time before the present; a person's previous experiences. PREP **1** to or on the further side of. **2** in front of, going from one side to the other. **3** no longer capable of or able to benefit from. ADV going past or beyond.
past it [INFORMAL] too old to be capable of anything.

P

pasta NOUN dried flour paste produced in various shapes, to be cooked in boiling water.

paste NOUN **1** a thick, moist substance. **2** an adhesive. **3** a glass-like substance used in imitation gems. VERB **1** fasten or coat with paste. **2** [INFORMAL] thrash.

pasteboard NOUN cardboard.

pastel NOUN **1** a chalk-like crayon; a drawing made with this. **2** a light delicate shade of colour.

pasteurize (also **pasteurise**) VERB sterilize by heating.
pasteurization NOUN

pastiche /pas-**teesh**/ NOUN a work in the style of another work, author, artist, or period.

pastille NOUN a small flavoured sweet; a lozenge.

pastime NOUN something done to pass time pleasantly.

past master NOUN an expert.

pastor NOUN a clergyman in charge of a church or congregation.

pastoral ADJ **1** of country life. **2** (of a farm etc.) keeping sheep and cattle. **3** of spiritual and moral guidance.

pastrami /pas-**trah**-mee/ NOUN seasoned smoked beef.

pastry NOUN (PL **pastries**) a dough made of flour, fat, and water, used for making pies etc.; an individual item of food made with this.

pasturage NOUN pasture land.

pasture NOUN grassy land suitable for grazing cattle. VERB put (animals) to graze.

pasty[1] /pas-ti/ NOUN (PL **pasties**) a pastry with a sweet or savoury filling, baked without a dish.

pasty[2] /pays-ti/ ADJ (**pastier, pastiest**) **1** of or like paste. **2** unhealthily pale.

pat VERB (**pats, patting, patted**) touch gently with the flat of the hand. NOUN **1** a patting movement or touch. **2** a small mass of a soft substance. ADJ unconvincingly quick and simple.
off pat known by heart.

patch NOUN a piece of cloth etc. put on something to mend or strengthen it; a part or area distinguished from the rest; a piece of drug-impregnated material worn on the skin so that the drug is gradually absorbed; a plot of land; [INFORMAL] a stretch of time with a particular character. VERB mend with patches.
not a patch on [INFORMAL] not nearly as good as.
patch up [INFORMAL] repair; settle (a quarrel).

patchwork NOUN needlework in which small pieces of cloth are joined to make a pattern; something made of assorted pieces.

patchy ADJ (**patchier, patchiest**) existing in patches; uneven in quality.
patchily ADV
patchiness NOUN

pâté /pa-tay/ NOUN a paste of meat etc.

patella NOUN (PL **patellae**) the kneecap.

patent ADJ **1** obvious. **2** patented. VERB obtain or hold a patent for. NOUN an official right to be the sole maker or user of an invention or process; an invention etc. protected by this.
patently ADV

patentee NOUN the holder of a patent.

patent leather NOUN leather with a glossy varnished surface.

paternal ADJ of a father; fatherly; related through one's father.
paternally ADV

paternalism NOUN a policy of making provision for people's needs but giving them no independence or responsibility.
paternalistic ADJ

paternity NOUN fatherhood.

path NOUN **1** a way by which people pass on foot; a line along which a person or thing moves. **2** a course of action.

pathetic ADJ arousing pity or sadness; [INFORMAL] miserably inadequate.
pathetically ADV

pathogenic ADJ causing disease.

pathology NOUN the study of disease.
pathological ADJ
pathologist NOUN

pathos NOUN a pathetic quality.

patience NOUN **1** calm endurance. **2** a card game for one player.

patient ADJ showing patience. NOUN a person receiving medical treatment.
patiently ADV

patina NOUN a sheen on a surface produced by age or use; a green film on bronze.

patio NOUN (PL **patios**) a paved outdoor area by a house.

patisserie /pă-tee-sě-ree/ NOUN fancy pastries; a shop selling these.

patois /pat-wah/ NOUN a dialect.

patriarch NOUN the male head of a family or tribe; a bishop of high rank in certain Churches.
patriarchal ADJ
patriarchate NOUN

patriarchy NOUN (PL **patriarchies**) a social organization in which a male is head of the family.

patricide NOUN the killing of one's own father; someone guilty of this.
patricidal ADJ

patrimony NOUN (PL **patrimonies**) heritage.

patriot NOUN a patriotic person.

patriotic ADJ loyally

supporting one's country.
patriotically ADV
patriotism NOUN

patrol VERB (**patrols**, **patrolling**, **patrolled**) walk or travel regularly through (an area or building) to see that all is well. NOUN the action of patrolling an area; a person or group patrolling.

patron /pay-trŏn/ NOUN **1** a person giving influential or financial support to a cause. **2** a customer.

patronage NOUN **1** a patron's support; regular custom; the power to control appointments and privileges. **2** patronizing behaviour.

patronize (also **patronise**) VERB **1** treat with apparent kindness that reveals one's sense of superiority. **2** be a customer of.
patronizing ADJ

patron saint NOUN a saint regarded as a protector.

patronymic /pat-rŏ-nim-ik/ NOUN a name derived from that of a father or ancestor.

patter VERB make a series of quick tapping sounds; run with short quick steps. NOUN **1** a pattering sound. **2** rapid glib speech.

pattern NOUN **1** a decorative design. **2** a model, design, or instructions showing how a thing is to be made; a sample of cloth etc.; an example to follow. **3** a regular sequence of events.
patterned ADJ

patty NOUN (PL **patties**) a small pie or pasty.

paucity NOUN lack, scarcity.

paunch NOUN a large protruding stomach.

pauper NOUN a very poor person.

pause NOUN a temporary stop. VERB make a pause.

pave VERB cover (a path, area, etc.) with flat stones or bricks.

pavement NOUN **1** a raised path at the side of a road. **2** [US] the hard surface of a road.

pavilion NOUN **1** a building on a sports ground for

use by players and spectators. **2** an ornamental building.

paw NOUN a foot of an animal that has claws. VERB touch with a paw; scrape (the ground) with a hoof; [INFORMAL] handle awkwardly or indecently.

pawn NOUN a chess piece of the smallest size and value; a person whose actions are controlled by others. VERB deposit with a pawnbroker as security for money borrowed.

pawnbroker NOUN a person licensed to lend money on the security of personal property deposited.

pawnshop NOUN a pawnbroker's premises.

pawpaw (also **papaw**, **papaya**) NOUN a tropical fruit.

pay VERB (**pays**, **paying**, **paid**) **1** give (money) to (someone) in return for goods or services; give what is owed; suffer (a penalty or misfortune) on account of one's actions. **2** be profitable or worthwhile. **3** give (attention etc.) to (someone or something). NOUN payment; wages.

pay off 1 pay (a debt) in full. **2** discharge (an employee). **3** [INFORMAL] be successful and profitable.

payer NOUN

payable ADJ which must or may be paid.

PAYE ABBREV pay as you earn, a system whereby tax is deducted from wages before payment.

payee NOUN a person to whom money is paid or is to be paid.

payload NOUN the part of a vehicle's load from which profit is derived.

payment NOUN the process of paying someone or of being paid; money etc. paid.

pay-off NOUN [INFORMAL] a payment on leaving a job; a bribe; a return on investment; a final outcome.

payola /pay-**oh**-lă/ NOUN a bribe offered for dishonest use of influence to promote a commercial product.

payroll NOUN a list of a firm's employees

receiving regular pay.

PC ABBREV **1** police constable. **2** personal computer. **3** (also **pc**) politically correct; political correctness.

p.d.q. ABBREV [INFORMAL] pretty damn quick.

PE ABBREV physical education.

pea NOUN a round seed growing in pods, used as a vegetable; the plant that yields these pods.

peace NOUN a state of freedom from war or disturbance.

peaceable ADJ avoiding conflict; peaceful. **peaceably** ADV

peace dividend NOUN public money made available when defence spending is reduced.

peaceful ADJ free from war or disturbance; not involving violence. **peacefully** ADV **peacefulness** NOUN

peacemaker NOUN a person who brings about peace.

peach NOUN a round fruit with yellow skin flushed with red and juicy flesh, with a rough stone; a pinkish-yellow colour.

peacock NOUN a male bird with splendid plumage and a long fan-like tail.

peahen NOUN the female of the peacock.

peak NOUN a pointed top, especially of a mountain; the projecting part of the edge of a cap; the point of highest value, intensity, etc. VERB reach a highest point. ADJ maximum. **peaked** ADJ

peaky ADJ (**peakier**, **peakiest**) looking pale and sickly.

peal NOUN the sound of ringing bells; a set of bells with different notes; a loud burst of thunder or laughter. VERB sound in a peal.

pean US spelling of **PAEAN**.

peanut NOUN **1** the oval seed of a South American plant, commonly eaten as a snack. **2** (**peanuts**) [INFORMAL] a trivial sum of money.

pear NOUN a rounded fruit tapering towards the

stalk.

pearl NOUN a round creamy-white gem formed inside the shell of certain oysters.
pearly ADJ

peasant NOUN a person working on the land, especially in the Middle Ages.

peasantry NOUN peasants collectively.

peat NOUN decomposed vegetable matter from bogs etc., used in horticulture or as fuel.
peaty ADJ

pebble NOUN a small smooth round stone.
pebbly ADJ

pecan NOUN a smooth pinkish-brown nut.

peccary NOUN (PL **peccaries**) a small wild pig.

peck VERB **1** (of a bird) strike, bite, or pick up with the beak. **2** kiss lightly and hastily. NOUN an act of pecking.
peck at [INFORMAL] eat (food) in small amounts and without enthusiasm.

pecker NOUN [US] [VULGAR SLANG] the penis.
keep your pecker up [INFORMAL] stay cheerful.

peckish ADJ [INFORMAL] hungry.

pectin NOUN a substance found in fruits which makes jam set.

pectoral ADJ of, in, or on the chest or breast. NOUN a pectoral fin or muscle.

peculiar ADJ **1** strange, eccentric. **2** belonging exclusively to one person or place or thing; special.
peculiarity NOUN
peculiarly ADV

pecuniary ADJ [FORMAL] of or in money.

pedagogue NOUN [FORMAL] a teacher.

pedal NOUN a lever operated by the foot. VERB (**pedals**, **pedalling**, **pedalled**; [US] **pedaling**, **pedaled**) operate by pedals; ride a bicycle.

pedalo NOUN (PL **pedalos** or **pedaloes**) a small pedal-operated pleasure boat.

pedantic ADJ insisting on strict observance of rules and details.
pedant NOUN
pedantically ADV

pedantry NOUN

peddle VERB sell (goods) as a pedlar.

peddler NOUN US spelling of **PEDLAR**.

pedestal NOUN a base supporting a column or statue etc.

pedestrian NOUN a person walking in a street. ADJ unimaginative, dull.

pediatrics etc. US spelling of **PAEDIATRICS** etc.

pedicure NOUN the care or treatment of the feet.

pedigree NOUN recorded ancestry; a line of descent. ADJ (of an animal) descended from a known line of animals of the same breed.

pediment NOUN a triangular part crowning the front of a building.

pedlar ([US] **peddler**) NOUN a person who sells small articles from door to door; a seller of illegal drugs.

pedometer NOUN a device for estimating the distance walked or run.

peduncle NOUN the stalk bearing a flower or fruit.

pee [INFORMAL] VERB urinate. NOUN urine.

peek VERB peep, glance. NOUN a peep.

peel NOUN the skin of certain fruits and vegetables. VERB remove the peel or skin from; strip off (an outer covering); (of skin etc.) come off in flakes or layers; lose skin etc. in this way.

peeler NOUN

peelings PLURAL NOUN

peep¹ VERB **1** look quickly and secretly. **2** (**peep out**) be just visible. NOUN a quick look.

peep² NOUN a short high-pitched sound. VERB make a peep.

peephole NOUN a small hole to peep through.

peeping Tom NOUN a furtive voyeur.

peer¹ VERB look searchingly or with difficulty or effort.

peer² NOUN **1** a duke, marquess, earl, viscount, or baron. **2** one who is the equal of another in rank, merit, age, etc.

peerage NOUN peers as a

group; the rank of peer or peeress.

peeress NOUN a female peer; a peer's wife.

peerless ADJ without equal, superb.

peeved ADJ [INFORMAL] annoyed.

peevish ADJ irritable.
peevishly ADV

peg NOUN a wooden or metal pin or stake as a fastening or to hang things on; a clip for holding clothes on a line. VERB (**pegs**, **pegging**, **pegged**) **1** fix or mark by means of pegs. **2** keep (wages or prices) at a fixed level.
off the peg (of clothes) ready-made. **take down a peg or two** make less arrogant.

p

pejorative ADJ expressing disapproval.

peke NOUN [INFORMAL] a Pekinese dog.

Pekinese (also **Pekingese**) NOUN a dog of a breed with short legs, a flat face, and silky hair.

pelican NOUN a waterbird with a pouch in its long bill for storing fish.

pelican crossing NOUN a pedestrian crossing with lights operated by pedestrians.

pellagra NOUN a disease involving cracking of the skin, caused by deficiencies in diet.

pellet NOUN a small round mass of a substance; a piece of small shot.
pelleted ADJ

pell-mell ADJ & ADV in a confused or rushed way.

pellucid ADJ very clear.

pelmet NOUN a border of cloth or wood above a window.

pelt VERB **1** throw missiles at. **2** [INFORMAL] run fast. NOUN an animal skin.
at full pelt as fast as possible.

pelvis NOUN the framework of bones round the body below the waist.
pelvic ADJ

pen NOUN **1** a device with a metal point for writing with ink. **2** a small fenced enclosure, especially for animals. **3** a female swan. VERB (**pens**, **penning**, **penned**) **1** write (a letter etc.). **2** shut in or as if in an animal pen.

penal /pee-năl/ ADJ of or involving punishment.

penalize (also **penalise**) VERB inflict a penalty on; put at a disadvantage.
penalization NOUN

penalty NOUN (PL **penalties**) a punishment for breaking a law, rule, or contract.

penance NOUN an act performed as an expression of penitence.

pence pl. of **PENNY**.

penchant /pahn-shahn/ NOUN a liking; a tendency.

pencil NOUN an instrument containing graphite, used for drawing or writing. VERB (**pencils**, **pencilling**, **pencilled**; [US] **penciling**, **penciled**) write, draw, or mark with a pencil.

pendant NOUN an ornament hung from a chain round the neck.

pendent (also **pendant**) ADJ hanging.

pending ADJ waiting to be decided or settled. PREP until, while waiting for.

pendulous ADJ hanging loosely.

pendulum NOUN a weight hung from a cord and swinging freely; a rod with a weighted end that regulates a clock's movement.

penetrate VERB make a way into or through, pierce; see into or through, understand.
penetrable ADJ
penetration NOUN

penetrating ADJ
1 showing great insight.
2 (of sound) piercing.

penfriend NOUN a friend to whom a person writes regularly without meeting.

penguin NOUN a flightless seabird of Antarctic regions.

penicillin NOUN an antibiotic obtained from mould fungi.

peninsula NOUN a piece of land almost surrounded by water.
peninsular ADJ

penis NOUN the organ by which a male mammal copulates and urinates.

penitent ADJ feeling or showing regret that one has done wrong. NOUN a penitent person.

p

penitence NOUN
penitently ADV

penitential ADJ of penitence or penance.

pen name NOUN an author's pseudonym.

pennant NOUN a long tapering flag.

penniless ADJ having no money.

pennon NOUN a pennant.

penny NOUN (PL **pennies** for separate coins, **pence** for a sum of money) a British bronze coin worth one-hundredth of £1; a former coin worth one-twelfth of a shilling.

penny-pinching ADJ niggardly, mean.

pen-pushing NOUN [DEROGATORY], [INFORMAL] clerical work.

pension[1] NOUN an income paid by the government, an ex-employer, or a private fund to a person who is retired, disabled, etc.
pension off dismiss with a pension.

pension[2] /pahn-si-ahn/ NOUN a guest house in Europe.

pensionable ADJ entitled or (of a job) entitling one to a pension.

pensioner NOUN a person who receives a pension.

pensive ADJ deep in thought.
pensively ADV
pensiveness NOUN

pentagon NOUN a geometric figure with five sides.
pentagonal ADJ

pentagram NOUN a five-pointed star.

pentathlon NOUN an athletic contest involving five events.

Pentecost NOUN the Jewish harvest festival; Whit Sunday.

penthouse NOUN a flat on the top floor of a tall building.

penultimate ADJ last but one.

penumbra NOUN (PL **penumbrae** or **penumbras**) an area of partial shadow; the shadow cast by the earth or moon in a partial eclipse.

penury NOUN poverty.
penurious ADJ

people PLURAL NOUN

1 human beings; the subjects of a state. **2** persons of ordinary rank, the common people. **3** a person's relatives. NOUN a race or nation. VERB fill with people, populate.

pep [INFORMAL] NOUN vigour. **pep up** (**peps**, **pepping**, **pepped**) make livelier or more vigorous.

pepper NOUN **1** a hot-tasting seasoning powder made from the dried berries of certain plants. **2** a capsicum. VERB sprinkle with pepper; scatter a large amount of something on or over; hit repeatedly with small missiles.
peppery ADJ

peppercorn NOUN a dried black berry from which pepper is made.

peppercorn rent NOUN a very low rent.

peppermint NOUN a mint producing a strong fragrant oil; a sweet flavoured with this.

pepsin NOUN an enzyme in gastric juice, helping in digestion.

pep talk NOUN [INFORMAL] a talk designed to encourage confidence and effort.

peptic ADJ of digestion.

per PREP **1** for each. **2** in accordance with.

perambulate VERB [FORMAL] walk through or round (an area).
perambulation NOUN

per annum ADV for each year.

per capita ADV & ADJ for each person.

perceive VERB become aware of; see, hear, etc.; regard in a particular way.

per cent ADV in or for every hundred.

percentage NOUN a rate or proportion per hundred; a proportion, a part.

perceptible ADJ able to be perceived.
perceptibly ADV

perception NOUN perceiving, the ability to perceive.

perceptive ADJ showing insight and understanding.
perceptively ADV
perceptiveness NOUN

perch[1] NOUN a branch or rod on which a bird lands and sits; a high seat. VERB (of a bird) land on a perch; sit somewhere; balance (something) on a narrow support.

perch[2] NOUN (PL **perch**) an edible freshwater fish.

percipient ADJ perceptive.
percipience NOUN

percolate VERB filter, especially through small holes; prepare (coffee) in a percolator.
percolation NOUN

percolator NOUN a coffee-making pot in which boiling water is circulated through ground coffee in a perforated drum.

percussion NOUN the playing of a musical instrument by striking it with a stick etc.; instruments played in this way.
percussive ADJ

perdition NOUN eternal damnation.

peregrinations PLURAL NOUN [ARCHAIC] travel or wandering from place to place.

peregrine NOUN a falcon.

peremptory ADJ imperious; insisting on obedience.
peremptorily ADV

perennial ADJ lasting a long or infinite time; constantly recurring; (of plants) living for several years. NOUN a perennial plant.
perennially ADV

perestroika /pe-ris-**troy**-kă/ NOUN (in the former USSR) reform of the economic and political system.

perfect ADJ /**per**-fekt/ **1** without faults or defects; excellent. **2** exact, total, absolute: *a perfect stranger.* VERB /per-**fekt**/ make perfect.
perfection NOUN
perfectly ADV

perfectionist NOUN a person who seeks perfection.
perfectionism NOUN

perfidious ADJ [LITERARY] treacherous, disloyal.
perfidy NOUN

perforate VERB pierce, make holes in.
perforation NOUN

perforce ADV [FORMAL] unavoidably, necessarily.

perform VERB **1** carry out (a task etc.); function. **2** present (a form of entertainment) to an audience; act, sing, etc., to entertain others.
performance NOUN
performer NOUN

perfume NOUN a sweet smell; a fragrant liquid for applying to the body. VERB give a sweet smell to.

perfumery NOUN the making and selling of perfumes; a shop selling perfumes.

perfunctory ADJ done without thought, effort, or enthusiasm.
perfunctorily ADV

pergola /per-gŏ-lă/ NOUN an arbour or walkway with arches covered in climbing plants.

perhaps ADV it may be, possibly.

pericardium NOUN (PL **pericardia**) the membranous sac enclosing the heart.

perigee /pe-ri-jee/ NOUN the point nearest to the earth in the moon's orbit.

peril NOUN serious danger.
perilous ADJ
perilously ADV

perimeter NOUN the outline of a geometric figure; the outer edge of an area; the length of this.

perinatal ADJ of the time immediately before and after birth.

period NOUN **1** a length or portion of time; a major division of geological time; a division of a school day. **2** an occurrence of menstruation. **3** a full stop in punctuation. ADJ (of dress or furniture) belonging to a past age.

periodic ADJ happening at intervals.
periodicity NOUN

periodical ADJ periodic. NOUN a magazine etc. published at regular intervals.
periodically ADV

peripatetic /pe-ri-pă-**te**-tik/ ADJ going from place to place.

peripheral ADJ of or on the periphery; of only minor importance.

p

periphery NOUN (PL **peripheries**) the outer limits of an area; the fringes of a subject.

periphrasis NOUN (PL **periphrases**) a roundabout phrase or way of speaking.

periscope NOUN a tube attached to a set of mirrors, enabling one to see things hidden behind others and otherwise out of sight.

perish VERB die, be destroyed; (of food, rubber, etc.) rot.
be perished [INFORMAL] feel very cold.

perishable ADJ liable to decay or go bad in a short time.

p

peritoneum /pe-ri-tŏ-nee-ŭm/ NOUN (PL **peritoneums** or **peritonea**) the membrane lining the abdominal cavity.

peritonitis NOUN inflammation of the peritoneum.

perjure VERB (**perjure oneself**) lie under oath.

perjury NOUN the deliberate giving of false evidence while under oath; this evidence.

perk NOUN [INFORMAL] a benefit to which an employee is entitled.
perk up make or become livelier, more cheerful, or more interesting.

perky ADJ (**perkier**, **perkiest**) lively and cheerful.
perkily ADV
perkiness NOUN

perm NOUN **1** a treatment giving hair a long-lasting artificial wave. **2** [INFORMAL] a permutation. VERB **1** treat (hair) with a perm. **2** [INFORMAL] select (a specified number) from a quantity.

permafrost NOUN permanently frozen subsoil in arctic regions.

permanent ADJ lasting indefinitely.
permanence NOUN
permanently ADV

permeable ADJ allowing liquid or gases to pass through it.
permeability NOUN

permeate VERB spread throughout, pervade.

permissible ADJ

allowable.

permission NOUN consent, authorization.

permissive ADJ tolerant, especially in social and sexual matters.
permissiveness NOUN

permit VERB /per-**mit**/ (**permits**, **permitting**, **permitted**) allow to do something or to be done or happen; make possible, provide an opportunity for. NOUN /**per**-mit/ a written order giving permission, especially for entry.

permutation NOUN one of several possible arrangements of things; a selection of a number of matches in a football pool.

pernicious ADJ harmful.

pernickety ADJ [INFORMAL] too fastidious, fussy.

peroration NOUN the concluding part of a speech.

peroxide NOUN a compound of hydrogen used to bleach hair.

perpendicular ADJ at an angle of 90° to a line or surface; upright, vertical. NOUN a perpendicular line or direction.
perpendicularly ADV

perpetrate VERB commit (a crime); make (an error).
perpetration NOUN
perpetrator NOUN

perpetual ADJ never ending or changing; very frequent.
perpetually ADV

perpetuate VERB cause to continue or be preserved indefinitely.
perpetuation NOUN

perpetuity NOUN the state of lasting forever; (**in perpetuity**) forever.

perplex VERB puzzle, baffle.

perplexity NOUN not knowing how to deal with something.

per pro. *see* **P.P.**

perquisite NOUN [FORMAL] a privilege or benefit given in addition to wages; a privilege derived from one's status.

perry NOUN a drink made from fermented pears.

per se ADV by or in itself; intrinsically.

persecute VERB treat with

hostility because of race or religion; harass.
persecution NOUN
persecutor NOUN

persevere VERB continue in spite of difficulties.
perseverance NOUN

persimmon NOUN a tropical fruit.

persist VERB continue in an opinion or course of action despite opposition; continue to exist.
persistence NOUN
persistent ADJ
persistently ADV

person NOUN (PL **people** or **persons**) **1** an individual human being; an individual with a particular character or tastes. **2** an individual's body. **3** [GRAMMAR] one of the three classes of personal pronouns and verb forms, referring to the person(s) speaking, spoken to, or referred to. **in person** oneself, physically present.

persona NOUN (PL **personas** or **personae**) the aspect of someone's character presented to others; a role adopted by someone.

personable ADJ attractive in appearance or manner.

personage NOUN a person, especially an important one.

personal ADJ **1** belonging to or affecting an individual; one's own, private. **2** concerning one's emotions, relationships, etc. **3** of a person's body. **4** done by a particular person, not delegated.
personally ADV

personal computer NOUN a computer designed for use by a single individual.

personal equity plan NOUN a scheme for tax-free personal investment.

personality NOUN (PL **personalities**) **1** a person's distinctive character; a person with distinctive qualities. **2** a celebrity.

personalize (also **personalise**) VERB **1** design to suit or identify as belonging to a particular individual. **2** cause (a discussion etc.) to be

concerned with personalities rather than abstract topics.
personalization NOUN

personal organizer NOUN a loose-leaf folder or pocket-sized computer for keeping details of meetings, phone numbers, addresses, etc.

personal pronoun *see* **PRONOUN**.

personify VERB (**personifies**, **personifying**, **personified**) represent in human form or as having human characteristics; embody in one's behaviour.
personification NOUN

personnel NOUN employees, staff.

perspective NOUN **1** the art of drawing so as to give an effect of solidity and relative position. **2** a particular attitude towards something; understanding of the relative importance of things.
in perspective drawn according to the rules of perspective; not distorting a thing's relative importance.

perspex NOUN [TRADE MARK] a tough light transparent plastic.

perspicacious /per-spi-kay-shŭs/ ADJ showing great insight.
perspicaciously ADV
perspicacity NOUN

perspicuous ADJ expressing things clearly.
perspicuity NOUN

perspire VERB sweat.
perspiration NOUN

persuade VERB cause (someone) to believe or do something by reasoning.
persuader NOUN

persuasion NOUN **1** the process of persuading or of being persuaded; persuasive argument. **2** a belief or set of beliefs.

persuasive ADJ able or trying to persuade people.
persuasively ADV
persuasiveness NOUN

pert ADJ impudent, especially in a lively and attractive way.
pertly ADV
pertness NOUN

pertain VERB be relevant;

belong as a part.

pertinacious ADJ [FORMAL] persistent and determined.
pertinaciously ADV
pertinacity NOUN

pertinent ADJ relevant.
pertinence NOUN
pertinently ADV

perturb VERB make anxious or uneasy.
perturbation NOUN

peruse VERB [FORMAL] read carefully.
perusal NOUN

pervade VERB spread throughout (a thing).
pervasive ADJ

perverse ADJ obstinate in unreasonable or unacceptable behaviour; contrary to reason or expectation.
perversely ADV
perversity NOUN

p

pervert VERB /pĕ-**vert**/ alter, distort, misuse or misapply; lead astray, corrupt. NOUN /**per**-vert/ a person whose sexual behaviour is regarded as abnormal and unacceptable.
perversion NOUN

pervious ADJ permeable; penetrable.

peseta NOUN a former unit of money in Spain.

peso NOUN (PL **pesos**) a unit of money in several South American countries.

pessary NOUN (PL **pessaries**) a vaginal suppository.

pessimism NOUN a tendency to take a gloomy view of things.
pessimist NOUN
pessimistic ADJ
pessimistically ADV

pest NOUN an insect or animal harmful to crops, stored food, etc.; [INFORMAL] an annoying person or thing.

pester VERB annoy continually, especially with requests or questions.

pesticide NOUN a substance used to destroy harmful insects etc.

pestilence NOUN [ARCHAIC] a deadly epidemic disease.
pestilential ADJ

pestle /**pess**-ĕl/ NOUN a club-shaped instrument for pounding things to powder.

pesto NOUN a sauce of basil, olive oil, Parmesan cheese, and pine nuts, often used on pasta.

pet NOUN **1** a tame animal kept for company and pleasure. **2** a favourite. ADJ **1** kept as a pet. **2** favourite. VERB (**pets**, **petting**, **petted**) stroke affectionately; treat affectionately and indulgently; kiss and caress.

petal NOUN one of the coloured outer parts of a flower head.

peter VERB (**peter out**) gradually come to an end or fade away.

pethidine NOUN a painkilling drug.

petite ADJ small and dainty.

petition NOUN a formal written request signed by many people. VERB present a petition to.

petrel NOUN a seabird.

petrify VERB (**petrifies**, **petrifying**, **petrified**) **1** change into a stony mass. **2** paralyse with astonishment or fear.
petrifaction NOUN

petrochemical NOUN a chemical substance obtained from petroleum or gas. ADJ of such a substance or the processing of it.

petrol NOUN an inflammable liquid made from petroleum for use as fuel in internal-combustion engines.

petroleum NOUN a mineral oil found underground, refined for use as fuel or in dry-cleaning etc.

petticoat NOUN a dress-length undergarment worn beneath a dress or skirt.

pettifogging ADJ trivial; quibbling about unimportant details.

pettish ADJ childishly bad-tempered.

petty ADJ (**pettier**, **pettiest**) unimportant, trivial; of relatively low rank; spitefully or unfairly critical of details.
pettily ADV
pettiness NOUN

petty cash NOUN money kept by an office etc. for small payments.

petulant ADJ sulky,

irritable.
petulance NOUN
petulantly ADV

pew NOUN a long bench-like seat in a church; [INFORMAL] a seat.

pewter NOUN a grey alloy of tin with lead or other metal.

pfennig NOUN a former German coin, one-hundredth of a mark.

PG ABBREV (in film classification) suitable for children subject to parental guidance.

pH NOUN a measure of acidity or alkalinity.

phalanx /fal-anks/ NOUN (PL **phalanxes**) a compact mass of people or things; a body of troops or police officers.

phallus NOUN (PL **phalluses** or **phalli**) a penis.
phallic ADJ

phantom NOUN a ghost.

Pharaoh /fair-oh/ NOUN the title of the kings of ancient Egypt.

pharmaceutical /fah-mă-syoo-tik-ăl/ ADJ of or engaged in pharmacy.

pharmacist NOUN a person skilled in pharmacy.

pharmacology NOUN the study of the action of drugs.
pharmacological ADJ
pharmacologist NOUN

pharmacopoeia /far-mă-kŏ-pee-ă/ NOUN an official list of medicinal drugs with their effects.

pharmacy NOUN (PL **pharmacies**) a shop or dispensary providing medicinal drugs; the preparation and dispensing of these drugs.

pharynx /fa-ringks/ NOUN the cavity at the back of the nose and throat.
pharyngeal ADJ

phase NOUN a distinct period in a process of change or development. VERB carry out (a programme etc.) in stages.
phase in or **out** bring gradually into or out of use.

PhD ABBREV Doctor of Philosophy, a higher degree.

pheasant NOUN a game bird with bright feathers in the male.

p

phenomenal ADJ extraordinary, remarkable.
phenomenally ADV

phenomenon NOUN (PL **phenomena**) **1** a fact, occurrence, or change perceived by the senses or the mind. **2** a remarkable person or thing.

pheromone NOUN a chemical secreted by an animal's body and influencing the behaviour of others of the same species when released into the air.

phial NOUN a small bottle.

philander VERB (of a man) engage in many casual love affairs.
philanderer NOUN

philanthropy NOUN benevolence, promotion of others' welfare.
philanthropic ADJ
philanthropist NOUN

philately NOUN stamp-collecting.
philatelic ADJ
philatelist NOUN

philistine NOUN an uncultured person.

philology NOUN the study of languages.
philological ADJ
philologist NOUN

philosopher NOUN a person who engages in philosophy.

philosophical ADJ **1** of philosophy. **2** bearing misfortune calmly.
philosophically ADV

philosophize (also **philosophise**) VERB theorize; moralize.

philosophy NOUN (PL **philosophies**) the study of the basic principles of existence, knowledge, morals, etc.; a particular system of beliefs about these; an outlook or set of principles.

philtre ([US] **philter**) NOUN a love potion.

phlegm /flem/ NOUN a thick mucus in the bronchial passages, ejected by coughing.

phlegmatic ADJ not excitable or emotional.
phlegmatically ADV

phobia NOUN an extreme or irrational fear or dislike.
phobic ADJ & NOUN

phoenix /fee-niks/ NOUN a

mythical Arabian bird said to burn itself and rise young again from its ashes.

phone NOUN a telephone. VERB telephone.

phonecard NOUN a card containing prepaid units for use in a public phone.

phone-in NOUN a broadcast programme in which listeners telephone the studio with questions and comments.

phonetic ADJ **1** of or representing speech sounds. **2** (of spelling) corresponding to pronunciation. NOUN (**phonetics**) the study or representation of speech sounds.
phonetically ADV
phonetician NOUN

phoney (also **phony**) [INFORMAL] ADJ false, sham. NOUN a phoney person or thing.

phonograph NOUN [US] a record player.

phosphate NOUN a compound of phosphorous, used especially in fertilizers.

phosphorescent ADJ luminous.
phosphorescence NOUN

phosphorus NOUN a chemical element; a wax-like form of this appearing luminous in the dark and igniting in air.

photo NOUN (PL **photos**) a photograph.

photocopier NOUN a machine for photocopying documents.

photocopy NOUN (PL **photocopies**) a photographic copy of a document. VERB (**photocopies**, **photocopying**, **photocopied**) make a photocopy of.

photoelectric cell NOUN an electronic device emitting an electric current when light falls on it.

photo finish NOUN a finish of a race so close that the winner has to be decided from a photograph.

photofit NOUN a likeness of a person made up of separate photographs of features.

p

photogenic ADJ looking attractive in photographs.

photograph NOUN a picture made using a camera, formed by the chemical action of light on sensitive material on to which an image is focused. VERB take a photograph of; come out (well or badly) when photographed.
photographer NOUN
photographic ADJ
photographically ADV
photography NOUN

photojournalism NOUN the reporting of news by photographs.

photon NOUN an indivisible unit of electromagnetic radiation.

photosensitive ADJ reacting to light.

photostat [TRADE MARK] NOUN a photocopier; a photocopy.
VERB (**photostats**, **photostatting**, **photostatted**) make a photocopy of.

photosynthesis NOUN the process by which green plants use sunlight to convert carbon dioxide and water into complex substances.
photosynthesize VERB (also **photosynthesise**)

phrase NOUN a group of words forming a unit; a short idiomatic expression; a unit in a melody. VERB **1** express in words. **2** divide (music) into phrases.
phrasal ADJ

phraseology NOUN (PL **phraseologies**) a mode of expression, a way of wording things.

phrenology NOUN the study of the shape of a person's skull, supposedly as an indication of their character.

phylum /fI-lŭm/ NOUN (PL **phyla**) a major division of the plant or animal kingdom.

physical ADJ **1** of the body; of things perceived by the senses. **2** of physics; of natural forces and laws.
physically ADV

physical education NOUN exercises and games as taught at school.

p

physical geography NOUN the study of the earth's natural features.

physical sciences PLURAL NOUN the sciences studying inanimate natural objects.

physician NOUN a doctor, especially one specializing in medicine as distinct from surgery.

physicist NOUN an expert in physics.

physics NOUN the study of the properties and interactions of matter and energy.

physiognomy NOUN (PL **physiognomies**) the features of a person's face.

p

physiology NOUN the study of the bodily functions of living organisms.
physiological ADJ
physiologist NOUN

physiotherapy NOUN treatment of an injury etc. by massage and exercises.
physiotherapist NOUN

physique /fi-zeek/ NOUN a person's physical build and muscular development.

pi NOUN a Greek letter (π) used as a symbol for the ratio of a circle's circumference to its diameter (about 3.14).

pianissimo ADV [MUSIC] very softly.

pianist NOUN a person who plays the piano.

piano NOUN (PL **pianos**) a musical instrument with strings struck by hammers operated by a keyboard. ADV [MUSIC] softly.

pianoforte NOUN [FORMAL] a piano.

piazza /pee-**at**-să/ NOUN a public square or market place.

picador NOUN a mounted bullfighter with a lance.

picaresque /pik-ă-**resk**/ ADJ (of fiction) recounting a series of adventures of a roguish hero.

piccalilli NOUN a pickle of chopped vegetables and hot spices.

piccaninny ([US] **pickaninny**) NOUN (PL **piccaninnies**, **pickaninnies**) [OFFENSIVE] a black child; an

Aboriginal child.

piccolo NOUN (PL **piccolos**) a small flute.

pick VERB **1** take hold of and pull or lift from its place. **2** select. **3** pull at something repeatedly with the fingers; make (a hole) in this way. NOUN **1** an act of choosing; the right to choose; [INFORMAL] the best of a group. **2** a pickaxe. **3** [INFORMAL] a plectrum.
pick a lock open a lock using something other than a key. **pick a pocket** steal from a pocket. **pick a quarrel** provoke a quarrel. **pick holes in** criticize. **pick off** single out and shoot. **pick on** unfairly single out for blame or criticism. **pick one's way** walk carefully over rough ground. **pick out 1** select. **2** mark, distinguish (a design etc.). **pick up 1** lift. **2** collect in a car. **3** become better or stronger. **4** [INFORMAL] casually become acquainted with someone, especially as a sexual overture.
picker NOUN

pickaback variant of **PIGGYBACK**.

pickaninny US spelling of **PICCANINNY**.

pickaxe ([US] **pickax**) NOUN a tool with a pointed iron bar at right angles to its handle, for breaking ground etc.

picket NOUN **1** people stationed outside a workplace to dissuade others from entering during a strike; a party of sentries. **2** a pointed stake set in the ground. VERB (**pickets**, **picketing**, **picketed**) form a picket outside (a workplace).

pickings PLURAL NOUN gains made easily or dishonestly.

pickle NOUN **1** vegetables preserved in vinegar or brine; this liquid. **2** [INFORMAL] a difficult or embarrassing situation. VERB preserve in pickle.

pickpocket NOUN a thief who steals from people's pockets.

pickup NOUN **1** a small van with low sides. **2** [INFORMAL] a casual encounter with

p

someone, especially a sexual one. **3** a device producing an electrical signal in response to a change, e.g. the stylus holder on a record player.

picnic NOUN an informal outdoor meal. VERB (**picnics**, **picnicking**, **picnicked**) take part in a picnic.
picnicker NOUN

pictograph NOUN a pictorial symbol used as a form of writing.

pictorial ADJ of, in, or like a picture or pictures; illustrated. NOUN a newspaper etc. with many pictures.
pictorially ADV

picture NOUN a representation made by painting, drawing, or photography; an idea, a mental image; (**the pictures**) the cinema. VERB represent, draw or paint; imagine.
be (or **look**) **a picture** be very beautiful. **get the picture** [INFORMAL] understand a situation.

picturesque ADJ forming a pleasant scene; (of words or a description) very expressive.

pidgin NOUN a simplified form of English or another language with elements of a local language.

pie NOUN a baked dish of meat, fish, or fruit covered with pastry.

piebald ADJ (of a horse) with irregular patches of white and black.

piece NOUN **1** a portion; a part; an item in a set. **2** something regarded as a unit. **3** a musical, literary, or artistic composition. **4** a small object used in board games.
of a piece of the same kind; consistent. **piece together** make by putting together pieces or parts.

pièce de résistance /pee-ess dě ray-zees-tahns/ NOUN (PL **pièces de résistance**) the most impressive feature, especially of a creative work.

piecemeal ADJ & ADV done at different times and in an inconsistent manner.

piecework NOUN work paid according to the

quantity done.

pie chart NOUN a diagram representing quantities as sectors of a circle.

pied ADJ particoloured.

pied-à-terre /pee-ayd a tair/ NOUN (PL **pieds-à-terre**) a small house for occasional use.

pie-eyed ADJ [INFORMAL] drunk.

pier NOUN **1** a structure built out into the sea, used as a landing stage or a promenade. **2** a pillar supporting an arch or bridge.

pierce VERB (of a sharp-pointed instrument) go into or through (something); make (a hole) in (something) in this way; force a way through.

piercing ADJ **1** (of cold or wind) penetrating sharply. **2** (of sound) shrilly audible.
piercingly ADV

piety NOUN the quality of being religious or reverent.

piffle NOUN [INFORMAL] nonsense.

pig NOUN **1** an omnivorous animal with cloven hooves and a blunt snout, domesticated for its meat. **2** [INFORMAL] a greedy or unpleasant person.

pigeon NOUN **1** a bird of the dove family. **2** [INFORMAL] a person's business or responsibility.

pigeonhole NOUN a small compartment where mail can be left for someone; a similar compartment for documents in a desk. VERB put (a document) in a pigeonhole; assign to a category, especially thoughtlessly.

piggery NOUN (PL **piggeries**) a pig-breeding establishment; a pigsty.

piggy ADJ like a pig.

piggyback (also **pickaback**) NOUN a ride on a person's back.

piggy bank NOUN a money box shaped like a pig.

pig-headed ADJ obstinate.

pig iron NOUN oblong blocks of crude iron from a smelting furnace.

piglet NOUN a young pig.

pigment NOUN colouring

p

matter.

pigmy variant of **PYGMY**.

pigsty NOUN (PL **pigsties**) a covered pen for pigs.

pigtail NOUN long hair worn in a plait at the back of the head.

pike NOUN **1** a spear with a long wooden shaft. **2** (PL **pike**) a large voracious freshwater fish.

pilaf (also **pilaff**, **pilau**) NOUN a dish of rice with meat, spices, etc.

pilaster NOUN a rectangular usually ornamental column.

pilchard NOUN a small sea fish.

pile NOUN **1** a number of things lying one on top of another; [INFORMAL] a large amount. **2** a large, imposing building. **3** a heavy beam driven vertically into the ground as a support for a building or bridge. **4** the surface of a carpet, velvet, etc., with many small projecting threads. **5** (**piles**) haemorrhoids. VERB **1** lay (things) on top of one another. **2** get into or out of a vehicle in a disorganized group.
pile up accumulate.

pile-up NOUN [INFORMAL] a collision of several vehicles.

pilfer VERB steal (small items or in small quantities).
pilferer NOUN

pilgrim NOUN a person who travels to a sacred place as an act of religious devotion.
pilgrimage NOUN

pill NOUN a small piece of medicinal substance for swallowing whole; (**the pill**) a contraceptive pill.

pillage VERB (in wartime) rob or steal with violence. NOUN the action of pillaging.

pillar NOUN a vertical structure used as a support or ornament.

pillar box NOUN a postbox.

pillbox NOUN **1** a small round hat. **2** a small concrete fort, partly underground.

pillion NOUN a passenger seat behind the driver of a motorcycle.

pillory NOUN (PL **pillories**) [HISTORICAL] a wooden frame with holes for the head and hands, in which offenders were locked and exposed to public ridicule. VERB (**pillories**, **pillorying**, **pilloried**) ridicule publicly.

pillow NOUN a cushion for supporting the head in bed. VERB rest (one's head) as though on a pillow.

pilot NOUN **1** a person who operates an aircraft's flying controls; a person qualified to steer ships into or out of a harbour. **2** a television programme made to test audience reaction; an experimental project or scheme. VERB (**pilots**, **piloting**, **piloted**) **1** act as pilot of (an aircraft or ship). **2** test (a project etc.).

pilot light NOUN **1** a small burning jet of gas which lights a larger burner. **2** an electric indicator light.

pimiento NOUN a sweet pepper.

pimp NOUN a man who finds clients for a prostitute or brothel.

pimple NOUN a small inflamed spot on the skin.
pimply ADJ

PIN ABBREV personal identification number.

pin NOUN **1** a short pointed piece of metal with a broadened head, used for fastening things together. **2** a peg or stake of wood or metal. **3** (**pins**) [INFORMAL] legs. VERB (**pins**, **pinning**, **pinned**) fasten or attach with pins; hold (someone) so that they are unable to move.
pin down force to be definite in a promise. **pin on** attach (blame) to someone. **pins and needles** a tingling sensation.

pinafore NOUN **1** an apron. **2** (in full **pinafore dress**) a sleeveless dress worn over a blouse or jumper.

pinball NOUN a game in which balls are propelled across a sloping board to strike targets.

pince-nez /panss-nay/ NOUN spectacles that clip on to the nose.

pincer NOUN a front claw of a lobster or similar shellfish; (**pincers**) a tool with pivoted jaws for gripping and pulling things.

pinch VERB **1** squeeze between two surfaces, especially between the finger and thumb. **2** [INFORMAL] steal. NOUN **1** an act of pinching. **2** a small amount.

at a pinch if really necessary. **feel the pinch** experience financial hardship.

pine¹ NOUN an evergreen tree with needle-shaped leaves.

pine² VERB become ill and weak through grief; miss someone or something intensely.

pineapple NOUN a large juicy tropical fruit.

ping NOUN a short sharp ringing sound. VERB make this sound.

pinger NOUN a device emitting short high-pitched sounds for detection, identification, or as a time signal.

ping-pong NOUN [INFORMAL] table tennis.

pinion NOUN **1** a bird's wing. **2** a small cogwheel. VERB restrain by holding or binding the arms or legs.

pink ADJ pale red. NOUN **1** a pink colour. **2** a garden plant with fragrant flowers. VERB **1** cut a zigzag edge on (fabric). **2** (of an engine) make rattling sounds when running imperfectly.

in the pink [INFORMAL] in very good health.

pinnacle NOUN a high pointed rock; a small ornamental turret; the highest point, the most successful moment.

pinpoint VERB locate precisely. ADJ absolutely precise.

pinstripe NOUN a very narrow stripe in cloth fabric.

pinstriped ADJ

pint NOUN a measure for liquids, one-eighth of a gallon (0.568 litre).

pin-up NOUN [INFORMAL] a poster of a famous or attractive person; such a person.

pioneer NOUN a person who is one of the first to explore a new region or subject. VERB be the first to explore, use, or develop.

pious ADJ devoutly religious; making a hypocritical display of virtue.
piously ADV
piousness NOUN

pip NOUN **1** a small seed in fruit. **2** a star showing rank on an army officer's uniform. **3** a short high-pitched sound. VERB (**pips**, **pipping**, **pipped**) [INFORMAL] defeat by a small margin.

pipe NOUN **1** a tube through which something can flow. **2** a wind instrument; (**pipes**) bagpipes. **3** a narrow tube with a bowl at one end for smoking tobacco. VERB **1** convey (water etc.) through pipe(s). **2** play (music) on a pipe. **3** utter in a shrill voice.
pipe down [INFORMAL] be quiet. **piping hot** very hot.

pipe dream NOUN an unrealistic hope or scheme.

pipeline NOUN a long pipe for conveying petroleum etc. over a distance; [COMPUTING] a channel of supply or information.
in the pipeline on the way, in preparation.

piper NOUN a player of pipes.

pipette NOUN a slender tube for transferring or measuring small amounts of liquid.

piquant /pee-kahnt/ ADJ pleasantly sharp in taste or smell; pleasantly ironic, mentally stimulating.
piquancy NOUN

pique /peek/ NOUN a feeling of hurt pride. VERB **1** stimulate (curiosity etc.). **2** hurt the pride of.

piquet /pee-kay/ NOUN a card game for two players.

piranha /pi-rah-nă, pir-ahn-yă/ NOUN a fierce tropical American freshwater fish.

pirate NOUN **1** a person on a ship who robs another ship at sea or raids a coast. **2** one who infringes copyright or business rights, or broadcasts without authorization. VERB reproduce (a book, video, etc.) without authorization.

piracy NOUN
piratical ADJ

pirouette /pi-roo-et/ NOUN a spin on one leg in ballet. VERB perform a pirouette.

piss [VULGAR SLANG] VERB urinate. NOUN urine.

pissed ADJ [VULGAR SLANG] drunk.

pistachio /pis-tash-i-oh/ NOUN (PL **pistachios**) a type of nut.

piste /peest/ NOUN a ski run.

pistil NOUN the seed-producing part of a flower.

pistol NOUN a small gun.

p

piston NOUN a sliding disc or cylinder inside a tube, especially as part of an engine or pump.

pit NOUN **1** a hole in the ground; a coal mine; a sunken area. **2** a place where racing cars are refuelled etc. during a race. **3** the stone of a fruit. VERB (**pits**, **pitting**, **pitted**) **1** make pits or depressions in. **2** set against in competition. **3** remove stones from olives etc.
be the pits [INFORMAL] be very bad or unpleasant.

pitch NOUN **1** an area of ground marked out for an outside game. **2** the degree of highness or lowness of a sound; the level of intensity of something. **3** the steepness of a slope. **4** a form of words used in trying to sell a product. **5** a place where a street trader or performer is stationed. **6** an act of throwing. **7** a dark tarry substance. VERB **1** throw; fall heavily. **2** set up (a tent). **3** set (one's voice, a piece of music) at a particular pitch; make suitable for a particular market, level of understanding, etc. **4** (of a ship) plunge forward and back alternately. **5** (**pitched**) (of a roof) sloping. **6** promote (a product).
pitch in [INFORMAL] vigorously join in a task.
pitch into [INFORMAL] attack; begin to deal with. **pitch up** [INFORMAL] arrive.

pitch-black (also **pitch-**

dark) ADJ completely black; with no light.

pitchblende NOUN a mineral ore (uranium oxide) yielding radium.

pitched battle NOUN a violent confrontation; a battle between large formations of troops.

pitcher NOUN **1** a baseball player who throws the ball to the batter. **2** a large usually earthenware jug.

pitchfork NOUN a long-handled fork for lifting and tossing hay.

piteous ADJ deserving or arousing pity.
piteously ADV

pitfall NOUN an unsuspected danger or difficulty.

pith NOUN **1** spongy tissue in stems or fruits. **2** the essence of something. **3** concise expressive language.

pithy ADJ (**pithier**, **pithiest**) **1** (of a plant) full of pith. **2** concise and expressive.
pithily ADV
pithiness NOUN

pitiful ADJ **1** deserving or arousing pity. **2** contemptibly small or inadequate.
pitifully ADV

piton /pee-ton/ NOUN a peg with a hole for a rope, used in rock-climbing.

pitta NOUN a flat bread, hollow inside.

pittance NOUN a very small allowance or wage.

pituitary gland NOUN a gland at the base of the brain, influencing bodily growth and functions.

pity NOUN (PL **pities**) a feeling of sorrow for another's suffering; a cause for regret: *what a pity you can't come.* VERB (**pities**, **pitying**, **pitied**) feel pity for.
take pity on try to help, show compassion.

pivot NOUN a central point or shaft on which a thing turns or swings; someone or something with a crucial role. VERB (**pivots**, **pivoting**, **pivoted**) turn on a pivot.

pivotal ADJ **1** of a pivot. **2** vitally important.

pixel NOUN any of the minute illuminated areas

making up the image on a VDU screen.

pixelate VERB divide (an image) into pixels; display an image of (someone) as a number of pixels.

pixie (also **pixy**) NOUN a small supernatural being in fairy tales.

pizza NOUN a layer of dough baked with a savoury topping.

pizzeria NOUN a pizza restaurant.

pizzicato /pit-si-**kah**-toh/ ADV plucking the strings of a violin etc. instead of using the bow.

placard NOUN a poster or similar notice. VERB put up placards on.

placate VERB make less angry, soothe. **placatory** ADJ

place NOUN **1** a particular portion of space or of an area; a particular town, district, building, etc. **2** a portion of space occupied by or available for someone; a person's rank; a position in a sequence; the behaviour appropriate to someone in a particular position: *not my place to argue.* VERB **1** put in a particular position; find a home, job, etc. for; cause to be in a specified situation. **2** identify, classify. **3** make (an order for goods). **be placed** (in a race) be among the first three. **in place** established, in the correct position. **out of place** in the wrong position; inappropriate, incongruous. **take place** occur.

placebo /pla-**see**-boh/ NOUN (PL **placebos**) a substance with little or no physical effect, given to a patient for the psychological benefit of being given medicine.

placement NOUN the action of placing; a temporary position given to someone in a workplace.

placenta NOUN (PL **placentae** or **placentas**) the organ in the womb that nourishes the foetus. **placental** ADJ

place setting NOUN a set of dishes or cutlery for one person at a table.

placid ADJ calm, not easily upset.
 placidity NOUN
 placidly ADV

placket NOUN an opening in a garment for fastenings or access to a pocket.

plagiarize /play-jiă-ryz/ (also **plagiarise**) VERB take and use (another's writings etc.) as one's own.
 plagiarism NOUN
 plagiarist NOUN

plague NOUN **1** a deadly contagious disease. **2** an infestation. VERB cause continual trouble to; annoy, pester.

plaice NOUN (PL **plaice**) an edible flatfish.

plaid /plad/ NOUN cloth with a tartan pattern; a long piece of such cloth worn as part of Scottish Highland dress.

plain ADJ **1** not elaborate or decorated, simple, ordinary; not patterned. **2** easy to perceive or understand; clear; frank, direct. **3** not beautiful or pretty. ADV clearly, directly; simply (used for emphasis): *plain wrong.* NOUN a large area of level country.
 plainly ADV
 plainness NOUN

plain clothes PLURAL NOUN civilian clothes, not a uniform.

plain sailing NOUN an activity free from difficulties.

plainsong (also **plainchant**) NOUN medieval church music for voices, without regular rhythm.

plaintiff NOUN a person bringing an action in a court of law.

plaintive ADJ sounding sad.
 plaintively ADV

plait /plat/ VERB weave (three or more strands) into one rope-like length. NOUN something plaited.

plan NOUN **1** an intention; a proposed means of achieving something. **2** a detailed diagram showing the relative positions of parts of a town etc. VERB (**plans**, **planning**, **planned**) **1** intend; work out the details of (an intended action). **2** draw a plan of.
 planner NOUN

plane NOUN **1** an aeroplane. **2** a level surface; a level of thought or development. **3** a tool for smoothing wood or metal by paring shavings from it. **4** a tall spreading tree with broad leaves. VERB smooth or pare (wood or metal) with a plane. ADJ level.

planet NOUN a celestial body orbiting round a star.
planetary ADJ

planetarium NOUN (PL **planetaria** or **planetariums**) a room with a domed ceiling on which lights are projected to show the positions of the stars and planets.

p

plangent ADJ [LITERARY] **1** loud and resonant. **2** sad, mournful.
plangency NOUN
plangently ADV

plank NOUN a long flat piece of timber.

plankton NOUN minute life forms floating in the sea, rivers, etc.

planning permission NOUN formal approval for construction of or changes to a building.

plant NOUN **1** a living organism such as a tree, grass, etc., with neither the power of movement nor special organs of digestion. **2** a factory; its machinery. **3** someone placed in a group as an informer; something placed in someone's belongings to incriminate them. VERB place in soil for growing; place in position.
planter NOUN

plantain NOUN **1** a tropical banana-like fruit. **2** a herb.

plantation NOUN an area planted with trees or cultivated plants; an estate on which cotton, tobacco, tea, etc. is cultivated.

planter NOUN **1** an owner or manager of a plantation. **2** a device for planting things. **3** a large container for plants.

plaque /plak, plahk/ NOUN **1** a commemorative plate fixed on a wall. **2** a film forming on teeth, encouraging harmful bacteria.

plasma NOUN **1** the colourless fluid part of blood. **2** a kind of gas. **plasmic** ADJ

plaster NOUN **1** a mixture of lime, sand, water, etc. used for coating walls. **2** a sticking plaster. VERB cover with plaster; coat, daub; display widely. **plasterer** NOUN

plasterboard NOUN board with a core of plaster, for making partitions etc.

plastered ADJ [INFORMAL] drunk.

plaster of Paris NOUN a white paste made from gypsum, for making moulds or casts.

plastic NOUN a synthetic substance that can be moulded to a permanent shape; [INFORMAL] credit cards or other plastic cards used to pay for things. ADJ **1** made of plastic. **2** easily moulded. **plasticity** NOUN

plastic bullet NOUN a solid plastic cylinder fired as a riot-control device rather than to kill.

plasticine NOUN [TRADE MARK] a soft material for modelling.

plastic surgery NOUN the reconstruction or repair of parts of the body for medical or cosmetic reasons.

plate NOUN **1** an almost flat usually circular utensil for holding food. **2** articles of gold, silver, or other metal. **3** a flat thin sheet of metal, glass, or other material. **4** an illustration on special paper in a book. **5** an orthodontic device. VERB cover or coat with metal. **plateful** NOUN

plateau /plat-oh/ NOUN (PL **plateaux** or **plateaus**) **1** an area of level high ground. **2** a state of little change following rapid progress.

plate glass NOUN thick glass for windows etc.

platelet NOUN a small disc in the blood, involved in clotting.

platen /pla-tĕn/ NOUN a plate in a printing press holding the paper against the type; the roller of a typewriter or printer.

platform NOUN **1** a raised level surface or area, especially for public speakers or performers; a raised structure beside a railway track at a station. **2** the declared policy on which a political party bases its campaign.

platinum NOUN a silver-white metal that does not tarnish.

platinum blonde NOUN a woman with silvery-blonde hair.

platitude NOUN a commonplace remark.
platitudinous ADJ

platonic ADJ involving affection but not sexual love.

platoon NOUN a subdivision of a military company.

platter NOUN a large plate for food.

platypus NOUN (PL **platypuses**) an Australian animal with a duck-like beak which lays eggs but suckles its young.

plaudits PLURAL NOUN praise; applause.

plausible ADJ seeming probable; persuasive but deceptive.
plausibility NOUN
plausibly ADV

play VERB **1** engage in activity for pleasure and relaxation rather than a practical purpose; take part in (a game or sport); compete against in a game; move (a piece) in a game. **2** act the part of. **3** perform on (a musical instrument); cause (a radio, recording, etc.) to produce sound. **4** move lightly and gently: *sunlight played on the ground.* NOUN **1** activity for relaxation and enjoyment; the action of playing in a sports match. **2** action, operation: *luck comes into play.* **3** a dramatic work. **4** freedom of operation. **make a play for** [INFORMAL] attempt to attract or attain. **make play of** draw attention to ostentatiously. **play along 1** perform a piece of music as it is being played on a record etc. **2** pretend to cooperate. **play at** do half-heartedly or frivolously. **play down** represent as unimportant. **play off**

bring into conflict for one's own advantage. **play on** exploit (weakness etc.). **play safe** avoid risks. **play the game** behave honourably. **play up** **1** [INFORMAL] cause pain or trouble; fail to work properly. **2** emphasize, represent as important. **player** NOUN

playboy NOUN a pleasure-loving usually rich man.

playful ADJ full of fun; for amusement, not serious. **playfully** ADV **playfulness** NOUN

playgroup NOUN a group of pre-school children who play regularly together under supervision.

playhouse NOUN a theatre.

playing card NOUN one of a set of (usually 52) pieces of card used in games.

playing field NOUN a field used for outdoor games.

playmate NOUN a child's companion in play.

playpen NOUN a portable enclosure for a young child to play in.

playwright NOUN a person who writes plays.

plaza NOUN a public square.

plc (also **PLC**) ABBREV Public Limited Company.

plea NOUN **1** an earnest or emotional request. **2** an excuse. **3** a defendant's answer to a charge in a law court.

plead VERB (**pleads**, **pleading**, **pleaded**; [SCOTTISH] & [US] **pled**) **1** give as one's plea; put forward (a case) in a law court. **2** make an appeal or entreaty. **3** put forward as an excuse.

pleasant ADJ giving pleasure; having an agreeable manner. **pleasantly** ADV **pleasantness** NOUN

pleasantry NOUN (PL **pleasantries**) a friendly or humorous remark.

please VERB **1** give pleasure to. **2** think fit, have the desire: *do as you please.* ADV a polite word of request. **please oneself** do as one chooses.

pleased ADJ feeling or

showing pleasure or satisfaction.

pleasurable ADJ causing pleasure.
pleasurably ADV

pleasure NOUN a feeling of satisfaction, enjoyment, or joy; a source of this.
at one's pleasure [FORMAL] whenever one wishes.

pleat NOUN a flat fold of cloth. VERB make a pleat or pleats in.

pleb NOUN [INFORMAL] a rough uncultured person.

plebeian ADJ of the lower social classes; uncultured.

plebiscite /pleb-i-syt/ NOUN a referendum.

plectrum NOUN (PL **plectrums** or **plectra**) a small piece of plastic etc. for plucking the strings of a musical instrument.

pledge NOUN a solemn promise; something deposited as a guarantee that a debt will be paid etc.; a token of something. VERB commit by a promise; give as a pledge.

plenary /pleen-ă-ri/ ADJ entire; attended by all members.

plenipotentiary NOUN (PL **plenipotentiaries**) a person given full power by a government to act on its behalf. ADJ (of power) complete.

plenitude NOUN [FORMAL] abundance; completeness.

plentiful ADJ existing in large amounts.
plentifully ADV

plenty PRON enough or more than enough. NOUN a situation where necessities are available in large quantities. ADV [INFORMAL] fully, plentifully.

plenteous ADJ [LITERARY] plentiful.

plethora /ple-thŏ-ră/ NOUN an oversupply or excess.

pleurisy NOUN inflammation of the membrane round the lungs.

pliable ADJ flexible; easily influenced.
pliability NOUN

pliant ADJ pliable.
pliancy NOUN

pliers PLURAL NOUN pincers with flat surfaces for gripping things.

plight NOUN a predicament.

plimsoll NOUN a canvas sports shoe.

Plimsoll line NOUN a mark on a ship's side showing the legal water level when loaded.

plinth NOUN a slab forming the base of a column or statue etc.

plod VERB (**plods**, **plodding**, **plodded**) walk doggedly, trudge; work slowly but steadily. **plodder** NOUN

plonk [INFORMAL] NOUN cheap or inferior wine. VERB set down heavily or carelessly.

plop NOUN a sound like something small dropping into water with no splash.

plot NOUN **1** a conspiracy, a secret plan. **2** the story in a play, novel, or film. **3** a small piece of land. VERB (**plots**, **plotting**, **plotted**) **1** secretly plan (an illegal action). **2** make a map of, mark (a route) on a map.

plough /plow/ ([US] **plow**) NOUN an implement for cutting furrows in soil and turning it up. VERB **1** cut or turn up (soil etc.) with a plough. **2** make one's way laboriously. **ploughman** NOUN

ploy NOUN a cunning manoeuvre.

pluck VERB pull at or out or off; pick (a flower etc.); strip (a dead bird) of its feathers. NOUN **1** a plucking movement. **2** courage.

plucky ADJ (**pluckier**, **pluckiest**) brave, spirited. **pluckily** ADV

plug NOUN **1** something fitting into and stopping or filling a hole or cavity. **2** a device for making an electrical connection, consisting of an insulated casing with metal pins that fit into a socket. VERB (**plugs**, **plugging**, **plugged**) **1** block or fill with a plug. **2** [INFORMAL] work steadily and laboriously. **3** [INFORMAL] promote (a product) by mentioning it publicly.
plug in connect electrically by putting a plug into a socket.

plum NOUN **1** a fruit with sweet pulp round a

pointed stone. **2** reddish purple. **3** [INFORMAL] something desirable, the best.

plumage NOUN a bird's feathers.

plumb /plum/ NOUN a lead weight hung on a cord **plumb line**, used for testing depths or verticality. ADV [INFORMAL] exactly; [US] completely. VERB **1** measure or test with a plumb line; reach (depths). **2** work or fit (things) as a plumber.

plumber /**plum**-er/ NOUN a person who fits and repairs plumbing.

plumbing /**plum**-ing/ NOUN a system of water and drainage pipes etc. in a building.

plume NOUN a feather, especially as an ornament; something resembling this.
plumed ADJ

plummet VERB (**plummets, plummeting, plummeted**) fall steeply or rapidly.

plump ADJ having a full rounded shape. VERB **1** make or become plump. **2** put down heavily.
plump for choose, decide on.
plumpness NOUN

plunder VERB rob. NOUN the action of plundering; goods etc. stolen.

plunge VERB **1** jump or dive; fall suddenly; decrease rapidly. **2** push or go forcefully into something. NOUN an act of plunging, a dive.

plunger NOUN a device that works with a plunging movement.

pluperfect ADJ [GRAMMAR] of the tense used to denote action completed before some past point of time, e.g. *we had arrived*.

plural NOUN the form of a noun or verb used in referring to more than one person or thing. ADJ of this form; of more than one.
plurality NOUN

plus PREP **1** with the addition of. **2** [INFORMAL] together with. ADJ **1** more than zero. **2** more than the amount indicated: *twenty plus*. NOUN **1** the symbol (+), indicating addition or a positive value. **2** [INFORMAL] an advantage.

plush NOUN cloth with a long soft nap. ADJ **1** made of plush. **2** [INFORMAL] luxurious.

plushy ADJ (**plushier**, **plushiest**) [INFORMAL] luxurious.

plutocracy NOUN government or control by the wealthy.
plutocrat NOUN
plutocratic ADJ

plutonium NOUN a radioactive substance used in nuclear weapons and reactors.

pluvial /ploo-vi-ăl/ ADJ of or caused by rain.

ply¹ NOUN (PL **plies**) **1** a thickness or layer of wood, cloth, etc. **2** plywood.

ply² VERB (**plies**, **plying**, **plied**) **1** use or wield (a tool etc.); work at (a trade). **2** travel regularly over a route for commercial purposes. **3** continually offer food etc. to.

plywood NOUN board made by gluing layers with the grain crosswise.

PM ABBREV Prime Minister.

p.m. ABBREV after noon (Latin *post meridiem*).

PMS ABBREV premenstrual syndrome.

PMT ABBREV premenstrual tension.

pneumatic /new-**ma**-tik/ ADJ filled with or operated by compressed air.
pneumatically ADV

pneumonia /new-**moh**-niă/ NOUN inflammation of the lungs.

PO ABBREV **1** Post Office. **2** postal order.

poach VERB **1** cook (an egg without its shell) in or over boiling water; simmer in a small amount of liquid. **2** take (game or fish) illegally; acquire unfairly.
poacher NOUN

pocket NOUN **1** a small bag-like part on a garment; a pouch-like compartment. **2** an isolated group or area. ADJ small enough to carry in one's pocket. VERB **1** put into one's pocket. **2** take dishonestly.

in or **out of pocket** having made a profit or loss.
pocketful NOUN

pocketbook NOUN **1** a notebook. **2** a small folding case for money or papers.

pocket money NOUN money for small personal expenses; money given regularly to children.

pockmarked ADJ marked by scars or pits.

poco ADV [MUSIC] a little, rather.

pod NOUN a long narrow seed case.

podgy ADJ (**podgier**, **podgiest**) [INFORMAL] short and fat.

podium NOUN (PL **podiums** or **podia**) a pedestal or platform.

poem NOUN a piece of creative writing expressing feelings etc. through diction, imagery, and sometimes rhyme and metre.

poet NOUN a person who writes poems.

poetic (also **poetical**) ADJ of or like poetry.
poetically ADV

poetry NOUN **1** poems; a poet's work. **2** a quality that pleases the mind in a poetic way.

po-faced ADJ [INFORMAL] solemn.

pogrom NOUN an organized massacre.

poignant ADJ evoking a keen sense of sadness.
poignancy NOUN
poignantly ADV

poinsettia /pwahn-set-i-ă/ NOUN a plant with large scarlet or cream bracts.

point NOUN **1** a tapered, sharp end; a tip. **2** a particular place or moment. **3** a single item in a discussion; an argument; a feature or characteristic: *her good points.* **4** advantage, purpose, reason to do something. **5** a unit of scoring. **6** a dot or other punctuation mark. **7** a promontory. **8** an electrical socket. **9** a movable rail for directing a train from one line to another. VERB **1** direct, aim (a weapon, finger, etc.); direct or attract attention in this way; have a particular direction:

pointing north; indicate a route etc.; emphasize: *point a moral.* **2** fill in (joints of brickwork) with mortar.
beside the point irrelevant. **make a point of** take special care to do. **on the point of** about to do. **point out** direct attention to. **point up** emphasize. **to the point** relevant.

point-blank ADJ & ADV **1** at very close range. **2** without explanation.

point duty NOUN traffic control by a policeman at a road junction.

pointed ADJ **1** tapering to a point. **2** (of a remark or manner) expressing criticism clearly.
pointedly ADV

pointer NOUN a thing that points to something; a dog that faces stiffly towards game which it scents.

pointing NOUN the mortar around the edges of bricks in a wall.

pointless ADJ having no purpose or meaning.
pointlessly ADV

point of view NOUN a way of considering an issue.

poise NOUN graceful bearing; self-assurance and dignity. VERB be or cause to be balanced.

poison NOUN a substance that can destroy life or harm health. VERB give poison to; put poison on or in; corrupt, fill with prejudice.
poisoner NOUN
poisonous ADJ

poison pen letter NOUN a malicious unsigned letter.

poke VERB **1** prod with one's finger, a stick, etc.; push forward or into something. **2** search, pry. NOUN an act of poking.
poke fun at ridicule.

poker NOUN **1** a stiff metal rod for stirring up a fire. **2** a gambling card game.

poker face NOUN an expression concealing one's feelings.

poky ADJ (**pokier, pokiest**) small and cramped.
pokiness NOUN

polar ADJ **1** of or near the North or South Pole. **2** of magnetic or electrical poles. **3** (of opposites) extreme, absolute.

polar bear NOUN a white bear of Arctic regions.

polarize (also **polarise**) VERB **1** confine similar vibrations of (light waves) to one direction or plane. **2** give magnetic poles to. **3** set at opposite extremes of opinion.
polarization NOUN

Polaroid NOUN [TRADE MARK] **1** a material that polarizes light passing through it, used in sunglasses. **2** a camera that prints a photograph as soon as it is taken.

Pole NOUN a Polish person.

pole NOUN **1** a long rod or post. **2** the north **North Pole** or south **South Pole** end of the earth's axis. **3** one of the opposite ends of a magnet or terminals of an electric cell or battery. VERB push along using a long rod.
poles apart having nothing in common.

polecat NOUN a small animal of the weasel family; [US] a skunk.

polemic NOUN a verbal attack on a belief or opinion.
polemical ADJ

polenta NOUN porridge made from maize meal.

pole position NOUN the most favourable starting position in a motor race.

pole star NOUN a star near the North Pole in the sky.

police NOUN a civil force responsible for keeping public order. VERB keep order in (a place) by means of police.

policeman (also **policewoman**) NOUN a member of the police force.

police state NOUN a country where political police supervise and control citizens' activities.

policy NOUN (PL **policies**) **1** a general plan of action. **2** an insurance contract.

polio NOUN poliomyelitis.

poliomyelitis NOUN an infectious disease causing temporary or permanent paralysis.

Polish NOUN the language of Poland. ADJ relating to Poland.

p

polish VERB make smooth and shiny by rubbing; refine, perfect. NOUN shininess; a substance for rubbing surfaces to make them shine; practised ease and elegance.
polish off finish off.
polisher NOUN

polished ADJ (of manner or performance) elegant, perfected.

polite ADJ having good manners, socially correct; refined.
politely ADV
politeness NOUN

politic ADJ showing good judgement.

political ADJ of the government and public affairs of a country; of or promoting a particular party.
politically ADV

political correctness NOUN avoidance of any expressions or behaviour that may be considered discriminatory.

politician NOUN an MP or other political representative.

politics NOUN the science and art of government; political affairs or life; (as PL) political principles.

polity NOUN (PL **polities**) a form of civil government; a society.

polka NOUN a lively dance for couples.

poll NOUN **1** the votes cast in an election; a place for this. **2** an estimate of public opinion made by questioning people. VERB record the opinions or votes of; receive a specified number of votes.

pollard VERB cut off the top and branches of (a tree) to produce a close head of young branches. NOUN a pollarded tree.

pollen NOUN a fertilizing powder produced by flowers.

pollen count NOUN a measurement of the amount of pollen in the air.

pollinate VERB fertilize with pollen.
pollination NOUN

pollster NOUN a person conducting an opinion poll.

poll tax NOUN a tax paid at the same rate by every

adult.

pollute VERB make dirty or impure; corrupt.
pollutant NOUN
pollution NOUN

polo NOUN a game like hockey played by teams on horseback.

polo neck NOUN a high turned-over collar on a jersey etc.

polonium NOUN a radioactive metallic element.

poltergeist NOUN a spirit believed to throw things about noisily.

polyandry NOUN a system of having more than one husband at a time.

p **polychrome** ADJ multicoloured.
polychromatic ADJ

polyester NOUN a synthetic resin or fibre.

polyethylene NOUN = **POLYTHENE.**

polygamy NOUN a system of having more than one wife or husband at a time.
polygamist NOUN
polygamous ADJ

polyglot ADJ knowing several languages.

polygon NOUN a geometric figure with many sides.
polygonal ADJ

polygraph NOUN a machine reading the pulse rate etc. used as a lie detector.

polyhedron NOUN (PL **polyhedra** or **polyhedrons**) a solid with many sides.
polyhedral ADJ

polymath NOUN a person with knowledge of many subjects.
polymathy NOUN

polymer NOUN a compound whose molecule is formed from a large number of simple molecules.

polymerize (also **polymerise**) VERB combine or cause to combine into a polymer.
polymerization NOUN

polynomial ADJ consisting of three or more terms.

polyp NOUN **1** a simple organism with a tube-shaped body. **2** an abnormal growth projecting from a mucous membrane.

polyphony NOUN (PL

polyphonies) combination of melodies; a composition in this style.
polyphonic ADJ

polystyrene NOUN a synthetic resin, a polymer of styrene.

polytechnic NOUN a college offering courses up to degree level.

polytheism NOUN belief in or worship of more than one god.
polytheist NOUN
polytheistic ADJ

polythene (also **polyethylene**) NOUN a tough light plastic.

polyunsaturated ADJ (of fat) not associated with the formation of cholesterol in the blood.

polyurethane NOUN a synthetic resin used in paint etc.

pomander NOUN a ball of mixed sweet-smelling substances.

pomegranate NOUN a tropical fruit with many seeds.

pommel /pum-ĕl/ NOUN a knob on the hilt of a sword; an upward projection on a saddle.

pomp NOUN stately and splendid ceremonial.

pompom (also **pompon**) NOUN a small woollen ball as a decoration on a hat.

pompous ADJ full of ostentatious dignity and self-importance.
pomposity NOUN
pompously ADV

ponce [INFORMAL] NOUN **1** a pimp. **2** [OFFENSIVE] an effeminate man, a homosexual. VERB (**ponce about/around**) behave in a time-wasting or silly way.

poncho NOUN (PL **ponchos**) a cloak like a blanket with a hole for the head.

pond NOUN a small area of still water.

ponder VERB be deep in thought; think over.

ponderous ADJ heavy, unwieldy; laborious.
ponderously ADV

pong [INFORMAL] NOUN a strong unpleasant smell. VERB smell strongly and unpleasantly.

pontiff NOUN the Pope.

pontificate VERB speak pompously and at

length.

pontoon NOUN **1** a flat-bottomed boat supporting a temporary bridge; such a bridge. **2** a card game.

pontoon bridge NOUN a temporary bridge supported on pontoons.

pony NOUN (PL **ponies**) a horse of any small breed.

ponytail NOUN long hair drawn back and tied to hang down.

poodle NOUN a dog with thick curly hair.

poof (also **poofter**) NOUN [INFORMAL], [OFFENSIVE] a homosexual or effeminate man.

p

pooh EXCLAMATION [INFORMAL] an exclamation of contempt.

pooh-pooh VERB [INFORMAL] dismiss (a subject) scornfully.

pool NOUN **1** a small area of still water; a puddle; a swimming pool. **2** a shared fund or supply. **3** a game resembling snooker. **4** (**the pools**) football pools. VERB put into a common fund or supply; share.

poop NOUN a raised deck at the stern of a ship.

pooper scooper NOUN a device for clearing up dog faeces.

poor ADJ **1** having little money or means. **2** not of high quality or standard. **3** deserving sympathy.

poorly ADV in a poor way, badly. ADJ unwell.

pop NOUN **1** a small explosive sound. **2** a fizzy drink. **3** pop music. VERB (**pops**, **popping**, **popped**) **1** make a sharp explosive sound; burst with this sound. **2** go or put something somewhere quickly. ADJ of popular music or culture; made intelligible and accessible to the general public.

popadom variant of **POPPADOM**.

popcorn NOUN maize heated to burst and form puffy balls.

Pope NOUN the head of the Roman Catholic Church.

poplar NOUN a tall slender tree.

poplin NOUN a plain woven usually cotton fabric.

pop music NOUN modern

music appealing to young people.

poppadom (also **popadom, poppadum**) NOUN a large thin crisp savoury Indian bread.

popper NOUN [INFORMAL] a press stud.

poppy NOUN (PL **poppies**) a plant with bright flowers on tall stems.

poppycock NOUN [INFORMAL] nonsense.

populace NOUN the general public.

popular ADJ liked, enjoyed, or used by many people; of or for the general public.
popularity NOUN
popularly ADV

popularize (also **popularise**) VERB **1** make generally liked. **2** present in an accessible non-technical form.

populate VERB fill with a population.

population NOUN the inhabitants of an area.

populous ADJ thickly populated.

porcelain NOUN fine china.

porch NOUN a roofed shelter over the entrance of a building.

porcine ADJ of or like a pig.

porcupine NOUN an animal covered with protective spines.

pore NOUN a tiny opening on skin or on a leaf, for giving off or taking in moisture.
pore over study closely.

pork NOUN unsalted pig meat.

porn NOUN [INFORMAL] pornography.

pornography NOUN writings or pictures intended to stimulate erotic feelings by portraying sexual activity.
pornographer NOUN
pornographic ADJ

porous ADJ letting through fluid or air.
porosity NOUN

porpoise NOUN a small whale.

porridge NOUN a food made by boiling oatmeal or other cereal in water or milk.

port NOUN **1** a harbour; a town with a harbour.

2 an opening for loading a ship, firing a gun from a tank or ship, etc.; a socket in a computer network into which a device can be plugged. **3** the left-hand side of a ship or aircraft. **4** strong sweet wine.

portable ADJ able to be carried.
portability NOUN

Portakabin NOUN [TRADE MARK] a small portable building.

portal NOUN a door or entrance, especially an imposing one.

portcullis NOUN a vertical grating lowered to block the gateway to a castle.

portend VERB foreshadow.

portent NOUN an omen, a sign of a future event.
portentous ADJ

porter NOUN **1** a person employed to carry luggage or goods. **2** a doorkeeper of a large building. **3** a dark beer.

portfolio NOUN (PL **portfolios**) **1** a case for loose sheets of paper. **2** a set of investments. **3** the area for which a Minister of State is responsible.

porthole NOUN a window in the side of a ship or aircraft.

portico NOUN (PL **porticoes** or **porticos**) a roof supported by columns forming a porch or similar structure.

portion NOUN a part, a share; an amount of food for one person.
VERB divide; distribute portions of.

portly ADJ (**portlier**, **portliest**) stout.
portliness NOUN

portmanteau /port-man-toh/ NOUN (PL **portmanteaus** or **portmanteaux**) a travelling bag opening into two equal parts. ADJ combining two or more separable elements, meanings, etc.

portrait NOUN a picture of a person or animal; a description.

portray VERB make a picture of; describe; represent in a play etc.
portrayal NOUN

Portuguese NOUN a person from Portugal;

the language of Portugal. ADJ relating to Portugal.

Portuguese man-of-war NOUN a jellyfish.

pose VERB **1** constitute or present (a problem). **2** adopt or place in a particular position, especially to be painted, photographed, etc.; pretend to be someone or something. NOUN an attitude in which someone is posed; a pretence.

poser NOUN **1** a puzzling problem. **2** a poseur.

poseur /poh-**zer**/ NOUN a person who behaves affectedly.

posh ADJ [INFORMAL] very smart, luxurious.

posit VERB assume, especially as the basis of an argument.

position NOUN **1** a place occupied by or intended for a person or thing. **2** a way in which someone or something stands, is arranged, etc. **3** a situation, a set of circumstances; a person's status; a job. **4** a point of view, an opinion about an issue. VERB place, arrange.
positional ADJ

positive ADJ
1 characterized by the presence of a quality rather than its absence; (of an utterance) affirmative, asserting; (of the results of a test) showing what was tested for to be present. **2** constructive, encouraging. **3** definite, not allowing doubt; convinced. **4** (of a battery terminal) through which electric current enters. **5** (of a photograph) showing lights and shades true to the original, not reversed. **6** (of a quantity) greater than zero. NOUN a positive quality, quantity, or photograph.
positively ADV

positive discrimination NOUN the policy of favouring members of groups often discriminated against when appointing to jobs etc.

positive pole NOUN the north-seeking pole of a magnet.

p

positive vetting NOUN an intensive enquiry into the background of an applicant for a job relating to security.

positron NOUN a particle with a positive electric charge.

posse /poss-ee/ NOUN [INFORMAL] a group or gang; [HISTORICAL] a body of law enforcers.

possess VERB **1** own; hold as belonging to oneself. **2** dominate the mind of.
possessor NOUN

possession NOUN the state of possessing something; something owned.
take possession of become the possessor of.

possessive ADJ **1** jealously guarding one's possessions; demanding someone's total attention. **2** [GRAMMAR] indicating possession.
possessively ADV
possessiveness NOUN

possessive pronoun *see* **PRONOUN**.

possible ADJ capable of existing, happening, being done, etc.
possibility NOUN
possibly ADV

possum NOUN a tree-living marsupial.
play possum pretend to be asleep; feign ignorance.

post NOUN **1** the official conveyance of letters etc.; the letters etc. conveyed. **2** a piece of timber, metal, etc. set upright to support or mark something. **3** a place of duty; a job; an outpost of soldiers; a trading station. VERB **1** send (letters etc.) by post. **2** put up (a notice); announce in this way. **3** send (someone) to take up employment in a particular place.
keep me posted keep me informed.

post- PREFIX after.

postage NOUN a charge for sending something by post.

postal ADJ of the post; by post.

postbox NOUN a box into which letters are put for sending by post.

postcard NOUN a card for sending messages by post without an envelope.

postcode NOUN a group of letters and figures in a postal address to assist sorting.

post-date VERB **1** put a date on (a cheque etc.) that is later than the actual date. **2** occur later than.

poster NOUN a large picture or notice used for decoration or for announcing or advertising something.

poste restante /pohst rest-**ahnt**/ NOUN a post office department where letters are kept until called for.

posterior ADJ situated behind or at the back. NOUN the buttocks.

posterity NOUN future generations.

postern NOUN a small back or side entrance to a fortress etc.

postgraduate NOUN a student studying for a higher degree.

post-haste ADV with great speed.

posthumous ADJ happening, awarded, published, etc. after a person's death.
posthumously ADV

postman (also **postwoman**) NOUN a person who collects and delivers post.

postmark NOUN an official mark stamped on something sent by post, giving place and date of marking. VERB mark with this.

postmaster NOUN a male official in charge of a post office.

postmistress NOUN a female official in charge of a post office.

post-mortem NOUN an examination of a body to determine the cause of death; an analysis of something that has happened.

post-natal ADJ after childbirth.

post office NOUN a building where postal business is carried on.

postpone VERB cause (an event) to take place later than was originally planned.
postponement NOUN

postprandial ADJ [FORMAL]

after lunch or dinner.

postscript NOUN an additional paragraph at the end of a letter etc.

post-traumatic stress disorder NOUN symptoms that typically occur after exposure to a stressful situation.

postulant NOUN a candidate for admission to a religious order.

postulate VERB assume to be true as a basis for reasoning.
postulation NOUN

posture NOUN the way a person stands, walks, etc. VERB assume a posture, especially for effect.
postural ADJ

p

posy NOUN (PL **posies**) a small bunch of flowers.

pot NOUN **1** a container for holding liquids or solids, or for cooking in. **2** [INFORMAL] cannabis. VERB (**pots**, **potting**, **potted**) **1** plant in a flowerpot. **2** preserve (food) in a pot. **3** send (a ball in billiards or snooker) into a pocket. **4** [INFORMAL] hit or kill by shooting.
go to pot [INFORMAL] deteriorate.

potable ADJ [FORMAL] drinkable.

potash NOUN potassium carbonate.

potassium NOUN a soft silvery-white metallic element.

potation NOUN [ARCHAIC] the action of drinking; a drink.

potato NOUN (PL **potatoes**) a plant with starchy tubers used as food; one of these tubers.

pot belly NOUN (PL **pot bellies**) a large protuberant belly.

potboiler NOUN [INFORMAL] a book, painting, etc. produced merely to make money.

poteen /poch-een/ NOUN illegally distilled whisky.

potent ADJ **1** having great natural power; having a strong effect. **2** (of a male) capable of sexual intercourse.
potency NOUN
potently ADV

potentate NOUN a monarch or ruler.

potential ADJ capable of being developed or used. NOUN an ability or

capacity for development.
potentiality NOUN
potentially ADV

pothole NOUN a hole formed underground by the action of water; a hole in a road surface.

potholing NOUN caving.
potholer NOUN

potion NOUN a liquid medicine or drug.

pot luck NOUN a situation in which one must take a chance that whatever is available will be acceptable.

pot-pourri /poh **poor**-ee/ NOUN a scented mixture of dried petals and spices; a medley or mixture.

pot roast NOUN a piece of meat cooked slowly in a covered dish.

potsherd NOUN a broken piece of earthenware.

potshot NOUN a shot aimed casually.

potted past and past participle of **POT**. ADJ **1** preserved in a pot. **2** abridged.

potter¹ NOUN a maker of pottery.

potter² ([US] **putter**) VERB work on trivial tasks in a leisurely way.

pottery NOUN (PL **potteries**) containers and other objects made of baked clay; a potter's work or workshop.

potty [INFORMAL] ADJ (**pottier**, **pottiest**) **1** mad, stupid. **2** enthusiastic. NOUN (PL **potties**) a chamber pot, especially for a child.

pouch NOUN a small bag or bag-like formation.

pouffe /poof/ NOUN a padded stool.

poult /pohlt/ NOUN a young domestic fowl or game bird.

poulterer NOUN a dealer in poultry.

poultice /**pohlt**-is/ NOUN a moist usually hot dressing applied to relieve inflammation.

poultry NOUN domestic fowls.

pounce VERB swoop down and grasp or attack. NOUN a pouncing movement.

pound¹ NOUN **1** a measure of weight, 16 oz. avoirdupois (0.454 kg) or 12 oz. troy (0.373 kg). **2** a unit of money in Britain and certain other countries.

pound² NOUN an enclosure where stray animals, or vehicles officially removed, are kept until claimed.

pound³ VERB beat or crush with repeated heavy strokes; (of the heart) beat loudly; run heavily.

poundage NOUN a charge or commission per £ or per pound weight.

pour VERB flow, cause to flow; rain heavily; come, go, or send in large quantities.

pout VERB push out one's lips. NOUN a pouting expression.

poverty NOUN **1** lack of money and resources; scarcity. **2** inferiority.

POW ABBREV prisoner of war.

powder NOUN a mass of fine dry particles; a medicine or cosmetic in this form; gunpowder. VERB cover or sprinkle with powder.
powdery ADJ

powder room NOUN a ladies' lavatory.

power NOUN **1** the ability to do something. **2** vigour, strength. **3** control, influence, authority; an influential person or country etc. **4** a product of a number multiplied by itself a given number of times. **5** mechanical or electrical energy; the electricity supply. VERB supply with mechanical or electrical power.

power dressing NOUN a style of dress for work intended to convey an impression of influence and efficiency.

powerful ADJ having great power or influence.
powerfully ADV

powerless ADJ without power to take action, wholly unable.

power of attorney NOUN legal authority to act for another person.

power station NOUN a building where electricity is generated for distribution.

pp ABBREV **1** (**pp.**) pages. **2** [MUSIC] pianissimo. **3** (also **p.p.**) used beside the name of someone signing a letter on someone else's behalf (Latin *per procurationem*).

PPS ABBREV **1** Parliamentary Private Secretary. **2** post postscript, an additional postscript.

PR ABBREV **1** public relations. **2** proportional representation.

practicable ADJ able to be done.
practicability NOUN

practical ADJ **1** involving activity rather than study or theory. **2** suitable for use rather than decorative; sensible in approaching problems, doing things, etc. **3** almost, so nearly as to be accepted as being (something specified): *a practical certainty*.
practicality NOUN

practical joke NOUN a humorous trick played on a person.

practically ADV **1** in a practical way. **2** virtually, almost.

practice NOUN **1** repeated exercise to improve skill. **2** action as opposed to theory. **3** a custom or habit. **4** a doctor's or lawyer's business. **in practice 1** in fact as opposed to wish or theory. **2** skilled through having practised. **out of practice** not having practised for a while.

practise ([US] **practice**) VERB **1** do something repeatedly or habitually. **2** (of a doctor or lawyer) perform professional work.

practised ([US] **practiced**) ADJ experienced; expert.

practitioner NOUN a professional worker, especially in medicine.

praesidium variant of **PRESIDIUM**.

pragmatic ADJ treating things from a practical point of view.
pragmatically ADV
pragmatism NOUN
pragmatist NOUN

prairie NOUN a large treeless area of grassland, especially in North America.

prairie dog NOUN a North American rodent that lives in burrows.

praise VERB express approval or admiration of; honour (God) in

p

words. NOUN the action of praising; words that show approval or admiration.

praiseworthy ADJ deserving praise.

praline NOUN a sweet substance made by crushing sweetened nuts.

pram NOUN a four-wheeled conveyance for a baby.

prance VERB move springily.

prang [INFORMAL] VERB crash (a vehicle). NOUN a crash or collision.

prank NOUN a piece of mischief.

prankster NOUN a person playing pranks.

p **praseodymium** /pray-zi-o-dI-mi-ŭm/ NOUN a metallic element.

prat NOUN [INFORMAL] a fool.

prattle VERB chatter in a childish way. NOUN childish chatter.

prawn NOUN an edible shellfish like a large shrimp.

pray VERB say prayers; entreat.

prayer NOUN a solemn request or thanksgiving to God; an act of praying; an entreaty.

pre- PREFIX before; beforehand.

preach VERB deliver a sermon; proclaim or teach (a religious belief); advocate (a course of action); talk in an annoyingly moralizing way.
preacher NOUN

preamble NOUN a preliminary statement, an introductory section.

pre-arrange VERB arrange beforehand.
pre-arrangement NOUN

precarious ADJ unsafe, not secure.
precariously ADV

precast ADJ (of concrete) cast in shape before use.

precaution NOUN something done in advance to avoid a risk.
precautionary ADJ

precede VERB come or go before in time, order, etc.

precedence NOUN the state of being more important than someone or something else.

precedent NOUN a previous case serving as an example to be followed.

precept NOUN a command or rule of conduct.

precinct NOUN **1** an area within a set of boundaries; a defined area round a cathedral etc. **2** an area closed to traffic in a town.

precious ADJ **1** of great value; beloved. **2** affectedly refined.

precipice NOUN a very steep face of a cliff or rock.

precipitate VERB /pri-**sip**-i-tayt/ **1** cause to happen suddenly or prematurely; cause to move suddenly and uncontrollably. **2** cause (a substance) to be deposited. **3** condense (vapour) into drops falling as rain etc. ADJ /pri-**sip**-i-tăt/ rash, hasty. NOUN /pri-**sip**-i-tăt/ a substance deposited from a solution.
precipitately ADV

precipitation NOUN **1** rain or snow. **2** the process of precipitating; the action of being precipitated.

precipitous ADJ very steep.

precis /pray-see/ NOUN (PL **precis**) a summary. VERB make a precis of.

precise ADJ exact, accurate over details.
precisely ADV
precision NOUN

preclude VERB exclude the possibility of, prevent.

precocious ADJ having developed earlier than is usual.
precociously ADV

precognition NOUN foreknowledge, especially supernatural.

preconceived ADJ (of an idea) formed beforehand.
preconception NOUN

precondition NOUN a condition that must be fulfilled beforehand.

precursor NOUN a forerunner.

pre-date VERB exist or occur at an earlier time than.

predator NOUN a predatory animal.

predatory /**pred**-ă-ter-i/ ADJ preying on others.

predecease VERB [FORMAL] die earlier than (another person).

predecessor NOUN a

person who held an office, position, etc. before one.

predestination NOUN the doctrine that everything has been determined in advance.

predicament NOUN a difficult situation.

predicate /pre-di-kăt/ NOUN [GRAMMAR] the part of a sentence that says something about the subject (e.g. *is short* in *life is short*).
predicative ADJ

predict VERB foretell.
predictable ADJ
predictably ADV
prediction NOUN
predictor NOUN

p

predictive ADJ foretelling or foreshowing something.

predilection NOUN a special liking.

predispose VERB make liable or inclined to a particular attitude, action, etc.
predisposition NOUN

predominate VERB be most numerous or powerful; exert control.
predominance NOUN
predominant ADJ
predominantly ADV

pre-eminent ADJ excelling others, outstanding.
pre-eminence NOUN
pre-eminently ADV

pre-empt VERB take action to prevent (an occurrence); forestall (someone); obtain (something) before anyone else can.
pre-emption NOUN
pre-emptive ADJ

preen VERB (of a bird) smooth (feathers) with the beak.
preen oneself groom oneself; show self-satisfaction.

prefabricate VERB manufacture in sections for assembly on a site.
prefabrication NOUN

preface NOUN an introductory statement. VERB **1** introduce with a preface. **2** lead up to (an event).

prefect NOUN **1** a senior pupil authorized to maintain discipline in a school. **2** an administrative official in certain countries.

prefecture NOUN

prefer VERB (**prefers, preferring, preferred**) **1** choose as more desirable, like better. **2** [FORMAL] put forward (an accusation).

preferable ADJ more desirable.
preferably ADV

preference NOUN **1** a greater liking for one person or thing than another; a thing preferred. **2** favour shown to one person over another.

preferential ADJ involving or showing favour or partiality.
preferentially ADV

preferment NOUN promotion.

prefix NOUN a word or syllable placed at the beginning of a word to change its meaning.
VERB add as a prefix or introduction; add a prefix to.

pregnant ADJ **1** having a child or young developing in the womb. **2** full of meaning.
pregnancy NOUN

prehensile ADJ (especially of an animal's tail) able to grasp things.

prehistoric ADJ of the ancient period before written records were made.
prehistorically ADV

prejudge VERB form a judgement on before knowing all the facts.

prejudice NOUN **1** a preconceived and irrational opinion; hostility and injustice based on this. **2** harm to someone's rights.
VERB **1** cause to have a prejudice. **2** cause harm to.
prejudiced ADJ

prejudicial ADJ harmful to rights or interests.
prejudicially ADV

prelate /pre-lăt/ NOUN a clergyman of high rank.
prelacy NOUN

preliminary ADJ preceding and preparing for a main action or event. NOUN (PL **preliminaries**) a preliminary action or event.

prelude NOUN an action or event leading up to

another; an introductory part or piece of music.

premarital ADJ before marriage.

premature ADJ coming or done before the usual or proper time.
prematurely ADV

pre-medication NOUN medication in preparation for an operation.

premeditated ADJ planned beforehand.
premeditation NOUN

premenstrual ADJ occurring before a menstrual period.

premier ADJ first in importance, order, or time. NOUN a prime minister, a head of government.
premiership NOUN

p

premiere /prem-i-air/ NOUN the first public performance of a play etc.

premise NOUN = **PREMISS**.

premises PLURAL NOUN a building and its grounds.

premiss NOUN a statement on which reasoning is based.

premium NOUN **1** an amount to be paid for an insurance policy. **2** a sum added to a usual price or charge.
at a premium 1 above the nominal or usual price. **2** scarce and in demand.

premonition NOUN a feeling that something (bad) will happen.
premonitory ADJ

preoccupation NOUN the state of being preoccupied; something that fills one's thoughts.

preoccupied ADJ so absorbed in or anxious about something that one is inattentive to other matters.

preparation NOUN the process of preparing; something done to prepare for something; a substance prepared for use.

preparatory ADJ preparing for something.
preparatory to as a preparation for.

preparatory school NOUN **1** a private school for pupils between seven and thirteen. **2** [US] a private school preparing pupils for university.

prepare VERB make ready for use, consumption, etc.; make ready to do or experience something; make oneself ready. **prepared to** willing to.

prepay VERB (**prepays**, **prepaying**, **prepaid**) pay for in advance.

preponderate VERB be greater in number, power, etc. **preponderance** NOUN **preponderant** ADJ

preposition NOUN [GRAMMAR] a word governing a noun or pronoun and indicating its relation to other words in the sentence (e.g. She came *after* dinner, We went *by* train). **prepositional** ADJ

prepossessing ADJ attractive.

preposterous ADJ utterly absurd, outrageous. **preposterously** ADV

prepuce /pree-pyoos/ NOUN the foreskin.

prerequisite NOUN something that is required before something else can happen.

prerogative NOUN a right or privilege.

presage VERB be an omen of. NOUN a sign, an omen, especially of something bad.

Presbyterian ADJ relating to a Protestant Church governed by elders of equal rank. NOUN a member of a Presbyterian Church. **Presbyterianism** NOUN

pre-school ADJ of the time before a child is old enough to go to school.

prescribe VERB **1** advise the use of (a medicine etc.). **2** lay down as a course or rule to be followed.

prescription NOUN the action of prescribing; a doctor's written instructions for the preparation and use of a medicine.

prescriptive ADJ imposing a rule to be followed.

presence NOUN the state of being present; a person or thing that is present without being seen; an impressive manner or bearing.

presence of mind ability to act sensibly in a crisis.

present[1] /pre-zĕnt/ ADJ **1** being in the place in question. **2** existing or being dealt with now. NOUN the present time, time now passing.
at present now. **for the present** for now, temporarily.

present[2] NOUN /pre-zĕnt/ a gift. VERB /pri-**zent**/ **1** give as a gift or award (to); cause (trouble, difficulty). **2** introduce (a broadcast); represent in a particular way.
present itself become apparent.
presentation NOUN
presenter NOUN

p

presentable ADJ clean, smart, etc. enough to be seen in public.
presentably ADV

presentiment NOUN a feeling of something about to happen, a foreboding.

presently ADV **1** soon. **2** [SCOTTISH] & [US] now, currently.

preservative ADJ preserving. NOUN a substance that preserves perishable food.

preserve VERB keep safe, unchanged, or in existence; treat (food) to prevent decay. NOUN **1** interests etc. regarded as one person's domain. **2** (also **preserves**) jam.
preservation NOUN
preserver NOUN

preside VERB be in authority or control.

president NOUN the head of an institution or club; the head of a republic.
presidency NOUN
presidential ADJ

presidium (also **praesidium**) NOUN the standing committee in a Communist organization.

press VERB **1** move or cause to move into contact with something by applying force; push downwards or inwards; squeeze; flatten; iron (clothes). **2** urge; try hard to persuade or influence; insist on (a point). **3** move in a specified direction by pushing. **4** bring into use as a makeshift. NOUN **1** a device for flattening or squeezing. **2** a machine for printing; newspapers and periodicals; people involved in making these; publicity of a specified kind: *a bad press.* **3** an act of pressing. **be pressed for** have barely enough of. **press on** continue in one's activity.

press conference NOUN an interview given to a number of reporters.

press cutting NOUN an article cut from a newspaper.

press-gang VERB force into service.

pressing ADJ urgent.

press stud NOUN a small fastener with two parts that are pressed together.

press-up NOUN an exercise of pressing on the hands to raise the body while lying face down.

pressure NOUN **1** exertion of force against a thing; this force. **2** influence or persuasion of an oppressive kind; stress. VERB pressurize (a person).

pressure cooker NOUN a pan for cooking things quickly by steam under pressure.

pressure group NOUN an organized group seeking to exert influence by concerted action.

pressurize (also **pressurise**) VERB **1** try to compel into an action. **2** maintain constant artificially raised pressure in (a gas or its container). **pressurization** NOUN

prestige NOUN respect resulting from good reputation or achievements.

prestigious ADJ having or bringing prestige.

presto ADV [MUSIC] very quickly.

prestressed ADJ (of concrete) strengthened by wires within it.

presumably ADV it may be presumed.

presume VERB **1** suppose to be true. **2** be presumptuous. **presume on/upon** take advantage of one's good relationship with someone. **presumption** NOUN

presumptuous ADJ impudently ignoring limits to one's rights, privileges, etc.
presumptuously ADV

presuppose VERB require as a precondition; assume at the beginning of an argument.
presupposition NOUN

pre-tax ADJ before tax has been deducted.

pretence ([US] **pretense**) NOUN **1** an act or the action of pretending. **2** a claim (e.g. to merit or knowledge).

pretend VERB **1** speak or behave so as to make something seem to be the case when it is not. **2** lay claim to something.
pretender NOUN

pretension NOUN **1** a claim or the assertion of it. **2** pretentiousness.

pretentious ADJ trying to appear more important, intelligent, etc., than is the case.
pretentiously ADV
pretentiousness NOUN

preternatural ADJ beyond what is natural.
preternaturally ADV

pretext NOUN a reason put forward to conceal one's true reason.

prettify VERB (**prettifies**, **prettifying**, **prettified**) make (something) look superficially attractive.

pretty ADJ (**prettier**, **prettiest**) attractive in a delicate way. ADV [INFORMAL] to a moderate extent: *pretty good.*
prettily ADV
prettiness NOUN

pretzel NOUN a knot-shaped salted biscuit.

prevail VERB **1** be victorious, gain mastery. **2** be widespread or current.
prevail on persuade.

prevalent ADJ existing generally, widespread.
prevalence NOUN

prevaricate VERB speak or act evasively or misleadingly.
prevarication NOUN

prevent VERB keep from happening; make unable to do something.
preventable ADJ
prevention NOUN

preventive (also **preventative**) ADJ

designed to prevent something from occurring.

previous ADJ coming before in time or order.
previously ADV

prey NOUN an animal hunted or killed by another for food; a victim.
bird of prey a bird that kills and eats birds and mammals. **prey on 1** kill and eat. **2** distress, worry.

price NOUN the amount of money for which something is bought or sold; an unpleasant experience etc. that is necessary to achieve something. VERB decide the price of.

priceless ADJ **1** invaluable. **2** [INFORMAL] very amusing or absurd.

prick VERB **1** pierce slightly; feel a pain as from this; provoke to action. **2** erect (the ears). NOUN **1** an act of pricking; a sensation of being pricked. **2** [VULGAR SLANG] someone's penis.
prick up one's ears listen intently.

prickle NOUN a small thorn or spine; a pricking sensation. VERB feel or cause a pricking sensation.

prickly ADJ (**pricklier, prickliest**) **1** having prickles. **2** easily offended.

pride NOUN **1** a feeling of pleasure or satisfaction about one's actions, qualities, or possessions or those of someone close to one; a source of this; a sense of dignity. **2** a group of lions.
pride of place the most prominent position. **pride oneself on** be proud of.

priest NOUN a member of the clergy; an official of a non-Christian religion.
priesthood NOUN
priestly ADJ

priestess NOUN a female priest of a non-Christian religion.

prig NOUN a self-righteous person.
priggish ADJ
priggishly ADV
priggishness NOUN

prim ADJ (**primmer, primmest**) very formal and proper, easily shocked or disgusted.
primly ADV

primness NOUN

prima ballerina NOUN a chief ballerina.

primacy NOUN pre-eminence.

prima donna NOUN **1** the chief female singer in an opera. **2** [INFORMAL] a temperamental and self-important person.

prima facie /pry-ma fay-shee/ ADV at first sight. ADJ based on first impressions.

primal ADJ **1** primitive, primeval. **2** fundamental.

primary ADJ **1** first in time, order, or importance. **2** (of a school or education) for children below the age of 11. NOUN (PL **primaries**) (in the USA) a preliminary election to choose delegates or candidates.
primarily ADV

primary colour NOUN a colour not made by mixing others, i.e. (for light) red, green, or blue, (for paint) red, blue, or yellow.

primate NOUN **1** an archbishop. **2** a member of the highly developed order of animals that includes humans, apes, and monkeys.

prime ADJ **1** most important, main. **2** excellent. NOUN a state or time of greatest strength, success, excellence, etc.: *past his prime.* VERB prepare for use or action; provide with information in preparation for something.

prime minister NOUN the head of a parliamentary government.

prime number NOUN a number that can be divided exactly only by itself and one.

primer NOUN **1** a substance used to prime a surface for painting. **2** an elementary textbook.

primeval ADJ of the earliest times of the world.

primitive ADJ of or at an early stage of evolution or civilization; simple, crude; fundamental.

primogeniture NOUN a system by which an eldest son inherits all his parents' property.

primordial ADJ primeval.

primrose NOUN a pale yellow spring flower; its colour.

prince NOUN a male member of a royal family; a sovereign's son or grandson.

princely ADJ of or appropriate to a prince; splendid; generous, lavish.

princess NOUN a female member of a royal family; a sovereign's daughter or granddaughter; a prince's wife.

principal ADJ first in rank or importance. NOUN **1** a person with the highest authority in an organization; the head of a school or college; a leading performer in a play, concert, etc. **2** a capital sum as distinct from interest or income.

principality NOUN (PL **principalities**) a country ruled by a prince.

principally ADV mainly.

principle NOUN a truth serving as the basis for a system of belief, reasoning, etc.; (**principles**) beliefs governing one's behaviour, moral standards; a scientific law applying across a wide field.
in principle 1 as a general idea. **2** theoretically though not necessarily in fact. **on principle** because of one's moral beliefs.

print VERB **1** press (a mark) on a surface, mark (a surface etc.) in this way; produce by applying inked type to paper. **2** write with unjoined letters. **3** produce a positive picture from (a photographic negative). NOUN a mark left by pressing; printed lettering or words; a printed design, picture, or fabric.

printed circuit NOUN an electric circuit with lines of conducting material printed on a flat sheet.

printer NOUN **1** a person who prints books, newspapers, etc. **2** a machine that prints.

printout NOUN printed material produced from a

computer printer or teleprinter.

prior ADJ coming before in time, order, or importance. NOUN a monk who is head of a religious community, or one ranking next below an abbot.

prioress NOUN a female prior.

prioritize (also **prioritise**) VERB treat as more important than other things; arrange in order of importance.
prioritization NOUN

priority NOUN (PL **priorities**) something regarded as more important than others; the state of being more important; the right to proceed before other traffic.

priory NOUN (PL **priories**) a monastery or nunnery governed by a prior or prioress.

prise ([US] **prize**) VERB force out or open by leverage.

prism NOUN a solid geometric shape with ends that are equal and parallel; a transparent object of this shape that separates white light into colours.

prismatic ADJ of or like a prism; (of colours) rainbow-like.

prison NOUN a building used to confine people convicted of crimes; a place of confinement.

prisoner NOUN a person kept in prison; a person in confinement.

prissy ADJ (**prissier**, **prissiest**) prim, prudish.
prissily ADV
prissiness NOUN

pristine ADJ in its original and unspoilt condition.

privacy NOUN a state in which one is not observed or disturbed by others.

private ADJ **1** belonging to a particular person or group, not public; confidential; free from intrusion. **2** not provided or owned by the state; not holding public office. NOUN a soldier of the lowest rank.
in private privately.
privately ADV

privation NOUN shortage of food etc.; hardship.

privatize (also **privatise**)

VERB transfer from state to private ownership.
privatization NOUN

privet NOUN a bushy evergreen shrub much used for hedges.

privilege NOUN a special right granted to a person or group; a great honour.
privileged ADJ

privy[1] NOUN (PL **privies**) [DATED] or [US] a lavatory, especially an outside one.

privy[2] ADJ (**privy to**) sharing in the knowledge of (something secret).

prize NOUN an award for victory or superiority; something that can be won. ADJ **1** having been or likely to be awarded a prize. **2** excellent. VERB **1** value highly. **2** US spelling of **PRISE**.

pro NOUN (PL **pros**) **1** [INFORMAL] a professional. **2** (in the phrase **pros and cons**) an advantage, an argument for something.

pro- PREFIX in favour of.

proactive ADJ gaining control by taking the initiative.

probable ADJ likely to happen or be true.
probability NOUN
probably ADV

probate NOUN the official process of proving that a will is valid; a certified copy of a will.

probation NOUN **1** observation to test someone's ability and suitability for a position. **2** the supervision of an offender by an official **probation officer** as an alternative to imprisonment.
probationary ADJ

probationer NOUN a person undergoing a probationary period in a new job.

probe NOUN a blunt surgical instrument for exploring a wound; an investigation; an unmanned exploratory spacecraft. VERB examine with a probe; conduct an inquiry.

probity NOUN honesty.

problem NOUN something difficult to deal with or understand; something to be solved or dealt with.
problematic, **problematical** ADJ

proboscis /prŏ-bos-is/ NOUN **1** a long flexible snout. **2** an insect's elongated mouthpart used for sucking things.

procedure NOUN a series of actions done to accomplish something, especially an established or official one.
procedural ADJ

proceed VERB **1** go forward or onward; continue. **2** start a lawsuit. **3** originate from a source.

proceedings PLURAL NOUN a series of activities, a formal procedure; a lawsuit; a published report of a conference.

proceeds PLURAL NOUN the profit from a sale, performance, etc.

process NOUN a series of actions to achieve an end; a natural series of events or changes; a series of operations performed in manufacturing something. VERB **1** change or preserve (something) by a series of mechanical or chemical operations. **2** deal with according to an official procedure.

procession NOUN a number of people or vehicles etc. going along in an orderly line.

processor NOUN a machine that processes things.

proclaim VERB announce publicly.
proclamation NOUN

proclivity NOUN (PL **proclivities**) a tendency, an inclination or preference.

procrastinate VERB postpone action.
procrastination NOUN

procreate VERB produce young, reproduce.
procreation NOUN

procurator fiscal NOUN (in Scotland) a public prosecutor and coroner.

procure VERB **1** obtain by care or effort, acquire. **2** act as procurer.
procurement NOUN

procurer NOUN a person who obtains a prostitute for someone else.

prod VERB (**prods**, **prodding**, **prodded**) **1** poke. **2** stimulate to action. NOUN **1** a prodding action; an instrument for prodding things. **2** a stimulus.

prodigal ADJ wasteful, extravagant.
prodigality NOUN
prodigally ADV

prodigious ADJ amazingly great, huge.
prodigiously ADV

prodigy NOUN (PL **prodigies**) a person with exceptional abilities; an amazing or unnatural thing.

produce VERB /prŏ-**dyoos**/ **1** make, manufacture; bring into being; grow, yield (crops); result in. **2** present for inspection. **3** administer the staging, financing, etc. of (a performance). NOUN /**pro**-dyoos/ things produced or grown.
production NOUN

producer NOUN **1** a person who produces something. **2** a person responsible for the schedule, expenditure, and quality of a film, play, broadcast, etc.

product NOUN **1** a thing produced. **2** a number obtained by multiplying.

productive ADJ producing things, especially in large quantities.

productivity NOUN efficiency in industrial production.

profane ADJ **1** not sacred. **2** not reverent, blasphemous. VERB treat irreverently.
profanely ADV
profanity NOUN

profess VERB **1** falsely claim to have or feel (an emotion etc.). **2** affirm faith in (a religion).

professed ADJ **1** self-acknowledged. **2** falsely claimed; falsely claiming to be something.
professedly ADV

profession NOUN **1** an occupation requiring advanced learning; the people engaged in this. **2** a declaration.

professional ADJ **1** belonging to a profession. **2** skilful and conscientious. **3** doing something for payment, not as a pastime. NOUN a professional worker or player.
professionalism NOUN
professionally ADV

professor NOUN a

p

university teacher of the highest rank; (in America) a university lecturer.
professorial ADJ

proffer VERB offer.

proficient ADJ competent, skilled.
proficiency NOUN
proficiently ADV

profile NOUN **1** a side view, especially of the face. **2** a short account of a person's character or career. **3** the extent to which someone or something attracts notice: *keep a low profile.*

profit NOUN money made in an enterprise or transaction; a gain, an advantage. VERB (**profits**, **profiting**, **profited**) make money; derive advantage.

profitable ADJ bringing profit.
profitability NOUN
profitably ADV

profiteer NOUN a person who makes excessive, unfair, or illegal profits.
profiteering NOUN

profligate ADJ wasteful, extravagant; dissolute. NOUN a profligate person.
profligacy NOUN

profound ADJ **1** (of an emotion, state, etc.) intense. **2** showing or needing great insight.
profoundly ADV
profundity NOUN

profuse ADJ lavish; plentiful.
profusely ADV
profusion NOUN

progenitor NOUN an ancestor.

progeny NOUN offspring.

progesterone NOUN a sex hormone that stimulates the uterus to prepare for pregnancy.

prognosis NOUN (PL **prognoses**) a forecast, especially of the course of a disease.
prognostic ADJ

prognosticate VERB forecast.
prognostication NOUN

program NOUN **1** US spelling of **PROGRAMME**. **2** a series of coded instructions for a computer. VERB (**programs**, **programming**, **programmed**) instruct (a computer) by means of a program.
programmer NOUN

programme ([US] **program**) NOUN **1** a planned series of future events or actions. **2** a sheet giving details of a performance and performers. **3** a radio or television broadcast. VERB arrange or include in a schedule.

progress NOUN /**proh**-gress/ forward or onward movement; development. VERB /prŏ-**gress**/ move forward or onward; develop.
in progress taking place.
progression NOUN

progressive ADJ **1** favouring progress or reform. **2** (of a disease) gradually increasing in its effect.
progressively ADV

prohibit VERB (**prohibits**, **prohibiting**, **prohibited**) forbid.
prohibition NOUN

prohibitive ADJ **1** (of a price) too high, impossible to pay. **2** forbidding something.

project NOUN /**pro**-jekt/ a plan, an undertaking; a piece of work involving research. VERB /prŏ-**jekt**/ **1** estimate; plan. **2** extend outwards beyond something else. **3** throw; cause (light etc.) to fall on a surface; make (one's voice) audible; present (an image of oneself); make (an impression).

projectile NOUN a missile.

projection NOUN **1** an estimate of future situations based on a study of present ones. **2** the presentation of an image on a screen; the presentation of a particular image of oneself etc. **3** something projecting from a surface.

projectionist NOUN a person who operates a projector.

projector NOUN an apparatus for projecting images on to a screen.

prolapse NOUN a condition in which an organ slips forward out of place.

proletariat NOUN working-class people.
proletarian ADJ & NOUN

pro-life ADJ opposed to abortion and euthanasia.

proliferate VERB

p

reproduce rapidly, multiply.
proliferation NOUN

prolific ADJ producing things abundantly.
prolifically ADV

prologue NOUN an introduction to a play, poem, etc.

prolong VERB lengthen in extent or duration.
prolongation NOUN

prolonged ADJ continuing for a long time.

prom NOUN [INFORMAL] **1** a promenade concert. **2** a promenade.

promenade NOUN a paved public walk (especially along a sea front).

promenade concert NOUN a concert where part of the audience is not seated and can move about.

promethium NOUN a radioactive metallic element.

prominent ADJ projecting from a surface; conspicuous; well known, famous.
prominence NOUN
prominently ADV

promiscuous ADJ **1** having sexual relations with many people. **2** indiscriminate.
promiscuity NOUN
promiscuously ADV

promise NOUN a declaration that one will give or do something; signs of future excellence; an indication that something specified is likely to happen. VERB **1** make a promise (to); say that one will do or give (a thing). **2** give reason to expect.

promising ADJ likely to turn out well.

promissory ADJ conveying a promise.

promontory NOUN (PL **promontories**) high land jutting out into the sea.

promote VERB **1** raise to a higher rank or office. **2** help the progress of; publicize in order to sell.
promoter NOUN
promotion NOUN

promotional ADJ of the publicizing of a product; of advertising.

prompt ADJ done or acting without delay. VERB **1** give rise to (a feeling or action). **2** assist (an actor)

by supplying forgotten words. ADV exactly (at a specified time).
promptly ADV
promptness NOUN

prompter NOUN a person positioned off stage to prompt actors.

promulgate VERB make widely known.
promulgation NOUN
promulgator NOUN

prone ADJ **1** lying face downwards. **2** likely to do or suffer something.

prong NOUN each of the pointed parts of a fork.
pronged ADJ

pronoun NOUN [GRAMMAR] a word used as a substitute for a noun: **demonstrative pronouns**, e.g. this, that; **interrogative pronouns**, e.g. who?, which?; **personal pronouns**, e.g. I, you, her, it; **possessive pronouns**, e.g. my, your, her, its; **reflexive pronouns**, e.g. myself, oneself; **relative pronouns**, e.g. who, which, that.
pronominal ADJ

pronounce VERB **1** utter (a sound or word) distinctly or in a certain way. **2** declare, announce.
pronunciation NOUN

pronounced ADJ noticeable.

pronouncement NOUN a declaration.

proof NOUN **1** evidence that something is true or exists. **2** a copy of printed matter for correction. ADJ able to resist penetration or damage: *proof against rain.* VERB make (fabric) proof against something (e.g. water).

proof-read VERB read and correct (printed proofs).
proof-reader NOUN

prop NOUN **1** a support to prevent something from falling, sagging, or failing. **2** [INFORMAL] a movable object used in a play or film. **3** [INFORMAL] a propeller. VERB (**props**, **propping**, **propped**) support with a prop.

propaganda NOUN publicity intended to persuade or convince people.

propagate VERB **1** breed or reproduce (a plant) from parent stock. **2** spread (news etc.); transmit.

propagation NOUN
propagator NOUN

propane NOUN a hydrocarbon fuel gas.

propel VERB (**propels**, **propelling**, **propelled**) push forwards or onwards.

propellant NOUN a gas which forces out the contents of an aerosol.

propeller NOUN a revolving device with blades, for propelling a ship or aircraft.

propensity NOUN (PL **propensities**) a tendency; an inclination.

proper ADJ **1** genuine, deserving a particular description: *a proper meal.* **2** of the required type, suitable. **3** according to or observing conventions of correct behaviour.
proper to belonging exclusively to.
properly ADV

proper name (also **proper noun**) NOUN [GRAMMAR] the name of an individual person, place, or organisation.

property NOUN (PL **properties**) **1** something owned; real estate, land. **2** a quality, a characteristic.

prophecy NOUN (PL **prophecies**) a prediction of future events.

prophesy VERB (**prophesies**, **prophesying**, **prophesied**) foretell (what will happen).

prophet NOUN **1** a person who foretells events. **2** a religious teacher inspired by God.

prophetic ADJ prophesying.

prophylactic /pro-fil-ak-tik/ ADJ preventing disease or misfortune. NOUN **1** a preventive medicine or action. **2** [US] a condom.
prophylaxis NOUN

propinquity NOUN nearness.

propitiate /prŏ-**pish**-i-ayt/ VERB win or regain the favour of.
propitiation NOUN
propitiatory ADJ

propitious /prŏ-**pish**-ŭs/ ADJ auspicious, favourable.
propitiously ADV
propitiousness NOUN

proponent NOUN a person putting forward a proposal.

proportion NOUN a fraction or share of a whole; a ratio; the correct relation in size or degree; (**proportions**) dimensions.
proportional ADJ
proportionally ADV

proportional representation NOUN an electoral system in which each party receives seats in proportion to the number of votes cast for its candidates.

proportionate ADJ in proportion, corresponding.
proportionately ADV

proposal NOUN **1** the proposing of something; something proposed. **2** an offer of marriage.

propose VERB **1** put forward (an idea etc.) for consideration; nominate for a position. **2** ask someone to marry one.
proposer NOUN

proposition NOUN **1** a statement or assertion. **2** a suggested plan. **3** a project considered in terms of the likelihood of success. **4** [INFORMAL] an offer of sexual intercourse. VERB [INFORMAL] make a proposal to; suggest intercourse to.

propound VERB put forward (an idea etc.) for consideration.

proprietary ADJ made and sold by a particular firm, usually under a patent; of an owner or ownership.

proprietor NOUN the owner of a business.
proprietorial ADJ

propriety NOUN correctness of behaviour.

propulsion NOUN the process of propelling or being propelled.

propylene NOUN a gaseous hydrocarbon.

pro rata ADJ proportional. ADV proportionally.

prorogue /proh-**rohg**/ VERB (**prorogues**, **proroguing**, **prorogued**) discontinue the meetings of (a parliament) without dissolving it.

prosaic ADJ plain and ordinary, unimaginative.
prosaically ADV

proscenium /prŏ-seen-i-ŭm/ NOUN (PL **prosceniums** or **proscenia**) the part of a theatre stage in front of the curtain.

proscribe VERB forbid.

prose NOUN written or spoken language without metre or other poetic elements.

prosecute VERB **1** take legal proceedings against (a person) for a crime. **2** continue with, carry on (a course of action).
prosecution NOUN
prosecutor NOUN

proselyte NOUN a recent convert to a religion.

proselytize (also **proselytise**) VERB seek to convert.

prospect NOUN /pross-pekt/ the likelihood of something's occurring; (**prospects**) chances of success. VERB /prŏ-**spekt**/ explore in search of something.
prospector NOUN

prospective ADJ expected to be or to occur; future, possible.

prospectus NOUN (PL **prospectuses**) a document giving details of a school, business, etc.

prosper VERB be successful, thrive.

prosperous ADJ financially successful.
prosperity NOUN

prostate gland NOUN the gland round the neck of the bladder in male mammals.

prosthesis NOUN (PL **prostheses**) an artificial body part.
prosthetic ADJ

prostitute NOUN a person who offers sexual intercourse for payment. VERB make a prostitute of; put (talent etc.) to an unworthy use.
prostitution NOUN

prostrate ADJ /pross-trayt/ **1** face downwards; lying horizontally. **2** overcome, exhausted. VERB /pross-**trayt**/ cause to be prostrate.
prostration NOUN

protactinium NOUN a radioactive metallic element.

protagonist NOUN **1** the chief person in a drama, story, etc. **2** a supporter of a cause etc.

protean /**proh**-ti-ăn/ ADJ variable; versatile.

protect VERB keep from harm or injury.
protection NOUN
protector NOUN

protectionism NOUN a policy of protecting home industries from competition by tariffs etc.
protectionist NOUN

protective ADJ protecting, giving protection.
protectively ADV

protectorate NOUN a country that is under the official protection and partial control of a stronger one.

protégé /**prot**-i-*zh*ay/ NOUN a person who is guided and supported by another.

protein NOUN an organic compound forming an essential part of humans' and animals' food.

pro tem ADJ & ADV for the time being.

protest NOUN /**proh**-test/ a statement or action indicating disapproval.
VERB /prŏ-**test**/ **1** express disapproval. **2** declare firmly: *protested her innocence.*

Protestant NOUN a member of any of the western Christian Churches that are separate from the Roman Catholic Church.
Protestantism NOUN

protestation NOUN a firm declaration.

protocol NOUN **1** official procedure governing affairs of state; accepted behaviour in a situation. **2** a draft of a treaty.

proton NOUN a particle of matter with a positive electric charge.

protoplasm NOUN the contents of a living cell.

prototype NOUN an original example from which others are developed.

protozoan /proh-tŏ-**zoh**-ăn/ NOUN (PL **protozoa** or **protozoans**) a one-celled microscopic animal.

protract VERB cause to last longer.
protraction NOUN

protractor NOUN an instrument for measuring angles.

protrude VERB project, stick out.
protrusion NOUN
protrusive ADJ

protuberance NOUN a bulging part.

protuberant ADJ bulging.

proud ADJ **1** feeling pride; giving cause for pride: *a proud history;* arrogant. **2** projecting slightly from a surface.
proudly ADV

prove VERB (**proves, proving, proved**; PAST PARTICIPLE **proved** or **proven**) **1** demonstrate to be true. **2** turn out to be of a specified kind. **3** (of dough) rise because of the action of yeast.

provenance NOUN a place of origin.

provender NOUN fodder.

proverb NOUN a short well-known saying.

proverbial ADJ **1** of or mentioned in a proverb. **2** well known.

provide VERB **1** supply, make available (to). **2** stipulate in a legal document.
provide for 1 supply with necessities. **2** make preparations for.
provider NOUN

provided CONJ on condition (that).

providence NOUN the protective care of God or of nature as a spiritual power.

provident ADJ showing wise forethought for future needs, thrifty.

providential ADJ happening very luckily.
providentially ADV

providing CONJ = **PROVIDED**.

province NOUN **1** an administrative division of a country. **2** (**the provinces**) all parts of a country outside its capital city. **3** a range of learning or responsibility.

provincial ADJ **1** of a province or provinces. **2** having limited interests and narrow-minded views. NOUN an inhabitant of a province.

provision NOUN **1** the process of providing things. **2** a stipulation in a treaty or contract etc. **3** (**provisions**) food and drink.

provisional ADJ arranged temporarily.
provisionally ADV

proviso /prŏ-vyz-oh/ NOUN (PL **provisos**) a condition attached to an agreement.

provisory ADJ provisional.

provoke VERB **1** make angry. **2** rouse to action; produce as a reaction.
provocation NOUN
provocative ADJ
provocatively ADV

provost NOUN the head of a college; the head of a cathedral chapter.

prow NOUN a projecting front part of a ship or boat.

prowess NOUN great ability or daring.

prowl VERB go about stealthily as though in search of prey.
on the prowl prowling.
prowler NOUN

proximate ADJ nearest.

proximity NOUN nearness.

proxy NOUN (PL **proxies**) a person authorized to represent or act for another; use of such a person.

prude NOUN a person who is too easily shocked, especially by references to sex etc.
prudery NOUN

prudent ADJ showing thought for the future.
prudence NOUN
prudently ADV

prudish ADJ easily shocked or offended.
prudishly ADV
prudishness NOUN

prune NOUN a dried plum. VERB trim (a tree etc.) by cutting away dead or unwanted parts; reduce.

prurient ADJ having or stimulating lustful thoughts.
prurience NOUN
pruriently ADV

pry VERB (**pries**, **prying**, **pried**) inquire too inquisitively into someone's private affairs.

PS ABBREV postscript.

psalm /sahm/ NOUN a sacred song.

psalter /sawl-ter/ NOUN a copy of the Book of Psalms.

psaltery /sawl-tĕ-ri/ NOUN

(PL **psalteries**) an ancient musical instrument.

psephology /sef-ol-ŏ-ji/ NOUN the study of trends in voting.
psephologist NOUN

pseudo- /syoo-doh/ COMBINING FORM false.

pseudonym /syoo-dŏ-nim/ NOUN a fictitious name used e.g. by an author.
pseudonymous ADJ

psoriasis /sŏ-ry-ă-sis/ NOUN a skin condition causing scaly red patches.

psyche /sy-kee/ NOUN the soul, the spirit; the mind.

psychedelic /sy-kĕ-del-ik/ ADJ **1** (of a drug) producing hallucinations. **2** with vivid colours or abstract patterns.

psychiatry /sy-ky-ă-tri/ NOUN the study and treatment of mental illness.
psychiatric ADJ
psychiatrist NOUN

psychic /sy-kik/ ADJ of the soul or mind; of or having apparently supernatural powers. NOUN a person having or claiming psychic powers.

psycho /sy-koh/ NOUN (PL **psychos**) [INFORMAL] a psychopath.

psychoanalyse ([US] **psychoanalyze**) VERB treat by psychoanalysis.
psychoanalyst NOUN

psychoanalysis NOUN a method of examining and treating mental conditions by investigating the interaction of conscious and unconscious elements.
psychoanalytical ADJ

psychology NOUN the study of the mind and how it works; a person's mental characteristics; the mental factors governing a situation or activity.
psychological ADJ
psychologically ADV
psychologist NOUN

psychopath NOUN a person suffering from a severe mental disorder resulting in antisocial or violent behaviour.
psychopathic ADJ

psychosis NOUN (PL **psychoses**) a severe mental disorder in which

the sufferer loses contact with reality.
psychotic ADJ & NOUN

psychosomatic ADJ (of illness) caused or aggravated by mental stress.

psychotherapy NOUN treatment of mental disorders by psychological rather than medical methods.
psychotherapist NOUN

PT ABBREV physical training.

pt. ABBREV **1** pint. **2** part. **3** point.

PTA ABBREV parent-teacher association.

ptarmigan /**tar**-mi-găn/ NOUN a bird of the grouse family.

pterodactyl /te-rŏ-**dak**-til/ NOUN an extinct reptile with wings.

PTO ABBREV please turn over.

pub NOUN [INFORMAL] a public house.

puberty NOUN the stage in life when a person reaches sexual maturity and becomes capable of reproduction.
pubertal ADJ

pubic ADJ of the abdomen at the lower front part of the pelvis.

public ADJ of, for, or known to people in general. NOUN members of a community in general; people interested in the work of a particular author, performer, etc.
publicly ADV

public address system NOUN a system of loudspeakers amplifying sound for an audience.

publican NOUN the keeper of a public house.

publication NOUN the action of publishing; a published book, newspaper, etc.

public convenience NOUN a public lavatory.

public house NOUN a building (other than a hotel) licensed to serve alcoholic drinks.

publicity NOUN attention given to someone or something by the media; material used for advertising or promotional purposes.

publicize (also **publicise**) VERB bring to the

attention of the public; promote, advertise. **publicist** NOUN

public relations PLURAL NOUN the promotion by a company or political party of a favourable public image.

public school NOUN **1** (in the UK) a private secondary school for fee-paying pupils. **2** (in the USA) a school supported by public funds.

public sector NOUN the part of the economy that is owned and controlled by the state.

public servant NOUN a state official, a civil servant, etc.

p

public-spirited ADJ showing readiness to do things for the benefit of people in general.

publish VERB **1** issue (a book etc.) for public sale. **2** make generally known. **publisher** NOUN

puce NOUN a brownish-purple colour.

puck NOUN a hard rubber disc used in ice hockey.

pucker VERB contract into wrinkles. NOUN a wrinkle.

pudding NOUN **1** a sweet cooked dish; the sweet course of a meal. **2** a savoury dish containing flour, suet, etc. **3** a kind of sausage.

puddle NOUN a small pool of rainwater or other liquid.

pudenda PLURAL NOUN the genitals.

puerile ADJ childish. **puerility** NOUN

puerperal ADJ of or resulting from childbirth.

puff NOUN **1** a short burst of breath or wind; smoke, etc., blown out by this. **2** a light pastry case with a filling. **3** a soft pad for applying powder to the skin. **4** [INFORMAL] an over-complimentary review of a book etc. VERB **1** emit or send out in puffs; breathe heavily, pant. **2** swell or cause to swell. **3** [INFORMAL] review with excessive praise.

puffball NOUN a ball-shaped fungus.

puffin NOUN a seabird with a short striped bill.

puff pastry NOUN very light flaky pastry.

puffy ADJ (**puffier**, **puffiest**) puffed out, swollen.
puffiness NOUN

pug NOUN a dog of a small breed with a flat nose and wrinkled face.

pugilist /pew-ji-list/ NOUN [DATED] a professional boxer.
pugilism NOUN

pugnacious ADJ eager to fight, aggressive.
pugnaciously ADV
pugnacity NOUN

puke [INFORMAL] VERB & NOUN vomit.

pukka ADJ [INFORMAL] real, genuine.

pull VERB **1** exert force on (someone or something that one is holding or attached to) so as to move it towards the source of the force; attract. **2** move steadily in a specified direction. **3** inhale deeply while smoking. **4** injure (a muscle etc.) by strain. NOUN **1** an act of pulling; a handle to hold while pulling. **2** an attraction; an influence or compulsion. **3** a deep drink. **4** a draw on a pipe etc. **5** an injury to a muscle etc.
pull down 1 demolish. **2** [INFORMAL] earn. **pull in** move to the side of a road; reach a station etc. **pull off** [INFORMAL] succeed in achieving. **pull out 1** leave a station; move out into the middle of a road. **2** withdraw from a contest etc. **pull through** come or bring through difficulty or danger. **pull to pieces** (or **apart**) criticize harshly. **pull up** stop.

pullet /puu-lit/ NOUN a young hen.

pulley NOUN (PL **pulleys**) a wheel over which a rope etc. passes, used in lifting things.

pullover NOUN a knitted garment covering the top half of the body.

pulmonary ADJ of the lungs.

pulp NOUN **1** a soft, moist, shapeless substance; the soft moist part of fruit. **2** writing of poor quality. VERB crush to pulp.
pulpy ADJ

pulpit NOUN a raised enclosed platform from

which a preacher speaks.

pulsar NOUN a star emitting regular pulses of radio waves.

pulsate VERB expand and contract rhythmically.
pulsation NOUN

pulse NOUN **1** the rhythmical throbbing of arteries as blood is propelled along them, as felt in the wrists or temples. **2** a single beat, throb, or vibration. **3** the edible seed of beans, peas, lentils, etc.
VERB pulsate.

pulverize (also **pulverise**) VERB crush to powder; [INFORMAL] defeat utterly.
pulverization NOUN

p

puma NOUN a large brown American animal of the cat family.

pumice (in full **pumice stone**) NOUN solidified lava used for scouring or polishing.

pummel VERB (**pummels**, **pummelling**, **pummelled**; [US] **pummeling**, **pummeled**) strike repeatedly, especially with the fists.

pump NOUN a machine for moving liquid, gas, or air. VERB **1** force (air etc.) in a particular direction using a pump; inflate or empty using a pump. **2** move vigorously up and down. **3** pour forth. **4** [INFORMAL] question persistently.

pumpkin NOUN a large round orange-coloured fruit.

pun NOUN a humorous use of a word to suggest another that sounds the same.
punning ADJ

punch VERB **1** strike with the fist. **2** cut (a hole etc.) with a device. **3** press (a key on a machine); enter (information) in this way. NOUN **1** a blow with the fist. **2** a device for cutting holes or impressing a design. **3** a drink made of wine or spirits mixed with fruit juices etc.

punch-drunk ADJ stupefied by repeated blows.

punchline NOUN words giving the climax of a joke.

punctilious ADJ attending

to details, especially of correct behaviour.
punctiliously ADV
punctiliousness NOUN

punctual ADJ arriving or doing things at the appointed time.
punctuality NOUN
punctually ADV

punctuate VERB **1** insert the appropriate marks in (written material) to separate sentences etc. **2** interrupt at intervals.
punctuation NOUN

puncture NOUN a small hole made by something sharp, especially in a tyre or other object containing air. VERB make a puncture in; suffer a puncture.

pundit NOUN an expert.

pungent ADJ having a strong sharp taste or smell.
pungency NOUN
pungently ADV

punish VERB cause (an offender) to suffer for his or her offence; inflict a penalty for (an offence); treat roughly.
punishment NOUN

punitive ADJ inflicting or intended to inflict punishment; (of a tax or charge) damagingly high.

punk NOUN **1** (in full **punk rock**) a deliberately outrageous type of rock music, popular in the 1970s; (in full **punk rocker**) a follower of this. **2** [INFORMAL] a hooligan, a lout.

punnet NOUN a small container for fruit etc.

punt[1] NOUN a shallow flat-bottomed boat with broad square ends. VERB propel (a punt) by pushing with a pole against the bottom of a river; travel in a punt.

punt[2] VERB kick (a dropped football) before it touches the ground. NOUN this kick.

punter NOUN [INFORMAL] **1** a person who gambles. **2** a customer.

puny ADJ (**punier**, **puniest**) small and weak.

pup NOUN a young dog; a young wolf, rat, or seal. VERB (**pups**, **pupping**, **pupped**) give birth to pups.

pupa /pyoo-pă/ NOUN (PL **pupae**) a chrysalis.

pupate VERB become a pupa.

pupil NOUN **1** a person who is taught by another. **2** the opening in the centre of the iris of the eye.

puppet NOUN a kind of doll made to move as an entertainment; a person, state, etc., controlled by another.

puppy NOUN (PL **puppies**) a young dog.

purchase VERB buy. NOUN **1** the act or process of buying; something bought. **2** a firm hold or grip; a pulley etc. to move heavy objects.
purchaser NOUN

p

purdah NOUN the Muslim or Hindu system of keeping women from the sight of men or strangers.

pure ADJ **1** not mixed with any other substances; uncontaminated; not immoral, innocent, chaste. **2** sheer, utter, simple: *pure chance.* **3** (of mathematics or sciences) dealing with theory rather than practical considerations.
purity NOUN

purée /pewr-ay/ NOUN pulped fruit or vegetables etc. VERB (**purées**, **puréeing**, **puréed**) make into a purée.

purely ADV **1** in a pure way. **2** entirely; only.

purgative ADJ strongly laxative. NOUN a laxative.

purgatory NOUN a place or condition of suffering, especially (in RC belief) in which souls undergo purification before going to heaven.

purge VERB **1** clear the bowels of by a purgative. **2** rid of undesirable people or things. NOUN the process of purging.

purify VERB (**purifies**, **purifying**, **purified**) make pure.
purification NOUN
purifier NOUN

purist NOUN a stickler for correctness.
purism NOUN

puritan NOUN a person who is strict in morals and regards certain pleasures as sinful.
puritanical ADJ

purl NOUN a knitting stitch. VERB **1** make this stitch.

2 [LITERARY] (of a stream) flow with a rippling sound.

purlieu /perl-yoo/ NOUN (PL **purlieus** or **purlieux**) the area surrounding a place.

purloin VERB [FORMAL] steal.

purple NOUN a colour made by mixing red and blue. ADJ of a purple colour.

purport NOUN /**per**-port/ the meaning or purpose of something. VERB /per-**port**/ appear or claim to be or do.
purportedly ADV

purpose NOUN the intended result of an action etc.; the reason something exists; a feeling of determination. VERB [FORMAL] intend.
on purpose intentionally. **to no purpose** pointlessly.

purpose-built ADJ designed and built for a particular purpose.

purposeful ADJ showing determination; having a useful purpose.
purposefully ADV

purposely ADV on purpose.

purr NOUN a low vibrant sound that a cat makes when pleased; any similar sound. VERB make this sound.

purse NOUN **1** a small pouch for carrying money. **2** [US] a handbag. **3** money available for use. VERB pucker (one's lips).

purser NOUN a ship's officer in charge of accounts.

pursuance NOUN [FORMAL] the performance (of duties etc.).

pursue VERB (**pursues**, **pursuing**, **pursued**) **1** follow; try to catch or attain. **2** continue along (a route); engage in (an activity).
pursuer NOUN

pursuit NOUN **1** the action of pursuing. **2** a leisure or sporting activity.

purulent /pewr-yuu-lĕnt/ ADJ of or containing pus.
purulence NOUN

purvey VERB supply (food etc.) as a trader.
purveyor NOUN

pus NOUN thick yellowish matter produced from an

infected wound.

push VERB **1** exert force on (someone or something) to move them away from the source of the force; move forward by exerting force. **2** make one's way forward forcibly. **3** press (a button or key). **4** make demands on; force to work hard. **5** [INFORMAL] promote the use or acceptance of; sell (drugs) illegally. NOUN **1** an act of pushing. **2** a vigorous effort; a military attack.
be pushed for [INFORMAL] have little of. **be pushing** [INFORMAL] approach (a specified age). **push ahead** carry on, proceed. **push off** [INFORMAL] go away.
pusher NOUN

p

pushchair NOUN a folding chair on wheels, in which a child can be pushed along.

pushy ADJ (**pushier**, **pushiest**) [INFORMAL] self-assertive; determined to get on.
pushiness NOUN

pusillanimous /pyoo-si-lan-i-mŭs/ ADJ cowardly.

puss (also **pussy**) NOUN [INFORMAL] a cat.

pussyfoot VERB [INFORMAL] move stealthily; act cautiously.

pussy willow NOUN a willow with furry catkins.

pustule NOUN a pimple or blister.

put VERB (**puts**, **putting**, **put**) **1** cause to be in a certain place, position, state, or relationship. **2** express, phrase. **3** throw (the shot or weight) as an athletic exercise. NOUN a throw of the shot or weight.
put by (or **aside**) save for future use. **put down** **1** snub; suppress. **2** kill (a sick animal). **3** record in writing. **4** pay (a deposit). **put down to** attribute to. **put off** **1** postpone. **2** discourage; repel. **put on** **1** put (a garment etc.) on one's body. **2** turn on (an electrical device etc.). **3** arrange (an event, entertainment, etc.). **put out** **1** [INFORMAL] annoy; inconvenience. **2** extinguish. **3** dislocate. **put up** **1** construct, erect.

2 raise (a price). 3 stay in or provide with temporary accommodation. **put upon** [INFORMAL] unfairly burdened. **put up with** tolerate.

putative ADJ reputed, supposed.
putatively ADV

putrefy VERB (**putrefies**, **putrefying**, **putrefied**) rot.
putrefaction NOUN

putrescent ADJ rotting.
putrescence NOUN

putrid ADJ rotten; stinking; [INFORMAL] very unpleasant.

putt VERB strike (a golf ball) gently to make it roll along the ground. NOUN this stroke.

putter NOUN a club used for putting. VERB US spelling of **POTTER**.

putty NOUN a soft paste that sets hard, used for fixing glass in frames, filling holes, etc.

put-up job NOUN [INFORMAL] a pre-arranged fraudulent scheme.

puzzle NOUN a difficult question or problem; a problem or toy designed to test knowledge or ingenuity. VERB cause to feel confused or bewildered; think or cause to think hard about a problem.
puzzlement NOUN

PVC ABBREV polyvinyl chloride, a synthetic resin used in flooring, sheeting, etc.

PW ABBREV policewoman.

pygmy (also **pigmy**) NOUN (PL **pygmies**, **pigmies**) a member of a black African people of very short stature; an unusually small person or thing.

pyjamas ([US] **pajamas**) PLURAL NOUN a loose jacket and trousers for sleeping in.

pylon NOUN a tall metal structure carrying electricity cables.

pyorrhoea /py-ŏ-ree-ă/ ([US] **pyorrhea**) NOUN a disease causing discharge of pus from the tooth-sockets.

pyramid NOUN a structure with triangular sloping sides that meet at the top.
pyramidal ADJ

p

pyre NOUN a pile of wood etc. for burning a dead body.

pyretic ADJ of or producing fever.

Pyrex NOUN [TRADE MARK] a hard heat-resistant glass.

pyrites /py-ry-teez/ NOUN a mineral sulphide of (copper and) iron.

pyromaniac NOUN a person with an uncontrollable impulse to set things on fire.

pyrotechnics PLURAL NOUN a firework display; a brilliant display or performance. **pyrotechnic** ADJ

Pyrrhic victory /pi-rik/ NOUN a victory gained at too great a cost to be worthwhile.

python NOUN a large snake that crushes its prey.

Qq

Q (also **q**) NOUN (PL **Qs** or **Q's**) the seventeenth letter of the alphabet.

QC ABBREV Queen's Counsel.

QED ABBREV used to convey that something proves the truth of one's claim (Latin *quod erat demonstrandum*).

qua /kway, kwah/ CONJ [FORMAL] in the capacity of, as.

quack NOUN **1** a duck's harsh cry. **2** a person who falsely claims to have medical skill. VERB (of a duck) make its harsh cry.

quad NOUN **1** quadrangle. **2** quadruplet.

quad bike NOUN a four-wheeled motorcycle used for racing.

quadrangle NOUN a four-sided courtyard bordered by large buildings.

quadrant NOUN **1** a quarter of a circle or of its circumference. **2** [HISTORICAL] a graduated instrument for taking angular measurements in astronomy.

quadraphonic (also **quadrophonic**) ADJ (of sound reproduction) using four transmission channels.

quadratic equation NOUN an equation involving the square (and no higher power) of an unknown quantity or variable.

quadrilateral NOUN a geometric figure with four sides.

quadrille /kwo-drill/ NOUN a square dance.

quadriplegia NOUN paralysis of both arms and legs.

quadrophonic variant of **QUADRAPHONIC**.

quadruped NOUN a four-footed animal.

quadruple ADJ having four parts or members; four times as much as. VERB increase by four times its amount.

quadruplet NOUN one of four children born at one birth.

quaff /kwoff/ VERB drink in large draughts.

quagmire NOUN a bog, a marsh; a situation full of hazards or difficulties.

quail NOUN a small game bird. VERB flinch, show fear.

quaint ADJ attractively strange or old-fashioned.
quaintly ADV
quaintness NOUN

quake VERB shake or tremble, especially with fear.

Quaker NOUN a member of the Society of Friends, a Christian sect with no written creed or ordained ministers.

qualification NOUN **1** the action of qualifying; a pass in an examination etc. qualifying someone for something; a quality making someone suitable for a job etc. **2** a restriction or condition on a statement, agreement, etc.

qualify VERB (**qualifies**, **qualifying**, **qualified**) **1** be entitled to a privilege or eligible for a competition; become or make an officially recognized practitioner of a profession etc. by meeting certain standards. **2** restrict, limit (a statement etc.).
qualifier NOUN

qualitative ADJ of or concerned with quality.

quality NOUN (PL **qualities**) **1** a degree of excellence. **2** a characteristic, a distinctive attribute of a person or thing.

qualm /kwahm/ NOUN an uneasy feeling of worry or fear.

quandary /kwon-dă-ri/ NOUN (PL **quandaries**) a state of perplexity; a difficult situation.

quango NOUN (PL **quangos**) an administrative body (outside the Civil Service) with senior members appointed by the government.

quantify VERB (**quantifies**, **quantifying**, **quantified**) express or measure the quantity of. **quantifiable** ADJ

quantitative ADJ of or concerned with quantity.

quantity NOUN (PL **quantities**) an amount or number of a substance or things; (**quantities**) large amounts.

quantity surveyor NOUN a person who measures and prices building work.

quantum leap NOUN a sudden great increase or advance.

quantum theory NOUN a theory of physics based on the assumption that energy exists in indivisible units.

quarantine NOUN isolation imposed on those who have been exposed to an infectious disease. VERB put into quarantine.

quark NOUN **1** a component of elementary particles. **2** low-fat curd cheese.

quarrel NOUN an angry argument; a reason for disagreement. VERB (**quarrels**, **quarrelling**, **quarrelled**; [US] **quarreling**, **quarreled**) engage in a quarrel.

quarrelsome ADJ liable to quarrel.

quarry NOUN (PL **quarries**) **1** an intended prey or victim; something sought or pursued. **2** an open excavation from which stone etc. is obtained. VERB (**quarries**, **quarrying**, **quarried**) obtain (stone etc.) from a quarry.

quart NOUN a quarter of a gallon, two pints (1.137 litres).

quarter NOUN **1** one of four equal parts of something. **2** three months, a fourth part of a year; a point of time 15 minutes before or after every hour. **3** [US] & [CANADA] a coin worth 25 cents. **4** a district of a town etc. having a particular characteristic; the direction of a point of the compass. **5** (**quarters**) accommodation. **6** mercy to a defeated enemy: *give no quarter*. VERB **1** divide into quarters. **2** put into lodgings.

quarterdeck NOUN the part of a ship's upper deck nearest the stern.

quarter-final NOUN a contest preceding a semi-final.

quarterly ADJ & ADV done, produced, or occurring once every quarter of a year. NOUN (PL **quarterlies**) a quarterly publication.

quartermaster NOUN a regimental officer in charge of stores etc.; a naval petty officer in charge of steering and signals.

quartet NOUN a group of four instruments or voices; music for these.

quartz /korts/ NOUN a hard mineral.

q

quartz clock NOUN a clock operated by electric vibrations of a quartz crystal.

quasar /kway-zah/ NOUN a star-like object that is the source of intense electromagnetic radiation.

quash /kwosh/ VERB reject as invalid; suppress, put an end to.

quasi- COMBINING FORM seeming to be but not really so.

quatrain /kwo-trayn/ NOUN a stanza or poem of four lines.

quaver VERB tremble, vibrate; speak or utter in a trembling voice. NOUN **1** a trembling sound. **2** a note in music, half a crochet.

quay /kee/ NOUN a landing place built for ships to load or unload alongside.
quayside NOUN

queasy ADJ (**queasier**, **queasiest**) feeling sick; causing nausea.
queasiness NOUN

queen NOUN **1** a female ruler of a country by right of birth; a king's wife; a woman or thing regarded as supreme in some way. **2** a piece in chess; a playing card bearing a picture of a queen. **3** a fertile female bee, ant, etc. **4** [INFORMAL] a male homosexual.
queenly ADJ

queen mother NOUN the widow of a king and mother of a reigning sovereign.

queer ADJ **1** strange, odd, eccentric. **2** [INFORMAL] slightly ill or faint. **3** [INFORMAL], [OFFENSIVE] homosexual. NOUN [INFORMAL], [OFFENSIVE] a homosexual. VERB spoil. **queer a person's pitch** spoil his or her chances.

quell VERB suppress.

quench VERB **1** satisfy (thirst). **2** extinguish (a fire); cool (red-hot metal) in water.

quern NOUN a hand mill for grinding corn.

querulous ADJ complaining peevishly. **querulously** ADV **querulousness** NOUN

query NOUN (PL **queries**) a question; a question mark. VERB (**queries**, **querying**, **queried**) ask a question or express doubt about.

quest NOUN a long search.

question NOUN a sentence requesting information; a matter for discussion or solution; a doubt. VERB ask (someone) questions; raise questions about. **in question** being discussed or disputed. **no question of** no possibility of. **out of the question** completely impracticable.

questionable ADJ open to doubt.

question mark NOUN a punctuation mark (?) placed after a question.

questionnaire NOUN a list of questions seeking information.

queue /kew/ NOUN a line of people waiting for something. VERB (**queues**, **queuing** or **queueing**, **queued**) wait in a queue.

quibble NOUN a petty objection. VERB make petty objections.

quiche /keesh/ NOUN an open tart with a savoury filling.

quick ADJ **1** moving or acting fast; taking only a short time. **2** able to learn or think quickly. **3** (of temper) easily roused. NOUN the sensitive flesh below the nails. **quickly** ADV **quickness** NOUN

quicken VERB make or become quicker or livelier.

quicklime NOUN = **LIME** (*sense* 1).

quicksand NOUN an area

of loose wet deep sand into which heavy objects will sink.

quicksilver NOUN mercury.

quickstep NOUN a ballroom dance.

quid [INFORMAL] NOUN (PL **quid**) £1.
quids in in a position of profit.

quid pro quo NOUN (PL **quid pro quos**) a favour etc. given in return for another.

quiescent ADJ inactive, quiet.
quiescence NOUN

quiet ADJ making little noise; free from disturbance; discreet, not elaborate or flamboyant. NOUN absence of noise or disturbance. VERB make or become quiet.
on the quiet [INFORMAL] secretly.
quietly ADV
quietness NOUN

quieten VERB make or become quiet.

quiff NOUN an upright tuft of hair.

quill NOUN **1** a large feather; a pen made from this. **2** each of a porcupine's spines.

quilt NOUN a padded bed-covering. VERB line with padding and fix with lines of stitching.

quin NOUN [INFORMAL] a quintuplet.

quince NOUN a hard yellowish fruit.

quinine NOUN a bitter-tasting drug used to treat malaria.

quinsy NOUN inflammation of the throat.

quintessence NOUN a perfect example of a quality; an essential characteristic or element.
quintessential ADJ
quintessentially ADV

quintet NOUN a group of five instruments or voices; music for these.

quintuple ADJ having five parts or members; five times as much as. VERB increase by five times its amount.

quintuplet NOUN one of five children born at one birth.

quip NOUN a witty or sarcastic remark. VERB (**quips**, **quipping**,

quipped) make a witty remark.

quire NOUN twenty-five (formerly twenty-four) sheets of writing paper.

quirk NOUN a peculiarity of behaviour; a trick of fate.

quisling NOUN a traitor who collaborates with occupying forces.

quit VERB (**quits**, **quitting**, **quitted** or **quit**) **1** leave; [INFORMAL] resign from (a job). **2** [US] [INFORMAL] cease, stop.

quite ADV **1** completely; exactly (expressing agreement). **2** to some extent, rather.
quite a few a considerable number.

quits ADJ on even terms after retaliation or repayment.

quiver VERB shake or vibrate with a slight rapid motion. NOUN **1** a quivering movement or sound. **2** a case for holding arrows.

quixotic ADJ idealistic; impractical.
quixotically ADV

quiz NOUN (PL **quizzes**) a series of questions testing knowledge, especially as an entertainment.
VERB (**quizzes**, **quizzing**, **quizzed**) interrogate.

quizzical ADJ done in a questioning way, especially humorously.
quizzically ADV

quoit /koyt/ NOUN a ring thrown to encircle a peg in the game of **quoits**.

quorate /kwor-ăt/ ADJ having a quorum present.

quorum /kwor-ŭm/ NOUN a minimum number of people that must be present for a valid meeting.

quota NOUN a fixed share; a maximum or minimum number or amount that may be admitted, manufactured, etc.

quotable ADJ worth quoting.

quotation NOUN the action of quoting; a passage or price quoted.

quotation mark NOUN each of a set of punctuation marks (‘ ’) or (“ ”) enclosing words quoted.

quote VERB **1** repeat or

copy words from a book or speech; refer to as evidence or authority for a statement. **2** estimate (a price) for (a job).

quotidian /kwot-**id**-i-ăn/ ADJ daily.

quotient /**kwoh**-shĕnt/ NOUN the result of a division sum.

q.v. ABBREV used to direct a reader to another part of a text (Latin *quod vide*).

qwerty ADJ denoting the standard layout of English-language keyboards.

q

Rr

R (also **r**) NOUN (PL **Rs** or **R's**) the eighteenth letter of the alphabet. ABBREV Regina, Rex: *Elizabeth R.*
the three Rs reading, writing, and arithmetic.

rabbi NOUN a religious leader of a Jewish congregation.

rabbinical ADJ of rabbis or Jewish doctrines or law.

rabbit NOUN a burrowing animal with long ears and a short furry tail. VERB (**rabbits**, **rabbiting**, **rabbited**) [INFORMAL] talk at length in a rambling way.

rabble NOUN a disorderly crowd.

rabid ADJ furious, fanatical; affected with rabies.
rabidity NOUN

rabies NOUN a contagious fatal virus disease of dogs etc., that causes madness and can be transmitted to humans.

RAC ABBREV Royal Automobile Club.

raccoon (also **racoon**) NOUN a small arboreal mammal of North America.

race NOUN **1** a contest of speed; (**the races**) a series of races for horses or dogs. **2** a large group of people with common ancestry and inherited physical characteristics; a genus, species, breed, or variety of animal or plant; the fact of belonging to a particular race, especially as grounds for division or discrimination. VERB compete in a race (with); move or operate at full or excessive speed.
racer NOUN

racecourse NOUN a ground where horse races are held.

raceme /ra-seem/ NOUN a flower cluster with flowers attached by short stalks along a central stem.

racetrack NOUN a racecourse; a track for motor racing.

racial ADJ of or based on race.
racially ADV

racialism NOUN racism.
racialist ADJ & NOUN

racism NOUN a belief in the superiority of a particular race; hostility or discrimination against members of a different race.
racist ADJ & NOUN

r

rack NOUN **1** a framework for hanging or placing things on. **2** a bar with teeth that engage with those of a wheel.
3 [HISTORICAL] an instrument of torture on which people were tied and stretched. VERB (also **wrack**) subject to suffering or stress.
rack and ruin destruction. **rack one's brains** try hard to think of something.

racket NOUN **1** (also **racquet**) a stringed bat used in tennis and similar games. **2** a din, a noisy fuss. **3** [INFORMAL] a fraudulent business or scheme.

racketeer NOUN a person who operates a fraudulent business etc.
racketeering NOUN

raconteur /rak-on-**ter**/ NOUN a person who is good at telling entertaining stories.

racoon variant of **RACCOON**.

racquet variant of **RACKET** (*sense* 1).

racy ADJ (**racier**, **raciest**) lively, entertaining, and mildly indecent.
racily ADV

rad NOUN a unit of absorbed dose of ionizing radiation.

RADA ABBREV Royal Academy of Dramatic Art.

radar NOUN a system for detecting objects by means of radio waves.

radial ADJ **1** of rays or

radii; having spokes or lines etc. that radiate from a central point. **2** (also **radial-ply**) (of a tyre) having the fabric layers parallel and the tread strengthened. NOUN a radial-ply tyre.
radially ADV

radian NOUN an SI unit of plane angle; the angle at the centre of a circle formed by the radii of an arc equal in length to the radius.

radiant ADJ **1** emitting rays of light or heat; emitted in rays. **2** looking very bright and happy.
radiance NOUN
radiantly ADV

radiate VERB **1** emit (energy) in rays; be emitted in rays. **2** spread outwards from a central point.

radiation NOUN **1** the process of radiating. **2** the sending out of rays and atomic particles characteristic of radioactive substances; these rays and particles.

radiator NOUN **1** an apparatus that radiates heat, especially a metal case through which steam or hot water circulates. **2** an engine-cooling apparatus in a motor vehicle.

radical ADJ **1** fundamental, of or affecting the basic nature of something. **2** extreme, thorough; advocating extreme political reform. NOUN someone holding radical views.
radically ADV

radicchio /ră-dee-ki-oh/ NOUN (PL **radicchios**) a variety of chicory with reddish leaves.

radicle NOUN an embryo root.

radii pl. of **RADIUS**.

radio NOUN (PL **radios**) the process of sending and receiving messages etc. by electromagnetic waves; a transmitter or receiver for this; sound broadcasting. ADJ of or involving radio. VERB (**radios**, **radioing**, **radioed**) transmit or communicate by radio.

radioactive ADJ emitting radiation caused by the decay of atomic nuclei.
radioactivity NOUN

radiocarbon NOUN a radioactive form of carbon used in carbon dating.

radiography NOUN the production of X-ray photographs.
radiographer NOUN

radiology NOUN a study of X-rays and similar radiation, especially of their use in medicine.
radiological ADJ
radiologist NOUN

radiophonic ADJ relating to electronically produced sound.

radiotherapy NOUN the treatment of disease by X-rays or similar radiation.
radiotherapist NOUN

radish NOUN a plant with a crisp root that is eaten raw.

radium NOUN a radioactive metallic element obtained from pitchblende.

radius NOUN (PL **radii** or **radiuses**) **1** a straight line from the centre to the circumference of a circle; its length. **2** the thicker long bone of the forearm.

radon NOUN a radioactive gas.

RAF ABBREV Royal Air Force.

raffia NOUN fibre from the leaves of a palm tree, used for making hats, mats, etc.

raffish ADJ slightly disreputable in appearance.
raffishness NOUN

raffle NOUN a lottery with an object as the prize. VERB offer as the prize in a raffle.

raft NOUN **1** a flat floating structure of timber etc., used as a boat. **2** a large collection.

rafter NOUN **1** one of the sloping beams forming the framework of a roof. **2** a person travelling on a raft.

rag NOUN **1** a torn or worn piece of cloth; (**rags**) old and torn clothes. **2** [INFORMAL] a newspaper, especially one of poor quality. **3** a students' carnival in aid of charity. VERB (**rags**, **ragging**, **ragged**) [INFORMAL] tease.

ragamuffin NOUN a person

in ragged dirty clothes.

rage NOUN **1** violent anger. **2** a fashion, something very popular: *his songs are all the rage.* VERB **1** show violent anger. **2** (of a storm or battle) continue furiously.

ragged ADJ (of clothes) old and torn; wearing ragged clothes; uneven, jagged.

raglan NOUN a sleeve that continues to the neck, without a shoulder seam.

ragout /ra-**goo**/ NOUN a stew of meat and vegetables.

raid NOUN a brief attack to destroy or seize something; a surprise visit by police etc. to arrest suspected people or seize illicit goods. VERB make a raid on.
raider NOUN

rail NOUN **1** a horizontal bar. **2** any of the lines of metal bars on which trains or trams run; the railway system. VERB **1** enclose or protect with a rail. **2** convey by rail. **3** utter angry reproaches.

railing NOUN a fence of rails supported on upright metal bars.

railroad NOUN [US] a railway. VERB [INFORMAL] force into hasty action.

railway NOUN a set of rails on which trains run; a system of transport using these.

raiment NOUN [ARCHAIC] clothing.

rain NOUN atmospheric moisture falling as drops; a fall of this; a shower of things. VERB send down or fall as or like rain.

rainbow NOUN an arch of colours formed in rain or spray by the sun's rays.

raincoat NOUN a rain-resistant coat.

raindrop NOUN a single drop of rain.

rainfall NOUN the total amount of rain falling in a given time.

rainforest NOUN dense wet tropical forest.

rainy ADJ (**rainier**, **rainiest**) in or on which much rain falls.

raise VERB **1** move or lift to a higher level; increase the amount or level of; promote; multiply (a number). **2** move to an upright position. **3** bring to people's attention, cause to be felt, noticed, etc. **4** collect, earn, or procure (a sum of money). **5** bring up (children). NOUN [US] an increase in salary.

raisin NOUN a dried grape.

raising agent NOUN a substance that makes bread etc. swell in cooking.

raison d'être /ray-zawn detr/ NOUN (PL **raisons d'être**) a reason for or purpose of a thing's existence.

Raj /rahj/ NOUN the period of British rule in India.

raja (also **rajah**) NOUN [HISTORICAL] an Indian king or prince.

rake NOUN **1** a tool with prongs for gathering leaves, smoothing loose soil, etc. **2** a backward slope of an object. **3** a man who lives an irresponsible and immoral life. VERB **1** gather or smooth with a rake; scratch and wound with a set of points; sweep with gunfire etc. **2** search; look over. **3** set (a stage etc.) at an angle.
rake up revive the memory of (an unpleasant incident).

rake-off NOUN [INFORMAL] a share of profits.

rakish ADJ dashing but slightly disreputable.

rallentando ADV [MUSIC] with a gradual decrease of speed.

rally VERB (**rallies**, **rallying**, **rallied**) **1** bring or come (back) together for a united effort. **2** revive; recover strength. NOUN (PL **rallies**) **1** a mass meeting in support of a cause or pursuit of an interest. **2** a long-distance driving competition over public roads. **3** a recovery. **4** a series of strokes in tennis.

RAM ABBREV [COMPUTING] random-access memory, a temporary working memory.

ram NOUN **1** an uncastrated male sheep. **2** a striking or plunging device. VERB (**rams**, **ramming**, **rammed**) strike or push heavily, crash against.

Ramadan NOUN the ninth month of the Muslim year, when Muslims fast during daylight hours.

ramble NOUN a walk taken for pleasure. VERB **1** take a ramble. **2** talk at length and in an incoherent way.

rambler NOUN

ramekin /ram-ĕ-kin/ NOUN a small individual baking dish.

ramification NOUN **1** a complex outcome of an action or event. **2** a subdivision of a complex structure.

ramify VERB (**ramifies, ramifying, ramified**) form branches or subdivisions.

ramp NOUN a slope joining two levels.

rampage VERB /ram-**payj**/ behave or race about violently. NOUN /**ram**- payj/ violent behaviour.

on the rampage rampaging.

rampant ADJ **1** flourishing uncontrollably, unrestrained. **2** (of an animal in heraldry) standing on one hind leg with the opposite foreleg raised.

rampart NOUN a broad-topped defensive wall or bank of earth.

ram raid NOUN a robbery in which a vehicle is crashed into a shop etc. VERB (**ram-raid**) rob in this way.

ramrod NOUN an iron rod formerly used for ramming a charge into guns.

ramshackle ADJ tumbledown, rickety.

ran past of **RUN**.

ranch NOUN a cattle-breeding establishment, especially in North America; a farm where certain other animals are bred. VERB operate a ranch.

rancher NOUN

rancid ADJ smelling or tasting like stale fat.

rancour ([US] **rancor**) NOUN a feeling of bitterness or ill will.

rancorous ADJ

rand NOUN a unit of money in South Africa.

R & B ABBREV rhythm and blues.

R & D ABBREV research and development.

random ADJ done or occurring without

method, planning, etc.
at random without a particular aim or purpose.
randomness NOUN

random-access ADJ (of a computer memory or file) with all parts directly accessible, so that it need not be read sequentially. *See also* **RAM**.

randy ADJ (**randier, randiest**) [INFORMAL] lustful, sexually aroused.

rang past of **RING**.

range NOUN **1** a set or series of similar or related things. **2** the limits between which something operates or varies. **3** the distance over which a thing can travel or be effective; the distance to an objective. **4** a large open area for grazing or hunting. **5** a place with targets for shooting practice. **6** a series of mountains or hills. VERB **1** vary or extend between specified limits. **2** place in rows or in order. **3** travel or wander over a wide area.

rangefinder NOUN a device for calculating the distance to a target etc.

ranger NOUN an official in charge of a park or forest; a mounted warden policing a thinly populated area.

rangy ADJ (**rangier, rangiest**) tall and thin.

rank NOUN **1** a position in a hierarchy, especially in the armed forces; high social position. **2** a line of people or things. **3** (**the ranks**) ordinary soldiers, not officers. VERB give a rank to; have a specified rank; arrange in ranks. ADJ **1** growing too thickly and coarsely. **2** foul-smelling; unmistakably bad.
rank and file the ordinary members of an organization.
rankness NOUN

rankle VERB cause lasting resentment.

ransack VERB search thoroughly or roughly; rob or pillage (a place).

ransom NOUN a price demanded or paid for the release of a captive. VERB demand or pay a ransom for.

rant VERB make a violent speech.

rap NOUN **1** a quick sharp blow; the sound of this; [INFORMAL] criticism. **2** a monologue recited rhythmically to music. VERB (**raps**, **rapping**, **rapped**) strike with a quick sharp blow; [INFORMAL] reprimand.
take the rap [INFORMAL] suffer the consequences.

rapacious ADJ grasping, violently greedy.
rapacity ADJ

rape[1] VERB have sexual intercourse with someone without consent. NOUN this act or crime; destruction or spoiling of a place.

rape[2] NOUN a plant with oil-rich seeds.

rapid ADJ quick, swift. NOUN (**rapids**) a swift current where a river bed slopes steeply.
rapidity NOUN
rapidly ADV

rapier NOUN a thin light sword.

rapist NOUN a person who commits rape.

rapport /ra-**por**/ NOUN a harmonious understanding or relationship.

rapprochement /ra-**prosh**-mahn/ NOUN a resumption of friendly relations.

rapt ADJ fascinated, absorbed.
raptly ADV

rapture NOUN intense delight.
rapturous ADJ
rapturously ADV

rare ADJ **1** very uncommon; exceptionally good. **2** (of meat) lightly cooked, still red inside.
rarely ADV
rareness NOUN
rarity NOUN

rarebit *see* **WELSH RABBIT**.

rarefied ADJ **1** (of the atmosphere) of low density, thin. **2** (of an idea etc.) very subtle; esoteric.
rarefaction NOUN

raring ADJ [INFORMAL] very eager: *raring to go.*

rascal NOUN a dishonest or mischievous person.
rascally ADV

rase variant of **RAZE**.

r

rash NOUN an eruption of spots or patches on the skin. ADJ acting or done without due consideration of the risks.
rashly ADV
rashness NOUN

rasher NOUN a slice of bacon or ham.

rasp NOUN **1** a coarse file. **2** a grating sound. VERB scrape with a rasp; utter with or make a grating sound.

raspberry NOUN (PL **raspberries**) **1** an edible red berry. **2** [INFORMAL] a vulgar sound of disapproval.

rasterize (also **rasterise**) VERB convert (an image) into a set of points on a grid for display on a computer screen.

r

rat NOUN **1** a rodent like a large mouse. **2** [INFORMAL] an unpleasant or treacherous person.
rat on (**rats**, **ratting**, **ratted**) [INFORMAL] desert or betray.

ratable variant of **RATEABLE**.

ratchet NOUN a bar or wheel with notches in which a device engages to prevent backward movement.

rate NOUN **1** a quantity, frequency, etc., measured against some other quantity. **2** a fixed price or charge; (**rates**) a tax levied according to the value of buildings and land. **3** a speed. VERB **1** estimate the worth or value of; consider, regard as. **2** deserve; be of or regarded as of a specified nature.
at any rate no matter what happens; at least.

rateable (also **ratable**) ADJ liable to rates.

rateable value NOUN the value at which a business etc. is assessed for rates.

rather ADV **1** by preference: *I'd rather not.* **2** to a certain extent. **3** on the contrary; more precisely. **4** emphatically yes.

ratify VERB (**ratifies**, **ratifying**, **ratified**) confirm (an agreement etc.) formally.
ratification NOUN

rating NOUN **1** the level at which a thing is rated. **2** a non-commissioned sailor.

ratio NOUN (PL **ratios**) the relationship between two amounts, reckoned as the number of times one contains the other.

ratiocinate VERB [FORMAL] reason logically.
ratiocination NOUN

ration NOUN a fixed allowance of food etc. VERB limit to a ration.

rational ADJ able to reason; sane; based on reasoning.
rationality NOUN
rationally ADV

rationale /rash-ŏ-**nahl**/ NOUN a fundamental reason; a logical basis.

rationalism NOUN the belief that opinions and actions should be based on reason and knowledge rather than on religious belief or emotions.
rationalist NOUN
rationalistic ADJ

rationalize (also **rationalise**) VERB **1** invent a rational explanation for. **2** make more efficient by reorganizing.
rationalization NOUN

rat race NOUN [INFORMAL] a fiercely competitive struggle for success.

rattan NOUN jointed stems of a palm, used in furniture making.

rattle VERB **1** make or cause to make a rapid series of short hard sounds. **2** [INFORMAL] make nervous or irritable. NOUN a rattling sound; a device for making this, especially as a baby's toy.
rattle off utter rapidly.

rattlesnake NOUN a poisonous American snake with a rattling tail.

raucous /**ror**-kŭs/ ADJ loud and harsh.
raucously ADV
raucousness NOUN

raunchy ADJ (**raunchier**, **raunchiest**) [INFORMAL] coarsely outspoken; sexually provocative.
raunchily ADV
raunchiness NOUN

ravage VERB do great damage to. NOUN (**ravages**) damage.

rave VERB talk wildly or furiously; speak with rapturous enthusiasm. NOUN [INFORMAL] **1** an all-night party with loud

r

music, attended by large numbers of young people. **2** a very enthusiastic review or reception.

ravel VERB (**ravels**, **ravelling**, **ravelled**; [US] **raveling**, **raveled**) complicate.
ravel out untangle.

raven NOUN a black bird with a hoarse cry. ADJ (of hair) glossy black.

ravenous ADJ very hungry.
ravenously ADV

ravine /ră-veen/ NOUN a deep narrow gorge.

raving ADJ **1** delirious. **2** [INFORMAL] utter, extreme: *a raving beauty*.

ravioli NOUN small square pasta cases containing a savoury filling.

r

ravish VERB [LITERARY] **1** rape. **2** delight.

ravishing ADJ enchanting, delightful.

raw ADJ **1** not cooked; not yet processed; inexperienced. **2** (of a part of the body) red and painful from friction. **3** (of weather) bleak, cold. **4** (of an emotion or quality) strong and undisguised.
rawness NOUN

raw deal NOUN unfair treatment.

rawhide NOUN untanned leather.

ray NOUN **1** a line or narrow beam of light or other radiation. **2** one of a set of things arranged radially. **3** a large marine flat fish. **4** [MUSIC] (also **re**) the second note of a major scale, or the note D.

rayon NOUN a synthetic fibre or fabric, made from cellulose.

raze (also **rase**) VERB tear down (a building).

razor NOUN a sharp-edged instrument used for shaving.

razzmatazz NOUN [INFORMAL] extravagant publicity and display.

RC ABBREV Roman Catholic.

Rd ABBREV Road.

RE ABBREV religious education.

re[1] PREP concerning.

re[2] variant of **RAY** (*sense* 4).

re- PREFIX once more; anew.

reach VERB **1** stretch out a hand to touch or take something. **2** arrive at; extend as far as; be able to touch; make contact with; achieve. NOUN **1** the distance over which someone or something can reach. **2** a section of a river.
out of reach too far away to be touched; unattainable.

react VERB cause or undergo a reaction.
reactive ADJ

reaction NOUN a response to a stimulus or act or situation etc.; a chemical change produced by substances acting on each other; an occurrence of one condition after a period of the opposite; a bad physical response to a drug.

reactionary ADJ opposed to progress and reform. NOUN (PL **reactionaries**) a person holding reactionary views.

reactor NOUN an apparatus for the production of nuclear energy.

read VERB (**reads, reading, read**) **1** look at and understand the meaning of (written or printed words or symbols); speak (such words etc.) aloud; study or discover by reading. **2** (of a passage of writing) have a certain wording. **3** (of an instrument) indicate as a measurement. **4** interpret mentally. **5** (of a computer) copy, extract, or transfer (data). NOUN a session of reading; [INFORMAL] a book considered in terms of its readability.
read into see (a meaning) as implied by a situation or utterance when in fact it is not.

readable ADJ **1** pleasant to read. **2** legible.
readably ADV

reader NOUN **1** a person who reads. **2** a senior lecturer at a university. **3** a device producing a readable image from a microfilm etc. **4** a book containing passages of a particular author's work or designed to give practice in reading.

readership NOUN **1** the

readers of a newspaper etc. **2** the position of a reader at a university.

readily ADV **1** willingly. **2** easily.

readjust VERB adjust again; adapt oneself again.
readjustment NOUN

ready ADJ (**readier, readiest**) **1** in a suitable state for action or use, prepared; available; willing; inclined to or on the point of; quick or prompt. VERB (**readies, readying, readied**) prepare. NOUN (**the ready**) [INFORMAL] cash.
readiness NOUN

reagent /ree-ay-jĕnt/ NOUN a substance used to produce a chemical reaction.

real ADJ existing as a thing or occurring as a fact; genuine, natural; actual, not assumed.

real estate NOUN immovable assets, i.e. buildings or land.

realign VERB align again; regroup in politics etc.

realism NOUN acceptance of things as they are; the presentation of things in a way that is true to life.
realist NOUN

realistic ADJ showing realism; practical.
realistically ADV

reality NOUN (PL **realities**) the quality of being real; something real and not imaginary; life and the world as they really are.

realize (also **realise**) VERB **1** be or become aware of; accept as a fact. **2** fulfil (a hope or plan). **3** convert (an asset) into money; make (a profit).
realization NOUN

really ADV **1** in fact. **2** thoroughly. **3** indeed; I assure you. **4** I protest.

realm NOUN **1** a kingdom. **2** a field of activity or interest.

realty /ree-ăl-ti/ NOUN real estate.

ream NOUN a quantity of paper (usually 500 sheets); (**reams**) a great quantity of written matter.

reap VERB **1** cut (grain etc.) as harvest. **2** receive as the consequence of actions.

reaper NOUN

reappear VERB appear again.

rear NOUN the back part. ADJ situated at the back. VERB **1** bring up (children); breed and look after (animals); cultivate (crops). **2** (of a horse etc.) raise itself on its hind legs. **3** (of a building etc.) extend to a great height.
bring up the rear be last.
rear one's head raise one's head; emerge.

rear admiral NOUN a naval officer next below vice admiral.

rearguard NOUN troops protecting an army's rear.

rearm VERB arm again.
rearmament NOUN

rearrange VERB arrange in a different way.
rearrangement NOUN

rearward ADJ directed towards the back. ADV (also **rearwards**) towards the back.

reason NOUN **1** a motive, cause, or justification. **2** the ability to think and draw conclusions; sanity; good sense or judgement. VERB use one's ability to think and draw conclusions.
reason with try to persuade by argument.

reasonable ADJ **1** ready to use or listen to reason; in accordance with reason, logical. **2** appropriate, moderate, not excessive.
reasonably ADV

reassemble VERB assemble again.

reassure VERB restore confidence to.
reassurance NOUN

rebate NOUN **1** a partial refund. **2** a step-shaped recess.

rebel NOUN /**re**-bĕl/ a person who rebels. VERB /ri-**bel**/ (**rebels**, **rebelling**, **rebelled**) fight against an established government; oppose authority or convention.
rebellion NOUN
rebellious ADJ

reboot VERB start up (a computer) again.

rebound VERB /ri-**bownd**/ spring back after impact. NOUN /**ree**-bownd/ the act of rebounding.
on the rebound while still grieving over a failed

r

relationship.

rebuff VERB reject ungraciously. NOUN a snub.

rebuild VERB (**rebuilds**, **rebuilding**, **rebuilt**) build again after destruction.

rebuke VERB reprove. NOUN a reproof.

rebus /ree-bŭs/ NOUN a representation of a word by pictures etc. suggesting its parts.

rebut VERB (**rebuts**, **rebutting**, **rebutted**) declare or show to be false.
rebuttal NOUN

recalcitrant ADJ obstinately disobedient.
recalcitrance NOUN

recall VERB **1** remember; remind someone of. **2** summon to return. NOUN **1** the action of remembering; the ability to remember. **2** an order for the return of someone or something.

recant VERB withdraw and reject (one's former statement or belief).
recantation NOUN

recap [INFORMAL] VERB (**recaps**, **recapping**, **recapped**) recapitulate. NOUN a recapitulation.

recapitulate VERB state again briefly.
recapitulation NOUN

recapture VERB capture again; experience again. NOUN the action of capturing again.

recce /re-kee/ NOUN [INFORMAL] a reconnaissance.

recede VERB move back from a position; diminish; slope backwards.

receipt /ri-seet/ NOUN the act of receiving; a written acknowledgement that something has been received or money paid.

receive VERB **1** acquire, accept, or take in. **2** experience, be treated with. **3** greet on arrival.

receiver NOUN **1** a person or thing that receives something. **2** a person who deals in stolen goods. **3** the earpiece of a telephone; an apparatus that receives electrical signals and converts them into sound or images. **4** (in full **official receiver**) an official who handles the affairs of a bankrupt person or company.

receivership NOUN the office of official receiver; the state of being dealt with by a receiver.

recent ADJ happening in a time shortly before the present.
recently ADV

receptacle NOUN a container.

reception NOUN **1** an act or process of receiving; a reaction to something. **2** an assembly held to receive guests. **3** an area in a hotel, office, etc. where guests and visitors are greeted on arrival.

receptionist NOUN a person employed to receive and direct clients or guests.

receptive ADJ quick to receive ideas.
receptiveness NOUN

receptor NOUN a bodily organ able to respond to a stimulus and transmit a signal through a nerve.

recess NOUN **1** a part or space set back from the line of a wall or room etc. **2** a temporary cessation from business.
VERB set (a light etc.) in a recess.

recession NOUN a temporary decline in economic activity.

recessive ADJ **1** (of a genetic characteristic) remaining latent when a dominant characteristic is present. **2** undergoing an economic recession.

recidivist /rĕ-**sid**-iv-ist/ NOUN a person who persistently relapses into crime.
recidivism NOUN

recipe /**ress**-i-pi/ NOUN directions for preparing a dish; something certain to lead to a particular outcome.

recipient NOUN a person who receives something.

reciprocal ADJ both given and received; given in return; (of an agreement) binding both parties equally.
reciprocally ADV
reciprocity NOUN

reciprocate VERB **1** respond to (an action etc.) with a corresponding one. **2** (of

part of a machine) move backwards and forwards.
reciprocation NOUN

recital NOUN **1** a musical entertainment. **2** a listing of names etc.

recitative /res-si-tă-**teev**/ NOUN a narrative part of an opera, sung in a rhythm imitating speech.

recite VERB repeat aloud from memory; state (facts) in order.
recitation NOUN

reckless ADJ wildly impulsive.
recklessly ADV
recklessness NOUN

reckon VERB **1** count; calculate. **2** [INFORMAL] have as one's opinion.
reckon on rely on.
reckon with take into account.

r

reclaim VERB **1** take action to recover possession of. **2** make (land) usable.
reclamation NOUN

recline VERB lie back with one's back supported.

recluse NOUN a person who avoids contact with other people.

recognition NOUN **1** the process of recognizing. **2** appreciation or acknowledgement.

recognizance /rĕ-kog-niz-ăns/ NOUN a pledge made to a law court or magistrate; surety for this.

recognize (also **recognise**) VERB **1** know again from one's previous experience; identify from knowledge. **2** acknowledge as genuine, valid, or worthy.
recognizable ADJ

recoil VERB **1** spring or shrink back in fear or disgust. **2** (of a gun) suddenly move backwards in response to the force of firing. **3** (**recoil on**) have an unpleasant effect on.
NOUN the act of recoiling.

recollect VERB remember, call to mind.
recollection NOUN

recommend VERB praise or suggest as suitable; advise; (of a quality etc.) make (the possessor) desirable.
recommendation NOUN

recompense VERB repay, compensate.

NOUN compensation.

reconcile VERB make friendly after an estrangement; induce to tolerate something unwelcome; make compatible.
reconciliation NOUN

recondite ADJ obscure, dealing with an obscure subject.

recondition VERB overhaul, repair.

reconnaissance /ri-**kon**-is-ăns/ NOUN a preliminary survey, especially exploration of an area for military purposes.

reconnoitre /rek-ŏn-**oy**-tĕ/ ([US] **reconnoiter**) VERB (**reconnoitres**, **reconnoitring**, **reconnoitred**; **reconnoiters**, **reconnoitering**, **reconnoitered**) make a reconnaissance of.

reconsider VERB consider again; consider changing.
reconsideration NOUN

reconstitute VERB reconstruct; restore (dried food) to its original form.
reconstitution NOUN

reconstruct VERB **1** rebuild after damage. **2** enact (a past event).
reconstruction NOUN

record VERB /ri-**kord**/ **1** set down in writing or other permanent form. **2** preserve (sound) on a disc or magnetic tape for later reproduction. **3** (of a measuring instrument) indicate, register. NOUN /**re**-kord/ **1** information set down in writing etc.; a document bearing this. **2** a disc bearing recorded sound. **3** facts known about a person's past. **4** the best performance or most remarkable event etc. of its kind. ADJ /**re**-kord/ the best or most extreme hitherto recorded.
off the record unofficially; not for publication.

recorder NOUN **1** a person or thing that records. **2** a barrister or solicitor serving as a part-time judge. **3** a simple woodwind instrument.

recount[1] VERB narrate, tell in detail.

recount[2] VERB count

again. NOUN a second or subsequent counting.

recoup VERB regain (something lost or spent); reimburse.

recourse NOUN a source of help to which one may turn.
have recourse to turn to for help.

recover VERB **1** regain possession or control of. **2** return to health.
recovery NOUN

recreation NOUN a pastime; relaxation.
recreational ADJ

recrimination NOUN an accusation in response to another.
recriminatory ADJ

recruit NOUN a new member, especially of the armed forces. VERB enlist (someone) as a recruit; form (an army etc.) from recruits.
recruitment NOUN

rectal ADJ of the rectum.

rectangle NOUN a geometric figure with four sides and four right angles, especially with adjacent sides unequal in length.
rectangular ADJ

rectifier NOUN an electrical device converting an alternating current to a direct one.

rectify VERB (**rectifies**, **rectifying**, **rectified**) **1** put right. **2** convert (an alternating current) to a direct one.
rectification NOUN

rectilinear ADJ consisting of or bounded by straight lines.

rectitude NOUN [FORMAL] correctness of behaviour or procedure.

rector NOUN **1** a clergyman in charge of a parish. **2** the head of certain schools, colleges, and universities.

rectory NOUN (PL **rectories**) the house of a rector.

rectum NOUN (PL **rectums** or **recta**) the last section of the intestine, between the colon and the anus.

recumbent ADJ lying down.

recuperate VERB recover from illness; regain.
recuperation NOUN
recuperative ADJ

recur VERB (**recurs**,

recurring, **recurred**) happen again or repeatedly.
recurrence NOUN
recurrent ADJ

recusant /rek-koo-zănt/ NOUN a person who refuses to submit or comply.

recycle VERB convert (waste material) for reuse.

red ADJ (**redder**, **reddest**) **1** of or like the colour of blood; flushed, especially with embarrassment; (of hair) reddish brown. **2** communist, favouring communism. NOUN **1** a red colour or thing. **2** a communist.
in the red overdrawn.
see red [INFORMAL] become very angry.
reddish ADJ
redness NOUN

red carpet NOUN privileged treatment for an important visitor.

redcurrant NOUN a small edible red berry.

redden VERB make or become red.

redeem VERB **1** compensate for the faults of; save from sin. **2** buy back; exchange (vouchers etc.) for goods. **3** fulfil (a promise).
redemption NOUN
redemptive ADJ

redeploy VERB send to a new place or task.
redeployment NOUN

red-handed ADJ in the act of committing a crime.

redhead NOUN a person with red hair.

red herring NOUN a misleading clue or diversion.

red-hot ADJ **1** glowing red from heat. **2** very exciting or popular.

redirect VERB direct or send to another place.
redirection NOUN

red-letter day NOUN a day that is memorable because of a success or happy event.

red light NOUN a signal to stop; a danger signal.

red-light district NOUN a district containing many brothels.

redolent ADJ **1** strongly reminiscent or suggestive. **2** smelling strongly of something.
redolence NOUN

redouble VERB increase or

intensify.

redoubtable ADJ formidable.

redress VERB set right. NOUN reparation, amends.

red tape NOUN excessive formalities in official transactions.

reduce VERB **1** make or become smaller or less; lose weight. **2** bring to a weaker or worse state. **3** convert to a simpler or more basic form; state simply. **4** demote (an officer).
be reduced to be forced by hardship to.
reducible ADJ
reduction NOUN

redundant ADJ superfluous; no longer needed; no longer in employment.
redundancy NOUN

redwood NOUN a very tall evergreen Californian tree.

reed NOUN **1** a water or marsh plant with tall hollow stems; its stem. **2** a vibrating part producing sound in certain wind instruments.

reedy ADJ (**reedier**, **reediest**) (of the voice) having a thin high tone.
reediness NOUN

reef NOUN **1** a ridge of rock or sand etc. reaching to or near the surface of water. **2** a part of a sail that can be drawn in when there is a high wind. VERB shorten (a sail).

reefer NOUN **1** a thick double-breasted jacket. **2** [INFORMAL] a cannabis cigarette.

reef knot NOUN a symmetrical double knot.

reek NOUN a strong unpleasant smell. VERB smell strongly.

reel NOUN **1** a cylinder on which something is wound. **2** a lively folk or Scottish dance. VERB **1** wind on or off a reel. **2** stagger.
reel off say rapidly without effort.

refectory NOUN (PL **refectories**) the dining room of a monastery or college etc.

refer VERB (**refers**, **referring**, **referred**)
refer to 1 mention. **2** pass

to an authority for decision; send to a specialist. **3** turn to for information.

referee NOUN **1** an umpire, especially in football and boxing; a person to whom disputes are referred for decision. **2** a person willing to testify to the character or ability of one applying for a job. VERB (**referees**, **refereeing**, **refereed**) act as referee in (a match etc.).

reference NOUN **1** a mention or allusion. **2** use of a source of information; consultation. **3** a letter from a previous employer testifying to someone's suitability for a job; someone providing this.
in or **with reference to** concerning.

reference book NOUN a book providing information.

reference library NOUN (PL **reference libraries**) a library containing books that can be consulted but not taken away.

referendum NOUN (PL **referendums** or **referenda**) the referring of a question to the people for decision by a general vote.

referral NOUN the action of referring someone to a specialist or higher authority.

refill VERB /ree-**fil**/ fill again. NOUN /**ree**- fil/ a second or later filling; material used for this.

refine VERB remove impurities or defects from; make small improvements to.

refined ADJ **1** with impurities removed. **2** elegant, cultured.

refinement NOUN **1** the action of refining. **2** elegance of behaviour. **3** an improvement added. **4** a fine distinction.

refinery NOUN (PL **refineries**) an establishment where crude substances are refined.

refit VERB (**refits**, **refitting**, **refitted**) renew or repair the fittings of.

reflate VERB restore (a financial system) after

deflation.
reflation NOUN
reflationary ADJ

reflect VERB **1** throw back (light, heat, or sound); show an image of; bring (credit or discredit). **2** think deeply.

reflection NOUN **1** the process of reflecting or being reflected. **2** a reflected image; reflected light etc. **3** thought; an idea.
a reflection on a source of discredit to.

reflective ADJ **1** reflecting (light etc.). **2** thoughtful.

reflector NOUN something that reflects light or heat.

reflex (also **reflex action**) NOUN an involuntary or instinctive movement in response to a stimulus.

reflex angle NOUN an angle of more than 180°.

reflexive ADJ [GRAMMAR] referring back to the subject of a verb or clause (e.g. *myself* in *I hurt myself*).

reflexology NOUN the massaging of points on the feet as a treatment for stress and other conditions.

reform VERB improve by removing faults; give up or cause to give up bad behaviour. NOUN the process or an act of reforming.
reformation NOUN
reformer NOUN
reformist NOUN

reformatory ADJ the action of reforming. NOUN (PL **reformatories**) [US] [HISTORICAL] an institution to which young offenders were sent to be reformed.

refract VERB (of water, air, or glass) make (a ray of light) change direction when it enters at an angle.
refraction NOUN
refractive ADJ
refractor NOUN

refractory ADJ [FORMAL] resisting control or discipline; resistant to treatment or heat.

refrain VERB keep oneself from doing something. NOUN recurring lines of a song; music for these.

refresh VERB **1** restore the vigour of by food, drink, or rest. **2** stimulate (a

r

person's memory).

refreshing ADJ **1** restoring vigour; cooling. **2** new and stimulating or welcome.
refreshingly ADV

refreshment NOUN **1** a light snack or drink. **2** the giving of fresh strength or energy.

refrigerate VERB make extremely cold, especially in order to preserve.
refrigeration NOUN

refrigerator NOUN a cabinet or room in which food is stored at a very low temperature.

refuge NOUN a shelter from pursuit or danger.

refugee NOUN a person who has left home and seeks refuge (e.g. from war or persecution).

refulgent ADJ [LITERARY] shining.

refund VERB /ri-**fund**/ pay back. NOUN /**ree**-fund/ a repayment, money refunded.

refurbish VERB make clean or bright again; redecorate.
refurbishment NOUN

refuse[1] /ri-**fewz**/ VERB say or show that one is unwilling to do something; show unwillingness to accept or grant (something offered or requested).
refusal NOUN

refuse[2] /**ref**-yooss/ NOUN waste material.

refute VERB prove (a statement or person) wrong.
refutation NOUN

regain VERB obtain again after loss; reach again.

regal ADJ like or fit for a king.
regality NOUN
regally ADV

regale VERB feed or entertain well.

regalia /ri-**gay**-li-ă/ PLURAL NOUN emblems of royalty or rank.

regard VERB **1** consider, think of as being of a specified kind. **2** look steadily at. NOUN **1** attention, concern. **2** liking, respect. **3** a steady gaze. **4** (**regards**) greetings conveyed in a message.
as regards (or **with regard to**) concerning.

r

regarding PREP with reference to.

regardless ADV despite; (**regardless of**) without regard for.

regatta NOUN boat races organized as a sporting event.

regency NOUN (PL **regencies**) rule by a regent; a period of this.

regenerate VERB regrow (new tissue); give new life or vigour to.
regeneration NOUN
regenerative ADJ

regent NOUN a person appointed to rule while the monarch is a minor or is unwell or absent.

reggae /reg-ay/ NOUN a West Indian style of music with a strong beat.

regicide NOUN the killing or killer of a king.

regime /ray-*zh*eem/ NOUN **1** a government. **2** a system of doing things; a regimen.

regimen NOUN a prescribed course of treatment etc.

regiment NOUN a permanent unit of an army. VERB organize rigidly.
regimentation NOUN

regimental ADJ of an army regiment.

Regina NOUN **1** a reigning queen: *Elizabeth Regina.* **2** [LAW] the Crown: *Regina v. Jones.*

region NOUN an area; an administrative division of a country; a part of a body or surface.
in the region of approximately.
regional ADJ

register NOUN **1** an official list. **2** a range of a voice or musical instrument; a level of formality in language. VERB **1** enter in a register; record in writing. **2** (of a measuring instrument) show (a reading); notice, be aware of; be noticed; convey (a feeling etc.).
registration NOUN

register office NOUN a place where records of births, marriages, and deaths are kept and civil marriages are performed.

registrar NOUN **1** an official responsible for keeping written records. **2** a hospital doctor ranking just below specialist.

registry NOUN (PL **registries**) **1** registration. **2** a place where written records are kept.

registry office NOUN a register office.

regress VERB /ri-**gress**/ return to an earlier or less advanced state. NOUN /**ree**-gress/ the action of regressing.
regression NOUN
regressive ADJ

regret NOUN a feeling of sorrow, annoyance, or repentance. VERB (**regrets**, **regretting**, **regretted**) feel or express sorrow or repentance.
regretful ADJ
regretfully ADV

regrettable ADJ unfortunate, undesirable.
regrettably ADV

regular ADJ **1** forming or following a definite pattern; occurring at uniform intervals; conforming to an accepted role or pattern. **2** frequent, repeated; doing something frequently. **3** even, symmetrical. **4** forming a country's permanent armed forces. NOUN **1** a regular customer or member of a team. **2** a regular soldier etc.
regularity NOUN
regularly ADV

regularize (also **regularise**) VERB make regular; make lawful or correct.
regularization NOUN

regulate VERB control (something) so that it functions properly; control by rules.
regulator NOUN

regulation NOUN a rule; the action of regulating.

regulo NOUN a point on the temperature scale of a gas oven: *cook at regulo 6.*

regurgitate VERB bring (swallowed food) up again to the mouth; repeat (facts) without understanding.
regurgitation NOUN

rehabilitate VERB restore to a normal life or good condition.
rehabilitation NOUN

rehash VERB /ree-**hash**/ put (old material) into a new form. NOUN /**ree**-hash/ the action of rehashing; something made of

r

rehashed material.

rehearse VERB practise (a play etc.) for later performance; state (a number of points that have already been made). **rehearsal** NOUN

rehouse VERB provide with new accommodation.

reign NOUN a sovereign's (period of) rule. VERB rule as king or queen; be supreme.

reimburse VERB repay (a person); refund. **reimbursement** NOUN

rein NOUN a long strap fastened to a bridle, used to guide or check a horse; a means of control. VERB control with reins; restrain.

r

reincarnation NOUN the rebirth of a soul in another body after death. **reincarnate** VERB

reindeer NOUN (PL **reindeer** or **reindeers**) a deer of Arctic regions.

reinforce VERB strengthen with additional people, material, or quantity. **reinforcement** NOUN

reinstate VERB restore to a previous position. **reinstatement** NOUN

reiterate VERB say or do again or repeatedly. **reiteration** NOUN

reject VERB /ri-**jekt**/ refuse to accept. NOUN /**ree**-jekt/ a person or thing rejected. **rejection** NOUN

rejig VERB (**rejigs**, **rejigging**, **rejigged**) **1** rearrange. **2** [DATED] re-equip with machinery.

rejoice VERB feel or show great joy.

rejoin VERB **1** join again. **2** retort.

rejoinder NOUN a reply, a retort.

rejuvenate VERB restore youthful appearance or vigour to. **rejuvenation** NOUN **rejuvenator** NOUN

relapse VERB fall back into a previous state; become ill again after a period of improvement. NOUN a return to ill health after a temporary improvement.

relate VERB **1** narrate. **2** show to be connected. **relate to 1** concern, be to do with. **2** feel sympathy with.

related ADJ having a common descent; causally connected; of a similar kind.

relation NOUN **1** a connection between people or things; people's behaviour towards one another. **2** a relative. **3** a narration. **4** (**relations**) sexual intercourse.
in relation to as concerns, in connection with.
relationship NOUN

relative ADJ considered in relation to something else; true only in comparison with something else. NOUN a person related to another by descent or marriage.
relatively ADV

relative pronoun *see* **PRONOUN**.

relativity NOUN **1** [PHYSICS] Einstein's theory of the universe, showing that all motion is relative and treating time as a fourth dimension related to space. **2** absence of absolute standards.

relax VERB make or become less tense; rest; make (a rule) less strict.
relaxation NOUN

relay NOUN /**ree**-lay/ **1** a group of workers etc., relieved after a fixed period by another group; a relay race. **2** a device activating an electrical circuit. **3** a device to receive and retransmit a broadcast; a broadcast transmitted by this. VERB /ri-**lay**/ receive and pass on or retransmit.

relay race NOUN a race between teams in which each person in turn covers part of the total distance.

release VERB **1** set free; remove from a fixed position. **2** make (information, a film or recording) available to the public. NOUN **1** the action of releasing; a handle or catch that releases part of a mechanism. **2** information or a film etc. released.
on release (of a film) being generally shown.

relegate VERB consign to a less important position or group.

relegation NOUN

relent VERB become less severe.

relentless ADJ oppressively constant; harsh, inflexible.
relentlessly ADV

relevant ADJ related to the matter in hand.
relevance NOUN

reliable ADJ able to be relied on; consistently good.
reliability NOUN
reliably ADV

reliance NOUN dependence on or trust in someone or something.
reliant ADJ

relic NOUN something that survives from earlier times; (**relics**) remains.

relief NOUN **1** relaxation following the removal of anxiety; alleviation of pain; a break in monotony or tension. **2** assistance to those in need. **3** a person replacing another on duty. **4** a carving etc. in which the design projects from a surface; a similar effect given by colour or shading.

relief road NOUN a road by which traffic can avoid a congested area.

relieve VERB give or bring relief to; release from a task, burden, or duty; raise the siege of.
relieve oneself urinate or defecate.

religion NOUN belief in and worship of a superhuman controlling power, especially a god; a system of this; an interest of supreme importance to someone.

religious ADJ **1** devout in religion; of religion. **2** (of a practice, belief, etc.) followed or held regularly or firmly.
religiously ADV

relinquish VERB give up, cease from.
relinquishment NOUN

reliquary NOUN (PL **reliquaries**) a receptacle for relics of a saint.

relish NOUN **1** great enjoyment of something. **2** a strong-tasting pickle, sauce, etc. VERB enjoy greatly.

relocate VERB move to a different place.
relocation NOUN

reluctant ADJ unwilling, grudging in one's consent.
reluctance NOUN
reluctantly ADV

rely VERB (**relies**, **relying**, **relied**)
rely on **1** have confidence in. **2** depend on for help etc.

REM ABBREV rapid eye movement (during sleep).

remain VERB stay; be left or left behind; continue in the same condition.

remainder NOUN the remaining people or things; a quantity left after subtraction or division. VERB dispose of unsold copies of (a book) at a reduced price.

remains PLURAL NOUN what remains, surviving parts; a dead body.

remand VERB send back (a prisoner) into custody while further evidence is sought.
on remand remanded.

remark NOUN a spoken or written comment. VERB **1** make a remark, say. **2** notice.

remarkable ADJ worth noticing, unusual.
remarkably ADV

remedial ADJ **1** providing a remedy. **2** (of teaching) for slow or disadvantaged pupils.

remedy NOUN (PL **remedies**) something that cures a condition or puts a matter right. VERB (**remedies**, **remedying**, **remedied**) set right.

remember VERB keep in one's mind and recall at will; act on a remembered instruction or need.
remembrance NOUN

remind VERB cause to remember.

reminder NOUN something that reminds someone; a letter sent for this purpose.

reminisce VERB think or talk about past events.

reminiscence NOUN the remembering of past events; an account of what one remembers.

reminiscent ADJ having characteristics that remind one (of something).

remiss ADJ negligent.

remission NOUN 1 cancellation of a debt or penalty. 2 a reduction of force or intensity; a temporary recovery from an illness.

remit VERB /ri-**mit**/ (**remits, remitting, remitted**) 1 cancel (a debt or punishment). 2 send (money). 3 refer (a matter for decision) to an authority. NOUN /**ree**-mit/ 1 a task or field assigned to someone. 2 an item referred for decision.

remittance NOUN the sending of money; money sent.

remnant NOUN a small remaining quantity; a surviving piece or trace.

r

remold US spelling of **REMOULD**.

remonstrate VERB make a protest.
remonstrance NOUN

remorse NOUN deep regret for one's wrongdoing.
remorseful ADJ
remorsefully ADV

remorseless ADJ pitiless; relentless.
remorselessly ADV

remote ADJ 1 far away in place or time; not close; aloof, unfriendly. 2 (of a possibility) very slight.
remotely ADV
remoteness NOUN

remould ([US] **remold**) VERB /ree-**mohld**/ mould again; reconstruct the tread of (a tyre). NOUN /**ree**-mohld/ a remoulded tyre.

remove VERB take off or away; dismiss from office; get rid of. NOUN a degree of remoteness or difference: *at one remove.*
removable ADJ
removal NOUN
remover NOUN

remunerate VERB pay or reward for services.
remuneration NOUN

remunerative ADJ giving good remuneration, profitable.

Renaissance NOUN a revival of art and learning in Europe in the 14th–16th centuries; (**renaissance**) any similar revival.

renal /ree-năl/ ADJ of the kidneys.

rend VERB (**rends, rending, rent**) tear.

render VERB **1** provide, give (help or service); submit (a bill etc.). **2** cause to become. **3** draw, represent; give a performance of. **4** translate. **5** melt down (fat).

rendezvous /ron-day-voo/ NOUN (PL **rendezvous**) a pre-arranged meeting or meeting place.
VERB (**rendezvouses, rendezvousing, rendezvoused**) meet at a rendezvous.

rendition NOUN the way something is rendered or performed.

renegade NOUN a person who deserts from a group, cause, etc.

renege /ri-nayg/ VERB fail to keep a promise or agreement.

renew VERB resume (an interrupted activity); repeat; replace with a new item of the same kind; extend the validity of (a licence etc.); give fresh life or vigour to.
renewal NOUN

rennet NOUN a substance used to curdle milk in making cheese.

renounce VERB give up formally; reject.
renouncement NOUN

renovate VERB repair, restore to good condition.
renovation NOUN

renown NOUN fame.

renowned ADJ famous.

rent[1] past and past participle of **REND**. NOUN a torn place.

rent[2] NOUN periodical payment for use of land, rooms, machinery, etc.
VERB pay or receive rent for.

rental NOUN rent; renting.

renunciation NOUN the action of renouncing.

reorganize (also **reorganise**) VERB organize in a new way.
reorganization NOUN

reorient VERB change the focus of.
reorient oneself find one's position in relation to one's surroundings again.

rep NOUN [INFORMAL] **1** a business firm's travelling representative.
2 repertory.

repair VERB **1** put right

damage to; undo (damage). **2** [FORMAL] go somewhere specified. NOUN **1** the process of repairing; a repaired place. **2** condition for use: *in good repair.*
repairer NOUN

repartee NOUN an exchange of witty remarks.

repast NOUN [FORMAL] a meal.

repatriate VERB send or bring back (a person) to his or her own country.
repatriation NOUN

repay VERB (**repays, repaying, repaid**) pay back.
repayable ADJ
repayment NOUN

repeal VERB withdraw (a law) officially. NOUN the repealing of a law.

repeat VERB say, do, or produce again; tell (a thing told to oneself) to another person. NOUN something that recurs or is repeated.
repeat itself occur again in the same way. **repeat oneself** say the same thing again.

repeatedly ADV again and again.

repel VERB (**repels, repelling, repelled**) **1** drive away; disgust. **2** be impervious to (a substance).

repellent ADJ causing disgust. NOUN a substance used to keep away pests or to make something impervious to water etc.

repent VERB feel regret about (a wrong or unwise action).
repentance NOUN
repentant ADJ

repercussion NOUN an unintended consequence.

repertoire /rep-er-twah/ NOUN a stock of songs, plays, etc., that a person or company is able to perform.

repertory NOUN (PL **repertories**) **1** the performance of several plays etc. by a company at regular short intervals. **2** a repertoire.

repetition NOUN the action of repeating; an instance of this.

repetitious ADJ repetitive.

repetitive ADJ characterized by

repetition, especially unnecessarily and tediously.
repetitively ADV

repine VERB /ri-**pIn**/ [LITERARY] be discontented.

replace VERB **1** put back in place. **2** provide or be a substitute for.
replacement NOUN

replay VERB /ree-**play**/ play again; repeat. NOUN /**ree**-play/ an instance of replaying.

replenish VERB refill; renew (a supply etc.).
replenishment NOUN

replete ADJ full; well supplied.

replica NOUN an exact copy.

replicate VERB make a replica of.
replication NOUN

reply VERB (**replies**, **replying**, **replied**) answer. NOUN (PL **replies**) an answer.

report VERB **1** give an account of; tell as news. **2** make a formal complaint about. **3** present oneself on arrival; be responsible to a superior. NOUN **1** a spoken or written account; a written statement about a pupil's work; a rumour. **2** an explosive sound.

reportage /re-por-**tah*zh***/ NOUN the reporting of news.

reported speech NOUN a speaker's words as reported by another person, not in the actual words.

reporter NOUN a person employed to report news for publication or broadcasting.

repose NOUN rest, sleep; tranquillity. VERB rest, lie.

repository NOUN (PL **repositories**) a storage place.

repossess VERB take back (goods etc.) when payments are not made.
repossession NOUN

reprehend VERB reproach.

reprehensible ADJ deserving reproach.
reprehensibly ADV

represent VERB **1** be entitled to speak or act on behalf of. **2** constitute, amount to; be an example of. **3** show in a picture etc.; act the part of; symbolize; describe as being of a particular nature.

representation NOUN
1 the action of representing; an image, model, etc. of something.
2 (**representations**) statements made as an appeal, protest, or allegation.

representative ADJ
1 typical of a group or class. **2** involving the representation of the public by elected spokesmen. NOUN a person's or firm's agent; a person chosen to represent others.

repress VERB subdue, control; restrain the expression of (emotions).
repression NOUN
repressive ADJ

reprieve NOUN a postponement or cancellation of punishment (especially a death sentence); a temporary relief from trouble. VERB give a reprieve to.

reprimand VERB reproach. NOUN a reproach.

reprint VERB /ree-**print**/ print again.
NOUN /**ree**-print/ a book reprinted.

reprisal NOUN an act of retaliation.

reproach VERB express one's disapproval of or disappointment with.
NOUN an expression of disapproval or disappointment.
reproachful ADJ
reproachfully ADV

reprobate NOUN an immoral or unprincipled person.

reproduce VERB produce again; produce a copy of; produce further members of the same species.
reproduction NOUN
reproductive ADJ

reproof NOUN an expression of condemnation for a fault.

reprove VERB give a reproof to.

reptile NOUN a member of the class of cold-blooded animals with a backbone and rough or scaly skin.
reptilian ADJ & NOUN

republic NOUN a country

in which the supreme power is held by the people's representatives, not by a monarch.

republican ADJ of or advocating a republic. NOUN a person advocating republican government.

repudiate VERB reject, disown; deny the truth of.
repudiation NOUN

repugnant ADJ distasteful, objectionable.
repugnance NOUN

repulse VERB drive back (an attacking force); reject, rebuff. NOUN a driving back; a rejection, a rebuff.

repulsion NOUN a strong feeling of distaste, revulsion.

repulsive ADJ arousing disgust.
repulsively ADV

reputable ADJ having a good reputation, respected.

reputation NOUN what is generally believed about a person or thing.

repute NOUN reputation.

reputed ADJ said or thought to be.

reputedly ADV by repute.

request NOUN an act of asking for something; something asked for. VERB ask for; ask (someone) to do something.

requiem /rek-wi-em/ NOUN a special Mass for the repose of the souls of the dead; music for this.

require VERB **1** need; depend on for success or fulfilment. **2** order, oblige.

requirement NOUN a need.

requisite ADJ required, necessary.
NOUN something needed.

requisition NOUN a formal written demand; an order laying claim to the use of property or materials. VERB demand or order by this.

requite VERB [FORMAL] make return for (a service or injury).

resale NOUN a sale to another person of something one has bought.

rescind /rĕ-sind/ VERB repeal or cancel (a law etc.).

rescue VERB save from danger or capture etc. NOUN an act of rescuing.
rescuer NOUN

research NOUN study and investigation to discover facts. VERB investigate; search for facts to use in (a book etc.).
researcher NOUN

resemble VERB be like.
resemblance NOUN

resent VERB feel bitter and indignant about.
resentful ADJ
resentfully ADV
resentment NOUN

reservation NOUN **1** reserving; reserved accommodation etc. **2** doubt. **3** an area of land set aside for a purpose.

reserve VERB put aside for future or special use; order or set aside for a particular person; retain; delay the expression of (an opinion). NOUN **1** a supply of something kept for emergencies; a body of troops outside the regular armed forces; a substitute player in a sporting team. **2** land set aside for special use, especially the protection of wildlife. **3** lack of friendliness or warmth. **4** the lowest acceptable price for an item at auction.
in reserve kept unused for emergencies.

reserved ADJ (of a person) showing reserve of manner.

reservist NOUN a member of a reserve force.

reservoir /rez-er-vwah/ NOUN a lake used as a store for a water supply; a container for a supply of fluid.

reshuffle VERB interchange; reorganize. NOUN a reorganization.

reside VERB live in a particular place; (**reside in**) be naturally present in; (of a right) belong to.

residence NOUN the fact of living somewhere; the place where a person lives.

resident ADJ residing, in residence. NOUN a permanent inhabitant; (at a hotel) a person staying overnight.

residential ADJ designed

for living in; lived in; providing accommodation.

residue NOUN what is left over.
residual ADJ

resign VERB give up (one's job, claim, etc.).
resign oneself to be ready to accept and endure.
resignation NOUN

resigned ADJ having resigned oneself.
resignedly ADV

resilient ADJ springing back when bent, pressed, etc.; readily recovering from shock or distress.
resilience NOUN

resin NOUN a sticky substance from plants and certain trees; a similar substance made synthetically, used in plastics.
resinous ADJ

resist VERB oppose strongly or forcibly; withstand; refrain from accepting or yielding to.
resistance NOUN
resistant ADJ
resistible ADJ

resistivity NOUN resistance to the passage of an electric current.

resistor NOUN a device having resistance to the passage of an electric current.

reskill VERB retrain (workers) in the skills required by a modern business.

resolute ADJ showing great determination.
resolutely ADV

resolution NOUN **1** a firm decision; determination; a formal statement of a committee's opinion. **2** the solving of a problem etc.

resolve VERB **1** find a solution to (a problem, dispute, etc.). **2** decide firmly on a course of action. **3** separate into constituent parts.
NOUN determination.

resonant ADJ deep, clear, and echoing; reinforcing sound, especially by vibration.
resonance NOUN

resonate VERB be filled with deep reverberating sound; be able to evoke images and memories.
resonator NOUN

resort VERB (**resort to**) adopt (a strategy or course of action) to resolve a difficult situation. NOUN **1** a popular holiday destination. **2** the action of resorting to something; a strategy or course of action.

resound VERB fill or be filled with sound; echo.

resource NOUN **1** a supply of an asset to be used when needed; (**resources**) available assets. **2** a strategy for dealing with difficulties. VERB provide with resources.

resourceful ADJ clever at finding ways of doing things.
resourcefully ADV
resourcefulness NOUN

r

respect NOUN **1** admiration or esteem; politeness, regard for others' rights and wishes. **2** an aspect of a situation etc. VERB feel or show respect for.
in respect of (or **with respect to**) regarding, concerning.

respectable ADJ **1** regarded as conventionally correct. **2** of some size, merit, or importance.
respectability NOUN
respectably ADV

respective ADJ belonging to each as an individual.

respectively ADV for each separately in the order mentioned.

respiration NOUN the process of breathing.

respirator NOUN a device worn over the nose and mouth to prevent the inhalation of smoke etc.; a device for giving artificial respiration.

respiratory ADJ of respiration.

respire VERB [FORMAL] breathe.

respite NOUN rest or relief from something unpleasant; a permitted delay before a punishment etc.

resplendent ADJ brilliant with colour or decorations.

respond VERB answer; react.

respondent NOUN a defendant in a lawsuit, especially in a divorce case.

response NOUN **1** an answer. **2** an act, feeling, or movement produced by a stimulus or another's action.

responsibility NOUN the state of being responsible; a duty resulting from one's job or position.

responsible ADJ **1** being the cause of something; deserving blame or credit for it. **2** reliable, fulfilling duties conscientiously. **3** (of a job etc.) involving important duties. **responsible for** having control or care over. **responsible to** having to report to (a superior).
responsibly ADV

responsive ADJ responding readily and positively.
responsiveness NOUN

rest VERB **1** stop work or movement in order to relax or recover strength. **2** place or be placed for support; be positioned. **3** (**rest on**) depend or be based on. **4** (**rest in** or **on**) place (trust, hope, etc.) in or on. **5** (**rest with**) (of power or responsibility) belong to. **6** (of a matter) be left without further action. NOUN **1** the action or a period of resting; a motionless or silent state. **2** a prop or support for an object.
the rest the remaining part; the others.

restaurant NOUN a place where meals can be bought and eaten.

restaurateur /res-tĕ-rĕ-**ter**/ NOUN a restaurant-keeper.

restful ADJ giving rest; relaxing.

restitution NOUN **1** the restoring of a thing to its proper owner or original state. **2** compensation.

restive ADJ restless; impatient.

restless ADJ too anxious etc. to rest or keep still.
restlessly ADV
restlessness NOUN

restorative ADJ restoring health or strength. NOUN a restorative food, medicine, or treatment.

restore VERB bring or give back (something lost or taken away); return to a

former place or position; repair, return to a former state.
restoration NOUN
restorer NOUN

restrain VERB hold back from movement or action; keep under control.
restraint NOUN

restrict VERB put a limit on, subject to limitations.
restriction NOUN
restrictive ADJ

result NOUN **1** what comes about because of an action etc.; the product of calculation. **2** a final score or mark in a contest or examination. VERB occur as a result.
result in have as a result.

resultant ADJ occurring as a result.

resume VERB begin to do or be done again after a pause; take again, return to using.
resumption NOUN

résumé /rez-yoo-may/ NOUN **1** a summary. **2** [US] = **CURRICULUM VITAE**.

resurface VERB **1** put a new surface on. **2** return to the surface; become evident again.

resurgent ADJ rising or arising again.
resurgence NOUN

resurrect VERB bring back to life or into use.

resurrection NOUN the action of resurrecting; (**the Resurrection**) Christ's rising from the dead.

resuscitate VERB restore to life or consciousness.
resuscitation NOUN

retail NOUN the sale of goods to the general public (rather than for resale). VERB sell or be sold by retail.
retailer NOUN

retain VERB keep in one's possession; absorb and hold; hold in place; keep in one's service.

retainer NOUN a fee paid to a barrister etc. to secure service when required.

retaliate VERB repay an injury, insult, etc. by inflicting one in return.
retaliation NOUN
retaliatory ADJ

retard VERB cause delay to.

retarded ADJ backward in mental or physical

development.

retch VERB strain one's throat as if vomiting.

retention NOUN the retaining of something.

retentive ADJ able to retain things.

rethink VERB (**rethinks**, **rethinking**, **rethought**) reconsider; plan again and differently.

reticent ADJ not revealing one's thoughts or feelings.
reticence NOUN

retina NOUN (PL **retinas** or **retinae**) a membrane at the back of the eyeball, sensitive to light.

retinue NOUN attendants accompanying an important person.

retire VERB **1** give up one's regular work because of age; cause (an employee) to do this. **2** withdraw; retreat; go to bed.
retirement NOUN

retiring ADJ shy, avoiding society.

retort VERB make (as) a witty or angry reply. NOUN **1** a reply of this kind. **2** a container or furnace for carrying out a chemical process on a large scale. **3** [HISTORICAL] a long-necked glass container used in distilling.

retouch VERB touch up (a picture or photograph).

retrace VERB go back over or repeat (a route).

retract VERB pull back; withdraw (an allegation etc.).
retractable ADJ
retraction NOUN
retractor NOUN

retractile ADJ able to be retracted.

retreat VERB withdraw after defeat or from an uncomfortable situation; recede, move back. NOUN **1** an act of retreating; a military signal for this. **2** a place of shelter or seclusion.

retrench VERB reduce costs or spending.
retrenchment NOUN

retrial NOUN a repeated trial.

retribution NOUN deserved punishment.

retrieve VERB **1** regain possession of; bring back; extract (information) from a computer. **2** rescue

from a state of difficulty.
retrieval NOUN

retriever NOUN a dog of a breed used to retrieve game.

retro ADJ imitative of a style from the recent past.

retroactive ADJ operating retrospectively.

retrograde ADJ going backwards; reverting to an inferior state.

retrogress VERB return to an earlier and worse state.
retrogression NOUN
retrogressive ADJ

retrospect NOUN (**in retrospect**) when looking back on a past event.

retrospective ADJ looking back on the past; (of a law etc.) made to apply to the past as well as the future. NOUN an exhibition showing the development of an artist's work.
retrospectively ADV

retroussé /ri-troo-say/ ADJ (of the nose) turned up.

retroverted ADJ turned backwards.
retroversion NOUN

retsina NOUN a Greek resin-flavoured wine.

return VERB **1** come or go back; bring, give, put, or send back. **2** make or yield (a profit). **3** elect to office. NOUN **1** an act of coming back etc.; a return ticket; a return match. **2** a profit. **3** an official report made by order.

return match NOUN a second match between the same opponents.

return ticket NOUN a ticket for a journey to a place and back again.

reunion NOUN a gathering of people who were formerly associated.

reunite VERB bring or come together again.

reusable ADJ able to be used again.

Rev. ABBREV Reverend.

rev [INFORMAL] NOUN a revolution of an engine. VERB (**revs**, **revving**, **revved**) cause (an engine) to run faster; (of an engine) increase speed.

revalue VERB reassess the value of.

r

revaluation NOUN

revamp VERB renovate, give a new appearance to.

Revd ABBREV Reverend.

reveal VERB make visible by uncovering; make known.

reveille /ri-va-li/ NOUN a military waking signal.

revel VERB (**revels**, **revelling**, **revelled**; [US] **reveling**, **reveled**) **1** enjoy oneself with others in a lively and noisy way. **2** (**revel in**) take great pleasure in. NOUN (**revels**) lively and noisy celebrations.
reveller NOUN
revelry NOUN

revelation NOUN the revealing of something; a surprising thing revealed.

revenge NOUN injury inflicted in return for what one has suffered. VERB avenge.

revenue NOUN income; a country's income from taxes; the department collecting this.

reverberate VERB be repeated as an echo; continue to have effects.
reverberation NOUN

revere VERB feel deep respect or religious veneration for.

reverence NOUN a feeling of awe and respect or veneration.
reverent ADJ
reverently ADV

reverend ADJ a title or form of address to members of the clergy.

reverie NOUN a daydream.

reversal NOUN a change to an opposite direction or position; an adverse change of fortune.

reverse VERB move backwards, cause to do this; undo, cancel; convert to its opposite; turn inside out or upside down etc. ADJ opposite in direction, nature, order, etc. NOUN **1** a change of direction; the opposite side. **2** a setback.
reversely ADV
reversible ADJ

revert VERB return to a former condition or habit; return to a subject in talk etc.; (of property etc.) return or pass to the original owner.

reversion NOUN

review NOUN **1** a general survey of events or a subject; revision or reconsideration; a critical report on a book, play, etc. **2** a ceremonial inspection of troops etc. VERB make or write a review of.

reviewer NOUN

revile VERB criticize angrily in abusive language.

revise VERB **1** re-examine and alter or correct. **2** reread work already done in preparation for an examination.

reviser NOUN

revision NOUN

revisory ADJ

revivalist NOUN person who seeks to promote religious fervour.

r

revivalism NOUN

revive VERB come or bring back to life, consciousness, or strength; restore interest in or use of.

revival NOUN

revivify VERB (**revivifies, revivifying, revivified**) give new life or strength to.

revoke VERB withdraw (a decree, licence, etc.).

revocable ADJ

revocation NOUN

revolt VERB **1** take part in a rebellion; be in a mood of protest or defiance. **2** cause strong disgust in. NOUN rebellion, refusal to submit or conform.

revolting ADJ **1** causing disgust. **2** in revolt.

revolution NOUN **1** the forcible overthrow of a government and installation of a new one; a complete change in methods etc. **2** an instance of revolving; a single complete orbit or rotation.

revolutionary ADJ of political revolution; involving dramatic change. NOUN (PL **revolutionaries**) a person who begins or supports a political revolution.

revolutionize (also **revolutionise**) VERB alter completely.

revolve VERB move in a circle on a central axis; move in an orbit.

revolver NOUN a type of pistol.

revue NOUN an entertainment consisting of a series of items.

revulsion NOUN strong disgust.

reward NOUN something given or received in return for service or merit; a sum offered for the detection of a criminal or return of property.
VERB give a reward to.

rewire VERB renew the electrical wiring of.

rewrite VERB (**rewrites**, **rewriting**, **rewrote**; PAST PARTICIPLE **rewritten**) write again in a different form or style.

Rex NOUN a reigning king.

RFC ABBREV Rugby Football Club.

rhapsodize (also **rhapsodise**) VERB talk or write about something very enthusiastically.

rhapsody NOUN (PL **rhapsodies**) **1** a very enthusiastic expression of feeling. **2** a romantic musical composition.
rhapsodic ADJ

rhenium NOUN a rare metallic element.

rheostat /ree-ŏ-stat/ NOUN a device for varying the resistance to electric current.

rhesus NOUN a small monkey.

rhesus factor NOUN a substance usually present in human blood.
rhesus-positive having this substance. **rhesus-negative** not having this substance.

rhetoric NOUN the art of using words impressively; impressive language.

rhetorical ADJ expressed so as to sound impressive.
rhetorically ADV

rhetorical question NOUN a question used for dramatic effect, not seeking an answer.

rheumatism NOUN a disease causing pain in the joints, muscles, or fibrous tissue.
rheumatic ADJ

rheumatoid ADJ having the character of rheumatism.

rhinestone NOUN an imitation diamond.

rhino NOUN (PL **rhino** or **rhinos**) [INFORMAL] a

rhinoceros.

rhinoceros NOUN (PL **rhinoceroses** or **rhinoceros**) a large thick-skinned animal with one horn (or occasionally two) on its nose.

rhizome NOUN an underground stem producing roots and shoots.

rhodium NOUN a metallic element.

rhododendron NOUN an evergreen shrub with large clusters of flowers.

rhombus NOUN a quadrilateral with opposite sides and angles equal (and not right angles).
rhomboid ADJ & NOUN

rhubarb NOUN a plant with red leaf-stalks used like fruit.

rhyme NOUN a similarity of sound between words or syllables; a word providing a rhyme to another; a poem with line-endings that rhyme. VERB have a similar or the same sound.

rhythm NOUN a strong, regular, repeated pattern of movement or sound; the arrangement of musical notes according to duration and stress; a recurring sequence of events.
rhythmic, **rhythmical** ADJ
rhythmically ADV

rhythm method NOUN contraception by avoiding sexual intercourse near the time of ovulation.

rib NOUN **1** one of the curved bones round the chest; a structural part resembling this. **2** a pattern of raised lines in knitting. VERB (**ribs**, **ribbing**, **ribbed**) **1** mark with raised lines. **2** [INFORMAL] tease.

ribald ADJ humorously rude or vulgar in discussing sexual matters.
ribaldry NOUN

riband NOUN [ARCHAIC] a ribbon.

ribbon NOUN a decorative narrow strip of fabric; a narrow strip of something.

riboflavin NOUN a B vitamin found in liver, milk, and eggs.

ribonucleic acid NOUN a substance controlling protein synthesis in cells.

rice NOUN a cereal plant grown in marshes in hot countries; its seeds used as food.

rich ADJ **1** having much money or many assets. **2** containing a large amount of something specified. **3** (of soil) fertile. **4** (of colour, sound, or smell) pleasantly deep and strong. NOUN (**riches**) wealth; valuable natural resources.
a bit rich [INFORMAL] (of a remark) unfair or unreasonable.
richness NOUN

richly ADV generously, plentifully, splendidly; fully, completely.

rick NOUN **1** a large stack of hay etc. **2** a slight sprain or strain. VERB sprain or strain slightly.

rickets NOUN a bone disease caused by vitamin D deficiency.

rickety ADJ shaky, insecure.

rickshaw NOUN a two-wheeled vehicle used in the Far East, pulled along by a person.

ricochet /rik-ŏ-shay/ VERB (**ricochets**, **ricocheting**, **ricocheted**) rebound from a surface after striking it with a glancing blow. NOUN a rebound of this kind.

ricotta NOUN a soft Italian cheese.

rid VERB (**rids**, **ridding**, **rid**) free from something unpleasant or unwanted.
get rid of cause to go away; free oneself of; discard.

ridden past participle of **RIDE**.

riddle NOUN **1** a question etc. designed to test ingenuity, especially for amusement; something puzzling or mysterious. **2** a coarse sieve. VERB **1** make many holes in; permeate. **2** pass through a coarse sieve.

ride VERB (**rides**, **riding**, **rode**; PAST PARTICIPLE **ridden**) sit on and be carried by (a horse or bicycle etc.); travel in a vehicle; be carried or supported by. NOUN **1** a spell of riding; a journey in a vehicle; a roller coaster or similar fairground amusement. **2** a path through woods for riding.

rider NOUN **1** a person who rides a horse etc. **2** an additional statement or condition.

ridge NOUN a long narrow hilltop; a narrow raised strip; a line where two upward slopes meet; an elongated region of high barometric pressure. **ridged** ADJ

ridicule NOUN mockery, derision. VERB subject to ridicule, make fun of.

ridiculous ADJ deserving to be laughed at, absurd. **ridiculously** ADV

rife ADJ occurring frequently, widespread. **rife with** full of.

r

riff NOUN a short repeated phrase in jazz etc.

riffle VERB flick through (pages etc.).

riff-raff NOUN rabble; disreputable people.

rifle NOUN a gun with a long barrel. VERB **1** search hurriedly through something. **2** cut spiral grooves in (a gun barrel) to make the bullets spin.

rift NOUN a cleft in earth or rock; a crack, a split; a breach in friendly relations.

rift valley NOUN a steep-sided valley formed by the earth's subsidence.

rig VERB (**rigs**, **rigging**, **rigged**) **1** fit (a ship) with rigging; set up (equipment), especially in a makeshift way. **2** manage or run fraudulently. NOUN **1** the way a ship's masts and sails etc. are arranged; an outfit, a style of dress. **2** an apparatus for drilling an oil well etc.

rigging NOUN ropes etc. used to support a ship's masts and sails.

right ADJ **1** morally good; in accordance with justice. **2** correct, true; suitable, appropriate to a need or purpose; satisfactory, in good condition. **3** of or on the side of the body which is on the east when one is facing north. **4** [INFORMAL] real, complete: *a right fool.* ADV **1** completely; directly, exactly. **2** correctly. **3** to

or on the right-hand side. NOUN **1** that which is morally good. **2** an entitlement, something to which one is entitled. **3** the right-hand side or direction. **4** a party or group favouring conservative views and capitalist policies. VERB restore to a normal or upright position; rectify, set right.
by rights according to strict fairness. **in one's own right** by one's own merit etc., not by association with another. **in the right** having truth or justice on one's side. **right away** immediately.
rightly ADV
rightness NOUN

right angle NOUN an angle of 90°.

righteous ADJ morally justifiable; doing what is right.
righteously ADV
righteousness NOUN

rightful ADJ having a right to something; just, legitimate.
rightfully ADV
rightfulness NOUN

right-handed ADJ using the right hand.

right-hand man NOUN an indispensable assistant.

right of way NOUN **1** the right to pass over another's land; a path subject to this. **2** the right to proceed while another vehicle must wait.

rigid ADJ unable to bend; strict, inflexible.
rigidity NOUN
rigidly ADV

rigmarole NOUN a long rambling statement.

rigor mortis NOUN stiffening of the body after death.

rigour ([US] **rigor**) NOUN the quality of being thorough and accurate; strictness, severity; harshness of weather etc.
rigorous ADJ
rigorously ADV
rigorousness NOUN

rile VERB [INFORMAL] annoy.

rill NOUN a small stream.

rim NOUN an edge or border, especially of something circular; the outer edge of a wheel. VERB (**rims, rimming, rimmed**) form a border to.

rime NOUN frost.

rind NOUN a tough outer layer on fruit, cheese, bacon, etc.

ring[1] NOUN **1** a small circular band worn on a finger; a circular outline; a circular device giving out heat on a gas or electric hob. **2** an enclosed area for a sport etc. **3** a group of people acting together dishonestly. VERB put a ring on; surround.

ring[2] VERB (**rings, ringing, rang**; PAST PARTICIPLE **rung**) give out a loud clear resonant sound; cause (a bell) to do this; ring a bell etc. as a signal; resound. NOUN **1** an act or sound of ringing. **2** a quality or impression conveyed by the tone of an utterance: *a ring of truth.* **3** [INFORMAL] a telephone call.
ring off end a telephone call. **ring the changes** vary things. **ring up** make a telephone call (to).

ringleader NOUN a person who leads others in wrongdoing.

ringlet NOUN a long spiralling curl of hair.

ringside NOUN the area beside a boxing ring.

ringside seat NOUN a position from which one has a clear view of the scene of action.

ringworm NOUN a fungal infection producing round scaly patches on the skin.

rink NOUN an area of ice for skating; an enclosed area for roller skating.

rinse VERB wash out soap etc. from; wash quickly. NOUN an act of rinsing; a mouthwash; a solution washed through hair to tint or condition it.

riot NOUN **1** a violent disturbance by a crowd of people. **2** a large and varied display. **3** [INFORMAL] a very amusing person or thing. VERB take part in a riot.
run riot behave in a violent and unrestrained way; grow in an uncontrolled way.

riotous ADJ disorderly, unruly; boisterous.

RIP ABBREV rest in peace.

rip VERB (**rips**, **ripping**, **ripped**) 1 tear apart; remove by pulling roughly; become torn. 2 rush along. NOUN an act of ripping; a torn place.
let rip [INFORMAL] act or speak without restraint. **rip into** [INFORMAL] attack verbally. **rip off** [INFORMAL] defraud; steal.

ripcord NOUN a cord for pulling to release a parachute.

ripe ADJ ready to be gathered and used; matured; ready for something; (of age) advanced.
ripeness NOUN

ripen VERB make or become ripe.

rip-off NOUN [INFORMAL] a swindle.

riposte /ri-posst/ NOUN a quick counterstroke or retort. VERB deliver a riposte.

ripple NOUN a small wave; a gentle sound that rises and falls. VERB form ripples.

rise VERB (**rises**, **rising**, **rose**; PAST PARTICIPLE **risen**) 1 move from a lower to a higher position; get up from lying or sitting. 2 become higher; increase in quantity, intensity, pitch, etc.; reach a higher rank or position. 3 rebel. 4 originate, have a source; (of the wind) start to blow. NOUN an act of rising; an increase, especially in pay; an upward slope.
give rise to cause.

risible ADJ ridiculous.
risibility NOUN
risibly ADV

risk NOUN a possibility of meeting danger or suffering harm; a person or thing representing a source of danger or harm. VERB expose to the chance of injury or loss; accept the risk of.

risky ADJ (**riskier**, **riskiest**) involving risk.
riskily ADV
riskiness NOUN

risotto NOUN (PL **risottos**) a dish of rice containing chopped meat, vegetables, etc.

risqué /riss-kay/ ADJ slightly indecent.

rissole NOUN a mixture of minced meat formed into a flat shape and fried.

rite NOUN a ritual.

ritual NOUN a series of actions used in a religious or other ceremony. ADJ of or done as a ritual.
ritually ADV

ritualism NOUN observance of ritual forms, especially without regard to content.
ritualistic ADJ

rival NOUN a person or thing that competes with or can equal another. ADJ being a rival or rivals. VERB (**rivals, rivalling, rivalled**; [US] **rivaling, rivaled**) be a rival of; seem as good as.
rivalry NOUN

river NOUN a large natural stream of water; a great flow.

r

rivet NOUN a bolt for holding pieces of metal together, with its end beaten to form a head when in place. VERB (**rivets, riveting, riveted**) **1** fasten with a rivet. **2** attract and hold the attention of, engross.

rivulet NOUN a small stream.

RN ABBREV Royal Navy.

RNA NOUN ribonucleic acid, a substance in living cells which carries instructions from DNA for controlling the synthesis of proteins.

road NOUN a prepared track along which people and vehicles may travel; a series of events or actions leading to a particular outcome.
on the road travelling.

road hog NOUN [INFORMAL] a reckless or inconsiderate driver.

roadie NOUN [INFORMAL] a person helping a touring band of musicians with their equipment.

road metal NOUN broken stone for making the foundation of a road or railway.

road rage NOUN aggressive behaviour by a driver, caused by the stress of driving in a heavy traffic etc.

roadster NOUN an open car with no rear seats.

roadway NOUN a road, especially as distinct from a footpath beside it.

roadworks PLURAL NOUN

screen separating the nave from the chancel in a church.

roof NOUN (PL **roofs**) the upper covering of a building, car, cavity, etc. VERB cover with a roof; be the roof of.

rook NOUN **1** a bird of the crow family. **2** a chess piece with a top shaped like battlements. VERB [INFORMAL] defraud.

rookery NOUN (PL **rookeries**) a colony of rooks.

room NOUN **1** a division of a building, separated off by walls. **2** space for occupying or moving in; scope to act or happen.

roomy ADJ (**roomier**, **roomiest**) having plenty of space.

roost NOUN a place where birds perch or rest. VERB perch, especially for sleep.

root NOUN **1** the part of a plant that grows into the earth and absorbs nourishment from the soil; the embedded part of a hair, tooth, etc. **2** the basis or origin of something. **3** a number in relation to another which it produces when multiplied by itself a specified number of times. **4** (**roots**) one's place of origin, especially as the object of emotional attachment. VERB **1** take or cause to take root; cause to stand fixed and unmoving. **2** (of an animal) turn up ground with the snout or beak in search of food; rummage, extract. **root for** [INFORMAL] support, cheer on. **root out** or **up** **1** drag or dig up by the roots; get rid of. **2** find by rummaging. **take root** send down roots; become established.
rootless ADJ

rope NOUN a strong thick cord. VERB fasten or secure with rope; fence off with rope.
know or **show the ropes** [INFORMAL] know or show the procedure. **on the ropes** near to defeat or collapse. **rope in** persuade to take part.

rosary NOUN (PL **rosaries**) a set series of prayers; a string of beads for

r

keeping count in this.

rose[1] NOUN **1** an ornamental usually fragrant flower. **2** a reddish-pink colour.

rose[2] past of **RISE**.

rosé /**roh**-zay/ NOUN a light pink wine.

rosemary NOUN a shrub with fragrant leaves used as a herb.

rosette NOUN a round badge or ornament made of ribbons.

rosewood NOUN a dark fragrant wood used for making furniture.

rosin NOUN a resin.

roster NOUN a list showing people's turns of duty etc.

rostrum NOUN (PL **rostra** or **rostrums**) a platform for standing on to make a speech, conduct an orchestra, etc.

rosy ADJ (**rosier**, **rosiest**) **1** deep pink. **2** promising, hopeful.

rot VERB (**rots**, **rotting**, **rotted**) decompose through chemical action caused by bacteria; deteriorate through lack of use, attention, or activity. NOUN **1** the process of rotting; a state of decomposition or decay. **2** [INFORMAL] nonsense.

rota NOUN a list of duties to be done or people to do them in rotation.

rotary ADJ acting by rotating.

rotate VERB revolve or cause to revolve; arrange, occur, or deal with in a recurrent series.
rotation NOUN
rotatory ADJ

rote NOUN (**by rote**) (with reference to learning something) by constant or mechanical repetition.

rotisserie /roh-**tees**-ĕ-ree/ NOUN a revolving spit for roasting.

rotor NOUN a rotating part of a machine.

rotten ADJ **1** decayed; breaking easily from age or use. **2** corrupt; [INFORMAL] very unpleasant.
rottenness NOUN

rotund ADJ plump; round or spherical.
rotundity NOUN

rotunda NOUN a circular domed building or hall.

rouble (also **ruble**) NOUN a

r

unit of money in Russia.

rouge NOUN a reddish cosmetic colouring for the cheeks. VERB colour with rouge.

rough ADJ **1** having an uneven or irregular surface; (of a voice) harsh. **2** not gentle or careful; violent; (of weather) stormy; (of water) with large waves; [INFORMAL] difficult, unpleasant. **3** not perfected or detailed; approximate; not refined or elegant. NOUN **1** a rough sketch. **2** long grass at the edge of a golf course. **3** a violent person.
in the rough not polished, elaborated, or refined. **rough it** [INFORMAL] do without comforts or conveniences. **rough out** plan or sketch roughly. **rough up** [INFORMAL] beat up.
roughly ADV
roughness NOUN

roughage NOUN dietary fibre.

rough and ready ADJ crude or simple but effective.

rough and tumble NOUN a haphazard struggle.

rough diamond NOUN a person of good nature but lacking polished manners.

roughen VERB make or become rough.

roughshod ADV
ride roughshod over treat inconsiderately or arrogantly.

roulette NOUN a gambling game played with a small ball on a revolving disc with numbered compartments.

round ADJ **1** curved, circular, spherical, or cylindrical. **2** (of a number) altered for convenience, e.g. to the nearest multiple of ten. NOUN **1** a circular piece of something. **2** a tour of visits or inspection; a recurring sequence of activities; one of a sequence of actions or events; one section of a competition. **3** a song for several voices starting the same tune at different times. **4** the amount of ammunition needed for one shot. ADV **1** in a circle or curve; so as to

surround someone or something; so as to cover a whole area or group. **2** so as to face in a different direction; facing in a particular way: *the wrong way round.* **3** to a place by a particular route: *the long way round;* [INFORMAL] to someone's home: *come round tonight.* PREP **1** so as to surround or enclose. **2** going past (an obstacle) and curving to go back along the other side. **3** visiting in a series; seeing the whole of. VERB **1** go round (a corner or obstacle). **2** alter (a number) for convenience. **3** make rounded.
in the round with all sides visible. **round about** nearby; approximately. **round off** complete. **round the clock** continuously through day and night. **round up** gather into one place.
roundness NOUN

roundabout NOUN **1** a revolving platform at a funfair, with model horses etc. to ride on. **2** a road junction with a circular island round which traffic has to pass in one direction.
ADJ indirect; circuitous.

roundel NOUN a small disc.

rounders NOUN a team game played with bat and ball, in which players have to run round a circuit.

Roundhead NOUN [HISTORICAL] a supporter of Parliament against Charles I in the English Civil War.

roundly ADV **1** emphatically; thoroughly; bluntly or severely. **2** in a rounded shape.

round robin NOUN a petition signed with names in a circle to conceal the order of writing.

round trip NOUN a circular tour; an outward and return journey.

round-up NOUN a systematic rounding up; a summary (of news etc.).

roundworm NOUN a parasitic worm with a

rounded body.

rouse VERB wake; cause to become active or excited.

rousing ADJ vigorous, stirring.

rout NOUN a complete defeat; a disorderly retreat. VERB **1** defeat completely; put to flight. **2** fetch (out); rummage.

route NOUN a course or way from starting point to finishing point.

route march NOUN a training march for troops.

router /roo-tĕ/ NOUN a device forwarding computer messages to the correct part of a network.

routine NOUN a standard procedure; a set sequence of movements. ADJ in accordance with routine.
routinely ADV

roux /roo/ NOUN (PL **roux**) a mixture of heated fat and flour as a basis for a sauce.

rove VERB wander.
rover NOUN

row¹ /roh/ NOUN people or things in a line.

row² /roh/ VERB propel (a boat) using oars; carry in a boat that one rows. NOUN a spell of rowing.
rowboat, **rowing boat** NOUN

row³ /*rhymes with* cow/ [INFORMAL] NOUN a loud noise; an angry argument. VERB quarrel, argue angrily.

rowan NOUN a tree bearing clusters of red berries.

rowdy ADJ (**rowdier**, **rowdiest**) noisy and disorderly. NOUN (PL **rowdies**) a rowdy person.
rowdily ADV
rowdiness NOUN

rowlock /rol-ŏk/ NOUN a device on the side of a boat for holding an oar.

royal ADJ **1** of or suited to a king or queen; of the family or in the service of royalty. **2** splendid. NOUN [INFORMAL] a member of a royal family.
royally ADV

royal blue NOUN a deep vivid blue.

royalist NOUN a person supporting or advocating monarchy.

royalty NOUN (PL **royalties**) **1** people of royal status;

one such person; royal status. **2** payment to an author, patentee, etc. for each copy, performance, or use of his or her work.

rpm ABBREV revolutions per minute.

RSI ABBREV repetitive strain injury.

RSJ ABBREV rolled steel joint, a load-bearing beam.

RSPB ABBREV Royal Society for the Protection of Birds.

RSPCA ABBREV Royal Society for the Prevention of Cruelty to Animals.

RSVP ABBREV please reply (French *répondez s'il vous plaît*).

r

Rt Hon. ABBREV Right Honourable.

rub VERB (**rubs**, **rubbing**, **rubbed**) press (one's hand, a cloth, etc.) against (a surface) and move to and fro; polish, clean, dry, or make sore in this way. NOUN an act of rubbing; an ointment to be rubbed on.
rub along [INFORMAL] manage without undue difficulty. **rub it in** [INFORMAL] constantly remind someone of something unpleasant.
rub out erase (pencil marks).

rubber NOUN **1** a tough elastic substance made from the juice of certain plants or synthetically; a piece of this for rubbing out pencil or ink marks. **2** [US] [INFORMAL] a condom.
rubber-stamp approve automatically without consideration.
rubbery ADJ

rubberize (also **rubberise**) VERB treat or coat with rubber.

rubbish NOUN waste or worthless material; nonsense.

rubble NOUN waste or rough fragments of stone, brick, etc.

rubella NOUN German measles.

rubidium NOUN a soft silvery metallic element.

ruble variant of **ROUBLE**.

rubric NOUN a heading; a set of rules or instructions.

ruby NOUN (PL **rubies**) a red

gem; a deep red colour. ADJ deep red.

ruby wedding NOUN a 40th wedding anniversary.

RUC ABBREV Royal Ulster Constabulary.

ruche /roosh/ NOUN a decorative frill of fabric.

ruck VERB crease, wrinkle. NOUN **1** a crease or wrinkle. **2** a tightly packed crowd; (in rugby) a loose scrum.

rucksack NOUN a bag carried on the back, used by walkers.

ructions PLURAL NOUN [INFORMAL] unpleasant arguments or protests.

rudder NOUN a vertical piece of metal or wood hinged to the stern of a boat or aircraft, used for steering.

ruddy ADJ (**ruddier**, **ruddiest**) reddish.

rude ADJ **1** impolite, showing no respect. **2** primitive, roughly made. **3** (of health) good, vigorous.
rudely ADV
rudeness NOUN

rudiment NOUN a basic principle or element; an undeveloped part.

rudimentary ADJ incompletely developed; basic, elementary.

rue NOUN a shrub with bitter leaves formerly used in medicine. VERB regret deeply.

rueful ADJ showing or feeling good-humoured regret.
ruefully ADV

ruff NOUN a pleated frill worn round the neck; a projecting or coloured ring of feathers or fur round a bird's or animal's neck.

ruffian NOUN a violent lawless person.

ruffle VERB disturb the calmness or smoothness of; annoy. NOUN a gathered frill.

rug NOUN a thick floor-mat; a piece of thick warm fabric used as a covering.

rugby (in full **rugby football**) NOUN a kind of football game played with an oval ball which may be kicked or carried.

rugged ADJ **1** uneven, irregular, craggy. **2** (of a man) having attractively

masculine features.
ruggedly ADV
ruggedness NOUN

rugger NOUN [INFORMAL] rugby football.

ruin NOUN destruction; complete loss of one's fortune or prospects; the damaged remains of a building etc.; a cause of ruin. VERB cause ruin to; reduce to ruins.
ruination NOUN

ruinous ADJ bringing ruin; in ruins, ruined.
ruinously ADV

rule NOUN **1** a statement or principle governing behaviour or describing a regular occurrence in nature etc.; a dominant custom; government, control. **2** a ruler used by carpenters etc. VERB **1** govern; keep under control; give an authoritative decision. **2** draw (a line) using a ruler.
as a rule usually. **rule of thumb** a rough practical method or procedure. **rule out** exclude.

ruler NOUN **1** a person who rules. **2** a straight strip used in measuring or for drawing straight lines.

ruling NOUN an authoritative decision.

rum NOUN an alcoholic spirit distilled from sugar cane or molasses. ADJ (**rummer**, **rummest**) [INFORMAL] strange, odd.

rumba NOUN a ballroom dance.

rumble VERB **1** make a low continuous sound. **2** [INFORMAL] detect, discover. NOUN a rumbling sound.

rumbustious ADJ [INFORMAL] boisterous, uproarious.

ruminant NOUN an animal that chews the cud. ADJ ruminating.

ruminate VERB **1** think deeply. **2** chew the cud.
rumination NOUN
ruminative ADJ

rummage VERB search clumsily. NOUN an untidy search through a number of things.

rummage sale NOUN [US] a jumble sale.

rummy NOUN a card game.

rumour ([US] **rumor**) NOUN a circulating story or report of doubtful truth.

be rumoured be spread as a rumour.

rump NOUN the buttocks; a bird's back near the tail.

rumple VERB make or become crumpled; make untidy.

rumpus NOUN [INFORMAL] an uproar, an angry dispute.

run VERB (**runs**, **running**, **ran**; PAST PARTICIPLE **run**) **1** move with quick steps with always at least one foot off the ground; do this for exercise or in a race; move around hurriedly. **2** move smoothly in a particular direction; flow; exude liquid; (of a road etc.) extend. **3** travel regularly along a route. **4** control, manage; function; continue, remain valid. **5** stand as a candidate in an election. **6** smuggle (goods). NOUN **1** a spell of running; a running pace; a journey. **2** a point scored in cricket or baseball. **3** a continuous spell or sequence: *a run of bad luck.* **4** unrestricted use of something: *the run of the house.* **5** an enclosed area where domestic animals can range. **6** a ladder in stockings etc. **in** or **out of the running** with a good or with no chance of winning. **in the long run** in the end; over a long period. **on the run** fleeing. **run across** happen to meet or find. **run a risk** take a risk. **run a temperature** be feverish. **run away** flee; leave secretly. **run down 1** reduce the numbers of. **2** speak of in a slighting way. **3** knock to the ground when driving. **run into** collide with; happen to meet. **run out** become used up; use up, have none left. **run over** knock down or crush with a vehicle. **run through** discuss or practise quickly. **run up** allow (a bill) to mount.

rundown NOUN a detailed analysis. ADJ (**run-down**) weak or exhausted.

rune NOUN any of the letters in an early Germanic alphabet.

rung¹ NOUN a crosspiece of a ladder etc.

rung² past participle of **RING²**.

runner NOUN **1** a person or animal that runs; a messenger. **2** a creeping stem that roots. **3** a groove, strip, or roller etc. for a thing to move on. **4** a long narrow strip of carpet or ornamental cloth.

runner-up NOUN one who finishes second in a competition.

runny ADJ (**runnier**, **runniest**) semi-liquid; tending to flow or exude fluid.

run-of-the-mill ADJ ordinary.

runt NOUN an undersized person or animal.

run-up NOUN the period leading up to an event.

runway NOUN a prepared surface on which aircraft may take off and land.

rupee NOUN a unit of money in India, Pakistan, etc.

rupture NOUN a breaking, a breach; an abdominal hernia. VERB burst, break; cause a hernia in.

rural ADJ of, in, or like the countryside.

ruse NOUN a deception, a trick.

rush[1] VERB move or cause to move with great speed; act or deal with hurriedly; force into hasty action; convey hurriedly; make a sudden assault on. NOUN a sudden quick movement; a very busy state or period; a sudden flow or surge.

rush[2] NOUN a marsh plant with a slender pithy stem.

rush hour NOUN one of the times of day when traffic is busiest.

rusk NOUN a biscuit, especially for babies.

russet ADJ soft reddish brown. NOUN a reddish-brown colour.

rust NOUN **1** a brownish corrosive coating formed on iron exposed to moisture. **2** a reddish-brown colour. VERB make or become rusty.

rustic ADJ of or like country life; simple, not sophisticated or elaborate; made of rough timber or untrimmed branches.

rustle VERB **1** make or

difficulties.

rock and roll NOUN rock music with elements of blues.

rock bottom NOUN the lowest or worst possible level. ADJ (**rock-bottom**) very low.

rocker NOUN **1** a person performing or dancing to rock music. **2** something that rocks; a pivoting switch.

rockery NOUN (PL **rockeries**) a bank containing large stones planted with rock plants.

rocket NOUN **1** a structure that flies by expelling burning gases; a spacecraft propelled in this way. **2** a firework that rises into the air and explodes. **3** [INFORMAL] a severe reprimand. VERB (**rockets**, **rocketing**, **rocketed**) move rapidly upwards or away.

rocketry NOUN the science or practice of rocket propulsion.

rock plant NOUN an alpine plant, a plant that grows among rocks.

rocky ADJ (**rockier**, **rockiest**) **1** of or like rock; full of rock. **2** unstable; [INFORMAL] full of problems.
rockily ADV
rockiness NOUN

rococo /rŏ-**koh-koh**/ ADJ of or in an elaborately ornate style of decoration popular in Europe in the 18th century.

rod NOUN a slender straight round stick or metal bar; a fishing rod.

rode past of **RIDE**.

rodent NOUN an animal with strong front teeth for gnawing things.

rodeo NOUN (PL **rodeos**) a competition or exhibition of cowboys' skill.

roe¹ NOUN a mass of eggs in a female fish's ovary.

roe² NOUN (PL **roe** or **roes**) a small deer.

roentgen /**runt**-yĕn/ NOUN a unit of ionizing radiation.

roger EXCLAMATION (in signalling) message received and understood.

rogue NOUN **1** a dishonest or mischievous person. **2** a wild animal living apart from the herd and

construction or repair of roads.

roadworthy ADJ (of a vehicle) fit to be used on a road.
roadworthiness NOUN

roam VERB wander.

roan ADJ (of a horse) having a brown or black coat sprinkled with lighter hairs. NOUN a roan horse.

roar NOUN a long deep sound made or like that made by a lion; a loud sound of laughter. VERB **1** give a roar. **2** (especially of a motor vehicle) move very fast.

roaring ADJ **1** noisy, giving a roar. **2** [INFORMAL] great and definite: *a roaring success.*

roast VERB **1** cook (meat etc.) in an oven; expose to great heat; undergo roasting. **2** reprimand severely. NOUN a roast joint of meat.

rob VERB (**robs**, **robbing**, **robbed**) steal from using violence; deprive unfairly of something.
robber NOUN
robbery NOUN

robe NOUN a long loose especially ceremonial garment. VERB dress in a robe.

robin NOUN a red-breasted bird.

robot NOUN a machine able to carry out a complex series of tasks automatically, especially when programmed by a computer.
robotic ADJ

robotics NOUN the study of robots and their design and operation.

robust ADJ sturdy; healthy.
robustly ADV
robustness NOUN

rock NOUN **1** the hard part of the earth's crust below the soil; a mass of this, a large stone. **2** a hard sugar sweet made in sticks. **3** modern popular music with a heavy beat. **4** a rocking movement. VERB **1** move or cause to move to and fro or from side to side. **2** shock, unsettle. **3** [INFORMAL] dance to rock music.
on the rocks 1 (of a drink) served with ice cubes. **2** [INFORMAL] in

unpredictably savage.

roguish ADJ dishonest; mischievously playful. **roguishly** ADV **roguishness** NOUN

roister VERB celebrate noisily.

role NOUN an actor's part; a person's or thing's function.

roll VERB **1** move or cause to move by turning over and over on an axis; move on wheels. **2** turn (something flexible) over on itself to form a ball or cylinder. **3** move in waves; undulate; rock, oscillate; (of a deep sound) reverberate. **4** flatten with a roller. NOUN **1** a cylinder of flexible material turned over and over on itself. **2** an act of rolling; an undulating shape. **3** a reverberating sound of thunder etc. **4** a small individual loaf of bread. **5** an official list or register. **be rolling (in money)** [INFORMAL] be very wealthy. **roll-on roll-off** (of a ferry) that vehicles can be driven on to and off.

roll-call NOUN the calling of a list of names to check that all are present.

rolled gold NOUN a thin coating of gold on another metal.

roller NOUN **1** a cylinder rolled over things to flatten or spread them, or on which something is wound. **2** a long swelling wave.

roller coaster NOUN a switchback at a fair.

roller skate NOUN a boot or frame with wheels, strapped to the foot for gliding across a hard surface. VERB move on roller skates.

rollicking ADJ full of boisterous high spirits.

rolling pin NOUN a roller for flattening dough.

rolling stock NOUN railway engines and carriages, wagons, etc.

rolling stone NOUN a person who does not settle in one place.

rollmop NOUN a rolled uncooked pickled herring fillet.

roly-poly NOUN (PL **roly-polies**) a pudding of suet pastry spread with jam, rolled up and boiled. ADJ [INFORMAL] plump, podgy.

ROM ABBREV [COMPUTING] read-only memory.

Roman ADJ relating to ancient Rome or its empire; relating to modern Rome. NOUN a person from Rome.

roman NOUN plain upright type.

Roman Catholic ADJ relating to the Church that acknowledges the Pope as its head. NOUN a member of this Church.

romance NOUN a romantic atmosphere or quality; a love affair or love story; an imaginative story. VERB **1** idealize, romanticise. **2** [INFORMAL] seek the favour of; [DATED] engage in a love affair.

Romance language NOUN a language descended from Latin.

Romanesque ADJ of or in a style of architecture characterized by rounded arches and vaulting, current in Europe about 900–1200.

Roman numeral NOUN any of the letters used as numbers in the system of ancient Rome.

romantic ADJ appealing to the emotions by its imaginative, heroic, or picturesque quality; involving a love affair; enjoying romantic situations etc. NOUN a romantic person. **romantically** ADV

romanticism NOUN romantic style.

romanticize (also **romanticise**) VERB idealize, regard or represent as better or more beautiful than is the case.

Romany NOUN (PL **Romanies**) a gypsy; the gypsy language.

romp VERB **1** play about in a lively way. **2** [INFORMAL] proceed to achieve something easily.

rondeau /ron-doh/ NOUN (PL **rondeaux**) a short poem with the opening words used as a refrain.

rondo NOUN (PL **rondos**) a piece of music with a recurring theme.

rood screen NOUN a

sacred ADJ venerated as connected with God or religion, holy; (of writing) embodying the doctrines of a religion; not to be tampered with.

sacred cow NOUN an idea etc. which its supporters will not allow to be criticized.

sacrifice NOUN the slaughter of a victim or presenting of a gift to win a god's favour; this victim or gift; the giving up of a valued thing for the sake of something else; the thing given up, a loss entailed. VERB offer, kill, or give up as a sacrifice.
sacrificial ADJ

sacrilege NOUN disrespect to a sacred thing.
sacrilegious ADJ

sacristan NOUN the person in charge of the sacred vessels etc. in a church.

sacristy NOUN (PL **sacristies**) the place where sacred vessels etc. are kept in a church.

sacrosanct ADJ too important or precious to be harmed or interfered with.

sacrum /say-krum/ NOUN (PL **sacrums** or **sacra**) the triangular bone at the base of the spine.

sad ADJ (**sadder, saddest**) feeling, causing, or expressing sorrow.
sadly ADV
sadness NOUN

sadden VERB make sad.

saddle NOUN **1** a seat for a rider. **2** a joint of meat consisting of the two loins. VERB put a saddle on (an animal); burden with a task.

saddler NOUN a person who makes or deals in saddles and harness.

sadism NOUN a tendency to derive pleasure from inflicting or watching cruelty.
sadist NOUN
sadistic ADJ
sadistically ADV

sae ABBREV stamped addressed envelope.

safari NOUN an expedition to observe or hunt wild animals.

safari park NOUN a park where exotic wild animals are kept in the

S

open for visitors to see.

safe ADJ not subject to risk or danger; not harmed; providing security. NOUN a strong lockable cupboard for valuables.
safely ADV

safe conduct NOUN immunity or protection from arrest or harm.

safe deposit NOUN a strongroom or safe in a hotel, bank, etc., where valuables may be deposited.

safeguard NOUN a means of protection.
VERB protect.

safe sex NOUN the use of condoms during sexual activity as a precaution against Aids etc.

safety NOUN the state of being safe; freedom from risk or danger.

S

safety belt NOUN a seat belt.

safety pin NOUN a pin with a point bent back towards the head and enclosed in a guard.

safety valve NOUN **1** a valve that opens automatically to relieve excessive pressure in a steam boiler. **2** a harmless outlet for emotion.

saffron NOUN orange food colouring and flavouring.

sag VERB (**sags**, **sagging**, **sagged**) gradually droop or sink. NOUN an instance of sagging.

saga NOUN a long story.

sagacious /să-gay-shŭs/ ADJ wise.
sagaciously ADV
sagacity NOUN

sage NOUN **1** a herb. **2** an old and wise man.
ADJ wise.
sagely ADV

sago NOUN the starchy pith of the sago palm, used in puddings.

said past and past participle of **SAY**.

sail NOUN **1** a piece of fabric spread to catch the wind and drive a boat along. **2** a journey by boat. **3** the arm of a windmill. VERB **1** travel by water; start on a sea voyage; control (a boat). **2** move smoothly.
sail through [INFORMAL] do or succeed in easily.
sailing ship NOUN

sailboard NOUN a board

with a mast and sail, used in windsurfing.
sailboarder NOUN
sailboarding NOUN

sailcloth NOUN canvas for sails; a canvas-like material for clothes.

sailor NOUN a member of a ship's crew.

saint NOUN a holy person, especially one venerated by the RC or Orthodox Church; a very good, patient, or unselfish person.
sainthood NOUN
saintly ADJ
saintliness NOUN

sake[1] NOUN (**for the sake of**) so as to achieve or keep; out of consideration for.

sake[2] /sah-ki/ NOUN a Japanese fermented liquor made from rice.

salaam /să-lahm/ NOUN an Oriental greeting meaning 'Peace'; a Muslim greeting consisting of a low bow.

salacious ADJ lewd, erotic.
salaciously ADV
salaciousness NOUN

salad NOUN a cold dish of (usually raw) vegetables etc.

salamander NOUN a lizard-like animal.

salami NOUN a strongly flavoured sausage, eaten cold.

salaried ADJ receiving a salary.

salary NOUN (PL **salaries**) a fixed regular (usually monthly) payment to an employee.

sale NOUN the exchange of something for money; an event at which goods are sold; the disposal of stock at reduced prices; (**sales**) the amount sold by a business or of a commodity.
for or **on sale** offered for purchase.

saleable ADJ fit to be sold, likely to find a purchaser.

salesman (also **saleswoman**) NOUN a person employed to sell or promote goods.

salesmanship NOUN skill at selling.

salient /say-lee-ĕnt/ ADJ prominent; most noticeable. NOUN a piece of land or fortification jutting out to form an angle.

saline ADJ salty, containing salt(s).
salinity NOUN

saliva NOUN the colourless liquid that forms in the mouth.
salivary ADJ

salivate VERB produce saliva.
salivation NOUN

sallow ADJ (of the complexion) yellowish.
NOUN a low-growing willow tree.

sally NOUN (PL **sallies**) a sudden charge from a besieged place; a witty remark or retort.
sally forth (**sallies**, **sallying**, **sallied**) rush out in attack; set out on a journey.

S

salmon /sa-mŏn/ NOUN (PL **salmon**) **1** a large fish with pinkish flesh. **2** (also **salmon pink**) pale yellowish pink.

salmonella NOUN a bacterium causing food poisoning.

salon NOUN a place where a hairdresser, couturier, etc. receives clients; an elegant room for receiving guests.

saloon NOUN **1** a public room, especially on board ship. **2** a saloon car.

saloon car NOUN a car with a separate boot, not a hatchback.

salsa NOUN **1** a style of music and dance of Cuban origin. **2** a spicy sauce.

salt NOUN **1** sodium chloride used to season and preserve food. **2** (**salts**) a substance resembling salt in form, especially a laxative. **3** a chemical compound of a metal and an acid.
ADJ tasting of salt; impregnated with salt.
VERB season with salt; preserve in salt.
take with a grain (or **pinch**) **of salt** regard sceptically. **worth one's salt** competent.
saltiness NOUN
salty ADJ

salt cellar NOUN a small container for salt used at meals.

saltpetre ([US] **saltpeter**)

NOUN a salty white powder used in gunpowder, in medicine, and in preserving meat.

salubrious ADJ health-giving.

salutary ADJ producing a beneficial or wholesome effect.

salutation NOUN a greeting.

salute NOUN a gesture of greeting or acknowledgement; a prescribed movement made in the armed forces etc. to show respect. VERB make a salute to.

salvage NOUN the recovery of a ship or its cargo from loss at sea, or of property from fire etc.; the items saved. VERB save, rescue from loss or destruction.
salvageable ADJ

salvation NOUN the state of being saved from sin; protection from loss or difficulty.

salve NOUN a soothing ointment; something that soothes. VERB soothe (conscience etc.).

salver NOUN a small tray.

salvo NOUN (PL **salvoes** or **salvos**) a simultaneous discharge of guns; a series of actions performed simultaneously or in quick succession.

sal volatile /sal vŏ-lat-i-li/ NOUN a solution of ammonium carbonate used as a remedy for faintness.

Samaritan NOUN a charitable or helpful person; a member of an organization counselling the distressed and suicidal.

samarium NOUN a metallic element.

samba NOUN a ballroom dance.

same ADJ identical; not changed or different. PRON the one already mentioned. ADV in the same way.
all the same nevertheless.
sameness NOUN

sami /sah-mi/ PLURAL NOUN the Lapps of northern Scandinavia.

samosa NOUN a fried triangular pastry containing spiced

vegetables or meat.

sampan NOUN a small flat-bottomed Chinese boat.

samphire NOUN a plant with edible fleshy leaves, growing by the sea.

sample NOUN a small part showing the quality of the whole; a specimen. VERB test by taking a sample of.

sampler NOUN a piece of embroidery worked in various stitches to show one's skill.

samurai /sam-yuu-rI/ NOUN (PL **samurai**) [HISTORICAL] a Japanese warrior.

sanatorium NOUN (PL **sanatoriums** or **sanatoria**) an establishment for treating chronic diseases or convalescents; a room for sick pupils in a school.

S

sanctify VERB (**sanctifies**, **sanctifying**, **sanctified**) make holy or sacred. **sanctification** NOUN

sanctimonious ADJ ostentatiously righteous, hypocritical. **sanctimoniously** ADV **sanctimoniousness** NOUN

sanction NOUN **1** permission, approval. **2** a penalty imposed on a country or organization. VERB **1** authorize. **2** impose a sanction on.

sanctity NOUN sacredness, holiness.

sanctuary NOUN (PL **sanctuaries**) **1** a place of refuge; a place where wildlife is protected. **2** a sacred place.

sanctum NOUN a sacred place; a private place.

sand NOUN very fine loose fragments of crushed rock; (**sands**) an expanse of sand, a sandbank. VERB **1** sprinkle with sand. **2** smooth with sandpaper or a sander.

sandal NOUN a light shoe with straps.

sandalwood NOUN a scented wood.

sandbag NOUN a bag filled with sand, used to protect a wall or building. VERB (**sandbags**, **sandbagging**, **sandbagged**) protect with sandbags.

sandbank NOUN a deposit

of sand forming a shallow area in a sea or river.

sandblast VERB treat or clean with a jet of sand driven by compressed air or steam.

sandcastle NOUN a model building of sand, made for fun.

sander NOUN a mechanical tool for smoothing surfaces.

sandpaper NOUN paper with a coating of sand or other abrasive substance, used for smoothing surfaces. VERB smooth with this.

sandstone NOUN rock formed of compressed sand.

sandstorm NOUN a desert storm of wind with blown sand.

sandwich NOUN two or more slices of bread with a layer of filling between; something arranged like this. VERB put between two other people or things.

sandy ADJ (**sandier**, **sandiest**) **1** like sand; covered with sand. **2** (of hair) yellowish red.

sane ADJ having a sound mind; rational.
sanely ADV

sang past of **SING**.

sangria NOUN a Spanish drink of red wine, lemonade, and fruit.

sanguinary ADJ full of bloodshed; bloodthirsty.

sanguine ADJ optimistic.

sanitarium NOUN (PL **sanitariums** or **sanitaria**) [US] a sanatorium.

sanitary ADJ of hygiene and health; clean, hygienic; of sanitation.

sanitary towel ([US] **sanitary napkin**) NOUN a pad worn to absorb blood during menstruation.

sanitation NOUN arrangements to protect public health, especially drainage and disposal of sewage.

sanitize (also **sanitise**) VERB clean, make hygienic; alter to make more palatable but less individual or authentic.

sanity NOUN the condition of being sane.

sank past of **SINK**.

S

sap NOUN **1** the food-carrying liquid in plants. **2** [INFORMAL] a foolish person. VERB (**saps, sapping, sapped**) exhaust gradually.

sapling NOUN a young tree.

sapphire NOUN a blue precious stone; its colour.

saprophyte /sap-rŏ-fIt/ NOUN a fungus or related plant living on decayed matter.

sarcasm NOUN ironically scornful language.
sarcastic ADJ
sarcastically ADV

sarcophagus /sah-ko-fă-gŭs/ NOUN (PL **sarcophagi**) a stone coffin.

sardine NOUN a young pilchard or similar small fish.

sardonic ADJ humorous in a grim or sarcastic way.
sardonically ADV

sari NOUN a length of cloth draped round the body, worn by Indian women.

sarong /să-rong/ NOUN a strip of cloth worn round the body, especially in Malaysia.

sartorial ADJ of tailoring, clothing, or style of dress.

SAS ABBREV Special Air Service.

sash NOUN **1** a strip of cloth worn round the waist or over one shoulder. **2** a frame holding a pane of a window and sliding up and down in grooves.

sash window NOUN a window opened and shut by sliding up and down in grooves.

sat past and past participle of **SIT**.

Satan NOUN the devil.

satanic ADJ **1** of Satan. **2** very evil or wicked.

Satanism NOUN the worship of Satan.
Satanist NOUN

satchel NOUN a bag for school books, hung over the shoulder.

sateen NOUN a closely woven cotton fabric resembling satin.

satellite NOUN **1** a heavenly or artificial body revolving round a planet. **2** a country that is dependent on another.

satellite dish NOUN a dish-shaped aerial for

receiving broadcasts transmitted by satellite.

satiate /say-shi-ayt/ VERB satisfy fully, glut.
satiation NOUN
satiety NOUN

satin NOUN a silky material that is glossy on one side. ADJ smooth as satin.

satire NOUN criticism through ridicule, irony, or sarcasm; a novel or play etc. that ridicules something.
satirical ADJ
satirically ADV

satirize (also **satirise**) VERB describe and criticize through satire.
satirist NOUN

satisfactory ADJ satisfying; adequate.
satisfactorily ADV

satisfy VERB (**satisfies**, **satisfying**, **satisfied**) fulfil the needs or wishes of; make pleased or contented; fulfil (a need, requirement, etc.).
satisfaction NOUN

satsuma NOUN a small variety of orange.

saturate VERB make thoroughly wet; fill or supply completely or to excess.
saturation NOUN

Saturday NOUN the day following Friday.

saturnine ADJ having a gloomy temperament or appearance.

satyr /sat-er/ NOUN a woodland god in classical mythology, with a goat's ears, tail, and legs.

sauce NOUN **1** a liquid food added for flavour. **2** [INFORMAL] impudence.

saucepan NOUN a metal cooking pot with a long handle.

saucer NOUN a shallow curved dish on which a cup stands; something shaped like this.

saucy ADJ (**saucier**, **sauciest**) [INFORMAL] impudent; mischievously or playfully provocative.
saucily ADV

sauerkraut /sow-er-krowt/ NOUN chopped pickled cabbage.

sauna /sor-nă/ NOUN a specially designed hot room for cleaning and refreshing the body.

saunter VERB walk in a slow, relaxed way. NOUN a

slow, relaxed walk.

sausage NOUN minced seasoned meat in a tubular case of thin skin.

sauté /soh-tay/ VERB (**sautés**, **sautéing**, **sautéd** or **sautéed**) fry quickly in shallow oil.

savage ADJ wild and fierce; cruel, hostile; primitive, uncivilized. NOUN a primitive or uncivilized person; a very cruel person. VERB maul, attack fiercely.
savagely ADV
savagery NOUN

savannah NOUN a grassy plain in hot regions.

save VERB **1** rescue or remove from harm or danger. **2** keep, store for future use; avoid wasting; keep money in this way. **3** prevent the scoring of (a goal). NOUN an act of saving in football etc.
saver NOUN

savings PLURAL NOUN money put aside for future use.

saviour ([US] **savior**) NOUN a person who rescues people from harm.

savoir faire /sav-wah **fair**/ NOUN knowledge of how to behave; social tact.

savory NOUN a herb. ADJ US spelling of **SAVOURY**.

savour ([US] **savor**) NOUN flavour; smell. VERB **1** enjoy fully, relish. **2** have a trace of a quality.

savoury ([US] **savory**) ADJ having an appetizing taste or smell; salty or piquant, not sweet. NOUN (PL **savouries**) a savoury dish or snack.

saw¹ past of **SEE**.

saw² NOUN a cutting tool with a zigzag edge. VERB (**saws**, **sawing**, **sawed**; PAST PARTICIPLE **sawn**) cut with a saw; make a to-and-fro movement.

saw³ NOUN a saying.

sawdust NOUN powdery fragments of wood, made in sawing timber.

sawmill NOUN a mill where timber is cut.

sawn past participle of **SAW²**.

sax NOUN [INFORMAL] a saxophone.

saxophone NOUN a brass wind instrument with

finger-operated keys. **saxophonist** NOUN

say VERB (**says**, **saying**, **said**) **1** utter (words); express, convey, state; have written or shown on the surface. **2** suppose as a possibility. NOUN the opportunity to express one's opinion or exert influence.

saying NOUN a well-known phrase or proverb.

scab NOUN **1** a crust forming over a cut; a skin disease or plant disease causing similar roughness. **2** [INFORMAL], [DEROGATORY] a blackleg. **scabby** ADJ

scabbard NOUN the sheath of a sword etc.

scabies NOUN a contagious skin disease causing itching.

scabrous /skay-brŭs/ ADJ **1** rough-surfaced. **2** indecent.

scaffold NOUN **1** a platform for the execution of criminals. **2** a structure of scaffolding.

scaffolding NOUN poles and planks providing platforms for people working on buildings etc.

scald VERB injure with hot liquid or steam; clean or peel using boiling water. NOUN an injury by scalding.

scale NOUN **1** an ordered series of units or qualities for measuring or classifying things; a series of marks at regular intervals, used in measuring. **2** relative size or extent. **3** (**scales**) an instrument for weighing. **4** a fixed series of notes in a system of music. **5** each of the overlapping plates of bony membrane protecting the skin of fish and reptiles; something resembling this. **6** a deposit caused in a kettle etc. by hard water; tartar on teeth. VERB **1** climb. **2** represent in proportion to the size of the original. **3** remove scale(s) from. **scaly** ADJ

scalene /skay-leen/ ADJ (of a triangle) having unequal sides.

scallion NOUN a shallot or spring onion.

scallop NOUN **1** a shellfish

with a hinged fan-shaped shell. **2** (**scallops**) semicircular curves as an ornamental edging.
scalloped ADJ

scallywag NOUN a rascal.

scalp NOUN the skin of the head excluding the face. VERB cut the scalp from.

scalpel NOUN a surgeon's or painter's small straight knife.

scam NOUN [INFORMAL] a dishonest scheme.

scamp NOUN a rascal.

scamper VERB run hastily or in play. NOUN a scampering run.

scampi PLURAL NOUN large prawns.

scan VERB (**scans, scanning, scanned**) **1** look at all parts of; read quickly. **2** pass a radar or electronic beam over; resolve (a picture) into elements of light and shade for transmission or reproduction. **3** (of verse) have a regular rhythm; analyse the rhythm of. NOUN scanning.
scanner NOUN

scandal NOUN an action or event causing outrage; such outrage; malicious gossip about such actions.
scandalous ADJ
scandalously ADV

scandalize (also **scandalise**) VERB shock; outrage.

scandalmonger NOUN a person who spreads scandal.

Scandinavian NOUN a person from Scandinavia. ADJ relating to Scandinavia.

scandium NOUN a metallic element.

scansion NOUN scanning of verse.

scant ADJ barely enough.

scanty ADJ (**scantier, scantiest**) small in amount or extent; barely enough.
scantily ADV
scantiness NOUN

scapegoat NOUN a person made to bear blame that should fall on others.

scapula NOUN (PL **scapulae** or **scapulas**) the shoulder blade.
scapular ADJ

scar NOUN the mark where

S

a wound has healed. VERB (**scars**, **scarring**, **scarred**) mark with a scar; form scar(s).

scarab NOUN a sacred beetle of ancient Egypt.

scarce ADJ not enough to supply a demand, rare.

scarcely ADV only just; only a short time before; surely or probably not.

scarcity NOUN (PL **scarcities**) a shortage.

scare VERB frighten; be frightened. NOUN a fright; widespread alarm.

scarecrow NOUN a figure dressed in old clothes and set up to scare birds away from crops.

scaremonger NOUN a person who spreads alarming rumours. **scaremongering** NOUN

scarf NOUN (PL **scarves** or **scarfs**) a piece or strip of material worn round the neck or over the head.

scarify VERB (**scarifies**, **scarifying**, **scarified**) **1** make cuts or scratches in; break up (grass or soil) with a rake. **2** criticize harshly.

scarlet NOUN a brilliant red colour.

scarlet fever NOUN an infectious fever producing a scarlet rash.

scarp NOUN a steep slope on a hillside.

SCART (also **Scart**) NOUN a 21-pin socket used to connect video equipment.

scary ADJ (**scarier**, **scariest**) [INFORMAL] frightening.

scathing ADJ (of criticism) very severe; scornful.

scatology NOUN an excessive interest in excrement. **scatological** ADJ

scatter VERB throw in various random directions; move off in different directions.

scatterbrain NOUN a careless or forgetful person. **scatterbrained** ADJ

scatty ADJ (**scattier**, **scattiest**) [INFORMAL] scatterbrained, disorganized.

scavenge VERB search for (usable objects) among rubbish etc.; (of animals) search for decaying flesh

as food.
scavenger NOUN

scenario NOUN (PL **scenarios**) **1** the script or summary of a film or play. **2** a possible or hypothetical sequence of events.

scene NOUN **1** the place where something occurs; a landscape, a place seen in a particular way; an event or episode characterized by a quality: *scenes of violence.* **2** a piece of continuous action in a play or film. **3** a display of temper or emotion. **4** one's area of interest or expertise: *not my scene.*
behind the scenes hidden from public view.

scenery NOUN the general (especially picturesque) appearance of a landscape; structures used on a theatre stage to represent the scene of action.

scenic ADJ picturesque.

scent NOUN a pleasant smell; liquid perfume; an animal's trail perceptible to a hound's sense of smell. VERB **1** apply scent to; make fragrant. **2** discover by smell; suspect or detect the presence of.
on the scent making progress in an investigation.

sceptic /skep-tik/ ([US] **skeptic**) NOUN a sceptical person.

sceptical /skep-tik-ăl/ ([US] **skeptical**) ADJ not easily convinced; having doubts.
sceptically ADV
scepticism NOUN

sceptre ([US] **scepter**) NOUN an ornamental rod carried as a symbol of sovereignty.

schadenfreude /shah-dĕn-froi-dĕ/ NOUN enjoyment of others' misfortunes.

schedule NOUN a programme or timetable of events. VERB **1** include in a schedule. **2** list (a building) for preservation.

scheduled flight NOUN a regular public flight, not a chartered flight.

schema NOUN (PL **schemata** or **schemas**) a summary, outline, or

S

diagram.

schematic ADJ in the form of a diagram; simplified or simplistic.
schematically ADV

schematize (also **schematise**) VERB put into schematic form.
schematization NOUN

scheme NOUN a plan of work or action; a system or arrangement.
VERB make plans, plot.
schemer NOUN

scherzo /**skair**-tsoh/ NOUN (PL **scherzos**) a lively piece of music.

schism /skizm/ NOUN division into opposing groups through a difference in belief or opinion.
schismatic ADJ & NOUN

schist /shist/ NOUN a rock formed in layers.

schizoid /**skits**-oid/ ADJ abnormally introverted; [INFORMAL] having contradictory characteristics. NOUN a schizoid person.

schizophrenia NOUN a mental disorder involving failures of perception and withdrawal from reality.
schizophrenic ADJ & NOUN

schmaltz /shmawlts/ NOUN sugary sentimentality.

schmuck NOUN [US] [INFORMAL] a foolish person.

schnapps NOUN a strong alcoholic spirit.

schnitzel /**shnit**-sĕl/ NOUN a fried cutlet.

scholar NOUN a learned person, especially in a particular field; a pupil; the holder of a scholarship.
scholarly ADJ
scholarliness NOUN

scholarship NOUN **1** academic study, learning. **2** a grant of money supporting a student's education.

scholastic ADJ of schools or education; academic.

school NOUN **1** an educational institution. **2** a group of people sharing the same ideas or following the same principles. **3** a shoal of fish. VERB train, discipline.
schoolboy NOUN
schoolchild NOUN

schoolgirl NOUN
schoolteacher NOUN

schooner NOUN **1** a sailing ship. **2** a measure for sherry.

sciatica /sI-at-ik-ă/ NOUN a condition causing pain in the hip and thigh.

science NOUN study or knowledge of the physical and natural world, based on observation and experiment.
scientific ADJ
scientifically ADV

science fiction NOUN fiction based on imagined future worlds.

scientist NOUN an expert in a science.

scimitar /sim-i-tă/ NOUN a short curved oriental sword.

scintilla /sin-til-ă/ NOUN a trace.

scintillating ADJ sparkling; witty, lively.

scion /sy-ŏn/ NOUN **1** a plant shoot cut for grafting. **2** a descendant.

scissors PLURAL NOUN a cutting instrument with two pivoted blades.

sclerosis NOUN abnormal hardening of body tissue.

scoff VERB **1** speak contemptuously, jeer. **2** [INFORMAL] eat greedily.

scold VERB rebuke (especially a child).
scolding NOUN

sconce NOUN an ornamental bracket on a wall, holding a light.

scone /skon, skohn/ NOUN a soft flat cake eaten buttered.

scoop NOUN **1** an implement like a spoon, with a long handle and a deep bowl; a short-handled deep shovel. **2** [INFORMAL] an item of news published by one newspaper before its rivals. VERB **1** lift or hollow with (or as if with) a scoop. **2** [INFORMAL] publish a news story before (a rival newspaper).

scoot VERB [INFORMAL] move or leave quickly.

scooter NOUN **1** a lightweight motorcycle. **2** a child's toy consisting of a footboard on wheels, propelled by the foot and steered by a long handle.

scope NOUN the range of a subject, activity, etc.;

opportunity.

scorch VERB burn or become burnt on the surface.

scorching ADJ very hot.

score NOUN **1** the number of points gained in a contest. **2** a set of twenty. **3** a line or mark cut into something. **4** written or printed music; music for a film or play. VERB **1** gain (points etc.) in a contest; keep a record of the score; [INFORMAL] achieve a success. **2** cut a line or mark into. **3** write or compose as a musical score.
score out cross out.
scorer NOUN

scorn NOUN the feeling that someone or something is worthless or despicable. VERB feel or show scorn for; reject with scorn.
scornful ADJ
scornfully ADV

scorpion NOUN a creature related to spiders, with lobster-like claws and a sting in its long tail.

Scot NOUN a person from Scotland.

Scotch ADJ [DATED] Scottish. NOUN Scotch whisky.

> In Scotland the adjectives **Scots** and **Scottish** are preferred to **Scotch**.

scotch VERB put an end to (a rumour).

scot-free ADV without injury or punishment.

Scots ADJ Scottish. NOUN the Scottish form of the English language.
Scotsman, Scotswoman NOUN

Scottish ADJ of Scotland or its people.

scoundrel NOUN a dishonest person.

scour VERB **1** clean by rubbing; clear out (a channel etc.) by flowing water. **2** search thoroughly. NOUN the action of scouring.
scourer NOUN

scourge /skerj/ NOUN **1** [HISTORICAL] a whip. **2** someone or something causing great suffering. VERB **1** [HISTORICAL] flog. **2** cause suffering to.

scout NOUN a person sent to gather information, especially about enemy movements. VERB act as a scout, search.

scowl NOUN a sullen or angry frown. VERB make a scowl.

scrabble VERB scratch or search busily with the hands, paws, etc.

scraggy ADJ (**scraggier**, **scraggiest**) thin and bony.

scragginess NOUN

scram VERB (**scrams**, **scramming**, **scrammed**) [INFORMAL] go away.

scramble VERB **1** climb with difficulty; move hastily or awkwardly; struggle to perform or achieve; (of a fighter aircraft) take off quickly for action. **2** mix, muddle; make (a transmission) unintelligible except by means of a special receiver; cook (eggs) by mixing and stirring. NOUN **1** a scrambling walk or movement; an eager struggle. **2** a motorcycle race over rough ground. **3** a disordered mixture.

scrambler NOUN

scrap NOUN **1** a fragment, especially one left after use, eating, etc. **2** discarded metal suitable for reprocessing. **3** [INFORMAL] a fight or quarrel. VERB (**scraps**, **scrapping**, **scrapped**) **1** discard as useless. **2** [INFORMAL] fight, quarrel.

scrapbook NOUN a book for newspaper cuttings or similar souvenirs.

scrape VERB **1** clean, smooth, or damage by passing a hard edge across a surface; make a harsh sound doing this. **2** achieve (something) or manage to get by with difficulty; be very economical. NOUN **1** a scraping movement or sound; a scraped place. **2** [INFORMAL] a predicament caused by unwise behaviour.

scraper NOUN

scrapie NOUN a disease of sheep causing loss of coordination.

scraping NOUN a fragment produced by scraping.

scrappy ADJ (**scrappier**, **scrappiest**) made up of scraps or disconnected elements.

scrappily ADV

S

scrappiness NOUN

scratch VERB **1** mark or wound with a pointed object; rub or scrape with claws or fingernails; make a thin scraping sound by doing this. **2** obtain with difficulty. **3** cancel; withdraw from a competition. NOUN a mark, wound, or sound made by scratching; a spell of scratching. ADJ collected from what is available; not of the highest quality.
from scratch from the very beginning or with no preparation. **up to scratch** up to the required standard.
scratchy ADJ

scratch card NOUN a card with sections coated in a waxy substance which may be scraped away to reveal whether one has won a prize.

scratchings PLURAL NOUN crisp residue of pork fat left after rendering lard.

scrawl VERB write in a hurried untidy way. NOUN bad handwriting.

scrawny ADJ (**scrawnier**, **scrawniest**) scraggy.

scream VERB give a piercing cry, especially of fear or pain; make a long piercing sound. NOUN **1** a screaming cry or sound. **2** [INFORMAL] a very amusing person or thing.

scree NOUN a mass of loose stones on a mountainside.

screech NOUN a harsh high-pitched scream or sound. VERB make a screech; move rapidly with a screech.

screed NOUN **1** a tiresomely long piece of writing or speech. **2** a thin layer of cement.

screen NOUN **1** an upright structure used to give shelter, divide a room, hide something, etc. **2** a windscreen. **3** the surface of a television, VDU, etc., on which images and data are displayed; a blank surface on to which an image is projected. VERB **1** shelter, protect, or separate with a screen. **2** show or broadcast (a film or television programme). **3** examine for the presence or absence of a disease, quality, etc.

screenplay NOUN the script of a film.

screen saver NOUN [COMPUTING] a program which, after a set time, replaces an unchanging screen display with a moving image to prevent damage.

screw NOUN **1** a metal pin with a spiral ridge round its length, fastened by turning; a thing twisted to tighten or press something; an act of twisting or tightening. **2** a propeller. **3** [INFORMAL] a prison officer. **4** [VULGAR SLANG] an act of sexual intercourse. VERB **1** fasten or tighten with screw(s); turn (a screw); twist, become twisted. **2** [INFORMAL] cheat; extort. **3** [VULGAR SLANG] have sexual intercourse with. **screw up 1** summon up (courage). **2** [INFORMAL] bungle (something); cause (someone) to be emotionally disturbed.

screwdriver NOUN a tool for turning screws.

scribble VERB write or draw hurriedly or carelessly. NOUN something scribbled.

scribe NOUN a person who (before the invention of printing) made copies of writings; (in New Testament times) a professional religious scholar.

scrimmage NOUN a confused struggle.

scrimp VERB economize, save.

script NOUN **1** handwriting; a style of printed characters resembling this. **2** the text of a play, broadcast talk, etc.

scripture NOUN sacred writings; (**the Scriptures**) those of the Christians or the Jews.
scriptural ADJ

scroll NOUN a roll of paper or parchment; an ornamental design in this shape. VERB move a display on a VDU screen up or down as the screen is filled.
scrollable ADJ

scrotum NOUN (PL **scrota** or **scrotums**) the pouch of skin enclosing the testicles.

scrounge VERB [INFORMAL] cadge; borrow; collect by foraging.
scrounger NOUN

scrub VERB (**scrubs**, **scrubbing**, **scrubbed**) rub hard to clean, especially with something coarse or bristly; [INFORMAL] cancel.
NOUN **1** an act of scrubbing; a semi-abrasive skin cleanser. **2** vegetation consisting of stunted trees and shrubs; land covered with this.

scruff NOUN the back of the neck.

scruffy ADJ (**scruffier**, **scruffiest**) [INFORMAL] shabby and untidy.
scruffily ADV
scruffiness NOUN

scrum NOUN a scrummage; [INFORMAL] a disorderly crowd.

scrummage NOUN a grouping of forwards in rugby football to struggle for possession of the ball by pushing.

scrumptious ADJ [INFORMAL] delicious.

scrunch VERB crunch; crush, crumple. NOUN a crunching noise.

scruple NOUN a doubt as to whether something is morally right; hesitation caused by this.
VERB hesitate because of scruples.

scrupulous ADJ very conscientious or careful.
scrupulously ADV
scrupulousness NOUN

scrutinize (also **scrutinise**) VERB examine carefully.

scrutiny NOUN (PL **scrutinies**) a careful look or examination.

scuba NOUN an aqualung (acronym from *s*elf-*c*ontained *u*nderwater *b*reathing *a*pparatus).
scuba-diving NOUN

scud VERB (**scuds**, **scudding**, **scudded**) move along fast and smoothly.

scuff VERB scrape the surface of (a shoe) against something; mark or scrape by doing this.

scuffle NOUN confused struggle or fight. VERB take part in a scuffle.

scull NOUN one of a pair of small oars; an oar that rests on a boat's stern, worked with a screw-like movement. VERB row with sculls.

scullery NOUN (PL **sculleries**) a room for washing dishes and similar work.

sculpt VERB sculpture.

sculptor NOUN a maker of sculptures.

sculpture NOUN the art of carving or modelling; work made in this way. VERB make or shape by carving or modelling. **sculptural** ADJ

scum NOUN a layer of impurities or froth etc. on the surface of a liquid; [INFORMAL] a worthless person.

scupper NOUN an opening in a ship's side to drain water from the deck. VERB sink (a ship) deliberately; [INFORMAL] thwart, spoil, stop.

scurf NOUN flakes of dry skin, especially from the scalp; similar scaly matter.

scurrilous ADJ making scandalous claims; humorously insulting. **scurrility** NOUN **scurrilously** ADV

scurry VERB (**scurries, scurrying, scurried**) run hurriedly, scamper. NOUN (PL **scurries**) a scurrying movement, a rush.

scurvy NOUN a disease caused by lack of vitamin C.

scuttle NOUN a box or bucket for fetching and holding coal. VERB **1** scurry. **2** sink (a ship) by letting in water.

scythe /*syth*/ NOUN an implement with a curved blade on a long handle, for cutting long grass.

SE ABBREV south-east; south-eastern.

sea NOUN the expanse of salt water surrounding the continents; a section of this; a large inland lake; the waves of the sea; a vast expanse. **at sea 1** in a ship on the sea. **2** perplexed.

seaboard NOUN the coast.

seaborgium NOUN a chemical element.

seafaring ADJ & NOUN working or travelling on the sea. **seafarer** NOUN

seafood NOUN fish or shellfish from the sea eaten as food.

seagoing ADJ of or for sea voyages.

seagull NOUN a gull.

sea horse NOUN a small fish with a horse-like head.

seal[1] NOUN **1** an engraved piece of metal used to stamp a design; its impression. **2** a device used to join things or close something firmly. **3** an action etc. regarded as guaranteeing something. VERB close or fasten securely; mark with a seal; settle (an agreement etc.).

seal[2] NOUN an amphibious sea animal with thick fur or bristles.

sealant NOUN a substance for coating a surface to make it airtight or watertight.

sea lion NOUN a large seal.

seam NOUN **1** a line where two pieces of fabric are sewn together; a join. **2** a layer of coal etc. in the ground. VERB join by a seam.

seaman NOUN a sailor; a person skilled in seafaring.
seamanship NOUN

seamless ADJ with no obvious joins; smooth and continuous.

seamstress NOUN a woman who sews, especially for a living.

seance /say-ahns/ NOUN a meeting where people try to make contact with the spirits of the dead.

seaplane NOUN an aeroplane designed to take off from and land on water.

sear VERB scorch, burn.

search VERB try to find something; hunt through or over (a place or person). NOUN the process of searching.

searching ADJ thorough.

searchlight NOUN an outdoor lamp with a powerful beam; its beam.

seascape NOUN a picture or view of the sea.

seasick ADJ made sick by the motion of a ship.
seasickness NOUN

seaside NOUN the coast as a place for holidays.

season NOUN one of the four divisions of the year associated with particular weather, length of daylight, etc.; the period when a specified event takes place or a specified food is plentiful. VERB 1 add salt etc. to (food). 2 dry or treat (timber) to prepare it for use.

seasonable ADJ suitable for the season.

seasonal ADJ of a season or seasons; varying with the seasons.
seasonally ADV

seasoned ADJ experienced.

seasoning NOUN a substance used to enhance the flavour of food.

season ticket NOUN a ticket valid for any number of journeys or performances in a specified period.

S

seat NOUN 1 a thing made or used for sitting on; a place as a member of parliament, a committee, etc.; the site or base of something. 2 a country house. 3 the buttocks; the part of a garment covering these. VERB cause to sit; have seats for.

seat belt NOUN a strap securing a person to a seat in a vehicle or aircraft.

sea urchin NOUN a sea animal with a round spiky shell.

seaweed NOUN large algae growing in the sea.

seaworthy ADJ (of ships) fit for a sea voyage.
seaworthiness NOUN

sebaceous /si-bay-shŭs/ ADJ secreting an oily or greasy substance.

secateurs PLURAL NOUN clippers for pruning plants.

secede VERB withdraw from membership.
secession NOUN

seclude VERB keep (a person) apart from others.

secluded ADJ (of a place) not much visited, private.

seclusion NOUN privacy.

second[1] /sek-ŏnd/ ADJ 1 next after the first. 2 inferior or subordinate. NOUN 1 a second class in an examination. 2 an

attendant at a duel or boxing match.
3 (**seconds**) goods of inferior quality.
4 (**seconds**) [INFORMAL] a second helping of food.
VERB formally support (a proposal etc.).
secondly ADV

second² /sek-ŏnd/ NOUN a sixtieth part of a minute of time or a degree of an angle.

second³ /si-**kond**/ VERB transfer temporarily to another job or department.
secondment NOUN

secondary ADJ **1** coming after or derived from what is primary. **2** (of schools or education) for children who have had primary education, usually between the ages of 11 and 18. NOUN a secondary thing.
secondarily ADV

second best ADJ next to the best in quality; inferior.

second class NOUN a group or division considered to be the second best. ADJ & ADV (**second-class**) relating to the second class; (of mail) costing less and delivered more slowly than first class.

second cousin *see* **COUSIN**.

second-hand ADJ bought after use by a previous owner; passed on from someone else.

second nature NOUN a habit or characteristic that has become automatic.

second-rate ADJ inferior in quality.

second sight NOUN the supposed power to foresee future events.

second thoughts PLURAL NOUN a change of mind after reconsideration.

second wind NOUN renewed capacity for effort.

secret ADJ kept from the knowledge of most people. NOUN something secret; a mystery; a means of achieving something: *the secret of success.*
in secret secretly.
secrecy NOUN
secretly ADV

secretariat NOUN an administrative office or department.

secretary NOUN (PL **secretaries**) a person employed to deal with correspondence and routine office work; an official in charge of an organization's correspondence; an ambassador's or government minister's chief assistant.
secretarial ADJ

Secretary General NOUN (PL **Secretary Generals**) a principal administrative officer.

secrete /si-kreet/ VERB **1** conceal, hide. **2** (of a cell, gland, etc.) produce and discharge (a substance).
secretion NOUN
secretor NOUN

S

secretive ADJ concealing information etc.
secretively ADV
secretiveness NOUN

secretory ADJ of physiological secretion.

sect NOUN a group with beliefs, especially religious ones, that differ from those generally accepted.

sectarian ADJ **1** of a sect or sects. **2** rigidly following the doctrines of a sect; promoting the interests of a sect.

section NOUN a distinct part; a cross section; a subdivision. VERB **1** divide into sections. **2** commit (a person) to a psychiatric hospital.

sectional ADJ of a section or sections; made in sections.

sector NOUN a part of an area; a branch of an activity; a section of a circular area between two lines drawn from centre to circumference.

secular ADJ of worldly (not religious or spiritual) matters.

secure ADJ tightly fixed or fastened, certain not to slip, come undone, etc.; safe; confident.
VERB **1** make secure, fasten securely; guarantee repayment of (a loan) by taking something as a pledge. **2** obtain.
securely ADV

security NOUN (PL **securities**) **1** the state of

being secure.
2 precautions taken against espionage, theft, etc. **3** something given as a pledge of fulfilment of an obligation or repayment of a loan. **4** a certificate showing ownership of financial stocks etc.

sedate[1] ADJ calm and dignified.
sedately ADV
sedateness NOUN

sedate[2] VERB treat with sedatives.
sedation NOUN

sedative ADJ having a calming effect. NOUN a sedative drug.

sedentary /sed-ĕnt-ă-ri/ ADJ seated; (of work) done while sitting.

sediment NOUN particles of solid matter in a liquid or deposited by water or wind.
sedimentary ADJ
sedimentation NOUN

sedition NOUN words or actions inciting rebellion.
seditious ADJ
seditiously ADV

seduce VERB tempt into wrong or unwise action; persuade into sexual intercourse.
seducer NOUN
seduction NOUN
seductive ADJ
seductress NOUN

sedulous /sed-yuu-lŭs/ ADJ diligent and persevering.
sedulously ADV

see[1] VERB (**sees**, **seeing**, **saw**; PAST PARTICIPLE **seen**) **1** perceive with the eyes; learn from something seen; watch, look.
2 understand; deduce.
3 meet; escort: *see you home.* **4** experience; be the time when (something) happens. **5** regard in a particular way. **6** ensure: *see it gets done.*
see about or **to** attend to. **seeing that** in view of the fact that. **see off** escort to the point of departure; drive away.
see through not be deceived by.

see[2] NOUN a bishop's or archbishop's seat of authority.

seed NOUN **1** a plant's fertilized ovule, from which a new plant may grow; semen; the origin of something. **2** one of the stronger players in a

S

sports tournament, scheduled to play in a particular order so they do not defeat one another early on.
VERB **1** plant with seeds; produce seeds. **2** remove seeds from (a fruit etc.). **3** give the status of seed to (a player).
go or **run to seed 1** cease flowering as seed develops. **2** deteriorate.

seedless ADJ not containing seeds.

seedling NOUN a very young plant.

seedy ADJ (**seedier**, **seediest**) sordid, disreputable.
seediness NOUN

seek VERB (**seeks**, **seeking**, **sought**) try to find or obtain; try (to do something).

S

seem VERB appear to be or exist or be true.
seemingly ADV

seen past participle of SEE[1].

seep VERB ooze slowly through porous material or small holes.
seepage NOUN

seer NOUN a prophet.

see-saw NOUN a long board balanced on a central support so that children sitting on each end can ride up and down; a situation with repeated changes from one state to another. VERB make this movement or change.

seethe VERB bubble as if boiling; be very agitated or excited.

segment NOUN a part cut off, marked off, or separable from others; a part of a circle or sphere cut off by a straight line or plane.
segmented ADJ

segregate VERB separate from others, isolate.
segregation NOUN

seine /sayn/ NOUN a fishing net that hangs from floats.

seismic /sIz-mik/ ADJ of earthquakes.

seismograph NOUN an instrument for recording earthquakes.

seismology NOUN the study of earthquakes.
seismological ADJ
seismologist NOUN

seize VERB **1** take hold of forcibly or suddenly; take possession of by force or legal right. **2** (of a sensation, emotion, etc.) affect (someone) suddenly and strongly.
seize on make use of eagerly. **seize up** (of a mechanism) become stuck, especially through overheating.

seizure NOUN an act of seizing; a sudden violent attack of an illness.

seldom ADV rarely, not often.

select VERB pick out as the best or most suitable. ADJ carefully chosen; exclusive.
selector NOUN

selection NOUN the action of selecting; a number of selected things; things from which to choose.

selective ADJ chosen or choosing carefully.
selectively ADV
selectivity NOUN

selenium NOUN a chemical element.

self NOUN (PL **selves**) a person's essential individual nature; a person as an individual; a person or thing as the object of reflexive action; one's own advantage or interests.

self- COMBINING FORM of or to or done by oneself or itself.

self-assured ADJ confident.

self-centred ADJ concerned primarily with one's own affairs and advantage.

self-confidence NOUN confidence in one's own worth and abilities.
self-confident ADJ

self-conscious ADJ embarrassed from knowing that one is observed.

self-contained ADJ **1** complete in itself; (of accommodation) having all the necessary rooms. **2** (of a person) quiet and independent.

self-control NOUN the ability to control one's feelings and act rationally.
self-controlled ADJ

self-denial NOUN deliberately going without things that one would like but thinks wrong or harmful.

self-determination NOUN a nation's choice of its own form of government, allegiances, etc.

self-evident ADJ obvious, needing no argument or proof.

self-interest NOUN one's own advantage as a motive.

self-interested ADJ pursuing one's own advantage.

selfish ADJ acting or done according to one's own interests without regard to those of others; keeping good things for oneself.
selfishly ADV
selfishness NOUN

S

selfless ADJ unselfish.
selflessly ADV

self-made ADJ having risen from poverty by one's own efforts.

self-possessed ADJ calm, controlled.
self-possession NOUN

self-respect NOUN regard for one's own dignity and standards.

self-righteous ADJ complacent about one's own virtue.

selfsame ADJ the very same.

self-satisfied ADJ excessively satisfied with one's qualities, achievements, etc.

self-seeking ADJ aiming at one's own advantage before that of others.

self-service ADJ (of a shop etc.) where customers help themselves and pay at a checkout.

self-styled ADJ using a title or description that one has adopted without right: *self-styled experts.*

self-sufficient ADJ able to provide what one needs without outside help.
self-sufficiency NOUN

self-willed ADJ obstinately doing what one wishes.

sell VERB (**sells, selling, sold**) **1** exchange (goods etc.) for money; keep (goods) for sale; (of goods) be sold, be for sale at a specified price.

2 persuade someone to accept. NOUN an act of selling or promoting. **sell off** dispose of by selling, especially at a reduced price. **sell out** **1** sell all of one's stock. **2** betray. **sell up** sell one's house or business.
seller NOUN

Sellotape NOUN [TRADE MARK] an adhesive usually transparent tape.

selvedge (also **selvage**) NOUN an edge of cloth woven so that it does not unravel.

semantic ADJ of meaning in language. NOUN (**semantics**) the study of meaning.
semantically ADV

semaphore NOUN a system of signalling with the arms.

semblance NOUN an outward appearance or form.

semen NOUN the sperm-bearing fluid produced by male animals.

semester NOUN a half-year course or university term.

semi- PREFIX half; partly.

semibreve NOUN a note in music, equal to two minims or half a breve.

semicircle NOUN half of a circle.
semicircular ADJ

semicolon NOUN a punctuation mark (;).

semiconductor NOUN a substance that conducts electricity in certain conditions.

semi-detached ADJ (of a house) joined to another on one side.

semi-final NOUN a match or round in a contest, preceding the final.
semi-finalist NOUN

seminal ADJ **1** of seed or semen. **2** giving rise to new developments.
seminally ADV

seminar NOUN a small class for discussion and research.

seminary NOUN (PL **seminaries**) a training college for priests or rabbis.

semi-precious ADJ (of gems) less valuable than those called precious.

semiquaver NOUN a note in music, equal to half a quaver.

Semite /see-mIt, sem-It/ NOUN a member of the group of races that includes Jews and Arabs. **Semitic** ADJ

semitone NOUN half a tone in music.

semolina NOUN hard particles left when wheat is ground and sifted, used to make puddings.

senate NOUN the upper house of certain parliaments; the governing body of certain universities.

senator NOUN a member of a senate.

send VERB (**sends**, **sending**, **sent**) **1** order or cause to go to a particular destination; propel; send a message. **2** bring into a specified state: *sends me crazy.* **send for** order to come or be brought. **send up** [INFORMAL] make fun of by imitating.

S

senile ADJ weak in body or mind because of old age. **senility** NOUN

senior ADJ **1** older; for children above a certain age. **2** holding a higher rank or position. NOUN a senior person; a member of a senior school. **seniority** NOUN

senior citizen NOUN an elderly person; an old-age pensioner.

senna NOUN dried pods or leaves of a tropical tree, used as a laxative.

sensation NOUN **1** a feeling produced by stimulation of a sense organ or of the mind. **2** excited interest; a person or thing producing this.

sensational ADJ causing great excitement or admiration. **sensationally** ADV

sensationalism NOUN use of or interest in exciting and shocking stories. **sensationalist** NOUN

sense NOUN **1** any of the special powers (sight, hearing, smell, taste, touch) by which a living thing becomes aware of the external world; the ability to perceive or be conscious of a thing. **2** a feeling that something is the case; awareness of or sensitivity to something; an impression received.

3 a sane and realistic outlook. 4 a meaning. 5 (**senses**) consciousness, sanity. VERB perceive by a sense or intuitively.
make sense have a meaning; be a sensible idea. **make sense of** find a meaning in.

senseless ADJ 1 foolish. 2 unconscious.

sensibility NOUN (PL **sensibilities**) sensitiveness.

sensible ADJ 1 having or showing good sense. 2 aware.
sensibly ADV

sensitive ADJ 1 readily receiving impressions or responding to stimuli; easily damaged, injured, or distressed; tactful, appreciating others' feelings. 2 (of information) likely to endanger security.
sensitively ADV
sensitivity NOUN

sensitize (also **sensitise**) VERB cause to respond readily to stimuli or a stimulus.
sensitization NOUN
sensitizer NOUN

sensor NOUN a device for detecting a particular physical property.

sensory ADJ of the senses; receiving and transmitting sensations.

sensual ADJ gratifying to the body; indulging oneself with physical pleasures.
sensualism NOUN
sensuality NOUN
sensually ADV

sensuous ADJ of the senses rather than the intellect; affecting the senses pleasantly.
sensuously ADV
sensuousness NOUN

sent past and past participle of **SEND**.

sentence NOUN 1 a series of words making a single complete statement. 2 a punishment decided by a law court. VERB pass sentence on (a person).

sententious ADJ moralizing pompously.
sententiously ADV
sententiousness NOUN

sentient ADJ capable of perceiving and feeling things.
sentience NOUN
sentiently ADV

S

sentiment NOUN **1** an opinion, view, or feeling. **2** sentimentality.

sentimental ADJ full of romantic or nostalgic feeling, especially excessively and self-indulgently so.
sentimental value value derived from something's emotional associations rather than its objective worth.
sentimentalism NOUN
sentimentality NOUN
sentimentally ADV

sentinel NOUN a sentry.

sentry NOUN (PL **sentries**) a soldier posted to keep watch and guard something.

sepal NOUN each of the leaf-like parts forming a calyx.

separate ADJ /sep-er-ăt/ not joined or united with others. VERB /sep-er-ayt/ divide; set, move, or keep apart; cease to live together as a married couple.
separability NOUN
separable ADJ
separately ADV
separation NOUN
separator NOUN

separatist NOUN a person who favours separation from a larger (especially political) unit.
separatism NOUN

sepia NOUN a reddish-brown colour or pigment.

sepsis NOUN septic condition.

September NOUN the ninth month.

septet NOUN a group of seven instruments or voices; music for these.

septic ADJ infected with harmful micro-organisms.

septicaemia /sep-ti-see-mi-a/ ([US] **septicemia**) NOUN blood poisoning.

septic tank NOUN a tank in which sewage is liquefied by bacterial activity.

septuagenarian /sept-ewr-jĕ-nair-i-ăn/ NOUN a person in his or her seventies.

sepulchre /sep-ŭl-ker/ ([US] **sepulcher**) NOUN a tomb.

sequel NOUN what follows, especially as a result; a novel or film etc.

continuing the story of an earlier one.

sequence NOUN **1** an order in which related items follow one another; a set of things belonging next to each other in a particular order. **2** a section dealing with one event or topic in a film.

sequential ADJ forming or following a logical sequence.
sequentially ADV

sequester VERB **1** isolate. **2** confiscate.

sequestrate VERB confiscate; take temporary possession of until a debt is paid etc.
sequestration NOUN

sequin NOUN a small shiny disc for decorating clothes.
sequinned ADJ

sequoia /si-**kwoi**-ă/ NOUN a Californian tree growing to a great height.

seraglio /si-**rahl**-yoh/ NOUN (PL **seraglios**) a harem.

seraph NOUN (PL **seraphim** or **seraphs**) a member of the highest order of angels.
seraphic ADJ

serenade NOUN music played for a lover, or suitable for this. VERB sing or play a serenade to.

serendipity NOUN the fortunate occurrence of events by coincidence or chance.
serendipitous ADJ

serene ADJ calm and cheerful.
serenely ADV
serenity NOUN

serf NOUN a medieval farm labourer forced to work for his landowner.
serfdom NOUN

serge NOUN strong twilled fabric.

sergeant /**sar**-jĕnt/ NOUN a non-commissioned army officer ranking just above corporal; a police officer ranking just below inspector.

serial NOUN a story presented in a series of instalments. ADJ of or forming part of a series; repeated, doing something repeatedly.
serially ADV

serialize (also **serialise**) VERB produce as a serial.
serialization NOUN

serial killer NOUN a person who murders repeatedly.

serial number NOUN a number identifying something by giving its position in a series.

series NOUN (PL **series**) a number of similar things occurring, arranged, or produced in order; a set of related television or radio programmes.

serious ADJ **1** solemn, thoughtful; sincere, in earnest. **2** requiring thought; important, not slight, significant; involving possible danger.
seriously ADV
seriousness NOUN

sermon NOUN a talk on a religious or moral subject, especially during a religious service.

sermonize (also **sermonise**) VERB give a long moralizing talk.

serpent NOUN a large snake.

serpentine ADJ twisting like a snake.

serrated ADJ having a series of small projections; saw-like.
serration NOUN

serried ADJ placed or standing close together.

serum NOUN (PL **sera** OR **serums**) fluid left when blood has clotted; this used for inoculation; a watery fluid from animal tissue.
serous ADJ

servant NOUN a person employed to do domestic work in a household or as an attendant; an employee.

serve VERB **1** perform duties or provide help for; be employed (in the army etc.). **2** be useful or suitable for something; help in achieving (a purpose). **3** present (food etc.) for others to consume; (of food) be enough for. **4** attend to (customers). **5** set the ball in play at tennis etc. **6** deliver (a legal writ etc.) to (a person). **7** spend (a period) in a post or in prison. NOUN a service in tennis etc.

server NOUN a computer or program managing access to a resource or service in a network.

service NOUN **1** an action helping someone; the action of working for someone, being employed; the activity of waiting on customers at a restaurant etc. **2** a system supplying a public need; a department run by the state. **3** (**the services**) the armed forces. **4** a religious ceremony. **5** a matching set of plates etc. **6** an act of serving in tennis etc. **7** maintenance and repair of machinery. VERB **1** perform maintenance work on (machinery). **2** provide services for. **3** pay interest on (a debt). **at someone's service** ready to assist someone when required. **be of service** assist someone.

serviceable ADJ useful, usable, functioning; hard-wearing.

service area NOUN an area beside a motorway where petrol and refreshments etc. are available.

service flat NOUN a rented flat where domestic service is provided.

serviceman (also **servicewoman**) NOUN a member of the armed forces.

service road NOUN a road giving access to houses etc. but not for use by through traffic.

service station NOUN a place beside a road selling petrol etc.

serviette NOUN a table napkin.

servile ADJ excessively submissive.
servility NOUN

servitude NOUN slavery; subjection to someone more powerful.

sesame /sess-ă-mi/ NOUN a tropical plant with seeds that yield oil or are used as food.

session NOUN a meeting or meetings for discussing something; a period spent in an activity; an academic year or term.

set VERB (**sets**, **setting**, **set**) **1** put, place, or fix in position or readiness; bring into a specified state; cause to start doing something. **2** represent (a story etc.) as taking place in a particular location. **3** fix or appoint (a date); assign as a task or problem; establish (an example, record, etc.). **4** adjust (a clock) to show the right time. **5** make or become hard, firm, or solid; become fixed. **6** (of the sun etc.) be brought below the horizon by the earth's movement. **7** (of a tide) move in a specified direction. NOUN **1** a group or collection of things or people that are alike or form a unit. **2** the way something is positioned or arranged. **3** a radio or television receiver. **4** a group of games forming a unit in a tennis match. **5** scenery for a play or film. **6** the process of styling hair. **7** variant of **SETT**.

be set on be determined to do. **set about 1** begin doing. **2** [INFORMAL] attack. **set back 1** delay the progress of. **2** [INFORMAL] cost (someone) a specified amount. **set in** (of bad weather etc.) begin and become established. **set off 1** begin a journey. **2** cause to explode. **3** make more noticeable or attractive by contrast. **set out** or **forth 1** begin a journey. **2** declare, state systematically. **set sail** begin a sea voyage. **set up 1** establish; erect. **2** [INFORMAL] cause (an innocent person) to appear guilty.

setback NOUN a delay in progress; a problem.

set piece NOUN a formal or elaborate construction.

set square NOUN a right-angled triangular drawing instrument.

sett (also **set**) NOUN **1** a badger's burrow. **2** a paving block.

settee NOUN a sofa.

setter NOUN a dog of a long-haired breed.

setting NOUN **1** the place where something is positioned or takes place. **2** a speed etc. to which a machine can be adjusted. **3** a set of cutlery or crockery laid for one person.

settle[1] VERB **1** arrange or resolve (a problem or dispute); pay (a bill); fix, decide on. **2** come to rest; adopt a more secure or steady lifestyle; place in position; become familiar with and at ease in new surroundings; come to live somewhere permanently; occupy (a previously unoccupied area). **3** become quieter or calmer. **4** bestow (property) legally.
settle for resign oneself to accepting. **settle up** pay what is owing.
settlement NOUN

settle[2] NOUN a wooden seat with a high back and arms.

settler NOUN a person who settles in unoccupied territory.

set-up NOUN [INFORMAL] an organization or arrangement; a trick.

seven ADJ & NOUN one more than six (7, VII).
seventh ADJ & NOUN

seventeen ADJ & NOUN one more than sixteen (17, XVII).
seventeenth ADJ & NOUN

seventy ADJ & NOUN seven times ten (70, LXX).
seventieth ADJ & NOUN

sever VERB cut or break off.
severance NOUN

several DETERMINER & PRON more than two but not many. ADJ separate or respective.

severally ADV separately.

severe ADJ **1** strict, harsh; (of something bad or unpleasant) intense. **2** (of style) plain, without decoration.
severely ADV
severity NOUN

sew /soh/ VERB (**sews**, **sewing**, **sewed**; PAST PARTICIPLE **sewn** or **sewed**) fasten by passing thread through material, using a needle etc.; make or fasten (a thing) by sewing.
sewer NOUN
sewing NOUN

sewage /soo-ij/ NOUN liquid waste drained from houses etc. for disposal.

sewer /soo-er/ NOUN a drain for carrying sewage.

sewerage NOUN a system

of sewers.

sewn past participle of **SEW**.

sex NOUN **1** either of the two main groups (**male** and **female**) into which living things are placed according to their reproductive functions; the fact of belonging to one of these. **2** sexual intercourse, sexual activity. VERB judge the sex of.

sexagenarian NOUN a person in his or her sixties.

sexist ADJ discriminating in favour of members of one sex; assuming a person's abilities and social functions are predetermined by his or her sex. NOUN a person who does this.

sexism NOUN

S

sexless ADJ **1** not involving sexual desire or activity. **2** neither male nor female.

sextant NOUN an instrument for finding one's position by measuring the height of the sun etc.

sextet NOUN a group of six instruments or voices; music for these.

sexton NOUN an official in charge of a church and churchyard.

sextuplet NOUN one of six children born at one birth.

sexual ADJ **1** of sex; (of reproduction) occurring by fusion of male and female cells. **2** of the two sexes.

sexually ADV

sexual intercourse NOUN sexual contact involving penetration, especially the insertion of the penis into the vagina.

sexuality NOUN capacity for sexual feelings; a person's sexual orientation.

sexy ADJ (**sexier**, **sexiest**) [INFORMAL] sexually attractive or stimulating.

sexily ADV

sexiness NOUN

shabby ADJ (**shabbier**, **shabbiest**) **1** worn; dilapidated; poorly dressed. **2** unfair, dishonourable.

shabbily ADV

shack NOUN a roughly built hut.

shackle NOUN one of a pair of metal rings joined by a chain, for fastening a prisoner's wrists or ankles. VERB put shackles on; impede, restrict.

shade NOUN **1** comparative darkness; a place sheltered from the sun; a screen or cover used to block or moderate light; (**shades**) sunglasses. **2** a colour, a degree of lightness or darkness in a colour; a slightly different variety of something; a trace, a slight amount. VERB **1** block the rays of; give shade to; darken (parts of a drawing etc.). **2** pass gradually into another colour or variety.

shadow NOUN **1** a dark area produced by an object coming between light and a surface; partial darkness; a dark patch. **2** gloom; something spoiling happiness. **3** a slight trace. **4** an inseparable companion or follower. VERB **1** cast shadow over. **2** follow and watch secretly.
shadower NOUN
shadowy ADJ

shadow-boxing NOUN boxing against an imaginary opponent as a form of training.

Shadow Cabinet NOUN members of the main opposition party in Parliament holding posts parallel to those of the government Cabinet.

shady ADJ (**shadier**, **shadiest**) **1** giving shade; situated in shade. **2** [INFORMAL] disreputable, not completely honest.
shadily ADV
shadiness NOUN

shaft NOUN **1** a long, slender, straight handle etc.; an arrow or spear; a ray or beam; a long rotating rod transmitting power in a machine; each of the two poles between which a horse is harnessed to a vehicle. **2** a vertical or sloping passage or opening.

shag NOUN **1** a shaggy mass. **2** a strong coarse tobacco. **3** a cormorant. ADJ (of a carpet) with a long rough pile.

shaggy ADJ (**shaggier**, **shaggiest**) having long rough hair or fibre; (of hair etc.) rough and thick.
shagginess NOUN

shaggy-dog story NOUN [INFORMAL] a long, inconsequential story or joke.

shah NOUN a title of the former ruler of Iran.

shake VERB (**shakes**, **shaking**, **shook**; PAST PARTICIPLE **shaken**) **1** tremble or vibrate, or cause to do so. **2** move quickly up and down or from side to side; dislodge by doing this. **3** shock or astonish; make (a belief or position) less firm. NOUN an act of shaking.
shake down become settled. **shake hands** clasp right hands in greeting, parting, or agreement. **shake off** [INFORMAL] get rid of. **shake on** [INFORMAL] confirm (an agreement) by shaking hands. **shake up 1** mix by shaking. **2** rouse by startling or shocking.
shaker NOUN

shake-up NOUN [INFORMAL] an upheaval, a reorganization.

shaky ADJ (**shakier**, **shakiest**) shaking; unstable; unreliable.
shakily ADV
shakiness NOUN

shale NOUN stone that splits easily.

shall AUXILIARY VERB used with *I* and *we* to express future tense, and with *you*, *he*, *she*, *it*, or *they* to express obligation or determination.

shallot NOUN a small onion-like plant.

shallow ADJ of little depth; not showing or requiring much thought, superficial. VERB become less deep. NOUN (**shallows**) a shallow area in a river etc.
shallowness NOUN

shalom /shă-**lom**/ NOUN a Jewish expression of greeting or leave-taking.

sham NOUN a pretence; something that is not genuine. ADJ pretended; not genuine. VERB (**shams**, **shamming**, **shammed**) pretend; fake.

shamble VERB walk or run in a shuffling or lazy way.

shambles NOUN [INFORMAL] a scene or condition of great disorder.

shame NOUN a painful mental feeling aroused by having done something dishonourable or ridiculous; the ability to feel this; loss of respect; a cause of this; something regrettable: *it's a shame you can't stay.* VERB cause to feel ashamed; provoke to action in this way.
shameful ADJ
shamefully ADV
shameless ADJ
shamelessly ADV

shamefaced ADJ looking ashamed.

shammy NOUN (PL **shammies**) [INFORMAL] a chamois leather.

shampoo NOUN a liquid used to wash hair; a preparation for cleaning upholstery etc.; the process of shampooing. VERB wash or clean with shampoo.

shamrock NOUN a clover-like plant.

shandy NOUN (PL **shandies**) a mixed drink of beer and lemonade or ginger beer.

shank NOUN a leg, especially from knee to ankle; the shaft or stem of a tool or implement.

shanty NOUN (PL **shanties**) **1** a shack. **2** a sailors' traditional song.

shanty town NOUN an area of makeshift housing of rough shacks.

shape NOUN **1** an area or form with a definite outline; structure, orderly arrangement. **2** the condition of something: *in good shape.* VERB give a shape to; influence the nature of.
shape up 1 develop in a particular way. **2** [INFORMAL] improve.
shapeless ADJ

shapely ADJ (**shapelier, shapeliest**) having an attractive shape.
shapeliness NOUN

shard NOUN a broken piece of pottery.

share NOUN **1** a part given to one person out of something divided among several; an amount that someone is entitled to or required to have. **2** one of the equal parts forming a business company's capital and entitling the holder to a proportion of the profits. VERB give or have a share (of).

sharer NOUN

shareholder NOUN an owner of shares in a company.

shareware NOUN computer programs freely available for trial, paid for by a fee to the author if used regularly.

shark NOUN **1** a large voracious sea fish. **2** [INFORMAL] an unscrupulous swindler or exploiter.

sharkskin NOUN a fabric with a slightly lustrous textured weave.

S

sharp ADJ **1** having a fine edge or point capable of cutting; tapering to a point; (of a remark etc.) hurtful, intended to hurt. **2** distinct, well-defined. **3** abrupt, sudden. **4** alert; perceiving keenly. **5** (of tastes or smells) causing a smarting sensation. **6** unscrupulous. **7** [MUSIC] above the correct or normal pitch; (of a note) a semitone higher than a specified note. ADV **1** punctually, exactly. **2** abruptly; at a sharp angle. **3** above the correct pitch. NOUN [MUSIC] (a sign indicating) a note raised by a semitone.

sharply ADV

sharpness NOUN

sharpen VERB make or become sharp or sharper.

sharpener NOUN

sharp practice NOUN barely honest dealings.

sharpshooter NOUN a skilled marksman.

shatter VERB break violently into small pieces; destroy utterly; distress greatly.

shave VERB **1** cut (growing hair) from (the face or other part of the body). **2** cut (a thin slice) from a surface. **3** pass very close to. NOUN an act of shaving hair from the face.

a close shave [INFORMAL] a narrow escape.

shaver NOUN

shaven ADJ shaved.

shaving NOUN a thin strip

of wood etc. shaved from a surface.

shawl NOUN a large piece of soft fabric worn round the shoulders or wrapped round a baby.

she PRON the female previously mentioned. NOUN a female.

s/he PRON a written representation of 'he or she'.

sheaf NOUN (PL **sheaves**) a bundle of corn stalks; a similar bundle.

shear VERB (**shears**, **shearing**, **sheared**; PAST PARTICIPLE **shorn** or **sheared**) **1** cut or trim with shears or some other sharp device. **2** break because of strain.
shearer NOUN

shears PLURAL NOUN a large cutting instrument shaped like scissors.

sheath /sheeth/ NOUN a close-fitting cover, especially for a blade or tool; a condom.

sheathe /shee*th*/ VERB put into a sheath; encase in a tight covering.

shed NOUN a building for storing things, or for use as a workshop. VERB (**sheds**, **shedding**, **shed**) lose (leaves etc.) by a natural falling; discard; lose (a load) accidentally.

sheen NOUN gloss, lustre.
sheeny ADJ

sheep NOUN (PL **sheep**) a grass-eating animal with a thick fleecy coat.

sheepdog NOUN a dog trained to guard and herd sheep.

sheepish ADJ feeling shy or foolish.
sheepishly ADV
sheepishness NOUN

sheepskin NOUN a sheep's skin with the fleece on.

sheer ADJ **1** pure, not mixed or qualified. **2** very steep. **3** (of fabric) very thin, transparent. ADV straight up or down. VERB swerve from a course.
sheerly ADV
sheerness NOUN

sheet NOUN **1** a piece of cotton or other fabric used to cover a bed. **2** a large thin piece of glass, metal, paper, etc. **3** an expanse of water, flame, etc. **4** a rope securing the lower corner of a sail.

sheet anchor NOUN a very dependable person or thing.

sheikh /shayk/ NOUN an Arab ruler.
sheikhdom NOUN

shekel NOUN a unit of money in Israel; (**shekels**) [INFORMAL] money, riches.

shelf NOUN (PL **shelves**) a flat piece of wood etc. fastened to a wall etc. for things to be placed on; a ledge of rock.
on the shelf [INFORMAL] not wanted, especially for marriage.

shelf life NOUN the time for which a stored thing remains usable.

shell NOUN **1** the hard outer covering of eggs, nut kernels, and of animals such as snails and tortoises; the outer structure or form of something, especially when hollow. **2** a metal case filled with explosive, fired from a large gun. VERB **1** remove the shell(s) of. **2** fire explosive shells at.
shell out [INFORMAL] pay (a sum of money).

shellac NOUN a resinous substance used in varnish. VERB (**shellacs, shellacking, shellacked**) coat with this.

shellfish NOUN (PL **shellfish**) an edible water animal that has a shell.

shell shock NOUN psychological disturbance from exposure to battle conditions.

shelter NOUN a structure that shields against danger, wind, rain, etc.; protection. VERB provide with shelter; find or take shelter.

shelve VERB **1** put on a shelf. **2** postpone or cancel. **3** slope.

shelving NOUN shelves.

shepherd NOUN a person who tends sheep. VERB guide (people).

shepherd's pie NOUN a pie of minced meat topped with mashed potato.

sherbet NOUN a sweet powder made into an effervescent drink.

sheriff NOUN the Crown's chief executive officer in

a county; a judge in Scotland; [US] the chief law-enforcing officer of a county.

Sherpa NOUN a member of a Himalayan people of Nepal and Tibet.

sherry NOUN (PL **sherries**) a fortified wine.

Shia /shee-ă/ NOUN (PL **Shia** or **Shias**) one of the two main branches of Islam; a Muslim who adheres to this branch of Islam.

shiatsu NOUN a Japanese therapy involving the application of pressure to points on the body.

shibboleth NOUN a principle etc. generally thought obsolete but considered essential by a particular group.

shield NOUN **1** a broad piece of metal etc. carried for protection; any source of protection. **2** a shield-shaped trophy.
VERB protect.

shift VERB move or cause to move from one place or position to another; transfer (blame etc.); [INFORMAL] move quickly; [INFORMAL] sell. NOUN **1** a slight change in position etc. **2** a set of workers who start work when another set finishes; the time for which they work.

shiftless ADJ lazy and inefficient.

shifty ADJ (**shiftier**, **shiftiest**) [INFORMAL] evasive; untrustworthy.
shiftily ADV
shiftiness NOUN

Shiite /shee-It/ NOUN a follower of the Shia branch of Islam.

shilly-shally VERB (**shilly-shallies**, **shilly-shallying**, **shilly-shallied**) be indecisive.

shim NOUN a thin wedge used to make parts of machinery fit together.

shimmer VERB shine with a soft wavering light. NOUN such a light.

shin NOUN the front of the leg below the knee; the lower foreleg.
shin up (**shins**, **shinning**, **shinned**) climb quickly.

shindig NOUN [INFORMAL] a lively party; a noisy disturbance.

shine VERB **1** (**shines**, **shining**, **shone**) give out

or reflect light, be bright; direct (a torch etc.) a particular way; be excellent or outstanding. **2** (**shined**, **shining**) polish. NOUN brightness.
take a shine to [INFORMAL] develop a liking for.

shingle NOUN **1** a mass of small round pebbles on a beach etc. **2** a wooden roof tile. **3** (**shingles**) a disease with a rash of small blisters.
shingly ADJ

Shinto NOUN a Japanese religion revering ancestors and nature spirits.
Shintoism NOUN

shiny ADJ (**shinier**, **shiniest**) shining, glossy.
shininess NOUN

ship NOUN a large seagoing vessel. VERB (**ships**, **shipping**, **shipped**) transport on a ship.
ship off take or send away.
shipper NOUN

shipmate NOUN a person travelling or working on the same ship as another.

shipment NOUN the shipping of goods; a consignment shipped.

shipping NOUN ships collectively.

shipshape ADJ in good order, tidy.

shipwreck NOUN the destruction of a ship by storm or striking rocks etc.
shipwrecked ADJ

shipyard NOUN an establishment where ships are built.

shire NOUN a county.

shire horse NOUN a horse of a heavy powerful breed.

shirk VERB avoid (duty or work etc.) selfishly.
shirker NOUN

shirt NOUN a lightweight garment for the upper part of the body.

shirty ADJ (**shirtier**, **shirtiest**) [INFORMAL] annoyed, angry.

shit [VULGAR SLANG] NOUN **1** faeces. **2** a contemptible person. VERB (**shits**, **shitting**, **shitted** or **shat** or **shit**) empty the bowels.

shiver VERB **1** tremble slightly, especially with cold or fear. **2** shatter. NOUN a shivering

movement.
shivery ADJ

shoal NOUN **1** a large number of fish swimming together. **2** a shallow place; an underwater sandbank. VERB form shoals.

shock NOUN **1** a sudden surprising and distressing experience, the feeling caused by this; acute weakness caused by injury, loss of blood, etc. **2** a violent impact or tremor. **3** a bushy mass of hair. VERB surprise and distress; scandalize.
shocker NOUN

shocking ADJ causing outrage or indignation; very surprising and distressing; [INFORMAL] very bad or unpleasant.

shod past and past participle of **SHOE**.

shoddy ADJ (**shoddier**, **shoddiest**) badly made or done.
shoddily ADV
shoddiness NOUN

shoe NOUN **1** an outer covering for a person's foot. **2** a horseshoe. **3** the part of a brake that presses against a wheel. VERB (**shoes, shoeing**, **shod**) fit with a shoe or shoes.

shoehorn NOUN a curved implement for easing one's heel into a shoe.

shoelace NOUN a cord for lacing up shoes.

shoeshine NOUN [US] an act of polishing someone's shoes.

shoestring NOUN **1** [INFORMAL] a barely adequate amount of money. **2** [US] a shoelace.

shoe tree NOUN a shaped block for keeping a shoe in shape.

shone past and past participle of **SHINE**.

shoo EXCLAMATION a sound uttered to frighten animals away.
VERB (**shoos, shooing**, **shooed**) drive away.

shook past of **SHAKE**.

shoot VERB (**shoots**, **shooting**, **shot**) **1** fire (a gun or missile); kill or wound with a missile from a gun etc.; hunt with a gun for sport. **2** move or propel swiftly and suddenly. **3** aim a ball at a goal. **4** film or

S

photograph. **5** (of a plant) put out shoots. NOUN a young branch or new growth of a plant.
shoot up rise suddenly; grow rapidly.
shooter NOUN

shooting star NOUN a small meteor seen to move quickly.

shooting stick NOUN a walking stick with a small folding seat in the handle.

shop NOUN **1** a building where goods or services are sold to the public. **2** a workshop. VERB (**shops**, **shopping**, **shopped**) **1** buy things from shops. **2** [INFORMAL] inform against.
shop around look for the best bargain. **talk shop** discuss one's work in a social setting.
shopper NOUN

shop floor NOUN workers as distinct from management.

shoplifter NOUN a person who steals goods from a shop.
shoplifting NOUN

shopping NOUN the action of buying goods in shops; the goods bought.

shop-soiled ADJ dirty or damaged from being on display in a shop.

shop steward NOUN a trade union official elected by workers as their spokesperson.

shore NOUN the land along the edge of the sea or a lake. VERB prop or support with a length of timber.

shorn past participle of **SHEAR**.

short ADJ **1** measuring little from end to end in space or time, or from head to foot. **2** not having enough of something; insufficient. **3** uncivilly curt. **4** (of pastry) crisp and easily crumbled. ADV not going far enough. NOUN **1** a small drink of spirits. **2** a short circuit. **3** (**shorts**) trousers reaching to the knee or thigh; [US] underpants. VERB short-circuit.

shortage NOUN a lack, an insufficiency.

shortbread (also **shortcake**) NOUN a rich sweet biscuit.

short-change VERB cheat,

S

especially by giving insufficient change.

short circuit NOUN a fault in an electrical circuit when current flows by a shorter route than the normal one. VERB (**short-circuit**) malfunction or cause to malfunction because of a short circuit; shorten or speed up (a process) improperly.

shortcoming NOUN failure to reach a required standard; a fault.

short cut NOUN a quicker route or method.

shorten VERB make or become shorter.

shortening NOUN fat used to make pastry etc.

shortfall NOUN a deficit.

shorthand NOUN a method of writing rapidly with quickly made symbols.

short-handed ADJ having insufficient workers.

shortlist NOUN a list of selected candidates from which a final choice will be made. VERB put on a shortlist.

shortly ADV **1** after a short time. **2** in a few words; curtly.

short-sighted ADJ able to see clearly only what is close; lacking foresight.

short ton *see* **TON**.

short wave NOUN a radio wave of frequency greater than 3 MHz.

shot[1] past and past participle of **SHOOT**.
shot through with suffused or interspersed with.

shot[2] NOUN **1** a firing of a gun etc., the sound of this; a person of specified skill in shooting. **2** an attempt to hit a target, put a ball in goal, etc.; a stroke in tennis etc.; [INFORMAL] an attempt. **3** a heavy ball used as a missile or thrown as a sport; ammunition. **4** a photograph. **5** [INFORMAL] a measure of spirits; an injection.
like a shot [INFORMAL] without hesitation.

shotgun NOUN a gun for firing small shot at close range.

should AUXILIARY VERB used to express duty or obligation, a possible or expected future event, or (with *I* and *we*) a polite statement or a conditional or indefinite clause.

shoulder NOUN the part of the body where the arm or foreleg is attached; an animal's upper foreleg as a joint of meat. VERB **1** assume (a burden or responsibility). **2** push with one's shoulder.

shoulder blade NOUN the large flat bone of the shoulder.

shout NOUN a loud cry or utterance. VERB utter a shout; call loudly.
shout down silence by shouting.

shove NOUN a rough push. VERB push roughly; make one's way by pushing; [INFORMAL] put down carelessly.
shove off 1 push away from the shore in a boat. **2** [INFORMAL] go away.

shovel NOUN a spade-like tool for moving sand, snow, etc. VERB (**shovels**, **shovelling**, **shovelled**; [US] **shoveling**, **shoveled**) shift or clear with or as if with a shovel; scoop or thrust roughly.

show VERB (**shows**, **showing**, **showed**; PAST PARTICIPLE **shown**) **1** allow or cause to be seen, present to view; visibly or clearly possess (a characteristic); be visible; represent, depict. **2** demonstrate or prove (something) to (someone). **3** treat (someone) with (a specified characteristic): *show him mercy*. **4** guide, lead. NOUN a spectacle; a public exhibition or performance; outward appearance, especially when misleading.
show off 1 display. **2** try to impress people. **show of hands** a vote by the raising of hands. **show up 1** make conspicuous; emphasize the failings of. **2** [INFORMAL] arrive.

show business NOUN the entertainment profession.

showdown NOUN a confrontation that settles an argument.

shower NOUN **1** a brief fall of rain or of snow, stones, etc. **2** a device spraying water over someone's body; a cubicle containing this; a wash in this. **3** a sudden influx of letters or gifts etc. **4** [US] a party for giving presents. VERB **1** fall or cause to fall in a shower; throw a number of things at or give a number of things to. **2** wash in a shower.

showerproof ADJ (of fabric) able to keep out light rain. VERB make showerproof.

showery ADJ with showers of rain.

showjumping NOUN the competitive sport of riding horses to jump over obstacles. **showjumper** NOUN

showman NOUN an organizer of circuses or theatrical entertainments.

showmanship NOUN skill in presenting entertainment or goods etc. well.

shown past participle of **SHOW**.

showpiece NOUN an excellent specimen used for exhibition.

showroom NOUN a room where goods are displayed for inspection.

showy ADJ (**showier**, **showiest**) striking; ostentatious or gaudy. **showily** ADV **showiness** NOUN

shrank past of **SHRINK**.

shrapnel NOUN pieces of metal scattered from an exploding bomb.

shred NOUN a small strip torn or cut from something; a small amount. VERB (**shreds**, **shredding**, **shredded**) tear or cut into shreds. **shredder** NOUN

shrew NOUN a small mouse-like animal.

shrewd ADJ showing sound judgement, clever. **shrewdly** ADV **shrewdness** NOUN

shriek NOUN a shrill cry or scream. VERB utter (with) a shriek.

shrill ADJ piercing and high-pitched in sound. **shrilly** ADV

shrimp NOUN **1** a small edible shellfish. **2** [INFORMAL] a very small person.

shrine NOUN a sacred or

revered place.

shrink VERB (**shrinks**, **shrinking**, **shrank**; PAST PARTICIPLE **shrunk**) **1** make or become smaller. **2** draw back in fear or disgust. NOUN [INFORMAL] a psychiatrist.

shrinkage NOUN the shrinking of textile fabric.

shrive VERB (**shrives**, **shriving**, **shrove**; PAST PARTICIPLE **shriven**) [ARCHAIC] hear the confession of and absolve.

shrivel VERB (**shrivels**, **shrivelling**, **shrivelled**; [US] **shriveling**, **shriveled**) shrink and wrinkle from heat or cold or lack of moisture.

shroud NOUN **1** a cloth wrapping a dead body for burial; something that conceals. **2** one of the ropes supporting a ship's mast. VERB wrap in a shroud; conceal.

shrub NOUN a woody plant smaller than a tree.

shrubbery NOUN (PL **shrubberies**) an area planted with shrubs.

shrug VERB (**shrugs**, **shrugging**, **shrugged**) raise (one's shoulders) as a gesture of indifference, doubt, or helplessness. NOUN this movement.

shrunk past participle of **SHRINK**.

shrunken ADJ having shrunk.

shudder VERB shiver or shake violently. NOUN this movement.

shuffle VERB **1** walk without lifting one's feet clear of the ground. **2** rearrange, jumble. NOUN **1** a shuffling movement or walk. **2** a rearrangement.
shuffle off avoid (a responsibility).

shun VERB (**shuns**, **shunning**, **shunned**) avoid.

shunt VERB move (a train) to a side track; divert.

shush [INFORMAL] EXCLAMATION & VERB hush.

shut VERB (**shuts**, **shutting**, **shut**) move (a door or window etc.) into position to block an opening; be moved in this way; block an opening into

(something); keep (someone or something) in a place by blocking an opening; bring together the sides of (a book etc.); make (a shop etc.) or become unavailable for business.
shut down stop or cease working or business. **shut off** stop the supply of.
shut up 1 close.
2 [INFORMAL] be quiet.

shut-eye NOUN [INFORMAL] sleep.

shutter NOUN a screen that can be closed over a window; a device that opens and closes the aperture of a camera.
shuttered ADJ

shuttle NOUN **1** a form of transport travelling frequently between places. **2** a spacecraft for repeated use. **3** a device carrying the weft thread in weaving. VERB move, travel, or send to and fro.

shuttlecock NOUN a small cone-shaped feathered object struck to and fro in badminton.

shy ADJ (**shyer**, **shyest**) nervous in company, lacking self-confidence. VERB (**shies**, **shying**, **shied**) **1** jump in alarm; avoid something through nervousness. **2** throw at a target.
shyly ADV
shyness NOUN

SI ABBREV Système International, the international system of units of measurement.

Siamese ADJ of Siam, the former name of Thailand.

Siamese cat NOUN a cat with pale fur and darker face, paws, and tail.

Siamese twins PLURAL NOUN twins whose bodies are joined at birth.

sibling NOUN a brother or sister.

sibyl NOUN a prophetess.

sic ADV thus (indicating that a quotation is exact though its wording or spelling appears wrong).

Sicilian NOUN a person from Sicily. ADJ relating to Sicily.

sick ADJ **1** unwell; suffering from nausea. **2** tired of or bored with something.
3 [INFORMAL] finding amusement in misfortune

or morbid subjects.

sicken VERB **1** become ill. **2** distress; disgust. **be sickening for** be in the first stages of (a disease).

sickle NOUN a curved blade used for cutting corn etc.

sickly ADJ (**sicklier**, **sickliest**) **1** often ill; weak. **2** causing nausea; distastefully sentimental. **sickliness** NOUN

sickness NOUN the state of being ill; nausea or vomiting.

side NOUN **1** a surface of an object, especially one that is not the top, bottom, front, back, or end; a bounding line of a plane figure; a slope of a hill or ridge. **2** a part near the edge and away from the middle. **3** a position to the left or right of someone or something; either of the halves into which something is divided; an aspect of a problem etc. **4** one of two opposing groups or teams. ADJ at or on the side.
on the side as a sideline; as a surreptitious activity. **side by side** close together. **side with** support in a dispute.

sideboard NOUN **1** a piece of dining-room furniture with drawers and cupboards for china etc. **2** (**sideboards**) [INFORMAL] sideburns.

sideburns PLURAL NOUN short whiskers on the cheeks.

side effect NOUN a secondary (usually bad) effect.

sidelight NOUN one of two small lights on either side of a vehicle.

sideline NOUN **1** something done in addition to one's main activity. **2** (**sidelines**) lines bounding the sides of a football pitch etc.; a place for spectators; a position etc. apart from the main action. VERB remove from the centre of activity or influence.

sidelong ADJ & ADV sideways.

sidereal /sy-**deer**-i-ăl/ ADJ of or measured by the stars.

side saddle NOUN a saddle on which a woman rider

S

sits with both legs on the same side of the horse. ADV (**side-saddle**) sitting in this way.

sideshow NOUN a small show forming part of a large one.

sidestep VERB (**sidesteps**, **sidestepping**, **sidestepped**) avoid by stepping sideways; evade.

sidetrack VERB divert; distract.

sidewalk NOUN [US] a pavement.

sideways ADV & ADJ to or from one side; with one side forward.

siding NOUN a short track by the side of a railway, used in shunting.

sidle VERB advance in a furtive or stealthy way.

siege NOUN the surrounding and blockading of a place by armed forces in order to capture it.

sienna NOUN a brownish clay used as colouring matter.

sierra /see-**air**-ă/ NOUN a chain of mountains with jagged peaks, especially in Spain or Spanish America.

siesta NOUN an afternoon nap or rest, especially in hot countries.

sieve /siv/ NOUN a utensil with a mesh through which liquids or fine particles can pass. VERB separate out by putting through a sieve.

sift VERB **1** sieve. **2** examine carefully and select or analyse.

sigh NOUN a long deep breath given out audibly in sadness, tiredness, relief, etc. VERB give or express with a sigh.

sight NOUN **1** the ability to see; the act of seeing; the distance within which one can see. **2** something seen or worth seeing; [INFORMAL] an unsightly thing. **3** a device looked through to aim or observe with a gun or telescope etc. VERB **1** see, catch sight of. **2** aim at with a sight.
at or **on sight** as soon as seen. **catch sight of** see, notice.

sightless ADJ blind.

sight-read VERB play or sing (music) without

preliminary study of the score.

sightseeing NOUN the activity of visiting places of interest.
sightseer NOUN

sign NOUN **1** something perceived that suggests the existence of a quality, a future occurrence, etc. **2** a notice displayed to give information or instructions. **3** an action or gesture conveying information etc. **4** any of the twelve divisions of the zodiac. VERB **1** write (one's name) on (a document); indicate agreement to (something) by doing this. **2** make a sign.
sign in sign a register on arrival. **sign on 1** take into one's employment. **2** register as unemployed. **sign up** commit oneself to a period of employment, education, etc.

S

signal NOUN **1** a sign or gesture giving information or a command; an apparatus indicating whether a railway line is clear. **2** a sequence of electrical impulses or radio waves transmitted or received. VERB (**signals**, **signalling**, **signalled**; [US] **signaling**, **signaled**) make a signal or signals; communicate with or announce in this way. ADJ noteworthy.
signaller NOUN
signally ADV

signal box NOUN a small railway building with signalling apparatus.

signalman NOUN a person responsible for operating railway signals.

signatory NOUN (PL **signatories**) one of the parties who sign an agreement.

signature NOUN **1** a person's name or initials written by himself or herself in signing something. **2** an indication of key or tempo at the beginning of a musical score.

signature tune NOUN a tune used to announce a particular performer or programme.

signet ring NOUN a finger ring with an engraved

design.

significance NOUN
1 importance. **2** the meaning of something.
significant ADJ
significantly ADV

signification NOUN meaning.

signify VERB (**signifies**, **signifying**, **signified**) indicate; have as a meaning; be important, matter.

signpost NOUN a post with arms showing the direction of and distance to certain places.

Sikh /seek/ NOUN a member of an Indian religious sect.
Sikhism NOUN

silage /sI-lij/ NOUN green fodder stored and fermented in a silo.

silence NOUN the absence of sound or of speaking; the withholding of information. VERB make silent.

silencer NOUN a device for reducing sound.

silent ADJ without sound; not speaking; not giving information.
silently ADV

silhouette /sil-oo-et/ NOUN a dark shadow or outline seen against a light background. VERB show as a silhouette.

silica NOUN a compound of silicon occurring as quartz and in sandstone etc.
siliceous ADJ

silicate NOUN a compound of silicon.

silicon NOUN a chemical element.

silicon chip NOUN a silicon microchip.

silicone NOUN an organic compound of silicon, used in paint, varnish, and lubricants.

silicosis NOUN a lung disease caused by inhaling dust that contains silica.

silk NOUN a fine strong soft fibre produced by silkworms; thread or cloth made from this.
silky ADJ

silken ADJ made of silk; soft and lustrous like silk.

silkworm NOUN a caterpillar which spins its cocoon of silk.

sill NOUN a strip of stone,

wood, or metal at the base of a doorway or window opening.

silly ADJ (**sillier**, **silliest**) lacking good sense, foolish; frivolous.
silliness NOUN

silo /sI-loh/ NOUN (PL **silos**) **1** a pit or airtight structure for holding silage. **2** a pit or tower for storing grain, cement, or radioactive waste. **3** an underground place where a missile is kept ready for firing.

silt NOUN sediment deposited by water in a channel or harbour etc. VERB block or become blocked with silt.

silvan variant of **SYLVAN**.

silver NOUN a white precious metal; articles made of this; coins made of an alloy resembling it; household cutlery; the colour of silver. ADJ made of or coloured like silver.

silverfish NOUN (PL **silverfish**) a small wingless insect.

silver jubilee NOUN the 25th anniversary of a significant event.

silverside NOUN a joint of beef cut from the haunch, below topside.

silver wedding NOUN the 25th anniversary of a wedding.

silvery ADJ **1** like silver. **2** having a clear gentle ringing sound.

simian /sim-ee-ăn/ ADJ monkey-like, ape-like.

similar ADJ alike but not identical.
similarity NOUN
similarly ADV

simile /sim-i-lee/ NOUN a figure of speech in which one thing is compared to another.

similitude NOUN similarity.

simmer VERB **1** boil very gently; cause to do this. **2** be in a state of barely suppressed anger or excitement.
simmer down become calmer or quieter.

simper VERB smile in an affected way. NOUN an affected smile.

simple ADJ **1** easy to understand or do, not complicated. **2** not elaborate or showy; not

proud or extravagant. 3 having only one element, not compound. 4 feeble-minded.
simplicity NOUN
simply ADV

simpleton NOUN a foolish or feeble-minded person.

simplify VERB (**simplifies**, **simplifying**, **simplified**) make easier or less complex.
simplification NOUN

simplistic ADJ oversimplified.
simplistically ADV

simulate VERB imitate; pretend to feel; produce a computer model of.
simulation NOUN
simulator NOUN

simultaneous ADJ occurring at the same time.
simultaneity NOUN
simultaneously ADV

sin NOUN the breaking of a religious or moral law; an act which does this. VERB (**sins**, **sinning**, **sinned**) commit a sin. ABBREV sine.
sinner NOUN

since PREP from (a specified time or event) until the present. CONJ 1 from the time that. 2 because. ADV since that time or event.

sincere ADJ without pretence or deceit.
sincerely ADV
sincerity NOUN

sine NOUN [MATHEMATICS] the ratio of the side opposite an angle (in a right-angled triangle) to the hypotenuse.

sinecure /sI-nĕ-kewr/ NOUN a profitable or prestigious position requiring no work.

sine qua non /sin-ay kwah **nohn**/ NOUN an indispensable condition.

sinew NOUN tough fibrous tissue joining muscle to bone; a tendon; (**sinews**) muscles, strength.
sinewy ADJ

sinful ADJ wicked.
sinfully ADV
sinfulness NOUN

sing VERB (**sings**, **singing**, **sang**; PAST PARTICIPLE **sung**) make musical sounds with the voice; perform (a song); make a humming sound; recount, celebrate.
singer NOUN

singe /sinj/ VERB (**singes**,

singeing, **singed**) burn slightly; burn the ends or edges of. NOUN a slight burn.

single ADJ **1** only one; individual and distinct; designed for one person; unmarried. **2** having only one part, not complex or multiple; (of a ticket) valid for an outward journey only. NOUN an individual person or thing; a room for one person; a single ticket; a pop record with one piece of music on each side; (**singles**) unmarried people; (**singles**) a game with one player on each side.
single out choose or distinguish from others.
singly ADV

single-handed ADJ & ADV done without help from others.

S

single market NOUN an association of countries trading without restrictions.

single-minded ADJ with one's mind set on a single purpose.

single parent NOUN a person bringing up a child or children without a partner.

singlet NOUN a sleeveless vest.

singleton NOUN a single thing or person of a particular kind.

sing-song ADJ with a monotonous rise and fall of the voice. NOUN informal singing by a group of people.

singular NOUN the form of a noun or verb used in referring to one person or thing. ADJ **1** of this form. **2** uncommon, extraordinary.
singularity NOUN
singularly ADV

sinister ADJ suggesting that something evil or harmful is at hand.

sink VERB (**sinks**, **sinking**, **sank**; PAST PARTICIPLE **sunk**) **1** go down below the surface of a liquid, cause to do this; become lower, move downwards; gradually penetrate the surface of something; decrease in amount or value. **2** send (a ball) into a pocket or hole. **3** invest (money). NOUN a fixed basin with taps and a

drainage pipe.
sink in be realized or understood.

sinker NOUN a weight used to sink a fishing line etc.

sinking fund NOUN money set aside regularly for repayment of a debt etc.

sinuous ADJ curving, undulating.

sinus /sy-nŭs/ NOUN a cavity in bone or tissue, especially that connecting with the nostrils.

sinusitis NOUN inflammation of the nasal sinus.

sip VERB (**sips**, **sipping**, **sipped**) drink in small mouthfuls. NOUN an amount sipped.

siphon NOUN a bent pipe or tube used for transferring liquid using atmospheric pressure; a bottle from which soda water etc. is forced out by pressure of gas. VERB draw out (liquid) through a siphon; take from a source, especially dishonestly.

sir NOUN a polite form of address to a man; (**Sir**) the title of a knight or baronet.

sire NOUN an animal's male parent. VERB be the sire of.

siren NOUN **1** a device that makes a loud prolonged sound as a signal or warning. **2** a dangerously fascinating woman.

sirloin NOUN the upper (best) part of a loin of beef.

sirocco NOUN (PL **siroccos**) a hot wind that reaches Italy from Africa.

sisal /sy-săl/ NOUN rope-fibre made from a tropical plant.

sissy NOUN (PL **sissies**) [INFORMAL] a weak or timid person.

sister NOUN **1** a daughter of the same parents as another person. **2** a woman who is a fellow member of a group. **3** a nun. **4** a senior female nurse.
sisterly ADJ

sisterhood NOUN **1** the relationship of sisters. **2** an order of nuns. **3** a group of women with common aims.

sister-in-law NOUN (PL

sisters-in-law) a sister of one's husband or wife; the wife of one's brother.

sit VERB (**sits**, **sitting**, **sat**) **1** take or be in a position with the body resting on the buttocks; cause to sit; (of animals) rest with legs bent and body on the ground; (of birds) perch; have room for (a specified number) to sit; pose for a portrait; (of birds) remain on the nest to hatch eggs. **2** be situated. **3** be a candidate; take (an examination); (of a committee etc.) hold a session.
sit tight [INFORMAL] remain firmly in place.

sitar NOUN a guitar-like Indian musical instrument.

sitcom NOUN [INFORMAL] a situation comedy.

site NOUN the place where something is, was, or is to be located. VERB locate, provide with a site.

sitter NOUN a babysitter; an artist's model.

sitting NOUN a period spent seated, especially while engaged in a particular activity; a session of a committee etc.; a scheduled period for a group to be served in a restaurant.

sitting room NOUN a room in a house used for relaxed sitting in.

sitting tenant NOUN a tenant already in occupation.

situated ADJ in a specified position or condition.
situate VERB

situation NOUN the place (with its surroundings) occupied by something; a set of circumstances; a position of employment.
situational ADJ

situation comedy NOUN (PL **situation comedies**) a broadcast comedy involving the same characters in a series of episodes.

six ADJ & NOUN one more than five (6, VI).
sixth ADJ & NOUN

sixteen ADJ & NOUN one more than fifteen (16, XVI).
sixteenth ADJ & NOUN

sixty ADJ & NOUN six times ten (60, LX).
sixtieth ADJ & NOUN

size¹ NOUN relative bigness, extent; largeness; one of a series of standard measurements in which things are made and sold.
size up estimate the size of; [INFORMAL] assess.

size² NOUN a gluey solution used to glaze paper or stiffen textiles.

sizeable (also **sizable**) ADJ large; fairly large.

sizzle VERB make a hissing sound like that of frying.

skate NOUN **1** a boot with a blade or wheels attached, for gliding over ice or a hard surface. **2** an edible flatfish. VERB move on skates.
skate over make only a passing reference to.
skater NOUN

skateboard NOUN a small board with wheels for riding on while standing. VERB ride on a skateboard.

skedaddle VERB [INFORMAL] leave hastily, run away.

skein /skayn/ NOUN **1** a loosely coiled bundle of yarn. **2** a flock of wild geese etc. in flight.

skeletal ADJ **1** of the skeleton. **2** very thin.

skeleton NOUN bones, cartilage, etc. forming the supporting structure of an animal body; the basic structure of something; the minimum number, structure, etc.

skeleton key NOUN a key made so as to fit many locks.

skeleton service, **skeleton staff** NOUN a service or staff reduced to the minimum.

skeptic US spelling of **SCEPTIC**.

sketch NOUN a rough drawing or painting; a brief account; a short usually comic play. VERB make a sketch or sketches (of).

sketchy ADJ (**sketchier**, **sketchiest**) rough and not detailed or substantial.
sketchily ADV
sketchiness NOUN

skew ADJ slanting, at an angle. VERB change direction; twist; distort, make biased.

skewbald ADJ (of an

animal) with irregular patches of white and another colour.

skewer NOUN a pin to hold pieces of food together while cooking. VERB pierce with a skewer.

ski NOUN one of a pair of long narrow strips of wood etc. fixed under the feet for travelling over snow. VERB (**skis**, **skiing**, **skied**) travel on skis.
skier NOUN

skid VERB (**skids**, **skidding**, **skidded**) slide uncontrollably off course. NOUN a skidding movement.
put the skids on [INFORMAL] hasten the decline of.

skidpan NOUN a surface used for practising control of skidding vehicles.

S

skiff NOUN a small light rowing boat.

skilful ([US] **skillful**) ADJ having or showing great skill.
skilfully ADV

skill NOUN ability to do something well.
skilled ADJ

skillet NOUN a long-handled cooking pot; [US] a frying pan.

skim VERB (**skims**, **skimming**, **skimmed**) **1** take (matter) from the surface of (liquid). **2** glide. **3** read quickly.

skim milk (also **skimmed milk**) NOUN milk from which the cream has been skimmed.

skimp VERB supply or use rather less than what is necessary.

skimpy ADJ (**skimpier**, **skimpiest**) scanty.
skimpily ADV
skimpiness NOUN

skin NOUN the tissue covering a human or other animal body; an animal skin used for clothing etc.; an outer covering; a film forming on hot milk etc.
VERB (**skins**, **skinning**, **skinned**) strip the skin from.

skin diving NOUN the sport of swimming under water with flippers and breathing apparatus.
skin diver NOUN

skinflint NOUN [INFORMAL] a miser.

skinny ADJ (**skinnier**, **skinniest**) [INFORMAL] very thin.

skint ADJ [INFORMAL] very short of money.

skip¹ VERB (**skips**, **skipping**, **skipped**) **1** move lightly with a hopping or bouncing step; jump with a skipping rope; jump over; [INFORMAL] omit, miss. **2** [INFORMAL] leave hastily or secretly. NOUN a skipping movement.

skip² NOUN a large open container for builders' rubbish etc.

skipper NOUN [INFORMAL] a captain.

skipping rope NOUN a rope turned over the head and under the feet while jumping.

skirmish NOUN a minor fight or conflict. VERB take part in a skirmish.

skirt NOUN **1** a woman's garment hanging from the waist; this part of a garment; any similar part. **2** a cut of beef from the lower flank. VERB form or go along the edge of; avoid (a subject).

skirting (in full **skirting board**) NOUN a narrow board round the bottom of the wall of a room.

skit NOUN a short parody or comedy sketch.

skittish ADJ lively and unpredictable.

skittle NOUN one of the wooden pins set up to be bowled down with a ball in the game of skittles.

skive VERB [INFORMAL] dodge a duty; play truant.

skulduggery NOUN trickery.

skulk VERB loiter stealthily.

skull NOUN the bony framework of the head.

skullcap NOUN a small cap with no peak, for the crown of the head.

skunk NOUN **1** a black and white animal able to spray an evil-smelling liquid. **2** [INFORMAL] a contemptible person.

sky NOUN (PL **skies**) the region of the clouds or upper air.

skydiving NOUN the sport of jumping from an aircraft and performing acrobatic movements in the sky before opening one's parachute.

skylark NOUN a lark that soars while singing. VERB [INFORMAL] play mischievously.

skylight NOUN a window set in a roof or ceiling.

skyscraper NOUN a very tall building.

slab NOUN a broad flat piece of something solid.

slack ADJ **1** not tight. **2** not busy; not fast; lazy or negligent. NOUN **1** a slack piece of rope. **2** coal dust. VERB **1** slacken. **2** [INFORMAL] work slowly or lazily.
slacker NOUN
slackness NOUN

slacken VERB make or become slack.

slacks PLURAL NOUN trousers for casual wear.

slag NOUN **1** solid waste left when metal has been smelted. **2** [INFORMAL] a promiscuous woman. VERB (also **slag off**) (**slags, slagging, slagged**) [INFORMAL] criticize, insult.

slag heap NOUN a mound of waste matter.

slain past participle of **SLAY.**

slake VERB **1** satisfy (thirst). **2** combine (lime) with water.

slalom /slah-lŏm/ NOUN a ski race down a zigzag course; an obstacle race in canoes etc.

slam VERB (**slams, slamming, slammed**) **1** shut forcefully and noisily; put or hit forcefully. **2** [INFORMAL] criticize severely. NOUN a slamming noise.

slander NOUN a false statement uttered maliciously that damages a person's reputation; the crime of uttering this. VERB utter slander about.
slanderer NOUN
slanderous ADJ

slang NOUN very informal words and phrases, used for vividness and often restricted to a particular group, activity, etc.

slant VERB **1** slope. **2** present (news etc.) from a particular point of view. NOUN **1** a slope. **2** a point of view, a bias.
slantwise ADV

slap VERB (**slaps, slapping, slapped**) strike with the open hand or with something flat; place forcefully or carelessly. NOUN a slapping blow. ADV [INFORMAL] suddenly and forcefully; directly.

slapdash ADJ hasty and careless.

slap-happy ADJ [INFORMAL] cheerfully casual.

slapstick NOUN boisterous comedy.

slap-up ADJ [INFORMAL] lavish, first class.

slash VERB cut with a sweeping stroke; [INFORMAL] reduce greatly. NOUN **1** a slashing stroke; a cut made by this. **2** an oblique line (/) used between alternatives.

slat NOUN a narrow strip of wood, metal, etc.

slate NOUN rock that splits easily into flat greyish plates; a piece of this used as roofing-material or (formerly) for writing on. VERB **1** cover with slates. **2** [INFORMAL] criticize severely.

slaughter VERB kill (animals) for food; kill ruthlessly or in great numbers. NOUN the action of killing in this way.

slaughterhouse NOUN a place where animals are killed for food.

Slav /slahv/ NOUN a member of a group of peoples of Europe who speak a Slavic language.

slave NOUN a person who is owned by and must work for another; a person dependent on or controlled by something; a mechanism directly controlled by another. VERB work very hard.

slave-driver NOUN [INFORMAL] a person who makes others work very hard.

slaver VERB have saliva flowing from the mouth.

slavery NOUN the state of being a slave; the system of ownership of slaves.

Slavic (also **Slavonic**) NOUN a group of languages that includes Russian, Polish, and Czech. ADJ relating to the Slavic languages or their speakers.

slavish ADJ excessively submissive or imitative. **slavishly** ADV

slay VERB (**slays**, **slaying**, **slew**; PAST PARTICIPLE **slain**) kill.

sleazy ADJ (**sleazier**, **sleaziest**) corrupt, immoral; squalid.
sleaze NOUN
sleaziness NOUN

sled NOUN [US] a sledge.

sledge NOUN a cart with runners instead of wheels, used on snow. VERB travel or convey in a sledge.

sledgehammer NOUN a large heavy hammer used with both hands.

sleek ADJ smooth and glossy; looking well fed and thriving.
sleekness NOUN

sleep NOUN the natural condition of rest with unconsciousness and relaxation of muscles; a spell of this. VERB (**sleeps**, **sleeping**, **slept**) **1** rest in this condition. **2** provide with sleeping accommodation.
sleep in sleep until late. **sleep off** dispel (sickness etc.) by sleeping.

sleeper NOUN **1** one who sleeps. **2** a railway coach fitted for sleeping in. **3** a beam on which the rails of a railway rest. **4** a ring worn in a pierced ear to keep the hole from closing. **5** a film etc. that achieves sudden success after initially being unnoticed.

sleeping bag NOUN a padded bag for sleeping in.

sleepwalk VERB walk about while asleep.
sleepwalker NOUN

sleepy ADJ (**sleepier**, **sleepiest**) feeling a desire to sleep; quiet, without stir or bustle.
sleepily ADV
sleepiness NOUN

sleet NOUN hail or snow and rain falling together. VERB fall as sleet.

sleeve NOUN the part of a garment covering the arm; a tube-like cover; the cover for a record.
up one's sleeve concealed but available.

sleigh /slay/ NOUN a sledge drawn by horses or reindeer.

sleight of hand /slyt/ NOUN skill in using the hands to perform conjuring tricks etc.

S

slender ADJ **1** slim and graceful. **2** small, barely enough.
slenderness NOUN

slept past and past participle of **SLEEP**.

sleuth /slooth/ NOUN [INFORMAL] a detective.

slew¹ past of **SLAY**.

slew² (also **slue**) VERB turn or swing round.

slice NOUN **1** a thin flat piece (or a wedge) cut from something; a portion; an implement for cutting and serving food. **2** a slicing stroke. VERB **1** cut, especially into slices. **2** strike (a ball) so that it spins away from the direction intended.
slicer NOUN

slick ADJ **1** efficient and effortless; glib, cunning. **2** smooth and glossy or slippery. NOUN a patch of oil on the sea; a smear of a glossy wet substance. VERB make sleek.

slide VERB (**slides**, **sliding**, **slid**) move or cause to move along a smooth surface, always remaining in contact with it; move or pass smoothly. NOUN **1** a smooth surface for sliding on; a structure with a smooth slope for children to slide down. **2** a piece of glass for holding an object under a microscope. **3** a picture for projecting on to a screen. **4** a hinged clip to hold hair in place.

sliding scale NOUN a scale of fees or taxes etc. that varies according to the variation of some standard.

slight ADJ not great or large; trivial, not profound; slender. VERB insult by treating with lack of respect; snub. NOUN a snub.
slightly ADV
slightness NOUN

slim ADJ (**slimmer**, **slimmest**) attractively thin; of small girth or thickness; very slight. VERB (**slims**, **slimming**, **slimmed**) make oneself thinner by dieting and exercise; make smaller.
slimness NOUN

slime NOUN an unpleasant thick liquid substance.

slimline ADJ of slender design.

slimy ADJ (**slimier**,

slimiest) **1** like slime; covered with slime. **2** [INFORMAL] insincerely flattering.
slimily ADV
sliminess NOUN

sling NOUN **1** a belt, chain, or bandage etc. looped round an object to support or lift it. **2** a looped strap used to throw a stone etc. VERB (**slings**, **slinging**, **slung**) **1** suspend (something) to hang loosely. **2** [INFORMAL] throw, put casually.

slink VERB (**slinks**, **slinking**, **slunk**) move in a stealthy or shamefaced way.

slinky ADJ (**slinkier**, **slinkiest**) smooth and sinuous.

slip VERB (**slips**, **slipping**, **slipped**) **1** slide accidentally; lose one's footing; fall or slide out of place. **2** move quietly and quickly, hand over (something) in this way; escape, elude; deteriorate gradually. NOUN **1** an act of slipping. **2** a slight mistake. **3** a small piece of paper. **4** a petticoat. **5** a liquid containing clay used in pottery.
give someone the slip [INFORMAL] evade or escape from someone. **let slip** reveal by mistake. **slip up** [INFORMAL] make a mistake.

slipped disc NOUN a disc of cartilage between vertebrae that has become displaced and causes pain.

slipper NOUN a light loose shoe for indoor wear.

slippery ADJ difficult to hold or stand on because smooth or wet; (of a person) not trustworthy.
slipperiness NOUN

slip road NOUN a road for entering or leaving a motorway.

slipshod ADJ done or doing things carelessly.

slipstream NOUN a current of air driven backward by a revolving propeller or jet engine.

slipway NOUN a sloping structure on which boats are landed or ships built or repaired.

slit NOUN a narrow straight cut or opening. VERB (**slits**, **slitting**, **slit**) cut a slit in; cut into strips.

slither VERB slide unsteadily.

sliver NOUN a small thin strip.

slob NOUN [INFORMAL] a lazy, untidy person.

slobber VERB slaver, dribble.

sloe NOUN a small bitter wild plum.

slog VERB (**slogs**, **slogging**, **slogged**) **1** work hard; walk with effort. **2** hit hard. NOUN **1** a spell of hard steady work or walking. **2** a hard hit.

slogan NOUN a word or phrase adopted as a motto or in advertising.

sloop NOUN a small ship with one mast.

slop VERB (**slops**, **slopping**, **slopped**) overflow; spill; splash. NOUN an unappetizing liquid; (**slops**) liquid refuse.

slope VERB lie or put at an angle from the horizontal or vertical. NOUN a sloping surface; the amount by which a thing slopes.
slope off [INFORMAL] leave unobtrusively.

sloppy ADJ (**sloppier**, **sloppiest**) **1** wet, slushy. **2** slipshod. **3** weakly sentimental.
sloppily ADV
sloppiness NOUN

slosh VERB **1** (of liquid) move with a splashing sound. **2** [INFORMAL] hit. NOUN **1** a splashing sound. **2** [INFORMAL] a heavy blow.

sloshed ADJ [INFORMAL] drunk.

slot NOUN **1** a narrow opening into or through which something is to be put. **2** a place assigned to something in a schedule etc. VERB (**slots**, **slotting**, **slotted**) fit into a slot.

sloth /slohth/ NOUN **1** laziness. **2** a slow-moving animal of tropical America.
slothful ADJ
slothfully ADV

slot machine NOUN a machine operated by inserting a coin into a slot.

slouch VERB stand, sit, or move in a lazy way. NOUN a slouching movement or posture.

slough[1] /*rhymes with* cow/ NOUN a swamp, a marsh.

slough² /sluf/ VERB shed (old or dead skin); be shed in this way.

slovenly /slu-vĕn-li/ ADJ careless and untidy.
slovenliness NOUN

slow ADJ not moving or working quickly; not learning quickly or easily; taking a long time; (of a clock) showing an earlier time than the correct one. ADV slowly. VERB reduce the speed (of).
slowly ADV
slowness NOUN

slowcoach NOUN [INFORMAL] a slow or lazy person.

slow-worm NOUN a legless lizard.

sludge NOUN thick mud.

slue variant of **SLEW²**.

slug NOUN **1** a small slimy creature like a snail without a shell. **2** a small lump of metal; a bullet. VERB (**slugs**, **slugging**, **slugged**) [INFORMAL] hit hard.

sluggard NOUN a slow or lazy person.

sluggish ADJ slow-moving, not lively.
sluggishly ADV
sluggishness NOUN

sluice /sloose/ NOUN a sliding gate controlling a flow of water; a channel carrying off water; an act of rinsing with water.

slum NOUN a squalid house or district.

slumber [LITERARY] VERB sleep. NOUN a sleep.

slump NOUN a sudden great fall in prices or demand. VERB **1** undergo a slump. **2** sit down heavily and limply.

slung past and past participle of **SLING**.

slunk past and past participle of **SLINK**.

slur VERB (**slurs**, **slurring**, **slurred**) **1** utter (words) with one sound running into the next. **2** pass over, attempt to conceal. **3** make damaging allegations about. NOUN **1** a damaging allegation. **2** a slurred sound. **3** a curved line showing that notes of music are to be played legato or sung to one syllable.

slurp VERB eat or drink with a loud sucking noise. NOUN a sound of slurping.

slurry NOUN (PL **slurries**) thin mud; thin liquid cement; fluid manure.

slush NOUN 1 partly melted snow on the ground. 2 [INFORMAL] silly sentimental talk or writing.
slushy ADJ

slush fund NOUN [INFORMAL] a fund of money for bribes etc.

slut NOUN a slovenly or immoral woman.
sluttish ADJ

sly ADJ (**slyer**, **slyest**) cunning, deceitful; (of an expression) suggesting that one has secret knowledge.
on the sly secretly.
slyly ADV
slyness NOUN

smack NOUN 1 a slap, the sound of this. 2 a loud kiss. 3 a flavour, a trace. 4 a single-masted boat. 5 [INFORMAL] heroin. VERB 1 slap, hit hard. 2 close and part (lips) noisily.
smack of taste of; suggest.

small ADJ of less than normal size, not large; not fully grown; unimportant. NOUN 1 the narrowest part (of the back). 2 (**smalls**) [INFORMAL] underwear. ADV into small pieces; in a small size.
smallness NOUN

smallholding NOUN a small farm.
smallholder NOUN

small hours PLURAL NOUN the period soon after midnight.

small-minded ADJ petty and narrow-minded.

smallpox NOUN a disease with pustules that often leave bad scars.

small talk NOUN social conversation on unimportant subjects.

small-time ADJ [INFORMAL] minor, unimportant.

smarmy ADJ (**smarmier**, **smarmiest**) [INFORMAL] distastefully flattering, fulsome.
smarmily ADV
smarminess NOUN

smart ADJ 1 neat and elegant; well dressed. 2 [INFORMAL] clever; (of a machine etc.) able to react independently of control. 3 brisk; sharp. VERB feel or cause a

stinging pain; feel distress.
smartly ADV
smartness NOUN

smarten VERB make or become smarter.

smash VERB break noisily into pieces; hit or collide with forcefully; destroy, ruin. NOUN an act or sound of smashing; a violent collision.
smash hit [INFORMAL] something very popular and successful.

smashing ADJ [INFORMAL] excellent.

smattering NOUN a slight knowledge; a small amount.

smear VERB **1** spread with a greasy or dirty substance. **2** damage the reputation of. NOUN **1** a mark made by smearing. **2** a slander.

S

smell NOUN the ability to perceive things with the sense organs of the nose; a quality perceived in this way; an act of smelling. VERB (**smells**, **smelling**, **smelt** or **smelled**) perceive the smell of; give off a smell.
smelly ADJ

smelt VERB heat and melt (ore) to extract metal; obtain (metal) in this way.

smidgen (also **smidgin**) NOUN [INFORMAL] a very small amount.

smile NOUN a facial expression indicating pleasure or amusement, with lips upturned. VERB give a smile; favour someone or something.

smirch VERB make dirty; discredit, disgrace.

smirk VERB smile in a smug or self-satisfied way. NOUN a smug or self-satisfied smile.

smite VERB (**smites**, **smiting**, **smote**; PAST PARTICIPLE **smitten**) [LITERARY] hit hard.

smith NOUN a person who makes things in metal; a blacksmith.

smithereens PLURAL NOUN [INFORMAL] small fragments.

smithy NOUN (PL **smithies**) a blacksmith's workshop.

smitten past participle of **SMITE**.

smock NOUN a loose shirt-like garment.

smog NOUN dense smoky fog.

smoke NOUN visible vapour given off by a burning substance; an act of smoking tobacco; [INFORMAL] a cigarette, a cigar. VERB **1** give out smoke; inhale and exhale the smoke of tobacco or a drug; do this habitually. **2** preserve (meat or fish) by exposure to smoke.
smokeless ADJ
smoky ADJ

smoker NOUN a person who habitually smokes cigarettes etc.

smokescreen NOUN something intended to disguise or conceal activities.

smolder US spelling of **SMOULDER**.

smooch VERB [INFORMAL] kiss and cuddle; dance slowly in a close hold.

smooth ADJ **1** having an even surface with no projections; not harsh in sound or taste; moving evenly without bumping; free from difficulties or setbacks. **2** polite but perhaps insincere. VERB make smooth.
smoothly ADV
smoothness NOUN

smorgasbord /smor-găs-bord/ NOUN a buffet meal with a variety of dishes.

smote past of **SMITE**.

smother VERB suffocate, stifle; cover thickly; suppress.

smoulder ([US] **smolder**) VERB **1** burn slowly with smoke but no flame. **2** show silent or suppressed anger etc.

smudge NOUN a dirty or blurred mark. VERB make a smudge on; become smudged; blur.
smudgy ADJ

smug ADJ (**smugger**, **smuggest**) self-satisfied.
smugly ADV
smugness NOUN

smuggle VERB convey (goods) illegally into or out of a country, avoiding customs duties; convey secretly.
smuggler NOUN

smut NOUN **1** a small flake of soot; a small black mark. **2** indecent pictures, stories, etc.
smutty ADJ

snack NOUN a small or casual meal.

snaffle NOUN a horse's bit without a curb. VERB [INFORMAL] take without permission.

snag NOUN **1** a problem, a drawback. **2** a jagged projection; a tear caused by this. VERB (**snags, snagging, snagged**) catch or tear on a snag.

snail NOUN a soft-bodied creature with a shell.

snake NOUN a reptile with a long narrow body and no legs. VERB move in a winding course.
snakeskin NOUN
snaky ADJ

snap VERB (**snaps, snapping, snapped**) **1** break or cause to break with a sharp sound; open or close with a brisk movement or sharp sound. **2** speak suddenly and irritably. **3** take a photograph of. NOUN **1** a snapping sound or movement. **2** a snapshot. ADJ done or happening at short notice.
snap up take eagerly.

snapper NOUN an edible sea fish.

snappy ADJ (**snappier, snappiest**) [INFORMAL] **1** irritable. **2** concise, pithy. **3** elegant.
make it snappy hurry up.
snappily ADV
snappiness NOUN

snapshot NOUN an informal photograph.

snare NOUN a trap, usually with a noose. VERB trap in a snare.

snarl VERB **1** growl angrily with bared teeth; speak or utter in a bad-tempered way. **2** become entangled. NOUN **1** an act or sound of snarling. **2** a tangle.

snarl-up NOUN [INFORMAL] a traffic jam; a muddle.

snatch VERB seize quickly or eagerly; [INFORMAL] steal. NOUN an act of snatching; a fragment.

snazzy ADJ (**snazzier, snazziest**) [INFORMAL] stylish.

sneak VERB **1** move or convey furtively; achieve or obtain furtively. **2** [INFORMAL] tell tales. NOUN [INFORMAL] a telltale.
sneaky ADJ

sneaking ADJ (of a feeling) persistent but

not openly acknowledged.

sneer NOUN a scornful expression or remark. VERB show contempt by a sneer.

sneeze VERB expel air suddenly and involuntarily through the nose and mouth. NOUN an act of sneezing.

snicker VERB **1** snigger. **2** (of a horse) neigh quietly.

snide ADJ sneering slyly.

sniff VERB draw air audibly through the nose; draw in as one breathes; try the smell of; [INFORMAL] make secret inquiries or investigations. NOUN the act or sound of sniffing.
sniffer NOUN

sniffle VERB sniff slightly or repeatedly. NOUN this act or sound.

snifter NOUN [INFORMAL] a small drink of alcohol.

snigger NOUN a half-suppressed laugh. VERB laugh in such a way.

snip VERB (**snips**, **snipping**, **snipped**) cut with scissors or shears in small quick strokes. NOUN **1** the act or sound of snipping. **2** [INFORMAL] a bargain.

snipe NOUN (PL **snipe** or **snipes**) a wading bird. VERB fire shots from a hiding place; make sly critical remarks.
sniper NOUN

snippet NOUN a small piece.

snivel VERB (**snivels**, **snivelling**, **snivelled**; [US] **sniveling**, **sniveled**) cry; complain in a whining way.

snob NOUN a person with an exaggerated respect for social position or wealth, despising those he or she considers inferior.
snobbery NOUN
snobbish ADJ

snood NOUN a loose bag-like ornamental net, holding a woman's hair at the back.

snooker NOUN a game played on a table, with 21 balls to be pocketed in a set order.

snoop VERB [INFORMAL] pry.
snooper NOUN

snooty ADJ (**snootier**, **snootiest**) [INFORMAL]

snobbishly aloof.

snootily ADV

snooze [INFORMAL] NOUN a short, light sleep. VERB have a snooze.

snore NOUN a snorting or grunting sound made during sleep. VERB make such sounds.

snorer NOUN

snorkel NOUN a tube by which an underwater swimmer can breathe. VERB (**snorkels**, **snorkelling**, **snorkelled**; [US] **snorkeling**, **snorkeled**) swim with a snorkel.

snort NOUN a sound made by forcing breath through the nose, especially in indignation. VERB make a snort; [INFORMAL] inhale (an illegal drug).

S

snout NOUN an animal's long projecting nose or nose and jaws.

snow NOUN frozen atmospheric vapour falling to earth in white flakes; a fall or layer of snow. VERB fall as or like snow.

snowed under overwhelmed with work etc.

snowstorm NOUN

snowy ADJ

snowball NOUN snow pressed into a compact mass for throwing. VERB increase in size or intensity.

snowblower NOUN a machine that clears snow from a road by blowing it to the side.

snowboarding NOUN the sport of sliding downhill over snow while standing on a single wide ski.

snowdrift NOUN a mass of snow piled up by the wind.

snowdrop NOUN a plant with white flowers blooming in spring.

snowman NOUN a figure made of snow.

snowplough ([US] **snowplow**) NOUN a device for clearing roads by pushing snow aside.

snub VERB (**snubs**, **snubbing**, **snubbed**) reject or ignore contemptuously. NOUN an act of snubbing. ADJ (of the nose) short and

turned up at the end.
snub-nosed ADJ

snuff NOUN powdered tobacco for sniffing up the nostrils. VERB put out (a candle).
snuff it [INFORMAL] die.
snuffer NOUN

snuffle VERB breathe with a noisy sniff. NOUN a snuffling sound.

snug ADJ (**snugger**, **snuggest**) cosy; close-fitting. NOUN a small comfortable room in a pub.
snugly ADJ

snuggle VERB settle into a warm, comfortable position.

so ADV **1** to such a great extent; to the same extent, to the extent indicated. **2** also: *so do I.* **3** in this way. CONJ **1** for that reason. **2** in order that; with the result that.
so as to in order to. **so that** with the aim or result that.

soak VERB place or lie in liquid so as to become thoroughly wet; (of liquid) penetrate. NOUN **1** a soaking. **2** [INFORMAL] a heavy drinker.
soak up absorb.

so-and-so NOUN (PL **so-and-sos**) **1** a person or thing that need not be named. **2** [INFORMAL] a person one dislikes.

soap NOUN **1** a substance used in washing things, made of fat or oil and an alkali. **2** [INFORMAL] a soap opera. VERB wash with soap.

soap opera NOUN a television or radio serial dealing with the daily lives of a group of characters.

soapsuds PLURAL NOUN froth of soapy water.

soapy ADJ (**soapier**, **soapiest**) of or like soap; containing or smeared with soap.
soapiness NOUN

soar VERB rise high, especially in flight.

sob NOUN an uneven drawing of breath when weeping or gasping. VERB (**sobs**, **sobbing**, **sobbed**) weep, breathe, or utter with sobs.

sober ADJ not drunk; serious and realistic; (of colour) not bright. VERB

S

make or become sober.
soberly ADV
sobriety NOUN

sobriquet /soh-brik-ay/ (also **soubriquet**) NOUN a nickname.

so-called ADJ called by a specified name, but perhaps wrongly.

soccer NOUN football, Association football.

sociable ADJ fond of company; characterized by friendly companionship.
sociability NOUN
sociably ADV

social ADJ **1** of society or its organization. **2** living in or suited to a community; of interaction between friends etc. NOUN a social gathering.
socially ADV

S

socialism NOUN a political and economic theory that resources, industries, and transport should be owned and managed by the state.
socialist NOUN
socialistic ADJ

socialite NOUN a person prominent in fashionable society.

socialize (also **socialise**) VERB **1** mix socially with others. **2** make (someone) behave in a way that is acceptable to society.
socialization NOUN

social security NOUN financial assistance from the state for people with little or no income.

social services NOUN welfare services provided by the State.

social worker NOUN a person trained to help people with social problems.

society NOUN (PL **societies**) **1** an ordered community; a particular system of ordering the community. **2** an organization or club. **3** wealthy and fashionable people. **4** company.

sociology NOUN the study of human society or of social problems.
sociological ADJ
sociologist NOUN

sock NOUN **1** a covering of wool, cotton, etc., for the foot; a removable inner sole for a shoe. **2** [INFORMAL] a heavy blow. VERB

[INFORMAL] hit forcefully.

socket NOUN a hollow into which something fits.

sod NOUN **1** turf; a piece of this. **2** [VULGAR SLANG] an unpleasant or awkward person or thing.

soda NOUN **1** a compound of sodium. **2** soda water.

soda water NOUN water made fizzy by being charged with carbon dioxide under pressure.

sodden ADJ very wet.

sodium NOUN a soft silver-white metallic element.

sodomy NOUN anal intercourse.
sodomite NOUN

sofa NOUN a long upholstered seat with a back.

sofa bed NOUN a sofa that can be converted into a bed.

soft ADJ **1** yielding to the touch, not hard or firm; smooth, not harsh. **2** not loud; subtle, not strongly marked; gentle. **3** lenient, not strict. **4** (of drinks) non-alcoholic; (of drugs) not likely to cause addiction. **5** (of currency) likely to fall suddenly in value.
soft-hearted ADJ
softly ADV
softness NOUN

softball NOUN a form of baseball using a large soft ball.

soften VERB make or become soft or softer.
softener NOUN

soft fruit NOUN any small stoneless fruit (e.g. raspberry).

soft furnishings PLURAL NOUN cushions, curtains, rugs, etc.

softie (also **softy**) NOUN [INFORMAL] a soft-hearted or sentimental person.

soft option NOUN an easy alternative.

soft-pedal VERB (**soft-pedals**, **soft-pedalling**, **soft-pedalled**; [US] **soft-pedaling**, **soft-pedaled**) refrain from emphasizing.

soft spot NOUN [INFORMAL] a feeling of affection.

software NOUN computer programs.

softwood NOUN the soft wood of coniferous trees.

softy variant of **SOFTIE**.

soggy ADJ (**soggier**,

soggiest) very wet and soft.

soh NOUN [MUSIC] the fifth note of a major scale, or the note G.

soigné /swahn-yay/ ADJ well groomed and sophisticated.

soil NOUN the upper layer of the earth; a nation's territory. VERB make dirty.

soirée /swah-ray/ NOUN a social gathering in the evening for music etc.

sojourn /so-jĕn/ NOUN a temporary stay. VERB stay temporarily.

solace NOUN comfort in time of distress. VERB give solace to.

solar ADJ of or from the sun; reckoned by the sun.

solar cell NOUN a device converting solar radiation into electricity.

solar plexus NOUN a network of nerves at the pit of the stomach.

solar system NOUN the sun with the planets etc. that revolve round it.

sold past and past participle of **SELL**.

solder NOUN a soft alloy used to cement metal parts together. VERB join with solder.

soldering iron NOUN a tool for melting and applying solder.

soldier NOUN a member of an army. VERB serve as a soldier.

soldier on [INFORMAL] persevere doggedly.

sole[1] NOUN **1** the undersurface of a foot; the part of a shoe etc. covering this. **2** a flatfish used as food. VERB put a sole on (a shoe).

sole[2] ADJ one and only; belonging exclusively to one person or group.

solely ADV

solemn ADJ serious, not smiling; formal and dignified.

solemnity NOUN

solemnly ADV

solemnize (also **solemnise**) VERB perform (a ceremony); mark with a ceremony.

solemnization NOUN

solenoid /so-lĕ-noid/ NOUN a coil of wire magnetized by electric current.

sol-fa NOUN the system of

S

syllables (*doh*, *ray*, *me*, etc.) representing the notes of a musical scale.

solicit VERB ask (someone) for (something); (of a prostitute) approach someone to offer sexual services.
solicitation NOUN

solicitor NOUN a lawyer who advises clients and instructs barristers.

solicitous ADJ anxious about a person's welfare or comfort.
solicitously ADV
solicitude NOUN

solid ADJ **1** keeping its shape, firm; not liquid or gas; strongly built; reliable. **2** not hollow; of a specified substance throughout: *solid gold;* (of time or an activity) uninterrupted. **3** three-dimensional; of three-dimensional objects. NOUN a solid substance, body, or food.
solidity NOUN
solidly ADV

solidarity NOUN unity resulting from common aims or interests etc.

solidify VERB (**solidifies**, **solidifying**, **solidified**) make or become solid.
solidification NOUN

solidus NOUN (PL **solidi**) an oblique stroke (/).

soliloquize (also **soliloquise**) VERB utter a soliloquy.

soliloquy NOUN (PL **soliloquies**) a speech made aloud to oneself.

solitaire NOUN **1** a gem set by itself. **2** a game for one person played on a board with pegs.

solitary ADJ alone; isolated; single, the only one. NOUN (PL **solitaries**) a recluse.

solitude NOUN the state of being solitary.

solo NOUN (PL **solos**) music for a single performer; an unaccompanied performance etc. ADJ & ADV unaccompanied, alone.

soloist NOUN the performer of a solo.

solstice NOUN either of the times (about 21 June and 22 Dec.) when the sun reaches its highest or lowest point in the sky at noon.

soluble ADJ **1** able to be dissolved. **2** able to be

solved.
solubility NOUN

solution NOUN 1 a liquid containing something dissolved; the process of dissolving. 2 the process of solving a problem etc.; the answer found.

solve VERB find the answer to.
solvable ADJ

solvent ADJ 1 having enough money to pay one's debts etc. 2 able to dissolve another substance. NOUN a liquid used for dissolving something.
solvency NOUN

somatic /soh-**mat**-ik/ ADJ of the body as distinct from the mind or spirit.

sombre ([US] **somber**) ADJ dark, gloomy.

sombrero /somb-**rair**-oh/ NOUN (PL **sombreros**) a hat with a very wide brim.

some DETERMINER 1 an unspecified amount or number of; unknown or unspecified: *some man called;* approximately: *some fifty people;* a considerable amount or number of. 2 [INFORMAL] used to express admiration. PRON a certain amount or number of people or things.

somebody NOUN & PRON 1 an unspecified person. 2 a person of importance.

somehow ADV in an unspecified or unexplained manner.

someone NOUN & PRON somebody.

somersault NOUN a leap or roll turning one's body upside down and over. VERB move in this way.

something NOUN & PRON 1 an unspecified thing; an approximate point or number. 2 a notable thing: *quite something.*

sometime ADV at an unspecified time. ADJ former.

sometimes ADV at some times but not all the time.

somewhat ADV to some extent.

somewhere ADV at, in, or to an unspecified place.

somnambulist NOUN a sleepwalker.
somnambulism NOUN

somnolent ADJ sleepy.

somnolence NOUN

son NOUN a male in relation to his parents.

sonar NOUN a device for detecting objects under water by reflection of sound waves.

sonata NOUN a musical composition for one instrument or two, usually in several movements.

son et lumière /son ay loom-**yair**/ NOUN a night-time entertainment dramatizing a historical event with lighting and sound effects.

song NOUN a set of words to be sung; the action of singing.
for a song [INFORMAL] very cheaply.

songbird NOUN a bird with a musical cry.

songster NOUN a singer.

sonic ADJ of sound waves.
sonically ADV

sonic boom NOUN a loud noise caused by an aircraft travelling faster than the speed of sound.

son-in-law NOUN (PL **sons-in-law**) a daughter's husband.

sonnet NOUN a poem of 14 lines.

sonorous ADJ resonant, with a deep powerful sound.
sonority NOUN
sonorously ADV

soon ADV **1** after a short time; early. **2** willingly, for preference.
sooner or later at some time, eventually.

soot NOUN a black powdery substance produced by burning.
sooty ADJ

soothe VERB calm; ease (pain or distress).
soothing ADJ

soothsayer NOUN a prophet.

sop NOUN a concession to pacify a troublesome person. VERB (**sops**, **sopping**, **sopped**) soak up (liquid) with something absorbent.

sophism NOUN sophistry.

sophisticated ADJ **1** characteristic of or experienced in fashionable life and its ways. **2** complicated, elaborate.
sophistication NOUN

sophistry NOUN clever and subtle but misleading reasoning.
sophist NOUN

soporific ADJ tending to cause sleep. NOUN a soporific drug etc.

sopping ADJ very wet, drenched.

soppy ADJ (**soppier**, **soppiest**) [INFORMAL] feebly or distastefully sentimental.
soppiness NOUN

soprano NOUN (PL **sopranos**) the highest female or boy's singing voice.

sorbet /sor-bay/ NOUN a flavoured water ice.

sorcerer NOUN a magician.
sorcery NOUN

sordid ADJ dishonourable, contemptible; dirty.
sordidly ADV
sordidness NOUN

S

sore ADJ **1** causing or suffering pain from injury or disease. **2** [INFORMAL] distressed, vexed. NOUN a sore place; a source of distress or annoyance.
soreness NOUN

sorely ADV very much, severely.

sorrel NOUN a sharp-tasting herb. ADJ reddish brown.

sorrow NOUN mental suffering caused by loss, disappointment, etc.; an event or fact causing this. VERB feel sorrow, grieve.
sorrowful ADJ
sorrowfully ADV

sorry ADJ (**sorrier**, **sorriest**) **1** feeling pity or distress. **2** feeling regret or repentance. **3** wretched, pitiful.

sort NOUN a kind or category; [INFORMAL] a person of a specified nature. VERB divide or arrange in classes, categories, etc.
sort out solve (problems).

sortie NOUN an attack by troops from a besieged place; a flight of an aircraft on a military operation.

SOS NOUN an international distress signal; an urgent appeal for help.

sot NOUN a habitual drunkard.

sotto voce /sott-oh

voh-chi/ ADV in an undertone.

sou /soo/ NOUN a former French coin of low value.

soubriquet variant of **SOBRIQUET**.

soufflé NOUN a light dish made with beaten egg white.

sough /sow, suf/ VERB (of the wind, sea, etc.) make a moaning or whispering sound.

sought past and past participle of **SEEK**.

souk /sook/ NOUN a marketplace in Muslim countries.

soul NOUN **1** the spiritual or immortal element in a person; a person's mental or emotional nature; a person. **2** someone embodying a quality: *the soul of discretion.* **3** (also **soul music**) black American music with elements of rhythm and blues, rock, and gospel.

soulful ADJ showing deep feeling, emotional.
soulfully ADV

soulless ADJ lacking interest or individuality; lacking feeling.

sound[1] NOUN vibrations of air detectable by the ear; the sensation produced by these; what is or may be heard. VERB **1** produce or cause to produce sound; utter, pronounce; give a specified impression when heard: *it sounded sweet.* **2** test the depth of (a river or sea etc.); examine with a probe. ADJ **1** in good condition, not damaged or diseased; (of reasoning) valid. **2** (of sleep) deep.
sound off express one's opinions loudly.
sounder NOUN
soundly ADV
soundness NOUN

sound[2] NOUN a strait.

sound barrier NOUN the high resistance of air to objects moving at speeds near that of sound.

sound bite NOUN a short, pithy quotation extracted from a recorded interview.

sounding board NOUN **1** a board to reflect sound or increase resonance. **2** a person used to test opinion.

S

soundproof ADJ not able to be penetrated by sound. VERB make soundproof.

soup NOUN liquid food made from meat, vegetables, etc.
soup up [INFORMAL] make more powerful or impressive.

soupçon /soop-son/ NOUN a very small quantity.

soup kitchen NOUN a place where soup etc. is served free to the poor.

soupy ADJ (**soupier, soupiest**) **1** like soup. **2** [INFORMAL] sentimental.

sour ADJ **1** tasting sharp; not fresh, tasting or smelling stale. **2** bad-tempered. VERB make or become sour.
sourly ADV
sourness NOUN

S

source NOUN the place from which something comes or is obtained; a river's starting point; a person or book etc. supplying information.

sourpuss NOUN [INFORMAL] a bad-tempered person.

souse VERB steep in pickle; drench.

south NOUN the point or direction to the right of a person facing east; a southern part or region. ADJ & ADV in or towards the south; (of wind) from the south.

south-east NOUN the direction or region halfway between south and east. ADJ & ADV in or towards the south-east; (of a wind) blowing from the south-east.
south-easterly NOUN & ADJ
south-eastern ADJ

southerly ADJ towards or blowing from the south. NOUN (PL **southerlies**) a wind blowing from the south.

southern ADJ of or in the south.

southerner NOUN a person from the south.

southernmost ADJ furthest south.

southpaw NOUN [INFORMAL] a left-handed person.

southward ADJ towards the south.
southwards ADV

south-west NOUN the direction or region halfway between south

and west. ADJ & ADV in or towards the south-west; (of a wind) blowing from the south-west.
south-westerly ADJ & NOUN
south-western ADJ

souvenir NOUN something serving as a reminder of an incident or place visited.

sou'wester NOUN a waterproof hat with a broad flap at the back.

sovereign NOUN **1** a king or queen who is the supreme ruler of a country. **2** a former British coin worth one pound. ADJ supreme; (of a state) independent.
sovereignty NOUN

soviet NOUN **1** (**Soviet**) a citizen of the former Soviet Union. **2** an elected council in the former Soviet Union. ADJ (**Soviet**) relating to the former Soviet Union.

sow[1] /soh/ VERB (**sows**, **sowing**, **sowed**; PAST PARTICIPLE **sown** or **sowed**) plant (seed, a particular type of seed) for growth; plant seeds in (land); suggest, give rise to.
sower NOUN

sow[2] /*rhymes with* cow/ NOUN an adult female pig.

soy NOUN = **SOYA**.

soya (in full **soya bean**) NOUN a plant from whose seed an edible oil and flour are obtained.

sozzled ADJ [INFORMAL] drunk.

spa NOUN a place with a curative mineral spring.

space NOUN **1** the boundless expanse in which all objects exist and move; the universe beyond the earth's atmosphere. **2** an unoccupied area; room to be or move; a blank patch; an interval of time. VERB arrange with gaps in between.
spaced out [INFORMAL] disorientated, dazed.

spacecraft NOUN a vehicle for travelling in outer space.

spaceship NOUN a spacecraft.

spacious ADJ providing much space, roomy.
spaciousness NOUN

spade NOUN **1** a tool for digging, with a broad metal blade on a handle.

S

2 (**spades**) one of the four suits in a pack of playing cards, marked with black figures shaped like an inverted heart with a small stem.

spadework NOUN hard preparatory work.

spaghetti NOUN pasta made in long strings.

span NOUN something's extent from end to end; the distance or part between the uprights of an arch or bridge. VERB (**spans**, **spanning**, **spanned**) bridge; extend across.

spangle NOUN a small piece of glittering material decorating a dress etc. VERB cover with spangles or sparkling objects.

Spaniard NOUN a person from Spain.

spaniel NOUN a dog with drooping ears and a silky coat.

Spanish NOUN the language of Spain. ADJ relating to Spain.

spank VERB slap on the buttocks.

spanking ADJ **1** brisk, lively. **2** [INFORMAL] striking; excellent.

spanner NOUN a tool for gripping and turning the nut on a screw etc.

spar NOUN a strong pole used as a ship's mast, yard, or boom. VERB (**spars**, **sparring**, **sparred**) box, especially for practice; quarrel, argue.

spare ADJ **1** additional to what is needed; not being used, kept in reserve. **2** thin. NOUN an extra thing kept in reserve. VERB **1** give from sufficient resources; be able to do without. **2** refrain from killing or hurting.
go spare [INFORMAL] become distraught. **to spare** additional to what is needed.

sparing ADJ economical, not generous or wasteful.

spark NOUN a fiery particle; a flash of light produced by an electrical discharge; a particle (of energy, genius, etc.). VERB give off spark(s).
spark off give rise to, provoke.

sparkle VERB shine with flashes of light; be lively or witty. NOUN a sparkling light.

sparkler NOUN a hand-held sparking firework.

sparkling ADJ (of wine or mineral water) effervescent, fizzy.

spark plug (also **sparking plug**) NOUN a device for making a spark in an internal-combustion engine.

sparrow NOUN a small brownish-grey bird.

sparse ADJ thinly scattered.
sparsely ADV
sparseness NOUN

spartan ADJ (of conditions) simple and sometimes harsh.

spasm NOUN a strong involuntary contraction of a muscle; a sudden brief spell of activity or emotion etc.

spasmodic ADJ occurring in brief irregular bursts; subject to spasms.
spasmodically ADV

spastic ADJ affected by cerebral palsy, which causes jerky, involuntary movements. NOUN a person with this condition.
spasticity NOUN

> The word **spastic** is frequently found offensive; it is better to say **affected by cerebral palsy** or **a person with cerebral palsy**.

spat[1] past and past participle of **SPIT**.

spat[2] NOUN [INFORMAL] a petty quarrel.

spate NOUN a sudden flood.

spatial ADJ of or existing in space.
spatially ADV

spatter VERB scatter or fall in small drops (on). NOUN a splash; the sound of spattering.

spatula NOUN a knife-like tool with a broad blunt blade; a medical instrument for pressing down the tongue.

spawn NOUN the eggs of fish, frogs, or shellfish. VERB **1** deposit spawn. **2** produce, generate.

spay VERB sterilize (a female animal) by

S

removing the ovaries.

speak VERB (**speaks**, **speaking**, **spoke**; PAST PARTICIPLE **spoken**) utter (words) in an ordinary voice; say something; have a conversation; be able to converse in (a language); express, be a sign of.
speak up for speak in defence of.

-speak COMBINING FORM jargon; *computerspeak*.

speaker NOUN **1** a person who speaks, one who makes a speech. **2** a loudspeaker.

spear NOUN a weapon with a long shaft and pointed tip; a pointed shoot or stem. VERB pierce with or as if with a spear.

spearhead NOUN the foremost part of an advancing force. VERB be the spearhead of.

S

spec NOUN [INFORMAL] **1** (**on spec**) without any specific preparation or plan. **2** a detailed working description.

special ADJ **1** better than or different from usual; outstanding. **2** for a particular purpose, recipient, etc.
specially ADV

specialist NOUN an expert in a particular branch of a subject.

speciality NOUN (PL **specialities**) a subject in which one specializes; something at which one excels.

specialize (also **specialise**) VERB **1** be or become a specialist. **2** adapt for a particular purpose.
specialization NOUN

species NOUN (PL **species**) a group of similar animals or plants which can interbreed.

specific ADJ particular; exact, not vague. NOUN a specific aspect.
specifically ADV

specification NOUN the action of specifying; details describing a thing to be made or done.

specify VERB (**specifies**, **specifying**, **specified**) identify precisely; include in specifications.

specimen NOUN a part or individual taken as an example or for examination or testing.

specious /spee-shŭs/ ADJ seeming good or sound but lacking real merit. **speciously** ADV **speciousness** NOUN

speck NOUN a small spot or particle.

speckle NOUN a small spot, especially as a natural marking. **speckled** ADJ

specs PLURAL NOUN [INFORMAL] a pair of spectacles.

spectacle NOUN **1** a visually striking performance, display, etc.; a ridiculous sight. **2** (**spectacles**) a pair of lenses in a frame, worn in front of the eyes to correct vision.

spectacular ADJ visually striking. NOUN an event designed to be visually striking. **spectacularly** ADV

spectator NOUN a person who watches a game, incident, etc.

spectral ADJ **1** of or like a ghost. **2** of the spectrum.

spectre ([US] **specter**) NOUN a ghost; a haunting fear.

spectrum NOUN (PL **spectra**) bands of colour or sound forming a series according to their wavelengths; an entire range of ideas etc.

speculate VERB **1** form opinions by guessing. **2** buy in the hope of making a profit. **speculation** NOUN **speculative** ADJ **speculator** NOUN

speculum NOUN (PL **specula**) a medical instrument for looking into bodily cavities.

sped past and past participle of **SPEED**.

speech NOUN the utterance of words; a formal talk delivered to an audience.

speechless ADJ unable to speak because of emotion or shock.

S

speed NOUN **1** the rate at which someone or something moves or operates; a fast rate, rapidity. **2** [INFORMAL] an amphetamine drug. VERB **1** (**speeds**, **speeding**, **sped**) move, pass, or send quickly. **2** (**speeds**, **speeding**, **speeded**)

drive at an illegal speed.
speed up accelerate.

speedboat NOUN a fast motor boat.

speedometer NOUN a device in a vehicle, showing its speed.

speedway NOUN **1** an arena for motorcycle racing; racing in this. **2** [US] a road for fast traffic.

speedy ADJ (**speedier**, **speediest**) rapid.
speedily ADV
speediness NOUN

speleology /spee-li-o-lŏ-ji/ NOUN the exploration and study of caves.
speleologist NOUN

spell VERB (**spells**, **spelling**, **spelt** or **spelled**) **1** give in correct order the letters that form (a word). **2** be a sign of; lead to inevitably. NOUN **1** words supposed to have magic power; their influence; a fascination, an attraction. **2** a period of time, weather, or activity.
spell out state explicitly.
speller NOUN

spellbound ADJ entranced.

spend VERB (**spends**, **spending**, **spent**) **1** pay out (money) in buying something. **2** use up; pass (time etc.).
spender NOUN

spendthrift NOUN a wasteful spender.

sperm NOUN (PL **sperms** or **sperm**) a male reproductive cell; semen.

spermatozoon /sper-mă-tŏ-zoh-ŏn/ NOUN (PL **spermatozoa**) the fertilizing cell of a male organism.

spermicidal ADJ killing sperm.

spew VERB **1** [INFORMAL] vomit. **2** cast out in a stream.

SPF ABBREV sun protection factor.

sphere NOUN **1** a perfectly round solid geometric figure or object. **2** a field of action or influence etc.

spherical ADJ shaped like a sphere.

sphincter NOUN a ring of muscle controlling an opening in the body.

sphinx NOUN **1** an ancient Egyptian statue with a

lion's body and human or ram's head. **2** an enigmatic person.

spice NOUN a flavouring substance with a strong taste or smell; interest, excitement. VERB flavour with spice.
spicy ADJ

spick and span ADJ neat and clean.

spider NOUN a small creature with a segmented body and eight legs.
spidery ADJ

spiel /shpeel/ NOUN [INFORMAL] a glib persuasive speech.

spigot NOUN a plug stopping the vent-hole of a cask or controlling the flow of a tap.

spike NOUN **1** a thin, pointed piece of metal, wood, etc. **2** a sharp increase. VERB **1** impale on a spike; form into spikes. **2** [INFORMAL] add alcohol to (a drink). **3** put an end to, frustrate.
spiky ADJ

spill VERB (**spills**, **spilling**, **spilt** or **spilled**) cause or allow to run over the edge of a container; overflow; spread outside an allotted space.
NOUN **1** an instance of something spilling; an amount spilled. **2** a fall from a mount. **3** a thin strip of wood or paper for lighting a fire etc.
spillage NOUN

spin VERB (**spins**, **spinning**, **spun**) **1** turn rapidly on an axis. **2** draw out and twist into threads; make (yarn etc.) in this way.
NOUN **1** a spinning movement. **2** [INFORMAL] a short drive for pleasure.
spin out prolong.
spinner NOUN

spina bifida NOUN a condition in which part of the spinal cord is exposed, often causing paralysis.

spinach NOUN a vegetable with green leaves.

spinal ADJ of the spine.

spindle NOUN a rod on which thread is wound in spinning; a revolving pin or axis.

spindly ADJ long or tall and thin.

spin doctor NOUN [INFORMAL] a spokesperson employed to present a favourable interpretation of events to the media.

spindrift NOUN sea spray.

spine NOUN **1** the backbone; the part of a book where the pages are hinged. **2** a needle-like projection on a plant or animal.

spineless ADJ **1** having no backbone. **2** lacking determination.

spinet NOUN a small harpsichord.

spinnaker NOUN a large extra sail on a racing yacht.

spinneret NOUN the thread-producing organ in a spider, silkworm, etc.

spinney NOUN (PL **spinneys**) a thicket.

spin-off NOUN an incidental benefit.

S **spinster** NOUN an unmarried woman.

spiny ADJ (**spinier**, **spiniest**) covered in spines.

spiracle NOUN an opening through which an insect breathes; the blowhole of a whale etc.

spiral ADJ forming a continuous curve round a central point or axis. NOUN **1** a spiral line or thing. **2** a progressive, usually harmful, increase or decrease. VERB (**spirals**, **spiralling**, **spiralled**; [US] **spiraling**, **spiraled**) **1** move in a spiral course. **2** increase or decrease progressively.
spirally ADV

spire NOUN a tall pointed structure especially on a church tower.

spirit NOUN **1** the mind as distinct from the body; the soul; a person's nature; something's characteristic quality; a person's mood; the prevailing mood at an event etc. **2** a ghost. **3** courage and determination. **4** the intended meaning of a law etc. **5** a strong distilled alcoholic drink. VERB (**spirits**, **spiriting**, **spirited**) carry off rapidly and secretly.

spirited ADJ courageous and determined.
spiritedly ADV

spirit level NOUN a sealed glass tube containing a bubble in liquid, used to test that a surface is level.

spiritual ADJ **1** of the human spirit or soul. **2** of the Church or religion. NOUN a religious folk song of American blacks.
spirituality NOUN
spiritually ADV

spiritualism NOUN attempted communication with spirits of the dead.
spiritualist NOUN
spiritualistic ADJ

spirituous ADJ [FORMAL] strongly alcoholic.

spit VERB (**spits**, **spitting**, **spat** or **spit**) **1** eject saliva; eject (food etc.) from the mouth; utter aggressively. **2** (of rain) fall lightly. NOUN **1** saliva; the act of spitting. **2** a metal spike holding meat while it is roasted. **3** a narrow strip of land projecting into the sea.

spite NOUN malicious desire to hurt or annoy someone. VERB hurt or annoy from spite.
in spite of not being prevented by.
spiteful ADJ
spitefully ADV
spitefulness NOUN

spitfire NOUN a hot-tempered person.

spittle NOUN saliva.

splash VERB **1** cause (liquid) to fall on something in drops; move, fall, or wet with such drops. **2** decorate with irregular patches of colour. **3** display (a story) prominently in a newspaper. NOUN **1** an act or the sound of splashing. **2** a patch of colour; a striking display.
splash out [INFORMAL] spend extravagantly.

splatter VERB splash, spatter. NOUN a splash.

splay VERB spread apart; become wider or more separate.

spleen NOUN **1** an abdominal organ involved in maintaining the proper condition of the blood. **2** bad temper; peevishness.

splendid ADJ brilliant, very impressive; [INFORMAL] excellent.
splendidly ADV

splendour ([US] **splendor**) NOUN a splendid

S

appearance.

splenetic ADJ bad-tempered, peevish.

splice VERB join by interweaving or overlapping the ends.

splint NOUN a rigid framework preventing a limb etc. from movement, e.g. while a broken bone heals. VERB secure with a splint.

splinter NOUN a thin sharp piece of broken wood etc. VERB break into splinters.

splinter group NOUN a small group that has broken away from a larger one.

split VERB (**splits**, **splitting**, **split**) break or come apart, especially lengthwise; divide, share; separate. NOUN an instance of splitting; a split thing or place; (**splits**) an acrobatic position with legs stretched fully apart.

split infinitive NOUN an infinitive with a word placed between *to* and the verb, e.g. *I want to really perfect my French*.

splotch (also **splodge**) [INFORMAL] NOUN a splash or blotch. VERB make a splash or blotch on.

splurge [INFORMAL] NOUN an act of spending extravagantly. VERB spend extravagantly.

splutter VERB make a rapid series of spitting sounds; speak or utter incoherently. NOUN a spluttering sound.

spoil VERB (**spoils**, **spoiling**, **spoilt** or **spoiled**) **1** make less good, pleasant, or useful; (of food) become unfit for eating. **2** harm the character of (especially a child) by being indulgent. NOUN (also **spoils**) plunder.
be spoiling for desire (a fight etc.) eagerly.

spoiler NOUN a device that slows down an aircraft by interrupting the air flow; a similar device on a vehicle, preventing it from being lifted off the road at speed.

spoilsport NOUN a person who spoils others' enjoyment.

spoke[1] NOUN any of the bars connecting the hub

S

to the rim of a wheel.

spoke² past of **SPEAK**.

spokesman (also **spokeswoman**) NOUN a person who speaks on behalf of a group.

spokesperson NOUN (PL **spokespersons** or **spokespeople**) a person who speaks on behalf of a group.

sponge NOUN **1** a water animal with a porous structure; its skeleton, or a similar substance, used for washing, cleaning, or padding. **2** (also **sponge cake**) a cake with a light, open texture. VERB **1** wipe or wash with a sponge. **2** [INFORMAL] live off the generosity of others.
spongeable ADJ
spongy ADJ

sponger NOUN [INFORMAL] a person who exploits others' generosity.

spongiform ADJ with a porous sponge-like texture.

sponsor NOUN **1** a person who provides funds for an artistic or sporting event etc.; one who sponsors another for charity. **2** a person introducing a proposal for legislation. **3** a godparent. VERB provide funds for; promise a sum of money to (someone) if they complete an activity raising funds for charity.
sponsorship NOUN

spontaneous ADJ not caused by outside influences; not rehearsed.
spontaneity NOUN
spontaneously ADV

spoof NOUN [INFORMAL] a hoax; a parody.

spook NOUN [INFORMAL] a ghost.
spooky ADJ

spool NOUN a reel on which something is wound. VERB wind on a spool.

spoon NOUN an eating and cooking utensil with a rounded bowl and a handle. VERB take or lift with a spoon.
spoonful NOUN

spoonerism NOUN the interchange of the initial sounds of two words, e.g. *he's a boiled sprat*.

spoon-feed VERB (**spoon-feeds**, **spoon-feeding**, **spoon-fed**) **1** feed from a spoon. **2** [INFORMAL] give excessive help to.

spoor NOUN a track or scent left by an animal.

sporadic ADJ occurring at irregular intervals or in a few places.
sporadically ADV

spore NOUN one of the tiny reproductive cells of fungi, ferns, etc.

sporran NOUN a pouch worn in front of a kilt.

sport NOUN **1** a physical activity engaged in for pleasure. **2** [INFORMAL] a sportsmanlike person. VERB **1** wear, display prominently. **2** play.

sporting ADJ **1** concerning or interested in sport. **2** fair and generous.

sporting chance NOUN a reasonable chance of success.

S

sportive ADJ playful.
sportively ADV

sports car NOUN an open low-built fast car.

sports jacket NOUN a man's jacket for informal wear.

sportsman (also **sportswoman**) NOUN **1** a person who takes part in a sport. **2** a person who behaves sportingly.

spot NOUN **1** a round mark or stain; a pimple. **2** a place. **3** [INFORMAL] a small amount. **4** a spotlight. VERB (**spots**, **spotting**, **spotted**) **1** notice, perceive. **2** mark with spots.
on the spot 1 at once. **2** at the scene of an action. **3** [INFORMAL] forced to answer or decide immediately.
spotter NOUN

spot check NOUN a random check.

spotless ADJ free from stain or blemish.
spotlessly ADJ

spotlight NOUN a lamp or its beam directed on a small area. VERB (**spotlights**, **spotlighting**, **spotlit** or **spotlighted**) direct a spotlight on; draw attention to.

spotty ADJ (**spottier**, **spottiest**) marked with spots.

spouse NOUN a husband or wife.

spout NOUN a projecting tube or lip through which liquid is poured or conveyed; a jet of liquid.

VERB **1** come or send out forcefully as a jet of liquid. **2** utter or speak lengthily.

sprain VERB injure by wrenching violently. NOUN this injury.

sprang past of **SPRING**.

sprat NOUN a small edible fish.

sprawl VERB sit, lie, or fall with arms and legs spread loosely; spread out irregularly. NOUN a sprawling attitude or arrangement.

spray NOUN **1** liquid dispersed in very small drops; a liquid for spraying; a device for spraying liquid. **2** a branch with leaves and flowers; a bunch of cut flowers. VERB come or send out in small drops; wet with liquid in this way.
sprayer NOUN

spray gun NOUN a device for spraying paint etc.

spread VERB (**spreads, spreading, spread**) **1** open out, make wider; stretch out (fingers, wings, etc.). **2** extend over a wide area or a specified period of time. **3** reach or cause to reach more and more people. **4** distribute. **5** apply in an even layer; be able to be applied. NOUN **1** the action of spreading; the extent to which something spreads; a range. **2** a paste for spreading on bread. **3** an article etc. covering several pages of a newspaper. **4** [INFORMAL] a lavish meal.

spreadeagled ADJ with arms and legs extended.

spreadsheet NOUN a computer program that manipulates figures in tables for calculation.

spree NOUN a period of unrestrained indulgence in an activity.

sprig NOUN a twig, a shoot.

sprightly ADJ (**sprightlier, sprightliest**) lively, full of energy.
sprightliness NOUN

spring VERB (**springs, springing, sprang**; PAST PARTICIPLE **sprung**) **1** jump; move rapidly; appear suddenly. **2** arise, originate. NOUN **1** the season after winter and before summer. **2** a device that reverts to its original shape or position after being pressed; elasticity, resilience. **3** a jump. **4** a place where water or oil flows naturally from the ground.

spring something on confront or present unexpectedly with something.

springboard NOUN a flexible board giving impetus to a gymnast or diver.

spring-clean VERB clean (one's home etc.) thoroughly.

spring roll NOUN a fried pancake filled with vegetables.

spring tide NOUN a tide when there is the largest rise and fall of water.

springy ADJ (**springier**, **springiest**) resilient, elastic; (of a step) bouncy.

springiness NOUN

sprinkle VERB scatter small particles of (a substance) over (a surface); fall in this way.

sprinkler NOUN a device for spraying water on plants or to put out fires.

sprinkling NOUN a small thinly distributed amount.

sprint VERB run at full speed. NOUN a fast run; a race over a short distance.

sprinter NOUN

sprite NOUN an elf, fairy, or goblin.

spritzer NOUN a drink of white wine and soda water.

sprocket NOUN a projection on a wheel, engaging with links on a chain etc.

sprout VERB (of plant shoots or hair) begin to grow or appear; put forth (shoots etc.). NOUN **1** a plant's shoot. **2** a Brussels sprout.

spruce ADJ neat, smart. VERB smarten. NOUN a fir tree.

sprucely ADV

sprung past participle of **SPRING**. ADJ fitted with springs.

spry ADJ (**spryer**, **spryest**) active, lively.

spryly ADV

spud NOUN **1** [INFORMAL] a potato. **2** a narrow spade.

spume NOUN [LITERARY] froth.

spun past and past participle of **SPIN**.

spur NOUN **1** a pricking device worn on a horse rider's heel; a stimulus, an incentive. **2** a projection. VERB (**spurs, spurring, spurred**) urge on (a horse) with one's spurs; urge on, incite; stimulate.
on the spur of the moment on impulse. **win one's spurs** prove one's ability.

spurious ADJ not genuine or authentic.
spuriously ADV
spuriousness NOUN

spurn VERB reject contemptuously.

spurt VERB gush; send out (liquid) suddenly; increase speed suddenly. NOUN a sudden gush; a sudden burst of activity or speed.

sputter VERB splutter. NOUN a spluttering sound.

sputum NOUN mixed saliva and mucus.

spy NOUN (PL **spies**) a person who secretly watches or gathers information. VERB (**spies, spying, spied**) work as a spy for a government etc.; observe, catch sight of.

sq ABBREV square.

squabble VERB quarrel pettily or noisily. NOUN a noisy and petty quarrel.

squad NOUN a small group working together.

squadron NOUN a division of a cavalry unit or an air force; a detachment of warships.

squalid ADJ dirty and unpleasant; morally degrading.
squalidly ADV
squalor NOUN

squall NOUN a sudden storm or wind.
squally ADJ

squander VERB spend wastefully.

square NOUN **1** a geometric figure with four equal sides and four right angles; an area or object shaped like this. **2** the product of a number multiplied by itself. **3** an instrument for testing right angles. ADJ **1** of

square shape. **2** right-angled; level, parallel. **3** of or using units expressing the measure of an area. **4** in good order; fair, honest. **5** [INFORMAL] old-fashioned. ADV directly, exactly. VERB **1** make square. **2** mark with squares. **3** multiply (a number) by itself. **4** make or be compatible; balance (an account). **5** [INFORMAL] bribe.
square up to face in a fighting attitude; face resolutely.
squarely ADV
squareness NOUN

square dance NOUN a dance in which four couples face inwards from four sides.

square meal NOUN a substantial meal.

S

square root NOUN the number of which a given number is the square.

squash VERB **1** crush; squeeze or become squeezed flat or into pulp. **2** suppress; silence with a crushing reply. NOUN **1** a crowd of people squashed together; a crowded place or state. **2** a fruit-flavoured soft drink. **3** (in full **squash rackets**) a game played with rackets and a small ball in a closed court. **4** a vegetable gourd.
squashy ADJ

squat VERB (**squats, squatting, squatted**) **1** crouch, sit on one's heels. **2** be a squatter. NOUN **1** a squatting posture. **2** a place occupied by squatters. ADJ short and stout.

squatter NOUN a person who takes unauthorized possession of an unoccupied building.

squawk VERB make a loud harsh cry. NOUN such a cry.

squeak NOUN a short high-pitched cry or sound. VERB make or utter with a squeak.
narrow squeak [INFORMAL] a narrow escape.
squeaky ADJ

squeal NOUN a long shrill cry or sound. VERB **1** make or utter with a squeal. **2** [INFORMAL] become an informer.

squeamish ADJ **1** easily sickened or disgusted.

2 scrupulous.
squeamishly ADV
squeamishness NOUN

squeeze VERB **1** press firmly; extract liquid from by doing this; obtain from someone with difficulty; [INFORMAL] extort money etc. from. **2** move or force into a tight space; crowd together. NOUN **1** an act of squeezing; an embrace; a crowded state. **2** liquid produced by squeezing. **3** restrictions on borrowing, spending, or investment.
squeezer NOUN

squelch VERB make a soft sucking sound such as that of treading in thick mud. NOUN a squelching sound.

squib NOUN a small exploding firework.

squid NOUN a sea creature with tentacles.

squiffy ADJ (**squiffier**, **squiffiest**) [INFORMAL] slightly drunk.

squiggle NOUN a short curly line.
squiggly ADJ

squint VERB have one eye turned abnormally from the line of gaze of the other; look sideways or through a small opening. NOUN a squinting condition of one eye; a sideways glance.

squire NOUN a country gentleman, especially a landowner.

squirm VERB wriggle; feel embarrassed.

squirrel NOUN a small tree-climbing animal with a bushy tail.

squirt VERB send out (liquid) or be sent out in a jet; wet in this way. NOUN **1** a jet of liquid. **2** [INFORMAL] a contemptible person.

squish VERB make a soft squelching sound. NOUN such a sound.
squishy ADJ

SS NOUN [HISTORICAL] the Nazi special police force. ABBREV **1** Saints. **2** steamship.

St ABBREV **1** Saint. **2** Street.

st ABBREV stone (in weight).

stab VERB (**stabs**, **stabbing**, **stabbed**) pierce, wound or kill with something pointed; poke. NOUN **1** a stabbing thrust; a sudden sharp sensation. **2** [INFORMAL] an attempt.

stabilize (also **stabilise**) VERB make or become stable.
stabilization NOUN

stabilizer (also **stabiliser**) NOUN a device to keep something steady or stable.

stable NOUN a building in which horses are kept; an establishment for training racehorses; the horses, people, etc. from the same establishment. VERB put or keep in a stable. ADJ firmly fixed or established, not easily shaken or destroyed.
stability NOUN
stably ADV

staccato ADV [MUSIC] with each sound sharply distinct.

S

stack NOUN **1** an orderly pile or heap; [INFORMAL] a large quantity. **2** a tall chimney. **3** a storage section of a library; a storage system in a computer. VERB **1** arrange in a stack; cover with stacks; cause (aircraft) to fly at different levels while waiting to land. **2** shuffle (cards) to allow one to cheat.

stadium NOUN a sports ground surrounded by tiers of seats for spectators.

staff NOUN **1** a stick used as a weapon, support, or symbol of authority. **2** the people employed by an organization. **3** a stave in music. VERB provide with a staff of people.

stag NOUN a fully grown male deer.

stage NOUN **1** a point reached in a process, journey, etc. **2** a raised floor or platform for theatrical performances etc.; acting as a profession. VERB present on the stage; organize and carry out.
go on the stage become an actor or actress.

stagecoach NOUN [HISTORICAL] a large horse-drawn coach running on a regular route by stages.

stage fright NOUN nervousness on facing an audience.

stage whisper NOUN a whisper meant to be overheard.

stagflation NOUN a state of inflation without an increase in demand and employment.

stagger VERB **1** move or go unsteadily. **2** surprise or shock deeply. **3** arrange so as not to coincide exactly. NOUN a staggering movement.

staggering ADJ astonishing.

staging NOUN **1** a presentation of a play. **2** a set of temporary platforms; a platform for plants in a greenhouse.

stagnant ADJ (of water) not flowing, still and stale; not active or developing.

stagnate VERB be or become stagnant.
stagnation NOUN

stag night NOUN an all-male party for a man about to marry.

staid ADJ steady and serious.

stain VERB discolour, mark with dirty patches; become discoloured; dye. NOUN **1** a mark caused by staining; a disgrace or blemish. **2** a dye.
stainless ADJ

stainless steel NOUN a steel alloy not liable to rust or tarnish.

stair NOUN one of a flight of fixed indoor steps; (**stairs**) a flight of these.

staircase NOUN a set of stairs with their supporting structure.

stairway NOUN a staircase.

stairwell NOUN the space for a staircase.

stake NOUN **1** a pointed stick or post for driving into the ground. **2** money etc. wagered; a share or interest in an enterprise etc. VERB **1** support on a stake; mark (an area) with stakes. **2** wager.
at stake being risked.
stake a claim claim a right to something. **stake out** [INFORMAL] place under surveillance.

stalactite NOUN a deposit of calcium carbonate hanging like an icicle.

stalagmite NOUN a deposit of calcium carbonate standing like a pillar.

stale ADJ not fresh;

unpleasant or uninteresting from lack of freshness; spoilt by too much practice. VERB make or become stale. **staleness** NOUN

stalemate NOUN a drawn position in chess; a situation where progress is impossible. VERB bring to such a state.

stalk NOUN a stem or similar supporting part. VERB **1** pursue stealthily; follow and harass. **2** walk stiffly or proudly. **stalker** NOUN

stalking horse NOUN a pretext concealing one's real intentions.

stall NOUN **1** a booth or stand for the display and sale of goods. **2** a stable or cowhouse; a compartment in this. **3** a fixed seat in a chancel. **4** (**stalls**) the ground floor seats in a theatre. **5** an engine's stalling. VERB **1** (of an engine) stop running; (of an aircraft) begin to drop because the speed is too low; stop making progress; be obstructive or evasive. **2** put or keep (an animal) in a stall.

stallion NOUN an uncastrated male horse.

stalwart ADJ loyal and hard-working. NOUN a stalwart person.

stamen NOUN the pollen-bearing part of a flower.

stamina NOUN the ability to withstand long physical or mental strain.

stammer VERB speak with involuntary pauses or repetitions of a syllable. NOUN this act or tendency.

stamp VERB **1** bring (one's foot) down heavily on the ground. **2** impress (a mark or pattern) on (a surface); mark out as having a particular characteristic. **3** fix a postage stamp to. NOUN **1** an instrument for stamping a mark; this mark; a characteristic quality. **2** a small adhesive label fixed to an envelope or document to show that postage or a fee has been paid. **3** an act of stamping the foot. **stamp out** suppress by force.

stampede NOUN a sudden rush of animals or people. VERB take part in a stampede.

stamping ground NOUN a place where someone regularly spends time.

stance NOUN a manner of standing.

stanch variant of **STAUNCH**.

stanchion /stan-shĕn/ NOUN an upright post or support.

stand VERB (**stands**, **standing**, **stood**) **1** have, keep, or take a stationary upright position; set upright; (of a building) be situated. **2** remain in a specified condition; remain undisturbed; remain valid or unaltered. **3** endure. **4** be a candidate in an election. **5** pay for (food, drinks) for (someone). NOUN **1** an attitude or policy; resistance to attack or pressure. **2** a support, a pedestal; a platform; a raised structure with seats at a sports ground; a stall for goods. **3** a stopping of motion or progress. **stand a chance** have a chance of success. **stand by 1** look on without interfering. **2** be ready for action. **3** support in difficulty; keep to (a promise). **stand down** withdraw. **stand for 1** represent; symbolize. **2** tolerate. **stand in** deputize. **stand one's ground** not yield. **stand out** be noticeable. **stand to reason** be logical. **stand up 1** get to one's feet; place upright. **2** [INFORMAL] fail to keep an appointment with. **stand up for** speak in defence of. **stand up to** resist courageously; be strong enough to endure.

standard NOUN **1** a thing against which something may be compared for testing or measurement; a level of quality or achievement reached or required. **2** a principle of conduct. **3** a flag. ADJ serving as or conforming to a standard; of average or usual quality, size, etc.

standardize (also **standardise**) VERB cause to conform to a standard.
standardization NOUN

standard lamp NOUN a

household lamp set on a tall support.

standby NOUN (PL **standbys**) readiness for action; a person or thing ready for use in emergency; a system of allocating unreserved tickets.

stand-in NOUN a deputy, a substitute.

standing NOUN **1** status. **2** the length of time that something has lasted.

standing order NOUN an instruction to a bank to make regular payments.

stand-offish ADJ [INFORMAL] cold or distant in manner.

standpipe NOUN a vertical pipe for fluid to rise in, especially for attachment to a water main.

S

standpoint NOUN a point of view.

standstill NOUN inability to proceed.

stank past of **STINK**.

stanza NOUN a verse of poetry.

staphylococcus /staf-il-ŏ-kok-ŭs/ NOUN (PL **staphylococci**) a pus-producing bacterium.

staple NOUN **1** a piece of wire driven into papers to fasten them together; a piece of bent metal used as a fastening. **2** a principal or standard food or product etc. ADJ principal, most important. VERB secure with staple(s).
stapler NOUN

star NOUN **1** a heavenly body appearing as a point of light. **2** a mark with points or rays representing a star, an asterisk; this as a mark of quality. **3** a famous actor, performer, etc. VERB (**stars**, **starring**, **starred**) **1** be a star performer; have as a star. **2** mark with an asterisk.

starboard NOUN the right-hand side of a ship or aircraft.

starch NOUN **1** a carbohydrate occurring in cereals, potatoes, etc. **2** a preparation for stiffening fabrics; stiffness of manner. VERB stiffen with starch.
starchy ADJ

stardom NOUN the state of being a famous actor,

musician, or sports player.

stare VERB gaze fixedly especially in astonishment. NOUN a staring gaze.

starfish NOUN a star-shaped sea creature.

stark NOUN **1** desolate, bare. **2** sharply evident; downright.
ADV completely.
starkly ADV
starkness NOUN

starling NOUN a bird with glossy black speckled feathers.

starry ADJ (**starrier**, **starriest**) set with stars; shining like stars.

starry-eyed ADJ romantically enthusiastic or idealistic.

start VERB **1** begin to do, be, or happen; begin to operate; cause to happen or operate. **2** begin to move or travel. **3** make a sudden movement, especially from pain or surprise. NOUN **1** an act of beginning; the point at which something begins. **2** an advantage gained or given at the beginning of a race etc. **3** a sudden movement of surprise.
starter NOUN

startle VERB shock, surprise.

starve VERB die or suffer acutely from lack of food; cause to do this; force by starvation; [INFORMAL] feel very hungry.
starvation NOUN

stash VERB [INFORMAL] store secretly.

state NOUN **1** the condition that someone or something is in; [INFORMAL] an agitated condition of mind. **2** a political community under one government or forming part of a federation; civil government. **3** grandeur, ceremony. ADJ **1** of or provided by the state. **2** ceremonial. VERB express in words; specify.

stateless ADJ not a citizen or subject of any country.

stately ADJ (**statelier**, **stateliest**) dignified, grand.
stateliness NOUN

statement NOUN a clear expression of something; an official account of an event; a written report of a financial account.

stateroom NOUN a room used on ceremonial occasions; a captain's or passenger's private compartment on a ship.

statesman (also **stateswoman**) NOUN an experienced and respected political leader.

static ADJ **1** not moving or changing. **2** [PHYSICS] of bodies at rest or forces in equilibrium. NOUN electrical disturbances in the air, causing interference in telecommunications; (in full **static electricity**) electricity present in a body, not flowing as current.

statics PLURAL NOUN the branch of mechanics concerned with bodies at rest or forces in equilibrium.

station NOUN **1** a place where trains stop for passengers to get on and off. **2** a place where a particular activity is carried on. **3** a broadcasting channel. **4** a place where someone stands, especially on duty; a person's status. VERB put at or in a certain place for a purpose.

stationary ADJ not moving; not movable.

stationer NOUN a dealer in stationery.

stationery NOUN writing paper, envelopes, labels, etc.

station wagon NOUN [US] an estate car.

statistic NOUN an item of information obtained by studying numerical data; (**statistics**) the science of collecting and interpreting numerical information.
statistical ADJ
statistically ADV

statistician NOUN an expert in statistics.

statue NOUN a sculptured, cast, or moulded figure.

statuesque ADJ like a statue in size, dignity, or stillness.

statuette NOUN a small statue.

stature NOUN bodily height; importance or reputation gained by ability or achievement.

status NOUN a person's position or rank in relation to others; high rank or prestige.

status quo NOUN the existing state of affairs.

statute NOUN a law passed by Parliament or a similar body.

statutory ADJ fixed, done, or required by statute.

staunch ADJ unshakeably loyal. VERB (also **stanch**) stop the flow of (blood) from a wound.
staunchly ADV

stave NOUN **1** a vertical wooden post; one of the strips of wood forming the side of a cask or tub. **2** a set of five horizontal lines on which music is written. VERB (**staves**, **staving**, **stove** or **staved**) dent, break a hole in.
stave off (**staved**) ward off.

stay VERB **1** remain in the same place; live temporarily; continue in the same state. **2** stop, postpone. NOUN **1** a period of staying somewhere. **2** a postponement.
stay the course be able to reach the end of it.

stead /sted/ NOUN (**in someone's** or **something's stead**) instead of someone or something.
stand in good stead be useful to (someone) in the future.

steadfast ADJ not changing or yielding.
steadfastly ADV

steady ADJ (**steadier**, **steadiest**) **1** firmly fixed; not shaking. **2** regular, not changing. **3** dependable, not excitable. VERB (**steadies**, **steadying**, **steadied**) make or become steady.
steadily ADV
steadiness NOUN

steak NOUN a thick slice of meat (especially beef) or fish.

steal VERB (**steals**, **stealing**, **stole**; PAST PARTICIPLE **stolen**) **1** take dishonestly. **2** move stealthily. NOUN [INFORMAL] a bargain.
steal the show outshine other performers.

stealth /stelth/ NOUN secrecy.

stealthy ADJ (**stealthier**, **stealthiest**) quiet and

S

cautious, avoiding notice.
stealthily ADV
stealthiness NOUN

steam NOUN vapour into which water is changed by boiling; this as motive power. VERB **1** give off steam; become or cause to become misted over with steam. **2** cook or treat with steam; move or function by the power of steam; [INFORMAL] move rapidly.
pick up steam move or work faster.
steamy ADJ

steamer NOUN **1** a steam-driven ship. **2** a container in which things are cooked or heated by steam.

steamroller NOUN a heavy engine with a large roller, used in road-making.

S

steed NOUN [LITERARY] a horse.

steel NOUN a very strong alloy of iron and carbon; a steel rod for sharpening knives.
steel oneself brace oneself to face difficulty or hardship etc.
steeliness NOUN
steely ADJ

steel wool NOUN a mass of fine shavings of steel used as an abrasive.

steep ADJ **1** sloping sharply, not gradually. **2** [INFORMAL] (of prices) unreasonably high. VERB soak in liquid; permeate thoroughly.
steeply ADV
steepness NOUN

steeple NOUN a tall tower with a spire, rising above a church roof.

steeplechase NOUN a race for horses or athletes, with fences to jump.
steeplechasing NOUN

steeplejack NOUN a person who climbs tall structures to do repairs.

steer[1] VERB direct the course of; follow (a course); guide.

steer[2] NOUN a bullock.

stellar ADJ of a star or stars.

stem NOUN **1** the supporting part of a plant; a long thin supporting section. **2** [GRAMMAR] the main part

of a noun or verb, to which endings are added. VERB (**stems**, **stemming**, **stemmed**) stop the flow of.
stem from have as its source.

stench NOUN a foul smell.

stencil NOUN a sheet of card etc. with a cut-out design, painted over to produce the design on the surface below; the design produced. VERB (**stencils**, **stencilling**, **stencilled**; [US] **stenciling**, **stenciled**) produce (a design) on (a surface) in this way.

stenography NOUN shorthand.
stenographer NOUN

stentorian ADJ (of a voice) extremely loud.

step VERB (**steps**, **stepping**, **stepped**) lift and set down a foot or alternate feet; move a short distance in this way. NOUN **1** a movement of a foot and leg in stepping; the distance covered in this way; a short distance; a movement of the feet and legs in dancing. **2** a level surface to place one's foot on in climbing; (**steps**) a stepladder. **3** one of a series of actions to achieve a goal; a stage in a process.
in step stepping in time with others; conforming. **mind** or **watch one's step** take care. **step down** resign from a position of power. **step in** intervene; enter. **step up** increase.

step- COMBINING FORM related by remarriage of a parent, as *stepfather*, *stepmother*, *stepson*, etc.

stepladder NOUN a short ladder with a supporting framework.

steppe NOUN a grassy plain, especially in south-east Europe and Siberia.

stepping stone NOUN a raised stone for stepping on in crossing a stream etc.; a stage in progress towards a goal.

stereo NOUN (PL **stereos**) stereophonic sound; a stereophonic player.

stereophonic ADJ (of sound recording and

S

transmission) using two transmission channels so as to give the effect of sound from more than one source.

stereoscope NOUN a device by which two photographs of the same object are viewed together to give an effect of depth.
stereoscopic ADJ

stereotype NOUN a standardized conventional idea or character etc. VERB regard or represent as a stereotype.
stereotypical ADJ

sterile ADJ **1** unable to produce fruit or young. **2** free from micro-organisms.
sterility NOUN

S

sterilize (also **sterilise**) VERB make sterile.
sterilization NOUN
sterilizer NOUN

sterling NOUN British money. ADJ of standard purity; excellent.

stern ADJ strict, severe. NOUN the rear of a ship or aircraft.
sternly ADV
sternness NOUN

sternum NOUN (PL **sternums** or **sterna**) the breastbone.

steroid NOUN any of a group of organic compounds that includes certain hormones.

stertorous /ster-tŏ-rŭs/ ADJ making a snoring or rasping sound.

stet VERB (placed by a word that has been crossed out etc.) ignore the alteration.

stethoscope NOUN a medical instrument for listening to a patient's heart or breathing.

stevedore NOUN a docker.

stew VERB **1** cook by simmering in a closed pot; (of tea) become strong. **2** [INFORMAL] worry. NOUN **1** a dish made by stewing meat etc. **2** [INFORMAL] a state of great anxiety.

steward NOUN **1** a person employed to manage an estate etc. **2** a passengers' attendant on a ship, aircraft, or train. **3** an official at a race meeting or show etc.

stewardess NOUN a female attendant on an aircraft, ship, etc.

stick VERB (**sticks**, **sticking**, **stuck**) **1** thrust (something sharp) into or through something; [INFORMAL] put. **2** cling or adhere; cause to do this; remain without moving; become unable to move or work, jam; be unable to make progress. **3** [INFORMAL] endure. NOUN **1** a thin piece of wood; a similar piece of other material; an implement used to propel the ball in hockey, polo, etc. **2** a threat of punishment; [INFORMAL] criticism.
stick out be prominent or conspicuous. **stick to** confine oneself to; remain faithful to. **stick together** [INFORMAL] remain loyal to one another. **stick to one's guns** refuse to yield. **stick up for** [INFORMAL] support.

sticker NOUN an adhesive label or sign.

sticking plaster NOUN an adhesive fabric for covering small cuts.

stick-in-the-mud NOUN [INFORMAL] a person who will not adopt new ideas etc.

stickleback NOUN a small fish with sharp spines on its back.

stickler NOUN a person who insists on a certain type of behaviour.

sticky ADJ (**stickier**, **stickiest**) **1** sticking to what is touched. **2** humid. **3** [INFORMAL] difficult.
stickily ADV
stickiness NOUN

stiff ADJ **1** not bending or moving easily; formal in manner. **2** severe; (of a wind) blowing strongly; difficult, requiring effort; (of a drink) strong. NOUN [INFORMAL] a corpse.
stiff with [INFORMAL] full of.
stiffly ADV
stiffness NOUN

stiffen VERB make or become stiff.
stiffener NOUN

stiff-necked ADJ obstinate.

stifle VERB feel or cause to feel unable to breathe; suppress.

stigma NOUN **1** a mark of

S

shame. **2** part of a flower pistil.

stigmata PLURAL NOUN marks corresponding to the Crucifixion marks on Christ's body.

stigmatize (also **stigmatise**) VERB brand as disgraceful.
stigmatization NOUN

stile NOUN steps or bars for people to climb over a fence.

stiletto NOUN (PL **stilettos**) a dagger with a narrow blade.

stiletto heel NOUN a long tapering heel of a shoe.

still ADJ **1** with little or no motion or sound. **2** (of drinks) not fizzy. NOUN **1** silence and calm. **2** a photograph taken from a cinema film. **3** a distilling apparatus. ADV **1** continuing the same up to the present or the time mentioned: *I'm still waiting.* **2** nevertheless. **3** even (used in comparisons): *still more.*
stillness NOUN

stillborn ADJ born dead.

still life NOUN a picture of inanimate objects.

stilted ADJ stiffly formal.

stilts PLURAL NOUN a pair of poles with footrests, enabling the user to walk above the ground; piles or posts supporting a building.

stimulant NOUN a substance that makes one feel more lively; an event or situation that encourages activity.

stimulate VERB rouse to action, make more active; motivate, encourage.
stimulation NOUN
stimulative ADJ
stimulator NOUN

stimulus NOUN (PL **stimuli**) something that rouses a person or thing to activity or energy.

sting NOUN a sharp wounding part of an insect etc.; a wound made by this; sharp bodily or mental pain. VERB (**stings**, **stinging**, **stung**) **1** wound or affect with a sting; feel or cause sharp pain; provoke by annoying or taunting. **2** [INFORMAL] overcharge, swindle.

stingy ADJ (**stingier**,

stingiest) spending or given grudgingly or in small amounts.
stingily ADV
stinginess NOUN

stink NOUN **1** an offensive smell. **2** [INFORMAL] a row or fuss. VERB (**stinks**, **stinking**, **stank** or **stunk**) **1** give off a stink. **2** [INFORMAL] seem very unpleasant or dishonest.

stinker NOUN [INFORMAL] an objectionable person; a difficult task.

stinking [INFORMAL] ADJ foul-smelling; unpleasant. ADV extremely: *stinking rich.*

stint VERB restrict to a small allowance; be thrifty or mean. NOUN an allotted period of work.

stipend /sty-pend/ NOUN a salary.

stipendiary ADJ receiving a stipend.

stipple VERB (in painting, engraving, etc.) mark with numerous small dots.

stipulate VERB demand or insist (on) as part of an agreement.
stipulation NOUN

stir VERB (**stirs**, **stirring**, **stirred**) **1** mix (a substance) by moving a spoon round in it. **2** move, begin to move; rouse, stimulate. NOUN **1** a slight movement. **2** a commotion. **3** an act of stirring.

stirrup NOUN a support for a rider's foot, hanging from the saddle.

stitch NOUN **1** a single movement of a thread in and out of fabric in sewing, or of a needle in knitting or crochet; the loop made in this way; a method of making a stitch. **2** a sudden pain in the side. VERB sew; join or close with stitches.
in stitches [INFORMAL] laughing uncontrollably.

stoat NOUN a weasel-like animal.

stock NOUN **1** goods kept in a shop etc. for sale; a supply of something. **2** livestock. **3** a business company's capital; a portion of this held by an investor. **4** reputation, status. **5** liquid made by stewing bones etc. **6** ancestry. **7** a plant into which a graft is inserted. **8** the handle of a rifle. **9** a cravat. **10** (**stocks**) a wooden frame with holes in which people had their feet locked as a punishment; a framework on which a ship rests during construction. ADJ stocked and regularly available; predictable, said or made regularly and without thought. VERB keep in stock; provide with a supply.

stockade NOUN a protective fence.

stockbroker NOUN a person who buys and sells shares for clients.

stock car NOUN a car used in races where deliberate bumping is allowed.

stock exchange NOUN the stock market.

stocking NOUN a close-fitting covering for the foot and leg.

stock-in-trade NOUN the commodity etc. used or traded in by a business; a characteristic quality.

stockist NOUN a firm that stocks certain goods.

stock market NOUN an institution for buying and selling stocks and shares; the transactions of this.

stockpile NOUN a large accumulated stock of goods or materials. VERB accumulate a stockpile of.

stock-still ADJ motionless.

stocktaking NOUN making an inventory of stock.

stocky ADJ (**stockier, stockiest**) short and solidly built.
stockiness NOUN

stodge NOUN [INFORMAL] stodgy food.

stodgy ADJ (**stodgier, stodgiest**) [INFORMAL] **1** (of food) heavy and filling. **2** dull.

stoic /stoh-ik/ NOUN a stoical person.

stoical ADJ calm and uncomplaining.
stoically ADV
stoicism NOUN

stoke VERB tend and put fuel on (a fire etc.).
stoker NOUN

stole[1] NOUN a woman's

wide scarf-like garment.

stole², **stolen** past and past participle of **STEAL**.

stolid ADJ not excitable.
stolidity NOUN
stolidly ADV

stomach NOUN the internal organ in which the first part of digestion occurs; the abdomen; appetite. VERB endure, tolerate.

stomp VERB tread heavily.

stone NOUN **1** a piece of rock; stones or rock as a substance or material. **2** a gem. **3** a hard substance formed in the bladder or kidney etc. **4** the hard case round the kernel of certain fruits. **5** (PL **stone**) a unit of weight, 14 lb. ADJ made of stone. VERB **1** pelt with stones. **2** remove stones from (fruit).

Stone Age NOUN a prehistoric period when weapons and tools were made of stone.

stoneground ADJ (of flour) ground with millstones.

stonemason NOUN a person who carves or builds in stone.

stonewall VERB obstruct (a process) by giving evasive replies.

stonewashed ADJ washed with abrasives to give a worn faded look.

stony ADJ (**stonier**, **stoniest**) **1** full of stones. **2** hard, unfeeling; unresponsive.
stonily ADV

stood past and past participle of **STAND**.

stooge NOUN a comedian's assistant; [DEROGATORY] a person working for and controlled by others.

stool NOUN **1** a movable seat without arms or raised back. **2** (**stools**) faeces.

stool pigeon NOUN a person acting as a decoy, especially to trap a criminal; an informer.

stoop VERB bend forwards and down; condescend; lower oneself morally. NOUN a stooping posture.

stop VERB (**stops**, **stopping**, **stopped**) **1** come or bring to an end; cease or cause to cease doing something;

cease or cause to cease moving. **2** prevent; prevent from doing something. **3** block, close. NOUN **1** a cessation from movement or activity; a place where a train or bus etc. stops regularly; something that stops or regulates motion. **2** a row of organ pipes of a particular tone and range of pitch; the knob etc. controlling these.

stopcock NOUN a valve regulating the flow in a pipe etc.

stopgap NOUN a temporary substitute.

stopover NOUN an overnight break in a journey.

stoppage NOUN an instance of stopping; an obstruction.

S

stopper NOUN a plug for closing a bottle etc.

stop press NOUN late news inserted in a newspaper after printing has begun.

stopwatch NOUN a watch that can be started and stopped, used for timing races etc.

storage NOUN the action of storing; a space for this.

storage heater NOUN an electric radiator accumulating heat in off-peak periods.

store NOUN **1** a supply of something available for use; a storehouse. **2** a large shop. VERB collect and keep for future use. **in store 1** kept in a safe place while not in use. **2** coming in the future. **set store by** value greatly.

storehouse NOUN a place where things are stored.

storey NOUN (PL **storeys** or **stories**) each horizontal section of a building. **storeyed** ADJ

stork NOUN a large bird with a long bill.

storm NOUN a disturbance of the atmosphere with strong winds and usually rain or snow; a heavy discharge of missiles; a violent outburst of feeling. VERB **1** move angrily and violently; be angry. **2** suddenly attack and capture. **stormy** ADJ

story NOUN (PL **stories**) an account of an incident (true or invented).

stout ADJ **1** fat; thick and strong. **2** brave and determined. NOUN a strong dark beer.
stoutly ADV
stoutness NOUN

stove[1] past and past participle of **STAVE**.

stove[2] NOUN an apparatus for cooking or heating, burning fuel or using electricity.

stow VERB place (something) somewhere for storage.
stow away conceal oneself as a stowaway.

stowaway NOUN a person who hides on a ship or aircraft so as to travel free of charge.

straddle VERB sit or stand with one leg on each side of (something); extend across.

strafe VERB attack with gunfire from the air. NOUN an act of strafing.

straggle VERB grow or spread untidily; wander separately; lag behind others.
straggler NOUN
straggly ADJ

straight ADJ **1** extending or moving in one direction, not curved or bent; level, even; tidy, ordered. **2** honest, frank, not evasive. **3** in continuous succession: *his fourth straight win.* **4** not modified, without additions. **5** [INFORMAL] heterosexual. ADV **1** in a straight line, directly; without delay. **2** clearly, without confusion. **3** frankly. NOUN the straight part of something, especially of a racecourse.
go straight live honestly after being a criminal.
straight away without delay. **straight off** [INFORMAL] without hesitation.
straightness NOUN

straighten VERB make or become straight.

straight face NOUN a serious expression.

straight fight NOUN a contest between only two opponents.

straightforward ADJ **1** simple, uncomplicated.

2 frank.
straightforwardly ADV

straightjacket variant of **STRAITJACKET**.

strain VERB **1** make taut; injure by excessive stretching or overexertion; make an intense effort (with). **2** sieve to separate solids from liquid. NOUN **1** a force stretching something; pressure, an excessive demand on strength etc.; an injury from straining. **2** a variety or breed of animal etc. **3** a tendency in someone's character. **4** the sound of music.
strainer NOUN

strained ADJ (of manner etc.) tense, not natural or relaxed.

strait NOUN **1** (also **straits**) a narrow stretch of water connecting two seas. **2** (**straits**) a difficult state of affairs.

straitened ADJ (of conditions) poverty-stricken.

straitjacket (also **straightjacket**) NOUN a strong garment put round a violent person to restrain his or her arms. VERB (**straitjackets**, **straitjacketing**, **straitjacketed**) restrict severely.

strait-laced ADJ having strict ideas about people's moral behaviour.

strand NOUN **1** a single thread, especially one woven or plaited with others; one element in a complex whole. **2** a shore. VERB run aground; leave in difficulties.

strange ADJ **1** unusual, odd. **2** not previously visited, seen, or encountered.
strangely ADV
strangeness NOUN

stranger NOUN a person one does not know; one who does not live in or know a place.

strangle VERB kill by squeezing the throat; suppress, restrict the growth of.
strangler NOUN

stranglehold NOUN a strangling grip; complete control.

strangulation NOUN **1** the action of strangling. **2** the cutting off of blood supply to part of the body.

strap NOUN a strip of leather or other flexible material for holding things together or in place, or supporting something. VERB (**straps, strapping, strapped**) secure or support with a strap.
strapped for [INFORMAL] short of.

straphanger NOUN [INFORMAL] a standing passenger in a bus or train.

strapping ADJ tall and robust.

strata pl. of **STRATUM**.

stratagem NOUN a cunning plan or scheme; a trick.

strategic ADJ **1** of strategy. **2** (of weapons) directed against an enemy's territory rather than used in battle.
strategically ADV

strategist NOUN an expert in strategy.

strategy NOUN (PL **strategies**) the planning and directing of the whole operation of a campaign or war; a plan for achieving a major goal.

stratify VERB (**stratifies, stratifying, stratified**) arrange in strata; classify.
stratification NOUN

stratosphere NOUN a layer of the atmosphere about 10–60 km above the earth's surface.

stratum NOUN (PL **strata**) one of a series of layers or levels.

straw NOUN **1** dry cut stalks of corn etc.; a single piece of this. **2** a narrow tube for sucking up liquid to drink.

strawberry NOUN (PL **strawberries**) a soft edible red fruit with seeds on the surface.

strawberry mark NOUN a red birthmark.

straw poll NOUN an unofficial poll as a test of general feeling.

stray VERB move from one's proper place; move idly or aimlessly; deviate from a subject. ADJ having strayed; occurring or appearing by chance. NOUN a stray domestic animal.

streak NOUN **1** a thin line or band of a colour or substance different from its surroundings; an element in someone's character. **2** a continuous period of luck etc. VERB **1** mark with streaks. **2** move very rapidly; [INFORMAL] run naked in a public place.
streaker NOUN
streaky ADJ

stream NOUN **1** a small river; a flow of liquid, things, or people; the direction of this. **2** a group into which schoolchildren of the same level of ability are placed. VERB **1** flow; move in a particular direction; float in the wind. **2** run with liquid. **3** arrange (schoolchildren) in streams.
on stream in active operation or production.

streamer NOUN a long narrow strip of material used for decoration.

streamline VERB make (something) with a smooth shape offering little resistance to movement through water or air; make more efficient by simplifying.

street NOUN a public road lined with buildings.

streetcar NOUN [US] a tram.

street cred (in full **street credibility**) NOUN [INFORMAL] acceptability among fashionable urban young people.

streetwise ADJ [INFORMAL] knowing how to survive in modern city life.

strength NOUN **1** the quality of being strong; the degree to which someone or something is strong or intense. **2** a good or advantageous quality. **3** the total number of people making up a group.
on the strength of relying on as a basis or support.

strengthen VERB make or become stronger.

strenuous ADJ making or requiring great effort.
strenuously ADV

streptococcus/strep-tŏ-kok-ŭs/ NOUN (PL **streptococci**) a

S

bacterium causing serious infections.

stress NOUN **1** pressure; mental or emotional strain. **2** emphasis; extra force given to a syllable or note. VERB **1** emphasize. **2** subject to pressure.
stressed ADJ
stressful ADJ

stretch VERB **1** pull out tightly or to a greater extent; become longer or wider without breaking; extend one's body or a limb. **2** extend over an area or period. **3** make demands on (a resource, ability, etc.). **4** exaggerate. NOUN **1** an act of stretching. **2** the ability to be stretched. **3** a continuous area or period. ADJ able to be stretched.
at a stretch
1 continuously. **2** only just, in extreme cases.
stretch a point agree to something not normally allowed.
stretchy ADJ

stretcher NOUN a framework for carrying a sick or injured person in a lying position.

strew VERB (**strews**, **strewing**, **strewed**; PAST PARTICIPLE **strewn** or **strewed**) scatter over a surface; cover with scattered things.

striation NOUN each of a series of lines or grooves.

stricken ADJ afflicted by an illness, shock, or grief.

strict ADJ **1** requiring obedience to rules; severe in enforcing rules. **2** exact; total, without exception.
strictly ADV
strictness NOUN

stricture NOUN **1** severe criticism. **2** a restriction; constriction of a duct in the body.

stride VERB (**strides**, **striding**, **strode**; PAST PARTICIPLE **stridden**) walk with long steps. NOUN a single long step; a manner of striding; (**strides**) progress.

strident ADJ loud and harsh.
stridency NOUN
stridently ADV

strife NOUN angry or bitter disagreement.

strike VERB (**strikes**,

striking, **struck**) 1 hit; knock; come into contact with. 2 attack suddenly, occur suddenly; afflict; come suddenly into the mind of. 3 stop work in protest. 4 ignite (a match) by friction. 5 indicate (the hour) by chiming. 6 agree on (a bargain). 7 find (oil, gold, etc.). 8 assume (a pose). 9 take down (a tent or flag). NOUN 1 a refusal by employees to work. 2 a sudden attack.
strike home deal an effective blow. **strike off** or **out** cross out. **strike up** begin playing or singing; start (a friendship etc.) casually.

strike-bound ADJ immobilized by a workers' strike.

S **striker** NOUN 1 a worker on strike. 2 a football player whose main function is to try to score goals.

striking ADJ sure to be noticed; impressive.
strikingly ADV

strimmer NOUN [TRADE MARK] a long-handled machine for cutting rough grass.

string NOUN 1 a narrow cord; a stretched piece of catgut or wire etc. in a musical instrument, vibrated to produce tones; (**strings**) stringed instruments. 2 a set of objects strung together; a series. 3 (**strings**) [INFORMAL] conditions or requirements. VERB (**strings**, **stringing**, **strung**) 1 hang up; thread on a string. 2 fit strings on (an instrument etc.).
pull strings [INFORMAL] use one's influence. **string along** [INFORMAL] allow (someone) to believe something that is not true. **string out** spread out on a line. **string up** hang up on strings; kill by hanging.

stringent ADJ strict, with firm restrictions.
stringency NOUN
stringently ADV

stringy ADJ (**stringier**, **stringiest**) like string; tall and thin; (of food) containing tough fibres.

strip VERB (**strips**, **stripping**, **stripped**) remove clothes or covers from; pull off; deprive of property, rank, etc. NOUN **1** an act of undressing. **2** a long narrow piece or area.

strip cartoon NOUN = **COMIC STRIP**.

stripe NOUN a long narrow band on a surface, differing in colour or texture from its surroundings; a chevron on a sleeve, indicating rank.
striped ADJ
stripy ADJ

strip light NOUN a tubular fluorescent lamp.

stripling NOUN a youth.

stripper NOUN **1** a device for stripping something. **2** a striptease performer.

striptease NOUN an entertainment in which a performer gradually undresses.

strive VERB (**strives**, **striving**, **strove**; PAST PARTICIPLE **striven**) **1** make great efforts. **2** struggle; compete.

stroboscope (also [INFORMAL] **strobe**) NOUN an apparatus for producing a rapidly flashing light.
stroboscopic ADJ

strode past of **STRIDE**.

stroganoff NOUN strips of meat etc. cooked in a sour cream sauce.

stroke VERB pass the hand gently along the surface of. NOUN **1** an act of striking something; the sound of a striking clock. **2** an act of stroking. **3** a mark made by a movement of a pen, paintbrush, etc. **4** a movement, a beat; a style of swimming. **5** a loss of consciousness due to an interruption in the supply of blood to the brain.
at a stroke by a single action.

stroll VERB walk in a leisurely way. NOUN a leisurely walk.

stroller NOUN [US] a pushchair.

strong ADJ **1** able to move heavy weights or resist great pressure; having skills, qualities, or numbers assisting survival or victory; (of an argument or position) valid; able to bear distress. **2** intense; concentrated; containing much alcohol. **3** having a specified number of members: *fifty strong*. **going strong** [INFORMAL] continuing to be healthy or successful. **strong language** swearing. **strong on** good at. **strongly** ADV

stronghold NOUN a fortified place; the centre of support for a cause.

strong-minded ADJ determined.

strongroom NOUN a room designed for safe storage of valuables.

strontium NOUN a silver-white metallic element.

strontium 90 NOUN a radioactive isotope of strontium.

strop NOUN a leather strip on which a razor is sharpened.

S

stroppy ADJ (**stroppier**, **stroppiest**) [INFORMAL] bad-tempered, awkward.

strove past of **STRIVE**.

struck past and past participle of **STRIKE**. **struck on** [INFORMAL] fond of, attracted to.

structure NOUN the way a thing is constructed or organized; a thing's supporting framework or essential parts; a constructed thing, a complex whole. **structural** ADJ **structurally** ADV

strudel NOUN flaky pastry filled with apple etc.

struggle VERB move violently to get free; make one's way or achieve something with difficulty; engage in conflict. NOUN a spell of struggling; a vigorous effort; a hard contest.

strum VERB (**strums**, **strumming**, **strummed**) play on (a stringed or keyboard instrument), especially unskilfully or monotonously. NOUN a sound made by strumming.

strumpet NOUN [ARCHAIC] a prostitute or promiscuous woman.

strung past and past participle of **STRING**.

strut NOUN **1** a bar of wood or metal supporting something. **2** a strutting walk. VERB (**struts**, **strutting**, **strutted**) walk stiffly and arrogantly.

strychnine /strik-neen/ NOUN a bitter highly poisonous substance.

stub NOUN **1** a short stump. **2** a counterfoil of a cheque or receipt etc. VERB (**stubs**, **stubbing**, **stubbed**) **1** strike (one's toe) against a hard object. **2** extinguish (a cigarette) by pressure.

stubble NOUN the lower ends of corn-stalks left in the ground after harvest; short stiff hair or bristles growing after shaving.
stubbly ADJ

stubborn ADJ obstinate, unyielding.
stubbornly ADV
stubbornness NOUN

stubby ADJ (**stubbier**, **stubbiest**) short and thick.
stubbiness NOUN

stucco NOUN plaster used for coating walls or moulding into decorations.
stuccoed ADJ

stuck past and past participle of **STICK**. ADJ unable to move or make progress.

stuck-up ADJ [INFORMAL] conceited, arrogantly aloof.

stud NOUN **1** a projecting nail-head or similar knob on a surface; a device for fastening e.g. a detachable shirt-collar. **2** an establishment where horses etc. are kept for breeding; these animals. VERB (**studs**, **studding**, **studded**) cover with studs or other small objects.

student NOUN a person who is studying at a college or university.

studied ADJ achieved by deliberate effort.

studio NOUN (PL **studios**) the workroom of a painter, photographer, etc.; premises where cinema films are made; a room from which broadcasts are transmitted or where recordings are made.

studio flat NOUN a one-room flat with a kitchen and bathroom.

studious ADJ spending much time in study; deliberate and careful.
studiously ADV

studiousness NOUN

study NOUN (PL **studies**) **1** effort and time spent in learning; a subject studied; a book or article on a topic. **2** a room for reading and writing. **3** a musical composition designed to develop a player's skill; a preliminary drawing. **4** an embodiment of a quality. VERB (**studies**, **studying**, **studied**) give one's attention to acquiring knowledge of (a subject); examine attentively.

stuff NOUN **1** [INFORMAL] matter, things; belongings. **2** the constituents or material for something. VERB fill tightly; force into a confined space; fill the skin of (a dead animal) to make it lifelike.

stuff oneself [INFORMAL] eat greedily.

stuffing NOUN padding used to fill something; a savoury mixture put inside poultry, vegetables, etc. before cooking.

stuffy ADJ (**stuffier**, **stuffiest**) **1** lacking fresh air or ventilation. **2** narrow-minded, old-fashioned.

stuffily ADV

stuffiness NOUN

stultify VERB (**stultifies**, **stultifying**, **stultified**) cause to lose enthusiasm and alertness.

stultification NOUN

stumble VERB trip and lose one's balance; walk with frequent stumbles; make mistakes in speaking etc. NOUN an act of stumbling.

stumble across encounter accidentally.

stumbling block NOUN an obstacle, a difficulty.

stump NOUN **1** the base of a tree left in the ground when the rest has gone; a similar remnant of something cut, broken, or worn down. **2** one of the uprights of a wicket in cricket. VERB **1** baffle; be too difficult for. **2** walk stiffly or noisily.

stump up [INFORMAL] pay over (money required).

stumpy ADJ (**stumpier**, **stumpiest**) short and thick.

stumpiness NOUN

S

stun VERB (**stuns**, **stunning**, **stunned**) knock unconscious; astonish.

stung past and past participle of **STING**.

stunk past and past participle of **STINK**.

stunning ADJ [INFORMAL] very attractive.
stunningly ADV

stunt NOUN an action displaying skill and daring; something done to attract attention. VERB hinder the growth or development of.

stupefy VERB (**stupefies**, **stupefying**, **stupefied**) make unable to think or feel; astound.
stupefaction NOUN

stupendous ADJ amazingly large or good.
stupendously ADV

stupid ADJ not clever; slow at learning or understanding; unable to think clearly.
stupidity NOUN
stupidly ADV

stupor NOUN a dazed condition.

sturdy ADJ (**sturdier**, **sturdiest**) strongly built, hardy, vigorous.
sturdily ADV
sturdiness NOUN

sturgeon NOUN a large shark-like fish.

stutter VERB stammer, especially repeating consonants. NOUN a stammer.

sty NOUN (PL **sties**) **1** a pigsty. **2** (also **stye**) an inflamed swelling on the edge of the eyelid.

style NOUN **1** a manner of writing, speaking, or doing something; a design, an appearance. **2** elegance. VERB design, shape, or arrange, especially fashionably.
in style elegantly, luxuriously.

stylish ADJ fashionable, elegant.
stylishly ADV
stylishness NOUN

stylist NOUN **1** a fashion designer; a hairdresser. **2** a person who writes or performs with good style.

stylistic ADJ of literary or artistic style.
stylistically ADV

stylized (also **stylised**) ADJ represented non-

S

realistically.

stylus NOUN (PL **styluses** or **styli**) a needle-like device for cutting or following a groove in a record.

stymie VERB (**stymies**, **stymieing** or **stymying**, **stymied**) [INFORMAL] obstruct, thwart.

styptic /stip-tik/ ADJ checking bleeding by causing blood vessels to contract.

styrene /stI-reen/ NOUN a liquid hydrocarbon used in plastics.

suave /swahv/ ADJ charming, confident, and elegant.
suavely ADV
suavity NOUN

sub NOUN [INFORMAL] **1** a submarine. **2** a subscription. **3** a substitute. **4** a subeditor.

S

sub- PREFIX under; subordinate.

subaltern /sub-ăl-tĕn/ NOUN an army officer below the rank of captain.

sub-aqua ADJ of underwater swimming.

subatomic ADJ smaller than an atom; occurring in an atom.

subcommittee NOUN a committee formed from some members of a main committee.

subconscious ADJ concerning the part of the mind of which one is not fully aware but which influences one's actions and feelings. NOUN this part of the mind.
subconsciously ADV

subcontinent NOUN a large land mass forming part of a continent.

subcontract VERB assign (work forming part of a contract) to someone outside one's company; undertake work in this way.
subcontractor NOUN

subculture NOUN a culture within a larger one.

subcutaneous /sub-kyoo-tay-ni-ŭs/ ADJ under the skin.

subdivide VERB divide (a part) into smaller parts.
subdivision NOUN

subdue VERB bring under control; make quieter or less intense.

subeditor NOUN a person who prepares newspaper

etc. text for printing.

subhuman ADJ less than human; not fully human.

subject NOUN /**sub**-jekt/ **1** a person or thing being discussed or treated; a branch of knowledge taught in schools, universities, etc. **2** a citizen, a person ruled by a government etc. **3** [GRAMMAR] the words in a sentence naming the person or thing performing the action of the verb. ADJ /**sub**-jekt/ not independent, ruled by another. VERB /sub-**jekt**/ cause to undergo an experience.
subject to /**sub**-jekt/ **1** liable to experience. **2** depending on. **3** under the authority of.
subjection NOUN

subjective ADJ **1** dependent on personal taste or views etc. **2** [GRAMMAR] of the form of a word used when it is the subject of a sentence.
subjectively ADV

subject matter NOUN the topic treated in a book or speech etc.

sub judice /sub **joo**-di-si/ ADJ under judicial consideration, not yet decided.

subjugate VERB bring under control or rule, especially by conquest.
subjugation NOUN

subjunctive ADJ [GRAMMAR] of the form of a verb expressing what is imagined, wished, or possible; e.g. *were* in *if I were you*.

sublet VERB (**sublets**, **subletting**, **sublet**) let (rooms etc. that one holds by lease) to a tenant.

sublimate VERB divert the energy of (an emotion or impulse) into a culturally higher activity.
sublimation NOUN

sublime ADJ of the highest excellence or beauty.
sublimely ADV

subliminal ADJ below the level of conscious awareness.

sub-machine gun NOUN a hand-held lightweight machine gun.

submarine ADJ under the surface of the sea. NOUN a

S

vessel that can operate under water.

submerge VERB go or cause to be under water; cover, obscure.
submersion NOUN

submersible ADJ designed to operate while submerged. NOUN a submersible craft.

submission NOUN **1** the action of submitting. **2** a proposal or application submitted for consideration.

submissive ADJ meek, obedient.
submissively ADV
submissiveness NOUN

submit VERB (**submits, submitting, submitted**) **1** yield to authority or power; subject to a particular treatment. **2** present for consideration.

subordinate ADJ /sub-**or**-di-năt/ of lesser importance or rank; working under another's authority. NOUN /sub-**or**-di-năt/ a subordinate person. VERB /sub-**or**-di-nayt/ treat as less important than something else.
subordination NOUN

suborn VERB induce by bribery to commit perjury or another unlawful act.
subornation NOUN

subpoena /sŭ-pee-nă/ NOUN a writ commanding a person to appear in a law court. VERB (**subpoenas, subpoenaing, subpoenaed**) summon with a subpoena.

subscribe VERB **1** pay in advance to receive a publication etc. regularly; contribute to a fund. **2** [FORMAL] sign.
subscribe to agree with, believe (a theory etc.).
subscriber NOUN

subscription NOUN a sum of money contributed; a fee for membership etc.; a process of subscribing.

subsequent ADJ occurring after something.
subsequently ADV

subservient ADJ **1** less important. **2** completely obedient.
subservience NOUN
subserviently ADV

subset NOUN a set of which all the elements

are contained in another set.

subside VERB sink to a lower or normal level; become less intense. **subsidence** NOUN

subsidiarity NOUN the principle that a central authority should perform only those functions not performed more efficiently at local level.

subsidiary ADJ of secondary importance; (of a business company) controlled by another. NOUN (PL **subsidiaries**) a subsidiary company.

subsidize (also **subsidise**) VERB pay a subsidy to or for.

subsidy NOUN (PL **subsidies**) money granted to support an industry and thus keep prices down; money granted to other enterprises.

subsist VERB keep oneself alive, exist. **subsistence** NOUN

subsoil NOUN the soil lying immediately below the surface layer.

subsonic ADJ of or flying at speeds less than that of sound.

substance NOUN **1** the matter of which something consists; a particular kind of matter. **2** an intoxicating or stimulating drug. **3** reality; importance. **4** something's essence or basic meaning.

substantial ADJ **1** solid, real; large, strong; important. **2** concerning the essence of something. **3** wealthy. **substantially** ADV

substantiate VERB support with evidence. **substantiation** NOUN

substantive ADJ genuine; existing in its own right.

substitute NOUN a person or thing that acts or serves in place of another. VERB use or serve as a substitute. **substitution** NOUN

subsume VERB bring or include under a particular classification.

subtenant NOUN a person to whom a room etc. is sublet.

subterfuge /sub-tĕ-fyooj/

NOUN deceit used to achieve an aim.

subterranean ADJ underground.

subtext NOUN an underlying theme.

subtitle NOUN **1** a caption displayed on a cinema or television screen to translate dialogue. **2** a subordinate title. VERB provide with subtitle(s).

subtle /sutt-ĕl/ ADJ (**subtler**, **subtlest**) **1** so slight or delicate as to be hard to analyse or identify. **2** making fine distinctions; ingenious.
subtlety NOUN
subtly ADV

subtotal NOUN the total of part of a group of figures.

subtract VERB remove (a part or quantity or number) from a greater one.
subtraction NOUN

subtropical ADJ of regions bordering on the tropics.

suburb NOUN a residential area outside the central part of a town.
suburban ADJ
suburbanite NOUN

suburbia NOUN suburbs and their inhabitants.

subvention NOUN a subsidy.

subvert VERB undermine the authority of, especially by weakening people's trust.
subversion NOUN
subversive ADJ

subway NOUN a tunnel under a road, used by pedestrians; [US] an underground railway.

succeed VERB **1** achieve one's aim or wish. **2** take the place previously filled by; come next in order.

success NOUN the attainment of one's aims, or of wealth, fame, or position; a successful person or thing.

successful ADJ accomplishing an aim; achieving wealth or popularity.
successfully ADV

succession NOUN a number of people or things following one after the other; the action or right of inheriting a position, title, etc.

in succession one after another.

successive ADJ following in succession.
successively ADV

successor NOUN a person who succeeds another.

succinct /suk-**sinkt**/ ADJ concise and clear.
succinctly ADV

succour ([US] **succor**) NOUN help and support given at a time of distress. VERB give such help to.

succulent ADJ juicy; (of plants) having thick fleshy leaves. NOUN a succulent plant.
succulence NOUN

succumb VERB give way to something overpowering.

such DETERMINER & PRON of the type previously mentioned or about to be mentioned; to so high a degree; so great.
as such in the precise sense. **such as** for example. **such that** with the result that.

such-and-such ADJ particular but not needing to be specified.

suchlike PRON things of the type mentioned. DETERMINER of the type mentioned.

suck VERB draw (liquid or air) into the mouth by contracting the lips to create a vacuum; draw liquid from in this way; hold in the mouth and roll with the tongue; draw in a particular direction. NOUN an act of sucking.
suck up to [INFORMAL] behave in a servile way to (someone) to gain advantage.

sucker NOUN **1** an organ or device that can adhere to a surface by suction. **2** [INFORMAL] a person who is easily deceived.
a sucker for [INFORMAL] very fond of or susceptible to.

suckle VERB feed at the breast.

suckling NOUN an unweaned child or animal.

sucrose NOUN sugar.

suction NOUN the production of a partial vacuum so that external atmospheric pressure forces fluid etc. into the vacant space or causes adhesion.

sudden ADJ happening or done quickly or without warning.
all of a sudden suddenly.
suddenly ADV
suddenness NOUN

sudorific /soo-dŏ-rif-ik/ ADJ causing sweating.

suds PLURAL NOUN soapsuds.

sue VERB (**sues**, **suing**, **sued**) take legal proceedings against.

suede /swayd/ NOUN leather with a velvety nap on one side.

suet NOUN hard white fat from round an animal's kidneys, used in cooking.

suffer VERB undergo (something unpleasant or harmful); experience pain or distress.
suffering NOUN

sufferance NOUN toleration rather than actual approval.

suffice VERB be enough (for).

sufficient ADJ enough.
sufficiency NOUN
sufficiently ADV

suffix NOUN letters added at the end of a word to make another word.

suffocate VERB kill by stopping the breathing; have or cause to have difficulty breathing.
suffocation NOUN

suffrage NOUN the right to vote in political elections.

suffragette NOUN [HISTORICAL] a woman who campaigned for the right to vote.

suffuse VERB spread throughout or over.
suffusion NOUN

sugar NOUN a sweet crystalline substance obtained from the juices of various plants. VERB sweeten; make more acceptable.
sugary ADJ

sugar beet NOUN white beet from which sugar is obtained.

sugar cane NOUN a tall tropical plant from which sugar is obtained.

sugar soap NOUN an abrasive cleaning compound.

suggest VERB put forward for consideration; imply;

cause someone to think of.

suggestible ADJ easily influenced.
suggestibility NOUN

suggestion NOUN **1** an idea or plan put forward for consideration. **2** a thing that suggests that something is the case; a slight trace.

suggestive ADJ conveying a suggestion; suggesting something indecent.
suggestively ADV

suicidal ADJ likely or wanting to commit suicide; very risky, likely to cause death or ruin.
suicidally ADV

suicide NOUN the intentional killing of oneself; a person who does this; an act destructive to one's own interests.

sui generis ADJ unique.

suit NOUN **1** a set of clothes to be worn together, especially jacket and trousers or skirt. **2** any of the four sets into which a pack of cards is divided. **3** a lawsuit. VERB **1** be convenient for or acceptable to. **2** (of clothes etc.) enhance the appearance of.

suitable ADJ right for the purpose or occasion.
suitability NOUN
suitably ADV

suitcase NOUN a rectangular case for carrying clothes.

suite /sweet/ NOUN **1** a set of rooms or furniture. **2** a group of attendants. **3** a set of musical pieces.

suitor NOUN a man who is courting a woman.

sulfur etc. US spelling of **SULPHUR** etc.

sulk VERB be quietly bad-tempered and sullen through annoyance or disappointment. NOUN (**a sulk** or **the sulks**) a period of sulking.
sulkily ADV
sulkiness NOUN
sulky ADJ

sullen ADJ bad-tempered; gloomy.
sullenly ADV
sullenness NOUN

sully VERB (**sullies**, **sullying**, **sullied**) stain, blemish.

sulphate ([US] **sulfate**)

NOUN a salt of sulphuric acid.

sulphide ([US] **sulfide**) NOUN a compound of sulphur and an element or radical.

sulphite ([US] **sulfite**) NOUN a salt of sulphurous acid.

sulphur ([US] **sulfur**) NOUN a pale yellow chemical element.
sulphurous ADJ

sulphuric acid ([US] **sulfuric acid**) NOUN a strong corrosive acid.

sultan NOUN a ruler of certain Muslim countries.

sultana NOUN **1** a seedless raisin. **2** a sultan's wife, mother, or daughter.

sultanate NOUN a sultan's territory.

sultry ADJ (**sultrier, sultriest**) hot and humid; (of someone's appearance) suggesting passion and sensuality.
sultriness NOUN

sum NOUN **1** an amount of money; a total. **2** an arithmetical problem.
sum up summarize; express an opinion of.

summarize (also **summarise**) VERB make or be a summary of.
summarization NOUN

summary NOUN (PL **summaries**) a brief statement of the main points of something.
ADJ **1** brief, without unnecessary detail. **2** without legal formalities.
summarily ADV

summation NOUN **1** the process of adding up. **2** the action of summarizing; a summary.

summer NOUN the warmest season of the year.
summery ADJ

summer time NOUN the time shown by clocks put forward in summer to give longer light evenings.

summit NOUN **1** the top of a mountain; the highest point. **2** a conference between heads of states.

summon VERB send for; order to appear in a law court; arrange (a meeting); produce (a reaction or quality) with effort.

summons NOUN a

command summoning a person; a written order to appear in a law court. VERB serve with a summons.

sumo /soo-moh/ NOUN Japanese wrestling.

sump NOUN a reservoir of oil in a petrol engine; a hole or low area into which liquid drains.

sumptuous ADJ splendid, lavish, costly.
sumptuously ADV
sumptuousness NOUN

sun NOUN the star around which the earth travels; the light or warmth from this; any fixed star. VERB (**suns**, **sunning**, **sunned**) expose to the sun.

sunbathe VERB lie in the sun, especially to tan one's skin.

sunbeam NOUN a ray of sun.

sunbed NOUN a device with ultraviolet lamps, for acquiring a tan artificially.

sunblock NOUN a cream protecting the skin against sunburn.

sunburn NOUN inflammation of the skin caused by exposure to sun. VERB suffer sunburn.
sunburnt ADJ

sundae /sun-day/ NOUN a dish of ice cream and fruit, nuts, syrup, etc.

Sunday NOUN the day after Saturday.

Sunday school NOUN a school for the religious instruction of Christian children, held on Sundays.

sunder VERB [LITERARY] break or tear apart.

sundial NOUN a device that shows the time by means of a shadow cast by the sun on a plate marked with the hours.

sundown NOUN sunset.

sundry ADJ various. NOUN (**sundries**) various small items.
all and sundry everyone.

sunflower NOUN a tall plant with large yellow flowers.

sung past participle of **SING**.

sunk past and past participle of **SINK**.

sunken ADJ lying below the level of the surrounding surface.

Sunni /suu-ni/ NOUN (PL **Sunni** or **Sunnis**) one of the two main branches of Islam; a Muslim who adheres to this branch of Islam.

sunny ADJ (**sunnier**, **sunniest**) **1** full of sunshine. **2** cheerful.
sunnily ADV

sunrise NOUN the rising of the sun.

sunset NOUN the setting of the sun; the sky full of colour at sunset.

sunshade NOUN a parasol; an awning.

sunshine NOUN direct sunlight.

sunspot NOUN a dark patch observed on the sun's surface.

sunstroke NOUN illness caused by too much exposure to sun.

S

super ADJ [INFORMAL] excellent, superb.

superannuation NOUN regular payment made by an employee towards a future pension.

superb ADJ of the most impressive or splendid kind.
superbly ADV

supercharge VERB increase the power of (an engine) by a device that forces extra air or fuel into it.
supercharger NOUN

supercilious ADJ haughty and superior.
superciliously ADV
superciliousness NOUN

supercomputer NOUN a very powerful computer.

superficial ADJ of or on the surface; shallow, not profound.
superficiality NOUN
superficially ADV

superfluous ADJ more than is required.
superfluity NOUN
superfluously ADV

superhighway NOUN an electronic network for the rapid transfer of information.

superhuman ADJ having or requiring more than ordinary human capacity.

superimpose VERB place on top of something else.

superintend VERB oversee.
superintendence NOUN

superintendent NOUN **1** a

supervisor. **2** a police officer next above inspector.

superior ADJ **1** of higher rank or quality; greater; thinking oneself better than others, haughty. **2** higher. NOUN a person or thing of higher rank or ability or quality.
superiority NOUN

superlative ADJ **1** of the highest quality. **2** of the grammatical form expressing 'most'. NOUN a superlative form of a word.
superlatively ADV

supermarket NOUN a large self-service store selling food and household goods.

supernatural ADJ of or attributed to a power outside the forces of nature.
supernaturally ADV

supernova NOUN (PL **supernovas** or **supernovae**) a star that suddenly increases in brightness because of an explosion.

supernumerary ADJ extra.

superphosphate NOUN a fertilizer containing soluble phosphates.

superpower NOUN an extremely powerful nation.

superscalar ADJ (of a computer microprocessor) able to execute more than one instruction at one time.

superscript ADJ written just above and to the right of a word etc.

supersede VERB take the place of; put or use in place of.

supersonic ADJ of or flying at speeds greater than that of sound.
supersonically ADV

superstition NOUN a belief in magical and similar influences; an idea or practice based on this.
superstitious ADJ

superstore NOUN a large supermarket.

superstructure NOUN a structure that rests on something else; the upper parts of a ship or building.

supervene VERB occur as an interruption or a change.

supervention NOUN

supervise VERB direct and inspect (workers etc.). **supervision** NOUN **supervisor** NOUN **supervisory** ADJ

supine /soo-pIn/ ADJ 1 lying face upwards. 2 weakly or idly failing to act.

supper NOUN an evening meal, especially a light or informal one.

supplant VERB oust and take the place of.

supple ADJ bending easily. **suppleness** NOUN **supply** ADV

supplement NOUN something added as an extra part or to make up for a deficiency. VERB provide or be a supplement to.

S

supplementary ADJ serving as a supplement.

suppliant /sup-li-ănt/ NOUN a person asking humbly for something.

supplicate VERB ask humbly for something. **supplication** NOUN

supply VERB (**supplies**, **supplying**, **supplied**) provide; make available to; satisfy (a need). NOUN (PL **supplies**) a stock to be used; the action of supplying; (**supplies**) necessary goods provided.

support VERB 1 bear the weight of. 2 assist financially; encourage, approve of; comfort; suggest the truth of. 3 endure. NOUN the act of supporting; a person or thing that supports. **supporter** NOUN **supportive** ADJ

suppose VERB assume, think; take as a hypothesis; presuppose. **be supposed to** be required to as a duty.

supposed ADJ thought to exist, often wrongly.

supposedly ADV according to what is generally thought or believed.

supposition NOUN the process of supposing; what is supposed.

suppository NOUN (PL **suppositories**) a solid medicinal substance placed in the rectum or vagina and left to melt.

suppress VERB 1 put an

end to the activity or existence of. **2** keep from being known.
suppression NOUN
suppressor NOUN

suppurate /sup-yuu-rayt/ VERB form pus, fester.
suppuration NOUN

supra- PREFIX above; beyond.

supreme ADJ highest in authority; greatest, most intense.
supremacy NOUN
supremely ADV

supremo NOUN (PL **supremos**) [INFORMAL] a person in overall charge of something; a person very skilled at something.

surcharge NOUN an additional charge. VERB exact a surcharge from (someone).

sure ADJ **1** confident, feeling no doubts. **2** reliable; certainly true or correct. ADV [INFORMAL] certainly.
make sure act so as to be certain. **sure to** certainly going to do something.
sureness NOUN

sure-footed ADJ never slipping or stumbling.

surely ADV **1** used to emphasize a belief that something is true. **2** (as an answer) of course. **3** confidently; securely.

surety NOUN (PL **sureties**) a guarantee; a guarantor of a person's promise.

surf NOUN white foam of breaking waves. VERB **1** ride on a surfboard. **2** move between sites on (the Internet).
surfer NOUN

surface NOUN the outside or uppermost layer of something; the top, the upper limit; an outward appearance. ADJ on the surface; (of mail etc.) carried by sea, not air. VERB **1** come to the surface of water etc.; become apparent. **2** put a specified surface on.

surfboard NOUN a narrow board for riding over surf.

surfeit /ser-fit/ NOUN an excessive amount, especially of food or drink. VERB satiate, give more than enough to.

surfing NOUN the sport of riding on a surfboard.

surge VERB move forward

in or like waves; increase in volume or intensity. NOUN a surging movement or increase.

surgeon NOUN a doctor qualified to perform surgical operations.

surgery NOUN (PL **surgeries**) **1** treatment by cutting or manipulation of affected parts of the body. **2** a place where (or times when) a doctor or dentist or an MP etc. is available for consultation.
surgical ADJ
surgically ADV

surly ADJ (**surlier**, **surliest**) bad-tempered and unfriendly.
surliness NOUN

surmise VERB guess, suppose. NOUN a guess, a supposition.

S

surmount VERB overcome (a difficulty or obstacle); be on the top of.
surmountable ADJ

surname NOUN a family name.

surpass VERB outdo; excel.

surplice NOUN a loose white garment worn by clergy and choir members.

surplus NOUN an amount left over after what is needed has been used.

surprise NOUN an emotion aroused by something sudden or unexpected; something causing this. VERB cause to feel surprise; approach or attack unexpectedly.

surreal ADJ bizarre; dreamlike.

surrealism NOUN a style of art and literature seeking to express what is in the subconscious mind, characterized by unusual images.
surrealist NOUN
surrealistic ADJ

surrender VERB cease to resist, submit to superior force etc.; hand over, give up. NOUN an act of surrendering.

surreptitious ADJ acting or done stealthily.
surreptitiously ADV

surrogate /su-rŏ-găt/ NOUN a deputy.
surrogacy NOUN

surrogate mother NOUN a woman who bears a

child on behalf of another.

surround VERB come, place, or be all round; encircle. NOUN a border.

surroundings PLURAL NOUN things or conditions around a person or place.

surtax NOUN an additional tax.

surveillance /ser-vay-lăns/ NOUN close observation.

survey VERB /ser-**vay**/ look at and take a general view of; examine the condition of (a building); measure and map out. NOUN /**ser**-vay/ a general look at or examination of something; a report or map produced by surveying.

surveyor NOUN a person whose job is to survey land or buildings.

survival NOUN surviving; something that has survived from an earlier time.

survive VERB continue to exist despite difficulty or danger; not be killed by; remain alive after the death of.

survivability NOUN
survivable ADJ
survivor NOUN

susceptible ADJ easily affected, influenced, or harmed.
susceptibility NOUN

sushi /soo-shi/ NOUN a Japanese dish of flavoured balls of cold rice usually garnished with fish.

suspect VERB /sŭ-**spekt**/ **1** feel that something may exist or be true. **2** believe (someone) to be guilty without proof. NOUN /**sus**-pekt/ a person suspected of a crime etc. ADJ /**sus**-pekt/ suspected, open to suspicion.

suspend VERB **1** hang up; keep from falling or sinking in air or liquid. **2** stop temporarily; deprive temporarily of a position or right; keep (a sentence) from being enforced if no further offence is committed within a specified period.

suspender NOUN an attachment to hold up a sock or stocking by its top; (**suspenders**) [US] braces.

suspense NOUN anxious uncertainty while awaiting an event etc.

suspension NOUN **1** the action of suspending. **2** the means by which a vehicle is supported on its axles.

suspension bridge NOUN a bridge suspended from cables that pass over supports at each end.

suspicion NOUN **1** an unconfirmed belief; a feeling that someone is guilty; distrust. **2** a slight trace.

suspicious ADJ feeling or causing suspicion. **suspiciously** ADV

suss VERB [INFORMAL] realize; discover the true nature of.

sussed ADJ [INFORMAL] well informed; clever.

sustain VERB **1** support; give strength to; keep alive or in existence. **2** undergo (injuries etc.). **3** uphold the validity of.

sustainable ADJ (of development etc.) able to be continued without damage to the environment.

sustenance NOUN food, nourishment.

suture /soo-cher/ NOUN surgical stitching of a wound; a stitch or thread used in this. VERB stitch (a wound).

suzerain /soo-zĕ-rayn/ NOUN a country or ruler with some authority over a self-governing country; an overlord.

svelte ADJ slender and graceful.

SW ABBREV south-west; south-western.

swab NOUN an absorbent pad for cleaning wounds or taking specimens; a specimen of a secretion taken on this; a mop. VERB (**swabs**, **swabbing**, **swabbed**) clean with a swab.

swaddle VERB swathe in wraps or warm garments.

swag NOUN **1** [INFORMAL] loot. **2** a decorative festoon of flowers, drapery, etc.

swagger VERB walk or behave with aggressive pride. NOUN this gait or manner.

Swahili NOUN a Bantu language widely used in

East Africa.

swallow VERB cause or allow to go down one's throat; work the throat muscles in doing this; absorb, engulf; accept, believe; resist expressing. NOUN **1** an act of swallowing; an amount swallowed. **2** a small migratory bird with a forked tail.

swam past of **SWIM**.

swami /swah-mi/ NOUN a Hindu male religious teacher.

swamp NOUN a marsh. VERB flood or overwhelm with water; overwhelm with a mass or number of things.
swampy ADJ

swan NOUN a large usually white waterbird.

swank [INFORMAL] VERB show off, try to impress others. NOUN such behaviour.

swansong NOUN a person's last performance or achievement etc.

swap (also **swop**) VERB (**swaps**, **swapping**, **swapped**) exchange. NOUN an exchange; a thing exchanged.

swarm NOUN a large cluster of people, insects, etc. VERB move in a swarm; be crowded.
swarm up climb by gripping with arms and legs.

swarthy ADJ (**swarthier**, **swarthiest**) having a dark complexion.
swarthiness NOUN

swashbuckling ADJ engaging in or full of daring and romantic adventures.
swashbuckler NOUN

swastika NOUN a symbol formed by a cross with ends bent at right angles.

swat VERB (**swats**, **swatting**, **swatted**) hit hard with something flat.
swatter NOUN

swatch NOUN a sample of cloth etc.

swath /swawth/ (also **swathe**) NOUN a strip cut in one sweep or passage by a scythe or mower.

swathe VERB wrap with layers of coverings. NOUN variant of **SWATH**.

sway VERB **1** move gently to and fro. **2** control, influence. NOUN **1** a

swaying movement.
2 influence.

swear VERB (**swears**, **swearing**, **swore**; PAST PARTICIPLE **sworn**) **1** state or promise on oath; state emphatically. **2** use a swear word.
swear by [INFORMAL] have great confidence in.

swear word NOUN a profane or indecent word used in anger etc.

sweat NOUN moisture given off by the body through the pores; a state of sweating; [INFORMAL] hard work; a state of anxiety. VERB give off sweat or as sweat; work hard; be very anxious.
sweaty ADJ

sweatband NOUN a band of material worn to absorb sweat.

sweated labour NOUN work with low pay and bad conditions; workers engaged in this.

sweater NOUN a jumper, a pullover.

sweatshirt NOUN a long-sleeved cotton sweater with a fleecy lining.

sweatshop NOUN a place employing sweated labour.

Swede NOUN a person from Sweden.

swede NOUN a large variety of turnip.

Swedish NOUN the language of Sweden. ADJ relating to Sweden.

sweep VERB (**sweeps**, **sweeping**, **swept**) **1** clean by brushing away dirt; clear away with a broom; drive or push forcefully. **2** move smoothly and swiftly or majestically. **3** extend in a continuous line. NOUN **1** an act of sweeping; a sweeping movement or line; a long expanse of land etc. **2** a chimney sweep. **3** [INFORMAL] a sweepstake.
sweep the board win all the prizes.
sweeper NOUN

sweeping ADJ comprehensive; making no exceptions.

sweepstake NOUN a form of gambling in which the money staked is divided among the winners.

sweet ADJ **1** tasting as if containing sugar.

2 pleasant to hear or smell; delightful; kind; charming. NOUN a small shaped piece of sweet substance; a sweet dish forming one course of a meal.

sweetly ADV
sweetness NOUN

sweetbread NOUN an animal's thymus gland or pancreas used as food.

sweetcorn NOUN sweet kernels of maize, eaten as a vegetable.

sweeten VERB make or become sweet or sweeter.

sweetener NOUN **1** a sweetening substance. **2** [INFORMAL] a bribe.

sweetheart NOUN a girlfriend or boyfriend; a term of affection.

sweetmeal NOUN sweetened wholemeal.

sweet tooth NOUN a liking for sweet food.

swell VERB (**swells**, **swelling**, **swelled**; PAST PARTICIPLE **swollen** or **swelled**) make or become larger from pressure within; curve outwards; make or become greater in amount or intensity. NOUN **1** a curving shape; a gradual increase. **2** the heaving movement of the sea. **3** [INFORMAL], [DATED] a person of wealth or high social position.

swelling NOUN a swollen place on the body.

swelter VERB be uncomfortably hot.

swept past and past participle of **SWEEP**.

swerve VERB turn aside from a straight course. NOUN a swerving movement or direction.

swift ADJ quick, rapid. NOUN a swiftly flying bird with narrow wings.

swiftly ADV

swill VERB **1** wash, rinse; cause (liquid) to swirl in a container. **2** [INFORMAL] drink greedily. NOUN kitchen refuse mixed with water and fed to pigs.

swim VERB (**swims**, **swimming**, **swam**; PAST PARTICIPLE **swum**) **1** travel through water by movements of the body. **2** be covered with liquid. **3** seem to be whirling or waving; be dizzy. NOUN an act or period of

swimming.
swimmer NOUN

swimming bath NOUN a building containing a public swimming pool.

swimmingly ADV [INFORMAL] easily and satisfactorily.

swimming pool NOUN an artificial pool for swimming in.

swindle VERB cheat, deprive of money etc. fraudulently. NOUN an act of swindling.
swindler NOUN

swine NOUN **1** (as PL) pigs. **2** (PL **swine** or **swines**) [INFORMAL] a very unpleasant person or thing.

swing VERB (**swings**, **swinging**, **swung**) **1** move or cause to move to and fro while suspended or on an axis. **2** move by grasping a support and jumping; move or cause to move in a smooth curve. **3** change or cause to change from one mood or opinion to another; influence decisively. NOUN **1** a swinging movement; a hanging seat for swinging on. **2** a style of jazz music; its rhythm. **3** a change in opinion etc.
in full swing with activity at its height.
swinger NOUN

swing bridge NOUN a bridge that can be swung aside for boats to pass.

swingeing ADJ severe; extreme.

swing-wing NOUN an aircraft wing that can be moved to slant backwards.

swipe [INFORMAL] VERB **1** hit with a swinging blow. **2** snatch, steal. NOUN a swinging blow.

swipe card NOUN a plastic card carrying magnetically encoded information which is read when the card is slid through an electronic device.

swirl VERB whirl, flow with a whirling movement.

swish VERB move with a hissing sound. NOUN this sound. ADJ [INFORMAL] smart, fashionable.

Swiss NOUN (PL **Swiss**) a person from Switzerland. ADJ relating to

Switzerland.

Swiss roll NOUN a thin flat sponge cake spread with jam etc. and rolled up.

switch NOUN **1** a device operated to turn electric current on or off. **2** a shift in opinion or method etc. **3** a flexible stick or rod, a whip. **4** a tress of false hair. VERB **1** change the direction or position of; change, exchange. **2** turn (an electrical device) on or off.

switchback NOUN a railway used for amusement at a fair etc., with alternate steep ascents and descents; a road with similar slopes.

switchboard NOUN a panel of switches for making telephone connections or operating electric circuits.

swivel NOUN a link or pivot enabling one part to revolve without turning another. VERB (**swivels**, **swivelling**, **swivelled**; [US] **swiveling**, **swiveled**) turn on or as if on a swivel.

swollen past participle of **SWELL**.

swoop VERB make a sudden downward rush; make a sudden attack. NOUN a swooping movement or attack.

swop variant of **SWAP**.

sword /sord/ NOUN a weapon with a long blade and a hilt.

swordfish NOUN (PL **swordfish**) an edible sea fish with a long sword-like upper jaw.

swore past of **SWEAR**.

sworn past participle of **SWEAR**. ADJ determined to remain as specified: *sworn enemies*.

swot [INFORMAL] VERB (**swots**, **swotting**, **swotted**) study hard. NOUN a person who studies hard.

swum past participle of **SWIM**.

swung past and past participle of **SWING**.

sybarite /sib-ă-rIt/ NOUN a person who is self-indulgently fond of luxury.
sybaritic ADJ

sycamore NOUN a large tree of the maple family.

S

sycophant /sik-ŏ-fant/ NOUN a person who tries to win favour by flattery. **sycophantic** ADJ **sycophantically** ADV

syllable NOUN a unit of sound in a word. **syllabic** ADJ

syllabub NOUN a dish of flavoured whipped cream.

syllabus NOUN (PL **syllabuses** or **syllabi**) the subjects to be covered by a course of study.

syllogism /sil-ŏ-jiz-ĕm/ NOUN an argument drawing a conclusion from two statements. **syllogistic** ADJ

sylph /silf/ NOUN a slender girl or woman; a spirit of the air.

sylvan (also **silvan**) ADJ of woods; wooded; rural.

S

symbiosis /sim-bI-**oh**-sis/ NOUN (PL **symbioses**) a relationship between two organisms living in close, usually mutually beneficial, association. **symbiotic** ADJ

symbol NOUN something representing something else; a written character etc. with a special meaning.

symbolic (also **symbolical**) ADJ of, using, or used as a symbol. **symbolically** ADV

symbolism NOUN the use of symbols to express things. **symbolist** NOUN

symbolize (also **symbolise**) VERB be a symbol of; represent by means of a symbol.

symmetry /sim-ĕt-ri/ NOUN the state of having parts that correspond in size, shape, and position on either side of a dividing line or round a centre. **symmetrical** ADJ **symmetrically** ADV

sympathetic ADJ feeling or showing sympathy; inspiring sympathy and affection; (of an effect) corresponding to or provoked by a similar action elsewhere. **sympathetically** ADV

sympathize (also **sympathise**) VERB feel or express sympathy. **sympathizer** NOUN

sympathy NOUN (PL **sympathies**) sorrow at

someone else's misfortune; understanding between people; support, approval.
in sympathy fitting in, in keeping.

symphony NOUN (PL **symphonies**) a long elaborate musical composition for a full orchestra.
symphonic ADJ

symposium /sim-**poh**-zi-ŭm/ NOUN (PL **symposia**) a meeting for discussing a particular subject.

symptom NOUN a sign of the existence of a condition, especially a disease.

symptomatic ADJ serving as a symptom.

synagogue NOUN a building for public Jewish worship.

synapse /**sI**-naps/ NOUN a junction of two nerve cells.

synchronic ADJ concerned with something as it exists at a particular time, not with its history.

synchronize (also **synchronise**) VERB cause to occur or operate at the same time; cause (clocks etc.) to show the same time.
synchronization NOUN

synchronous ADJ occurring or existing at the same time.

syncopate VERB change the accents in (music) so that weak beats become strong and vice versa.
syncopation NOUN

syndicate NOUN /**sin**-di-kăt/ a group of people or firms combining to achieve a common interest. VERB /**sin**-di-kayt/ control or manage by a syndicate; arrange publication in many newspapers etc. simultaneously.
syndication NOUN

syndrome NOUN a combination of signs, symptoms, etc. characteristic of a specified condition.

synod /**sin**-ŏd/ NOUN a council of clergy and officials to discuss church policy, teaching, etc.

synonym NOUN a word or phrase meaning the same

as another in the same language.
synonymous ADJ

synopsis /sin-op-sis/ NOUN (PL **synopses**) a summary, a brief general survey.

synovial /sin-oh-vi-ăl/ ADJ (of a joint) surrounded by a membrane secreting a thick lubricating fluid.

syntax NOUN the way words are arranged to form phrases and sentences.
syntactic ADJ
syntactically ADV

synthesis NOUN (PL **syntheses**) **1** the combination of components to form a connected whole. **2** the production of chemical compounds by reaction from simpler substances.

S

synthesize (also **synthesise**) VERB **1** make by chemical synthesis. **2** combine into a coherent whole.

synthesizer (also **synthesiser**) NOUN an electronic musical instrument able to produce a great variety of sounds.

synthetic ADJ made by synthesis; not natural or genuine. NOUN a synthetic substance or fabric.
synthetically ADV

syphilis /si-fi-lis/ NOUN a venereal disease.
syphilitic ADJ

syringe NOUN a tube with a nozzle and piston, for sucking in and ejecting liquid. VERB wash out or spray with a syringe.

syrup NOUN a thick sweet liquid.
syrupy ADJ

system NOUN **1** a set of connected things that form a whole or work together; the animal body as a whole; a set of rules or practices used together; orderliness. **2** a method of classification, notation, or measurement.

systematic ADJ methodical.
systematically ADV

systematize (also **systematise**) VERB arrange according to a system.

systemic ADJ of or affecting an entire system.

Tt

T (also **t**) NOUN (PL **Ts** or **T's**) the twentieth letter of the alphabet.
to a T [INFORMAL] exactly; to perfection.

ta EXCLAMATION [INFORMAL] thank you.

tab NOUN a small projecting flap or strip.
keep tabs on [INFORMAL] keep under observation.

tabard NOUN a short sleeveless tunic-like garment.

tabby NOUN (PL **tabbies**) a cat with grey or brown fur and dark stripes.

tabernacle /tab-ĕ-nak-ĕl/ NOUN (in the Bible) a light hut, a portable shrine; (in the RC Church) a receptacle for the Eucharist; a meeting place for worship, used by Nonconformists or Mormons.

table NOUN **1** a piece of furniture with a flat top supported on one or more legs. **2** food provided. **3** a list of facts or figures arranged in columns. VERB submit (a motion or report) for discussion.

tableau /tab-loh/ NOUN (PL **tableaux**) a silent motionless group arranged to represent a scene.

table d'hôte /tahbl doht/ NOUN a restaurant meal at a fixed price and with a set menu.

tableland NOUN a plateau of land.

tablespoon NOUN a large spoon for serving food.
tablespoonful NOUN

tablet NOUN **1** a slab bearing an inscription etc. **2** a measured amount of a drug compressed into a solid form.

table tennis NOUN a game played with bats and a light hollow ball on a table.

tabloid NOUN a small-sized newspaper, often sensational in style.

taboo (also **tabu**) NOUN a ban or prohibition made by religion or social custom. ADJ prohibited by a taboo.

tabular ADJ arranged in a table or list.

tabulate VERB arrange in tabular form.
tabulation NOUN

tachograph /tak-ŏ-grahf/ NOUN a device in a vehicle to record speed and travel time.

tachometer /tak-o-mi-tĕ/ NOUN an instrument measuring the speed of an engine.

tacit ADJ implied or understood without being put into words.
tacitly ADJ

taciturn ADJ saying very little.
taciturnity NOUN

tack NOUN **1** a small broad-headed nail. **2** a long stitch as a temporary fastening. **3** a change of course in sailing; an approach to a problem. **4** equipment used in horse riding. VERB **1** nail with tacks. **2** stitch with tacks. **3** change course by turning a boat into the wind; do this repeatedly.
tack on add as an extra item.

tackle NOUN **1** a set of ropes and pulleys for lifting etc. **2** equipment for a task or sport. **3** an act of tackling in football etc. VERB **1** try to deal with or overcome (an opponent or problem). **2** intercept (an opponent who has the ball in football etc.).

tacky ADJ (**tackier**, **tackiest**) **1** (of paint etc.) sticky, not quite dry. **2** [INFORMAL] tasteless, vulgar.
tackiness NOUN

taco /ta-koh, **tah**-koh/ NOUN (PL **tacos**) a folded tortilla with a savoury filling.

tact NOUN skill in avoiding offence or in winning goodwill.
tactful ADJ
tactfully ADV

tactless ADJ
tactlessly ADV

tactic NOUN an action to achieve a particular end; (**tactics**) the organization of forces in battle and of operations; steps towards an overall goal.

tactical ADJ of tactics; (of weapons) for use in a battle or at close quarters.
tactically ADV

tactical voting NOUN voting for the candidate most likely to defeat the leading candidate.

tactician NOUN an expert in tactics.

tactile ADJ of or using the sense of touch.

tadpole NOUN the larva of a frog or toad etc. at the stage when it has gills and a tail.

taffeta NOUN a shiny silk-like fabric.

tag NOUN **1** a label; an electronic device attached to someone or something so that they can be monitored. **2** a metal point on a shoelace etc. **3** a much-used phrase or quotation. VERB (**tags**, **tagging**, **tagged**) attach a label or electronic tag to.
tag along follow without being invited. **tag on** add at the end.

tagliatelle /tal-yă-**tel**-li/ NOUN pasta in ribbon-shaped strips.

t'ai chi /ty **chee**/ NOUN a Chinese martial art and system of exercises.

tail NOUN **1** an animal's hindmost part, especially when extending beyond its body; the rear or end of something. **2** [INFORMAL] a person tailing another. **3** (**tails**) the reverse of a coin as a choice when tossing. **4** (**tails**) [INFORMAL] a tailcoat. VERB [INFORMAL] follow and observe.
tail off become fewer, smaller, or slighter; end inconclusively.

tailback NOUN a queue of traffic extending back from an obstruction.

tailboard NOUN a hinged or removable back of a lorry etc.

tailcoat NOUN a man's formal coat with a long divided flap at the back.

tailgate NOUN a rear door

in a motor vehicle; a tailboard.

tail light NOUN a light at the back of a motor vehicle or train etc.

tailor NOUN a maker of men's clothes, especially to order. VERB **1** make (clothes) as a tailor. **2** make or adapt for a special purpose.
tailor-made ADJ

tailplane NOUN the horizontal part of an aeroplane's tail.

tailspin NOUN an aircraft's spinning dive.

taint NOUN a trace of decay, infection, or other bad quality. VERB contaminate, pollute, spoil.

take VERB (**takes**, **taking**, **took**; PAST PARTICIPLE **taken**) **1** get hold of; receive and keep; steal; capture. **2** cause to go with one, convey, remove; escort, guide. **3** accept; endure; react to, interpret. **4** measure (temperature etc.). **5** perform, make (a decision, an action); act on (an opportunity). **6** study or teach (a subject). **7** require (time etc.). **8** make (a photograph). NOUN **1** a sequence of film or sound recorded at one time. **2** the amount of something gained from a source.
be taken ill become ill. **be taken with** or **by** find attractive. **take after** resemble (a parent). **take back** withdraw (a statement). **take down** write from dictation. **take in 1** make (a garment) smaller. **2** realize fully. **3** include. **4** deceive. **take off 1** become airborne. **2** [INFORMAL] mimic humorously. **take on 1** undertake; engage as an opponent. **2** employ. **take one's time** not hurry. **take out on** relieve (anger etc.) by mistreating (someone not to blame). **take over** take control of. **take part** join in an activity. **take place** occur. **take sides** support one party against another. **take to 1** develop a liking or ability for. **2** develop as a habit. **3** go to (a place) for refuge. **take up 1** adopt as

t

a hobby. **2** use (time). **3** accept (an offer or the person making it). **take up with** begin to associate with.
taker NOUN

takeaway NOUN a restaurant or shop selling cooked food to be eaten elsewhere; a meal of such food.

take-off NOUN **1** a piece of humorous mimicry. **2** the process of becoming airborne.

takeover NOUN the gaining of control of a business etc.

takings PLURAL NOUN money taken in business.

talc NOUN talcum powder; magnesium silicate used as a lubricator.

talcum powder NOUN talc powdered and usually perfumed, for use on the skin.

tale NOUN a narrative, a story.

talent NOUN a special ability; people possessing such ability.

talented ADJ having talent.

talisman NOUN (PL **talismans**) an object supposed to bring good luck.

talk VERB convey or exchange ideas by spoken words; have the power of speech; (**talk over** or **through**) discuss thoroughly. NOUN a conversation; an address or lecture; (**talks**) formal discussions; rumour. **the talk of** widely discussed among.
talker NOUN

talkative ADJ talking very much.

talking book NOUN a recorded reading of a book.

talking shop NOUN [INFORMAL] a place for unproductive talk.

talking-to NOUN [INFORMAL] a reproof or reprimand.

tall ADJ of great or specified height.
tallness NOUN

tall order NOUN a difficult task.

tallow NOUN animal fat used to make candles, lubricants, etc.

tall story NOUN (PL **tall stories**) [INFORMAL] a

fanciful and incredible account.

tally NOUN (PL **tallies**) a total score etc.; a record of this. VERB (**tallies**, **tallying**, **tallied**) agree, correspond.

Talmud NOUN the ancient writings on Jewish law and tradition.
Talmudic ADJ

talon NOUN a bird's large claw.

tambourine NOUN a percussion instrument with jingling metal discs.

tame ADJ (of an animal) domesticated, not fierce towards or frightened of humans; unexciting.
VERB make tame or manageable.
tamely ADV
tameness NOUN

Tamil NOUN a member of a people of south India and Sri Lanka; their language.

tamp VERB pack down tightly.

tamper VERB (**tamper with**) meddle or interfere with.

tampon NOUN a plug of absorbent material inserted into the body, especially to absorb menstrual blood.

tan VERB (**tans**, **tanning**, **tanned**) **1** make or become brown by exposure to sun.
2 convert (hide) into leather. **3** [INFORMAL] thrash.
NOUN yellowish brown; the brown colour of suntanned skin.
ADJ yellowish brown.
ABBREV tangent.

tandem NOUN a bicycle for two people one behind another. ADV together.
in tandem arranged one behind another; alongside each other.

tandoori NOUN a style of Indian cooking.

tang NOUN a strong taste or smell.
tangy ADJ

tangent NOUN [MATHEMATICS] **1** a straight line that touches the outside of a curve without intersecting it. **2** (in a right-angled triangle) the ratio of the sides (other than the hypotenuse) opposite and adjacent to an angle.
go off at a tangent diverge suddenly from a

line of thought etc.
tangential ADJ

tangerine NOUN a small orange.

tangible ADJ able to be perceived by touch; clear and definite, real.
tangibility NOUN
tangibly ADV

tangle VERB twist into a confused mass. NOUN a tangled mass or condition.
tangle with [INFORMAL] come into conflict with.

tango NOUN (PL **tangos**) a ballroom dance.

tank NOUN **1** a large container for liquid or gas. **2** an armoured fighting vehicle moving on a continuous metal track.

tankard NOUN a one-handled usually metal drinking container.

tanker NOUN a ship, aircraft, or vehicle for carrying liquid in bulk.

tanner NOUN **1** a person who tans hides. **2** [INFORMAL] a sixpence.

tannery NOUN (PL **tanneries**) a place where hides are tanned into leather.

tannic acid NOUN tannin.

tannin NOUN a substance (found in tree-barks and also in tea) used in tanning and dyeing.

tannoy NOUN [TRADE MARK] a public address system.

tantalize (also **tantalise**) VERB torment by the sight of something desired but kept out of reach or withheld.

tantalum NOUN a hard white metallic element.
tantalic ADJ

tantamount ADJ equivalent.

tantra NOUN a Hindu or Buddhist mystical or magical text.
tantric ADJ

tantrum NOUN an outburst of bad temper.

tap NOUN **1** a device for drawing liquid in a controlled flow. **2** a light blow; the sound of this. **3** a connection for tapping a telephone. VERB (**taps**, **tapping**, **tapped**) **1** knock gently. **2** draw liquid from through a tap; exploit (a resource). **3** fit a device in (a

telephone), enabling one to listen secretly to conversations. **4** cut a thread in (something) to accept a screw.
on tap [INFORMAL] readily available.

tapas PLURAL NOUN small Spanish-style savoury dishes.

tap dance NOUN a dance in which the feet tap an elaborate rhythm.

tape NOUN **1** a narrow strip of material for tying, fastening, or labelling things. **2** magnetic tape; a tape recording. **3** a tape measure. VERB **1** record on magnetic tape. **2** fasten with tape.
have something taped [INFORMAL] understand and be able to deal with something.

tape deck NOUN a machine for playing and recording audiotapes.

tape measure NOUN a strip of tape or flexible metal marked for measuring length.

taper NOUN a thin candle. VERB make or become gradually narrower.
taper off become gradually less.

tape recorder NOUN an apparatus for recording and playing sounds on magnetic tape.
tape recording NOUN

tapestry NOUN (PL **tapestries**) a textile fabric woven or embroidered ornamentally.

tapeworm NOUN a ribbon-like worm living as a parasite in intestines.

tapioca NOUN starchy grains obtained from cassava, used in making puddings.

tapir /tay-peer/ NOUN a pig-like animal with a flexible snout.

taproom NOUN a room in a pub with alcoholic drinks (especially beer) on tap.

taproot NOUN a plant's chief root.

tar NOUN a thick dark liquid distilled from coal etc.; a similar substance formed by burning tobacco. VERB (**tars**, **tarring**, **tarred**) coat with tar.

taramasalata NOUN a

t

pâté made from the roe of mullet or smoked cod.

tarantella NOUN a whirling Italian dance.

tarantula NOUN a large black hairy spider.

tardy ADJ (**tardier**, **tardiest**) late; slow.
tardily ADV
tardiness NOUN

tare NOUN **1** a cornfield weed. **2** an allowance for the weight of the container or vehicle weighed with the goods it holds.

target NOUN an object or mark to be hit in shooting etc.; the object of criticism; an objective. VERB (**targets**, **targeted**, **targeting**) aim at; direct.

tariff NOUN a list of fixed charges; a duty to be paid.

tarmac NOUN [TRADE MARK] broken stone or slag mixed with tar; an area surfaced with this.
tarmacked ADJ

tarn NOUN a small mountain lake.

tarnish VERB cause (metal) to lose its shine by exposure to air or damp; blemish (a reputation). NOUN a film or stain formed on exposed metal.

tarot /ta-roh/ NOUN a pack of 78 cards mainly used for fortune-telling.

tarpaulin NOUN a waterproof canvas.

tarragon NOUN an aromatic herb.

tarsus NOUN (PL **tarsi**) the set of small bones forming the ankle and upper foot.
tarsal ADJ

tart NOUN **1** a pie or flan with a sweet filling. **2** [INFORMAL] a prostitute. ADJ sour; sharp and sarcastic.
tart up [INFORMAL] dress gaudily; smarten up; decorate.
tartly ADV
tartness NOUN

tartan NOUN a checked pattern (originally of a Scottish clan); cloth marked with this.

tartar NOUN **1** a hard deposit forming on teeth; a deposit formed in a wine cask by fermentation. **2** (**Tartar**) [HISTORICAL] a member of a group of central Asian peoples. **3** a bad-tempered or difficult person.

tartare sauce NOUN a cold savoury sauce.

tartaric acid NOUN an acid used in baking powder.

tartrazine NOUN a yellow dye from tartaric acid, used as food colouring.

task NOUN a piece of work to be done.
take to task rebuke.

task force NOUN a group organized for a special task.

taskmaster NOUN a person who makes others work hard.

tassel NOUN an ornamental bunch of hanging threads.
tasselled ADJ

taste NOUN **1** the sensation caused in the tongue by things placed on it; the ability to perceive this; a small quantity of food or drink tried as a sample; a slight experience. **2** a liking; a tendency to like certain things. **3** the ability to perceive beauty or quality. VERB **1** discover or test the flavour of; have a certain flavour. **2** experience.

tasteful ADJ showing good judgement of quality.
tastefully ADV

tasteless ADJ **1** having no flavour. **2** showing poor judgement of quality.
tastelessly ADV
tastelessness NOUN

taster NOUN **1** a person who judges teas, wines, etc. by tasting them. **2** a small sample.

tasty ADJ (**tastier**, **tastiest**) having a pleasant flavour.

tat NOUN [INFORMAL] tasteless ornaments etc.

tattered ADJ ragged.

tatters PLURAL NOUN torn pieces.

tatting NOUN lace made by hand with a small shuttle.

tattle VERB chatter idly, reveal private information in this way. NOUN idle chatter.

tattoo VERB mark (skin) by puncturing it and inserting pigments; make (a pattern) in this way.

NOUN **1** a tattooed pattern. **2** a military display or pageant. **3** a rhythmic tapping sound.

tatty ADJ (**tattier**, **tattiest**) [INFORMAL] ragged, shabby and untidy.
tattily ADV
tattiness NOUN

taught past and past participle of **TEACH**.

taunt VERB jeer at provocatively. NOUN a taunting remark.

taupe /tohp/ NOUN pale greyish brown.

taut ADJ stretched tightly, not slack.

tauten VERB make or become taut.

tautology NOUN saying the same thing in different ways unnecessarily (e.g. *free, gratis, and for nothing*).
tautological ADJ
tautologous ADJ

tavern NOUN [ARCHAIC] an inn, a pub.

taverna NOUN a Greek restaurant.

tawdry ADJ (**tawdrier**, **tawdriest**) showy but tasteless and worthless.
tawdrily ADV
tawdriness NOUN

tawny ADJ orange brown.

tax NOUN money compulsorily paid to the state; a strain or demand on strength etc. VERB impose a tax on; strain, make heavy demands on.
taxable ADJ
taxation NOUN

tax evasion NOUN illegal non-payment of tax.

taxi NOUN (also **taxicab**) a car with a driver which may be hired. VERB (**taxis**, **taxiing**, **taxied**) (of an aircraft) move along the ground under its own power.

taxidermy NOUN the process of preparing, stuffing, and mounting the skins of animals in lifelike form.
taxidermist NOUN

taxonomy NOUN the scientific classification of organisms.
taxonomical ADJ
taxonomist NOUN

tax return NOUN a form declaring income and expenditure for a particular year, used for tax assessment.

TB ABBREV tuberculosis (from *tubercle bacillus*).

t.b.a. ABBREV to be announced.

T-bone NOUN a piece of loin steak containing a T-shaped bone.

tbsp ABBREV tablespoonful.

te NOUN [MUSIC] the seventh note of a major scale, or the note B.

tea NOUN **1** a drink made by infusing the dried leaves of a tropical plant in boiling water; these leaves. **2** an afternoon or evening meal at which tea is drunk.

tea bag NOUN a small porous sachet holding tea for infusion.

teacake NOUN a flat sweet yeasted bun served toasted and buttered.

teach VERB (**teaches**, **teaching**, **taught**) impart information or skill to (a person) or about (a subject).
teacher NOUN

tea chest NOUN a light metal-lined wooden box in which tea is exported.

tea cloth NOUN a tea towel.

teacup NOUN a cup from which tea etc. is drunk.

teak NOUN strong heavy wood of an Asian evergreen tree.

team NOUN a group of players forming one side in a competitive sport; a set of people or animals working together. VERB combine into a team or set.

teamster NOUN **1** a driver of a team of animals. **2** [US] a lorry driver.

teamwork NOUN organized cooperation.

teapot NOUN a container with a spout, for brewing and pouring tea.

tear¹ /tair/ VERB (**tears**, **tearing**, **tore**; PAST PARTICIPLE **torn**) **1** pull forcibly apart or to pieces; make (a hole) in (something) in this way; become torn. **2** [INFORMAL] move hurriedly. NOUN a hole etc. torn.

tear² /teer/ NOUN a drop of liquid forming in and falling from the eye.
in tears crying.

tearaway NOUN an unruly young person.

tearful ADJ crying or about to cry.
tearfully ADV

tear gas NOUN a gas causing severe irritation of the eyes.

tea room NOUN a tea shop.

tease VERB **1** try to provoke in a playful or unkind way. **2** pick into separate strands. NOUN a person fond of teasing others.

teasel NOUN a plant with bristly heads.

tea set NOUN a set of cups and plates etc. for serving tea.

tea shop NOUN a small restaurant serving tea and light refreshments.

teaspoon NOUN a small spoon for stirring tea etc.
teaspoonful NOUN

teat NOUN a nipple on a milk-secreting organ; a device of rubber etc. on a feeding bottle, through which the contents are sucked.

tea towel NOUN a cloth for drying washed crockery etc.

technetium /tek-nee-shŭm/ NOUN an artificial radioactive element.

technical ADJ **1** of a particular subject, craft, etc.; requiring specialized knowledge to be understood. **2** of applied science and mechanical arts. **3** according to a strict legal interpretation.

technicality NOUN (PL **technicalities**) a small detail of a set of rules or of interpretation.

technically ADV **1** according to the facts, strictly. **2** with regard to technique or technology.

technician NOUN **1** an expert in the techniques of a subject or craft. **2** a person employed to look after technical equipment.

Technicolor NOUN [TRADE MARK] a process of producing films in colour; [INFORMAL] vivid colour.

technique NOUN a method of doing something; skill in an activity.

technocrat NOUN a technical expert perceived as having great social or political

influence.
technocracy NOUN

technology NOUN (PL **technologies**) the application of scientific knowledge in industry etc.; equipment developed in this way.
technological ADJ
technologically ADV
technologist NOUN

teddy (in full **teddy bear**) NOUN (PL **teddies**) a soft toy bear.

tedious ADJ tiresome because of length, slowness, or dullness.
tediously ADV
tediousness NOUN
tedium NOUN

tee NOUN a cleared space from which a golf ball is driven at the start of play; a small peg for supporting this ball. VERB (**tees**, **teeing**, **teed**) place a ball on a tee.
tee off make the first stroke in golf.

teem VERB be full of; be present in large numbers; (of water or rain) pour.

teenager NOUN a person in his or her teens.
teenage ADJ
teenaged ADJ

teens PLURAL NOUN the years of age from 13 to 19.

teeny ADJ (**teenier**, **teeniest**) [INFORMAL] tiny.

teepee variant of **TEPEE**.

tee shirt variant of **T-SHIRT**.

teeter VERB balance or move unsteadily.

teeth pl. of **TOOTH**.

teethe VERB (of a baby) have its first teeth appear through the gums.

teething troubles PLURAL NOUN [INFORMAL] problems in the early stages of an enterprise.

teetotal ADJ abstaining completely from alcohol.
teetotaller NOUN

Teflon NOUN [TRADE MARK] a non-stick coating for saucepans etc.

tele- COMBINING FORM **1** at a distance. **2** by telephone. **3** television.

telecommunications PLURAL NOUN communication by telephone, radio, cable, etc.

telegram NOUN a message sent by telegraph.

telegraph NOUN a system or apparatus for sending

messages, especially by electrical impulses along wires. VERB send (a message) to (someone) in this way.

telegraphic ADJ **1** of telegraphs. **2** concise, omitting inessential words.
telegraphically ADJ

telegraphy NOUN communication by telegraph.
telegraphist NOUN

telekinesis NOUN the supposed ability to move things without touching them.

telemarketing NOUN the marketing of goods or services by means of telephone calls.

telemessage NOUN a message sent by telephone or telex, delivered in printed form.

telemeter NOUN an apparatus for recording the readings of an instrument and transmitting them by radio.
telemetry NOUN

telepathy NOUN supposed communication by means other than the senses.
telepathic ADJ

telephone NOUN a device for transmitting speech by wire or radio. VERB speak to (a person) by telephone; send (a message) by telephone.
telephonic ADJ
telephonically ADV
telephony NOUN

telephonist NOUN an operator of a telephone switchboard.

telephoto lens NOUN a photographic lens producing a large image of a distant object.

teleprinter NOUN a device for transmitting, receiving, and printing telegraph messages.

teleprompter NOUN [US] an autocue.

telesales PLURAL NOUN the selling of goods or services over the telephone.

telescope NOUN an optical instrument for making distant objects appear larger. VERB make or become shorter by sliding each section inside the next; compress

or become compressed forcibly.
telescopic ADJ
telescopically ADV

teletext NOUN a service transmitting news and information to television screens.

telethon NOUN a long television programme broadcast to raise money for charity.

televise VERB transmit by television.

television NOUN a system for reproducing on a screen a view of scenes etc. by radio transmission; televised programmes; (in full **television set**) an apparatus for receiving these.
televisual ADJ

telework NOUN work from home, communicating with an office by fax, modem, etc.

t

telex NOUN a system of telegraphy using teleprinters and public transmission lines. VERB send a message to (a person) by telex.

tell VERB (**tells, telling, told**) **1** communicate information, ideas, etc. to (someone) in words; order, instruct; narrate; reveal a secret. **2** perceive, recognize; distinguish: *tell them apart.* **3** have an effect.
tell off [INFORMAL] reprimand. **tell on** [INFORMAL] report the misdoings of. **tell tales** reveal secrets.

teller NOUN **1** a narrator. **2** a person appointed to count votes. **3** a bank cashier.

telling ADJ having a noticeable effect.

telltale ADJ revealing something. NOUN a person who reveals secrets.

tellurium NOUN an element used in semiconductors.

telly NOUN (PL **tellies**) [INFORMAL] a television.

temerity NOUN audacity, rashness.

temp NOUN [INFORMAL] a temporary employee.

temper NOUN **1** a state of mind as regards calmness or anger. **2** a fit of anger. VERB **1** reheat and cool (metal) to increase its strength and elasticity. **2** moderate, neutralize. **keep** or **lose one's temper** remain or fail to remain calm under provocation.

tempera NOUN a method of painting using colours mixed with egg.

temperament NOUN a person's nature as it controls his or her behaviour.

temperamental ADJ of or relating to temperament; liable to unreasonable changes of mood.
temperamentally ADV

temperance NOUN self-restraint, moderation; total abstinence from alcohol.

temperate ADJ **1** (of a climate) without extremes. **2** self-restrained.
temperately ADV

temperature NOUN the degree of heat or cold; a body temperature above normal.

tempest NOUN a violent storm.

tempestuous ADJ stormy.

template NOUN a pattern or gauge, especially for cutting shapes.

temple NOUN **1** a building dedicated to the worship of a god or gods. **2** the flat part between the forehead and the ear.

tempo NOUN (PL **tempos** or **tempi**) the speed of a piece of music; the rate of motion or activity.

temporal ADJ **1** secular. **2** of or denoting time. **3** of the temple(s) of the head.

temporary ADJ lasting for a limited time.
temporarily ADV

temporize (also **temporise**) VERB avoid committing oneself in order to gain time.
temporization NOUN

tempt VERB persuade or try to persuade, especially to do something wrong, by the prospect of pleasure or advantage; arouse a desire in.
temptation NOUN
tempter NOUN
temptress NOUN

ten ADJ & NOUN one more

than nine (10, X).
tenth ADJ & NOUN

tenable ADJ able to be defended or held.
tenability NOUN

tenacious ADJ determined in holding a position etc.
tenaciously ADV
tenacity NOUN

tenancy NOUN (PL **tenancies**) the use of land or a building as a tenant.

tenant NOUN a person who rents land or a building from a landlord.

tend VERB **1** take care of. **2** have a specified tendency.

tendency NOUN (PL **tendencies**) the way a person or thing is likely to be or behave; an inclination.

tendentious ADJ promoting a controversial point of view.
tendentiously ADV

tender ADJ **1** not tough or hard; delicate; painful when touched. **2** gentle and loving. NOUN **1** a formal offer to supply goods or carry out work at a stated price. **2** a container or vehicle conveying goods or passengers to and from a larger one. **3** a truck attached to a steam locomotive and carrying fuel and water etc. VERB offer formally; make a tender for a piece of work.
legal tender currency that must, by law, be accepted in payment.
tenderly ADV
tenderness NOUN

tendon NOUN a strip of strong tissue connecting a muscle to a bone etc.

tendril NOUN a thread-like part by which a climbing plant clings; a slender curl of hair etc.

tenement NOUN a large house let in portions to tenants.

tenet NOUN a firm belief or principle.

tenner NOUN [INFORMAL] a ten-pound note.

tennis NOUN a game in which players strike a ball over a net with rackets, with a soft ball on an open court **lawn**

tennis, or with a hard ball in a walled court **real tennis**.

tenon NOUN a projection shaped to fit into a mortise.

tenor NOUN **1** general meaning; a settled course or character. **2** the highest ordinary male singing voice. ADJ of tenor pitch.

tense ADJ stretched tightly; nervous, anxious. VERB make or become tense. NOUN [GRAMMAR] any of the forms of a verb that indicate the time of the action.
tensely ADV
tenseness NOUN

tensile ADJ of tension; capable of being stretched.

tension NOUN **1** the state of being stretched tight; strain caused by forces working in opposition; electromagnetic force. **2** anxiety, mental strain.

tent NOUN a portable shelter or dwelling made of canvas etc.

tentacle NOUN a slender flexible part of certain animals, used for feeling or grasping.

tentative ADJ hesitant; not certain.
tentatively ADJ

tenterhook NOUN (**on tenterhooks**) in a state of nervous suspense.

tenuous ADJ very slight; very thin.
tenuousness NOUN

tenure NOUN the holding of an office or of land or accommodation etc.

tepee /tee-pee/ (also **teepee**) NOUN a conical tent used by North American Indians.

tepid ADJ slightly warm, lukewarm.

tequila /te-kee-lă/ NOUN a Mexican liquor.

terbium NOUN a metallic element.

tercentenary NOUN a 300th anniversary.

tergiversate /ter-ji-vĕ-sayt/ VERB **1** change one's party or principles. **2** make conflicting or evasive statements.

term NOUN **1** a fixed or limited period; a period of weeks during which a school etc. is open or in which a law court holds sessions. **2** a word or phrase; each quantity or expression in a mathematical series or ratio etc. **3** (**terms**) conditions offered or accepted; relations between people: *on good terms.*

come to terms with reconcile oneself to (a difficulty etc.).

termagant NOUN a bullying woman.

terminal ADJ **1** of or forming an end. **2** (of a disease) leading to death; of such a disease. NOUN **1** a terminus. **2** a building where air passengers arrive and depart. **3** a point of connection in an electric circuit. **4** an apparatus with a VDU and keyboard connected to a large computer etc.

terminally ADV

t

terminate VERB come or bring to an end.

terminator NOUN

termination NOUN **1** the process of coming or bringing to an end. **2** an induced abortion.

terminology NOUN (PL **terminologies**) the technical terms of a subject.

terminological ADJ

terminus NOUN (PL **termini** or **terminuses**) the end; the last stopping place on a rail or bus route.

termite NOUN a small insect that is destructive to timber.

tern NOUN a seabird.

ternary ADJ composed of three parts.

terrace NOUN **1** a raised level place; a paved area beside a house. **2** a row of houses joined by party walls.

terracotta NOUN brownish-red unglazed pottery; its colour.

terra firma NOUN dry land, the ground.

terrain NOUN land with regard to its natural features.

terrapin NOUN a freshwater turtle.

terrarium /tĕ-rair-i-ŭm/ NOUN (PL **terrariums** or **terraria**) **1** a place for keeping small land animals. **2** a sealed glass container with growing plants inside.

terrestrial ADJ of the earth; of or living on land; (of television) broadcast by land-based equipment, not satellite.

terrible ADJ shockingly bad or serious; very unpleasant.
terribly ADV

terrier NOUN a small dog.

terrific ADJ **1** very great or intense. **2** [INFORMAL] excellent, wonderful.
terrifically ADV

terrify VERB (**terrifies, terrifying, terrified**) fill with terror.

terrine NOUN a kind of pâté.

territorial ADJ of territory or its ownership.

Territorial Army NOUN a volunteer reserve force.

territory NOUN (PL **territories**) **1** land under the control of a person, state, city, etc.; an area with a particular characteristic. **2** a sphere of action or thought.

terror NOUN **1** extreme fear; someone or something causing this; control by intimidation. **2** [INFORMAL] a very annoying person.

terrorism NOUN the use of violence and intimidation for political purposes.
terrorist NOUN

terrorize (also **terrorise**) VERB fill with terror; coerce by terrorism.

terry NOUN (PL **terries**) a looped cotton fabric used for towels.

terse ADJ concise, curt.
tersely ADV
terseness NOUN

tertiary /ter-sher-i/ ADJ third in order or level.

tessellated ADJ decorated with or resembling mosaic.

test NOUN **1** something done to discover a person's or thing's qualities or abilities etc.; an examination (especially in a school) on a limited subject; a procedure to determine the presence or absence of a disease, quality, etc. **2** a test match.
VERB subject to a test.
tester NOUN

testament NOUN **1** a will. **2** evidence, proof.
Old Testament the books of the Bible telling the

history and beliefs of the Jews. **New Testament** the books of the Bible telling the life and teachings of Christ.

testate ADJ having left a valid will at death.

testator NOUN a person who has made a will.

testatrix NOUN (PL **testatrices** or **testatrixes**) a woman who has made a will.

testes pl. of **TESTIS**.

testicle NOUN a male organ that secretes sperm-bearing fluid.

testify VERB (**testifies**, **testifying**, **testified**) give evidence in court; bear witness to something.

testimonial NOUN a formal statement testifying to character, abilities, etc.; a public tribute.

testimony NOUN (PL **testimonies**) a formal statement (especially one given in a court of law); evidence or proof.

testis NOUN (PL **testes**) a testicle.

test match NOUN one of a series of international cricket or rugby matches.

testosterone NOUN a male sex hormone.

test tube NOUN a tube of thin glass with one end closed, used to hold material in laboratory tests.

test-tube baby NOUN [INFORMAL] a baby conceived by in vitro fertilization.

testy ADJ (**testier**, **testiest**) irritable.
testily ADV

tetanus NOUN a bacterial disease causing painful muscular spasms and rigidity.

tête-à-tête /tet-a-**tet**/ NOUN a private conversation between two people.

tether NOUN a rope or chain for tying an animal to a spot. VERB fasten with a tether.
at the end of one's tether having reached the limit of one's endurance.

tetrahedron NOUN (PL **tetrahedra** or **tetrahedrons**) a solid with four triangular sides.

Teutonic /Tyoo-**ton**-ik/ ADJ of Germanic peoples or their languages.

text NOUN **1** a written work; the main body of a book as distinct from illustrations etc. **2** a passage from the Scriptures used as the subject of a sermon. VERB send (someone) a text message.
textual ADJ

textbook NOUN a book of information for use in studying a subject.

textile NOUN a woven or machine-knitted fabric. ADJ of textiles.

text message NOUN an electronic communication sent and received via mobile phone.

texture NOUN the feel of a substance; the combination of threads or elements.
textural ADJ

textured ADJ having a noticeable texture; (of a yarn or fabric) crimped, curled, or looped.

thalidomide NOUN a sedative drug found to have caused malformation of babies whose mothers took it during pregnancy.

thallium NOUN a toxic metallic element.

than CONJ & PREP used to introduce the second element in a comparison.

thank VERB express gratitude to. NOUN (**thanks**) an expression of gratitude.
thank you a polite expression of thanks.

thankful ADJ feeling or expressing gratitude.

thankfully ADV **1** in a thankful way. **2** let us be thankful that.

thankless ADJ unpleasant and unlikely to inspire gratitude.
thanklessness NOUN

thanksgiving NOUN an expression of gratitude, especially to God.

that PRON & DETERMINER **1** (PL **those**) used to refer to a person or thing seen or heard or already mentioned. **2** (PL **those**) referring to the more distant of two things. PRON used to introduce a clause that defines or identifies something. ADV to such a degree. CONJ introducing a statement or suggestion.

thatch NOUN a roof made of straw or reeds etc. VERB cover (a roof) with thatch.
thatcher NOUN

thaw VERB make or become unfrozen; become friendlier or less formal. NOUN a period of warm weather melting ice etc.

the DETERMINER **1** used with a noun denoting someone or something specific and known; identifying something unique. **2** identifying a class or group rather than an individual: *I play the piano.* **3** emphasizing importance or fame.

theatre ([US] **theater**) NOUN **1** a place for the performance of plays etc.; plays and acting. **2** a lecture hall with seats in tiers. **3** a room where surgical operations are performed.

theatrical ADJ of or for the theatre; exaggerated for effect. NOUN (**theatricals**) theatrical performances or behaviour.
theatricality NOUN
theatrically ADV

thee PRON [ARCHAIC] the objective case of *thou.*

theft NOUN the action of stealing.

their ADJ of or belonging to them.

theirs POSSESSIVE PRONOUN belonging to them.

theism /thee-izm/ NOUN belief in a god or gods, especially as creator of the world.
theist NOUN
theistic ADJ

them PRON the objective case of *they.*

theme NOUN **1** a subject being discussed. **2** a melody which is repeated in a work.
thematic ADJ

theme park NOUN a park with amusements organized round one theme.

themselves PRON the emphatic and reflexive form of *they* and *them.*

then ADV **1** at that time. **2** next, afterwards. **3** in that case.

thence ADV [FORMAL] from that place or source.

thenceforth ADV [FORMAL] from then on.

theocracy NOUN (PL **theocracies**) government by priests in the name of a divine being. **theocratic** ADJ

theodolite NOUN a surveying instrument for measuring angles.

theology NOUN (PL **theologies**) the study of God; a system of religious beliefs. **theologian** NOUN **theological** ADJ

theorem NOUN a mathematical statement to be proved by reasoning.

theoretical ADJ concerning or based on theory rather than practice. **theoretically** ADV

theoretician NOUN a person who develops the theoretical framework of a subject.

theorist NOUN a person who theorizes.

theorize (also **theorise**) VERB form theories.

theory NOUN (PL **theories**) a set of ideas formulated to explain something; the principles on which an activity is based.

theosophy NOUN a system of philosophy that aims at direct intuitive knowledge of God. **theosophical** ADJ

therapeutic /the-ră-pew-tik/ ADJ contributing to the relief or curing of a disease etc. **therapeutically** ADV

therapist NOUN a specialist in therapy.

therapy NOUN (PL **therapies**) a treatment for physical or mental disorders.

there ADV in, at, or to that place; at that point; in that respect.

thereabouts ADV near there; approximately then.

thereafter ADV after that.

thereby ADV by that means.

therefore ADV for that reason.

therein ADV [FORMAL] in that place or point.

t

thereof ADV [FORMAL] of that.

thereto ADV [FORMAL] to that.

thereupon ADV [FORMAL] immediately after that.

thermal ADJ of or using heat; (of a garment) made of a special insulating fabric. NOUN a rising current of hot air.

thermodynamics NOUN the science of the relationship between heat and other forms of energy.

thermoelectric ADJ producing electricity by a difference of temperatures.

thermometer NOUN an instrument for measuring temperature.

thermonuclear ADJ of or using nuclear reactions that occur only at very high temperatures.

t

thermoplastic ADJ (of a substance) becoming soft when heated.

thermos (in full **thermos flask**) NOUN [TRADE MARK] a vacuum flask.

thermosetting ADJ (of plastics) setting permanently when heated.

thermostat NOUN a device that regulates temperature automatically. **thermostatic** ADJ **thermostatically** ADV

thesaurus /thi-sor-ŭs/ NOUN (PL **thesauri** or **thesauruses**) a dictionary of synonyms.

these pl. of **THIS**.

thesis NOUN (PL **theses**) **1** a theory put forward and supported by reasoning. **2** a lengthy written essay submitted for a university degree.

thespian ADJ of the theatre. NOUN an actor or actress.

theta NOUN the eighth letter of the Greek alphabet (**Θ**, **θ**).

they PRON the people already referred to; people in general; unspecified people.

thiamine (also **thiamin**) NOUN a vitamin of the B complex found in unrefined cereals.

thick ADJ **1** of a great or specified distance between opposite

surfaces. **2** composed of many closely-packed elements; fairly stiff in consistency. **3** [INFORMAL] stupid. **4** [INFORMAL] friendly. ADV thickly. NOUN (**the thick**) the busiest or most intense part.
thickly ADV
thickness NOUN

thicken VERB make or become thicker.

thicket NOUN a close group of shrubs or small trees.

thickset ADJ stocky, burly.

thick-skinned ADJ not sensitive to criticism or snubs.

thief NOUN (PL **thieves**) a person who steals.
thievish ADJ

thieve VERB be a thief; steal.
thievery NOUN

thigh NOUN the upper part of the leg, between the hip and the knee.

thimble NOUN a hard cap worn to protect the end of the finger in sewing.

thin ADJ (**thinner**, **thinnest**) **1** not thick; lean, not plump. **2** inadequate, lacking substance; (of a sound) faint and high-pitched. ADV thinly. VERB (**thins**, **thinning**, **thinned**) make or become thinner.
thinly ADV
thinness NOUN

thine [ARCHAIC] ADJ & POSSESSIVE PRONOUN belonging to thee.

thing NOUN **1** an object of unspecified type; an action, utterance, etc.; an inanimate object. **2** (**things**) belongings. **3** (**the thing**) an important fact about a situation; (**things**) circumstances, life in general.

think VERB (**thinks**, **thinking**, **thought**) **1** have a belief or opinion. **2** use one's mind to form ideas, solve problems, etc. NOUN [INFORMAL] an act of thinking.
think better of it change a decision after thought.
think of **1** call to mind, remember. **2** have an opinion of. **think up** [INFORMAL] devise ingeniously.
thinker NOUN

think tank NOUN a group providing ideas and

t

advice on national or commercial problems.

thinner NOUN a substance for thinning paint.

third ADJ next after second. NOUN **1** a third thing, class, etc. **2** one of three equal parts.
the third degree long and severe questioning.
thirdly ADV

third-degree burn NOUN a burn of the most severe kind.

third party NOUN (PL **third parties**) a person involved in a situation besides the two principals.

third-party insurance NOUN insurance covering injury by the person insured to someone else.

third-rate ADJ of very poor quality.

t

Third World NOUN the developing countries of Asia, Africa, and Latin America.

thirst NOUN the feeling caused by a desire to drink; any strong desire. VERB feel a strong desire.
thirstily ADV
thirsty ADJ

thirteen ADJ & NOUN one more than twelve (13, XIII).
thirteenth ADJ & NOUN

thirty ADJ & NOUN three times ten (30, XXX).
thirtieth ADJ & NOUN

this PRON & DETERMINER (PL **these**) used to identify a specific person or thing close at hand, just mentioned, or being indicated or experienced; referring to the nearer of two things. ADV to the degree or extent indicated.

thistle NOUN a prickly plant.

thistledown NOUN the fluff on thistle seeds.

thither ADV [ARCHAIC] to or towards that place.

thong NOUN **1** a strip of leather used as a fastening or lash etc. **2** a pair of very skimpy knickers.

thorax NOUN (PL **thoraces** or **thoraxes**) the part of the body between the neck and the abdomen.
thoracic ADJ

thorium NOUN a radioactive metallic

element.

thorn NOUN a small sharp projection on a plant; a thorn-bearing tree or shrub.
thorny ADJ

thorough ADJ complete in every way; detailed, careful.
thoroughly ADV
thoroughness NOUN

thoroughbred ADJ of pure breed. NOUN a thoroughbred animal.

thoroughfare NOUN the main route between two places.

those pl. of **THAT**.

thou PRON [ARCHAIC] you.

though CONJ in spite of the fact that, even supposing. ADV however.

thought past and past participle of **THINK**. NOUN an idea; the process of thinking; attention, consideration.

thoughtful ADJ **1** thinking deeply; thought out carefully. **2** considerate.
thoughtfully ADV
thoughtfulness NOUN

thoughtless ADJ careless; inconsiderate.
thoughtlessly ADV
thoughtlessness NOUN

thousand ADJ & NOUN ten hundred (1000, M).
thousandth ADJ & NOUN

thrall NOUN (**in thrall**) in someone's power.

thrash VERB beat violently and repeatedly; [INFORMAL] defeat thoroughly; move wildly or convulsively.
thrash out discuss thoroughly.

thread NOUN **1** a thin length of spun cotton or wool etc.; a long or continuous strand of this. **2** the spiral ridge of a screw. VERB **1** pass a thread through (a needle etc.); string together on a thread. **2** move between crowded obstacles. **3** cut a thread in (a screw).
lose the thread forget the sequence of a story, argument, etc.

threadbare ADJ (of cloth) thin and tattered with age; shabbily dressed.

threat NOUN an expression of intention to punish, hurt, or harm; a person or thing thought likely to bring harm or danger.

threaten VERB make or be a threat (to).

three ADJ & NOUN one more than two (3, III).

three-dimensional ADJ having or appearing to have length, breadth, and depth.

threesome NOUN a group of three people.

thresh VERB beat out (grain) from husks of corn; make flailing movements.

threshold NOUN **1** a piece of wood or stone forming the bottom of a doorway; a point of entry. **2** the lowest limit at which a stimulus is perceptible.

threw past of **THROW**.

thrice ADV [LITERARY] three times.

thrift NOUN economical management of resources.
thriftily ADV
thrifty ADJ

thrill NOUN a sudden feeling of excitement; something causing this; a wave of emotion.
VERB excite; be excited.

thriller NOUN an exciting story or play etc., especially involving crime.

thrive VERB (**thrives**, **thriving**, **throve** or **thrived**; PAST PARTICIPLE **thriven** or **thrived**) grow or develop well; prosper.

throat NOUN the passage from the back of the mouth to the oesophagus or lungs; the front of the neck.

throaty ADJ (**throatier**, **throatiest**) uttered deep in the throat; hoarse.
throatily ADV

throb VERB (**throbs**, **throbbing**, **throbbed**) beat or pulsate with a strong rhythm; feel regular bursts of pain.
NOUN a regular pulsation.

throes PLURAL NOUN severe or violent pain or struggle.
in the throes of struggling in the midst of.

thrombosis NOUN (PL **thromboses**) the formation of a clot of blood in a blood vessel or organ of the body.

throne NOUN a ceremonial seat for a monarch, bishop, etc.; sovereign power.

throng NOUN a crowded mass of people. VERB crowd (a place); move in a crowd.

throttle NOUN a device controlling the flow of fuel or steam etc. to an engine. VERB strangle.

through PREP **1** from end to end or side to side of; from start to finish of. **2** by the agency, means, or fault of. ADV **1** from end to end or side to side; from beginning to end; entering at one point and coming out at another. **2** so as to have finished; so as to have passed (an examination). **3** so as to be connected by telephone. ADJ going through a place without stopping; (of a means of transport etc.) going to one's final destination. **through and through** completely.

throughout PREP & ADV right through; from beginning to end (of).

throughput NOUN the amount of material processed.

throve past of **THRIVE**.

throw VERB (**throws**, **throwing**, **threw**; PAST PARTICIPLE **thrown**) **1** propel through the air from one's hand; push forcefully in a specified direction; put (clothes) on or off hastily. **2** cause to be in a specified state; [INFORMAL] disconcert; have (a fit or tantrum). **3** operate (a switch or lever). **4** give (a party). **5** shape (pottery) on a wheel. NOUN an act of throwing; the distance something is thrown. **throw away** discard as useless or unwanted; fail to make use of. **throw in the towel** admit defeat or failure. **throw out 1** expel; discard. **2** cause (calculations) to become inadequate. **throw over** reject (a lover). **throw up 1** vomit. **2** bring to notice. **3** give up.
thrower NOUN

throwback NOUN an animal etc. showing characteristics of an earlier ancestor.

thru US = **THROUGH**.

thrum VERB (**thrums**, **thrumming**, **thrummed**) make a rhythmic humming sound; strum.

thrush NOUN **1** a songbird with a speckled breast. **2** a fungal infection of the mouth, throat, or vagina.

thrust VERB (**thrusts**, **thrusting**, **thrust**) push forcibly; make a forward stroke with a sword etc. NOUN a thrusting movement or force.

thud NOUN a dull low sound like that of a blow. VERB (**thuds**, **thudding**, **thudded**) make or fall with a thud.

thug NOUN a violent criminal.
thuggery NOUN

thulium NOUN a metallic element.

thumb NOUN the short thick finger set apart from the other four. VERB **1** touch or turn (pages etc.) with the thumbs. **2** request (a lift) by signalling with one's thumb.
under the thumb of completely under the influence of.

thumbnail NOUN the nail of the thumb. ADJ brief, concise.

thump VERB strike heavily; set down heavily and noisily; thud. NOUN a heavy blow; a sound of thumping.

thunder NOUN the loud rumbling or crashing noise that accompanies lightning; any similar sound. VERB sound with or like thunder; utter loudly or angrily.
steal a person's thunder forestall him or her.
thundery ADJ

thunderbolt NOUN **1** a lightning flash. **2** a sudden unexpected event or piece of news.

thunderclap NOUN a crash of thunder.

thundering ADJ [INFORMAL] great, extreme.

thunderous ADJ of or like thunder; threatening.

thunderstorm NOUN a storm accompanied by thunder.

thunderstruck ADJ amazed.

Thursday NOUN the day after Wednesday.

thus ADV [FORMAL] in this way; as a result of this; to this extent.

thwack VERB strike with a heavy blow. NOUN this blow or sound.

thwart /thwort/ VERB prevent from doing what is intended; frustrate. NOUN a rower's bench across a boat.

thy ADJ [ARCHAIC] belonging to thee.

thyme /tym/ NOUN a fragrant herb.

thymus NOUN (PL **thymi**) the ductless gland near the base of the neck.

thyroid (in full **thyroid gland**) NOUN a large gland in the neck producing hormones which regulate growth and development.

thyself PRON the emphatic and reflexive form of *thou* and *thee.*

tiara NOUN a woman's jewelled semicircular headdress.

tibia NOUN (PL **tibiae**) the inner shin bone.

tic NOUN an involuntary muscular twitch.

tick NOUN **1** a regular clicking sound, especially made by a clock or watch. **2** [INFORMAL] a moment. **3** a mark (✓) used to show that an answer is correct or an item on a list has been dealt with. **4** a blood-sucking mite or parasitic insect. VERB **1** (of a clock etc.) make a series of ticks. **2** mark with a tick.
on tick [INFORMAL] on credit, with payment deferred. **tick off** [INFORMAL] reprimand. **tick over** (of an engine) run in neutral.

ticket NOUN **1** a marked piece of card or paper entitling the holder to a certain right (e.g. to travel by train etc.). **2** a label. **3** notification of a traffic offence. **4** a certificate of qualification as a ship's master or pilot etc. **5** a list of candidates for office. VERB (**tickets, ticketing, ticketed**) give a ticket to; mark with a ticket.
just the ticket [INFORMAL] exactly what is wanted or needed.

ticking NOUN strong fabric used for covering mattresses, pillows, etc.

tickle VERB **1** touch or

stroke lightly so as to cause a slight tingling sensation. **2** feel this sensation; amuse, please. NOUN the act or sensation of tickling.

ticklish ADJ **1** sensitive to tickling. **2** (of a problem) requiring careful handling.

tic-tac NOUN a system of semaphore signals used by racecourse bookmakers.

tidal ADJ of or affected by tides.

tidbit NOUN [US] a titbit.

tiddler NOUN [INFORMAL] a small fish.

tiddly ADJ (**tiddlier**, **tiddliest**) [INFORMAL] **1** very small. **2** slightly drunk.

tiddlywinks NOUN a game involving flicking small counters into a cup.

t

tide NOUN **1** the sea's regular rise and fall. **2** a trend of feeling or events etc.

tide over help temporarily.

tidemark NOUN a mark made by the tide at high water; a line left round a bath by dirty water.

tidings PLURAL NOUN [LITERARY] news.

tidy ADJ (**tidier**, **tidiest**) neat and orderly. VERB (**tidies**, **tidying**, **tidied**) make tidy.

tidily ADV

tidiness NOUN

tie VERB (**ties**, **tying**, **tied**) **1** attach or fasten with cord etc.; form into a knot or bow; link, connect. **2** restrict, limit. **3** make the same score as another competitor. NOUN **1** a cord etc. used for tying; something that unites; a restriction. **2** a strip of cloth worn round the collar and knotted at the front of the neck. **3** an equal score between competitors. **4** a sports match in which the winners proceed to the next round of a competition.

tie in link or (of information etc.) be connected with something else. **tie up** **1** fasten with cord etc. **2** make (money etc.) not readily available for use. **3** [INFORMAL] occupy fully.

tie-break NOUN a means of

deciding the winner when competitors have tied.

tied ADJ **1** (of a public house) bound to supply a particular brewer's beer. **2** (of a house) for occupation only by a person working for its owner.

tiepin NOUN an ornamental pin for holding a necktie in place.

tier /teer/ NOUN any of a series of rows or levels of a structure placed one above the other.

tie-up NOUN a connection, a link.

tiff NOUN [INFORMAL] a petty quarrel.

tiger NOUN a large striped animal of the cat family.

tight ADJ **1** held or fastened firmly; stretched taut, not slack; fitting closely or too closely; leaving little room. **2** strict, thorough. **3** limited; [INFORMAL] stingy.
4 [INFORMAL] drunk.
ADV tightly.
a tight corner a difficult situation.
tightly ADV
tightness NOUN

tighten VERB make or become tighter.

tight-fisted ADJ [INFORMAL] stingy.

tightrope NOUN a rope strung tightly high above the ground, on which acrobats balance.

tights PLURAL NOUN a garment closely covering the legs and lower part of the body.

tigress NOUN a female tiger.

tike variant of **TYKE**.

tilde /til-dĕ/ NOUN a mark (˜) put over a letter to mark a change in its pronunciation.

tile NOUN a thin slab of baked clay etc. used for covering roofs, walls, or floors. VERB cover with tiles.

till[1] PREP & CONJ up to (a specified time, event, etc.); until.

till[2] NOUN a cash register or drawer for money in a shop etc.

till[3] VERB cultivate (land) for crops.

tiller NOUN a bar by which the rudder of a boat is turned.

tilt VERB move or cause to move into a sloping position. NOUN a sloping position.
at full tilt at full speed or force.

timber NOUN wood prepared for use in building or carpentry; trees suitable for this; a wooden beam used in constructing a house or ship.

timbered ADJ 1 constructed of timber or with a timber framework. 2 (of land) wooded.

timbre /tambr/ NOUN the characteristic quality of the sound of a voice or instrument.

time NOUN 1 the dimension in which events etc. continue or succeed one another; past, present, and future; a period of this; a point of this measured in hours and minutes; an occasion. 2 a person's lifetime or prime. 3 rhythm in music. 4 (**times**) expressing multiplication.
VERB 1 arrange when (something) should happen. 2 measure the time taken by.
behind the times out of date. **for the time being** until another arrangement is made. **from time to time** at intervals. **in time** 1 not late. 2 eventually. **on time** punctually.

time-and-motion study NOUN (PL **time-and-motion studies**) a procedure measuring efficiency in an industrial operation.

time bomb NOUN a bomb that can be set to explode at a particular time.

time-honoured ADJ respected because of antiquity; traditional.

time lag NOUN an interval between two connected events.

timeless ADJ not affected by the passage of time.
timelessness NOUN

timely ADJ occurring at a favourable time.
timeliness NOUN

timepiece NOUN a clock or watch.

t

timeshare NOUN a share in a property that allows use by several joint owners at agreed different times.

time switch NOUN a switch operating automatically at a set time.

timetable NOUN a list showing the times at which trains, buses, or aeroplanes arrive and depart or at which events are scheduled to take place.

time zone NOUN a region (between parallels of longitude) where a common standard time is used.

timid ADJ lacking courage or confidence.
timidity NOUN
timidly ADV

timing NOUN **1** the deciding of when to do something for greatest benefit. **2** (in an engine) the times when the valves open and close.

timorous ADJ timid.
timorously ADV
timorousness NOUN

timpani (also **tympani**) PLURAL NOUN kettledrums.
timpanist NOUN

tin NOUN **1** a silvery-white metal. **2** a metal box or other container; one in which food is sealed for preservation. VERB (**tins**, **tinning**, **tinned**) **1** seal (food) in a tin. **2** coat with tin.

tincture NOUN **1** a solution of a medicinal substance in alcohol. **2** a slight tinge.

tinder NOUN any dry substance that catches fire easily.

tine NOUN a prong or point of a fork, harrow, or antler.

tinge VERB (**tinges**, **tingeing**, **tinged**) colour slightly; give a slight trace of an element or quality to. NOUN a slight colouring or trace.

tingle VERB have a slight pricking or stinging sensation. NOUN this sensation.

tinker NOUN **1** a travelling mender of pots and pans. **2** [INFORMAL] a mischievous child. VERB work at something casually, trying to repair or improve it.

t

tinkle NOUN a series of short light ringing sounds. VERB make or cause to make this sound.

tinnitus /tin-i-tŭs, tin-I-tŭs/ NOUN ringing or buzzing in the ears.

tinny ADJ (**tinnier**, **tinniest**) (of metal objects) flimsy; (of sound) thin and metallic.

tinpot ADJ [INFORMAL] lacking value or power.

tinsel NOUN glittering decorative metallic strips or threads.

tint NOUN a variety or slight trace of a colour. VERB colour slightly.

tiny ADJ (**tinier**, **tiniest**) very small.

tip VERB (**tips**, **tipping**, **tipped**) **1** overbalance or cause to overbalance and fall; spill (contents) by doing this. **2** give a small present of money to (someone) in return for services. **3** name as a likely winner. **4** put a substance on the end of (something small or tapering). NOUN **1** a small money present. **2** a useful piece of advice. **3** the end of something slender or tapering. **4** a place where rubbish etc. is tipped.
tip off [INFORMAL] give a warning or hint to.
tipper NOUN

tip-off NOUN [INFORMAL] a warning or hint.

tippet NOUN a small cape or collar of fur with hanging ends.

tipple VERB drink alcohol habitually. NOUN [INFORMAL] an alcoholic drink.

tipster NOUN a person who gives tips, especially about likely winners in racing.

tipsy ADJ (**tipsier**, **tipsiest**) slightly drunk.

tiptoe VERB (**tiptoes**, **tiptoeing**, **tiptoed**) walk very quietly or carefully with one's weight on the balls of one's feet.

tip-top ADJ [INFORMAL] first-rate.

tirade NOUN a long angry speech.

tire VERB make or become tired; become bored. NOUN US spelling of **TYRE**.

tired ADJ feeling a desire to sleep or rest.
tired of bored or

impatient with.

tireless ADJ not tiring easily.
tirelessly ADV
tirelessness NOUN

tiresome ADJ annoying; tedious.

tiro variant of **TYRO**.

tissue NOUN **1** a substance forming an animal or plant body. **2** tissue paper; a piece of soft absorbent paper used as a handkerchief etc.

tissue paper NOUN thin soft paper used for packing things.

tit NOUN **1** a small songbird. **2** [VULGAR SLANG] someone's breast.
tit for tat blow for blow.

titanic ADJ enormous.

titanium NOUN a grey metallic element.

titbit ([US] **tidbit**) NOUN a small choice bit of food or item of information.

tithe NOUN one-tenth of income or produce, formerly paid to the Church.

titillate VERB excite or stimulate pleasantly.
titillation NOUN

titivate VERB [INFORMAL] smarten up, put finishing touches to.
titivation NOUN

title NOUN **1** the name of a book, poem, picture, etc. **2** a word denoting rank or office, or used in speaking of or to someone with a particular rank or office. **3** the position of champion in a sporting contest. **4** the legal right to ownership of property.

titled ADJ having a title indicating high rank.

title deed NOUN a legal document proving a person's right to a property.

title role NOUN the part in a play etc. from which the title is taken.

titter NOUN a short, quiet laugh. VERB give a titter.

tittle-tattle NOUN gossip. VERB engage in gossip.

titular ADJ having a title but no real power.

tizzy NOUN (PL **tizzies**) [INFORMAL] a state of nervous agitation or confusion.

T-junction NOUN a junction where one road

meets another at right angles but does not cross it.

TNT ABBREV trinitrotoluene, a powerful explosive.

to PREP **1** towards; as far as; becoming: *the lights changed to green.* **2** affecting; for (someone) to hold or possess: *give it to me;* so as to be connected: *tied to a tree.* **3** resulting in (an emotion etc.). **4** in comparison with; as regarded by. **5** (with a verb) forming an infinitive; expressing purpose; used alone when the infinitive is understood: *come if you want to.* ADV into a closed position.
to and fro backwards and forwards.

toad NOUN a frog-like animal living chiefly on land.

toad-in-the-hole NOUN sausages baked in batter.

toadstool NOUN a mushroom-like fungus, often poisonous.

toady NOUN (PL **toadies**) a person who flatters in order to gain advantage. VERB (**toadies**, **toadying**, **toadied**) behave in this way.

toast VERB **1** brown (bread) by heating on a grill etc. **2** drink in honour of (someone or something); express good wishes before drinking. NOUN **1** toasted bread. **2** an act of toasting someone; a person or thing toasted.

toaster NOUN an electrical device for toasting bread.

tobacco NOUN a plant with leaves that are used for smoking or snuff; its prepared leaves.

tobacconist NOUN a shopkeeper who sells cigarettes etc.

toboggan NOUN a small sledge used for sliding downhill.
tobogganing NOUN

tocsin NOUN an alarm bell or signal.

today ADV on this present day; at the present period of time. NOUN this present day; the present period of time.

toddle VERB (of a young child) walk with short unsteady steps.

toddler NOUN a child who has only recently learnt to walk.

toddy NOUN (PL **toddies**) a sweetened drink of spirits and hot water.

to-do NOUN [INFORMAL] a fuss or commotion.

toe NOUN any of the divisions (five in humans) of the front part of the foot; part of a shoe or stocking covering the toes. VERB touch with the toe(s).
be on one's toes be alert or eager. **toe the line** conform; obey orders.

toehold NOUN **1** a slight foothold. **2** a position from which one can progress.

toff NOUN [INFORMAL] a rich or upper-class person.

toffee NOUN a sweet made with heated butter and sugar.

toffee apple NOUN a toffee-coated apple on a stick.

tofu NOUN curd from crushed soya beans.

tog NOUN **1** a unit for measuring the warmth of duvets or clothing. **2** (**togs**) [INFORMAL] clothes.
tog out or **up** (**togs, togging, togged**) [INFORMAL] be or get fully dressed.

toga NOUN a loose outer garment worn by men in ancient Rome.

together ADV in company or conjunction; at the same time; so as to meet.

toggle NOUN **1** a short piece of wood etc. passed through a loop to fasten a garment. **2** a switch on a computer that turns a function on and off alternately.

toil VERB work or move laboriously.
NOUN laborious work.

toilet NOUN **1** a lavatory. **2** (also **toilette**) the process of dressing and grooming oneself.

toiletries PLURAL NOUN articles used in washing and grooming oneself.

toilet water NOUN a light perfume.

token NOUN **1** something representing or expressing something else. **2** a voucher that can be exchanged for goods;

t

a disc used as money in a slot machine etc. ADJ for the sake of appearances, not important in itself.

tokenism NOUN the making of concessions to a minority etc. that improves appearances rather than the situation.

told past and past participle of **TELL**.
all told counting everything or everyone.

tolerable ADJ **1** endurable. **2** fairly good.
tolerably ADV

tolerance NOUN **1** willingness to tolerate. **2** an allowable variation in the size of machine parts etc.
tolerant ADJ
tolerantly ADV

tolerate VERB permit without protest or interference; endure.
toleration NOUN

t

toll NOUN **1** a tax paid for the use of a public road etc. **2** loss or damage caused by a disaster. **3** a stroke of a tolling bell. VERB (of a bell) ring with slow strokes, especially to mark a death.

toll gate NOUN a barrier preventing passage on a road etc. until a toll is paid.

tom (in full **tomcat**) NOUN a male cat.

tomahawk NOUN a light axe used by North American Indians.

tomato NOUN (PL **tomatoes**) a red fruit used as a vegetable.

tomb NOUN a grave or other place of burial.

tombola NOUN a lottery with tickets drawn for immediate prizes.

tomboy NOUN a girl who enjoys rough and noisy activities.

tombstone NOUN a memorial stone set up over a grave.

tome NOUN a large book.

tomfoolery NOUN foolish behaviour.

tommyrot NOUN [INFORMAL], [DATED] nonsense.

tomorrow ADV on the day after today; in the near future. NOUN the day after today; the near future.

tom-tom NOUN a medium-sized cylindrical drum.

ton NOUN a measure of weight, either 2,240 lb

long ton or 2,000 lb **short ton** or 1,000 kg **metric ton**; a unit of volume in shipping; [INFORMAL] a great weight or large number.

tone NOUN **1** the quality of a musical or vocal sound; a musical note; an expression of an emotion or quality; the general character of an event or place. **2** an interval of a major second in music (e.g. between C and D). **3** a shade of colour. **4** proper firmness of muscles. VERB **1** give firmness to (muscles). **2** harmonize.
tone down make less intense.
tonal ADJ
tonality NOUN
tonally ADV

tone-deaf ADJ unable to perceive differences of musical pitch.

toneless ADJ without positive tone, not expressive.
tonelessly ADV

tone poem NOUN an orchestral composition illustrating a poetic idea.

toner NOUN an ink-like substance used in a photocopier, printer, etc.

tongs PLURAL NOUN an instrument with two arms used for grasping things.

tongue NOUN **1** the muscular organ in the mouth, used in tasting and speaking; the tongue of an ox etc. as food. **2** a language. **3** a projecting strip; a tapering jet of flame.

tongue-in-cheek ADJ ironic, insincere.

tongue-tied ADJ silent from shyness etc.

tongue-twister NOUN a sequence of words difficult to pronounce quickly and correctly.

tonic NOUN **1** a medicine increasing energy and well-being. **2** tonic water. **3** a keynote in music. ADJ invigorating.

tonic sol-fa NOUN the system of representing the notes of a musical scale by the syllables *doh, ray, me,* etc.

tonic water NOUN a carbonated soft drink flavoured with quinine.

tonight ADV on the present or approaching evening or night. NOUN the evening or night of the present day.

tonnage NOUN weight of cargo etc. in tons; a ship's carrying capacity expressed in tons.

tonne NOUN a metric ton, 1000 kg.

tonsil NOUN either of two small organs near the root of the tongue.

tonsillitis NOUN inflammation of the tonsils.

tonsorial ADJ [FORMAL] of hairdressing.

tonsure NOUN a circular area on a monk's or priest's head where the hair is shaved off. **tonsured** ADJ

too ADV **1** to a greater extent than is desirable; [INFORMAL] very. **2** also.

took past of **TAKE**.

tool NOUN an implement used for a particular task; a person controlled and exploited by another. VERB **1** impress a design on (leather). **2** equip with tools.

toolbar NOUN [COMPUTING] a strip of icons used to call up various functions when clicked on with a mouse.

toot NOUN a short sound produced by a horn or whistle. VERB make or cause to make a toot.

tooth NOUN (PL **teeth**) each of the white bony structures in the jaws, used in biting and chewing; a tooth-like part or projection; (**teeth**) power, effectiveness. **toothed** ADJ

toothpaste NOUN paste for cleaning the teeth.

toothpick NOUN a small pointed instrument for removing food from between the teeth.

toothy ADJ (**toothier**, **toothiest**) having or showing many prominent teeth.

top NOUN **1** the highest point, part, or position; the upper surface; something forming the upper part or covering. **2** a garment for the upper part of the body. **3** the highest level of volume etc. **4** a toy that spins on

its point when set in motion. ADJ highest in position or rank etc. VERB (**tops**, **topping**, **topped**) **1** be more than; be at the highest place in (a ranking etc.); reach the top of. **2** put a top or cover on.
on top of in addition to.
top up fill up (something half empty).

topaz NOUN a semi-precious stone of various colours, especially yellow.

topcoat NOUN **1** an overcoat. **2** a final coat of paint etc.

top dog NOUN [INFORMAL] the master or victor.

top-dress VERB apply fertilizer on the top of (soil).

top hat NOUN a man's tall hat worn with formal dress.

top-heavy ADJ liable to fall over because excessively heavy at the top.

topiary NOUN the art of clipping shrubs into ornamental shapes.
topiarist NOUN

topic NOUN the subject of a discussion or written work.

topical ADJ having reference to current events.
topicality NOUN
topically ADV

topknot NOUN a tuft, crest, or bow on top of the head.

topless ADJ wearing nothing on top, having the breasts bare.

topmost ADJ highest.

top-notch ADJ [INFORMAL] of the highest quality.

topography NOUN local geography, the position of the rivers, roads, buildings, etc., of a place or district.
topographical ADJ

topology NOUN the study of geometrical properties unaffected by changes of shape or size.

topper NOUN [INFORMAL] a top hat.

topple VERB overbalance or cause to overbalance and fall.

top secret ADJ of the highest category of secrecy.

topside NOUN beef from

the upper part of the haunch.

topsoil NOUN the top layer of the soil.

topspin NOUN a spinning motion given to a ball by hitting it forward and upward.

topsy-turvy ADV & ADJ upside down; in or into great disorder.

tor NOUN a hill or rocky peak.

torch NOUN a small hand-held electric lamp; a burning piece of wood etc. carried as a light.
torchlight NOUN

tore past of **TEAR**[1].

toreador NOUN a bullfighter (especially on horseback).

torment NOUN /**tor**-ment/ severe suffering; a cause of this. VERB /tor-**ment**/ subject to torment; tease, annoy.
tormentor NOUN

torn past participle of **TEAR**[1].

tornado NOUN (PL **tornadoes** or **tornados**) a violent destructive whirlwind.

torpedo NOUN (PL **torpedoes**) an explosive underwater missile. VERB (**torpedoes**, **torpedoing**, **torpedoed**) attack or destroy with a torpedo.

torpid ADJ sluggish and inactive.
torpidity NOUN

torpor NOUN a sluggish condition.

torque /tork/ NOUN a force that produces rotation.

torr NOUN (PL **torr**) a unit of pressure.

torrent NOUN a fast and powerful stream of liquid; an outpouring.
torrential ADJ

torrid ADJ intensely hot and dry; passionate.

torsion NOUN the action of twisting or the state of being twisted.

torso NOUN (PL **torsos**) the trunk of the human body.

tort NOUN [LAW] any private or civil wrong (other than breach of contract) for which damages may be claimed.

tortilla /tor-tee-yă/ NOUN **1** a Mexican flat maize cake. **2** a Spanish omelette.

tortoise NOUN a slow-moving reptile with a hard shell.

tortoiseshell NOUN the mottled yellowish-brown shell of certain turtles, used for making combs etc.

tortuous ADJ full of twists and turns; complex.
tortuously ADV

torture NOUN the infliction of pain on someone as a punishment or means of coercion; extreme pain. VERB inflict severe pain on.
torturer NOUN

Tory NOUN (PL **Tories**) a member or supporter of the Conservative Party.

toss VERB throw lightly; throw up (a coin) to settle a question by the way it falls; roll about or cause to roll about from side to side; coat (food) by gently shaking it in dressing etc. NOUN an act of tossing.
toss off **1** drink rapidly. **2** produce rapidly and easily. **toss up** toss a coin to decide a choice etc.

toss-up NOUN [INFORMAL] an act of tossing a coin to settle an issue; a situation where two outcomes are equally likely.

tot NOUN **1** a small child. **2** a small quantity of spirits.
tot up (**tots**, **totting**, **totted**) add up.

total ADJ including everything or everyone; complete. NOUN a total amount. VERB (**totals**, **totalling**, **totalled**; [US] **totaling**, **totaled**) **1** amount to. **2** calculate the total of.
totality NOUN
totally ADV

totalitarian ADJ of a regime in which no rival parties or loyalties are permitted.
totalitarianism NOUN

totalizator (also **totalisator**, **totalizer**) NOUN a device that automatically registers bets, so that the total amount can be divided among the winners.

tote [INFORMAL] NOUN a system of betting using a totalizator. VERB [US] carry.

totem NOUN a natural object adopted as a tribal emblem.

totem pole NOUN a pole

decorated with totems.

totter VERB walk or rock unsteadily. NOUN a tottering walk or movement.
tottery ADJ

toucan NOUN a tropical American bird with an immense beak.

touch VERB **1** be, come, or bring into contact; feel or stroke; press or strike lightly. **2** handle, especially so as to damage or harm. **3** affect; rouse sympathy or gratitude in. **4** [INFORMAL] request a gift or loan from. NOUN **1** an act, fact, or manner of touching; the ability to perceive things through touching them. **2** a slight trace; a detail. **3** a manner of dealing with something. **a touch** slightly. **in touch** in contact or communication. **lose touch** lose contact. **touch down 1** touch the ball on the ground behind the goal line in rugby. **2** (of an aircraft) land. **touch off** cause to explode; start (a process). **touch on** mention briefly. **touch up 1** make small improvements to. **2** [INFORMAL] touch sexually.

touch-and-go ADJ uncertain as regards the result.

touché /too-**shay**/ EXCLAMATION an acknowledgement of a hit in fencing, or of a valid criticism.

touching ADJ rousing pity, affection, or gratitude.
PREP concerning.

touchline NOUN the side limit of a football field.

touchstone NOUN a standard or criterion.

touchy ADJ (**touchier, touchiest**) easily offended.
touchiness NOUN

tough NOUN **1** strong, withstanding rough treatment or conditions; hard to chew or break; strong-minded, resolute, uncompromising. **2** prone to violence. **3** difficult; unpleasant, unfair. NOUN a rough violent person.
toughness NOUN

toughen VERB make or become tough or

tougher.

toupee /too-pay/ NOUN a small wig.

tour NOUN a journey, visiting things of interest or giving performances. VERB make a tour (of). **on tour** touring.

tour de force NOUN (PL **tours de force**) a feat of strength or skill.

tourism NOUN the commercial organization of holidays and services for tourists.

tourist NOUN a person visiting a place for recreation.

tourmaline NOUN a mineral with unusual electric properties.

tournament NOUN a sporting contest consisting of a series of matches.

tourniquet /toor-ni-kay/ NOUN a strip of material pulled tightly round a limb to stop the flow of blood from an artery.

tousle VERB make (hair etc.) untidy by ruffling.

tout VERB **1** sell (tickets etc.) by pestering people. **2** spy on (racehorses in training). NOUN a person who buys up tickets for popular events and resells them at high prices; a person who touts.

tow VERB pull along behind. NOUN **1** the act of towing. **2** coarse fibres of flax or hemp.

towards (also **toward**) PREP **1** in the direction of. **2** in relation to. **3** as a contribution to.

towel NOUN a piece of absorbent material for drying things. VERB (**towels**, **towelling**, **towelled**; [US] **toweling**, **toweled**) rub with a towel.

towelling ([US] **toweling**) NOUN fabric for towels.

tower NOUN a tall narrow building; a tall pile or structure. VERB be very tall.

tower block NOUN a tall building with many storeys.

tower of strength NOUN a person who gives strong reliable support.

town NOUN a collection of houses, shops, etc. (larger

than a village); its inhabitants; a central business and shopping area.
go to town [INFORMAL] do something enthusiastically or extravagantly.
townsman NOUN
townswoman NOUN

town hall NOUN a building containing local government offices etc.

township NOUN a small town; [SOUTH AFRICAN] [HISTORICAL] an urban area set aside for black people under apartheid.

towpath NOUN a path beside a canal or river, originally for horses towing barges.

toxaemia /tok-see-mi-ă/ ([US] **toxemia**) NOUN **1** blood poisoning. **2** abnormally high blood pressure in pregnancy.

t

toxic ADJ poisonous; of or caused by poison.
toxicity NOUN

toxicology NOUN the study of poisons.
toxicologist NOUN

toxin NOUN a poison produced by a living organism.

toy NOUN a thing to play with. ADJ (of a dog) of a small variety.
toy with handle idly; deal with (a thing) without seriousness.

toy boy NOUN [INFORMAL] a woman's much younger male lover.

trace NOUN **1** a track or mark left behind; a sign of what has existed or occurred. **2** a very small quantity; a slight sign or appearance. **3** each of the two side-straps by which a horse draws a vehicle.
VERB **1** follow or discover by observing marks or other evidence. **2** copy (a design etc.) by drawing over it on transparent paper; give an outline of.
kick over the traces become insubordinate or reckless.
traceable ADJ
tracer NOUN

trace element NOUN a chemical element occurring or required only in minute amounts.

tracery NOUN (PL **traceries**) a decorative pattern of interlacing lines, especially in stone.

trachea /tră-kee-ă/ NOUN (PL **tracheae** or **tracheas**) the windpipe.

tracheotomy /tra-ki-ot-ŏ-mi/ NOUN (PL **tracheotomies**) a surgical opening made in the trachea.

tracing NOUN a copy of a map or drawing etc. made by tracing it.

tracing paper NOUN transparent paper used for making tracings.

track NOUN **1** a rough path or road; a railway line; a racecourse. **2** marks left by a moving person or thing; a course followed. **3** a section on a CD, tape, etc. **4** a continuous band round the wheels of a tank, tractor etc. VERB follow or find by observing marks left in moving.
keep or **lose track of** keep or fail to keep oneself informed about.
tracker NOUN

tracksuit NOUN a loose warm suit worn for exercise etc.

tract NOUN **1** a stretch of land. **2** a system of connected parts of the body, along which something passes. **3** a pamphlet with a short essay, especially on a religious subject.

tractable ADJ easy to deal with or control.
tractability NOUN

traction NOUN **1** the action of pulling something along a surface. **2** the grip of wheels on the ground. **3** the use of weights etc. to exert a steady pull, maintaining an injured limb in position.

tractor NOUN a powerful vehicle for pulling farm equipment etc.

trad ADJ [INFORMAL] traditional.

trade NOUN **1** the buying and selling of goods and services; a commercial activity of a particular kind: *the tourist trade.* **2** a job requiring manual skills and special training. VERB engage in trade, buy and sell; exchange (goods) in trading.
trade in give (a used article) as partial payment for a new one.
trade off exchange as a

compromise. **trade on** take advantage of.
trader NOUN

trade mark (also **trademark**) NOUN a company's registered emblem or name etc. used to identify its goods.

tradesman NOUN a person engaged in trading or a trade.

trade union NOUN an organized association of employees formed to protect and promote their common interests.
trade unionist NOUN

trade wind NOUN a constant wind blowing towards the equator.

tradition NOUN a belief or custom handed down from one generation to another; a long-established procedure.
traditional ADJ
traditionally ADV

traditionalist NOUN a person who upholds traditional beliefs etc.
traditionalism NOUN

traduce VERB misrepresent in an unfavourable way.
traducement NOUN

traffic NOUN **1** vehicles, ships, or aircraft moving along a route. **2** the action of trading in something illegal. VERB (**traffics**, **trafficking**, **trafficked**) trade in something illegal.
trafficker NOUN

traffic warden NOUN an official who enforces parking restrictions for road vehicles.

tragedian NOUN a writer of tragedies; an actor in tragedy.

tragedienne NOUN an woman who acts in tragedy.

tragedy NOUN (PL **tragedies**) a serious drama with unhappy events or a sad ending; an event causing great suffering and sadness.

tragic ADJ causing or suffering extreme grief; of dramatic tragedy.
tragically ADV

tragicomedy NOUN (PL **tragicomedies**) a drama of mixed tragic and comic events.

trail VERB **1** draw or be drawn along the ground behind someone or something; hang loosely; move slowly, lag behind. **2** track. NOUN **1** a track, a mark left by movement; a line of people or things; a beaten path. **2** something hanging or drawn behind someone or something.

trailer NOUN **1** an unpowered vehicle designed to be hauled by another. **2** a short extract from a film etc., shown in advance to advertise it. **3** a trailing plant. VERB advertise with a trailer.

train NOUN **1** a railway engine drawing a set of trucks or carriages. **2** a line of pack animals or vehicles; a retinue; a sequence of events. **3** part of a long robe, trailing behind the wearer. VERB **1** teach a particular skill to (someone); practise and exercise to reach a peak of fitness. **2** cause (a plant) to grow in a particular direction. **3** aim (a gun).
in train in progress.

trainee NOUN a person being trained.

trainer NOUN **1** a person who trains horses or athletes etc. **2** (**trainers**) soft sports or running shoes.

traipse VERB move laboriously or by an unnecessarily long route.

trait /tray, trayt/ NOUN a characteristic.

traitor NOUN a person who behaves disloyally, especially to his or her country.
traitorous ADJ

trajectory NOUN (PL **trajectories**) the path of a projectile.

tram NOUN a public passenger vehicle powered by electricity and running on rails laid in the road.

tramcar NOUN a tram.

tramlines PLURAL NOUN **1** rails on which a tram runs. **2** [INFORMAL] a pair of parallel sidelines in tennis etc.

trammel VERB (**trammels**, **trammelling**, **trammelled**; [US] **trammeling**, **trammeled**) hamper, restrain.

tramp VERB walk with

heavy footsteps; go on foot across (an area); trample. NOUN **1** a vagrant. **2** the sound of heavy footsteps. **3** a long walk. **4** a cargo boat that does not travel a regular route. **5** [INFORMAL] a promiscuous woman.

trample VERB tread repeatedly, crush or harm by treading.

trampoline NOUN a sheet of canvas attached by springs to a frame, used for jumping on in acrobatic leaps. VERB use a trampoline.

trance NOUN a sleep-like or dreamy state.

tranquil ADJ peaceful, untroubled.
tranquillity NOUN
tranquilly ADV

tranquillize (also **tranquillise**; [US] **tranquilize**) VERB make calm.

tranquillizer (also **tranquilliser**; [US] **tranquilizer**) NOUN a drug used to relieve anxiety and tension.

transact VERB perform or carry out (business etc.).
transaction NOUN

transatlantic ADJ on or from the other side of the Atlantic; crossing the Atlantic.

transceiver NOUN a radio transmitter and receiver.

transcend VERB go beyond the range of (experience, belief, etc.); surpass.
transcendence NOUN
transcendent ADJ

transcendental ADJ of a spiritual or non-physical realm; mystical.

transcontinental ADJ crossing or extending across a continent.

transcribe VERB put into written form; write out (notes etc.) in full; arrange (music) for a different instrument etc.
transcription NOUN

transcript NOUN a written version of a broadcast etc.

transducer NOUN a device that converts variations in a physical medium into an electrical signal or vice versa.

transept NOUN a part lying at right angles to the nave in a church.

t

transexual variant of **TRANSSEXUAL**.

transfer VERB /trans-**fer**/ (**transfers**, **transferring**, **transferred**) move from one position etc. to another. NOUN /**trans**-fer/ an act of transferring; a conveyance of property from one person to another; a design for transferring from one surface to another.
transferable ADJ
transference NOUN

transfigure VERB transform into something nobler or more beautiful.
transfiguration NOUN

transfix VERB **1** pierce through, impale. **2** make motionless with fear or astonishment.

transform VERB **1** change completely or strikingly in appearance or nature. **2** change the voltage of (electric current).
transformation NOUN

transformer NOUN an apparatus for changing the voltage of an alternating current.

transfuse VERB **1** give a transfusion of or to. **2** permeate; imbue.

transfusion NOUN an injection of blood or other fluid into a blood vessel.

transgenic ADJ of an organism into which DNA from an unrelated organism has been artificially introduced.

transgress VERB break (a rule or law).
transgression NOUN
transgressor NOUN

transient ADJ passing away quickly.
transience NOUN

transistor NOUN a very small semiconductor device which controls the flow of an electric current; a portable radio set using transistors.

transit NOUN the process of travelling or conveying someone or something across an area.

transition NOUN the process of changing from one state to another.
transitional ADJ

transitive ADJ [GRAMMAR] (of a verb) used with a direct object.

transitory ADJ lasting

t

only briefly.

translate VERB **1** express in another language or other words; be able to be translated. **2** transfer.
translation NOUN
translator NOUN

transliterate VERB convert to the letters of another alphabet.
transliteration NOUN

translucent ADJ allowing light to pass through but not transparent.
translucence NOUN

transmigrate VERB (of the soul) pass into another body after a person's death.
transmigration NOUN

transmission NOUN **1** the action of transmitting; a broadcast. **2** the gear transmitting power from engine to axle in a motor vehicle.

t

transmit VERB (**transmits**, **transmitting**, **transmitted**) **1** pass on from one person, place, or thing to another. **2** send out (a signal or programme etc.) by cable or radio waves.
transmissible, **transmittable** ADJ
transmitter NOUN

transmogrify VERB (**transmogrifies**, **transmogrifying**, **transmogrified**) transform in a surprising or magical way.

transmute VERB change in form or substance.
transmutation NOUN

transom NOUN **1** a horizontal bar across the top of a door or window. **2** the flat surface forming the stern of a boat.

transparency NOUN (PL **transparencies**) **1** the condition of being transparent. **2** a photographic slide.

transparent ADJ **1** able to be seen through. **2** easily understood or detected.
transparently ADV

transpire VERB **1** become known. **2** (of plants) give off vapour from leaves etc.
transpiration NOUN

transplant VERB /trans-**plahnt**/ remove and replant or establish elsewhere; transfer (an organ or tissue) to another body or part of the body.

NOUN /**trans**-plahnt/ an operation in which an organ or tissue is transplanted; something transplanted.
transplantation NOUN

transport VERB /trans-**port**/ convey from one place to another. NOUN /**trans**-port/ **1** a means of conveying people or goods; the process of transporting. **2** (**transports**) strong emotion: *transports of joy*.
transportation NOUN
transporter NOUN

transpose VERB **1** cause (two or more things) to change places; move to a new position. **2** put (music) into a different key.
transposition NOUN

transsexual (also **transexual**) NOUN a person who feels himself or herself to be a member of the opposite sex; a person who has had a sex change.

transubstantiation NOUN the doctrine that the bread and wine in the Eucharist are converted by consecration into the body and blood of Christ.

transuranic ADJ having a higher atomic number than uranium.

transverse ADJ crosswise.

transvestite NOUN a person who dresses in the clothes of the opposite sex for sexual pleasure.
transvestism NOUN

trap NOUN **1** a device for capturing an animal; a scheme for tricking or catching a person. **2** a curved section of a pipe holding liquid to prevent gases from coming upwards. **3** a compartment from which a dog is released in racing; a trapdoor. **4** [INFORMAL] the mouth. **5** a two-wheeled horse-drawn carriage. VERB (**traps**, **trapping**, **trapped**) catch or hold in a trap.

trapdoor NOUN a door in a floor, ceiling, or roof.

trapeze NOUN a suspended swinging bar on which acrobatics are performed.

trapezium NOUN (PL **trapezia** or **trapeziums**) **1** a quadrilateral with only two opposite sides parallel. 2 [US] a trapezoid.

trapezoid NOUN 1 a quadrilateral with no sides parallel. 2 [US] a trapezium.

trapper NOUN a person who traps animals, especially for furs.

trappings PLURAL NOUN accessories; symbols of status.

trash NOUN worthless stuff. VERB [INFORMAL] discard; damage, ruin.
trashy ADJ

trash can NOUN [US] a dustbin.

trattoria /trat-ŏ-ree-ă/ NOUN an Italian restaurant.

trauma NOUN an injury; an emotional shock having a lasting effect.
traumatic ADJ
traumatize VERB (also **traumatise**)

t

travail (also **travails**) NOUN [LITERARY] painful or laborious effort.

travel VERB (**travels**, **travelling**, **travelled**; [US] **traveling**, **traveled**) go from one place to another; journey along or through. NOUN the action of travelling; (**travels**) journeys, especially abroad.

traveller ([US] **traveler**) NOUN a person who travels; a person living the life of a gypsy.

traveller's cheque NOUN a cheque for a fixed amount, able to be cashed in other countries.

travelogue NOUN a book, film, etc., about someone's travels.

traverse VERB travel or extend across. NOUN 1 an act of traversing. 2 a part of a structure that lies across another.

travesty NOUN (PL **travesties**) a distorted or absurd imitation. VERB (**travesties**, **travestying**, **travestied**) imitate in such away.

trawl NOUN a large wide-mouthed fishing net. VERB fish with a trawl; search thoroughly.

trawler NOUN a boat used in trawling.

tray NOUN a board with a rim for carrying small articles; an open receptacle for office correspondence.

treacherous ADJ showing treachery; not to be relied on, deceptive.
treacherously ADV

treachery NOUN (PL **treacheries**) betrayal, disloyalty; an act of betrayal.

treacle NOUN a thick sticky liquid produced when sugar is refined.
treacly ADJ

tread VERB (**treads, treading, trod**; PAST PARTICIPLE **trodden**) set one's foot down, walk; walk on (a road etc.); press or crush with the feet. NOUN **1** the manner or sound of walking. **2** a horizontal surface of a stair. **3** the part of a tyre that touches the ground.
tread water keep upright in water by making treading movements.

treadle NOUN a lever worked by the foot to drive a wheel.

treadmill NOUN **1** a mill-wheel formerly turned by people treading on steps round its edge.
2 monotonous routine work.

treason NOUN treachery towards one's country.

treasonable ADJ involving treason.

treasure NOUN a collection of precious metals or gems; [INFORMAL] a highly valued object or person. VERB value highly; store as precious.

treasurer NOUN a person in charge of the funds of an institution.

treasure trove NOUN treasure of unknown ownership, found hidden.

treasury NOUN (PL **treasuries**) **1** the revenue of a state, institution, etc.; the department managing this. **2** a place where treasure is stored.

treat VERB **1** act or behave towards or deal with in a specified way; give medical treatment to; subject to a chemical or other process. **2** buy something for (a person) in order to give pleasure. NOUN something special that gives pleasure.

treatise NOUN a written work dealing with one subject.

t

treatment NOUN **1** a manner of dealing with a person or thing. **2** something done to relieve illness etc.

treaty NOUN (PL **treaties**) a formal agreement, especially between countries.

treble ADJ **1** three times as much or as many. **2** (of a voice) high-pitched, soprano. NOUN **1** a treble quantity or thing. **2** a treble voice, a person with this.
trebly ADV

tree NOUN a perennial plant with a single thick woody stem, usually tall and having branches.

trefoil NOUN a plant with leaves divided into three parts; a design resembling this.

trek NOUN a long arduous journey. VERB (**treks**, **trekking**, **trekked**) make a trek.

trellis NOUN a light framework of crossing strips of wood etc.

tremble VERB shake, shiver; be very frightened. NOUN a trembling movement.
trembly ADJ

tremendous ADJ immense; [INFORMAL] excellent.
tremendously ADV

tremolo NOUN (PL **tremolos**) a trembling effect in music.

tremor NOUN a slight trembling movement; a thrill of fear etc.

tremulous ADJ trembling, quivering.
tremulously ADV

trench NOUN a deep ditch.

trenchant ADJ (of comments, policies, etc.) strong and effective.

trend NOUN a general tendency; a fashion.

trendsetter NOUN a person who leads the way in fashion etc.

trendy ADJ (**trendier**, **trendiest**) [INFORMAL] fashionable.
trendily ADV
trendiness NOUN

trepidation NOUN nervousness.

trespass VERB enter land or property unlawfully; intrude. NOUN the act of trespassing.
trespasser NOUN

tress NOUN a lock of hair.

trestle table NOUN a board held on a set of supports with sloping legs, forming a table.

trews PLURAL NOUN trousers.

tri- COMBINING FORM three times, triple.

triad NOUN **1** a group of three. **2** a Chinese secret society.

trial NOUN **1** an examination of evidence by a judge in a law court. **2** a test of quality or performance. **3** a person or thing that tries one's patience.
on trial being tested and assessed.

triangle NOUN a geometric figure with three sides and three angles; a triangular steel rod used as a percussion instrument.

triangular ADJ **1** shaped like a triangle. **2** involving three people.

triangulation NOUN the measurement or mapping of an area by means of a network of triangles.

tribe NOUN a community in a traditional society, consisting of a group of linked or related families.
tribal ADJ
tribesman NOUN

tribulation NOUN trouble, suffering.

tribunal NOUN a board of officials appointed to pass judgement on a particular problem.

tributary NOUN (PL **tributaries**) a river or stream flowing into a larger river or a lake.

tribute NOUN **1** something said or done as a mark of respect. **2** a payment that one country or ruler was formerly obliged to pay to another more powerful one.

trice NOUN (**in a trice**) in an instant.

trichology /tri-kol-ŏ-ji/ NOUN the study of hair and its diseases.
trichologist NOUN

trick NOUN **1** something done to deceive or outwit someone; a mischievous act. **2** a clever act performed for entertainment; an illusion. **3** a mannerism. VERB deceive, outwit.

do the trick [INFORMAL] achieve what is required.

trickery NOUN skilful deception.

trickle VERB flow or cause to flow in a thin stream; come or go gradually. NOUN a trickling flow.

tricky ADJ (**trickier**, **trickiest**) **1** difficult. **2** deceitful.
trickiness NOUN

tricolour ([US] **tricolor**) NOUN a flag with three colours in stripes.

tricycle NOUN a three-wheeled pedal-driven vehicle.

trident NOUN a three-pronged spear.

triennial ADJ happening every third year; lasting three years.

trier NOUN a person who tries hard.

t

trifle NOUN **1** something of only slight value or importance; a very small amount. **2** a sweet dish of sponge cake and jelly etc. topped with custard and cream.
trifle with treat without seriousness or respect.
trifler NOUN

trifling ADJ trivial.

trigger NOUN a lever for releasing a spring, especially to fire a gun. VERB (also **trigger off**) set in action, cause.

trigger-happy ADJ apt to shoot on slight provocation.

trigonometry NOUN a branch of mathematics dealing with the relationship of sides and angles of triangles.

trilateral ADJ having three sides or three participants.

trilby NOUN (PL **trilbies**) a man's soft felt hat.

trill NOUN a vibrating sound, especially in music or singing. VERB sound or sing with a trill.

trillion NOUN a million million; [DATED] a million million million.

trilobite NOUN a fossil marine creature.

trilogy NOUN (PL **trilogies**) a group of three related books, plays, etc.

trim VERB (**trims**, **trimming**, **trimmed**) **1** cut untidy edges from; shorten and

neaten. **2** decorate. **3** adjust (a sail); balance (a boat) by rearranging the cargo. NOUN **1** decoration. **2** an act of cutting. **3** good condition: *everything is in trim.* ADJ (**trimmer**, **trimmest**) neat, smart, orderly.
trimly ADV
trimness NOUN

trimaran NOUN a boat like a catamaran, with three hulls.

trimming NOUN **1** decoration; (**trimmings**) [INFORMAL] traditional accompaniments, extra items. **2** (**trimmings**) pieces cut off when trimming something.

trinity NOUN (PL **trinities**) a group of three; (**the Trinity**) the three members of the Christian deity (Father, Son, Holy Spirit) as constituting one God.

trinket NOUN a small ornament or piece of jewellery.

trio NOUN (PL **trios**) a group or set of three; music for three instruments or voices.

trip VERB (**trips**, **tripping**, **tripped**) **1** catch one's foot on something and fall; cause to do this. **2** move with quick light steps. **3** activate (a mechanism) by releasing a switch etc. NOUN **1** a journey or excursion, especially for pleasure. **2** an act of stumbling. **3** [INFORMAL] a hallucinatory experience caused by a drug. **4** a device for tripping a mechanism.
trip up make a mistake.

tripartite ADJ consisting of three parts.

tripe NOUN **1** the stomach of an ox etc. as food. **2** [INFORMAL] nonsense.

triple ADJ having three parts or members; three times as much or as many. VERB increase by three times its amount.

triplet NOUN one of three children born at one birth; a set of three.

triplex ADJ having three parts.

triplicate ADJ existing in three examples. VERB make three copies of.
in triplicate as three identical copies.

tripod NOUN a three-legged stand.

tripos NOUN the final examination for the BA degree at Cambridge University.

tripper NOUN [INFORMAL] a person who goes on a pleasure trip.

triptych /trip-tik/ NOUN a picture or carving on three panels fixed or hinged side by side.

trite ADJ unoriginal, overused.

tritium NOUN a radioactive isotope of hydrogen.

triumph NOUN a great victory or achievement; joy at this. VERB be successful or victorious; rejoice at this.

triumphal ADJ celebrating or commemorating a triumph.

t

triumphant ADJ victorious, successful; exultant.
triumphantly ADV

triumvirate NOUN a group of three powerful people.

trivet NOUN a metal stand for a kettle or hot dish.

trivia PLURAL NOUN trivial things, trifles.

trivial ADJ of only small value or importance.
triviality NOUN
trivially ADV

trod, **trodden** past and past participle of **TREAD**.

troglodyte /trog-lŏ-dIt/ NOUN a cave dweller.

troika NOUN **1** a Russian vehicle pulled by a team of three horses. **2** an administrative group of three people.

troll NOUN a giant or dwarf in Scandinavian folklore.

trolley NOUN (PL **trolleys**) a basket or frame on wheels for transporting goods; a small table on wheels.

trollop NOUN [DATED] a promiscuous or disreputable woman.

trombone NOUN a large brass wind instrument with a sliding tube.

trompe l'oeil /tromp loi/ NOUN a painting on a wall designed to give an illusion of reality.

troop NOUN a body of soldiers; a group of people or animals. VERB move in a group, especially a large one.

trooper NOUN a soldier in a cavalry or armoured unit; [US] & [AUSTRALIAN] a mounted or state police officer.

trophy NOUN (PL **trophies**) something taken in war or hunting etc. as a souvenir of success; an object awarded as a prize.

tropic NOUN a line of latitude 23°27′ north or south of the equator; (**the tropics**) the region between these, with a hot climate.
tropical ADJ

troposphere NOUN the layer of the atmosphere between the earth's surface and the stratosphere.

trot NOUN a horse's pace faster than a walk; a moderate running pace. VERB (**trots**, **trotting**, **trotted**) move or cause to move at a trot.
on the trot [INFORMAL] **1** in continuous succession. **2** constantly busy. **trot out** [INFORMAL] produce (a frequently repeated excuse etc.).

troth NOUN [ARCHAIC] faithfulness to a promise.

trotter NOUN a pig's foot, especially as food.

troubadour /troo-bă-door/ NOUN a medieval romantic poet.

trouble NOUN **1** difficulty, inconvenience; a cause of this; an unfortunate situation. **2** unrest, violence. VERB **1** disturb, cause inconvenience to. **2** worry, distress. **3** make the effort to do something.

troubleshooter NOUN a person employed to deal with faults or problems.

troublesome ADJ causing trouble.

trough /troff/ NOUN **1** a long open receptacle, especially for animals' food or water. **2** a depression between two waves or ridges; a region of low atmospheric pressure.

trounce VERB defeat heavily.

troupe NOUN a company of actors or other performers.

trouper NOUN **1** a member of a troupe. **2** a reliable person.

t

trousers PLURAL NOUN a two-legged outer garment reaching from the waist usually to the ankles.

trousseau /troo-soh/ NOUN (PL **trousseaux** or **trousseaus**) a bride's collection of clothing etc. for her marriage.

trout NOUN (PL **trout** or **trouts**) a freshwater fish valued as food.

trowel NOUN a small garden tool for digging; a similar tool for spreading mortar etc.

troy weight NOUN a system of weights used for precious metals and gems.

truant NOUN a pupil who stays away from school without leave.
play truant stay away as a truant.
truancy NOUN

t

truce NOUN an agreement to cease hostilities temporarily.

truck NOUN an open container on wheels for transporting loads; an open railway wagon; a lorry.

trucker NOUN a lorry driver.

truculent ADJ defiant and aggressive.
truculence NOUN
truculently ADV

trudge VERB walk laboriously. NOUN a laborious walk.

true ADJ **1** in accordance with fact; accurate; genuine. **2** loyal. **3** (**true to**) conforming to.
come true be fulfilled, actually happen.

truffle NOUN **1** a rich-flavoured underground fungus valued as a delicacy. **2** a soft chocolate sweet.

trug NOUN a shallow wooden basket.

truism NOUN a statement that is obviously true, especially a hackneyed one.

truly ADV **1** genuinely, really. **2** truthfully. **3** [ARCHAIC] loyally.

trump NOUN **1** (in card games) a card of a suit chosen to rank above the others. **2** [INFORMAL], [DATED] a helpful or admirable person.
trump up invent

fraudulently. **turn up trumps** [INFORMAL] be successful or helpful.

trumpet NOUN a metal wind instrument with a flared tube; something shaped like this. VERB (**trumpets**, **trumpeting**, **trumpeted**) proclaim loudly; (of an elephant) make a loud sound through its trunk. **trumpeter** NOUN

truncate VERB shorten by cutting off the end. **truncation** NOUN

truncheon NOUN a short thick stick carried as a weapon.

trundle VERB roll along, move along heavily on wheels.

trunk NOUN **1** a tree's main stem. **2** the body apart from the head and limbs. **3** a large box with a hinged lid, for transporting or storing clothes etc. **4** an elephant's long flexible nose. **5** [US] the boot of a car. **6** (**trunks**) men's shorts for swimming etc.

trunk road NOUN an important main road.

truss NOUN **1** a framework supporting a roof etc.; a surgical support for a hernia. **2** a cluster of flowers or fruit. VERB tie up securely.

trust NOUN **1** firm belief in the reliability, strength, or truth of someone or something; confident expectation. **2** responsibility; something for which one is responsible. **3** a legal arrangement whereby someone is made the nominal owner of property to use it for another's benefit; an organization administering funds to promote or protect something specified. VERB **1** feel trust in; expect confidently. **2** entrust. **in trust** held by a legal trust. **on trust** without question or investigation. **trustful** ADJ **trustfully** ADV **trustworthiness** NOUN **trustworthy** ADJ

trustee NOUN a person who administers property held as a trust; one of a group managing the business affairs of an

t

institution.

trusty ADJ (**trustier**, **trustiest**) loyal, faithful.

truth NOUN the quality of being true; something that is true.

truthful ADJ habitually telling the truth; accurate, realistic.
truthfully ADV
truthfulness NOUN

try VERB (**tries**, **trying**, **tried**) **1** attempt. **2** test the quality, taste, etc., of. **3** be a strain on. **4** subject to legal trial. NOUN **1** an attempt. **2** a touchdown in rugby, entitling the player's side to a kick at goal.
try on put on (a garment) to see if it fits.
try out test by use.

trying ADJ annoying.

tsar (also **czar**) NOUN the title of the former emperors of Russia.

t

tsetse NOUN an African fly that transmits disease by its bite.

T-shirt (also **tee shirt**) NOUN a short-sleeved casual cotton top.

tsp ABBREV teaspoonful.

T-square NOUN a large T-shaped ruler used in technical drawing.

tsunami NOUN a long high sea wave caused by an earthquake.

tub NOUN a wide, open, usually round container for liquids etc.; a small container for food.

tuba NOUN a large low-pitched brass wind instrument.

tubby ADJ (**tubbier**, **tubbiest**) [INFORMAL] short and fat.
tubbiness NOUN

tube NOUN **1** a long hollow glass or metal cylinder; a similarly shaped container or vessel. **2** a cathode ray tube. **3** (**the Tube**) [TRADE MARK] the underground railway system in London.

tuber NOUN a short thick rounded root or underground stem from which shoots will grow.

tubercle NOUN a small rounded swelling.

tubercular ADJ of or affected with tuberculosis.

tuberculosis NOUN an infectious wasting

disease, especially affecting lungs.

tuberous ADJ of or like a tuber; bearing tubers.

tubing NOUN tubular pieces of metal etc.

tubular ADJ tube-shaped.

TUC ABBREV Trades Union Congress.

tuck NOUN a flat fold stitched in a garment etc. VERB fold or put (an edge of material) into or under something so that it is concealed or held in place; hide or put away neatly.

tuck in [INFORMAL] eat heartily.

tuck shop NOUN [INFORMAL] a shop selling cakes and sweets etc. to schoolchildren.

Tudor ADJ relating to the English royal dynasty which held the throne from 1485 to 1603.

Tuesday NOUN the day after Monday.

tufa NOUN porous rock formed round springs of mineral water.

tuft NOUN a bunch of threads, grass, hair, etc., held or growing together at the base.

tufted ADJ

tufty ADJ

tug VERB (**tugs**, **tugging**, **tugged**) pull vigorously; tow. NOUN **1** a vigorous pull. **2** a small powerful boat for towing others.

tug of war NOUN a contest of strength with two teams pulling opposite ways on a rope.

tuition NOUN teaching or instruction, especially of an individual or small group.

tulip NOUN a garden plant with a cup-shaped flower.

tumble VERB **1** fall headlong; move in an uncontrolled way; rumple, disarrange. **2** perform somersaults etc. NOUN **1** a fall. **2** an untidy mass or state.

tumble to [INFORMAL] understand, grasp.

tumbledown ADJ dilapidated.

tumble-dryer NOUN a machine for drying washing in a heated rotating drum.

tumbler NOUN **1** a drinking

glass with no handle or stem. **2** an acrobat. **3** a pivoted piece in a lock, holding the bolt.

tumbril (also **tumbrel**) NOUN [HISTORICAL] an open cart, especially used to take condemned people to the guillotine.

tumescent ADJ swollen. **tumescence** NOUN

tummy NOUN (PL **tummies**) [INFORMAL] the stomach.

tumour ([US] **tumor**) NOUN a swelling of part of the body, caused by abnormal growth of tissue.

tumult /tyoo-mŭlt/ NOUN a loud confused noise; confusion, disorder.

tumultuous ADJ making an uproar.

tun NOUN a large cask; a fermenting vat.

tuna NOUN (PL **tuna** or **tunas**) a large edible sea fish.

tundra NOUN a vast level Arctic region where the subsoil is frozen.

tune NOUN a melody. VERB **1** put (a musical instrument) in tune. **2** set (a radio) to the desired wavelength. **3** adjust (an engine) to run smoothly. **in tune 1** playing or singing at the correct musical pitch. **2** in harmony or agreement. **out of tune** not in tune.

tuneful ADJ melodious.

tuner NOUN **1** a person who tunes pianos etc. **2** a radio receiver as part of a hi-fi system.

tungsten NOUN a heavy grey metallic element.

tunic NOUN a close-fitting jacket worn as part of a uniform; a loose garment reaching to the knees.

tunnel NOUN an underground passage. VERB (**tunnels**, **tunnelling**, **tunnelled**; [US] **tunneling**, **tunneled**) make a passage underground or through something; move forward in this way.

tunny NOUN (PL **tunnies**) = **TUNA**.

tup NOUN a ram.

turban NOUN a Muslim or Sikh man's headdress of cloth wound round the head; a woman's hat resembling this.

turbid ADJ (of a liquid) muddy, cloudy; confused, unclear. **turbidity** NOUN

turbine NOUN a machine or motor driven by a wheel that is turned by a flow of water or gas.

turbo- COMBINING FORM using a turbine; driven by such engines.

turbot NOUN a large edible flatfish.

turbulent ADJ characterized by commotion, unrest, or violence; moving unevenly. **turbulence** NOUN **turbulently** ADV

turd NOUN [VULGAR SLANG] a lump of excrement.

tureen NOUN a deep covered dish from which soup is served.

turf NOUN (PL **turfs** or **turves**) **1** short grass and the soil just below it; a piece of this. **2** (**the turf**) horse racing and race courses. VERB cover (ground) with turf. **turf out** [INFORMAL] force to leave.

turf accountant NOUN [FORMAL] a bookmaker.

turgid ADJ swollen; (of language) pompous. **turgidity** NOUN

Turk NOUN a person from Turkey.

turkey NOUN (PL **turkeys**) a large bird bred for eating.

Turkish NOUN the language of Turkey. ADJ relating to Turkey.

Turkish bath NOUN a hot-air or steam bath followed by massage etc.

Turkish delight NOUN a sweet of flavoured gelatin coated in powdered sugar.

turmeric NOUN a bright yellow spice.

turmoil NOUN a state of great disturbance or confusion.

turn VERB **1** move or cause to move in a circular direction round a point or axis; change or cause to change direction or position; aim, direct; pass round (a corner etc.). **2** change or cause to change in nature, appearance, etc., reach a specified state; shape (wood) on a lathe;

express elegantly; become or make (milk) sour. **3** pass (a specified age or time). NOUN **1** an act of turning; a change of direction; a new development in events; a bend in a road etc. **2** an opportunity or obligation coming to each of a group in succession: *it's my turn to pay.* **3** a short performance in an entertainment. **4** [INFORMAL] a shock; a brief feeling of illness. **5** a short walk. **a good** or **bad turn** a service or disservice. **in turn** in succession. **on the turn** about to turn or change. **out of turn** before or after one's proper turn; inappropriately. **take turns** (of two or more people) do something alternately or in succession. **to a turn** so as to be perfectly cooked. **turn against** make or become hostile to. **turn down 1** reject. **2** reduce the volume of. **turn in 1** hand over to an authority. **2** [INFORMAL] go to bed. **turn off 1** stop (a machine etc.) working. **2** [INFORMAL] cause to lose interest. **turn on 1** start (a machine etc.). **2** [INFORMAL] excite, especially sexually. **turn out 1** prove to be the case. **2** go somewhere to attend or do something. **3** switch off (a light). **4** expel; empty, search, clean. **5** produce. **6** equip, dress. **turn the tables** reverse a situation so that one is in a superior position to those previously superior. **turn to 1** resort to for help. **2** move on to do or consider. **turn up 1** appear, be found; discover. **2** increase the volume of.

turncoat NOUN a person who changes sides in a dispute etc.

turner NOUN a person who works with a lathe.

turning NOUN a point where a road branches off another.

turning point NOUN a point at which a decisive change takes place.

turnip NOUN a plant with a round white root used as a vegetable.

t

turnout NOUN **1** the number of people attending or taking part in an event. **2** the way in which someone is dressed or equipped. **3** an act of clearing and tidying a room etc.

turnover NOUN **1** the amount of money taken in a business. **2** the rate at which employees leave or goods are sold and are replaced. **3** a small pie of pastry folded over a filling.

turnpike NOUN [HISTORICAL] a toll gate; a road on which tolls were levied.

turnstile NOUN a revolving barrier for admitting people one at a time.

turntable NOUN a circular revolving platform.

turn-up NOUN **1** the lower end of a trouser leg folded upwards. **2** [INFORMAL] an unexpected event.

turpentine NOUN oil used for thinning paint and as a solvent.

turpitude NOUN [FORMAL] wickedness.

turps NOUN [INFORMAL] turpentine.

turquoise NOUN a blue-green precious stone; its colour.

turret NOUN a small tower; a revolving tower for a gun on a warship or tank.
turreted ADJ

turtle NOUN a sea creature like a tortoise.
turn turtle capsize.

turtle dove NOUN a wild dove noted for its soft cooing.

turtleneck NOUN a high round close-fitting neckline.

tusk NOUN a long pointed tooth projecting from the mouth of an elephant, walrus, etc.

tussle NOUN a struggle, a conflict.

tussock NOUN a tuft or clump of grass.

tutelage /tyoo-tĕ-lij/ NOUN guardianship; tuition.

tutor NOUN a private teacher; a teacher at a university. VERB act as tutor to.

tutorial ADJ of a tutor. NOUN a student's session with a tutor.

t

tutti ADV [MUSIC] with all voices or instruments together.

tut-tut EXCLAMATION an exclamation of annoyance, impatience, or rebuke.

tutu NOUN a dancer's short skirt made of layers of frills.

tuxedo /tuk-see-doh/ NOUN (PL **tuxedos** or **tuxedoes**) [US] a dinner jacket.

TV ABBREV television.

twaddle NOUN [INFORMAL] nonsense.

twang NOUN **1** a sharp ringing sound like that made by a tense wire when plucked. **2** a nasal intonation. VERB make or cause to make a twang.

tweak VERB **1** pull or twist sharply. **2** [INFORMAL] make fine adjustments to. NOUN a sharp pull.

twee ADJ (**tweer**, **tweest**) affectedly pretty or sentimental.

tweed NOUN a thick woollen fabric; (**tweeds**) clothes made of tweed.
tweedy ADJ

tweet NOUN the chirp of a small or young bird. VERB make a chirping noise.

tweeter NOUN a small loudspeaker for reproducing high-frequency signals.

tweezers PLURAL NOUN small pincers for handling very small things.

twelve ADJ & NOUN one more than eleven (12, XII).
twelfth ADJ & NOUN

twenty ADJ & NOUN twice ten.
twentieth ADJ & NOUN

twerp NOUN [INFORMAL] a stupid person.

twice ADV two times; in double amount or degree.

twiddle VERB twist idly about. NOUN an act of twiddling.
twiddle one's thumbs have nothing to do.

twig NOUN a small shoot growing from a branch or stem. VERB (**twigs**, **twigging**, **twigged**) [INFORMAL] realize or understand something.

twilight NOUN light from the sky after sunset; the period of this.

twill NOUN fabric woven so that parallel diagonal lines are produced.
twilled ADJ

twin NOUN one of two children or animals born at one birth; one of a pair that are exactly alike. ADJ being a twin or twins. VERB (**twins**, **twinning**, **twinned**) combine as a pair; link with (another town) for cultural and social exchange.

twine NOUN strong thread or string. VERB twist; wind or coil.

twinge NOUN a slight or brief pang.

twinkle VERB shine with a flickering light. NOUN a twinkling light.
twinkly ADJ

twirl VERB spin round lightly or rapidly. NOUN a twirling movement; a spiralling shape.
twirly ADJ

twist VERB **1** bend; distort; shape by turning both ends; pervert the meaning of. **2** cause to move round each other or something stationary; wind (strands) round each other to form a single cord; wind, bend. NOUN an act of twisting; a twisted shape, a spiral; a distortion; an unexpected development in a story etc.

twister NOUN **1** [INFORMAL] a swindler. **2** [US] a tornado.

twit [INFORMAL] NOUN a stupid person. VERB (**twits**, **twitting**, **twitted**) [DATED] tease.

twitch VERB give a short jerking or convulsive movement; pull sharply in a particular direction. NOUN a twitching movement.

twitcher NOUN [INFORMAL] a birdwatcher who tries to see as many species as possible.

twitter VERB make light chirping sounds; talk rapidly in a high-pitched voice or in a trivial way. NOUN a twittering sound.

two ADJ & NOUN one more than one (2, II).

two-dimensional ADJ having or appearing to have length and breadth but no depth.

two-faced ADJ insincere,

deceitful.

twosome NOUN two together, a pair.

two-time VERB [INFORMAL] be unfaithful to (a lover).

tycoon NOUN a wealthy influential industrialist.

tying present participle of **TIE**.

tyke (also **tike**) NOUN **1** [INFORMAL] a small mischievous child. **2** [DATED] a coarse or unpleasant man.

tympani variant of **TIMPANI**.

tympanum NOUN (PL **tympana** or **tympanums**) **1** the eardrum. **2** a recessed triangular area above a door.

type NOUN **1** a kind, a category; [INFORMAL] a person of a specified nature. **2** a perfect example of something. **3** printed characters or letters; a piece of metal with a raised character, used in printing. VERB **1** write using a typewriter. **2** classify according to type.

typecast VERB (**typecasts**, **typecasting**, **typecast**) cast (an actor or actress) repeatedly in the same type of role.

typeface NOUN a set of printing types in one design.

typescript NOUN a typewritten document.

typesetter NOUN a person or machine that sets type for printing.

typewriter NOUN a machine for producing print-like characters on paper by pressing keys.
typewritten ADJ

typhoid (in full **typhoid fever**) NOUN a serious infectious feverish disease.

typhoon NOUN a tropical storm.

typhus NOUN an infectious feverish disease transmitted by parasites.

typical ADJ having the distinctive qualities of a particular type of person or thing.
typically ADV

typify VERB (**typifies**, **typifying**, **typified**) be a typical example of.

typist NOUN a person who types.

t

typography NOUN the art or style of printing.
typographical ADJ

tyrannize (also **tyrannise**) VERB exercise power cruelly.

tyrannosaurus (also **tyrannosaur**) NOUN a large flesh-eating dinosaur.

tyranny NOUN (PL **tyrannies**) cruel exercise of power; absolute and arbitrary rule.
tyrannical ADJ
tyrannically ADV
tyrannous ADJ

tyrant NOUN a ruler or other person who uses power in a harsh or oppressive way.

tyre ([US] **tire**) NOUN a rubber covering round the rim of a wheel to absorb shocks.

tyro /tI-roh/ (also **tiro**) NOUN (PL **tyros**) a beginner.

tzatziki NOUN a Greek dish of yogurt and cucumber.

Uu

U (also **u**) NOUN (PL **Us** or **U's**) the twenty-first letter of the alphabet. ABBREV (in film classification) universal (indicating suitability for all ages).

ubiquitous ADJ found everywhere.
ubiquity NOUN

UCAS ABBREV Universities and Colleges Admissions Service.

UDA ABBREV Ulster Defence Association.

udder NOUN a bag-like milk-secreting organ of a cow, goat, etc.

UDR ABBREV Ulster Defence Regiment.

UEFA ABBREV Union of European Football Associations.

UFO ABBREV unidentified flying object.

ugly ADJ (**uglier, ugliest**) unpleasant to look at or hear; threatening, hostile.
ugliness NOUN

UHF ABBREV ultra-high frequency.

UHT ABBREV ultra heat treated (of milk).

UK ABBREV United Kingdom.

ukulele /yoo-kŭ-**lay**-li/ NOUN a small four-stringed guitar.

ulcer NOUN an open sore.
ulcerous ADJ

ulcerated ADJ affected with an ulcer.
ulceration NOUN

ulna NOUN (PL **ulnae** or **ulnas**) the thinner long bone of the forearm.
ulnar ADJ

ulterior ADJ beyond what is obvious or admitted.

ultimate ADJ final; extreme; fundamental.
ultimately ADV

ultimatum NOUN (PL

ultimatums or **ultimata**) a final demand, with a threat of hostile action if this is rejected.

ultimo ADJ [DATED] of last month.

ultra- PREFIX beyond; extremely.

ultra-high ADJ (of a frequency) between 300 and 3000 megahertz.

ultramarine NOUN a brilliant deep blue colour.

ultrasonic ADJ above the range of normal human hearing.

ultrasound NOUN ultrasonic waves.

ultraviolet ADJ of or using radiation with a wavelength shorter than that of visible light rays.

ululate /ul-yuu-layt, yoo-yuu-layt/ VERB howl, wail.
ululation NOUN

umbel NOUN a broad flat flower cluster.

umber NOUN a brownish natural pigment.

umbilical ADJ of the navel.

umbilical cord NOUN a flexible tube connecting the placenta to the navel of a foetus.

umbra NOUN (PL **umbrae** or **umbras**) an area of total shadow cast by the moon or earth in an eclipse.

umbrage NOUN annoyance.
take umbrage be offended.

umbrella NOUN a circle of fabric on a folding framework of spokes on a central stick, used as a protection against rain.

umlaut /uum-lowt/ NOUN a mark (¨) over a vowel indicating a change in pronunciation, used especially in Germanic languages.

umpire NOUN a person appointed to supervise a sporting contest and see that rules are observed.
VERB act as umpire in.

umpteen ADJ [INFORMAL] very many.
umpteenth ADJ

UN ABBREV United Nations.

un- PREFIX not; reversing the action indicated by a verb, e.g. *unlock*. (*The number of verbs taking this* *prefix is almost unlimited and many of those whose meaning is obvious are not listed below.)*

unaccountable ADJ **1** not explicable or predictable. **2** not having to justify one's actions.
unaccountably ADV

unadulterated ADJ not mixed or diluted; absolute.

unalloyed ADJ not spoiled or qualified; pure.

unanimous ADJ with everyone's agreement.
unanimity NOUN
unanimously ADV

unarmed ADJ without weapons.

unassuming ADJ not arrogant, unpretentious.

unattended ADJ not supervised or guarded; not dealt with.

unavoidable ADJ unable to be avoided.
unavoidably ADV

u

unawares ADV not realizing something, not aware.

unbalanced ADJ **1** not balanced; not impartial. **2** mentally unstable.

unbeknown (also **unbeknownst**) ADJ (**unbeknown to**) without the knowledge of.

unbend VERB (**unbends, unbending, unbent**) **1** change from a bent position. **2** become relaxed or affable.

unbending ADJ inflexible, refusing to alter one's demands.

unbidden ADJ not commanded or invited.

unblock VERB remove an obstruction from.

unbolt VERB open (a door) by drawing back the bolt.

unborn ADJ not yet born.

unbounded ADJ without limits.

unbridled ADJ unrestrained.

unburden VERB (**unburden oneself**) confide in someone about a worry or problem.

uncalled for ADJ given or done impertinently or unjustifiably.

uncanny ADJ (**uncannier, uncanniest**) mysterious and frightening; eerie.
uncannily ADV

uncared for ADJ neglected.

unceasing ADJ continuous.

unceremonious ADJ without proper formality or dignity.

uncertain ADJ not definitely known, not dependable; not knowing certainly.

uncle NOUN a brother or brother-in-law of one's father or mother.

unclean ADJ not clean; ritually impure.

uncoil VERB unwind.

uncommon ADJ not common, unusual.

uncompromising ADJ not allowing or not seeking compromise, inflexible.

unconcern NOUN lack of concern.

unconditional ADJ not subject to conditions. **unconditionally** ADV

unconscionable ADJ not right or reasonable; excessive.

unconscious ADJ not conscious; not aware; done without conscious intention. **unconsciously** ADV **unconsciousness** NOUN

unconsidered ADJ 1 disregarded. 2 said or done without thought.

uncork VERB pull the cork from.

uncouple VERB disconnect (train carriages etc.).

uncouth ADJ awkward in manner, boorish.

uncover VERB remove a covering from; reveal, expose.

unction NOUN [FORMAL] 1 the smearing of someone with oil as a religious rite. 2 effusive politeness.

unctuous ADJ flattering, ingratiating. **unctuously** ADV **unctuousness** NOUN

undeceive VERB free (a person) from a misconception.

undecided ADJ not having made a decision; not settled or answered.

undeniable ADJ undoubtedly true. **undeniably** ADV

under PREP 1 extending below. 2 at or to a position or rank lower than; below (a surface); less than. 3 governed or controlled by; affected

by, undergoing. **4** subject to the rules of; in accordance with. ADV **1** in or to a position directly below something; under water. **2** in or into a state of unconsciousness. **3** below a required or specified number or amount.
under age not old enough, especially for some legal right; not yet of adult status. **under way** making progress.

under- PREFIX **1** below; lower, subordinate. **2** insufficiently.

underarm ADJ & ADV (of a throw or stroke in sport) made with the arm below shoulder level. NOUN a person's armpit.

underbelly NOUN (PL **underbellies**) the soft underside of an animal; an area vulnerable to attack.

u

undercarriage NOUN an aircraft's landing wheels and their supports; the supporting framework of a vehicle.

underclass NOUN the lowest and poorest social class in a country.

undercliff NOUN a terrace or lower cliff formed by a landslip.

underclothes PLURAL NOUN underwear.
underclothing NOUN

undercoat NOUN a layer of paint used under a finishing coat.

undercover ADJ done or doing things secretly.

undercurrent NOUN a current flowing below a surface; an underlying feeling, influence, or trend.

undercut VERB (**undercuts**, **undercutting**, **undercut**) **1** offer goods or services for a lower price than (a competitor). **2** cut away the part below (a cliff edge etc.); weaken, undermine.

underdog NOUN a person etc. in an inferior or subordinate position.

underdone ADJ not thoroughly cooked.

underestimate VERB make too low an estimate (of).

underfelt NOUN felt for laying under a carpet.

underfoot ADV **1** on the ground. **2** getting in the way.

underfunded ADJ provided with insufficient funds.

undergo VERB (**undergoes**, **undergoing**, **underwent**; PAST PARTICIPLE **undergone**) experience; be subjected to.

undergraduate NOUN a university student who has not yet taken a degree.

underground ADJ & ADV beneath the surface of the ground; in secrecy or hiding. NOUN an underground railway.

undergrowth NOUN thick growth of shrubs and bushes under trees.

underhand ADJ **1** done or doing things slyly or secretly. **2** underarm.

underlay NOUN material laid under another as a support. VERB past of **UNDERLIE**.

underlie VERB (**underlies**, **underlying**, **underlay**; PAST PARTICIPLE **underlain**) be the cause or basis of. **underlying** ADJ

underline VERB **1** draw a line under. **2** emphasize.

underling NOUN a subordinate.

undermanned ADJ having too few staff or crew etc.

undermine VERB weaken gradually; weaken the foundations of.

underneath PREP & ADV below; hidden by (a surface).

underpants PLURAL NOUN an undergarment covering the lower part of the body and having two holes for the legs.

underpass NOUN a road passing under another.

underpay VERB (**underpays**, **underpaying**, **underpaid**) pay (a person) too little.

underpin VERB (**underpins**, **underpinning**, **underpinned**) support, strengthen from beneath.

underprivileged ADJ not having the normal standard of living or rights.

underrate VERB underestimate.

underscore VERB

underline.

underseal VERB coat the lower surface of (a vehicle) with a protective layer. NOUN this coating.

undersell VERB (**undersells**, **underselling**, **undersold**) sell at a lower price than (a competitor).

undershoot VERB (**undershoots**, **undershooting**, **undershot**) fall short of (a target); land short of (a runway).

undersigned ADJ who has or have signed this document.

underskirt NOUN a petticoat.

understand VERB (**understands**, **understanding**, **understood**) **1** grasp the meaning, nature, or cause of; see the significance of. **2** infer; assume without being told; interpret in a particular way.

understandable ADJ able to be understood; able to be accepted or excused. **understandably** ADV

understanding ADJ showing insight or sympathy. NOUN **1** ability to understand; sympathetic insight. **2** an agreement; a thing agreed.

understate VERB represent as smaller, less good, etc., than is the case. **understatement** NOUN

understated ADJ subtle, not exaggerated or flamboyant.

understudy NOUN (PL **understudies**) an actor who studies another's part in order to be able to take his or her place if necessary. VERB (**understudies**, **understudying**, **understudied**) be an understudy for.

undertake VERB (**undertakes**, **undertaking**, **undertook**; PAST PARTICIPLE **undertaken**) commit oneself to (an action); promise to do something.

undertaker NOUN a person whose business is to organize funerals.

undertaking NOUN **1** work

etc. undertaken. **2** a promise, a guarantee.

undertone NOUN **1** a low or subdued tone. **2** an underlying quality or feeling.

undertow NOUN an undercurrent moving in the opposite direction to the surface current.

underwear NOUN garments worn under indoor clothing, next to the skin.

underwent past of **UNDERGO**.

underworld NOUN **1** a part of society habitually involved in crime. **2** (in mythology) the abode of the spirits of the dead, under the earth.

underwrite VERB (**underwrites**, **underwriting**, **underwrote**; PAST PARTICIPLE **underwritten**) accept liability under (an insurance policy); undertake to finance. **underwriter** NOUN

undesirable ADJ harmful or unpleasant. **undesirably** ADV

undies PLURAL NOUN [INFORMAL] women's underwear.

undo VERB (**undoes**, **undoing**, **undid**; PAST PARTICIPLE **undone**) **1** unfasten, unwrap. **2** cancel the effect of. **3** [FORMAL] cause disaster to.

undone ADJ **1** not fastened or tied. **2** not done.

undoubted ADJ not disputed. **undoubtedly** ADV

undreamed (also **undreamt**) ADJ not imagined, not thought to be possible.

undress VERB take clothes off.

undue ADJ excessive.

undulate VERB move with a wave-like motion; have a wave-like shape. **undulation** NOUN

unduly ADV excessively.

undying ADJ everlasting.

unearned income NOUN income from interest on investments, rent from tenants, etc.

unearth VERB uncover or bring out from the ground; find by searching.

unearthly ADJ

1 supernatural; mysterious. 2 [INFORMAL] absurdly early or inconvenient.

uneasy ADJ (**uneasier**, **uneasiest**) anxious; uncomfortable; awkward.
unease NOUN
uneasily ADV
uneasiness NOUN

uneatable ADJ not fit to be eaten.

uneconomic ADJ not profitable.

unemployable ADJ not fit for paid employment.

unemployed ADJ 1 without a paid job. 2 not in use.
unemployment NOUN

unending ADJ endless.

unequalled ([US] **unequaled**) ADJ without an equal; supreme.

unequivocal ADJ clear and not ambiguous.
unequivocally ADV

u

unerring ADJ making no mistake.

uneven ADJ not level or smooth; not regular.
unevenly ADV
unevenness NOUN

unexampled ADJ [FORMAL] without precedent.

unexceptionable ADJ entirely satisfactory.

unexceptional ADJ not unusual or outstanding.

unexpected ADJ not expected; surprising.
unexpectedly ADV

unfailing ADJ constant; never stopping or going wrong.
unfailingly ADV

unfair ADJ not impartial, not in accordance with justice.
unfairly ADV
unfairness NOUN

unfaithful ADJ not loyal; having committed adultery.
unfaithfully ADV
unfaithfulness NOUN

unfeeling ADJ unsympathetic, callous.
unfeelingly ADV

unfit ADJ 1 unsuitable. 2 not in perfect physical condition.

unflappable ADJ [INFORMAL] remaining calm in a crisis.

unfold VERB 1 open, spread out. 2 reveal; be revealed.

unforeseen ADJ not predicted.

unforgettable ADJ

impossible to forget.
unforgettably ADV

unfortunate ADJ having bad luck; regrettable.
unfortunately ADV

unfounded ADJ with no basis in fact.

unfrock VERB dismiss (a priest) from the priesthood.

unfurl VERB unroll; spread out.

ungainly ADJ awkward-looking, not graceful.
ungainliness NOUN

ungodly ADJ **1** irreligious; wicked. **2** [INFORMAL] unreasonably inconvenient or early.
ungodliness NOUN

ungovernable ADJ uncontrollable.

ungracious ADJ not courteous or kind.
ungraciously ADV

unguarded ADJ **1** not guarded. **2** incautious.

unguent /ung-wĕnt/ NOUN an ointment, a lubricant.

ungulate NOUN a hoofed animal.

unhand VERB [ARCHAIC] let go of.

unhappy ADJ (**unhappier**, **unhappiest**) **1** not happy, sad. **2** unfortunate. **3** not satisfied.
unhappily ADV
unhappiness NOUN

unhealthy ADJ (**unhealthier**, **unhealthiest**) not healthy; harmful to health.
unhealthily ADV

unheard of ADJ not previously known of or done.

unhinged ADJ mentally unbalanced.

unholy ADJ (**unholier**, **unholiest**) **1** wicked, irreverent. **2** [INFORMAL] dreadful, outrageous.

unicorn NOUN a mythical horse-like animal with one straight horn on its forehead.

uniform NOUN distinctive clothing identifying the wearer as a member of an organization or group. ADJ always the same; not differing from one another.
uniformity NOUN
uniformly ADV

unify VERB (**unifies**, **unifying**, **unified**) unite.
unification NOUN

unilateral ADJ done by or affecting only one person or group out of several. **unilaterally** ADV

unimpeachable ADJ completely trustworthy.

uninterested ADJ not interested; showing no concern.

uninviting ADJ unattractive, repellent.

union NOUN **1** the action of uniting or the fact of being united; a whole formed by uniting parts. **2** an association; a trade union.

unionist NOUN **1** a member of a trade union; a supporter of trade unions. **2** one who favours union, especially someone in Northern Ireland favouring union with Great Britain.

unionize (also **unionise**) VERB organize into or cause to join a union. **unionization** NOUN

Union Jack NOUN the national flag of the UK.

unique ADJ **1** the only one of its kind; belonging only to one place, person, etc. **2** extraordinary. **uniquely** ADV

unisex ADJ suitable for people of either sex.

unison NOUN the fact of two or more things being said or happening at the same time.

unit NOUN **1** an individual thing, person, or group, especially as part of a complex whole. **2** a fixed quantity used as a standard of measurement. **3** a piece of furniture or equipment; part of an institution, having a specialized function.

Unitarian NOUN a person who believes that God is not a Trinity but one person.

unitary ADJ single; of a single whole.

unite VERB join together, make or become one; act together, cooperate.

United Kingdom NOUN Great Britain and Northern Ireland.

unit trust NOUN a trust managing a number of securities, in which small investors can buy units.

unity NOUN (PL **unities**) the state of being united or coherent; agreement; a complex whole.

universal ADJ of, for, or done by all.
universally ADV

universe NOUN all existing things, including the earth and its creatures and all the stars and planets.

university NOUN (PL **universities**) an educational institution for advanced learning and research.

unkempt ADJ looking untidy or neglected.

unkind ADJ cruel, harsh, hurtful.
unkindly ADV
unkindness NOUN

unknown ADJ not known. NOUN an unknown person, thing, or place.

unleaded ADJ (of petrol etc.) without added lead.

unleash VERB release, let loose.

unleavened ADJ (of bread) made without yeast or other raising agent.

unless CONJ except when; except on condition that.

unlettered ADJ illiterate.

unlike ADJ different. PREP different or differently from.

unlikely ADJ (**unlikelier**, **unlikeliest**) improbable, not likely to happen, be true, etc.

unlimited ADJ not limited; very great in number.

unlisted ADJ not included in a (published) list.

unload VERB **1** remove (a cargo) from (a vehicle etc.); [INFORMAL] get rid of. **2** remove ammunition from (a gun).

unlock VERB release the lock of (a door etc.); make accessible or available.

unlooked for ADJ unexpected.

unmanned ADJ operated without a crew.

unmask VERB expose the true nature of; remove a mask from.

unmentionable ADJ too shocking to be spoken of.

unmistakable ADJ clear, not able to be doubted or mistaken for another.

unmistakably ADV

unmitigated ADJ not modified, absolute.

unmoved ADJ not affected by emotion; not changed in intention.

unnatural ADJ not natural; not normal.
unnaturally ADV

unnecessary ADJ not needed; excessive.
unnecessarily ADV

unnerve VERB cause to lose courage or determination.

unnumbered ADJ **1** not marked with a number. **2** countless.

unobtrusive ADJ not making oneself or itself noticed.
unobtrusively ADV

unpack VERB open and remove the contents of (a suitcase etc.); take out from its packaging.

unparalleled ADJ never yet equalled.

unpick VERB undo the stitching of.

unplaced ADJ not placed as one of the first three in a race etc.

unpleasant ADJ causing distaste or distress.
unpleasantly ADV
unpleasantness NOUN

unplumbed ADJ not fully investigated or understood.

unpopular ADJ not popular; disliked.
unpopularity NOUN

unprecedented ADJ not done or known before; unparalleled.

unprepared ADJ not ready or equipped for something; not prepared.

unprepossessing ADJ unattractive, not making a good impression.

unpretentious ADJ not trying to impress by artifice.

unprincipled ADJ without good moral principles, unscrupulous.

unprintable ADJ too indecent or libellous etc. to be printed.

unprofessional ADJ contrary to the standards of behaviour for members of a profession.
unprofessionally ADV

unprofitable ADJ not profitable; useless.
unprofitably ADV

unprompted ADJ

spontaneous.

unqualified ADJ **1** lacking official qualifications. **2** absolute, unmodified.

unquestionable ADJ too clear to be doubted. **unquestionably** ADV

unravel VERB (**unravels**, **unravelling**, **unravelled**; [US] **unraveling**, **unraveled**) disentangle; undo (knitted fabric); become disentangled.

unready ADJ **1** not ready or prepared for something. **2** [ARCHAIC] slow to act.

unreal ADJ imaginary, not real; [INFORMAL] incredible, amazing.

unreasonable ADJ not guided by reason; unfair, excessive. **unreasonably** ADV

unrelenting ADJ not becoming less intense, severe, or strict.

unremitting ADJ not ceasing.

unrequited ADJ (especially of love) not returned or rewarded.

unreservedly ADV without reservation, completely.

unrest NOUN disturbance, violent disorder; dissatisfaction.

unrivalled ([US] **unrivaled**) ADJ having no equal incomparable.

unroll VERB open out (something rolled).

unruly ADJ (**unrulier**, **unruliest**) not easy to control, disorderly. **unruliness** NOUN

unsaid ADJ not spoken or expressed.

unsaturated ADJ (of fat or oil) capable of further reaction by combining with hydrogen.

unsavoury ([US] **unsavory**) ADJ disagreeable to the taste or smell; morally disgusting.

unscathed ADJ without suffering any injury.

unscramble VERB sort out; make (a scrambled transmission) intelligible.

unscrew VERB unfasten (a lid etc.); unfasten by removing screws.

unscripted ADJ without a prepared script.

unscrupulous ADJ lacking moral scruples or

principles.

unseasonable ADJ not seasonable; untimely.

unseat VERB dislodge (a rider); remove from a position of authority.

unseen ADJ not seen, invisible; (of translation) done without preparation.

unselfish ADJ not selfish; considering others' needs before one's own.
unselfishly ADV
unselfishness NOUN

unsettle VERB make uneasy, disturb.

unsettled ADJ lacking stability; changeable; uneasy, anxious.

unshakeable (also **unshakable**) ADJ firm.

unsightly ADJ not pleasant to look at, ugly.
unsightliness NOUN

unskilled ADJ not having or needing skill or special training.

u

unsociable ADJ disliking company.

unsocial ADJ **1** (of working hours) inconvenient because not conforming to the normal working day. **2** antisocial, disturbing to others.

unsolicited ADJ not requested.

unsophisticated ADJ simple and natural or naive.

unsound ADJ not safe or strong; faulty, unreliable, invalid.
of unsound mind insane.

unsparing ADJ giving lavishly.

unspeakable ADJ too bad to be described in words.

unstable ADJ not stable; mentally or emotionally unbalanced.

unstick VERB (**unsticks**, **unsticking**, **unstuck**) detach (what is stuck).
come unstuck [INFORMAL] suffer disaster, fail.

unstinting ADJ given freely and generously.

unstudied ADJ natural in manner, spontaneous.

unsung ADJ not acknowledged or honoured.

unsuspecting ADJ not expecting or aware of something.

unswerving ADJ not turning aside; unchanging.

untenable ADJ (of a theory or position) not valid because of strong arguments against it.

unthinkable ADJ too bad or too unlikely to be thought about.

unthinking ADJ thoughtless.

untidy ADJ (**untidier**, **untidiest**) in disorder; not keeping things neat.
untidily ADV
untidiness NOUN

untie VERB (**unties**, **untying**, **untied**) unfasten; release from being tied up.

until PREP & CONJ up to (a specified time, event, etc.), till.

untimely ADJ happening at an unsuitable time; premature.
untimeliness NOUN

unto PREP [ARCHAIC] to.

untold ADJ **1** not told. **2** too much or too many to be counted.

untouchable ADJ not able or not allowed to be touched. NOUN a member of the lowest Hindu social group.

untoward ADJ unexpected and inconvenient.

untried ADJ not yet tried or tested.

untruth NOUN a lie; the quality of being false.
untruthful ADJ
untruthfully ADV

unusual ADJ not usual; remarkable, rare.
unusually ADV

unutterable ADJ too great to be expressed in words.
unutterably ADV

unvarnished ADJ not varnished; plain and straightforward.

unveil VERB remove a veil or drapery from; reveal, make known.

unwaged ADJ not doing paid work.

unwarranted ADJ unjustified, unauthorized.

unwary ADJ not cautious.

unwell ADJ not in good health.

unwieldy ADJ (**unwieldier**, **unwieldiest**) awkward to move or control because of its size, shape, or weight.

unwilling ADJ reluctant.

unwind VERB (**unwinds**, **unwinding**, **unwound**)

draw out or become drawn out from being wound; [INFORMAL] relax from work or tension.

unwise ADJ not sensible, foolish.
unwisely ADV

unwitting ADJ unaware; unintentional.
unwittingly ADV

unwonted /un-**wohn**-tid/ ADJ not customary, not usual.

unworldly ADJ spiritually-minded, not materialistic.
unworldliness NOUN

unworthy ADJ (**unworthier**, **unworthiest**) not deserving something; beneath someone's character; discreditable; worthless.

unwrap VERB (**unwraps**, **unwrapping**, **unwrapped**) remove the wrapping from; open, unfold.

unwritten ADJ not written down; based on custom not statute.

unzip VERB (**unzips**, **unzipping**, **unzipped**) open by the undoing of a zip fastener.

up ADV **1** to, in, or at a higher place or state; to a larger size or higher level of intensity, volume, etc. **2** to a vertical position; out of bed. **3** towards or as far as a stated place, position, etc. **4** so as to be closed or finished: *do up the buttons.* **5** [INFORMAL] happening, amiss: *what's up?* PREP upwards along, through, or into; to or at a higher part of. ADJ **1** moving or directed upwards. **2** (of a train) travelling towards the capital or a major station. **3** (of a computer system) functioning. VERB (**ups**, **upping**, **upped**) [INFORMAL] **1** do something suddenly: *she upped and went.* **2** raise; increase. **it's all up with someone** [INFORMAL] someone is ruined or killed. **up against** [INFORMAL] confronted by (a difficulty). **up on** well informed about. **ups and downs** alternate good and bad fortune. **up to** **1** as far as; as much as. **2** capable of, fit for. **3** the responsibility or choice of. **4** [INFORMAL] doing, occupied with.

upbeat NOUN [MUSIC] an unaccented beat preceding an accented one. ADJ [INFORMAL] cheerful, optimistic.

upbraid VERB reproach.

upbringing NOUN training and education during childhood.

update VERB bring up to date.

upend VERB set on end or upside down.

upgrade VERB raise to a higher grade; improve (equipment etc.).

upheaval NOUN a sudden violent change or movement.

uphill ADJ & ADV going or sloping upwards.

uphold VERB (**upholds, upholding, upheld**) support.

upholster VERB put a fabric covering, padding, etc. on (furniture).

upholstery NOUN the practice of upholstering; the soft padded covering used to upholster furniture.

upkeep NOUN the process of keeping something in good condition and repair; the process of supporting someone financially; the cost of these.

upland (also **uplands**) NOUN an area of high or hilly land.

uplift VERB **1** raise. **2** make more hopeful or happy. NOUN **1** an act of uplifting; an upward movement of the earth's surface. **2** a feeling of fresh hope or happiness.

upmarket ADJ & ADV of or towards higher prices and quality.

upon PREP on.

upper ADJ higher in place, position, or rank. NOUN the part of a shoe above the sole.
the upper hand mastery, dominance.

upper case NOUN capital letters in printing or typing.

upper class NOUN the highest social class.
upper-class ADJ

upper crust NOUN [INFORMAL] the aristocracy.

uppermost ADJ & ADV in, on, or to the top or most

prominent position.

uppish (also **uppity**) ADJ [INFORMAL] self-assertive; arrogant.

upright ADJ **1** in a vertical position. **2** strictly honest or honourable. NOUN a vertical part or support.

uprising NOUN a rebellion.

uproar NOUN an outburst of noise and excitement or anger.

uproarious ADJ noisy; with loud laughter. **uproariously** ADV

uproot VERB pull out of the ground together with its roots; force to leave an established home.

upset VERB /up-set/ (**upsets**, **upsetting**, **upset**) **1** distress, worry. **2** knock over; disrupt; disturb the digestion of. NOUN /**up**-set/ a state of distress or disruption.

upshot NOUN an outcome.

u

upside down ADV & ADJ with the upper part underneath; in or into great disorder.

upstage ADV & ADJ at or towards the back of a theatre stage. VERB divert attention from; outshine.

upstairs ADV & ADJ to or on a higher floor.

upstanding ADJ **1** honest, respectable. **2** strong, healthy.

upstart NOUN a person newly risen to a high position, especially one who behaves arrogantly.

upstream ADJ & ADV towards the source of a stream or river, against the current.

upsurge NOUN an upward surge, a rise.

upswing NOUN an increase; an upward trend.

uptake NOUN the action of taking up or making use of something.
be quick on the uptake [INFORMAL] be quick to understand.

uptight ADJ [INFORMAL] nervously tense; annoyed.

up to date ADJ modern, fashionable.

upturn /**up**-tern/ NOUN an improvement or upward trend. VERB turn upwards or upside down.

upward ADJ moving or leading up. ADV (also **upwards**) towards a higher place etc.

upwind ADJ & ADV in the direction from which the wind is blowing, into the wind.

uranium NOUN a heavy grey metal used as a source of nuclear energy.

urban ADJ of a city or town.

urbane /er-**bayn**/ ADJ courteous; having elegant manners.
urbanely ADV
urbanity NOUN

urbanize (also **urbanise**) VERB change (a place) into an urban area.
urbanization NOUN

urchin NOUN a mischievous child.

Urdu /**oor**-doo/ NOUN a language related to Hindi.

ureter /yoo-**ree**-ter/ NOUN the duct from the kidney to the bladder.

urethra /yoo-**ree**-thră/ NOUN the duct which carries urine from the body.

urge VERB encourage, advise strongly; recommend strongly; guide hurriedly. NOUN a strong desire or impulse.

urgent ADJ needing or calling for immediate attention or action.
urgency NOUN
urgently ADV

urinal NOUN a receptacle or structure for receiving urine.

urinate VERB discharge urine from the body.
urination NOUN

urine NOUN waste liquid which collects in the bladder and is discharged from the body.
urinary ADJ

URL ABBREV uniform (or universal) resource locator (the address of a World Wide Web page).

urn NOUN **1** a vase, especially for holding a cremated person's ashes. **2** a large metal container with a tap, for keeping water etc. hot.

ursine /**er**-sIn/ ADJ of or like a bear.

US ABBREV United States.

us PRON the objective case of *we*.

USA ABBREV United States of America.

usable ADJ able or fit to be used.

usage NOUN **1** the action of using something; the way in which something is used. **2** customary practice.

use VERB /yooz/ **1** cause to serve one's purpose or achieve one's end; exploit selfishly. **2** treat in a specified way. **3** (**used to**) did repeatedly or existed in the past. NOUN /yooss/ the action of using or the state of being used; the power to control and use something; a purpose for which something is used.
use up use all or the remains of, finish.

used /yoozd/ ADJ second-hand.

useful ADJ fit for a practical purpose; able to produce good results.
usefully ADV
usefulness NOUN

useless ADJ unable to serve a practical purpose; [INFORMAL] hopelessly incompetent.
uselessly ADV
uselessness NOUN

user NOUN a person who uses something.

user-friendly ADJ easy for a user to understand and operate.

usher NOUN a person who shows people to their seats in a public hall etc. VERB lead, escort.

usherette NOUN a woman who ushers people to seats in a cinema etc.

USSR ABBREV [HISTORICAL] Union of Soviet Socialist Republics.

usual ADJ such as happens or is done or used etc. in many or most instances.
usually ADV

usurp /yoo-**serp**/ VERB take (power, a position, or right) wrongfully or by force.
usurpation NOUN
usurper NOUN

usury NOUN the lending of money at excessively high rates of interest.
usurer NOUN

utensil NOUN an instrument or container, especially for domestic use.

uterus NOUN the womb.
uterine ADJ

utilitarian ADJ useful rather than decorative or luxurious.

utilitarianism NOUN the theory that actions are justified if they benefit the majority.

utility NOUN (PL **utilities**) **1** the state of being useful. **2** (also **public utility**) a company supplying water, gas, electricity, etc. to the community. ADJ severely practical.

utility room NOUN a room with appliances for washing etc.

utilize (also **utilise**) VERB make use of.
utilization NOUN

utmost ADJ furthest, greatest, extreme. NOUN the furthest point or degree etc.

Utopia NOUN an imaginary place or state where all is perfect.
Utopian ADJ

utter¹ ADJ complete, absolute.
utterly ADV

utter² VERB make (a sound or words) with the mouth or voice; speak.
utterance NOUN

uttermost ADJ & NOUN = **UTMOST**.

U-turn NOUN the driving of a vehicle in a U-shaped course to reverse its direction; a reversal of policy or opinion.

UV ABBREV ultraviolet.

uvula /yoov-yoo-lă/ NOUN (PL **uvulae**) the small fleshy projection hanging at the back of the throat.
uvular ADJ

uxorious /uk-sor-i-ŭs/ ADJ excessively fond of one's wife.

Vv

V (also **v**) NOUN (PL **Vs** or **V's**) **1** the twenty-second letter of the alphabet. **2** the Roman numeral for 5. ABBREV **1** volts. **2** (**v**) versus.

vac NOUN [INFORMAL] **1** a vacation. **2** a vacuum cleaner.

vacancy NOUN (PL **vacancies**) an unoccupied position or job; empty space; emptiness.

vacant ADJ **1** unoccupied. **2** showing no interest or understanding.
vacantly ADV

vacate VERB cease to occupy.

V

vacation NOUN **1** an interval between terms in universities and law courts; [US] a holiday. **2** the action of vacating a place or position.

vaccinate VERB inoculate with a vaccine.
vaccination NOUN

vaccine /vak-seen/ NOUN a substance used to stimulate the production of antibodies giving immunity against a disease by causing a mild form of it.

vacillate VERB keep changing one's mind.
vacillation NOUN

vacuous ADJ unintelligent, inane; expressionless.
vacuity NOUN
vacuously ADV

vacuum NOUN (PL **vacuums** or **vacua**) a space from which air has been removed; a gap, a blank. VERB [INFORMAL] clean with a vacuum cleaner.

vacuum cleaner NOUN an electrical apparatus that takes up dust by suction.

vacuum flask NOUN a

container for keeping liquids hot or cold.

vacuum-packed ADJ sealed after removal of air.

vagabond NOUN a wanderer; a vagrant.

vagary NOUN (PL **vagaries**) an unpredictable change or action.

vagina NOUN the passage leading from the vulva to the womb.
vaginal ADJ

vagrant NOUN a person without a settled home.
vagrancy NOUN

vague ADJ not clearly explained or perceived; not expressing oneself clearly.
vaguely ADV
vagueness NOUN

vain ADJ **1** excessively proud of one's appearance, abilities, etc. **2** useless, futile.
in vain uselessly, without success.
vainly ADV

vainglory NOUN [LITERARY] great pride in oneself.
vainglorious ADJ

valance /val-ăns/ NOUN a short curtain or hanging frill.

vale NOUN [LITERARY] a valley.

valediction NOUN a farewell.
valedictory ADJ

valence /vay-lĕns/ (also **valency**) NOUN the combining power of an atom as compared with that of the hydrogen atom.

valentine NOUN a romantic greetings card sent, often anonymously, on St Valentine's Day (14 Feb.); a person to whom one sends this.

valet /val-ay/ NOUN a man's personal attendant. VERB (**valets**, **valeting**, **valeted**) **1** act as valet to. **2** clean (a car) thoroughly.

valetudinarian NOUN a person of poor health or unduly anxious about health.

valiant ADJ brave.
valiantly ADV

valid ADJ **1** having legal force, legally acceptable. **2** actually supporting the intended conclusion, logically sound.
validity NOUN

validate VERB check the

validity of; demonstrate the truth of; make valid. **validation** NOUN

valise NOUN a small suitcase.

valley NOUN (PL **valleys**) a low area between hills or mountains.

valour ([US] **valor**) NOUN bravery.

valuable ADJ of great value or worth. NOUN (**valuables**) valuable things.

valuation NOUN estimation or an estimate of a thing's worth.

value NOUN **1** the amount of money etc. considered equivalent to something; the extent to which something is considered useful, important, etc. **2** (**values**) moral principles, standards that one considers important. VERB **1** consider precious. **2** estimate the value of.

V

value added tax NOUN a tax on the amount by which a thing's value has been increased at each stage of its production.

value judgement NOUN a subjective estimate of quality etc.

valuer NOUN a person who estimates values professionally.

valve NOUN **1** a device controlling flow through a pipe; a structure allowing blood to flow in one direction only. **2** each half of the hinged shell of an oyster etc. **valvular** ADJ

vamoose VERB [INFORMAL] depart hurriedly.

vamp NOUN the upper front part of a boot or shoe. VERB play a short simple passage of music repeatedly.

vampire NOUN a ghost or reanimated body believed to suck blood from living humans.

van NOUN **1** a covered vehicle for transporting goods etc.; a railway carriage for luggage or goods. **2** the leading part, the front.

vanadium NOUN a hard grey metallic element.

vandal NOUN a person who damages things wilfully. **vandalism** NOUN

vandalize (also

vandalise) VERB damage wilfully.

vane NOUN **1** a weathervane. **2** the blade of a propeller, sail of a windmill, etc.

vanguard NOUN the foremost part of an advancing army etc.

vanilla NOUN a sweetish flavouring. ADJ [INFORMAL] ordinary, not elaborate or special.

vanish VERB disappear completely.

vanity NOUN (PL **vanities**) **1** conceit. **2** futility.

vanity case NOUN a small case for carrying cosmetics etc.

vanquish VERB conquer.

vantage point NOUN a position giving a good view.

vapid ADJ insipid, uninteresting.
vapidity NOUN
vapidly ADV

vaporize (also **vaporise**) VERB convert or be converted into vapour.
vaporization NOUN

vapour ([US] **vapor**) NOUN moisture suspended in air, into which certain liquids or solids are converted by heating.
vaporous ADJ

variable ADJ changeable, not constant. NOUN a part or element liable to change.
variability NOUN

variance NOUN the amount by which something changes or is different from something else.
at variance in disagreement.

variant NOUN a form of something differing from others or from a standard. ADJ differing in this way.

variation NOUN a change, a slight difference; a variant; a repetition of a musical theme with changes and ornamentation.

varicose ADJ (of veins) permanently swollen.

varied ADJ of different sorts.

variegated ADJ having irregular patches of colours.
variegation NOUN

variety NOUN (PL **varieties**)

1 not being uniform or monotonous; a selection of different things of the same type. 2 a sort or kind. 3 light entertainment made up of a series of short unrelated performances.

various ADJ of different kinds or sorts. DETERMINER & PRON more than one; individual and separate.
variously ADV

varlet NOUN [ARCHAIC] 1 a menial servant. 2 a rascal.

varnish NOUN a liquid that dries to form a shiny transparent coating. VERB coat with varnish.

vary VERB (**varies**, **varying**, **varied**) make or be or become different.

vascular ADJ of vessels or ducts for conveying blood or sap.

vase NOUN a decorative jar for holding cut flowers.

vasectomy NOUN (PL **vasectomies**) a surgical removal of part of the ducts that carry semen from the testicles, especially as a method of birth control.

Vaseline NOUN [TRADE MARK] a thick oily cream made from petroleum, used as an ointment or lubricant.

vassal NOUN a person or country subordinate to another.

vast ADJ very great in area or size.
vastly ADV
vastness NOUN

VAT ABBREV value added tax.

vat NOUN a large tank for liquids.

vault NOUN 1 an arched roof. 2 an underground storage room; a burial chamber. 3 an act of vaulting. VERB jump, especially with the help of the hands or a pole.
vaulted ADJ

vaunt VERB boast about. NOUN a boast.

VC ABBREV Victoria Cross.

V-chip NOUN a computer chip to be installed in a television receiver to block violent or sexually explicit material.

VCR ABBREV video cassette recorder.

VD ABBREV venereal disease.

VDU ABBREV visual display unit.

veal NOUN calf's flesh as food.

vector NOUN **1** a quantity (e.g. velocity) that has both magnitude and direction. **2** the carrier of an infectious agent.

veer VERB change direction.

veg [INFORMAL] NOUN vegetables. VERB (**vegges**, **vegging**, **vegged**) relax totally.

vegan /vee-găn/ NOUN a person who eats no meat or animal products.

vegetable NOUN a plant grown for food. ADJ of or from plants.

vegetarian NOUN a person who eats no meat or fish. ADJ of or for such people.
vegetarianism NOUN

vegetate VERB live an uneventful life.

vegetation NOUN plants collectively.

vehement ADJ showing strong feeling.
vehemence NOUN
vehemently ADV

vehicle NOUN a conveyance for transporting passengers or goods on land or in space; a means by which something is expressed or displayed.
vehicular ADJ

veil NOUN a piece of fabric concealing or protecting the face; something that conceals. VERB cover with or as if with a veil.

vein NOUN **1** any of the blood vessels conveying blood towards the heart. **2** a narrow streak or stripe; a narrow layer of ore etc. **3** a mood or style: *something in a lighter vein.*
veined ADJ

Velcro NOUN [TRADE MARK] a fastener consisting of two strips of fabric which cling together when pressed.

veld (also **veldt**) NOUN open grassland in South Africa.

vellum NOUN fine parchment; smooth writing paper.

velocity NOUN (PL **velocities**) speed.

velour /vĕ-loor/ (also **velours**) NOUN a plush fabric resembling velvet.

velvet NOUN **1** a woven fabric with a thick short pile on one side; a cotton

fabric resembling velvet. **2** soft downy skin that covers a deer's antler while it is growing.
velvety ADJ

venal ADJ susceptible to or influenced by bribery.
venality NOUN

vend VERB sell, offer for sale.

vendetta NOUN a feud.

vending machine NOUN a slot machine where small articles can be bought.

vendor NOUN a seller.

veneer NOUN a thin covering layer of fine wood; a superficial show of a quality. VERB cover with a veneer.

venerable ADJ worthy of great respect; (**Venerable**) the title of an archdeacon.

venerate VERB respect deeply.
veneration NOUN

venereal ADJ (of infections) contracted by sexual intercourse with an infected person.

V

Venetian NOUN a person from Venice. ADJ relating to Venice.

venetian blind NOUN a window blind of adjustable horizontal slats.

vengeance NOUN retaliation, revenge.
with a vengeance in an extreme degree.

vengeful ADJ seeking vengeance.

venial ADJ (of a sin) pardonable, not serious.
veniality NOUN

venison NOUN deer's flesh as food.

Venn diagram NOUN a diagram using overlapping circles etc. to show relationships between sets.

venom NOUN **1** a poisonous fluid secreted by snakes etc. **2** bitter feeling or language.
venomous ADJ

venous /vee-nŭs/ ADJ of veins.

vent NOUN **1** an opening allowing gas or liquid to pass through. **2** a slit at the lower edge of a coat. VERB give vent to.
give vent to give an outlet to (feelings).

ventilate VERB **1** cause air to enter or circulate

freely in. **2** discuss or examine publicly.
ventilation NOUN

ventilator NOUN **1** a device for ventilating a room etc. **2** a respirator.

ventral ADJ of or on the abdomen.

ventricle NOUN a cavity, especially in the heart or brain.
ventricular ADJ

ventriloquist NOUN an entertainer who can produce voice sounds so that they seem to come from a puppet etc.
ventriloquism NOUN

venture NOUN an undertaking that involves risk. VERB dare to do something or go somewhere; dare to say; expose to risk of loss.
venturesome ADJ

venue NOUN an appointed place for a meeting, concert, etc.

veracious ADJ [FORMAL] truthful; true.
veraciously ADV
veracity NOUN

veranda NOUN a roofed terrace.

verb NOUN a word indicating an action, state, or occurrence.

verbal ADJ **1** of or in words; spoken. **2** of a verb.
verbally ADV

verbalize (also **verbalise**) VERB express in words; be verbose.
verbalization NOUN

verbatim /ver-**bay**-tim/ ADV & ADJ in exactly the same words.

verbiage /**ver**-bee-ij/ NOUN an excessive number of words.

verbose ADJ using more words than are needed.
verbosely ADV
verbosity NOUN

verdant ADJ (of grass etc.) green.

verdict NOUN a decision reached by a jury; a decision or opinion reached after testing something.

verdigris /**ver**-di-gree/ NOUN a green deposit forming on copper or brass.

verdure NOUN green vegetation.

verge NOUN the extreme edge, the brink; a grass edging of a road etc.

verge on come close to being.

verger NOUN a church caretaker.

verify VERB (**verifies**, **verifying**, **verified**) check the truth or correctness of.
verification NOUN

verisimilitude NOUN the appearance of being true.

veritable ADJ deserving a specified description: *the book is a veritable gold mine.*

vermicelli /ver-mi-**chel**-li/ NOUN pasta made in slender threads.

vermilion NOUN a bright red colour.

vermin NOUN (PL **vermin**) an animal or insect regarded as a pest.
verminous ADJ

vernacular NOUN the ordinary language of a country or district.

vernal ADJ of or occurring in spring.

V

verruca /vĕ-**roo**-kă/ NOUN (PL **verrucas** or **verrucae**) an infectious wart on the foot.

versatile ADJ able to do or be used for many different things.
versatility NOUN

verse NOUN poetry, a poem; a group of lines forming a unit in a poem or hymn; a numbered division of a Bible chapter.

versed ADJ (**versed in**) skilled or experienced in.

versify VERB (**versifies**, **versifying**, **versified**) express in verse; compose verse.
versification NOUN

version NOUN a particular form of something, differing from others; an account of events from a particular viewpoint; a translation or edition.

verso NOUN (PL **versos**) the left-hand page of a book; the back of a leaf of manuscript.

versus PREP against.

vertebra NOUN (PL **vertebrae**) any of the small bones forming the backbone.

vertebrate NOUN an animal having a backbone. ADJ relating to vertebrates.

vertex NOUN (PL **vertices** or **vertexes**) the highest point of a hill etc.; an apex.

vertical ADJ perpendicular to the horizontal, upright. NOUN a vertical line or position. **vertically** ADV

vertiginous /ver-**tij**-in-ŭs/ ADJ causing vertigo.

vertigo NOUN dizziness, especially caused by heights.

verve NOUN enthusiasm, vigour.

very ADV to a high degree, extremely; absolutely: *the very best.* ADJ **1** actual, precise: *this very moment.* **2** mere: *the very thought.* **very well** an expression of consent.

vesicle /ves-ik-ĕl, **vees**-ik-ĕl/ NOUN a sac, especially containing liquid; a blister.

vessel NOUN **1** a receptacle, especially for liquid. **2** a ship, a boat. **3** a tube-like structure conveying blood or other fluid in the body of an animal or plant.

vest NOUN an undergarment covering the trunk; [US] a waistcoat. VERB confer (power) as a legal right.

vested interest NOUN a personal interest in a state of affairs, usually with an expectation of gain.

vestibule NOUN an entrance hall; a porch.

vestige NOUN a small amount or trace. **vestigial** ADJ

vestment NOUN a ceremonial garment, especially of clergy or a church choir.

vet NOUN **1** a veterinary surgeon. **2** [US] [INFORMAL] a military veteran. VERB (**vets**, **vetting**, **vetted**) examine critically for faults etc.

veteran NOUN a person with long experience, especially in the armed forces.

veterinarian NOUN [US] a veterinary surgeon.

veterinary ADJ of or for the treatment of diseases and disorders of animals.

veterinary surgeon NOUN a person qualified to treat animal diseases and disorders.

veto NOUN (PL **vetoes**) an authoritative rejection of something proposed; the right to make this. VERB (**vetoes**, **vetoing**, **vetoed**) reject by a veto.

vex VERB annoy.
vexation NOUN
vexatious ADJ

vexed question NOUN a problem that is much discussed.

VHF ABBREV very high frequency.

via PREP by way of, through.

viable ADJ capable of working successfully, or of living or surviving.
viability NOUN

viaduct NOUN a long bridge carrying a road etc. over a valley.

vial NOUN a small bottle.

viands /vI-ăndz/ PLURAL NOUN [ARCHAIC] articles of food.

vibes PLURAL NOUN [INFORMAL] **1** an emotional state communicated to others; an atmosphere. **2** a vibraphone.

vibrant ADJ full of energy and enthusiasm; quivering; resonant.

vibraphone NOUN a percussion instrument like a xylophone but with a vibrating effect.

vibrate VERB move rapidly and continuously to and fro; sound with rapid slight variation of pitch.
vibrator NOUN
vibratory ADJ

vibration NOUN **1** an instance of the state of vibrating. **2** (**vibrations**) [INFORMAL] mental influences; an atmosphere or feeling communicated.

vibrato NOUN [MUSIC] a rapid slight fluctuation in the pitch of a note.

vicar NOUN a member of the clergy in charge of a parish.

vicarage NOUN the house of a vicar.

vicarious /vik-air-i-ŭs/ ADJ felt through sharing imaginatively in the feelings or activities etc. of another person; acting or done etc. for another.
vicariously ADV

vice NOUN **1** great wickedness; criminal and immoral practices. **2** ([US] **vise**) a tool with two jaws for holding things firmly.

vice- COMBINING FORM a substitute or deputy for; next in rank to.

viceroy NOUN a person governing a colony etc. as the sovereign's representative.
viceregal ADJ

vice versa ADV reversing the order of the items just mentioned.

vicinity NOUN (PL **vicinities**) the surrounding district.
in the vicinity (of) near.

vicious ADJ deliberately cruel or spiteful; savage, dangerous.
viciously ADV

vicious circle NOUN a bad situation producing effects that intensify its original cause.

vicissitude /vi-sis-i-tyood/ NOUN a change of circumstances or luck.

victim NOUN a person injured or killed or made to suffer.

victimize (also **victimise**) VERB single out to suffer ill treatment.
victimization NOUN

victor NOUN a winner in a battle or competition.

Victorian ADJ relating to the reign of Queen Victoria (1837–1901). NOUN a person who lived during this period.

victorious ADJ having gained victory.

victory NOUN (PL **victories**) success achieved by winning a battle or contest.

victualler /vit-ler/ ([US] **victualer**) NOUN a person licensed to sell alcohol.

victuals PLURAL NOUN [DATED] food, provisions.

video NOUN (PL **videos**) a recording or broadcasting of pictures; an apparatus for this; a videotape. VERB (**videoes**, **videoing**, **videoed**) make a video of.

videotape NOUN magnetic tape for recording visual images and sound; a video cassette; a film recorded on this. VERB record on videotape.

videotex (also **videotext**) NOUN teletext or viewdata.

vie VERB (**vies**, **vying**, **vied**) carry on a rivalry,

V

compete.

view NOUN **1** the ability to see something or to be seen from a particular place; what can be seen from a particular place, especially considered aesthetically. **2** an attitude or opinion. VERB **1** look at, inspect; watch (a television programme). **2** regard in a particular way.
in view visible. **in view of** because of, considering. **on view** displayed for inspection. **with a view to** with the hope or intention of.
viewer NOUN

viewdata NOUN a news and information service from a computer source to which a television screen is connected by a telephone link.

viewfinder NOUN a device on a camera showing the extent of the area being photographed.

V

viewpoint NOUN **1** a point of view. **2** a place from which there is a good view.

vigil NOUN a period of staying awake to keep watch or pray.

vigilant ADJ watchful.
vigilance NOUN
vigilantly ADV

vigilante /vi-ji-**lan**-ti/ NOUN a member of a self-appointed group trying to prevent crime etc.

vignette /veen-**yet**/ NOUN a short written description.

vigour ([US] **vigor**) NOUN active physical or mental strength; forcefulness.
vigorous ADJ
vigorously ADV
vigorousness NOUN

Viking NOUN an ancient Scandinavian trader and pirate.

vile ADJ extremely disgusting or wicked.
vilely ADV
vileness NOUN

vilify VERB (**vilifies, vilifying, vilified**) disparage, blacken the reputation of.
vilification NOUN
vilifier NOUN

villa NOUN a large country residence; a house in a residential district; a rented holiday home.

village NOUN a collection of houses and other

buildings in a country district.
villager NOUN

villain NOUN a wicked person.
villainous ADJ
villainy NOUN

villein NOUN [HISTORICAL] a feudal tenant subject to a lord.

vim NOUN [INFORMAL] vigour.

vinaigrette NOUN a salad dressing of oil and vinegar.

vindicate VERB clear of blame; justify.
vindication NOUN

vindictive ADJ showing a strong or excessive desire for vengeance.
vindictively ADV
vindictiveness NOUN

vine NOUN a climbing plant on which grapes grow.

vinegar NOUN a sour liquid made from wine, malt, etc., by fermentation.
vinegary ADJ

vineyard NOUN a plantation of vines for winemaking.

vintage NOUN **1** the year in which a wine was produced; wine of high quality from a particular year; the date of something's origin. ADJ of high quality, especially from a past period.

vintner NOUN a wine-merchant.

vinyl /vy-nil/ NOUN a kind of plastic.

viola¹ /vi-**oh**-lă/ NOUN an instrument like a violin but of lower pitch.

viola² /**vy**-ŏ-lă/ NOUN a plant of the genus to which violets and pansies belong.

violate VERB break (a rule, promise, etc.); fail to respect (a right); treat irreverently; rape.
violation NOUN
violator NOUN

violent ADJ involving great force or intensity; using excessive physical force.
violence NOUN
violently ADV

violet NOUN a small plant, often with purple flowers; a bluish-purple colour. ADJ bluish purple.

violin NOUN a musical instrument with four strings of treble pitch,

played with a bow.
violinist NOUN

violoncello NOUN (PL **violoncellos**) a cello.

VIP ABBREV very important person.

viper NOUN a type of poisonous snake.

virago /vi-rah-goh/ NOUN (PL **viragos**) an aggressive woman.

viral /vy-răl/ ADJ of a virus.

virgin NOUN **1** a person (especially a woman) who has never had sexual intercourse; (**the Virgin**) Mary, mother of Christ. **2** a person lacking experience in a specified area. ADJ **1** never having had sexual intercourse. **2** untouched, not yet used.
virginal ADJ
virginity NOUN

virile ADJ having masculine strength or procreative power.
virility NOUN

virology NOUN the study of viruses.
virologist NOUN

virtual ADJ almost existing or being as described, but not strictly or officially so.
virtually ADV

virtual reality NOUN a computer-generated simulation of reality.

virtue NOUN moral excellence of character or behaviour; an excellent characteristic; a good or useful quality; [ARCHAIC] chastity.
by or **in virtue of** because of, on the strength of.

virtuoso NOUN (PL **virtuosos** or **virtuosi**) an expert performer.
virtuosity NOUN

virtuous ADJ morally good.
virtuously ADV
virtuousness NOUN

virulent ADJ (of poison or disease) extremely strong or violent; bitterly hostile.
virulence NOUN
virulently ADV

virus NOUN **1** a minute organism capable of causing disease. **2** a destructive code hidden in a computer program.

visa /vee-ză/ NOUN an official mark on a passport, permitting the holder to enter a specified country.

visage /viz-ij/ NOUN [LITERARY] a person's face.

vis-à-vis /veez-ah-**vee**/ PREP in relation to; in comparison to.

viscera /viss-er-ă/ PLURAL NOUN the internal organs of the body.
visceral ADJ

viscid /vi-sid/ ADJ thick and sticky.
viscidity NOUN

viscose NOUN viscous cellulose; a fabric made from this.

viscount /vy-kownt/ NOUN a nobleman ranking between earl and baron.

viscountess NOUN a woman holding the rank of viscount; a viscount's wife or widow.

viscous /vis-kŭs/ ADJ thick and gluey.
viscosity NOUN

vise US spelling of **VICE** (*sense* 2).

visibility NOUN the state of being visible; the distance one can see under certain weather conditions etc.

visible ADJ able to be seen or noticed.
visibly ADV

vision NOUN **1** the ability to see; inspired and idealistic ideas about the future. **2** a dream, an apparition; an extraordinarily beautiful person.

visionary ADJ idealistic; imaginative. NOUN (PL **visionaries**) a person with visionary ideas.

visit VERB **1** go or come to see; stay temporarily with or at. **2** inflict (harm) on someone. NOUN an act of visiting.
visitor NOUN

visitation NOUN **1** an official visit or inspection. **2** trouble regarded as divine punishment.

visor /vy-zer/ (also **vizor**) NOUN a movable front part of a helmet, covering the face; a shading device at the top of a vehicle's windscreen.

vista NOUN an extensive view, especially seen through a long opening.

visual ADJ of or used in seeing.
visually ADV

visual display unit NOUN a device displaying a computer output or input on a screen.

visualize (also **visualise**) VERB form a mental picture of.
visualization NOUN

vital ADJ **1** essential to life; essential to a thing's existence or success. **2** full of vitality. NOUN (**vitals**) the important internal organs of the body, such as the heart and brain.
vitally ADV

vitality NOUN liveliness, persistent energy.

vital statistics PLURAL NOUN [INFORMAL] the measurements of a woman's bust, waist, and hips.

vitamin NOUN an organic compound present in food and essential for growth and nutrition.

vitiate /vish-i-ayt/ VERB [FORMAL] make imperfect or ineffective.
vitiation NOUN

viticulture NOUN the cultivation of vines for wine production.

vitreous ADJ like glass in texture, finish, etc.

vitrify VERB (**vitrifies**, **vitrifying**, **vitrified**) change into a glassy substance.
vitrifaction NOUN

vitriol NOUN **1** [ARCHAIC] sulphuric acid. **2** savagely hostile remarks.
vitriolic ADJ

vituperate VERB [ARCHAIC] insult, abuse.
vituperation NOUN
vituperative ADJ

viva[1] /vI-vă/ NOUN [INFORMAL] a viva voce examination.

viva[2] /vee-vă/ EXCLAMATION long live (someone or something).

vivace /vi-vah-chi/ ADV [MUSIC] in a lively manner.

vivacious ADJ lively, high-spirited.
vivaciously ADV
vivacity NOUN

vivarium NOUN (PL **vivaria**) a place for keeping living animals etc. in natural conditions.

viva voce /vy-vă **voh**-chi/ NOUN an oral university examination.

vivid ADJ bright, intense; clear; (of imagination) lively.

V

vividly ADV
vividness NOUN

vivify VERB (**vivifies**, **vivifying**, **vivified**) put life into.

viviparous /vi-vi-pă-rŭs/ ADJ bringing forth young alive, not egg-laying.

vivisection NOUN performance of experiments on living animals.

vixen NOUN a female fox.

viz. ADV in other words; that is; namely.

vizor variant of **VISOR**.

V-neck NOUN a V-shaped neckline on a pullover etc.

vocabulary NOUN (PL **vocabularies**) the words known by a person or group, or used in a particular field; a list of words and their meanings.

vocal ADJ **1** of or for the voice. **2** expressing opinions freely; talking a great deal. NOUN a piece of sung music.
vocally ADV

vocalist NOUN a singer.

vocalize (also **vocalise**) VERB utter.
vocalization NOUN

vocation NOUN a strong desire or feeling of fitness for a certain career; a trade or profession.
vocational ADJ

vociferate VERB say loudly, shout.
vociferation NOUN

vociferous ADJ making a great outcry.
vociferously ADV

vodka NOUN an alcoholic spirit distilled chiefly from rye.

vogue NOUN current fashion; popularity.
in vogue in fashion.

voice NOUN sounds formed in the larynx and uttered by the mouth; an expressed opinion, the right to express an opinion. VERB express; utter.

voicemail NOUN an electronic system for storing messages left by telephone or transmitted through a digital computer network.

voice-over NOUN a narration in a film etc. without a picture of the speaker.

void ADJ **1** empty. **2** not valid. NOUN an empty space, emptiness. VERB make void; excrete.

voile /voil, vwahl/ NOUN a very thin dress fabric.

volatile ADJ **1** evaporating rapidly. **2** liable to change unpredictably; changing quickly in mood.
volatility NOUN

vol-au-vent /vol-oh-von/ NOUN a small puff pastry case filled with a savoury mixture.

volcano NOUN (PL **volcanoes**) a mountain with a vent through which lava is expelled.
volcanic ADJ

vole NOUN a small rodent.

volition NOUN the exercise of one's will.

volley NOUN (PL **volleys**) **1** a simultaneous discharge of missiles etc.; an outburst of questions or other words. **2** a return of the ball in tennis etc. before it touches the ground. VERB send in a volley.

volleyball NOUN a game for two teams sending a large ball by hand over a net.

volt NOUN a unit of electromotive force.

voltage NOUN electromotive force expressed in volts.

volte-face /volt-fass/ NOUN a complete change of attitude to something.

voltmeter NOUN an instrument measuring electrical potential in volts.

voluble ADJ talking easily and at length.
volubility NOUN
volubly ADV

volume NOUN **1** a book. **2** the amount of space held or occupied by a container or object; an amount, the quantity of something. **3** the loudness of a sound.

voluminous ADJ having great volume, bulky; copious.

voluntary ADJ done, given, or acting by choice; working or done without payment; maintained by voluntary contributions.
voluntarily ADV

volunteer NOUN a person

who offers to do something; one who works for no pay; one who enrols voluntarily for military service. VERB freely offer to do something; offer (something) voluntarily.

voluptuary NOUN (PL **voluptuaries**) a person fond of luxury and sensual pleasure.

voluptuous ADJ **1** full of or fond of sensual pleasure. **2** (of a woman) having a full attractive figure.
voluptuously ADV
voluptuousness NOUN

vomit VERB (**vomits**, **vomiting**, **vomited**) eject (matter) from the stomach through the mouth; emit in vast quantities. NOUN vomited matter.

voodoo NOUN a form of religion based on witchcraft.
voodooism NOUN

voracious ADJ greedy; ravenous; insatiable.
voraciously ADV
voracity NOUN

vortex NOUN (PL **vortexes** or **vortices**) a whirlpool or whirlwind.

vote NOUN a formal expression of one's opinion or choice on a matter under discussion; a choice etc. expressed in this way; the right to vote. VERB express one's choice by a vote; elect to a position by votes.
voter NOUN

votive ADJ given to fulfil a vow.

vouch VERB (**vouch for**) guarantee the accuracy or reliability etc. of.

voucher NOUN a document exchangeable for certain goods or services; a receipt.

vouchsafe VERB give or grant.

vow NOUN a solemn promise. VERB make a vow.

vowel NOUN a speech sound made without audible stopping of the breath; the letter representing this, e.g. *a* or *e*.

vox pop NOUN [INFORMAL] popular opinion represented by informal comments from the public.

voyage NOUN a journey made by water or in space. VERB make a voyage.
voyager NOUN

voyeur /vwah-yer/ NOUN a person who gets sexual pleasure from watching others having sex or undressing.

vs ABBREV versus.

V-sign NOUN a sign of abuse made with the first two fingers pointing up and the back of the hand facing out; a similar sign with the palm facing outwards as a symbol of victory.

VSO ABBREV voluntary service overseas.

vulcanite NOUN hard black vulcanized rubber.

vulcanize (also **vulcanise**) VERB strengthen (rubber) by treating with sulphur.
vulcanization NOUN

vulgar ADJ lacking refinement or good taste.
vulgarity NOUN
vulgarly ADV

vulgar fraction NOUN a fraction represented by numbers above and below a line (rather than decimally).

vulgarian NOUN a coarse person, especially one with newly acquired wealth.

vulgarism NOUN a coarse word or expression.

vulnerable ADJ able to be hurt or injured; exposed to danger or criticism.
vulnerability NOUN

vulture NOUN a large bird of prey that lives on the flesh of dead animals.

vulva NOUN the external parts of the female genital organs.

vying present participle of **VIE**.

Ww

W (also **w**) NOUN (PL **Ws** or **W's**) the twenty-third letter of the alphabet. ABBREV **1** west, western. **2** watts.

wacky ADJ (**wackier**, **wackiest**) [INFORMAL] mad, eccentric.

wad NOUN **1** a pad of soft material. **2** a bunch of papers or banknotes. VERB (**wads**, **wadding**, **wadded**) line, pad.

wadding NOUN padding.

waddle VERB walk with short steps and a swaying movement. NOUN a waddling gait.

wade VERB walk through water or mud; proceed slowly and laboriously (through work etc.).

wader NOUN **1** a long-legged waterbird. **2** (**waders**) high waterproof boots worn in fishing etc.

wadi /wo-di, wah-di/ NOUN a rocky watercourse, dry except in the rainy season.

wafer NOUN a thin light biscuit; a very thin slice.

waffle NOUN **1** [INFORMAL] lengthy but vague or trivial speech or writing. **2** a small cake of batter eaten hot, cooked in a **waffle iron**. VERB [INFORMAL] talk or write waffle.

waft VERB carry or travel lightly through air or over water. NOUN a gentle movement of air; a scent carried on it.

wag VERB (**wags**, **wagging**, **wagged**) move or cause to move briskly to and fro. NOUN **1** a wagging movement. **2** [INFORMAL] a humorous person.

wage NOUN (also **wages**) regular payment to an employee for his or her work. VERB engage in (war).

waged ADJ having paid employment.

wager NOUN a bet. VERB make a bet.

waggle [INFORMAL] VERB wag. NOUN a waggling motion.
waggly ADJ

wagon (also **waggon**) NOUN a four-wheeled vehicle for heavy loads; an open railway truck.
on the wagon [INFORMAL] abstaining from alcohol.

waif NOUN a homeless child; a thin and vulnerable person.

wail NOUN a long sad cry. VERB utter a wail.

wainscot (also **wainscoting**) NOUN wooden panelling on the lower part of a room's walls.

waist NOUN the part of the human body between ribs and hips; a narrow middle part.

W

waistcoat NOUN a close-fitting waist-length sleeveless jacket.

waistline NOUN the outline or size of the waist.

wait VERB **1** stay where one is or refrain from acting until a specified time or event; expect someone or something, especially when they are late; be left until later. **2** serve at table. NOUN an act or period of waiting.
wait on serve food and drink to (a person) at a meal; fetch and carry things for.

waiter NOUN a man employed to serve customers in a restaurant etc.

waitress NOUN a woman employed to serve customers in a restaurant etc.

waive VERB refrain from using (a right etc.).
waiver NOUN

wake[1] VERB (**wakes**, **waking**, **woke** or **waked**; PAST PARTICIPLE **woken** or **waked**) **1** cease to sleep; cause to cease sleeping. **2** evoke. NOUN a gathering held beside the body of someone who has died; a party held after a funeral.
wake up wake; make or become alert.

wake[2] NOUN a trail of disturbed water left by a ship.
in the wake of behind; following.

wakeful ADJ unable to sleep; sleepless.
wakefulness NOUN

waken VERB wake.

walk VERB progress by setting down one foot and then lifting the other(s) in turn; travel along (a path etc.) in this way; accompany in walking. NOUN a journey on foot; a manner or style of walking; a place or route for walking.
walk of life social rank; occupation. **walk out** depart suddenly and angrily; go on strike suddenly. **walk out on** desert.
walker NOUN

walkabout NOUN an informal stroll among a crowd by royalty etc.

walkie-talkie NOUN a small portable radio transmitter and receiver.

walking stick NOUN a stick carried or used as a support when walking.

walkout NOUN a sudden angry departure, especially as a strike.

walkover NOUN an easy victory.

wall NOUN a continuous upright structure forming one side of a building or room or enclosing an area of land; a barrier; something that divides or encloses. VERB surround or enclose with a wall.

wallaby NOUN (PL **wallabies**) a marsupial like a small kangaroo.

wallet NOUN a small folding case for banknotes or documents.

wallflower NOUN **1** a garden plant. **2** [INFORMAL] a girl who has no-one to dance with at a party.

wallop [INFORMAL] VERB (**wallops**, **walloping**, **walloped**) thrash, hit hard. NOUN a heavy blow.

wallow VERB roll in mud or water etc. NOUN an act of wallowing.
wallow in take unrestrained pleasure in.

wallpaper NOUN decorative paper for covering the interior walls of rooms.

wally NOUN (PL **wallies**) [INFORMAL] a stupid person.

walnut NOUN a nut containing a wrinkled edible kernel.

walrus NOUN a large seal-like Arctic animal with long tusks.

waltz NOUN a ballroom dance; the music for this. VERB dance a waltz; [INFORMAL] move easily and casually.

wan ADJ pale, pallid.
wanly ADV
wanness NOUN

wand NOUN a slender rod, especially associated with the working of magic.

wander VERB go from place to place with no settled route or purpose; stray; digress. NOUN an act of wandering.
wanderer NOUN

wanderlust NOUN a strong desire to travel.

wane VERB decrease in vigour or importance; (of the moon) show a decreasing bright area after being full.
on the wane waning.

wangle VERB [INFORMAL] obtain or arrange by trickery or scheming.

wannabe /won-ă-bee/ NOUN [INFORMAL] a person who aspires to be like someone famous.

want VERB **1** desire, wish for or to; need. **2** lack, fall short of. NOUN a desire; something desired or needed.

wanted ADJ (of a suspected criminal) sought by the police.

wanting ADJ lacking, deficient.

wanton ADJ irresponsible, lacking proper restraint.

WAP ABBREV Wireless Application Protocol (enabling a mobile phone to connect to the Internet).

war NOUN a state of armed conflict between nations, states, or groups; open hostility; conflict. VERB (**wars**, **warring**, **warred**) make war.

warble VERB sing, especially with a gentle trilling note. NOUN a warbling sound.

ward NOUN **1** a room with beds for patients in a

W

hospital. **2** a division of a city or town, electing a councillor to represent it. **3** a child under the care of a guardian or law court.
ward off keep at a distance; repel.

warden NOUN an official with supervisory duties.

warder NOUN a prison officer.

wardrobe NOUN a large cupboard for storing hanging clothes; a stock of clothes or costumes.

ware NOUN manufactured goods of the kind specified; (**wares**) articles offered for sale.

warehouse NOUN a building for storing goods or furniture; a large wholesale or retail store.

warfare NOUN the activity of fighting a war.

warhead NOUN the explosive head of a missile.

warlike ADJ aggressive; threatening war.

warm ADJ **1** moderately hot; providing warmth. **2** readily feeling and expressing affection; enthusiastic, heartfelt.
VERB make or become warm.
warm to become friendlier towards (someone) or more enthusiastic about (something). **warm up** **1** heat or reheat; become livelier. **2** prepare for exercise by stretching muscles etc.
warmly ADV
warmness NOUN

warm-blooded ADJ having blood that remains at a constant temperature.

warmonger NOUN a person who seeks to bring about war.

warmth NOUN warmness.

warn VERB inform about a present or future danger or difficulty etc., advise about action in this.
warn off tell (a person) to keep away or to avoid (a thing).

warning NOUN something that serves to warn a person.

warp VERB make or become bent by uneven shrinkage or expansion;

distort, pervert. NOUN **1** a distortion, a warped state. **2** the lengthwise threads in a loom.

warrant NOUN a document giving legal authorization for an action; a voucher; justification. VERB justify; guarantee.

warranty NOUN (PL **warranties**) a guarantee of repair or replacement of a purchased article.

warren NOUN a series of burrows where rabbits live.

warrior NOUN a person who fights in a battle.

wart NOUN a small hard abnormal growth on the skin.

warthog NOUN an African wild pig with wart-like lumps on its face.

wary ADJ (**warier**, **wariest**) cautious, suspicious.
warily ADV
wariness NOUN

was 1st and 3rd person singular present of **BE**.

wash VERB **1** clean with water or other liquid; wash oneself or clothes etc.; be washable. **2** flow past, against, or over; carry by flowing. **3** coat thinly with paint. **4** [INFORMAL] be convincing or persuasive: *that idea won't wash with him.* NOUN **1** the process of washing or being washed; clothes etc. to be washed; a solution for washing. **2** disturbed water or air behind a moving ship or aircraft etc. **3** a thin coating of paint.
wash down accompany (food) with a drink. **wash one's hands of** refuse to take responsibility for. **wash out** (of heavy rain) make (a sporting event) impossible. **wash up** **1** wash dishes etc. after use. **2** cast on the shore.

washable ADJ able to be washed without suffering damage.

washbasin NOUN a bowl (usually fixed to a wall) for washing one's hands and face.

washed out ADJ faded; pallid.

washer NOUN a ring of rubber or metal etc. placed under a nut or bolt or in a tap to give tightness.

washing NOUN clothes etc. to be washed.

washing-up NOUN dishes etc. for washing after use; the process of washing these.

washout NOUN [INFORMAL] a failure.

washroom NOUN [US] a room with a lavatory.

washy ADJ (**washier**, **washiest**) [INFORMAL] (of food) watery; lacking vigour.

Wasp NOUN a middle-class American white Protestant.

wasp NOUN a stinging insect with a black and yellow striped body.

waspish ADJ making sharp or irritable comments.

wassail [ARCHAIC] NOUN revelry with a lot of drinking. VERB celebrate in this way; sing carols.

wastage NOUN loss or diminution by waste; loss of employees by retirement or resignation.

waste VERB **1** use more of (something) than is needed; use or spend to no purpose; fail to make use of. **2** become thinner and weaker. ADJ left or thrown away because not wanted; (of land) unfit for use. NOUN **1** an act or process of wasting; waste material; a waste pipe. **2** a large expanse of usually barren land.

waster NOUN

wasteful ADJ extravagant.

wastefully ADV

wastefulness NOUN

waste pipe NOUN a pipe carrying off used or superfluous water or steam.

watch VERB **1** look at attentively, observe; spy on; be careful about. **2** [ARCHAIC] stay awake for prayer etc. NOUN **1** a small device indicating the time, usually worn on the wrist. **2** an act of observing or guarding. **3** a spell of duty worked by a sailor, police officer, etc.

on the watch alertly looking out for something. **watch out** be careful.

watcher NOUN

watchdog NOUN a dog

kept to guard property; a guardian of people's rights etc.

watchful ADJ vigilant, observant, alert.
watchfully ADV
watchfulness NOUN

watchman NOUN a person employed to guard a building etc.

watchtower NOUN a tower from which observation can be kept.

watchword NOUN a word or phrase expressing a group's principles.

water NOUN **1** a colourless odourless tasteless liquid that is a compound of hydrogen and oxygen; this as supplied for domestic use. **2** a watery secretion; urine. **3** a lake or other stretch of water; (**waters**) an area of sea controlled by a particular country; the level of the tide: *high water*. VERB **1** sprinkle water over; give a drink of water to. **2** produce tears or saliva.
by water in a boat etc.
water down dilute; make less forceful.

waterbed NOUN a mattress of rubber etc. filled with water.

water biscuit NOUN a thin unsweetened biscuit.

water butt NOUN a barrel used to catch rainwater.

water cannon NOUN a device giving a powerful jet of water to dispel a crowd etc.

water chestnut NOUN the edible corm from a sedge.

water closet NOUN [DATED] a lavatory flushed by water.

watercolour ([US] **watercolor**) NOUN artists' paint mixed with water (not oil); a painting done with this.

watercourse NOUN a stream, brook, or artificial waterway; its channel.

watercress NOUN a kind of cress that grows in streams and ponds.

waterfall NOUN a stream that falls from a height.

waterfront NOUN part of a town that borders on a river, lake, or sea.

water ice NOUN frozen flavoured water.

watering can NOUN a container with a spout for watering plants.

watering place NOUN a pool where animals drink; a spa, a seaside resort.

water lily NOUN (PL **water lilies**) a plant with broad floating leaves and flowers.

waterline NOUN the level normally reached by water on a ship's side.

waterlogged ADJ saturated with water.

water main NOUN a main pipe in a water supply system.

watermark NOUN a manufacturer's design in paper, visible when the paper is held against light.

water meadow NOUN a meadow that is flooded periodically by a stream.

watermelon NOUN a melon with watery red pulp.

watermill NOUN a mill worked by a waterwheel.

water power NOUN power obtained from flowing or falling water.

waterproof ADJ unable to be penetrated by water. NOUN a waterproof garment. VERB make waterproof.

water rat NOUN a small rodent living beside a lake or stream.

watershed NOUN a line of high land separating two river systems; a turning point in the course of events.

waterskiing NOUN the sport of skimming over water on skis while towed by a motor boat.

waterspout NOUN a rotating column of water formed by a whirlwind over the sea.

water table NOUN the level below which the ground is saturated with water.

watertight ADJ **1** made or fastened so that water cannot get in or out. **2** impossible to disprove.

waterway NOUN a navigable channel, a canal.

waterwheel NOUN a wheel turned by a flow of water to work machinery.

water wings PLURAL NOUN floats worn on the shoulders by a person learning to swim.

waterworks NOUN an establishment with machinery etc. for supplying water to a district.

watery ADJ of or like water; containing too much water; pale, weak.

watt NOUN a unit of electric power.

wattage NOUN an amount of electric power expressed in watts.

wattle NOUN **1** interwoven sticks used as material for fences, walls, etc. **2** a fold of skin hanging from the neck of a turkey etc.

wave NOUN **1** a moving ridge of water; a curved shape compared to this. **2** an act of waving. **3** a slight curl in hair. **4** a burst of feeling; a sequence of a type of event: *a wave of strikes.* **5** a wave-like motion by which heat, light, sound, or electricity is spread; a single curve in this. VERB **1** move one's hand or arm to and fro as a greeting or signal; move to and fro with a swaying motion while fixed to one point. **2** style (hair) so that it curls slightly.

waveband NOUN a range of wavelengths.

wavelength NOUN the distance between corresponding points in a sound wave or electromagnetic wave. **on the same wavelength** in sympathy, understanding each other.

waver VERB be or become unsteady; be undecided. **waverer** NOUN

wavy ADJ (**wavier**, **waviest**) having waves or curves.

wax NOUN a soft fatty solid used for polishing, making models, etc. VERB **1** coat or polish with wax; use wax to remove unwanted hair from (part of the body). **2** (of the moon) show an increasingly large bright area until becoming full; [LITERARY] become stronger; speak in a specified way.

W

waxy ADJ

waxwork NOUN a wax model, especially of a person.

way NOUN **1** a method or manner of doing something; someone's characteristic manner; (**ways**) habits. **2** a route, a path, a line of communication; progress: *make one's way;* a direction: *go the other way.* **3** a distance: *a long way to go.* **4** a respect or aspect: *wrong in every way.* ADV [INFORMAL] by a great deal, extremely: *way too much.* **by the way** incidentally, as an unconnected remark. **by way of 1** via. **2** as a form of, serving as. **have one's way** achieve what one wants. **in a way** to some extent, in a sense. **in the way** forming an obstacle. **make** or **give way** allow someone to pass. **on one's way** travelling somewhere. **on the way** travelling; (of a baby) conceived but not yet born. **out of one's way** not on one's intended route; going to particular trouble.

waybill NOUN a list of the passengers or goods being carried by a vehicle.

wayfarer NOUN [LITERARY] a traveller.

waylay VERB (**waylays**, **waylaying**, **waylaid**) lie in wait for.

waymark (also **waymarker**) NOUN an arrow showing the direction of a footpath.

wayside NOUN the side of a road or path.

wayward ADJ self-willed and hard to control or predict.

WC ABBREV water closet.

we PRON used by a person referring to himself or herself and another or others; used instead of 'I' in newspaper editorials and by a royal person in formal proclamations.

weak ADJ lacking physical strength or social etc. power; breaking easily; unconvincing; irresolute, easily influenced; much diluted; not bright or intense.
weakly ADV

weaken VERB make or become weaker.

weakling NOUN a feeble person or animal.

weakness NOUN the state or condition of being weak; a vulnerable point; a self-indulgent liking.

weal NOUN a ridge raised on flesh especially by the stroke of a rod or whip.

wealth NOUN money and valuable possessions; possession of these; a great quantity.
wealthy ADJ

wean VERB accustom (a baby) to take food other than milk; cause to give up something gradually.

weapon NOUN a thing designed or used for inflicting harm or damage; a means of coercing someone.

wear VERB (**wears**, **wearing**, **wore**; PAST PARTICIPLE **worn**) **1** have on the body as clothing or ornament. **2** damage or become damaged by friction or use. **3** endure continued use: *the carpet has worn well.* NOUN **1** the action of wearing or the state of being worn; clothes of a specified type: *formal wear.* **2** damage by friction etc.
wear down overcome (opposition) by persistence. **wear off** pass off gradually. **wear on** (of time) pass slowly. **wear out 1** use or be used until no longer usable. **2** tire out.
wearable ADJ
wearer NOUN

wearisome ADJ causing weariness.

weary ADJ (**wearier**, **weariest**) very tired; tiring, tedious. VERB (**wearies**, **wearying**, **wearied**) make or become weary.
wearily ADV
weariness NOUN

weasel NOUN a small slender carnivorous wild mammal.

weather NOUN the state of the atmosphere with reference to sunshine, rain, wind, etc. VERB **1** wear away or change by exposure to the weather. **2** come safely through (a storm).
make heavy weather of [INFORMAL] have difficulty

W

in doing. **under the weather** [INFORMAL] feeling unwell or depressed.

weather-beaten ADJ bronzed or worn by exposure to the weather.

weatherboard NOUN a sloping board at the bottom of a door, for keeping out rain.

weathervane (also **weathercock**) NOUN a revolving pointer to show the direction of the wind.

weave VERB (**weaves, weaving, wove**; PAST PARTICIPLE **woven**) **1** make (fabric etc.) by passing crosswise threads or strips under and over lengthwise ones; form (thread etc.) into fabric in this way. **2** compose (a story etc.). **3** move in an intricate course. NOUN a style or pattern of weaving.
weaver NOUN

web NOUN **1** a network of fine strands made by a spider etc.; a complex system of interconnected elements. **2** (**the Web**) the World Wide Web. **3** skin filling the spaces between the toes of ducks, frogs, etc.
webbed ADJ

webbing NOUN a strong band of woven fabric used in upholstery.

webcam (also **Webcam**) NOUN [TRADE MARK IN THE US] a video camera connected to a computer, so that the film produced may be viewed on the Internet.

web page NOUN a document forming part of the World Wide Web.

web site NOUN a location connected to the Internet that maintains one or more web pages.

wed VERB (**weds, wedding, wedded**) marry; unite, combine.

wedding NOUN a marriage ceremony and festivities.

wedge NOUN a piece of solid substance thick at one end and tapering to a thin edge at the other. VERB force apart or fix in position with a wedge; force into a narrow space.

wedlock NOUN the married state.

Wednesday NOUN the day after Tuesday.

wee ADJ [SCOTTISH] little. NOUN & VERB [INFORMAL] = **WEE-WEE**.

weed NOUN **1** a wild plant growing where it is not wanted. **2** [INFORMAL] a thin or feeble person. VERB uproot and remove weeds from.
weed out remove as inferior or undesirable.
weedy ADJ

week NOUN a period of seven successive days, especially from Monday to Sunday or Sunday to Saturday; the weekdays of this; the working period during a week.

weekday NOUN a day other than Sunday or other than the weekend.

weekend NOUN Saturday and Sunday.

weekly ADJ & ADV done, produced, or occurring once a week. NOUN (PL **weeklies**) a newspaper or magazine issued every week.

weeny ADJ (**weenier**, **weeniest**) [INFORMAL] tiny.

weep VERB (**weeps**, **weeping**, **wept**) shed tears; (of a sore etc.) exude liquid. NOUN a spell of weeping.

weeping ADJ (of a tree) having drooping branches.

weepy ADJ (**weepier**, **weepiest**) prone to crying; inducing tears, sentimental.

weevil NOUN a small beetle that feeds on grain etc.

wee-wee [INFORMAL] VERB urinate. NOUN urine, the act of urinating.

weft NOUN the crosswise threads in weaving.

weigh VERB **1** find how heavy (someone or something) is; have a specified weight. **2** consider the relative importance or desirability of; have influence. **3** be a burden.
weigh anchor raise the anchor and start a voyage. **weigh down** be a burden to; oppress, depress. **weigh up** form an estimate of.

weighbridge NOUN a weighing machine with a plate set in a road etc. for weighing vehicles.

weight NOUN **1** an object's mass, the heaviness of a person or thing; a unit or system of units for expressing this; a piece of metal of known weight used in weighing; a heavy object or load. **2** influence. VERB **1** attach a weight to; hold down with a weight; burden. **2** attach importance to; bias.
weightless ADJ
weightlessness NOUN

weighting NOUN extra pay or allowances given in special cases.

weighty ADJ (**weightier**, **weightiest**) heavy; serious, important; influential.

weir NOUN a small dam built to regulate the flow of a river.

weird ADJ uncanny, bizarre.
weirdly ADV
weirdness NOUN

welch variant of **WELSH**.

welcome ADJ gladly received; much wanted or needed. NOUN a kind greeting; a manner of receiving someone. VERB greet kindly; be glad to receive. EXCLAMATION a pleased greeting.
welcome to willingly given the use of.

weld VERB unite or fuse (pieces of metal) by heating or pressure; unite into a whole. NOUN a welded joint.
welder NOUN

welfare NOUN well-being; organized efforts to ensure people's well-being.

welfare state NOUN a system attempting to ensure the welfare of all citizens by means of state operated social services.

well[1] NOUN a shaft sunk into the ground to obtain water, oil, etc.; an enclosed shaft-like space. VERB (of liquid) rise to the surface.

well[2] ADV (**better**, **best**) **1** in a good or satisfactory way; in an appropriate or right way; in an advantageous way. **2** kindly; favourably. **3** thoroughly; extremely. **4** possibly, probably: *it may well be so.* ADJ in good health; satisfactory. EXCLAMATION expressing

W

surprise, relief, or resignation etc., or said when one is hesitating. **as well 1** in addition. **2** prudent, advisable. **as well as** in addition to. **might as well** have no reason not to.

well appointed ADJ well equipped or furnished.

well-being NOUN good health, happiness, and prosperity.

well disposed ADJ having sympathetic or favourable feelings.

well-heeled ADJ [INFORMAL] wealthy.

wellington NOUN a boot of rubber or other waterproof material.

well meaning (also **well meant**) ADJ acting or done with good intentions.

well-nigh ADV almost.

well off ADJ in a satisfactory or good situation; fairly rich.

well read ADJ having read much literature.

W

well spoken ADJ speaking in a cultured way.

well-to-do ADJ fairly rich.

Welsh NOUN the language of Wales. ADJ relating to Wales.

welsh (also **welch**) VERB fail to keep a promise or pay a debt.
welsher NOUN

Welsh rabbit (also **Welsh rarebit**) NOUN melted cheese on toast.

welt NOUN **1** a leather rim attaching the top of a boot or shoe to the sole. **2** a ribbed or strengthened border of a knitted garment. **3** a weal. VERB **1** provide with a welt. **2** raise weals on, thrash.

welter NOUN a turmoil; a disorderly mixture.

welterweight NOUN a boxing weight between lightweight and middleweight.

wen NOUN a benign tumour on the skin.

wend VERB (**wend one's way**) go slowly or by an indirect route.

went past of **GO**.

wept past and past participle of **WEEP**.

were 2nd person singular past, plural past, and past subjunctive of **BE**.

werewolf NOUN (PL **werewolves**) (in myths) a

person who at times turns into a wolf.

west NOUN the point on the horizon where the sun sets; the direction in which this lies; a western part or region. ADJ & ADV in or towards the west; (of a wind) from the west.
go west [INFORMAL] be destroyed, lost, or killed.

westerly ADJ towards the west; blowing from the west.

western ADJ of or in the west. NOUN a film or novel about cowboys in western North America.

westerner NOUN a person from the west.

westernize (also **westernise**) VERB cause (a country etc.) to adopt European or North American economic, cultural, or political systems.
westernization NOUN

westernmost ADJ furthest west.

westward ADJ towards the west.
westwards ADV

wet ADJ (**wetter**, **wettest**) **1** soaked or covered with water or other liquid; rainy; (of paint etc.) not having dried. **2** [INFORMAL] feeble, ineffectual. VERB (**wets**, **wetting**, **wetted**) make wet. NOUN wet weather; wetness.
wetly ADV
wetness NOUN

wet blanket NOUN [INFORMAL] someone who spoils others' pleasure by being gloomy.

wether NOUN a castrated ram.

wet nurse NOUN a woman employed to suckle another's child. VERB (**wet-nurse**) act as wet nurse to.

wetsuit NOUN a rubber garment worn for warmth by divers, windsurfers, etc.

whack [INFORMAL] VERB strike with a sharp blow. NOUN **1** a sharp blow. **2** an attempt. **3** an amount; a contribution.

whacked ADJ [INFORMAL] exhausted.

whale NOUN a very large sea mammal.
a whale of a [INFORMAL] an example of an exceedingly great or

good thing.

whalebone NOUN a horny substance from the upper jaw of whales, formerly used as stiffening in corsets etc.

whaler NOUN a whaling ship; a seaman hunting whales.

whaling NOUN hunting whales.

wham [INFORMAL] EXCLAMATION & NOUN the sound of a forcible impact.

wharf /whorf/ NOUN (PL **wharfs** or **wharves**) a landing stage where ships load and unload.

what PRON & DETERMINER **1** asking for information specifying something. **2** whatever. **3** used to emphasize something remarkable. PRON **1** asking someone to repeat something. **2** the thing that. ADV to what extent?

whatever PRON & DETERMINER everything or anything that; no matter what. PRON used for emphasis instead of *what* in questions. ADV at all; of any kind.

whatnot NOUN [INFORMAL] unspecified objects felt to form part of a group or series.

whatsoever ADJ & PRON whatever.

wheat NOUN grain from which flour is made; the plant producing this.

wheaten ADJ made from wheat.

wheatmeal NOUN wholemeal wheat flour.

wheedle VERB coax.

wheel NOUN a disc or circular frame that revolves on a shaft passing through its centre, used to move a vehicle, as part of a machine, etc.; a turn or rotation. VERB **1** push or pull (a cart or bicycle etc.) along. **2** turn; move in circles or curves.
at the wheel driving a vehicle, directing a ship; in control of affairs.
wheel and deal engage in scheming to exert influence.

wheelbarrow NOUN an open container with a wheel at one end and handles at the other, for moving small loads.

wheelbase NOUN the distance between a vehicle's front and rear axles.

wheelchair NOUN a chair on wheels for a person who cannot walk.

wheel-clamp VERB immobilize (an illegally parked car etc.).

wheelwright NOUN a maker and repairer of wooden wheels.

wheeze VERB breathe with a hoarse whistling sound. NOUN **1** this sound. **2** [INFORMAL] a clever scheme.
wheezy ADJ

whelk NOUN a shellfish with a spiral shell.

whelp NOUN a young dog, a pup. VERB give birth to (whelps).

when ADV **1** at what time? **2** in what circumstances? **3** at which time or in which situation. CONJ **1** at or during the time that; at any time that, whenever; **2** in view of the fact that. **3** although.

whence ADV [FORMAL] from where; from which.

whenever CONJ at whatever time or on whatever occasion; every time that. ADV used for emphasis instead of *when* in questions.

where ADV **1** in or to what place or position? **2** in what direction or respect? **3** at, in, or to which. **4** the place or situation in which. **5** in or to a place or situation in which.

whereabouts ADV in or near what place. NOUN a person's or thing's approximate location.

whereas CONJ **1** in contrast with the fact that. **2** [FORMAL] seeing that.

whereby ADV by which.

whereupon CONJ immediately after which.

wherever ADV **1** in or to whatever place. **2** used for emphasis instead of *where* in questions. CONJ in every case when.

wherewithal NOUN the things (especially money) needed for a purpose.

wherry NOUN (PL **wherries**) a light rowing boat; a large light barge.

whet VERB (**whets**, **whetting**, **whetted**) sharpen (a knife etc.) by rubbing against a stone; stimulate (appetite or interest).

whether CONJ introducing a choice between alternatives; expressing a question or investigation: *I'll see whether he's in.*

whetstone NOUN a shaped hard stone used for sharpening tools.

whey NOUN the watery liquid left when milk forms curds.

which PRON & DETERMINER **1** asking for information specifying one or more people or things from a definite set. **2** used to introduce further information about something just referred to.

whichever DETERMINER & PRON any which, no matter which.

whiff NOUN a puff of air or odour.

W

Whig NOUN [HISTORICAL] a member of the political party in the 17th–19th centuries opposed to the Tories.

while CONJ **1** during the time that; at the same time as. **2** although; whereas. NOUN a period of time.
the while meanwhile.
while away pass (time) in an interesting way.

whilst CONJ while.

whim NOUN a sudden fancy.

whimper VERB make feeble crying sounds. NOUN a whimpering sound.

whimsical ADJ impulsive and playful; fanciful, quaint; wryly humorous; capricious.
whimsicality NOUN
whimsically ADV

whine VERB make a long high complaining cry or a similar shrill sound; complain peevishly. NOUN a whining sound or complaint.
whiner NOUN

whinge VERB [INFORMAL] whine, complain.

whinny NOUN (PL **whinnies**) a gentle or joyful neigh. VERB (**whinnies**, **whinnying**, **whinnied**) utter a whinny.

whip NOUN **1** a cord or strip of leather on a handle, used for striking a person or animal. **2** a dessert made with whipped cream etc. **3** an official maintaining discipline in a political party. VERB (**whips**, **whipping**, **whipped**) **1** strike with a whip. **2** beat into a froth. **3** move rapidly; [INFORMAL] steal.
have the whip hand have control. **whip up** incite.

whipcord NOUN **1** a cord of tightly twisted strands. **2** ribbed twilled fabric.

whiplash NOUN **1** the stroke of a whip. **2** injury caused by a jerk to the head.

whippet NOUN a small dog resembling a greyhound.

whipping boy NOUN a scapegoat.

whippy ADJ flexible, springy.

whip-round NOUN [INFORMAL] a collection of money from a group.

whirl VERB spin or cause to spin round and round; move with bewildering speed. NOUN a whirling movement; a confused state; a state of activity.
give something a whirl [INFORMAL] try something.

whirlpool NOUN a current of water whirling in a circle.

whirlwind NOUN a mass of air whirling rapidly about a central point.

whirr VERB make a continuous low buzzing or vibrating sound. NOUN such a sound.

whisk VERB **1** convey or go rapidly; brush away lightly. **2** beat into a froth. NOUN **1** a whisking movement. **2** an instrument for beating eggs etc.; a bunch of bristles etc. for brushing or flicking things.

whisker NOUN a long hair-like bristle on the face of a cat etc.; (**whiskers**) hairs growing on a man's cheek.
whiskered ADJ
whiskery ADJ

whisky ([IRISH] & [US] **whiskey**) NOUN a spirit distilled from malted grain (especially barley).

whisper VERB speak or utter softly, not using the vocal cords; rustle.

NOUN a very soft tone; a whispered remark.

whist NOUN a card game usually for two pairs of players.

whistle NOUN a shrill sound made by blowing through a narrow opening between the lips; a similar sound; an instrument for producing this. VERB make such a sound; produce (a tune) in this way.
whistler NOUN

whistle-stop ADJ (of a tour) hurried, with only short stops.

Whit ADJ of or close to **Whit Sunday**, the seventh Sunday after Easter.

white ADJ **1** of the colour of snow or common salt; having a light-coloured skin; pale from illness, fear, etc. **2** (of coffee or tea) served with milk. NOUN **1** a white colour or thing; a member of a race with light-coloured skin. **2** the transparent substance round egg yolk; the pale part of the eyeball around the iris.
whiteness NOUN

white ant NOUN a termite.

whitebait NOUN (PL **whitebait**) very small fish used as food.

whiteboard NOUN a white board which can be written on with coloured pens and wiped clean.

white-collar worker NOUN a person not engaged in manual labour.

white elephant NOUN a useless possession.

white gold NOUN gold mixed with platinum.

white hope NOUN a person expected to achieve much.

white horses PLURAL NOUN white-crested waves on the sea.

white-hot ADJ (of metal) glowing white after heating.

white lie NOUN a lie told to avoid hurting someone's feelings.

whiten VERB make or become white or whiter.
whitener NOUN

white noise NOUN noise containing many frequencies with equal intensities, a harsh hissing sound.

White Paper NOUN a government report giving information.

white sale NOUN a sale of household linen.

white spirit NOUN light petroleum used as a solvent.

whitewash NOUN **1** a liquid containing quicklime or powdered chalk, used for painting walls or ceilings etc. **2** deliberate concealment of mistakes. VERB **1** paint with whitewash. **2** conceal (mistakes); present as blameless.

whither ADV [ARCHAIC] to what place.

whiting NOUN (PL **whiting**) a small sea fish used as food.

whitlow NOUN an inflammation near a fingernail or toenail.

Whitsun NOUN Whit Sunday and the days close to it.
Whitsuntide NOUN

whittle VERB trim (wood) by cutting thin slices from the surface; gradually reduce by removing parts or elements.

whizz (also **whiz**) VERB (**whizzes**, **whizzing**, **whizzed**) make a hissing or whistling sound like something moving fast through air; move very quickly. NOUN a whizzing sound.

whizz-kid (also **whiz-kid**) NOUN [INFORMAL] a brilliant or successful young person.

who PRON **1** what or which person or people? **2** introducing more information about someone just referred to.

whodunnit ([US] **whodunit**) NOUN [INFORMAL] a detective story or play.

whoever PRON **1** the person or people who; any person who. **2** used for emphasis instead of *who* in questions.

whole ADJ with no part removed or left out; not injured or broken. NOUN the full amount, all parts or members; a complete system made up of parts. **on the whole** considering everything; in general.

wholefood NOUN food which has not been unnecessarily processed.

wholehearted ADJ without doubts or reservations.
wholeheartedly ADV

wholemeal ADJ made from the whole grain of wheat etc.

whole number NOUN a number consisting of one or more units with no fractions.

wholesale NOUN the selling of goods in large quantities to be retailed by others. ADJ & ADV **1** in the wholesale trade. **2** on a large scale.
wholesaler NOUN

wholesome ADJ good for health or well-being.
wholesomeness NOUN

wholly ADV entirely, fully, totally.

whom PRON the objective case of *who*.

whoop VERB utter a loud cry of excitement. NOUN such a cry.

whooping cough NOUN an infectious disease especially of children, with a violent convulsive cough.

whopper NOUN [INFORMAL] something very large; a great lie.

whore NOUN a prostitute.

whorl /werl, worl/ NOUN a coiled form, one turn of a spiral; a circle of ridges in a fingerprint; a ring of leaves or petals.

who's CONTRACTION who is, who has.

whose PRON & ADJ belonging to whom or to which.

whosoever PRON whoever.

why ADV for what reason or purpose; on account of which. EXCLAMATION an exclamation of surprised discovery or recognition.

wick NOUN a length of thread in a candle or lamp etc., by which the flame is kept supplied with melted grease or fuel.

wicked ADJ **1** morally bad, evil; [INFORMAL] very harsh or unpleasant. **2** playfully mischievous. **3** [INFORMAL] excellent.
wickedly ADV
wickedness NOUN

wicker NOUN osiers or thin canes interwoven to make furniture, baskets, etc.
wickerwork NOUN

wicket NOUN a set of three stumps with two bails across the top, used in cricket; the part of a cricket ground between or near the two wickets.

wide ADJ **1** having a great or a specified distance between its sides. **2** including a variety of people or things. **3** far from the target. ADV widely; to the full extent.
wide awake fully awake; [INFORMAL] alert.
widely ADV
wideness NOUN

widen VERB make or become wider.

widespread ADJ found or distributed over a wide area.

widow NOUN a woman whose husband has died and who has not remarried.
widowhood NOUN

widowed ADJ made a widow or widower.

widower NOUN a man whose wife has died and who has not remarried.

width NOUN the extent of something from side to side; a piece of something at its full extent from side to side.

wield VERB hold and use (a tool etc.); have and use (power).

wife NOUN (PL **wives**) a married woman in relation to her husband.
wifely ADJ

wig NOUN a covering of hair worn on the head.

wiggle VERB move repeatedly from side to side, wriggle. NOUN an act of wiggling.
wiggly ADJ

wigwam NOUN a conical tent used by some North American Indians.

wild ADJ **1** not domesticated, tame, or cultivated; not civilized; desolate, bleak. **2** uncontrolled; unrestrained, unreasonable; [INFORMAL] very enthusiastic; [INFORMAL] very angry. **3** random: *a wild guess.* NOUN (**the wild, the wilds**) desolate places.
wildly ADV

W

wildness NOUN

wildcat ADJ (of a strike) sudden and unofficial.

wildebeest NOUN (PL **wildebeest** or **wildebeests**) a gnu.

wilderness NOUN an uncultivated and uninhabited area.

wildfire NOUN (**spread like wildfire**) spread very fast.

wildfowl PLURAL NOUN birds hunted as game.

wild goose chase NOUN a useless quest.

wildlife NOUN wild animals and plants.

wiles PLURAL NOUN trickery, cunning.

wilful ([US] **willful**) ADJ intentional, not accidental; stubbornly self-willed.
wilfully ADV
wilfulness NOUN

will[1] AUXILIARY VERB used with *I* and *we* to express promises or obligations, and with other words to express a future tense.

will[2] NOUN **1** the mental faculty by which a person decides on and controls his or her actions; determination; a person's attitude in wishing good or bad to others. **2** a legal document with instructions for the disposal of someone's property after their death. VERB **1** exercise one's will power, influence by doing this. **2** bequeath by a will.
at will whenever one pleases. **have one's will** get what one desires.

willie variant of **WILLY**.

willing ADJ ready to do what is asked; given or done readily.
willingly ADV
willingness NOUN

will-o'-the-wisp NOUN **1** a phosphorescent light seen on marshy ground. **2** a hope or aim that can never be fulfilled.

willow NOUN a tree or shrub with flexible branches.

willowy ADJ slender and supple.

will power NOUN determination used to achieve something or restrain one's impulses.

willy (also **willie**) NOUN (PL **willies**) [INFORMAL] the penis.

willy-nilly ADV whether one desires it or not.

wilt VERB (of a plant) droop through lack of water; (of a person) become limp from exhaustion.

wily ADJ (**wilier**, **wiliest**) cunning.
wiliness NOUN

wimp NOUN [INFORMAL] a feeble or ineffective person.

win VERB (**wins**, **winning**, **won**) defeat an opponent in (a contest), be victorious; obtain as the result of a contest etc., or by effort. NOUN a victory, especially in a game.
win over gain the favour of.

wince VERB make a slight movement from pain or embarrassment etc. NOUN this movement.

winch NOUN a machine for hoisting or pulling things by a cable that winds round a revolving drum. VERB hoist or pull with a winch.

wind¹ /wind/ NOUN **1** a natural current of air; breath as needed for exertion. **2** gas in the stomach or intestines. **3** empty talk. **4** an orchestra's wind instruments. VERB **1** cause to be out of breath. **2** detect by smell.
get wind of [INFORMAL] hear a hint or rumour of. **in the wind** happening or about to happen. **put the wind up** [INFORMAL] frighten. **take the wind out of a person's sails** take away an advantage, frustrate.

wind² /wynd/ VERB (**winds**, **winding**, **wound**) move in a twisting or spiral course; wrap (something) repeatedly around something else or round on itself; operate by turning a key, handle, etc.; hoist with a windlass etc.
wind down [INFORMAL] become calmer, relax after stress. **wind up 1** set (a clock etc.) going by tightening its spring. **2** bring or come to an end; settle the affairs of and close (a business company). **3** [INFORMAL]

provoke by teasing.
winder NOUN

windbag NOUN [INFORMAL] a person who talks at unnecessary length.

windbreak NOUN a screen shielding something from the wind.

wind chill NOUN the cooling effect of the wind.

windfall NOUN **1** fruit blown off a tree by the wind. **2** an unexpected gain, especially a sum of money.

wind farm NOUN a group of energy-producing windmills or wind turbines.

wind instrument NOUN a musical instrument sounded by a current of air, especially by the player's breath.

windlass NOUN a winch-like device using a rope or chain that winds round a horizontal roller.

windmill NOUN a building with projecting sails or vanes that produce energy for grinding etc. when turned by the wind.

window NOUN **1** an opening in a wall etc. to admit light and air, usually filled with glass; this glass; a space behind the window of a shop for displaying goods. **2** a framed area on a computer screen for viewing information.

window box NOUN a trough fixed outside a window, for growing flowers etc.

window dressing NOUN the arrangement of a display in a shop window; the presentation of something in a misleadingly favourable way.

window-shopping NOUN the action of looking at goods displayed in shop windows without buying.

windpipe NOUN the air passage from the throat to the bronchial tubes.

windscreen ([US] **windshield**) NOUN the glass in the window at the front of a vehicle.

windsock NOUN a canvas cylinder flown at an airfield to show the direction of the wind.

windsurfing NOUN the

sport of surfing on a board to which a sail is fixed.
windsurfer NOUN

windswept ADJ exposed to strong winds.

wind tunnel NOUN an enclosed tunnel in which winds can be created for testing the resistance of buildings etc.

windward ADJ & ADV in or towards the direction from which the wind blows. NOUN this side or region.

wine NOUN **1** fermented grape juice as an alcoholic drink; a fermented drink made from other fruits or plants. **2** dark red.
wine and dine entertain with food and drink.

wine bar NOUN a bar or small restaurant serving wine as the main drink.

wing NOUN **1** each of a pair of projecting parts by which a bird, insect, etc., is able to fly; each of the projections on an aircraft supporting it in the air. **2** a projecting part; the bodywork above the wheel of a car; a side or projecting part of a large building; (**wings**) the sides of a theatre stage. **3** either end of a battle array; a player at either end of the forward line in football or hockey etc., the side part of the playing area in these games; an extreme section of a political party. VERB **1** travel on wings; move very quickly. **2** wound in the wing or arm.
on the wing flying. **take wing** fly away. **under one's wing** under one's protection.

winged ADJ having wings.

winger NOUN a wing player in football etc.

wingspan NOUN the measurement across wings from one tip to the other.

wink VERB rapidly close and open one eye as a signal; (of a light) shine or flash intermittently. NOUN an act of winking.
not a wink no sleep at all.

winkle NOUN an edible sea snail.
winkle out extract, prise

W

out.

winner NOUN a person or thing that wins; [INFORMAL] something successful.

winning ADJ charming, persuasive. NOUN (**winnings**) money won in betting etc.

winnow VERB fan or toss (grain) to free it of chaff.

wino NOUN (PL **winos**) [INFORMAL] an alcoholic.

winsome ADJ charming.

winter NOUN the coldest season of the year. VERB spend the winter in a particular place.
wintry ADJ

wipe VERB rub (a surface) to clean or dry it; remove (dirt etc.) in this way; spread (liquid) over a surface by rubbing. NOUN an act of wiping; a piece of material for wiping.
wipe out destroy completely.

wiper NOUN a device that automatically wipes rain etc. from a windscreen.

W

wire NOUN a strand of metal; a length of this used for fencing, conducting electric current, etc. VERB **1** install electric wires in. **2** fasten or strengthen with wire.

wired ADJ [INFORMAL] **1** using computers and information technology to transmit and receive information. **2** tense, nervous.

wiring NOUN a system of electric wires in a building, vehicle, etc.

wiry ADJ (**wirier**, **wiriest**) like wire; thin but strong.
wiriness NOUN

wisdom NOUN the quality of being wise; soundness of judgement; wise sayings.

wisdom tooth NOUN a hindmost molar tooth, not usually cut before the age of 20.

wise ADJ having experience, knowledge, and sound judgement; sensible, prudent.
wise to [INFORMAL] alert to, aware of.
wisely ADV

wiseacre NOUN a person who pretends to have great wisdom.

wisecrack [INFORMAL] NOUN a witty remark or joke. VERB make a wisecrack.

wish NOUN a desire, a hope; an expression of a desire, a request or instruction; (**wishes**) expressions of friendly feeling. VERB feel a desire; desire or express a desire for (something) to happen to (someone).

wishbone NOUN a forked bone between a bird's neck and breast.

wishful thinking NOUN supposing that something desired but impossible or improbable is the case.

wishy-washy ADJ weak in colour, character, etc.

wisp NOUN a small separate bunch; a small streak of smoke etc.
wispiness NOUN
wispy ADJ

wistful ADJ full of sad or vague longing.
wistfully ADV
wistfulness NOUN

wit NOUN amusing ingenuity in expressing words or ideas; a person who has this; intelligence.
at one's wits' end worried and not knowing what to do.

witch NOUN a person (especially a woman) who practises witchcraft; a fascinatingly attractive woman.

witchcraft NOUN the practice of magic.

witch doctor NOUN a magician and healer in traditional tribal societies.

witch hazel NOUN an astringent lotion made from a shrub.

witch-hunt NOUN [INFORMAL] persecution of people thought to be holders of unpopular views.

with PREP **1** accompanied by or accompanying. **2** having; characterized by; showing (a mood, emotion, etc). **3** using; employed by. **4** towards, in relation to: *I'm angry with her.* **5** indicating opposition or separation: *I won't part with this.* **6** affected by; because of: *weak with hunger.* **7** sharing the opinion of.
with it [INFORMAL] **1** up to date in one's knowledge or behaviour. **2** alert.

withdraw VERB (**withdraws**, **withdrawing**,

withdrew; PAST PARTICIPLE **withdrawn**) **1** take back; remove (deposited money) from a bank etc.; cancel (a statement). **2** go away from a place or from company.
withdrawal NOUN

withdrawn ADJ (of a person) not communicative or sociable.

wither VERB **1** shrivel, lose freshness or vitality. **2** subdue by scorn.

withhold VERB (**withholds**, **withholding**, **withheld**) refuse to give; suppress (a reaction etc.).

within PREP inside; not beyond the limit or scope of; in a time no longer than. ADV inside.

without PREP not having; in the absence of; not doing (a specified action). ADV outside.

withstand VERB (**withstands**, **withstanding**, **withstood**) endure successfully.

W

witless ADJ stupid.

witness NOUN a person who sees or hears something; one who gives evidence in a law court; one who watches the signing of a document and signs to confirm this; something that serves as evidence. VERB be a witness of.

witter VERB [INFORMAL] speak lengthily about something trivial.

witticism NOUN a witty remark.

witty ADJ (**wittier**, **wittiest**) clever, inventive, and funny.
wittily ADV
wittiness NOUN

wives pl. of **WIFE**.

wizard NOUN a male witch, a magician; a person with great skill in a particular field.
wizardry NOUN

wizened /wiz-ĕnd/ ADJ full of wrinkles, shrivelled with age.

woad NOUN a blue dye obtained from a plant.

wobble VERB stand or move unsteadily; quiver. NOUN a wobbling movement; a quiver.

wobbly ADJ (**wobblier**, **wobbliest**) unsteady; quivering.

throw a wobbly [INFORMAL] have a fit of annoyance or panic.

wodge NOUN [INFORMAL] a large slice or lump.

woe NOUN [LITERARY] sorrow, distress; trouble causing this, misfortune.
woeful ADJ
woefully ADV

woebegone ADJ looking unhappy.

wog NOUN [INFORMAL], [OFFENSIVE] a person who is not white.

wok NOUN a large bowl-shaped frying pan used especially in Chinese cookery.

woke, **woken** past and past participle of **WAKE**.

wold NOUN (especially **wolds**) an area of open upland country.

wolf NOUN (PL **wolves**) a wild animal of the dog family. VERB eat quickly and greedily.
cry wolf raise false alarms.
wolfish ADJ

wolfram NOUN tungsten or its ore.

wolf whistle NOUN a rising and falling whistle, expressing sexual admiration.

woman NOUN (PL **women**) an adult female person; women in general.

womanhood NOUN the state of being a woman; women collectively.

womanize (also **womanise**) VERB (of a man) engage in many casual affairs with women.
womanizer NOUN

womankind NOUN women in general.

womanly ADJ having qualities considered appropriate to a woman.
womanliness NOUN

womb /woom/ NOUN the hollow organ in female mammals in which the young develop before birth.

wombat NOUN a burrowing Australian marsupial like a small bear.

women pl. of **WOMAN**.

womenfolk NOUN women in general; the women of one's family.

won past and past participle of **WIN**.

wonder NOUN a feeling of

surprise and admiration; an extraordinary and beautiful or admirable thing, person, etc. VERB **1** feel curiosity. **2** feel amazement and admiration.

wonderful ADJ very good; excellent, delightful.
wonderfully ADV

wonderland NOUN a place full of wonderful things.

wonderment NOUN a feeling of wonder.

wonky ADJ (**wonkier**, **wonkiest**) [INFORMAL] crooked; unsteady; not working.

wont /wohnt/ [ARCHAIC] ADJ accustomed to do something. NOUN one's usual practice.

woo VERB seek to marry; seek the favour of.

wood NOUN the tough fibrous substance of a tree; this cut for use; (also **woods**) trees growing fairly densely over an area of ground.
out of the wood clear of danger or difficulty.

woodbine NOUN wild honeysuckle.

woodcut NOUN a print made from a design cut in a block of wood.

wooded ADJ covered with trees.

wooden ADJ **1** made of wood. **2** stiff; showing no emotion.
woodenly ADV

woodland NOUN wooded country.

woodlouse NOUN (PL **woodlice**) a small wingless creature living in decaying wood etc.

woodpecker NOUN a bird that taps tree trunks with its beak to discover insects.

woodwind NOUN wind instruments made (or formerly made) of wood, e.g. the clarinet.

woodwork NOUN the art or practice of making things from wood; wooden parts of a room.

woodworm NOUN the larva of a kind of beetle that bores in wood.

woody ADJ (**woodier**, **woodiest**) **1** wooded. **2** like or consisting of wood.

woof NOUN a dog's gruff bark. VERB make this

sound.

woofer NOUN a loudspeaker for reproducing low-frequency signals.

wool NOUN the soft hair from sheep or goats etc.; yarn or fabric made from this.
pull the wool over someone's eyes deceive someone.

woollen ([US] **woolen**) ADJ made of wool.
NOUN (**woollens**) woollen garments.

woolly ADJ (**woollier, woolliest**) **1** covered with wool; like wool, woollen. **2** vague, confused. NOUN (PL **woollies**) [INFORMAL] woollen garment.
woolliness NOUN

woozy ADJ (**woozier, wooziest**) [INFORMAL] dizzy, dazed.

word NOUN a unit of sound expressing a meaning independently and forming a basic element of speech; this represented by letters or symbols; something said; a message, news; a promise; a command.
VERB express in a particular style.
have a word with speak briefly to. **have words** quarrel. **word of mouth** spoken, not written, words.

wording NOUN the way a thing is worded.

word-perfect ADJ knowing every word of a speech etc.

word processor NOUN a computer or program designed for producing and altering text and documents.

wordy ADJ (**wordier, wordiest**) using too many words.

wore past of **WEAR**.

work NOUN **1** the use of bodily or mental power in order to do or make something; such activity as a means of earning money; a task to be done. **2** something produced by work; a literary or musical composition; embroidery or other decorative articles of a particular kind. **3** (**works**) a factory; the operative parts of a machine; a defensive structure. **4** (**the works**)

W

[INFORMAL] everything required or available. VERB **1** perform work; be employed. **2** operate (a machine etc.); function. **3** bring about, accomplish: *working miracles.* **4** shape (material); produce, create; bring or come into a specified state. **work off** get rid of by activity. **work one's way** or **passage** fund oneself or pay for a journey by working. **work out 1** find or solve by calculation; plan the details of. **2** have a specified outcome. **3** take exercise. **work to rule** cause delay by over-strict observance of rules, as a form of protest. **work up 1** bring gradually to a more developed state; progress to a climax. **2** excite or make anxious.

workable ADJ feasible, able to be put into practice.

W

workaday ADJ ordinary, everyday; practical.

workbook NOUN a book with exercises for practice in a subject.

worker NOUN **1** a person who works; a member of the working class. **2** a neuter bee or ant etc. that does the work of the hive or colony.

workhouse NOUN a former public institution where people unable to support themselves were housed in return for work.

working ADJ **1** having paid employment; doing manual work. **2** functioning. **3** serving as a basis for work or argument. NOUN **1** a mine or part of a mine. **2** (**workings**) the way in which a system operates.

working class NOUN the class of people who are employed for wages, especially in manual or industrial work. **working-class** ADJ

working knowledge NOUN knowledge adequate to work with.

workman NOUN a person employed to do manual labour.

workmanlike ADJ efficient, practical.

workmanship NOUN skill in working or in a thing

produced.

workout NOUN a session of physical exercise or training.

workshop NOUN **1** a room or building in which manual work or manufacture etc. is carried on. **2** a meeting for discussion or practice of a particular subject or activity.

workstation NOUN **1** a computer terminal and keyboard; a desk with this. **2** the location of a stage in a manufacturing process.

worktop NOUN a flat surface for working on, especially in a kitchen.

world NOUN **1** the earth; all the people, creatures, etc., on it; everything. **2** an aspect of life; the people involved in a particular activity etc. **think the world of** respect highly.

worldly ADJ of or concerned with earthly life or material gains, not spiritual.
worldliness NOUN

worldwide ADJ extending through the whole world.

World Wide Web NOUN a system of linked and cross-referenced documents for accessing information on the Internet.

worm NOUN **1** a creature with a long soft body and no backbone or limbs; (**worms**) internal parasites. **2** [INFORMAL] a feeble or contemptible person. **3** a spiral part of a mechanical device. VERB **1** make one's way with twisting movements; insinuate oneself; obtain by crafty persistence. **2** rid (an animal) of parasitic worms.
wormy ADJ

worm cast NOUN a pile of earth cast up by an earthworm.

worm-eaten ADJ full of holes made by insect larvae.

wormwood NOUN a woody plant with a bitter flavour.

worn past participle of **WEAR**. ADJ damaged or altered by use or wear; looking exhausted.

worn out ADJ exhausted;

damaged and thin from use.

worried ADJ feeling or showing worry.

worry VERB (**worries, worrying, worried**) **1** feel anxious; cause anxiety to; annoy, trouble. **2** seize with the teeth and shake or pull about. NOUN (PL **worries**) anxiety, unease; something about which one worries.
worrier NOUN

worse ADJ less good or satisfactory; more serious or severe. ADV less well; more seriously or severely. NOUN something worse.
worse off less fortunate or wealthy.

worsen VERB make or become worse.

worship NOUN reverence and respect paid to a god; adoration of or devotion to a person or thing. VERB (**worships, worshipping, worshipped**; [US] **worshiping, worshiped**) honour as a god; take part in an act of worship; idolize, treat with adoration.
worshipper NOUN

worst ADJ most bad, severe, or serious. ADV most severely or seriously; least well. NOUN the worst part, feature, event, etc.

worsted /wuu-stid/ NOUN a smooth woollen yarn or fabric.

worth ADJ having a specified value; good enough for a specified treatment; likely to repay a specified treatment; possessing a specified sum as wealth. NOUN value, merit, usefulness; the amount that a specified sum will buy.
for all one is worth [INFORMAL] with all one's energy. **worth one's while** worth the time or effort needed.

worthless ADJ having no value or merit.
worthlessness NOUN

worthwhile ADJ worth the time or effort spent.

worthy ADJ (**worthier, worthiest**) having great merit; deserving. NOUN (PL **worthies**) a worthy person.
worthily ADV

worthiness NOUN

would AUXILIARY VERB used in senses corresponding to *will*[1] in the past tense, conditional statements, questions, polite requests and statements, and to express probability or something that happens from time to time.

would-be ADJ desiring or pretending to be.

wound¹ /woond/ NOUN an injury done to tissue by violence; injury to feelings. VERB inflict a wound on.

wound² /wownd/ past and past participle of **WIND²**.

wove, **woven** past and past participle of **WEAVE**.

wow EXCLAMATION an exclamation of astonishment. NOUN [INFORMAL] a sensational success.

WPC ABBREV woman police constable.

wrack NOUN seaweed. VERB variant of **RACK**.

wraith NOUN a ghost, a spectral apparition of a living person.

wrangle VERB argue or quarrel noisily. NOUN a noisy argument.

wrap VERB (**wraps**, **wrapping**, **wrapped**) arrange (a soft or flexible covering) round (a person or thing). NOUN a shawl.
be wrapped up in have one's attention deeply occupied by. **wrap up** **1** dress warmly. **2** [INFORMAL] complete, conclude.

wrapper NOUN a cover of paper etc. wrapped round something.

wrapping NOUN material for wrapping things.

wrath NOUN anger, indignation.
wrathful ADJ
wrathfully ADV

wreak VERB cause (damage); exact (revenge).

wreath /reeth/ NOUN a decorative ring of flowers, leaves, and stems.

wreathe /ree*th*/ VERB encircle; twist into a wreath; wind, curve.

wreck NOUN the destruction especially of a ship by storms or accident; a ship that has

suffered this; something ruined or dilapidated; a person whose health or spirits have been destroyed. VERB destroy; ruin; involve in shipwreck.
wrecker NOUN

wreckage NOUN the remains of something that has been badly damaged.

wren NOUN a very small bird.

wrench VERB twist or pull violently round; damage or pull by twisting. NOUN **1** a violent twisting pull. **2** pain caused by parting. **3** an adjustable spanner-like tool.

wrest VERB wrench away; obtain by force or effort.

wrestle VERB fight (especially as a sport) by grappling with and trying to throw an opponent to the ground; struggle with a task or problem.

wretch NOUN a despicable person; a miserable person.

wretched ADJ **1** very unhappy. **2** contemptible; infuriating.
wretchedly ADV
wretchedness NOUN

wriggle VERB move with short twisting movements; escape (out of a difficulty etc.) cunningly. NOUN a wriggling movement.

wring VERB (**wrings**, **wringing**, **wrung**) twist and squeeze, especially to remove liquid; squeeze (someone's hand) firmly or forcibly; (**wring from** or **out of**) obtain with difficulty from.

wrinkle NOUN **1** a small furrow in the skin, cloth, etc.; [INFORMAL] a minor fault or problem. **2** [INFORMAL] a useful hint or knack. VERB make or become wrinkled.
wrinkly ADJ

wrist NOUN the joint connecting the hand and forearm; part of a garment covering this.

writ NOUN a formal written authoritative command; someone's power or influence.

write VERB (**writes**, **writing**, **wrote**; PAST PARTICIPLE **written**) make letters or

other symbols on a surface, especially with a pen or pencil; compose in written form, especially for publication; be an author; write and send a letter; write the necessary details on (a cheque etc.); [COMPUTING] enter (data) into a storage medium.
write off 1 dismiss as insignificant. **2** acknowledge the loss of. **write up** write an account of; write entries in (a diary etc.).

write-off NOUN something written off as lost; a vehicle too damaged to be worth repairing.

writer NOUN a person who writes; an author.

writer's cramp NOUN cramp in the muscles of the hand.

write-up NOUN a published account of something, a review.

writhe VERB twist one's body continually, especially in pain; suffer from embarrassment.

writing NOUN handwriting; literary work.
in writing in written form.

writing paper NOUN paper for writing (especially letters) on.

written past participle of **WRITE**.

wrong ADJ **1** not true or correct; mistaken. **2** morally bad; unjust, dishonest. **3** unsuitable, undesirable; not the one desired or needed. ADV **1** mistakenly, incorrectly. **2** unjustly, wickedly. NOUN an immoral or unjust action. VERB treat unjustly.
in the wrong not having truth or justice on one's side.
wrongly ADV

wrongdoer NOUN a person who behaves illegally or immorally.
wrongdoing NOUN

wrongful ADJ contrary to what is right or legal.
wrongfully ADV

wrote past of **WRITE**.

wrought /rawt/ ADJ (of metals) shaped by hammering.
wrought up tense, distressed.

wrought iron NOUN a pure

form of iron used for decorative work.

wrung past and past participle of **WRING**.

wry ADJ (**wryer**, **wryest** or **wrier**, **wriest**) **1** (of the face) contorted in disgust or disappointment. **2** (of humour) dry, mocking.

wryly ADV

wryness NOUN

www ABBREV World Wide Web.

Xx

X (also **x**) NOUN (PL **Xs** or **X's**) **1** the twenty-fourth letter of the alphabet. **2** an x-shaped symbol, indicating an incorrect answer or representing a kiss. **3** the Roman numeral for ten.

X certificate NOUN (formerly) a classification of a film as suitable for adults only.

X chromosome NOUN a sex chromosome, of which female cells have twice as many as males.

xenon /zen-on/ NOUN a colourless, odourless gas.

xenophobia /zen-ŏ-foh-bi-ă/ NOUN a strong dislike or distrust of foreigners.

xenotransplantation NOUN the grafting or transplanting of tissues or organs between different species.

Xerox /zeer-oks/ NOUN [TRADE MARK] a machine for producing photocopies; a photocopy.
VERB photocopy.

Xmas NOUN [INFORMAL] Christmas.

X-ray NOUN a photograph or examination made by electromagnetic radiation **X-rays** that can penetrate solids. VERB photograph, examine, or treat by X-rays.

xylophone /zI-lŏ-fohn/ NOUN a musical instrument with flat wooden bars struck with small hammers.

Yy

Y (also **y**) NOUN (PL **Ys** or **Y's**) the twenty-fifth letter of the alphabet.

yacht /yot/ NOUN a light sailing vessel for racing; a vessel used for private pleasure excursions.
yachting NOUN
yachtsman NOUN
yachtswoman NOUN

yak NOUN a long-haired Asian ox.

yam NOUN the edible tuber of a tropical plant; a sweet potato.

yang NOUN (in Chinese philosophy) the active male principle.

yank [INFORMAL] VERB pull sharply. NOUN **1** a sharp pull. **2** (**Yank**) an American.

yap NOUN a shrill bark. VERB (**yaps**, **yapping**, **yapped**) bark shrilly.

y

yard NOUN **1** a measure of length, 3 feet (0.9144 metre). **2** a piece of enclosed ground, especially attached to a building. **3** a pole slung from a mast to support a sail.

yardage NOUN length measured in yards.

yardstick NOUN a standard of comparison.

yarmulke /yar-muul-kă/ (also **yarmulka**) NOUN a skullcap worn by Jewish men.

yarn NOUN **1** any spun thread. **2** [INFORMAL] a story.

yashmak NOUN a veil worn by Muslim women in certain countries.

yaw VERB (of a ship or aircraft) fail to hold a straight course.

yawn VERB open the mouth wide and draw in breath, as when sleepy or bored; have a wide opening. NOUN the act of yawning.

Y chromosome NOUN a sex chromosome occurring only in males.

yd ABBREV yard.

year NOUN the time taken by the earth to orbit the sun (365¼ days); (also **calendar year**) the period of 365 days (or 366 days in a leap year) from 1 January to 31 December; any consecutive period of twelve months.

yearbook NOUN an annual publication listing events or aspects of the previous year.

yearling NOUN an animal between 1 and 2 years old.

yearly ADJ happening, published, or payable once a year. ADV annually.

yearn VERB feel great longing.

yeast NOUN a fungus used to cause fermentation in making beer and wine and as a raising agent.

yell NOUN a loud, sharp cry. VERB shout loudly.

yellow ADJ **1** coloured like buttercups or ripe lemons. **2** [INFORMAL] cowardly. **3** (of reporting etc.) sensational. NOUN a yellow colour or thing. VERB turn yellow.
yellowish ADJ

yelp NOUN a short sharp cry. VERB make a yelp or yelps.

yen NOUN **1** (PL **yen**) the basic monetary unit in Japan. **2** [INFORMAL] a longing, a yearning.

yeoman /yoh-măn/ NOUN [HISTORICAL] a man who owned and farmed a small estate.

yes EXCLAMATION & NOUN an affirmative reply; an expression of agreement or consent, or of reply to a summons etc.

yes-man NOUN [INFORMAL] a person who is always ready to agree with a superior.

yesterday ADV on the day before today. NOUN the day before today; the recent past.

yet ADV **1** up to the present or a specified time; this soon; for some time into the future. **2** even (used with comparatives): *yet more vain.* CONJ nevertheless, in spite of that.

yeti NOUN a large manlike animal said to exist in the Himalayas.

yew NOUN an evergreen tree with dark needle-like leaves.

Y-fronts PLURAL NOUN [TRADE MARK] men's briefs with a Y-shaped seam at the front.

YHA ABBREV Youth Hostels Association.

Yiddish NOUN the language used by Jews from eastern Europe.

yield VERB **1** produce as a fruit, outcome of effort, etc. **2** surrender; hand over to another; move or give way when pushed or pressed. NOUN an amount yielded or produced.

yin NOUN (in Chinese philosophy) the passive female principle.

yippee EXCLAMATION an exclamation of delight or excitement.

YMCA ABBREV Young Men's Christian Association.

y

yob NOUN [INFORMAL] an aggressive and coarse person.

yodel VERB (**yodels**, **yodelling**, **yodelled**; [US] **yodeling**, **yodeled**) sing with a quickly alternating change of pitch. NOUN a yodelling cry.

yodeller NOUN

yoga NOUN a Hindu system of meditation and self-control; exercises used in this.

yogurt (also **yoghurt**) NOUN food made of milk that has been thickened by the action of bacteria.

yoke NOUN **1** a wooden crosspiece fastened over the necks of two oxen pulling a plough etc.; a frame fitting over someone's shoulders and holding a load at each end; part of a garment fitting over the shoulders. **2** oppressive rule. VERB harness with a yoke; join, link.

yokel NOUN a country person regarded as stupid or uneducated.

yolk NOUN the round yellow internal part of an egg.

yonder [ARCHAIC] ADV over there. DETERMINER that or

those.

yonks PLURAL NOUN [INFORMAL] a long time.

yore NOUN (**of yore**) [LITERARY] in the past; long ago.

Yorkshire pudding NOUN a baked batter pudding eaten with gravy or meat.

you PRON **1** the person(s) addressed. **2** one, people in general.

young ADJ having lived or existed for only a short time; energetic and enthusiastic; immature. NOUN an animal's offspring.

youngster NOUN a young person, a child.

your ADJ of or belonging to you.

yours POSSESSIVE PRONOUN belonging to you.

yourself PRON (PL **yourselves**) the emphatic and reflexive form of *you*.

youth NOUN **1** the state or period of being young. **2** a young man; young people.

youth club NOUN a club providing leisure activities for young people.

youthful ADJ young; characteristic of young people.
youthfulness NOUN

youth hostel NOUN a hostel providing cheap accommodation for walkers or holidaymakers.

yowl NOUN a loud cry of pain or distress.
VERB make such a cry.

yo-yo NOUN (PL **yo-yos**) [TRADE MARK] a disc-shaped toy that can be made to rise and fall on a string that winds round it in a groove. VERB (**yo-yoes**, **yo-yoing**, **yo-yoed**) fluctuate, move up and down rapidly.

YTS ABBREV Youth Training Scheme.

ytterbium /it-er-bi-ŭm/ NOUN a metallic element.

yttrium /it-ri-ŭm/ NOUN a metallic element.

yuan NOUN (PL **yuan**) the chief monetary unit in China.

yuck (also **yuk**) EXCLAMATION [INFORMAL] an expression of disgust.

Yuletide NOUN [ARCHAIC] the Christmas festival.

yummy ADJ (**yummier**, **yummiest**) [INFORMAL] delicious.

yuppie (also **yuppy**) NOUN [INFORMAL] a young middle-class professional person working in a city.

YWCA ABBREV Young Women's Christian Association.

Zz

Z (also **z**) NOUN (PL **Zs** or **Z's**) the twenty-sixth letter of the alphabet.

zany ADJ (**zanier**, **zaniest**) crazily funny. NOUN (PL **zanies**) a zany person.

zap [INFORMAL] VERB (**zaps**, **zapping**, **zapped**) **1** destroy. **2** move or propel suddenly. NOUN a burst of energy.

zeal NOUN enthusiasm, hearty and persistent effort.
zealous ADJ
zealously ADV

zealot /zel-ŏt/ NOUN a person who is fanatical in support of a cause.

zebra NOUN an African horse-like animal with black and white stripes.

zebra crossing NOUN a pedestrian crossing where the road is marked with broad white stripes.

Zen NOUN a form of Buddhism.

zenith NOUN the part of the sky that is directly overhead; the highest point.

zephyr NOUN [LITERARY] a soft gentle wind.

zero NOUN (PL **zeros**) nought, the figure 0; nil; a point marked 0 on a graduated scale, a temperature corresponding to this.
zero in on (**zeroes**, **zeroing**, **zeroed**) take aim at; focus attention on.

zero-emission ADJ (of a vehicle) not emitting pollutant gases in its exhaust.

zero hour NOUN the hour at which something is timed to begin.

zest NOUN **1** keen enjoyment or interest. **2** orange or lemon peel as

flavouring.
zestful ADJ
zestfully ADV

zigzag NOUN a line or course turning right and left alternately at sharp angles. ADJ & ADV as or in a zigzag. VERB (**zigzags**, **zigzagging**, **zigzagged**) move in a zigzag.

zilch NOUN [INFORMAL] nothing.

zinc NOUN a white metallic element.

zing [INFORMAL] NOUN vigour. VERB move swiftly.

Zionism NOUN a movement that campaigned for a Jewish homeland in Palestine.
Zionist NOUN

zip NOUN **1** a fastening device with teeth that interlock when brought together by a sliding tab. **2** [INFORMAL] energy. VERB (**zips**, **zipping**, **zipped**) **1** fasten with a zip fastener. **2** [INFORMAL] move with vigour or at high speed.

Zip code NOUN [US] a postal code.

zipper NOUN a zip fastener.

zircon NOUN a bluish-white gem cut from a translucent mineral.

zirconium NOUN grey metallic element.

zit NOUN [INFORMAL] a pimple.

zither NOUN a stringed instrument played with the fingers.

zloty NOUN (PL **zloty** or **zlotys**) the unit of money in Poland.

zodiac NOUN (in astrology) a band of the sky divided into twelve equal parts **signs of the zodiac** each named from a constellation.
zodiacal ADJ

zombie NOUN **1** (in voodoo) a corpse said to have been revived by witchcraft. **2** [INFORMAL] a person apparently without awareness, will, or energy.

zone NOUN an area with particular characteristics, purpose, or use.
VERB divide into zones.
zonal ADJ

zoo NOUN a place where wild animals are kept for exhibition, conservation, and study.

zoology NOUN the study of

Z

animals.
zoological ADJ
zoologist NOUN

zoom VERB **1** move very quickly; increase sharply. **2** (in photography) make a distant object appear gradually closer by means of a zoom lens.

zoophyte /zoo-ŏ-fIt/ NOUN a plant-like animal, especially a coral, sea anemone, or sponge.

zucchini /zoo-kee-ni/ NOUN (PL **zucchini** or **zucchinis**) [US] a courgette.

Zulu NOUN a member of a Bantu people of South Africa; their language.

zygote /zI-goht/ NOUN a cell formed by the union of two gametes.